# INTERNATIONAL LEGAL MATERIALS ON INTELLECTUAL PROPERTY

## 2021 Edition

**PAUL GOLDSTEIN**
*Lillick Professor of Law*
*Stanford Law School*

**MARKETA TRIMBLE**
*Lionel Professor of Intellectual Property Law*
*University of Nevada, Las Vegas*

FOUNDATION
PRESS

© 2000, 2002 FOUNDATION PRESS
© 2006 By THOMSON REUTERS/FOUNDATION PRESS
© 2011 By THOMSON REUTERS
© 2014 LEG, Inc. d/b/a West Academic
© 2021 LEG, Inc. d/b/a West Academic
     444 Cedar Street, Suite 700
     St. Paul, MN 55101
     1-877-888-1330

Printed in the United States of America

**ISBN:** 978-1-63659-021-9

# ACKNOWLEDGMENT

We are grateful to the World Intellectual Property Organization for permission to reproduce its compilations of treaty parties.

P.G.

M.T.

# TABLE OF CONTENTS

## PATENTS AND PLANT VARIETY PROTECTION

## TRADEMARKS AND GEOGRAPHICAL INDICATIONS

## INDUSTRIAL DESIGN

## EUROPEAN UNION DIRECTIVES AND REGULATIONS

# INTERNATIONAL LEGAL MATERIALS ON INTELLECTUAL PROPERTY

## 2021 Edition

# TRADE AGREEMENTS AND TREATY ORGANIZATIONS

———

## 1. AGREEMENT ON TRADE-RELATED ASPECTS OF INTELLECTUAL PROPERTY RIGHTS, INCLUDING TRADE IN COUNTERFEIT GOODS

(A Portion of the Agreement Amending the General Agreement on Tariffs and Trade and Creating the World Trade Organization)

Signed by the Members of GATT, April 15, 1994 at Marrakesh, Morocco

*TABLE OF CONTENTS*

———

*Members,*

*Desiring* to reduce distortions and impediments to international trade, and taking into account the need to promote effective and adequate protection of intellectual property rights, and to ensure that measures and procedures to enforce intellectual property rights do not themselves become barriers to legitimate trade;

*Recognizing*, to this end, the need for new rules and disciplines concerning:

(a) the applicability of the basic principles of GATT 1994 and of relevant international intellectual property agreements or conventions;

(b) the provision of adequate standards and principles concerning the availability, scope and use of trade-related intellectual property rights;

1

(c)    the provision of effective and appropriate means for the enforcement of trade-related intellectual property rights, taking into account differences in national legal systems;

(d)    the provision of effective and expeditious procedures for the multilateral prevention and settlement of disputes between governments; and

(e)    transitional arrangements aiming at the fullest participation in the results of the negotiations;

*Recognizing* the need for a multilateral framework of principles, rules and disciplines dealing with international trade in counterfeit goods;

*Recognizing* that intellectual property rights are private rights;

*Recognizing* the underlying public policy objectives of national systems for the protection of intellectual property, including developmental and technological objectives;

*Recognizing* also the special needs of the least-developed country Members in respect of maximum flexibility in the domestic implementation of laws and regulations in order to enable them to create a sound and viable technological base;

*Emphasizing* the importance of reducing tensions by reaching strengthened commitments to resolve disputes on trade-related intellectual property issues through multilateral procedures;

*Desiring* to establish a mutually supportive relationship between the WTO and the World Intellectual Property Organization (referred to in this Agreement as "WIPO") as well as other relevant international organizations;

*Hereby agree* as follows:

PART I
GENERAL PROVISIONS AND BASIC PRINCIPLES

*Article 1*
*Nature and Scope of Obligations*

1.    Members shall give effect to the provisions of this Agreement. Members may, but shall not be obliged to, implement in their law more extensive protection than is required by this Agreement, provided that such protection does not contravene the provisions of this Agreement. Members shall be free to determine the appropriate method of implementing the provisions of this Agreement within their own legal system and practice.

2.    For the purposes of this Agreement, the term "intellectual property" refers to all categories of intellectual property that are the subject of Sections 1 through 7 of Part II.

3.    Members shall accord the treatment provided for in this Agreement to the nationals of other Members.[1] In respect of the relevant intellectual property right, the nationals of other Members shall be understood as those natural or legal persons that would meet the criteria for eligibility for protection provided for in the Paris Convention (1967), the Berne Convention (1971), the Rome Convention and the Treaty on Intellectual Property in Respect of Integrated Circuits, were all Members of the WTO members of those conventions.[2] Any Member availing itself of the possibilities

---

[1]    When "nationals" are referred to in this Agreement, they shall be deemed, in the case of a separate customs territory Member of the WTO, to mean persons, natural or legal, who are domiciled or who have a real and effective industrial or commercial establishment in that customs territory.

[2]    In this Agreement, "Paris Convention" refers to the Paris Convention for the Protection of Industrial Property; "Paris Convention (1967)" refers to the Stockholm Act of this Convention of 14 July 1967. "Berne Convention" refers to the Berne Convention for the Protection of Literary and Artistic Works; "Berne Convention (1971)" refers to the Paris Act of this Convention of 24 July 1971. "Rome Convention" refers to the International Convention for the Protection of Performers, Producers of Phonograms and Broadcasting Organizations, adopted at Rome on 26 October 1961. "Treaty on Intellectual Property in Respect of Integrated Circuits" (IPIC Treaty) refers to the Treaty on Intellectual Property in

2

provided in paragraph 3 of Article 5 or paragraph 2 of Article 6 of the Rome Convention shall make a notification as foreseen in those provisions to the Council for Trade-Related Aspects of Intellectual Property Rights (the "Council for TRIPS").

## Article 2
### Intellectual Property Conventions

1.    In respect of Parts II, III and IV of this Agreement, Members shall comply with Articles 1 through 12, and Article 19, of the Paris Convention (1967).

2.    Nothing in Parts I to IV of this Agreement shall derogate from existing obligations that Members may have to each other under the Paris Convention, the Berne Convention, the Rome Convention and the Treaty on Intellectual Property in Respect of Integrated Circuits.

## Article 3
### National Treatment

1.    Each Member shall accord to the nationals of other Members treatment no less favourable than that it accords to its own nationals with regard to the protection[3] of intellectual property, subject to the exceptions already provided in, respectively, the Paris Convention (1967), the Berne Convention (1971), the Rome Convention or the Treaty on Intellectual Property in Respect of Integrated Circuits. In respect of performers, producers of phonograms and broadcasting organizations, this obligation only applies in respect of the rights provided under this Agreement. Any Member availing itself of the possibilities provided in Article 6 of the Berne Convention (1971) or paragraph 1(b) of Article 16 of the Rome Convention shall make a notification as foreseen in those provisions to the Council for TRIPS.

2.    Members may avail themselves of the exceptions permitted under paragraph 1 in relation to judicial and administrative procedures, including the designation of an address for service or the appointment of an agent within the jurisdiction of a Member, only where such exceptions are necessary to secure compliance with laws and regulations which are not inconsistent with the provisions of this Agreement and where such practices are not applied in a manner which would constitute a disguised restriction on trade.

## Article 4
### Most-Favoured-Nation Treatment

With regard to the protection of intellectual property, any advantage, favour, privilege or immunity granted by a Member to the nationals of any other country shall be accorded immediately and unconditionally to the nationals of all other Members. Exempted from this obligation are any advantage, favour, privilege or immunity accorded by a Member:

(a)    deriving from international agreements on judicial assistance or law enforcement of a general nature and not particularly confined to the protection of intellectual property;

(b)    granted in accordance with the provisions of the Berne Convention (1971) or the Rome Convention authorizing that the treatment accorded be a function not of national treatment but of the treatment accorded in another country;

(c)    in respect of the rights of performers, producers of phonograms and broadcasting organizations not provided under this Agreement;

(d)    deriving from international agreements related to the protection of intellectual property which entered into force prior to the entry into force of the WTO Agreement, provided that

---

Respect of Integrated Circuits, adopted at Washington on 26 May 1989. "WTO Agreement" refers to the Agreement Establishing the WTO.

    [3]    For the purposes of Articles 3 and 4, "protection" shall include matters affecting the availability, acquisition, scope, maintenance and enforcement of intellectual property rights as well as those matters affecting the use of intellectual property rights specifically addressed in this Agreement.

such agreements are notified to the Council for TRIPS and do not constitute an arbitrary or unjustifiable discrimination against nationals of other Members.

*Article 5*
*Multilateral Agreements on Acquisition or Maintenance of Protection*

The obligations under Articles 3 and 4 do not apply to procedures provided in multilateral agreements concluded under the auspices of WIPO relating to the acquisition or maintenance of intellectual property rights.

*Article 6*
*Exhaustion*

For the purposes of dispute settlement under this Agreement, subject to the provisions of Articles 3 and 4 nothing in this Agreement shall be used to address the issue of the exhaustion of intellectual property rights.

*Article 7*
*Objectives*

The protection and enforcement of intellectual property rights should contribute to the promotion of technological innovation and to the transfer and dissemination of technology, to the mutual advantage of producers and users of technological knowledge and in a manner conducive to social and economic welfare, and to a balance of rights and obligations.

*Article 8*
*Principles*

1.　Members may, in formulating or amending their laws and regulations, adopt measures necessary to protect public health and nutrition, and to promote the public interest in sectors of vital importance to their socio-economic and technological development, provided that such measures are consistent with the provisions of this Agreement.

2.　Appropriate measures, provided that they are consistent with the provisions of this Agreement, may be needed to prevent the abuse of intellectual property rights by right holders or the resort to practices which unreasonably restrain trade or adversely affect the international transfer of technology.

PART II
STANDARDS CONCERNING THE AVAILABILITY, SCOPE
AND USE OF INTELLECTUAL PROPERTY RIGHTS
SECTION 1: COPYRIGHT AND RELATED RIGHTS

*Article 9*
*Relation to the Berne Convention*

1.　Members shall comply with Articles 1 through 21 of the Berne Convention (1971) and the Appendix thereto. However, Members shall not have rights or obligations under this Agreement in respect of the rights conferred under Article 6*bis* of that Convention or of the rights derived therefrom.

2.　Copyright protection shall extend to expressions and not to ideas, procedures, methods of operation or mathematical concepts as such.

*Article 10*
*Computer Programs and Compilations of Data*

1.　Computer programs, whether in source or object code, shall be protected as literary works under the Berne Convention (1971).

4

2.     Compilations of data or other material, whether in machine readable or other form, which by reason of the selection or arrangement of their contents constitute intellectual creations shall be protected as such. Such protection, which shall not extend to the data or material itself, shall be without prejudice to any copyright subsisting in the data or material itself.

## Article 11
### Rental Rights

In respect of at least computer programs and cinematographic works, a Member shall provide authors and their successors in title the right to authorize or to prohibit the commercial rental to the public of originals or copies of their copyright works. A Member shall be excepted from this obligation in respect of cinematographic works unless such rental has led to widespread copying of such works which is materially impairing the exclusive right of reproduction conferred in that Member on authors and their successors in title. In respect of computer programs, this obligation does not apply to rentals where the program itself is not the essential object of the rental.

## Article 12
### Term of Protection

Whenever the term of protection of a work, other than a photographic work or a work of applied art, is calculated on a basis other than the life of a natural person, such term shall be no less than 50 years from the end of the calendar year of authorized publication, or, failing such authorized publication within 50 years from the making of the work, 50 years from the end of the calendar year of making.

## Article 13
### Limitations and Exceptions

Members shall confine limitations or exceptions to exclusive rights to certain special cases which do not conflict with a normal exploitation of the work and do not unreasonably prejudice the legitimate interests of the right holder.     *Three step test*

## Article 14
### Protection of Performers, Producers of Phonograms
### (Sound Recordings) and Broadcasting Organizations

1.     In respect of a fixation of their performance on a phonogram, performers shall have the possibility of preventing the following acts when undertaken without their authorization: the fixation of their unfixed performance and the reproduction of such fixation. Performers shall also have the possibility of preventing the following acts when undertaken without their authorization: the broadcasting by wireless means and the communication to the public of their live performance.

2.     Producers of phonograms shall enjoy the right to authorize or prohibit the direct or indirect reproduction of their phonograms.

3.     Broadcasting organizations shall have the right to prohibit the following acts when undertaken without their authorization: the fixation, the reproduction of fixations, and the rebroadcasting by wireless means of broadcasts, as well as the communication to the public of television broadcasts of the same. Where Members do not grant such rights to broadcasting organizations, they shall provide owners of copyright in the subject matter of broadcasts with the possibility of preventing the above acts, subject to the provisions of the Berne Convention (1971).

4.     The provisions of Article 11 in respect of computer programs shall apply *mutatis mutandis* to producers of phonograms and any other right holders in phonograms as determined in a Member's law. If on 15 April 1994 a Member has in force a system of equitable remuneration of right holders in respect of the rental of phonograms, it may maintain such system provided that the commercial rental of phonograms is not giving rise to the material impairment of the exclusive rights of reproduction of right holders.

5.    The term of the protection available under this Agreement to performers and producers of phonograms shall last at least until the end of a period of **50** years computed from the end of the calendar year in which the fixation was made or the performance took place. The term of protection granted pursuant to paragraph 3 shall last for at least **20** years from the end of the calendar year in which the broadcast took place.

6.    Any Member may, in relation to the rights conferred under paragraphs 1, 2 and 3, provide for conditions, limitations, exceptions and reservations to the extent permitted by the Rome Convention. However, the provisions of Article 18 of the Berne Convention (1971) shall also apply, *mutatis mutandis*, to the rights of performers and producers of phonograms in phonograms.

SECTION 2: TRADEMARKS

*Article 15*
*Protectable Subject Matter*

1.    Any sign, or any combination of signs, capable of distinguishing the goods or services of one undertaking from those of other undertakings, shall be capable of constituting a trademark. Such signs, in particular words including personal names, letters, numerals, figurative elements and combinations of colours as well as any combination of such signs, shall be eligible for registration as trademarks. Where signs are not inherently capable of distinguishing the relevant goods or services, Members may make registrability depend on distinctiveness acquired through use. Members may require, as a condition of registration, that signs be visually perceptible.

2.    Paragraph 1 shall not be understood to prevent a Member from denying registration of a trademark on other grounds, provided that they do not derogate from the provisions of the Paris Convention (1967).

3.    Members may make registrability depend on use. However, actual use of a trademark shall not be a condition for filing an application for registration. An application shall not be refused solely on the ground that intended use has not taken place before the expiry of a period of three years from the date of application.

4.    The nature of the goods or services to which a trademark is to be applied shall in no case form an obstacle to registration of the trademark.

5.    Members shall publish each trademark either before it is registered or promptly after it is registered and shall afford a reasonable opportunity for petitions to cancel the registration. In addition, Members may afford an opportunity for the registration of a trademark to be opposed.

*Article 16*
*Rights Conferred*

1.    The owner of a registered trademark shall have the exclusive right to prevent all third parties not having the owner's consent from using in the course of trade identical or similar signs for goods or services which are identical or similar to those in respect of which the trademark is registered where such use would result in a likelihood of confusion. In case of the use of an identical sign for identical goods or services, a likelihood of confusion shall be presumed. The rights described above shall not prejudice any existing prior rights, nor shall they affect the possibility of Members making rights available on the basis of use.

2.    Article 6*bis* of the Paris Convention (1967) shall apply, *mutatis mutandis*, to services. In determining whether a trademark is well-known, Members shall take account of the knowledge of the trademark in the relevant sector of the public, including knowledge in the Member concerned which has been obtained as a result of the promotion of the trademark.

3.    Article 6*bis* of the Paris Convention (1967) shall apply, *mutatis mutandis*, to goods or services which are not similar to those in respect of which a trademark is registered, provided that use of that trademark in relation to those goods or services would indicate a connection between those goods or

services and the owner of the registered trademark and provided that the interests of the owner of the registered trademark are likely to be damaged by such use.

*Article 17*
*Exceptions*

Members may provide limited exceptions to the rights conferred by a trademark, such as fair use of descriptive terms, provided that such exceptions take account of the legitimate interests of the owner of the trademark and of third parties.

*Article 18*
*Term of Protection*

Initial registration, and each renewal of registration, of a trademark shall be for a term of no less than seven years. The registration of a trademark shall be renewable indefinitely.

*Article 19*
*Requirement of Use*

1.   If use is required to maintain a registration, the registration may be cancelled only after an uninterrupted period of at least three years of non-use, unless valid reasons based on the existence of obstacles to such use are shown by the trademark owner. Circumstances arising independently of the will of the owner of the trademark which constitute an obstacle to the use of the trademark, such as import restrictions on or other government requirements for goods or services protected by the trademark, shall be recognized as valid reasons for non-use.

2.   When subject to the control of its owner, use of a trademark by another person shall be recognized as use of the trademark for the purpose of maintaining the registration.

*Article 20*
*Other Requirements*

The use of a trademark in the course of trade shall not be unjustifiably encumbered by special requirements, such as use with another trademark, use in a special form or use in a manner detrimental to its capability to distinguish the goods or services of one undertaking from those of other undertakings. This will not preclude a requirement prescribing the use of the trademark identifying the undertaking producing the goods or services along with, but without linking it to, the trademark distinguishing the specific goods or services in question of that undertaking.

*Article 21*
*Licensing and Assignment*

Members may determine conditions on the licensing and assignment of trademarks, it being understood that the compulsory licensing of trademarks shall not be permitted and that the owner of a registered trademark shall have the right to assign the trademark with or without the transfer of the business to which the trademark belongs.

## SECTION 3: GEOGRAPHICAL INDICATIONS

*Article 22*
*Protection of Geographical Indications*

1.   Geographical indications are, for the purposes of this Agreement, indications which identify a good as originating in the territory of a Member, or a region or locality in that territory, where a given quality, reputation or other characteristic of the good is essentially attributable to its geographical origin.

2.   In respect of geographical indications, Members shall provide the legal means for interested parties to prevent:

(a)  the use of any means in the designation or presentation of a good that indicates or suggests that the good in question originates in a geographical area other than the true place of origin in a manner which misleads the public as to the geographical origin of the good;

(b)  any use which constitutes an act of unfair competition within the meaning of Article 10*bis* of the Paris Convention (1967).

3.  A Member shall, *ex officio* if its legislation so permits or at the request of an interested party, refuse or invalidate the registration of a trademark which contains or consists of a geographical indication with respect to goods not originating in the territory indicated, if use of the indication in the trademark for such goods in that Member is of such a nature as to mislead the public as to the true place of origin.

4.  The protection under paragraphs 1, 2 and 3 shall be applicable against a geographical indication which, although literally true as to the territory, region or locality in which the goods originate, falsely represents to the public that the goods originate in another territory.

### Article 23
### Additional Protection for Geographical Indications for Wines and Spirits

1.  Each Member shall provide the legal means for interested parties to prevent use of a geographical indication identifying wines for wines not originating in the place indicated by the geographical indication in question or identifying spirits for spirits not originating in the place indicated by the geographical indication in question, even where the true origin of the goods is indicated or the geographical indication is used in translation or accompanied by expressions such as "kind", "type", "style", "imitation" or the like.[4]

2.  The registration of a trademark for wines which contains or consists of a geographical indication identifying wines or for spirits which contains or consists of a geographical indication identifying spirits shall be refused or invalidated, *ex officio* if a Member's legislation so permits or at the request of an interested party, with respect to such wines or spirits not having this origin.

3.  In the case of homonymous geographical indications for wines, protection shall be accorded to each indication, subject to the provisions of paragraph 4 of Article 22. Each Member shall determine the practical conditions under which the homonymous indications in question will be differentiated from each other, taking into account the need to ensure equitable treatment of the producers concerned and that consumers are not misled.

4.  In order to facilitate the protection of geographical indications for wines, negotiations shall be undertaken in the Council for TRIPS concerning the establishment of a multilateral system of notification and registration of geographical indications for wines eligible for protection in those Members participating in the system.

### Article 24
### International Negotiations; Exceptions

1.  Members agree to enter into negotiations aimed at increasing the protection of individual geographical indications under Article 23. The provisions of paragraphs 4 through 8 below shall not be used by a Member to refuse to conduct negotiations or to conclude bilateral or multilateral agreements. In the context of such negotiations, Members shall be willing to consider the continued applicability of these provisions to individual geographical indications whose use was the subject of such negotiations.

2.  The Council for TRIPS shall keep under review the application of the provisions of this Section; the first such review shall take place within two years of the entry into force of the WTO Agreement. Any matter affecting the compliance with the obligations under these provisions may be drawn to the

---

[4]  Notwithstanding the first sentence of Article 42, Members may, with respect to these obligations, instead provide for enforcement by administrative action.

attention of the Council, which, at the request of a Member, shall consult with any Member or Members in respect of such matter in respect of which it has not been possible to find a satisfactory solution through bilateral or plurilateral consultations between the Members concerned. The Council shall take such action as may be agreed to facilitate the operation and further the objectives of this Section.

3.    In implementing this Section, a Member shall not diminish the protection of geographical indications that existed in that Member immediately prior to the date of entry into force of the WTO Agreement.

4.    Nothing in this Section shall require a Member to prevent continued and similar use of a particular geographical indication of another Member identifying wines or spirits in connection with goods or services by any of its nationals or domiciliaries who have used that geographical indication in a continuous manner with regard to the same or related goods or services in the territory of that Member either (*a*) for at least 10 years preceding 15 April 1994 or (*b*) in good faith preceding that date.

5.    Where a trademark has been applied for or registered in good faith, or where rights to a trademark have been acquired through use in good faith either:

(a)   before the date of application of these provisions in that Member as defined in Part VI; or

(b)   before the geographical indication is protected in its country of origin;

measures adopted to implement this Section shall not prejudice eligibility for or the validity of the registration of a trademark, or the right to use a trademark, on the basis that such a trademark is identical with, or similar to, a geographical indication.

6.    Nothing in this Section shall require a Member to apply its provisions in respect of a geographical indication of any other Member with respect to goods or services for which the relevant indication is identical with the term customary in common language as the common name for such goods or services in the territory of that Member. Nothing in this Section shall require a Member to apply its provisions in respect of a geographical indication of any other Member with respect to products of the vine for which the relevant indication is identical with the customary name of a grape variety existing in the territory of that Member as of the date of entry into force of the WTO Agreement.

7.    A Member may provide that any request made under this Section in connection with the use or registration of a trademark must be presented within five years after the adverse use of the protected indication has become generally known in that Member or after the date of registration of the trademark in that Member provided that the trademark has been published by that date, if such date is earlier than the date on which the adverse use became generally known in that Member, provided that the geographical indication is not used or registered in bad faith.

8.    The provisions of this Section shall in no way prejudice the right of any person to use, in the course of trade, that person's name or the name of that person's predecessor in business, except where such name is used in such a manner as to mislead the public.

9.    There shall be no obligation under this Agreement to protect geographical indications which are not or cease to be protected in their country of origin, or which have fallen into disuse in that country.

## SECTION 4: INDUSTRIAL DESIGNS

*Article 25*
*Requirements for Protection*

1.    Members shall provide for the protection of independently created industrial designs that are new or original. Members may provide that designs are not new or original if they do not significantly differ from known designs or combinations of known design features. Members may provide that such protection shall not extend to designs dictated essentially by technical or functional considerations.

2.    Each Member shall ensure that requirements for securing protection for textile designs, in particular in regard to any cost, examination or publication, do not unreasonably impair the

opportunity to seek and obtain such protection. Members shall be free to meet this obligation through industrial design law or through copyright law.

*Article 26*
*Protection*

1. The owner of a protected industrial design shall have the right to prevent third parties not having the owner's consent from making, selling or importing articles bearing or embodying a design which is a copy, or substantially a copy, of the protected design, when such acts are undertaken for commercial purposes.

2. Members may provide limited exceptions to the protection of industrial designs, provided that such exceptions do not unreasonably conflict with the normal exploitation of protected industrial designs and do not unreasonably prejudice the legitimate interests of the owner of the protected design, taking account of the legitimate interests of third parties.

3. The duration of protection available shall amount to at least 10 years.

## SECTION 5: PATENTS

*Article 27*
*Patentable Subject Matter*

1. Subject to the provisions of paragraphs 2 and 3, patents shall be available for any inventions, whether products or processes, in all fields of technology, provided that they are new, involve an inventive step and are capable of industrial application.[5] Subject to paragraph 4 of Article 65, paragraph 8 of Article 70 and paragraph 3 of this Article, patents shall be available and patent rights enjoyable without discrimination as to the place of invention, the field of technology and whether products are imported or locally produced. — Shouldn't discriminate / deny patent just because something is being import.

2. Members may exclude from patentability inventions, the prevention within their territory of the commercial exploitation of which is necessary to protect *ordre public* or morality, including to protect human, animal or plant life or health or to avoid serious prejudice to the environment, provided that such exclusion is not made merely because the exploitation is prohibited by their law.

3. Members may also exclude from patentability:

    (a) diagnostic, therapeutic and surgical methods for the treatment of humans or animals;

    (b) plants and animals other than micro-organisms, and essentially biological processes for the production of plants or animals other than non-biological and microbiological processes. However, Members shall provide for the protection of plant varieties either by patents or by an effective *sui generis* system or by any combination thereof. The provisions of this subparagraph shall be reviewed four years after the date of entry into force of the WTO Agreement.

*Article 28*
*Rights Conferred*

1. A patent shall confer on its owner the following exclusive rights:

    (a) where the subject matter of a patent is a product, to prevent third parties not having the owner's consent from the acts of: making, using, offering for sale, selling, or importing[6] for these purposes that product;

---

  [5] For the purposes of this Article, the terms "inventive step" and "capable of industrial application" may be deemed by a Member to be synonymous with the terms "non-obvious" and "useful" respectively.

  [6] This right, like all other rights conferred under this Agreement in respect of the use, sale, importation or other distribution of goods, is subject to the provisions of Article 6.

(b)   where the subject matter of a patent is a process, to prevent third parties not having the owner's consent from the act of using the process, and from the acts of: using, offering for sale, selling, or importing for these purposes at least the product obtained directly by that process.

2.   Patent owners shall also have the right to assign, or transfer by succession, the patent and to conclude licensing contracts.

*Article 29*
*Conditions on Patent Applicants*

1.   Members shall require that an applicant for a patent shall disclose the invention in a manner sufficiently clear and complete for the invention to be carried out by a person skilled in the art and may require the applicant to indicate the best mode for carrying out the invention known to the inventor at the filing date or, where priority is claimed, at the priority date of the application.

2.   Members may require an applicant for a patent to provide information concerning the applicant's corresponding foreign applications and grants.

*Article 30*
*Exceptions to Rights Conferred*

Members may provide limited exceptions to the exclusive rights conferred by a patent, provided that such exceptions do not unreasonably conflict with a normal exploitation of the patent and do not unreasonably prejudice the legitimate interests of the patent owner, taking account of the legitimate interests of third parties.

*Article 31*
*Other Use Without Authorization of the Right Holder*

Where the law of a Member allows for other use[7] of the subject matter of a patent without the authorization of the right holder, including use by the government or third parties authorized by the government, the following provisions shall be respected:

(a)   authorization of such use shall be considered on its individual merits;

(b)   such use may only be permitted if, prior to such use, the proposed user has made efforts to obtain authorization from the right holder on reasonable commercial terms and conditions and that such efforts have not been successful within a reasonable period of time. This requirement may be waived by a Member in the case of a national emergency or other circumstances of extreme urgency or in cases of public non-commercial use. In situations of national emergency or other circumstances of extreme urgency, the right holder shall, nevertheless, be notified as soon as reasonably practicable. In the case of public non-commercial use, where the government or contractor, without making a patent search, knows or has demonstrable grounds to know that a valid patent is or will be used by or for the government, the right holder shall be informed promptly;

(c)   the scope and duration of such use shall be limited to the purpose for which it was authorized, and in the case of semi-conductor technology shall only be for public non-commercial use or to remedy a practice determined after judicial or administrative process to be anti-competitive;

(d)   such use shall be non-exclusive;

(e)   such use shall be non-assignable, except with that part of the enterprise or goodwill which enjoys such use;

---

7   "Other use" refers to use other than that allowed under Article 30.

(f) any such use shall be authorized predominantly for the supply of the domestic market of the Member authorizing such use;

(g) authorization for such use shall be liable, subject to adequate protection of the legitimate interests of the persons so authorized, to be terminated if and when the circumstances which led to it cease to exist and are unlikely to recur. The competent authority shall have the authority to review, upon motivated request, the continued existence of these circumstances;

(h) the right holder shall be paid adequate remuneration in the circumstances of each case, taking into account the economic value of the authorization;

(i) the legal validity of any decision relating to the authorization of such use shall be subject to judicial review or other independent review by a distinct higher authority in that Member;

(j) any decision relating to the remuneration provided in respect of such use shall be subject to judicial review or other independent review by a distinct higher authority in that Member;

(k) Members are not obliged to apply the conditions set forth in subparagraphs (b) and (f) where such use is permitted to remedy a practice determined after judicial or administrative process to be anti-competitive. The need to correct anti-competitive practices may be taken into account in determining the amount of remuneration in such cases. Competent authorities shall have the authority to refuse termination of authorization if and when the conditions which led to such authorization are likely to recur;

(l) where such use is authorized to permit the exploitation of a patent ("the second patent") which cannot be exploited without infringing another patent ("the first patent"), the following additional conditions shall apply:

  (i) the invention claimed in the second patent shall involve an important technical advance of considerable economic significance in relation to the invention claimed in the first patent;

  (ii) the owner of the first patent shall be entitled to a cross-licence on reasonable terms to use the invention claimed in the second patent; and

  (iii) the use authorized in respect of the first patent shall be non-assignable except with the assignment of the second patent.

### Article 31bis

1. The obligations of an exporting Member under Article 31(f) shall not apply with respect to the grant by it of a compulsory licence to the extent necessary for the purposes of production of a pharmaceutical product(s) and its export to an eligible importing Member(s) in accordance with the terms set out in paragraph 2 of the Annex to this Agreement.

2. Where a compulsory licence is granted by an exporting Member under the system set out in this Article and the Annex to this Agreement, adequate remuneration pursuant to Article 31(h) shall be paid in that Member taking into account the economic value to the importing Member of the use that has been authorized in the exporting Member. Where a compulsory licence is granted for the same products in the eligible importing Member, the obligation of that Member under Article 31(h) shall not apply in respect of those products for which remuneration in accordance with the first sentence of this paragraph is paid in the exporting Member.

3. With a view to harnessing economies of scale for the purposes of enhancing purchasing power for, and facilitating the local production of, pharmaceutical products: where a developing or least developed country WTO Member is a party to a regional trade agreement within the meaning of Article XXIV of the GATT 1994 and the Decision of 28 November 1979 on Differential and More Favourable Treatment Reciprocity and Fuller Participation of Developing Countries (L/4903), at least half of the current membership of which is made up of countries presently on the United Nations list of least developed countries, the obligation of that Member under Article 31(f) shall not apply to the extent

necessary to enable a pharmaceutical product produced or imported under a compulsory licence in that Member to be exported to the markets of those other developing or least developed country parties to the regional trade agreement that share the health problem in question. It is understood that this will not prejudice the territorial nature of the patent rights in question.

4.    Members shall not challenge any measures taken in conformity with the provisions of this Article and the Annex to this Agreement under subparagraphs 1(b) and 1(c) of Article XXIII of GATT 1994.

5.    This Article and the Annex to this Agreement are without prejudice to the rights, obligations and flexibilities that Members have under the provisions of this Agreement other than paragraphs (f) and (h) of Article 31, including those reaffirmed by the Declaration on the TRIPS Agreement and Public Health (WT/MIN(01)/DEC/2), and to their interpretation. They are also without prejudice to the extent to which pharmaceutical products produced under a compulsory licence can be exported under the provisions of Article 31(f).

### Article 32
### *Revocation/Forfeiture*

An opportunity for judicial review of any decision to revoke or forfeit a patent shall be available.

### Article 33
### *Term of Protection*

The term of protection available shall not end before the expiration of a period of twenty years counted from the filing date.[8]

### Article 34
### *Process Patents: Burden of Proof*

1.    For the purposes of civil proceedings in respect of the infringement of the rights of the owner referred to in paragraph 1(b) of Article 28, if the subject matter of a patent is a process for obtaining a product, the judicial authorities shall have the authority to order the defendant to prove that the process to obtain an identical product is different from the patented process. Therefore, Members shall provide, in at least one of the following circumstances, that any identical product when produced without the consent of the patent owner shall, in the absence of proof to the contrary, be deemed to have been obtained by the patented process:

(a)    if the product obtained by the patented process is new;

(b)    if there is a substantial likelihood that the identical product was made by the process and the owner of the patent has been unable through reasonable efforts to determine the process actually used.

2.    Any Member shall be free to provide that the burden of proof indicated in paragraph 1 shall be on the alleged infringer only if the condition referred to in subparagraph (a) is fulfilled or only if the condition referred to in subparagraph (b) is fulfilled.

3.    In the adduction of proof to the contrary, the legitimate interests of defendants in protecting their manufacturing and business secrets shall be taken into account.

### SECTION 6: LAYOUT-DESIGNS (TOPOGRAPHIES) OF INTEGRATED CIRCUITS

### Article 35
### *Relation to the IPIC Treaty*

Members agree to provide protection to the layout-designs (topographies) of integrated circuits (referred to in this Agreement as "layout-designs") in accordance with Articles 2 through 7 (other than

---

[8]    It is understood that those Members which do not have a system of original grant may provide that the term of protection shall be computed from the filing date in the system of original grant.

paragraph 3 of Article 6), Article 12 and paragraph 3 of Article 16 of the Treaty on Intellectual Property in Respect of Integrated Circuits and, in addition, to comply with the following provisions.

## Article 36
### Scope of the Protection

Subject to the provisions of paragraph 1 of Article 37, Members shall consider unlawful the following acts if performed without the authorization of the right holder:[9] importing, selling, or otherwise distributing for commercial purposes a protected layout-design, an integrated circuit in which a protected layout-design is incorporated, or an article incorporating such an integrated circuit only in so far as it continues to contain an unlawfully reproduced layout-design.

## Article 37
### Acts Not Requiring the Authorization of the Right Holder

1.    Notwithstanding Article 36, no Member shall consider unlawful the performance of any of the acts referred to in that Article in respect of an integrated circuit incorporating an unlawfully reproduced layout-design or any article incorporating such an integrated circuit where the person performing or ordering such acts did not know and had no reasonable ground to know, when acquiring the integrated circuit or article incorporating such an integrated circuit, that it incorporated an unlawfully reproduced layout-design. Members shall provide that, after the time that such person has received sufficient notice that the layout-design was unlawfully reproduced, that person may perform any of the acts with respect to the stock on hand or ordered before such time, but shall be liable to pay to the right holder a sum equivalent to a reasonable royalty such as would be payable under a freely negotiated licence in respect of such a layout-design.

2.    The conditions set out in subparagraphs (a) through (k) of Article 31 shall apply *mutatis mutandis* in the event of any non-voluntary licensing of a layout-design or of its use by or for the government without the authorization of the right holder.

## Article 38
### Term of Protection

1.    In Members requiring registration as a condition of protection, the term of protection of layout-designs shall not end before the expiration of a period of 10 years counted from the date of filing an application for registration or from the first commercial exploitation wherever in the world it occurs.

2.    In Members not requiring registration as a condition for protection, layout-designs shall be protected for a term of no less than 10 years from the date of the first commercial exploitation wherever in the world it occurs.

3.    Notwithstanding paragraphs 1 and 2, a Member may provide that protection shall lapse 15 years after the creation of the layout-design.

### SECTION 7: PROTECTION OF UNDISCLOSED INFORMATION

## Article 39

1.    In the course of ensuring effective protection against unfair competition as provided in Article 10*bis* of the Paris Convention (1967), Members shall protect undisclosed information in accordance with paragraph 2 and data submitted to governments or governmental agencies in accordance with paragraph 3.

---

[9]    The term "right holder" in this Section shall be understood as having the same meaning as the term "holder of the right" in the IPIC Treaty.

2.    Natural and legal persons shall have the possibility of preventing information lawfully within their control from being disclosed to, acquired by, or used by others without their consent in a manner contrary to honest commercial practices[10] so long as such information:

(a)    is secret in the sense that it is not, as a body or in the precise configuration and assembly of its components, generally known among or readily accessible to persons within the circles that normally deal with the kind of information in question;

(b)    has commercial value because it is secret; and

(c)    has been subject to reasonable steps under the circumstances, by the person lawfully in control of the information, to keep it secret.

3.    Members, when requiring, as a condition of approving the marketing of pharmaceutical or of agricultural chemical products which utilize new chemical entities, the submission of undisclosed test or other data, the origination of which involves a considerable effort, shall protect such data against unfair commercial use. In addition, Members shall protect such data against disclosure, except where necessary to protect the public, or unless steps are taken to ensure that the data are protected against unfair commercial use.

## SECTION 8: CONTROL OF ANTI-COMPETITIVE PRACTICES IN CONTRACTUAL LICENCES

### *Article 40*

1.    Members agree that some licensing practices or conditions pertaining to intellectual property rights which restrain competition may have adverse effects on trade and may impede the transfer and dissemination of technology.

2.    Nothing in this Agreement shall prevent Members from specifying in their legislation licensing practices or conditions that may in particular cases constitute an abuse of intellectual property rights having an adverse effect on competition in the relevant market. As provided above, a Member may adopt, consistently with the other provisions of this Agreement, appropriate measures to prevent or control such practices, which may include for example exclusive grantback conditions, conditions preventing challenges to validity and coercive package licensing, in the light of the relevant laws and regulations of that Member.

3.    Each Member shall enter, upon request, into consultations with any other Member which has cause to believe that an intellectual property right owner that is a national or domiciliary of the Member to which the request for consultations has been addressed is undertaking practices in violation of the requesting Member's laws and regulations on the subject matter of this Section, and which wishes to secure compliance with such legislation, without prejudice to any action under the law and to the full freedom of an ultimate decision of either Member. The Member addressed shall accord full and sympathetic consideration to, and shall afford adequate opportunity for, consultations with the requesting Member, and shall cooperate through supply of publicly available non-confidential information of relevance to the matter in question and of other information available to the Member, subject to domestic law and to the conclusion of mutually satisfactory agreements concerning the safeguarding of its confidentiality by the requesting Member.

4.    A Member whose nationals or domiciliaries are subject to proceedings in another Member concerning alleged violation of that other Member's laws and regulations on the subject matter of this Section shall, upon request, be granted an opportunity for consultations by the other Member under the same conditions as those foreseen in paragraph 3.

---

[10]   For the purpose of this provision, "a manner contrary to honest commercial practices" shall mean at least practices such as breach of contract, breach of confidence and inducement to breach, and includes the acquisition of undisclosed information by third parties who knew, or were grossly negligent in failing to know, that such practices were involved in the acquisition.

## PART III
## ENFORCEMENT OF INTELLECTUAL PROPERTY RIGHTS
### SECTION 1: GENERAL OBLIGATIONS

*Article 41* •

1.    Members shall ensure that enforcement procedures as specified in this Part are available under their law so as to permit effective action against any act of infringement of intellectual property rights covered by this Agreement, including expeditious remedies to prevent infringements and remedies which constitute a deterrent to further infringements. These procedures shall be applied in such a manner as to avoid the creation of barriers to legitimate trade and to provide for safeguards against their abuse.

2.    Procedures concerning the enforcement of intellectual property rights shall be fair and equitable. They shall not be unnecessarily complicated or costly, or entail unreasonable time-limits or unwarranted delays.

3.    Decisions on the merits of a case shall preferably be in writing and reasoned. They shall be made available at least to the parties to the proceeding without undue delay. Decisions on the merits of a case shall be based only on evidence in respect of which parties were offered the opportunity to be heard.

4.    Parties to a proceeding shall have an opportunity for review by a judicial authority of final administrative decisions and, subject to jurisdictional provisions in a Member's law concerning the importance of a case, of at least the legal aspects of initial judicial decisions on the merits of a case. However, there shall be no obligation to provide an opportunity for review of acquittals in criminal cases.

5.    It is understood that this Part does not create any obligation to put in place a judicial system for the enforcement of intellectual property rights distinct from that for the enforcement of law in general, nor does it affect the capacity of Members to enforce their law in general. Nothing in this Part creates any obligation with respect to the distribution of resources as between enforcement of intellectual property rights and the enforcement of law in general.

### SECTION 2: CIVIL AND ADMINISTRATIVE
### PROCEDURES AND REMEDIES

*Article 42*
*Fair and Equitable Procedures*

Members shall make available to right holders[11] civil judicial procedures concerning the enforcement of any intellectual property right covered by this Agreement. Defendants shall have the right to written notice which is timely and contains sufficient detail, including the basis of the claims. Parties shall be allowed to be represented by independent legal counsel, and procedures shall not impose overly burdensome requirements concerning mandatory personal appearances. All parties to such procedures shall be duly entitled to substantiate their claims and to present all relevant evidence. The procedure shall provide a means to identify and protect confidential information, unless this would be contrary to existing constitutional requirements.

*Article 43*
*Evidence*

1.    The judicial authorities shall have the authority, where a party has presented reasonably available evidence sufficient to support its claims and has specified evidence relevant to substantiation of its claims which lies in the control of the opposing party, to order that this evidence be produced by

---

[11]  For the purpose of this Part, the term "right holder" includes federations and associations having legal standing to assert such rights.

the opposing party, subject in appropriate cases to conditions which ensure the protection of confidential information.

2.    In cases in which a party to a proceeding voluntarily and without good reason refuses access to, or otherwise does not provide necessary information within a reasonable period, or significantly impedes a procedure relating to an enforcement action, a Member may accord judicial authorities the authority to make preliminary and final determinations, affirmative or negative, on the basis of the information presented to them, including the complaint or the allegation presented by the party adversely affected by the denial of access to information, subject to providing the parties an opportunity to be heard on the allegations or evidence.

*Article 44 ·*
*Injunctions*

1.    The judicial authorities shall have the authority to order a party to desist from an infringement, *inter alia* to prevent the entry into the channels of commerce in their jurisdiction of imported goods that involve the infringement of an intellectual property right, immediately after customs clearance of such goods. Members are not obliged to accord such authority in respect of protected subject matter acquired or ordered by a person prior to knowing or having reasonable grounds to know that dealing in such subject matter would entail the infringement of an intellectual property right.

2.    Notwithstanding the other provisions of this Part and provided that the provisions of Part II specifically addressing use by governments, or by third parties authorized by a government, without the authorization of the right holder are complied with, Members may limit the remedies available against such use to payment of remuneration in accordance with subparagraph (h) of Article 31. In other cases, the remedies under this Part shall apply or, where these remedies are inconsistent with a Member's law, declaratory judgments and adequate compensation shall be available.

*Article 45 ·*
*Damages*

1.    The judicial authorities shall have the authority to order the infringer to pay the right holder damages adequate to compensate for the injury the right holder has suffered because of an infringement of that person's intellectual property right by an infringer who knowingly, or with reasonable grounds to know, engaged in infringing activity.

2.    The judicial authorities shall also have the authority to order the infringer to pay the right holder expenses, which may include appropriate attorney's fees. In appropriate cases, Members may authorize the judicial authorities to order recovery of profits and/or payment of pre-established damages even where the infringer did not knowingly, or with reasonable grounds to know, engage in infringing activity.

*Article 46 ·*
*Other Remedies*

In order to create an effective deterrent to infringement, the judicial authorities shall have the authority to order that goods that they have found to be infringing be, without compensation of any sort, disposed of outside the channels of commerce in such a manner as to avoid any harm caused to the right holder, or, unless this would be contrary to existing constitutional requirements, destroyed. The judicial authorities shall also have the authority to order that materials and implements the predominant use of which has been in the creation of the infringing goods be, without compensation of any sort, disposed of outside the channels of commerce in such a manner as to minimize the risks of further infringements. In considering such requests, the need for proportionality between the seriousness of the infringement and the remedies ordered as well as the interests of third parties shall be taken into account. In regard to counterfeit trademark goods, the simple removal of the trademark unlawfully affixed shall not be sufficient, other than in exceptional cases, to permit release of the goods into the channels of commerce.

17

*Article 47*
*Right of Information*

Members may provide that the judicial authorities shall have the authority, unless this would be out of proportion to the seriousness of the infringement, to order the infringer to inform the right holder of the identity of third persons involved in the production and distribution of the infringing goods or services and of their channels of distribution.

*Article 48*
*Indemnification of the Defendant*

1. The judicial authorities shall have the authority to order a party at whose request measures were taken and who has abused enforcement procedures to provide to a party wrongfully enjoined or restrained adequate compensation for the injury suffered because of such abuse. The judicial authorities shall also have the authority to order the applicant to pay the defendant expenses, which may include appropriate attorney's fees.

2. In respect of the administration of any law pertaining to the protection or enforcement of intellectual property rights, Members shall only exempt both public authorities and officials from liability to appropriate remedial measures where actions are taken or intended in good faith in the course of the administration of that law.

*Article 49*
*Administrative Procedures*

To the extent that any civil remedy can be ordered as a result of administrative procedures on the merits of a case, such procedures shall conform to principles equivalent in substance to those set forth in this Section.

SECTION 3: PROVISIONAL MEASURES

*Article 50*

1. The judicial authorities shall have the authority to order prompt and effective provisional measures:

   (a) to prevent an infringement of any intellectual property right from occurring, and in particular to prevent the entry into the channels of commerce in their jurisdiction of goods, including imported goods immediately after customs clearance;

   (b) to preserve relevant evidence in regard to the alleged infringement.

2. The judicial authorities shall have the authority to adopt provisional measures *inaudita altera parte* where appropriate, in particular where any delay is likely to cause irreparable harm to the right holder, or where there is a demonstrable risk of evidence being destroyed.

3. The judicial authorities shall have the authority to require the applicant to provide any reasonably available evidence in order to satisfy themselves with a sufficient degree of certainty that the applicant is the right holder and that the applicant's right is being infringed or that such infringement is imminent, and to order the applicant to provide a security or equivalent assurance sufficient to protect the defendant and to prevent abuse.

4. Where provisional measures have been adopted *inaudita altera parte*, the parties affected shall be given notice, without delay after the execution of the measures at the latest. A review, including a right to be heard, shall take place upon request of the defendant with a view to deciding, within a reasonable period after the notification of the measures, whether these measures shall be modified, revoked or confirmed.

5. The applicant may be required to supply other information necessary for the identification of the goods concerned by the authority that will execute the provisional measures.

6.    Without prejudice to paragraph 4, provisional measures taken on the basis of paragraphs 1 and 2 shall, upon request by the defendant, be revoked or otherwise cease to have effect, if proceedings leading to a decision on the merits of the case are not initiated within a reasonable period, to be determined by the judicial authority ordering the measures where a Member's law so permits or, in the absence of such a determination, not to exceed 20 working days or 31 calendar days, whichever is the longer.

7.    Where the provisional measures are revoked or where they lapse due to any act or omission by the applicant, or where it is subsequently found that there has been no infringement or threat of infringement of an intellectual property right, the judicial authorities shall have the authority to order the applicant, upon request of the defendant, to provide the defendant appropriate compensation for any injury caused by these measures.

8.    To the extent that any provisional measure can be ordered as a result of administrative procedures, such procedures shall conform to principles equivalent in substance to those set forth in this Section.

### SECTION 4: SPECIAL REQUIREMENTS
### RELATED TO BORDER MEASURES[12]

*Article 51*
*Suspension of Release by Customs Authorities*

Members shall, in conformity with the provisions set out below, adopt procedures[13] to enable a right holder, who has valid grounds for suspecting that the importation of counterfeit trademark or pirated copyright goods[14] may take place, to lodge an application in writing with competent authorities, administrative or judicial, for the suspension by the customs authorities of the release into free circulation of such goods. Members may enable such an application to be made in respect of goods which involve other infringements of intellectual property rights, provided that the requirements of this Section are met. Members may also provide for corresponding procedures concerning the suspension by the customs authorities of the release of infringing goods destined for exportation from their territories.

*Article 52*
*Application*

Any right holder initiating the procedures under Article 51 shall be required to provide adequate evidence to satisfy the competent authorities that, under the laws of the country of importation, there is *prima facie* an infringement of the right holder's intellectual property right and to supply a sufficiently detailed description of the goods to make them readily recognizable by the customs authorities. The competent authorities shall inform the applicant within a reasonable period whether they have accepted the application and, where determined by the competent authorities, the period for which the customs authorities will take action.

---

   [12]   Where a Member has dismantled substantially all controls over movement of goods across its border with another Member with which it forms part of a customs union, it shall not be required to apply the provisions of this Section at that border.

   [13]   It is understood that there shall be no obligation to apply such procedures to imports of goods put on the market in another country by or with the consent of the right holder, or to goods in transit.

   [14]   For the purposes of this Agreement:

(a) "counterfeit trademark goods" shall mean any goods, including packaging, bearing without authorization a trademark which is identical to the trademark validly registered in respect of such goods, or which cannot be distinguished in its essential aspects from such a trademark, and which thereby infringes the rights of the owner of the trademark in question under the law of the country of importation;

(b) "pirated copyright goods" shall mean any goods which are copies made without the consent of the right holder or person duly authorized by the right holder in the country of production and which are made directly or indirectly from an article where the making of that copy would have constituted an infringement of a copyright or a related right under the law of the country of importation.

*Article 53*
*Security or Equivalent Assurance*

1.   The competent authorities shall have the authority to require an applicant to provide a security or equivalent assurance sufficient to protect the defendant and the competent authorities and to prevent abuse. Such security or equivalent assurance shall not unreasonably deter recourse to these procedures.

2.   Where pursuant to an application under this Section the release of goods involving industrial designs, patents, layout-designs or undisclosed information into free circulation has been suspended by customs authorities on the basis of a decision other than by a judicial or other independent authority, and the period provided for in Article 55 has expired without the granting of provisional relief by the duly empowered authority, and provided that all other conditions for importation have been complied with, the owner, importer, or consignee of such goods shall be entitled to their release on the posting of a security in an amount sufficient to protect the right holder for any infringement. Payment of such security shall not prejudice any other remedy available to the right holder, it being understood that the security shall be released if the right holder fails to pursue the right of action within a reasonable period of time.

*Article 54*
*Notice of Suspension*

The importer and the applicant shall be promptly notified of the suspension of the release of goods according to Article 51.

*Article 55*
*Duration of Suspension*

If, within a period not exceeding 10 working days after the applicant has been served notice of the suspension, the customs authorities have not been informed that proceedings leading to a decision on the merits of the case have been initiated by a party other than the defendant, or that the duly empowered authority has taken provisional measures prolonging the suspension of the release of the goods, the goods shall be released, provided that all other conditions for importation or exportation have been complied with; in appropriate cases, this time-limit may be extended by another 10 working days. If proceedings leading to a decision on the merits of the case have been initiated, a review, including a right to be heard, shall take place upon request of the defendant with a view to deciding, within a reasonable period, whether these measures shall be modified, revoked or confirmed. Notwithstanding the above, where the suspension of the release of goods is carried out or continued in accordance with a provisional judicial measure, the provisions of paragraph 6 of Article 50 shall apply.

*Article 56*
*Indemnification of the Importer and of the Owner of the Goods*

Relevant authorities shall have the authority to order the applicant to pay the importer, the consignee and the owner of the goods appropriate compensation for any injury caused to them through the wrongful detention of goods or through the detention of goods released pursuant to Article 55.

*Article 57*
*Right of Inspection and Information*

Without prejudice to the protection of confidential information, Members shall provide the competent authorities the authority to give the right holder sufficient opportunity to have any goods detained by the customs authorities inspected in order to substantiate the right holder's claims. The competent authorities shall also have authority to give the importer an equivalent opportunity to have any such goods inspected. Where a positive determination has been made on the merits of a case, Members may provide the competent authorities the authority to inform the right holder of the names and addresses of the consignor, the importer and the consignee and of the quantity of the goods in question.

## Article 58
### Ex Officio Action

Where Members require competent authorities to act upon their own initiative and to suspend the release of goods in respect of which they have acquired *prima facie* evidence that an intellectual property right is being infringed:

(a) the competent authorities may at any time seek from the right holder any information that may assist them to exercise these powers;

(b) the importer and the right holder shall be promptly notified of the suspension. Where the importer has lodged an appeal against the suspension with the competent authorities, the suspension shall be subject to the conditions, *mutatis mutandis*, set out at Article 55;

(c) Members shall only exempt both public authorities and officials from liability to appropriate remedial measures where actions are taken or intended in good faith.

## Article 59
### Remedies

Without prejudice to other rights of action open to the right holder and subject to the right of the defendant to seek review by a judicial authority, competent authorities shall have the authority to order the destruction or disposal of infringing goods in accordance with the principles set out in Article 46. In regard to counterfeit trademark goods, the authorities shall not allow the re-exportation of the infringing goods in an unaltered state or subject them to a different customs procedure, other than in exceptional circumstances.

## Article 60
### De Minimis Imports

Members may exclude from the application of the above provisions small quantities of goods of a non-commercial nature contained in travellers' personal luggage or sent in small consignments.

## SECTION 5: CRIMINAL PROCEDURES

### Article 61

Members shall provide for criminal procedures and penalties to be applied at least in cases of wilful trademark counterfeiting or copyright piracy on a commercial scale. Remedies available shall include imprisonment and/or monetary fines sufficient to provide a deterrent, consistently with the level of penalties applied for crimes of a corresponding gravity. In appropriate cases, remedies available shall also include the seizure, forfeiture and destruction of the infringing goods and of any materials and implements the predominant use of which has been in the commission of the offence. Members may provide for criminal procedures and penalties to be applied in other cases of infringement of intellectual property rights, in particular where they are committed wilfully and on a commercial scale.

## PART IV
## ACQUISITION AND MAINTENANCE OF INTELLECTUAL PROPERTY RIGHTS AND RELATED *INTER-PARTES* PROCEDURES

### Article 62

1. Members may require, as a condition of the acquisition or maintenance of the intellectual property rights provided for under Sections 2 through 6 of Part II, compliance with reasonable procedures and formalities. Such procedures and formalities shall be consistent with the provisions of this Agreement.

2.     Where the acquisition of an intellectual property right is subject to the right being granted or registered, Members shall ensure that the procedures for grant or registration, subject to compliance with the substantive conditions for acquisition of the right, permit the granting or registration of the right within a reasonable period of time so as to avoid unwarranted curtailment of the period of protection.

3.     Article 4 of the Paris Convention (1967) shall apply *mutatis mutandis* to service marks.

4.     Procedures concerning the acquisition or maintenance of intellectual property rights and, where a Member's law provides for such procedures, administrative revocation and *inter partes* procedures such as opposition, revocation and cancellation, shall be governed by the general principles set out in paragraphs 2 and 3 of Article 41.

5.     Final administrative decisions in any of the procedures referred to under paragraph 4 shall be subject to review by a judicial or quasi-judicial authority. However, there shall be no obligation to provide an opportunity for such review of decisions in cases of unsuccessful opposition or administrative revocation, provided that the grounds for such procedures can be the subject of invalidation procedures.

PART V
DISPUTE PREVENTION AND SETTLEMENT
*Article 63*
*Transparency*

1.     Laws and regulations, and final judicial decisions and administrative rulings of general application, made effective by a Member pertaining to the subject matter of this Agreement (the availability, scope, acquisition, enforcement and prevention of the abuse of intellectual property rights) shall be published, or where such publication is not practicable made publicly available, in a national language, in such a manner as to enable governments and right holders to become acquainted with them. Agreements concerning the subject matter of this Agreement which are in force between the government or a governmental agency of a Member and the government or a governmental agency of another Member shall also be published.

2.     Members shall notify the laws and regulations referred to in paragraph 1 to the Council for TRIPS in order to assist that Council in its review of the operation of this Agreement. The Council shall attempt to minimize the burden on Members in carrying out this obligation and may decide to waive the obligation to notify such laws and regulations directly to the Council if consultations with WIPO on the establishment of a common register containing these laws and regulations are successful. The Council shall also consider in this connection any action required regarding notifications pursuant to the obligations under this Agreement stemming from the provisions of Article 6*ter* of the Paris Convention (1967).

3.     Each Member shall be prepared to supply, in response to a written request from another Member, information of the sort referred to in paragraph 1. A Member, having reason to believe that a specific judicial decision or administrative ruling or bilateral agreement in the area of intellectual property rights affects its rights under this Agreement, may also request in writing to be given access to or be informed in sufficient detail of such specific judicial decisions or administrative rulings or bilateral agreements.

4.     Nothing in paragraphs 1, 2 and 3 shall require Members to disclose confidential information which would impede law enforcement or otherwise be contrary to the public interest or would prejudice the legitimate commercial interests of particular enterprises, public or private.

## Article 64
### Dispute Settlement

1.  The provisions of Articles XXII and XXIII of GATT 1994 as elaborated and applied by the Dispute Settlement Understanding shall apply to consultations and the settlement of disputes under this Agreement except as otherwise specifically provided herein.

2.  Subparagraphs 1(b) and 1(c) of Article XXIII of GATT 1994 shall not apply to the settlement of disputes under this Agreement for a period of five years from the date of entry into force of the WTO Agreement.

3.  During the time period referred to in paragraph 2, the Council for TRIPS shall examine the scope and modalities for complaints of the type provided for under subparagraphs 1(b) and 1(c) of Article XXIII of GATT 1994 made pursuant to this Agreement, and submit its recommendations to the Ministerial Conference for approval. Any decision of the Ministerial Conference to approve such recommendations or to extend the period in paragraph 2 shall be made only by consensus, and approved recommendations shall be effective for all Members without further formal acceptance process.

## PART VI
## TRANSITIONAL ARRANGEMENTS
### Article 65

### Transitional Arrangements

1.  Subject to the provisions of paragraphs 2, 3 and 4, no Member shall be obliged to apply the provisions of this Agreement before the expiry of a general period of one year following the date of entry into force of the WTO Agreement.

2.  A developing country Member is entitled to delay for a further period of four years the date of application, as defined in paragraph 1, of the provisions of this Agreement other than Articles 3, 4 and 5.

3.  Any other Member which is in the process of transformation from a centrally-planned into a market, free-enterprise economy and which is undertaking structural reform of its intellectual property system and facing special problems in the preparation and implementation of intellectual property laws and regulations, may also benefit from a period of delay as foreseen in paragraph 2.

4.  To the extent that a developing country Member is obliged by this Agreement to extend product patent protection to areas of technology not so protectable in its territory on the general date of application of this Agreement for that Member, as defined in paragraph 2, it may delay the application of the provisions on product patents of Section 5 of Part II to such areas of technology for an additional period of five years.

5.  A Member availing itself of a transitional period under paragraphs 1, 2, 3 or 4 shall ensure that any changes in its laws, regulations and practice made during that period do not result in a lesser degree of consistency with the provisions of this Agreement.

## Article 66
### Least-Developed Country Members

1.  In view of the special needs and requirements of least-developed country Members, their economic, financial and administrative constraints, and their need for flexibility to create a viable technological base, such Members shall not be required to apply the provisions of this Agreement, other than Articles 3, 4 and 5, for a period of 10 years from the date of application as defined under paragraph 1 of Article 65. The Council for TRIPS shall, upon duly motivated request by a least-developed country Member, accord extensions of this period.

2.     Developed country Members shall provide incentives to enterprises and institutions in their territories for the purpose of promoting and encouraging technology transfer to least-developed country Members in order to enable them to create a sound and viable technological base.

### Article 67
### Technical Cooperation

In order to facilitate the implementation of this Agreement, developed country Members shall provide, on request and on mutually agreed terms and conditions, technical and financial cooperation in favour of developing and least-developed country Members. Such cooperation shall include assistance in the preparation of laws and regulations on the protection and enforcement of intellectual property rights as well as on the prevention of their abuse, and shall include support regarding the establishment or reinforcement of domestic offices and agencies relevant to these matters, including the training of personnel.

## PART VII
## INSTITUTIONAL ARRANGEMENTS; FINAL PROVISIONS

### Article 68
### Council for Trade-Related Aspects of Intellectual Property Rights

The Council for TRIPS shall monitor the operation of this Agreement and, in particular, Members' compliance with their obligations hereunder, and shall afford Members the opportunity of consulting on matters relating to the trade-related aspects of intellectual property rights. It shall carry out such other responsibilities as assigned to it by the Members, and it shall, in particular, provide any assistance requested by them in the context of dispute settlement procedures. In carrying out its functions, the Council for TRIPS may consult with and seek information from any source it deems appropriate. In consultation with WIPO, the Council shall seek to establish, within one year of its first meeting, appropriate arrangements for cooperation with bodies of that Organization.

### Article 69
### International Cooperation

Members agree to cooperate with each other with a view to eliminating international trade in goods infringing intellectual property rights. For this purpose, they shall establish and notify contact points in their administrations and be ready to exchange information on trade in infringing goods. They shall, in particular, promote the exchange of information and cooperation between customs authorities with regard to trade in counterfeit trademark goods and pirated copyright goods.

### Article 70
### Protection of Existing Subject Matter

1.     This Agreement does not give rise to obligations in respect of acts which occurred before the date of application of the Agreement for the Member in question.

2.     Except as otherwise provided for in this Agreement, this Agreement gives rise to obligations in respect of all subject matter existing at the date of application of this Agreement for the Member in question, and which is protected in that Member on the said date, or which meets or comes subsequently to meet the criteria for protection under the terms of this Agreement. In respect of this paragraph and paragraphs 3 and 4, copyright obligations with respect to existing works shall be solely determined under Article 18 of the Berne Convention (1971), and obligations with respect to the rights of producers of phonograms and performers in existing phonograms shall be determined solely under Article 18 of the Berne Convention (1971) as made applicable under paragraph 6 of Article 14 of this Agreement.

3.     There shall be no obligation to restore protection to subject matter which on the date of application of this Agreement for the Member in question has fallen into the public domain.

4. In respect of any acts in respect of specific objects embodying protected subject matter which become infringing under the terms of legislation in conformity with this Agreement, and which were commenced, or in respect of which a significant investment was made, before the date of acceptance of the WTO Agreement by that Member, any Member may provide for a limitation of the remedies available to the right holder as to the continued performance of such acts after the date of application of this Agreement for that Member. In such cases the Member shall, however, at least provide for the payment of equitable remuneration.

5. A Member is not obliged to apply the provisions of Article 11 and of paragraph 4 of Article 14 with respect to originals or copies purchased prior to the date of application of this Agreement for that Member.

6. Members shall not be required to apply Article 31, or the requirement in paragraph 1 of Article 27 that patent rights shall be enjoyable without discrimination as to the field of technology, to use without the authorization of the right holder where authorization for such use was granted by the government before the date this Agreement became known.

7. In the case of intellectual property rights for which protection is conditional upon registration, applications for protection which are pending on the date of application of this Agreement for the Member in question shall be permitted to be amended to claim any enhanced protection provided under the provisions of this Agreement. Such amendments shall not include new matter.

8. Where a Member does not make available as of the date of entry into force of the WTO Agreement patent protection for pharmaceutical and agricultural chemical products commensurate with its obligations under Article 27, that Member shall:

(a) notwithstanding the provisions of Part VI, provide as from the date of entry into force of the WTO Agreement a means by which applications for patents for such inventions can be filed;

(b) apply to these applications, as of the date of application of this Agreement, the criteria for patentability as laid down in this Agreement as if those criteria were being applied on the date of filing in that Member or, where priority is available and claimed, the priority date of the application; and

(c) provide patent protection in accordance with this Agreement as from the grant of the patent and for the remainder of the patent term, counted from the filing date in accordance with Article 33 of this Agreement, for those of these applications that meet the criteria for protection referred to in subparagraph (b).

9. Where a product is the subject of a patent application in a Member in accordance with paragraph 8(a), exclusive marketing rights shall be granted, notwithstanding the provisions of Part VI, for a period of five years after obtaining marketing approval in that Member or until a product patent is granted or rejected in that Member, whichever period is shorter, provided that, subsequent to the entry into force of the WTO Agreement, a patent application has been filed and a patent granted for that product in another Member and marketing approval obtained in such other Member.

*Article 71*
*Review and Amendment*

1. The Council for TRIPS shall review the implementation of this Agreement after the expiration of the transitional period referred to in paragraph 2 of Article 65. The Council shall, having regard to the experience gained in its implementation, review it two years after that date, and at identical intervals thereafter. The Council may also undertake reviews in the light of any relevant new developments which might warrant modification or amendment of this Agreement.

2. Amendments merely serving the purpose of adjusting to higher levels of protection of intellectual property rights achieved, and in force, in other multilateral agreements and accepted under those agreements by all Members of the WTO may be referred to the Ministerial Conference for action in

accordance with paragraph 6 of Article X of the WTO Agreement on the basis of a consensus proposal from the Council for TRIPS.

### Article 72
### Reservations

Reservations may not be entered in respect of any of the provisions of this Agreement without the consent of the other Members.

### Article 73
### Security Exceptions

Nothing in this Agreement shall be construed:

(a)  to require a Member to furnish any information the disclosure of which it considers contrary to its essential security interests; or

(b)  to prevent a Member from taking any action which it considers necessary for the protection of its essential security interests;

   (i)  relating to fissionable materials or the materials from which they are derived;

   (ii)  relating to the traffic in arms, ammunition and implements of war and to such traffic in other goods and materials as is carried on directly or indirectly for the purpose of supplying a military establishment;

   (iii)  taken in time of war or other emergency in international relations; or

(c)  to prevent a Member from taking any action in pursuance of its obligations under the United Nations Charter for the maintenance of international peace and security.

# 2. MEMBERS OF THE WORLD TRADE ORGANIZATION

164 members on May 4, 2021, with dates of membership

| Members | Membership Date | Members | Membership Date |
|---|---|---|---|
| Afghanistan | 29 July 2016 | Czech Republic | 1 January 1995 |
| Albania | 8 September 2000 | Democratic Republic of the Congo | 1 January 1997 |
| Angola | 23 November 1996 | Denmark | 1 January 1995 |
| Antigua and Barbuda | 1 January 1995 | Djibouti | 31 May 1995 |
| Argentina | 1 January 1995 | Dominica | 1 January 1995 |
| Armenia | 5 February 2003 | Dominican Republic | 9 March 1995 |
| Australia | 1 January 1995 | Ecuador | 21 January 1996 |
| Austria | 1 January 1995 | Egypt | 30 June 1995 |
| Bahrain, Kingdom of | 1 January 1995 | El Salvador | 7 May 1995 |
| Bangladesh | 1 January 1995 | Estonia | 13 November 1999 |
| Barbados | 1 January 1995 | Eswatini | 1 January 1995 |
| Belgium | 1 January 1995 | European Union (formerly EC) | 1 January 1995 |
| Belize | 1 January 1995 | Fiji | 14 January 1996 |
| Benin | 22 February 1996 | Finland | 1 January 1995 |
| Bolivia, Plurinational State of | 12 September 1995 | France | 1 January 1995 |
| Botswana | 31 May 1995 | Gabon | 1 January 1995 |
| Brazil | 1 January 1995 | Gambia | 23 October 1996 |
| Brunei Darussalam | 1 January 1995 | Georgia | 14 June 2000 |
| Bulgaria | 1 December 1996 | Germany | 1 January 1995 |
| Burkina Faso | 3 June 1995 | Ghana | 1 January 1995 |
| Burundi | 23 July 1995 | Greece | 1 January 1995 |
| Cabo Verde | 23 July 2008 | Grenada | 22 February 1996 |
| Cambodia | 13 October 2004 | Guatemala | 21 July 1995 |
| Cameroon | 13 December 1995 | Guinea | 25 October 1995 |
| Canada | 1 January 1995 | Guinea-Bissau | 31 May 1995 |
| Central African Republic | 31 May 1995 | Guyana | 1 January 1995 |
| Chad | 19 October 1996 | Haiti | 30 January 1996 |
| Chile | 1 January 1995 | Honduras | 1 January 1995 |
| China | 11 December 2001 | Hong Kong, China | 1 January 1995 |
| Colombia | 30 April 1995 | Hungary | 1 January 1995 |
| Congo | 27 March 1997 | Iceland | 1 January 1995 |
| Costa Rica | 1 January 1995 | India | 1 January 1995 |
| Côte d'Ivoire | 1 January 1995 | Indonesia | 1 January 1995 |
| Croatia | 30 November 2000 | Ireland | 1 January 1995 |
| Cuba | 20 April 1995 | Israel | 21 April 1995 |
| Cyprus | 30 July 1995 | | |

## MEMBERS OF THE WTO

| Members | Membership Date | Members | Membership Date |
| --- | --- | --- | --- |
| Italy | 1 January 1995 | Nicaragua | 3 September 1995 |
| Jamaica | 9 March 1995 | Niger | 13 December 1996 |
| Japan | 1 January 1995 | Nigeria | 1 January 1995 |
| Jordan | 11 April 2000 | North Macedonia | 4 April 2003 |
| Kazakhstan | 30 November 2015 | Norway | 1 January 1995 |
| Kenya | 1 January 1995 | Oman | 9 November 2000 |
| Korea, Republic of | 1 January 1995 | Pakistan | 1 January 1995 |
| Kuwait, the State of | 1 January 1995 | Panama | 6 September 1997 |
| Kyrgyz Republic | 20 December 1998 | Papua New Guinea | 9 June 1996 |
| Lao People's Democratic Republic | 2 February 2013 | Paraguay | 1 January 1995 |
| Latvia | 10 February 1999 | Peru | 1 January 1995 |
| Lesotho | 31 May 1995 | Philippines | 1 January 1995 |
| Liberia | 14 July 2016 | Poland | 1 July 1995 |
| Liechtenstein | 1 September 1995 | Portugal | 1 January 1995 |
| Lithuania | 31 May 2001 | Qatar | 13 January 1996 |
| Luxembourg | 1 January 1995 | Romania | 1 January 1995 |
| Macao, China | 1 January 1995 | Russian Federation | 22 August 2012 |
| Madagascar | 17 November 1995 | Rwanda | 22 May 1996 |
| Malawi | 31 May 1995 | Saint Kitts and Nevis | 21 February 1996 |
| Malaysia | 1 January 1995 | Saint Lucia | 1 January 1995 |
| Maldives | 31 May 1995 | Saint Vincent and the Grenadines | 1 January 1995 |
| Mali | 31 May 1995 | Samoa | 10 May 2012 |
| Malta | 1 January 1995 | Saudi Arabia, Kingdom of | 11 December 2005 |
| Mauritania | 31 May 1995 | Senegal | 1 January 1995 |
| Mauritius | 1 January 1995 | Seychelles | 26 April 2015 |
| Mexico | 1 January 1995 | Sierra Leone | 23 July 1995 |
| Moldova, Republic of | 26 July 2001 | Singapore | 1 January 1995 |
| Mongolia | 29 January 1997 | Slovak Republic | 1 January 1995 |
| Montenegro | 29 April 2012 | Slovenia | 30 July 1995 |
| Morocco | 1 January 1995 | Solomon Islands | 26 July 1996 |
| Mozambique | 26 August 1995 | South Africa | 1 January 1995 |
| Myanmar | 1 January 1995 | Spain | 1 January 1995 |
| Namibia | 1 January 1995 | Sri Lanka | 1 January 1995 |
| Nepal | 23 April 2004 | Suriname | 1 January 1995 |
| Netherlands | 1 January 1995 | Sweden | 1 January 1995 |
| New Zealand | 1 January 1995 | | |

## MEMBERS OF THE WTO

| Members | Membership Date | Members | Membership Date |
| --- | --- | --- | --- |
| Switzerland | 1 July 1995 | Ukraine | 16 May 2008 |
| Chinese Taipei | 1 January 2002 | United Arab Emirates | 10 April 1996 |
| Tajikistan | 2 March 2013 | United Kingdom | 1 January 1995 |
| Tanzania | 1 January 1995 | United States | 1 January 1995 |
| Thailand | 1 January 1995 | Uruguay | 1 January 1995 |
| Togo | 31 May 1995 | Vanuatu | 24 August 2012 |
| Tonga | 27 July 2007 | Venezuela, Bolivarian Republic of | 1 January 1995 |
| Trinidad and Tobago | 1 March 1995 | Viet Nam | 11 January 2007 |
| Tunisia | 29 March 1995 | Yemen | 26 June 2014 |
| Turkey | 26 March 1995 | Zambia | 1 January 1995 |
| Uganda | 1 January 1995 | Zimbabwe | 5 March 1995 |

# 3. AGREEMENT ESTABLISHING THE WORLD TRADE ORGANIZATION, ANNEX 2— DISPUTE SETTLEMENT

ANNEX 2
UNDERSTANDING ON RULES AND PROCEDURES
GOVERNING THE SETTLEMENT OF DISPUTES

*Members* hereby *agree* as follows:

*Article 1*
*Coverage and Application*

1.    The rules and procedures of this Understanding shall apply to disputes brought pursuant to the consultation and dispute settlement provisions of the agreements listed in Appendix 1 to this Understanding (referred to in this Understanding as the "covered agreements"). The rules and procedures of this Understanding shall also apply to consultations and the settlement of disputes between Members concerning their rights and obligations under the provisions of the Agreement Establishing the World Trade Organization (referred to in this Understanding as the "WTO Agreement") and of this Understanding taken in isolation or in combination with any other covered agreement.

2.    The rules and procedures of this Understanding shall apply subject to such special or additional rules and procedures on dispute settlement contained in the covered agreements as are identified in Appendix 2 to this Understanding. To the extent that there is a difference between the rules and procedures of this Understanding and the special or additional rules and procedures set forth in Appendix 2, the special or additional rules and procedures in Appendix 2 shall prevail. In disputes involving rules and procedures under more than one covered agreement, if there is a conflict between special or additional rules and procedures of such agreements under review, and where the parties to the dispute cannot agree on rules and procedures within 20 days of the establishment of the panel, the Chairman of the Dispute Settlement Body provided for in paragraph 1 of Article 2 (referred to in this Understanding as the "DSB"), in consultation with the parties to the dispute, shall determine the rules and procedures to be followed within 10 days after a request by either Member. The Chairman shall be guided by the principle that special or additional rules and procedures should be used where possible, and the rules and procedures set out in this Understanding should be used to the extent necessary to avoid conflict.

*Article 2*
*Administration*

1.    The Dispute Settlement Body is hereby established to administer these rules and procedures and, except as otherwise provided in a covered agreement, the consultation and dispute settlement provisions of the covered agreements. Accordingly, the DSB shall have the authority to establish panels, adopt panel and Appellate Body reports, maintain surveillance of implementation of rulings and recommendations, and authorize suspension of concessions and other obligations under the covered agreements. With respect to disputes arising under a covered agreement which is a Plurilateral Trade Agreement, the term "Member" as used herein shall refer only to those Members that are parties to the relevant Plurilateral Trade Agreement. Where the DSB administers the dispute settlement provisions of a Plurilateral Trade Agreement, only those Members that are parties to that Agreement may participate in decisions or actions taken by the DSB with respect to that dispute.

2.    The DSB shall inform the relevant WTO Councils and Committees of any developments in disputes related to provisions of the respective covered agreements.

3.    The DSB shall meet as often as necessary to carry out its functions within the time-frames provided in this Understanding.

4. Where the rules and procedures of this Understanding provide for the DSB to take a decision, it shall do so by consensus.[1]

*Article 3*
*General Provisions*

1. Members affirm their adherence to the principles for the management of disputes heretofore applied under Articles XXII and XXIII of GATT 1947, and the rules and procedures as further elaborated and modified herein.

2. The dispute settlement system of the WTO is a central element in providing security and predictability to the multilateral trading system. The Members recognize that it serves to preserve the rights and obligations of Members under the covered agreements, and to clarify the existing provisions of those agreements in accordance with customary rules of interpretation of public international law. Recommendations and rulings of the DSB cannot add to or diminish the rights and obligations provided in the covered agreements.

3. The prompt settlement of situations in which a Member considers that any benefits accruing to it directly or indirectly under the covered agreements are being impaired by measures taken by another Member is essential to the effective functioning of the WTO and the maintenance of a proper balance between the rights and obligations of Members.

4. Recommendations or rulings made by the DSB shall be aimed at achieving a satisfactory settlement of the matter in accordance with the rights and obligations under this Understanding and under the covered agreements.

5. All solutions to matters formally raised under the consultation and dispute settlement provisions of the covered agreements, including arbitration awards, shall be consistent with those agreements and shall not nullify or impair benefits accruing to any Member under those agreements, nor impede the attainment of any objective of those agreements.

6. Mutually agreed solutions to matters formally raised under the consultation and dispute settlement provisions of the covered agreements shall be notified to the DSB and the relevant Councils and Committees, where any Member may raise any point relating thereto.

7. Before bringing a case, a Member shall exercise its judgement as to whether action under these procedures would be fruitful. The aim of the dispute settlement mechanism is to secure a positive solution to a dispute. A solution mutually acceptable to the parties to a dispute and consistent with the covered agreements is clearly to be preferred. In the absence of a mutually agreed solution, the first objective of the dispute settlement mechanism is usually to secure the withdrawal of the measures concerned if these are found to be inconsistent with the provisions of any of the covered agreements. The provision of compensation should be resorted to only if the immediate withdrawal of the measure is impracticable and as a temporary measure pending the withdrawal of the measure which is inconsistent with a covered agreement. The last resort which this Understanding provides to the Member invoking the dispute settlement procedures is the possibility of suspending the application of concessions or other obligations under the covered agreements on a discriminatory basis vis-à-vis the other Member, subject to authorization by the DSB of such measures.

8. In cases where there is an infringement of the obligations assumed under a covered agreement, the action is considered *prima facie* to constitute a case of nullification or impairment. This means that there is normally a presumption that a breach of the rules has an adverse impact on other Members parties to that covered agreement, and in such cases, it shall be up to the Member against whom the complaint has been brought to rebut the charge.

---

[1] The DSB shall be deemed to have decided by consensus on a matter submitted for its consideration, if no Member, present at the meeting of the DSB when the decision is taken, formally objects to the proposed decision.

9.    The provisions of this Understanding are without prejudice to the rights of Members to seek authoritative interpretation of provisions of a covered agreement through decision-making under the WTO Agreement or a covered agreement which is a Plurilateral Trade Agreement.

10.    It is understood that requests for conciliation and the use of the dispute settlement procedures should not be intended or considered as contentious acts and that, if a dispute arises, all Members will engage in these procedures in good faith in an effort to resolve the dispute. It is also understood that complaints and counter-complaints in regard to distinct matters should not be linked.

11.    This Understanding shall be applied only with respect to new requests for consultations under the consultation provisions of the covered agreements made on or after the date of entry into force of the WTO Agreement. With respect to disputes for which the request for consultations was made under GATT 1947 or under any other predecessor agreement to the covered agreements before the date of entry into force of the WTO Agreement, the relevant dispute settlement rules and procedures in effect immediately prior to the date of entry into force of the WTO Agreement shall continue to apply.[2]

12.    Notwithstanding paragraph 11, if a complaint based on any of the covered agreements is brought by a developing country Member against a developed country Member, the complaining party shall have the right to invoke, as an alternative to the provisions contained in Articles 4, 5, 6 and 12 of this Understanding, the corresponding provisions of the Decision of 5 April 1966 (BISD 14S/18), except that where the Panel considers that the time-frame provided for in paragraph 7 of that Decision is insufficient to provide its report and with the agreement of the complaining party, that time-frame may be extended. To the extent that there is a difference between the rules and procedures of Articles 4, 5, 6 and 12 and the corresponding rules and procedures of the Decision, the latter shall prevail.

*Article 4*
*Consultations*

1.    Members affirm their resolve to strengthen and improve the effectiveness of the consultation procedures employed by Members.

2.    Each Member undertakes to accord sympathetic consideration to and afford adequate opportunity for consultation regarding any representations made by another Member concerning measures affecting the operation of any covered agreement taken within the territory of the former.[3]

3.    If a request for consultations is made pursuant to a covered agreement, the Member to which the request is made shall, unless otherwise mutually agreed, reply to the request within 10 days after the date of its receipt and shall enter into consultations in good faith within a period of no more than 30 days after the date of receipt of the request, with a view to reaching a mutually satisfactory solution. If the Member does not respond within 10 days after the date of receipt of the request, or does not enter into consultations within a period of no more than 30 days, or a period otherwise mutually agreed, after the date of receipt of the request, then the Member that requested the holding of consultations may proceed directly to request the establishment of a panel.

4.    All such requests for consultations shall be notified to the DSB and the relevant Councils and Committees by the Member which requests consultations. Any request for consultations shall be submitted in writing and shall give the reasons for the request, including identification of the measures at issue and an indication of the legal basis for the complaint.

---

[2]    This paragraph shall also be applied to disputes on which panel reports have not been adopted or fully implemented.

[3]    Where the provisions of any other covered agreement concerning measures taken by regional or local governments or authorities within the territory of a Member contain provisions different from the provisions of this paragraph, the provisions of such other covered agreement shall prevail.

5.    In the course of consultations in accordance with the provisions of a covered agreement, before resorting to further action under this Understanding, Members should attempt to obtain satisfactory adjustment of the matter.

6.    Consultations shall be confidential, and without prejudice to the rights of any Member in any further proceedings.

7.    If the consultations fail to settle a dispute within 60 days after the date of receipt of the request for consultations, the complaining party may request the establishment of a panel. The complaining party may request a panel during the 60-day period if the consulting parties jointly consider that consultations have failed to settle the dispute.

8.    In cases of urgency, including those which concern perishable goods, Members shall enter into consultations within a period of no more than 10 days after the date of receipt of the request. If the consultations have failed to settle the dispute within a period of 20 days after the date of receipt of the request, the complaining party may request the establishment of a panel.

9.    In cases of urgency, including those which concern perishable goods, the parties to the dispute, panels and the Appellate Body shall make every effort to accelerate the proceedings to the greatest extent possible.

10.    During consultations Members should give special attention to the particular problems and interests of developing country Members.

11.    Whenever a Member other than the consulting Members considers that it has a substantial trade interest in consultations being held pursuant to paragraph 1 of Article XXII of GATT 1994, paragraph 1 of Article XXII of GATS, or the corresponding provisions in other covered agreements,[4] such Member may notify the consulting Members and the DSB, within 10 days after the date of the circulation of the request for consultations under said Article, of its desire to be joined in the consultations. Such Member shall be joined in the consultations, provided that the Member to which the request for consultations was addressed agrees that the claim of substantial interest is well-founded. In that event they shall so inform the DSB. If the request to be joined in the consultations is not accepted, the applicant Member shall be free to request consultations under paragraph 1 of Article XXII or paragraph 1 of Article XXIII of GATT 1994, paragraph 1 of Article XXII or paragraph 1 of Article XXIII of GATS, or the corresponding provisions in other covered agreements.

### Article 5
### *Good Offices, Conciliation and Mediation*

1.    Good offices, conciliation and mediation are procedures that are undertaken voluntarily if the parties to the dispute so agree.

2.    Proceedings involving good offices, conciliation and mediation, and in particular positions taken by the parties to the dispute during these proceedings, shall be confidential, and without prejudice to the rights of either party in any further proceedings under these procedures.

3.    Good offices, conciliation or mediation may be requested at any time by any party to a dispute. They may begin at any time and be terminated at any time. Once procedures for good offices,

---

[4] The corresponding consultation provisions in the covered agreements are listed hereunder: Agreement on Agriculture, Article 19; Agreement on the Application of Sanitary and Phytosanitary Measures, paragraph 1 of Article 11; Agreement on Textiles and Clothing, paragraph 4 of Article 8; Agreement on Technical Barriers to Trade, paragraph 1 of Article 14; Agreement on Trade-Related Investment Measures, Article 8; Agreement on Implementation of Article VI of GATT 1994, paragraph 2 of Article 17; Agreement on Implementation of Article VII of GATT 1994, paragraph 2 of Article 19; Agreement on Preshipment Inspection, Article 7; Agreement on Rules of Origin, Article 7; Agreement on Import Licensing Procedures, Article 6; Agreement on Subsidies and Countervailing Measures, Article 30; Agreement on Safeguards, Article 14; Agreement on Trade-Related Aspects of Intellectual Property Rights, Article 64.1; and any corresponding consultation provisions in Plurilateral Trade Agreements as determined by the competent bodies of each Agreement and as notified to the DSB.

conciliation or mediation are terminated, a complaining party may then proceed with a request for the establishment of a panel.

4.     When good offices, conciliation or mediation are entered into within 60 days after the date of receipt of a request for consultations, the complaining party must allow a period of 60 days after the date of receipt of the request for consultations before requesting the establishment of a panel. The complaining party may request the establishment of a panel during the 60-day period if the parties to the dispute jointly consider that the good offices, conciliation or mediation process has failed to settle the dispute.

5.     If the parties to a dispute agree, procedures for good offices, conciliation or mediation may continue while the panel process proceeds.

6.     The Director-General may, acting in an *ex officio* capacity, offer good offices, conciliation or mediation with the view to assisting Members to settle a dispute.

## Article 6
### Establishment of Panels

1.     If the complaining party so requests, a panel shall be established at the latest at the DSB meeting following that at which the request first appears as an item on the DSB's agenda, unless at that meeting the DSB decides by consensus not to establish a panel.[5]

2.     The request for the establishment of a panel shall be made in writing. It shall indicate whether consultations were held, identify the specific measures at issue and provide a brief summary of the legal basis of the complaint sufficient to present the problem clearly. In case the applicant requests the establishment of a panel with other than standard terms of reference, the written request shall include the proposed text of special terms of reference.

## Article 7
### Terms of Reference of Panels

1.     Panels shall have the following terms of reference unless the parties to the dispute agree otherwise within 20 days from the establishment of the panel:

"To examine, in the light of the relevant provisions in (name of the covered agreement(s) cited by the parties to the dispute), the matter referred to the DSB by (name of party) in document . . . and to make such findings as will assist the DSB in making the recommendations or in giving the rulings provided for in that/those agreement(s)."

2.     Panels shall address the relevant provisions in any covered agreement or agreements cited by the parties to the dispute.

3.     In establishing a panel, the DSB may authorize its Chairman to draw up the terms of reference of the panel in consultation with the parties to the dispute, subject to the provisions of paragraph 1. The terms of reference thus drawn up shall be circulated to all Members. If other than standard terms of reference are agreed upon, any Member may raise any point relating thereto in the DSB.

## Article 8
### Composition of Panels

1.     Panels shall be composed of well-qualified governmental and/or non-governmental individuals, including persons who have served on or presented a case to a panel, served as a representative of a Member or of a contracting party to GATT 1947 or as a representative to the Council or Committee of any covered agreement or its predecessor agreement, or in the Secretariat,

---

[5]     If the complaining party so requests, a meeting of the DSB shall be convened for this purpose within 15 days of the request, provided that at least 10 days' advance notice of the meeting is given.

taught or published on international trade law or policy, or served as a senior trade policy official of a Member.

2.      Panel members should be selected with a view to ensuring the independence of the members, a sufficiently diverse background and a wide spectrum of experience.

3.      Citizens of Members whose governments[6] are parties to the dispute or third parties as defined in paragraph 2 of Article 10 shall not serve on a panel concerned with that dispute, unless the parties to the dispute agree otherwise.

4.      To assist in the selection of panelists, the Secretariat shall maintain an indicative list of governmental and non-governmental individuals possessing the qualifications outlined in paragraph 1, from which panelists may be drawn as appropriate. That list shall include the roster of non-governmental panelists established on 30 November 1984 (BISD 31S/9), and other rosters and indicative lists established under any of the covered agreements, and shall retain the names of persons on those rosters and indicative lists at the time of entry into force of the WTO Agreement. Members may periodically suggest names of governmental and non-governmental individuals for inclusion on the indicative list, providing relevant information on their knowledge of international trade and of the sectors or subject matter of the covered agreements, and those names shall be added to the list upon approval by the DSB. For each of the individuals on the list, the list shall indicate specific areas of experience or expertise of the individuals in the sectors or subject matter of the covered agreements.

5.      Panels shall be composed of three panelists unless the parties to the dispute agree, within 10 days from the establishment of the panel, to a panel composed of five panelists. Members shall be informed promptly of the composition of the panel.

6.      The Secretariat shall propose nominations for the panel to the parties to the dispute. The parties to the dispute shall not oppose nominations except for compelling reasons.

7.      If there is no agreement on the panelists within 20 days after the date of the establishment of a panel, at the request of either party, the Director-General, in consultation with the Chairman of the DSB and the Chairman of the relevant Council or Committee, shall determine the composition of the panel by appointing the panelists whom the Director-General considers most appropriate in accordance with any relevant special or additional rules or procedures of the covered agreement or covered agreements which are at issue in the dispute, after consulting with the parties to the dispute. The Chairman of the DSB shall inform the Members of the composition of the panel thus formed no later than 10 days after the date the Chairman receives such a request.

8.      Members shall undertake, as a general rule, to permit their officials to serve as panelists.

9.      Panelists shall serve in their individual capacities and not as government representatives, nor as representatives of any organization. Members shall therefore not give them instructions nor seek to influence them as individuals with regard to matters before a panel.

10.     When a dispute is between a developing country Member and a developed country Member the panel shall, if the developing country Member so requests, include at least one panelist from a developing country Member.

11.     Panelists' expenses, including travel and subsistence allowance, shall be met from the WTO budget in accordance with criteria to be adopted by the General Council, based on recommendations of the Committee on Budget, Finance and Administration.

*Article 9*
*Procedures for Multiple Complainants*

1.      Where more than one Member requests the establishment of a panel related to the same matter, a single panel may be established to examine these complaints taking into account the rights

---

[6]    In the case where customs unions or common markets are parties to a dispute, this provision applies to citizens of all member countries of the customs unions or common markets.

of all Members concerned. A single panel should be established to examine such complaints whenever feasible.

2.    The single panel shall organize its examination and present its findings to the DSB in such a manner that the rights which the parties to the dispute would have enjoyed had separate panels examined the complaints are in no way impaired. If one of the parties to the dispute so requests, the panel shall submit separate reports on the dispute concerned. The written submissions by each of the complainants shall be made available to the other complainants, and each complainant shall have the right to be present when any one of the other complainants presents its views to the panel.

3.    If more than one panel is established to examine the complaints related to the same matter, to the greatest extent possible the same persons shall serve as panelists on each of the separate panels and the timetable for the panel process in such disputes shall be harmonized.

## Article 10
### Third Parties

1.    The interests of the parties to a dispute and those of other Members under a covered agreement at issue in the dispute shall be fully taken into account during the panel process.

2.    Any Member having a substantial interest in a matter before a panel and having notified its interest to the DSB (referred to in this Understanding as a "third party") shall have an opportunity to be heard by the panel and to make written submissions to the panel. These submissions shall also be given to the parties to the dispute and shall be reflected in the panel report.

3.    Third parties shall receive the submissions of the parties to the dispute to the first meeting of the panel.

4.    If a third party considers that a measure already the subject of a panel proceeding nullifies or impairs benefits accruing to it under any covered agreement, that Member may have recourse to normal dispute settlement procedures under this Understanding. Such a dispute shall be referred to the original panel wherever possible.

## Article 11
### Function of Panels

The function of panels is to assist the DSB in discharging its responsibilities under this Understanding and the covered agreements. Accordingly, a panel should make an objective assessment of the matter before it, including an objective assessment of the facts of the case and the applicability of and conformity with the relevant covered agreements, and make such other findings as will assist the DSB in making the recommendations or in giving the rulings provided for in the covered agreements. Panels should consult regularly with the parties to the dispute and give them adequate opportunity to develop a mutually satisfactory solution.

## Article 12
### Panel Procedures

1.    Panels shall follow the Working Procedures in Appendix 3 unless the panel decides otherwise after consulting the parties to the dispute.

2.    Panel procedures should provide sufficient flexibility so as to ensure high-quality panel reports, while not unduly delaying the panel process.

3.    After consulting the parties to the dispute, the panelists shall, as soon as practicable and whenever possible within one week after the composition and terms of reference of the panel have been agreed upon, fix the timetable for the panel process, taking into account the provisions of paragraph 9 of Article 4, if relevant.

4.    In determining the timetable for the panel process, the panel shall provide sufficient time for the parties to the dispute to prepare their submissions.

5.　　Panels should set precise deadlines for written submissions by the parties and the parties should respect those deadlines.

6.　　Each party to the dispute shall deposit its written submissions with the Secretariat for immediate transmission to the panel and to the other party or parties to the dispute. The complaining party shall submit its first submission in advance of the responding party's first submission unless the panel decides, in fixing the timetable referred to in paragraph 3 and after consultations with the parties to the dispute, that the parties should submit their first submissions simultaneously. When there are sequential arrangements for the deposit of first submissions, the panel shall establish a firm time-period for receipt of the responding party's submission. Any subsequent written submissions shall be submitted simultaneously.

7.　　Where the parties to the dispute have failed to develop a mutually satisfactory solution, the panel shall submit its findings in the form of a written report to the DSB. In such cases, the report of a panel shall set out the findings of fact, the applicability of relevant provisions and the basic rationale behind any findings and recommendations that it makes. Where a settlement of the matter among the parties to the dispute has been found, the report of the panel shall be confined to a brief description of the case and to reporting that a solution has been reached.

8.　　In order to make the procedures more efficient, the period in which the panel shall conduct its examination, from the date that the composition and terms of reference of the panel have been agreed upon until the date the final report is issued to the parties to the dispute, shall, as a general rule, not exceed six months. In cases of urgency, including those relating to perishable goods, the panel shall aim to issue its report to the parties to the dispute within three months.

9.　　When the panel considers that it cannot issue its report within six months, or within three months in cases of urgency, it shall inform the DSB in writing of the reasons for the delay together with an estimate of the period within which it will issue its report. In no case should the period from the establishment of the panel to the circulation of the report to the Members exceed nine months.

10.　　In the context of consultations involving a measure taken by a developing country Member, the parties may agree to extend the periods established in paragraphs 7 and 8 of Article 4. If, after the relevant period has elapsed, the consulting parties cannot agree that the consultations have concluded, the Chairman of the DSB shall decide, after consultation with the parties, whether to extend the relevant period and, if so, for how long. In addition, in examining a complaint against a developing country Member, the panel shall accord sufficient time for the developing country Member to prepare and present its argumentation. The provisions of paragraph 1 of Article 20 and paragraph 4 of Article 21 are not affected by any action pursuant to this paragraph.

11.　　Where one or more of the parties is a developing country Member, the panel's report shall explicitly indicate the form in which account has been taken of relevant provisions on differential and more-favourable treatment for developing country Members that form part of the covered agreements which have been raised by the developing country Member in the course of the dispute settlement procedures.

12.　　The panel may suspend its work at any time at the request of the complaining party for a period not to exceed 12 months. In the event of such a suspension, the time-frames set out in paragraphs 8 and 9 of this Article, paragraph 1 of Article 20, and paragraph 4 of Article 21 shall be extended by the amount of time that the work was suspended. If the work of the panel has been suspended for more than 12 months, the authority for establishment of the panel shall lapse.

*Article 13*
*Right to Seek Information*

1.　　Each panel shall have the right to seek information and technical advice from any individual or body which it deems appropriate. However, before a panel seeks such information or advice from any individual or body within the jurisdiction of a Member it shall inform the authorities of that Member. A Member should respond promptly and fully to any request by a panel for such information as the panel considers necessary and appropriate. Confidential information which is provided shall not be revealed without formal authorization from the individual, body, or authorities of the Member providing the information.

2. Panels may seek information from any relevant source and may consult experts to obtain their opinion on certain aspects of the matter. With respect to a factual issue concerning a scientific or other technical matter raised by a party to a dispute, a panel may request an advisory report in writing from an expert review group. Rules for the establishment of such a group and its procedures are set forth in Appendix 4.

## Article 14
### Confidentiality

1. Panel deliberations shall be confidential.

2. The reports of panels shall be drafted without the presence of the parties to the dispute in the light of the information provided and the statements made.

3. Opinions expressed in the panel report by individual panelists shall be anonymous.

## Article 15
### Interim Review Stage

1. Following the consideration of rebuttal submissions and oral arguments, the panel shall issue the descriptive (factual and argument) sections of its draft report to the parties to the dispute. Within a period of time set by the panel, the parties shall submit their comments in writing.

2. Following the expiration of the set period of time for receipt of comments from the parties to the dispute, the panel shall issue an interim report to the parties, including both the descriptive sections and the panel's findings and conclusions. Within a period of time set by the panel, a party may submit a written request for the panel to review precise aspects of the interim report prior to circulation of the final report to the Members. At the request of a party, the panel shall hold a further meeting with the parties on the issues identified in the written comments. If no comments are received from any party within the comment period, the interim report shall be considered the final panel report and circulated promptly to the Members.

3. The findings of the final panel report shall include a discussion of the arguments made at the interim review stage. The interim review stage shall be conducted within the time-period set out in paragraph 8 of Article 12.

## Article 16
### Adoption of Panel Reports

1. In order to provide sufficient time for the Members to consider panel reports, the reports shall not be considered for adoption by the DSB until 20 days after the date they have been circulated to the Members.

2. Members having objections to a panel report shall give written reasons to explain their objections for circulation at least 10 days prior to the DSB meeting at which the panel report will be considered.

3. The parties to a dispute shall have the right to participate fully in the consideration of the panel report by the DSB, and their views shall be fully recorded.

4. Within 60 days after the date of circulation of a panel report to the Members, the report shall be adopted at a DSB meeting[7] unless a party to the dispute formally notifies the DSB of its decision to appeal or the DSB decides by consensus not to adopt the report. If a party has notified its decision to

---

[7] If a meeting of the DSB is not scheduled within this period at a time that enables the requirements of paragraphs 1 and 4 of Article 16 to be met, a meeting of the DSB shall be held for this purpose.

appeal, the report by the panel shall not be considered for adoption by the DSB until after completion of the appeal. This adoption procedure is without prejudice to the right of Members to express their views on a panel report.

*Article 17*
*Appellate Review*

*Standing Appellate Body*

1.     A standing Appellate Body shall be established by the DSB. The Appellate Body shall hear appeals from panel cases. It shall be composed of seven persons, three of whom shall serve on any one case. Persons serving on the Appellate Body shall serve in rotation. Such rotation shall be determined in the working procedures of the Appellate Body.

2.     The DSB shall appoint persons to serve on the Appellate Body for a four-year term, and each person may be reappointed once. However, the terms of three of the seven persons appointed immediately after the entry into force of the WTO Agreement shall expire at the end of two years, to be determined by lot. Vacancies shall be filled as they arise. A person appointed to replace a person whose term of office has not expired shall hold office for the remainder of the predecessor's term.

3.     The Appellate Body shall comprise persons of recognized authority, with demonstrated expertise in law, international trade and the subject matter of the covered agreements generally. They shall be unaffiliated with any government. The Appellate Body membership shall be broadly representative of membership in the WTO. All persons serving on the Appellate Body shall be available at all times and on short notice, and shall stay abreast of dispute settlement activities and other relevant activities of the WTO. They shall not participate in the consideration of any disputes that would create a direct or indirect conflict of interest.

4.     Only parties to the dispute, not third parties, may appeal a panel report. Third parties which have notified the DSB of a substantial interest in the matter pursuant to paragraph 2 of Article 10 may make written submissions to, and be given an opportunity to be heard by, the Appellate Body.

5.     As a general rule, the proceedings shall not exceed 60 days from the date a party to the dispute formally notifies its decision to appeal to the date the Appellate Body circulates its report. In fixing its timetable the Appellate Body shall take into account the provisions of paragraph 9 of Article 4, if relevant. When the Appellate Body considers that it cannot provide its report within 60 days, it shall inform the DSB in writing of the reasons for the delay together with an estimate of the period within which it will submit its report. In no case shall the proceedings exceed 90 days.

6.     An appeal shall be limited to issues of law covered in the panel report and legal interpretations developed by the panel.

7.     The Appellate Body shall be provided with appropriate administrative and legal support as it requires.

8.     The expenses of persons serving on the Appellate Body, including travel and subsistence allowance, shall be met from the WTO budget in accordance with criteria to be adopted by the General Council, based on recommendations of the Committee on Budget, Finance and Administration.

*Procedures for Appellate Review*

9.     Working procedures shall be drawn up by the Appellate Body in consultation with the Chairman of the DSB and the Director-General, and communicated to the Members for their information.

10.     The proceedings of the Appellate Body shall be confidential. The reports of the Appellate Body shall be drafted without the presence of the parties to the dispute and in the light of the information provided and the statements made.

11.     Opinions expressed in the Appellate Body report by individuals serving on the Appellate Body shall be anonymous.

12.   The Appellate Body shall address each of the issues raised in accordance with paragraph 6 during the appellate proceeding.

13.   The Appellate Body may uphold, modify or reverse the legal findings and conclusions of the panel.

*Adoption of Appellate Body Reports*

14.   An Appellate Body report shall be adopted by the DSB and unconditionally accepted by the parties to the dispute unless the DSB decides by consensus not to adopt the Appellate Body report within 30 days following its circulation to the Members.[8] This adoption procedure is without prejudice to the right of Members to express their views on an Appellate Body report.

## Article 18
### Communications with the Panel or Appellate Body

1.   There shall be no *ex parte* communications with the panel or Appellate Body concerning matters under consideration by the panel or Appellate Body.

2.   Written submissions to the panel or the Appellate Body shall be treated as confidential, but shall be made available to the parties to the dispute. Nothing in this Understanding shall preclude a party to a dispute from disclosing statements of its own positions to the public. Members shall treat as confidential information submitted by another Member to the panel or the Appellate Body which that Member has designated as confidential. A party to a dispute shall also, upon request of a Member, provide a non-confidential summary of the information contained in its written submissions that could be disclosed to the public.

## Article 19
### Panel and Appellate Body Recommendations

1.   Where a panel or the Appellate Body concludes that a measure is inconsistent with a covered agreement, it shall recommend that the Member concerned[9] bring the measure into conformity with that agreement.[10] In addition to its recommendations, the panel or Appellate Body may suggest ways in which the Member concerned could implement the recommendations.

2.   In accordance with paragraph 2 of Article 3, in their findings and recommendations, the panel and Appellate Body cannot add to or diminish the rights and obligations provided in the covered agreements.

## Article 20
### Time-frame for DSB Decisions

Unless otherwise agreed to by the parties to the dispute, the period from the date of establishment of the panel by the DSB until the date the DSB considers the panel or appellate report for adoption shall as a general rule not exceed nine months where the panel report is not appealed or 12 months where the report is appealed. Where either the panel or the Appellate Body has acted, pursuant to paragraph 9 of Article 12 or paragraph 5 of Article 17, to extend the time for providing its report, the additional time taken shall be added to the above periods.

---

[8]   If a meeting of the DSB is not scheduled during this period, such a meeting of the DSB shall be held for this purpose.

[9]   The "Member concerned" is the party to the dispute to which the panel or Appellate Body recommendations are directed.

[10]   With respect to recommendations in cases not involving a violation of GATT 1994 or any other covered agreement, see Article 26.

*Article 21*
*Surveillance of Implementation of Recommendations and Rulings*

1.    Prompt compliance with recommendations or rulings of the DSB is essential in order to ensure effective resolution of disputes to the benefit of all Members.

2.    Particular attention should be paid to matters affecting the interests of developing country Members with respect to measures which have been subject to dispute settlement.

3.    At a DSB meeting held within 30 days[11] after the date of adoption of the panel or Appellate Body report, the Member concerned shall inform the DSB of its intentions in respect of implementation of the recommendations and rulings of the DSB. If it is impracticable to comply immediately with the recommendations and rulings, the Member concerned shall have a reasonable period of time in which to do so. The reasonable period of time shall be:

(a)    the period of time proposed by the Member concerned, provided that such period is approved by the DSB; or, in the absence of such approval,

(b)    a period of time mutually agreed by the parties to the dispute within 45 days after the date of adoption of the recommendations and rulings; or, in the absence of such agreement,

(c)    a period of time determined through binding arbitration within 90 days after the date of adoption of the recommendations and rulings.[12] In such arbitration, a guideline for the arbitrator[13] should be that the reasonable period of time to implement panel or Appellate Body recommendations should not exceed 15 months from the date of adoption of a panel or Appellate Body report. However, that time may be shorter or longer, depending upon the particular circumstances.

4.    Except where the panel or the Appellate Body has extended, pursuant to paragraph 9 of Article 12 or paragraph 5 of Article 17, the time of providing its report, the period from the date of establishment of the panel by the DSB until the date of determination of the reasonable period of time shall not exceed 15 months unless the parties to the dispute agree otherwise. Where either the panel or the Appellate Body has acted to extend the time of providing its report, the additional time taken shall be added to the 15-month period; provided that unless the parties to the dispute agree that there are exceptional circumstances, the total time shall not exceed 18 months.

5.    Where there is disagreement as to the existence or consistency with a covered agreement of measures taken to comply with the recommendations and rulings such dispute shall be decided through recourse to these dispute settlement procedures, including wherever possible resort to the original panel. The panel shall circulate its report within 90 days after the date of referral of the matter to it. When the panel considers that it cannot provide its report within this time frame, it shall inform the DSB in writing of the reasons for the delay together with an estimate of the period within which it will submit its report.

6.    The DSB shall keep under surveillance the implementation of adopted recommendations or rulings. The issue of implementation of the recommendations or rulings may be raised at the DSB by any Member at any time following their adoption. Unless the DSB decides otherwise, the issue of implementation of the recommendations or rulings shall be placed on the agenda of the DSB meeting after six months following the date of establishment of the reasonable period of time pursuant to paragraph 3 and shall remain on the DSB's agenda until the issue is resolved. At least 10 days prior to each such DSB meeting, the Member concerned shall provide the DSB with a status report in writing of its progress in the implementation of the recommendations or rulings.

---

[11]  If a meeting of the DSB is not scheduled during this period, such a meeting of the DSB shall be held for this purpose.

[12]  If the parties cannot agree on an arbitrator within ten days after referring the matter to arbitration, the arbitrator shall be appointed by the Director-General within ten days, after consulting the parties.

[13]  The expression "arbitrator" shall be interpreted as referring either to an individual or a group.

7.    If the matter is one which has been raised by a developing country Member, the DSB shall consider what further action it might take which would be appropriate to the circumstances.

8.    If the case is one brought by a developing country Member, in considering what appropriate action might be taken, the DSB shall take into account not only the trade coverage of measures complained of, but also their impact on the economy of developing country Members concerned.

*Article 22*
*Compensation and the Suspension of Concessions*

1.    Compensation and the suspension of concessions or other obligations are temporary measures available in the event that the recommendations and rulings are not implemented within a reasonable period of time. However, neither compensation nor the suspension of concessions or other obligations is preferred to full implementation of a recommendation to bring a measure into conformity with the covered agreements. Compensation is voluntary and, if granted, shall be consistent with the covered agreements.

2.    If the Member concerned fails to bring the measure found to be inconsistent with a covered agreement into compliance therewith or otherwise comply with the recommendations and rulings within the reasonable period of time determined pursuant to paragraph 3 of Article 21, such Member shall, if so requested, and no later than the expiry of the reasonable period of time, enter into negotiations with any party having invoked the dispute settlement procedures, with a view to developing mutually acceptable compensation. If no satisfactory compensation has been agreed within 20 days after the date of expiry of the reasonable period of time, any party having invoked the dispute settlement procedures may request authorization from the DSB to suspend the application to the Member concerned of concessions or other obligations under the covered agreements.

3.    In considering what concessions or other obligations to suspend, the complaining party shall apply the following principles and procedures:

(a)    the general principle is that the complaining party should first seek to suspend concessions or other obligations with respect to the same sector(s) as that in which the panel or Appellate Body has found a violation or other nullification or impairment;

(b)    if that party considers that it is not practicable or effective to suspend concessions or other obligations with respect to the same sector(s), it may seek to suspend concessions or other obligations in other sectors under the same agreement;

(c)    if that party considers that it is not practicable or effective to suspend concessions or other obligations with respect to other sectors under the same agreement, and that the circumstances are serious enough, it may seek to suspend concessions or other obligations under another covered agreement;

(d)    in applying the above principles, that party shall take into account:

(i)    the trade in the sector or under the agreement under which the panel or Appellate Body has found a violation or other nullification or impairment, and the importance of such trade to that party;

(ii)    the broader economic elements related to the nullification or impairment and the broader economic consequences of the suspension of concessions or other obligations;

(e)    if that party decides to request authorization to suspend concessions or other obligations pursuant to subparagraphs (b) or (c), it shall state the reasons therefor in its request. At the same time as the request is forwarded to the DSB, it also shall be forwarded to the relevant Councils and also, in the case of a request pursuant to subparagraph (b), the relevant sectoral bodies;

(f)    for purposes of this paragraph, "sector" means:

(i)    with respect to goods, all goods;

(ii) with respect to services, a principal sector as identified in the current "Services Sectoral Classification List" which identifies such sectors;[14]

(iii) with respect to trade-related intellectual property rights, each of the categories of intellectual property rights covered in Section 1, or Section 2, or Section 3, or Section 4, or Section 5, or Section 6, or Section 7 of Part II, or the obligations under Part III, or Part IV of the Agreement on TRIPS;

(g) for purposes of this paragraph, "agreement" means:

(i) with respect to goods, the agreements listed in Annex 1A of the WTO Agreement, taken as a whole as well as the Plurilateral Trade Agreements in so far as the relevant parties to the dispute are parties to these agreements;

(ii) with respect to services, the GATS;

(iii) with respect to intellectual property rights, the Agreement on TRIPS.

4. The level of the suspension of concessions or other obligations authorized by the DSB shall be equivalent to the level of the nullification or impairment.

5. The DSB shall not authorize suspension of concessions or other obligations if a covered agreement prohibits such suspension.

6. When the situation described in paragraph 2 occurs, the DSB, upon request, shall grant authorization to suspend concessions or other obligations within 30 days of the expiry of the reasonable period of time unless the DSB decides by consensus to reject the request. However, if the Member concerned objects to the level of suspension proposed, or claims that the principles and procedures set forth in paragraph 3 have not been followed where a complaining party has requested authorization to suspend concessions or other obligations pursuant to paragraph 3(b) or (c), the matter shall be referred to arbitration. Such arbitration shall be carried out by the original panel, if members are available, or by an arbitrator[15] appointed by the Director-General and shall be completed within 60 days after the date of expiry of the reasonable period of time. Concessions or other obligations shall not be suspended during the course of the arbitration.

7. The arbitrator[16] acting pursuant to paragraph 6 shall not examine the nature of the concessions or other obligations to be suspended but shall determine whether the level of such suspension is equivalent to the level of nullification or impairment. The arbitrator may also determine if the proposed suspension of concessions or other obligations is allowed under the covered agreement. However, if the matter referred to arbitration includes a claim that the principles and procedures set forth in paragraph 3 have not been followed, the arbitrator shall examine that claim. In the event the arbitrator determines that those principles and procedures have not been followed, the complaining party shall apply them consistent with paragraph 3. The parties shall accept the arbitrator's decision as final and the parties concerned shall not seek a second arbitration. The DSB shall be informed promptly of the decision of the arbitrator and shall upon request, grant authorization to suspend concessions or other obligations where the request is consistent with the decision of the arbitrator, unless the DSB decides by consensus to reject the request.

8. The suspension of concessions or other obligations shall be temporary and shall only be applied until such time as the measure found to be inconsistent with a covered agreement has been removed, or the Member that must implement recommendations or rulings provides a solution to the nullification or impairment of benefits, or a mutually satisfactory solution is reached. In accordance with paragraph 6 of Article 21, the DSB shall continue to keep under surveillance the implementation of adopted recommendations or rulings, including those cases where compensation has been provided

---

[14] The list in document MTN.GNS/W/120 identifies eleven sectors.

[15] The expression "arbitrator" shall be interpreted as referring either to an individual or a group.

[16] The expression "arbitrator" shall be interpreted as referring either to an individual or a group or to the members of the original panel when serving in the capacity of arbitrator.

or concessions or other obligations have been suspended but the recommendations to bring a measure into conformity with the covered agreements have not been implemented.

9.    The dispute settlement provisions of the covered agreements may be invoked in respect of measures affecting their observance taken by regional or local governments or authorities within the territory of a Member. When the DSB has ruled that a provision of a covered agreement has not been observed, the responsible Member shall take such reasonable measures as may be available to it to ensure its observance. The provisions of the covered agreements and this Understanding relating to compensation and suspension of concessions or other obligations apply in cases where it has not been possible to secure such observance.[17]

### Article 23
### Strengthening of the Multilateral System

1.    When Members seek the redress of a violation of obligations or other nullification or impairment of benefits under the covered agreements or an impediment to the attainment of any objective of the covered agreements, they shall have recourse to, and abide by, the rules and procedures of this Understanding.

2.    In such cases, Members shall:

(a)    not make a determination to the effect that a violation has occurred, that benefits have been nullified or impaired or that the attainment of any objective of the covered agreements has been impeded, except through recourse to dispute settlement in accordance with the rules and procedures of this Understanding, and shall make any such determination consistent with the findings contained in the panel or Appellate Body report adopted by the DSB or an arbitration award rendered under this Understanding;

(b)    follow the procedures set forth in Article 21 to determine the reasonable period of time for the Member concerned to implement the recommendations and rulings; and

(c)    follow the procedures set forth in Article 22 to determine the level of suspension of concessions or other obligations and obtain DSB authorization in accordance with those procedures before suspending concessions or other obligations under the covered agreements in response to the failure of the Member concerned to implement the recommendations and rulings within that reasonable period of time.

### Article 24
### Special Procedures Involving Least-Developed Country Members

1.    At all stages of the determination of the causes of a dispute and of dispute settlement procedures involving a least-developed country Member, particular consideration shall be given to the special situation of least-developed country Members. In this regard, Members shall exercise due restraint in raising matters under these procedures involving a least-developed country Member. If nullification or impairment is found to result from a measure taken by a least-developed country Member, complaining parties shall exercise due restraint in asking for compensation or seeking authorization to suspend the application of concessions or other obligations pursuant to these procedures.

2.    In dispute settlement cases involving a least-developed country Member, where a satisfactory solution has not been found in the course of consultations the Director-General or the Chairman of the DSB shall, upon request by a least-developed country Member offer their good offices, conciliation and mediation with a view to assisting the parties to settle the dispute, before a request

---

[17] Where the provisions of any covered agreement concerning measures taken by regional or local governments or authorities within the territory of a Member contain provisions different from the provisions of this paragraph, the provisions of such covered agreement shall prevail.

for a panel is made. The Director-General or the Chairman of the DSB, in providing the above assistance, may consult any source which either deems appropriate.

*Article 25*
*Arbitration*

1.    Expeditious arbitration within the WTO as an alternative means of dispute settlement can facilitate the solution of certain disputes that concern issues that are clearly defined by both parties.

2.    Except as otherwise provided in this Understanding, resort to arbitration shall be subject to mutual agreement of the parties which shall agree on the procedures to be followed. Agreements to resort to arbitration shall be notified to all Members sufficiently in advance of the actual commencement of the arbitration process.

3.    Other Members may become party to an arbitration proceeding only upon the agreement of the parties which have agreed to have recourse to arbitration. The parties to the proceeding shall agree to abide by the arbitration award. Arbitration awards shall be notified to the DSB and the Council or Committee of any relevant agreement where any Member may raise any point relating thereto.

4.    Articles 21 and 22 of this Understanding shall apply *mutatis mutandis* to arbitration awards.

*Article 26*

1.    *Non-Violation Complaints of the Type Described in Paragraph 1(b) of Article XXIII of GATT 1994*

Where the provisions of paragraph 1(b) of Article XXIII of GATT 1994 are applicable to a covered agreement, a panel or the Appellate Body may only make rulings and recommendations where a party to the dispute considers that any benefit accruing to it directly or indirectly under the relevant covered agreement is being nullified or impaired or the attainment of any objective of that Agreement is being impeded as a result of the application by a Member of any measure, whether or not it conflicts with the provisions of that Agreement. Where and to the extent that such party considers and a panel or the Appellate Body determines that a case concerns a measure that does not conflict with the provisions of a covered agreement to which the provisions of paragraph 1(b) of Article XXIII of GATT 1994 are applicable, the procedures in this Understanding shall apply, subject to the following:

    (a)    the complaining party shall present a detailed justification in support of any complaint relating to a measure which does not conflict with the relevant covered agreement;

    (b)    where a measure has been found to nullify or impair benefits under, or impede the attainment of objectives, of the relevant covered agreement without violation thereof, there is no obligation to withdraw the measure. However, in such cases, the panel or the Appellate Body shall recommend that the Member concerned make a mutually satisfactory adjustment;

    (c)    notwithstanding the provisions of Article 21, the arbitration provided for in paragraph 3 of Article 21, upon request of either party, may include a determination of the level of benefits which have been nullified or impaired, and may also suggest ways and means of reaching a mutually satisfactory adjustment; such suggestions shall not be binding upon the parties to the dispute;

    (d)    notwithstanding the provisions of paragraph 1 of Article 22, compensation may be part of a mutually satisfactory adjustment as final settlement of the dispute.

2.    *Complaints of the Type Described in Paragraph 1(c) of Article XXIII of GATT 1994*

Where the provisions of paragraph 1(c) of Article XXIII of GATT 1994 are applicable to a covered agreement, a panel may only make rulings and recommendations where a party considers that any benefit accruing to it directly or indirectly under the relevant covered agreement is being nullified or impaired or the attainment of any objective of that Agreement is being impeded as a result of the existence of any situation other than those to which the provisions of paragraphs 1(a) and 1(b) of

Article XXIII of GATT 1994 are applicable. Where and to the extent that such party considers and a panel determines that the matter is covered by this paragraph, the procedures of this Understanding shall apply only up to and including the point in the proceedings where the panel report has been circulated to the Members. The dispute settlement rules and procedures contained in the Decision of 12 April 1989 (BISD 36S/61–67) shall apply to consideration for adoption, and surveillance and implementation of recommendations and rulings. The following shall also apply:

(a)   the complaining party shall present a detailed justification in support of any argument made with respect to issues covered under this paragraph;

(b)   in cases involving matters covered by this paragraph, if a panel finds that cases also involve dispute settlement matters other than those covered by this paragraph, the panel shall circulate a report to the DSB addressing any such matters and a separate report on matters falling under this paragraph.

*Article 27*
*Responsibilities of the Secretariat*

1.   The Secretariat shall have the responsibility of assisting panels, especially on the legal, historical and procedural aspects of the matters dealt with, and of providing secretarial and technical support.

2.   While the Secretariat assists Members in respect of dispute settlement at their request, there may also be a need to provide additional legal advice and assistance in respect of dispute settlement to developing country Members. To this end, the Secretariat shall make available a qualified legal expert from the WTO technical cooperation services to any developing country Member which so requests. This expert shall assist the developing country Member in a manner ensuring the continued impartiality of the Secretariat.

3.   The Secretariat shall conduct special training courses for interested Members concerning these dispute settlement procedures and practices so as to enable Members' experts to be better informed in this regard.

APPENDIX 1
AGREEMENTS COVERED BY THE UNDERSTANDING

(A)   Agreement Establishing the World Trade Organization

(B)   Multilateral Trade Agreements

Annex 1A: Multilateral Agreements on Trade in Goods

Annex 1B: General Agreement on Trade in Services

Annex 1C: Agreement on Trade-Related Aspects of Intellectual Property Rights

Annex 2: Understanding on Rules and Procedures Governing the Settlement of Disputes

(C)   Plurilateral Trade Agreements

Annex 4: Agreement on Trade in Civil Aircraft

Agreement on Government Procurement

International Dairy Agreement

International Bovine Meat Agreement

The applicability of this Understanding to the Plurilateral Trade Agreements shall be subject to the adoption of a decision by the parties to each agreement setting out the terms for the application of the Understanding to the individual agreement, including any special or additional rules or procedures for inclusion in Appendix 2, as notified to the DSB.

## APPENDIX 2
### SPECIAL OR ADDITIONAL RULES AND PROCEDURES
### CONTAINED IN THE COVERED AGREEMENTS

*Agreement Rules and Procedures*

Agreement on the Application of Sanitary and Phytosanitary Measures 11.2

Agreement on Textiles and Clothing 2.14, 2.21, 4.4, 5.2, 5.4, 5.6, 6.9, 6.10, 6.11, 8.1 through 8.12

Agreement on Technical Barriers to Trade 14.2 through 14.4, Annex 2

Agreement on Implementation of Article VI of GATT 1994 17.4 through 17.7

Agreement on Implementation of Article VII of GATT 1994 19.3 through 19.5, Annex II.2(f), 3, 9, 21

Agreement on Subsidies and Countervailing Measures 4.2 through 4.12, 6.6, 7.2 through 7.10, 8.5, footnote 35, 24.4, 27.7, Annex V

General Agreement on Trade in Services XXII:3, XXIII:3

Annex on Financial Services 4

Annex on Air Transport Services 4

Decision on Certain Dispute Settlement Procedures for the GATS 1 through 5

The list of rules and procedures in this Appendix includes provisions where only a part of the provision may be relevant in this context.

Any special or additional rules or procedures in the Plurilateral Trade Agreements as determined by the competent bodies of each agreement and as notified to the DSB.

### APPENDIX 3
### WORKING PROCEDURES

1.   In its proceedings the panel shall follow the relevant provisions of this Understanding. In addition, the following working procedures shall apply.

2.   The panel shall meet in closed session. The parties to the dispute, and interested parties, shall be present at the meetings only when invited by the panel to appear before it.

3.   The deliberations of the panel and the documents submitted to it shall be kept confidential. Nothing in this Understanding shall preclude a party to a dispute from disclosing statements of its own positions to the public. Members shall treat as confidential information submitted by another Member to the panel which that Member has designated as confidential. Where a party to a dispute submits a confidential version of its written submissions to the panel, it shall also, upon request of a Member, provide a non-confidential summary of the information contained in its submissions that could be disclosed to the public.

4.   Before the first substantive meeting of the panel with the parties, the parties to the dispute shall transmit to the panel written submissions in which they present the facts of the case and their arguments.

5.   At its first substantive meeting with the parties, the panel shall ask the party which has brought the complaint to present its case. Subsequently, and still at the same meeting, the party against which the complaint has been brought shall be asked to present its point of view.

6.   All third parties which have notified their interest in the dispute to the DSB shall be invited in writing to present their views during a session of the first substantive meeting of the panel set aside for that purpose. All such third parties may be present during the entirety of this session.

7.    Formal rebuttals shall be made at a second substantive meeting of the panel. The party complained against shall have the right to take the floor first to be followed by the complaining party. The parties shall submit, prior to that meeting, written rebuttals to the panel.

8.    The panel may at any time put questions to the parties and ask them for explanations either in the course of a meeting with the parties or in writing.

9.    The parties to the dispute and any third party invited to present its views in accordance with Article 10 shall make available to the panel a written version of their oral statements.

10.    In the interest of full transparency, the presentations, rebuttals and statements referred to in paragraphs 5 to 9 shall be made in the presence of the parties. Moreover, each party's written submissions, including any comments on the descriptive part of the report and responses to questions put by the panel, shall be made available to the other party or parties.

11.    Any additional procedures specific to the panel.

12.    Proposed timetable for panel work:

   (a)    Receipt of first written submissions of the parties:

   (1)    complaining Party: _____ 3–6 weeks

   (2)    Party complained against: _____ 2–3 weeks

   (b)    Date, time and place of first substantive meeting with the parties; third party session: _____ 1–2 weeks

   (c)    Receipt of written rebuttals of the parties: _____ 2–3 weeks

   (d)    Date, time and place of second substantive meeting with the parties: _____ 1–2 weeks

   (e)    Issuance of descriptive part of the report to the parties: _____ 2–4 weeks

   (f)    Receipt of comments by the parties on the descriptive part of the report: _____ 2 weeks

   (g)    Issuance of the interim report, including the findings and conclusions, to the parties: _____ 2–4 weeks

   (h)    Deadline for party to request review of part(s) of report: _____ 1 week

   (i)    Period of review by panel, including possible additional meeting with parties: _____ 2 weeks

   (j)    Issuance of final report to parties to dispute: _____ 2 weeks

   (k)    Circulation of the final report to the Members: _____ 3 weeks

   The above calendar may be changed in the light of unforeseen developments. Additional meetings with the parties shall be scheduled if required.

## APPENDIX 4
## EXPERT REVIEW GROUPS

   The following rules and procedures shall apply to expert review groups established in accordance with the provisions of paragraph 2 of Article 13.

1.    Expert review groups are under the panel's authority. Their terms of reference and detailed working procedures shall be decided by the panel, and they shall report to the panel.

2.    Participation in expert review groups shall be restricted to persons of professional standing and experience in the field in question.

3.    Citizens of parties to the dispute shall not serve on an expert review group without the joint agreement of the parties to the dispute, except in exceptional circumstances when the panel considers that the need for specialized scientific expertise cannot be fulfilled otherwise. Government officials of

parties to the dispute shall not serve on an expert review group. Members of expert review groups shall serve in their individual capacities and not as government representatives, nor as representatives of any organization. Governments or organizations shall therefore not give them instructions with regard to matters before an expert review group.

4.     Expert review groups may consult and seek information and technical advice from any source they deem appropriate. Before an expert review group seeks such information or advice from a source within the jurisdiction of a Member, it shall inform the government of that Member. Any Member shall respond promptly and fully to any request by an expert review group for such information as the expert review group considers necessary and appropriate.

5.     The parties to a dispute shall have access to all relevant information provided to an expert review group, unless it is of a confidential nature. Confidential information provided to the expert review group shall not be released without formal authorization from the government, organization or person providing the information. Where such information is requested from the expert review group but release of such information by the expert review group is not authorized, a non-confidential summary of the information will be provided by the government, organization or person supplying the information.

6.     The expert review group shall submit a draft report to the parties to the dispute with a view to obtaining their comments, and taking them into account, as appropriate, in the final report, which shall also be issued to the parties to the dispute when it is submitted to the panel. The final report of the expert review group shall be advisory only.

### DECISION ON THE APPLICATION AND REVIEW OF THE UNDERSTANDING ON RULES AND PROCEDURES GOVERNING THE SETTLEMENT OF DISPUTES

*Ministers,*

*Recalling* the Decision of 22 February 1994 that existing rules and procedures of GATT 1947 in the field of dispute settlement shall remain in effect until the date of entry into force of the Agreement Establishing the World Trade Organization;

*Invite* the relevant Councils and Committees to decide that they shall remain in operation for the purpose of dealing with any dispute for which the request for consultation was made before that date;

*Invite* the Ministerial Conference to complete a full review of dispute settlement rules and procedures under the World Trade Organization within four years after the entry into force of the Agreement Establishing the World Trade Organization, and to take a decision on the occasion of its first meeting after the completion of the review, whether to continue, modify or terminate such dispute settlement rules and procedures.

# 4. CONVENTION ESTABLISHING THE WORLD INTELLECTUAL PROPERTY ORGANIZATION

Signed at Stockholm on July 14, 1967 and
as amended on September 28, 1979

*The Contracting Parties,*

*Desiring to contribute to better understanding and cooperation among States for their mutual benefit on the basis of respect for their sovereignty and equality,*

*Desiring, in order to encourage creative activity, to promote the protection of intellectual property throughout the world,*

*Desiring to modernize and render more efficient the administration of the Unions established in the fields of the protection of industrial property and the protection of literary and artistic works, while fully respecting the independence of each of the Unions,*

*Agree as follows:*

## Article 1

### Establishment of the Organization

The World Intellectual Property Organization is hereby established.

## Article 2

### Definitions

For the purposes of this Convention:

(i)   "Organization" shall mean the World Intellectual Property Organization (WIPO);

(ii)   "International Bureau" shall mean the International Bureau of Intellectual Property;

(iii)   "Paris Convention" shall mean the Convention for the Protection of Industrial Property signed on March 20, 1883, including any of its revisions;

(iv)   "Berne Convention" shall mean the Convention for the Protection of Literary and Artistic Works signed on September 9, 1886, including any of its revisions;

(v)   "Paris Union" shall mean the International Union established by the Paris Convention;

(vi)   "Berne Union" shall mean the International Union established by the Berne Convention;

(vii)  "Unions" shall mean the Paris Union, the Special Unions and Agreements established in relation with that Union, the Berne Union, and any other international agreement designed to promote the protection of intellectual property whose administration is assumed by the Organization according to Article 4(iii);

(viii) "intellectual property" shall include the rights relating to:

— literary, artistic and scientific works,

— performances of performing artists, phonograms, and broadcasts,

— inventions in all fields of human endeavor,

— scientific discoveries,

— industrial designs,

— trademarks, service marks, and commercial names and designations,

— protection against unfair competition,

and all other rights resulting from intellectual activity in the industrial, scientific, literary or artistic fields.

## Article 3

### Objectives of the Organization

The objectives of the Organization are:

(i) to promote the protection of intellectual property throughout the world through cooperation among States and, where appropriate, in collaboration with any other international organization,

(ii) to ensure administrative cooperation among the Unions.

## Article 4

### Functions

In order to attain the objectives described in Article 3, the Organization, through its appropriate organs, and subject to the competence of each of the Unions:

(i) shall promote the development of measures designed to facilitate the efficient protection of intellectual property throughout the world and to harmonize national legislation in this field;

(ii) shall perform the administrative tasks of the Paris Union, the Special Unions established in relation with that Union, and the Berne Union;

(iii) may agree to assume, or participate in, the administration of any other international agreement designed to promote the protection of intellectual property;

(iv) shall encourage the conclusion of international agreements designed to promote the protection of intellectual property;

(v) shall offer its cooperation to States requesting legal-technical assistance in the field of intellectual property;

(vi) shall assemble and disseminate information concerning the protection of intellectual property, carry out and promote studies in this field, and publish the results of such studies;

(vii) shall maintain services facilitating the international protection of intellectual property and, where appropriate, provide for registration in this field and the publication of the data concerning the registrations;

(viii) shall take all other appropriate action.

## Article 5

### Membership

(1) Membership in the Organization shall be open to any State which is a member of any of the Unions as defined in Article 2(vii).

(2) Membership in the Organization shall be equally open to any State not a member of any of the Unions, provided that:

(i) it is a member of the United Nations, any of the Specialized Agencies brought into relationship with the United Nations, or the International Atomic Energy Agency, or is a party to the Statute of the International Court of Justice, or

(ii) it is invited by the General Assembly to become a party to this Convention.

## Article 6

### General Assembly

(1)

(a)  There shall be a General Assembly consisting of the States party to this Convention which are members of any of the Unions.

(b)  The Government of each State shall be represented by one delegate, who may be assisted by alternate delegates, advisors, and experts.

(c)  The expenses of each delegation shall be borne by the Government which has appointed it.

(2)  The General Assembly shall:

(i)  appoint the Director General upon nomination by the Coordination Committee;

(ii)  review and approve reports of the Director General concerning the Organization and give him all necessary instructions;

(iii)  review and approve the reports and activities of the Coordination Committee and give instructions to such Committee;

(iv)  adopt the biennial budget of expenses common to the Unions;

(v)  approve the measures proposed by the Director General concerning the administration of the international agreements referred to in Article 4(iii);

(vi)  adopt the financial regulations of the Organization;

(vii)  determine the working languages of the Secretariat, taking into consideration the practice of the United Nations;

(viii) invite States referred to under Article 5(2)(ii) to become party to this Convention;

(ix)  determine which States not Members of the Organization and which intergovernmental and international non-governmental organizations shall be admitted to its meetings as observers;

(x)  exercise such other functions as are appropriate under this Convention.

(3)

(a)  Each State, whether member of one or more Unions, shall have one vote in the General Assembly.

(b)  One-half of the States members of the General Assembly shall constitute a quorum.

(c)  Notwithstanding the provisions of subparagraph (b), if, in any session, the number of States represented is less than one-half but equal to or more than one-third of the States members of the General Assembly, the General Assembly may make decisions but, with the exception of decisions concerning its own procedure, all such decisions shall take effect only if the following conditions are fulfilled. The International Bureau shall communicate the said decisions to the States members of the General Assembly which were not represented and shall invite them to express in writing their vote or abstention within a period of three months from the date of the communication. If, at the expiration of this period, the number of States having thus expressed their vote or abstention attains the number of States which was lacking for attaining the quorum in the session itself, such decisions shall take effect provided that at the same time the required majority still obtains.

(d)  Subject to the provisions of subparagraphs (e) and (f), the General Assembly shall make its decisions by a majority of two-thirds of the votes cast.

(e) The approval of measures concerning the administration of international agreements referred to in Article 4(iii) shall require a majority of three-fourths of the votes cast.

(f) The approval of an agreement with the United Nations under Articles 57 and 63 of the Charter of the United Nations shall require a majority of nine-tenths of the votes cast.

(g) For the appointment of the Director General (paragraph (2)(i)), the approval of measures proposed by the Director General concerning the administration of international agreements (paragraph (2)(v)), and the transfer of headquarters (Article 10), the required majority must be attained not only in the General Assembly but also in the Assembly of the Paris Union and the Assembly of the Berne Union.

(h) Abstentions shall not be considered as votes.

(i) A delegate may represent, and vote in the name of, one State only.

(4)

(a) The General Assembly shall meet once in every second calendar year in ordinary session, upon convocation by the Director General.

(b) The General Assembly shall meet in extraordinary session upon convocation by the Director General either at the request of the Coordination Committee or at the request of one-fourth of the States members of the General Assembly.

(c) Meetings shall be held at the headquarters of the Organization.

(5) States party to this Convention which are not members of any of the Unions shall be admitted to the meetings of the General Assembly as observers.

(6) The General Assembly shall adopt its own rules of procedure.

## Article 7

### Conference

(1)

(a) There shall be a Conference consisting of the States party to this Convention whether or not they are members of any of the Unions.

(b) The Government of each State shall be represented by one delegate, who may be assisted by alternate delegates, advisors, and experts.

(c) The expenses of each delegation shall be borne by the Government which has appointed it.

(2) The Conference shall:

(i) discuss matters of general interest in the field of intellectual property and may adopt recommendations relating to such matters, having regard for the competence and autonomy of the Unions;

(ii) adopt the biennial budget of the Conference;

(iii) within the limits of the budget of the Conference, establish the biennial program of legal-technical assistance;

(iv) adopt amendments to this Convention as provided in Article 17;

(v) determine which States not Members of the Organization and which intergovernmental and international non-governmental organizations shall be admitted to its meetings as observers;

(vi) exercise such other functions as are appropriate under this Convention.

(3)

    (a)    Each Member State shall have one vote in the Conference.

    (b)    One-third of the Member States shall constitute a quorum.

    (c)    Subject to the provisions of Article 17, the Conference shall make its decisions by a majority of two-thirds of the votes cast.

    (d)    The amounts of the contributions of States party to this Convention not members of any of the Unions shall be fixed by a vote in which only the delegates of such States shall have the right to vote.

    (e)    Abstentions shall not be considered as votes.

    (f)    A delegate may represent, and vote in the name of, one State only.

(4)

    (a)    The Conference shall meet in ordinary session, upon convocation by the Director General, during the same period and at the same place as the General Assembly.

    (b)    The Conference shall meet in extraordinary session, upon convocation by the Director General, at the request of the majority of the Member States.

(5)    The Conference shall adopt its own rules of procedure.

## Article 8

### Coordination Committee

(1)

    (a)    There shall be a Coordination Committee consisting of the States party to this Convention which are members of the Executive Committee of the Paris Union, or the Executive Committee of the Berne Union, or both. However, if either of these Executive Committees is composed of more than one-fourth of the number of the countries members of the Assembly which elected it, then such Executive Committee shall designate from among its members the States which will be members of the Coordination Committee, in such a way that their number shall not exceed the one-fourth referred to above, it being understood that the country on the territory of which the Organization has its headquarters shall not be included in the computation of the said one-fourth.

    (b)    The Government of each State member of the Coordination Committee shall be represented by one delegate, who may be assisted by alternate delegates, advisors, and experts.

    (c)    Whenever the Coordination Committee considers either matters of direct interest to the program or budget of the Conference and its agenda, or proposals for the amendment of this Convention which would affect the rights or obligations of States party to this Convention not members of any of the Unions, one-fourth of such States shall participate in the meetings of the Coordination Committee with the same rights as members of that Committee. The Conference shall, at each of its ordinary sessions, designate these States.

    (d)    The expenses of each delegation shall be borne by the Government which has appointed it.

(2)    If the other Unions administered by the Organization wish to be represented as such in the Coordination Committee, their representatives must be appointed from among the States members of the Coordination Committee.

(3)    The Coordination Committee shall:

    (i)    give advice to the organs of the Unions, the General Assembly, the Conference, and the Director General, on all administrative, financial and other matters of common interest either to two or more of the Unions, or to one or more of the Unions and the Organization, and in particular on the budget of expenses common to the Unions;

(ii)  prepare the draft agenda of the General Assembly;

(iii)  prepare the draft agenda and the draft program and budget of the Conference;

(iv)  [deleted]

(v)  when the term of office of the Director General is about to expire, or when there is a vacancy in the post of the Director General, nominate a candidate for appointment to such position by the General Assembly; if the General Assembly does not appoint its nominee, the Coordination Committee shall nominate another candidate; this procedure shall be repeated until the latest nominee is appointed by the General Assembly;

(vi)  if the post of the Director General becomes vacant between two sessions of the General Assembly, appoint an Acting Director General for the term preceding the assuming of office by the new Director General;

(vii)  perform such other functions as are allocated to it under this Convention.

(4)

(a)  The Coordination Committee shall meet once every year in ordinary session, upon convocation by the Director General. It shall normally meet at the headquarters of the Organization.

(b)  The Coordination Committee shall meet in extraordinary session, upon convocation by the Director General, either on his own initiative, or at the request of its Chairman or one-fourth of its members.

(5)

(a)  Each State whether a member of one or both of the Executive Committees referred to in paragraph (1)(a), shall have one vote in the Coordination Committee.

(b)  One-half of the members of the Coordination Committee shall constitute a quorum.

(c)  A delegate may represent, and vote in the name of, one State only.

(6)

(a)  The Coordination Committee shall express its opinions and make its decisions by a simple majority of the votes cast. Abstentions shall not be considered as votes.

(b)  Even if a simple majority is obtained, any member of the Coordination Committee may, immediately after the vote, request that the votes be the subject of a special recount in the following manner: two separate lists shall be prepared, one containing the names of the States members of the Executive Committee of the Paris Union and the other the names of the States members of the Executive Committee of the Berne Union; the vote of each State shall be inscribed opposite its name in each list in which it appears. Should this special recount indicate that a simple majority has not been obtained in each of those lists, the proposal shall not be considered as carried.

(7)  Any State Member of the Organization which is not a member of the Coordination Committee may be represented at the meetings of the Committee by observers having the right to take part in the debates but without the right to vote.

(8)  The Coordination Committee shall establish its own rules of procedure.

## Article 9

### International Bureau

(1)  The International Bureau shall be the Secretariat of the Organization.

(2)  The International Bureau shall be directed by the Director General, assisted by two or more Deputy Directors General.

(3)  The Director General shall be appointed for a fixed term, which shall be not less than six years. He shall be eligible for reappointment for fixed terms. The periods of the initial appointment and possible subsequent appointments, as well as all other conditions of the appointment, shall be fixed by the General Assembly.

(4)

    (a)  The Director General shall be the chief executive of the Organization.

    (b)  He shall represent the Organization.

    (c)  He shall report to, and conform to the instructions of, the General Assembly as to the internal and external affairs of the Organization.

(5)  The Director General shall prepare the draft programs and budgets and periodical reports on activities. He shall transmit them to the Governments of the interested States and to the competent organs of the Unions and the Organization.

(6)  The Director General and any staff member designated by him shall participate, without the right to vote, in all meetings of the General Assembly, the Conference, the Coordination Committee, and any other committee or working group. The Director General or a staff member designated by him shall be *ex officio* secretary of these bodies.

(7)  The Director General shall appoint the staff necessary for the efficient performance of the tasks of the International Bureau. He shall appoint the Deputy Directors General after approval by the Coordination Committee. The conditions of employment shall be fixed by the staff regulations to be approved by the Coordination Committee on the proposal of the Director General. The paramount consideration in the employment of the staff and in the determination of the conditions of service shall be the necessity of securing the highest standards of efficiency, competence, and integrity. Due regard shall be paid to the importance of recruiting the staff on as wide a geographical basis as possible.

(8)  The nature of the responsibilities of the Director General and of the staff shall be exclusively international. In the discharge of their duties they shall not seek or receive instructions from any Government or from any authority external to the Organization. They shall refrain from any action which might prejudice their position as international officials. Each Member State undertakes to respect the exclusively international character of the responsibilities of the Director General and the staff, and not to seek to influence them in the discharge of their duties.

## Article 10

### Headquarters

(1)  The headquarters of the Organization shall be at Geneva.

(2)  Its transfer may be decided as provided for in Article 6(3)(d) and Article (6)(3)(g).

## Article 11

### Finances

(1)  The Organization shall have two separate budgets: the budget of expenses common to the Unions, and the budget of the Conference.

(2)

    (a)    The budget of expenses common to the Unions shall include provision for expenses of interest to several Unions.

    (b)    This budget shall be financed from the following sources:

        (i)    contributions of the Unions, provided that the amount of the contribution of each Union shall be fixed by the Assembly of that Union, having regard to the interest the Union has in the common expenses;

        (ii)    charges due for services performed by the International Bureau not in direct relation with any of the Unions or not received for services rendered by the International Bureau in the field of legal-technical assistance;

        (iii)    sale of, or royalties on, the publications of the International Bureau not directly concerning any of the Unions;

        (iv)    gifts, bequests, and subventions, given to the Organization, except those referred to in paragraph (3)(b)(iv);

        (v)    rents, interests, and other miscellaneous income, of the Organization.

(3)

    (a)    The budget of the Conference shall include provision for the expenses of holding sessions of the Conference and for the cost of the legal-technical assistance program.

    (b)    This budget shall be financed from the following sources:

        (i)    contributions of States party to this Convention not members of any of the Unions;

        (ii)    any sums made available to this budget by the Unions, provided that the amount of the sum made available by each Union shall be fixed by the Assembly of that Union and that each Union shall be free to abstain from contributing to the said budget;

        (iii)    sums received for services rendered by the International Bureau in the field of legal-technical assistance;

        (iv)    gifts, bequests, and subventions, given to the Organization for the purposes referred to in subparagraph (a).

(4)

    (a)    For the purpose of establishing its contribution towards the budget of the Conference, each State party to this Convention not member of any of the Unions shall belong to a class, and shall pay its annual contributions on the basis of a number of units fixed as follows:

Class A. . . . 10

Class B. . . . 3

Class C. . . . 1

    (b)    Each such State shall, concurrently with taking action as provided in Article 14(1), indicate the class to which it wishes to belong. Any such State may change class. If it chooses a lower class, the State must announce it to the Conference at one of its ordinary sessions. Any such change shall take effect at the beginning of the calendar year following the session.

    (c)    The annual contribution of each such State shall be an amount in the same proportion to the total sum to be contributed to the budget of the Conference by all such States as the number of its units is to the total of the units of all the said States.

    (d)    Contributions shall become due on the first of January of each year.

(e)   If the budget is not adopted before the beginning of a new financial period the budget shall be at the same level as the budget of the previous year, in accordance with the financial regulations.

(5)   Any State party to this Convention not member of any of the Unions which is in arrears in the payment of its financial contributions under the present Article, and any State party to this Convention member of any of the Unions which is in arrears in the payment of its contributions to any of the Unions, shall have no vote in any of the bodies of the Organization of which it is a member, if the amount of its arrears equals or exceeds the amount of the contributions due from it for the preceding two full years. However, any of these bodies may allow such a State to continue to exercise its vote in that body if, and as long as, it is satisfied that the delay in payment arises from exceptional and unavoidable circumstances.

(6)   The amount of the fees and charges due for services rendered by the International Bureau in the field of legal-technical assistance shall be established, and shall be reported to the Coordination Committee, by the Director General.

(7)   The Organization, with the approval of the Coordination Committee, may receive gifts, bequests, and subventions, directly from Governments, public or private institutions, associations or private persons.

(8)

(a)   The Organization shall have a working capital fund which shall be constituted by a single payment made by the Unions and by each State party to this Convention not member of any Union. If the fund becomes insufficient, it shall be increased.

(b)   The amount of the single payment of each Union and its possible participation in any increase shall be decided by its Assembly.

(c)   The amount of the single payment of each State party to this Convention not member of any Union and its part in any increase shall be a proportion of the contribution of that State for the year in which the fund is established or the increase decided. The proportion and the terms of payment shall be fixed by the Conference on the proposal of the Director General and after it has heard the advice of the Coordination Committee.

(9)

(a)   In the headquarters agreement concluded with the State on the territory of which the Organization has its headquarters, it shall be provided that, whenever the working capital fund is insufficient, such State shall grant advances. The amount of these advances and the conditions on which they are granted shall be the subject of separate agreements, in each case, between such State and the Organization. As long as it remains under the obligation to grant advances, such State shall have an ex officio seat on the Coordination Committee.

(b)   The State referred to in subparagraph (a) and the Organization shall each have the right to denounce the obligation to grant advances, by written notification. Denunciation shall take effect three years after the end of the year in which it has been notified.

(10)  The auditing of the accounts shall be effected by one or more Member States, or by external auditors, as provided in the financial regulations. They shall be designated, with their agreement, by the General Assembly.

## Article 12

### Legal Capacity; Privileges and Immunities

(1)   The Organization shall enjoy on the territory of each Member State, in conformity with the laws of that State, such legal capacity as may be necessary for the fulfilment of the Organization's objectives and for the exercise of its functions.

(2) The Organization shall conclude a headquarters agreement with the Swiss Confederation and with any other State in which the headquarters may subsequently be located.

(3) The Organization may conclude bilateral or multilateral agreements with the other Member States with a view to the enjoyment by the Organization, its officials, and representatives of all Member States, of such privileges and immunities as may be necessary for the fulfilment of its objectives and for the exercise of its functions.

(4) The Director General may negotiate and, after approval by the Coordination Committee, shall conclude and sign on behalf of the Organization the agreements referred to in paragraphs (2) and (3).

## Article 13

### Relations with Other Organizations

(1) The Organization shall, where appropriate, establish working relations and cooperate with other intergovernmental organizations. Any general agreement to such effect entered into with such organizations shall be concluded by the Director General after approval by the Coordination Committee.

(2) The Organization may, on matters within its competence, make suitable arrangements for consultation and cooperation with international non-governmental organizations and, with the consent of the Governments concerned, with national organizations, governmental or non-governmental. Such arrangements shall be made by the Director General after approval by the Coordination Committee.

## Article 14

### Becoming Party to the Convention

(1) States referred to in Article 5 may become party to this Convention and Member of the Organization by:

(i) signature without reservation as to ratification, or

(ii) signature subject to ratification followed by the deposit of an instrument of ratification, or

(iii) deposit of an instrument of accession.

(2) Notwithstanding any other provision of this Convention, a State party to the Paris Convention, the Berne Convention, or both Conventions, may become party to this Convention only if it concurrently ratifies or accedes to, or only after it has ratified or acceded to:

— either the Stockholm Act of the Paris Convention in its entirety or with only the limitation set forth in Article 20(1)(b)(i) thereof,

— or the Stockholm Act of the Berne Convention in its entirety or with only the limitation set forth in Article 28(1)(b)(i) thereof.

(3) Instruments of ratification or accession shall be deposited with the Director General.

## Article 15

### Entry into Force of the Convention

(1) This Convention shall enter into force three months after ten States members of the Paris Union and seven States members of the Berne Union have taken action as provided in Article 14(1), it being understood that, if a State is a member of both Unions, it will be counted in both groups. On that date, this Convention shall enter into force also in respect of States which, not being members of either of the two Unions, have taken action as provided in Article 14(1) three months or more prior to that date.

(2) In respect to any other State, this Convention shall enter into force three months after the date on which such State takes action as provided in Article 14(1).

## Article 16

### Reservations

No reservations to this Convention are permitted.

## Article 17

### Amendments

(1) Proposals for the amendment of this Convention may be initiated by any Member State, by the Coordination Committee, or by the Director General. Such proposals shall be communicated by the Director General to the Member States at least six months in advance of their consideration by the Conference.

(2) Amendments shall be adopted by the Conference. Whenever amendments would affect the rights and obligations of States party to this Convention not members of any of the Unions, such States shall also vote. On all other amendments proposed, only States party to this Convention members of any Union shall vote. Amendments shall be adopted by a simple majority of the votes cast, provided that the Conference shall vote only on such proposals for amendments as have previously been adopted by the Assembly of the Paris Union and the Assembly of the Berne Union according to the rules applicable in each of them regarding the adoption of amendments to the administrative provisions of their respective Conventions.

(3) Any amendment shall enter into force one month after written notifications of acceptance, effected in accordance with their respective constitutional processes, have been received by the Director General from three-fourths of the States Members of the Organization, entitled to vote on the proposal for amendment pursuant to paragraph (2), at the time the Conference adopted the amendment. Any amendments thus accepted shall bind all the States which are Members of the Organization at the time the amendment enters into force or which become Members at a subsequent date, provided that any amendment increasing the financial obligations of Member States shall bind only those States which have notified their acceptance of such amendment.

## Article 18

### Denunciation

(1) Any Member State may denounce this Convention by notification addressed to the Director General.

(2) Denunciation shall take effect six months after the day on which the Director General has received the notification.

## Article 19

### Notifications

The Director General shall notify the Governments of all Member States of:

(i) the date of entry into force of the Convention,

(ii) signatures and deposits of instruments of ratification or accession,

(iii) acceptances of an amendment to this Convention, and the date upon which the amendment enters into force,

(iv) denunciations of this Convention.

## Article 20

### Final Provisions

(1)

    (a)   This Convention shall be signed in a single copy in English, French, Russian and Spanish, all texts being equally authentic, and shall be deposited with the Government of Sweden.

    (b)   This Convention shall remain open for signature at Stockholm until January 13, 1968.

(2)   Official texts shall be established by the Director General, after consultation with the interested Governments, in German, Italian and Portuguese, and such other languages as the Conference may designate.

(3)   The Director General shall transmit two duly certified copies of this Convention and of each amendment adopted by the Conference to the Governments of the States members of the Paris or Berne Unions, to the Government of any other State when it accedes to this Convention, and, on request, to the Government of any other State. The copies of the signed text of the Convention transmitted to the Governments shall be certified by the Government of Sweden.

(4)   The Director General shall register this Convention with the Secretariat of the United Nations.

## Article 21

### Transitional Provisions

(1)   Until the first Director General assumes office, references in this Convention to the International Bureau or to the Director General shall be deemed to be references to the United International Bureaux for the Protection of Industrial, Literary and Artistic Property (also called the United International Bureaux for the Protection of Intellectual Property (BIRPI)), or its Director, respectively.

(2)

    (a)   States which are members of any of the Unions but which have not become party to this Convention may, for five years from the date of entry into force of this Convention, exercise, if they so desire, the same rights as if they had become party to this Convention. Any State desiring to exercise such rights shall give written notification to this effect to the Director General; this notification shall be effective on the date of its receipt. Such States shall be deemed to be members of the General Assembly and the Conference until the expiration of the said period.

    (b)   Upon expiration of this five-year period, such States shall have no right to vote in the General Assembly, the Conference, and the Coordination Committee.

    (c)   Upon becoming party to this Convention, such States shall regain such right to vote.

(3)

    (a)   As long as there are States members of the Paris or Berne Unions which have not become party to this Convention, the International Bureau and the Director General shall also function as the United International Bureaux for the Protection of Industrial, Literary and Artistic Property, and its Director, respectively.

    (b)   The staff in the employment of the said Bureaux on the date of entry into force of this Convention shall, during the transitional period referred to in subparagraph (a), be considered as also employed by the International Bureau.

(4)

    (a)   Once all the States members of the Paris Union have become Members of the Organization, the rights, obligations, and property, of the Bureau of that Union shall devolve on the International Bureau of the Organization.

    (b)   Once all the States members of the Berne Union have become Members of the Organization, the rights, obligations, and property, of the Bureau of that Union shall devolve on the International Bureau of the Organization.

# 5. PARTIES TO THE CONVENTION ESTABLISHING THE WORLD INTELLECTUAL PROPERTY ORGANIZATION*

WIPO Convention (1967), amended in 1979

**Status on May 4, 2021**

| State | Date on which State became member of WIPO | Paris Union (P) and/or Berne Union (B) | |
|---|---|---|---|
| Afghanistan | December 13, 2005 | P | B |
| Albania | June 30, 1992 | P | B |
| Algeria | April 16, 1975 | P | B |
| Andorra | October 28, 1994 | P | B |
| Angola | April 15, 1985 | P | – |
| Antigua and Barbuda | March 17, 2000 | P | B |
| Argentina | October 8, 1980 | P | B |
| Armenia | April 22, 1993 | P | B |
| Australia | August 10, 1972 | P | B |
| Austria | August 11, 1973 | P | B |
| Azerbaijan | December 25, 1995 | P | B |
| Bahamas | January 4, 1977 | P | B |
| Bahrain | June 22, 1995 | P | B |
| Bangladesh | May 11, 1985 | P | B |
| Barbados | October 5, 1979 | P | B |
| Belarus | April 26, 1970 | P | B |
| Belgium | January 31, 1975 | P | B |
| Belize | June 17, 2000 | P | B |
| Benin | March 9, 1975 | P | B |
| Bhutan | March 16, 1994 | P | B |
| Bolivia (Plurinational State of) | July 6, 1993 | P | B |
| Bosnia and Herzegovina | March 1, 1992 | P | B |
| Botswana | April 15, 1998 | P | B |
| Brazil | March 20, 1975 | P | B |
| Brunei Darussalam | April 21, 1994 | P | B |
| Bulgaria | May 19, 1970 | P | B |
| Burkina Faso | August 23, 1975 | P | B |
| Burundi | March 30, 1977 | P | B |
| Cabo Verde | July 7, 1997 | – | B |
| Cambodia | July 25, 1995 | P | – |
| Cameroon | November 3, 1973 | P | B |

---

* Document originally produced by the World Intellectual Property Organization (WIPO), the owner of the copyright. Published with the permission of the World Intellectual Property Organization.

## PARTIES TO THE CONVENTION ESTABLISHING WIPO

| State | Date on which State became member of WIPO | Paris Union (P) and/or Berne Union (B) | |
|---|---|---|---|
| Canada | June 26, 1970 | P | B |
| Central African Republic | August 23, 1978 | P | B |
| Chad | September 26, 1970 | P | B |
| Chile | June 25, 1975 | P | B |
| China | June 3, 1980 | P | B |
| Colombia | May 4, 1980 | P | B |
| Comoros | April 3, 2005 | P | B |
| Congo | December 2, 1975 | P | B |
| Cook Islands | October 27, 2016 | – | B |
| Costa Rica | June 10, 1981 | P | B |
| Côte d'Ivoire | May 1, 1974 | P | B |
| Croatia | October 8, 1991 | P | B |
| Cuba | March 27, 1975 | P | B |
| Cyprus | October 26, 1984 | P | B |
| Czech Republic | January 1, 1993 | P | B |
| Democratic People's Republic of Korea | August 17, 1974 | P | B |
| Democratic Republic of the Congo | January 28, 1975 | P | B |
| Denmark | April 26, 1970 | P | B |
| Djibouti | May 13, 2002 | P | B |
| Dominica | September 26, 1998 | P | B |
| Dominican Republic | June 27, 2000 | P | B |
| Ecuador | May 22, 1988 | P | B |
| Egypt | April 21, 1975 | P | B |
| El Salvador | September 18, 1979 | P | B |
| Equatorial Guinea | June 26, 1997 | P | B |
| Eritrea | February 20, 1997 | – | – |
| Estonia | February 5, 1994 | P | B |
| Eswatini | August 18, 1988 | P | B |
| Ethiopia | February 19, 1998 | – | – |
| Fiji | March 11, 1972 | – | B |
| Finland | September 8, 1970 | P | B |
| France | October 18, 1974 | P | B |
| Gabon | June 6, 1975 | P | B |
| Gambia | December 10, 1980 | P | B |
| Georgia | December 25, 1991 | P | B |
| Germany | September 19, 1970 | P | B |
| Ghana | June 12, 1976 | P | B |
| Greece | March 4, 1976 | P | B |
| Grenada | September 22, 1998 | P | B |
| Guatemala | April 30, 1983 | P | B |

## PARTIES TO THE CONVENTION ESTABLISHING WIPO

| State | Date on which State became member of WIPO | Paris Union (P) and/or Berne Union (B) | |
|---|---|---|---|
| Guinea | November 13, 1980 | P | B |
| Guinea-Bissau | June 28, 1988 | P | B |
| Guyana | October 25, 1994 | P | B |
| Haiti | November 2, 1983 | P | B |
| Holy See | April 20, 1975 | P | B |
| Honduras | November 15, 1983 | P | B |
| Hungary | April 26, 1970 | P | B |
| Iceland | September 13, 1986 | P | B |
| India | May 1, 1975 | P | B |
| Indonesia | December 18, 1979 | P | B |
| Iran (Islamic Republic of) | March 14, 2002 | P | – |
| Iraq | January 21, 1976 | P | – |
| Ireland | April 26, 1970 | P | B |
| Israel | April 26, 1970 | P | B |
| Italy | April 20, 1977 | P | B |
| Jamaica | December 25, 1978 | P | B |
| Japan | April 20, 1975 | P | B |
| Jordan | July 12, 1972 | P | B |
| Kazakhstan | December 25, 1991 | P | B |
| Kenya | October 5, 1971 | P | B |
| Kiribati | July 19, 2013 | – | B |
| Kuwait | July 14, 1998 | P | B |
| Kyrgyzstan | December 25, 1991 | P | B |
| Lao People's Democratic Republic | January 17, 1995 | P | B |
| Latvia | January 21, 1993 | P | B |
| Lebanon | December 30, 1986 | P | B |
| Lesotho | November 18, 1986 | P | B |
| Liberia | March 8, 1989 | P | B |
| Libya | September 28, 1976 | P | B |
| Liechtenstein | May 21, 1972 | P | B |
| Lithuania | April 30, 1992 | P | B |
| Luxembourg | March 19, 1975 | P | B |
| Madagascar | December 22, 1989 | P | B |
| Malawi | June 11, 1970 | P | B |
| Malaysia | January 1, 1989 | P | B |
| Maldives | May 12, 2004 | – | – |
| Mali | August 14, 1982 | P | B |
| Malta | December 7, 1977 | P | B |
| Marshall Islands | December 11, 2017 | – | – |
| Mauritania | September 17, 1976 | P | B |

## PARTIES TO THE CONVENTION ESTABLISHING WIPO

| State | Date on which State became member of WIPO | Paris Union (P) and/or Berne Union (B) | |
|---|---|---|---|
| Mauritius | September 21, 1976 | P | B |
| Mexico | June 14, 1975 | P | B |
| Monaco | March 3, 1975 | P | B |
| Mongolia | February 28, 1979 | P | B |
| Montenegro | June 3, 2006 | P | B |
| Morocco | July 27, 1971 | P | B |
| Mozambique | December 23, 1996 | P | B |
| Myanmar | May 15, 2001 | – | – |
| Namibia | December 23, 1991 | P | B |
| Nauru | May 11, 2020 | – | B |
| Nepal | February 4, 1997 | P | B |
| Netherlands | January 9, 1975 | P | B |
| New Zealand | June 20, 1984 | P | B |
| Nicaragua | May 5, 1985 | P | B |
| Niger | May 18, 1975 | P | B |
| Nigeria | April 9, 1995 | P | B |
| Niue | January 8, 2015 | – | B |
| North Macedonia | September 8, 1991 | P | B |
| Norway | June 8, 1974 | P | B |
| Oman | February 19, 1997 | P | B |
| Pakistan | January 6, 1977 | P | B |
| Panama | September 17, 1983 | P | B |
| Papua New Guinea | July 10, 1997 | P | – |
| Paraguay | June 20, 1987 | P | B |
| Peru | September 4, 1980 | P | B |
| Philippines | July 14, 1980 | P | B |
| Poland | March 23, 1975 | P | B |
| Portugal | April 27, 1975 | P | B |
| Qatar | September 3, 1976 | P | B |
| Republic of Korea | March 1, 1979 | P | B |
| Republic of Moldova | December 25, 1991 | P | B |
| Romania | April 26, 1970 | P | B |
| Russian Federation | April 26, 1970[2] | P | B |
| Rwanda | February 3, 1984 | P | B |
| Saint Kitts and Nevis | November 16, 1995 | P | B |
| Saint Lucia | August 21, 1993 | P | B |
| Saint Vincent and the Grenadines | August 29, 1995 | P | B |
| Samoa | October 11, 1997 | P | B |
| San Marino | June 26, 1991 | P | B |
| Sao Tome and Principe | May 12, 1998 | P | B |

## PARTIES TO THE CONVENTION ESTABLISHING WIPO

| State | Date on which State became member of WIPO | Paris Union (P) and/or Berne Union (B) | |
|---|---|---|---|
| Saudi Arabia | May 22, 1982 | P | B |
| Senegal | April 26, 1970 | P | B |
| Serbia[3] | April 27, 1992 | P | B |
| Seychelles | March 16, 2000 | P | – |
| Sierra Leone | May 18, 1986 | P | – |
| Singapore | December 10, 1990 | P | B |
| Slovakia | January 1, 1993 | P | B |
| Slovenia | June 25, 1991 | P | B |
| Solomon Islands | July 4, 2019 | – | B |
| Somalia | November 18, 1982 | – | – |
| South Africa | March 23, 1975 | P | B |
| Spain | April 26, 1970 | P | B |
| Sri Lanka | September 20, 1978 | P | B |
| Sudan | February 15, 1974 | P | B |
| Suriname | November 25, 1975 | P | B |
| Sweden | April 26, 1970 | P | B |
| Switzerland | April 26, 1970 | P | B |
| Syrian Arab Republic | November 18, 2004 | P | B |
| Tajikistan | December 25, 1991 | P | B |
| Thailand | December 25, 1989 | P | B |
| Timor-Leste | December 12, 2017 | – | – |
| Togo | April 28, 1975 | P | B |
| Tonga | June 14, 2001 | P | B |
| Trinidad and Tobago | August 16, 1988 | P | B |
| Tunisia | November 28, 1975 | P | B |
| Turkey | May 12, 1976 | P | B |
| Turkmenistan | December 25, 1991 | P | B |
| Tuvalu | June 4, 2014 | – | B |
| Uganda | October 18, 1973 | P | – |
| Ukraine | April 26, 1970 | P | B |
| United Arab Emirates | September 24, 1974 | P | B |
| United Kingdom | April 26, 1970 | P | B |
| United Republic of Tanzania | December 30, 1983 | P | B |
| United States of America | August 25, 1970 | P | B |
| Uruguay | December 21, 1979 | P | B |
| Uzbekistan | December 25, 1991 | P | B |
| Vanuatu | March 2, 2012 | – | B |
| Venezuela (Bolivarian Republic of) | November 23, 1984 | P | B |
| Viet Nam | July 2, 1976 | P | B |
| Yemen | March 29, 1979 | P | B |

## PARTIES TO THE CONVENTION ESTABLISHING WIPO

| State | Date on which State became member of WIPO | Paris Union (P) and/or Berne Union (B) | |
|---|---|---|---|
| Zambia | May 14, 1977 | P | B |
| Zimbabwe | December 29, 1981 | P | B |

(Total: 193 States)

---

[1] "P" means that the State is also a member of the International Union for the Protection of Industrial Property (Paris Union), founded by the Paris Convention for the Protection of Industrial Property.

"B" means that the State is also a member of the International Union for the Protection of Literary and Artistic Works (Berne Union), founded by the Berne Convention for the Protection of Literary and Artistic Works.

[2] Date of ratification of the Soviet Union, continued by the Russian Federation as from December 25, 1991.

[3] Serbia is the continuing State from Serbia and Montenegro as from June 3, 2006.

# 6. WTO MINISTERIAL DECLARATION

Adopted on 14 November 2001
Ministerial Conference, Fourth Session, Doha, 9–14 November 2001
(WT/MIN(01)/DEC/1 20 November 2001)

1.   The multilateral trading system embodied in the World Trade Organization has contributed significantly to economic growth, development and employment throughout the past fifty years. We are determined, particularly in the light of the global economic slowdown, to maintain the process of reform and liberalization of trade policies, thus ensuring that the system plays its full part in promoting recovery, growth and development. We therefore strongly reaffirm the principles and objectives set out in the Marrakesh Agreement Establishing the World Trade Organization, and pledge to reject the use of protectionism.

2.   International trade can play a major role in the promotion of economic development and the alleviation of poverty. We recognize the need for all our peoples to benefit from the increased opportunities and welfare gains that the multilateral trading system generates. The majority of WTO Members are developing countries. We seek to place their needs and interests at the heart of the Work Programme adopted in this Declaration. Recalling the Preamble to the Marrakesh Agreement, we shall continue to make positive efforts designed to ensure that developing countries, and especially the least-developed among them, secure a share in the growth of world trade commensurate with the needs of their economic development. In this context, enhanced market access, balanced rules, and well targeted, sustainably financed technical assistance and capacity-building programmes have important roles to play.

3.   We recognize the particular vulnerability of the least-developed countries and the special structural difficulties they face in the global economy. We are committed to addressing the marginalization of least-developed countries in international trade and to improving their effective participation in the multilateral trading system. We recall the commitments made by Ministers at our meetings in Marrakesh, Singapore and Geneva, and by the international community at the Third UN Conference on Least-Developed Countries in Brussels, to help least-developed countries secure beneficial and meaningful integration into the multilateral trading system and the global economy. We are determined that the WTO will play its part in building effectively on these commitments under the Work Programme we are establishing.

4.   We stress our commitment to the WTO as the unique forum for global trade rule-making and liberalization, while also recognizing that regional trade agreements can play an important role in promoting the liberalization and expansion of trade and in fostering development.

5.   We are aware that the challenges Members face in a rapidly changing international environment cannot be addressed through measures taken in the trade field alone. We shall continue to work with the Bretton Woods institutions for greater coherence in global economic policy-making.

6.   We strongly reaffirm our commitment to the objective of sustainable development, as stated in the Preamble to the Marrakesh Agreement. We are convinced that the aims of upholding and safeguarding an open and non-discriminatory multilateral trading system, and acting for the protection of the environment and the promotion of sustainable development can and must be mutually supportive. We take note of the efforts by Members to conduct national environmental assessments of trade policies on a voluntary basis. We recognize that under WTO rules no country should be prevented from taking measures for the protection of human, animal or plant life or health, or of the environment at the levels it considers appropriate, subject to the requirement that they are not applied in a manner which would constitute a means of arbitrary or unjustifiable discrimination between countries where the same conditions prevail, or a disguised restriction on international trade, and are otherwise in accordance with the provisions of the WTO Agreements. We welcome the WTOs continued cooperation with UNEP and other inter-governmental environmental organizations. We encourage efforts to promote cooperation between the WTO and relevant international environmental

and developmental organizations, especially in the lead-up to the World Summit on Sustainable Development to be held in Johannesburg, South Africa, in September 2002. [. . .]

11.   In view of these considerations, we hereby agree to undertake the broad and balanced Work Programme set out below. This incorporates both an expanded negotiating agenda and other important decisions and activities necessary to address the challenges facing the multilateral trading system.

## WORK PROGRAMME

### IMPLEMENTATION-RELATED ISSUES AND CONCERNS

12.   We attach the utmost importance to the implementation-related issues and concerns raised by Members and are determined to find appropriate solutions to them. In this connection, and having regard to the General Council Decisions of 3 May and 15 December 2000, we further adopt the Decision on Implementation-Related Issues and Concerns in document WT/MIN(01)/17 to address a number of implementation problems faced by Members. We agree that negotiations on outstanding implementation issues shall be an integral part of the Work Programme we are establishing, and that agreements reached at an early stage in these negotiations shall be treated in accordance with the provisions of paragraph 47 below. In this regard, we shall proceed as follows: (a) where we provide a specific negotiating mandate in this Declaration, the relevant implementation issues shall be addressed under that mandate; (b) the other outstanding implementation issues shall be addressed as a matter of priority by the relevant WTO bodies, which shall report to the Trade Negotiations Committee, established under paragraph 46 below, by the end of 2002 for appropriate action. [. . .]

### TRADE-RELATED ASPECTS OF INTELLECTUAL PROPERTY RIGHTS

17.   We stress the importance we attach to implementation and interpretation of the Agreement on Trade-Related Aspects of Intellectual Property Rights (TRIPS Agreement) in a manner supportive of public health, by promoting both access to existing medicines and research and development into new medicines and, in this connection, are adopting a separate Declaration.

18.   With a view to completing the work started in the Council for Trade-Related Aspects of Intellectual Property Rights (Council for TRIPS) on the implementation of Article 23.4, we agree to negotiate the establishment of a multilateral system of notification and registration of geographical indications for wines and spirits by the Fifth Session of the Ministerial Conference. We note that issues related to the extension of the protection of geographical indications provided for in Article 23 to products other than wines and spirits will be addressed in the Council for TRIPS pursuant to paragraph 12 of this Declaration.

19.   We instruct the Council for TRIPS, in pursuing its work programme including under the review of Article 27.3(b), the review of the implementation of the TRIPS Agreement under Article 71.1 and the work foreseen pursuant to paragraph 12 of this Declaration, to examine, inter alia, the relationship between the TRIPS Agreement and the Convention on Biological Diversity, the protection of traditional knowledge and folklore, and other relevant new developments raised by Members pursuant to Article 71.1. In undertaking this work, the TRIPS Council shall be guided by the objectives and principles set out in Articles 7 and 8 of the TRIPS Agreement and shall take fully into account the development dimension. [. . .]

### DISPUTE SETTLEMENT UNDERSTANDING

30.   We agree to negotiations on improvements and clarifications of the Dispute Settlement Understanding. The negotiations should be based on the work done thus far as well as any additional proposals by Members, and aim to agree on improvements and clarifications not later than May 2003, at which time we will take steps to ensure that the results enter into force as soon as possible thereafter. [. . .]

ELECTRONIC COMMERCE

34.   We take note of the work which has been done in the General Council and other relevant bodies since the Ministerial Declaration of 20 May 1998 and agree to continue the Work Programme on Electronic Commerce. The work to date demonstrates that electronic commerce creates new challenges and opportunities for trade for Members at all stages of development, and we recognize the importance of creating and maintaining an environment which is favourable to the future development of electronic commerce. We instruct the General Council to consider the most appropriate institutional arrangements for handling the Work Programme, and to report on further progress to the Fifth Session of the Ministerial Conference. We declare that Members will maintain their current practice of not imposing customs duties on electronic transmissions until the Fifth Session. [. . .]

TRADE AND TRANSFER OF TECHNOLOGY

37.   We agree to an examination, in a Working Group under the auspices of the General Council, of the relationship between trade and transfer of technology, and of any possible recommendations on steps that might be taken within the mandate of the WTO to increase flows of technology to developing countries. The General Council shall report to the Fifth Session of the Ministerial Conference on progress in the examination.

TECHNICAL COOPERATION AND CAPACITY BUILDING

38.   We confirm that technical cooperation and capacity building are core elements of the development dimension of the multilateral trading system, and we welcome and endorse the New Strategy for WTO Technical Cooperation for Capacity Building, Growth and Integration. We instruct the Secretariat, in coordination with other relevant agencies, to support domestic efforts for mainstreaming trade into national plans for economic development and strategies for poverty reduction. The delivery of WTO technical assistance shall be designed to assist developing and least-developed countries and low-income countries in transition to adjust to WTO rules and disciplines, implement obligations and exercise the rights of membership, including drawing on the benefits of an open, rules-based multilateral trading system. Priority shall also be accorded to small, vulnerable, and transition economies, as well as to Members and Observers without representation in Geneva. We reaffirm our support for the valuable work of the International Trade Centre, which should be enhanced.

39.   We underscore the urgent necessity for the effective coordinated delivery of technical assistance with bilateral donors, in the OECD Development Assistance Committee and relevant international and regional intergovernmental institutions, within a coherent policy framework and timetable. In the coordinated delivery of technical assistance, we instruct the Director-General to consult with the relevant agencies, bilateral donors and beneficiaries, to identify ways of enhancing and rationalizing the Integrated Framework for Trade-Related Technical Assistance to Least-Developed Countries and the Joint Integrated Technical Assistance Programme (JITAP).

40.   We agree that there is a need for technical assistance to benefit from secure and predictable funding. We therefore instruct the Committee on Budget, Finance and Administration to develop a plan for adoption by the General Council in December 2001 that will ensure long-term funding for WTO technical assistance at an overall level no lower than that of the current year and commensurate with the activities outlined above.

41.   We have established firm commitments on technical cooperation and capacity building in various paragraphs in this Ministerial Declaration. We reaffirm these specific commitments contained in paragraphs 16, 21, 24, 26, 27, 33, 38–40, 42 and 43, and also reaffirm the understanding in paragraph 2 on the important role of sustainably financed technical assistance and capacity-building programmes. We instruct the Director-General to report to the Fifth Session of the Ministerial Conference, with an interim report to the General Council in December 2002 on the implementation and adequacy of these commitments in the identified paragraphs.

LEAST-DEVELOPED COUNTRIES

42. We acknowledge the seriousness of the concerns expressed by the least-developed countries (LDCs) in the Zanzibar Declaration adopted by their Ministers in July 2001. We recognize that the integration of the LDCs into the multilateral trading system requires meaningful market access, support for the diversification of their production and export base, and trade-related technical assistance and capacity building. We agree that the meaningful integration of LDCs into the trading system and the global economy will involve efforts by all WTO Members. We commit ourselves to the objective of duty-free, quota-free market access for products originating from LDCs. In this regard, we welcome the significant market access improvements by WTO Members in advance of the Third UN Conference on LDCs (LDC-III), in Brussels, May 2001. We further commit ourselves to consider additional measures for progressive improvements in market access for LDCs. Accession of LDCs remains a priority for the Membership. We agree to work to facilitate and accelerate negotiations with acceding LDCs. We instruct the Secretariat to reflect the priority we attach to LDCs' accessions in the annual plans for technical assistance. We reaffirm the commitments we undertook at LDC-III, and agree that the WTO should take into account, in designing its work programme for LDCs, the trade-related elements of the Brussels Declaration and Programme of Action, consistent with the WTO's mandate, adopted at LDC-III. We instruct the Sub-Committee for Least-Developed Countries to design such a work programme and to report on the agreed work programme to the General Council at its first meeting in 2002.

43. We endorse the Integrated Framework for Trade-Related Technical Assistance to Least-Developed Countries (IF) as a viable model for LDCs' trade development. We urge development partners to significantly increase contributions to the IF Trust Fund and WTO extra-budgetary trust funds in favour of LDCs. We urge the core agencies, in coordination with development partners, to explore the enhancement of the IF with a view to addressing the supply-side constraints of LDCs and the extension of the model to all LDCs, following the review of the IF and the appraisal of the ongoing Pilot Scheme in selected LDCs. We request the Director-General, following coordination with heads of the other agencies, to provide an interim report to the General Council in December 2002 and a full report to the Fifth Session of the Ministerial Conference on all issues affecting LDCs.

SPECIAL AND DIFFERENTIAL TREATMENT

44. We reaffirm that provisions for special and differential treatment are an integral part of the WTO Agreements. We note the concerns expressed regarding their operation in addressing specific constraints faced by developing countries, particularly least-developed countries. In that connection, we also note that some Members have proposed a Framework Agreement on Special and Differential Treatment (WT/GC/W/442). We therefore agree that all special and differential treatment provisions shall be reviewed with a view to strengthening them and making them more precise, effective and operational. In this connection, we endorse the work programme on special and differential treatment set out in the Decision on Implementation-Related Issues and Concerns.

ORGANIZATION AND MANAGEMENT OF THE WORK PROGRAMME

45. The negotiations to be pursued under the terms of this Declaration shall be concluded not later than 1 January 2005. The Fifth Session of the Ministerial Conference will take stock of progress in the negotiations, provide any necessary political guidance, and take decisions as necessary. When the results of the negotiations in all areas have been established, a Special Session of the Ministerial Conference will be held to take decisions regarding the adoption and implementation of those results.

46. The overall conduct of the negotiations shall be supervised by a Trade Negotiations Committee under the authority of the General Council. The Trade Negotiations Committee shall hold its first meeting not later than 31 January 2002. It shall establish appropriate negotiating mechanisms as required and supervise the progress of the negotiations.

47. With the exception of the improvements and clarifications of the Dispute Settlement Understanding, the conduct, conclusion and entry into force of the outcome of the negotiations shall be treated as parts of a single undertaking. However, agreements reached at an early stage may be

implemented on a provisional or a definitive basis. Early agreements shall be taken into account in assessing the overall balance of the negotiations.

48. Negotiations shall be open to:

    (i)   all Members of the WTO; and

    (ii)  States and separate customs territories currently in the process of accession and those that inform Members, at a regular meeting of the General Council, of their intention to negotiate the terms of their membership and for whom an accession working party is established.

Decisions on the outcomes of the negotiations shall be taken only by WTO Members.

49. The negotiations shall be conducted in a transparent manner among participants, in order to facilitate the effective participation of all. They shall be conducted with a view to ensuring benefits to all participants and to achieving an overall balance in the outcome of the negotiations.

50. The negotiations and the other aspects of the Work Programme shall take fully into account the principle of special and differential treatment for developing and least-developed countries embodied in: Part IV of the GATT 1994; the Decision of 28 November 1979 on Differential and More Favourable Treatment, Reciprocity and Fuller Participation of Developing Countries; the Uruguay Round Decision on Measures in Favour of Least-Developed Countries; and all other relevant WTO provisions.

51. The Committee on Trade and Development and the Committee on Trade and Environment shall, within their respective mandates, each act as a forum to identify and debate developmental and environmental aspects of the negotiations, in order to help achieve the objective of having sustainable development appropriately reflected.

52. Those elements of the Work Programme which do not involve negotiations are also accorded a high priority. They shall be pursued under the overall supervision of the General Council, which shall report on progress to the Fifth Session of the Ministerial Conference.

# 7. DECLARATION ON THE TRIPS AGREEMENT AND PUBLIC HEALTH

Adopted on 14 November 2001
Ministerial Conference, Fourth Session, Doha, 9–14 November 2001
(WT/MIN(01)/DEC/2 20 November 2001)

1.　We recognize the gravity of the public health problems afflicting many developing and least-developed countries, especially those resulting from HIV/AIDS, tuberculosis, malaria and other epidemics.

2.　We stress the need for the WTO Agreement on Trade-Related Aspects of Intellectual Property Rights (TRIPS Agreement) to be part of the wider national and international action to address these problems.

3.　We recognize that intellectual property protection is important for the development of new medicines. We also recognize the concerns about its effects on prices.

4.　We agree that the TRIPS Agreement does not and should not prevent Members from taking measures to protect public health. Accordingly, while reiterating our commitment to the TRIPS Agreement, we affirm that the Agreement can and should be interpreted and implemented in a manner supportive of WTO Members' right to protect public health and, in particular, to promote access to medicines for all.

In this connection, we reaffirm the right of WTO Members to use, to the full, the provisions in the TRIPS Agreement, which provide flexibility for this purpose.

5.　Accordingly and in the light of paragraph 4 above, while maintaining our commitments in the TRIPS Agreement, we recognize that these flexibilities include:

(a)　In applying the customary rules of interpretation of public international law, each provision of the TRIPS Agreement shall be read in the light of the object and purpose of the Agreement as expressed, in particular, in its objectives and principles.

(b)　Each Member has the right to grant compulsory licences and the freedom to determine the grounds upon which such licences are granted.

(c)　Each Member has the right to determine what constitutes a national emergency or other circumstances of extreme urgency, it being understood that public health crises, including those relating to HIV/AIDS, tuberculosis, malaria and other epidemics, can represent a national emergency or other circumstances of extreme urgency.

(d)　The effect of the provisions in the TRIPS Agreement that are relevant to the exhaustion of intellectual property rights is to leave each Member free to establish its own regime for such exhaustion without challenge, subject to the MFN and national treatment provisions of Articles 3 and 4.

6.　We recognize that WTO Members with insufficient or no manufacturing capacities in the pharmaceutical sector could face difficulties in making effective use of compulsory licensing under the TRIPS Agreement. We instruct the Council for TRIPS to find an expeditious solution to this problem and to report to the General Council before the end of 2002.

7.　We reaffirm the commitment of developed-country Members to provide incentives to their enterprises and institutions to promote and encourage technology transfer to least-developed country Members pursuant to Article 66.2. We also agree that the least-developed country Members will not be obliged, with respect to pharmaceutical products, to implement or apply Sections 5 and 7 of Part II of the TRIPS Agreement or to enforce rights provided for under these Sections until 1 January 2016, without prejudice to the right of least-developed country Members to seek other extensions of the transition periods as provided for in Article 66.1 of the TRIPS Agreement. We instruct the Council for TRIPS to take the necessary action to give effect to this pursuant to Article 66.1 of the TRIPS Agreement.

# 8.  GENERAL COUNCIL DECISION ON THE IMPLEMENTATION OF PARAGRAPH 6 OF THE DOHA DECLARATION ON THE TRIPS AGREEMENT AND PUBLIC HEALTH

Adopted on 30 August 2003
(WT/L/540 and Corr.1 1 September 2003)

The General Council,

*Having regard* to paragraphs 1, 3 and 4 of Article IX of the Marrakesh Agreement Establishing the World Trade Organization ("the WTO Agreement");

*Conducting* the functions of the Ministerial Conference in the interval between meetings pursuant to paragraph 2 of Article IV of the WTO Agreement;

*Noting* the Declaration on the TRIPS Agreement and Public Health (WT/MIN(01)/DEC/2) (the "Declaration") and, in particular, the instruction of the Ministerial Conference to the Council for TRIPS contained in paragraph 6 of the Declaration to find an expeditious solution to the problem of the difficulties that WTO Members with insufficient or no manufacturing capacities in the pharmaceutical sector could face in making effective use of compulsory licensing under the TRIPS Agreement and to report to the General Council before the end of 2002;

*Recognizing*, where eligible importing Members seek to obtain supplies under the system set out in this Decision, the importance of a rapid response to those needs consistent with the provisions of this Decision;

*Noting* that, in the light of the foregoing, exceptional circumstances exist justifying waivers from the obligations set out in paragraphs (f) and (h) of Article 31 of the TRIPS Agreement with respect to pharmaceutical products;

*Decides* as follows:

1.  For the purposes of this Decision:

(a)  "pharmaceutical product" means any patented product, or product manufactured through a patented process, of the pharmaceutical sector needed to address the public health problems as recognized in paragraph 1 of the Declaration. It is understood that active ingredients necessary for its manufacture and diagnostic kits needed for its use would be included;[1]

(b)  "eligible importing Member" means any least-developed country Member, and any other Member that has made a notification[2] to the Council for TRIPS of its intention to use the system as an importer, it being understood that a Member may notify at any time that it will use the system in whole or in a limited way, for example only in the case of a national emergency or other circumstances of extreme urgency or in cases of public non-commercial use. It is noted that some Members will not use the system set out in this Decision as importing Members[3] and that some other Members have stated that, if they use the system, it would be in no more than situations of national emergency or other circumstances of extreme urgency;

---

[1]  This subparagraph is without prejudice to subparagraph 1(b).

[2]  It is understood that this notification does not need to be approved by a WTO body in order to use the system set out in this Decision.

[3]  Australia, Austria, Belgium, Canada, Denmark, Finland, France, Germany, Greece, Iceland, Ireland, Italy, Japan, Luxembourg, Netherlands, New Zealand, Norway, Portugal, Spain, Sweden, Switzerland, United Kingdom and United States of America.

(c)   "exporting Member" means a Member using the system set out in this Decision to produce pharmaceutical products for, and export them to, an eligible importing Member.

2.    The obligations of an exporting Member under Article 31(f) of the TRIPS Agreement shall be waived with respect to the grant by it of a compulsory licence to the extent necessary for the purposes of production of a pharmaceutical product(s) and its export to an eligible importing Member(s) in accordance with the terms set out below in this paragraph:

(a)   the eligible importing Member(s)[4] has made a notification[2] to the Council for TRIPS, that:

(i)    specifies the names and expected quantities of the product(s) needed[5];

(ii)   confirms that the eligible importing Member in question, other than a least developed country Member, has established that it has insufficient or no manufacturing capacities in the pharmaceutical sector for the product(s) in question in one of the ways set out in the Annex to this Decision; and

(iii)  confirms that, where a pharmaceutical product is patented in its territory, it has granted or intends to grant a compulsory licence in accordance with Article 31 of the TRIPS Agreement and the provisions of this Decision[6];

(b)   the compulsory licence issued by the exporting Member under this Decision shall contain the following conditions:

(i)    only the amount necessary to meet the needs of the eligible importing Member(s) may be manufactured under the licence and the entirety of this production shall be exported to the Member(s) which has notified its needs to the Council for TRIPS;

(ii)   products produced under the licence shall be clearly identified as being produced under the system set out in this Decision through specific labelling or marking. Suppliers should distinguish such products through special packaging and/or special colouring/shaping of the products themselves, provided that such distinction is feasible and does not have a significant impact on price; and

(iii)  before shipment begins, the licensee shall post on a website[7] the following information:

—    the quantities being supplied to each destination as referred to in indent (i) above; and

—    the distinguishing features of the product(s) referred to in indent (ii) above;

(c)   the exporting Member shall notify[8] the Council for TRIPS of the grant of the licence, including the conditions attached to it.[9] The information provided shall include the name and address of the licensee, the product(s) for which the licence has been granted, the quantity(ies) for which it has been granted, the country(ies) to which the product(s) is (are) to be supplied and the duration of the licence. The notification shall also indicate the address of the website referred to in subparagraph (b)(iii) above.

3.    Where a compulsory licence is granted by an exporting Member under the system set out in this Decision, adequate remuneration pursuant to Article 31(h) of the TRIPS Agreement shall be paid in

---

[4]   Joint notifications providing the information required under this subparagraph may be made by the regional organizations referred to in paragraph 6 of this Decision on behalf of eligible importing Members using the system that are parties to them, with the agreement of those parties.

[5]   The notification will be made available publicly by the WTO Secretariat through a page on the WTO website dedicated to this Decision.

[6]   This subparagraph is without prejudice to Article 66.1 of the TRIPS Agreement.

[7]   The licensee may use for this purpose its own website or, with the assistance of the WTO Secretariat, the page on the WTO website dedicated to this Decision.

[8]   It is understood that this notification does not need to be approved by a WTO body in order to use the system set out in this Decision.

[9]   The notification will be made available publicly by the WTO Secretariat through a page on the WTO website dedicated to this Decision.

that Member taking into account the economic value to the importing Member of the use that has been authorized in the exporting Member. Where a compulsory licence is granted for the same products in the eligible importing Member, the obligation of that Member under Article 31(h) shall be waived in respect of those products for which remuneration in accordance with the first sentence of this paragraph is paid in the exporting Member.

4.    In order to ensure that the products imported under the system set out in this Decision are used for the public health purposes underlying their importation, eligible importing Members shall take reasonable measures within their means, proportionate to their administrative capacities and to the risk of trade diversion to prevent re-exportation of the products that have actually been imported into their territories under the system. In the event that an eligible importing Member that is a developing country Member or a least-developed country Member experiences difficulty in implementing this provision, developed country Members shall provide, on request and on mutually agreed terms and conditions, technical and financial cooperation in order to facilitate its implementation.

5.    Members shall ensure the availability of effective legal means to prevent the importation into, and sale in, their territories of products produced under the system set out in this Decision and diverted to their markets inconsistently with its provisions, using the means already required to be available under the TRIPS Agreement. If any Member considers that such measures are proving insufficient for this purpose, the matter may be reviewed in the Council for TRIPS at the request of that Member.

6.    With a view to harnessing economies of scale for the purposes of enhancing purchasing power for, and facilitating the local production of, pharmaceutical products:

(i)    where a developing or least-developed country WTO Member is a party to a regional trade agreement within the meaning of Article XXIV of the GATT 1994 and the Decision of 28 November 1979 on Differential and More Favourable Treatment Reciprocity and Fuller Participation of Developing Countries (L/4903), at least half of the current membership of which is made up of countries presently on the United Nations list of least developed countries, the obligation of that Member under Article 31(f) of the TRIPS Agreement shall be waived to the extent necessary to enable a pharmaceutical product produced or imported under a compulsory licence in that Member to be exported to the markets of those other developing or least developed country parties to the regional trade agreement that share the health problem in question. It is understood that this will not prejudice the territorial nature of the patent rights in question;

(ii)   it is recognized that the development of systems providing for the grant of regional patents to be applicable in the above Members should be promoted. To this end, developed country Members undertake to provide technical cooperation in accordance with Article 67 of the TRIPS Agreement, including in conjunction with other relevant intergovernmental organizations.

7.    Members recognize the desirability of promoting the transfer of technology and capacity building in the pharmaceutical sector in order to overcome the problem identified in paragraph 6 of the Declaration. To this end, eligible importing Members and exporting Members are encouraged to use the system set out in this Decision in a way which would promote this objective. Members undertake to cooperate in paying special attention to the transfer of technology and capacity building in the pharmaceutical sector in the work to be undertaken pursuant to Article 66.2 of the TRIPS Agreement, paragraph 7 of the Declaration and any other relevant work of the Council for TRIPS.

8.    The Council for TRIPS shall review annually the functioning of the system set out in this Decision with a view to ensuring its effective operation and shall annually report on its operation to the General Council. This review shall be deemed to fulfil the review requirements of Article IX:4 of the WTO Agreement.

9.    This Decision is without prejudice to the rights, obligations and flexibilities that Members have under the provisions of the TRIPS Agreement other than paragraphs (f) and (h) of Article 31, including those reaffirmed by the Declaration, and to their interpretation. It is also without prejudice to the

extent to which pharmaceutical products produced under a compulsory licence can be exported under the present provisions of Article 31(f) of the TRIPS Agreement.

10.   Members shall not challenge any measures taken in conformity with the provisions of the waivers contained in this Decision under subparagraphs 1(b) and 1(c) of Article XXIII of GATT 1994.

11.   This Decision, including the waivers granted in it, shall terminate for each Member on the date on which an amendment to the TRIPS Agreement replacing its provisions takes effect for that Member. The TRIPS Council shall initiate by the end of 2003 work on the preparation of such an amendment with a view to its adoption within six months, on the understanding that the amendment will be based, where appropriate, on this Decision and on the further understanding that it will not be part of the negotiations referred to in paragraph 45 of the Doha Ministerial Declaration (WT/MIN(01)/DEC/1).

**Annex**

**Assessment of Manufacturing Capacities in the Pharmaceutical Sector**

Least-developed country Members are deemed to have insufficient or no manufacturing capacities in the pharmaceutical sector.

For other eligible importing Members insufficient or no manufacturing capacities for the product(s) in question may be established in either of the following ways:

(i)   the Member in question has established that it has no manufacturing capacity in the pharmaceutical sector;

or

(ii)   where the Member has some manufacturing capacity in this sector, it has examined this capacity and found that, excluding any capacity owned or controlled by the patent owner, it is currently insufficient for the purposes of meeting its needs. When it is established that such capacity has become sufficient to meet the Member's needs, the system shall no longer apply.

# 9. PROTOCOL AMENDING THE TRIPS AGREEMENT

Adopted on 6 December 2005
(WT/L/641 8 December 2005)

*Members of the World Trade Organization;*

*Having regard* to the Decision of the General Council in document WT/L/641, adopted pursuant to paragraph 1 of Article X of the Marrakesh Agreement Establishing the World Trade Organization ("the WTO Agreement");

*Hereby agree* as follows:

1. The Agreement on Trade-Related Aspects of Intellectual Property Rights (the "TRIPS Agreement") shall, upon the entry into force of the Protocol pursuant to paragraph 4, be amended as set out in the Annex to this Protocol, by inserting Article 31bis after Article 31 and by inserting the Annex to the TRIPS Agreement after Article 73.

2. Reservations may not be entered in respect of any of the provisions of this Protocol without the consent of the other Members.

3. This Protocol shall be open for acceptance by Members until 1 December 2007 or such later date as may be decided by the Ministerial Conference.

4. This Protocol shall enter into force in accordance with paragraph 3 of Article X of the WTO Agreement.

5. This Protocol shall be deposited with the Director-General of the World Trade Organization who shall promptly furnish to each Member a certified copy thereof and a notification of each acceptance thereof pursuant to paragraph 3.

6. This Protocol shall be registered in accordance with the provisions of Article 102 of the Charter of the United Nations.

*Done* at Geneva this sixth day of December two thousand and five, in a single copy in the English, French and Spanish languages, each text being authentic.

**Annex to the Protocol**

## Article 31bis

1. The obligations of an exporting Member under Article 31(f) shall not apply with respect to the grant by it of a compulsory licence to the extent necessary for the purposes of production of a pharmaceutical product(s) and its export to an eligible importing Member(s) in accordance with the terms set out in paragraph 2 of the Annex to this Agreement.

2. Where a compulsory licence is granted by an exporting Member under the system set out in this Article and the Annex to this Agreement, adequate remuneration pursuant to Article 31(h) shall be paid in that Member taking into account the economic value to the importing Member of the use that has been authorized in the exporting Member. Where a compulsory licence is granted for the same products in the eligible importing Member, the obligation of that Member under Article 31(h) shall not apply in respect of those products for which remuneration in accordance with the first sentence of this paragraph is paid in the exporting Member.

3. With a view to harnessing economies of scale for the purposes of enhancing purchasing power for, and facilitating the local production of, pharmaceutical products: where a developing or least developed country WTO Member is a party to a regional trade agreement within the meaning of Article XXIV of the GATT 1994 and the Decision of 28 November 1979 on Differential and More Favourable Treatment Reciprocity and Fuller Participation of Developing Countries (L/4903), at least half of the current membership of which is made up of countries presently on the United Nations list of least developed countries, the obligation of that Member under Article 31(f) shall not apply to the extent

necessary to enable a pharmaceutical product produced or imported under a compulsory licence in that Member to be exported to the markets of those other developing or least developed country parties to the regional trade agreement that share the health problem in question. It is understood that this will not prejudice the territorial nature of the patent rights in question.

4.     Members shall not challenge any measures taken in conformity with the provisions of this Article and the Annex to this Agreement under subparagraphs 1(b) and 1(c) of Article XXIII of GATT 1994.

5.     This Article and the Annex to this Agreement are without prejudice to the rights, obligations and flexibilities that Members have under the provisions of this Agreement other than paragraphs (f) and (h) of Article 31, including those reaffirmed by the Declaration on the TRIPS Agreement and Public Health (WT/MIN(01)/DEC/2), and to their interpretation. They are also without prejudice to the extent to which pharmaceutical products produced under a compulsory licence can be exported under the provisions of Article 31(f).

**Annex to the TRIPS Agreement**

1.     For the purposes of Article 31bis and this Annex:

(a)   "pharmaceutical product" means any patented product, or product manufactured through a patented process, of the pharmaceutical sector needed to address the public health problems as recognized in paragraph 1 of the Declaration on the TRIPS Agreement and Public Health (WT/MIN(01)/DEC/2). It is understood that active ingredients necessary for its manufacture and diagnostic kits needed for its use would be included[1];

(b)   "eligible importing Member" means any least-developed country Member, and any other Member that has made a notification[2] to the Council for TRIPS of its intention to use the system set out in Article 31bis and this Annex ("system") as an importer, it being understood that a Member may notify at any time that it will use the system in whole or in a limited way, for example only in the case of a national emergency or other circumstances of extreme urgency or in cases of public non-commercial use. It is noted that some Members will not use the system as importing Members[3] and that some other Members have stated that, if they use the system, it would be in no more than situations of national emergency or other circumstances of extreme urgency;

(c)   "exporting Member" means a Member using the system to produce pharmaceutical products for, and export them to, an eligible importing Member.

2.     The terms referred to in paragraph 1 of Article 31bis are that:

(a)   the eligible importing Member(s)[4] has made a notification[2] to the Council for TRIPS, that:

(i)   specifies the names and expected quantities of the product(s) needed;[5]

(ii)   confirms that the eligible importing Member in question, other than a least developed country Member, has established that it has insufficient or no manufacturing capacities in the pharmaceutical sector for the product(s) in question in one of the ways set out in the Appendix to this Annex; and

---

[1]   This subparagraph is without prejudice to subparagraph 1(b).

[2]   It is understood that this notification does not need to be approved by a WTO body in order to use the system.

[3]   Australia, Canada, the European Communities with, for the purposes of Article 31bis and this Annex, its member States, Iceland, Japan, New Zealand, Norway, Switzerland, and the United States.

[4]   Joint notifications providing the information required under this subparagraph may be made by the regional organizations referred to in paragraph 3 of Article 31bis on behalf of eligible importing Members using the system that are parties to them, with the agreement of those parties.

[5]   The notification will be made available publicly by the WTO Secretariat through a page on the WTO website dedicated to the system.

(iii) confirms that, where a pharmaceutical product is patented in its territory, it has granted or intends to grant a compulsory licence in accordance with Articles 31 and 31bis of this Agreement and the provisions of this Annex;[6]

(b)    the compulsory licence issued by the exporting Member under the system shall contain the following conditions:

(i)    only the amount necessary to meet the needs of the eligible importing Member(s) may be manufactured under the licence and the entirety of this production shall be exported to the Member(s) which has notified its needs to the Council for TRIPS;

(ii)    products produced under the licence shall be clearly identified as being produced under the system through specific labelling or marking. Suppliers should distinguish such products through special packaging and/or special colouring/shaping of the products themselves, provided that such distinction is feasible and does not have a significant impact on price; and

(iii)    before shipment begins, the licensee shall post on a website[7] the following information:

—    the quantities being supplied to each destination as referred to in indent (i) above; and

—    the distinguishing features of the product(s) referred to in indent (ii) above;

(c)    the exporting Member shall notify[8] the Council for TRIPS of the grant of the licence, including the conditions attached to it.[9] The information provided shall include the name and address of the licensee, the product(s) for which the licence has been granted, the quantity(ies) for which it has been granted, the country(ies) to which the product(s) is (are) to be supplied and the duration of the licence. The notification shall also indicate the address of the website referred to in subparagraph (b)(iii) above.

3.    In order to ensure that the products imported under the system are used for the public health purposes underlying their importation, eligible importing Members shall take reasonable measures within their means, proportionate to their administrative capacities and to the risk of trade diversion to prevent re-exportation of the products that have actually been imported into their territories under the system. In the event that an eligible importing Member that is a developing country Member or a least-developed country Member experiences difficulty in implementing this provision, developed country Members shall provide, on request and on mutually agreed terms and conditions, technical and financial cooperation in order to facilitate its implementation.

4.    Members shall ensure the availability of effective legal means to prevent the importation into, and sale in, their territories of products produced under the system and diverted to their markets inconsistently with its provisions, using the means already required to be available under this Agreement. If any Member considers that such measures are proving insufficient for this purpose, the matter may be reviewed in the Council for TRIPS at the request of that Member.

5.    With a view to harnessing economies of scale for the purposes of enhancing purchasing power for, and facilitating the local production of, pharmaceutical products, it is recognized that the development of systems providing for the grant of regional patents to be applicable in the Members described in paragraph 3 of Article 31bis should be promoted. To this end, developed country Members undertake to provide technical cooperation in accordance with Article 67 of this Agreement, including in conjunction with other relevant intergovernmental organizations.

---

[6]    This subparagraph is without prejudice to Article 66.1 of this Agreement.

[7]    The licensee may use for this purpose its own website or, with the assistance of the WTO Secretariat, the page on the WTO website dedicated to the system.

[8]    It is understood that this notification does not need to be approved by a WTO body in order to use the system.

[9]    The notification will be made available publicly by the WTO Secretariat through a page on the WTO website dedicated to the system.

6.    Members recognize the desirability of promoting the transfer of technology and capacity building in the pharmaceutical sector in order to overcome the problem faced by Members with insufficient or no manufacturing capacities in the pharmaceutical sector. To this end, eligible importing Members and exporting Members are encouraged to use the system in a way which would promote this objective. Members undertake to cooperate in paying special attention to the transfer of technology and capacity building in the pharmaceutical sector in the work to be undertaken pursuant to Article **66.2** of this Agreement, paragraph 7 of the Declaration on the TRIPS Agreement and Public Health and any other relevant work of the Council for TRIPS.

7.    The Council for TRIPS shall review annually the functioning of the system with a view to ensuring its effective operation and shall annually report on its operation to the General Council.

**Appendix to the Annex to the TRIPS Agreement**

**Assessment of Manufacturing Capacities in the Pharmaceutical Sector**

Least-developed country Members are deemed to have insufficient or no manufacturing capacities in the pharmaceutical sector.

For other eligible importing Members insufficient or no manufacturing capacities for the product(s) in question may be established in either of the following ways:

(i)    the Member in question has established that it has no manufacturing capacity in the pharmaceutical sector;

or

(ii)    where the Member has some manufacturing capacity in this sector, it has examined this capacity and found that, excluding any capacity owned or controlled by the patent owner, it is currently insufficient for the purposes of meeting its needs. When it is established that such capacity has become sufficient to meet the Member's needs, the system shall no longer apply.

# COPYRIGHT AND NEIGHBORING RIGHTS

---

## 10. INTERNATIONAL COPYRIGHT RELATIONS OF THE UNITED STATES

### United States Copyright Office Circular 38A

### . . . Relations as of February 2021

This publication documents the countries that are parties to specific multilateral copyright conventions or agreements, as well as those that have specific bilateral relationships with the United States. The relevant agreements and their abbreviations are listed below. A list of countries follows, indicating which agreements each country has signed and the date each agreement took effect.

### *Agreements and Treaties*

**BAC**  Buenos Aires Convention of 1910. U.S. ratification deposited with the government of Argentina, May 1, 1911; proclaimed by the president of the United States, July 13, 1914.

**Berne**  Berne Convention for the Protection of Literary and Artistic Works. The Berne Convention, which was first accepted in 1886, has been revised numerous times. Notable revisions were made at Berlin on November 13, 1908; at Rome on June 2, 1928; at Brussels on June 26, 1948; at Stockholm on July 14, 1967; and at Paris on July 27, 1971 (which were subsequently amended on September 28, 1979). Accordingly, the list of countries includes in a parenthetical the latest act of the convention to which the country is party. For example, the substantive provisions of Berne (Paris) include articles 1 to 21 and the appendix; articles 22 to 38 deal with administrative provisions of the convention. The effective date for U.S. adherence to the Berne Convention is March 1, 1989.

**Bilateral**  Bilateral copyright relations with the United States by virtue of a proclamation or treaty. Where there is more than one proclamation or treaty, only the date of the first one is given.

**FTA**  Free Trade Agreement. The United States has concluded comprehensive free trade agreements (many bilaterally, some regionally) with multiple countries. With the exception of the United States-Israel agreement, the FTAs contain chapters on intellectual property rights, which include substantive copyright law and enforcement obligations.

**NAFTA**  North American Free Trade Agreement. The effective date for the United States is January 1, 1994, the date the agreement entered into force. NAFTA was renegotiated and replaced with the United States-Mexico-Canada Agreement (USMCA), which entered into force on July 1, 2020.

**None**  No known copyright relations with the United States.

**Phonograms**  Convention for the Protection of Producers of Phonograms Against Unauthorized Duplication of Their Phonograms, Geneva, 1971. The effective date for the United States is March 10, 1974.

**SAT**  Convention Relating to the Distribution of Programme-Carrying Signals Transmitted by Satellite, Brussels, 1974. The effective date for the United States is March 7, 1985.

**UCC Geneva**  Universal Copyright Convention, Geneva, 1952. The effective date for the United States is September 16, 1955, the date the treaty entered into force.

**UCC Paris** Universal Copyright Convention as revised at Paris, 1971. The effective date for the United States is July 10, 1974, the date the treaty entered into force.

**Unclear** Copyright relations status is unclear; a country may not have established copyright relations with the United States but may be honoring obligations incurred under a former political status, including possible relationships as a territory.

**USMCA** United States-Mexico-Canada Agreement. The USMCA entered into force on July 1, 2020, replacing NAFTA.

**VIP[2]** The Marrakesh Treaty to Facilitate Access to Published Works for Persons Who Are Blind, Visually Impaired, or Otherwise Print Disabled. This treaty entered into force on September 30, 2016 after twenty eligible parties, including countries or certain intergovernmental organizations, ratified it. Because the European Union has ratified this treaty, all 28 members of the EU are covered by this treaty's obligations. The effective date for the United States is May 8, 2019.

**WCT** World Intellectual Property Organization (WIPO) Copyright Treaty, Geneva, 1996. The effective date for the United States is March 6, 2002, the date the treaty entered into force.

**WPPT** WIPO Performances and Phonograms Treaty, Geneva, 1996. The effective date for the United States is May 20, 2002, the date the treaty entered into force.

**WTO** World Trade Organization (WTO), established pursuant to the Marrakesh Agreement of April 15, 1994, to implement the Uruguay Round Agreements. The Agreement on Trade-Related Aspects of Intellectual Property Rights (TRIPS) is one of the WTO agreements. It includes substantive obligations for the protection of copyright and other intellectual property rights as well as their enforcement. The effective date of United States membership in the WTO is January 1, 1995.

The United States has not yet acceded to the treaty below.

**BTAP[3]** Beijing Treaty on Audiovisual Performances. On June 26, 2012, the United States and forty-seven other nations signed the treaty. It entered into force on April 28, 2020.

. . .

### Countries[4]

**Afghanistan** *WTO* July 29, 2016; *Berne (Paris)* Jun. 2, 2018; *VIP* Oct. 26, 2018; *WCT* Feb. 9, 2021; *WPPT* Feb. 9, 2021

**Albania** *Berne (Paris)* Mar. 6, 1994; *WTO* Sept. 8, 2000; *Phonograms* June 26, 2001; *WPPT* May 20, 2002; *UCC Geneva* Feb. 4, 2004; *UCC Paris* Feb. 4, 2004; *WCT* Aug. 6, 2005

**Algeria** *UCC Geneva* Aug. 28, 1973; *UCC Paris* July 10, 1974; *Berne (Paris)* Apr. 19, 1998; *WCT* Jan. 31, 2014; *WPPT* Jan. 31, 2014

**Andorra** *UCC Geneva* Sept. 16, 1955; *Berne (Paris)* June 2, 2004

**Angola** *WTO* Nov. 23, 1996

**Antigua and Barbuda** *WTO* Jan. 1, 1995; *Berne (Paris)* Mar. 17, 2000

**Argentina**  *Bilateral* Aug. 23, 1934; *BAC* Apr. 19, 1950; *UCC Geneva* Feb. 13, 1958; *Berne (Paris)* June 10, 1967; *Phonograms* June 30, 1973; *WTO* Jan. 1, 1995; *WCT* Mar. 6, 2002; *WPPT* May 20, 2002; *VIP* Sept. 30, 2016

**Armenia**  *SAT* Dec. 13, 1993; *Berne (Paris)* Oct. 19, 2000; *Phonograms* Jan. 31, 2003; *WTO* Feb. 5, 2003; *WCT* Mar. 6, 2005; *WPPT* Mar. 6, 2005

**Australia**  *Bilateral* Mar. 15, 1918; *Berne (Paris)* Apr. 14, 1928; *UCC Geneva* May 1, 1969; *Phonograms* June 22, 1974; *UCC Paris* Feb. 29, 1978; *SAT* Oct. 26, 1990; *WTO* Jan. 1, 1995; *FTA* Jan. 1, 2005[5]; *WCT* July 26, 2007; *WPPT* July 26, 2007; *VIP* Sept. 30, 2016

**Austria**  *Bilateral* Sept. 20, 1907; *Berne (Paris)* Oct. 1, 1920; *UCC Geneva* July 2, 1957; *SAT* Aug. 6, 1982; *UCC Paris* Aug. 14, 1982; *Phonograms* Aug. 21, 1982; *WTO* Jan. 1, 1995; *WCT* Mar. 14, 2010; *WPPT* Mar. 14, 2010; *VIP* Jan. 1, 2019

**Azerbaijan**[6]  *UCC Geneva* Apr. 7, 1997; *Berne (Paris)* June 4, 1999; *Phonograms* Sept. 1, 2001; *WCT* Apr. 11, 2006; *WPPT* Apr. 11, 2006; *VIP* Dec. 24, 2018

**Bahamas**  *Berne (Brussels)* July 10, 1973; *UCC Geneva* July 13, 1976; *UCC Paris* Dec. 27, 1976

**Bahrain**  *WTO* Jan. 1, 1995; *Berne (Paris)* Mar. 2, 1997; *WCT* Dec. 15, 2005; *WPPT* Dec. 15, 2005; *FTA* Jan. 11, 2006[7]; *SAT* May 1, 2007

**Bangladesh**  *UCC Geneva* Aug. 5, 1975; *UCC Paris* Aug. 5, 1975; *WTO* Jan. 1, 1995; *Berne (Paris)* May 4, 1999

**Barbados**  *UCC Geneva* June 18, 1983; *UCC Paris* June 18, 1983; *Berne (Paris)* July 30, 1983; *Phonograms* July 29, 1983; *WTO* Jan. 1, 1995; *WCT* Dec. 13, 2019; *WPPT* Dec. 13, 2019

**Belarus**[6]  *UCC Geneva* Mar. 29, 1994; *Berne (Paris)* Dec. 12, 1997; *WCT* Mar. 6, 2002; *WPPT* May 20, 2002; *Phonograms* Apr. 17, 2003; *VIP* Oct. 22, 2020

**Belgium**  *Berne (Paris)* Dec. 5, 1887; *Bilateral* July 1, 1891[8]; *UCC Geneva* Aug. 31, 1960; *WTO* Jan. 1, 1995; *WCT* Aug. 30, 2006; *WPPT* Aug. 30, 2006; *VIP* Jan. 1, 2019

**Belize**  *UCC Geneva* Dec. 1, 1982; *WTO* Jan. 1, 1995; *Berne (Paris)* June 17, 2000; *WCT* Feb. 9, 2019; *WPPT* Feb. 9, 2019; *VIP* Feb. 9, 2019

**Benin**  *Berne (Paris)* Jan. 3, 1961; *WTO* Feb. 22, 1996; *WCT* Apr. 16, 2006; *WPPT* Apr. 16, 2006; *SAT* Aug. 17, 2017

**Bhutan**  *Berne (Paris)* Nov. 25, 2004

**Bolivia**  *BAC* May 15, 1914; *UCC Geneva* Mar. 22, 1990; *UCC Paris* Mar. 22, 1990; *Berne (Paris)* Nov. 4, 1993; *WTO* Sept. 12, 1995; *VIP* June 12, 2019

**Bosnia and Herzegovina**   *Berne (Paris)* Mar. 1, 1992; *UCC Geneva* July 12, 1993; *UCC Paris* July 12, 1993; *SAT* Jan. 12, 1994; *Phonograms* May 25, 2009; *WCT* Nov. 25, 2009; *WPPT* Nov. 25, 2009; *VIP* Apr. 20, 2021

**Botswana**   *WTO* May 31, 1995; *Berne (Paris)* Apr. 15, 1998; *WCT* Jan. 27, 2005; *WPPT* Jan. 27, 2005; *VIP* Jan. 5, 2017

**Brazil**   *BAC* Aug. 31, 1915; *Berne (Paris)* Feb. 9, 1922; *Bilateral* Apr. 2, 1957; *UCC Geneva* Jan. 13, 1960; *Phonograms* Nov. 28, 1975; *UCC Paris* Dec. 11, 1975; *WTO* Jan. 1, 1995; *VIP* Sept. 30, 2016

**Brunei Darussalam**   *WTO* Jan. 1, 1995; *Berne (Paris)* Aug. 30, 2006; *WCT* May 2, 2017; *WPPT* May 2, 2017

**Bulgaria**   *Berne (Paris)* Dec. 5, 1921; *UCC Geneva* June 7, 1975; *UCC Paris* June 7, 1975; *Phonograms* Sept. 6, 1995; *WTO* Dec. 1, 1996; *WCT* Mar. 6, 2002; *WPPT* May 20, 2002; *VIP* Jan. 1, 2019

**Burkina Faso**   *Berne (Paris)* Aug. 19, 1963; *Phonograms* Jan. 30, 1988; *WTO* June 3, 1995; *WCT* Mar. 6, 2002; *WPPT* May 20, 2002; *VIP* Oct. 31, 2017

**Burundi**   *WTO* July 23, 1995; *Berne (Paris)* Apr. 12, 2016; *WCT* Apr. 12, 2016

**Cambodia**   *UCC Geneva* Sept. 16, 1955; *WTO* Oct. 13, 2004

**Cameroon**   *Berne (Paris)* Sept. 21, 1964; *UCC Geneva* May 1, 1973; *UCC Paris* July 10, 1974; *WTO* Dec. 13, 1995

**Canada**   *Bilateral* Jan. 1, 1924; *Berne (Paris)* Apr. 10, 1928; *UCC Geneva* Aug. 10, 1962; *FTA* Jan. 1, 1989[9]; *NAFTA* Jan. 1, 1994[10]; *WTO* Jan. 1, 1995; *WCT* Aug. 13, 2014; *WPPT* Aug. 13, 2014; *VIP* Sept. 30, 2016; *USMCA* July 1, 2020

**Cape Verde**   *Berne (Paris)* July 7, 1997; *WTO* July 23, 2008; *VIP* May 22, 2019; *WCT* May 22, 2019; *WPPT* May 22, 2019

**Central African Republic**   *Berne (Paris)* Sept. 3, 1977; *WTO* May 31, 1995; *VIP* Nov. 19, 2020

**Chad**   *Berne (Brussels/Stockholm)* Nov. 25, 1971; *WTO* Oct. 19, 1996

**Chile**   *Bilateral* May 25, 1896; *BAC* June 14, 1955; *UCC Geneva* Sept. 16, 1955; *Berne (Paris)* June 5, 1970; *Phonograms* Mar. 24, 1977; *WTO* Jan. 1, 1995; *WCT* Mar. 6, 2002; *WPPT* May 20, 2002; *FTA* Jan. 1, 2004[11]; *SAT* June 8, 2011; *VIP* Sept. 30, 2016

**China**   *Bilateral* Jan. 13, 1904[12]; *Bilateral* Nov. 30, 1948; *Bilateral* Mar. 17, 1992[14]; *Berne (Paris)* Oct. 15, 1992; *UCC Geneva* Oct. 30, 1992; *UCC Paris* Oct. 30, 1992; *Phonograms* Apr. 30, 1993; *WTO* Dec. 11, 2001; *WCT* June 9, 2007; *WPPT* June 9, 2007

**Colombia**   *BAC* Dec. 23, 1936; *UCC Geneva* June 18, 1976; *UCC Paris* June 18, 1976; *Berne (Paris)* Mar. 7, 1988; *Phonograms* May 16, 1994; *WTO* Apr. 30, 1995; *WCT* Mar. 6, 2002; *WPPT* May 20, 2002; *FTA*[13] May 15, 2012; *SAT* Mar. 20, 2014

**Comoros**   *Berne (Paris)* Apr. 17, 2005; *WCT* Apr. 25, 2021; *WPPT* Apr. 25, 2021; *VIP* Apr. 25, 2021

**Congo, Democratic Republic of the**   *Berne (Paris)* Oct. 8, 1963; *WTO* Jan. 1, 1997; *Phonograms* Nov. 29, 1977

**Congo**   *Berne (Paris)* May 8, 1962; *WTO* Mar. 27, 1997

**Cook Islands**   *Berne (Paris)* Aug. 3, 2017; *VIP* June 19, 2019; *WCT* June 19, 2019; *WPPT* June 19, 2019

**Costa Rica**[15]   *Bilateral* Oct. 19, 1899; *BAC* Nov. 30, 1916; *UCC Geneva* Sept. 16, 1955; *Berne (Paris)* June 10, 1978; *UCC Paris* Mar. 7, 1980; *Phonograms* June 17, 1982; *WTO* Jan. 1, 1995; *SAT* June 25, 1999; *WCT* Mar. 6, 2002; *WPPT* May 20, 2002; *FTA* Jan. 1, 2009[16]; *VIP* Jan. 9, 2019

**Cote d'Ivoire**   *Berne (Paris)* Jan. 1, 1962; *WTO* Jan. 1, 1995; *VIP* Dec. 17, 2020

**Croatia**   *Berne (Paris)* Oct. 8, 1991; *UCC Paris* July 6, 1992; *UCC Geneva* July 6, 1992; *SAT* July 26, 1993; *Phonograms* Apr. 20, 2000; *WTO* Nov. 30, 2000; *WCT* Mar. 6, 2002; *WPPT* May 20, 2002; *VIP* Jan. 1, 2019

**Cuba**   *Bilateral* Nov. 17, 1903; *BAC* May 28, 1913; *UCC Geneva* June 18, 1957; *WTO* Apr. 20, 1995; *Berne (Paris)* Feb. 20, 1997

**Cyprus**   *Berne (Paris)* Feb. 24, 1964; *UCC Geneva* Dec. 19, 1990; *UCC Paris* Dec. 19, 1990; *Phonograms* Sept. 30, 1993; *WTO* July 30, 1995; *WCT* Nov. 4, 2003; *WPPT* Dec. 2, 2005; *VIP* Jan. 1, 2019

**Czech Republic**   *Berne (Paris)* Jan. 1, 1993; *Phonograms* Jan. 1, 1993; *UCC Geneva* Mar. 26, 1993; *UCC Paris* Mar. 26, 1993; *WTO* Jan. 1, 1995; *WCT* Mar. 6, 2002; *WPPT* May 20, 2002; *VIP* Jan. 1, 2019

**Denmark**   *Bilateral* May 8, 1893; *Berne (Paris)* July 1, 1903; *UCC Geneva* Feb. 9, 1962; *Phonograms* Mar. 24, 1977; *UCC Paris* July 11, 1979; *WTO* Jan. 1, 1995; *WCT* Mar. 14, 2010; *WPPT* Mar. 14, 2010; *VIP* Jan. 1, 2019

**Djibouti**   *WTO* May 31, 1995; *Berne (Paris)* May 13, 2002

**Dominica**   *WTO* Jan. 1, 1995; *Berne (Paris)* Aug. 7, 1999

**Dominican Republic**[15]   *BAC* Oct. 31, 1912; *UCC Geneva* May 8, 1983; *UCC Paris* May 8, 1983; *WTO* Mar. 9, 1995; *Berne (Paris)* Dec. 24, 1997; *WCT* Jan. 10, 2006; *WPPT* Jan. 10, 2006; *FTA* Mar. 1, 2007[16]; *VIP* Sept. 5, 2018

**Ecuador**   *BAC* Aug. 31, 1914; *UCC Geneva* June 5, 1957; *Phonograms* Sept. 14, 1974; *UCC Paris* Sept. 6, 1991; *Berne (Paris)* Oct. 9, 1991; *WTO* Jan. 21, 1996; *WCT* Mar. 6, 2002; *WPPT* May 20, 2002; *VIP* Sept. 30, 2016

**Egypt**   *Berne (Paris)* June 7, 1977; *Phonograms* Apr. 23, 1978; *WTO* June 30, 1995

**El Salvador**   *Bilateral* June 30, 1908[17]; *Phonograms* Feb. 9, 1979; *UCC Geneva* Mar. 29, 1979; *UCC Paris* Mar. 29, 1979; *Berne (Paris)* Feb. 19, 1994; *WTO* May 7, 1995; *WCT* Mar. 6, 2002; *WPPT* May 20, 2002; *FTA* Mar. 1, 2006[16]; *SAT* July 22, 2008; *VIP* Sept. 30, 2016

**Equatorial Guinea**   *Berne (Paris)* June 26, 1997

**Eritrea**   *None*

**Estonia**   *Berne (Paris)* Oct. 26, 1994; *WTO* Nov. 13, 1999; *Phonograms* May 28, 2000; *WCT* Mar. 14, 2010; *WPPT* Mar. 14, 2010; *VIP* Jan. 1, 2019

**Eswatini (formerly Swaziland)**   *WTO* Jan. 1, 1995; *Berne (Paris)* Dec. 14, 1998

**Ethiopia**   *VIP* Feb. 2, 2021

**European Union**[18]   *WTO* Jan. 1, 1995; *WCT* Mar. 14, 2010; *WPPT* Mar. 14, 2010; *VIP* Jan. 1, 2019

**Fiji**   *Berne (Brussels)* Dec. 1, 1971; *UCC Geneva* Dec. 13, 1971; *Phonograms* Apr. 18, 1973; *WTO* Jan. 14, 1996

**Finland**   *Berne (Paris)* Apr. 1, 1928; *Bilateral* Jan. 1, 1929; *UCC Geneva* Apr. 16, 1963; *Phonograms* Apr. 18, 1973; *UCC Paris* Nov. 1, 1986; *WTO* Jan. 1, 1995; *WCT* Mar. 14, 2010; *WPPT* Mar. 14, 2010; *VIP* Jan. 1, 2019

**France**   *Berne (Paris)* Dec. 5, 1887; *Bilateral* July 1, 1891[8]; *UCC Geneva* Jan. 14, 1956; *Phonograms* Apr. 18, 1973; *UCC Paris* July 10, 1974; *WTO* Jan. 1, 1995; *WCT* Mar. 14, 2010; *WPPT* Mar. 14, 2010; *VIP* Jan. 1, 2019

**Gabon**   *Berne (Paris)* Mar. 26, 1962; *WTO* Jan. 1, 1995; *WCT* Mar. 6, 2002; *WPPT* May 20, 2002

**Gambia, The**   *Berne (Paris)* Mar. 7, 1993; *WTO* Oct. 23, 1996

**Georgia**   *Berne (Paris)* May 16, 1995; *WTO* June 14, 2000; *WCT* Mar. 6, 2002; *WPPT* May 20, 2002

**Germany**[19]  *Berne (Paris)* Dec. 5, 1887[20]; *Bilateral* Apr. 15, 1892; *UCC Geneva* Sept. 16, 1955; *Bilateral* July 12, 1967[21]; *Phonograms* May 18, 1974; *UCC Paris* July 10, 1974; *SAT* Aug. 25, 1979; *WTO* Jan. 1, 1995; *WCT* Mar. 14, 2010; *WPPT* Mar. 14, 2010; *VIP* Jan. 1, 2019

**Ghana**  *UCC Geneva* Aug. 22, 1962; *Berne (Paris)* Oct. 11, 1991; *WTO* Jan. 1, 1995; *WCT* Nov. 18, 2006; *WPPT* Feb. 16, 2013; *Phonograms* Feb. 10, 2017; *VIP* Aug. 11, 2018

**Greece**  *Berne (Paris)* Nov. 9, 1920; *Bilateral* Mar. 1, 1932; *UCC Geneva* Aug. 24, 1963; *SAT* Oct. 22, 1991; *Phonograms* Feb. 9, 1994; *WTO* Jan. 1, 1995; *WCT* Mar. 14, 2010; *WPPT* Mar. 14, 2010; *VIP* Jan. 1, 2019

**Grenada**  *WTO* Feb. 22, 1996; *Berne (Paris)* Sept. 22, 1998

**Guatemala**[15]  *BAC* Mar. 28, 1913; *UCC Geneva* Oct. 28, 1964; *Phonograms* Feb. 1, 1977; *WTO* July 21, 1995; *Berne (Paris)* July 28, 1997; *WPPT* Jan. 8, 2003; *WCT* Feb. 4, 2003; *FTA* July 1, 2006[16]; *VIP* Sept. 30, 2016

**Guinea**  *Berne (Paris)* Nov. 20, 1980; *UCC Geneva* Nov. 13, 1981; *UCC Paris* Nov. 13, 1981; *WTO* Oct. 25, 1995; *WCT* May 25, 2002; *WPPT* May 25, 2002

**Guinea-Bissau**  *Berne (Paris)* July 22, 1991; *WTO* May 31, 1995

**Guyana**  *Berne (Paris)* Oct. 25, 1994; *WTO* Jan. 1, 1995

**Haiti**  *BAC* Nov. 27, 1919; *UCC Geneva* Sept. 16, 1955; *Berne (Paris)* Jan. 11, 1996; *WTO* Jan. 30, 1996

**Holy See**  *Berne (Paris)* Sept. 12, 1935; *UCC Geneva* Oct. 5, 1955; *Phonograms* July 18, 1977; *UCC Paris* May 6, 1980

**Honduras**[15]  *BAC* Apr. 27, 1914; *Berne (Paris)* Jan. 25, 1990; *Phonograms* Mar. 6, 1990; *WTO* Jan. 1, 1995; *WCT* May 20, 2002 ; *WPPT* May 20, 2002; *FTA* Apr. 1, 2006[16]; *SAT* Apr. 7, 2008; *VIP* June 29, 2017

**Hong Kong, China**[22]  *WTO* Jan. 1, 1995; *Berne (Paris)* July 1, 1997; *Phonograms* July 1, 1997

**Hungary**  *Bilateral* Oct. 16, 1912; *Berne (Paris)* Feb. 14, 1922; *UCC Geneva* Jan. 23, 1971; *UCC Paris* July 10, 1974; *Phonograms* May 28, 1975; *WTO* Jan. 1, 1995; *WCT* Mar. 6, 2002; *WPPT* May 20, 2002; *VIP* Jan. 1, 2019

**Iceland**  *Berne (Paris)* Sept. 7, 1947; *UCC Geneva* Dec. 18, 1956; *WTO* Jan. 1, 1995

**India**  *Berne (Paris)* Apr. 1, 1928; *Bilateral* Aug. 15, 1947; *UCC Geneva* Jan. 21, 1958; *Phonograms* Feb. 12, 1975; *UCC Paris* Apr. 7, 1988; *WTO* Jan. 1, 1995; *WCT* Dec. 25, 2018; *WPPT* Dec. 25, 2018; *VIP* Sept. 30, 2016

**Indonesia**  *Bilateral* Aug. 1, 1989; *WTO* Jan. 1, 1995; *Berne (Paris)* Sept. 5, 1997; *WCT* Mar. 6, 2002; *WPPT* Feb. 15, 2005; *VIP* Apr. 28, 2020

**Iran**  *None*

**Iraq**  *None*

**Ireland**  *Berne (Paris)* Oct. 5, 1927; *Bilateral* Oct. 1, 1929; *UCC Geneva* Jan. 20, 1959; *WTO* Jan. 1, 1995; *WCT* Mar. 14, 2010; *WPPT* Mar. 14, 2010; *VIP* Jan. 1, 2019

**Israel**  *Bilateral* May 15, 1948; *Berne (Paris)* Mar. 24, 1950; *UCC Geneva* Sept. 16, 1955; *Phonograms* May 1, 1978; *FTA* Aug. 19, 1985; *Bilateral* Sept. 1, 1985; *WTO* Apr. 21, 1995; *VIP* Sept. 30, 2016

**Italy**  *Berne (Paris)* Dec. 5, 1887; *Bilateral* Oct. 31, 1892; *Bilateral* May 1, 1915; *UCC Geneva* Jan. 24, 1957; *Phonograms* Mar. 24, 1977; *UCC Paris* Jan. 25, 1980; *SAT* July 7, 1981; *WTO* Jan. 1, 1995; *WCT* Mar. 14, 2010; *WPPT* Mar. 14, 2010; *VIP* Jan. 1, 2019

**Jamaica**  *Berne (Paris)* Jan. 1, 1994; *Phonograms* Jan. 11, 1994; *WTO* Mar. 9, 1995; *SAT* Jan. 12, 2000; *WCT* June 12, 2002; *WPPT* June 12, 2002

**Japan**[23]  *Berne (Paris)* July 15, 1899; *Bilateral* May 10, 1906; *UCC Geneva* Apr. 28, 1956; *UCC Paris* Oct. 21, 1977; *Phonograms* Oct. 14, 1978; *WTO* Jan. 1, 1995; *WCT* Mar. 6, 2002; *WPPT* Oct. 9, 2002; *VIP* Jan. 1, 2019

**Jordan**  *Berne (Paris)* July 28, 1999; *WTO* Apr. 11, 2000; *FTA* Dec. 17, 2001[24]; *WCT* Apr. 27, 2004; *WPPT* May 24, 2004; *VIP* Sept. 26, 2018

**Kazakhstan**[6]  *UCC Geneva* Aug. 6, 1992; *Berne (Paris)* Apr. 12, 1999; *Phonograms* Aug. 3, 2001; *WCT* Nov. 12, 2004; *WPPT* Nov. 12, 2004; *WTO* Nov. 30, 2015

**Kenya**  *UCC Geneva* Sept. 7, 1966; *UCC Paris* July 10, 1974; *Phonograms* Apr. 21, 1976; *SAT* Aug. 25, 1979; *Berne (Paris)* June 11, 1993; *WTO* Jan. 1, 1995; *VIP* Sept. 2, 2017

**Kiribati**  *Berne (Paris)* Jan. 2, 2018; *VIP* Oct. 31, 2019

**Korea, Democratic People's Republic of North**  *Berne (Paris)* Apr. 28, 2003; *VIP* Sept. 30, 2016

**Korea, Republic of**  *UCC Geneva* Oct. 1, 1987; *UCC Paris* Oct. 1, 1987; *Phonograms* Oct. 10, 1987; *WTO* Jan. 1, 1995; *Berne (Paris)* Aug. 21, 1996; *WCT* June 24, 2004; *WPPT* Mar. 18, 2009; *FTA* Mar. 15, 2012; *SAT* Mar. 19, 2012; *VIP* Sept. 30, 2016

**Kuwait**  *WTO* Jan. 1, 1995; *Berne (Paris)* Dec. 2, 2014

**Kyrgyz Republic** *WTO* Dec. 20, 1998; *Berne (Paris)* July 8, 1999; *WCT* Mar. 6, 2002; *WPPT* Aug. 15, 2002; *Phonograms* Oct. 12, 2002; *VIP* Aug. 15, 2017

**Lao People's Democratic Republic** *UCC Geneva* Sept. 16, 1955; *Berne (Paris)* Mar. 14, 2012; *WTO* Feb. 2, 2013

**Latvia** *Berne (Paris)* Aug. 11, 1995; *Phonograms* Aug. 23, 1997; *WTO* Feb. 10, 1999; *WCT* Mar. 6, 2002; *WPPT* May 20, 2002; *VIP* Jan. 1, 2019

**Lebanon** *Berne (Rome)* Sept. 30, 1947; *UCC Geneva* Oct. 17, 1959

**Lesotho** *Berne (Paris)* Sept. 28, 1989; *WTO* May 31, 1995; *VIP* July 30, 2018

**Liberia** *UCC Geneva* July 27, 1956; *Berne (Paris)* Mar. 8, 1989; *Phonograms* Dec. 16, 2005; *WTO* July 14, 2016; *VIP* Jan. 6, 2017

**Libya** *Berne (Paris)* Sept. 28, 1976

**Liechtenstein** *Berne (Paris)* July 30, 1931; *UCC Geneva* Jan. 22, 1959; *WTO* Sept. 1, 1995; *Phonograms* Oct. 12, 1999; *UCC Paris* Nov. 11, 1999; *WCT* Apr. 30, 2007; *WPPT* Apr. 30, 2007

**Lithuania** *Berne (Paris)* Dec. 14, 1994; *Phonograms* Jan. 27, 2000; *WTO* May 31, 2001; *WCT* Mar. 6, 2002; *WPPT* May 20, 2002; *VIP* Jan. 1, 2019

**Luxembourg** *Berne (Paris)* June 20, 1888; *Bilateral (two)* June 29, 1910; *UCC Geneva* Oct. 15, 1955; *Phonograms* Mar. 8, 1976; *WTO* Jan. 1, 1995; *WCT* Mar. 14, 2010; *WPPT* Mar. 14, 2010; *VIP* Jan. 1, 2019

**Macau, China**[25] *WTO* Jan. 1, 1995

**Madagascar** *Berne (Brussels)* Jan. 1, 1966; *WTO* Nov. 17, 1995; *WCT* Feb. 24, 2015; *WPPT* Feb. 24, 2015

**Malawi** *UCC Geneva* Oct. 26, 1965; *Berne (Paris)* Oct. 12, 1991; *WTO* May 31, 1995; *VIP* Oct. 14, 2017

**Malaysia** *Berne (Paris)* Oct. 1, 1990; *WTO* Jan. 1, 1995; *WCT* Dec. 27, 2012; *WPPT* Dec. 27, 2012

**Maldives** *WTO* May 31, 1995

**Mali** *Berne (Rome)* Mar. 19, 1962; *WTO* May 31, 1995; *WCT* Apr. 24, 2002; *WPPT* May 20, 2002; *VIP* Sept. 30, 2016

**Malta**  *Berne (Rome)* Sept. 21, 1964; *UCC Geneva* Nov. 19, 1968; *WTO* Jan. 1, 1995; *WCT* Mar. 14, 2010; *WPPT* Mar. 14, 2010; *VIP* Jan. 1, 2019

**Marshall Islands**  *VIP* May 8, 2019

**Mauritania**  *Berne (Paris)* Feb. 6, 1973; *WTO* May 31, 1995

**Mauritius**  *UCC Geneva* Aug. 20, 1970; *Berne (Paris)* May 10, 1989; *WTO* Jan. 1, 1995; *VIP* Apr. 11, 2021

**Mexico**  *Bilateral* Feb. 27, 1896; *UCC Geneva* May 12, 1957; *BAC* Apr. 24, 1964; *Berne (Paris)* June 11, 1967; *Phonograms* Dec. 21, 1973; *UCC Paris* Oct. 31, 1975; *SAT* Aug. 25, 1979; *NAFTA* Jan. 1, 1994[10]; *WTO* Jan. 1, 1995; *WCT* Mar. 6, 2002; *WPPT* May 20, 2002; *VIP* Sept. 30, 2016; *USMCA* July 1, 2020

**Micronesia, Federated States of**  *Berne (Paris)* Oct. 7, 2003

**Moldova**[6]  *UCC Geneva* June 23, 1997; *Berne (Paris)* Nov. 2, 1995; *Phonograms* July 17, 2000; *WTO* July 26, 2001; *WCT* Mar. 6, 2002; *WPPT* May 20, 2002; *SAT* Oct. 28, 2008; *VIP* May 19, 2018

**Monaco**  *Berne (Paris)* May 30, 1889; *Bilateral* Oct. 15, 1952; *UCC Geneva* Sept. 16, 1955; *Phonograms* Dec. 2, 1974; *UCC Paris* Dec. 13, 1974

**Mongolia**  *WTO* Jan. 29, 1997; *Berne (Paris)* Mar. 12, 1998; *WCT* Oct. 25, 2002; *WPPT* Oct. 25, 2002; *VIP* Sept. 30, 2016

**Montenegro**  *Berne (Paris)* June 3, 2006; *Phonograms* June 3, 2006; *WCT* June 3, 2006; *WPPT* June 3, 2006; *SAT* Oct. 23, 2006; *UCC Geneva* Apr. 26, 2007; *UCC Paris* Apr. 26, 2007; *WTO* Apr. 29, 2012

**Morocco**  *Berne (Paris)* June 16, 1917; *UCC Geneva* May 8, 1972; *UCC Paris* Jan. 28, 1976; *SAT* June 30, 1983; *WTO* Jan. 1, 1995; *FTA* Jan. 1, 2006[26]; *WCT* July 20, 2011; *WPPT* July 20, 2011; *VIP* Aug. 15, 2019

**Mozambique**  *WTO* Aug. 26, 1995; *Berne (Paris)* Nov. 22, 2013

**Myanmar, Union of**  *WTO* Jan. 1, 1995

**Namibia**  *Berne (Paris)* Mar. 21, 1990; *WTO* Jan. 1, 1995

**Nauru**  *Berne (Paris)* May 11, 2020; *WCT* Aug. 11, 2020

**Nepal**  *WTO* Apr. 23, 2004; *Berne (Paris)* Jan. 11, 2006

**Netherlands**[27]   *Bilateral* Nov. 20, 1899; *Berne (Paris)* Nov. 1, 1912; *UCC Geneva* June 22, 1967; *UCC Paris* Nov. 30, 1985; *Phonograms* Oct. 12, 1993; *WTO* Jan. 1, 1995; *WCT* Mar. 14, 2010; *WPPT* Mar. 14, 2010; *VIP* Jan. 1, 2019

**New Zealand**   *Bilateral* Dec. 1, 1916; *Berne (Paris)* Apr. 24, 1928; *UCC Geneva* Sept. 11, 1964; *Phonograms* Aug. 13, 1976; *WTO* Jan. 1, 1995; *WCT* Mar. 17, 2019; *WPPT* Mar. 17, 2019; *VIP* Jan. 4, 2020

**Nicaragua**[15]   *BAC* Dec. 15, 1913; *UCC Geneva* Aug. 16, 1961; *SAT* Aug. 25, 1979; *WTO* Sept. 3, 1995; *Phonograms* Aug. 10, 2000; *Berne (Paris)* Aug. 23, 2000; *WCT* Mar. 6, 2003; *WPPT* Mar. 6, 2003; *FTA* Apr. 1, 2006[16]; *VIP* Apr. 16, 2020

**Niger**   *Berne (Paris)* May 2, 1962; *UCC Geneva* May 15, 1989; *UCC Paris* May 15, 1989; *WTO* Dec. 13, 1996

**Nigeria**   *UCC Geneva* Feb. 14, 1962; *Berne (Paris)* Sept. 14, 1993; *WTO* Jan. 1, 1995; *WCT* Jan. 4, 2018; *WPPT* Jan. 4, 2018; *VIP* Jan. 4, 2018

**Niue**   *Berne (Paris)* Sept. 24, 2016

**North Macedonia**   *Berne (Paris)* Sept. 8, 1991; *SAT* Sept. 2, 1977; *UCC Geneva* Apr. 30, 1997; *UCC Paris* Apr. 30, 1997; *Phonograms* Mar. 2, 1998; *WTO* Apr. 4, 2003; *WCT* Feb. 4, 2004; *WPPT* Mar. 20, 2005

**Norway**   *Berne (Paris)* Apr. 13, 1896; *Bilateral* July 1, 1905; *UCC Geneva* Jan. 23, 1963; *UCC Paris* Aug. 7, 1974; *Phonograms* Aug. 1, 1978; *WTO* Jan. 1, 1995

**Oman**   *Berne (Paris)* July 14, 1999; *WTO* Nov. 9, 2000; *WCT* Sept. 20, 2005; *WPPT* Sept. 20, 2005; *SAT* Mar. 18, 2008; *FTA* Jan. 1, 2009[28]

**Pakistan**   *Berne (Rome)* July 5, 1948; *UCC Geneva* Sept. 16, 1955; *WTO* Jan. 1, 1995

**Palau**   *Unclear*

**Panama**   *BAC* Nov. 25, 1913; *UCC Geneva* Oct. 17, 1962; *Phonograms* June 29, 1974; *UCC Paris* Sept. 3, 1980; *SAT* Sept. 25, 1985; *Berne (Paris)* June 8, 1996; *WTO* Sept. 6, 1997; *WCT* Mar. 6, 2002; *WPPT* May 20, 2002; *FTA* Oct. 21, 2012[29]; *VIP* May 10, 2017

**Papua New Guinea**   *WTO* June 9, 1996

**Paraguay**   *BAC* Sept. 20, 1917; *UCC Geneva* Mar. 11, 1962; *Phonograms* Feb. 13, 1979; *Berne (Paris)* Jan. 2, 1992; *WTO* Jan. 1, 1995; *WCT* Mar. 6, 2002; *WPPT* May 20, 2002; *VIP* Sept. 30, 2016

**Peru**  *BAC* Apr. 30, 1920; *UCC Geneva* Oct. 16, 1963; *UCC Paris* July 22, 1985; *SAT* Aug. 7, 1985; *Phonograms* Aug. 24, 1985; *Berne (Paris)* Aug. 20, 1988; *WTO* Jan. 1, 1995; *WCT* Mar. 6, 2002; *WPPT* July 18, 2002; *FTA* Feb. 1, 2009[30]; *VIP* Sept. 30, 2016

**Philippines**  *Bilateral* Oct. 21, 1948; *Berne (Paris)* Aug. 1, 1951; *WTO* Jan. 1, 1995; *WCT* Oct. 4, 2002; *WPPT* Oct. 4, 2002; *VIP* Mar. 18, 2019

**Poland**  *Berne (Paris)* Jan. 28, 1920; *Bilateral* Feb. 16, 1927; *UCC Geneva* Mar. 9, 1977; *UCC Paris* Mar. 9, 1977; *WTO* July 1, 1995; *WPPT* Oct. 21, 2003; *WCT* Mar. 23, 2004; *VIP* Jan. 1, 2019

**Portugal**  *Bilateral* July 20, 1893; *Berne (Paris)* Mar. 29, 1911; *UCC Geneva* Dec. 25, 1956; *UCC Paris* July 30, 1981; *WTO* Jan. 1, 1995; *SAT* Mar. 11, 1996; *WCT* Mar. 14, 2010; *WPPT* Mar. 14, 2010; *VIP* Jan. 1, 2019

**Qatar**  *WTO* Jan. 13, 1996; *Berne (Paris)* July 5, 2000; *WCT* Oct. 28, 2005; *WPPT* Oct. 28, 2005; *VIP* Jan. 24, 2019

**Romania**  *Berne (Paris)* Jan. 1, 1927; *Bilateral* May 14, 1928; *WTO* Jan. 1, 1995; *Phonograms* Oct. 1, 1998; *WCT* Mar. 6, 2002; *WPPT* May 20, 2002; *VIP* Jan. 1, 2019

**Russian Federation**[6]  *UCC Geneva* May 27, 1973; *SAT* Jan. 20, 1989; *UCC Paris* Mar. 9, 1995; *Berne (Paris)* Mar. 13, 1995; *Phonograms* Mar. 13, 1995; *WCT* Feb. 5, 2009; *WPPT* Feb. 5, 2009; *WTO* Aug. 22, 2012; *VIP* May 8, 2018

**Rwanda**  *Berne (Paris)* Mar. 1, 1984; *UCC Geneva* Nov. 10, 1989; *UCC Paris* Nov. 10, 1989; *WTO* May 22, 1996; *SAT* July 25, 2001

**Saint Kitts and Nevis**  *Berne (Paris)* Apr. 9, 1995; *WTO* Feb. 21, 1996

**Saint Lucia**  *Berne (Paris)* Aug. 24, 1993; *WTO* Jan. 1, 1995; *Phonograms* Apr. 2, 2001; *WCT* Mar. 6, 2002; *WPPT* May 20, 2002; *VIP* Sept. 11, 2020

**Saint Vincent and the Grenadines**  *UCC Geneva* Jan. 22, 1985; *UCC Paris* Jan. 22, 1985; *WTO* Jan. 1, 1995; *Berne (Paris)* Aug. 29, 1995; *WPPT* Feb. 12, 2011; *VIP* Dec. 5, 2016

**Samoa**[31]  *Berne (Paris)* July 21, 2006; *WTO* May 10, 2012

**San Marino**  *Berne (Paris)* Sept. 2, 2020; *VIP* Sept. 2, 2020; *WCT* Sept. 2, 2020; *WPPT* Sept. 2, 2020

**São Tomé and Principe**  *Berne (Paris)* June 14, 2016; *WCT* Apr. 27, 2020; *WPPT* Apr. 27, 2020; *VIP* Jan. 15, 2021

**Saudi Arabia**  *UCC Geneva* July 13, 1994; *UCC Paris* July 13, 1994; *Berne (Paris)* Mar. 11, 2004; *WTO* Dec. 11, 2005; *VIP* Feb. 21, 2019

**Senegal**  *Berne (Paris)* Aug. 25, 1962; *UCC Geneva* July 9, 1974; *UCC Paris* July 10, 1974; *WTO* Jan. 1, 1995; *WCT* May 18, 2002; *WPPT* May 20, 2002

**Serbia**  *Berne (Paris)* Apr. 27, 1992; *SAT* Mar. 12, 2001; *UCC Paris* Sept. 11, 2001; *UCC Geneva* Nov. 11, 2001; *Phonograms* June 10, 2003; *WCT* June 13, 2003; *WPPT* June 13, 2003; *VIP* May 24, 2020

**Seychelles**  *WTO* Apr. 26, 2015

**Sierra Leone**  *WTO* July 23, 1995

**Singapore**  *Bilateral* May 18, 1987; *WTO* Jan. 1, 1995; *Berne (Paris)* Dec. 21, 1998; *FTA* Jan. 1, 2004[32]; *WCT* Apr. 17, 2005; *WPPT* Apr. 17, 2005; *SAT* Apr. 27, 2005; *VIP* Sept. 30, 2016

**Slovakia**  *Berne (Paris)* Jan. 1, 1993; *Phonograms* Jan. 1, 1993; *UCC Geneva* Mar. 31, 1993; *UCC Paris* Mar. 31, 1993; *WTO* Jan. 1, 1995; *WCT* Mar. 6, 2002; *WPPT* May 20, 2002; *VIP* Jan. 1, 2019

**Slovenia**  *Berne (Paris)* June 25, 1991; *SAT* Nov. 3, 1992; *UCC Geneva* Nov. 5, 1992; *UCC Paris* Nov. 5, 1992; *WTO* July 30, 1995; *Phonograms* Oct. 15, 1996; *WCT* Mar. 6, 2002; *WPPT* May 20, 2002; *VIP* Jan. 1, 2019

**Solomon Islands**  *WTO* July 26, 1996; *Berne (Paris)* July 4, 2019

**Somalia**  *Unclear*

**South Africa**  *Bilateral* July 1, 1924; *Berne (Brussels)* Oct. 3, 1928; *WTO* Jan. 1, 1995

**Spain**  *Berne (Paris)* Dec. 5, 1887; *Bilateral* July 10, 1895; *UCC Geneva* Sept. 16, 1955; *UCC Paris* July 10, 1974; *Phonograms* Aug. 24, 1974; *WTO* Jan. 1, 1995; *WCT* Mar. 14, 2010; *WPPT* Mar. 14, 2010; *VIP* Jan. 1, 2019

**Sri Lanka**  *Berne (Rome)* July 20, 1959; *UCC Geneva* Jan. 25, 1984; *UCC Paris* Jan. 25, 1984; *WTO* Jan. 1, 1995; *VIP* Jan. 5, 2017

**Sudan**  *Berne (Paris)* Dec. 28, 2000

**Sudan, Republic of South**  *Unclear*

**Suriname**  *Berne (Paris)* Feb. 23, 1977; *WTO* Jan. 1, 1995

**Sweden**  *Berne (Paris)* Aug. 1, 1904; *Bilateral* June 1, 1911; *UCC Geneva* July 1, 1961; *Phonograms* Apr. 18, 1973; *UCC Paris* July 10, 1974; *WTO* Jan. 1, 1995; *WCT* Mar. 14, 2010; *WPPT* Mar. 14, 2010; *VIP* Jan. 1, 2019

**Switzerland** *Berne (Paris)* Dec. 5, 1887; *Bilateral* July 1, 1891[8]; *UCC Geneva* Mar. 30, 1956; *UCC Paris* Sept. 21, 1993; *SAT* Sept. 24, 1993; *Phonograms* Sept. 30, 1993; *WTO* July 1, 1995; *WCT* July 1, 2008; *WPPT* July 1, 2008; *VIP* May 11, 2020

**Syria** *Berne (Paris)* June 11, 2004

**Taiwan (Chinese Taipei)**[12] *WTO* Jan. 1, 2002

**Tajikistan**[6] *UCC Geneva* Aug. 28, 1992; *Berne (Paris)* Mar. 9, 2000; *WCT* Apr. 5, 2009; *WPPT* Aug. 24, 2011; *Phonograms* Feb. 26, 2013; *WTO* Mar. 2, 2013; *VIP* May 27, 2019

**Tanzania** *Berne (Paris)* July 25, 1994; *WTO* Jan. 1, 1995; *VIP* July 8, 2020

**Timor Leste** *Unclear*

**Thailand** *Bilateral* Sept. 1, 1921; *Berne (Paris)* July 17, 1931; *Bilateral* June 8, 1968; *WTO* Jan. 1, 1995; *VIP* Apr. 28, 2019

**Togo** *Berne (Paris)* Apr. 30, 1975; *WTO* May 31, 1995; *WCT* May 21, 2003; *WPPT* May 21, 2003; *UCC Geneva* May 28, 2003; *UCC Paris* May 28, 2003; *Phonograms* June 10, 2003; *SAT* June 10, 2003

**Tonga** *Berne (Paris)* June 14, 2001; *WTO* July 27, 2007

**Trinidad and Tobago** *Berne (Paris)* Aug. 16, 1988; *UCC Geneva* Aug. 19, 1988; *UCC Paris* Aug. 19, 1988; *Phonograms* Oct. 1, 1988; *WTO* Mar. 1, 1995; *SAT* Nov. 1, 1996; *WCT* Nov. 28, 2008; *WPPT* Nov. 28, 2008; *VIP* Jan. 4, 2020

**Tunisia** *Berne (Paris)* Dec. 5, 1887; *UCC Geneva* June 19, 1969; *UCC Paris* June 10, 1975; *WTO* Mar. 29, 1995; *VIP* Dec. 7, 2016

**Turkey** *Berne (Paris)* Jan. 1, 1952; *WTO* Mar. 26, 1995; *WCT* Nov. 28, 2008; *WPPT* Nov. 28, 2008

**Turkmenistan** *Berne (Paris)* May 29, 2016; *VIP* Jan. 15, 2021

**Tuvalu** *Berne (Paris)* Jun. 2, 2017

**Uganda** *WTO* Jan. 1, 1995; *VIP* July 23, 2018

**Ukraine**[6] *UCC Geneva* Jan. 17, 1994; *Berne (Paris)* Oct. 25, 1995; *Phonograms* Feb. 18, 2000; *WCT* Mar. 6, 2002; *WPPT* May 20, 2002; *WTO* May 16, 2008

**United Arab Emirates** *WTO* Apr. 10, 1996; *Berne (Paris)* July 14, 2004; *WCT* July 14, 2004; *WPPT* June 9, 2005; *VIP* Sept. 30, 2016

**United Kingdom**  *Berne (Paris)* Dec. 5, 1887; *Bilateral* July 1, 1891[8]; *UCC Geneva* Sept. 27, 1957; *Phonograms* Apr. 18, 1973; *UCC Paris* July 10, 1974; *WTO* Jan. 1, 1995; *WCT* Mar. 14, 2010; *WPPT* Mar. 14, 2010; *VIP* Jan. 1, 2021

**United States of America**  *UCC Geneva* Sept. 16, 1955; *Phonograms* Mar. 10, 1974; *UCC Paris* July 10, 1974; *SAT* Mar. 7, 1985; *WTO* Jan. 1, 1995; *Berne (Paris)* Mar. 1, 1989; *WCT* Mar. 6, 2002; *WPPT* May 20, 2002; *VIP* May 8, 2019

**Uruguay**  *BAC* Mar. 18, 1920; *Berne (Paris)* July 10, 1967; *Phonograms* Jan. 18, 1983; *UCC Geneva* Apr. 12, 1993; *UCC Paris* Apr. 12, 1993; *WTO* Jan. 1, 1995; *WPPT* Aug. 28, 2008; *WCT* June 5, 2009; *VIP* Sept. 30, 2016

**Uzbekistan**  *Berne (Paris)* Apr. 19, 2005; *Phonograms* Apr. 25, 2019; *WCT* July 17, 2019; *WPPT* July 17, 2019

**Vanuatu**  *Berne (Paris)* Dec. 27, 2012; *WTO* Aug. 24, 2012; *VIP* Aug. 6, 2020; *WCT* Aug. 6, 2020; *WPPT* Aug. 6, 2020

**Venezuela**  *UCC Geneva* Sept. 30, 1966; *Phonograms* Nov. 18, 1982; *Berne (Paris)* Dec. 30, 1982; *WTO* Jan. 1, 1995; *UCC Paris* Apr. 11, 1996; *VIP* Jan. 2, 2020

**Viet Nam**  *Bilateral* Dec. 23, 1998[33]; *Bilateral* Dec. 10, 2001; *Berne (Paris)* Oct. 26, 2004; *Phonograms* July 6, 2005; *SAT* Jan. 12, 2006; *WTO* Jan. 11, 2007

**Yemen**  *Berne (Paris)* July 14, 2008; *WTO* June 26, 2014

**Zambia**  *UCC Geneva* June 1, 1965; *Berne (Paris)* Jan. 2, 1992; *WTO* Jan. 1, 1995

**Zimbabwe**  *Berne (Rome)* Apr. 18, 1980; *WTO* Mar. 5, 1995; *VIP* Dec. 12, 2019

. . .

*Notes*

. . .

2.    The Marrakesh Treaty requires contracting parties to adopt national law provisions that permit the reproduction, distribution, and making available of published works in accessible formats through limitations and exceptions to the rights of copyright holders. It also provides for the exchange of these accessible-format works across borders by organizations that serve persons who are blind, visually impaired, and print disabled.

3.    The Beijing Treaty updates the international legal framework for audiovisual performers to provide rights and protections similar to those already provided for musical performers under the WPPT. Included in the Beijing Treaty are articles requiring national treatment for audiovisual performers in other countries, exclusive rights for audiovisual performers, and safeguards for technological protection measures.

4.    In certain cases, the United States may have had copyright relations with former territories or colonies of countries such as France, the Netherlands, Portugal, the Soviet Union, Spain, and the United Kingdom before those countries and their territories gained independence and joined international copyright treaties

and conventions and bilateral agreements in their own right. The legal situations involved may be fact-specific, and the scope of copyright protection for U.S. works in such situations may be complex.

5.    Copyright relations between Australia and the United States were further developed pursuant to the United States-Australia Free Trade Agreement, effective Jan. 1, 2005.

6.    Each of the Commonwealth of Independent States (CIS) countries listed in this circular is a successor to the Soviet Union's copyright treaty obligations, in particular those under UCC Geneva; accordingly, each is a member of UCC Geneva effective May 27, 1973, the date the Soviet Union became a party. The successor status of each country was confirmed in a bilateral trade agreement between each country and the United States, effective on the following dates: Armenia (Apr. 2, 1992); Azerbaijan (Apr. 21, 1995); Belarus (Feb. 16, 1993); Georgia (Aug. 13, 1993); Kazakhstan (Feb. 18, 1993); Kyrgyz Republic (Aug. 21, 1992); Moldova (July 2, 1992); Russia (June 17, 1992); Tajikistan (Nov. 24, 1993); Turkmenistan (Oct. 25, 1993); Ukraine (June 23, 1992); Uzbekistan (Jan. 13, 1994). However, only the countries listed in this circular as parties to the UCC have filed notices of succession with the United Nations Educational, Scientific, and Cultural Organization, which administers UCC Geneva. The notices of succession are effective on the dates specified.

7.    Copyright relations between the United States and Bahrain were further developed pursuant to the United States-Bahrain Free Trade Agreement, effective Jan. 11, 2006.

8.    Copyright relations between the United States and Belgium, France, the United Kingdom, and Switzerland were established by Presidential Proclamation No. 3. of July 1, 1891, 27 Stat. 981 (1891), effective that same date, under the authority of the Chase Act of 1891.

9.    Relations between Canada and the United States were further developed pursuant to the Canada-U.S. Free Trade Agreement, effective Jan. 1, 1989.

10.    Relations between Canada, Mexico, and the United States were further developed pursuant to the North American Free Trade Agreement (NAFTA), effective Jan. 1, 1994. NAFTA was renegotiated and replaced with the United States-Mexico-Canada Agreement (USMCA), which entered into force on July 1, 2020.

11.    Copyright relations between Chile and the United States were further developed pursuant to the United States-Chile Free Trade Agreement, effective Jan. 1, 2004

12.    The government of the People's Republic of China views the 1904 treaty as not binding. In the territory administered by the authorities on Taiwan, the treaty is considered to be in force.

13.    Copyright relations between Colombia and the United States were further developed pursuant to the United States-Colombia Trade Promotion Agreement, effective May 15, 2012.

14.    Copyright relations between the People's Republic of China and the United States of America were established, effective Mar. 17, 1992, by a presidential proclamation of the same date, under the authority of section 104 of Title 17 of the United States Code, as amended on Oct. 31, 1988 (Public Law 100–568, 102 Stat. 2853, 2855).

15.    This country became a party to the Mexico City Convention, 1902, effective June 30, 1908, to which the United States also became a party, effective on the same date. As regards copyright relations with the United States, this convention is considered to have been superseded by adherence of this country and the United States to the Buenos Aires Convention of 1910.

16.    Copyright relations between the United States and Costa Rica, the Dominican Republic, El Salvador, Guatemala, Honduras, and Nicaragua were further developed pursuant to the Dominican Republic-Central American Free Trade Agreement (CAFTA-DR). All countries signed CAFTA-DR on Aug. 5, 2004. CAFTA-DR entered into force for each country on the dates specified in this circular.

17.    This country became a party to the Mexico City Convention, 1902, effective June 30, 1908, to which the United States also became a party, effective on the same date.

18.    Formerly European Communities. The effective date of the name change from European Communities to European Union is December 1, 2009. Member countries are Austria, Belgium, Bulgaria, Cyprus, Czech Republic, Denmark, Estonia, Finland, France, Germany, Greece, Hungary, Ireland, Italy, Latvia, Lithuania,

Luxembourg, Malta, Netherlands, Poland, Portugal, Romania, Slovakia, Slovenia, Spain, and Sweden. The European Commission is the European Union's executive arm.

19.    The dates of adherence by Germany to multilateral treaties include adherence by the Federal Republic of Germany when that country was divided into the Federal Republic of Germany and the German Democratic Republic. However, through the accession, effective Oct. 3, 1990, of the German Democratic Republic to the Federal Republic of Germany, in accordance with the German Unification Treaty of Aug. 31, 1990, the German Democratic Republic ceased, on the said date, to be a sovereign state. Previously, the German Democratic Republic had become party to the Paris Act of the Berne Convention for the Protection of Literary and Artistic Works on Feb. 18, 1978, but ceased to be a party to the said convention on Oct. 3, 1990. The German Democratic Republic had also been a member of the Universal Copyright Convention, having become party to the Geneva text of the convention on Oct. 5, 1973, and party to the revised Paris text of the same convention on Dec. 10, 1980.

20.    Date on which the accession by the German Empire became effective.

21.    Copyright relations between the United States and Germany were established effective July 12, 1967, by Presidential Proclamation No. 3792 of that same date, at 32 FR 10341, under the authority of the Copyright Act of 1909 as amended at 55 Stat. 732.

22.    Prior to the return of Hong Kong to China, bilateral copyright relations existed with Hong Kong through the United Kingdom (from Aug. 1, 1973), and Phonogram Convention Membership existed through the United Kingdom (from Mar. 4, 1975). The Berne Convention for the Protection of Literary and Artistic Works of Sept. 9, 1886, as amended in 1979, applies to Hong Kong, China, through the People's Republic of China (PRC), effective July 1, 1997. The Convention for the Protection of Producers of Phonograms Against Unauthorized Duplication of Their Phonograms applies to Hong Kong, China, through the PRC, effective July 1, 1997.

23.    Copyright relations between Japan and the United States, which were formulated effective May 10, 1906, are considered to have been abrogated and superseded by the adherence of Japan to the UCC Geneva, effective Apr. 28, 1956.

24.    Copyright relations between the Hashemite Kingdom of Jordan and the United States were further developed pursuant to the United States-Jordan Free Trade Agreement, effective Dec. 17, 2001.

25.    Prior to the return of Macau to the People's Republic of China (PRC), Macau was a member of Berne (Paris) through Portugal. The Berne Convention for the Protection of Literary and Artistic Works of Sept. 9, 1886, applies to Macau, China, effective Dec. 20, 1999, through the PRC.

26.    Copyright relations between the United States and Morocco were further developed pursuant to the United States-Morocco Free Trade Agreement, effective Jan. 1, 2006.

27.    Refers to the country in Europe and the Netherland Antilles.

28.    Copyright relations between the United States and Oman were further developed pursuant to the United States-Oman Free Trade Agreement, effective Jan. 1, 2009.

29.    Copyright relations between the United States and Panama were further developed pursuant to the United States-Panama Trade Promotion Agreement, effective Oct. 21, 2012.

30.    Copyright relations between the United States and Peru were further developed pursuant to the United States-Peru Trade Promotion Agreement, effective Feb. 1, 2009.

31.    U.S. federal copyright law applies in the U.S. Virgin Islands, Guam, and the Northern Mariana Islands but not in American Samoa.

32.    Copyright relations between the United States and Singapore were further developed pursuant to the United States-Singapore Free Trade Agreement, effective Jan. 1, 2004.

33.    Copyright relations between the Socialist Republic of Viet Nam and the United States were established effective December 23, 1998, by Presidential Proclamation No. 7161 of that same date, at 63 FR 71571 (1998), under the authority of sections 104(b)(5) and 104A(g) of Title 17 of the United States Code, as amended.

# 11. BERNE CONVENTION FOR THE PROTECTION OF LITERARY AND ARTISTIC WORKS

Paris Act of July 24, 1971, as amended on September 28, 1979

Berne Convention for the Protection of Literary and Artistic Works of September 9, 1886, completed at PARIS on May 4, 1896, revised at BERLIN on November 13, 1908, completed at BERNE on March 20, 1914, revised at ROME on June 2, 1928, at BRUSSELS on June 26, 1948, at STOCKHOLM on July 14, 1967, and at PARIS on July 24, 1971, and amended on September 28, 1979.

The countries of the Union, being equally animated by the desire to protect, in as effective and uniform a manner as possible, the rights of authors in their literary and artistic works,

Recognizing the importance of the work of the Revision Conference held at Stockholm in 1967,

Have resolved to revise the Act adopted by the Stockholm Conference, while maintaining without change Articles 1 to 20 and 22 to 26 of that Act.

Consequently, the undersigned Plenipotentiaries, having presented their full powers, recognized as in good and due form, have agreed as follows:

## Article 1

The countries to which this Convention applies constitute a Union for the protection of the rights of authors in their literary and artistic works.

## Article 2

(1)   The expression "literary and artistic works" shall include every production in the literary, scientific and artistic domain, whatever may be the mode or form of its expression, such as books, pamphlets and other writings; lectures, addresses, sermons and other works of the same nature; dramatic or dramatico-musical works; choreographic works and entertainments in dumb show; musical compositions with or without words; cinematographic works to which are assimilated works expressed by a process analogous to cinematography; works of drawing, painting, architecture, sculpture, engraving and lithography; photographic works to which are assimilated works expressed by a process analogous to photography; works of applied art; illustrations, maps, plans, sketches and three-dimensional works relative to geography, topography, architecture or science.

(2)   It shall, however, be a matter for legislation in the countries of the Union to prescribe that works in general or any specified categories of works shall not be protected unless they have been fixed in some material form. - *Fixation*

(3)   Translations, adaptations, arrangements of music and other alterations of a literary or artistic work shall be protected as original works without prejudice to the copyright in the original work.

(4)   It shall be a matter for legislation in the countries of the Union to determine the protection to be granted to official texts of a legislative, administrative and legal nature, and to official translations of such texts.

(5)   Collections of literary or artistic works such as encyclopaedias and anthologies which, by reason of the selection and arrangement of their contents, constitute intellectual creations shall be protected as such, without prejudice to the copyright in each of the works forming part of such collections.

(6)   The works mentioned in this Article shall enjoy protection in all countries of the Union. This protection shall operate for the benefit of the author and his successors in title.

(7)   Subject to the provisions of Article 7(4) of this Convention, it shall be a matter for legislation in the countries of the Union to determine the extent of the application of their laws to works of applied art and industrial designs and models, as well as the conditions under which such works, designs and

models shall be protected. Works protected in the country of origin solely as designs and models shall be entitled in another country of the Union only to such special protection as is granted in that country to designs and models; however, if no such special protection is granted in that country, such works shall be protected as artistic works.

(8)    The protection of this Convention shall not apply to news of the day or to miscellaneous facts having the character of mere items of press information.

## Article 2*bis*

(1)    It shall be a matter for legislation in the countries of the Union to exclude, wholly or in part, from the protection provided by the preceding Article political speeches and speeches delivered in the course of legal proceedings.

(2)    It shall also be a matter for legislation in the countries of the Union to determine the conditions under which lectures, addresses and other works of the same nature which are delivered in public may be reproduced by the press, broadcast, communicated to the public by wire and made the subject of public communication as envisaged in Article 11*bis*(1) of this Convention, when such use is justified by the informatory purpose.

(3)    Nevertheless, the author shall enjoy the exclusive right of making a collection of his works mentioned in the preceding paragraphs.

## Article 3

(1)    The protection of this Convention shall apply to:

(a)    authors who are nationals of one of the countries of the Union, for their works, whether published or not;

(b)    authors who are not nationals of one of the countries of the Union, for their works first published in one of those countries, or simultaneously in a country outside the Union and in a country of the Union.

(2)    Authors who are not nationals of one of the countries of the Union but who have their habitual residence in one of them shall, for the purposes of this Convention, be assimilated to nationals of that country.

(3)    The expression "published works" means works published with the consent of their authors, whatever may be the means of manufacture of the copies, provided that the availability of such copies has been such as to satisfy the reasonable requirements of the public, having regard to the nature of the work. The performance of a dramatic, dramatico-musical, cinematographic or musical work, the public recitation of a literary work, the communication by wire or the broadcasting of literary or artistic works, the exhibition of a work of art and the construction of a work of architecture shall not constitute publication.

(4)    A work shall be considered as having been published simultaneously in several countries if it has been published in two or more countries within thirty days of its first publication.

## Article 4

The protection of this Convention shall apply, even if the conditions of Article 3 are not fulfilled, to:

(a)    authors of cinematographic works the maker of which has his headquarters or habitual residence in one of the countries of the Union;

(b)    authors of works of architecture erected in a country of the Union or of other artistic works incorporated in a building or other structure located in a country of the Union.

## Article 5

(1)    Authors shall enjoy, in respect of works for which they are protected under this Convention, in countries of the Union other than the country of origin, the rights which their respective laws do now or may hereafter grant to their nationals, as well as the rights specially granted by this Convention.

(2)    The enjoyment and the exercise of these rights shall not be subject to any formality; such enjoyment and such exercise shall be independent of the existence of protection in the country of origin of the work. Consequently, apart from the provisions of this Convention, the extent of protection, as well as the means of redress afforded to the author to protect his rights, shall be governed exclusively by the laws of the country where protection is claimed.

(3)    Protection in the country of origin is governed by domestic law. However, when the author is not a national of the country of origin of the work for which he is protected under this Convention, he shall enjoy in that country the same rights as national authors.

(4)    The country of origin shall be considered to be:

(a)    in the case of works first published in a country of the Union, that country; in the case of works published simultaneously in several countries of the Union which grant different terms of protection, the country whose legislation grants the shortest term of protection;

(b)    in the case of works published simultaneously in a country outside the Union and in a country of the Union, the latter country;

(c)    in the case of unpublished works or of works first published in a country outside the Union, without simultaneous publication in a country of the Union, the country of the Union of which the author is a national, provided that:

(i)    when these are cinematographic works the maker of which has his headquarters or his habitual residence in a country of the Union, the country of origin shall be that country, and

(ii)    when these are works of architecture erected in a country of the Union or other artistic works incorporated in a building or other structure located in a country of the Union, the country of origin shall be that country.

## Article 6

(1)    Where any country outside the Union fails to protect in an adequate manner the works of authors who are nationals of one of the countries of the Union, the latter country may restrict the protection given to the works of authors who are, at the date of the first publication thereof, nationals of the other country and are not habitually resident in one of the countries of the Union. If the country of first publication avails itself of this right, the other countries of the Union shall not be required to grant to works thus subjected to special treatment a wider protection than that granted to them in the country of first publication.

(2)    No restrictions introduced by virtue of the preceding paragraph shall affect the rights which an author may have acquired in respect of a work published in a country of the Union before such restrictions were put into force.

(3)    The countries of the Union which restrict the grant of copyright in accordance with this Article shall give notice thereof to the Director General of the World Intellectual Property Organization (hereinafter designated as "the Director General") by a written declaration specifying the countries in regard to which protection is restricted, and the restrictions to which rights of authors who are nationals of those countries are subjected. The Director General shall immediately communicate this declaration to all the countries of the Union.

## Article 6*bis*

(1)   Independently of the author's economic rights, and even after the transfer of the said rights, the author shall have the right to claim authorship of the work and to object to any distortion, mutilation or other modification of, or other derogatory action in relation to, the said work, which would be prejudicial to his honor or reputation.

(2)   The rights granted to the author in accordance with the preceding paragraph shall, after his death, be maintained, at least until the expiry of the economic rights, and shall be exercisable by the persons or institutions authorized by the legislation of the country where protection is claimed. However, those countries whose legislation, at the moment of their ratification of or accession to this Act, does not provide for the protection after the death of the author of all the rights set out in the preceding paragraph may provide that some of these rights may, after his death, cease to be maintained.

(3)   The means of redress for safeguarding the rights granted by this Article shall be governed by the legislation of the country where protection is claimed.

## Article 7

(1)   The term of protection granted by this Convention shall be the life of the author and fifty years after his death.

(2)   However, in the case of cinematographic works, the countries of the Union may provide that the term of protection shall expire fifty years after the work has been made available to the public with the consent of the author, or, failing such an event within fifty years from the making of such a work, fifty years after the making.

(3)   In the case of anonymous or pseudonymous works, the term of protection granted by this Convention shall expire fifty years after the work has been lawfully made available to the public. However, when the pseudonym adopted by the author leaves no doubt as to his identity, the term of protection shall be that provided in paragraph (1). If the author of an anonymous or pseudonymous work discloses his identity during the above-mentioned period, the term of protection applicable shall be that provided in paragraph (1). The countries of the Union shall not be required to protect anonymous or pseudonymous works in respect of which it is reasonable to presume that their author has been dead for fifty years.

(4)   It shall be a matter for legislation in the countries of the Union to determine the term of protection of photographic works and that of works of applied art in so far as they are protected as artistic works; however, this term shall last at least until the end of a period of twenty-five years from the making of such a work.

(5)   The term of protection subsequent to the death of the author and the terms provided by paragraph (2), paragraph (3) and paragraph (4) shall run from the date of death or of the event referred to in those paragraphs, but such terms shall always be deemed to begin on the first of January of the year following the death or such event.

(6)   The countries of the Union may grant a term of protection in excess of those provided by the preceding paragraphs.

(7)   Those countries of the Union bound by the Rome Act of this Convention which grant, in their national legislation in force at the time of signature of the present Act, shorter terms of protection than those provided for in the preceding paragraphs shall have the right to maintain such terms when ratifying or acceding to the present Act.

(8)   In any case, the term shall be governed by the legislation of the country where protection is claimed; however, unless the legislation of that country otherwise provides, the term shall not exceed the term fixed in the country of origin of the work.

### Article 7*bis*

The provisions of the preceding Article shall also apply in the case of a work of joint authorship, provided that the terms measured from the death of the author shall be calculated from the death of the last surviving author.

### Article 8

Authors of literary and artistic works protected by this Convention shall enjoy the exclusive right of making and of authorizing the translation of their works throughout the term of protection of their rights in the original works.

### Article 9

(1)   Authors of literary and artistic works protected by this Convention shall have the exclusive right of authorizing the reproduction of these works, in any manner or form.

(2)   It shall be a matter for legislation in the countries of the Union to permit the reproduction of such works in certain special cases, provided that such reproduction does not conflict with a normal exploitation of the work and does not unreasonably prejudice the legitimate interests of the author.

(3)   Any sound or visual recording shall be considered as a reproduction for the purposes of this Convention.

### Article 10

(1)   It shall be permissible to make quotations from a work which has already been lawfully made available to the public, provided that their making is compatible with fair practice, and their extent does not exceed that justified by the purpose, including quotations from newspaper articles and periodicals in the form of press summaries.

(2)   It shall be a matter for legislation in the countries of the Union, and for special agreements existing or to be concluded between them, to permit the utilization, to the extent justified by the purpose, of literary or artistic works by way of illustration in publications, broadcasts or sound or visual recordings for teaching, provided such utilization is compatible with fair practice.

(3)   Where use is made of works in accordance with the preceding paragraphs of this Article, mention shall be made of the source, and of the name of the author if it appears thereon.

### Article 10*bis*

(1)   It shall be a matter for legislation in the countries of the Union to permit the reproduction by the press, the broadcasting or the communication to the public by wire of articles published in newspapers or periodicals on current economic, political or religious topics, and of broadcast works of the same character, in cases in which the reproduction, broadcasting or such communication thereof is not expressly reserved. Nevertheless, the source must always be clearly indicated; the legal consequences of a breach of this obligation shall be determined by the legislation of the country where protection is claimed.

(2)   It shall also be a matter for legislation in the countries of the Union to determine the conditions under which, for the purpose of reporting current events by means of photography, cinematography, broadcasting or communication to the public by wire, literary or artistic works seen or heard in the course of the event may, to the extent justified by the informatory purpose, be reproduced and made available to the public.

### Article 11

(1)   Authors of dramatic, dramatico-musical and musical works shall enjoy the exclusive right of authorizing:

(i)    the public performance of their works, including such public performance by any means or process;

(ii)    any communication to the public of the performance of their works.

(2)    Authors of dramatic or dramatico-musical works shall enjoy, during the full term of their rights in the original works, the same rights with respect to translations thereof.

## Article 11*bis*

(1)    Authors of literary and artistic works shall enjoy the exclusive right of authorizing:

(i)    the broadcasting of their works or the communication thereof to the public by any other means of wireless diffusion of signs, sounds or images;

(ii)    any communication to the public by wire or by rebroadcasting of the broadcast of the work, when this communication is made by an organization other than the original one;

(iii)    the public communication by loudspeaker or any other analogous instrument transmitting, by signs, sounds or images, the broadcast of the work.

(2)    It shall be a matter for legislation in the countries of the Union to determine the conditions under which the rights mentioned in the paragraph 1 may be exercised, but these conditions shall apply only in the countries where they have been prescribed. They shall not in any circumstances be prejudicial to the moral rights of the author, nor to his right to obtain equitable remuneration which, in the absence of agreement, shall be fixed by competent authority.

(3)    In the absence of any contrary stipulation, permission granted in accordance with paragraph (1) of this Article shall not imply permission to record, by means of instruments recording sounds or images, the work broadcast. It shall, however, be a matter for legislation in the countries of the Union to determine the regulations for ephemeral recordings made by a broadcasting organization by means of its own facilities and used for its own broadcasts. The preservation of these recordings in official archives may, on the ground of their exceptional documentary character, be authorized by such legislation.

## Article 11*ter*

(1)    Authors of literary works shall enjoy the exclusive right of authorizing:

(i)    the public recitation of their works, including such public recitation by any means or process;

(ii)    any communication to the public of the recitation of their works.

(2)    Authors of literary works shall enjoy, during the full term of their rights in the original works, the same rights with respect to translations thereof.

## Article 12

Authors of literary or artistic works shall enjoy the exclusive right of authorizing adaptations, arrangements and other alterations of their works.

## Article 13

(1)    Each country of the Union may impose for itself reservations and conditions on the exclusive right granted to the author of a musical work and to the author of any words, the recording of which together with the musical work has already been authorized by the latter, to authorize the sound recording of that musical work, together with such words, if any; but all such reservations and conditions shall apply only in the countries which have imposed them and shall not, in any circumstances, be prejudicial to the rights of these authors to obtain equitable remuneration which, in the absence of agreement, shall be fixed by competent authority.

(2)    Recordings of musical works made in a country of the Union in accordance with Article 13(3) of the Conventions signed at Rome on June 2, 1928, and at Brussels on June 26, 1948, may be reproduced in that country without the permission of the author of the musical work until a date two years after that country becomes bound by this Act.

(3)    Recordings made in accordance with paragraph (1) and paragraph (2) of this Article and imported without permission from the parties concerned into a country where they are treated as infringing recordings shall be liable to seizure.

## Article 14

(1)    Authors of literary or artistic works shall have the exclusive right of authorizing:

(i)    the cinematographic adaptation and reproduction of these works, and the distribution of the works thus adapted or reproduced;

(ii)    the public performance and communication to the public by wire of the works thus adapted or reproduced.

(2)    The adaptation into any other artistic form of a cinematographic production derived from literary or artistic works shall, without prejudice to the authorization of the author of the cinematographic production, remain subject to the authorization of the authors of the original works.

(3)    The provisions of Article 13(1) shall not apply.

## Article 14*bis*

(1)    Without prejudice to the copyright in any work which may have been adapted or reproduced, a cinematographic work shall be protected as an original work. The owner of copyright in a cinematographic work shall enjoy the same rights as the author of an original work, including the rights referred to in the preceding Article.

(2)

(a)    Ownership of copyright in a cinematographic work shall be a matter for legislation in the country where protection is claimed.

(b)    However, in the countries of the Union which, by legislation, include among the owners of copyright in a cinematographic work authors who have brought contributions to the making of the work, such authors, if they have undertaken to bring such contributions, may not, in the absence of any contrary or special stipulation, object to the reproduction, distribution, public performance, communication to the public by wire, broadcasting or any other communication to the public, or to the subtitling or dubbing of texts, of the work.

(c)    The question whether or not the form of the undertaking referred to above should, for the application of the preceding subparagraph (b), be in a written agreement or a written act of the same effect shall be a matter for the legislation of the country where the maker of the cinematographic work has his headquarters or habitual residence. However, it shall be a matter for the legislation of the country of the Union where protection is claimed to provide that the said undertaking shall be in a written agreement or a written act of the same effect. The countries whose legislation so provides shall notify the Director General by means of a written declaration, which will be immediately communicated by him to all the other countries of the Union.

(d)    By "contrary or special stipulation" is meant any restrictive condition which is relevant to the aforesaid undertaking.

(3)    Unless the national legislation provides to the contrary, the provisions of paragraph (2)(b) above shall not be applicable to authors of scenarios, dialogues and musical works created for the making of the cinematographic work, or to the principal director thereof. However, those countries of the Union whose legislation does not contain rules providing for the application of the said paragraph (2)(b) to

such director shall notify the Director General by means of a written declaration, which will be immediately communicated by him to all the other countries of the Union.

## Article 14*ter*

(1)    The author, or after his death the persons or institutions authorized by national legislation, shall, with respect to original works of art and original manuscripts of writers and composers, enjoy the inalienable right to an interest in any sale of the work subsequent to the first transfer by the author of the work.

(2)    The protection provided by the preceding paragraph may be claimed in a country of the Union only if legislation in the country to which the author belongs so permits, and to the extent permitted by the country where this protection is claimed.

(3)    The procedure for collection and the amounts shall be matters for determination by national legislation.

## Article 15

(1)    In order that the author of a literary or artistic work protected by this Convention shall, in the absence of proof to the contrary, be regarded as such, and consequently be entitled to institute infringement proceedings in the countries of the Union, it shall be sufficient for his name to appear on the work in the usual manner. This paragraph shall be applicable even if this name is a pseudonym, where the pseudonym adopted by the author leaves no doubt as to his identity.

(2)    The person or body corporate whose name appears on a cinematographic work in the usual manner shall, in the absence of proof to the contrary, be presumed to be the maker of the said work.

(3)    In the case of anonymous and pseudonymous works, other than those referred to in paragraph (1) above, the publisher whose name appears on the work shall, in the absence of proof to the contrary, be deemed to represent the author, and in this capacity he shall be entitled to protect and enforce the author's rights. The provisions of this paragraph shall cease to apply when the author reveals his identity and establishes his claim to authorship of the work.

(4)

(a)    In the case of unpublished works where the identity of the author is unknown, but where there is every ground to presume that he is a national of a country of the Union, it shall be a matter for legislation in that country to designate the competent authority which shall represent the author and shall be entitled to protect and enforce his rights in the countries of the Union.

(b)    Countries of the Union which make such designation under the terms of this provision shall notify the Director General by means of a written declaration giving full information concerning the authority thus designated. The Director General shall at once communicate this declaration to all other countries of the Union.

## Article 16

(1)    Infringing copies of a work shall be liable to seizure in any country of the Union where the work enjoys legal protection.

(2)    The provisions of the preceding paragraph shall also apply to reproductions coming from a country where the work is not protected, or has ceased to be protected.

(3)    The seizure shall take place in accordance with the legislation of each country.

## Article 17

The provisions of this Convention cannot in any way affect the right of the Government of each country of the Union to permit, to control, or to prohibit, by legislation or regulation, the circulation, presentation, or exhibition of any work or production in regard to which the competent authority may find it necessary to exercise that right.

## Article 18

(1)   This Convention shall apply to all works which, at the moment of its coming into force, have not yet fallen into the public domain in the country of origin through the expiry of the term of protection.

(2)   If, however, through the expiry of the term of protection which was previously granted, a work has fallen into the public domain of the country where protection is claimed, that work shall not be protected anew.

(3)   The application of this principle shall be subject to any provisions contained in special conventions to that effect existing or to be concluded between countries of the Union. In the absence of such provisions, the respective countries shall determine, each in so far as it is concerned, the conditions of application of this principle.

(4)   The preceding provisions shall also apply in the case of new accessions to the Union and to cases in which protection is extended by the application of Article 7 or by the abandonment of reservations.

## Article 19

The provisions of this Convention shall not preclude the making of a claim to the benefit of any greater protection which may be granted by legislation in a country of the Union.

## Article 20

The Governments of the countries of the Union reserve the right to enter into special agreements among themselves, in so far as such agreements grant to authors more extensive rights than those granted by the Convention, or contain other provisions not contrary to this Convention. The provisions of existing agreements which satisfy these conditions shall remain applicable.

## Article 21

(1)   Special provisions regarding developing countries are included in the Appendix.

(2)   Subject to the provisions of Article 28(1)(b), the Appendix forms an integral part of this Act.

## Article 22

(1)

(a)   The Union shall have an Assembly consisting of those countries of the Union which are bound by Article 22 to Article 26.

(b)   The Government of each country shall be represented by one delegate, who may be assisted by alternate delegates, advisors, and experts.

(c)   The expenses of each delegation shall be borne by the Government which has appointed it.

(2)

(a)   The Assembly shall:

(i)   deal with all matters concerning the maintenance and development of the Union and the implementation of this Convention;

(ii) give directions concerning the preparation for conferences of revision to the International Bureau of Intellectual Property (hereinafter designated as "the International Bureau") referred to in the Convention Establishing the World Intellectual Property Organization (hereinafter designated as "the Organization"), due account being taken of any comments made by those countries of the Union which are not bound by Article 22 to Article 26;

(iii) review and approve the reports and activities of the Director General of the Organization concerning the Union, and give him all necessary instructions concerning matters within the competence of the Union;

(iv) elect the members of the Executive Committee of the Assembly;

(v) review and approve the reports and activities of its Executive Committee, and give instructions to such Committee;

(vi) determine the program and adopt the biennial budget of the Union, and approve its final accounts;

(vii) adopt the financial regulations of the Union;

(viii) establish such committees of experts and working groups as may be necessary for the work of the Union;

(ix) determine which countries not members of the Union and which intergovernmental and international non-governmental organizations shall be admitted to its meetings as observers;

(x) adopt amendments to Article 22 to Article 26;

(xi) take any other appropriate action designed to further the objectives of the Union;

(xii) exercise such other functions as are appropriate under this Convention;

(xiii) subject to its acceptance, exercise such rights as are given to it in the Convention establishing the Organization.

(b) With respect to matters which are of interest also to other Unions administered by the Organization, the Assembly shall make its decisions after having heard the advice of the Coordination Committee of the Organization.

(3)

(a) Each country member of the Assembly shall have one vote.

(b) One-half of the countries members of the Assembly shall constitute a quorum.

(c) Notwithstanding the provisions of subparagraph (b), if, in any session, the number of countries represented is less than one-half but equal to or more than one-third of the countries members of the Assembly, the Assembly may make decisions but, with the exception of decisions concerning its own procedure, all such decisions shall take effect only if the following conditions are fulfilled. The International Bureau shall communicate the said decisions to the countries members of the Assembly which were not represented and shall invite them to express in writing their vote or abstention within a period of three months from the date of the communication. If, at the expiration of this period, the number of countries having thus expressed their vote or abstention attains the number of countries which was lacking for attaining the quorum in the session itself, such decisions shall take effect provided that at the same time the required majority still obtains.

(d) Subject to the provisions of Article 26(2), the decisions of the Assembly shall require two-thirds of the votes cast.

(e) Abstentions shall not be considered as votes.

(f) A delegate may represent, and vote in the name of, one country only.

(g) Countries of the Union not members of the Assembly shall be admitted to its meetings as observers.

(4)

(a)   The Assembly shall meet once in every second calendar year in ordinary session upon convocation by the Director General and, in the absence of exceptional circumstances, during the same period and at the same place as the General Assembly of the Organization.

(b)   The Assembly shall meet in extraordinary session upon convocation by the Director General, at the request of the Executive Committee or at the request of one-fourth of the countries members of the Assembly.

(5)   The Assembly shall adopt its own rules of procedure.

## Article 23

(1)   The Assembly shall have an Executive Committee.

(2)

(a)   The Executive Committee shall consist of countries elected by the Assembly from among countries members of the Assembly. Furthermore, the country on whose territory the Organization has its headquarters shall, subject to the provisions of Article 25(7)(b), have an ex officio seat on the Committee.

(b)   The Government of each country member of the Executive Committee shall be represented by one delegate, who may be assisted by alternate delegates, advisors, and experts.

(c)   The expenses of each delegation shall be borne by the Government which has appointed it.

(3)   The number of countries members of the Executive Committee shall correspond to one-fourth of the number of countries members of the Assembly. In establishing the number of seats to be filled, remainders after division by four shall be disregarded.

(4)   In electing the members of the Executive Committee, the Assembly shall have due regard to an equitable geographical distribution and to the need for countries party to the Special Agreements which might be established in relation with the Union to be among the countries constituting the Executive Committee.

(5)

(a)   Each member of the Executive Committee shall serve from the close of the session of the Assembly which elected it to the close of the next ordinary session of the Assembly.

(b)   Members of the Executive Committee may be re-elected, but not more than two-thirds of them.

(c)   The Assembly shall establish the details of the rules governing the election and possible re-election of the members of the Executive Committee.

(6)

(a)   The Executive Committee shall:

(i)   prepare the draft agenda of the Assembly;

(ii)   submit proposals to the Assembly respecting the draft program and biennial budget of the Union prepared by the Director General;

(iii)   [deleted]

(iv)   submit, with appropriate comments, to the Assembly the periodical reports of the Director General and the yearly audit reports on the accounts;

(v)   in accordance with the decisions of the Assembly and having regard to circumstances arising between two ordinary sessions of the Assembly, take all necessary measures to ensure the execution of the program of the Union by the Director General;

(vi) perform such other functions as are allocated to it under this Convention.

(b) With respect to matters which are of interest also to other Unions administered by the Organization, the Executive Committee shall make its decisions after having heard the advice of the Coordination Committee of the Organization.

(7)

(a) The Executive Committee shall meet once a year in ordinary session upon convocation by the Director General, preferably during the same period and at the same place as the Coordination Committee of the Organization.

(b) The Executive Committee shall meet in extraordinary session upon convocation by the Director General, either on his own initiative, or at the request of its Chairman or one-fourth of its members.

(8)

(a) Each country member of the Executive Committee shall have one vote.

(b) One-half of the members of the Executive Committee shall constitute a quorum.

(c) Decisions shall be made by a simple majority of the votes cast.

(d) Abstentions shall not be considered as votes.

(e) A delegate may represent, and vote in the name of, one country only.

(9) Countries of the Union not members of the Executive Committee shall be admitted to its meetings as observers.

(10) The Executive Committee shall adopt its own rules of procedure.

## Article 24

(1)

(a) The administrative tasks with respect to the Union shall be performed by the International Bureau, which is a continuation of the Bureau of the Union united with the Bureau of the Union established by the International Convention for the Protection of Industrial Property.

(b) In particular, the International Bureau shall provide the secretariat of the various organs of the Union.

(c) The Director General of the Organization shall be the chief executive of the Union and shall represent the Union.

(2) The International Bureau shall assemble and publish information concerning the protection of copyright. Each country of the Union shall promptly communicate to the International Bureau all new laws and official texts concerning the protection of copyright.

(3) The International Bureau shall publish a monthly periodical.

(4) The International Bureau shall, on request, furnish information to any country of the Union on matters concerning the protection of copyright.

(5) The International Bureau shall conduct studies, and shall provide services, designed to facilitate the protection of copyright.

(6) The Director General and any staff member designated by him shall participate, without the right to vote, in all meetings of the Assembly, the Executive Committee and any other committee of experts or working group. The Director General, or a staff member designated by him, shall be ex officio secretary of these bodies.

(7)

(a)   The International Bureau shall, in accordance with the directions of the Assembly and in cooperation with the Executive Committee, make the preparations for the conferences of revision of the provisions of the Convention other than Article 22 to Article 26.

(b)   The International Bureau may consult with intergovernmental and international non-governmental organizations concerning preparations for conferences of revision.

(c)   The Director General and persons designated by him shall take part, without the right to vote, in the discussions at these conferences.

(8)   The International Bureau shall carry out any other tasks assigned to it.

## Article 25

(1)

(a)   The Union shall have a budget.

(b)   The budget of the Union shall include the income and expenses proper to the Union, its contribution to the budget of expenses common to the Unions, and, where applicable, the sum made available to the budget of the Conference of the Organization.

(c)   Expenses not attributable exclusively to the Union but also to one or more other Unions administered by the Organization shall be considered as expenses common to the Unions. The share of the Union in such common expenses shall be in proportion to the interest the Union has in them.

(2)   The budget of the Union shall be established with due regard to the requirements of coordination with the budgets of the other Unions administered by the Organization.

(3)   The budget of the Union shall be financed from the following sources:

(i)   contributions of the countries of the Union;

(ii)   fees and charges due for services performed by the International Bureau in relation to the Union;

(iii) sale of, or royalties on, the publications of the International Bureau concerning the Union;

(iv)  gifts, bequests, and subventions;

(v)   rents, interests, and other miscellaneous income.

(4)

(a)   For the purpose of establishing its contribution towards the budget, each country of the Union shall belong to a class, and shall pay its annual contributions on the basis of a number of units fixed as follows:

| Class I | 25 |
|---------|----|
| Class II | 20 |
| Class III | 15 |
| Class IV | 10 |
| Class V | 5 |
| Class VI | 3 |
| Class VII | 1 |

(b) Unless it has already done so, each country shall indicate, concurrently with depositing its instrument of ratification or accession, the class to which it wishes to belong. Any country may change class. If it chooses a lower class, the country must announce it to the Assembly at one of its ordinary sessions. Any such change shall take effect at the beginning of the calendar year following the session.

(c) The annual contribution of each country shall be an amount in the same proportion to the total sum to be contributed to the annual budget of the Union by all countries as the number of its units is to the total of the units of all contributing countries.

(d) Contributions shall become due on the first of January of each year.

(e) A country which is in arrears in the payment of its contributions shall have no vote in any of the organs of the Union of which it is a member if the amount of its arrears equals or exceeds the amount of the contributions due from it for the preceding two full years. However, any organ of the Union may allow such a country to continue to exercise its vote in that organ if, and as long as, it is satisfied that the delay in payment is due to exceptional and unavoidable circumstances.

(f) If the budget is not adopted before the beginning of a new financial period, it shall be at the same level as the budget of the previous year, in accordance with the financial regulations.

(5) The amount of the fees and charges due for services rendered by the International Bureau in relation to the Union shall be established, and shall be reported to the Assembly and the Executive Committee, by the Director General.

(6)

(a) The Union shall have a working capital fund which shall be constituted by a single payment made by each country of the Union. If the fund becomes insufficient, an increase shall be decided by the Assembly.

(b) The amount of the initial payment of each country to the said fund or of its participation in the increase thereof shall be a proportion of the contribution of that country for the year in which the fund is established or the increase decided.

(c) The proportion and the terms of payment shall be fixed by the Assembly on the proposal of the Director General and after it has heard the advice of the Coordination Committee of the Organization.

(7)

(a) In the headquarters agreement concluded with the country on the territory of which the Organization has its headquarters, it shall be provided that, whenever the working capital fund is insufficient, such country shall grant advances. The amount of these advances and the conditions on which they are granted shall be the subject of separate agreements, in each case, between such country and the Organization. As long as it remains under the obligation to grant advances, such country shall have an ex officio seat on the Executive Committee.

(b) The country referred to in subparagraph (a) and the Organization shall each have the right to denounce the obligation to grant advances, by written notification. Denunciation shall take effect three years after the end of the year in which it has been notified.

(8) The auditing of the accounts shall be effected by one or more of the countries of the Union or by external auditors, as provided in the financial regulations. They shall be designated, with their agreement, by the Assembly.

### Article 26

(1) Proposals for the amendment of Article 22, Article 23, Article 24, Article 25, and the present Article, may be initiated by any country member of the Assembly, by the Executive Committee, or by

the Director General. Such proposals shall be communicated by the Director General to the member countries of the Assembly at least six months in advance of their consideration by the Assembly.

(2)   Amendments to the Articles referred to in paragraph (1) shall be adopted by the Assembly. Adoption shall require three-fourths of the votes cast, provided that any amendment of Article 22, and of the present paragraph, shall require four-fifths of the votes cast.

(3)   Any amendment to the Articles referred to in paragraph (1) shall enter into force one month after written notifications of acceptance, effected in accordance with their respective constitutional processes, have been received by the Director General from three-fourths of the countries members of the Assembly at the time it adopted the amendment. Any amendment to the said Articles thus accepted shall bind all the countries which are members of the Assembly at the time the amendment enters into force, or which become members thereof at a subsequent date, provided that any amendment increasing the financial obligations of countries of the Union shall bind only those countries which have notified their acceptance of such amendment.

### Article 27

(1)   This Convention shall be submitted to revision with a view to the introduction of amendments designed to improve the system of the Union.

(2)   For this purpose, conferences shall be held successively in one of the countries of the Union among the delegates of the said countries.

(3)   Subject to the provisions of Article 26 which apply to the amendment of Article 22 to Article 26, any revision of this Act, including the Appendix, shall require the unanimity of the votes cast.

### Article 28

(1)

(a)   Any country of the Union which has signed this Act may ratify it, and, if it has not signed it, may accede to it. Instruments of ratification or accession shall be deposited with the Director General.

(b)   Any country of the Union may declare in its instrument of ratification or accession that its ratification or accession shall not apply to Article 1 to Article 21 and the Appendix, provided that, if such country has previously made a declaration under Article VI(1) of the Appendix, then it may declare in the said instrument only that its ratification or accession shall not apply to Article 1 to Article 20.

(c)   Any country of the Union which, in accordance with subparagraph (b), has excluded provisions therein referred to from the effects of its ratification or accession may at any later time declare that it extends the effects of its ratification or accession to those provisions. Such declaration shall be deposited with the Director General.

(2)

(a)   Article 1 to Article 21 and the Appendix shall enter into force three months after both of the following two conditions are fulfilled:

(i)   at least five countries of the Union have ratified or acceded to this Act without making a declaration under paragraph (1)(b),

(ii)   France, Spain, the United Kingdom of Great Britain and Northern Ireland, and the United States of America, have become bound by the Universal Copyright Convention as revised at Paris on July 24, 1971.

(b)   The entry into force referred to in subparagraph (a) shall apply to those countries of the Union which, at least three months before the said entry into force, have deposited instruments of ratification or accession not containing a declaration under paragraph (1)(b).

(c)    With respect to any country of the Union not covered by subparagraph (b) and which ratifies or accedes to this Act without making a declaration under paragraph (1)(b), Article 1 to Article 21 and the Appendix shall enter into force three months after the date on which the Director General has notified the deposit of the relevant instrument of ratification or accession, unless a subsequent date has been indicated in the instrument deposited. In the latter case, Article 1 to Article 21 and the Appendix shall enter into force with respect to that country on the date thus indicated.

(d)    The provisions of subparagraph (a) to subparagraph (c) do not affect the application of Article VI of the Appendix.

(3)    With respect to any country of the Union which ratifies or accedes to this Act with or without a declaration made under paragraph (1)(b), Article 22 to Article 38 shall enter into force three months after the date on which the Director General has notified the deposit of the relevant instrument of ratification or accession, unless a subsequent date has been indicated in the instrument deposited. In the latter case, Article 22 to Article 38 shall enter into force with respect to that country on the date thus indicated.

### Article 29

(1)    Any country outside the Union may accede to this Act and thereby become party to this Convention and a member of the Union. Instruments of accession shall be deposited with the Director General.

(2)

(a)    Subject to subparagraph (b), this Convention shall enter into force with respect to any country outside the Union three months after the date on which the Director General has notified the deposit of its instrument of accession, unless a subsequent date has been indicated in the instrument deposited. In the latter case, this Convention shall enter into force with respect to that country on the date thus indicated.

(b)    If the entry into force according to subparagraph (a) precedes the entry into force of Article 1 to Article 21 and the Appendix according to Article 28(2)(a), the said country shall, in the meantime, be bound, instead of by Article 1 to Article 21 and the Appendix, by Article 1 to Article 20 of the Brussels Act of this Convention.

### Article 29*bis*

Ratification of or accession to this Act by any country not bound by Article 22 to Article 38 of the Stockholm Act of this Convention shall, for the sole purposes of Article 14(2) of the Convention establishing the Organization, amount to ratification of or accession to the said Stockholm Act with the limitation set forth in Article 28(1)(b)(i) thereof.

### Article 30

(1)    Subject to the exceptions permitted by paragraph (2) of this Article, by Article 28(1)(b), by Article 33(2), and by the Appendix, ratification or accession shall automatically entail acceptance of all the provisions and admission to all the advantages of this Convention.

(2)

(a)    Any country of the Union ratifying or acceding to this Act may, subject to Article V(2) of the Appendix, retain the benefit of the reservations it has previously formulated on condition that it makes a declaration to that effect at the time of the deposit of its instrument of ratification or accession.

(b)    Any country outside the Union may declare, in acceding to this Convention and subject to Article V(2) of the Appendix, that it intends to substitute, temporarily at least, for Article 8 of this Act concerning the right of translation, the provisions of Article 5 of the Union Convention of 1886, as completed at Paris in 1896, on the clear understanding that the said provisions are applicable only to translations into a language in general use in the said country. Subject to Article I(6)(b) of the Appendix, any country has the right to apply, in relation to the right of translation of works whose country of origin is a country availing itself of such a reservation, a protection which is equivalent to the protection granted by the latter country.

(c)   Any country may withdraw such reservations at any time by notification addressed to the Director General.

## Article 31

(1)   Any country may declare in its instrument of ratification or accession, or may inform the Director General by written notification at any time thereafter, that this Convention shall be applicable to all or part of those territories, designated in the declaration or notification, for the external relations of which it is responsible.

(2)   Any country which has made such a declaration or given such a notification may, at any time, notify the Director General that this Convention shall cease to be applicable to all or part of such territories.

(3)

(a)   Any declaration made under paragraph (1) shall take effect on the same date as the ratification or accession in which it was included, and any notification given under that paragraph shall take effect three months after its notification by the Director General.

(b)   Any notification given under paragraph (2) shall take effect twelve months after its receipt by the Director General.

(4)   This Article shall in no way be understood as implying the recognition or tacit acceptance by a country of the Union of the factual situation concerning a territory to which this Convention is made applicable by another country of the Union by virtue of a declaration under paragraph (1).

## Article 32

(1)   This Act shall, as regards relations between the countries of the Union, and to the extent that it applies, replace the Berne Convention of September 9, 1886, and the subsequent Acts of revision. The Acts previously in force shall continue to be applicable, in their entirety or to the extent that this Act does not replace them by virtue of the preceding sentence, in relations with countries of the Union which do not ratify or accede to this Act.

(2)   Countries outside the Union which become party to this Act shall, subject to paragraph (3), apply it with respect to any country of the Union not bound by this Act or which, although bound by this Act, has made a declaration pursuant to Article 28(1)(b). Such countries recognize that the said country of the Union, in its relations with them:

(i)   may apply the provisions of the most recent Act by which it is bound, and

(ii)   subject to Article I(6) of the Appendix, has the right to adapt the protection to the level provided for by this Act.

(3)   Any country which has availed itself of any of the faculties provided for in the Appendix may apply the provisions of the Appendix relating to the faculty or faculties of which it has availed itself in its relations with any other country of the Union which is not bound by this Act, provided that the latter country has accepted the application of the said provisions.

## Article 33

(1)　Any dispute between two or more countries of the Union concerning the interpretation or application of this Convention, not settled by negotiation, may, by any one of the countries concerned, be brought before the International Court of Justice by application in conformity with the Statute of the Court, unless the countries concerned agree on some other method of settlement. The country bringing the dispute before the Court shall inform the International Bureau; the International Bureau shall bring the matter to the attention of the other countries of the Union.

(2)　Each country may, at the time it signs this Act or deposits its instrument of ratification or accession, declare that it does not consider itself bound by the provisions of paragraph (1). With regard to any dispute between such country and any other country of the Union, the provisions of paragraph (1) shall not apply.

(3)　Any country having made a declaration in accordance with the provisions of paragraph (2) may, at any time, withdraw its declaration by notification addressed to the Director General.

## Article 34

(1)　Subject to Article 29*bis*, no country may ratify or accede to earlier Acts of this Convention once Article 1 to Article 21 and the Appendix have entered into force.

(2)　Once Article 1 to Article 21 and the Appendix have entered into force, no country may make a declaration under Article 5 of the Protocol Regarding Developing Countries attached to the Stockholm Act.

## Article 35

(1)　This Convention shall remain in force without limitation as to time.

(2)　Any country may denounce this Act by notification addressed to the Director General. Such denunciation shall constitute also denunciation of all earlier Acts and shall affect only the country making it, the Convention remaining in full force and effect as regards the other countries of the Union.

(3)　Denunciation shall take effect one year after the day on which the Director General has received the notification.

(4)　The right of denunciation provided by this Article shall not be exercised by any country before the expiration of five years from the date upon which it becomes a member of the Union.

## Article 36

(1)　Any country party to this Convention undertakes to adopt, in accordance with its constitution, the measures necessary to ensure the application of this Convention.

(2)　It is understood that, at the time a country becomes bound by this Convention, it will be in a position under its domestic law to give effect to the provisions of this Convention.

## Article 37

(1)

(a)　This Act shall be signed in a single copy in the French and English languages and, subject to paragraph (2), shall be deposited with the Director General.

(b)　Official texts shall be established by the Director General, after consultation with the interested Governments, in the Arabic, German, Italian, Portuguese and Spanish languages, and such other languages as the Assembly may designate.

(c)   In case of differences of opinion on the interpretation of the various texts, the French text shall prevail.

(2)   This Act shall remain open for signature until January 31, 1972. Until that date, the copy referred to in paragraph (1)(a) shall be deposited with the Government of the French Republic.

(3)   The Director General shall certify and transmit two copies of the signed text of this Act to the Governments of all countries of the Union and, on request, to the Government of any other country.

(4)   The Director General shall register this Act with the Secretariat of the United Nations.

(5)   The Director General shall notify the Governments of all countries of the Union of signatures, deposits of instruments of ratification or accession and any declarations included in such instruments or made pursuant to Article 28(1)(c), Article 30(2)(a) and Article 30(2)(b), and Article 33(2), entry into force of any provisions of this Act, notifications of denunciation, and notifications pursuant to Article 30(2)(c), Article 31(1) and Article 31(2), Article 33(3), and Article 38(1), as well as the Appendix.

## Article 38

(1)   Countries of the Union which have not ratified or acceded to this Act and which are not bound by Article 22 to Article 26 of the Stockholm Act of this Convention may, until April 26, 1975, exercise, if they so desire, the rights provided under the said Articles as if they were bound by them. Any country desiring to exercise such rights shall give written notification to this effect to the Director General; this notification shall be effective on the date of its receipt. Such countries shall be deemed to be members of the Assembly until the said date.

(2)   As long as all the countries of the Union have not become Members of the Organization, the International Bureau of the Organization shall also function as the Bureau of the Union, and the Director General as the Director of the said Bureau.

(3)   Once all the countries of the Union have become Members of the Organization, the rights, obligations, and property, of the Bureau of the Union shall devolve on the International Bureau of the Organization.

## APPENDIX

### SPECIAL PROVISIONS REGARDING DEVELOPING COUNTRIES

### Article I

(1)   Any country regarded as a developing country in conformity with the established practice of the General Assembly of the United Nations which ratifies or accedes to this Act, of which this Appendix forms an integral part, and which, having regard to its economic situation and its social or cultural needs, does not consider itself immediately in a position to make provision for the protection of all the rights as provided for in this Act, may, by a notification deposited with the Director General at the time of depositing its instrument of ratification or accession or, subject to Article V(1)(c), at any time thereafter, declare that it will avail itself of the faculty provided for in Article II, or of the faculty provided for in Article III, or of both of those faculties. It may, instead of availing itself of the faculty provided for in Article II, make a declaration according to Article V(1)(a).

(2)

(a)   Any declaration under paragraph (1) notified before the expiration of the period of ten years from the entry into force of Article 1 to Article 21 and this Appendix according to Article 28(2) shall be effective until the expiration of the said period. Any such declaration may be renewed in whole or in part for periods of ten years each by a notification deposited with the Director General not more than fifteen months and not less than three months before the expiration of the ten-year period then running.

(b)   Any declaration under paragraph (1) notified after the expiration of the period of ten years from the entry into force of Article 1 to Article 21 and this Appendix according to Article 28(2) shall be effective until the expiration of the ten-year period then running. Any such declaration may be renewed as provided for in the second sentence of subparagraph (a).

(3)   Any country of the Union which has ceased to be regarded as a developing country as referred to in paragraph (1) shall no longer be entitled to renew its declaration as provided in paragraph (2), and, whether or not it formally withdraws its declaration, such country shall be precluded from availing itself of the faculties referred to in paragraph (1) from the expiration of the ten-year period then running or from the expiration of a period of three years after it has ceased to be regarded as a developing country, whichever period expires later.

(4)   Where, at the time when the declaration made under paragraph (1) or paragraph (2) ceases to be effective, there are copies in stock which were made under a license granted by virtue of this Appendix, such copies may continue to be distributed until their stock is exhausted.

(5)   Any country which is bound by the provisions of this Act and which has deposited a declaration or a notification in accordance with Article 31(1) with respect to the application of this Act to a particular territory, the situation of which can be regarded as analogous to that of the countries referred to in paragraph (1), may, in respect of such territory, make the declaration referred to in paragraph (1) and the notification of renewal referred to in paragraph (2). As long as such declaration or notification remains in effect, the provisions of this Appendix shall be applicable to the territory in respect of which it was made.

(6)

(a)   The fact that a country avails itself of any of the faculties referred to in paragraph (1) does not permit another country to give less protection to works of which the country of origin is the former country than it is obliged to grant under Article 1 to Article 20.

(b)   The right to apply reciprocal treatment provided for in Article 30(2)(b), second sentence, shall not, until the date on which the period applicable under Article I(3) expires, be exercised in respect of works the country of origin of which is a country which has made a declaration according to Article V(1)(a).

## Article II

(1)   Any country which has declared that it will avail itself of the faculty provided for in this Article shall be entitled, so far as works published in printed or analogous forms of reproduction are concerned, to substitute for the exclusive right of translation provided for in Article 8 a system of non-exclusive and non-transferable licenses, granted by the competent authority under the following conditions and subject to Article IV.

(2)

(a)   Subject to paragraph (3), if, after the expiration of a period of three years, or of any longer period determined by the national legislation of the said country, commencing on the date of the first publication of the work, a translation of such work has not been published in a language in general use in that country by the owner of the right of translation, or with his authorization, any national of such country may obtain a license to make a translation of the work in the said language and publish the translation in printed or analogous forms of reproduction.

(b)   A license under the conditions provided for in this Article may also be granted if all the editions of the translation published in the language concerned are out of print.

(3)

(a)   In the case of translations into a language which is not in general use in one or more developed countries which are members of the Union, a period of one year shall be substituted for the period of three years referred to in paragraph (2)(a).

(b)   Any country referred to in paragraph (1) may, with the unanimous agreement of the developed countries which are members of the Union and in which the same language is in general use, substitute, in the case of translations into that language, for the period of three years referred to in paragraph (2)(a) a shorter period as determined by such agreement but not less than one year. However, the provisions of the foregoing sentence shall not apply where the language in question is English, French or Spanish. The Director General shall be notified of any such agreement by the Governments which have concluded it.

(4)

(a)   No license obtainable after three years shall be granted under this Article until a further period of six months has elapsed, and no license obtainable after one year shall be granted under this Article until a further period of nine months has elapsed

(i)   from the date on which the applicant complies with the requirements mentioned in Article IV(1), or

(ii)   where the identity or the address of the owner of the right of translation is unknown, from the date on which the applicant sends, as provided for in Article IV(2), copies of his application submitted to the authority competent to grant the license.

(b)   If, during the said period of six or nine months, a translation in the language in respect of which the application was made is published by the owner of the right of translation or with his authorization, no license under this Article shall be granted.

(5)   Any license under this Article shall be granted only for the purpose of teaching, scholarship or research.

(6)   If a translation of a work is published by the owner of the right of translation or with his authorization at a price reasonably related to that normally charged in the country for comparable works, any license granted under this Article shall terminate if such translation is in the same language and with substantially the same content as the translation published under the license. Any copies already made before the license terminates may continue to be distributed until their stock is exhausted.

(7)   For works which are composed mainly of illustrations, a license to make and publish a translation of the text and to reproduce and publish the illustrations may be granted only if the conditions of Article III are also fulfilled.

(8)   No license shall be granted under this Article when the author has withdrawn from circulation all copies of his work.

(9)

(a)   A license to make a translation of a work which has been published in printed or analogous forms of reproduction may also be granted to any broadcasting organization having its headquarters in a country referred to in paragraph (1), upon an application made to the competent authority of that country by the said organization, provided that all of the following conditions are met:

(i)   the translation is made from a copy made and acquired in accordance with the laws of the said country;

(ii)   the translation is only for use in broadcasts intended exclusively for teaching or for the dissemination of the results of specialized technical or scientific research to experts in a particular profession;

(iii)   the translation is used exclusively for the purposes referred to in condition (ii) through broadcasts made lawfully and intended for recipients on the territory of the said country, including broadcasts made through the medium of sound or visual recordings lawfully and exclusively made for the purpose of such broadcasts;

(iv)   all uses made of the translation are without any commercial purpose.

(b)   Sound or visual recordings of a translation which was made by a broadcasting organization under a license granted by virtue of this paragraph may, for the purposes and subject to the conditions referred to in subparagraph (a) and with the agreement of that organization, also be used by any other broadcasting organization having its headquarters in the country whose competent authority granted the license in question.

(c)   Provided that all of the criteria and conditions set out in subparagraph (a) are met, a license may also be granted to a broadcasting organization to translate any text incorporated in an audio-visual fixation where such fixation was itself prepared and published for the sole purpose of being used in connection with systematic instructional activities.

(d)   Subject to subparagraphs (a) to (c), the provisions of the preceding paragraphs shall apply to the grant and exercise of any license granted under this paragraph.

## Article III

(1)   Any country which has declared that it will avail itself of the faculty provided for in this Article shall be entitled to substitute for the exclusive right of reproduction provided for in Article 9 a system of non-exclusive and non-transferable licenses, granted by the competent authority under the following conditions and subject to Article IV.

(2)

(a)   If, in relation to a work to which this Article applies by virtue of paragraph (7), after the expiration of

(i)   the relevant period specified in paragraph (3), commencing on the date of first publication of a particular edition of the work, or

(ii)   any longer period determined by national legislation of the country referred to in paragraph (1), commencing on the same date,

copies of such edition have not been distributed in that country to the general public or in connection with systematic instructional activities, by the owner of the right of reproduction or with his authorization, at a price reasonably related to that normally charged in the country for comparable works, any national of such country may obtain a license to reproduce and publish such edition at that or a lower price for use in connection with systematic instructional activities.

(b)   A license to reproduce and publish an edition which has been distributed as described in subparagraph (a) may also be granted under the conditions provided for in this Article if, after the expiration of the applicable period, no authorized copies of that edition have been on sale for a period of six months in the country concerned to the general public or in connection with systematic instructional activities at a price reasonably related to that normally charged in the country for comparable works.

(3)   The period referred to in paragraph (2)(a)(i) shall be five years, except that

(i)   for works of the natural and physical sciences, including mathematics, and of technology, the period shall be three years;

(ii)   for works of fiction, poetry, drama and music, and for art books, the period shall be seven years.

(4)

(a)   No license obtainable after three years shall be granted under this Article until a period of six months has elapsed

(i)   from the date on which the applicant complies with the requirements mentioned in Article IV(1), or

(ii)  where the identity or the address of the owner of the right of reproduction is unknown, from the date on which the applicant sends, as provided for in Article IV(2), copies of his application submitted to the authority competent to grant the license.

(b)  Where licenses are obtainable after other periods and Article IV(2) is applicable, no license shall be granted until a period of three months has elapsed from the date of the dispatch of the copies of the application.

(c)  If, during the period of six or three months referred to in subparagraph (a) and subparagraph (b), a distribution as described in paragraph (2)(a) has taken place, no license shall be granted under this Article.

(d)  No license shall be granted if the author has withdrawn from circulation all copies of the edition for the reproduction and publication of which the license has been applied for.

(5)  A license to reproduce and publish a translation of a work shall not be granted under this Article in the following cases:

(i)  where the translation was not published by the owner of the right of translation or with his authorization, or

(ii)  where the translation is not in a language in general use in the country in which the license is applied for.

(6)  If copies of an edition of a work are distributed in the country referred to in paragraph (1) to the general public or in connection with systematic instructional activities, by the owner of the right of reproduction or with his authorization, at a price reasonably related to that normally charged in the country for comparable works, any license granted under this Article shall terminate if such edition is in the same language and with substantially the same content as the edition which was published under the said license. Any copies already made before the license terminates may continue to be distributed until their stock is exhausted.

(7)

(a)  Subject to subparagraph (b), the works to which this Article applies shall be limited to works published in printed or analogous forms of reproduction.

(b)  This Article shall also apply to the reproduction in audio-visual form of lawfully made audio-visual fixations including any protected works incorporated therein and to the translation of any incorporated text into a language in general use in the country in which the license is applied for, always provided that the audio-visual fixations in question were prepared and published for the sole purpose of being used in connection with systematic instructional activities.

## Article IV

(1)  A license under Article II or Article III may be granted only if the applicant, in accordance with the procedure of the country concerned, establishes either that he has requested, and has been denied, authorization by the owner of the right to make and publish the translation or to reproduce and publish the edition, as the case may be, or that, after due diligence on his part, he was unable to find the owner of the right. At the same time as making the request, the applicant shall inform any national or international information center referred to in paragraph (2).

(2)  If the owner of the right cannot be found, the applicant for a license shall send, by registered airmail, copies of his application, submitted to the authority competent to grant the license, to the publisher whose name appears on the work and to any national or international information center which may have been designated, in a notification to that effect deposited with the Director General, by the Government of the country in which the publisher is believed to have his principal place of business.

(3)  The name of the author shall be indicated on all copies of the translation or reproduction published under a license granted under Article II or Article III. The title of the work shall appear on all such copies. In the case of a translation, the original title of the work shall appear in any case on all the said copies.

(4)

(a)  No license granted under Article II or Article III shall extend to the export of copies, and any such license shall be valid only for publication of the translation or of the reproduction, as the case may be, in the territory of the country in which it has been applied for.

(b)  For the purposes of subparagraph (a), the notion of export shall include the sending of copies from any territory to the country which, in respect of that territory, has made a declaration under Article I(5).

(c)  Where a governmental or other public entity of a country which has granted a license to make a translation under Article II into a language other than English, French or Spanish sends copies of a translation published under such license to another country, such sending of copies shall not, for the purposes of subparagraph (a), be considered to constitute export if all of the following conditions are met:

(i)  the recipients are individuals who are nationals of the country whose competent authority has granted the license, or organizations grouping such individuals;

(ii)  the copies are to be used only for the purpose of teaching, scholarship or research;

(iii)  the sending of the copies and their subsequent distribution to recipients is without any commercial purpose; and

(iv)  the country to which the copies have been sent has agreed with the country whose competent authority has granted the license to allow the receipt, or distribution, or both, and the Director General has been notified of the agreement by the Government of the country in which the license has been granted.

(5)  All copies published under a license granted by virtue of Article II or Article III shall bear a notice in the appropriate language stating that the copies are available for distribution only in the country or territory to which the said license applies.

(6)

(a)  Due provision shall be made at the national level to ensure

(i)  that the license provides, in favour of the owner of the right of translation or of reproduction, as the case may be, for just compensation that is consistent with standards of royalties normally operating on licenses freely negotiated between persons in the two countries concerned, and

(ii)  payment and transmittal of the compensation: should national currency regulations intervene, the competent authority shall make all efforts, by the use of international machinery, to ensure transmittal in internationally convertible currency or its equivalent.

(b)  Due provision shall be made by national legislation to ensure a correct translation of the work, or an accurate reproduction of the particular edition, as the case may be.

## Article V

(1)

(a)  Any country entitled to make a declaration that it will avail itself of the faculty provided for in Article II may, instead, at the time of ratifying or acceding to this Act:

(i)  if it is a country to which Article 30(2)(a) applies, make a declaration under that provision as far as the right of translation is concerned;

    (ii)   if it is a country to which Article 30(2)(a) does not apply, and even if it is not a country outside the Union, make a declaration as provided for in Article 30(2)(b), first sentence.

(b)   In the case of a country which ceases to be regarded as a developing country as referred to in Article I(1), a declaration made according to this paragraph shall be effective until the date on which the period applicable under Article I(3) expires.

(c)   Any country which has made a declaration according to this paragraph may not subsequently avail itself of the faculty provided for in Article II even if it withdraws the said declaration.

(2)   Subject to paragraph (3), any country which has availed itself of the faculty provided for in Article II may not subsequently make a declaration according to paragraph (1).

(3)   Any country which has ceased to be regarded as a developing country as referred to in Article I(1) may, not later than two years prior to the expiration of the period applicable under Article I(3), make a declaration to the effect provided for in Article 30(2)(b), first sentence, notwithstanding the fact that it is not a country outside the Union. Such declaration shall take effect at the date on which the period applicable under Article I(3) expires.

## Article VI

(1)   Any country of the Union may declare, as from the date of this Act, and at any time before becoming bound by Article 1 to Article 21 and this Appendix:

    (i)   if it is a country which, were it bound by Article 1 to Article 21 and this Appendix, would be entitled to avail itself of the faculties referred to in Article I(1), that it will apply the provisions of Article II or of Article III or of both to works whose country of origin is a country which, pursuant to (ii) below, admits the application of those Articles to such works, or which is bound by Article 1 to Article 21 and this Appendix; such declaration may, instead of referring to Article II, refer to Article V;

    (ii)   that it admits the application of this Appendix to works of which it is the country of origin by countries which have made a declaration under (i) above or a notification under Article I.

(2)   Any declaration made under paragraph (1) shall be in writing and shall be deposited with the Director General. The declaration shall become effective from the date of its deposit.

# 12. PARTIES TO THE BERNE CONVENTION FOR THE PROTECTION OF LITERARY AND ARTISTIC WORKS*

Berne Convention (1886), completed at Paris (1896),
revised at Berlin (1908), completed at Berne (1914),
revised at Rome (1928), at Brussels (1948),
at Stockholm (1967) and at Paris (1971),
and amended in 1979 (Berne Union)

**Status on May 4, 2021**

| State | Date on which State became party to the Convention | Latest Act[1] of the Convention to which State is party and date on which State became party to that Act | |
|---|---|---|---|
| Afghanistan | June 2, 2018 | Paris: | June 2, 2018 |
| Albania | March 6, 1994 | Paris: | March 6, 1994 |
| Algeria | April 19, 1998 | Paris: | April 19, 1998[2, 3] |
| Andorra | June 2, 2004 | Paris: | June 2, 2004 |
| Antigua and Barbuda | March 17, 2000 | Paris: | March 17, 2000 |
| Argentina | June 10, 1967 | Paris: | Articles 1 to 21: February 19, 2000 |
| | | Paris: | Articles 22 to 38: October 8, 1980 |
| Armenia | October 19, 2000 | Paris: | October 19, 2000 |
| Australia | April 14, 1928 | Paris: | March 1, 1978 |
| Austria | October 1, 1920 | Paris: | August 21, 1982 |
| Azerbaijan | June 4, 1999 | Paris: | June 4, 1999 |
| Bahamas | July 10, 1973 | Brussels: | July 10, 1973 |
| | | Paris: | Articles 22 to 38: January 8, 1977[2] |
| Bahrain | March 2, 1997 | Paris: | March 2, 1997 |
| Bangladesh | May 4, 1999 | Paris: | May 4, 1999[3] |
| Barbados | July 30, 1983 | Paris: | July 30, 1983 |
| Belarus | December 12, 1997 | Paris: | December 12, 1997 |
| Belgium | December 5, 1887 | Paris: | September 29, 1999 |
| Belize | June 17, 2000 | Paris: | June 17, 2000 |
| Benin | January 3, 1961[4] | Paris: | March 12, 1975 |
| Bhutan | November 25, 2004 | Paris: | November 25, 2004 |
| Bolivia (Plurinational State of) | November 4, 1993 | Paris: | November 4, 1993 |
| Bosnia and Herzegovina | March 1, 1992 | Paris: | March 1, 1992[5] |
| Botswana | April 15, 1998 | Paris: | April 15, 1998 |
| Brazil | February 9, 1922 | Paris: | April 20, 1975 |
| Brunei Darussalam | August 30, 2006 | Paris: | August 30, 2006 |
| Bulgaria | December 5, 1921 | Paris: | December 4, 1974 |
| Burkina Faso | August 19, 1963[6] | Paris: | January 24, 1976 |
| Burundi | April 12, 2016 | Paris: | April 12, 2016 |
| Cabo Verde | July 7, 1997 | Paris: | July 7, 1997 |
| Cameroon | September 21, 1964[4] | Paris: | Articles 1 to 21: October 10, 1974 |
| | | Paris: | Articles 22 to 38: November 10, 1973 |
| Canada | April 10, 1928 | Paris: | June 26, 1998 |
| Central African Republic | September 3, 1977 | Paris: | September 3, 1977 |

---

\*    Document originally produced by the World Intellectual Property Organization (WIPO), the owner of the copyright. Published with the permission of the World Intellectual Property Organization.

| State | Date on which State became party to the Convention | Latest Act[1] of the Convention to which State is party and date on which State became party to that Act | |
|---|---|---|---|
| Chad............................................... | November 25, 1971 | Brussels: | November 25, 1971[7,8] |
| | | Stockholm: | Articles 22 to 38: November 25, 1971 |
| Chile............................................... | June 5, 1970 | Paris: | July 10, 1975 |
| China.............................................. | October 15, 1992 | Paris: | October 15, 1992[9] |
| Colombia ........................................ | March 7, 1988 | Paris: | March 7, 1988 |
| Comoros ......................................... | April 17, 2005 | Paris: | April 17, 2005 |
| Cook Islands................................... | August 3, 2017 | Paris: | August 3, 2017[19] |
| Congo ............................................. | May 8, 1962[4] | Paris: | December 5, 1975 |
| Costa Rica ...................................... | June 10, 1978 | Paris: | June 10, 1978 |
| Côte d'Ivoire ................................... | January 1, 1962 | Paris: | Articles 1 to 21: October 10, 1974 |
| | | Paris: | Articles 22 to 38: May 4, 1974 |
| Croatia ........................................... | October 8, 1991 | Paris: | October 8, 1991 |
| Cuba................................................ | February 20, 1997 | Paris: | February 20, 1997[2, 3] |
| Cyprus............................................. | February 24, 1964[4] | Paris: | July 27, 1983[5] |
| Czech Republic................................ | January 1, 1993 | Paris: | January 1, 1993 |
| Democratic People's Republic of Korea.... | April 28, 2003 | Paris: | April 28, 2003[2] |
| Democratic Republic of the Congo .......... | October 8, 1963[4] | Paris: | January 31, 1975 |
| Denmark.......................................... | July 1, 1903 | Paris: | June 30, 1979 |
| Djibouti .......................................... | May 13, 2002 | Paris: | May 13, 2002 |
| Dominica......................................... | August 7, 1999 | Paris: | August 7, 1999 |
| Dominican Republic.......................... | December 24, 1997 | Paris: | December 24, 1997 |
| Ecuador........................................... | October 9, 1991 | Paris: | October 9, 1991 |
| Egypt............................................... | June 7, 1977 | Paris: | June 7, 1977[2] |
| El Salvador ..................................... | February 19, 1994 | Paris: | February 19, 1994 |
| Equatorial Guinea ........................... | June 26, 1997 | Paris: | June 26, 1997 |
| Estonia............................................ | October 26, 1994[10] | Paris: | October 26, 1994 |
| Eswatini.......................................... | December 14, 1998 | Paris: | December 14, 1998 |
| Fiji.................................................. | December 1, 1971[4] | Brussels: | December 1, 1971 |
| | | Stockholm: | Articles 22 to 38: March 15, 1972 |
| Finland............................................ | April 1, 1928 | Paris: | November 1, 1986 |
| France ............................................ | December 5, 1887 | Paris: | Articles 1 to 21: October 10, 1974 |
| | | Paris: | Articles 22 to 38: December 15, 1972 |
| Gabon.............................................. | March 26, 1962 | Paris: | June 10, 1975 |
| Gambia............................................ | March 7, 1993 | Paris: | March 7, 1993 |
| Georgia............................................ | May 16, 1995 | Paris: | May 16, 1995 |
| Germany ......................................... | December 5, 1887 | Paris: | Articles 1 to 21: October 10, 1974[11] |
| | | Paris: | Articles 22 to 38: January 22, 1974 |
| Ghana ............................................. | October 11, 1991 | Paris: | October 11, 1991 |
| Greece ............................................ | November 9, 1920 | Paris: | March 8, 1976 |
| Grenada .......................................... | September 22, 1998 | Paris: | September 22, 1998 |
| Guatemala ...................................... | July 28, 1997 | Paris: | July 28, 1997[2] |
| Guinea............................................. | November 20, 1980 | Paris: | November 20, 1980 |
| Guinea-Bissau................................. | July 22, 1991 | Paris: | July 22, 1991 |
| Guyana............................................ | October 25, 1994 | Paris: | October 25, 1994 |
| Haiti................................................ | January 11, 1996 | Paris: | January 11, 1996 |
| Holy See .......................................... | September 12, 1935 | Paris: | April 24, 1975 |
| Honduras ........................................ | January 25, 1990 | Paris: | January 25, 1990 |
| Hungary.......................................... | February 14, 1922 | Paris: | Articles 1 to 21: October 10, 1974 |
| | | Paris: | Articles 22 to 38: December 15, 1972 |
| Iceland ........................................... | September 7, 1947 | Paris: | Article 1 to 21: August 25, 1999 |
| | | Paris: | Articles 22 to 38: December 28, 1984 |

| State | Date on which State became party to the Convention | Latest Act[1] of the Convention to which State is party and date on which State became party to that Act | |
|---|---|---|---|
| India.......................................... | April 1, 1928 | Paris: | Articles 1 to 21: May 6, 1984[3, 12, 13] |
| | | Paris: | Articles 22 to 38: January 10, 1975[2] |
| Indonesia.................................... | September 5, 1997 | Paris: | September 5, 1997[2] |
| Ireland ...................................... | October 5, 1927 | Paris: | March 2, 2005 |
| Israel......................................... | March 24, 1950 | Paris: | January 1, 2004[2] |
| Italy........................................... | December 5, 1887 | Paris: | November 14, 1979 |
| Jamaica...................................... | January 1, 1994 | Paris: | January 1, 1994 |
| Japan ........................................ | July 15, 1899 | Paris: | April 24, 1975 |
| Jordan ....................................... | July 28, 1999 | Paris: | July 28, 1999[2, 3] |
| Kazakhstan................................. | April 12, 1999 | Paris: | April 12, 1999 |
| Kenya......................................... | June 11, 1993 | Paris: | June 11, 1993 |
| Kiribati...................................... | January 2, 2018 | Paris: | January 2, 2018 |
| Kuwait ....................................... | December 2, 2014 | Paris: | December 2, 2014[3] |
| Kyrgyzstan.................................. | July 8, 1999 | Paris: | July 8, 1999 |
| Lao People's Democratic Republic .......... | March 14, 2012 | Paris: | March 14, 2012 |
| Latvia......................................... | August 11, 1995[14] | Paris: | August 11, 1995 |
| Lebanon ..................................... | September 30, 1947 | Rome: | September 30, 1947 |
| Lesotho....................................... | September 28, 1989 | Paris: | September 28, 1989[2] |
| Liberia........................................ | March 8, 1989 | Paris: | March 8, 1989[2] |
| Libya .......................................... | September 28, 1976 | Paris: | September 28, 1976[2] |
| Liechtenstein .............................. | July 30, 1931 | Paris: | September 23, 1999 |
| Lithuania ................................... | December 14, 1994 | Paris: | December 14, 1994[2] |
| Luxembourg................................. | June 20, 1888 | Paris: | April 20, 1975 |
| Madagascar................................. | January 1, 1966 | Brussels: | January 1, 1966 |
| Malawi ....................................... | October 12, 1991 | Paris: | October 12, 1991 |
| Malaysia..................................... | October 1, 1990 | Paris: | October 1, 1990 |
| Mali........................................... | March 19, 1962[4] | Paris: | December 5, 1977 |
| Malta.......................................... | September 21, 1964 | Rome: | September 21, 1964 |
| | | Paris: | Articles 22 to 38: December 12, 1977[2] |
| Mauritania.................................. | February 6, 1973 | Paris: | September 21, 1976 |
| Mauritius.................................... | May 10, 1989 | Paris: | May 10, 1989[2] |
| Mexico........................................ | June 11, 1967 | Paris: | December 17, 1974 |
| Micronesia (Federated States of)............ | October 7, 2003 | Paris: | October 7, 2003 |
| Monaco....................................... | May 30, 1889 | Paris: | November 23, 1974 |
| Mongolia .................................... | March 12, 1998 | Paris: | March 12, 1998[2] |
| Montenegro ................................. | June 3, 2006 | Paris: | June 3, 2006 |
| Morocco ..................................... | June 16, 1917 | Paris: | May 17, 1987 |
| Mozambique................................. | November 22, 2013 | Paris: | November 22, 2013 |
| Namibia ..................................... | March 21, 1990 | Paris: | December 24, 1993 |
| Nauru ........................................ | May 11, 2020 | Paris: | May 11, 2020 |
| Nepal.......................................... | January 11, 2006 | Paris: | January 11, 2006[2] |
| Netherlands ................................ | November 1, 1912 | Paris: | Articles 1 to 21: January 30, 1986[15] |
| | | Paris: | Articles 22 to 38: January 10, 1975[16] |
| New Zealand ................................ | April 24, 1928 | Paris: | March 17, 2019[17] |
| Nicaragua.................................... | August 23, 2000 | Paris: | August 23, 2000 |
| Niger ......................................... | May 2, 1962[4] | Paris: | May 21, 1975 |
| Nigeria....................................... | September 14, 1993 | Paris: | September 14, 1993 |
| Niue........................................... | September 24, 2016 | Paris: | September 24, 2016 |
| North Macedonia .......................... | September 8, 1991 | Paris: | September 8, 1991 |
| Norway....................................... | April 13, 1896 | Paris: | Articles 1 to 21: October 11, 1995[11] |
| | | Paris: | Articles 22 to 38: June 13, 1974 |
| Oman ......................................... | July 14, 1999 | Paris: | July 14, 1999[2] |

| State | Date on which State became party to the Convention | Latest Act[1] of the Convention to which State is party and date on which State became party to that Act | |
|---|---|---|---|
| Pakistan.................................................. | July 5, 1948 | Rome: | July 5, 1948[7] |
| | | Stockholm: | Articles 22 to 38: January 29 or February 26, 1970 |
| Panama.................................................. | June 8, 1996 | Paris: | June 8, 1996 |
| Paraguay............................................... | January 2, 1992 | Paris: | January 2, 1992 |
| Peru....................................................... | August 20, 1988 | Paris: | August 20, 1988 |
| Philippines........................................... | August 1, 1951 | Paris: | Articles 1 to 21: June 18, 1997 |
| | | Paris: | Articles 22 to 38: July 16, 1980 |
| Poland................................................... | January 28, 1920 | Paris: | Articles 1 to 21: October 22, 1994 |
| | | Paris: | Articles 22 to 38: August 4, 1990 |
| Portugal................................................ | March 29, 1911 | Paris: | January 12, 1979[18] |
| Qatar..................................................... | July 5, 2000 | Paris: | July 5, 2000 |
| Republic of Korea................................ | August 21, 1996 | Paris: | August 21, 1996 |
| Republic of Moldova............................ | November 2, 1995 | Paris: | November 2, 1995 |
| Romania................................................ | January 1, 1927 | Paris: | September 9, 1998 |
| Russian Federation.............................. | March 13, 1995 | Paris: | March 13, 1995 |
| Rwanda.................................................. | March 1, 1984 | Paris: | March 1, 1984 |
| Saint Kitts and Nevis .......................... | April 9, 1995 | Paris: | April 9, 1995 |
| Saint Lucia........................................... | August 24, 1993 | Paris: | August 24, 1993[2] |
| Saint Vincent and the Grenadines ......... | August 29, 1995 | Paris: | August 29, 1995 |
| Samoa ................................................... | July 21, 2006 | Paris: | July 21, 2006 |
| San Marino ........................................... | September 2, 2020 | Paris: | September 2, 2020 |
| Sao Tome and Principe ......................... | June 14, 2016 | Paris: | June 14, 2016 |
| Saudi Arabia........................................ | March 11, 2004 | Paris: | March 11, 2004 |
| Senegal.................................................. | August 25, 1962 | Paris: | August 12, 1975 |
| Serbia[19] | April 27, 1992 | Paris: | April 27, 1992[5] |
| Singapore ............................................. | December 21, 1998 | Paris: | December 21, 1998 |
| Slovakia ................................................ | January 1, 1993 | Paris: | January 1, 1993 |
| Slovenia................................................ | June 25, 1991 | Paris: | June 25, 1991[5] |
| Solomon Islands................................... | July 4, 2019 | Paris: | July 4, 2019 |
| South Africa.......................................... | October 3, 1928 | Brussels: | August 1, 1951 |
| | | Paris: | Articles 22 to 38: March 24, 1975[2] |
| Spain..................................................... | December 5, 1887 | Paris: | Articles 1 to 21: October 10, 1974 |
| | | Paris: | Articles 22 to 38: February 19, 1974 |
| Sri Lanka .............................................. | July 20, 1959[4] | Paris: | Articles 1 to 21: December 27, 2005 |
| | | Paris: | Articles 22 to 38: September 23, 1978 |
| Sudan..................................................... | December 28, 2000 | Paris: | December 28, 2000 |
| Suriname ............................................... | February 23, 1977 | Paris: | February 23, 1977 |
| Sweden.................................................. | August 1, 1904 | Paris: | Articles 1 to 21: October 10, 1974 |
| | | Paris: | Articles 22 to 38: September 20, 1973 |
| Switzerland........................................... | December 5, 1887 | Paris: | September 25, 1993 |
| Syrian Arab Republic........................... | June 11, 2004 | Paris: | June 11, 2004 |
| Tajikistan.............................................. | March 9, 2000 | Paris: | March 9, 2000 |
| Thailand................................................ | July 17, 1931 | Paris: | Articles 1 to 21: September 2, 1995[20] |
| | | Paris: | Articles 22 to 38: December 29, 1980[2] |
| Togo....................................................... | April 30, 1975 | Paris: | April 30, 1975 |
| Tonga ..................................................... | June 14, 2001 | Paris: | June 14, 2001 |
| Trinidad and Tobago............................ | August 16, 1988 | Paris: | August 16, 1988 |
| Tunisia................................................... | December 5, 1887 | Paris: | August 16, 1975[2] |
| Turkey................................................... | January 1, 1952 | Paris: | January 1, 1996[2] |
| Turkmenistan ....................................... | May 29, 2016 | Paris: | May 29, 2016[2] |
| Tuvalu.................................................... | June 2, 2017 | Paris: | June 2, 2017 |
| Ukraine.................................................. | October 25, 1995 | Paris: | October 25, 1995 |

| State | Date on which State became party to the Convention | Latest Act[1] of the Convention to which State is party and date on which State became party to that Act | |
|---|---|---|---|
| United Arab Emirates ............................. | July 14, 2004 | Paris: | July 14, 2004[3] |
| United Kingdom........................................ | December 5, 1887 | Paris: | January 2, 1990[11, 21, 22] |
| United Republic of Tanzania ................... | July 25, 1994 | Paris: | July 25, 1994[2] |
| United States of America......................... | March 1, 1989 | Paris: | March 1, 1989 |
| Uruguay.................................................... | July 10, 1967 | Paris: | December 28, 1979 |
| Uzbekistan............................................... | April 19, 2005 | Paris: | April 19, 2005 |
| Vanuatu.................................................... | December 27, 2012 | Paris: | December 27, 2012 |
| Venezuela (Bolivarian Republic of).......... | December 30, 1982 | Paris: | December 30, 1982[2] |
| Viet Nam.................................................. | October 26, 2004 | Paris: | October 26, 2004[2, 3] |
| Yemen ...................................................... | July 14, 2008 | Paris: | July 14, 2008[3] |
| Zambia ..................................................... | January 2, 1992 | Paris: | January 2, 1992 |
| Zimbabwe.................................................. | April 18, 1980 | Rome: | April 18, 1980 |
| | | Paris: | Articles 22 to 38: December 30, 1981 |

(Total: 179 States)

---

[1]    "Paris" means the Berne Convention for the Protection of Literary and Artistic Works as revised at Paris on July 24, 1971 (Paris Act); "Stockholm" means the said Convention as revised at Stockholm on July 14, 1967 (Stockholm Act); "Brussels" means the said Convention as revised at Brussels on June 26, 1948 (Brussels Act); "Rome" means the said Convention as revised at Rome on June 2, 1928 (Rome Act); "Berlin" means the said Convention as revised at Berlin on November 13, 1908 (Berlin Act).

[2]    With the declaration provided for in Article 33(2) relating to the International Court of Justice.

[3]    Pursuant to Article I of the Appendix of the Paris Act, this State availed itself of the faculties provided for in Articles II and III of the Appendix. The relevant declaration is effective until October 10, 2024.

[4]    Date on which the declaration of continued adherence was sent, after the accession of the State to independence.

[5]    Subject to the reservation concerning the right of translation.

[6]    Burkina Faso, which had acceded to the Berne Convention (Brussels Act) as from August 19, 1963, denounced the said Convention as from September 20, 1970. Later on, Burkina Faso acceded again to the Berne Convention (Paris Act); this accession took effect on January 24, 1976.

[7]    This State deposited its instrument of ratification of (or of accession to) the Stockholm Act in its entirety; however, Articles 1 to 21 (substantive clauses) of the said Act have not entered into force.

[8]    In accordance with the provision of Article 29 of the Stockholm Act applicable to the States outside the Union which accede to the said Act, this State is bound by Articles 1 to 20 of the Brussels Act.

[9]    The Paris Act applies also to Hong Kong, China with effect from July 1, 1997, and to Macao, China with effect from December 20, 1999.

[10]    Estonia acceded to the Berne Convention (Berlin Act, 1908) with effect from June 9, 1927. It lost its independence on August 6, 1940, and regained it on August 20, 1991.

[11]    This State has declared that it admits the application of the Appendix of the Paris Act to works of which it is the State of origin by States which have made a declaration under Article VI(1)(i) of the Appendix or a notification under Article I of the Appendix. The declarations took effect on October 18, 1973, for Germany, on March 8, 1974, for Norway and on September 27, 1971, for the United Kingdom.

[12]    This State declared that its ratification shall not apply to the provisions of Article 14bis(2)(b) of the Paris Act (presumption of legitimation for some authors who have brought contributions to the making of the cinematographic work).

[13]    This State notified the designation of the competent authority provided by Article 15(4) of the Paris Act.

[14]    Latvia acceded to the Berne Convention (Rome Act, 1928) with effect from May 15, 1937. It lost its independence on July 21, 1940, and regained it on August 21, 1991.

[15]    Ratification for the Kingdom in Europe.

[16]    Ratification for the Kingdom in Europe. Articles 22 to 38 of the Paris Act apply also to the Netherlands Antilles and Aruba. The Netherlands Antilles ceased to exist on October 10, 2010. As from that date, Articles 22 to 38 continue to apply to Curaçao and Sint Maarten. Articles 22 to 38 also continue to apply to the islands of Bonaire, Sint Eustatius and Saba which, with effect from October 10, 2010, have become part of the territory of the Kingdom of the Netherlands in Europe.

[17]    The accession by New Zealand to the Paris Act shall extend to Tokelau.

[18]    Pursuant to the provisions of Article 14*bis*(2)(c) of the Paris Act, this State has made a declaration to the effect that the undertaking by authors to bring contributions to the making of a cinematographic work must be in a written agreement. This declaration was received on November 5, 1986.

[19]    Serbia is the continuing State from Serbia and Montenegro as from June 3, 2006.

[20]    Pursuant to Article I of the Appendix of the Paris Act, this State availed itself of the faculty provided for in Article II of the said Appendix. The relevant declaration is effective until October 10, 2024.

[21]    The United Kingdom extended the application of the Paris Act to the Isle of Man with effect from March 18, 1996, to the territory of the Bailiwick of Jersey with effect from January 31, 2014, and to the territory of the Bailiwick of Guernsey with effect from November 21, 2014.

[22]    The United Kingdom extended the application of the Convention to the territory of Gibraltar with effect from January 1, 2021

# 13. UNIVERSAL COPYRIGHT CONVENTION

Paris Text, 1971

The Contracting States,

Moved by the desire to ensure in all countries copyright protection of literary, scientific and artistic works,

Convinced that a system of copyright protection appropriate to all nations of the world and expressed in a universal convention, additional to, and without impairing international systems already in force, will ensure respect for the rights of the individual and encourage the development of literature, the sciences and the arts,

Persuaded that such a universal copyright system will facilitate a wider dissemination of works of the human mind and increase international understanding,

Have resolved to revise the Universal Copyright Convention as signed at Geneva on 6 September 1952 (hereinafter called "the 1952 Convention"), and consequently,

Have agreed as follows:

## Article I

Each Contracting State undertakes to provide for the adequate and effective protection of the rights of authors and other copyright proprietors in literary, scientific and artistic works, including writings, musical, dramatic and cinematographic works, and paintings, engravings and sculpture.

## Article II

1.    Published works of nationals of any Contracting State and works first published in that State shall enjoy in each other Contracting State the same protection as that other State accords to works of its nationals first published in its own territory, as well as the protection specially granted by this Convention.

2.    Unpublished works of nationals of each Contracting State shall enjoy in each other Contracting State the same protection as that other State accords to unpublished works of its own nationals, as well as the protection specially granted by this Convention.

3.    For the purpose of this Convention any Contracting State may, by domestic legislation, assimilate to its own nationals any person domiciled in that State.

## Article III

1.    Any Contracting State which, under its domestic law, requires as a condition of copyright, compliance with formalities such as deposit, registration, notice, notarial certificates, payment of fees or manufacture or publication in that Contracting State, shall regard these requirements as satisfied with respect to all works protected in accordance with this Convention and first published outside its territory and the author of which is not one of its nationals, if from the time of the first publication all the copies of the work published with the authority of the author or other copyright proprietor bear the symbol © accompanied by the name of the copyright proprietor and the year of first publication placed in such manner and location as to give reasonable notice of claim of copyright.

2.    The provisions of paragraph 1 shall not preclude any Contracting State from requiring formalities or other conditions for the acquisition and enjoyment of copyright in respect of works first published in its territory or works of its nationals wherever published.

3.    The provisions of paragraph 1 shall not preclude any Contracting State from providing that a person seeking judicial relief must, in bringing the action, comply with procedural requirements,

such as that the complainant must appear through domestic counsel or that the complainant must deposit with the court or an administrative office, or both, a copy of the work involved in the litigation; provided that failure to comply with such requirements shall not affect the validity of the copyright, nor shall any such requirement be imposed upon a national of another Contracting State if such requirement is not imposed on nationals of the State in which protection is claimed.

4.     In each Contracting State there shall be legal means of protecting without formalities the unpublished works of nationals of other Contracting States.

5.     If a Contracting State grants protection for more than one term of copyright and the first term is for a period longer than one of the minimum periods prescribed in Article IV, such State shall not be required to comply with the provisions of paragraph 1 of this Article in respect of the second or any subsequent term of copyright.

## Article IV

1.     The duration of protection of a work shall be governed, in accordance with the provisions of Article II and this Article, by the law of the Contracting State in which protection is claimed.

2.     (a)    The term of protection for works protected under this Convention shall not be less than the life of the author and twenty-five years after his death. However, any Contracting State which, on the effective date of this Convention in that State, has limited this term for certain classes of works to a period computed from the first publication of the work, shall be entitled to maintain these exceptions and to extend them to other classes of works. For all these classes the term of protection shall not be less than twenty-five years from the date of first publication.

(b)    Any Contracting State which, upon the effective date of this Convention in that State, does not compute the term of protection upon the basis of the life of the author, shall be entitled to compute the term of protection from the date of the first publication of the work or from its registration prior to publication, as the case may be, provided the term of protection shall not be less than twenty-five years from the date of first publication or from its registration prior to publication, as the case may be.

(c)    If the legislation of a Contracting State grants two or more successive terms of protection, the duration of the first term shall not be less than one of the minimum periods specified in sub-paragraphs (a) and (b).

3.     The provisions of paragraph 2 shall not apply to photographic works or to works of applied art; provided, however, that the term of protection in those Contracting States which protect photographic works, or works of applied art in so far as they are protected as artistic works, shall not be less than ten years for each of said classes of works.

4.     (a) No Contracting State shall be obliged to grant protection to a work for a period longer than that fixed for the class of works to which the work in question belongs, in the case of unpublished works by the law of the Contracting State of which the author is a national, and in the case of published works by the law of the Contracting State in which the work has been first published.

(b)    For the purposes of the application of sub-paragraph (a), if the law of any Contracting State grants two or more successive terms of protection, the period of protection of that State shall be considered to be the aggregate of those terms. However, if a specified work is not protected by such State during the second or any subsequent term for any reason, the other Contracting States shall not be obliged to protect it during the second or any subsequent term.

5.     For the purposes of the application of paragraph 4, the work of a national of a Contracting State, first published in a non-Contracting State, shall be treated as though first published in the Contracting State of which the author is a national.

6.    For the purposes of the application of paragraph 4, in case of simultaneous publication in two or more Contracting States, the work shall be treated as though first published in the State which affords the shortest term; any work published in two or more Contracting States within thirty days of its first publication shall be considered as having been published simultaneously in said Contracting States.

## Article IV*bis*

1.    The rights referred to in Article I shall include the basic rights ensuring the author's economic interests, including the exclusive right to authorize reproduction by any means, public performance and broadcasting. The provisions of this Article shall extend to works protected under this Convention either in their original form or in any form recognizably derived from the original.

2.    However, any Contracting State may, by its domestic legislation, make exceptions that do not conflict with the spirit and provisions of this Convention, to the rights mentioned in paragraph 1 of this Article. Any State whose legislation so provides, shall nevertheless accord a reasonable degree of effective protection to each of the rights to which exception has been made.

## Article V

1.    The rights referred to in Article I shall include the exclusive right of the author to make, publish and authorize the making and publication of translations of works protected under this Convention.

2.    However, any Contracting State may, by its domestic legislation, restrict the right of translation of writings, but only subject to the following provisions:

(a)    If, after the expiration of a period of seven years from the date of the first publication of a writing, a translation of such writing has not been published in a language in general use in the Contracting State, by the owner of the right of translation or with his authorization, any national of such Contracting State may obtain a non-exclusive licence from the competent authority thereof to translate the work into that language and publish the work so translated.

(b)    Such national shall in accordance with the procedure of the State concerned, establish either that he has requested, and been denied, authorization by the proprietor of the right to make and publish the translation, or that, after due diligence on his part, he was unable to find the owner of the right. A licence may also be granted on the same conditions if all previous editions of a translation in a language in general use in the Contracting State are out of print.

(c)    If the owner of the right of translation cannot be found, then the applicant for a licence shall send copies of his application to the publisher whose name appears on the work and, if the nationality of the owner of the right of translation is known, to the diplomatic or consular representative of the State of which such owner is a national, or to the organization which may have been designated by the government of that State. The licence shall not be granted before the expiration of a period of two months from the date of the dispatch of the copies of the application.

(d)    Due provision shall be made by domestic legislation to ensure to the owner of the right of translation a compensation which is just and conforms to international standards, to ensure payment and transmittal of such compensation, and to ensure a correct translation of the work.

(e)    The original title and the name of the author of the work shall be printed on all copies of the published translation. The licence shall be valid only for publication of the translation in the territory of the Contracting State where it has been applied for. Copies so published may be imported and sold in another Contracting State if a language in general use in such other State is the same language as that into which the work has been so translated, and if the domestic law in such other State makes provision for such licences and does not prohibit such importation and sale. Where the foregoing conditions do not exist, the importation and sale of such copies in a

Contracting State shall be governed by its domestic law and its agreements. The licence shall not be transferred by the licensee.

(f)    The licence shall not be granted when the author has withdrawn from circulation all copies of the work.

### Article V*bis*

1.    Any Contracting State regarded as a developing country in conformity with the established practice of the General Assembly of the United Nations may, by a notification deposited with the Director-General of the United Nations Educational, Scientific and Cultural Organization (hereinafter called "the Director-General") at the time of its ratification, acceptance or accession or thereafter, avail itself of any or all of the exceptions provided for in Articles V*ter* and V*quater*.

2.    Any such notification shall be effective for ten years from the date of coming into force of this Convention, or for such part of that ten-year period as remains at the date of deposit of the notification, and may be renewed in whole or in part for further periods of ten years each if, not more than fifteen or less than three months before the expiration of the relevant ten-year period, the Contracting State deposits a further notification with the Director-General. Initial notifications may also be made during these further periods of ten years in accordance with the provisions of this Article.

3.    Notwithstanding the provisions of paragraph 2, a Contracting State that has ceased to be regarded as a developing country as referred to in paragraph 1 shall no longer be entitled to renew its notification made under the provisions of paragraph 1 or 2, and whether or not it formally withdraws the notification such State shall be precluded from availing itself of the exceptions provided for in Articles V*ter* and V*quater* at the end of the current ten-year period, or at the end of three years after it has ceased to be regarded as a developing country, whichever period expires later.

4.    Any copies of a work already made under the exceptions provided for in Articles V*ter* and V*quater* may continue to be distributed after the expiration of the period for which notifications under this Article were effective until their stock is exhausted.

5.    Any Contracting State that has deposited a notification in accordance with Article XIII with respect to the application of this Convention to a particular country or territory, the situation of which can be regarded as analogous to that of the States referred to in paragraph 1 of this Article, may also deposit notifications and renew them in accordance with the provisions of this Article with respect to any such country or territory. During the effective period of such notifications, the provisions of Articles V*ter* and V*quater* may be applied with respect to such country or territory. The sending of copies from the country or territory to the Contracting State shall be considered as export within the meaning of Articles V*ter* and V*quater*.

### Article V*ter*

1.    (a)   Any Contracting State to which Article V*bis*(1) applies may substitute for the period of seven years provided for in Article V(2) a period of three years or any longer period prescribed by its legislation. However, in the case of a translation into a language not in general use in one or more developed countries that are party to this Convention or only the 1952 Convention, the period shall be one year instead of three.

(b)   A Contracting State to which Article *Vbis*(1) applies may, with the unanimous agreement of the developed countries party to this Convention or only the 1952 Convention and in which the same language is in general use, substitute, in the case of translation into that language, for the period of three years provided for in sub-paragraph (a) another period as determined by such agreement but not shorter than one year. However, this sub-paragraph shall not apply where the language in question is English, French or Spanish. Notification of any such agreement shall be made to the Director-General.

(c)   The licence may only be granted if the applicant, in accordance with the procedure of the State concerned, establishes either that he has requested, and been denied, authorization by the owner of the right of translation, or that, after due diligence on his part, he was unable to find the owner of the right. At the same time as he makes his request he shall inform either the International Copyright Information Centre established by the United Nations Educational, Scientific and Cultural Organization or any national or regional information centre which may have been designated in a notification to that effect deposited with the Director-General by the government of the State in which the publisher is believed to have his principal place of business.

(d)   If the owner of the right of translation cannot be found, the applicant for a licence shall send, by registered airmail, copies of his application to the publisher whose name appears on the work and to any national or regional information centre as mentioned in sub-paragraph (c). If no such centre is notified he shall also send a copy to the international copyright information centre established by the United Nations Educational, Scientific and Cultural Organization.

2.   (a)   Licences obtainable after three years shall not be granted under this Article until a further period of six months has elapsed and licences obtainable after one year until a further period of nine months has elapsed. The further period shall begin either from the date of the request for permission to translate mentioned in paragraph 1(c) or, if the identity or address of the owner of the right of translation is not known, from the date of dispatch of the copies of the application for a licence mentioned in paragraph 1(d).

(b)   Licences shall not be granted if a translation has been published by the owner of the right of translation or with his authorization during the said period of six or nine months.

3.   Any licence under this Article shall be granted only for the purpose of teaching, scholarship or research.

4.   (a)   Any licence granted under this Article shall not extend to the export of copies and shall be valid only for publication in the territory of the Contracting State where it has been applied for.

(b)   Any copy published in accordance with a licence granted under this Article shall bear a notice in the appropriate language stating that the copy is available for distribution only in the Contracting State granting the licence. If the writing bears the notice specified in Article III(1) the copies shall bear the same notice.

(c)   The prohibition of export provided for in sub-paragraph (a) shall not apply where a governmental or other public entity of a State which has granted a licence under this Article to translate a work into a language other than English, French or Spanish sends copies of a translation prepared under such licence to another country if:

(i)   the recipients are individuals who are nationals of the Contracting State granting the licence, or organizations grouping such individuals;

(ii)   the copies are to be used only for the purpose of teaching, scholarship or research;

(iii)   the sending of the copies and their subsequent distribution to recipients is without the object of commercial purpose; and

(iv)   the country to which the copies have been sent has agreed with the Contracting State to allow the receipt, distribution or both and the Director-General has been notified of such agreement by any one of the governments which have concluded it.

5.   Due provision shall be made at the national level to ensure:

(a)   that the licence provides for just compensation that is consistent with standards of royalties normally operating in the case of licences freely negotiated between persons in the two countries concerned; and

(b) payment and transmittal of the compensation; however, should national currency regulations intervene, the competent authority shall make all efforts, by the use of international machinery, to ensure transmittal in internationally convertible currency or its equivalent.

6. Any licence granted by a Contracting State under this Article shall terminate if a translation of the work in the same language with substantially the same content as the edition in respect of which the licence was granted is published in the said State by the owner of the right of translation or with his authorization, at a price reasonably related to that normally charged in the same State for comparable works. Any copies already made before the licence is terminated may continue to be distributed until their stock is exhausted.

7. For works which are composed mainly of illustrations a licence to translate the text and to reproduce the illustrations may be granted only if the conditions of Article V*quater* are also fulfilled.

8. (a) A licence to translate a work protected under this Convention, published in printed or analogous forms of reproduction, may also be granted to a broadcasting organization having its headquarters in a Contracting State to which Article V*bis*(1) applies, upon an application made in that State by the said organization under the following conditions:

   (i) the translation is made from a copy made and acquired in accordance with the laws of the Contracting State;

   (ii) the translation is for use only in broadcasts intended exclusively for teaching or for the dissemination of the results of specialized technical or scientific research to experts in a particular profession;

   (iii) the translation is used exclusively for the purposes set out in condition (ii), through broadcasts lawfully made which are intended for recipients on the territory of the Contracting State, including broadcasts made through the medium of sound or visual recordings lawfully and exclusively made for the purpose of such broadcasts;

   (iv) sound or visual recordings of the translation may be exchanged only between broadcasting organizations having their headquarters in the Contracting State granting the licence; and

   (v) all uses made of the translation are without any commercial purpose.

   (b) Provided all of the criteria and conditions set out in sub-paragraph (a) are met, a licence may also be granted to a broadcasting organization to translate any text incorporated in an audio-visual fixation which was itself prepared and published for the sole purpose of being used in connexion with systematic instructional activities.

   (c) Subject to sub-paragraphs (a) and (b), the other provisions of this Article shall apply to the grant and exercise of the licence.

9. Subject to the provisions of this Article, any licence granted under this Article shall be governed by the provisions of Article V, and shall continue to be governed by the provisions of Article V and of this Article, even after the seven-year period provided for in Article V(2) has expired. However, after the said period has expired, the licensee shall be free to request that the said licence be replaced by a new licence governed exclusively by the provisions of Article V.

### Article V*quater*

1. Any Contracting State to which Article V*bis*(1) applies may adopt the following provisions:

(a) If, after the expiration of (i) the relevant period specified in sub-paragraph (c) commencing from the date of first publication of a particular edition of a literary, scientific or artistic work referred to in paragraph 3, or (ii) any longer period determined by national legislation of the State, copies of such edition have not been distributed in that State to the general public or in connexion with systematic instructional activities at a price reasonably related to that normally charged in the State for comparable works, by the owner of the right of reproduction or with his authorization, any national of such State may obtain a non-exclusive licence from the competent authority to publish such edition at that or a lower price for use in connexion with systematic instructional activities. The licence may only be granted if such national, in accordance with the procedure of the State concerned, establishes either that he has requested, and been denied, authorization by the proprietor of the right to publish such work, or that, after due diligence on his part, he was unable to find the owner of the right. At the same time as he makes his request he shall inform either the international copyright information centre established by the United Nations Educational, Scientific and Cultural Organization or any national or regional information centre referred to in sub-paragraph (d).

(b)   A licence may also be granted on the same conditions if, for a period of six months, no authorized copies of the edition in question have been on sale in the State concerned to the general public or in connexion with systematic instructional activities at a price reasonably related to that normally charged in the State for comparable works.

(c)   The period referred to in subparagraph (a) shall be five years except that:

   (i)   for works of the natural and physical sciences, including mathematics, and of technology, the period shall be three years;

   (ii)   for works of fiction, poetry, drama and music, and for art books, the period shall be seven years.

(d)   If the owner of the right of reproduction cannot be found, the applicant for a licence shall send, by registered air mail, copies of his application to the publisher whose name appears on the work and to any national or regional information centre identified as such in a notification deposited with the Director-General by the State in which the publisher is believed to have his principal place of business. In the absence of any such notification, he shall also send a copy to the international copyright information centre established by the United Nations Educational, Scientific and Cultural Organization. The licence shall not be granted before the expiration of a period of three months from the date of dispatch of the copies of the application.

(e)   Licences obtainable after three years shall not be granted under this Article:

   (i)   until a period of six months has elapsed from the date of the request for permission referred to in sub-paragraph (a) or, if the identity or address of the owner of the right of reproduction is unknown, from the date of the dispatch of the copies of the application for a licence referred to in sub-paragraph (d);

   (ii)   if any such distribution of copies of the edition as is mentioned in sub-paragraph (a) has taken place during that period.

(f)   The name of the author and the title of the particular edition of the work shall be printed on all copies of the published reproduction. The licence shall not extend to the export of copies and shall be valid only for publication in the territory of the Contracting State where it has been applied for. The licence shall not be transferable by the licensee.

(g)   Due provision shall be made by domestic legislation to ensure an accurate reproduction of the particular edition in question.

(h)   A licence to reproduce and publish a translation of a work shall not be granted under this Article in the following cases:

   (i)   where the translation was not published by the owner of the right of translation or with his authorization;

   (ii)   where the translation is not in a language in general use in the State with power to grant the licence.

2.    The exceptions provided for in paragraph 1 are subject to the following additional provisions:

(a)    Any copy published in accordance with a licence granted under this Article shall bear a notice in the appropriate language stating that the copy is available for distribution only in the Contracting State to which the said licence applies. If the edition bears the notice specified in Article III(1), the copies shall bear the same notice.

(b)    Due provision shall be made at the national level to ensure:

(i)    that the licence provides for just compensation that is consistent with standards of royalties normally operating in the case of licences freely negotiated between persons in the two countries concerned; and

(ii)    payment and transmittal of the compensation; however, should national currency regulations intervene, the competent authority shall make all efforts, by the use of international machinery, to ensure transmittal in internationally convertible currency or its equivalent.

(c)    Whenever copies of an edition of a work are distributed in the Contracting State to the general public or in connexion with systematic instructional activities, by the owner of the right of reproduction or with his authorization, at a price reasonably related to that normally charged in the State for comparable works, any licence granted under this Article shall terminate if such edition is in the same language and is substantially the same in content as the edition published under the licence. Any copies already made before the licence is terminated may continue to be distributed until their stock is exhausted.

(d)    No licence shall be granted when the author has withdrawn from circulation all copies of the edition in question.

3.    (a)    Subject to sub-paragraph (b), the literary, scientific or artistic works to which this Article applies shall be limited to works published in printed or analogous forms of reproduction.

(b)    The provisions of this Article shall also apply to reproduction in audio-visual form of lawfully made audio-visual fixations including any protected works incorporated therein and to the translation of any incorporated text into a language in general use in the State with power to grant the licence; always provided that the audio-visual fixations in question were prepared and published for the sole purpose of being used in connexion with systematic instructional activities.

## Article VI

"Publication," as used in this Convention, means the reproduction in tangible form and the general distribution to the public of copies of a work from which it can be read or otherwise visually perceived.

## Article VII

This Convention shall not apply to works or rights in works which, at the effective date of this Convention in a Contracting State where protection is claimed, are permanently in the public domain in the said Contracting State.

## Article VIII

1.    This Convention, which shall bear the date of 24 July 1971, shall be deposited with the Director-General and shall remain open for signature by all States party to the 1952 Convention for a period of 120 days after the date of this Convention. It shall be subject to ratification or acceptance by the signatory States.

2.    Any State which has not signed this Convention may accede thereto.

3.    Ratification, acceptance or accession shall be effected by the deposit of an instrument to that effect with the Director-General.

## Article IX

1.    This Convention shall come into force three months after the deposit of twelve instruments of ratification, acceptance or accession.

2.    Subsequently, this Convention shall come into force in respect of each State three months after that State has deposited its instrument of ratification, acceptance or accession.

3.    Accession to this Convention by a State not party to the 1952 Convention shall also constitute accession to that Convention; however, if its instrument of accession is deposited before this Convention comes into force, such State may make its accession to the 1952 Convention conditional upon the coming into force of this Convention. After the coming into force of this Convention, no State may accede solely to the 1952 Convention.

4.    Relations between States party to this Convention and States that are party only to the 1952 Convention, shall be governed by the 1952 Convention. However, any State party only to the 1952 Convention may, by a notification deposited with the Director-General, declare that it will admit the application of the 1971 Convention to works of its nationals or works first published in its territory by all States party to this Convention.

## Article X

1.    Each Contracting State undertakes to adopt, in accordance with its Constitution, such measures as are necessary to ensure the application of this Convention.

2.    It is understood that at the date this Convention comes into force in respect of any State, that State must be in a position under its domestic law to give effect to the terms of this Convention.

## Article XI

1.    An Intergovernmental Committee is hereby established with the following duties:

(a)   to study the problems concerning the application and operation of the Universal Copyright Convention;

(b)   to make preparation for periodic revisions of this Convention;

(c)   to study any other problems concerning the international protection of copyright, in co-operation with the various interested international organizations, such as the United Nations Educational, Scientific and Cultural Organization, the International Union for the Protection of Literary and Artistic Works and the Organization of American States;

(d)   to inform States party to the Universal Copyright Convention as to its activities.

2.    The Committee shall consist of the representatives of eighteen States party to this Convention or only to the 1952 Convention.

3.    The Committee shall be selected with due consideration to a fair balance of national interests on the basis of geographical location, population, languages and stage of development.

4.    The Director-General of the United Nations Educational, Scientific and Cultural Organization, the Director-General of the World Intellectual Property Organization and the Secretary-General of the Organization of American States, or their representatives, may attend meetings of the Committee in an advisory capacity.

## Article XII

The Intergovernmental Committee shall convene a conference for revision whenever it deems necessary, or at the request of at least ten States party to this Convention.

## Article XIII

1.    Any Contracting State may, at the time of deposit of its instrument of ratification, acceptance or accession, or at any time thereafter, declare by notification addressed to the Director-General that this Convention shall apply to all or any of the countries or territories for the international relations of which it is responsible and this Convention shall thereupon apply to the countries or territories named in such notification after the expiration of the term of three months provided for in Article IX. In the absence of such notification, this Convention shall not apply to any such country or territory.

2.    However, nothing in this Article shall be understood as implying the recognition or tacit acceptance by a Contracting State of the factual situation concerning a country or territory to which this Convention is made applicable by another Contracting State in accordance with the provisions of this Article.

## Article XIV

1.    Any Contracting State may denounce this Convention in its own name or on behalf of all or any of the countries or territories with respect to which a notification has been given under Article XIII. The denunciation shall be made by notification addressed to the Director-General. Such denunciation shall also constitute denunciation of the 1952 Convention.

2.    Such denunciation shall operate only in respect of the State or of the country or territory on whose behalf it was made and shall not take effect until twelve months after the date of receipt of the notification.

## Article XV

A dispute between two or more Contracting States concerning the interpretation or application of this Convention, not settled by negotiation, shall, unless the States concerned agree on some other method of settlement, be brought before the International Court of Justice for determination by it.

## Article XVI

1.    This Convention shall be established in English, French and Spanish. The three texts shall be signed and shall be equally authoritative.

2.    Official texts of this Convention shall be established by the Director-General, after consultation with the governments concerned, in Arabic, German, Italian and Portuguese.

3.    Any Contracting State or group of Contracting States shall be entitled to have established by the Director-General other texts in the language of its choice by arrangement with the Director-General.

4.    All such texts shall be annexed to the signed texts of this Convention.

## Article XVII

1.    This Convention shall not in any way affect the provisions of the Berne Convention for the Protection of Literary and Artistic Works or membership in the Union created by that Convention.

2.    In application of the foregoing paragraph, a declaration has been annexed to the present Article. This declaration is an integral part of this Convention for the States bound by the Berne Convention on 1 January 1951, or which have or may become bound to it at a later date. The signature

of this Convention by such States shall also constitute signature of the said declaration, and ratification, acceptance or accession by such States shall include the declaration, as well as this Convention.

## Article XVIII

This Convention shall not abrogate multilateral or bilateral copyright conventions or arrangements that are or may be in effect exclusively between two or more American Republics. In the event of the difference either between the provisions of such existing conventions or arrangements and the provisions of this Convention, or between the provisions of this Convention and those of any new convention or arrangement which may be formulated between two or more American Republics after this Convention comes into force, the convention or arrangement most recently formulated shall prevail between the parties thereto. Rights in works acquired in any Contracting State under existing conventions or arrangements before the date this Convention comes into force in such State shall not be affected.

## Article XIX

This Convention shall not abrogate multilateral or bilateral conventions or arrangements in effect between two or more Contracting States. In the event of any difference between the provisions of such existing conventions or arrangements and the provisions of this Convention, the provisions of this Convention shall prevail. Rights in works acquired in any Contracting State under existing conventions or arrangements before the date on which this Convention comes into force in such State shall not be affected. Nothing in this Article shall affect the provisions of Articles XVII and XVIII.

## Article XX

Reservations to this Convention shall not be permitted.

## Article XXI

1.   The Director-General shall send duly certified copies of this Convention to the States interested and to the Secretary-General of the United Nations for registration by him.

2.   He shall also inform all interested States of the ratifications, acceptances and accessions which have been deposited, the date on which this Convention comes into force, the notifications under this Convention and denunciations under Article XIV.

## Appendix Declaration Relating to Article XVII

The States which are members of the International Union for the Protection of Literary and Artistic Works (hereinafter called "the Berne Union") and which are signatories to this Convention,

Desiring to reinforce their mutual relations on the basis of the said Union and to avoid any conflict which might result from the co-existence of the Berne Convention and the Universal Copyright Convention,

Recognizing the temporary need of some States to adjust their level of copyright protection in accordance with their stage of cultural, social and economic development,

Have, by common agreement, accepted the terms of the following declaration:

(a)   Except as provided by paragraph (b), works which, according to the Berne Convention, have as their country of origin a country which has withdrawn from the Berne Union after 1 January 1951, shall not be protected by the Universal Copyright Convention in the countries of the Berne Union;

(b)   Where a Contracting State is regarded as a developing country in conformity with the established practice of the General Assembly of the United Nations, and has deposited with the

Director-General of the United Nations Educational, Scientific and Cultural Organization, at the time of its withdrawal from the Berne Union, a notification to the effect that it regards itself as a developing country, the provisions of paragraph (a) shall not be applicable as long as such State may avail itself of the exceptions provided for by this Convention in accordance with Article V*bis;*

(c)   The Universal Copyright Convention shall not be applicable to the relationships among countries of the Berne Union in so far as it relates to the protection of works having as their country of origin, within the meaning of the Berne Convention, a country of the Berne Union.

## Resolution Concerning Article XI

The Conference for Revision of the Universal Copyright Convention,

Having considered the problems relating to the Intergovernmental Committee provided for in Article XI of this Convention, to which this resolution is annexed, Resolves that:

1.   At its inception, the Committee shall include representatives of the twelve States members of the Intergovernmental Committee established under Article XI of the 1952 Convention and the resolution annexed to it, and, in addition, representatives of the following States: Algeria, Australia, Japan, Mexico, Senegal and Yugoslavia.

2.   Any States that are not party to the 1952 Convention and have not acceded to this Convention before the first ordinary session of the Committee following the entry into force of this Convention shall be replaced by other States to be selected by the Committee at its first ordinary session in conformity with the provisions of Article XI(2) and (3).

3.   As soon as this Convention comes into force the Committee as provided for in paragraph 1 shall be deemed to be constituted in accordance with Article XI of this Convention.

4.   A session of the Committee shall take place within one year after the coming into force of this Convention; thereafter the Committee shall meet in ordinary session at intervals of not more than two years.

5.   The Committee shall elect its Chairman and two Vice-Chairmen. It shall establish its Rules of Procedure having regard to the following principles:

(a)   The normal duration of the term of office of the members represented on the Committee shall be six years with one-third retiring every two years, it being however understood that, of the original terms of office, one-third shall expire at the end of the Committee's second ordinary session which will follow the entry into force of this Convention, a further third at the end of its third ordinary session, and the remaining third at the end of its fourth ordinary session;

(b)   The rules governing the procedure whereby the Committee shall fill vacancies, the order in which terms of membership expire, eligibility for re-election, and election procedures, shall be based upon a balancing of the needs for continuity of membership and rotation of representation, as well as the considerations set out in Article XI(3).

Expresses the wish that the United Nations Educational, Scientific and Cultural Organization provide its Secretariat.

In faith whereof the undersigned, having deposited their respective full powers, have signed this Convention.

Done at Paris, this twenty-fourth day of July 1971, in a single copy.

## *Protocol 1*

### *Annexed to The Universal Copyright Convention as Revised at Paris on 24 July 1971 Concerning the Application of that Convention to Works of Stateless Persons and Refugees*

The States party hereto, being also party to the Universal Copyright Convention as revised at Paris on 24 July 1971 (hereinafter called "the 1971 Convention"),

Have accepted the following provisions:

1.    Stateless persons and refugees who have their habitual residence in a State party to this Protocol shall, for the purposes of the 1971 Convention, be assimilated to the nationals of that State.

2.    (a)   This Protocol shall be signed and shall be subject to ratification or acceptance, or may be acceded to, as if the provisions of Article VIII of the 1971 Convention applied hereto.

(b)   This Protocol shall enter into force in respect of each State, on the date of deposit of the instrument of ratification, acceptance or accession of the State concerned or on the date of entry into force of the 1971 Convention with respect to such State, whichever is the later.

(c)   On the entry into force of this Protocol in respect of a State not party to Protocol 1 annexed to the 1952 Convention, the latter Protocol shall be deemed to enter into force in respect of such State.

In faith whereof the undersigned, being duly authorized thereto, have signed this Protocol.

Done at Paris this twenty-fourth day of July 1971, in the English, French and Spanish languages, the three texts being equally authoritative, in a single copy which shall be deposited with the Director-General of the United Nations Educational, Scientific and Cultural Organization. The Director-General shall send certified copies to the signatory States, and to the Secretary-General of the United Nations for registration.

## *Protocol 2*

### *Annexed to the Universal Copyright Convention as Revised at Paris on 24 July 1971 Concerning the Application of that Convention to the Works of Certain International Organizations*

The States party hereto, being also party to the Universal Copyright Convention as revised at Paris on 24 July 1971 (hereinafter called "the 1971 Convention"),

Have accepted the following provisions:

1.    (a)   The protection provided for in Article II(1) of the 1971 Convention shall apply to works published for the first time by the United Nations, by the Specialized Agencies in relationship therewith, or by the Organization of American States.

(b)   Similarly, Article II(2) of the 1971 Convention shall apply to the said organization or agencies.

2.    (a)   This Protocol shall be signed and shall be subject to ratification or acceptance, or may be acceded to, as if the provisions of Article VIII of the 1971 Convention applied hereto.

(b)   This Protocol shall enter into force for each State on the date of deposit of the instrument of ratification, acceptance or accession of the State concerned or on the date of entry into force of the 1971 Convention with respect to such State, whichever is the later.

In faith whereof the undersigned, being duly authorized thereto, have signed this Protocol.

Done at Paris, this twenty-fourth day of July 1971, in the English, French and Spanish languages, the three texts being equally authoritative, in a single copy which shall be deposited with the Director-General of the United Nations Educational, Scientific and Cultural Organization. The Director-General shall send certified copies to the signatory States, and to the Secretary-General of the United Nations for registration.

# 14. PARTIES TO THE UNIVERSAL COPYRIGHT CONVENTION*

Revised at Paris (1971)

**Status on May 4, 2021**

| CONTRACTING PARTIES/ SIGNATORIES | INSTRUMENT | IN FORCE |
|---|---|---|
| Albania | Accession: November 4, 2003 | February 4, 2004 |
| Algeria | Accession: May 28, 1973 | August 28, 1973 |
| Andorra | Ratification: December 31, 1952 | September 16, 1955 |
| Argentina | Ratification: November 13, 1957 | February 13, 1958 |
| Australia | Ratification: February 1, 1969 | May 1, 1969 |
| Austria | Ratification: April 2, 1957 | July 2, 1957 |
| Azerbaijan | Declaration/Notification of Succession: April 7, 1997 | October 18, 1991 |
| Bahamas | Declaration/Notification of Succession: July 13, 1976 | July 13, 1976 |
| Bangladesh | Accession: May 5, 1975 | August 5, 1975 |
| Barbados | Accession: March 18, 1983 | June 18, 1983 |
| Belarus | Declaration/Notification of Succession: March 29, 1994 | July 27, 1991 |
| Belgium | Ratification: May 31, 1960 | August 31, 1960 |
| Belize | Declaration/Notification of Succession: December 1, 1982 | September 21, 1981 |
| Bolivia (Plurinational State of) | Accession: December 22, 1989 | March 22, 1990 |
| Bosnia and Herzegovina | Declaration/Notification of Succession: July 12, 1993 | March 6, 1992 |
| Brazil | Ratification: October 13, 1959 | January 13, 1960 |
| Bulgaria | Accession: March 7, 1975 | June 7, 1975 |
| Cambodia | Accession: August 3, 1953 | September 16, 1955 |
| Cameroon | Accession: February 1, 1973 | May 1, 1973 |
| Canada | Ratification: May 10, 1962 | August 10, 1962 |
| Chile | Ratification: January 18, 1955 | September 16, 1955 |
| China | Accession: July 30, 1992 | October 30, 1992 |
| Colombia | Accession: March 18, 1976 | June 18, 1976 |
| Costa Rica | Accession: December 7, 1954 | September 16, 1955 |
| Croatia | Declaration/Notification of Succession: July 6, 1992 | October 8, 1991 |

*   Document originally produced by the World Intellectual Property Organization (WIPO), the owner of the copyright. Published with the permission of the World Intellectual Property Organization.

| CONTRACTING PARTIES/ SIGNATORIES | INSTRUMENT | IN FORCE |
|---|---|---|
| Cuba | Ratification: March 18, 1957 | June 18, 1957 |
| Cyprus | Accession: September 19, 1990 | December 19, 1990 |
| Czech Republic | Declaration/Notification of Succession: March 26, 1993 | January 1, 1993 |
| Denmark | Ratification: November 9, 1961 | February 9, 1962 |
| Dominican Republic | Accession: February 8, 1983 | May 8, 1983 |
| Ecuador | Accession: March 5, 1957 | June 5, 1957 |
| El Salvador | Accession: December 29, 1978 | March 29, 1979 |
| Fiji | Declaration/Notification of Succession: December 13, 1971 | October 10, 1970 |
| Finland | Ratification: January 16, 1963 | April 16, 1963 |
| France | Ratification: October 14, 1955 | January 14, 1956 |
| Germany | Ratification: June 3, 1955 | September 16, 1955 |
| Ghana | Accession: May 22, 1962 | August 22, 1962 |
| Greece | Accession: May 24, 1963 | August 24, 1963 |
| Guatemala | Ratification: July 28, 1964 | October 28, 1964 |
| Guinea | Accession: August 13, 1981 | November 13, 1981 |
| Haiti | Ratification: September 1, 1954 | September 16, 1955 |
| Holy See | Ratification: July 5, 1955 | October 5, 1955 |
| Honduras | [Signature: September 6, 1952] | |
| Hungary | Accession: October 23, 1970 | January 23, 1971 |
| Iceland | Accession: September 18, 1956 | December 18, 1956 |
| India | Ratification: October 21, 1957 | January 21, 1958 |
| Ireland | Ratification: October 20, 1958 | January 20, 1959 |
| Israel | Ratification: April 6, 1955 | September 16, 1955 |
| Italy | Ratification: October 24, 1956 | January 24, 1957 |
| Japan | Ratification: January 28, 1956 | April 28, 1956 |
| Kazakhstan | Declaration/Notification of Succession: August 6, 1992 | December 16, 1991 |
| Kenya | Accession: June 7, 1966 | June 7, 1966 |
| Lao People's Democratic Republic | Accession: August 19, 1954 | September 16, 1955 |
| Lebanon | Accession: July 17, 1959 | October 17, 1959 |
| Liberia | Ratification: April 27, 1956 | July 27, 1956 |
| Liechtenstein | Accession: October 22, 1958 | January 22, 1959 |
| Luxembourg | Ratification: July 15, 1955 | October 15, 1955 |
| Malawi | Accession: July 26, 1965 | October 26, 1965 |
| Malta | Accession: August 19, 1968 | November 19, 1968 |

## PARTIES TO THE UNIVERSAL COPYRIGHT CONVENTION

| CONTRACTING PARTIES/ SIGNATORIES | INSTRUMENT | IN FORCE |
|---|---|---|
| Mauritius | Declaration/Notification of Succession: August 20, 1970 | March 12, 1968 |
| Mexico | Ratification: February 12, 1957 | May 12, 1957 |
| Monaco | Ratification: June 16, 1955 | September 16, 1955 |
| Montenegro | Declaration/Notification of Succession: April 26, 2007 | June 3, 2006 |
| Morocco | Accession: February 8, 1972 | May 8, 1972 |
| Netherlands | Ratification: March 22, 1967 | June 22, 1967 |
| New Zealand | Accession: June 11, 1964 | September 11, 1964 |
| Nicaragua | Ratification: May 16, 1961 | August 16, 1961 |
| Niger | Accession: February 15, 1989 | May 15, 1989 |
| Nigeria | Accession: November 14, 1961 | February 14, 1962 |
| Norway | Ratification: October 23, 1962 | January 23, 1962 |
| Pakistan | Accession: April 28, 1954 | September 16, 1955 |
| Panama | Accession: July 17, 1962 | October 17, 1962 |
| Paraguay | Accession: December 11, 1961 | March 11, 1962 |
| Peru | Ratification: July 16, 1963 | October 16, 1963 |
| Philippines | Accession: August 19, 1955 | November 19, 1955 |
| Poland | Accession: December 9, 1976 | March 9, 1977 |
| Portugal | Ratification: September 25, 1956 | December 25, 1956 |
| Republic of Korea | Accession: July 1, 1987 | October 1, 1987 |
| Republic of Moldova | Declaration/Notification of Succession: June 23, 1997 | May 27, 1973 |
| Russian Federation | Accession: February 27, 1973 | May 27, 1973 |
| Rwanda | Accession: August 10, 1989 | November 10, 1989 |
| Saint Vincent and the Grenadines | Declaration/Notification of Succession: January 22, 1985 | October 27, 1979 |
| San Marino | [Signature: September 6, 1952] | |
| Saudi Arabia | Accession: April 13, 1994 | July 13, 1994 |
| Senegal | Accession: April 9, 1974 | July 9, 1974 |
| Serbia | Declaration/Notification of Succession: September 11, 2001 | April 28, 1992 |
| Slovakia | Declaration/Notification of Succession: March 31, 1993 | January 1, 1993 |
| Slovenia | Declaration/Notification of Succession: November 5, 1992 | June 25, 1991 |
| Spain | Ratification: October 27, 1954 | September 16, 1955 |
| Sri Lanka | Accession: October 25, 1983 | January 25, 1984 |
| Sweden | Ratification: April 1, 1961 | July 1, 1961 |

## PARTIES TO THE UNIVERSAL COPYRIGHT CONVENTION

| CONTRACTING PARTIES/ SIGNATORIES | INSTRUMENT | IN FORCE |
|---|---|---|
| Switzerland | Ratification: December 30, 1955 | March 30, 1956 |
| Tajikistan | Declaration/Notification of Succession: August 28, 1992 | September 9, 1991 |
| The former Yugoslav Republic of Macedonia | Declaration/Notification of Succession: April 30, 1997 | November 17, 1991 |
| Togo | Accession: February 28, 2003 | May 28, 2003 |
| Trinidad and Tobago | Accession: May 19, 1988 | August 19, 1988 |
| Tunisia | Accession: March 19, 1969 | June 19, 1969 |
| Ukraine | Declaration/Notification of Succession: January 17, 1994 | August 24, 1991 |
| United Kingdom | Ratification: June 27, 1957 | September 27, 1957 |
| United States of America | Ratification: December 6, 1954 | September 16, 1955 |
| Uruguay | Ratification: January 12, 1993 | April 12, 1993 |
| Venezuela (Bolivarian Republic of) | Accession: June 30, 1966 | September 30, 1966 |

(Total: **100** states)

# 15. WIPO COPYRIGHT TREATY

(with Agreed Statements Concerning the WIPO Copyright Treaty)
Adopted by the Diplomatic Conference on December 20, 1996

## Contents

---

## Preamble

### *The Contracting Parties,*

*Desiring* to develop and maintain the protection of the rights of authors in their literary and artistic works in a manner as effective and uniform as possible,

*Recognizing* the need to introduce new international rules and clarify the interpretation of certain existing rules in order to provide adequate solutions to the questions raised by new economic, social, cultural and technological developments,

*Recognizing* the profound impact of the development and convergence of information and communication technologies on the creation and use of literary and artistic works,

*Emphasizing* the outstanding significance of copyright protection as an incentive for literary and artistic creation,

*Recognizing* the need to maintain a balance between the rights of authors and the larger public interest, particularly education, research and access to information, as reflected in the Berne Convention,

*Have agreed as follows:*

## Article 1

### Relation to the Berne Convention

(1)   This Treaty is a special agreement within the meaning of Article 20 of the Berne Convention for the Protection of Literary and Artistic Works, as regards Contracting Parties that are countries of the Union established by that Convention. This Treaty shall not have any connection with treaties other than the Berne Convention, nor shall it prejudice any rights and obligations under any other treaties.

(2)   Nothing in this Treaty shall derogate from existing obligations that Contracting Parties have to each other under the Berne Convention for the Protection of Literary and Artistic Works.

(3)   Hereinafter, "Berne Convention" shall refer to the Paris Act of July 24, 1971 of the Berne Convention for the Protection of Literary and Artistic Works.

(4)   Contracting Parties shall comply with Articles 1 to 21 and the Appendix of the Berne Convention.

## Article 2

### Scope of Copyright Protection

Copyright protection extends to expressions and not to ideas, procedures, methods of operation or mathematical concepts as such.

## Article 3

### Application of Articles 2 to 6 of the Berne Convention

Contracting Parties shall apply *mutatis mutandis* the provisions of Articles 2 to 6 of the Berne Convention in respect of the protection provided for in this Treaty.

## Article 4

### Computer Programs

Computer programs are protected as literary works within the meaning of Article 2 of the Berne Convention. Such protection applies to computer programs, whatever may be the mode or form of their expression.

## Article 5

### Compilations of Data (Databases)

Compilations of data or other material, in any form, which by reason of the selection or arrangement of their contents constitute intellectual creations, are protected as such. This protection does not extend to the data or the material itself and is without prejudice to any copyright subsisting in the data or material contained in the compilation.

## Article 6

### Right of Distribution

(1)   Authors of literary and artistic works shall enjoy the exclusive right of authorizing the making available to the public of the original and copies of their works through sale or other transfer of ownership.

(2)   Nothing in this Treaty shall affect the freedom of Contracting Parties to determine the conditions, if any, under which the exhaustion of the right in paragraph (1) applies after the first sale or other transfer of ownership of the original or a copy of the work with the authorization of the author.

## Article 7

### Right of Rental

(1) Authors of

    (i)   computer programs;

    (ii)  cinematographic works; and

    (iii) works embodied in phonograms, as determined in the national law of Contracting Parties,

shall enjoy the exclusive right of authorizing commercial rental to the public of the originals or copies of their works.

(2) Paragraph (1) shall not apply

    (i)   in the case of computer programs, where the program itself is not the essential object of the rental; and

    (ii)  in the case of cinematographic works, unless such commercial rental has led to widespread copying of such works materially impairing the exclusive right of reproduction.

(3) Notwithstanding the provisions of paragraph (1), a Contracting Party that, on April 15, 1994, had and continues to have in force a system of equitable remuneration of authors for the rental of copies of their works embodied in phonograms may maintain that system provided that the commercial rental of works embodied in phonograms is not giving rise to the material impairment of the exclusive right of reproduction of authors.

## Article 8

### Right of Communication to the Public

Without prejudice to the provisions of Articles 11(1)(ii), 11*bis*(1)(i) and (ii), 11*ter*(1)(ii), 14(1)(ii) and 14*bis*(1) of the Berne Convention, authors of literary and artistic works shall enjoy the exclusive right of authorizing any communication to the public of their works, by wire or wireless means, including the making available to the public of their works in such a way that members of the public may access these works from a place and at a time individually chosen by them.

## Article 9

### Duration of the Protection of Photographic Works

In respect of photographic works, the Contracting Parties shall not apply the provisions of Article 7(4) of the Berne Convention.

## Article 10

### Limitations and Exceptions

(1) Contracting Parties may, in their national legislation, provide for limitations of or exceptions to the rights granted to authors of literary and artistic works under this Treaty in certain special cases that do not conflict with a normal exploitation of the work and do not unreasonably prejudice the legitimate interests of the author.

(2) Contracting Parties shall, when applying the Berne Convention, confine any limitations of or exceptions to rights provided for therein to certain special cases that do not conflict with a normal exploitation of the work and do not unreasonably prejudice the legitimate interests of the author.

## Article 11

### Obligations concerning Technological Measures

Contracting Parties shall provide adequate legal protection and effective legal remedies against the circumvention of effective technological measures that are used by authors in connection with the exercise of their rights under this Treaty or the Berne Convention and that restrict acts, in respect of their works, which are not authorized by the authors concerned or permitted by law.

## Article 12

### Obligations concerning Rights Management Information

(1)   Contracting Parties shall provide adequate and effective legal remedies against any person knowingly performing any of the following acts knowing, or with respect to civil remedies having reasonable grounds to know, that it will induce, enable, facilitate or conceal an infringement of any right covered by this Treaty or the Berne Convention:

(i)   to remove or alter any electronic rights management information without authority;

(ii)   to distribute, import for distribution, broadcast or communicate to the public, without authority, works or copies of works knowing that electronic rights management information has been removed or altered without authority.

(2)   As used in this Article, "rights management information" means information which identifies the work, the author of the work, the owner of any right in the work, or information about the terms and conditions of use of the work, and any numbers or codes that represent such information, when any of these items of information is attached to a copy of a work or appears in connection with the communication of a work to the public.

## Article 13

### Application in Time

Contracting Parties shall apply the provisions of Article 18 of the Berne Convention to all protection provided for in this Treaty.

## Article 14

### Provisions on Enforcement of Rights

(1)   Contracting Parties undertake to adopt, in accordance with their legal systems, the measures necessary to ensure the application of this Treaty.

(2)   Contracting Parties shall ensure that enforcement procedures are available under their law so as to permit effective action against any act of infringement of rights covered by this Treaty, including expeditious remedies to prevent infringements and remedies which constitute a deterrent to further infringements.

## Article 15

### Assembly

(1)   (a)   The Contracting Parties shall have an Assembly.

(b)   Each Contracting Party shall be represented by one delegate who may be assisted by alternate delegates, advisors and experts.

(c)   The expenses of each delegation shall be borne by the Contracting Party that has appointed the delegation. The Assembly may ask the World Intellectual Property Organization (hereinafter referred to as "WIPO") to grant financial assistance to facilitate the participation of delegations of Contracting Parties that are regarded as developing countries in conformity with the established practice of the General Assembly of the United Nations or that are countries in transition to a market economy.

(2) (a) The Assembly shall deal with matters concerning the maintenance and development of this Treaty and the application and operation of this Treaty.

(b) The Assembly shall perform the function allocated to it under Article 17(2) in respect of the admission of certain intergovernmental organizations to become party to this Treaty.

(c) The Assembly shall decide the convocation of any diplomatic conference for the revision of this Treaty and give the necessary instructions to the Director General of WIPO for the preparation of such diplomatic conference.

(3) (a) Each Contracting Party that is a State shall have one vote and shall vote only in its own name.

(b) Any Contracting Party that is an intergovernmental organization may participate in the vote, in place of its Member States, with a number of votes equal to the number of its Member States which are party to this Treaty. No such intergovernmental organization shall participate in the vote if any one of its Member States exercises its right to vote and *vice versa*.

(4) The Assembly shall meet in ordinary session once every two years upon convocation by the Director General of WIPO.

(5) The Assembly shall establish its own rules of procedure, including the convocation of extraordinary sessions, the requirements of a quorum and, subject to the provisions of this Treaty, the required majority for various kinds of decisions.

## Article 16

### International Bureau

The International Bureau of WIPO shall perform the administrative tasks concerning the Treaty.

## Article 17

### Eligibility for Becoming Party to the Treaty

(1) Any Member State of WIPO may become party to this Treaty.

(2) The Assembly may decide to admit any intergovernmental organization to become party to this Treaty which declares that it is competent in respect of, and has its own legislation binding on all its Member States on, matters covered by this Treaty and that it has been duly authorized, in accordance with its internal procedures, to become party to this Treaty.

(3) The European Community, having made the declaration referred to in the preceding paragraph in the Diplomatic Conference that has adopted this Treaty, may become party to this Treaty.

## Article 18

### Rights and Obligations under the Treaty

Subject to any specific provisions to the contrary in this Treaty, each Contracting Party shall enjoy all of the rights and assume all of the obligations under this Treaty.

## Article 19

### Signature of the Treaty

This Treaty shall be open for signature until December 31, 1997, by any Member State of WIPO and by the European Community.

## Article 20

### Entry into Force of the Treaty

This Treaty shall enter into force three months after 30 instruments of ratification or accession by States have been deposited with the Director General of WIPO.

## Article 21

### Effective Date of Becoming Party to the Treaty

This Treaty shall bind

(i)   the 30 States referred to in Article 20, from the date on which this Treaty has entered into force;

(ii)   each other State from the expiration of three months from the date on which the State has deposited its instrument with the Director General of WIPO;

(iii)   the European Community, from the expiration of three months after the deposit of its instrument of ratification or accession if such instrument has been deposited after the entry into force of this Treaty according to Article 20, or, three months after the entry into force of this Treaty if such instrument has been deposited before the entry into force of this Treaty;

(iv)   any other intergovernmental organization that is admitted to become party to this Treaty, from the expiration of three months after the deposit of its instrument of accession.

## Article 22

### No Reservations to the Treaty

No reservation to this Treaty shall be admitted.

## Article 23

### Denunciation of the Treaty

This Treaty may be denounced by any Contracting Party by notification addressed to the Director General of WIPO. Any denunciation shall take effect one year from the date on which the Director General of WIPO received the notification.

## Article 24

### Languages of the Treaty

(1)   This Treaty is signed in a single original in English, Arabic, Chinese, French, Russian and Spanish languages, the versions in all these languages being equally authentic.

(2)   An official text in any language other than those referred to in paragraph (1) shall be established by the Director General of WIPO on the request of an interested party, after consultation with all the interested parties. For the purposes of this paragraph, "interested party" means any Member State of WIPO whose official language, or one of whose official languages, is involved and the European Community, and any other intergovernmental organization that may become party to this Treaty, if one of its official languages is involved.

## Article 25

### Depositary

The Director General of WIPO is the depositary of this Treaty.

## AGREED STATEMENTS CONCERNING THE WIPO COPYRIGHT TREATY

*adopted by the Diplomatic Conference on December 20, 1996*

### Concerning Article 1(4)

The reproduction right, as set out in Article 9 of the Berne Convention, and the exceptions permitted thereunder, fully apply in the digital environment, in particular to the use of works in digital form. It is understood that the storage of a protected work in digital form in an electronic medium constitutes a reproduction within the meaning of Article 9 of the Berne Convention.

### Concerning Article 3

It is understood that in applying Article 3 of this Treaty, the expression "country of the Union" in Articles 2 to 6 of the Berne Convention will be read as if it were a reference to a Contracting Party to this Treaty, in the application of those Berne Articles in respect of protection provided for in this Treaty. It is also understood that the expression "country outside the Union" in those Articles in the Berne Convention will, in the same circumstances, be read as if it were a reference to a country that is not a Contracting Party to this Treaty, and that "this Convention" in Articles 2(8), 2*bis*(2), 3, 4 and 5 of the Berne Convention will be read as if it were a reference to the Berne Convention and this Treaty. Finally, it is understood that a reference in Articles 3 to 6 of the Berne Convention to a "national of one of the countries of the Union" will, when these Articles are applied to this Treaty, mean, in regard to an intergovernmental organization that is a Contracting Party to this Treaty, a national of one of the countries that is member of that organization.

### Concerning Article 4

The scope of protection for computer programs under Article 4 of this Treaty, read with Article 2, is consistent with Article 2 of the Berne Convention and on a par with the relevant provisions of the TRIPS Agreement.

### Concerning Article 5

The scope of protection for compilations of data (databases) under Article 5 of this Treaty, read with Article 2, is consistent with Article 2 of the Berne Convention and on a par with the relevant provisions of the TRIPS Agreement.

### Concerning Articles 6 and 7

As used in these Articles, the expressions "copies" and "original and copies," being subject to the right of distribution and the right of rental under the said Articles, refer exclusively to fixed copies that can be put into circulation as tangible objects.

### Concerning Article 7

It is understood that the obligation under Article 7(1) does not require a Contracting Party to provide an exclusive right of commercial rental to authors who, under that Contracting Party's law, are not granted rights in respect of phonograms. It is understood that this obligation is consistent with Article 14(4) of the TRIPS Agreement.

### Concerning Article 8

It is understood that the mere provision of physical facilities for enabling or making a communication does not in itself amount to communication within the meaning of this Treaty or the

Berne Convention. It is further understood that nothing in Article 8 precludes a Contracting Party from applying Article 11*bis*(2).

### Concerning Article 10

It is understood that the provisions of Article 10 permit Contracting Parties to carry forward and appropriately extend into the digital environment limitations and exceptions in their national laws which have been considered acceptable under the Berne Convention. Similarly, these provisions should be understood to permit Contracting Parties to devise new exceptions and limitations that are appropriate in the digital network environment.

It is also understood that Article 10(2) neither reduces nor extends the scope of applicability of the limitations and exceptions permitted by the Berne Convention.

### Concerning Article 12

It is understood that the reference to "infringement of any right covered by this Treaty or the Berne Convention" includes both exclusive rights and rights of remuneration.

It is further understood that Contracting Parties will not rely on this Article to devise or implement rights management systems that would have the effect of imposing formalities which are not permitted under the Berne Convention or this Treaty, prohibiting the free movement of goods or impeding the enjoyment of rights under this Treaty.

# 16.  PARTIES TO THE WIPO COPYRIGHT TREATY*

(Geneva, 1996)

**Status on May 4, 2021**

| State/IGO | Date on which State/IGO became party to the Treaty |
| --- | --- |
| Afghanistan | February 9, 2021 |
| Albania | August 6, 2005 |
| Algeria | January 31, 2014 |
| Argentina | March 6, 2002 |
| Armenia | March 6, 2005 |
| Australia | July 26, 2007 |
| Austria | March 14, 2010 |
| Azerbaijan | April 11, 2006 |
| Bahrain | December 15, 2005 |
| Barbados | December 13, 2019 |
| Belarus | March 6, 2002 |
| Belgium | August 30, 2006 |
| Belize | February 9, 2019 |
| Benin | April 16, 2006 |
| Bosnia and Herzegovina | November 25, 2009 |
| Botswana | January 27, 2005 |
| Brunei Darussalam | May 2, 2017 |
| Bulgaria | March 6, 2002 |
| Burkina Faso | March 6, 2002 |
| Burundi | April 12, 2016 |
| Cabo Verde | May 22, 2019 |
| Canada | August 13, 2014 |
| Chile | March 6, 2002 |
| China[1,2] | June 9, 2007 |
| Colombia | March 6, 2002 |
| Comoros | April 25, 2021 |
| Cook Islands | June 19, 2019 |
| Costa Rica | March 6, 2002 |
| Croatia | March 6, 2002 |
| Cyprus | November 4, 2003 |
| Czech Republic | March 6, 2002 |
| Denmark[3] | March 14, 2010 |
| Dominican Republic | January 10, 2006 |

---

| State/IGO | Date on which State/IGO became party to the Treaty |
|---|---|
| Ecuador | March 6, 2002 |
| El Salvador | March 6, 2002 |
| Estonia | March 14, 2010 |
| European Union | March 14, 2010 |
| Finland | March 14, 2010 |
| France | March 14, 2010 |
| Gabon | March 6, 2002 |
| Georgia | March 6, 2002 |
| Germany | March 14, 2010 |
| Ghana | November 18, 2006 |
| Greece | March 14, 2010 |
| Guatemala | February 4, 2003 |
| Guinea | May 25, 2002 |
| Honduras | May 20, 2002 |
| Hungary | March 6, 2002 |
| India | December 25, 2018 |
| Indonesia | March 6, 2002 |
| Ireland | March 14, 2010 |
| Italy | March 14, 2010 |
| Jamaica | June 12, 2002 |
| Japan | March 6, 2002 |
| Jordan | April 27, 2004 |
| Kazakhstan | November 12, 2004 |
| Kiribati | June 22, 2021 |
| Kyrgyzstan | March 6, 2002 |
| Latvia | March 6, 2002 |
| Liechtenstein | April 30, 2007 |
| Luxembourg | March 14, 2010 |
| Lithuania | March 6, 2002 |
| Madagascar | February 24, 2015 |
| Malaysia | December 27, 2012 |
| Mali | April 24, 2002 |
| Malta | March 14, 2010 |
| Mexico | March 6, 2002 |
| Mongolia | October 25, 2002 |
| Montenegro | June 3, 2006 |
| Morocco | July 20, 2011 |
| Nauru | August 11, 2020 |
| Netherlands | March 14, 2010 |
| New Zealand[4] | March 17, 2019 |
| Nicaragua | March 6, 2003 |

## PARTIES TO THE WIPO COPYRIGHT TREATY

| State/IGO | Date on which State/IGO became party to the Treaty |
| --- | --- |
| Nigeria | January 4, 2018 |
| North Macedonia | February 4, 2004 |
| Oman | September 20, 2005 |
| Panama | March 6, 2002 |
| Paraguay | March 6, 2002 |
| Peru | March 6, 2002 |
| Philippines | October 4, 2002 |
| Poland | March 23, 2004 |
| Portugal | March 14, 2010 |
| Qatar | October 28, 2005 |
| Republic of Korea | June 24, 2004 |
| Republic of Moldova | March 6, 2002 |
| Romania | March 6, 2002 |
| Russian Federation | February 5, 2009 |
| Saint Lucia | March 6, 2002 |
| San Marino | September 2, 2020 |
| Sao Tome and Principe | April 27, 2020 |
| Senegal | May 18, 2002 |
| Serbia[5] | June 13, 2003 |
| Singapore | April 17, 2005 |
| Slovakia | March 6, 2002 |
| Slovenia | March 6, 2002 |
| Spain | March 14, 2010 |
| Sweden | March 14, 2010 |
| Switzerland | July 1, 2008 |
| Tajikistan | April 5, 2009 |
| Togo | May 21, 2003 |
| Trinidad and Tobago | November 28, 2008 |
| Turkey | November 28, 2008 |
| Ukraine | March 6, 2002 |
| United Arab Emirates | July 14, 2004 |
| United Kingdom | March 14, 2010 |
| United States of America | March 6, 2002 |
| Uruguay | June 5, 2009 |
| Uzbekistan | July 17, 2019 |
| Vanuatu | August 6, 2020 |

(Total: 110)

---

[1]  In accordance with the Basic Law of Hong Kong, China, the Government of the People's Republic of China has decided that the Treaty will apply to Hong Kong, China with effect from October 1, 2008.

2    In accordance with the Basic Law of the Macao Special Administrative Region of the People's Republic of China (PRC), the Government of the PRC decides that the Treaty shall apply to the Macao Special Administrative Region. The declaration took effect on November 6, 2013.

3    Applicable to the Faroe Islands as of April 30, 2018.

4    The accession by New Zealand shall extend to Tokelau.

5    Serbia is the continuing State from Serbia and Montenegro as from June 3, 2006.

# 17. WIPO PERFORMANCES AND PHONOGRAMS TREATY

(with Agreed Statements Concerning the WIPO
Performances and Phonograms Treaty)

Adopted by the Diplomatic Conference on December 20, 1996

*Contents*

## Preamble

*The Contracting Parties,*

*Desiring* to develop and maintain the protection of the rights of performers and producers of phonograms in a manner as effective and uniform as possible,

*Recognizing* the need to introduce new international rules in order to provide adequate solutions to the questions raised by economic, social, cultural and technological developments,

*Recognizing* the profound impact of the development and convergence of information and communication technologies on the production and use of performances and phonograms,

*Recognizing* the need to maintain a balance between the rights of performers and producers of phonograms and the larger public interest, particularly education, research and access to information,

*Have agreed* as follows:

## CHAPTER I
## GENERAL PROVISIONS

### Article 1

### Relation to Other Conventions

(1)   Nothing in this Treaty shall derogate from existing obligations that Contracting Parties have to each other under the International Convention for the Protection of Performers, Producers of Phonograms and Broadcasting Organizations done in Rome, October 26, 1961 (hereinafter the "Rome Convention").

(2)   Protection granted under this Treaty shall leave intact and shall in no way affect the protection of copyright in literary and artistic works. Consequently, no provision of this Treaty may be interpreted as prejudicing such protection.

(3)   This Treaty shall not have any connection with, nor shall it prejudice any rights and obligations under, any other treaties.

### Article 2

### Definitions

For the purposes of this Treaty:

(a)   "performers" are actors, singers, musicians, dancers, and other persons who act, sing, deliver, declaim, play in, interpret, or otherwise perform literary or artistic works or expressions of folklore;

(b)   "phonogram" means the fixation of the sounds of a performance or of other sounds, or of a representation of sounds, other than in the form of a fixation incorporated in a cinematographic or other audiovisual work;

(c)   "fixation" means the embodiment of sounds, or of the representations thereof, from which they can be perceived, reproduced or communicated through a device;

(d)   "producer of a phonogram" means the person, or the legal entity, who or which takes the initiative and has the responsibility for the first fixation of the sounds of a performance or other sounds, or the representations of sounds;

(e)   "publication" of a fixed performance or a phonogram means the offering of copies of the fixed performance or the phonogram to the public, with the consent of the rightholder, and provided that copies are offered to the public in reasonable quantity;

(f)   "broadcasting" means the transmission by wireless means for public reception of sounds or of images and sounds or of the representations thereof; such transmission by satellite is also "broadcasting"; transmission of encrypted signals is "broadcasting" where the means for decrypting are provided to the public by the broadcasting organization or with its consent;

(g)   "communication to the public" of a performance or a phonogram means the transmission to the public by any medium, otherwise than by broadcasting, of sounds of a performance or the sounds or the representations of sounds fixed in a phonogram. For the purposes of Article 15, "communication to the public" includes making the sounds or representations of sounds fixed in a phonogram audible to the public.

## Article 3

### Beneficiaries of Protection under this Treaty

(1)   Contracting Parties shall accord the protection provided under this Treaty to the performers and producers of phonograms who are nationals of other Contracting Parties.

(2)   The nationals of other Contracting Parties shall be understood to be those performers or producers of phonograms who would meet the criteria for eligibility for protection provided under the Rome Convention, were all the Contracting Parties to this Treaty Contracting States of that Convention. In respect of these criteria of eligibility, Contracting Parties shall apply the relevant definitions in Article 2 of this Treaty.

(3)   Any Contracting Party availing itself of the possibilities provided in Article 5(3) of the Rome Convention or, for the purposes of Article 5 of the same Convention, Article 17 thereof shall make a notification as foreseen in those provisions to the Director General of the World Intellectual Property Organization (WIPO).

## Article 4

### National Treatment

(1)   Each Contracting Party shall accord to nationals of other Contracting Parties, as defined in Article 3(2), the treatment it accords to its own nationals with regard to the exclusive rights specifically granted in this Treaty, and to the right to equitable remuneration provided for in Article 15 of this Treaty.

(2)   The obligation provided for in paragraph (1) does not apply to the extent that another Contracting Party makes use of the reservations permitted by Article 15(3) of this Treaty.

## CHAPTER II
## RIGHTS OF PERFORMERS

## Article 5

### Moral Rights of Performers

(1)   Independently of a performer's economic rights, and even after the transfer of those rights, the performer shall, as regards his live aural performances or performances fixed in phonograms, have the right to claim to be identified as the performer of his performances, except where omission is dictated by the manner of the use of the performance, and to object to any distortion, mutilation or other modification of his performances that would be prejudicial to his reputation.

(2)   The rights granted to a performer in accordance with paragraph (1) shall, after his death, be maintained, at least until the expiry of the economic rights, and shall be exercisable by the persons or

institutions authorized by the legislation of the Contracting Party where protection is claimed. However, those Contracting Parties whose legislation, at the moment of their ratification of or accession to this Treaty, does not provide for protection after the death of the performer of all rights set out in the preceding paragraph may provide that some of these rights will, after his death, cease to be maintained.

(3) The means of redress for safeguarding the rights granted under this Article shall be governed by the legislation of the Contracting Party where protection is claimed.

## Article 6

### Economic Rights of Performers in their Unfixed Performances

Performers shall enjoy the exclusive right of authorizing, as regards their performances:

(i) the broadcasting and communication to the public of their unfixed performances except where the performance is already a broadcast performance; and

(ii) the fixation of their unfixed performances.

## Article 7

### Right of Reproduction

Performers shall enjoy the exclusive right of authorizing the direct or indirect reproduction of their performances fixed in phonograms, in any manner or form.

## Article 8

### Right of Distribution

(1) Performers shall enjoy the exclusive right of authorizing the making available to the public of the original and copies of their performances fixed in phonograms through sale or other transfer of ownership.

(2) Nothing in this Treaty shall affect the freedom of Contracting Parties to determine the conditions, if any, under which the exhaustion of the right in paragraph (1) applies after the first sale or other transfer of ownership of the original or a copy of the fixed performance with the authorization of the performer.

## Article 9

### Right of Rental

(1) Performers shall enjoy the exclusive right of authorizing the commercial rental to the public of the original and copies of their performances fixed in phonograms as determined in the national law of Contracting Parties, even after distribution of them by, or pursuant to, authorization by the performer.

(2) Notwithstanding the provisions of paragraph (1), a Contracting Party that, on April 15, 1994, had and continues to have in force a system of equitable remuneration of performers for the rental of copies of their performances fixed in phonograms, may maintain that system provided that the commercial rental of phonograms is not giving rise to the material impairment of the exclusive right of reproduction of performers.

## Article 10

### Right of Making Available of Fixed Performances

Performers shall enjoy the exclusive right of authorizing the making available to the public of their performances fixed in phonograms, by wire or wireless means, in such a way that members of the public may access them from a place and at a time individually chosen by them.

## CHAPTER III
## RIGHTS OF PRODUCERS OF PHONOGRAMS

## Article 11

### Right of Reproduction

Producers of phonograms shall enjoy the exclusive right of authorizing the direct or indirect reproduction of their phonograms, in any manner or form.

## Article 12

### Right of Distribution

(1)　Producers of phonograms shall enjoy the exclusive right of authorizing the making available to the public of the original and copies of their phonograms through sale or other transfer of ownership.

(2)　Nothing in this Treaty shall affect the freedom of Contracting Parties to determine the conditions, if any, under which the exhaustion of the right in paragraph (1) applies after the first sale or other transfer of ownership of the original or a copy of the phonogram with the authorization of the producer of the phonogram.

## Article 13

### Right of Rental

(1)　Producers of phonograms shall enjoy the exclusive right of authorizing the commercial rental to the public of the original and copies of their phonograms, even after distribution of them by or pursuant to authorization by the producer.

(2)　Notwithstanding the provisions of paragraph (1), a Contracting Party that, on April 15, 1994, had and continues to have in force a system of equitable remuneration of producers of phonograms for the rental of copies of their phonograms, may maintain that system provided that the commercial rental of phonograms is not giving rise to the material impairment of the exclusive rights of reproduction of producers of phonograms.

## Article 14

### Right of Making Available of Phonograms

Producers of phonograms shall enjoy the exclusive right of authorizing the making available to the public of their phonograms, by wire or wireless means, in such a way that members of the public may access them from a place and at a time individually chosen by them.

## CHAPTER IV
## COMMON PROVISIONS

### Article 15

### Right to Remuneration for Broadcasting
### and Communication to the Public

(1)   Performers and producers of phonograms shall enjoy the right to a single equitable remuneration for the direct or indirect use of phonograms published for commercial purposes for broadcasting or for any communication to the public.

(2)   Contracting Parties may establish in their national legislation that the single equitable remuneration shall be claimed from the user by the performer or by the producer of a phonogram or by both. Contracting Parties may enact national legislation that, in the absence of an agreement between the performer and the producer of a phonogram, sets the terms according to which performers and producers of phonograms shall share the single equitable remuneration.

(3)   Any Contracting Party may in a notification deposited with the Director General of WIPO, declare that it will apply the provisions of paragraph (1) only in respect of certain uses, or that it will limit their application in some other way, or that it will not apply these provisions at all.

(4)   For the purposes of this Article, phonograms made available to the public by wire or wireless means in such a way that members of the public may access them from a place and at a time individually chosen by them shall be considered as if they had been published for commercial purposes.

### Article 16

### Limitations and Exceptions

(1)   Contracting Parties may, in their national legislation, provide for the same kinds of limitations or exceptions with regard to the protection of performers and producers of phonograms as they provide for, in their national legislation, in connection with the protection of copyright in literary and artistic works.

(2)   Contracting Parties shall confine any limitations of or exceptions to rights provided for in this Treaty to certain special cases which do not conflict with a normal exploitation of the performance or phonogram and do not unreasonably prejudice the legitimate interests of the performer or of the producer of the phonogram.

### Article 17

### Term of Protection

(1)   The term of protection to be granted to performers under this Treaty shall last, at least, until the end of a period of 50 years computed from the end of the year in which the performance was fixed in a phonogram.

(2)   The term of protection to be granted to producers of phonograms under this Treaty shall last, at least, until the end of a period of 50 years computed from the end of the year in which the phonogram was published, or failing such publication within 50 years from fixation of the phonogram, 50 years from the end of the year in which the fixation was made.

### Article 18

### Obligations Concerning Technological Measures

Contracting Parties shall provide adequate legal protection and effective legal remedies against the circumvention of effective technological measures that are used by performers or producers of phonograms in connection with the exercise of their rights under this Treaty and that restrict acts, in respect of their performances or phonograms, which are not authorized by the performers or the producers of phonograms concerned or permitted by law.

## Article 19

### Obligations Concerning Rights Management Information

(1)   Contracting Parties shall provide adequate and effective legal remedies against any person knowingly performing any of the following acts knowing, or with respect to civil remedies having reasonable grounds to know, that it will induce, enable, facilitate or conceal an infringement of any right covered by this Treaty:

    (i)   to remove or alter any electronic rights management information without authority;

    (ii)   to distribute, import for distribution, broadcast, communicate or make available to the public, without authority, performances, copies of fixed performances or phonograms knowing that electronic rights management information has been removed or altered without authority.

(2)   As used in this Article, "rights management information" means information which identifies the performer, the performance of the performer, the producer of the phonogram, the phonogram, the owner of any right in the performance or phonogram, or information about the terms and conditions of use of the performance or phonogram, and any numbers or codes that represent such information, when any of these items of information is attached to a copy of a fixed performance or a phonogram or appears in connection with the communication or making available of a fixed performance or a phonogram to the public.

## Article 20

### Formalities

The enjoyment and exercise of the rights provided for in this Treaty shall not be subject to any formality.

## Article 21

### Reservations

Subject to the provisions of Article 15(3), no reservations to this Treaty shall be permitted.

## Article 22

### Application in Time

(1)   Contracting Parties shall apply the provisions of Article 18 of the Berne Convention, *mutatis mutandis*, to the rights of performers and producers of phonograms provided for in this Treaty.

(2)   Notwithstanding paragraph (1), a Contracting Party may limit the application of Article 5 of this Treaty to performances which occurred after the entry into force of this Treaty for that Party.

## Article 23

### Provisions on Enforcement of Rights

(1)   Contracting Parties undertake to adopt, in accordance with their legal systems, the measures necessary to ensure the application of this Treaty.

(2)   Contracting Parties shall ensure that enforcement procedures are available under their law so as to permit effective action against any act of infringement of rights covered by this Treaty, including expeditious remedies to prevent infringements and remedies which constitute a deterrent to further infringements.

## CHAPTER V
## ADMINISTRATIVE AND FINAL CLAUSES

### Article 24

### Assembly

(1)  (a)  The Contracting Parties shall have an Assembly.

(b)  Each Contracting Party shall be represented by one delegate who may be assisted by alternate delegates, advisors and experts.

(c)  The expenses of each delegation shall be borne by the Contracting Party that has appointed the delegation. The Assembly may ask WIPO to grant financial assistance to facilitate the participation of delegations of Contracting Parties that are regarded as developing countries in conformity with the established practice of the General Assembly of the United Nations or that are countries in transition to a market economy.

(2)  (a)  The Assembly shall deal with matters concerning the maintenance and development of this Treaty and the application and operation of this Treaty.

(b)  The Assembly shall perform the function allocated to it under Article 26(2) in respect of the admission of certain intergovernmental organizations to become party to this Treaty.

(c)  The Assembly shall decide the convocation of any diplomatic conference for the revision of this Treaty and give the necessary instructions to the Director General of WIPO for the preparation of such diplomatic conference.

(3)  (a)  Each Contracting Party that is a State shall have one vote and shall vote only in its own name.

(b)  Any Contracting Party that is an intergovernmental organization may participate in the vote, in place of its Member States, with a number of votes equal to the number of its Member States which are party to this Treaty. No such intergovernmental organization shall participate in the vote if any one of its Member States exercises its right to vote and vice versa.

(4)  The Assembly shall meet in ordinary session once every two years upon convocation by the Director General of WIPO.

(5)  The Assembly shall establish its own rules of procedure, including the convocation of extraordinary sessions, the requirements of a quorum and, subject to the provisions of this Treaty, the required majority for various kinds of decisions.

### Article 25

### International Bureau

The International Bureau of WIPO shall perform the administrative tasks concerning the Treaty.

### Article 26

### Eligibility for Becoming Party to the Treaty

(1)  Any Member State of WIPO may become party to this Treaty.

(2)  The Assembly may decide to admit any intergovernmental organization to become party to this Treaty which declares that it is competent in respect of, and has its own legislation binding on all its Member States on, matters covered by this Treaty and that it has been duly authorized, in accordance with its internal procedures, to become party to this Treaty.

(3)   The European Community, having made the declaration referred to in the preceding paragraph in the Diplomatic Conference that has adopted this Treaty, may become party to this Treaty.

## Article 27

### Rights and Obligations under the Treaty

Subject to any specific provisions to the contrary in this Treaty, each Contracting Party shall enjoy all of the rights and assume all of the obligations under this Treaty.

## Article 28

### Signature of the Treaty

This Treaty shall be open for signature until December 31, 1997, by any Member State of WIPO and by the European Community.

## Article 29

### Entry into Force of the Treaty

This Treaty shall enter into force three months after 30 instruments of ratification or accession by States have been deposited with the Director General of WIPO.

## Article 30

### Effective Date of Becoming Party to the Treaty

This Treaty shall bind

(i)   the 30 States referred to in Article 29, from the date on which this Treaty has entered into force;

(ii)   each other State from the expiration of three months from the date on which the State has deposited its instrument with the Director General of WIPO;

(iii) the European Community, from the expiration of three months after the deposit of its instrument of ratification or accession if such instrument has been deposited after the entry into force of this Treaty according to Article 29, or, three months after the entry into force of this Treaty if such instrument has been deposited before the entry into force of this Treaty;

(iv)   any other intergovernmental organization that is admitted to become party to this Treaty, from the expiration of three months after the deposit of its instrument of accession.

## Article 31

### Denunciation of the Treaty

This Treaty may be denounced by any Contracting Party by notification addressed to the Director General of WIPO. Any denunciation shall take effect one year from the date on which the Director General of WIPO received the notification.

## Article 32

### Languages of the Treaty

(1)   This Treaty is signed in a single original in English, Arabic, Chinese, French, Russian and Spanish languages, the versions in all these languages being equally authentic.

(2)   An official text in any language other than those referred to in paragraph (1) shall be established by the Director General of WIPO on the request of an interested party, after consultation

with all the interested parties. For the purposes of this paragraph, "interested party" means any Member State of WIPO whose official language, or one of whose official languages, is involved and the European Community, and any other intergovernmental organization that may become party to this Treaty, if one of its official languages is involved.

## Article 33

### Depositary

The Director General of WIPO is the depositary of this Treaty.

## AGREED STATEMENTS CONCERNING THE WIPO PERFORMANCES AND PHONOGRAMS TREATY

*adopted by the Diplomatic Conference on December 20, 1996*

### Concerning Article 1

It is understood that Article 1(2) clarifies the relationship between rights in phonograms under this Treaty and copyright in works embodied in the phonograms. In cases where authorization is needed from both the author of a work embodied in the phonogram and a performer or producer owning rights in the phonogram, the need for the authorization of the author does not cease to exist because the authorization of the performer or producer is also required, and vice versa.

It is further understood that nothing in Article 1(2) precludes a Contracting Party from providing exclusive rights to a performer or producer of phonograms beyond those required to be provided under this Treaty.

### Concerning Article 2(b)

It is understood that the definition of phonogram provided in Article 2(b) does not suggest that rights in the phonogram are in any way affected through their incorporation into a cinematographic or other audiovisual work.

### Concerning Articles 2(e), 8, 9, 12, and 13

As used in these Articles, the expressions "copies" and "original and copies," being subject to the right of distribution and the right of rental under the said Articles, refer exclusively to fixed copies that can be put into circulation as tangible objects.

### Concerning Article 3

It is understood that the reference in Articles 5(a) and 16(a)(iv) of the Rome Convention to "national of another Contracting State" will, when applied to this Treaty, mean, in regard to an intergovernmental organization that is a Contracting Party to this Treaty, a national of one of the countries that is a member of that organization.

### Concerning Article 3(2)

For the application of Article 3(2), it is understood that fixation means the finalization of the master tape ("bande-mère").

### Concerning Articles 7, 11 and 16

The reproduction right, as set out in Articles 7 and 11, and the exceptions permitted thereunder through Article 16, fully apply in the digital environment, in particular to the use of performances and phonograms in digital form. It is understood that the storage of a protected performance or phonogram in digital form in an electronic medium constitutes a reproduction within the meaning of these Articles.

### Concerning Article 15

It is understood that Article 15 does not represent a complete resolution of the level of rights of broadcasting and communication to the public that should be enjoyed by performers and phonogram producers in the digital age. Delegations were unable to achieve consensus on differing proposals for aspects of exclusivity to be provided in certain circumstances or for rights to be provided without the possibility of reservations, and have therefore left the issue to future resolution.

### Concerning Article 15

It is understood that Article 15 does not prevent the granting of the right conferred by this Article to performers of folklore and producers of phonograms recording folklore where such phonograms have not been published for commercial gain.

### Concerning Article 16

The agreed statement concerning Article 10 (on Limitations and Exceptions) of the WIPO Copyright Treaty is applicable *mutatis mutandis* also to Article 16 (on Limitations and Exceptions) of the WIPO Performances and Phonograms Treaty.

### Concerning Article 19

The agreed statement concerning Article 12 (on Obligations concerning Rights Management Information) of the WIPO Copyright Treaty is applicable *mutatis mutandis* also to Article 19 (on Obligations concerning Rights Management Information) of the WIPO Performances and Phonograms Treaty.

# 18. PARTIES TO THE WIPO PERFORMANCES AND PHONOGRAMS TREATY*

(Geneva, 1996)

**Status on May 4, 2021**

| State/IGO | Date on which State/IGO became party to the Treaty |
|---|---|
| Afghanistan | February 9, 2021 |
| Albania | May 20, 2002 |
| Algeria | January 31, 2014 |
| Argentina | May 20, 2002 |
| Armenia | March 6, 2005 |
| Australia[1, 2] | July 26, 2007 |
| Austria | March 14, 2010 |
| Azerbaijan | April 11, 2006 |
| Bahrain | December 15, 2005 |
| Barbados | December 13, 2019 |
| Belarus | May 20, 2002 |
| Belgium | August 30, 2006[2] |
| Belize | February 9, 2019 |
| Benin | April 16, 2006 |
| Bosnia and Herzegovina | November 25, 2009 |
| Botswana | January 27, 2005 |
| Brunei Darussalam | May 2, 2017 |
| Bulgaria | May 20, 2002 |
| Burkina Faso | May 20, 2002 |
| Cabo Verde | May 22, 2019 |
| Canada[3, 4, 5] | August 13, 2014 |
| Chile[6] | May 20, 2002 |
| China[7, 8, 9] | June 9, 2007 |
| Colombia | May 20, 2002 |
| Comoros | April 25, 2021 |
| Cook Islands | June 19, 2019 |
| Costa Rica | May 20, 2002 |
| Croatia | May 20, 2002 |
| Cyprus | December 2, 2005 |
| Czech Republic | May 20, 2002 |
| Denmark[2, 10] | March 14, 2010 |
| Dominican Republic | January 10, 2006 |

---

* Document originally produced by the World Intellectual Property Organization (WIPO), the owner of the copyright. Published with the permission of the World Intellectual Property Organization.

## PARTIES TO THE WIPO PERFORMANCES
## & PHONOGRAMS TREATY

| State/IGO | Date on which State/IGO became party to the Treaty |
|---|---|
| Ecuador | May 20, 2002 |
| El Salvador | May 20, 2002 |
| Estonia | March 14, 2010 |
| European Union | March 14, 2010 |
| Finland[11] | March 14, 2010 |
| France[2] | March 14, 2010 |
| Gabon | May 20, 2002 |
| Georgia | May 20, 2002 |
| Germany[24] | March 14, 2010 |
| Ghana | February 16, 2013 |
| Greece | March 14, 2010 |
| Guatemala | January 8, 2003 |
| Guinea | May 25, 2002 |
| Honduras | May 20, 2002 |
| Hungary | May 20, 2002 |
| India[12, 13] | December 25, 2018 |
| Indonesia | February 15, 2005 |
| Ireland | March 14, 2010 |
| Italy | March 14, 2010 |
| Jamaica | June 12, 2002 |
| Japan | October 9, 2002[2, 14] |
| Jordan | May 24, 2004 |
| Kazakhstan | November 12, 2004 |
| Kiribati | June 22, 2021 |
| Kyrgyzstan | August 15, 2002 |
| Latvia | May 20, 2002 |
| Liechtenstein | April 30, 2007 |
| Lithuania | May 20, 2002 |
| Luxembourg | March 14, 2010 |
| Madagascar | February 24, 2015 |
| Malaysia | December 27, 2012 |
| Mali | May 20, 2002 |
| Malta | March 14, 2010 |
| Mexico | May 20, 2002 |
| Mongolia | October 25, 2002 |
| Montenegro | June 3, 2006 |
| Morocco | July 20, 2011 |
| Netherlands | March 14, 2010 |
| New Zealand[15, 16] | March 17, 2019 |
| Nicaragua | March 6, 2003 |
| Nigeria | January 4, 2018 |

## PARTIES TO THE WIPO PERFORMANCES
## & PHONOGRAMS TREATY

| State/IGO | Date on which State/IGO became party to the Treaty |
|---|---|
| North Macedonia | March 20, 2005[2, 17] |
| Oman | September 20, 2005 |
| Panama | May 20, 2002 |
| Paraguay | May 20, 2002 |
| Peru | July 18, 2002 |
| Philippines | October 4, 2002 |
| Poland | October 21, 2003 |
| Portugal | March 14, 2010 |
| Qatar | October 28, 2005 |
| Republic of Korea | March 18, 2009[2, 18, 19] |
| Republic of Moldova | May 20, 2002 |
| Romania | May 20, 2002 |
| Russian Federation[20] | February 5, 2009 |
| Saint Lucia | May 20, 2002 |
| Saint Vincent and the Grenadines | February 12, 2011 |
| San Marino | September 2, 2020 |
| Sao Tome and Principe | April 27, 2020 |
| Senegal | May 20, 2002 |
| Serbia[21] | June 13, 2003 |
| Singapore | April 17, 2005[22] |
| Slovakia | May 20, 2002 |
| Slovenia | May 20, 2002 |
| Spain | March 14, 2010 |
| Sweden[23] | March 14, 2010 |
| Switzerland | July 1, 2008[24] |
| Tajikistan | August 24, 2011 |
| Togo | May 21, 2003 |
| Trinidad and Tobago | November 28, 2008 |
| Turkey | November 28, 2008 |
| Ukraine | May 20, 2002 |
| United Arab Emirates | June 9, 2005 |
| United Kingdom | March 14, 2010 |
| United States of America | May 20, 2002[25] |
| Uruguay | August 28, 2008 |
| Uzbekistan | July 17, 2019 |
| Vanuatu | August 6, 2020 |

(Total: 109)

---

[1]  Pursuant to Article 15(3), Australia will not apply the provisions of Article 15(1) in respect of:

(a)  the use of phonograms for (i) radio broadcasting, and (ii) radio communication to the public within the meaning of the first sentence of Article 2(g), and

(b)  the communication to the public of phonograms by way of making the sounds of the phonograms audible to the public by means of the operation of equipment to receive a broadcast or other transmission of the phonograms.

2   In accordance with Article 3(3) of the Treaty, this State has declared that it will not apply the criterion of publication concerning the protection of phonograms.

3   Pursuant to Article 3(3) of the Treaty, Canada will not apply the criterion of fixation with regard to exclusive rights of producers of phonograms.

4   Pursuant to Article 3(3) of the Treaty, Canada will not apply the criterion of publication with regard to the remuneration right of Article 15(1) of the Treaty.

5   Pursuant to Article 15(3) of the Treaty, Canada will not apply Article 15(1) of the Treaty with regard to the retransmission of phonograms.

6   Pursuant to Article 15, paragraph 3 of the Treaty, the Republic of Chile will apply the provisions of Article 15, paragraph 1 of the Treaty only in respect of direct uses of phonograms published for commercial purposes for broadcasting or for any communication to the public. Pursuant to Article 15, paragraph 3 of the Treaty, as regards phonograms the producer or performer of which is a national of another Contracting Party which has made a declaration under Article 15, paragraph 3 of the Treaty, the Republic of Chile will apply, notwithstanding the provisions of the preceding declaration, the provisions of Article 15, paragraph 1 of the Treaty to the extent that Party grants the protection provided for by the provisions of Article 15, paragraph 1 of the Treaty.

7   Pursuant to Article 15(3) of the Treaty, the People's Republic of China will not apply the provisions of Article 15(1).

8   In accordance with the *Basic Law of Hong Kong, China*, the Government of the People's Republic of China has decided that the Treaty will apply to Hong Kong, China, with effect from October 1, 2008. Hong Kong, China, does not consider itself bound by Article 15(1) of the Treaty with regard to the right of the performers. With respect to the right of the producers of phonograms stipulated in Article 15(1) of the Treaty, relevant laws of Hong Kong, China shall apply.

9   In accordance with the Basic Law of the Macao, China, the Government of the People's Republic of China decides that the *Treaty* shall apply to Macao, China. Macao, China, shall not be bound by Article 15(1) of the Treaty with regard to the right of producers of phonograms. With respect to the right of performers stipulated in Article 15(1) of the *Treaty*, relevant laws of Macao, China, shall apply.

10  Applicable to the Faroe Islands as of April 30, 2018.

11  Pursuant to Article 3(3) of the Treaty the Republic of Finland, availing itself of the possibilities provided in Article 5(3) of the Rome Convention, declares that it will not apply the criterion of publication.

12  In accordance with Article 3(3) of the Treaty, the Republic of India availing itself of the possibilities provided in Article 5(3) of the Rome Convention, will not apply the criterion of fixation while granting national treatment to phonograms producers.

13  In accordance with Article 15(3) of the Treaty, the Republic of India will not apply the provisions of Article 15(1) relating to a single equitable remuneration for performers and producers of phonograms.

14  Pursuant to Article 15(3) Japan will apply, as regards phonograms the producer of which is a national of another Contracting Party, the provisions of Article 15(1) to the extent that Contracting Party grants the protection provided for by these provisions; Japan will apply the provisions of Article 15(1) in respect of the direct or indirect use of the phonograms published for commercial purposes for broadcasting, cablecasting or "automatic public transmission of unfixed information"; and in respect of the direct or indirect use of phonograms made available to the public, by wire or wireless means, in such a way that members of the public may access them from a place and at a time individually chosen by them for broadcasting, cablecasting (wire diffusion) or "automatic public transmission of unfixed information".

15  In accordance with Article 15(3) of the Treaty, the provision of Article 15(1) will not be applied in New Zealand.

16  The accession by New Zealand shall extend to Tokelau.

17  Pursuant to Article 15(3) of the WPPT, the Republic of Macedonia does not apply the provision on single equitable remuneration for the performers and for the phonogram producers for direct or indirect use of phonograms published for commercial purposes for broadcasting or for any other communication to the public, in relation to the expressed reservation of the then former Yugoslav Republic of Macedonia on Article 16 (1)(a)(i) of the Rome Convention.

## PARTIES TO THE WIPO PERFORMANCES
## & PHONOGRAMS TREATY

18  In accordance with Article 15(3) of the Treaty, the Republic of Korea will apply the provision of Article 15(1) thereof in respect of the use of phonograms published for commercial purposes for broadcasting or transmission by wire. Transmission by wire does not include transmission over the Internet.

19  In accordance with 15(3) of the Treaty, as regards phonograms the producer or performer of which is a national of another Contracting Party which has made a declaration under Article 15(3) thereof, the Republic of Korea will apply the provisions of Article 15(1) thereof to the extent to which, and to the term for which, the other Contracting Party grants protection to phonograms the producer or performer of which is a national of the Republic of Korea under the provisions of Article 15(1) thereof.

20  In accordance with Article 15(3) of the WPPT, the Russian Federation shall not apply the provisions of Article 15(1) of the said Treaty in relation to phonograms, the producer of which is not a citizen or legal person of another Contracting Party; shall limit the protection granted, in accordance with Article 15(1) of the WPPT, in relation to phonograms, the producer of which is a citizen or legal person of another Contracting Party, within the scope and on the conditions provided for by this Contracting Party for phonograms first recorded by a citizen or legal person of the Russian Federation; and In accordance with Article 3(3) of the WPPT, the Russian Federation notifies that when it acceded to the International Convention for the Protection of Performers, Producers of Phonograms and Broadcasting Organisations (Rome Convention) of October 26, 1961, the Russian Federation in accordance with Article 5(3) of the Rome Convention, declared that it shall not apply the fixation criterion provided for in Article 5(1)(b) of the Rome Convention.

21  Serbia is the continuing State from Serbia and Montenegro as from June 3, 2006.

22  Pursuant to Article 15(3), Singapore will limit the provisions of Article 15(1) in the following ways: (i) Producers of phonograms have the exclusive right to make available to the public a sound recording by means of, or as part of, a digital audio transmission; and (ii) Performers can bring an action of unauthorized communication of a live performance to the public (on a network or otherwise) in such a way that the recording may be accessed by any person from a place and at a time chosen by him. In this context, "communication" includes broadcasting, inclusion in a cable programme service and the making available of the live performance in such a way that the performance may be accessed by any person from a place and at a time chosen by him.

23  In accordance with Article 3(3) of WPPT, the Kingdom of Sweden has declared that it will not apply the criterion of publication, with the exception of the reproduction right for phonogram producers.

24  In accordance with Article 3(3) of the Treaty, this State has declared that it will not apply the criterion of fixation concerning the protection of phonograms.

25  Pursuant to Article 15(3) of the WIPO Performances and Phonograms Treaty, the United States will apply the provisions of Article 15(1) of the WIPO Performances and Phonograms Treaty only in respect of certain acts of broadcasting and communication to the public by digital means for which a direct or indirect fee is charged for reception, and for other retransmissions and digital phonorecord deliveries, as provided under the United States law.

# 19. INTERNATIONAL CONVENTION FOR THE PROTECTION OF PERFORMERS, PRODUCERS OF PHONOGRAMS AND BROADCASTING ORGANISATIONS

Done at Rome on October 26, 1961

(Rome Convention)

*The Contracting States, moved by the desire to protect the rights of performers, producers of phonograms, and broadcasting organisations,*

*Have agreed as follows:*

## Article 1

Protection granted under this Convention shall leave intact and shall in no way affect the protection of copyright in literary and artistic works. Consequently, no provision of this Convention may be interpreted as prejudicing such protection.

## Article 2

1. For the purposes of this Convention, national treatment shall mean the treatment accorded by the domestic law of the Contracting State in which protection is claimed:

   (a) to performers who are its nationals, as regards performances taking place, broadcast, or first fixed, on its territory;

   (b) to producers of phonograms who are its nationals, as regards phonograms first fixed or first published on its territory;

   (c) to broadcasting organisations which have their headquarters on its territory, as regards broadcasts transmitted from transmitters situated on its territory.

2. National treatment shall be subject to the protection specifically guaranteed, and the limitations specifically provided for, in this Convention.

## Article 3

For the purposes of this Convention:

(a) "performers" means actors, singers, musicians, dancers, and other persons who act, sing, deliver, declaim, play in, or otherwise perform literary or artistic works;

(b) "phonogram" means any exclusively aural fixation of sounds of a performance or of other sounds;

(c) "producer of phonograms" means the person who, or the legal entity which, first fixes the sounds of a performance or other sounds;

(d) "publication" means the offering of copies of a phonogram to the public in reasonable quantity;

(e) "reproduction" means the making of a copy or copies of a fixation;

(f) "broadcasting" means the transmission by wireless means for public reception of sounds or of images and sounds;

(g) "rebroadcasting" means the simultaneous broadcasting by one broadcasting organisation of the broadcast of another broadcasting organisation.

## Article 4

Each Contracting State shall grant national treatment to performers if any of the following conditions is met:

   (a)   the performance takes place in another Contracting State;

   (b)   the performance is incorporated in a phonogram which is protected under Article 5 of this Convention;

   (c)   the performance, not being fixed on a phonogram, is carried by a broadcast which is protected by Article 6 of this Convention.

## Article 5

1.   Each Contracting State shall grant national treatment to producers of phonograms if any of the following conditions is met:

   (a)   the producer of the phonogram is a national of another Contracting State (criterion of nationality);

   (b)   the first fixation of the sound was made in another Contracting State (criterion of fixation);

   (c)   the phonogram was first published in another Contracting State (criterion of publication).

2.   If a phonogram was first published in a non-contracting State but if it was also published, within thirty days of its first publication, in a Contracting State (simultaneous publication), it shall be considered as first published in the Contracting State.

3.   By means of a notification deposited with the Secretary-General of the United Nations, any Contracting State may declare that it will not apply the criterion of publication or, alternatively, the criterion of fixation. Such notification may be deposited at the time of ratification, acceptance or accession, or at any time thereafter; in the last case, it shall become effective six months after it has been deposited.

## Article 6

1.   Each Contracting State shall grant national treatment to broadcasting organisations if either of the following conditions is met:

   (a)   the headquarters of the broadcasting organisation is situated in another Contracting State;

   (b)   the broadcast was transmitted from a transmitter situated in another Contracting State.

2.   By means of a notification deposited with the Secretary-General of the United Nations, any Contracting State may declare that it will protect broadcasts only if the headquarters of the broadcasting organisation is situated in another Contracting State and the broadcast was transmitted from a transmitter situated in the same Contracting State. Such notification may be deposited at the time of ratification, acceptance or accession, or at any time thereafter; in the last case, it shall become effective six months after it has been deposited.

## Article 7

1.   The protection provided for performers by this Convention shall include the possibility of preventing:

   (a)   the broadcasting and the communication to the public, without their consent, of their performance, except where the performance used in the broadcasting or the public communication is itself already a broadcast performance or is made from a fixation;

   (b)   the fixation, without their consent, of their unfixed performance;

   (c)   the reproduction, without their consent, of a fixation of their performance:

(i)   if the original fixation itself was made without their consent;

(ii)  if the reproduction is made for purposes different from those for which the performers gave their consent;

(iii) if the original fixation was made in accordance with the provisions of Article 15, and the reproduction is made for purposes different from those referred to in those provisions.

2.

(1) If broadcasting was consented to by the performers, it shall be a matter for the domestic law of the Contracting State where protection is claimed to regulate the protection against rebroadcasting, fixation for broadcasting purposes and the reproduction of such fixation for broadcasting purposes.

(2) The terms and conditions governing the use by broadcasting organisations of fixations made for broadcasting purposes shall be determined in accordance with the domestic law of the Contracting State where protection is claimed.

(3) However, the domestic law referred to in sub-paragraphs (1) and (2) of this paragraph shall not operate to deprive performers of the ability to control, by contract, their relations with broadcasting organisations.

## Article 8

Any Contracting State may, by its domestic laws and regulations, specify the manner in which performers will be represented in connexion with the exercise of their rights if several of them participate in the same performance.

## Article 9

Any Contracting State may, by its domestic laws and regulations, extend the protection provided for in this Convention to artists who do not perform literary or artistic works.

## Article 10

Producers of phonograms shall enjoy the right to authorise or prohibit the direct or indirect reproduction of their phonograms.

## Article 11

If, as a condition of protecting the rights of producers of phonograms, or of performers, or both, in relation to phonograms, a Contracting State, under its domestic law, requires compliance with formalities, these shall be considered as fulfilled if all the copies in commerce of the published phonogram or their containers bear a notice consisting of the symbol (P), accompanied by the year date of the first publication, placed in such a manner as to give reasonable notice of claim of protection; and if the copies or their containers do not identify the producer or the licensee of the producer (by carrying his name, trade mark or other appropriate designation), the notice shall also include the name of the owner of the rights of the producer; and, furthermore, if the copies or their containers do not identify the principal performers, the notice shall also include the name of the person who, in the country in which the fixation was effected, owns the rights of such performers.

## Article 12

If a phonogram published for commercial purposes, or a reproduction of such phonogram, is used directly for broadcasting or for any communication to the public, a single equitable remuneration shall be paid by the user to the performers, or to the producers of the phonograms, or to both. Domestic law may, in the absence of agreement between these parties, lay down the conditions as to the sharing of this remuneration.

## Article 13

Broadcasting organisations shall enjoy the right to authorise or prohibit:

(a)  the rebroadcasting of their broadcasts;

(b)  the fixation of their broadcasts;

(c)  the reproduction:

   (i)   of fixations, made without their consent, of their broadcasts;

   (ii)  of fixations, made in accordance with the provisions of Article 15, of their broadcasts, if the reproduction is made for purposes different from those referred to in those provisions;

(d)  the communication to the public of their television broadcasts if such communication is made in places accessible to the public against payment of an entrance fee; it shall be a matter for the domestic law of the State where protection of this right is claimed to determine the conditions under which it may be exercised.

## Article 14

The term of protection to be granted under this Convention shall last at least until the end of a period of twenty years computed from the end of the year in which:

(a)  the fixation was made-for phonograms and for performances incorporated therein;

(b)  the performance took place-for performances not incorporated in phonograms;

(c)  the broadcast took place-for broadcasts.

## Article 15

1.  Any Contracting State may, in its domestic laws and regulations, provide for exceptions to the protection guaranteed by this Convention as regards:

(a)  private use;

(b)  use of short excerpts in connexion with the reporting of current events;

(c)  ephemeral fixation by a broadcasting organisation by means of its own facilities and for its own broadcasts;

(d)  use solely for the purposes of teaching or scientific research.

2.  Irrespective of paragraph 1 of this Article, any Contracting State may, in its domestic laws and regulations, provide for the same kinds of limitations with regard to the protection of performers, producers of phonograms and broadcasting organisations, as it provides for, in its domestic laws and regulations, in connexion with the protection of copyright in literary and artistic works. However, compulsory licenses may be provided for only to the extent to which they are compatible with this Convention.

## Article 16

1.  Any State, upon becoming party to this Convention, shall be bound by all the obligations and shall enjoy all the benefits thereof. However, a State may at any time, in a notification deposited with the Secretary-General of the United Nations, declare that:

(a)  as regards Article 12:

(i)    it will not apply the provisions of that Article;

(ii)   it will not apply the provisions of that Article in respect of certain uses;

(iii)  as regards phonograms the producer of which is not a national of another Contracting State, it will not apply that Article;

(iv)   as regards phonograms the producer of which is a national of another Contracting State, it will limit the protection provided for by that Article to the extent to which, and to the term for which, the latter State grants protection to phonograms first fixed by a national of the State making the declaration; however, the fact that the Contracting State of which the producer is a national does not grant the protection to the same beneficiary or beneficiaries as the State making the declaration shall not be considered as a difference in the extent of the protection;

(b)    as regards Article 13, it will not apply item 13(d); if a Contracting State makes such a declaration, the other Contracting States shall not be obliged to grant the right referred to in Article 13(d), to broadcasting organisations whose headquarters are in that State.

2.   If the notification referred to in paragraph 1 of this Article is made after the date of the deposit of the instrument of ratification, acceptance or accession, the declaration will become effective six months after it has been deposited.

## Article 17

Any State which, on October 26, 1961, grants protection to producers of phonograms solely on the basis of the criterion of fixation may, by a notification deposited with the Secretary-General of the United Nations at the time of ratification, acceptance or accession, declare that it will apply, for the purposes of Article 5, the criterion of fixation alone and, for the purposes of paragraph 16.1(a)(iii) and 16.1(a)(iv), the criterion of fixation instead of the criterion of nationality.

## Article 18

Any State which has deposited a notification under Article 5.3, Article 6.2, Article 16.1 or Article 17, may, by a further notification deposited with the Secretary-General of the United Nations, reduce its scope or withdraw it.

## Article 19

Notwithstanding anything in this Convention, once a performer has consented to the incorporation of his performance in a visual or audio-visual fixation, Article 7 shall have no further application.

## Article 20

1.   This Convention shall not prejudice rights acquired in any Contracting State before the date of coming into force of this Convention for that State.

2.   No Contracting State shall be bound to apply the provisions of this Convention to performances or broadcasts which took place, or to phonograms which were fixed, before the date of coming into force of this Convention for that State.

## Article 21

The protection provided for in this Convention shall not prejudice any protection otherwise secured to performers, producers of phonograms and broadcasting organisations.

## Article 22

Contracting States reserve the right to enter into special agreements among themselves in so far as such agreements grant to performers, producers of phonograms or broadcasting organisations more extensive rights than those granted by this Convention or contain other provisions not contrary to this Convention.

## Article 23

This Convention shall be deposited with the Secretary-General of the United Nations. It shall be open until June 30, 1962, for signature by any State invited to the Diplomatic Conference on the International Protection of Performers, Producers of Phonograms and Broadcasting Organisations which is a party to the Universal Copyright Convention or a member of the International Union for the Protection of Literary and Artistic Works.

## Article 24

1.   This Convention shall be subject to ratification or acceptance by the signatory States.

2.   This Convention shall be open for accession by any State invited to the Conference referred to in Article 23, and by any State Member of the United Nations, provided that in either case such State is a party to the Universal Copyright Convention or a member of the International Union for the Protection of Literary and Artistic Works.

3.   Ratification, acceptance or accession shall be effected by the deposit of an instrument to that effect with the Secretary-General of the United Nations.

## Article 25

1.   This Convention shall come into force three months after the date of deposit of the sixth instrument of ratification, acceptance or accession.

2.   Subsequently, this Convention shall come into force in respect of each State three months after the date of deposit of its instrument of ratification, acceptance or accession.

## Article 26

1.   Each Contracting State undertakes to adopt, in accordance with its Constitution, the measures necessary to ensure the application of this Convention.

2.   At the time of deposit of its instrument of ratification, acceptance or accession, each State must be in a position under its domestic law to give effect to the terms of this Convention.

## Article 27

1.   Any State may, at the time of ratification, acceptance or accession, or at any time thereafter, declare by notification addressed to the Secretary-General of the United Nations that this Convention shall extend to all or any of the territories for whose international relations it is responsible, provided that the Universal Copyright Convention or the International Convention for the Protection of Literary and Artistic Works applies to the territory or territories concerned. This notification shall take effect three months after the date of its receipt.

2.   The notifications referred to in Article 5.3, Article 6.2, Article 16.1 and Articles 17 and 18, may be extended to cover all or any of the territories referred to in paragraph 1 of this Article.

## Article 28

1.   Any Contracting State may denounce this Convention, on its own behalf or on behalf of all or any of the territories referred to in Article 27.

2.  The denunciation shall be effected by a notification addressed to the Secretary-General of the United Nations and shall take effect twelve months after the date of receipt of the notification.

3.  The right of denunciation shall not be exercised by a Contracting State before the expiry of a period of five years from the date on which the Convention came into force with respect to that State.

4.  A Contracting State shall cease to be a party to this Convention from that time when it is neither a party to the Universal Copyright Convention nor a member of the International Union for the Protection of Literary and Artistic Works.

5.  This Convention shall cease to apply to any territory referred to in Article 27 from that time when neither the Universal Copyright Convention nor the International Convention for the Protection of Literary and Artistic Works applies to that territory.

## Article 29

1.  After this Convention has been in force for five years, any Contracting State may, by notification addressed to the Secretary-General of the United Nations, request that a conference be convened for the purpose of revising the Convention. The Secretary-General shall notify all Contracting States of this request. If, within a period of six months following the date of notification by the Secretary-General of the United Nations, not less than one half of the Contracting States notify him of their concurrence with the request, the Secretary-General shall inform the Director-General of the International Labour Office, the Director-General of the United Nations Educational, Scientific and Cultural Organization and the Director of the Bureau of the International Union for the Protection of Literary and Artistic Works, who shall convene a revision conference in co-operation with the Intergovernmental Committee provided for in Article 32.

2.  The adoption of any revision of this Convention shall require an affirmative vote by two-thirds of the States attending the revision conference, provided that this majority includes two-thirds of the States which, at the time of the revision conference, are parties to the Convention.

3.  In the event of adoption of a Convention revising this Convention in whole or in part, and unless the revising Convention provides otherwise:

    (a)  this Convention shall cease to be open to ratification, acceptance or accession as from the date of entry into force of the revising Convention;

    (b)  this Convention shall remain in force as regards relations between or with Contracting States which have not become parties to the revising Convention.

## Article 30

Any dispute which may arise between two or more Contracting States concerning the interpretation or application of this Convention and which is not settled by negotiation shall, at the request of any one of the parties to the dispute, be referred to the International Court of Justice for decision, unless they agree to another mode of settlement.

## Article 31

Without prejudice to the provisions of Article 5.3, Article 6.2, Article 16.1 and Article 17, no reservation may be made to this Convention.

## Article 32

1.  An Intergovernmental Committee is hereby established with the following duties:

    (a)  to study questions concerning the application and operation of this Convention; and

(b)   to collect proposals and to prepare documentation for possible revision of this Convention.

2.   The Committee shall consist of representatives of the Contracting States, chosen with due regard to equitable geographical distribution. The number of members shall be six if there are twelve Contracting States or less, nine if there are thirteen to eighteen Contracting States and twelve if there are more than eighteen Contracting States.

3.   The Committee shall be constituted twelve months after the Convention comes into force by an election organised among the Contracting States, each of which shall have one vote, by the Director-General of the International Labour Office, the Director-General of the United Nations Educational, Scientific and Cultural Organization and the Director of the Bureau of the International Union for the Protection of Literary and Artistic Works, in accordance with rules previously approved by a majority of all Contracting States.

4.   The Committee shall elect its Chairman and officers. It shall establish its own rules of procedure. These rules shall in particular provide for the future operation of the Committee and for a method of selecting its members for the future in such a way as to ensure rotation among the various Contracting States.

5.   Officials of the International Labour Office, the United Nations Educational, Scientific and Cultural Organization and the Bureau of the International Union for the Protection of Literary and Artistic Works, designated by the Directors-General and the Director thereof, shall constitute the Secretariat of the Committee.

6.   Meetings of the Committee, which shall be convened whenever a majority of its members deems it necessary, shall be held successively at the headquarters of the International Labour Office, the United Nations Educational, Scientific and Cultural Organization and the Bureau of the International Union for the Protection of Literary and Artistic Works.

7.   Expenses of members of the Committee shall be borne by their respective Governments.

## Article 33

1.   The present Convention is drawn up in English, French and Spanish, the three texts being equally authentic.

2.   In addition, official texts of the present Convention shall be drawn up in German, Italian and Portuguese.

## Article 34

1.   The Secretary-General of the United Nations shall notify the States invited to the Conference referred to in Article 23 and every State Member of the United Nations, as well as the Director-General of the International Labour Office, the Director-General of the United Nations Educational, Scientific and Cultural Organization and the Director of the Bureau of the International Union for the Protection of Literary and Artistic Works:

(a)   of the deposit of each instrument of ratification, acceptance or accession;

(b)   of the date of entry into force of the Convention;

(c)   of all notifications, declarations or communications provided for in this Convention;

(d)   if any of the situations referred to in paragraphs 28.4 and 28.5 arise.

2.   The Secretary-General of the United Nations shall also notify the Director-General of the International Labour Office, the Director-General of the United Nations Educational, Scientific and Cultural Organization and the Director of the Bureau of the International Union for the Protection of Literary and Artistic Works of the requests communicated to him in accordance with Article 29, as well as of any communication received from the Contracting States concerning the revision of the Convention.

# 20. PARTIES TO THE INTERNATIONAL CONVENTION FOR THE PROTECTION OF PERFORMERS, PRODUCERS OF PHONOGRAMS AND BROADCASTING ORGANISATIONS*

Rome Convention (1961)

**Status on May 4, 2021**

| State | Date on which State became party to the Convention |
| --- | --- |
| Albania | September 1, 2000 |
| Algeria | April 22, 2007 |
| Andorra | May 25, 2004 |
| Argentina | March 2, 1992 |
| Armenia | January 31, 2003 |
| Australia[1] | September 30, 1992 |
| Austria[1] | June 9, 1973 |
| Azerbaijan | October 8, 2005 |
| Bahrain | January 18, 2006 |
| Barbados | September 18, 1983 |
| Belarus[1] | May 27, 2003 |
| Belgium[1] | October 2, 1999 |
| Belize | February 9, 2019 |
| Bolivia (Plurinational State of) | November 24, 1993 |
| Bosnia and Herzegovina | May 19, 2009 |
| Brazil | September 29, 1965 |
| Bulgaria[1] | August 31, 1995 |
| Burkina Faso | January 14, 1988 |
| Cabo Verde | July 3, 1997 |
| Canada[1] | June 4, 1998 |
| Chile | September 5, 1974 |
| Colombia | September 17, 1976 |
| Congo[1] | May 18, 1964 |
| Costa Rica | September 9, 1971 |
| Croatia[1] | April 20, 2000 |
| Cyprus | June 17, 2009 |
| Czech Republic[1] | January 1, 1993 |
| Denmark[1] | September 23, 1965 |
| Dominica | November 9, 1999 |
| Dominican Republic | January 27, 1987 |

---

* Document originally produced by the World Intellectual Property Organization (WIPO), the owner of the copyright. Published with the permission of the World Intellectual Property Organization.

| State | Date on which State became party to the Convention |
| --- | --- |
| Ecuador | May 18, 1964 |
| El Salvador | June 29, 1979 |
| Estonia[1] | April 28, 2000 |
| Fiji[1] | April 11, 1972 |
| Finland[1] | October 21, 1983 |
| France[1] | July 3, 1987 |
| Georgia | August 14, 2004 |
| Germany[1] | October 21, 1966 |
| Greece | January 6, 1993 |
| Guatemala | January 14, 1977 |
| Honduras | February 16, 1990 |
| Hungary | February 10, 1995 |
| Iceland[1] | June 15, 1994 |
| Ireland[1] | September 19, 1979 |
| Israel[1] | December 30, 2002 |
| Italy[1] | April 8, 1975 |
| Jamaica | January 27, 1994 |
| Japan[1] | October 26, 1989 |
| Kazakhstan | June 30, 2012 |
| Kyrgyzstan | August 13, 2003 |
| Latvia[1] | August 20, 1999 |
| Lebanon | August 12, 1997 |
| Lesotho[1] | January 26, 1990 |
| Liberia | December 16, 2005 |
| Liechtenstein[1] | October 12, 1999 |
| Lithuania[1] | July 22, 1999 |
| Luxembourg[1] | February 25, 1976 |
| Mexico | May 18, 1964 |
| Monaco | December 6, 1985 |
| Montenegro[2] | June 3, 2006 |
| Netherlands[1,3] | October 7, 1993 |
| Nicaragua | August 10, 2000 |
| Niger[1] | May 18, 1964 |
| Nigeria[1] | October 29, 1993 |
| North Macedonia[1] | March 2, 1998 |
| Norway[1] | July 10, 1978 |
| Panama | September 2, 1983 |
| Paraguay | February 26, 1970 |
| Peru | August 7, 1985 |
| Philippines | September 25, 1984 |
| Poland[1] | June 13, 1997 |

## PARTIES TO THE ROME CONVENTION

| State | Date on which State became party to the Convention |
| --- | --- |
| Portugal | July 17, 2002 |
| Qatar | September 23, 2017 |
| Republic of Korea[1] | March 18, 2009 |
| Republic of Moldova[1] | December 5, 1995 |
| Romania[1] | October 22, 1998 |
| Russian Federation[1] | May 26, 2003 |
| Saint Lucia[1] | August 17, 1996 |
| Serbia | June 10, 2003 |
| Slovakia[1] | January 1, 1993 |
| Slovenia[1] | October 9, 1996 |
| Spain[1] | November 14, 1991 |
| Sweden[1] | May 18, 1964 |
| Switzerland[1] | September 24, 1993 |
| Syrian Arab Republic | May 13, 2006 |
| Tajikistan | May 19, 2008 |
| Togo | June 10, 2003 |
| Trinidad and Tobago | March 9, 2020 |
| Turkey | April 8, 2004 |
| Turkmenistan | November 30, 2020 |
| Ukraine | June 12, 2002 |
| United Arab Emirates | January 14, 2005 |
| United Kingdom[1,4] | May 18, 1964 |
| Uruguay | July 4, 1977 |
| Venezuela (Bolivarian Republic of) | January 30, 1996 |
| Viet Nam[5] | March 1, 2007 |

(Total: 96 States)

---

*    The secretariat tasks relating to this Convention are performed jointly with the International Labour Office and UNESCO.

[1]    The instruments of ratification or accession, or subsequent notifications, deposited with the Secretary-General of the United Nations by the following States contain declarations made under the articles mentioned hereafter (with reference to publication in *Le Droit d'auteur* (Copyright) for the years 1962 to 1964, in *Copyright* for the years 1965 to 1994, in *Industrial Property and Copyright* until May 1998 and, in *Intellectual Property Laws and Treaties* from June 1998 until December 2001):

Algeria, Articles 5(3) (concerning Article 5(1)(c)), Article 6(2) and 16(1)(a)(iii) and (iv);

Australia, Articles 5(3) (concerning Article 5(1)(c)), 6(2), 16(1)(a)(i) and 16(1)(b) [1992, p. 301];

Austria, Article 16(1)(a)(iii) and (iv) and 1(b) [1973, p. 67];

Belarus, Articles 5(3) (concerning Article 5(1)(b)), 6(2), 16(1)(a)(iii) and (iv);

Belgium, Articles 5(3) (concerning Article 5(1)(c)), 6(2), 16(1)(a)(iii) and (iv) [1999, p. 119];

Bulgaria, Article 16(1)(a)(iii) and (iv) [1995, p. 262];

Canada, Article 5(3) (concerning Articles 5(1)(b) and (c)), 6(2) (concerning Article 6(1)) and 16(1)(a)(iv) [1998, p. 42]

Congo, Articles 5(3) (concerning Article 5(1)(c)) and 16(1)(a)(i) [1964, p. 127];

Croatia, Articles 5(3) (concerning Article 5(1)(b)) and 16(1)(a)(iii) and (iv) [2000, p.14];

Czech Republic, Article 16(1)(a)(iii) and (iv) [1964, p. 110];

Denmark, Articles 5(3) (concerning Article 5(1)(c)), 6(2), 16(1)(a)(ii) and (iv) [1965, p. 214];

Estonia, Articles 5(3) (concerning Article 5(1)(c)), and 6(2), and as from October 9, 2003, Article 16(1)(a)(iv);

Fiji, Articles 5(3) (concerning Article 5(1)(b)), 6(2) and 16(1)(a)(i) [1972, pp. 88 and 178];

Finland, Articles 16(1)(a)(i), (ii) and (iv) and 17 [1983, p. 287 and 1994, p. 152];

France, Articles 5(3) (concerning Article 5(1)(c)) and 16(1)(a)(iii) and (iv) [1987, p. 184];

Germany, Articles 5(3) (concerning Article 5(1)(b)) and 16(1)(a)(iv) [1966, p. 237];

Iceland, Articles 5(3) (concerning Article 5(1)(b)), 6(2) and 16(1)(a)(i), (ii), (iii) and (iv) [1994, p. 152];

Ireland, Articles 5(3) (concerning Article 5(1)(b)), 6(2) and 16(1)(a)(ii) [1979, p. 218];

Israel, Articles 5(3) (concerning Article 5(1)(b)), 6(2) (concerning Article 6(1)) and 16(1)(a)(iii), (iv) and 16(1)(b);

Italy, Articles 6(2), 16(1)(a)(ii), (iii) and (iv), 16(1)(b) and 17 [1975, p. 44];

Japan, Articles 5(3) (concerning Article 5(1)(c)) and 16(1)(a)(ii) and (iv) [1989, p. 288];

Latvia, Article 16(1)(a)(iii) [1999, p. 76];

Lesotho, Article 16(1)(a)(ii) and (1)(b) [1990, p. 95];

Liechtenstein, Article 5(3) (concerning Article 5(1)(b)) and Article 16(1)(a)(iii) and (iv) [1999, p. 119];

Lithuania, Article 16(1)(a)(iii) [1999, p. 76];

Luxembourg, Articles 5(3) (concerning Article 5(1)(c)), 16(1)(a)(i) and 16(1)(b) [1976, p. 24];

Monaco, Articles 5(3) (concerning Article 5(1)(c)), 16(1)(a)(i) and 16(1)(b) [1985, p. 422];

Netherlands, Article 16(1)(a)(iii) and (iv) [1993, p. 253];

Niger, Articles 5(3) (concerning Article 5(1)(c)) and 16(1)(a)(i) [1963, p. 155];

Nigeria, Articles 5(3) (concerning Article 5(1)(c)), 6(2) and 16(1)(a)(ii), (iii) and (iv) [1993, p. 253];

North Macedonia, Articles 5(3) (concerning Article 5(1)(c)) and 16(1)(a)(i) [1998, p. 42];

Norway, Articles 6(2) and 16(1)(a)(iii) and (iv) [1978, p. 133; in respect of 16(1)(a)(ii) modified: 1989, p. 288];

Poland, Articles 5(3) (concerning Article 5(1)(c)), 6(2), 16(1)(a)(i), (iii) and (iv) and 16(1)(b) [1997 p. 170];

Republic of Korea, Articles 5(3), 6(2), 16(1)(a)(ii), (iii) and (iv) and 16(1)(b);

Republic of Moldova, Articles 5(3) (concerning Article 5(1)(b)), 6(2), 16(1)(a)(ii), (iii) and (iv) [1996, p. 40];

Romania, Articles 5(3), 6(2), 16(1)(a)(iii) and (iv) [1998, p. 54];

Russian Federation, Articles 5(3) (concerning Article 5(1)(b)), 6(2) and 16(1)(a)(iii) and (iv);

Saint Lucia, Articles 5(3) (concerning Article 5(1)(c)) and 16(1)(a)(iii);

Slovakia, Article 16(1)(a)(iii) and (iv) [1964, p. 110];

Slovenia, Articles 5(3) (concerning Article 5(1)(c)) and 16(1)(a)(i) [1996, p. 318];

Spain, Articles 5(3) (concerning Article 5(1)(c)), 6(2) and 16(1)(a)(iii) and (iv) [1991, p. 221];

Sweden, Article 16(1)(a)(iv) [1962, p. 211; 1986, p. 382];

Switzerland, Articles 5(3) (concerning Article 5(1)(b)) and 16(1)(a)(iii) and (iv) [1993, p. 254];

United Kingdom, Articles 5(3) (concerning Article 5(1)(b)), 6(2) and 16(1)(a)(ii), (iii) and (iv) [1963, p. 244]; the same declarations were made for Gibraltar and Bermuda [1967, p. 36; 1970, p. 108].

²    Deposited declaration on October 23, 2006, with effect from June 3, 2006, the date of State succession.

# PARTIES TO THE ROME CONVENTION

[3] Accession for the Kingdom in Europe.

[4] The United Kingdom extended the application of the Rome Convention to the Isle of Man with effect from July 28, 1999.

[5] This State has declared that in accordance with Articles 16(1)(a)(i) and 16(1)(b), it will not apply the provisions of Articles 12 and 13(d).

# 21. CONVENTION FOR THE PROTECTION OF PRODUCERS OF PHONOGRAMS AGAINST UNAUTHORIZED DUPLICATION OF THEIR PHONOGRAMS

of October 29, 1971

(Geneva Phonograms Convention)

*The Contracting States,*

*concerned at the widespread and increasing unauthorized duplication of phonograms and the damage this is occasioning to the interests of authors, performers and producers of phonograms;*

*convinced that the protection of producers of phonograms against such acts will also benefit the performers whose performances, and the authors whose works, are recorded on the said phonograms;*

*recognizing the value of the work undertaken in this field by the United Nations Educational, Scientific and Cultural Organization and the World Intellectual Property Organization;*

*anxious not to impair in any way international agreements already in force and in particular in no way to prejudice wider acceptance of the Rome Convention of October 26, 1961, which affords protection to performers and to broadcasting organizations as well as to producers of phonograms;*

*have agreed as follows:*

## Article 1

For the purposes of this Convention:

(a) "phonogram" means any exclusively aural fixation of sounds of a performance or of other sounds;

(b) "producer of phonograms" means the person who, or the legal entity which, first fixes the sounds of a performance or other sounds;

(c) "duplicate" means an article which contains sounds taken directly or indirectly from a phonogram and which embodies all or a substantial part of the sounds fixed in that phonogram;

(d) "distribution to the public" means any act by which duplicates of a phonogram are offered, directly or indirectly, to the general public or any section thereof.

## Article 2

Each Contracting State shall protect producers of phonograms who are nationals of other Contracting States against the making of duplicates without the consent of the producer and against the importation of such duplicates, provided that any such making or importation is for the purpose of distribution to the public, and against the distribution of such duplicates to the public.

## Article 3

The means by which this Convention is implemented shall be a matter for the domestic law of each Contracting State and shall include one or more of the following: protection by means of the grant of a copyright or other specific right; protection by means of the law relating to unfair competition; protection by means of penal sanctions.

## Article 4

The duration of the protection given shall be a matter for the domestic law of each Contracting State. However, if the domestic law prescribes a specific duration for the protection, that duration shall not be less than twenty years from the end either of the year in which the sounds embodied in the phonogram were first fixed or of the year in which the phonogram was first published.

## Article 5

If, as a condition of protecting the producers of phonograms, a Contracting State, under its domestic law, requires compliance with formalities, these shall be considered as fulfilled if all the authorized duplicates of the phonogram distributed to the public or their containers bear a notice consisting of the symbol (P), accompanied by the year date of the first publication, placed in such manner as to give reasonable notice of claim of protection; and, if the duplicates or their containers do not identify the producer, his successor in title or the exclusive licensee (by carrying his name, trademark or other appropriate designation), the notice shall also include the name of the producer, his successor in title or the exclusive licensee.

## Article 6

Any Contracting State which affords protection by means of copyright or other specific right, or protection by means of penal sanctions, may in its domestic law provide, with regard to the protection of producers of phonograms, the same kinds of limitations as are permitted with respect to the protection of authors of literary and artistic works. However, no compulsory licenses may be permitted unless all of the following conditions are met:

(a)  the duplication is for use solely for the purpose of teaching or scientific research;

(b)  the license shall be valid for duplication only within the territory of the Contracting State whose competent authority has granted the license and shall not extend to the export of duplicates;

(c)  the duplication made under the license gives rise to an equitable remuneration fixed by the said authority taking into account, inter alia, the number of duplicates which will be made.

## Article 7

(1)  This Convention shall in no way be interpreted to limit or prejudice the protection otherwise secured to authors, to performers, to producers of phonograms or to broadcasting organizations under any domestic law or international agreement.

(2)  It shall be a matter for the domestic law of each Contracting State to determine the extent, if any, to which performers whose performances are fixed in a phonogram are entitled to enjoy protection and the conditions for enjoying any such protection.

(3)  No Contracting State shall be required to apply the provisions of this Convention to any phonogram fixed before this Convention entered into force with respect to that State.

(4)  Any Contracting State which, on October 29, 1971, affords protection to producers of phonograms solely on the basis of the place of first fixation may, by a notification deposited with the Director General of the World Intellectual Property Organization, declare that it will apply this criterion instead of the criterion of the nationality of the producer.

## Article 8

(1)  The International Bureau of the World Intellectual Property Organization shall assemble and publish information concerning the protection of phonograms. Each Contracting State shall promptly communicate to the International Bureau all new laws and official texts on this subject.

(2)  The International Bureau shall, on request, furnish information to any Contracting State on matters concerning this Convention, and shall conduct studies and provide services designed to facilitate the protection provided for therein.

(3)  The International Bureau shall exercise the functions enumerated in paragraph (1) and paragraph (2) above in cooperation, for matters within their respective competence, with the

United Nations Educational, Scientific and Cultural Organization and the International Labour Organisation.

## Article 9

(1) This Convention shall be deposited with the Secretary-General of the United Nations. It shall be open until April 30, 1972, for signature by any State that is a member of the United Nations, any of the Specialized Agencies brought into relationship with the United Nations, or the International Atomic Energy Agency, or is a party to the Statute of the International Court of Justice.

(2) This Convention shall be subject to ratification or acceptance by the signatory States. It shall be open for accession by any State referred to in paragraph (1) of this Article.

(3) Instruments of ratification, acceptance or accession shall be deposited with the Secretary-General of the United Nations.

(4) It is understood that, at the time a State becomes bound by this Convention, it will be in a position in accordance with its domestic law to give effect to the provisions of the Convention.

## Article 10

No reservations to this Convention are permitted.

## Article 11

(1) This Convention shall enter into force three months after deposit of the fifth instrument of ratification, acceptance or accession.

(2) For each State ratifying, accepting or acceding to this Convention after the deposit of the fifth instrument of ratification, acceptance or accession, the Convention shall enter into force three months after the date on which the Director General of the World Intellectual Property Organization informs the States, in accordance with Article 13(4), of the deposit of its instrument.

(3) Any State may, at the time of ratification, acceptance or accession or at any later date, declare by notification addressed to the Secretary-General of the United Nations that this Convention shall apply to all or any one of the territories for whose international affairs it is responsible. This notification will take effect three months after the date on which it is received.

(4) However, the preceding paragraph may in no way be understood as implying the recognition or tacit acceptance by a Contracting State of the factual situation concerning a territory to which this Convention is made applicable by another Contracting State by virtue of the said paragraph.

## Article 12

(1) Any Contracting State may denounce this Convention, on its own behalf or on behalf of any of the territories referred to in Article 11(3), by written notification addressed to the Secretary-General of the United Nations.

(2) Denunciation shall take effect twelve months after the date on which the Secretary-General of the United Nations has received the notification.

## Article 13

(1) This Convention shall be signed in a single copy in English, French, Russian and Spanish, the four texts being equally authentic.

(2) Official texts shall be established by the Director General of the World Intellectual Property Organization, after consultation with the interested Governments, in the Arabic, Dutch, German, Italian and Portuguese languages.

(3) The Secretary-General of the United Nations shall notify the Director General of the World Intellectual Property Organization, the Director-General of the United Nations Educational, Scientific and Cultural Organization and the Director-General of the International Labour Office of:

(a) signatures to this Convention;

(b) the deposit of instruments of ratification, acceptance or accession;

(c) the date of entry into force of this Convention;

(d) any declaration notified pursuant to Article 11(3);

(e) the receipt of notifications of denunciation.

(4) The Director General of the World Intellectual Property Organization shall inform the States referred to in Article 9(1), of the notifications received pursuant to the preceding paragraph and of any declarations made under Article 7(4). He shall also notify the Director-General of the United Nations Educational, Scientific and Cultural Organization and the Director-General of the International Labour Office of such declarations.

(5) The Secretary-General of the United Nations shall transmit two certified copies of this Convention to the States referred to in Article 9(1).

# 22. PARTIES TO THE CONVENTION FOR THE PROTECTION OF PRODUCERS OF PHONOGRAMS AGAINST UNAUTHORIZED DUPLICATION OF THEIR PHONOGRAMS*

Phonograms Convention (Geneva, 1971)

**Status on May 4, 2021**

| State | Date on which State became party to the Convention |
|---|---|
| Albania | June 26, 2001 |
| Argentina | June 30, 1973 |
| Armenia | January 31, 2003 |
| Australia | June 22, 1974 |
| Austria | August 21, 1982 |
| Azerbaijan | September 1, 2001 |
| Barbados | July 29, 1983 |
| Belarus | April 17, 2003 |
| Bosnia and Herzegovina | May 25, 2009 |
| Brazil | November 28, 1975 |
| Bulgaria | September 6, 1995 |
| Burkina Faso | January 30, 1988 |
| Chile | March 24, 1977 |
| China[1] | April 30, 1993 |
| Colombia | May 16, 1994 |
| Costa Rica | June 17, 1982 |
| Croatia | April 20, 2000 |
| Cyprus | September 30, 1993 |
| Czech Republic | January 1, 1993 |
| Democratic Republic of the Congo | November 29, 1977 |
| Denmark | March 24, 1977 |
| Ecuador | September 14, 1974 |
| Egypt | April 23, 1978 |
| El Salvador | February 9, 1979 |
| Estonia | May 28, 2000 |
| Fiji | April 18, 1973 |
| Finland[2] | April 18, 1973 |
| France | April 18, 1973 |
| Germany | May 18, 1974 |
| Ghana | February 10, 2017 |

---

## PARTIES TO THE GENEVA CONVENTION

| State | Date on which State became party to the Convention |
|---|---|
| Greece | February 9, 1994 |
| Guatemala | February 1, 1977 |
| Holy See | July 18, 1977 |
| Honduras | March 6, 1990 |
| Hungary | May 28, 1975 |
| India | February 12, 1975 |
| Israel | May 1, 1978 |
| Italy[2] | March 24, 1977 |
| Jamaica | January 11, 1994 |
| Japan | October 14, 1978 |
| Kazakhstan | August 3, 2001 |
| Kenya | April 21, 1976 |
| Kyrgyzstan | October 12, 2002 |
| Latvia | August 23, 1997 |
| Liberia | December 16, 2005 |
| Liechtenstein | October 12, 1999 |
| Lithuania | January 27, 2000 |
| Luxembourg | March 8, 1976 |
| Mexico | December 21, 1973 |
| Monaco | December 2, 1974 |
| Montenegro[3] | June 3, 2006 |
| Netherlands[4] | October 12, 1993 |
| New Zealand | August 13, 1976 |
| Nicaragua | August 10, 2000 |
| North Macedonia | March 2, 1998 |
| Norway | August 1, 1978 |
| Panama | June 29, 1974 |
| Paraguay | February 13, 1979 |
| Peru | August 24, 1985 |
| Republic of Korea | October 10, 1987 |
| Republic of Moldova | July 17, 2000 |
| Romania | October 1, 1998 |
| Russian Federation | March 13, 1995 |
| Saint Lucia | April 2, 2001 |
| Serbia | June 10, 2003 |
| Slovakia | January 1, 1993 |
| Slovenia | October 15, 1996 |
| Spain | August 24, 1974 |
| Sweden | April 18, 1973 |
| Switzerland | September 30, 1993 |
| Tajikistan | February 26, 2013 |

## PARTIES TO THE GENEVA CONVENTION

| State | Date on which State became party to the Convention |
| --- | --- |
| Togo | June 10, 2003 |
| Trinidad and Tobago | October 1, 1988 |
| Ukraine | February 18, 2000 |
| United Kingdom | April 18, 1973 |
| United States of America | March 10, 1974 |
| Uruguay | January 18, 1983 |
| Uzbekistan | April 25, 2019 |
| Venezuela (Bolivarian Republic of) | November 18, 1982 |
| Viet Nam | July 6, 2005 |

(Total: 80 States)

---

[1]   The Phonograms Convention applies also to Hong Kong, China with effect from July 1, 1997.

[2]   This State has declared, in accordance with Article 7(4) of the Convention, that it will apply the criterion according to which it affords protection to producers of phonograms solely on the basis of the place of first fixation instead of the criterion of the nationality of the producer.

[3]   Deposited declaration on October 23, 2006, with effect June 3, 2006, the date of State succession.

[4]   Accession for the Kingdom in Europe.

# 23. CONVENTION RELATING TO THE DISTRIBUTION OF PROGRAMME-CARRYING SIGNALS TRANSMITTED BY SATELLITE

Done at Brussels on May 21, 1974

(Brussels Satellite Convention)

*The Contracting States,*

*Aware that the use of satellites for the distribution of programme-carrying signals is rapidly growing both in volume and geographical coverage;*

*Concerned that there is no world-wide system to prevent distributors from distributing programme-carrying signals transmitted by satellite which were not intended for those distributors, and that this lack is likely to hamper the use of satellite communications;*

*Recognizing, in this respect, the importance of the interests of authors, performers, producers of phonograms and broadcasting organizations;*

*Convinced that an international system should be established under which measures would be provided to prevent distributors from distributing programme-carrying signals transmitted by satellite which were not intended for those distributors;*

*Conscious of the need not to impair in any way international agreements already in force, including the International Telecommunication Convention and the Radio Regulations annexed to that Convention, and in particular in no way to prejudice wider acceptance of the Rome Convention of October 26, 1961, which affords protection to performers, producers of phonograms and broadcasting organizations,*

*Have agreed as follows:*

## Article 1

For the purposes of this Convention:

(i) "signal" is an electronically-generated carrier capable of transmitting programmes;

(ii) "programme" is a body of live or recorded material consisting of images, sounds or both, embodied in signals emitted for the purpose of ultimate distribution;

(iii) "satellite" is any device in extraterrestrial space capable of transmitting signals;

(iv) "emitted signal" or "signal emitted" is any programme-carrying signal that goes to or passes through a satellite;

(v) "derived signal" is a signal obtained by modifying the technical characteristics of the emitted signal, whether or not there have been one or more intervening fixations;

(vi) "originating organization" is the person or legal entity that decides what programme the emitted signals will carry;

(vii) "distributor" is the person or legal entity that decides that the transmission of the derived signals to the general public or any section thereof should take place;

(viii)"distribution" is the operation by which a distributor transmits derived signals to the general public or any section thereof.

## Article 2

(1) Each Contracting State undertakes to take adequate measures to prevent the distribution on or from its territory of any programme-carrying signal by any distributor for whom the signal emitted to or passing through the satellite is not intended. This obligation shall apply where the originating organization is a national of another Contracting State and where the signal distributed is a derived signal.

(2) In any Contracting State in which the application of the measures referred to in paragraph (1) is limited in time, the duration thereof shall be fixed by its domestic law. The Secretary-General of the United Nations shall be notified in writing of such duration at the time of ratification, acceptance or accession, or if the domestic law comes into force or is changed thereafter, within six months of the coming into force of that law or of its modification.

(3) The obligation provided for in paragraph (1) shall not apply to the distribution of derived signals taken from signals which have already been distributed by a distributor for whom the emitted signals were intended.

## Article 3

This Convention shall not apply where the signals emitted by or on behalf of the originating organization are intended for direct reception from the satellite by the general public.

## Article 4

No Contracting State shall be required to apply the measures referred to in Article 2(1) where the signal distributed on its territory by a distributor for whom the emitted signal is not intended

(i) carries short excerpts of the programme carried by the emitted signal, consisting of reports of current events, but only to the extent justified by the informatory purpose of such excerpts, or

(ii) carries, as quotations, short excerpts of the programme carried by the emitted signal, provided that such quotations are compatible with fair practice and are justified by the informatory purpose of such quotations, or

(iii) carries, where the said territory is that of a Contracting State regarded as a developing country in conformity with the established practice of the General Assembly of the United Nations, a programme carried by the emitted signal, provided that the distribution is solely for the purpose of teaching, including teaching in the framework of adult education, or scientific research.

## Article 5

No Contracting State shall be required to apply this Convention with respect to any signal emitted before this Convention entered into force for that State.

## Article 6

This Convention shall in no way be interpreted to limit or prejudice the protection secured to authors, performers, producers of phonograms, or broadcasting organizations, under any domestic law or international agreement.

## Article 7

This Convention shall in no way be interpreted as limiting the right of any Contracting State to apply its domestic law in order to prevent abuses of monopoly.

## Article 8

(1) Subject to paragraph (2) and paragraph (3), no reservation to this Convention shall be permitted.

(2) Any Contracting State whose domestic law, on May 21, 1974, so provides may, by a written notification deposited with the Secretary-General of the United Nations, declare that, for its purposes, the words "where the originating organization is a national of another Contracting State" appearing in Article 2(1) shall be considered as if they were replaced by the words "where the signal is emitted from the territory of another Contracting State."

(3)

    (a) Any Contracting State which, on May 21, 1974, limits or denies protection with respect to the distribution of programme-carrying signals by means of wires, cable or other similar communications channels to subscribing members of the public may, by a written notification deposited with the Secretary-General of the United Nations, declare that, to the extent that and as long as its domestic law limits or denies protection, it will not apply this Convention to such distributions.

    (b) Any State that has deposited a notification in accordance with subparagraph (a) shall notify the Secretary-General of the United Nations in writing, within six months of their coming into force, of any changes in its domestic law whereby the reservation under that subparagraph becomes inapplicable or more limited in scope.

## Article 9

(1) This Convention shall be deposited with the Secretary-General of the United Nations. It shall be open until March 31, 1975, for signature by any State that is a member of the United Nations, any of the Specialized Agencies brought into relationship with the United Nations, or the International Atomic Energy Agency, or is a party to the Statute of the International Court of Justice.

(2) This Convention shall be subject to ratification or acceptance by the signatory States. It shall be open for accession by any State referred to in paragraph (1).

(3) Instruments of ratification, acceptance or accession shall be deposited with the Secretary-General of the United Nations.

(4) It is understood that, at the time a State becomes bound by this Convention, it will be in a position in accordance with its domestic law to give effect to the provisions of the Convention.

## Article 10

(1) This Convention shall enter into force three months after the deposit of the fifth instrument of ratification, acceptance or accession.

(2) For each State ratifying, accepting or acceding to this Convention after the deposit of the fifth instrument of ratification, acceptance or accession, this Convention shall enter into force three months after the deposit of its instrument.

## Article 11

(1) Any Contracting State may denounce this Convention by written notification deposited with the Secretary-General of the United Nations.

(2) Denunciation shall take effect twelve months after the date on which the notification referred to in paragraph (1) is received.

## Article 12

(1) This Convention shall be signed in a single copy in English, French, Russian and Spanish, the four texts being equally authentic.

(2) Official texts shall be established by the Director-General of the United Nations Educational, Scientific and Cultural Organization and the Director General of the World Intellectual Property Organization, after consultation with the interested Governments, in the Arabic, Dutch, German, Italian and Portuguese languages.

(3) The Secretary-General of the United Nations shall notify the States referred to in Article 9(1), as well as the Director-General of the United Nations Educational, Scientific and Cultural Organization, the Director General of the World Intellectual Property Organization, the Director-General of the International Labour Office and the Secretary-General of the International Telecommunication Union, of

   (i) signatures to this Convention;

   (ii) the deposit of instruments of ratification, acceptance or accession;

   (iii) the date of entry into force of this Convention under Article 10(1);

   (iv) the deposit of any notification relating to Article 2(2), Article 8(2) or Article 8(3), together with its text;

   (v) the receipt of notifications of denunciation.

(4) The Secretary-General of the United Nations shall transmit two certified copies of this Convention to all States referred to in Article 9(1).

# 24. PARTIES TO THE CONVENTION RELATING TO THE DISTRIBUTION OF PROGRAMME-CARRYING SIGNALS TRANSMITTED BY SATELLITE*

Satellites Convention (Brussels, 1974)

**Status on May 4, 2021**

| State | Date on which State became party to the Convention |
| --- | --- |
| Armenia | December 13, 1993 |
| Australia | October 26, 1990 |
| Austria | August 6, 1982 |
| Bahrain | May 1, 2007 |
| Benin | August 18, 2017 |
| Bosnia and Herzegovina | March 6, 1992 |
| Chile | June 8, 2011 |
| Colombia | March 20, 2014 |
| Costa Rica | June 25, 1999 |
| Croatia | October 8, 1991 |
| El Salvador[1] | July 22, 2008 |
| Germany[2] | August 25, 1979 |
| Greece | October 22, 1991 |
| Honduras | April 7, 2008 |
| Italy[2] | July 7, 1981 |
| Jamaica | January 12, 2000 |
| Kenya | August 25, 1979 |
| Mexico | August 25, 1979 |
| Montenegro | June 3, 2006[3] |
| Morocco | June 30, 1983 |
| Nicaragua | August 25, 1979 |
| North Macedonia | November 17, 1991 |
| Panama | September 25, 1985 |
| Peru | August 7, 1985 |
| Portugal | March 11, 1996 |
| Republic of Korea | March 19, 2012 |
| Republic of Moldova | October 28, 2008 |
| Russian Federation | January 20, 1989[4] |
| Rwanda | July 25, 2001 |
| Serbia | April 27, 1992 |
| Singapore | April 27, 2005 |

## *PARTIES TO THE BRUSSELS SATELLITE CONVENTION*

| State | Date on which State became party to the Convention |
|---|---|
| Slovenia | June 25, 1991 |
| Switzerland | September 24, 1993 |
| Togo | June 10, 2003 |
| Trinidad and Tobago[5] | November 1, 1996 |
| United States of America | March 7, 1985 |
| Viet Nam | January 12, 2006 |

(Total: 38 States)

---

[1]   With a declaration, pursuant to Article 2(2) of the Convention, the Salvadorian law does not set a limit on the length of authorization for the distribution of a programme-carrying signal and leaves it open for the owner of the programme to determine the length of authorization when granting the permit or authorization.

[2]   With a declaration, pursuant to Article 2(2) of the Convention, that the protection accorded under Article 2(1) is restricted in its territory to a period of 25 years after the expiry of the calendar year in which the transmission by satellite has occurred.

[3]   Deposited declaration, on October 23, 2006, with effect from June 3, 2006, the date of State succession.

[4]   Date of accession by the Soviet Union, continued by the Russian Federation as from December 25, 1991.

[5]   With a declaration, pursuant to Article 2(2) of the Convention, that the protection accorded under Article 2(1) is restricted in its territory to a period of 20 years after the expiry of the calendar year in which the transmission by satellite has occurred.

# 25. TREATY ON THE INTERNATIONAL REGISTRATION OF AUDIOVISUAL WORKS

Adopted at Geneva April 18, 1989

*Contents*

**Preamble**

## CHAPTER 1: SUBSTANTIVE PROVISIONS

## CHAPTER II: ADMINISTRATIVE PROVISIONS

## CHAPTER III: REVISION AND AMENDMENT

## CHAPTER IV: FINAL PROVISIONS

---

The Contracting States

*Desirous* to increase the legal security in transactions relating to audiovisual works and thereby to enhance the creation of audiovisual works and the international flow of such works and to contribute to the fight against piracy of audiovisual works and contributions contained therein;

*Have agreed* as follows:

## CHAPTER I
## SUBSTANTIVE PROVISIONS

### Article 1

### Establishment of the Union

The States party to this Treaty (hereinafter called "the Contracting States") constitute a Union for the international registration of audiovisual works (hereinafter referred to as "the Union").

213

## Article 2

### "Audiovisual Work"

For the purposes of this Treaty, "audiovisual work" means any work that consists of a series of fixed related images, with or without accompanying sound, susceptible of being made visible and, where accompanied by sound, susceptible of being made audible.

## Article 3

### The International Register

(1)  The International Register of Audiovisual Works (hereinafter referred to as "the International Register") is hereby established for the purpose of the registration of statements concerning audiovisual works and rights in such works, including, in particular, rights relating to their exploitation.

(2)  The International Registry of Audiovisual Works (hereinafter referred to as "the International Registry") is hereby set up for the purpose of keeping the International Register. It is an administrative unit of the International Bureau of the World Intellectual Property Organization (hereinafter referred to as "the International Bureau" and "the Organization," respectively).

(3)  The International Registry shall be located in Austria as long as a treaty to that effect between the Republic of Austria and the Organization is in force. Otherwise, it shall be located in Geneva.

(4)  The registration of any statement in the International Register shall be based on an application filed to this effect, with the prescribed contents, in the prescribed form and subject to the payment of the prescribed fee, by a natural person or legal entity entitled to file an application.

(5)  *(a)*  Subject to subparagraph *(b)*, the following shall be entitled to file an application:

    (i)  any natural person who is a national of, is domiciled in, has his habitual residence in, or has a real and effective industrial or commercial establishment in, a Contracting State.

    (ii)  any legal entity which is organized under the laws of, or has a real and effective industrial or commercial establishment in, a Contracting State.

*(b)*  If the application concerns a registration already effected, it may also be filed by a natural person or legal entity not satisfying the conditions referred to in subparagraph *(a)*.

## Article 4

### Legal Effect of the International Register

(1)  Each Contracting State undertakes to recognize that a statement recorded in the International Register shall be considered as true until the contrary is proved, except

    (i)  where the statement cannot be valid under the copyright law, or any other law concerning intellectual property rights in audiovisual works, of that State, or

    (ii)  where the statement is contradicted by another statement recorded in the International Register.

(2)  No provision of this Treaty shall be interpreted as affecting the copyright law, or any other law concerning intellectual property rights in audiovisual works, of any Contracting State or, if that State is party to the Berne Convention for the Protection of Literary and Artistic Works or any other treaty concerning intellectual property rights in audiovisual works, the rights and obligations of the said State under the said Convention or treaty.

## CHAPTER II
## ADMINISTRATIVE PROVISIONS

### Article 5

### Assembly

(1)  *(a)*  The Union shall have an Assembly that shall consist of the Contracting States.

*(b)*  The Government of each Contracting State shall be represented by one delegate, who may be assisted by alternate delegates, advisors and experts.

(2)  The expenses of each delegation shall be borne by the Government which has appointed it, except for the travel expenses and the subsistence allowance of one delegate for each Contracting State, which shall be paid from the funds of the Union.

(3)  *(a)*  The Assembly shall:

(i)  deal with all matters concerning the maintenance and development of the Union and the implementation of this Treaty;

(ii)  exercise such tasks as are specially assigned to it under this Treaty;

(iii)  give directions to the Director General of the Organization (hereinafter referred to as "the Director General"), concerning the preparation for revision conferences;

(iv)  review and approve the reports and activities of the Director General concerning the Union, and give him all necessary instructions concerning matters within the competence of the Union;

(v)  determine the program and adopt the biennial budget of the Union, and approve its final accounts;

(vi)  adopt the financial regulations of the Union;

(vii) establish, and decide from time to time the membership of, a consultative committee consisting of representatives of interested non-governmental organizations and such other committees and working groups as it deems appropriate to facilitate the work of the Union and of its organs;

(viii) control the system and amounts of the fees determined by the Director General;

(ix) determine which States other than Contracting States and which intergovernmental and non-governmental organizations shall be admitted to its meetings as observers;

(x)  take any other appropriate action designed to further the objectives of the Union and perform such other functions as are appropriate under this Treaty.

*(b)*  With respect to matters which are of interest also to other Unions administered by the Organization, the Assembly shall make its decisions after having heard the advice of the Coordination Committee of the Organization.

(4)  A delegate may represent, and vote in the name of, one State only.

(5)  Each Contracting State shall have one vote.

(6)  *(a)*  One-half of the Contracting States shall constitute a quorum.

*(b)*  In the absence of the quorum, the Assembly may make decisions but, with the exception of the decisions concerning its own procedure, all such decisions shall take effect only if the quorum and the required majority are attained through voting by correspondence.

(7)  *(a)*  Subject to Article 8(2)*(b)* and Article 10(2)*(b)*, the decisions of the Assembly shall require a majority of the votes cast.

*(b)*   Abstentions shall not be considered as votes.

(8)   *(a)*   The Assembly shall meet once in every second calendar year in ordinary session upon convocation by the Director General and, in the absence of exceptional circumstances, during the same period and at the same place as the General Assembly of the Organization.

*(b)*   The Assembly shall meet in extraordinary session upon convocation by the Director General, either at the request of one-fourth of the Contracting States or on the Director General's own initiative.

(9)   The Assembly shall adopt its own rules of procedure.

## Article 6

### International Bureau

(1)   The International Bureau shall:

(i)   perform, through the International Registry, all the tasks related to the keeping of the International Register;

(ii)   provide the secretariat of revision conferences, of the Assembly, of the committees and working groups established by the Assembly, and of any other meeting convened by the Director General and dealing with matters of concern to the Union;

(iii)   perform all other tasks specially assigned to it under this Treaty and the Regulations referred to in Article 8 or by the Assembly.

(2)   The Director General shall be the chief executive of the Union and shall represent the Union.

(3)   The Director General shall convene any committee and working group established by the Assembly and all other meetings dealing with matters of concern to the Union.

(4)   *(a)*   The Director General and any staff member designated by him shall participate, without the right to vote, in all meetings of the Assembly, the committees and working groups established by the Assembly, and any other meeting convened by the Director General and dealing with matters of concern to the Union.

*(b)*   The Director General or a staff member designated by him shall be *ex officio* secretary of the Assembly, and of the committees, working groups and other meetings referred to in sub-paragraph *(a)*.

(5)   *(a)*   The Director General shall, in accordance with the directions of the Assembly, make the preparations for revision conferences.

*(b)*   The Director General may consult with intergovernmental and non-governmental organizations concerning the said preparations.

*(c)*   The Director General and staff members designated by him shall take part, without the right to vote, in the discussions at revision conferences.

*(d)*   The Director General or a staff member designated by him shall be *ex officio* secretary of any revision conference.

## Article 7

### Finances

(1)   *(a)*   The Union shall have a budget.

*(b)*   The budget of the Union shall include the income and expenses proper to the Union, and its contribution to the budget of expenses common to the Unions administered by the Organization.

*(c)* Expenses not attributable exclusively to the Union but also to one or more other Unions administered by the Organization shall be considered as expenses common to the Unions. The share of the Union in such common expenses shall be in proportion to the interest the Union has in them.

(2) The budget of the Union shall be established with due regard to the requirements of coordination with the budgets of the other Unions administered by the Organization.

(3) The budget of the Union shall be financed from the following sources:

   (i) fees due for registrations and other services rendered by the International Registry;

   (ii) sale of, or royalties on, the publications of the International Registry;

   (iii) donations, particularly by associations of rights holders in audiovisual works;

   (iv) gifts, bequests, and subventions;

   (v) rents, interests, and other miscellaneous income.

(4) The amounts of fees due to the International Registry and the prices of its publications shall be so fixed that they, together with any other income, should be sufficient to cover the expenses connected with the administration of this Treaty.

(5) If the budget is not adopted before the beginning of a new financial period, it shall be at the same level as the budget of the previous period, as provided in the financial regulations. If the income exceeds the expenses, the difference shall be credited to a reserve fund.

(6) The Union shall have a working capital fund which shall be constituted from the income of the Union.

(7) The auditing of the accounts shall be effected by one or more of the Contracting States or by external auditors, as provided in the financial regulations. They shall be designated, with their agreement, by the Assembly.

## Article 8

### Regulations

(1) The Regulations adopted at the same time as this Treaty are annexed to this Treaty.

(2) *(a)* The Assembly may amend the Regulations.

   *(b)* Any amendment of the Regulations shall require two-thirds of the votes cast.

(3) In the case of conflict between the provisions of this Treaty and those of the Regulations, the former shall prevail.

(4) The Regulations provide for the establishment of Administrative Instructions.

## CHAPTER III
## REVISION AND AMENDMENT

### Article 9

### Revision of the Treaty

(1) This Treaty may be revised by a conference of the Contracting States.

(2) The convocation of any revision conference shall be decided by the Assembly.

(3) The provisions referred to in Article 10(1)*(a)* may be amended either by a revision conference or according to Article 10.

## Article 10

### Amendment of Certain Provisions of the Treaty

(1)   *(a)*   Proposals for the amendment of Article 5(6) and (8), Article 6(4) and (5) and Article 7(1) to (3) and (5) to (7) may be initiated by any Contracting State or by the Director General.

*(b)*   Such proposals shall be communicated by the Director General to the Contracting States at least six months in advance of their consideration by the Assembly.

(2)   *(a)*   Amendments to the provisions referred to in paragraph (1) shall be adopted by the Assembly.

*(b)*   Adoption shall require three-fourths of the votes cast.

(3)   *(a)*   Any amendment to the provisions referred to in paragraph (1) shall enter into force one month after written notifications of acceptance, effected in accordance with their respective constitutional processes, have been received by the Director General from three-fourths of the Contracting States members of the Assembly at the time the Assembly adopted the amendment.

*(b)*   Any amendment to the said Articles thus accepted shall bind all the Contracting States which were Contracting States at the time the amendment was adopted by the Assembly.

*(c)*   Any amendment which has been accepted and which has entered into force in accordance with subparagraph *(a)* shall bind all States which become Contracting States after the date on which the amendment was adopted by the Assembly.

## CHAPTER IV
## FINAL PROVISIONS

## Article 11

### Becoming Party to the Treaty

(1)   Any State member of the Organization may become party to this Treaty by:

(i)   signature followed by the deposit of an instrument of ratification, acceptance or approval, or

(ii)   the deposit of an instrument of accession.

(2)   The instruments referred to in paragraph (I) shall be deposited with the Director General.

## Article 12

### Entry Into Force of the Treaty

(1)   This Treaty shall enter into force, with respect to the first five States which have deposited their instruments of ratification, acceptance, approval or accession, three months after the date on which the fifth instrument of ratification, acceptance, approval or accession has been deposited.

(2)   This Treaty shall enter into force with respect to any State not covered by paragraph (1) three months after the date on which that State has deposited its instrument of ratification, acceptance, approval or accession unless a later date has been indicated in the instrument of ratification, acceptance, approval or accession. In the latter case, this Treaty shall enter into force with respect to the said State on the date thus indicated.

## Article 13

### Reservations to the Treaty

(1)   Subject to paragraph (2), no reservation may be made to this Treaty.

(2)   Any State, upon becoming party to this Treaty, may, in a notification deposited with the Director General, declare that it will not apply the provisions of Article 4(1) in respect of statements which do not concern the exploitation of intellectual property rights in audiovisual works. Any State that has made such a declaration may, by a notification deposited with the Director General, withdraw it.

## Article 14

### Denunciation of the Treaty

(1)   Any Contracting State may denounce this Treaty by notification addressed to the Director General,

(2)   Denunciation shall take effect one year after the day on which the Director General has received the notification.

(3)   The right of denouncing this Treaty provided for in paragraph (1) shall not be exercised by any Contracting State before the expiration of five years from the date on which this Treaty enters into force with respect to it.

## Article 15

### Signature and Languages of the Treaty

(1)   This Treaty shall be signed in a single original in the English and French languages, both texts being equally authentic.

(2)   Official texts shall be established by the Director General, after consultation with the interested Governments, in the Arabic, German, Italian, Japanese, Portuguese, Russian and Spanish languages, and such other languages as the Assembly may designate.

(3)   This Treaty shall remain open for signature at the International Bureau until December 31, 1989.

## Article 16

### Depositary Functions

(1)   The original of this Treaty and the Regulations shall be deposited with the Director General.

(2)   The Director General shall transmit two copies, certified by him, of this Treaty and the Regulations, to the Governments of States entitled to sign this Treaty.

(3)   The Director General shall register this Treaty with the Secretariat of the United Nations.

(4)   The Director General shall transmit two copies, certified by him, of any amendment to this Treaty and the Regulations to the Governments of the Contracting States and, on request, to the Government of any other State.

## Article 17

### Notifications

The Director General shall notify the Governments of the States members of the Organization of any of the events referred to in Articles 8(2), 10(2) and (3), 11, 12, 13 and 14.

# 26. PARTIES TO THE TREATY ON THE INTERNATIONAL REGISTRATION OF AUDIOVISUAL WORKS*

Film Register Treaty (Geneva, 1989)

(FRT Union)

**Status on May 4, 2021**

| Contracting Party | Signature | Instrument | Entry into Force |
|---|---|---|---|
| Argentina | - | Accession: April 29, 1992 | June 29, 1992 |
| Austria | April 20, 1989 | Ratification: August 6, 1990 | February 27, 1991 |
| Brazil | December 7, 1989 | Ratification: March 26, 1993 | June 26, 1993 |
| Burkina Faso | April 20, 1989 | Ratification: June 11, 1990 | February 27, 1991 |
| Canada | December 21, 1989 | - | - |
| Chile | April 20, 1989 | Ratification: September 29, 1993 | December 29, 1993 |
| Colombia | - | Accession: February 9, 1994 | May 9, 1994 |
| Czechoslovakia | - | Accession: November 27, 1990 | February 27, 1991 |
| Czech Republic | - | Continued application: December 18, 1992 | January 1, 1993 |
| Egypt | May 3, 1989 | - | - |
| France | April 20, 1989 | Approval: August 14, 1990 | February 27, 1991 |
| Greece | December 29, 1989 | - | - |
| Guinea | April 20, 1989 | - | - |
| Hungary | April 20, 1989 | Ratification: May 7, 1998 | August 7, 1998 |
| India | April 20, 1989 | - | - |
| Mexico | July 6, 1989 | Ratification: October 9, 1990 | February 27, 1991 |
| Peru | - | Accession: April 27, 1994 | July 27, 1994 |
| Philippines | April 25, 1989 | - | - |
| Poland | December 29, 1989 | - | - |
| Senegal | May 2, 1989 | Ratification: January 3, 1994 | April 3, 1994 |
| Slovakia | - | Continued application: December 30, 1992 | January 1, 1993 |

## PARTIES TO THE TREATY ON THE INTERNATIONAL REGISTRATION OF AUDIOVISUAL WORKS

| Contracting Party | Signature | Instrument | Entry into Force |
|---|---|---|---|
| United States of America | April 20, 1989 | - | - |
| Yugoslavia | December 29, 1989 | - | - |

At the 1993 Assembly meeting of the Film Register Treaty Union, it was decided that until any further decision by the Assembly of the Film Register Treaty Union, the application of the Treaty be suspended. At the General Assemblies, in 2000, the Assembly of the Film Register Treaty Union decided that it would not be reconvened unless there was a specific request to convene the Assembly.

# 27. BEIJING TREATY ON AUDIOVISUAL PERFORMANCES

Adopted at Beijing June 24, 2012

## Preamble

The Contracting Parties,

Desiring to develop and maintain the protection of the rights of performers in their audiovisual performances in a manner as effective and uniform as possible,

Recalling the importance of the Development Agenda recommendations, adopted in 2007 by the General Assembly of the Convention Establishing the World Intellectual Property Organization (WIPO), which aim to ensure that development considerations form an integral part of the Organization's work,

Recognizing the need to introduce new international rules in order to provide adequate solutions to the questions raised by economic, social, cultural and technological developments,

Recognizing the profound impact of the development and convergence of information and communication technologies on the production and use of audiovisual performances,

Recognizing the need to maintain a balance between the rights of performers in their audiovisual performances and the larger public interest, particularly education, research and access to information,

Recognizing that the WIPO Performances and Phonograms Treaty (WPPT) done in Geneva on December 20, 1996, does not extend protection to performers in respect of their performances fixed in audiovisual fixations,

Referring to the Resolution concerning Audiovisual Performances adopted by the Diplomatic Conference on Certain Copyright and Neighboring Rights Questions on December 20, 1996,

Have agreed as follows:

## Article 1

### Relation to Other Conventions and Treaties

(1)   Nothing in this Treaty shall derogate from existing obligations that Contracting Parties have to each other under the WPPT or the International Convention for the Protection of Performers, Producers of Phonograms and Broadcasting Organizations done in Rome on October 26, 1961.

(2)   Protection granted under this Treaty shall leave intact and shall in no way affect the protection of copyright in literary and artistic works. Consequently, no provision of this Treaty may be interpreted as prejudicing such protection.

(3)   This Treaty shall not have any connection with treaties other than the WPPT, nor shall it prejudice any rights and obligations under any other treaties.[1,2]

---

[1]   Agreed statement concerning Article 1: It is understood that nothing in this Treaty affects any rights or obligations under the WIPO Performances and Phonograms Treaty (WPPT) or their interpretation and it is further understood that paragraph 3 does not create any obligations for a Contracting Party to this Treaty to ratify or accede to the WPPT or to comply with any of its provisions.

[2]   Agreed statement concerning Article 1(3): It is understood that Contracting Parties who are members of the World Trade Organization (WTO) acknowledge all the principles and objectives of the Agreement on Trade-Related Aspects of Intellectual Property Rights (TRIPS Agreement) and understand that nothing in this Treaty affects the provisions of the TRIPS Agreement, including, but not limited to, the provisions relating to anti-competitive practices.

## Article 2

### Definitions

For the purposes of this Treaty:

(a)   "performers" are actors, singers, musicians, dancers, and other persons who act, sing, deliver, declaim, play in, interpret, or otherwise perform literary or artistic works or expressions of folklore;[3]

(b)   "audiovisual fixation" means the embodiment of moving images, whether or not accompanied by sounds or by the representations thereof, from which they can be perceived, reproduced or communicated through a device;[4]

(c)   "broadcasting" means the transmission by wireless means for public reception of sounds or of images or of images and sounds or of the representations thereof; such transmission by satellite is also "broadcasting"; transmission of encrypted signals is "broadcasting" where the means for decrypting are provided to the public by the broadcasting organization or with its consent;

(d)   "communication to the public" of a performance means the transmission to the public by any medium, otherwise than by broadcasting, of an unfixed performance, or of a performance fixed in an audiovisual fixation. For the purposes of Article 11, "communication to the public" includes making a performance fixed in an audiovisual fixation audible or visible or audible and visible to the public.

## Article 3

### Beneficiaries of Protection

(1)   Contracting Parties shall accord the protection granted under this Treaty to performers who are nationals of other Contracting Parties.

(2)   Performers who are not nationals of one of the Contracting Parties but who have their habitual residence in one of them shall, for the purposes of this Treaty, be assimilated to nationals of that Contracting Party.

## Article 4

### National Treatment

(1)   Each Contracting Party shall accord to nationals of other Contracting Parties the treatment it accords to its own nationals with regard to the exclusive rights specifically granted in this Treaty and the right to equitable remuneration provided for in Article 11 of this Treaty.

(2)   A Contracting Party shall be entitled to limit the extent and term of the protection accorded to nationals of another Contracting Party under paragraph (1), with respect to the rights granted in Article 11(1) and 11(2) of this Treaty, to those rights that its own nationals enjoy in that other Contracting Party.

(3)   The obligation provided for in paragraph (1) does not apply to a Contracting Party to the extent that another Contracting Party makes use of the reservations permitted by Article 11(3) of this Treaty, nor does it apply to a Contracting Party, to the extent that it has made such reservation.

---

[3]   Agreed statement concerning Article 2(a): It is understood that the definition of "performers" includes those who perform a literary or artistic work that is created or first fixed in the course of a performance.

[4]   Agreed statement concerning Article 2(b): It is hereby confirmed that the definition of "audiovisual fixation" contained in Article 2(b) is without prejudice to Article 2(c) of the WPPT.

## Article 5

## Moral Rights

(1)   Independently of a performer's economic rights, and even after the transfer of those rights, the performer shall, as regards his live performances or performances fixed in audiovisual fixations, have the right:

(i)   to claim to be identified as the performer of his performances, except where omission is dictated by the manner of the use of the performance; and

(ii)   to object to any distortion, mutilation or other modification of his performances that would be prejudicial to his reputation, taking due account of the nature of audiovisual fixations.

(2)   The rights granted to a performer in accordance with paragraph (1) shall, after his death, be maintained, at least until the expiry of the economic rights, and shall be exercisable by the persons or institutions authorized by the legislation of the Contracting Party where protection is claimed. However, those Contracting Parties whose legislation, at the moment of their ratification of or accession to this Treaty, does not provide for protection after the death of the performer of all rights set out in the preceding paragraph may provide that some of these rights will, after his death, cease to be maintained.

(3)   The means of redress for safeguarding the rights granted under this Article shall be governed by the legislation of the Contracting Party where protection is claimed.[5]

## Article 6

## Economic Rights of Performers in their Unfixed Performances

Performers shall enjoy the exclusive right of authorizing, as regards their performances:

(i)   the broadcasting and communication to the public of their unfixed performances except where the performance is already a broadcast performance; and

(ii)   the fixation of their unfixed performances.

## Article 7

## Right of Reproduction

Performers shall enjoy the exclusive right of authorizing the direct or indirect reproduction of their performances fixed in audiovisual fixations, in any manner or form.[6]

---

[5]   Agreed statement concerning Article 5: For the purposes of this Treaty and without prejudice to any other treaty, it is understood that, considering the nature of audiovisual fixations and their production and distribution, modifications of a performance that are made in the normal course of exploitation of the performance, such as editing, compression, dubbing, or formatting, in existing or new media or formats, and that are made in the course of a use authorized by the performer, would not in themselves amount to modifications within the meaning of Article 5(1)(ii). Rights under Article 5(1)(ii) are concerned only with changes that are objectively prejudicial to the performer's reputation in a substantial way. It is also understood that the mere use of new or changed technology or media, as such, does not amount to modification within the meaning of Article 5(1)(ii).

[6]   Agreed statement concerning Article 7: The reproduction right, as set out in Article 7, and the exceptions permitted thereunder through Article 13, fully apply in the digital environment, in particular to the use of performances in digital form. It is understood that the storage of a protected performance in digital form in an electronic medium constitutes a reproduction within the meaning of this Article.

## Article 8

### Right of Distribution

(1)   Performers shall enjoy the exclusive right of authorizing the making available to the public of the original and copies of their performances fixed in audiovisual fixations through sale or other transfer of ownership.

(2)   Nothing in this Treaty shall affect the freedom of Contracting Parties to determine the conditions, if any, under which the exhaustion of the right in paragraph (1) applies after the first sale or other transfer of ownership of the original or a copy of the fixed performance with the authorization of the performer.[7]

## Article 9

### Right of Rental

(1)   Performers shall enjoy the exclusive right of authorizing the commercial rental to the public of the original and copies of their performances fixed in audiovisual fixations as determined in the national law of Contracting Parties, even after distribution of them by, or pursuant to, authorization by the performer.

(2)   Contracting Parties are exempt from the obligation of paragraph (1) unless the commercial rental has led to widespread copying of such fixations materially impairing the exclusive right of reproduction of performers.[8]

## Article 10

### Right of Making Available of Fixed Performances

Performers shall enjoy the exclusive right of authorizing the making available to the public of their performances fixed in audiovisual fixations, by wire or wireless means, in such a way that members of the public may access them from a place and at a time individually chosen by them.

## Article 11

### Right of Broadcasting and Communication to the Public

(1)   Performers shall enjoy the exclusive right of authorizing the broadcasting and communication to the public of their performances fixed in audiovisual fixations.

(2)   Contracting Parties may in a notification deposited with the Director General of WIPO declare that, instead of the right of authorization provided for in paragraph (1), they will establish a right to equitable remuneration for the direct or indirect use of performances fixed in audiovisual fixations for broadcasting or for communication to the public. Contracting Parties may also declare that they will set conditions in their legislation for the exercise of the right to equitable remuneration.

(3)   Any Contracting Party may declare that it will apply the provisions of paragraphs (1) or (2) only in respect of certain uses, or that it will limit their application in some other way, or that it will not apply the provisions of paragraphs (1) and (2) at all.

---

   [7]   Agreed statement concerning Articles 8 and 9: As used in these Articles, the expression "original and copies," being subject to the right of distribution and the right of rental under the said Articles, refers exclusively to fixed copies that can be put into circulation as tangible objects.

   [8]   Agreed statement concerning Articles 8 and 9: As used in these Articles, the expression "original and copies," being subject to the right of distribution and the right of rental under the said Articles, refers exclusively to fixed copies that can be put into circulation as tangible objects.

## Article 12

### Transfer of Rights

(1)   A Contracting Party may provide in its national law that once a performer has consented to fixation of his or her performance in an audiovisual fixation, the exclusive rights of authorization provided for in Articles 7 to 11 of this Treaty shall be owned or exercised by or transferred to the producer of such audiovisual fixation subject to any contract to the contrary between the performer and the producer of the audiovisual fixation as determined by the national law.

(2)   A Contracting Party may require with respect to audiovisual fixations produced under its national law that such consent or contract be in writing and signed by both parties to the contract or by their duly authorized representatives.

(3)   Independent of the transfer of exclusive rights described above, national laws or individual, collective or other agreements may provide the performer with the right to receive royalties or equitable remuneration for any use of the performance, as provided for under this Treaty including as regards Articles 10 and 11.

## Article 13

### Limitations and Exceptions

(1)   Contracting Parties may, in their national legislation, provide for the same kinds of limitations or exceptions with regard to the protection of performers as they provide for, in their national legislation, in connection with the protection of copyright in literary and artistic works.

(2)   Contracting Parties shall confine any limitations of or exceptions to rights provided for in this Treaty to certain special cases which do not conflict with a normal exploitation of the performance and do not unreasonably prejudice the legitimate interests of the performer.[9]

## Article 14

### Term of Protection

The term of protection to be granted to performers under this Treaty shall last, at least, until the end of a period of 50 years computed from the end of the year in which the performance was fixed.

## Article 15

### Obligations concerning Technological Measures

Contracting Parties shall provide adequate legal protection and effective legal remedies against the circumvention of effective technological measures that are used by performers in connection with the exercise of their rights under this Treaty and that restrict acts, in respect of their performances, which are not authorized by the performers concerned or permitted by law.[10, 11]

---

[9]   Agreed statement concerning Article 13: The Agreed statement concerning Article 10 (on Limitations and Exceptions) of the WIPO Copyright Treaty (WCT) is applicable *mutatis mutandis* also to Article 13 (on Limitations and Exceptions) of the Treaty.

[10]   Agreed statement concerning Article 15 as it relates to Article 13: It is understood that nothing in this Article prevents a Contracting Party from adopting effective and necessary measures to ensure that a beneficiary may enjoy limitations and exceptions provided in that Contracting Party's national law, in accordance with Article 13, where technological measures have been applied to an audiovisual performance and the beneficiary has legal access to that performance, in circumstances such as where appropriate and effective measures have not been taken by rights holders in relation to that performance to enable the beneficiary to enjoy the limitations and exceptions under that Contracting Party's national law. Without prejudice to the legal protection of an audiovisual work in which a performance is fixed, it is further understood that the obligations under Article 15 are not applicable to performances unprotected or no longer protected under the national law giving effect to this Treaty.

[11]   Agreed statement concerning Article 15: The expression "technological measures used by performers" should, as this is the case regarding the WPPT, be construed broadly, referring also to those acting on behalf of performers, including

## Article 16

### Obligations concerning Rights Management Information

(1)   Contracting Parties shall provide adequate and effective legal remedies against any person knowingly performing any of the following acts knowing, or with respect to civil remedies having reasonable grounds to know, that it will induce, enable, facilitate, or conceal an infringement of any right covered by this Treaty:

(i) to remove or alter any electronic rights management information without authority;

(ii) to distribute, import for distribution, broadcast, communicate or make available to the public, without authority, performances or copies of performances fixed in audiovisual fixations knowing that electronic rights management information has been removed or altered without authority.

(2)   As used in this Article, "rights management information" means information which identifies the performer, the performance of the performer, or the owner of any right in the performance, or information about the terms and conditions of use of the performance, and any numbers or codes that represent such information, when any of these items of information is attached to a performance fixed in an audiovisual fixation.[12]

## Article 17

### Formalities

The enjoyment and exercise of the rights provided for in this Treaty shall not be subject to any formality.

## Article 18

### Reservations and Notifications

(1)   Subject to provisions of Article 11(3), no reservations to this Treaty shall be permitted.

(2)   Any notification under Article 11(2) or 19(2) may be made in instruments of ratification or accession, and the effective date of the notification shall be the same as the date of entry into force of this Treaty with respect to the Contracting Party having made the notification. Any such notification may also be made later, in which case the notification shall have effect three months after its receipt by the Director General of WIPO or at any later date indicated in the notification.

## Article 19

### Application in Time

(1)   Contracting Parties shall accord the protection granted under this Treaty to fixed performances that exist at the moment of the entry into force of this Treaty and to all performances that occur after the entry into force of this Treaty for each Contracting Party.

(2)   Notwithstanding the provisions of paragraph (1), a Contracting Party may declare in a notification deposited with the Director General of WIPO that it will not apply the provisions of Articles 7 to 11 of this Treaty, or any one or more of those, to fixed performances that existed at the moment of the entry into force of this Treaty for each Contracting Party. In respect of such Contracting Party, other Contracting Parties may limit the application of the said Articles to performances that occurred after the entry into force of this Treaty for that Contracting Party.

---

their representatives, licensees or assignees, including producers, service providers, and persons engaged in communication or broadcasting using performances on the basis of due authorization.

[12]   Agreed statement concerning Article 16: The Agreed statement concerning Article 12 (on Obligations concerning Rights Management Information) of the WCT is applicable *mutatis mutandis* also to Article 16 (on Obligations concerning Rights Management Information) of the Treaty.

(3)   The protection provided for in this Treaty shall be without prejudice to any acts committed, agreements concluded or rights acquired before the entry into force of this Treaty for each Contracting Party.

(4)   Contracting Parties may in their legislation establish transitional provisions under which any person who, prior to the entry into force of this Treaty, engaged in lawful acts with respect to a performance, may undertake with respect to the same performance acts within the scope of the rights provided for in Articles 5 and 7 to 11 after the entry into force of this Treaty for the respective Contracting Parties.

## Article 20

### Provisions on Enforcement of Rights

(1)   Contracting Parties undertake to adopt, in accordance with their legal systems, the measures necessary to ensure the application of this Treaty.

(2)   Contracting Parties shall ensure that enforcement procedures are available under their law so as to permit effective action against any act of infringement of rights covered by this Treaty, including expeditious remedies to prevent infringements and remedies which constitute a deterrent to further infringements.

## Article 21

### Assembly

(1)   (a) The Contracting Parties shall have an Assembly.

(b) Each Contracting Party shall be represented in the Assembly by one delegate who may be assisted by alternate delegates, advisors and experts.

(c) The expenses of each delegation shall be borne by the Contracting Party that has appointed the delegation. The Assembly may ask WIPO to grant financial assistance to facilitate the participation of delegations of Contracting Parties that are regarded as developing countries in conformity with the established practice of the General Assembly of the United Nations or that are countries in transition to a market economy.

(2)   (a) The Assembly shall deal with matters concerning the maintenance and development of this Treaty and the application and operation of this Treaty.

(b) The Assembly shall perform the function allocated to it under Article 23(2) in respect of the admission of certain intergovernmental organizations to become party to this Treaty.

(c) The Assembly shall decide the convocation of any diplomatic conference for the revision of this Treaty and give the necessary instructions to the Director General of WIPO for the preparation of such diplomatic conference.

(3)   (a) Each Contracting Party that is a State shall have one vote and shall vote only in its own name.

(b) Any Contracting Party that is an intergovernmental organization may participate in the vote, in place of its Member States, with a number of votes equal to the number of its Member States which are party to this Treaty. No such intergovernmental organization shall participate in the vote if any one of its Member States exercises its right to vote and vice versa.

(4)   The Assembly shall meet upon convocation by the Director General and, in the absence of exceptional circumstances, during the same period and at the same place as the General Assembly of WIPO.

(5)   The Assembly shall endeavor to take its decisions by consensus and shall establish its own rules of procedure, including the convocation of extraordinary sessions, the requirements of a quorum and, subject to the provisions of this Treaty, the required majority for various kinds of decisions.

## Article 22

### International Bureau

The International Bureau of WIPO shall perform the administrative tasks concerning the Treaty.

## Article 23

### Eligibility for Becoming Party to the Treaty

(1)　Any Member State of WIPO may become party to this Treaty.

(2)　The Assembly may decide to admit any intergovernmental organization to become party to this Treaty which declares that it is competent in respect of, and has its own legislation binding on all its Member States on, matters covered by this Treaty and that it has been duly authorized, in accordance with its internal procedures, to become party to this Treaty.

(3)　The European Union, having made the declaration referred to in the preceding paragraph in the Diplomatic Conference that has adopted this Treaty, may become party to this Treaty.

## Article 24

### Rights and Obligations under the Treaty

Subject to any specific provisions to the contrary in this Treaty, each Contracting Party shall enjoy all of the rights and assume all of the obligations under this Treaty.

## Article 25

### Signature of the Treaty

This Treaty shall be open for signature at the headquarters of WIPO by any eligible party for one year after its adoption.

## Article 26

### Entry into Force of the Treaty

This Treaty shall enter into force three months after 30 eligible parties referred to in Article 23 have deposited their instruments of ratification or accession.

## Article 27

### Effective Date of Becoming Party to the Treaty

This Treaty shall bind:

(i)　the 30 eligible parties referred to in Article 26, from the date on which this Treaty has entered into force;

(ii)　each other eligible party referred to in Article 23, from the expiration of three months from the date on which it has deposited its instrument of ratification or accession with the Director General of WIPO.

## Article 28

### Denunciation of the Treaty

This Treaty may be denounced by any Contracting Party by notification addressed to the Director General of WIPO. Any denunciation shall take effect one year from the date on which the Director General of WIPO received the notification.

## Article 29

### Languages of the Treaty

(1)   This Treaty is signed in a single original in English, Arabic, Chinese, French, Russian and Spanish languages, the versions in all these languages being equally authentic.

(2)   An official text in any language other than those referred to in paragraph (1) shall be established by the Director General of WIPO on the request of an interested party, after consultation with all the interested parties. For the purposes of this paragraph, "interested party" means any Member State of WIPO whose official language, or one of whose official languages, is involved and the European Union, and any other intergovernmental organization that may become party to this Treaty, if one of its official languages is involved.

## Article 30

### Depositary

The Director General of WIPO is the depositary of this Treaty.

# 28. PARTIES TO THE BEIJING TREATY ON AUDIOVISUAL PERFORMANCES*

Beijing Treaty (Beijing, 2012)

**Status on May 4, 2021**

| State | Date on which State became party to the Treaty |
|---|---|
| Algeria | April 28, 2020 |
| Armenia | March 17, 2021 |
| Belize | April 28, 2020 |
| Botswana | April 28, 2020 |
| Burkina Faso | April 28, 2020 |
| Cambodia | April 28, 2020 |
| Central African Republic | November 19, 2020 |
| Chile | April 28, 2020 |
| China[1,2] | April 28, 2020 |
| Comoros | April 25, 2021 |
| Cook Islands | April 28, 2020 |
| Costa Rica | February 13, 2021 |
| Democratic People's Republic of Korea | April 28, 2020 |
| Dominican Republic | April 28, 2020 |
| El Salvador | April 28, 2020 |
| Gabon | April 28, 2020 |
| Indonesia | April 28, 2020 |
| Japan[3] | April 28, 2020 |
| Kenya | April 28, 2020 |
| Kiribati | June 22, 2021 |
| Mali | April 28, 2020 |
| Marshall Islands | April 28, 2020 |
| Nigeria | April 28, 2020 |
| Peru[4] | April 28, 2020 |
| Qatar | April 28, 2020 |
| Republic of Korea[5] | July 22, 2020 |
| Republic of Moldova | April 28, 2020 |
| Russian Federation | April 28, 2020 |
| Saint Vincent and the Grenadines | April 28, 2020 |
| Samoa[6] | April 28, 2020 |
| Sao Tome and Principe | January 15, 2021 |
| Slovakia[7] | April 28, 2020 |
| Switzerland[8] | May 11, 2020 |

---

* Document originally produced by the World Intellectual Property Organization (WIPO), the owner of the copyright. Published with the permission of the World Intellectual Property Organization.

## PARTIES TO THE BEIJING TREATY

| State | Date on which State became party to the Treaty |
|---|---|
| Syrian Arab Republic | April 28, 2020 |
| Togo | April 20, 2021 |
| Trinidad and Tobago | April 28, 2020 |
| Tunisia | April 28, 2020 |
| United Arab Emirates | April 28, 2020 |
| Vanuatu | August 6, 2020 |
| Zimbabwe | April 28, 2020 |

(Total: 40 States)

---

[1]     The People's Republic of China shall not be bound by Article 11(1) and (2) of the Treaty.

[2]     The Treaty shall not apply for the time being to Hong Kong, China until otherwise notified by the Government of the People's Republic of China.

[3]     Pursuant to Article 11(2) of the Treaty, Japan will establish a right to equitable remuneration, instead of the right of authorization provided for in Article 11(1) for the broadcasting of a performance by:

(a)    a broadcasting organization, using the audiovisual fixation that it made for the broadcasting under the authorization of the person entitled to the right to broadcast the performance;

(b)    a person to whom the broadcasting organization referred to in (a) provided the audiovisual fixations referred to in (a), using those audiovisual fixations; or

(c)    a person to whom the broadcasting organization referred to in (a) otherwise supplied a broadcasting program pertaining to the authorization referred to in (a), using that broadcasting program;

Pursuant to Article 11(2) of the Treaty, Japan will also establish a right to equitable remuneration, instead of the right of authorization provided for in Article 11(1) of the Treaty, for the simultaneous cablecasting of a broadcast performance and for the "automatic public transmission of unfixed information" made in order that a broadcast performance be received simultaneously with the original broadcasting exclusively in the broadcasting service area pertaining to the original broadcasting;

"automatic public transmission of unfixed information" shall mean transmission by means of inputting information into an automatic public transmission server already connected with a telecommunication line that is provided for use by the public, which is carried out automatically in response to a request from the public and which is intended for direct receipt by the public;

Pursuant to Article 11, paragraph 3 of the Treaty, Japan will not apply the provisions of Article 11 paragraphs (1) and (2) of the Treaty to the communication to the public of a performance fixed in audiovisual fixations done by means other than cablecasting or "automatic public transmission of unfixed information".

[4]     In accordance with Article 11(2) of the Treaty, the Republic of Peru opts for the right to equitable remuneration for the direct or indirect use of performances fixed in audiovisual fixations for broadcasting or for communication to the public.

[5]     In accordance with Article 11(3) of the Treaty, the Republic of Korea will apply the provision of Article 11(1) thereof only in respect of the performances fixed in audiovisual fixation for broadcasting or transmission by wire. Transmission by wire does not include transmission over the Internet.

[6]     Pursuant to Article 11(3) of the Treaty, the provisions under Articles 11(1) and (2) do not apply to the Independent State of Samoa, until such time that the national laws have been reformed.

[7]     In accordance with Article 11(2) of the Treaty, the Slovak Republic has set conditions in its legislation for the exercise of the right to equitable remuneration.

[8]     Pursuant to Article 11(2) and (3), instead of the exclusive right of authorization referred to in Article 11(1), Switzerland shall grant a right to remuneration subject to collective management and to the principle of reciprocity for the broadcasting, retransmission or public reception of an audiovisual fixation where it is made from a commercially available audiovisual fixation.

# 29. MARRAKESH TREATY TO FACILITATE ACCESS TO PUBLISHED WORKS FOR PERSONS WHO ARE BLIND, VISUALLY IMPAIRED, OR OTHERWISE PRINT DISABLED

Adopted at Marrakesh June 27, 2013

## Preamble

The Contracting Parties,

*Recalling* the principles of non-discrimination, equal opportunity, accessibility and full and effective participation and inclusion in society, proclaimed in the Universal Declaration of Human Rights and the United Nations Convention on the Rights of Persons with Disabilities,

*Mindful* of the challenges that are prejudicial to the complete development of persons with visual impairments or with other print disabilities, which limit their freedom of expression, including the freedom to seek, receive and impart information and ideas of all kinds on an equal basis with others, including through all forms of communication of their choice, their enjoyment of the right to education, and the opportunity to conduct research,

*Emphasizing* the importance of copyright protection as an incentive and reward for literary and artistic creations and of enhancing opportunities for everyone, including persons with visual impairments or with other print disabilities, to participate in the cultural life of the community, to enjoy the arts and to share scientific progress and its benefits,

*Aware* of the barriers of persons with visual impairments or with other print disabilities to access published works in achieving equal opportunities in society, and the need to both expand the number of works in accessible formats and to improve the circulation of such works,

*Taking into account* that the majority of persons with visual impairments or with other print disabilities live in developing and least-developed countries,

*Recognizing* that, despite the differences in national copyright laws, the positive impact of new information and communication technologies on the lives of persons with visual impairments or with other print disabilities may be reinforced by an enhanced legal framework at the international level,

*Recognizing* that many Member States have established limitations and exceptions in their national copyright laws for persons with visual impairments or with other print disabilities, yet there is a continuing shortage of available works in accessible format copies for such persons, and that considerable resources are required for their effort of making works accessible to these persons, and that the lack of possibilities of cross-border exchange of accessible format copies has necessitated duplication of these efforts,

*Recognizing* both the importance of rightholders' role in making their works accessible to persons with visual impairments or with other print disabilities and the importance of appropriate limitations and exceptions to make works accessible to these persons, particularly when the market is unable to provide such access,

*Recognizing* the need to maintain a balance between the effective protection of the rights of authors and the larger public interest, particularly education, research and access to information, and that such a balance must facilitate effective and timely access to works for the benefit of persons with visual impairments or with other print disabilities,

*Reaffirming* the obligations of Contracting Parties under the existing international treaties on the protection of copyright and the importance and flexibility of the three-step test for limitations and exceptions established in Article 9(2) of the Berne Convention for the Protection of Literary and Artistic Works and other international instruments,

*Recalling* the importance of the Development Agenda recommendations, adopted in 2007 by the General Assembly of the World Intellectual Property Organization (WIPO), which aim to ensure that development considerations form an integral part of the Organization's work,

*Recognizing* the importance of the international copyright system and desiring to harmonize limitations and exceptions with a view to facilitating access to and use of works by persons with visual impairments or with other print disabilities,

Have agreed as follows:

## Article 1

### Relation to Other Conventions and Treaties

Nothing in this Treaty shall derogate from any obligations that Contracting Parties have to each other under any other treaties, nor shall it prejudice any rights that a Contracting Party has under any other treaties.

## Article 2

### Definitions

For the purposes of this Treaty:

(a) "works" means literary and artistic works within the meaning of Article 2(1) of the Berne Convention for the Protection of Literary and Artistic Works, in the form of text, notation and/or related illustrations, whether published or otherwise made publicly available in any media;[1]

(b) "accessible format copy" means a copy of a work in an alternative manner or form which gives a beneficiary person access to the work, including to permit the person to have access as feasibly and comfortably as a person without visual impairment or other print disability. The accessible format copy is used exclusively by beneficiary persons and it must respect the integrity of the original work, taking due consideration of the changes needed to make the work accessible in the alternative format and of the accessibility needs of the beneficiary persons;

(c) "authorized entity" means an entity that is authorized or recognized by the government to provide education, instructional training, adaptive reading or information access to beneficiary persons on a non-profit basis. It also includes a government institution or non-profit organization that provides the same services to beneficiary persons as one of its primary activities or institutional obligations.[2]

An authorized entity establishes and follows its own practices:

(i) to establish that the persons it serves are beneficiary persons;

(ii) to limit to beneficiary persons and/or authorized entities its distribution and making available of accessible format copies;

(iii) to discourage the reproduction, distribution and making available of unauthorized copies; and

(iv) to maintain due care in, and records of, its handling of copies of works, while respecting the privacy of beneficiary persons in accordance with Article 8.

---

[1] Agreed statement concerning Article 2(a): For the purposes of this Treaty, it is understood that this definition includes such works in audio form, such as audiobooks.

[2] Agreed statement concerning Article 2(c): For the purposes of this Treaty, it is understood that "entities recognized by the government" may include entities receiving financial support from the government to provide education, instructional training, adaptive reading or information access to beneficiary persons on a non-profit basis.

## Article 3

### Beneficiary Persons

A beneficiary person is a person who:

(a)   is blind;

(b)   has a visual impairment or a perceptual or reading disability which cannot be improved to give visual function substantially equivalent to that of a person who has no such impairment or disability and so is unable to read printed works to substantially the same degree as a person without an impairment or disability; or[3]

(c)   is otherwise unable, through physical disability, to hold or manipulate a book or to focus or move the eyes to the extent that would be normally acceptable for reading; regardless of any other disabilities.

## Article 4

### National Law Limitations and Exceptions
### Regarding Accessible Format Copies

1.   (a) Contracting Parties shall provide in their national copyright laws for a limitation or exception to the right of reproduction, the right of distribution, and the right of making available to the public as provided by the WIPO Copyright Treaty (WCT), to facilitate the availability of works in accessible format copies for beneficiary persons. The limitation or exception provided in national law should permit changes needed to make the work accessible in the alternative format.

(b) Contracting Parties may also provide a limitation or exception to the right of public performance to facilitate access to works for beneficiary persons.

2.   A Contracting Party may fulfill Article 4(1) for all rights identified therein by providing a limitation or exception in its national copyright law such that:

(a)   Authorized entities shall be permitted, without the authorization of the copyright rightholder, to make an accessible format copy of a work, obtain from another authorized entity an accessible format copy, and supply those copies to beneficiary persons by any means, including by non-commercial lending or by electronic communication by wire or wireless means, and undertake any intermediate steps to achieve those objectives, when all of the following conditions are met:

(i)    the authorized entity wishing to undertake said activity has lawful access to that work or a copy of that work;

(ii)   the work is converted to an accessible format copy, which may include any means needed to navigate information in the accessible format, but does not introduce changes other than those needed to make the work accessible to the beneficiary person;

(iii)   such accessible format copies are supplied exclusively to be used by beneficiary persons; and

(iv)   the activity is undertaken on a non-profit basis;

and

(b)   A beneficiary person, or someone acting on his or her behalf including a primary caretaker or caregiver, may make an accessible format copy of a work for the personal use of the beneficiary person or otherwise may assist the beneficiary person to make and use accessible format copies where the beneficiary person has lawful access to that work or a copy of that work.

---

[3]   Agreed statement concerning Article 3(b): Nothing in this language implies that "cannot be improved" requires the use of all possible medical diagnostic procedures and treatments.

3.    A Contracting Party may fulfill Article 4(1) by providing other limitations or exceptions in its national copyright law pursuant to Articles 10 and 11.[4]

4.    A Contracting Party may confine limitations or exceptions under this Article to works which, in the particular accessible format, cannot be obtained commercially under reasonable terms for beneficiary persons in that market. Any Contracting Party availing itself of this possibility shall so declare in a notification deposited with the Director General of WIPO at the time of ratification of, acceptance of or accession to this Treaty or at any time thereafter.[5]

5.    It shall be a matter for national law to determine whether limitations or exceptions under this Article are subject to remuneration.

## Article 5

## Cross-Border Exchange of Accessible Format Copies

1.    Contracting Parties shall provide that if an accessible format copy is made under a limitation or exception or pursuant to operation of law, that accessible format copy may be distributed or made available by an authorized entity to a beneficiary person or an authorized entity in another Contracting Party.[6]

2.    A Contracting Party may fulfill Article 5(1) by providing a limitation or exception in its national copyright law such that:

(a)   authorized entities shall be permitted, without the authorization of the rightholder, to distribute or make available for the exclusive use of beneficiary persons accessible format copies to an authorized entity in another Contracting Party; and

(b)   authorized entities shall be permitted, without the authorization of the rightholder and pursuant to Article 2(c), to distribute or make available accessible format copies to a beneficiary person in another Contracting Party;

provided that prior to the distribution or making available the originating authorized entity did not know or have reasonable grounds to know that the accessible format copy would be used for other than beneficiary persons.[7]

3.    A Contracting Party may fulfill Article 5(1) by providing other limitations or exceptions in its national copyright law pursuant to Articles 5(4), 10 and 11.

4.    (a) When an authorized entity in a Contracting Party receives accessible format copies pursuant to Article 5(1) and that Contracting Party does not have obligations under Article 9 of the Berne Convention, it will ensure, consistent with its own legal system and practices, that the accessible format copies are only reproduced, distributed or made available for the benefit of beneficiary persons in that Contracting Party's jurisdiction.

(b)   The distribution and making available of accessible format copies by an authorized entity pursuant to Article 5(1) shall be limited to that jurisdiction unless the Contracting Party is a Party to the WIPO Copyright Treaty or otherwise limits limitations and exceptions implementing this Treaty to the right of distribution and the right of making available to the public to certain

---

[4]   Agreed statement concerning Article 4(3): It is understood that this paragraph neither reduces nor extends the scope of applicability of limitations and exceptions permitted under the Berne Convention, as regards the right of translation, with respect to persons with visual impairments or with other print disabilities.

[5]   Agreed statement concerning Article 4(4): It is understood that a commercial availability requirement does not prejudge whether or not a limitation or exception under this Article is consistent with the three-step test.

[6]   Agreed statement concerning Article 5(1): It is further understood that nothing in this Treaty reduces or extends the scope of exclusive rights under any other treaty.

[7]   Agreed statement concerning Article 5(2): It is understood that, to distribute or make available accessible format copies directly to a beneficiary person in another Contracting Party, it may be appropriate for an authorized entity to apply further measures to confirm that the person it is serving is a beneficiary person and to follow its own practices as described in Article 2(c).

special cases which do not conflict with a normal exploitation of the work and do not unreasonably prejudice the legitimate interests of the rightholder.[8, 9]

(c)   Nothing in this Article affects the determination of what constitutes an act of distribution or an act of making available to the public.

5.   Nothing in this Treaty shall be used to address the issue of exhaustion of rights.

## Article 6

### Importation of Accessible Format Copies

To the extent that the national law of a Contracting Party would permit a beneficiary person, someone acting on his or her behalf, or an authorized entity, to make an accessible format copy of a work, the national law of that Contracting Party shall also permit them to import an accessible format copy for the benefit of beneficiary persons, without the authorization of the rightholder.[10]

## Article 7

### Obligations Concerning Technological Measures

Contracting Parties shall take appropriate measures, as necessary, to ensure that when they provide adequate legal protection and effective legal remedies against the circumvention of effective technological measures, this legal protection does not prevent beneficiary persons from enjoying the limitations and exceptions provided for in this Treaty.[11]

## Article 8

### Respect for Privacy

In the implementation of the limitations and exceptions provided for in this Treaty, Contracting Parties shall endeavor to protect the privacy of beneficiary persons on an equal basis with others.

## Article 9

### Cooperation to Facilitate Cross-Border Exchange

1.   Contracting Parties shall endeavor to foster the cross-border exchange of accessible format copies by encouraging the voluntary sharing of information to assist authorized entities in identifying one another. The International Bureau of WIPO shall establish an information access point for this purpose.

2.   Contracting Parties undertake to assist their authorized entities engaged in activities under Article 5 to make information available regarding their practices pursuant to Article 2(c), both through the sharing of information among authorized entities, and through making available information on their policies and practices, including related to cross-border exchange of accessible format copies, to interested parties and members of the public as appropriate.

---

   [8]   Agreed statement concerning Article 5(4)(b): It is understood that nothing in this Treaty requires or implies that a Contracting Party adopt or apply the three-step test beyond its obligations under this instrument or under other international treaties.

   [9]   Agreed statement concerning Article 5(4)(b): It is understood that nothing in this Treaty creates any obligations for a Contracting Party to ratify or accede to the WCT or to comply with any of its provisions and nothing in this Treaty prejudices any rights, limitations and exceptions contained in the WCT.

   [10]   Agreed statement concerning Article 6: It is understood that the Contracting Parties have the same flexibilities set out in Article 4 when implementing their obligations under Article 6.

   [11]   Agreed statement concerning Article 7: It is understood that authorized entities, in various circumstances, choose to apply technological measures in the making, distribution and making available of accessible format copies and nothing herein disturbs such practices when in accordance with national law.

3. The International Bureau of WIPO is invited to share information, where available, about the functioning of this Treaty.

4. Contracting Parties recognize the importance of international cooperation and its promotion, in support of national efforts for realization of the purpose and objectives of this Treaty.[12]

## Article 10

### General Principles on Implementation

1. Contracting Parties undertake to adopt the measures necessary to ensure the application of this Treaty.

2. Nothing shall prevent Contracting Parties from determining the appropriate method of implementing the provisions of this Treaty within their own legal system and practice.[13]

3. Contracting Parties may fulfill their rights and obligations under this Treaty through limitations or exceptions specifically for the benefit of beneficiary persons, other limitations or exceptions, or a combination thereof, within their national legal system and practice. These may include judicial, administrative or regulatory determinations for the benefit of beneficiary persons as to fair practices, dealings or uses to meet their needs consistent with the Contracting Parties' rights and obligations under the Berne Convention, other international treaties, and Article 11.

## Article 11

### General Obligations on Limitations and Exceptions

In adopting measures necessary to ensure the application of this Treaty, a Contracting Party may exercise the rights and shall comply with the obligations that that Contracting Party has under the Berne Convention, the Agreement on Trade-Related Aspects of Intellectual Property Rights and the WIPO Copyright Treaty, including their interpretative agreements so that:

(a) in accordance with Article 9(2) of the Berne Convention, a Contracting Party may permit the reproduction of works in certain special cases provided that such reproduction does not conflict with a normal exploitation of the work and does not unreasonably prejudice the legitimate interests of the author;

(b) in accordance with Article 13 of the Agreement on Trade-Related Aspects of Intellectual Property Rights, a Contracting Party shall confine limitations or exceptions to exclusive rights to certain special cases which do not conflict with a normal exploitation of the work and do not unreasonably prejudice the legitimate interests of the rightholder;

(c) in accordance with Article 10(1) of the WIPO Copyright Treaty, a Contracting Party may provide for limitations of or exceptions to the rights granted to authors under the WCT in certain special cases, that do not conflict with a normal exploitation of the work and do not unreasonably prejudice the legitimate interests of the author;

(d) in accordance with Article 10(2) of the WIPO Copyright Treaty, a Contracting Party shall confine, when applying the Berne Convention, any limitations of or exceptions to rights to certain special cases that do not conflict with a normal exploitation of the work and do not unreasonably prejudice the legitimate interests of the author.

---

[12] Agreed statement concerning Article 9: It is understood that Article 9 does not imply mandatory registration for authorized entities nor does it constitute a precondition for authorized entities to engage in activities recognized under this Treaty; but it provides for a possibility for sharing information to facilitate the cross-border exchange of accessible format copies.

[13] Agreed statement concerning Article 10(2): It is understood that when a work qualifies as a work under Article 2(a), including such works in audio form, the limitations and exceptions provided for by this Treaty apply *mutatis mutandis* to related rights as necessary to make the accessible format copy, to distribute it and to make it available to beneficiary persons.

## Article 12

### Other Limitations and Exceptions

1.    Contracting Parties recognize that a Contracting Party may implement in its national law other copyright limitations and exceptions for the benefit of beneficiary persons than are provided by this Treaty having regard to that Contracting Party's economic situation, and its social and cultural needs, in conformity with that Contracting Party's international rights and obligations, and in the case of a least-developed country taking into account its special needs and its particular international rights and obligations and flexibilities thereof.

2.    This Treaty is without prejudice to other limitations and exceptions for persons with disabilities provided by national law.

## Article 13

### Assembly

1.    (a) The Contracting Parties shall have an Assembly.

(b)    Each Contracting Party shall be represented in the Assembly by one delegate who may be assisted by alternate delegates, advisors and experts.

(c)    The expenses of each delegation shall be borne by the Contracting Party that has appointed the delegation. The Assembly may ask WIPO to grant financial assistance to facilitate the participation of delegations of Contracting Parties that are regarded as developing countries in conformity with the established practice of the General Assembly of the United Nations or that are countries in transition to a market economy.

2.    (a) The Assembly shall deal with matters concerning the maintenance and development of this Treaty and the application and operation of this Treaty.

(b)    The Assembly shall perform the function allocated to it under Article 15 in respect of the admission of certain intergovernmental organizations to become party to this Treaty.

(c)    The Assembly shall decide the convocation of any diplomatic conference for the revision of this Treaty and give the necessary instructions to the Director General of WIPO for the preparation of such diplomatic conference.

3.    (a) Each Contracting Party that is a State shall have one vote and shall vote only in its own name.

(b)    Any Contracting Party that is an intergovernmental organization may participate in the vote, in place of its Member States, with a number of votes equal to the number of its Member States which are party to this Treaty. No such intergovernmental organization shall participate in the vote if any one of its Member States exercises its right to vote and vice versa.

4.    The Assembly shall meet upon convocation by the Director General and, in the absence of exceptional circumstances, during the same period and at the same place as the General Assembly of WIPO.

5.    The Assembly shall endeavor to take its decisions by consensus and shall establish its own rules of procedure, including the convocation of extraordinary sessions, the requirements of a quorum and, subject to the provisions of this Treaty, the required majority for various kinds of decisions.

## Article 14

### International Bureau

The International Bureau of WIPO shall perform the administrative tasks concerning this Treaty.

## Article 15

### Eligibility for Becoming Party to the Treaty

1.    Any Member State of WIPO may become party to this Treaty.

2.    The Assembly may decide to admit any intergovernmental organization to become party to this Treaty which declares that it is competent in respect of, and has its own legislation binding on all its Member States on, matters covered by this Treaty and that it has been duly authorized, in accordance with its internal procedures, to become party to this Treaty.

3.    The European Union, having made the declaration referred to in the preceding paragraph at the Diplomatic Conference that has adopted this Treaty, may become party to this Treaty.

## Article 16

### Rights and Obligations Under the Treaty

Subject to any specific provisions to the contrary in this Treaty, each Contracting Party shall enjoy all of the rights and assume all of the obligations under this Treaty.

## Article 17

### Signature of the Treaty

This Treaty shall be open for signature at the Diplomatic Conference in Marrakesh, and thereafter at the headquarters of WIPO by any eligible party for one year after its adoption.

## Article 18

### Entry into Force of the Treaty

This Treaty shall enter into force three months after 20 eligible parties referred to in Article 15 have deposited their instruments of ratification or accession.

## Article 19

### Effective Date of Becoming Party to the Treaty

This Treaty shall bind:

(a)    the 20 eligible parties referred to in Article 18, from the date on which this Treaty has entered into force;

(b)    each other eligible party referred to in Article 15, from the expiration of three months from the date on which it has deposited its instrument of ratification or accession with the Director General of WIPO.

## Article 20

### Denunciation of the Treaty

This Treaty may be denounced by any Contracting Party by notification addressed to the Director General of WIPO. Any denunciation shall take effect one year from the date on which the Director General of WIPO received the notification.

## Article 21

### Languages of the Treaty

1.    This Treaty is signed in a single original in English, Arabic, Chinese, French, Russian and Spanish languages, the versions in all these languages being equally authentic.

2.     An official text in any language other than those referred to in Article 21(1) shall be established by the Director General of WIPO on the request of an interested party, after consultation with all the interested parties. For the purposes of this paragraph, "interested party" means any Member State of WIPO whose official language, or one of whose official languages, is involved and the European Union, and any other intergovernmental organization that may become party to this Treaty, if one of its official languages is involved.

## Article 22

### Depositary

The Director General of WIPO is the depositary of this Treaty.

# 30. PARTIES TO THE MARRAKESH TREATY TO FACILITATE ACCESS TO PUBLISHED WORKS FOR PERSONS WHO ARE BLIND, VISUALLY IMPAIRED, OR OTHERWISE PRINT DISABLED*

Marrakesh Treaty (Marrakesh, 2013)

**Status on May 4, 2021**

| State/IGO | Date on which State/IGO became party to the Treaty |
|---|---|
| Afghanistan | October 26, 2018 |
| Argentina | September 30, 2016 |
| Australia[1] | September 30, 2016 |
| Azerbaijan[2] | December 24, 2018 |
| Belarus | October 22, 2020 |
| Belize | February 9, 2019 |
| Bolivia (Plurinational State of) | June 12, 2019 |
| Bosnia and Herzegovina | April 20, 2021 |
| Botswana | January 5, 2017 |
| Brazil | September 30, 2016 |
| Burkina Faso | October 31, 2017 |
| Canada[1] | September 30, 2016 |
| Cabo Verde | May 22, 2019 |
| Central African Republic | November 19, 2020 |
| Chile | September 30, 2016 |
| Comoros | April 25, 2021 |
| Cook Islands | June 19, 2019 |
| Costa Rica | January 9, 2018 |
| Côte d'Ivoire | December 17, 2020 |
| Democratic People's Republic of Korea | September 30, 2016 |
| Dominican Republic | September 5, 2018 |
| Ecuador | September 30, 2016 |
| El Salvador | September 30, 2016 |
| Ethiopia | February 2, 2021 |
| European Union | January 1, 2019 |
| Ghana | August 11, 2018 |
| Guatemala | September 30, 2016 |
| Honduras | June 29, 2017 |
| India | September 30, 2016 |
| Indonesia | April 28, 2020 |

---

| State/IGO | Date on which State/IGO became party to the Treaty |
|---|---|
| Israel | September 30, 2016 |
| Japan[1] | January 1, 2019 |
| Jordan | September 26, 2018 |
| Kenya | September 2, 2017 |
| Kiribati | October 31, 2019 |
| Kyrgyzstan | August 15, 2017 |
| Lesotho | July 30, 2018 |
| Liberia | January 6, 2017 |
| Malawi | October 14, 2017 |
| Mali | September 30, 2016 |
| Marshall Islands | May 8, 2019 |
| Mauritius | April 25, 2021 |
| Mexico | September 30, 2016 |
| Mongolia | September 30, 2016 |
| Morocco | August 15, 2019 |
| New Zealand[3] | January 4, 2020 |
| Nicaragua | April 16, 2020 |
| Nigeria | January 4, 2018 |
| Panama | May 10, 2017 |
| Paraguay | September 30, 2016 |
| Peru | September 30, 2016 |
| Philippines | March 18, 2019 |
| Qatar | January 24, 2019 |
| Republic of Korea | September 30, 2016 |
| Republic of Moldova | May 19, 2018 |
| Russian Federation | May 8, 2018 |
| Saint Lucia | September 11, 2020 |
| Saint Vincent and the Grenadines | December 5, 2016 |
| San Marino | September 2, 2020 |
| Sao Tome and Principe | January 15, 2021 |
| Saudi Arabia | February 21, 2019 |
| Serbia | May 24, 2020 |
| Singapore | September 30, 2016 |
| Sri Lanka | January 5, 2017 |
| Switzerland | May 11, 2020 |
| Tajikistan | May 27, 2019 |
| Thailand | April 28, 2019 |
| Trinidad and Tobago | January 4, 2020 |
| Tunisia | December 7, 2016 |
| Turkmenistan | January 15, 2021 |
| Uganda | July 23, 2018 |

## PARTIES TO THE MARRAKESH TREATY

| State/IGO | Date on which State/IGO became party to the Treaty |
|---|---|
| United Arab Emirates | September 30, 2016 |
| United Kingdom[4] | January 1, 2021 |
| United Republic of Tanzania | July 8, 2020 |
| United States of America | May 8, 2019 |
| Uruguay | September 30, 2016 |
| Vanuatu | August 6, 2020 |
| Venezuela (Bolivarian Republic of) | January 2, 2020 |
| Zimbabwe | December 12, 2019 |

(Total: 79)

---

[1]   With the declaration under Article 4(4).

[2]   The Republic of Azerbaijan declares that the provisions of the Marrakesh Treaty to Facilitate Access to Published Works for Persons Who Are Blind, Visually Impaired or Otherwise Print Disabled shall not be applied by the Republic of Azerbaijan in respect of the Republic of Armenia in the future; and

The Republic of Azerbaijan declares that it is unable to guarantee the implementation of the provisions of the Marrakesh Treaty to Facilitated Access to Published Works for Persons Who Are Blind, Visually Impaired or Otherwise Print Disabled in its territories occupied by the Republic of Armenia (the Nagorno-Karabakh region of the Republic of Azerbaijan and its seven districts surrounding that region) until the liberation of those territories from the occupation and complete elimination of the consequences of that occupation.

[3]   The accession by New Zealand shall extend to Tokelau.

[4]   Ratification in respect of the United Kingdom, and the Bailiwick of Guernsey, the Bailiwick of Jersey, Gibraltar and the Isle of Man.

# PATENTS AND PLANT VARIETY PROTECTION

---

## 31. PARIS CONVENTION FOR THE PROTECTION OF INDUSTRIAL PROPERTY

of March 20, 1883, as revised

at BRUSSELS on December 14, 1900, at WASHINGTON on June 2, 1911, at THE HAGUE on November 6, 1925, at LONDON on June 2, 1934, at LISBON on October 31, 1958, and at STOCKHOLM on July 14, 1967

### Article 1

### [Establishment of the Union; Scope of Industrial Property]

(1)   The countries to which this Convention applies constitute a Union for the protection of industrial property.

(2)   The protection of industrial property has as its object patents, utility models, industrial designs, trademarks, service marks, trade names, indications of source or appellations of origin, and the repression of unfair competition.

(3)   Industrial property shall be understood in the broadest sense and shall apply not only to industry and commerce proper, but likewise to agricultural and extractive industries and to all manufactured or natural products, for example, wines, grain, tobacco leaf, fruit, cattle, minerals, mineral waters, beer, flowers, and flour.

(4)   Patents shall include the various kinds of industrial patents recognized by the laws of the countries of the Union, such as patents of importation, patents of improvement, patents and certificates of addition, etc.

### Article 2

### [National Treatment for Nationals of Countries of the Union]

(1)   Nationals of any country of the Union shall, as regards the protection of industrial property, enjoy in all the other countries of the Union the advantages that their respective laws now grant, or may hereafter grant, to nationals; all without prejudice to the rights specially provided for by this Convention. Consequently, they shall have the same protection as the latter, and the same legal remedy against any infringement of their rights, provided that the conditions and formalities imposed upon nationals are complied with.

(2)   However, no requirement as to domicile or establishment in the country where protection is claimed may be imposed upon nationals of countries of the Union for the enjoyment of any industrial property rights.

(3)   The provisions of the laws of each of the countries of the Union relating to judicial and administrative procedure and to jurisdiction, and to the designation of an address for service or the appointment of an agent, which may be required by the laws on industrial property are expressly reserved.

## Article 3

### [Same Treatment for Certain Categories of Persons as for Nationals of Countries of the Union]

Nationals of countries outside the Union who are domiciled or who have real and effective industrial or commercial establishments in the territory of one of the countries of the Union shall be treated in the same manner as nationals of the countries of the Union.

## Article 4

### [A to I. *Patents, Utility Models, Industrial Designs, Marks, Inventors' Certificates*: Right of Priority.—G. *Patents*: Division of the Application]

A.—

(1)   Any person who has duly filed an application for a patent, or for the registration of a utility model, or of an industrial design, or of a trademark, in one of the countries of the Union, or his successor in title, shall enjoy, for the purpose of filing in the other countries, a right of priority during the periods hereinafter fixed.

(2)   Any filing that is equivalent to a regular national filing under the domestic legislation of any country of the Union or under bilateral or multilateral treaties concluded between countries of the Union shall be recognized as giving rise to the right of priority.

(3)   By a regular national filing is meant any filing that is adequate to establish the date on which the application was filed in the country concerned, whatever may be the subsequent fate of the application.

B.—Consequently, any subsequent filing in any of the other countries of the Union before the expiration of the periods referred to above shall not be invalidated by reason of any acts accomplished in the interval, in particular, another filing, the publication or exploitation of the invention, the putting on sale of copies of the design, or the use of the mark, and such acts cannot give rise to any third-party right or any right of personal possession. Rights acquired by third parties before the date of the first application that serves as the basis for the right of priority are reserved in accordance with the domestic legislation of each country of the Union.

C.—

(1)   The periods of priority referred to above shall be twelve months for patents and utility models, and six months for industrial designs and trademarks.

(2)   These periods shall start from the date of filing of the first application; the day of filing shall not be included in the period.

(3)   If the last day of the period is an official holiday, or a day when the Office is not open for the filing of applications in the country where protection is claimed, the period shall be extended until the first following working day.

(4)   A subsequent application concerning the same subject as a previous first application within the meaning of paragraph (2), above, filed in the same country of the Union, shall be considered as the first application, of which the filing date shall be the starting point of the period of priority, if, at the time of filing the subsequent application, the said previous application has been withdrawn, abandoned, or refused, without having been laid open to public inspection and without leaving any rights outstanding, and if it has not yet served as a basis for claiming a right of priority. The previous application may not thereafter serve as a basis for claiming a right of priority.

D.—

(1)   Any person desiring to take advantage of the priority of a previous filing shall be required to make a declaration indicating the date of such filing and the country in which it was made. Each country shall determine the latest date on which such declaration must be made.

(2)   These particulars shall be mentioned in the publications issued by the competent authority, and in particular in the patents and the specifications relating thereto.

(3)   The countries of the Union may require any person making a declaration of priority to produce a copy of the application (description, drawings, etc.) previously filed. The copy, certified as correct by the authority which received such application, shall not require any authentication, and may in any case be filed, without fee, at any time within three months of the filing of the subsequent application. They may require it to be accompanied by a certificate from the same authority showing the date of filing, and by a translation.

(4)   No other formalities may be required for the declaration of priority at the time of filing the application. Each country of the Union shall determine the consequences of failure to comply with the formalities prescribed by this Article, but such consequences shall in no case go beyond the loss of the right of priority.

(5)   Subsequently, further proof may be required.

Any person who avails himself of the priority of a previous application shall be required to specify the number of that application; this number shall be published as provided for by paragraph (2), above.

E.—

(1)   Where an industrial design is filed in a country by virtue of a right of priority based on the filing of a utility model, the period of priority shall be the same as that fixed for industrial designs.

(2)   Furthermore, it is permissible to file a utility model in a country by virtue of a right of priority based on the filing of a patent application, and vice versa.

F.—No country of the Union may refuse a priority or a patent application on the ground that the applicant claims multiple priorities, even if they originate in different countries, or on the ground that an application claiming one or more priorities contains one or more elements that were not included in the application or applications whose priority is claimed, provided that, in both cases, there is unity of invention within the meaning of the law of the country.

With respect to the elements not included in the application or applications whose priority is claimed, the filing of the subsequent application shall give rise to a right of priority under ordinary conditions.

G.—

(1)   If the examination reveals that an application for a patent contains more than one invention, the applicant may divide the application into a certain number of divisional applications and preserve as the date of each the date of the initial application and the benefit of the right of priority, if any.

(2)   The applicant may also, on his own initiative, divide a patent application and preserve as the date of each divisional application the date of the initial application and the benefit of the right of priority, if any. Each country of the Union shall have the right to determine the conditions under which such division shall be authorized.

H.—Priority may not be refused on the ground that certain elements of the invention for which priority is claimed do not appear among the claims formulated in the application in the country of origin, provided that the application documents as a whole specifically disclose such elements.

I.—

(1) Applications for inventors' certificates filed in a country in which applicants have the right to apply at their own option either for a patent or for an inventor's certificate shall give rise to the right of priority provided for by this Article, under the same conditions and with the same effects as applications for patents.

(2) In a country in which applicants have the right to apply at their own option either for a patent or for an inventor's certificate, an applicant for an inventor's certificate shall, in accordance with the provisions of this Article relating to patent applications, enjoy a right of priority based on an application for a patent, a utility model, or an inventor's certificate.

## Article 4bis

### [*Patents*: Independence of Patents Obtained for the Same Invention in Different Countries]

(1) Patents applied for in the various countries of the Union by nationals of countries of the Union shall be independent of patents obtained for the same invention in other countries, whether members of the Union or not.

(2) The foregoing provision is to be understood in an unrestricted sense, in particular, in the sense that patents applied for during the period of priority are independent, both as regards the grounds for nullity and forfeiture, and as regards their normal duration.

(3) The provision shall apply to all patents existing at the time when it comes into effect.

(4) Similarly, it shall apply, in the case of the accession of new countries, to patents in existence on either side at the time of accession.

(5) Patents obtained with the benefit of priority shall, in the various countries of the Union, have a duration equal to that which they would have, had they been applied for or granted without the benefit of priority.

## Article 4ter

### [*Patents*: Mention of the Inventor in the Patent]

The inventor shall have the right to be mentioned as such in the patent.

## Article 4quater

### [*Patents*: Patentability in Case of Restrictions of Sale by Law]

The grant of a patent shall not be refused and a patent shall not be invalidated on the ground that the sale of the patented product or of a product obtained by means of a patented process is subject to restrictions or limitations resulting from the domestic law.

## Article 5

### [A. *Patents*: Importation of Articles; Failure to Work or Insufficient Working; Compulsory Licenses.—B. *Industrial Designs*: Failure to Work; Importation of Articles.—C. *Marks*: Failure to Use; Different Forms; Use by Co-proprietors. —D. *Patents, Utility Models, Marks, Industrial Designs*: Marking]

A.—

(1) Importation by the patentee into the country where the patent has been granted of articles manufactured in any of the countries of the Union shall not entail forfeiture of the patent.

(2)   Each country of the Union shall have the right to take legislative measures providing for the grant of compulsory licenses to prevent the abuses which might result from the exercise of the exclusive rights conferred by the patent, for example, failure to work.

(3)   Forfeiture of the patent shall not be provided for except in cases where the grant of compulsory licenses would not have been sufficient to prevent the said abuses. No proceedings for the forfeiture or revocation of a patent may be instituted before the expiration of two years from the grant of the first compulsory license.

(4)   A compulsory license may not be applied for on the ground of failure to work or insufficient working before the expiration of a period of four years from the date of filing of the patent application or three years from the date of the grant of the patent, whichever period expires last; it shall be refused if the patentee justifies his inaction by legitimate reasons. Such a compulsory license shall be non-exclusive and shall not be transferable, even in the form of the grant of a sub-license, except with that part of the enterprise or goodwill which exploits such license.

(5)   The foregoing provisions shall be applicable, *mutatis mutandis*, to utility models.

B.—The protection of industrial designs shall not, under any circumstance, be subject to any forfeiture, either by reason of failure to work or by reason of the importation of articles corresponding to those which are protected.

C.—

(1)   If, in any country, use of the registered mark is compulsory, the registration may be cancelled only after a reasonable period, and then only if the person concerned does not justify his inaction.

(2)   Use of a trademark by the proprietor in a form differing in elements which do not alter the distinctive character of the mark in the form in which it was registered in one of the countries of the Union shall not entail invalidation of the registration and shall not diminish the protection granted to the mark.

(3)   Concurrent use of the same mark on identical or similar goods by industrial or commercial establishments considered as co-proprietors of the mark according to the provisions of the domestic law of the country where protection is claimed shall not prevent registration or diminish in any way the protection granted to the said mark in any country of the Union, provided that such use does not result in misleading the public and is not contrary to the public interest.

D.—No indication or mention of the patent, of the utility model, of the registration of the trademark, or of the deposit of the industrial design, shall be required upon the goods as a condition of recognition of the right to protection.

## Article 5bis

### [*All Industrial Property Rights*: Period of Grace for the Payment of Fees for the Maintenance of Rights; *Patents*: Restoration]

(1)   A period of grace of not less than six months shall be allowed for the payment of the fees prescribed for the maintenance of industrial property rights, subject, if the domestic legislation so provides, to the payment of a surcharge.

(2)   The countries of the Union shall have the right to provide for the restoration of patents which have lapsed by reason of non-payment of fees.

Article 5ter  — *very limited.*
*Mainly abathship.*

**[*Patents*: Patented Devices Forming Part of Vessels, Aircraft, or Land Vehicles]**

In any country of the Union the following shall not be considered as infringements of the rights of a patentee:

1.    the use on board vessels of other countries of the Union of devices forming the subject of his patent in the body of the vessel, in the machinery, tackle, gear and other accessories, when such vessels temporarily or accidentally enter the waters of the said country, provided that such devices are used there exclusively for the needs of the vessel;

2.    the use of devices forming the subject of the patent in the construction or operation of aircraft or land vehicles of other countries of the Union, or of accessories of such aircraft or land vehicles, when those aircraft or land vehicles temporarily or accidentally enter the said country.

## Article 5quater

**[*Patents*: Importation of Products Manufactured by
a Process Patented in the Importing Country]**

When a product is imported into a country of the Union where there exists a patent protecting a process of manufacture of the said product, the patentee shall have all the rights, with regard to the imported product, that are accorded to him by the legislation of the country of importation, on the basis of the process patent, with respect to products manufactured in that country.

*patent Rights attach to
product, processes, &
products made by process.*

## Article 5quinquies

**[*Industrial Designs*]**

Industrial designs shall be protected in all the countries of the Union.

## Article 6

**[*Marks*: Conditions of Registration; Independence of
Protection of Same Mark in Different Countries]**

(1)    The conditions for the filing and registration of trademarks shall be determined in each country of the Union by its domestic legislation.

(2)    However, an application for the registration of a mark filed by a national of a country of the Union in any country of the Union may not be refused, nor may a registration be invalidated, on the ground that filing, registration, or renewal, has not been effected in the country of origin.

(3)    A mark duly registered in a country of the Union shall be regarded as independent of marks registered in the other countries of the Union, including the country of origin.

## Article 6bis

**[*Marks*: Well-Known Marks]**

(1)    The countries of the Union undertake, *ex officio* if their legislation so permits, or at the request of an interested party, to refuse or to cancel the registration, and to prohibit the use, of a trademark which constitutes a reproduction, an imitation, or a translation, liable to create confusion, of a mark considered by the competent authority of the country of registration or use to be well known in that country as being already the mark of a person entitled to the benefits of this Convention and used for identical or similar goods. These provisions shall also apply when the essential part of the mark constitutes a reproduction of any such well-known mark or an imitation liable to create confusion therewith.

(2)   A period of at least five years from the date of registration shall be allowed for requesting the cancellation of such a mark. The countries of the Union may provide for a period within which the prohibition of use must be requested.

(3)   No time limit shall be fixed for requesting the cancellation or the prohibition of the use of marks registered or used in bad faith.

**Article 6ter**

**[*Marks*: Prohibitions Concerning State Emblems, Official Hallmarks, and Emblems of Intergovernmental Organizations]**

(1)

(*a*)   The countries of the Union agree to refuse or to invalidate the registration, and to prohibit by appropriate measures the use, without authorization by the competent authorities, either as trademarks or as elements of trademarks, of armorial bearings, flags, and other State emblems, of the countries of the Union, official signs and hallmarks indicating control and warranty adopted by them, and any imitation from a heraldic point of view.

(*b*)   The provisions of subparagraph (*a*), above, shall apply equally to armorial bearings, flags, other emblems, abbreviations, and names, of international intergovernmental organizations of which one or more countries of the Union are members, with the exception of armorial bearings, flags, other emblems, abbreviations, and names, that are already the subject of international agreements in force, intended to ensure their protection.

(*c*)   No country of the Union shall be required to apply the provisions of subparagraph (*b*), above, to the prejudice of the owners of rights acquired in good faith before the entry into force, in that country, of this Convention. The countries of the Union shall not be required to apply the said provisions when the use or registration referred to in subparagraph (*a*), above, is not of such a nature as to suggest to the public that a connection exists between the organization concerned and the armorial bearings, flags, emblems, abbreviations, and names, or if such use or registration is probably not of such a nature as to mislead the public as to the existence of a connection between the user and the organization.

(2)   Prohibition of the use of official signs and hallmarks indicating control and warranty shall apply solely in cases where the marks in which they are incorporated are intended to be used on goods of the same or a similar kind.

(3)

(*a*)   For the application of these provisions, the countries of the Union agree to communicate reciprocally, through the intermediary of the International Bureau, the list of State emblems, and official signs and hallmarks indicating control and warranty, which they desire, or may hereafter desire, to place wholly or within certain limits under the protection of this Article, and all subsequent modifications of such list. Each country of the Union shall in due course make available to the public the lists so communicated.

Nevertheless such communication is not obligatory in respect of flags of States.

(*b*)   The provisions of subparagraph (*b*) of paragraph (1) of this Article shall apply only to such armorial bearings, flags, other emblems, abbreviations, and names, of international intergovernmental organizations as the latter have communicated to the countries of the Union through the intermediary of the International Bureau.

(4)   Any country of the Union may, within a period of twelve months from the receipt of the notification, transmit its objections, if any, through the intermediary of the International Bureau, to the country or international intergovernmental organization concerned.

(5)   In the case of State flags, the measures prescribed by paragraph (1), above, shall apply solely to marks registered after November 6, 1925.

(6)   In the case of State emblems other than flags, and of official signs and hallmarks of the countries of the Union, and in the case of armorial bearings, flags, other emblems, abbreviations, and names, of international intergovernmental organizations, these provisions shall apply only to marks registered more than two months after receipt of the communication provided for in paragraph (3), above.

(7)   In cases of bad faith, the countries shall have the right to cancel even those marks incorporating State emblems, signs, and hallmarks, which were registered before November 6, 1925.

(8)   Nationals of any country who are authorized to make use of the State emblems, signs, and hallmarks, of their country may use them even if they are similar to those of another country.

(9)   The countries of the Union undertake to prohibit the unauthorized use in trade of the State armorial bearings of the other countries of the Union, when the use is of such a nature as to be misleading as to the origin of the goods.

(10) The above provisions shall not prevent the countries from exercising the right given in paragraph (3) of Article 6quinquies, Section B, to refuse or to invalidate the registration of marks incorporating, without authorization, armorial bearings, flags, other State emblems, or official signs and hallmarks adopted by a country of the Union, as well as the distinctive signs of international intergovernmental organizations referred to in paragraph (1), above.

## Article 6quater

### [*Marks:* Assignment of Marks]

(1)   When, in accordance with the law of a country of the Union, the assignment of a mark is valid only if it takes place at the same time as the transfer of the business or goodwill to which the mark belongs, it shall suffice for the recognition of such validity that the portion of the business or goodwill located in that country be transferred to the assignee, together with the exclusive right to manufacture in the said country, or to sell therein, the goods bearing the mark assigned.

(2)   The foregoing provision does not impose upon the countries of the Union any obligation to regard as valid the assignment of any mark the use of which by the assignee would, in fact, be of such a nature as to mislead the public, particularly as regards the origin, nature, or essential qualities, of the goods to which the mark is applied.

## Article 6quinquies

### [*Marks:* Protection of Marks Registered in One Country of the Union in the Other Countries of the Union]

A.—

(1)   Every trademark duly registered in the country of origin shall be accepted for filing and protected as is in the other countries of the Union, subject to the reservations indicated in this Article. Such countries may, before proceeding to final registration, require the production of a certificate of registration in the country of origin, issued by the competent authority. No authentication shall be required for this certificate.

(2)   Shall be considered the country of origin the country of the Union where the applicant has a real and effective industrial or commercial establishment, or, if he has no such establishment within the Union, the country of the Union where he has his domicile, or, if he has no domicile within the Union but is a national of a country of the Union, the country of which he is a national.

B.—Trademarks covered by this Article may be neither denied registration nor invalidated except in the following cases:

1.     when they are of such a nature as to infringe rights acquired by third parties in the country where protection is claimed;

2.     when they are devoid of any distinctive character, or consist exclusively of signs or indications which may serve, in trade, to designate the kind, quality, quantity, intended purpose, value, place of origin, of the goods, or the time of production, or have become customary in the current language or in the bona fide and established practices of the trade of the country where protection is claimed;

3.     when they are contrary to morality or public order and, in particular, of such a nature as to deceive the public. It is understood that a mark may not be considered contrary to public order for the sole reason that it does not conform to a provision of the legislation on marks, except if such provision itself relates to public order.

This provision is subject, however, to the application of Article 10$^{bis}$.

C.—

(1)     In determining whether a mark is eligible for protection, all the factual circumstances must be taken into consideration, particularly the length of time the mark has been in use.

(2)     No trademark shall be refused in the other countries of the Union for the sole reason that it differs from the mark protected in the country of origin only in respect of elements that do not alter its distinctive character and do not affect its identity in the form in which it has been registered in the said country of origin.

D.—No person may benefit from the provisions of this Article if the mark for which he claims protection is not registered in the country of origin.

E.—However, in no case shall the renewal of the registration of the mark in the country of origin involve an obligation to renew the registration in the other countries of the Union in which the mark has been registered.

F.—The benefit of priority shall remain unaffected for applications for the registration of marks filed within the period fixed by Article 4, even if registration in the country of origin is effected after the expiration of such period.

## Article 6<sup>sexies</sup>

### [*Marks*: Service Marks]

The countries of the Union undertake to protect service marks. They shall not be required to provide for the registration of such marks.

## Article 6<sup>septies</sup>

### [*Marks*: Registration in the Name of the Agent or Representative of the Proprietor Without the Latter's Authorization]

(1)     If the agent or representative of the person who is the proprietor of a mark in one of the countries of the Union applies, without such proprietor's authorization, for the registration of the mark in his own name, in one or more countries of the Union, the proprietor shall be entitled to oppose the registration applied for or demand its cancellation or, if the law of the country so allows, the assignment in his favor of the said registration, unless such agent or representative justifies his action.

(2)     The proprietor of the mark shall, subject to the provisions of paragraph (1), above, be entitled to oppose the use of his mark by his agent or representative if he has not authorized such use.

(3)   Domestic legislation may provide an equitable time limit within which the proprietor of a mark must exercise the rights provided for in this Article.

## Article 7

### [*Marks*: Nature of the Goods to which the Mark is Applied]

The nature of the goods to which a trademark is to be applied shall in no case form an obstacle to the registration of the mark.

## Article 7bis

### [*Marks*: Collective Marks]

(1)   The countries of the Union undertake to accept for filing and to protect collective marks belonging to associations the existence of which is not contrary to the law of the country of origin, even if such associations do not possess an industrial or commercial establishment.

(2)   Each country shall be the judge of the particular conditions under which a collective mark shall be protected and may refuse protection if the mark is contrary to the public interest.

(3)   Nevertheless, the protection of these marks shall not be refused to any association the existence of which is not contrary to the law of the country of origin, on the ground that such association is not established in the country where protection is sought or is not constituted according to the law of the latter country.

## Article 8

### [*Trade Names*]

A trade name shall be protected in all the countries of the Union without the obligation of filing or registration, whether or not it forms part of a trademark.

## Article 9

### [*Marks, Trade Names*: Seizure, on Importation, etc., of Goods Unlawfully Bearing a Mark or Trade Name]

(1)   All goods unlawfully bearing a trademark or trade name shall be seized on importation into those countries of the Union where such mark or trade name is entitled to legal protection.

(2)   Seizure shall likewise be effected in the country where the unlawful affixation occurred or in the country into which the goods were imported.

(3)   Seizure shall take place at the request of the public prosecutor, or any other competent authority, or any interested party, whether a natural person or a legal entity, in conformity with the domestic legislation of each country.

(4)   The authorities shall not be bound to effect seizure of goods in transit.

(5)   If the legislation of a country does not permit seizure on importation, seizure shall be replaced by prohibition of importation or by seizure inside the country.

(6)   If the legislation of a country permits neither seizure on importation nor prohibition of importation nor seizure inside the country, then, until such time as the legislation is modified accordingly, these measures shall be replaced by the actions and remedies available in such cases to nationals under the law of such country.

## Article 10

### [*False Indications*: Seizure, on Importation, etc., of Goods Bearing False Indications as to their Source or the Identity of the Producer]

(1)   The provisions of the preceding Article shall apply in cases of direct or indirect use of a false indication of the source of the goods or the identity of the producer, manufacturer, or merchant.

(2)   Any producer, manufacturer, or merchant, whether a natural person or a legal entity, engaged in the production or manufacture of or trade in such goods and established either in the locality falsely indicated as the source, or in the region where such locality is situated, or in the country falsely indicated, or in the country where the false indication of source is used, shall in any case be deemed an interested party.

## Article 10<sup>bis</sup>

### [*Unfair Competition*]

(1)   The countries of the Union are bound to assure to nationals of such countries effective protection against unfair competition.

(2)   Any act of competition contrary to honest practices in industrial or commercial matters constitutes an act of unfair competition.

(3)   The following in particular shall be prohibited:

1.   all acts of such a nature as to create confusion by any means whatever with the establishment, the goods, or the industrial or commercial activities, of a competitor;

2.   false allegations in the course of trade of such a nature as to discredit the establishment, the goods, or the industrial or commercial activities, of a competitor;

3.   indications or allegations the use of which in the course of trade is liable to mislead the public as to the nature, the manufacturing process, the characteristics, the suitability for their purpose, or the quantity, of the goods.

## Article 10<sup>ter</sup>

### [*Marks, Trade Names, False Indications, Unfair Competition*: Remedies, Right to Sue]

(1)   The countries of the Union undertake to assure to nationals of the other countries of the Union appropriate legal remedies effectively to repress all the acts referred to in Articles 9, 10, and 10<sup>bis</sup>.

(2)   They undertake, further, to provide measures to permit federations and associations representing interested industrialists, producers, or merchants, provided that the existence of such federations and associations is not contrary to the laws of their countries, to take action in the courts or before the administrative authorities, with a view to the repression of the acts referred to in Articles 9, 10, and 10<sup>bis</sup>, in so far as the law of the country in which protection is claimed allows such action by federations and associations of that country.

## Article 11

### [*Inventions, Utility Models, Industrial Designs, Marks*: Temporary Protection at Certain International Exhibitions]

(1)   The countries of the Union shall, in conformity with their domestic legislation, grant temporary protection to patentable inventions, utility models, industrial designs, and trademarks, in respect of goods exhibited at official or officially recognized international exhibitions held in the territory of any of them.

(2) Such temporary protection shall not extend the periods provided by Article 4. If, later, the right of priority is invoked, the authorities of any country may provide that the period shall start from the date of introduction of the goods into the exhibition.

(3) Each country may require, as proof of the identity of the article exhibited and of the date of its introduction, such documentary evidence as it considers necessary.

## Article 12

### [Special National Industrial Property Services]

(1) Each country of the Union undertakes to establish a special industrial property service and a central office for the communication to the public of patents, utility models, industrial designs, and trademarks.

(2) This service shall publish an official periodical journal. It shall publish regularly:

(*a*) the names of the proprietors of patents granted, with a brief designation of the inventions patented;

(*b*) the reproductions of registered trademarks.

## Article 13

### [Assembly of the Union]

(1)

(*a*) The Union shall have an Assembly consisting of those countries of the Union which are bound by Articles 13 to 17.

(*b*) The Government of each country shall be represented by one delegate, who may be assisted by alternate delegates, advisors, and experts.

(*c*) The expenses of each delegation shall be borne by the Government which has appointed it.

(2)

(*a*) The Assembly shall:

(i) deal with all matters concerning the maintenance and development of the Union and the implementation of this Convention;

(ii) give directions concerning the preparation for conferences of revision to the International Bureau of Intellectual Property (hereinafter designated as "the International Bureau") referred to in the Convention establishing the World Intellectual Property Organization (hereinafter designated as "the Organization"), due account being taken of any comments made by those countries of the Union which are not hound by Articles 13 to 17;

(iii) review and approve the reports and activities of the Director General of the Organization concerning the Union, and give him all necessary instructions concerning matters within the competence of the Union;

(iv) elect the members of the Executive Committee of the Assembly;

(v) review and approve the reports and activities of its Executive Committee, and give instructions to such Committee;

(vi) determine the program and adopt the biennial budget of the Union, and approve its final accounts;

(vii) adopt the financial regulations of the Union;

(viii) establish such committees of experts and working groups as it deems appropriate to achieve the objectives of the Union;

(ix) determine which countries not members of the Union and which intergovernmental and international nongovernmental organizations shall be admitted to its meetings as observers;

(x) adopt amendments to Articles 13 to 17;

(xi) take any other appropriate action designed to further the objectives of the Union;

(xii) perform such other functions as are appropriate under this Convention;

(xiii) subject to its acceptance, exercise such rights as are given to it in the Convention establishing the Organization.

(*b*) With respect to matters which are of interest also to other Unions administered by the Organization, the Assembly shall make its decisions after having heard the advice of the Coordination Committee of the Organization.

(3)

(*a*) Subject to the provisions of subparagraph (b), a delegate may represent one country only.

(*b*) Countries of the Union grouped under the terms of a special agreement in a common office possessing for each of them the character of a special national service of industrial property as referred to in Article 12 may be jointly represented during discussions by one of their number.

(4)

(*a*) Each country member of the Assembly shall have one vote.

(*b*) One-half of the countries members of the Assembly shall constitute a quorum.

(*c*) Notwithstanding the provisions of subparagraph (b), if, in any session, the number of countries represented is less than one-half but equal to or more than one-third of the countries members of the Assembly, the Assembly may make decisions but, with the exception of decisions concerning its own procedure, all such decisions shall take effect only if the conditions, set forth hereinafter are fufilled. The International Bureau shall communicate the said decisions to the countries members of the Assembly which were not represented and shall invite them to express in writing their vote or abstention within a period of three months from the date of the communication. If, at the expiration of this period, the number of countries having thus expressed their vote or abstention attains the number of countries which was lacking for attaining the quorum in the session itself, such decisions shall take effect provided that at the same time the required majority still obtains.

(*d*) Subject to the provisions of Article 17(2), the decisions of the Assembly shall require two-thirds of the votes cast.

(*e*) Abstentions shall not be considered as votes.

(5)

(*a*) Subject to the provisions of subparagraph (b), a delegate may vote in the name of one country only.

(*b*) The countries of the Union referred to in paragraph (3)(b) shall, as a general rule, endeavor to send their own delegations to the sessions of the Assembly. If, however, for exceptional reasons, any such country cannot send its own delegation, it may give to the delegation of another such country the power to vote in its name, provided that each delegation may vote by proxy for one country only. Such power to vote shall be granted in a document signed by the Head of State or the competent Minister.

(6) Countries of the Union not members of the Assembly shall be admitted to the meetings of the latter as observers.

(7)

(*a*) The Assembly shall meet once in every second calendar year in ordinary session upon convocation by the Director General and, in the absence of exceptional circumstances, during the same period and at the same place as the General Assembly of the Organization.

(*b*) The Assembly shall meet in extraordinary session upon convocation by the Director General, at the request of the Executive Committee or at the request of one-fourth of the countries members of the Assembly.

(8) The Assembly shall adopt its own rules of procedure.

## Article 14

### [Executive Committee]

(1) The Assembly shall have an Executive Committee.

(2)

(*a*) The Executive Committee shall consist of countries elected by the Assembly from among countries members of the Assembly. Furthermore, the country on whose territory the Organization has its headquarters shall, subject to the provisions of Article 16(7)(b), have an *ex officio* seat on the Committee.

(*b*) The Government of each country member of the Executive Committee shall be represented by one delegate, who may be assisted by alternate delegates, advisors, and experts.

(*c*) The expenses of each delegation shall be borne by the Government which has appointed it.

(3) The number of countries members of the Executive Committee shall correspond to one-fourth of the number of countries members of the Assembly. In establishing the number of seats to be filled, remainders after division by four shall be disregarded.

(4) In electing the members of the Executive Committee, the Assembly shall have due regard to an equitable geographical distribution and to the need for countries party to the Special Agreements established in relation with the Union to be among the countries constituting the Executive Committee.

(5)

(*a*) Each member of the Executive Committee shall serve from the close of the session of the Assembly which elected it to the close of the next ordinary session of the Assembly.

(*b*) Members of the Executive Committee may be re-elected, but only up to a maximum of two-thirds of such members.

(*c*) The Assembly shall establish the details of the rules governing the election and possible re-election of the members of the Executive Committee.

(6)

(*a*) The Executive Committee shall:

(i) prepare the draft agenda of the Assembly;

(ii) submit proposals to the Assembly in respect of the draft program and biennial budget of the Union prepared by the Director General;

(iii) deleted

(iv)  submit, with appropriate comments, to the Assembly the periodical reports of the Director General and the yearly audit reports on the accounts;

(v)  take all necessary measures to ensure the execution of the program of the Union by the Director General, in accordance with the decisions of the Assembly and having regard to circumstances arising between two ordinary sessions of the Assembly;

(vi)  perform such other functions as are allocated to it under this Convention.

(b)  With respect to matters which are of interest also to other Unions administered by the Organization, the Executive Committee shall make its decisions after having heard the advice of the Coordination Committee of the Organization.

(7)

(a)  The Executive Committee shall meet once a year in ordinary session upon convocation by the Director General, preferably during the same period and at the same place as the Coordination Committee of the Organization.

(b)  The Executive Committee shall meet in extraordinary session upon convocation by the Director General, either on his own initiative, or at the request of its Chairman or one-fourth of its members.

(8)

(a)  Each country member of the Executive Committee shall have one vote.

(b)  One-half of the members of the Executive Committee shall constitute a quorum.

(c)  Decisions shall be made by a simple majority of the votes cast.

(d)  Abstentions shall not be considered as votes.

(e)  A delegate may represent, and vote in the name of, one country only.

(9)  Countries of the Union not members of the Executive Committee shall be admitted to its meetings as observers.

(10)  The Executive Committee shall adopt its own rules of procedure.

## Article 15

### [International Bureau]

(1)

(a)  Administrative tasks concerning the Union shall be performed by the International Bureau, which is a continuation of the Bureau of the Union united with the Bureau of the Union established by the International Convention for the Protection of Literary and Artistic Works.

(b)  In particular, the International Bureau shall provide the secretariat of the various organs of the Union.

(c)  The Director General of the Organization shall be the chief executive of the Union and shall represent the Union.

(2)  The International Bureau shall assemble and publish information concerning the protection of industrial property. Each country of the Union shall promptly communicate to the International Bureau all new laws and official texts concerning the protection of industrial property. Furthermore, it shall furnish the International Bureau with all the publications of its industrial property service of direct concern to the protection of industrial property which the International Bureau may find useful in its work.

(3)  The International Bureau shall publish a monthly periodical.

(4)   The International Bureau shall, on request, furnish any country of the Union with information on matters concerning the protection of industrial property.

(5)   The International Bureau shall conduct Studies, and shall provide services, designed to facilitate the protection of industrial property.

(6)   The Director General and any staff member designated by him shall participate, without the right to vote, in all meetings of the Assembly, the Executive Committee, and any other committee of experts or working group. The Director General, or a staff member designated by him, shall be ex officio secretary of these bodies.

(7)

(a)   The International Bureau shall, in accordance with the directions of the Assembly and in cooperation with the Executive Committee, make the preparations for the conferences of revision of the provisions of the Convention other than Articles 13 to 17.

(b)   The International Bureau may consult with intergovernmental and international non-governmental organizations concerning preparations for conferences of revision.

(c)   The Director General and persons designated by him shall take part, without the right to vote, in the discussions at these conferences.

(8)   International Bureau shall carry out any other tasks assigned to it.

## Article 16

### [Finances]

(1)

(a)   The Union shall have a budget.

(b)   The budget of the Union shall include the income and expenses proper to the Union, its contribution to the budget of expenses common to the Unions, and, where applicable, the sum made available to the budget of the Conference of the Organization.

(c)   Expenses not attributable exclusively to the Union but also to one or more other Unions administered by the Organization shall be considered as expenses common to the Unions. The share of the Union in such common expenses shall be in proportion to the interest the Union has in them.

(2)   The budget of the Union shall be established with due regard to the requirements of coordination with the budgets of the other Unions administered by the Organization.

(3)   The budget of the Union shall be financed from the following sources:

(i)   contributions of the countries of the Union;

(ii)   fees and charges due for services rendered by the International Bureau in relation to the Union;

(iii)   sale of, or royalties on, the publications of the International Bureau concerning the Union;

(iv)   gifts, bequests, and subventions;

(v)   rents, interests, and other miscellaneous income.

(4)

(a)   For the purpose of establishing its contribution towards the budget, each country of the Union shall belong to a class, and shall pay its annual contributions on the basis of a number of units fixed as follows:

Class I ... 5

Class II ... 20

Class III ... 15

Class IV ... 10

Class V ... 5

Class VI ... 3

Class VII ... 1

(*b*)   Unless it has already done so, each country shall indicate, concurrently with depositing its instrument of ratification or accession, the class to which it wishes to belong. Any country may change class. If it chooses a lower class, the country must announce such change to the Assembly at one of its ordinary sessions. Any such change shall take effect at the beginning of the calendar year following the said session.

(*c*)   The annual contribution of each country shall be an amount in the same proportion to the total sum to be contributed to the budget of the Union by all countries as the number of its units is to the total of the units of all contributing countries.

(*d*)   Contributions shall become due on the first of January of each year.

(*e*)   A country which is in arrears in the payment of its contributions may not exercise its right to vote in any of the organs of the Union of which it is a member if the amount of its arrears equals or exceeds the amount of the contributions due from it for the preceding two full years. However, any organ of the Union may allow such a country to continue to exercise its right to vote in that organ if, and as long as, it is satisfied that the delay in payment is due to exceptional and unavoidable circumstances.

(*f*)   If the budget is not adopted before the beginning of a new financial period, it shall be at the same level as the budget of the previous year, as provided in the financial regulations

(5)   The amount of the fees and charges due for services rendered by the International Bureau in relation to the Union shall be established, and shall be reported to the Assembly and the Executive Committee, by the Director General.

(6)

(*a*)   The Union shall have a working capital fund which shall be constituted by a single payment made by each country of the Union. If the fund becomes insufficient, the Assembly shall decide to increase it.

(*b*)   The amount of the initial payment of each country to the said fund or of its participation in the increase thereof shall be a proportion of the contribution of that country for the year in which the fund is established or the decision to increase it is made.

(*c*)   The proportion and the terms of payment shall be fixed by the Assembly on the proposal of the Director General and after it has heard the advice of the Coordination Committee of the Organization.

(7)

(*a*)   In the headquarters agreement concluded with the country on the territory of which the Organization has its headquarters, it shall be provided that, whenever the working capital fund is insufficient, such country shall grant advances. The amount of these advances and the conditions on which they are granted shall be the subject of separate agreements, in each case, between such country and the Organization. As long as it remains under the obligation to grant advances, such country shall have an *ex* officio seat on the Executive Committee.

(*b*) The country referred to in subparagraph (a) and the Organization shall each have the right to denounce the obligation to grant advances, by written notification. Denunciation shall take effect three years after the end of the year in which it has been notified.

(8) The auditing of the accounts shall be effected by one or more of the countries of the Union or by external auditors, as provided in the financial regulations. They shall be designated, with their agreement, by the Assembly.

## Article 17

### [Amendment of Articles 13 to 17]

(1) Proposals for the amendment of Articles 13, 14, 15, 16, and the present Article, may be initiated by any country member of the Assembly, by the Executive Committee, or by the Director General. Such proposals shall be communicated by the Director General to the member countries of the Assembly at least six months in advance of their consideration by the Assembly.

(2) Amendments to the Articles referred to in paragraph (1) shall be adopted by the Assembly. Adoption shall require three-fourths of the votes cast, provided that any amendment to Article 13, and to the present paragraph, shall require four-fifths of the votes cast.

(3) Any amendment to the Articles referred to in paragraph (1) shall enter into force one month after written notifications of acceptance, effected in accordance with their respective constitutional processes, have been received by the Director General from three-fourths of the countries members of the Assembly at the time it adopted the amendment. Any amendment to the said Articles thus accepted shall bind all the countries which are members of the Assembly at the time the amendment enters into force, or which become members thereof at a subsequent date, provided that any amendment increasing the financial obligations of countries of the Union shall bind only those countries which have notified their acceptance of such amendment.

## Article 18

### [Revision of Articles 1 to 12 and 18 to 30]

(1) This Convention shall be submitted to revision with a view to the introduction of amendments designed to improve the system of the Union.

(2) For that purpose, conferences shall be held successively in one of the countries of the Union among the delegates of the said countries.

(3) Amendments to Articles 13 to 17 are governed by the provisions of Article 17.

## Article 19

### [Special Agreements]

It is understood that the countries of the Union reserve the right to make separately between themselves special agreements for the protection of industrial property, in so far as these agreements do not contravene the provisions of this Convention.

## Article 20

### [Ratification or Accession by Countries of the Union; Entry Into Force]

(1)

(*a*) Any country of the Union which has signed this Act may ratify it, and, if it has not signed it, may accede to it. Instruments of ratification and accession shall be deposited with the Director General.

(*b*)   Any country of the Union may declare in its instrument of ratification or accession that its ratification or accession shall not apply:

(i)   to Articles 1 to 12, or

(ii)   to Articles 13 to 17.

(*c*)   Any country of the Union which, in accordance with subparagraph (b), has excluded from the effects of its ratification or accession one of the two groups of Articles referred to in that subparagraph may at any later time declare that it extends the effects of its ratification or accession to that group of Articles. Such declaration shall be deposited with the Director General.

(2)

(*a*)   Articles 1 to 12 shall enter into force, with respect to the first ten countries of the Union which have deposited instruments of ratification or accession without making the declaration permitted under paragraph (1)(b)(i), three months after the deposit of the tenth such instrument of ratification or accession.

(*b*)   Articles 13 to 17 shall enter into force, with respect to the first ten countries of the Union which have deposited instruments of ratification or accession without making the declaration permitted under paragraph (1)(b)(ii), three months after the deposit of the tenth such instrument of ratification or accession.

(*c*)   Subject to the initial entry into force, pursuant to the provisions of subparagraphs (a) and (b), of each of the two groups of Articles referred to in paragraph (1)(b)(i) and (1)(b)(ii), and subject to the provisions of paragraph (1)(b), Articles 1 to 17 shall, with respect to any country of the Union, other than those referred to in subparagraphs (a) and (b), which deposits an instrument of ratification or accession or any country of the Union which deposits a declaration pursuant to paragraph (1)(c), enter into force three months after the date of notification by the Director General of such deposit, unless a subsequent date has been indicated in the instrument or declaration deposited. In the latter case, this Act shall enter into force with respect to that country on the date thus indicated.

(3)   With respect to any country of the Union which deposits an instrument of ratification or accession, Articles 18 to 30 shall enter into force on the earlier of the dates on which any of the groups of Articles referred to in paragraph (1)(b) enters into force with respect to that country pursuant to paragraph (2)(a), (2)(b), or (2)(c).

## Article 21

### [Accession by Countries Outside the Union; Entry Into Force]

(1)   Any country outside the Union may accede to this Act and thereby become a member of the Union. Instruments of accession shall be deposited with the Director General.

(2)

(*a*)   With respect to any country outside the Union which deposits its instrument of accession one month or more before the date of entry into force of any provisions of the present Act, this Act shall enter into force, unless a subsequent date has been indicated in the instrument of accession, on the date upon which provisions first enter into force pursuant to Article 20(2)(a) or 20(2)(b); provided that:

(i)   if Articles 1 to 12 do not enter into force on that date, such country shall, during the interim period before the entry into force of such provisions, and in substitution therefor, be bound by Articles 1 to 12 of the Lisbon Act.

(ii)   if Articles 13 to 17 do not enter into force on that date, such country shall, during the interim period before the entry into force of such provisions, and in substitution therefor, be bound by Articles 13 and 14(3), 14(4), and 14(5), of the Lisbon Act.

If a country indicates a subsequent date in its instrument of accession, this Act shall enter into force with respect to that country on the date thus indicated.

(*b*) With respect to any country outside the Union which deposits its instrument of accession on a date which is subsequent to, or precedes by less than one month, the entry into force of one group of Articles of the present Act, this Act shall, subject to the proviso of subparagraph (a), enter into force three months after the date on which its accession has been notified by the Director General, unless a subsequent date has been indicated in the instrument of accession. In the latter case, this Act shall enter into force with respect to that country on the date thus indicated.

(3) With respect to any country outside the Union which deposits its instrument of accession after the date of entry into force of the present Act in its entirety, or less than one month before such date, this Act shall enter into force three months after the date on which its accession has been notified by the Director General, unless a subsequent date has been indicated in the instrument of accession. In the latter case, this Act shall enter into force with respect to that country on the date thus indicated.

## Article 22

### [Consequences of Ratification or Accession]

Subject to the possibilities of exceptions provided for in Articles 20(1)(b) and 28(2), ratification or accession shall automatically entail acceptance of all the clauses and admission to all the advantages of this Act.

## Article 23

### [Accession to Earlier Acts]

After the entry into force of this Act in its entirety, a country may not accede to earlier Acts of this Convention.

## Article 24

### [Territories]

(1) Any country may declare in its instrument of ratification or accession, or may inform the Director General by written notification any time thereafter, that this Convention shall be applicable to all or part of those territories, designated in the declaration or notification, for the external relations of which it is responsible.

(2) Any country which has made such a declaration or given such a notification may, at any time, notify the Director General that this Convention shall cease to be applicable to all or part of such territories.

(3)

(*a*) Any declaration made under paragraph (1) shall take effect on the same date as the ratification or accession in the instrument of which it was included, and any notification given under such paragraph shall take effect three months after its notification by the Director General.

(*b*) Any notification given under paragraph (2) shall take effect twelve months after its receipt by the Attorney General.

## Article 25

### [Implementation of the Convention on the Domestic Level]

(1) Any country party to this Convention undertakes to adopt, in accordance with its constitution, the measures necessary to ensure the application of this Convention.

(2)   It is understood that, at the time a country deposits its instrument of ratification or accession, it will be in a position under its domestic law to give effect to the provisions of this Convention.

## Article 26

### [Denunciation]

(1)   This Convention shall remain in force without limitation as to time.

(2)   Any country may denounce this Act by notification addressed to the Director General. Such denunciation shall constitute also denunciation of all earlier Acts and shall affect only the country making it, the Convention remaining in full force and effect as regards the other countries of the Union.

(3)   Denunciation shall take effect one year after the day on which the Director General has received the notification.

(4)   The right of denunciation provided by this Article shall not be exercised by any country before the expiration of five years from the date upon which it becomes a member of the Union.

## Article 27

### [Application of Earlier Acts]

(1)   The present Act shall, as regards the relations between the countries to which it applies, and to the extent that it applies, replace the Convention of Paris of March 20, 1883 and the subsequent Acts of revision.

(2)

   (*a*)   As regards the countries to which the present Act does not apply, or does not apply in its entirety, but to which the Lisbon Act of October 31, 1958, applies, the latter shall remain in force in its entirety or to the extent that the present Act does not replace it by virtue of paragraph (1).

   (*b*)   Similarly, as regards the countries to which neither the present Act, nor portions thereof, nor the Lisbon Act applies, the London Act of June 2, 1934, shall remain in force in its entirety or to the extent that the present Act does not replace it by virtue of paragraph (1).

   (*c*)   Similarly, as regards the countries to which neither the present Act, nor portions thereof, nor the Lisbon Act, nor the London Act applies, the Hague Act of November 6, 1925, shall remain in force in its entirety or to the extent that the present Act does not replace it by virtue of paragraph (1).

(3)   Countries outside the Union which become party to this Act shall apply it with respect to any country of the Union not party to this Act or which, although party to this Act, has made a declaration pursuant to Article 20(1)(b)(i). Such countries recognize that the said country of the Union may apply, in its relations with them, the provisions of the most recent Act to which it is party.

## Article 28

### [Disputes]

(1)   Any dispute between two or more countries of the Union concerning the interpretation or application of this Convention, not settled by negotiation, may, by any one of the countries concerned, be brought before the International Court of Justice by application in conformity with the Statute of the Court, unless the countries concerned agree on some other method of settlement. The country bringing the dispute before the Court shall inform the International Bureau; the International Bureau shall bring the matter to the attention of the other countries of the Union.

(2)   Each country may, at the time it signs this Act or deposits its instrument of ratification or accession, declare that it does not consider itself hound by the provisions of paragraph (1). With regard to any dispute between such country and any other country of the Union, the provisions of paragraph (1) shall not apply.

(3)   Any country having made a declaration in accordance with the provisions of paragraph (2) may, at any time, withdraw its declaration by notification addressed to the Director General.

## Article 29

### [Signature, Languages, Depositary Functions]

(1)

(*a*)   This Act shall be signed in a single copy in the French language and shall be deposited with the Government of Sweden.

(*b*)   Official texts shall be established by the Director General, after consultation with the interested Governments, in the English, German, Italian, Portuguese, Russian and Spanish languages, and such other languages as the Assembly may designate.

(*c*)   In case of differences of opinion on the interpretation of the various texts, the French text shall prevail.

(2)   This Act shall remain open for signature at Stockholm until January 13, 1968.

(3)   The Director General shall transmit two copies, certified by the Government of Sweden, of the signed text of this Act to the Governments of all countries of the Union and, on request, to the Government of any other country.

(4)   The Director General shall register this Act with the Secretariat of the United Nations.

(5)   The Director General shall notify the Governments of all countries of the Union of signatures, deposits of instruments of ratification or accession and any declarations included in such instruments or made pursuant to Article 20(1)(c), entry into force of any provisions of this Act, notifications of denunciation, and notifications pursuant to Article 24.

## Article 30

### [Transitional Provisions]

(1)   Until the first Director General assumes office, references in this Act to the International Bureau of the Organization or to the Director General shall be deemed to be references to the Bureau of the Union or its Director, respectively.

(2)   Countries of the Union not bound by Articles 13 to 17 may, until five years after the entry into force of the Convention establishing the Organization, exercise, if they so desire. The rights provided under Articles 13 to 17 of this Act as if they were hound by those Articles. Any country desiring to exercise such rights shall give written notification to that effect to the Director General; such notification shall be effective from the date of its receipt. Such countries shall be deemed to be members of the Assembly until the expiration of the said period.

(3)   As long as all the countries of the Union have not become Members of the Organization, the International Bureau of the Organization shall also function as the Bureau of the Union, and the Director General as the Director of the said Bureau.

(4)   Once all the countries of the Union have become Members of the Organization, the rights, obligations, and property, of the Bureau of the Union shall devolve on the International Bureau of the Organization.

# 32. PATENT COOPERATION TREATY

Done at Washington on June 19, 1970, amended on
October 2, 1979, and modified on February 3, 1984,
and on October 3, 2001

The Contracting States,

Desiring to make a contribution to the progress of science and technology,

Desiring to perfect the legal protection of inventions,

Desiring to simplify and render more economical the obtaining of protection for inventions where protection is sought in several countries,

Desiring to facilitate and accelerate access by the public to the technical information contained in documents describing new inventions,

Desiring to foster and accelerate the economic development of developing countries through the adoption of measures designed to increase the efficiency of their legal systems, whether national or regional, instituted for the protection of inventions by providing easily accessible information on the availability of technological solutions applicable to their special needs and by facilitating access to the ever expanding volume of modern technology,

Convinced that cooperation among nations will greatly facilitate the attainment of these aims,

Have concluded the present Treaty.

## INTRODUCTORY PROVISIONS

### Article 1

### Establishment of a Union

(1)  The States party to this Treaty (hereinafter called "the Contracting States") constitute a Union for cooperation in the filing, searching, and examination, of applications for the protection of inventions, and for rendering special technical services. The Union shall be known as the International Patent Cooperation Union.

(2)  No provision of this Treaty shall be interpreted as diminishing the rights under the Paris Convention for the Protection of Industrial Property of any national or resident of any country party to that Convention.

### Article 2

### Definitions

For the purposes of this Treaty and the Regulations and unless expressly stated otherwise:

(i)  "application" means an application for the protection of an invention; references to an "application" shall be construed as references to applications for patents for inventions, inventors' certificates, utility certificates, utility models, patents or certificates of addition, inventors' certificates of addition, and utility certificates of addition;

(ii)  references to a "patent" shall be construed as references to patents for inventions, inventors' certificates, utility certificates, utility models, patents or certificates of addition, inventors' certificates of addition, and utility certificates of addition;

(iii)  "national patent" means a patent granted by a national authority;

(iv)  "regional patent" means a patent granted by a national or an intergovernmental authority having the power to grant patents effective in more than one State;

(v) "regional application" means an application for a regional patent;

(vi) references to a "national application" shall be construed as references to applications for national patents and regional patents, other than applications filed under this Treaty;

(vii) "international application" means an application filed under this Treaty;

(viii) references to an "application" shall be construed as references to international applications and national applications;

(ix) references to a "patent" shall be construed as references to national patents and regional patents;

(x) references to "national law" shall be construed as references to the national law of a Contracting State or, where a regional application or a regional patent is involved, to the treaty providing for the filing of regional applications or the granting of regional patents;

(xi) "priority date," for the purposes of computing time limits, means:

    (a) where the international application contains a priority claim under Article 8, the filing date of the application whose priority is so claimed;

    (b) where the international application contains several priority claims under Article 8, the filing date of the earliest application whose priority is so claimed;

    (c) where the international application does not contain any priority claim under Article 8, the international filing date of such application;

(xii) "national Office" means the government authority of a Contracting State entrusted with the granting of patents; references to a "national Office" shall be construed as referring also to any intergovernmental authority which several States have entrusted with the task of granting regional patents, provided that at least one of those States is a Contracting State, and provided that the said States have authorized that authority to assume the obligations and exercise the powers which this Treaty and the Regulations provide for in respect of national Offices;

(xiii) "designated Office" means the national Office of or acting for the State designated by the applicant under Chapter I of this Treaty;

(xiv) "elected Office" means the national Office of or acting for the State elected by the applicant under Chapter II of this Treaty;

(xv) "receiving Office" means the national Office or the intergovernmental organization with which the international application has been filed;

(xvi) "Union" means the International Patent Cooperation Union;

(xvii) "Assembly" means the Assembly of the Union;

(xviii) "Organization" means the World Intellectual Property Organization;

(xix) "International Bureau" means the International Bureau of the Organization and, as long as it subsists, the United International Bureaux for the Protection of Intellectual Property (BIRPI);

(xx) "Director General" means the Director General of the Organization and, as long as BIRPI subsists, the Director of BIRPI.

## CHAPTER I
## INTERNATIONAL APPLICATION AND INTERNATIONAL SEARCH

### Article 3

### The International Application

(1)  Applications for the protection of inventions in any of the Contracting States may be filed as international applications under this Treaty.

(2)  An international application shall contain, as specified in this Treaty and the Regulations, a request, a description, one or more claims, one or more drawings (where required), and an abstract.

(3)  The abstract merely serves the purpose of technical information and cannot be taken into account for any other purpose, particularly not for the purpose of interpreting the scope of the protection sought.

(4)  The international application shall:

  (i)  be in a prescribed language;

  (ii)  comply with the prescribed physical requirements;

  (iii)  comply with the prescribed requirement of unity of invention;

  (iv)  be subject to the payment of the prescribed fees.

### Article 4

### The Request

(1)  The request shall contain:

  (i)  a petition to the effect that the international application be processed according to tis Treaty;

  (ii)  the designation of the Contracting State or States in which protection for the invention is desired on the basis of the international application ("designated States"); if for any designated State a regional patent is available and the applicant wishes to obtain a regional patent rather than a national patent, the request shall so indicate; if, under a treaty concerning a regional patent, the applicant cannot limit his application to certain of the States party to that treaty, designation of one of those States and the indication of the wish to obtain the regional patent shall be treated as designation of all the States party to that treaty; if, under the national law of the designated State, the designation of that State has the effect of an application for a regional patent, the designation of the said State shall be treated as an indication of the wish to obtain the regional patent;

  (iii)  the name of and other prescribed data concerning the applicant and the agent (if any);

  (iv)  the title of the invention;

  (v)  the name of and other prescribed data concerning the inventor where the national law of at least one of the designated States requires that these indications be furnished at the time of filing a national application. Otherwise, the said indications may be furnished either in the request or in separate notices addressed to each designated Office whose national law requires the furnishing of the said indications but allows that they be furnished at a time later than that of the filing of a national application.

(2)  Every designation shall be subject to the payment of the prescribed fee within the prescribed time limit.

(3) Unless the applicant asks for any of the other kinds of protection referred to in Article 43, designation shall mean that the desired protection consists of the grant of a patent by or for the designated State. For the purposes of this paragraph, Article 2(ii) shall not apply.

(4) Failure to indicate in the request the name and other prescribed data concerning the inventor shall have no consequence in any designated State whose national law requires the furnishing of the said indications but allows that they be furnished at a time later than that of the filing of a national application. Failure to furnish the said indications in a separate notice shall have no consequence in any designated State whose national law does not require the furnishing of the said indications.

## Article 5

### The Description

The description shall disclose the invention in a manner sufficiently clear and complete for the invention to be carried out by a person skilled in the art.

## Article 6

### The Claims

The claim or claims shall define the matter for which protection is sought. Claims shall be clear and concise. They shall be fully supported by the description.

## Article 7

### The Drawings

(1) Subject to the provisions of paragraph (2)(ii), drawings shall be required when they are necessary for the understanding of the invention.

(2) Where, without being necessary for the understanding of the invention, the nature of the invention admits of illustration by drawings:

    (i) the applicant may include such drawings in the international application when filed,

    (ii) any designated Office may require that the applicant file such drawings with it within the prescribed time limit.

## Article 8

### Claiming Priority

(1) The international application may contain a declaration, as prescribed in the Regulations, claiming the priority of one or more earlier applications filed in or for any country party to the Paris Convention for the Protection of Industrial Property.

(2) (a) Subject to the provisions of subparagraph (b), the conditions for, and the effect of, any priority claim declared under paragraph (1) shall be as provided in Article 4 of the Stockholm Act of the Paris Convention for the Protection of Industrial Property.

    (b) The international application for which the priority of one or more earlier applications filed in or for a Contracting State is claimed may contain the designation of that State. Where, in the international application, the priority of one or more national applications filed in or for a designated State is claimed, or where the priority of an international application having designated only one State is claimed, the conditions for, and the effect of, the priority claim in that State shall be governed by the national law of that State.

## Article 9

### The Applicant

(1) Any resident or national of a Contracting State may file an international application.

(2) The Assembly may decide to allow the residents and the nationals of any country party to the Paris Convention for the Protection of Industrial Property which is not party to this Treaty to file international applications.

(3) The concepts of residence and nationality, and the application of those concepts in cases where there are several applicants or where the applicants are not the same for all the designated States, are defined in the Regulations.

## Article 10

### The Receiving Office

The international application shall be filed with the prescribed receiving Office, which will check and process it as provided in this Treaty and the Regulations.

## Article 11

### Filing Date and Effects of the International Application

(1) The receiving Office shall accord as the international filing date the date of receipt of the international application, provided that that Office has found that, at the time of receipt:

    (i) the applicant does not obviously lack, for reasons of residence or nationality, the right to file an international application with the receiving Office,

    (ii) the international application is in the prescribed language,

    (iii) the international application contains at least the following elements:

        (a) an indication that it is intended as an international application,

        (b) the designation of at least one Contracting State,

        (c) the name of the applicant, as prescribed,

        (d) a part which on the face of it appears to be a description,

        (e) a part which on the face of it appears to be a claim or claims.

(2) (a) If the receiving Office finds that the international application did not, at the time of receipt, fulfill the requirements listed in paragraph (1), it shall, as provided in the Regulations, invite the applicant to file the required correction.

    (b) If the applicant complies with the invitation, as provided in the Regulations, the receiving Office shall accord as the international filing date the date of receipt of the required correction.

(3) Subject to Article 64(4), any international application fulfilling the requirements listed in items (i) to (iii) of paragraph (1) and accorded an international filing date shall have the effect of a regular national application in each designated State as of the international filing date, which date shall be considered to be the actual filing date in each designated State.

(4) Any international application fulfilling the requirements listed in items (i) to (iii) of paragraph (1) shall be equivalent to a regular national filing within the meaning of the Paris Convention for the Protection of Industrial Property.

## Article 12

### Transmittal of the International Application to the International Bureau and the International Searching Authority

(1) One copy of the international application shall be kept by the receiving Office ("home copy"), one copy ("record copy") shall be transmitted to the International Bureau, and another copy ("search copy") shall be transmitted to the competent International Searching Authority referred to in Article 16, as provided in the Regulations.

(2) The record copy shall be considered the true copy of the international application.

(3) The international application shall be considered withdrawn if the record copy has not been received by the International Bureau within the prescribed time limit.

## Article 13

### Availability of Copy of the International Application to Designated Offices

(1) Any designated Office may ask the International Bureau to transmit to it a copy of the international application prior to the communication provided for in Article 20, and the International Bureau shall transmit such copy to the designated Office as soon as possible after the expiration of one year from the priority date.

(2) (a) The applicant may, at any time, transmit a copy of his international application to any designated Office.

(b) The applicant may, at any time, ask the International Bureau to transmit a copy of his international application to any designated Office, and the International Bureau shall transmit such copy to the designated Office as soon as possible.

(c) Any national Office may notify the International Bureau that it does not wish to receive copies as provided for in subparagraph (b), in which case that subparagraph shall not be applicable in respect of that Office.

## Article 14

### Certain Defects in the International Application

(1) (a) The receiving Office shall check whether the international application contains any of the following defects, that is to say:

   (i) it is not signed as provided in the Regulations;

   (ii) it does not contain the prescribed indications concerning the applicant;

   (iii) it does not contain a title;

   (iv) it does not contain an abstract;

   (v) it does not comply to the extent provided in the Regulations with the prescribed physical requirements.

(b) If the receiving Office finds any of the said defects, it shall invite the applicant to correct the international application within the prescribed time limit, failing which that application shall be considered withdrawn and the receiving Office shall so declare.

(2) If the international application refers to drawings which, in fact, are not included in that application, the receiving Office shall notify the applicant accordingly and he may furnish them within the prescribed time limit and, if he does, the international filing date shall be the date on which the drawings are received by the receiving Office. Otherwise, any reference to the said drawings shall be considered non-existent.

(3) (a) If the receiving Office finds that, within the prescribed time limits, the fees prescribed under Article 3(4)(iv) have not been paid, or no fee prescribed under Article 4(2) has been paid in respect of any of the designated States, the international application shall be considered withdrawn and the receiving Office shall so declare.

(b) If the receiving Office finds that the fee prescribed under Article 4(2) has been paid in respect of one or more (but less than all) designated States within the prescribed time limit, the designation of those States in respect of which it has not been paid within the prescribed time limit shall be considered withdrawn and the receiving Office shall so declare.

(4) If, after having accorded an international filing date to the international application, the receiving Office finds, within the prescribed time limit, that any of the requirements listed in items (i) to (iii) of Article 11(1) was not complied with at that date, the said application shall be considered withdrawn and the receiving Office shall so declare.

## Article 15

### The International Search

(1) Each international application shall be the subject of international search.

(2) The objective of the international search is to discover relevant prior art.

(3) International search shall be made on the basis of the claims, with due regard to the description and the drawings (if any).

(4) The International Searching Authority referred to in Article 16 shall endeavor to discover as much of the relevant prior art as its facilities permit, and shall, in any case, consult the documentation specified in the Regulations.

(5) (a) If the national law of the Contracting State so permits, the applicant who files a national application with the national Office of or acting for such State may, subject to the conditions provided for in such law, request that a search similar to an international search ("international-type search") be carried out on such application.

(b) If the national law of the Contracting State so permits, the national Office of or acting for such State may subject any national application filed with it to an international-type search.

(c) The international-type search shall be carried out by the International Searching Authority referred to in Article 16 which would be competent for an international search if the national application were an international application and were filed with the Office referred to in subparagraphs (a) and (b). If the national application is in a language which the International Searching Authority considers it is not equipped to handle, the international-type search shall be carried out on a translation prepared by the applicant in a language prescribed for international applications and which the International Searching Authority has undertaken to accept for international applications. The national application and the translation, when required, shall be presented in the form prescribed for international applications.

## Article 16

### The International Searching Authority

(1) International search shall be carried out by an International Searching Authority, which may be either a national Office or an intergovernmental organization, such as the International Patent Institute, whose tasks include the establishing of documentary search reports on prior art with respect to inventions which are the subject of applications.

(2) If, pending the establishment of a single International Searching Authority, there are several International Searching Authorities, each receiving Office shall, in accordance with the

provisions of the applicable agreement referred to in paragraph (3)(b), specify the International Searching Authority or Authorities competent for the searching of international applications filed with such Office.

(3) (a) International Searching Authorities shall be appointed by the Assembly. Any national Office and any intergovernmental organization satisfying the requirements referred to in subparagraph (c) may be appointed as International Searching Authority.

   (b) Appointment shall be conditional on the consent of the national Office or intergovernmental organization to be appointed and the conclusion of an agreement, subject to approval by the Assembly, between such Office or organization and the International Bureau. The agreement shall specify the rights and obligations of the parties, in particular, the formal undertaking by the said Office or organization to apply and observe all the common rules of international search.

   (c) The Regulations prescribe the minimum requirements, particularly as to manpower and documentation, which any Office or organization must satisfy before it can be appointed and must continue to satisfy while it remains appointed.

   (d) Appointment shall be for a fixed period of time and may be extended for further periods.

   (e) Before the Assembly makes a decision on the appointment of any national Office or intergovernmental organization, or on the extension of its appointment, or before it allows any such appointment to lapse, the Assembly shall hear the interested Office or organization and seek the advice of the Committee for Technical Cooperation referred to in Article 56 once that Committee has been established.

## Article 17

### Procedure before the International Searching Authority

(1) Procedure before the International Searching Authority shall be governed by the provisions of this Treaty, the Regulations, and the agreement which the International Bureau shall conclude, subject to this Treaty and the Regulations, with the said Authority.

(2) (a) If the International Searching Authority considers

   (i) that the international application relates to a subject matter which the International Searching Authority is not required, under the Regulations, to search, and in the particular case decides not to search, or

   (ii) that the description, the claims, or the drawings, fail to comply with the prescribed requirements to such an extent that a meaningful search could not be carried out, the said Authority shall so declare and shall notify the applicant and the International Bureau that no international search report will be established.

   (b) If any of the situations referred to in subparagraph (a) is found to exist in connection with certain claims only, the international search report shall so indicate in respect of such claims, whereas, for the other claims, the said report shall be established as provided in Article 18.

(3) (a) If the International Searching Authority considers that the international application does not comply with the requirement of unity of invention as set forth in the Regulations, it shall invite the applicant to pay additional fees. The International Searching Authority shall establish the international search report on those parts of the international application which relate to the invention first mentioned in the claims ("main invention") and, provided the required additional fees have been paid within the prescribed time limit, on those parts of the international application which relate to inventions in respect of which the said fees were paid.

(b)     The national law of any designated State may provide that, where the national Office of that State finds the invitation, referred to in subparagraph (a), of the International Searching Authority justified and where the applicant has not paid all additional fees, those parts of the international application which consequently have not been searched shall, as far as effects in that State are concerned, be considered withdrawn unless a special fee is paid by the applicant to the national Office of that State.

## Article 18

### The International Search Report

(1)     The international search report shall be established within the prescribed time limit and in the prescribed form.

(2)     The international search report shall, as soon as it has been established, be transmitted by the International Searching Authority to the applicant and the International Bureau.

(3)     The international search report or the declaration referred to in Article 17(2)(a) shall be translated as provided in the Regulations. The translations shall be prepared by or under the responsibility of the International Bureau.

## Article 19

### Amendment of the Claims before the International Bureau

(1)     The applicant shall, after having received the international search report, be entitled to one opportunity to amend the claims of the international application by filing amendments with the International Bureau within the prescribed time limit. He may, at the same time, file a brief statement, as provided in the Regulations, explaining the amendments and indicating any impact that such amendments might have on the description and the drawings.

(2)     The amendments shall not go beyond the disclosure in the international application as filed.

(3)     If the national law of any designated State permits amendments to go beyond the said disclosure, failure to comply with paragraph (2) shall have no consequence in that State.

## Article 20

### Communication to Designated Offices

(1)     (a)     The international application, together with the international search report (including any indication referred to in Article 17(2)(b)) or the declaration referred to in Article 17(2)(a), shall be communicated to each designated Office, as provided in the Regulations, unless the designated Office waives such requirement in its entirety or in part.

   (b)     The communication shall include the translation (as prescribed) of the said report or declaration.

(2)     If the claims have been amended by virtue of Article 19(1), the communication shall either contain the full text of the claims both as filed and as amended or shall contain the full text of the claims as filed and specify the amendments, and shall include the statement, if any, referred to in Article 19(1).

(3)     At the request of the designated Office or the applicant, the International Searching Authority shall send to the said Office or the applicant, respectively, copies of the documents cited in the international search report, as provided in the Regulations.

## Article 21

### International Publication

(1)  The International Bureau shall publish international applications.

(2)  (a)  Subject to the exceptions provided for in subparagraph (b) and in Article 64(3), the international publication of the international application shall be effected promptly after the expiration of 18 months from the priority date of that application.

   (b)  The applicant may ask the International Bureau to publish his international application any time before the expiration of the time limit referred to in subparagraph (a). The International Bureau shall proceed accordingly, as provided in the Regulations.

(3)  The international search report or the declaration referred to in Article 17(2)(a) shall be published as prescribed in the Regulations.

(4)  The language and form of the international publication and other details are governed by the Regulations.

(5)  There shall be no international publication if the international application is withdrawn or is considered withdrawn before the technical preparations for publication have been completed.

(6)  If the international application contains expressions or drawings which, in the opinion of the International Bureau, are contrary to morality or public order, or if, in its opinion, the international application contains disparaging statements as defined in the Regulations, it may omit such expressions, drawings, and statements, from its publications, indicating the place and number of words or drawings omitted, and furnishing, upon request, individual copies of the passages omitted.

## Article 22

### Copy, Translation, and Fee, to Designated Offices

(1)  The applicant shall furnish a copy of the international application (unless the communication provided for in Article 20 has already taken place) and a translation thereof (as prescribed), and pay the national fee (if any), to each designated Office not later than at the expiration of 30 months from the priority date. Where the national law of the designated State requires the indication of the name of and other prescribed data concerning the inventor but allows that these indications be furnished at a time later than that of the filing of a national application, the applicant shall, unless they were contained in the request, furnish the said indications to the national Office of or acting for the State not later than at the expiration of 30 months from the priority date.

(2)  Where the International Searching Authority makes a declaration, under Article 17(2)(a), that no international search report will be established, the time limit for performing the acts referred to in paragraph (1) of this Article shall be the same as that provided for in paragraph (1).

(3)  Any national law may, for performing the acts referred to in paragraphs (1) or (2), fix time limits which expire later than the time limit provided for in those paragraphs.

## Article 23

### Delaying of National Procedure

(1)  No designated Office shall process or examine the international application prior to the expiration of the applicable time limit under Article 22.

(2)  Notwithstanding the provisions of paragraph (1), any designated Office may, on the express request of the applicant, process or examine the international application at any time.

## Article 24

### Possible Loss of Effect in Designated States

(1)   Subject, in case (ii) below, to the provisions of Article 25, the effect of the international application provided for in Article 11(3) shall cease in any designated State with the same consequences as the withdrawal of any national application in that State:

(i)   if the applicant withdraws his international application or the designation of that State;

(ii)   if the international application is considered withdrawn by virtue of Articles 12(3), 14(1)(b), 14(3)(a), or 14(4), or if the designation of that State is considered withdrawn by virtue of Article 14(3)(b);

(iii)   if the applicant fails to perform the acts referred to in Article 22 within the applicable time limit.

(2)   Notwithstanding the provisions of paragraph (1), any designated Office may maintain the effect provided for in Article 11(3) even where such effect is not required to be maintained by virtue of Article 25(2).

## Article 25

### Review by Designated Offices

(1)   (a)   Where the receiving Office has refused to accord an international filing date or has declared that the international application is considered withdrawn, or where the International Bureau has made a finding under Article 12(3), the International Bureau shall promptly send, at the request of the applicant, copies of any document in the file to any of the designated Offices named by the applicant.

(b)   Where the receiving Office has declared that the designation of any given State is considered withdrawn, the International Bureau shall promptly send, at the request of the applicant, copies of any document in the file to the national Office of such State.

(c)   The request under subparagraphs (a) or (b) shall be presented within the prescribed time limit.

(2)   (a)   Subject to the provisions of subparagraph (b), each designated Office shall, provided that the national fee (if any) has been paid and the appropriate translation (as prescribed) has been furnished within the prescribed time limit, decide whether the refusal, declaration, or finding, referred to in paragraph (1) was justified under the provisions of this Treaty and the Regulations, and, if it finds that the refusal or declaration was the result of an error or omission on the part of the receiving Office or that the finding was the result of an error or omission on the part of the International Bureau, it shall, as far as effects in the State of the designated Office are concerned, treat the international application as if such error or omission had not occurred.

(b)   Where the record copy has reached the International Bureau after the expiration of the time limit prescribed under Article 12(3) on account of any error or omission on the part of the applicant, the provisions of subparagraph (a) shall apply only under the circumstances referred to in Article 48(2).

## Article 26

### Opportunity to Correct before Designated Offices

No designated Office shall reject an international application on the grounds of non-compliance with the requirements of this Treaty and the Regulations without first giving the applicant the opportunity to correct the said application to the extent and according to the procedure provided by the national law for the same or comparable situations in respect of national applications.

## Article 27

### National Requirements

(1)   No national law shall require compliance with requirements relating to the form or contents of the international application different from or additional to those which are provided for in this Treaty and the Regulations.

(2)   The provisions of paragraph (1) neither affect the application of the provisions of Article 7(2) nor preclude any national law from requiring, once the processing of the international application has started in the designated Office, the furnishing:

    (i)   when the applicant is a legal entity, of the name of an officer entitled to represent such legal entity,

    (ii)   of documents not part of the international application but which constitute proof of allegations or statements made in that application, including the confirmation of the international application by the signature of the applicant when that application, as filed, was signed by his representative or agent.

(3)   Where the applicant, for the purposes of any designated State, is not qualified according to the national law of that State to file a national application because he is not the inventor, the international application may be rejected by the designated Office.

(4)   Where the national law provides, in respect of the form or contents of national applications, for requirements which, from the viewpoint of applicants, are more favorable than the requirements provided for by this Treaty and the Regulations in respect of international applications, the national Office, the courts and any other competent organs of or acting for the designated State may apply the former requirements, instead of the latter requirements, to international applications, except where the applicant insists that the requirements provided for by this Treaty and the Regulations be applied to his international application.

(5)   Nothing in this Treaty and the Regulations is intended to be construed as prescribing anything that would limit the freedom of each Contracting State to prescribe such substantive conditions of patentability as it desires. In particular, any provision in this Treaty and the Regulations concerning the definition of prior art is exclusively for the purposes of the international procedure and, consequently, any Contracting State is free to apply, when determining the patentability of an invention claimed in an international application, the criteria of its national law in respect of prior art and other conditions of patentability not constituting requirements as to the form and contents of applications.

(6)   The national law may require that the applicant furnish evidence in respect of any substantive condition of patentability prescribed by such law.

(7)   Any receiving Office or, once the processing of the international application has started in the designated Office, that Office may apply the national law as far as it relates to any requirement that the applicant be represented by an agent having the right to represent applicants before the said Office and/or that the applicant have an address in the designated State for the purpose of receiving notifications.

(8)   Nothing in this Treaty and the Regulations is intended to be construed as limiting the freedom of any Contracting State to apply measures deemed necessary for the preservation of its national security or to limit, for the protection of the general economic interests of that State, the right of its own residents or nationals to file international applications.

## Article 28

### Amendment of the Claims, the Description, and the Drawings, before Designated Offices

(1) The applicant shall be given the opportunity to amend the claims, the description, and the drawings, before each designated Office within the prescribed time limit. No designated Office shall grant a patent, or refuse the grant of a patent, before such time limit has expired except with the express consent of the applicant.

(2) The amendments shall not go beyond the disclosure in the international application as filed unless the national law of the designated State permits them to go beyond the said disclosure.

(3) The amendments shall be in accordance with the national law of the designated State in all respects not provided for in this Treaty and the Regulations.

(4) Where the designated Office requires a translation of the international application, the amendments shall be in the language of the translation.

## Article 29

### Effects of the International Publication

(1) As far as the protection of any rights of the applicant in a designated State is concerned, the effects, in that State, of the international publication of an international application shall, subject to the provisions of paragraphs (2) to (4), be the same as those which the national law of the designated State provides for the compulsory national publication of unexamined national applications as such.

(2) If the language in which the international publication has been effected is different from the language in which publications under the national law are effected in the designated State, the said national law may provide that the effects provided for in paragraph (1) shall be applicable only from such time as:

(i) a translation into the latter language has been published as provided by the national law, or

(ii) a translation into the latter language has been made available to the public, by laying open for public inspection as provided by the national law, or

(iii) a translation into the latter language has been transmitted by the applicant to the actual or prospective unauthorized user of the invention claimed in the international application, or

(iv) both the acts described in (i) and (iii), or both the acts described in (ii) and (iii), have taken place.

(3) The national law of any designated State may provide that, where the international publication has been effected, on the request of the applicant, before the expiration of 18 months from the priority date, the effects provided for in paragraph (1) shall be applicable only from the expiration of 18 months from the priority date.

(4) The national law of any designated State may provide that the effects provided for in paragraph (1) shall be applicable only from the date on which a copy of the international application as published under Article 21 has been received in the national Office of or acting for such State. The said Office shall publish the date of receipt in its gazette as soon as possible.

## Article 30

### Confidential Nature of the International Application

(1) (a) Subject to the provisions of subparagraph (b), the International Bureau and the International Searching Authorities shall not allow access by any person or authority to the international application before the international publication of that application, unless requested or authorized by the applicant.

(b) The provisions of subparagraph (a) shall not apply to any transmittal to the competent International Searching Authority, to transmittals provided for under Article 13, and to communications provided for under Article 20.

(2) (a) No national Office shall allow access to the international application by third parties, unless requested or authorized by the applicant, before the earliest of the following dates:

(i) date of the international publication of the international application,

(ii) date of the receipt of the communication of the international application under Article 20,

(iii) date of the receipt of a copy of the international application under Article 22.

(b) The provisions of subparagraph (a) shall not prevent any national Office from informing third parties that it has been designated, or from publishing that fact. Such information or publication may, however, contain only the following data: identification of the receiving Office, name of the applicant, international filing date, international application number, and title of the invention.

(c) The provisions of subparagraph (a) shall not prevent any designated Office from allowing access to the international application for the purposes of the judicial authorities.

(3) The provisions of paragraph (2)(a) shall apply to any receiving Office except as far as transmittals provided for under Article 12(1) are concerned.

(4) For the purposes of this Article, the term "access" covers any means by which third parties may acquire cognizance, including individual communication and general publication, provided, however, that no national Office shall generally publish an international application or its translation before the international publication or, if international publication has not taken place by the expiration of 20 months from the priority date, before the expiration of 20 months from the said priority date.

## CHAPTER II
## INTERNATIONAL PRELIMINARY EXAMINATION

### Article 31

### Demand for International Preliminary Examination

(1) On the demand of the applicant, his international application shall be the subject of an international preliminary examination as provided in the following provisions and the Regulations.

(2) (a) Any applicant who is a resident or national, as defined in the Regulations, of a Contracting State bound by Chapter II, and whose international application has been filed with the receiving Office of or acting for such State, may make a demand for international preliminary examination.

(b) The Assembly may decide to allow persons entitled to file international applications to make a demand for international preliminary examination even if they are residents or nationals of a State not party to this Treaty or not bound by Chapter II.

(3) The demand for international preliminary examination shall be made separately from the international application. The demand shall contain the prescribed particulars and shall be in the prescribed language and form.

(4) (a) The demand shall indicate the Contracting State or States in which the applicant intends to use the results of the international preliminary examination ("elected States"). Additional Contracting States may be elected later. Election may relate only to Contracting States already designated under Article 4.

    (b) Applicants referred to in paragraph (2)(a) may elect any Contracting State bound by Chapter II. Applicants referred to in paragraph (2)(b) may elect only such Contracting States bound by Chapter II as have declared that they are prepared to be elected by such applicants.

(5) The demand shall be subject to the payment of the prescribed fees within the prescribed time limit.

(6) (a) The demand shall be submitted to the competent International Preliminary Examining Authority referred to in Article 32.

    (b) Any later election shall be submitted to the International Bureau.

(7) Each elected Office shall be notified of its election.

## Article 32

### The International Preliminary Examining Authority

(1) International preliminary examination shall be carried out by the International Preliminary Examining Authority.

(2) In the case of demands referred to in Article 31(2)(a), the receiving Office, and, in the case of demands referred to in Article 31(2)(b), the Assembly, shall, in accordance with the applicable agreement between the interested International Preliminary Examining Authority or Authorities and the International Bureau, specify the International Preliminary Examining Authority or Authorities competent for the preliminary examination.

(3) The provisions of Article 16(3) shall apply, *mutatis mutandis*, in respect of International Preliminary Examining Authorities.

## Article 33

### The International Preliminary Examination

(1) The objective of the international preliminary examination is to formulate a preliminary and non-binding opinion on the questions whether the claimed invention appears to be novel, to involve an inventive step (to be non-obvious), and to be industrially applicable.

(2) For the purposes of the international preliminary examination, a claimed invention shall be considered novel if it is not anticipated by the prior art as defined in the Regulations.

(3) For the purposes of the international preliminary examination, a claimed invention shall be considered to involve an inventive step if, having regard to the prior art as defined in the Regulations, it is not, at the prescribed relevant date, obvious to a person skilled in the art.

(4) For the purposes of the international preliminary examination, a claimed invention shall be considered industrially applicable if, according to its nature, it can be made or used (in the technological sense) in any kind of industry. "Industry" shall be understood in its broadest sense, as in the Paris Convention for the Protection of Industrial Property.

(5) The criteria described above merely serve the purposes of international preliminary examination. Any Contracting State may apply additional or different criteria for the purpose of deciding whether, in that State, the claimed invention is patentable or not.

(6) The international preliminary examination shall take into consideration all the documents cited in the international search report. It may take into consideration any additional documents considered to be relevant in the particular case.

# Article 34

## Procedure before the International Preliminary Examining Authority

(1) Procedure before the International Preliminary Examining Authority shall be governed by the provisions of this Treaty, the Regulations, and the agreement which the International Bureau shall conclude, subject to this Treaty and the Regulations, with the said Authority.

(2) (a) The applicant shall have a right to communicate orally and in writing with the International Preliminary Examining Authority.

(b) The applicant shall have a right to amend the claims, the description, and the drawings, in the prescribed manner and within the prescribed time limit, before the international preliminary examination report is established. The amendment shall not go beyond the disclosure in the international application as filed.

(c) The applicant shall receive at least one written opinion from the International Preliminary Examining Authority unless such Authority considers that all of the following conditions are fulfilled:

(i) the invention satisfies the criteria set forth in Article 33(1),

(ii) the international application complies with the requirements of this Treaty and the Regulations in so far as checked by that Authority,

(iii) no observations are intended to be made under Article 35(2), last sentence.

(d) The applicant may respond to the written opinion.

(3) (a) If the International Preliminary Examining Authority considers that the international application does not comply with the requirement of unity of invention as set forth in the Regulations, it may invite the applicant, at his option, to restrict the claims so as to comply with the requirement or to pay additional fees.

(b) The national law of any elected State may provide that, where the applicant chooses to restrict the claims under subparagraph (a), those parts of the international application which, as a consequence of the restriction, are not to be the subject of international preliminary examination shall, as far as effects in that State are concerned, be considered withdrawn unless a special fee is paid by the applicant to the national Office of that State.

(c) If the applicant does not comply with the invitation referred to in subparagraph (a) within the prescribed time limit, the International Preliminary Examining Authority shall establish an international preliminary examination report on those parts of the international application which relate to what appears to be the main invention and shall indicate the relevant facts in the said report. The national law of any elected State may provide that, where its national Office finds the invitation of the International Preliminary Examining Authority justified, those parts of the international application which do not relate to the main invention shall, as far as effects in that State are concerned, be considered withdrawn unless a special fee is paid by the applicant to that Office.

(4) (a) If the International Preliminary Examining Authority considers

(i) that the international application relates to a subject matter on which the International Preliminary Examining Authority is not required, under the Regulations, to carry out an international preliminary examination, and in the particular case decides not to carry out such examination, or

(ii) that the description, the claims, or the drawings, are so unclear, or the claims are so inadequately supported by the description, that no meaningful opinion can be formed on the novelty, inventive step (non-obviousness), or industrial applicability, of the claimed invention, the said Authority shall not go into the questions referred to in Article 33(1) and shall inform the applicant of this opinion and the reasons therefor.

(b) If any of the situations referred to in subparagraph (a) is found to exist in, or in connection with, certain claims only, the provisions of that subparagraph shall apply only to the said claims.

## Article 35

### The International Preliminary Examination Report

(1) The international preliminary examination report shall be established within the prescribed time limit and in the prescribed form.

(2) The international preliminary examination report shall not contain any statement on the question whether the claimed invention is or seems to be patentable or unpatentable according to any national law. It shall state, subject to the provisions of paragraph (3), in relation to each claim, whether the claim appears to satisfy the criteria of novelty, inventive step (non-obviousness), and industrial applicability, as defined for the purposes of the international preliminary examination in Article 33(1) to (4). The statement shall be accompanied by the citation of the documents believed to support the stated conclusion with such explanations as the circumstances of the case may require. The statement shall also be accompanied by such other observations as the Regulations provide for.

(3) (a) If, at the time of establishing the international preliminary examination report, the International Preliminary Examining Authority considers that any of the situations referred to in Article 34(4)(a) exists, that report shall state this opinion and the reasons therefor. It shall not contain any statement as provided in paragraph (2).

(b) If a situation under Article 34(4)(b) is found to exist, the international preliminary examination report shall, in relation to the claims in question, contain the statement as provided in subparagraph (a), whereas, in relation to the other claims, it shall contain the statement as provided in paragraph (2).

## Article 36

### Transmittal, Translation, and Communication, of the International Preliminary Examination Report

(1) The international preliminary examination report, together with the prescribed annexes, shall be transmitted to the applicant and to the International Bureau.

(2) (a) The international preliminary examination report and its annexes shall be translated into the prescribed languages.

(b) Any translation of the said report shall be prepared by or under the responsibility of the International Bureau, whereas any translation of the said annexes shall be prepared by the applicant.

(3) (a) The international preliminary examination report, together with its translation (as prescribed) and its annexes (in the original language), shall be communicated by the International Bureau to each elected Office.

(b) The prescribed translation of the annexes shall be transmitted within the prescribed time limit by the applicant to the elected Offices.

(4) The provisions of Article 20(3) shall apply, *mutatis mutandis*, to copies of any document which is cited in the international preliminary examination report and which was not cited in the international search report.

## Article 37

### Withdrawal of Demand or Election

(1) The applicant may withdraw any or all elections.

(2) If the election of all elected States is withdrawn, the demand shall be considered withdrawn.

(3) (a) Any withdrawal shall be notified to the International Bureau.

    (b) The elected Offices concerned and the International Preliminary Examining Authority concerned shall be notified accordingly by the International Bureau.

(4) (a) Subject to the provisions of subparagraph (b), withdrawal of the demand or of the election of a Contracting State shall, unless the national law of that State provides otherwise, be considered to be withdrawal of the international application as far as that State is concerned.

    (b) Withdrawal of the demand or of the election shall not be considered to be withdrawal of the international application if such withdrawal is effected prior to the expiration of the applicable time limit under Article 22; however, any Contracting State may provide in its national law that the aforesaid shall apply only if its national Office has received, within the said time limit, a copy of the international application, together with a translation (as prescribed), and the national fee.

## Article 38

### Confidential Nature of the International Preliminary Examination

(1) Neither the International Bureau nor the International Preliminary Examining Authority shall, unless requested or authorized by the applicant, allow access within the meaning, and with the proviso, of Article 30(4) to the file of the international preliminary examination by any person or authority at any time, except by the elected Offices once the international preliminary examination report has been established.

(2) Subject to the provisions of paragraph (1) and Articles 36(1) and (3) and 37(3)(b), neither the International Bureau nor the International Preliminary Examining Authority shall, unless requested or authorized by the applicant, give information on the issuance or nonissuance of an international preliminary examination report and on the withdrawal or nonwithdrawal of the demand or of any election.

## Article 39

### Copy, Translation, and Fee, to Elected Offices

(1) (a) If the election of any Contracting State has been effected prior to the expiration of the 19th month from the priority date, the provisions of Article 22 shall not apply to such State and the applicant shall furnish a copy of the international application (unless the communication under Article 20 has already taken place) and a translation thereof (as prescribed), and pay the national fee (if any), to each elected Office not later than at the expiration of 30 months from the priority date.

    (b) Any national law may, for performing the acts referred to in subparagraph (a), fix time limits which expire later than the time limit provided for in that subparagraph.

(2) The effect provided for in Article 11(3) shall cease in the elected State with the same consequences as the withdrawal of any national application in that State if the applicant fails to perform the acts referred to in paragraph (1)(a) within the time limit applicable under paragraph (1)(a) or (b).

(3) Any elected Office may maintain the effect provided for in Article 11(3) even where the applicant does not comply with the requirements provided for in paragraph (1)(a) or (b).

## Article 40

## Delaying of National Examination and Other Processing

(1) If the election of any Contracting State has been effected prior to the expiration of the 19th month from the priority date, the provisions of Article 23 shall not apply to such State and the national Office of or acting for that State shall not proceed, subject to the provisions of paragraph (2), to the examination and other processing of the international application prior to the expiration of the applicable time limit under Article 39.

(2) Notwithstanding the provisions of paragraph (1), any elected Office may, on the express request of the applicant, proceed to the examination and other processing of the international application at any time.

## Article 41

## Amendment of the Claims, the Description, and the Drawings, before Elected Offices

(1) The applicant shall be given the opportunity to amend the claims, the description, and the drawings, before each elected Office within the prescribed time limit. No elected Office shall grant a patent, or refuse the grant of a patent, before such time limit has expired, except with the express consent of the applicant.

(2) The amendments shall not go beyond the disclosure in the international application as filed, unless the national law of the elected State permits them to go beyond the said disclosure.

(3) The amendments shall be in accordance with the national law of the elected State in all respects not provided for in this Treaty and the Regulations.

(4) Where an elected Office requires a translation of the international application, the amendments shall be in the language of the translation.

## Article 42

## Results of National Examination in Elected Offices

No elected Office receiving the international preliminary examination report may require that the applicant furnish copies, or information on the contents, of any papers connected with the examination relating to the same international application in any other elected Office.

## CHAPTER III
## COMMON PROVISIONS

## Article 43

## Seeking Certain Kinds of Protection

In respect of any designated or elected State whose law provides for the grant of inventors' certificates, utility certificates, utility models, patents or certificates of addition, inventors' certificates of addition, or utility certificates of addition, the applicant may indicate, as prescribed in the Regulations, that his international application is for the grant, as far as that State is concerned, of an inventor's certificate, a utility certificate, or a utility model, rather than a patent, or that it is for the grant of a patent or certificate of addition, an inventor's certificate of addition, or a utility certificate of addition, and the ensuing effect shall be governed by the applicant's choice. For the purposes of this Article and any Rule thereunder, Article 2(ii) shall not apply.

## Article 44

### Seeking Two Kinds of Protection

In respect of any designated or elected State whose law permits an application, while being for the grant of a patent or one of the other kinds of protection referred to in Article 43, to be also for the grant of another of the said kinds of protection, the applicant may indicate, as prescribed in the Regulations, the two kinds of protection he is seeking, and the ensuing effect shall be governed by the applicant's indications. For the purposes of this Article, Article 2(ii) shall not apply.

## Article 45

### Regional Patent Treaties

(1) Any treaty providing for the grant of regional patents ("regional patent treaty"), and giving to all persons who, according to Article 9, are entitled to file international applications the right to file applications for such patents, may provide that international applications designating or electing a State party to both the regional patent treaty and the present Treaty may be filed as applications for such patents.

(2) The national law of the said designated or elected State may provide that any designation or election of such State in the international application shall have the effect of an indication of the wish to obtain a regional patent under the regional patent treaty.

## Article 46

### Incorrect Translation of the International Application

If, because of an incorrect translation of the international application, the scope of any patent granted on that application exceeds the scope of the international application in its original language, the competent authorities of the Contracting State concerned may accordingly and retroactively limit the scope of the patent, and declare it null and void to the extent that its scope has exceeded the scope of the international application in its original language.

## Article 47

### Time Limits

(1) The details for computing time limits referred to in this Treaty are governed by the Regulations.

(2) (a) All time limits fixed in Chapters I and II of this Treaty may, outside any revision under Article 60, be modified by a decision of the Contracting States.

  (b) Such decisions shall be made in the Assembly or through voting by correspondence and must be unanimous.

  (c) The details of the procedure are governed by the Regulations.

## Article 48

### Delay in Meeting Certain Time Limits

(1) Where any time limit fixed in this Treaty or the Regulations is not met because of interruption in the mail service or unavoidable loss or delay in the mail, the time limit shall be deemed to be met in the cases and subject to the proof and other conditions prescribed in the Regulations.

(2) (a) Any Contracting State shall, as far as that State is concerned, excuse, for reasons admitted under its national law, any delay in meeting any time limit.

  (b) Any Contracting State may, as far as that State is concerned, excuse, for reasons other than those referred to in subparagraph (a), any delay in meeting any time limit.

## Article 49

### Right to Practice before International Authorities

Any attorney, patent agent, or other person, having the right to practice before the national Office with which the international application was filed, shall be entitled to practice before the International Bureau and the competent International Searching Authority and competent International Preliminary Examining Authority in respect of that application.

## CHAPTER IV
## TECHNICAL SERVICES

## Article 50

### Patent Information Services

(1) The International Bureau may furnish services by providing technical and any other pertinent information available to it on the basis of published documents, primarily patents and published applications (referred to in this Article as "the information services").

(2) The International Bureau may provide these information services either directly or through one or more International Searching Authorities or other national or international specialized institutions, with which the International Bureau may reach agreement.

(3) The information services shall be operated in a way particularly facilitating the acquisition by Contracting States which are developing countries of technical knowledge and technology, including available published know-how.

(4) The information services shall be available to Governments of Contracting States and their nationals and residents. The Assembly may decide to make these services available also to others.

(5) (a) Any service to Governments of Contracting States shall be furnished at cost, provided that, when the Government is that of a Contracting State which is a developing country, the service shall be furnished below cost if the difference can be covered from profit made on services furnished to others than Governments of Contracting States or from the sources referred to in Article 51(4).

(b) The cost referred to in subparagraph (a) is to be understood as cost over and above costs normally incident to the performance of the services of a national Office or the obligations of an International Searching Authority.

(6) The details concerning the implementation of the provisions of this Article shall be governed by decisions of the Assembly and, within the limits to be fixed by the Assembly, such working groups as the Assembly may set up for that purpose.

(7) The Assembly shall, when it considers it necessary, recommend methods of providing financing supplementary to those referred to in paragraph (5).

## Article 51

### Technical Assistance

(1) The Assembly shall establish a Committee for Technical Assistance (referred to in this Article as "the Committee").

(2) (a) The members of the Committee shall be elected among the Contracting States, with due regard to the representation of developing countries.

(b) The Director General shall, on his own initiative or at the request of the Committee, invite representatives of intergovernmental organizations concerned with technical assistance to developing countries to participate in the work of the Committee.

(3)  (a)  The task of the Committee shall be to organize and supervise technical assistance for Contracting States which are developing countries in developing their patent systems individually or on a regional basis.

   (b)  The technical assistance shall comprise, among other things, the training of specialists, the loaning of experts, and the supply of equipment both for demonstration and for operational purposes.

(4)  The International Bureau shall seek to enter into agreements, on the one hand, with international financing organizations and intergovernmental organizations, particularly the United Nations, the agencies of the United Nations, and the Specialized Agencies connected with the United Nations concerned with technical assistance, and, on the other hand, with the Governments of the States receiving the technical assistance, for the financing of projects pursuant to this Article.

(5)  The details concerning the implementation of the provisions of this Article shall be governed by decisions of the Assembly and, within the limits to be fixed by the Assembly, such working groups as the Assembly may set up for that purpose.

## Article 52

### Relations with Other Provisions of the Treaty

Nothing in this Chapter shall affect the financial provisions contained in any other Chapter of this Treaty. Such provisions are not applicable to the present Chapter or to its implementation.

## CHAPTER V
## ADMINISTRATIVE PROVISIONS

## Article 53

### Assembly

(1)  (a)  The Assembly shall, subject to Article 57(8), consist of the Contracting States.

   (b)  The Government of each Contracting State shall be represented by one delegate, who may be assisted by alternate delegates, advisors, and experts.

(2)  (a)  The Assembly shall:

   (i)   deal with all matters concerning the maintenance and development of the Union and the implementation of this Treaty;

   (ii)  perform such tasks as are specifically assigned to it under other provisions of this Treaty;

   (iii) give directions to the International Bureau concerning the preparation for revision conferences;

   (iv)  review and approve the reports and activities of the Director General concerning the Union, and give him all necessary instructions concerning matters within the competence of the Union;

   (v)   review and approve the reports and activities of the Executive Committee established under paragraph (9), and give instructions to such Committee;

   (vi)  determine the program and adopt the triennial budget of the Union, and approve its final accounts;

   (vii) adopt the financial regulations of the Union;

   (viii) establish such committees and working groups as it deems appropriate to achieve the objectives of the Union;

(ix) determine which States other than Contracting States and, subject to the provisions of paragraph (8), which intergovernmental and international non-governmental organizations shall be admitted to its meetings as observers;

(x) take any other appropriate action designed to further the objectives of the Union and perform such other functions as are appropriate under this Treaty.

(b) With respect to matters which are of interest also to other Unions administered by the Organization, the Assembly shall make its decisions after having heard the advice of the Coordination Committee of the Organization.

(3) A delegate may represent, and vote in the name of, one State only.

(4) Each Contracting State shall have one vote.

(5) (a) One-half of the Contracting States shall constitute a quorum.

(b) In the absence of the quorum, the Assembly may make decisions but, with the exception of decisions concerning its own procedure, all such decisions shall take effect only if the quorum and the required majority are attained through voting by correspondence as provided in the Regulations.

(6) (a) Subject to the provisions of Articles 47(2)(b), 58(2)(b), 58(3) and 61(2)(b), the decisions of the Assembly shall require two-thirds of the votes cast.

(b) Abstentions shall not be considered as votes.

(7) In connection with matters of exclusive interest to States bound by Chapter II, any reference to Contracting States in paragraphs (4), (5), and (6), shall be considered as applying only to States bound by Chapter II.

(8) Any intergovernmental organization appointed as International Searching or Preliminary Examining Authority shall be admitted as observer to the Assembly.

(9) When the number of Contracting States exceeds forty, the Assembly shall establish an Executive Committee. Any reference to the Executive Committee in this Treaty and the Regulations shall be construed as references to such Committee once it has been established.

(10) Until the Executive Committee has been established, the Assembly shall approve, within the limits of the program and triennial budget, the annual programs and budgets prepared by the Director General.

(11) (a) The Assembly shall meet in every second calendar year in ordinary session upon convocation by the Director General and, in the absence of exceptional circumstances, during the same period and at the same place as the General Assembly of the Organization.

(b) The Assembly shall meet in extraordinary session upon convocation by the Director General, at the request of the Executive Committee, or at the request of one-fourth of the Contracting States.

(12) The Assembly shall adopt its own rules of procedure.

## Article 54

### Executive Committee

(1) When the Assembly has established an Executive Committee, that Committee shall be subject to the provisions set forth hereinafter.

(2) (a) The Executive Committee shall, subject to Article 57(8), consist of States elected by the Assembly from among States members of the Assembly.

(b) The Government of each State member of the Executive Committee shall be represented by one delegate, who may be assisted by alternate delegates, advisors, and experts.

(3)   The number of States members of the Executive Committee shall correspond to one-fourth of the number of States members of the Assembly. In establishing the number of seats to be filled, remainders after division by four shall be disregarded.

(4)   In electing the members of the Executive Committee, the Assembly shall have due regard to an equitable geographical distribution.

(5)   (a)   Each member of the Executive Committee shall serve from the close of the session of the Assembly which elected it to the close of the next ordinary session of the Assembly.

(b)   Members of the Executive Committee may be re-elected but only up to a maximum of two-thirds of such members.

(c)   The Assembly shall establish the details of the rules governing the election and possible re-election of the members of the Executive Committee.

(6)   (a)   The Executive Committee shall:

(i)     prepare the draft agenda of the Assembly;

(ii)    submit proposals to the Assembly in respect of the draft program and biennial budget of the Union prepared by the Director General;

(iii)   deleted

(iv)    submit, with appropriate comments, to the Assembly the periodical reports of the Director General and the yearly audit reports on the accounts;

(v)     take all necessary measures to ensure the execution of the program of the Union by the Director General, in accordance with the decisions of the Assembly and having regard to circumstances arising between two ordinary sessions of the Assembly;

(vi)    perform such other functions as are allocated to it under this Treaty.

(b)   With respect to matters which are of interest also to other Unions administered by the Organization, the Executive Committee shall make its decisions after having heard the advice of the Coordination Committee of the Organization.

(7)   (a)   The Executive Committee shall meet once a year in ordinary session upon convocation by the Director General, preferably during the same period and at the same place as the Coordination Committee of the Organization.

(b)   The Executive Committee shall meet in extraordinary session upon convocation by the Director General, either on his own initiative or at the request of its Chairman or one-fourth of its members.

(8)   (a)   Each State member of the Executive Committee shall have one vote.

(b)   One-half of the members of the Executive Committee shall constitute a quorum.

(c)   Decisions shall be made by a simple majority of the votes cast.

(d)   Abstentions shall not be considered as votes.

(e)   A delegate may represent, and vote in the name of, one State only.

(9)   Contracting States not members of the Executive Committee shall be admitted to its meetings as observers, as well as any intergovernmental organization appointed as International Searching or Preliminary Examining Authority.

(10)   The Executive Committee shall adopt its own rules of procedure.

## Article 55

### International Bureau

(1) Administrative tasks concerning the Union shall be performed by the International Bureau.

(2) The International Bureau shall provide the secretariat of the various organs of the Union.

(3) The Director General shall be the chief executive of the Union and shall represent the Union.

(4) The International Bureau shall publish a Gazette and other publications provided for by the Regulations or required by the Assembly.

(5) The Regulations shall specify the services that national Offices shall perform in order to assist the International Bureau and the International Searching and Preliminary Examining Authorities in carrying out their tasks under this Treaty.

(6) The Director General and any staff member designated by him shall participate, without the right to vote, in all meetings of the Assembly, the Executive Committee and any other committee or working group established under this Treaty or the Regulations. The Director General, or a staff member designated by him, shall be *ex officio* secretary of these bodies.

(7) (a) The International Bureau shall, in accordance with the directions of the Assembly and in cooperation with the Executive Committee, make the preparations for the revision conferences.

(b) The International Bureau may consult with intergovernmental and international non-governmental organizations concerning preparations for revision conferences.

(c) The Director General and persons designated by him shall take part, without the right to vote, in the discussions at revision conferences.

(8) The International Bureau shall carry out any other tasks assigned to it.

## Article 56

### Committee for Technical Cooperation

(1) The Assembly shall establish a Committee for Technical Cooperation (referred to in this Article as "the Committee").

(2) (a) The Assembly shall determine the composition of the Committee and appoint its members, with due regard to an equitable representation of developing countries.

(b) The International Searching and Preliminary Examining Authorities shall be *ex officio* members of the Committee. In the case where such an Authority is the national Office of a Contracting State, that State shall not be additionally represented on the Committee.

(c) If the number of Contracting States so allows, the total number of members of the Committee shall be more than double the number of *ex officio* members.

(d) The Director General shall, on his own initiative or at the request of the Committee, invite representatives of interested organizations to participate in discussions of interest to them.

(3) The aim of the Committee shall be to contribute, by advice and recommendations:

(i) to the constant improvement of the services provided for under this Treaty,

(ii) to the securing, so long as there are several International Searching Authorities and several International Preliminary Examining Authorities, of the maximum degree of uniformity in their documentation and working methods and the maximum degree of uniformly high quality in their reports, and

(iii) on the initiative of the Assembly or the Executive Committee, to the solution of the technical problems specifically involved in the establishment of a single International Searching Authority.

(4) Any Contracting State and any interested international organization may approach the Committee in writing on questions which fall within the competence of the Committee.

(5) The Committee may address its advice and recommendations to the Director General or, through him, to the Assembly, the Executive Committee, all or some of the International Searching and Preliminary Examining Authorities, and all or some of the receiving Offices.

(6) (a) In any case, the Director General shall transmit to the Executive Committee the texts of all the advice and recommendations of the Committee. He may comment on such texts.

(b) The Executive Committee may express its views on any advice, recommendation, or other activity of the Committee, and may invite the Committee to study and report on questions falling within its competence. Executive Committee may submit to the Assembly, with appropriate comments, the advice, recommendations and report of the Committee.

(7) Until the Executive Committee has been established, references in paragraph (6) to the Executive Committee shall be construed as references to the Assembly.

(8) The details of the procedure of the Committee shall be governed by the decisions of the Assembly.

## Article 57

### Finances

(1) (a) The Union shall have a budget.

(b) The budget of the Union shall include the income and expenses proper to the Union and its contribution to the budget of expenses common to the Unions administered by the Organization.

(c) Expenses not attributable exclusively to the Union but also to one or more other Unions administered by the Organization shall be considered as expenses common to the Unions. The share of the Union in such common expenses shall be in proportion to the interest the Union has in them.

(2) The budget of the Union shall be established with due regard to the requirements of coordination with the budgets of the other Unions administered by the Organization.

(3) Subject to the provisions of paragraph (5), the budget of the Union shall be financed from the following sources:

(i) fees and charges due for services rendered by the International Bureau in relation to the Union;

(ii) sale of, or royalties on, the publications of the International Bureau concerning the Union;

(iii) gifts, bequests, and subventions;

(iv) rents, interests, and other miscellaneous income.

(4) The amounts of fees and charges due to the International Bureau and the prices of its publications shall be so fixed that they should, under normal circumstances, be sufficient to cover all the expenses of the International Bureau connected with the administration of this Treaty.

(5) (a) Should any financial year close with a deficit, the Contracting States shall, subject to the provisions of subparagraphs (b) and (c), pay contributions to cover such deficit.

(b)    The amount of the contribution of each Contracting State shall be decided by the Assembly with due regard to the number of international applications which has emanated from each of them in the relevant year.

(c)    If other means of provisionally covering any deficit or any part thereof are secured, the Assembly may decide that such deficit be carried forward and that the Contracting States should not be asked to pay contributions.

(d)    If the financial situation of the Union so permits, the Assembly may decide that any contributions paid under subparagraph (a) be reimbursed to the Contracting States which have paid them.

(e)    A Contracting State which has not paid, within two years of the due date as established by the Assembly, its contribution under subparagraph (b) may not exercise its right to vote in any of the organs of the Union. However, any organ of the Union may allow such a State to continue to exercise its right to vote in that organ so long as it is satisfied that the delay in payment is due to exceptional and unavoidable circumstances.

(6)    If the budget is not adopted before the beginning of a new financial period, it shall be at the same level as the budget of the previous year, as provided in the financial regulations.

(7)    (a)    The Union shall have a working capital fund which shall be constituted by a single payment made by each Contracting State. If the fund becomes insufficient, the Assembly shall arrange to increase it. If part of the fund is no longer needed, it shall be reimbursed.

(b)    The amount of the initial payment of each Contracting State to the said fund or of its participation in the increase thereof shall be decided by the Assembly on the basis of principles similar to those provided for under paragraph (5)(b).

(c)    The terms of payment shall be fixed by the Assembly on the proposal of the Director General and after it has heard the advice of Coordination committee of the Organization.

(d)    Any reimbursement shall be proportionate to the amounts paid by each Contracting State, taking into account the dates at which they were paid.

(8)    (a)    In the headquarters agreement concluded with the State on the territory of which the Organization has its headquarters, it shall be provided that, whenever the working capital fund is insufficient, such State shall grant advances. The amount of these advances and the conditions on which they are granted shall be the subject of separate agreements, in each case, between such State and the Organization. As long as it remains under the obligation to grant advances, such State shall have an *ex officio* seat in the Assembly and on the Executive Committee.

(b)    The State referred to in subparagraph (a) and the Organization shall each have the right to denounce the obligation to grant advances, by written notification. Denunciation shall take effect three years after the end of the year in which it has been notified.

(9)    The auditing of the accounts shall be effected by one or more of the Contracting States or by external auditors, as provided in the financial regulations. They shall be designated, with their agreement, by the Assembly.

## Article 58

### Regulations

(1)    The Regulations annexed to this Treaty provide Rules:

(i)    concerning matters in respect of which this Treaty expressly refers to the Regulations or expressly provides that they are or shall be prescribed,

(ii)    concerning any administrative requirements, matters, or procedures,

        (iii)  concerning any details useful in the implementation of the provisions of this Treaty.

(2)  (a)  The Assembly may amend the Regulations.

     (b)  Subject to the provisions of paragraph (3), amendments shall require three-fourths of the votes cast.

(3)  (a)  The Regulations specify the rules which may be amended

        (i)  only by unanimous consent, or

        (ii)  only if none of the Contracting States whose national Office acts as an International Searching or Preliminary Examining Authority dissents, and, where such Authority is an intergovernmental organization, if the Contracting State member of that organization authorized for that purpose by the other member States within the competent body of such organization does not dissent.

     (b)  Exclusion, for the future, of any such Rules from the applicable requirement shall require the fulfillment of the conditions referred to in subparagraph (a)(i) or (a)(ii), respectively.

     (c)  Inclusion, for the future, of any Rule in one or the other of the requirements referred to in subparagraph (a) shall require unanimous consent.

(4)  The Regulations provide for the establishment, under the control of the Assembly, of Administrative Instructions by the Director General.

(5)  In the case of conflict between the provisions of the Treaty and those of the Regulations, the provisions of the Treaty shall prevail.

## CHAPTER VI
## DISPUTES

### Article 59

### Disputes

Subject to Article 64(5), any dispute between two or more Contracting States concerning the interpretation or application of this Treaty or the Regulations, not settled by negotiation, may, by any one of the States concerned, be brought before the International Court of Justice by application in conformity with the Statute of the Court, unless the States concerned agree on some other method of settlement. The Contracting State bringing the dispute before the Court shall inform the International Bureau; the International Bureau shall bring the matter to the attention of the other Contracting States.

## CHAPTER VII
## REVISION AND AMENDMENT

### Article 60

### Revision of the Treaty

(1)  This Treaty may be revised from time to time by a special conference of the Contracting States.

(2)  The convocation of any revision conference shall be decided by the Assembly.

(3)  Any intergovernmental organization appointed as International Searching or Preliminary Examining Authority shall be admitted as observer to any revision conference.

(4)  Articles 53(5), (9) and (11), 54, 55(4) to (8), 56, and 57, may be amended either by a revision conference or according to the provisions of Article 61.

## Article 61

### Amendment of Certain Provisions of the Treaty

(1) (a) Proposals for the amendment of Articles 53(5), 53(9) and 53(11), 54, 55(4) to 55(8), 56, and 57, may be initiated by any State member of the Assembly, by the Executive Committee, or by the Director General.

(b) Such proposals shall be communicated by the Director General to the Contracting States at least six months in advance of their consideration by the Assembly.

(2) (a) Amendments to the Articles referred to in paragraph (1) shall be adopted by the Assembly.

(b) Adoption shall require three-fourths of the votes cast.

(3) (a) Any amendment to the Articles referred to in paragraph (1) shall enter into force one month after written notifications of acceptance, effected in accordance with their respective constitutional processes, have been received by the Director General from three-fourths of the States members of the Assembly at the time it adopted the amendment.

(b) Any amendment to the said Articles thus accepted shall bind all the States which are members of the Assembly at the time the amendment enters into force, provided that any amendment increasing the financial obligations of the Contracting States shall bind only those States which have notified their acceptance of such amendment.

(c) Any amendment accepted in accordance with the provisions of subparagraph (a) shall bind all States which become members of the Assembly after the date on which the amendment entered into force in accordance with the provisions of subparagraph (a).

## CHAPTER VIII
## FINAL PROVISIONS

## Article 62

### Becoming Party to the Treaty

(1) Any State member of the International Union for the Protection of Industrial Property may become party to this Treaty by:

(i) signature followed by the deposit of an instrument of ratification, or

(ii) deposit of an instrument of accession.

(2) Instruments of ratification or accession shall be deposited the Director General.

(3) The provisions of Article 24 of the Stockholm Act of the Paris Convention for the Protection of Industrial Property shall apply to this Treaty.

(4) Paragraph (3) shall in no way be understood as implying the recognition or tacit acceptance by a Contracting State of the factual situation concerning a territory to which this Treaty is made applicable by another Contracting State by virtue of the said paragraph.

## Article 63

### Entry into Force of the Treaty

(1) (a) Subject to the provisions of paragraph (3), this Treaty shall enter into force three months after eight States have deposited their instruments of ratification or accession, provided that at least four of those States each fulfill any of the following conditions:

(i) the number of applications filed in the State has exceeded 40,000 according to the most recent annual statistics published by the International Bureau,

(ii) the nationals or residents of the State have filed at least **1,000** applications in one foreign country according to the most recent annual statistics published by the International Bureau,

(iii) the national Office of the State has received at least **10,000** applications from nationals or residents of foreign countries according to the most recent annual statistics published by the International Bureau.

(b) For the purposes of this paragraph, the term "applications" does not include applications for utility models.

(2) Subject to the provisions of paragraph (3), any State which does not become party to this Treaty upon entry into force under paragraph (1) shall become bound by this Treaty three months after the date on which such State has deposited its instrument of ratification or accession.

(3) The provisions of Chapter II and the corresponding provisions of the Regulations annexed to this Treaty shall become applicable, however, only on the date on which three States each of which fulfill at least one of the three requirements specified in paragraph (1) become party to this Treaty without declaring, as provided in Article 64(1), that they do not intend to be bound by the provisions of Chapter II. That date shall not, however, be prior to that of the initial entry into force under paragraph (1).

## Article 64

### Reservations

(1) (a) Any State may declare that it shall not be bound by the provisions of Chapter II.

(b) States making a declaration under subparagraph (a) shall not be bound by the provisions of Chapter II and the corresponding provisions of the Regulations.

(2) (a) Any State not having made a declaration under paragraph (1)(a) may declare that:

(i) it shall not be bound by the provisions of Article 39(1) with respect to the furnishing of a copy of the international application and a translation thereof (as prescribed),

(ii) the obligation to delay national processing, as provided for under Article 40, shall not prevent publication, by or through its national Office, of the international application or a translation thereof, it being understood, however, that it is not exempted from the limitations provided for in Articles 30 and 38.

(b) States making such a declaration shall be bound accordingly.

(3) (a) Any State may declare that, as far as it is concerned, international publication of international applications is not required.

(b) Where, at the expiration of 18 months from the priority date, the international application contains the designation only of such States as have made declarations under subparagraph (a), the international application shall not be published by virtue of Article 21(2).

(c) Where the provisions of subparagraph (b) apply, the international application shall nevertheless be published by the International Bureau:

(i) at the request of the applicant, as provided in the Regulations,

(ii) when a national application or a patent based on the international application is published by or on behalf of the national Office of any designated State having made a declaration under subparagraph (a), promptly after such publication but not before the expiration of 18 months from the priority date.

(4) (a) Any State whose national law provides for prior art effect of its patents as from a date before publication, but does not equate for prior art purposes the priority date claimed under the Paris Convention for the Protection of Industrial Property to the actual filing date in that

State, may declare that the filing outside that State of an international application designating that State is not equated to an actual filing in that State for prior art purposes.

(b) Any State making a declaration under subparagraph (a) shall to that extent not be bound by the provisions of Article 11(3).

(c) Any State making a declaration under subparagraph (a) shall, at the same time, state in writing the date from which, and the conditions under which, the prior art effect of any international application designating that State becomes effective in that State. This statement may be modified at any time by notification addressed to the Director General.

(5) Each State may declare that it does not consider itself bound by Article 59. With regard to any dispute between any Contracting State having made such a declaration and any other Contracting State, the provisions of Article 59 shall not apply.

(6) (a) Any declaration made under this Article shall be made in writing. It may be made at the time of signing this Treaty, at the time of depositing the instrument of ratification or accession, or, except in the case referred to in paragraph (5), at any later time by notification addressed to the Director General. In the case of the said notification, the declaration shall take effect six months after the day on which the Director General has received the notification, and shall not affect international applications filed prior to the expiration of the said six-month period.

(b) Any declaration made under this Article may be withdrawn at any time by notification addressed to the Director General. Such withdrawal shall take effect three months after the day on which the Director General has received the notification and, in the case of the withdrawal of a declaration made under paragraph (3), shall not affect international applications filed prior to the expiration of the said three-month period.

(7) No reservations to this Treaty other than the reservations under paragraphs (1) to (5) are permitted.

## Article 65

### Gradual Application

(1) If the agreement with any International Searching or Preliminary Examining Authority provides, transitionally, for limits on the number or kind of international applications that such Authority undertakes to process, the Assembly shall adopt the measures necessary for the gradual application of this Treaty and the Regulations in respect of given categories of international applications. This provision shall also apply to requests for an international type search under Article 15(5).

(2) The Assembly shall fix the dates from which, subject to the provision of paragraph (1), international applications may be filed and demands for international preliminary examination may be submitted. Such dates shall not be later than six months after this Treaty has entered into force according to the provisions of Article 63(1), or after Chapter II has become applicable under Article 63(3), respectively.

## Article 66

### Denunciation

(1) Any Contracting State may denounce this Treaty by notification addressed to the Director General.

(2) Denunciation shall take effect six months after receipt of the said notification by the Director General. It shall not affect the effects of the international application in the denouncing State if the international application was filed, and, where the denouncing State has been elected, the election was made, prior to the expiration of the said six-month period.

## Article 67

### Signature and Languages

(1)   (a)   This Treaty shall be signed in a single original in the English and French languages, both texts being equally authentic.

      (b)   Official texts shall be established by the Director General, after consultation with the interested Governments, in the German, Japanese, Portuguese, Russian and Spanish languages, and such other languages as the Assembly may designate.

(2)   This Treaty shall remain open for signature at Washington until December 31, 1970.

## Article 68

### Depositary Functions

(1)   The original of this Treaty, when no longer open for signature, shall be deposited with the Director General.

(2)   The Director General shall transmit two copies, certified by him, of this Treaty and the Regulations annexed hereto to the Governments of all States party to the Paris Convention for the Protection Industrial Property and, on request, to the Government of any other State.

(3)   The Director General shall register this Treaty with the Secretariat of the United Nations.

(4)   The Director General shall transmit two copies, certified by him, of any amendment to this Treaty and the Regulations to the Governments of all Contracting States and, on request, to the Government of any other State.

## Article 69

### Notifications

The Director General shall notify the Governments of all States party to the Paris Convention for the Protection of Industrial Property of:

  (i)   signatures under Article 62,

  (ii)   deposits of instruments of ratification or accession under Article 62,

  (iii)   the date of entry into force of this Treaty and the date from which Chapter II is applicable in accordance with Article 63(3),

  (iv)   any declarations made under Article 64(1) to 64(5),

  (v)   withdrawals of any declarations made under Article 64(6)(b),

  (vi)   denunciations received under Article 66, and

  (vii)   any declarations made under Article 31(4).

# 33. PARTIES TO THE PARIS CONVENTION AND THE PATENT COOPERATION TREATY*

**Status on May 4, 2021**

| States/Members | PCT (153) | Paris (177) | WTO² (164) |
|---|---|---|---|
| Andorra | – | X | – |
| United Arab Emirates | X | X | X |
| Afghanistan | – | X | X |
| Antigua and Barbuda | X | X | X |
| Albania | X | X | X |
| Armenia | X | X | X |
| Angola | X | X | X |
| Argentina | – | X | X |
| Austria | X | X | X |
| Australia | X | X | X |
| Azerbaijan | X | X | – |
| Bosnia and Herzegovina | X | X | – |
| Barbados | X | X | X |
| Bangladesh | – | X | X |
| Belgium | X | X | X |
| Burkina Faso | X | X | X |
| Bulgaria | X | X | X |
| Bahrain | X | X | X |
| Burundi | – | X | X |

| States/Members | PCT (153) | Paris (177) | WTO² (164) |
|---|---|---|---|
| Benin | X | X | X |
| Brunei Darussalam | X | X | X |
| Bolivia (Plurinational State of) | – | X | X |
| Brazil | X | X | X |
| Bahamas | – | X | – |
| Bhutan | – | X | – |
| Botswana | X | X | X |
| Belarus | X | X | – |
| Belize | X | X | X |
| Canada | X | X | X |
| Democratic Republic of the Congo | – | X | X |
| Central African Republic | X | X | X |
| Congo | X | X | X |
| Switzerland | X | X | X |
| Côte d'Ivoire | X | X | X |
| Chile | X | X | X |
| Cameroon | X | X | X |

## PARTIES TO THE PARIS CONVENTION & THE PCT

| States/Members | PCT (153) | Paris (177) | WTO[2] (164) |
|---|---|---|---|
| China | X[3] | X[3, 4] | X |
| Colombia | X | X | X |
| Costa Rica | X | X | X |
| Cuba | X | X | X |
| Cabo Verde | – | – | X |
| Cyprus | X | X | X |
| Czechia | X | X | X |
| Germany | X | X | X |
| Djibouti | X | X | X |
| Denmark | X | X | X |
| Dominica | X | X | X |
| Dominican Republic | X | X | X |
| Algeria | X | X | – |
| Ecuador | X | X | X |
| Estonia | X | X | X |
| Egypt | X | X | X |
| Spain | X | X | X |
| European Union | – | – | X |
| Finland | X | X | X |
| Fiji | – | – | X |
| France | X | X | X |
| Gabon | X | X | X |
| United Kingdom | X | X | X |
| Grenada | X | X | X |
| Georgia | X | X | X |

| States/Members | PCT (153) | Paris (177) | WTO[2] (164) |
|---|---|---|---|
| Ghana | X | X | X |
| Gambia | X | X | X |
| Guinea | X | X | X |
| Equatorial Guinea | X | X | – |
| Greece | X | X | X |
| Guatemala | X | X | X |
| Guinea-Bissau | X | X | X |
| Guyana | – | X | X |
| Hong Kong, China | –[3] | –[3] | X |
| Honduras | X | X | X |
| Croatia | X | X | X |
| Haiti | – | X | X |
| Hungary | X | X | X |
| Indonesia | X | X | X |
| Ireland | X | X | X |
| Israel | X | X | X |
| India | X | X | X |
| Iraq | – | X | – |
| Iran (Islamic Republic of) | X | X | – |
| Iceland | X | X | X |
| Italy | X | X | X |
| Jamaica | – | X | X |
| Jordan | X | X | X |
| Japan | X | X | X |

## PARTIES TO THE PARIS CONVENTION & THE PCT

| States/Members | PCT (153) | Paris (177) | WTO[2] (164) |
|---|---|---|---|
| Kenya | X | X | X |
| Kyrgyzstan | X | X | X |
| Cambodia | X | X | X |
| Comoros | X | X | – |
| Saint Kitts and Nevis | X | X | X |
| Democratic People's Republic of Korea | X | X | – |
| Republic of Korea | X | X | X |
| Kuwait | X | X | X |
| Kazakhstan | X | X | X |
| Lao People's Democratic Republic | X | X | X |
| Lebanon | – | X | – |
| Saint Lucia | X | X | X |
| Liechtenstein | X | X | X |
| Sri Lanka | X | X | X |
| Liberia | X | X | X |
| Lesotho | X | X | X |
| Lithuania | X | X | X |
| Luxembourg | X | X | X |
| Latvia | X | X | X |
| Libya | X | X | – |
| Morocco | X | X | X |
| Monaco | X | X | – |

| States/Members | PCT (153) | Paris (177) | WTO[2] (164) |
|---|---|---|---|
| Republic of Moldova | X | X | X |
| Montenegro | X | X | X |
| Madagascar | X | X | X |
| North Macedonia | X | X | X |
| Mali | X | X | X |
| Myanmar | – | – | X |
| Mongolia | X | X | X |
| Macao, China | – | –[4] | X |
| Mauritania | X | X | X |
| Malta | X | X | X |
| Mauritius | – | X | X |
| Maldives | – | – | X |
| Malawi | X | X | X |
| Mexico | X | X | X |
| Malaysia | X | X | X |
| Mozambique | X | X | X |
| Namibia | X | X | X |
| Niger | X | X | X |
| Nigeria | X | X | X |
| Nicaragua | X | X | X |
| Netherlands | X | X | X |
| Norway | X | X | X |
| Nepal | – | X | X |
| New Zealand | X | X | X |
| Oman | X | X | X |

| States/Members | PCT (153) | Paris (177) | WTO[2] (164) |
|---|---|---|---|
| Panama | X | X | X |
| Peru | X | X | X |
| Papua New Guinea | X | X | X |
| Philippines | X | X | X |
| Pakistan | – | X | X |
| Poland | X | X | X |
| Portugal | X | X | X |
| Paraguay | – | X | X |
| Qatar | X | X | X |
| Romania | X | X | X |
| Serbia | X | X | – |
| Russian Federation | X | X | X |
| Rwanda | X | X | X |
| Saudi Arabia | X | X | X |
| Solomon Islands | – | – | X |
| Seychelles | X | X | X |
| Sudan | X | X | – |
| Sweden | X | X | X |
| Singapore | X | X | X |
| Slovenia | X | X | X |
| Slovakia | X | X | X |
| Sierra Leone | X | X | X |
| San Marino | X | X | – |
| Senegal | X | X | X |

| States/Members | PCT (153) | Paris (177) | WTO[2] (164) |
|---|---|---|---|
| Suriname | – | X | X |
| Sao Tome and Principe | X | X | – |
| El Salvador | X | X | X |
| Syrian Arab Republic | X | X | – |
| Eswatini | X | X | X |
| Chad | X | X | X |
| Togo | X | X | X |
| Thailand | X | X | X |
| Tajikistan | X | X | X |
| Turkmenistan | X | X | – |
| Tunisia | X | X | X |
| Tonga | – | X | X |
| Turkey | X | X | X |
| Trinidad and Tobago | X | X | X |
| Taiwan Province of China[5] | – | – | X |
| United Republic of Tanzania | X | X | X |
| Ukraine | X | X | X |
| Uganda | X | X | X |
| United States of America | X | X | X |
| Uruguay | – | X | X |
| Uzbekistan | X | X | – |
| Holy See | – | X | – |

## PARTIES TO THE PARIS CONVENTION & THE PCT

| States/Members | PCT (153) | Paris (177) | WTO² (164) |
|---|---|---|---|
| Saint Vincent and the Grenadines | X | X | X |
| Venezuela (Bolivarian Republic of) | – | X | X |
| Viet Nam | X | X | X |
| Vanuatu | – | – | X |

| States/Members | PCT (153) | Paris (177) | WTO² (164) |
|---|---|---|---|
| Samoa | X | X | X |
| Yemen | – | X | X |
| South Africa | X | X | X |
| Zambia | X | X | X |
| Zimbabwe | X | X | X |

1. Under PCT Rule 4.10(a), it is possible to claim in an international application the priority of one or more earlier applications filed in or for any country party to the Paris Convention for the Protection of Industrial Property, or in or for any Member of the World Trade Organization (WTO) that is not party to that Convention.

2. WTO Members cannot necessarily become party to the Paris Convention or the PCT.

3. China has notified the Director General of WIPO that the Paris Convention and the PCT apply also to Hong Kong, China.

4. China has notified the Director General of WIPO that the Paris Convention applies also to Macao, China.

5. Also referred to by the WTO as "Chinese Taipei" or "Separate Customs Territory of Taiwan, Penghu, Kinmen and Matsu".

# 34. CONVENTION ON THE GRANT OF EUROPEAN PATENTS

(EUROPEAN PATENT CONVENTION)

of 5 October 1973 (Including the Protocol on Recognition)

text as amended by the act revising Article 63 EPC of 17 December 1991, the Act revising the EPC of 29 November 2000 and by decisions of the Administrative Council of the European Patent Organisation of 21 December 1978, 13 December 1994, 20 October 1995, 5 December 1996, 10 December 1998 and 27 October 2005.

## PREAMBLE

### The Contracting States,

DESIRING to strengthen co-operation between the States of Europe in respect of the protection of inventions,

DESIRING that such protection may be obtained in those States by a single procedure for the grant of patents and by the establishment of certain standard rules governing patents so granted,

DESIRING, for this purpose, to conclude a Convention which establishes a European Patent Organisation and which constitutes a special agreement within the meaning of Article 19 of the Convention for the Protection of Industrial Property, signed in Paris on 20 March 1883 and last revised on 14 July 1967, and a regional patent treaty within the meaning of Article 45, paragraph 1, of the Patent Cooperation Treaty of 19 June 1970,

HAVE AGREED on the following provisions:

## PART I—GENERAL AND INSTITUTIONAL PROVISIONS

### Chapter I—General provisions

### Article 1—European law for the grant of patents

A system of law, common to the Contracting States, for the grant of patents for invention is hereby established by this Convention.

### Article 2—European patent

**(1)** Patents granted under this Convention shall be called European patents.

**(2)** The European patent shall, in each of the Contracting States for which it is granted, have the effect of and be subject to the same conditions as a national patent granted by that State, unless provides otherwise this Convention.

### Article 3—Territorial effect

The grant of a European patent may be requested for one or more of the Contracting States.

### Article 4—European Patent Organisation

**(1)** A European Patent Organisation, hereinafter referred to as the Organisation, is established by this Convention. It shall have administrative and financial autonomy.

**(2)** The organs of the Organisation shall be:

(a) the European Patent Office;

(b) the Administrative Council.

**(3)** The task of the Organisation shall be to grant European patents. This shall be carried out by the European Patent Office supervised by the Administrative Council.

### Article 4a—Conference of ministers of the Contracting States

A conference of ministers of the Contracting States responsible for patent matters shall meet at least every five years to discuss issues pertaining to the Organisation and to the European patent system.

## Chapter II—The European Patent Organisation

### Article 5—Legal status

**(1)** The Organisation shall have legal personality.

**(2)** In each of the Contracting States, the Organisation shall enjoy the most extensive legal capacity accorded to legal persons under the national law of that State; it may in particular acquire or dispose of movable and immovable property and may be a party to legal proceedings.

**(3)** The President of the European Patent Office shall represent the Organisation.

### Article 6—Headquarters

**(1)** The Organisation shall have its headquarters in Munich.

**(2)** The European Patent Office shall be located in Munich. It shall have a branch at The Hague.

### Article 7—Sub-offices of the European Patent Office

By decision of the Administrative Council, sub-offices of the European Patent Office may be created, if need be, for the purpose of information and liaison, in the Contracting States and with intergovernmental organisations in the field of industrial property, subject to the approval of the Contracting State or organisation concerned.

### Article 8—Privileges and immunities

The Protocol on Privileges and Immunities annexed to this Convention shall define the conditions under which the Organisation, the members of the Administrative Council, the employees of the European Patent Office and such other persons specified in that Protocol as take part in the work of the Organisation, shall enjoy, in each Contracting State, the privileges and immunities necessary for the performance of their duties.

### Article 9—Liability

**(1)** The contractual liability of the Organisation shall be governed by the law applicable to the contract in question.

**(2)** The non-contractual liability of the Organisation in respect of any damage caused by it or by the employees of the European Patent Office in the performance of their duties shall be governed by the provisions of the law of the Federal Republic of Germany. Where the damage is caused by the branch at The Hague or a sub-office or employees attached thereto, the provisions of the law of the Contracting State in which such branch or sub-office is located shall apply.

**(3)** The personal liability of the employees of the European Patent Office towards the Organisation shall be governed by their Service Regulations or conditions of employment.

**(4)** The courts with jurisdiction to settle disputes under paragraphs 1 and 2 shall be:

(a)   for disputes under paragraph 1, the courts of the Federal Republic of Germany, unless the contract concluded between the parties designates a court of another State;

(b)    for disputes under paragraph 2, the courts of the Federal Republic of Germany, or the State in which the branch or sub-office is located.

## Chapter III—The European Patent Office

### Article 10—Management

**(1)**    The European Patent Office shall be managed by the President who shall be responsible for its activities to the Administrative Council.

**(2)**    To this end, the President shall have in particular the following functions and powers:

(a)    he shall take all necessary steps, to ensure the functioning of the European Patent Office, including the adoption of internal administrative instructions and information the public;

(b)    unless this Convention provides otherwise, he shall prescribe which acts are to be performed out at the European Patent Office at Munich and its branch at The Hague respectively;

(c)    he may submit to the Administrative Council any proposal for amending this Convention, for general regulations, or for decisions which come within the competence of the Administrative Council;

(d)    he shall prepare and implement the budget and any amending or supplementary budget;

(e)    he shall submit a management report to the Administrative Council each year;

(f)    he shall exercise supervisory authority over the staff;

(g)    subject to Article 11, he shall appoint the employees and decide on their promotion;

(h)    he shall exercise disciplinary authority over the employees other than those referred to in Article 11, and may propose disciplinary action to the Administrative Council with regard to employees referred to in Article 11, paragraphs 2 and 3;

(i)    he may delegate his functions and powers.

**(3)**    The President shall be assisted by a number of Vice-Presidents. If the President is absent or indisposed, one of the Vice-Presidents shall take his place in accordance with the procedure laid down by the Administrative Council.

### Article 11—Appointment of senior employees

**(1)**    The President of the European Patent Office shall be appointed by the Administrative Council.

**(2)**    The Vice-Presidents shall be appointed by the Administrative Council after the President of the European Patent Office has been consulted.

**(3)**    The members, including the Chairmen, of the Boards of Appeal and of the Enlarged Board of Appeal shall be appointed by the Administrative Council on a proposal from the President of the European Patent Office. They may be re-appointed by the Administrative Council after the President of the European Patent Office has been consulted.

**(4)**    The Administrative Council shall exercise disciplinary authority over the employees referred to in paragraphs 1 to 3.

**(5)**    The Administrative Council, after consulting the President of the European Patent Office, may also appoint as members of the Enlarged Board of Appeal legally qualified members of the national courts or quasi-judicial authorities of the Contracting States, who may continue their judicial activities at the national level. They shall be appointed for a term of three years and may be re-appointed.

## Article 12—Duties of office

Employees of the European Patent Office shall be bound, even after the termination of their employment, neither to disclose nor to make use of information which by its nature is a professional secret.

## Article 13—Disputes between the Organisation and the employees of the European Patent Office

**(1)** Employees and former employees of the European Patent Office or their successors in title may apply to the Administrative Tribunal of the International Labour Organisation in the case of disputes with the European Patent Organisation in accordance with the Statute of the Tribunal and within the limits and subject to the conditions laid down in the Service Regulations for permanent employees or the Pension Scheme Regulations or arising from the conditions of employment of other employees.

**(2)** An appeal shall only be admissible if the person concerned has exhausted such other means of appeal as are available to him under the Service Regulations, the Pension Scheme Regulations or the conditions of employment.

## Article 14—Languages of the European Patent Office, European patent applications and other documents

**(1)** The official languages of the European Patent Office shall be English, French and German.

**(2)** A European patent application shall be filed in one of the official languages or, if filed in any other language, translated into one of the official languages in accordance with the Implementing Regulations. Throughout the proceedings before the European Patent Office, such translation may be brought into conformity with the application as filed. If a required translation is not filed in due time, the application shall be deemed to be withdrawn.

**(3)** The official language of the European Patent Office in which the European patent application is filed or into which it is translated shall be used as the language of the proceedings in all proceedings before the European Patent Office, unless the Implementing Regulations provide otherwise.

**(4)** Natural or legal persons having their residence or principal place of business within a Contracting State having a language other than English, French or German as an official language, and nationals of that State who are resident abroad, may file documents which have to be filed within a time limit in an official language of that State. They shall, however, file a translation in an official language of the European Patent Office in accordance with the Implementing Regulations. If any document, other than those documents making up the European patent application, is not filed in the prescribed language, or if any required translation is not filed in due time, the document shall be deemed not to have been filed.

**(5)** European patent applications shall be published in the language of the proceedings.

**(6)** Specifications of European patents shall be published in the language of the proceedings and shall include a translation of the claims in the other two official languages of the European Patent Office.

**(7)** The following shall be published in the three official languages of the European Patent Office:

(a)    the European Patent Bulletin;

(b)    the Official Journal of the European Patent Office.

**(8)** Entries in the European Patent Register shall be made in the three official languages of the European Patent Office. In cases of doubt, the entry in the language of the proceedings shall be authentic.

## Article 15—Departments entrusted with the procedure

To carry out the following the procedures laid down in this Convention, there shall be set up within the European Patent Office:

(a)   a Receiving Section;

(b)   Search Divisions;

(c)   Examining Divisions;

(d)   Opposition Divisions;

(e)   a Legal Division;

(f)   Boards of Appeal;

(g)   an Enlarged Board of Appeal.

## Article 16—Receiving Section

The Receiving Section shall be responsible for the examination on filing and the examination as to formal requirements of European patent applications.

## Article 17—Search Divisions

The Search Divisions shall be responsible for drawing up European search reports.

## Article 18—Examining Divisions

**(1)** The Examining Divisions shall be responsible for the examination of European patent applications.

**(2)** An Examining Division shall consist of three technically qualified examiners. However, before a decision is taken on a European patent application, its examination shall, as a general rule, be entrusted to one member of the Examining Division. Oral proceedings shall be before the Examining Division itself. If the Examining Division considers that the nature of the decision so requires, it shall be enlarged by the addition of a legally qualified examiner. In the event of parity of votes, the vote of the Chairman of the Examining Division shall be decisive.

## Article 19—Opposition Divisions

**(1)** An Opposition Division shall be responsible for the examination of oppositions against any European patent.

**(2)** An Opposition Division shall consist of three technically qualified examiners, at least two of whom shall not have taken part in the proceedings for grant of the patent to which the opposition relates. An examiner who has taken part in the proceedings for the grant of the European patent may not be the Chairman. Before a decision is taken on the opposition, the Opposition Division may entrust the examination of the opposition to one of its members. Oral proceedings shall be before the Opposition Division itself. If the Opposition Division considers that the nature of the decision so requires, it shall be enlarged by the addition of a legally qualified examiner who shall not have taken part in the proceedings for grant of the patent. In the event of parity of votes, the vote of the Chairman of the Opposition Division shall be decisive.

## Article 20—Legal Division

**(1)** The Legal Division shall be responsible for decisions in respect of entries in the Register of European Patents and in respect of registration on, and deletion from, the list of professional representatives.

**(2)** Decisions of the Legal Division shall be taken by one legally qualified member.

## Article 21—Boards of Appeal

**(1)** The Boards of Appeal shall be responsible for the examination of appeals from decisions of the Receiving Section, the Examining Divisions and Opposition Divisions, and the Legal Division.

**(2)** For appeals from decisions of the Receiving Section or the Legal Division, a Board of Appeal shall consist of three legally qualified members.

**(3)** For appeals from a decision of an Examining Division, a Board of Appeal shall consist of:

(a)   two technically qualified members and one legally qualified member, when the decision concerns the refusal of a European patent application or the grant, limitation or revocation of a European patent, and was taken by an Examining Division consisting of less than four members;

(b)   three technically and two legally qualified members, when the decision was taken by an Examining Division consisting of four members, or when the Board of Appeal considers that the nature of the appeal so requires;

(c)   three legally qualified members in all other cases.

**(4)** For appeals from a decision of an Opposition Division, a Board of Appeal shall consist of:

(a)   two technically qualified members and one legally qualified member, when the decision was taken by an Opposition Division consisting of three members;

(b)   three technically and two legally qualified members, when the decision was taken by an Opposition Division consisting of four members, or when the Board of Appeal considers that the nature of the appeal so requires.

## Article 22—Enlarged Board of Appeal

**(1)** The Enlarged Board of Appeal shall be responsible for:

(a)   deciding on points of law referred to it by Boards of Appeal under Article 112;

(b)   giving opinions on points of law referred to it by the President of the European Patent Office under Article 112;

(c)   deciding on petitions for review of decisions of the Boards of Appeal under Article 112a.

**(2)** In proceedings under paragraph 1(a) and (b), the Enlarged Board of Appeal shall consist of five legally and two technically qualified members. In proceedings under paragraph 1(c), the Enlarged Board of Appeal shall consist of three or five members as laid down in the Implementing Regulations. In all proceedings, a legally qualified member shall be the Chairman.

## Article 23—Independence of the members of the Boards

**(1)** The members of the Enlarged Board of Appeal and of the Boards of Appeal shall be appointed for a term of five years and may not be removed from office during this term, except if there are serious grounds for such removal and if the Administrative Council, on a proposal from the Enlarged Board of Appeal, takes a decision to this effect. Notwithstanding sentence 1, the term of office of members of the Boards shall end if they resign or are retired in accordance with the Service Regulations for permanent employees of the European Patent Office.

**(2)** The members of the Boards may not be members of the Receiving Section, Examining Divisions, Opposition Divisions or Legal Division.

**(3)** In their decisions the members of the Boards shall not be bound by any instructions and shall comply only with the provisions of this Convention.

**(4)** The Rules of Procedure of the Boards of Appeal and the Enlarged Board of Appeal shall be adopted in accordance with the Implementing Regulations. They shall be subject to the approval of the Administrative Council.

### Article 24—Exclusion and objection

**(1)** Members of the Boards of Appeal or of the Enlarged Board of Appeal may not take part in a case in which they have any personal interest, or if they have previously been involved as representatives of one of the parties, or if they participated in the decision under appeal.

**(2)** If, for one of the reasons mentioned in paragraph 1, or for any other reason, a member of a Board of Appeal or of the Enlarged Board of Appeal considers that he should not take part in any appeal, he shall inform the Board accordingly.

**(3)** Members of a Board of Appeal or of the Enlarged Board of Appeal may be objected to by any party for one of the reasons mentioned in paragraph 1, or if suspected of partiality. An objection shall not be admissible if, while being aware of a reason for objection, the party has taken a procedural step. An objection may not be based upon the nationality of members.

**(4)** The Boards of Appeal and the Enlarged Board of Appeal shall decide as to the action to be taken in the cases specified in paragraphs 2 and 3 without the participation of the member concerned. For the purposes of taking this decision the member objected to shall be replaced by his alternate.

### Article 25—Technical opinion

At the request of the competent national court hearing an infringement or revocation action, the European Patent Office shall be obliged, against payment of an appropriate fee, to give a technical opinion concerning the European patent which is the subject of the action. The Examining Division shall be responsible for the issue of such opinions.

### Chapter IV—The Administrative Council

### Article 26—Membership

**(1)** The Administrative Council shall be composed of the Representatives and the alternate Representatives of the Contracting States. Each Contracting State shall be entitled to appoint one Representative and one alternate Representative to the Administrative Council.

**(2)** The members of the Administrative Council may, in accordance with the Rules of Procedure of the Administrative Council, be assisted by advisers or experts.

### Article 27—Chairmanship

**(1)** The Administrative Council shall elect a Chairman and a Deputy Chairman from among the Representatives and alternate Representatives of the Contracting States. The Deputy Chairman shall *ex officio* replace the Chairman if he is prevented from carrying out his duties.

**(2)** The terms of office of the Chairman and the Deputy Chairman shall be three years. They may not be re-elected.

### Article 28—Board

**(1)** When there are at least eight Contracting States, the Administrative Council may set up a Board composed of five of its members.

**(2)** The Chairman and the Deputy Chairman of the Administrative Council shall be members of the Board *ex officio*; the other three members shall be elected by the Administrative Council.

**(3)** The term of office of the members elected by the Administrative Council shall be three years. They may not be re-elected.

**(4)** The Board shall perform the duties assigned to it by the Administrative Council in accordance with the Rules of Procedure.

## Article 29—Meetings

**(1)** Meetings of the Administrative Council shall be convened by its Chairman.

**(2)** The President of the European Patent Office shall take part in the deliberations of the Administrative Council.

**(3)** The Administrative Council shall hold an ordinary meeting once each year. In addition, it shall meet on the initiative of its Chairman or at the request of one-third of the Contracting States.

**(4)** The deliberations of the Administrative Council shall be based on an agenda, and shall be held in accordance with its Rules of Procedure.

**(5)** The provisional agenda shall contain any question whose inclusion is requested by any Contracting State in accordance with the Rules of Procedure.

## Article 30—Attendance of observers

**(1)** The World Intellectual Property Organization shall be represented at the meetings of the Administrative Council, in accordance with an agreement between the Organisation and the World Intellectual Property Organization.

**(2)** Any other inter-governmental organisation charged with the implementation of international procedures in the field of patents with which the Organisation has concluded an agreement shall be represented at the meetings of the Administrative Council, in accordance with any provisions contained in such agreement.

**(3)** Any other inter-governmental and international non-governmental organisations exercising an activity of interest to the Organisation may be invited by the Administrative Council to arrange to be represented at its meetings during any discussion of matters of mutual interest.

## Article 31—Languages of the Administrative Council

**(1)** The languages in use in the deliberations of the Administrative Council shall be English, French and German.

**(2)** Documents submitted to the Administrative Council, and the minutes of its deliberations, shall be drawn up in the three languages mentioned in paragraph 1.

## Article 32—Staff, premises and equipment

The European Patent Office shall place at the disposal of the Administrative Council and any body established by it such staff, premises and equipment as may be necessary for the performance of their duties.

## Article 33—Competence of the Administrative Council in certain cases

**(1)** The Administrative Council shall be competent to amend:

(a) the time limits laid down in this Convention;

(b) Parts II to VIII and Part X of this Convention, to bring them into line with an international treaty relating to patents or European Community legislation relating to patents;

(c)    the Implementing Regulations.

**(2)**    The Administrative Council shall be competent, in conformity with this Convention, to adopt or amend:

(a)    the Financial Regulations;

(b)    the Service Regulations for permanent employees and the conditions of employment of other employees of the European Patent Office, the salary scales of the said permanent and other employees, and also the nature of any supplementary benefits and the rules for granting them;

(c)    the Pension Scheme Regulations and any appropriate increases in existing pensions to correspond to increases in salaries;

(d)    the Rules relating to Fees;

(e)    its Rules of Procedure.

**(3)**    Notwithstanding Article 18, paragraph 2, the Administrative Council shall be competent to decide, in the light of experience, that in certain categories of cases Examining Divisions shall consist of one technically qualified examiner only. Such decision may be rescinded.

**(4)**    The Administrative Council shall be competent to authorise the President of the European Patent Office to negotiate and, subject to its approval, to conclude agreements on behalf of the European Patent Organisation with States, with intergovernmental organisations and with documentation centres set up on the basis of agreements with such organisations.

**(5)**    The Administrative Council may not take a decision under paragraph 1(b):

—    concerning an international treaty, before its entry into force;

—    concerning European Community legislation, before its entry into force or, where that legislation lays down a period for its implementation, before the expiry of that period.

### Article 34—Voting rights

**(1)**    The right to vote in the Administrative Council shall be restricted to the Contracting States.

**(2)**    Each Contracting State shall have one vote, except where Article 36 applies.

### Article 35—Voting rules

**(1)**    The Administrative Council shall take its decisions, other than those referred to in paragraphs 2 and 3, by a simple majority of the Contracting States represented and voting.

**(2)**    A majority of three-quarters of the votes of the Contracting States represented and voting shall be required for the decisions which the Administrative Council is empowered to take under Article 7, Article 11, paragraph 1, Article 33, paragraphs 1(a) and (c), and 2 to 4, Article 39, paragraph 1, Article 40, paragraphs 2 and 4, Article 46, Article 134a, Article 149a, paragraph 2, Article 152, Article 153, paragraph 7, Article 166 and Article 172.

**(3)**    Unanimity of the Contracting States voting shall be required for the decisions which the Administrative Council is empowered to take under Article 33, paragraph 1(b). The Administrative Council shall take such decisions only if all the Contracting States are represented. A decision taken on the basis of Article 33, paragraph 1(b), shall not take effect if a Contracting State declares, within twelve months of the date of the decision, that it does not wish to be bound by that decision.

**(4)**    Abstentions shall not be considered as votes.

### Article 36—Weighting of votes

**(1)**    In respect of the adoption or amendment of the Rules relating to Fees and, if the financial contribution to be made by the Contracting States would thereby be increased, the adoption of the budget of the Organisation and of any amending or supplementary budget, any Contracting State may require, following a first ballot in which each Contracting State shall have one vote, and whatever the result of this ballot, that a second ballot be taken immediately, in which votes shall be given to the States in accordance with paragraph 2. The decision shall be determined by the result of this second ballot.

(2)   The number of votes that each Contracting State shall have in the second ballot shall be calculated as follows:

(a)   the percentage obtained for each Contracting State in respect of the scale for the special financial contributions, pursuant to Article 40, paragraphs 3 and 4, shall be multiplied by the number of Contracting States and divided by five;

(b)   the number of votes thus given shall be rounded upwards to the next whole number;

(c)   five additional votes shall be added to this number;

(d)   nevertheless no Contracting State shall have more than 30 votes.

### Chapter V—Financial provisions

### Article 37—Budgetary funding

The budget of the Organisation shall be financed:

(a)   by the Organisation's own resources;

(b)   by payments made by the Contracting States in respect of renewal fees for European patents levied in these States;

(c)   where necessary, by special financial contributions made by the Contracting States;

(d)   where appropriate, by the revenue provided for in Article 146;

(e)   where appropriate, and for tangible assets only, by third-party borrowings secured on land or buildings;

(f)   where appropriate, by third-party funding for specific projects.

### Article 38—The Organisation's own resources

The Organisation's own resources shall comprise:

(a)   all income from fees and other sources and also the reserves of the Organisation;

(b)   the resources of the Pension Reserve Fund, which shall be treated as a special class of asset of the Organisation, designed to support the Organisation's pension scheme by providing the appropriate reserves.

### Article 39—Payments by the Contracting States in respect of renewal fees for European patents

(1)   Each Contracting State shall pay to the Organisation in respect of each renewal fee received for a European patent in that State an amount equal to a proportion of that fee, to be fixed by the Administrative Council; the proportion shall not exceed 75% and shall be the same for all Contracting States. However, if the said proportion corresponds to an amount which is less than a uniform minimum amount fixed by the Administrative Council, the Contracting State shall pay that minimum to the Organisation.

(2)   Each Contracting State shall communicate to the Organisation such information as the Administrative Council considers to be necessary to determine the amount of these payments.

(3)   The due dates for these payments shall be determined by the Administrative Council.

**(4)** If a payment is not remitted fully by the due date, the Contracting State shall pay interest from the due date on the amount remaining unpaid.

### Article 40—Level of fees and payments—Special financial contributions

**(1)** The amounts of the fees referred to in Article 38 and the proportion referred to in Article 39 shall be fixed at such a level as to ensure that the revenue in respect thereof is sufficient for the budget of the Organisation to be balanced.

**(2)** However, if the Organisation is unable to balance its budget under the conditions laid down in paragraph 1, the Contracting States shall remit to the Organisation special financial contributions, the amount of which shall be determined by the Administrative Council for the accounting period in question.

**(3)** These special financial contributions shall be determined in respect of any Contracting State on the basis of the number of patent applications filed in the last year but one prior to that of entry into force of this Convention, and calculated in the following manner:

    (a)   one half in proportion to the number of patent applications filed in that Contracting State;

    (b)   one half in proportion to the second highest number of patent applications filed in the other Contracting States by natural or legal persons having their residence or principal place of business in that Contracting State.

However, the amounts to be contributed by States in which the number of patent applications filed exceeds 25 000 shall then be taken as a whole and a new scale drawn up in proportion to the total number of patent applications filed in these States.

**(4)** Where the scale position of any Contracting State cannot be established in accordance with paragraph 3, the Administrative Council shall, with the consent of that State, decide its scale position.

**(5)** Article 39, paragraphs 3 and 4, shall apply *mutatis mutandis* to the special financial contributions.

**(6)** The special financial contributions shall be repaid with interest at a rate which shall be the same for all Contracting States. Repayments shall be made in so far as it is possible to provide for this purpose in the budget; the amount thus provided shall be distributed among the Contracting States in accordance with the scale referred to in paragraphs 3 and 4.

**(7)** The special financial contributions remitted in any accounting period shall be repaid in full before any such contributions or parts thereof remitted in any subsequent accounting period are repaid.

### Article 41—Advances

**(1)** At the request of the President of the European Patent Office, the Contracting States shall grant advances to the Organisation, on account of their payments and contributions, within the limit of the amount fixed by the Administrative Council. The amount of such advances shall be determined in proportion to the amounts due from the Contracting States for the accounting period in question.

**(2)** Article 39, paragraphs 3 and 4, shall apply *mutatis mutandis* to the advances.

### Article 42—Budget

**(1)** The budget of the Organisation shall be balanced. It shall be drawn up in accordance with the generally accepted accounting principles laid down in the Financial Regulations. If necessary, there may be amending or supplementary budgets.

**(2)** The budget shall be drawn up in the unit of account fixed in the Financial Regulations.

### Article 43—Authorisation for expenditure

**(1)** The expenditure entered in the budget shall be authorised for the duration of one accounting period, unless the Financial Regulations provide otherwise.

**(2)** Subject to the conditions to be laid down in the Financial Regulations, any appropriations, other than those relating to staff costs, which are unexpended at the end of the accounting period may be carried forward, but not beyond the end of the following accounting period.

**(3)** Appropriations shall be set out under different headings according to type and purpose of the expenditure and subdivided, as far as necessary, in accordance with the Financial Regulations.

### Article 44—Appropriations for unforeseeable expenditure

**(1)** The budget of the Organisation may contain appropriations for unforeseeable expenditure.

**(2)** The employment of these appropriations by the Organisation shall be subject to the prior approval of the Administrative Council.

### Article 45—Accounting period

The accounting period shall commence on 1 January and end on 31 December.

### Article 46—Preparation and adoption of the budget

**(1)** The President of the European Patent Office shall lay the draft budget before the Administrative Council not later than the date prescribed in the Financial Regulations.

**(2)** The budget and any amending or supplementary budget shall be adopted by the Administrative Council.

### Article 47—Provisional budget

**(1)** If, at the beginning of the accounting period, the budget has not been adopted by the Administrative Council, expenditures may be effected on a monthly basis per heading or other division of the budget, according to the provisions of the Financial Regulations, up to one-twelfth of the budget appropriations for the preceding accounting period, provided that the appropriations thus made available to the President of the European Patent Office shall not exceed one-twelfth of those provided for in the draft budget.

**(2)** The Administrative Council may, subject to the observance of the other provisions laid down in paragraph 1, authorise expenditure in excess of one-twelfth of the appropriations.

**(3)** The payments referred to in Article 37, sub-paragraph (b), shall continue to be made, on a provisional basis, under the conditions determined under Article 39 for the year preceding that to which the draft budget relates.

**(4)** The Contracting States shall pay each month, on a provisional basis and in accordance with the scale referred to in Article 40, paragraphs 3 and 4, any special financial contributions necessary to ensure implementation of paragraphs 1 and 2. Article 39, paragraph 4, shall apply mutatis mutandis to these contributions.

### Article 48—Budget implementation

**(1)** The President of the European Patent Office shall implement the budget and any amending or supplementary budget on his own responsibility and within the limits of the allocated appropriations.

**(2)** Within the budget, the President of the European Patent Office may, in accordance with the Financial Regulations, transfer funds as between the various headings or sub-headings.

### Article 49—Auditing of accounts

**(1)** The income and expenditure account and a balance sheet of the Organisation shall be examined by auditors whose independence is beyond doubt, appointed by the Administrative Council for a period of five years, which shall be renewable or extensible.

**(2)** The audit shall be based on vouchers and shall take place, if necessary, in situ. The audit shall ascertain whether all income has been received and all expenditure effected in a lawful and proper manner and whether the financial management is sound. The auditors shall draw up a report containing a signed audit opinion after the end of each accounting period.

**(3)** The President of the European Patent Office shall annually submit to the Administrative Council the accounts of the preceding accounting period in respect of the budget and the balance sheet showing the assets and liabilities of the Organisation together with the report of the auditors.

**(4)** The Administrative Council shall approve the annual accounts together with the report of the auditors and shall discharge the President of the European Patent Office in respect of the implementation of the budget.

### Article 50—Financial Regulations

The Financial Regulations shall lay down in particular:

(a)　the arrangements relating to the establishment and implementation of the budget and for the rendering and auditing of accounts;

(b)　the method and procedure whereby the payments and contributions provided for in Article 37 and the advances provided for in Article 41 are to be made available to the Organisation by the Contracting States;

(c)　the rules concerning the responsibilities of authorising and accounting officers and the arrangements for their supervision;

(d)　the rates of interest provided for in Articles 39, 40 and 47;

(e)　the method of calculating the contributions payable by virtue of Article 146;

(f)　the composition of and duties to be assigned to a Budget and Finance Committee which should be set up by the Administrative Council;

(g)　the generally accepted accounting principles on which the budget and the annual financial statements shall be based.

### Article 51—Fees

**(1)** The European Patent Office may levy fees for any official task or procedure carried out under this Convention.

**(2)** Time limits for the payment of fees other than those fixed by this Convention shall be laid down in the Implementing Regulations.

**(3)** Where the Implementing Regulations provide that a fee shall be paid, they shall also lay down the legal consequences of failure to pay such fee in due time.

**(4)** The Rules relating to Fees shall determine in particular the amounts of the fees and the ways in which they are to be paid.

## PART II—SUBSTANTIVE PATENT LAW
### Chapter I—Patentability

### Article 52—Patentable inventions

**(1)** European patents shall be granted for any inventions, in all fields of technology, provided that they are new, involve an inventive step and are susceptible of industrial application.

**(2)** The following in particular shall not be regarded as inventions within the meaning of paragraph 1:

    (a)    discoveries, scientific theories and mathematical methods;

    (b)    aesthetic creations;

    (c)    schemes, rules and methods for performing mental acts, playing games or doing business, and programs for computers;

    (d)    presentations of information.

**(3)** Paragraph 2 shall exclude the patentability of the subject-matter or activities referred to therein only to the extent to which a European patent application or European patent relates to such subject-matter or activities as such.

### Article 53—Exceptions to patentability

European patents shall not be granted in respect of:

    (a)    inventions the commercial exploitation of which would be contrary to "ordre public" or morality; such exploitation shall not be deemed to be so contrary merely because it is prohibited by law or regulation in some or all of the Contracting States;

    (b)    plant or animal varieties or essentially biological processes for the production of plants or animals; this provision shall not apply to microbiological processes or the products thereof;

    (c)    methods for treatment of the human or animal body by surgery or therapy and diagnostic methods practised on the human or animal body; this provision shall not apply to products, in particular substances or compositions, for use in any of these methods.

### Article 54—Novelty

**(1)** An invention shall be considered to be new if it does not form part of the state of the art.

**(2)** The state of the art shall be held to comprise everything made available to the public by means of a written or oral description, by use, or in any other way, before the date of filing of the European patent application.

**(3)** Additionally, the content of European patent applications as filed, the dates of filing of which are prior to the date referred to in paragraph 2 and which were published on or after that date, shall be considered as comprised in the state of the art.

**(4)** Paragraphs 2 and 3 shall not exclude the patentability of any substance or composition, comprised in the state of the art, for use in a method referred to in Article 53(c), provided that its use for any such method is not comprised in the state of the art.

**(5)** Paragraphs 2 and 3 shall also not exclude the patentability of any substance or composition referred to in paragraph 4 for any specific use in a method referred to in Article 53(c), provided that such use is not comprised in the state of the art.

### Article 55—Non-prejudicial disclosures

**(1)** For the application of Article 54 a disclosure of the invention shall not be taken into consideration if it occurred no earlier than six months preceding the filing of the European patent application and if it was due to, or in consequence of:

(a)  an evident abuse in relation to the applicant or his legal predecessor, or

(b)  the fact that the applicant or his legal predecessor has displayed the invention at an official, or officially recognised, international exhibition falling within the terms of the Convention on international exhibitions signed at Paris on 22 November 1928 and last revised on 30 November 1972.

**(2)** In the case of paragraph 1(b), paragraph 1 shall apply only if the applicant states, when filing the European patent application, that the invention has been so displayed and files a supporting certificate within the time limit and under the conditions laid down in the Implementing Regulations.

### Article 56—Inventive step

An invention shall be considered as involving an inventive step if, having regard to the state of the art, it is not obvious to a person skilled in the art. If the state of the art also includes documents within the meaning of Article 54, paragraph 3, these documents shall not be considered in deciding whether there has been an inventive step.

### Article 57—Industrial application

An invention shall be considered as susceptible of industrial application if it can be made or used in any kind of industry, including agriculture.

### Chapter II—Persons entitled to apply for and obtain a European patent— Mention of the inventor

### Article 58—Entitlement to file a European patent application

A European patent application may be filed by any natural or legal person, or any body equivalent to a legal person by virtue of the law governing it.

### Article 59—Multiple applicants

A European patent application may also be filed either by joint applicants or by two or more applicants designating different Contracting States.

### Article 60—Right to a European patent

**(1)** The right to a European patent shall belong to the inventor or his successor in title. If the inventor is an employee, the right to a European patent shall be determined in accordance with the law of the State in which the employee is mainly employed; if the State in which the employee is mainly employed cannot be determined, the law to be applied shall be that of the State in which the employer has the place of business to which the employee is attached.

**(2)** If two or more persons have made an invention independently of each other, the right to a European patent therefor shall belong to the person whose European patent application has the earliest date of filing, provided that this first application has been published.

**(3)** In proceedings before the European Patent Office, the applicant shall be deemed to be entitled to exercise the right to a European patent.

### Article 61—European patent applications filed by non-entitled persons

**(1)** If by a final decision it is adjudged that a person other than the applicant is entitled to the grant of the European patent, that person may, in accordance with the Implementing Regulations:

(a) prosecute the European patent application as his own application in place of the applicant;

(b) file a new European patent application in respect of the same invention; or

(c) request that the European patent application be refused.

**(2)** Article 76, paragraph 1, shall apply mutatis mutandis to a new European patent application filed under paragraph 1(b).

### Article 62—Right of the inventor to be mentioned

The inventor shall have the right, *vis-à-vis* the applicant for or proprietor of a European patent, to be mentioned as such before the European Patent Office.

## Chapter III—Effects of the European patent and the European patent application

### Article 63—Term of the European patent

**(1)** The term of the European patent shall be 20 years from the date of filing of the application.

**(2)** Nothing in the preceding paragraph shall limit the right of a Contracting State to extend the term of a European patent, or to grant corresponding protection which follows immediately on expiry of the term of the patent, under the same conditions as those applying to national patents:

(a) in order to take account of a state of war or similar emergency conditions affecting that State;

(b) if the subject-matter of the European patent is a product or a process of manufacturing a product or a use of a product which has to undergo an administrative authorisation procedure required by law before it can be put on the market in that State.

**(3)** Paragraph 2 shall apply *mutatis mutandis* to European patents granted jointly for a group of Contracting States in accordance with Article 142.

**(4)** A Contracting State which makes provision for extension of the term or corresponding protection under paragraph 2(b) may, in accordance with an agreement concluded with the Organisation, entrust to the European Patent Office tasks associated with implementation of the relevant provisions.

### Article 64—Rights conferred by a European patent

**(1)** A European patent shall, subject to the provisions of paragraph 2, confer on its proprietor from the date on which the mention of its grant is published in the European Patent Bulletin, in each Contracting State in respect of which it is granted, the same rights as would be conferred by a national patent granted in that State.

**(2)** If the subject-matter of the European patent is a process, the protection conferred by the patent shall extend to the products directly obtained by such process.

**(3)** Any infringement of a European patent shall be dealt with by national law.

### Article 65—Translation of the European patent

**(1)** Any Contracting State may, if the European patent as granted, amended or limited by the European Patent Office is not drawn up in one of its official languages, prescribe that the proprietor of the patent shall supply to its central industrial property office a translation of the patent as granted, amended or limited in one of its official languages at his option or, where that State has prescribed the use of one specific official language, in that language. The period for supplying the translation shall end three months after the date on which the mention of the grant, maintenance in amended form or limitation of the European patent is published in the European Patent Bulletin, unless the State concerned prescribes a longer period.

**(2)** Any Contracting State which has adopted provisions pursuant to paragraph 1 may prescribe that the proprietor of the patent must pay all or part of the costs of publication of such translation within a period laid down by that State.

**(3)** Any Contracting State may prescribe that in the event of failure to observe the provisions adopted in accordance with paragraphs 1 and 2, the European patent shall be deemed to be void ab initio in that State.

### Article 66—Equivalence of European filing with national filing

A European patent application which has been accorded a date of filing shall, in the designated Contracting States, be equivalent to a regular national filing, where appropriate with the priority claimed for the European patent application.

### Article 67—Rights conferred by a European patent application after publication

**(1)** A European patent application shall, from the date of its publication, provisionally confer upon the applicant the protection provided for by Article 64, in the Contracting States designated in the application.

**(2)** Any Contracting State may prescribe that a European patent application shall not confer such protection as is conferred by Article 64. However, the protection attached to the publication of the European patent application may not be less than that which the laws of the State concerned attach to the compulsory publication of unexamined national patent applications. In any event, each State shall ensure at least that, from the date of publication of a European patent application, the applicant can claim compensation reasonable in the circumstances from any person who has used the invention in that State in circumstances where that person would be liable under national law for infringement of a national patent.

**(3)** Any Contracting State which does not have as an official language the language of the proceedings may prescribe that provisional protection in accordance with paragraphs 1 and 2 above shall not be effective until such time as a translation of the claims in one of its official languages at the option of the applicant or, where that State has prescribed the use of one specific official language, in that language:

(a) has been made available to the public in the manner prescribed by national law, or

(b) has been communicated to the person using the invention in the said State.

**(4)** The European patent application shall be deemed never to have had the effects set out in paragraphs 1 and 2 when it has been withdrawn, deemed to be withdrawn or finally refused. The same shall apply in respect of the effects of the European patent application in a Contracting State the designation of which is withdrawn or deemed to be withdrawn.

### Article 68—Effect of revocation or limitation of the European patent

The European patent application and the resulting European patent shall be deemed not to have had, from the outset, the effects specified in Articles 64 and 67, to the extent that the patent has been revoked or limited in opposition, limitation or revocation proceedings.

## Article 69—Extent of protection

**(1)** The extent of the protection conferred by a European patent or a European patent application shall be determined by the claims. Nevertheless, the description and drawings shall be used to interpret the claims.

**(2)** For the period up to grant of the European patent, the extent of the protection conferred by the European patent application shall be determined by the claims contained in the application as published. However, the European patent as granted or as amended in opposition, limitation or revocation proceedings shall determine retroactively the protection conferred by the application, in so far as such protection is not thereby extended.

## Article 70—Authentic text of a European patent application or European patent

**(1)** The text of a European patent application or a European patent in the language of the proceedings shall be the authentic text in any proceedings before the European Patent Office and in any Contracting State.

**(2)** If, however, the European patent application has been filed in a language which is not an official language of the European Patent Office, that text shall be the application as filed within the meaning of this Convention.

**(3)** Any Contracting State may provide that a translation into one of its official languages, as prescribed by it according to this Convention, shall in that State be regarded as authentic, except for revocation proceedings, in the event of the European patent application or European patent in the language of the translation conferring protection which is narrower than that conferred by it in the language of the proceedings.

**(4)** Any Contracting State which adopts a provision under paragraph 3:

(a)   shall allow the applicant for or proprietor of the patent to file a corrected translation of the European patent application or European patent. Such corrected translation shall not have any legal effect until any conditions established by the Contracting State under Article 65, paragraph 2, or Article 67, paragraph 3, have been complied with;

(b)   may prescribe that any person who, in that State, in good faith has used or has made effective and serious preparations for using an invention the use of which would not constitute infringement of the application or patent in the original translation, may, after the corrected translation takes effect, continue such use in the course of his business or for the needs thereof without payment.

### Chapter IV—The European patent application as an object of property

### Article 71—Transfer and constitution of rights

A European patent application may be transferred or give rise to rights for one or more of the designated Contracting States.

### Article 72—Assignment

An assignment of a European patent application shall be made in writing and shall require the signature of the parties to the contract.

### Article 73—Contractual licensing

A European patent application may be licensed in whole or in part for the whole or part of the territories of the designated Contracting States.

### Article 74—Law applicable

Unless this Convention provides otherwise, the European patent application as an object of property shall, in each designated Contracting State and with effect for such State, be subject to the law applicable in that State to national patent applications.

## PART III—THE EUROPEAN PATENT APPLICATION

### Chapter I—Filing and requirements of the European patent application

### Article 75—Filing of a European patent application

**(1)**   A European patent application may be filed:

(a)   with the European Patent Office, or

(b)   if the law of a Contracting State so permits, and subject to Article 76, paragraph 1, with the central industrial property office or other competent authority of that State. Any application filed in this way shall have the same effect as if it had been filed on the same date with the European Patent Office.

**(2)**   Paragraph 1 shall not preclude the application of legislative or regulatory provisions which, in any Contracting State:

(a)   govern inventions which, owing to the nature of their subject-matter, may not be communicated abroad without the prior authorisation of the competent authorities of that State, or

(b)   prescribe that any application is to be filed initially with a national authority, or make direct filing with another authority subject to prior authorisation.

### Article 76—European divisional applications

**(1)**   A European divisional application shall be filed directly with the European Patent Office in accordance with the Implementing Regulations. It may be filed only in respect of subject-matter which does not extend beyond the content of the earlier application as filed; in so far as this requirement is complied with, the divisional application shall be deemed to have been filed on the date of filing of the earlier application and shall enjoy any right of priority.

**(2)**   All the Contracting States designated in the earlier application at the time of filing of a European divisional application shall be deemed to be designated in the divisional application.

### Article 77—Forwarding of European patent applications

**(1)**   The central industrial property office of a Contracting State shall forward to the European Patent Office any European patent application filed with it or any other competent authority in that State, in accordance with the Implementing Regulations.

**(2)**   A European patent application the subject of which has been made secret shall not be forwarded to the European Patent Office.

**(3)**   A European patent application not forwarded to the European Patent Office in due time shall be deemed to be withdrawn.

### Article 78—Requirements of a European patent application

**(1)**   A European patent application shall contain:

(a)   a request for the grant of a European patent;

(b)   a description of the invention;

(c)   one or more claims;

(d)  any drawings referred to in the description or the claims;

(e)  an abstract,

and satisfy the requirements laid down in the Implementing Regulations.

**(2)**  A European patent application shall be subject to the payment of the filing fee and the search fee. If the filing fee or the search fee is not paid in due time, the application shall be deemed to be withdrawn.

## Article 79—Designation of Contracting States

**(1)**  All the Contracting States party to this Convention at the time of filing of the European patent application shall be deemed to be designated in the request for grant of a European patent.

**(2)**  The designation of a Contracting State may be subject to the payment of a designation fee.

**(3)**  The designation of a Contracting State may be withdrawn at any time up to the grant of the European patent.

## Article 80—Date of filing

The date of filing of a European patent application shall be the date on which the requirements laid down in the Implementing Regulations are fulfilled.

## Article 81—Designation of the inventor

The European patent application shall designate the inventor. If the applicant is not the inventor or is not the sole inventor, the designation shall contain a statement indicating the origin of the right to the European patent.

## Article 82—Unity of invention

The European patent application shall relate to one invention only or to a group of inventions so linked as to form a single general inventive concept.

## Article 83—Disclosure of the invention

The European patent application must disclose the invention in a manner sufficiently clear and complete for it to be carried out by a person skilled in the art.

## Article 84—The claims

The claims shall define the matter for which protection is sought. They shall be clear and concise and be supported by the description.

## Article 85—Abstract

The abstract shall serve the purpose of technical information only; it may not be taken into account for any other purpose, in particular for the purpose of interpreting the scope of the protection sought or applying Article 54, paragraph 3.

## Article 86—Renewal fees for European patent application

**(1)**  Renewal fees for the European patent application shall be paid to the European Patent Office in accordance with the Implementing Regulations. These fees shall be due in respect of the third year and each subsequent year, calculated from the date of filing of the application. If a renewal fee is not paid in due time, the application shall be deemed to be withdrawn.

**(2)** The obligation to pay renewal fees shall terminate with the payment of the renewal fee due in respect of the year in which the mention of the grant of the European patent is published in the European Patent Bulletin.

## Chapter II—Priority

### Article 87—Priority right

**(1)** Any person who has duly filed, in or for

(a) any State party to the Paris Convention for the Protection of Industrial Property or

(b) any Member of the World Trade Organization,

an application for a patent, a utility model or a utility certificate, or his successor in title, shall enjoy, for the purpose of filing a European patent application in respect of the same invention, a right of priority during a period of twelve months from the date of filing of the first application.

**(2)** Every filing that is equivalent to a regular national filing under the national law of the State where it was made or under bilateral or multilateral agreements, including this Convention, shall be recognised as giving rise to a right of priority.

**(3)** A regular national filing shall mean any filing that is sufficient to establish the date on which the application was filed, whatever the outcome of the application may be.

**(4)** A subsequent application in respect of the same subject-matter as a previous first application and filed in or for the same State shall be considered as the first application for the purposes of determining priority, provided that, at the date of filing the subsequent application, the previous application has been withdrawn, abandoned or refused, without being open to public inspection and without leaving any rights outstanding, and has not served as a basis for claiming a right of priority. The previous application may not thereafter serve as a basis for claiming a right of priority.

**(5)** If the first filing has been made with an industrial property authority which is not subject to the Paris Convention for the Protection of Industrial Property or the Agreement Establishing the World Trade Organization, paragraphs 1 to 4 shall apply if that authority, according to a communication issued by the President of the European Patent Office, recognises that a first filing made with the European Patent Office gives rise to a right of priority under conditions and with effects equivalent to those laid down in the Paris Convention.

### Article 88—Claiming priority

**(1)** An applicant desiring to take advantage of the priority of a previous application shall file a declaration of priority and any other document required, in accordance with the Implementing Regulations.

**(2)** Multiple priorities may be claimed in respect of a European patent application, notwithstanding the fact that they originated in different countries. Where appropriate, multiple priorities may be claimed for any one claim. Where multiple priorities are claimed, time limits which run from the date of priority shall run from the earliest date of priority.

**(3)** If one or more priorities are claimed in respect of a European patent application, the right of priority shall cover only those elements of the European patent application which are included in the application or applications whose priority is claimed.

**(4)** If certain elements of the invention for which priority is claimed do not appear among the claims formulated in the previous application, priority may nonetheless be granted, provided that the documents of the previous application as a whole specifically disclose such elements.

### Article 89—Effect of priority right

The right of priority shall have the effect that the date of priority shall count as the date of filing of the European patent application for the purposes of Article 54, paragraphs 2 and 3, and Article 60, paragraph 2.

## PART IV—PROCEDURE UP TO GRANT

### Article 90—Examination on filing and examination as to formal requirements

**(1)** The European Patent Office shall examine, in accordance with the Implementing Regulations, whether the application satisfies the requirements for the accordance of a date of filing.

**(2)** If a date of filing cannot be accorded following the examination under paragraph 1, the application shall not be dealt with as a European patent application.

**(3)** If the European patent application has been accorded a date of filing, the European Patent Office shall examine, in accordance with the Implementing Regulations, whether the requirements in Articles 14, 78 and 81, and, where applicable, Article 88, paragraph 1, and Article 133, paragraph 2, as well as any other requirement laid down in the Implementing Regulations, have been satisfied.

**(4)** Where the European Patent Office in carrying out the examination under paragraphs 1 or 3 notes that there are deficiencies which may be corrected, it shall give the applicant an opportunity to correct them.

**(5)** If any deficiency noted in the examination under paragraph 3 is not corrected, the European patent application shall be refused unless a different legal consequence is provided for by this Convention. Where the deficiency concerns the right of priority, this right shall be lost for the application.

### Article 91

(deleted)

### Article 92—Drawing up of the European search report

The European Patent Office shall, in accordance with the Implementing Regulations, draw up and publish a European search report in respect of the European patent application on the basis of the claims, with due regard to the description and any drawings.

### Article 93—Publication of the European patent application

**(1)** The European Patent Office shall publish the European patent application as soon as possible

(a) after the expiry of a period of eighteen months from the date of filing or, if priority has been claimed, from the date of priority, or

(b) at the request of the applicant, before the expiry of that period.

**(2)** The European patent application shall be published at the same time as the specification of the European patent when the decision to grant the patent becomes effective before the expiry of the period referred to in paragraph 1(a).

### Article 94—Examination of the European patent application

**(1)** The European Patent Office shall, in accordance with the Implementing Regulations, examine on request whether the European patent application and the invention to which it relates meet the requirements of this Convention. The request shall not be deemed to be filed until the examination fee has been paid.

**(2)** If no request for examination has been made in due time, the application shall be deemed to be withdrawn.

**(3)** If the examination reveals that the application or the invention to which it relates does not meet the requirements of this Convention, the Examining Division shall invite the applicant, as often as necessary, to file his observations and, subject to Article 123, paragraph 1, to amend the application.

**(4)** If the applicant fails to reply in due time to any communication from the Examining Division, the application shall be deemed to be withdrawn.

## Articles 95–96

(deleted)

### Article 97—Grant or refusal

**(1)** If the Examining Division is of the opinion that the European patent application and the invention to which it relates meet the requirements of this Convention, it shall decide to grant a European patent, provided that the conditions laid down in the Implementing Regulations are fulfilled.

**(2)** If the Examining Division is of the opinion that the European patent application or the invention to which it relates does not meet the requirements of this Convention, it shall refuse the application unless this Convention provides for a different legal consequence.

**(3)** The decision to grant a European patent shall take effect on the date on which the mention of the grant is published in the European Patent Bulletin.

### Article 98—Publication of the specification of the European patent

The European Patent Office shall publish the specification of the European patent as soon as possible after the mention of the grant of the European patent has been published in the European Patent Bulletin.

## PART V—OPPOSITION AND LIMITATION PROCEDURE

### Article 99—Opposition

**(1)** Within nine months of the publication of the mention of the grant of the European patent in the European Patent Bulletin, any person may give notice to the European Patent Office of opposition to that patent, in accordance with the Implementing Regulations. Notice of opposition shall not be deemed to have been filed until the opposition fee has been paid.

**(2)** The opposition shall apply to the European patent in all the Contracting States in which that patent has effect.

**(3)** Opponents shall be parties to the opposition proceedings as well as the proprietor of the patent.

**(4)** Where a person provides evidence that in a Contracting State, following a final decision, he has been entered in the patent register of such State instead of the previous proprietor, such person shall, at his request, replace the previous proprietor in respect of such State. Notwithstanding Article 118, the previous proprietor and the person making the request shall not be regarded as joint proprietors unless both so request.

### Article 100—Grounds for opposition

Opposition may only be filed on the grounds that:

(a)   the subject-matter of the European patent is not patentable under Articles 52 to 57;

(b)   the European patent does not disclose the invention in a manner sufficiently clear and complete for it to be carried out by a person skilled in the art;

(c)   the subject-matter of the European patent extends beyond the content of the application as filed, or, if the patent was granted on a divisional application or on a new application filed under Article 61, beyond the content of the earlier application as filed.

### Article 101—Examination of the opposition—Revocation or maintenance of the European patent

**(1)**   If the opposition is admissible, the Opposition Division shall examine, in accordance with the Implementing Regulations, whether at least one ground for opposition under Article 100 prejudices the maintenance of the European patent. During this examination, the Opposition Division shall invite the parties, as often as necessary, to file observations on communications from another party or issued by itself.

**(2)**   If the Opposition Division is of the opinion that at least one ground for opposition prejudices the maintenance of the European patent, it shall revoke the patent. Otherwise, it shall reject the opposition.

**(3)**   If the Opposition Division is of the opinion that, taking into consideration the amendments made by the proprietor of the European patent during the opposition proceedings, the patent and the invention to which it relates

(a)   meet the requirements of this Convention, it shall decide to maintain the patent as amended, provided that the conditions laid down in the Implementing Regulations are fulfilled;

(b)   do not meet the requirements of this Convention, it shall revoke the patent.

### Article 102

(deleted)

### Article 103—Publication of a new specification of the European patent

If the European patent is maintained as amended under Article 101, paragraph 3(a), the European Patent Office shall publish a new specification of the European patent as soon as possible after the mention of the opposition decision has been published in the European Patent Bulletin.

### Article 104—Costs

**(1)**   Each party to the opposition proceedings shall bear the costs it has incurred, unless the Opposition Division, for reasons of equity, orders, in accordance with the Implementing Regulations, a different apportionment of costs.

**(2)**   The procedure for fixing costs shall be laid down in the Implementing Regulations.

**(3)**   Any final decision of the European Patent Office fixing the amount of costs shall be dealt with, for the purpose of enforcement in the Contracting States, in the same way as a final decision given by a civil court of the State in which enforcement is to take place. Verification of such decision shall be limited to its authenticity.

### Article 105—Intervention of the assumed infringer

**(1)** Any third party may, in accordance with the Implementing Regulations, intervene in opposition proceedings after the opposition period has expired, if the third party proves that

(a) proceedings for infringement of the same patent have been instituted against him, or

(b) following a request of the proprietor of the patent to cease alleged infringement, the third party has instituted proceedings for a ruling that he is not infringing the patent.

**(2)** An admissible intervention shall be treated as an opposition.

### Article 105a—Request for limitation or revocation

**(1)** At the request of the proprietor, the European patent may be revoked or be limited by an amendment of the claims. The request shall be filed with the European Patent Office in accordance with the Implementing Regulations. It shall not be deemed to have been filed until the limitation or revocation fee has been paid.

**(2)** The request may not be filed while opposition proceedings in respect of the European patent are pending.

### Article 105b—Limitation or revocation of the European patent

**(1)** The European Patent Office shall examine whether the requirements laid down in the Implementing Regulations for limiting or revoking the European patent have been met.

**(2)** If the European Patent Office considers that the request for limitation or revocation of the European patent meets these requirements, it shall decide to limit or revoke the European patent in accordance with the Implementing Regulations. Otherwise, it shall reject the request.

**(3)** The decision to limit or revoke the European patent shall apply to the European patent in all the Contracting States in respect of which it has been granted. It shall take effect on the date on which the mention of the decision is published in the European Patent Bulletin.

### Article 105c—Publication of the amended specification of the European patent

If the European patent is limited under Article 105b, paragraph 2, the European Patent Office shall publish the amended specification of the European patent as soon as possible after the mention of the limitation has been published in the European Patent Bulletin.

## PART VI—APPEALS PROCEDURE

### Article 106—Decisions subject to appeal

**(1)** An appeal shall lie from decisions of the Receiving Section, Examining Divisions, Opposition Divisions and the Legal Division. It shall have suspensive effect.

**(2)** A decision which does not terminate proceedings as regards one of the parties can only be appealed together with the final decision, unless the decision allows a separate appeal.

**(3)** The right to file an appeal against decisions relating to the apportionment or fixing of costs in opposition proceedings may be restricted in the Implementing Regulations.

### Article 107—Persons entitled to appeal and to be parties to appeal proceedings

Any party to proceedings adversely affected by a decision may appeal. Any other parties to the proceedings shall be parties to the appeal proceedings as of right.

### Article 108—Time limit and form

Notice of appeal shall be filed, in accordance with the Implementing Regulations, at the European Patent Office within two months of notification of the decision. Notice of appeal shall not be deemed to have been filed until the fee for appeal has been paid. Within four months of notification of the decision, a statement setting out the grounds of appeal shall be filed in accordance with the Implementing Regulations.

### Article 109—Interlocutory revision

**(1)** If the department whose decision is contested considers the appeal to be admissible and well founded, it shall rectify its decision. This shall not apply where the appellant is opposed by another party to the proceedings.

**(2)** If the appeal is not allowed within three months of receipt of the statement of grounds, it shall be remitted to the Board of Appeal without delay, and without comment as to its merit.

### Article 110—Examination of appeals

If the appeal is admissible, the Board of Appeal shall examine whether the appeal is allowable. The examination of the appeal shall be conducted in accordance with the Implementing Regulations.

### Article 111—Decision in respect of appeals

**(1)** Following the examination as to the allowability of the appeal, the Board of Appeal shall decide on the appeal. The Board of Appeal may either exercise any power within the competence of the department which was responsible for the decision appealed or remit the case to that department for further prosecution.

**(2)** If the Board of Appeal remits the case for further prosecution to the department whose decision was appealed, that department shall be bound by the *ratio decidendi* of the Board of Appeal, in so far as the facts are the same. If the decision under appeal was taken by the Receiving Section, the Examining Division shall also be bound by the ratio decidendi of the Board of Appeal.

### Article 112—Decision or opinion of the Enlarged Board of Appeal

**(1)** In order to ensure uniform application of the law, or if a point of law of fundamental importance arises:

(a)   the Board of Appeal shall, during proceedings on a case and either of its own motion or following a request from a party to the appeal, refer any question to the Enlarged Board of Appeal if it considers that a decision is required for the above purposes. If the Board of Appeal rejects the request, it shall give the reasons in its final decision;

(b)   the President of the European Patent Office may refer a point of law to the Enlarged Board of Appeal where two Boards of Appeal have given different decisions on that question.

**(2)** In the cases referred to in paragraph 1(a) the parties to the appeal proceedings shall be parties to the proceedings before the Enlarged Board of Appeal.

**(3)** The decision of the Enlarged Board of Appeal referred to in paragraph 1(a) shall be binding on the Board of Appeal in respect of the appeal in question.

### Article 112a—Petition for review by the Enlarged Board of Appeal

**(1)** Any party to appeal proceedings adversely affected by the decision of the Board of Appeal may file a petition for review of the decision by the Enlarged Board of Appeal.

**(2)** The petition may only be filed on the grounds that:

(a) a member of the Board of Appeal took part in the decision in breach of Article 24, paragraph 1, or despite being excluded pursuant to a decision under Article 24, paragraph 4;

(b) the Board of Appeal included a person not appointed as a member of the Boards of Appeal;

(c) a fundamental violation of Article 113 occurred;

(d) any other fundamental procedural defect defined in the Implementing Regulations occurred in the appeal proceedings; or

(e) a criminal act established under the conditions laid down in the Implementing Regulations may have had an impact on the decision.

**(3)** The petition for review shall not have suspensive effect.

**(4)** The petition for review shall be filed in a reasoned statement, in accordance with the Implementing Regulations. If based on paragraph 2(a) to (d), the petition shall be filed within two months of notification of the decision of the Board of Appeal. If based on paragraph 2(e), the petition shall be filed within two months of the date on which the criminal act has been established and in any event no later than five years from notification of the decision of the Board of Appeal. The petition shall not be deemed to have been filed until after the prescribed fee has been paid.

**(5)** The Enlarged Board of Appeal shall examine the petition for review in accordance with the Implementing Regulations. If the petition is allowable, the Enlarged Board of Appeal shall set aside the decision and shall re-open proceedings before the Boards of Appeal in accordance with the Implementing Regulations.

**(6)** Any person who, in a designated Contracting State, has in good faith used or made effective and serious preparations for using an invention which is the subject of a published European patent application or a European patent in the period between the decision of the Board of Appeal and publication in the European Patent Bulletin of the mention of the decision of the Enlarged Board of Appeal on the petition, may without payment continue such use in the course of his business or for the needs thereof.

## PART VII—COMMON PROVISIONS
### Chapter I—Common provisions governing procedure

### Article 113—Right to be heard and basis of decisions

**(1)** The decisions of the European Patent Office may only be based on grounds or evidence on which the parties concerned have had an opportunity to present their comments.

**(2)** The European Patent Office shall examine, and decide upon the European patent application or the European patent only in the text submitted to it, or agreed, by the applicant for or proprietor of the patent.

### Article 114—Examination by the European Patent Office of its own motion

**(1)** In proceedings before it, the European Patent Office shall examine the facts of its own motion; it shall not be restricted in this examination to the facts, evidence and arguments provided by the parties and the relief sought.

**(2)** The European Patent Office may disregard facts or evidence which are not submitted in due time by the parties concerned.

### Article 115—Observations by third parties

In proceedings before the European Patent Office, following the publication of the European patent application, any third party may, in accordance with the Implementing Regulations, present observations concerning the patentability of the invention to which the application or patent relates. That person shall not be a party to the proceedings.

## Article 116—Oral proceedings

**(1)** Oral proceedings shall take place either at the instance of the European Patent Office if it considers this to be expedient or at the request of any party to the proceedings. However, the European Patent Office may reject a request for further oral proceedings before the same department where the parties and the subject of the proceedings are the same.

**(2)** Nevertheless, oral proceedings shall take place before the Receiving Section at the request of the applicant only where the Receiving Section considers this to be expedient or where it intends to refuse the European patent application.

**(3)** Oral proceedings before the Receiving Section, the Examining Divisions and the Legal Division shall not be public.

**(4)** Oral proceedings, including delivery of the decision, shall be public, as regards the Boards of Appeal and the Enlarged Board of Appeal, after publication of the European patent application, and also before the Opposition Divisions, in so far as the department before which the proceedings are taking place does not decide otherwise in cases where admission of the public could have serious and unjustified disadvantages, in particular for a party to the proceedings.

## Article 117—Means and taking of evidence

**(1)** In proceedings before the European Patent Office the means of giving or obtaining evidence shall include the following:

    (a)   hearing the parties;

    (b)   requests for information;

    (c)   production of documents;

    (d)   hearing witnesses;

    (e)   opinions by experts;

    (f)   inspection;

    (g)   sworn statements in writing.

**(2)** The procedure for taking such evidence shall be laid down in the Implementing Regulations.

## Article 118—Unity of the European patent application or European patent

Where the applicants for or proprietors of a European patent are not the same in respect of different designated Contracting States, they shall be regarded as joint applicants or proprietors for the purposes of proceedings before the European Patent Office. The unity of the application or patent in these proceedings shall not be affected; in particular the text of the application or patent shall be uniform for all designated Contracting States, unless this Convention provides otherwise.

## Article 119—Notification

Decisions, summonses, notices and communications shall be notified by the European Patent Office of its own motion in accordance with the Implementing Regulations. Notification may, where exceptional circumstances so require, be effected through the intermediary of the central industrial property offices of the Contracting States.

## Article 120—Time limits

The Implementing Regulations shall specify:

(a) the time limits which are to be observed in proceedings before the European Patent Office and are not fixed by this Convention;

(b) the manner of computation of time limits and the conditions under which time limits may be extended;

(c) the minima and maxima for time limits to be determined by the European Patent Office.

## Article 121—Further processing of the European patent application

**(1)** If an applicant fails to observe a time limit vis-à-vis the European Patent Office, he may request further processing of the European patent application.

**(2)** The European Patent Office shall grant the request, provided that the requirements laid down in the Implementing Regulations are met. Otherwise, it shall reject the request.

**(3)** If the request is granted, the legal consequences of the failure to observe the time limit shall be deemed not to have ensued.

**(4)** Further processing shall be ruled out in respect of the time limits in Article 87, paragraph 1, Article 108 and Article 112a, paragraph 4, as well as the time limits for requesting further processing or re-establishment of rights. The Implementing Regulations may rule out further processing for other time limits.

## Article 122—Re-establishment of rights

**(1)** An applicant for or proprietor of a European patent who, in spite of all due care required by the circumstances having been taken, was unable to observe a time limit vis-à-vis the European Patent Office shall have his rights re-established upon request if the non-observance of this time limit has the direct consequence of causing the refusal of the European patent application or of a request, or the deeming of the application to have been withdrawn, or the revocation of the European patent, or the loss of any other right or means of redress.

**(2)** The European Patent Office shall grant the request, provided that the conditions of paragraph 1 and any other requirements laid down in the Implementing Regulations are met. Otherwise, it shall reject the request.

**(3)** If the request is granted, the legal consequences of the failure to observe the time limit shall be deemed not to have ensued.

**(4)** Re-establishment of rights shall be ruled out in respect of the time limit for requesting re-establishment of rights. The Implementing Regulations may rule out re-establishment for other time limits.

**(5)** Any person who, in a designated Contracting State, has in good faith used or made effective and serious preparations for using an invention which is the subject of a published European patent application or a European patent in the period between the loss of rights referred to in paragraph 1 and publication in the European Patent Bulletin of the mention of re-establishment of those rights, may without payment continue such use in the course of his business or for the needs thereof.

**(6)** Nothing in this Article shall limit the right of a Contracting State to grant re-establishment of rights in respect of time limits provided for in this Convention and to be observed vis-à-vis the authorities of such State.

### Article 123—Amendments

**(1)** The European patent application or European patent may be amended in proceedings before the European Patent Office, in accordance with the Implementing Regulations. In any event, the applicant shall be given at least one opportunity to amend the application of his own volition.

**(2)** The European patent application or European patent may not be amended in such a way that it contains subject-matter which extends beyond the content of the application as filed.

**(3)** The European patent may not be amended in such a way as to extend the protection it confers.

### Article 124—Information on prior art

**(1)** The European Patent Office may, in accordance with the Implementing Regulations, invite the applicant to provide information on prior art taken into consideration in national or regional patent proceedings and concerning an invention to which the European patent application relates.

**(2)** If the applicant fails to reply in due time to an invitation under paragraph 1, the European patent application shall be deemed to be withdrawn.

### Article 125—Reference to general principles

In the absence of procedural provisions in this Convention, the European Patent Office shall take into account the principles of procedural law generally recognised in the Contracting States.

### Article 126

(deleted)

### Chapter II—Information to the public or to official authorities

### Article 127—European Patent Register

The European Patent Office shall keep a European Patent Register, in which the particulars specified in the Implementing Regulations shall be recorded. No entry shall be made in the European Patent Register before the publication of the European patent application. The European Patent Register shall be open to public inspection.

### Article 128—Inspection of files

**(1)** Files relating to European patent applications which have not yet been published shall not be made available for inspection without the consent of the applicant.

**(2)** Any person who can prove that the applicant has invoked the rights under the European patent application against him may obtain inspection of the files before the publication of that application and without the consent of the applicant.

**(3)** Where a European divisional application or a new European patent application filed under Article 61, paragraph 1, is published, any person may obtain inspection of the files of the earlier application before the publication of that application and without the consent of the applicant.

**(4)** After the publication of the European patent application, the files relating to the application and the resulting European patent may be inspected on request, subject to the restrictions laid down in the Implementing Regulations.

**(5)** Even before the publication of the European patent application, the European Patent Office may communicate to third parties or publish the particulars specified in the Implementing Regulations.

## Article 129—Periodical publications

The European Patent Office shall periodically publish:

(a) a European Patent Bulletin containing the particulars the publication of which is prescribed by this Convention, the Implementing Regulations or the President of the European Patent Office;

(b) an Official Journal containing notices and information of a general character issued by the President of the European Patent Office, as well as any other information relevant to this Convention or its implementation.

## Article 130—Exchange of information

(1) Unless this Convention or national laws provide otherwise, the European Patent Office and the central industrial property office of any Contracting State shall, on request, communicate to each other any useful information regarding European or national patent applications and patents and any proceedings concerning them.

(2) Paragraph 1 shall apply to the communication of information by virtue of working agreements between the European Patent Office and

(a) the central industrial property offices of other States;

(b) any intergovernmental organisation entrusted with the task of granting patents;

(c) any other organisation.

(3) Communications under paragraphs 1 and 2(a) and (b) shall not be subject to the restrictions laid down in Article 128. The Administrative Council may decide that communications under paragraph 2(c) shall not be subject to such restrictions, provided that the organisation concerned treats the information communicated as confidential until the European patent application has been published.

## Article 131—Administrative and legal co-operation

(1) Unless this Convention or national laws provide otherwise, the European Patent Office and the courts or authorities of Contracting States shall on request give assistance to each other by communicating information or opening files for inspection. Where the European Patent Office makes files available for inspection by courts, Public Prosecutors' Offices or central industrial property offices, the inspection shall not be subject to the restrictions laid down in Article 128.

(2) At the request of the European Patent Office, the courts or other competent authorities of Contracting States shall undertake, on behalf of the Office and within the limits of their jurisdiction, any necessary enquiries or other legal measures.

## Article 132—Exchange of publications

(1) The European Patent Office and the central industrial property offices of the Contracting States shall despatch to each other on request and for their own use one or more copies of their respective publications free of charge.

(2) The European Patent Office may conclude agreements relating to the exchange or supply of publications.

## Chapter III—Representation

## Article 133—General principles of representation

(1) Subject to paragraph 2, no person shall be compelled to be represented by a professional representative in proceedings established by this Convention.

**(2)** Natural or legal persons not having their residence or principal place of business in a Contracting State shall be represented by a professional representative and act through him in all proceedings established by this Convention, other than in filing a European patent application; the Implementing Regulations may permit other exceptions.

**(3)** Natural or legal persons having their residence or principal place of business in a Contracting State may be represented in proceedings established by this Convention by an employee, who need not be a professional representative but who shall be authorised in accordance with the Implementing Regulations. The Implementing Regulations may provide whether and under what conditions an employee of a legal person may also represent other legal persons which have their principal place of business in a Contracting State and which have economic connections with the first legal person.

**(4)** The Implementing Regulations may lay down special provisions concerning the common representation of parties acting in common.

### Article 134—Representation before the European Patent Office

**(1)** Representation of natural or legal persons in proceedings established by this Convention may only be undertaken by professional representatives whose names appear on a list maintained for this purpose by the European Patent Office.

**(2)** Any natural person who

(a) is a national of a Contracting State,

(b) has his place of business or employment in a Contracting State and

(c) has passed the European qualifying examination

may be entered on the list of professional representatives.

**(3)** During a period of one year from the date on which the accession of a State to this Convention takes effect, entry on that list may also be requested by any natural person who

(a) is a national of a Contracting State,

(b) has his place of business or employment in the State having acceded to the Convention and

(c) is entitled to represent natural or legal persons in patent matters before the central industrial property office of that State. Where such entitlement is not conditional upon the requirement of special professional qualifications, the person shall have regularly so acted in that State for at least five years.

**(4)** Entry shall be effected upon request, accompanied by certificates indicating that the conditions laid down in paragraph 2 or 3 are fulfilled.

**(5)** Persons whose names appear on the list of professional representatives shall be entitled to act in all proceedings established by this Convention.

**(6)** For the purpose of acting as a professional representative, any person whose name appears on the list of professional representatives shall be entitled to establish a place of business in any Contracting State in which proceedings established by this Convention may be conducted, having regard to the Protocol on Centralisation annexed to this Convention. The authorities of such State may remove that entitlement in individual cases only in application of legal provisions adopted for the purpose of protecting public security and law and order. Before such action is taken, the President of the European Patent Office shall be consulted.

**(7)** The President of the European Patent Office may grant exemption from:

(a) the requirement of paragraphs 2(a) or 3(a) in special circumstances;

(b)   the requirement of paragraph 3(c), second sentence, if the applicant furnishes proof that he has acquired the requisite qualification in another way.

**(8)**   Representation in proceedings established by this Convention may also be undertaken, in the same way as by a professional representative, by any legal practitioner qualified in a Contracting State and having his place of business in that State, to the extent that he is entitled in that State to act as a professional representative in patent matters. Paragraph 6 shall apply mutatis mutandis.

### Article 134a—Institute of Professional Representatives before the European Patent Office

**(1)**   The Administrative Council shall be competent to adopt and amend provisions governing:

(a)   the Institute of Professional Representatives before the European Patent Office, hereinafter referred to as the Institute;

(b)   the qualifications and training required of a person for admission to the European qualifying examination and the conduct of such examination;

(c)   the disciplinary power exercised by the Institute or the European Patent Office in respect of professional representatives;

(d)   the obligation of confidentiality on the professional representative and the privilege from disclosure in proceedings before the European Patent Office in respect of communications between a professional representative and his client or any other person.

**(2)**   Any person entered on the list of professional representatives referred to in Article 134, paragraph 1, shall be a member of the Institute.

## PART VIII—IMPACT ON NATIONAL LAW

### Chapter I—Conversion into a national patent application

### Article 135—Request for conversion

**(1)**   The central industrial property office of a designated Contracting State shall, at the request of the applicant for or proprietor of a European patent, apply the procedure for the grant of a national patent in the following circumstances:

(a)   where the European patent application is deemed to be withdrawn under Article 77, paragraph 3;

(b)   in such other cases as are provided for by the national law, in which the European patent application is refused or withdrawn or deemed to be withdrawn, or the European patent is revoked under this Convention.

**(2)**   In the case referred to in paragraph 1(a), the request for conversion shall be filed with the central industrial property office with which the European patent application has been filed. That office shall, subject to the provisions governing national security, transmit the request directly to the central industrial property offices of the Contracting States specified therein.

**(3)**   In the cases referred to in paragraph 1(b), the request for conversion shall be submitted to the European Patent Office in accordance with the Implementing Regulations. It shall not be deemed to be filed until the conversion fee has been paid. The European Patent Office shall transmit the request to the central industrial property offices of the Contracting States specified therein.

**(4)**   The effect of the European patent application referred to in Article 66 shall lapse if the request for conversion is not submitted in due time.

## Article 136

(deleted)

### Article 137—Formal requirements for conversion

**(1)** A European patent application transmitted in accordance with Article 135, paragraph 2 or 3, shall not be subjected to formal requirements of national law which are different from or additional to those provided for in this Convention.

**(2)** Any central industrial property office to which the European patent application is transmitted may require that the applicant shall, within a period of not less than two months:

(a) pay the national application fee; and

(b) file a translation of the original text of the European patent application in an official language of the State in question and, where appropriate, of the text as amended during proceedings before the European Patent Office which the applicant wishes to use as the basis for the national procedure.

### Chapter II—Revocation and prior rights

### Article 138—Revocation of European patents

**(1)** Subject to Article 139, a European patent may be revoked with effect for a Contracting State only on the grounds that:

(a) the subject-matter of the European patent is not patentable under Articles 52 to 57;

(b) the European patent does not disclose the invention in a manner sufficiently clear and complete for it to be carried out by a person skilled in the art;

(c) the subject-matter of the European patent extends beyond the content of the application as filed or, if the patent was granted on a divisional application or on a new application filed under Article 61, beyond the content of the earlier application as filed;

(d) the protection conferred by the European patent has been extended; or

(e) the proprietor of the European patent is not entitled under Article 60, paragraph 1.

**(2)** If the grounds for revocation affect the European patent only in part, the patent shall be limited by a corresponding amendment of the claims and revoked in part.

**(3)** In proceedings before the competent court or authority relating to the validity of the European patent, the proprietor of the patent shall have the right to limit the patent by amending the claims. The patent as thus limited shall form the basis for the proceedings.

### Article 139—Prior rights and rights arising on the same date

**(1)** In any designated Contracting State a European patent application and a European patent shall have with regard to a national patent application and a national patent the same prior right effect as a national patent application and a national patent.

**(2)** A national patent application and a national patent in a Contracting State shall have with regard to a European patent designating that Contracting State the same prior right effect as if the European patent were a national patent.

**(3)** Any Contracting State may prescribe whether and on what terms an invention disclosed in both a European patent application or patent and a national application or patent having the same date of filing or, where priority is claimed, the same date of priority, may be protected simultaneously by both applications or patents.

## Chapter III—Miscellaneous effects

### Article 140—National utility models and utility certificates

Articles 66, 124, 135, 137 and 139 shall apply to utility models and utility certificates and to applications for utility models and utility certificates registered or deposited in the Contracting States whose laws make provision for such models or certificates.

### Article 141—Renewal fees for European patents

**(1)** Renewal fees for a European patent may only be imposed for the years which follow that referred to in Article 86, paragraph 2.

**(2)** Any renewal fees falling due within two months of the publication in the European Patent Bulletin of the mention of the grant of the European patent shall be deemed to have been validly paid if they are paid within that period. Any additional fee provided for under national law shall not be charged.

## PART IX—SPECIAL AGREEMENTS

### Article 142—Unitary patents

**(1)** Any group of Contracting States, which has provided by a special agreement that a European patent granted for those States has a unitary character throughout their territories, may provide that a European patent may only be granted jointly in respect of all those States.

**(2)** Where any group of Contracting States has availed itself of the authorisation given in paragraph 1, the provisions of this Part shall apply.

### Article 143—Special departments of the European Patent Office

**(1)** The group of Contracting States may give additional tasks to the European Patent Office.

**(2)** Special departments common to the Contracting States in the group may be set up within the European Patent Office in order to carry out the additional tasks. The President of the European Patent Office shall direct such special departments; Article 10, paragraphs 2 and 3, shall apply *mutatis mutandis*.

### Article 144—Representation before special departments

The group of Contracting States may lay down special provisions to govern representation of parties before the departments referred to in Article 143, paragraph 2.

### Article 145—Select committee of the Administrative Council

**(1)** The group of Contracting States may set up a select committee of the Administrative Council for the purpose of supervising the activities of the special departments set up under Article 143, paragraph 2; the European Patent Office shall place at its disposal such staff, premises and equipment as may be necessary for the performance of its duties. The President of the European Patent Office shall be responsible for the activities of the special departments to the select committee of the Administrative Council.

**(2)** The composition, powers and functions of the select committee shall be determined by the group of Contracting States.

### Article 146—Cover for expenditure for carrying out special tasks

Where additional tasks have been given to the European Patent Office under Article 143, the group of Contracting States shall bear the expenses incurred by the Organisation in carrying out these tasks. Where special departments have been set up in the European Patent Office to carry out these additional tasks, the group shall bear the expenditure on staff, premises and equipment chargeable in respect of these departments. Article 39, paragraphs 3 and 4, Article 41 and Article 47 shall apply *mutatis mutandis.*

### Article 147—Payments in respect of renewal fees for unitary patents

If the group of Contracting States has fixed a common scale of renewal fees in respect of European patents, the proportion referred to in Article 39, paragraph 1, shall be calculated on the basis of the common scale; the minimum amount referred to in Article 39, paragraph 1, shall apply to the unitary patent. Article 39, paragraphs 3 and 4, shall apply *mutatis mutandis.*

### Article 148—The European patent application as an object of property

**(1)**   Article 74 shall apply unless the group of Contracting States has specified otherwise.

**(2)**   The group of Contracting States may provide that a European patent application for which these Contracting States are designated may only be transferred, mortgaged or subjected to any legal means of execution in respect of all the Contracting States of the group and in accordance with the provisions of the special agreement.

### Article 149—Joint designation

**(1)**   The group of Contracting States may provide that these States may only be designated jointly, and that the designation of one or some only of such States shall be deemed to constitute the designation of all the States of the group.

**(2)**   Where the European Patent Office acts as a designated Office under Article 153, paragraph 1, paragraph 1 shall apply if the applicant has indicated in the international application that he wishes to obtain a European patent for one or more of the designated States of the group. The same shall apply if the applicant designates in the international application one of the Contracting States in the group, whose national law provides that the designation of that State shall have the effect of the application being for a European patent.

### Article 149a—Other agreements between the Contracting States

**(1)**   Nothing in this Convention shall be construed as limiting the right of some or all of the Contracting States to conclude special agreements on any matters concerning European patent applications or European patents which under this Convention are subject to and governed by national law, such as, in particular

(a)   an agreement establishing a European patent court common to the Contracting States party to it;

(b)   an agreement establishing an entity common to the Contracting States party to it to deliver, at the request of national courts or quasi-judicial authorities, opinions on issues of European or harmonised national patent law;

(c)   an agreement under which the Contracting States party to it dispense fully or in part with translations of European patents under Article 65;

(d)   an agreement under which the Contracting States party to it provide that translations of European patents as required under Article 65 may be filed with, and published by, the European Patent Office.

**(2)**   The Administrative Council shall be competent to decide that:

(a)   the members of the Boards of Appeal or the Enlarged Board of Appeal may serve on a European patent court or a common entity and take part in proceedings before that court or entity in accordance with any such agreement;

(b)   the European Patent Office shall provide a common entity with such support staff, premises and equipment as may be necessary for the performance of its duties, and the expenses incurred by that entity shall be borne fully or in part by the Organisation.

## PART X—INTERNATIONAL APPLICATIONS UNDER THE PATENT COOPERATION TREATY—EURO-PCT APPLICATIONS

### Article 150—Application of the Patent Cooperation Treaty

**(1)**   The Patent Cooperation Treaty of 19 June 1970, hereinafter referred to as the PCT, shall be applied in accordance with the provisions of this Part.

**(2)**   International applications filed under the PCT may be the subject of proceedings before the European Patent Office. In such proceedings, the provisions of the PCT and its Regulations shall be applied, supplemented by the provisions of this Convention. In case of conflict, the provisions of the PCT or its Regulations shall prevail.

### Article 151—The European Patent Office as a receiving Office

The European Patent Office shall act as a receiving Office within the meaning of the PCT, in accordance with the Implementing Regulations. Article 75, paragraph 2, shall apply.

### Article 152—The European Patent Office as an International Searching Authority or International Preliminary Examining Authority

The European Patent Office shall act as an International Searching Authority and International Preliminary Examining Authority within the meaning of the PCT, in accordance with an agreement between the Organisation and the International Bureau of the World Intellectual Property Organization, for applicants who are residents or nationals of a State party to this Convention. This agreement may provide that the European Patent Office shall also act for other applicants.

### Article 153—The European Patent Office as a designated Office or elected Office

**(1)**   The European Patent Office shall be

(a)   a designated Office for any State party to this Convention in respect of which the PCT is in force, which is designated in the international application and for which the applicant wishes to obtain a European patent, and

(b)   an elected Office, if the applicant has elected a State designated pursuant to letter (a).

**(2)**   An international application for which the European Patent Office is a designated or elected Office, and which has been accorded an international date of filing, shall be equivalent to a regular European application (Euro-PCT application).

**(3)**   The international publication of a Euro-PCT application in an official language of the European Patent Office shall take the place of the publication of the European patent application and shall be mentioned in the European Patent Bulletin.

**(4)**   If the Euro-PCT application is published in another language, a translation into one of the official languages shall be filed with the European Patent Office, which shall publish it. Subject to Article 67, paragraph 3, the provisional protection under Article 67, paragraphs 1 and 2, shall be effective from the date of that publication.

**(5)**   The Euro-PCT application shall be treated as a European patent application and shall be considered as comprised in the state of the art under Article 54, paragraph 3, if the conditions laid down in paragraph 3 or 4 and in the Implementing Regulations are fulfilled.

**(6)** The international search report drawn up in respect of a Euro-PCT application or the declaration replacing it, and their international publication, shall take the place of the European search report and the mention of its publication in the European Patent Bulletin.

**(7)** A supplementary European search report shall be drawn up in respect of any Euro-PCT application under paragraph 5. The Administrative Council may decide that the supplementary search report is to be dispensed with or that the search fee is to be reduced.

### Articles 154–158

(deleted)

## PART XI—TRANSITIONAL PROVISIONS

### Articles 159–163

(deleted)

## PART XII—FINAL PROVISIONS

### Article 164—Implementing Regulations and Protocols

**(1)** The Implementing Regulations, the Protocol on Recognition, the Protocol on Privileges and Immunities, the Protocol on Centralisation, the Protocol on the Interpretation of Article 69 and the Protocol on Staff Complement shall be integral parts of this Convention.

**(2)** In case of conflict between the provisions of this Convention and those of the Implementing Regulations, the provisions of this Convention shall prevail.

### Article 165—Signature—Ratification

**(1)** This Convention shall be open for signature until 5 April 1974 by the States which took part in the Inter-Governmental Conference for the setting up of a European System for the Grant of Patents or were informed of the holding of that conference and offered the option of taking part therein.

**(2)** This Convention shall be subject to ratification; instruments of ratification shall be deposited with the Government of the Federal Republic of Germany.

### Article 166—Accession

**(1)** This Convention shall be open to accession by:

    (a)   the States referred to in Article 165, paragraph 1;

    (b)   any other European State at the invitation of the Administrative Council.

**(2)** Any State which has been a party to the Convention and has ceased to be so as a result of the application of Article 172, paragraph 4, may again become a party to the Convention by acceding to it.

**(3)** Instruments of accession shall be deposited with the Government of the Federal Republic of Germany.

### Article 167

(deleted)

### Article 168—Territorial field of application

**(1)** Any Contracting State may declare in its instrument of ratification or accession, or may inform the Government of the Federal Republic of Germany by written notification any time thereafter, that this Convention shall be applicable to one or more of the territories for the external relations of which it is responsible. European patents granted for that Contracting State shall also have effect in the territories for which such a declaration has taken effect.

**(2)** If the declaration referred to in paragraph 1 is contained in the instrument of ratification or accession, it shall take effect on the same date as the ratification or accession; if the declaration is notified after the deposit of the instrument of ratification or accession, such notification shall take effect six months after the date of its receipt by the Government of the Federal Republic of Germany.

**(3)** Any Contracting State may at any time declare that the Convention shall cease to apply to some or to all of the territories in respect of which it has given a notification pursuant to paragraph 1. Such declaration shall take effect one year after the date on which the Government of the Federal Republic of Germany received notification thereof.

## Article 169—Entry into force

**(1)** This Convention shall enter into force three months after the deposit of the last instrument of ratification or accession by six States on whose territory the total number of patent applications filed in 1970 amounted to at least 180,000 for all the said States.

**(2)** Any ratification or accession after the entry into force of this Convention shall take effect on the first day of the third month after the deposit of the instrument of ratification or accession.

## Article 170—Initial contribution

**(1)** Any State which ratifies or accedes to this Convention after its entry into force shall pay to the Organisation an initial contribution, which shall not be refunded.

**(2)** The initial contribution shall be 5% of an amount calculated by applying the percentage obtained for the State in question, on the date on which ratification or accession takes effect, in accordance with the scale provided for in Article 40, paragraphs 3 and 4, to the sum of the special financial contributions due from the other Contracting States in respect of the accounting periods preceding the date referred to above.

**(3)** In the event that special financial contributions were not required in respect of the accounting period immediately preceding the date referred to in paragraph 2, the scale of contributions referred to in that paragraph shall be the scale that would have been applicable to the State concerned in respect of the last year for which financial contributions were required.

## Article 171—Duration of the Convention

The present Convention shall be of unlimited duration.

## Article 172—Revision

**(1)** This Convention may be revised by a Conference of the Contracting States.

**(2)** The Conference shall be prepared and convened by the Administrative Council. The Conference shall not be validly constituted unless at least three-quarters of the Contracting States are represented at it. Adoption of the revised text shall require a majority of three-quarters of the Contracting States represented and voting at the Conference. Abstentions shall not be considered as votes.

**(3)** The revised text shall enter into force when it has been ratified or acceded to by the number of Contracting States specified by the Conference, and at the time specified by that Conference.

**(4)** Such States as have not ratified or acceded to the revised text of the Convention at the time of its entry into force shall cease to be parties to this Convention as from that time.

### Article 173—Disputes between Contracting States

**(1)** Any dispute between Contracting States concerning the interpretation or application of the present Convention which is not settled by negotiation shall be submitted, at the request of one of the States concerned, to the Administrative Council, which shall endeavour to bring about agreement between the States concerned.

**(2)** If such agreement is not reached within six months from the date when the dispute was referred to the Administrative Council, any one of the States concerned may submit the dispute to the International Court of Justice for a binding decision.

### Article 174—Denunciation

Any Contracting State may at any time denounce this Convention. Denunciation shall be notified to the Government of the Federal Republic of Germany. It shall take effect one year after the date of receipt of such notification.

### Article 175—Preservation of acquired rights

**(1)** In the event of a State ceasing to be party to this Convention in accordance with Article 172, paragraph 4, or Article 174, rights already acquired pursuant to this Convention shall not be impaired.

**(2)** A European patent application which is pending when a designated State ceases to be party to the Convention shall be processed by the European Patent Office, as far as that State is concerned, as if the Convention in force thereafter were applicable to that State.

**(3)** Paragraph 2 shall apply to European patents in respect of which, on the date mentioned in that paragraph, an opposition is pending or the opposition period has not expired.

**(4)** Nothing in this Article shall affect the right of any State that has ceased to be a party to this Convention to treat any European patent in accordance with the text to which it was a party.

### Article 176—Financial rights and obligations of former Contracting States

**(1)** Any State which has ceased to be a party to this Convention in accordance with Article 172, paragraph 4, or Article 174, shall have the special financial contributions which it has paid pursuant to Article 40, paragraph 2, refunded to it by the Organisation only at the time when and under the conditions whereby the Organisation refunds special financial contributions paid by other States during the same accounting period.

**(2)** The State referred to in paragraph 1 shall, even after ceasing to be a party to this Convention, continue to pay the proportion pursuant to Article 39 of renewal fees in respect of European patents remaining in force in that State, at the rate current on the date on which it ceased to be a party.

### Article 177—Languages of the Convention

**(1)** This Convention, drawn up in a single original, in the English, French and German languages, shall be deposited in the archives of the Government of the Federal Republic of Germany, the three texts being equally authentic.

**(2)** The texts of this Convention drawn up in official languages of Contracting States other than those referred to in paragraph 1 shall, if they have been approved by the Administrative Council, be considered as official texts. In the event of disagreement on the interpretation of the various texts, the texts referred to in paragraph 1 shall be authentic.

### Article 178—Transmission and notifications

**(1)** The Government of the Federal Republic of Germany shall draw up certified true copies of this Convention and shall transmit them to the Governments of all signatory or acceding States.

**(2)** The Government of the Federal Republic of Germany shall notify to the Governments of the States referred to in paragraph 1:

(a) the deposit of any instrument of ratification or accession;

(b) any declaration or notification received pursuant to Article 168;

(c) any denunciation received pursuant to the provisions of Article 174 and the date on which such denunciation comes into force.

**(3)** The Government of the Federal Republic of Germany shall register this Convention with the Secretariat of the United Nations.

IN WITNESS WHEREOF, the Plenipotentiaries authorised thereto, having presented their Full Powers, found to be in good and due form, have signed this Convention.

Done at Munich this fifth day of October one thousand nine hundred and seventy-three

## PROTOCOL ON JURISDICTION AND THE RECOGNITION OF DECISIONS IN RESPECT OF THE RIGHT TO THE GRANT OF A EUROPEAN PATENT (PROTOCOL ON RECOGNITION)

### of 5 October 1973

### Section I—Jurisdiction

### Article 1

**(1)** The courts of the Contracting States shall, in accordance with Articles 2 to 6, have jurisdiction to decide claims, against the applicant, to the right to the grant of a European patent in respect of one or more of the Contracting States designated in the European patent application.

**(2)** For the purposes of this Protocol, the term "courts" shall include authorities which, under the national law of a Contracting State, have jurisdiction to decide the claims referred to in paragraph 1. Any Contracting State shall notify the European Patent Office of the identity of any authority on which such a jurisdiction is conferred, and the European Patent Office shall inform the other Contracting States accordingly.

**(3)** For the purposes of this Protocol, the term "Contracting State" refers to a Contracting State which has not excluded application of this Protocol pursuant to Article 167 of the Convention.

### Article 2

Subject to Articles 4 and 5, if an applicant for a European patent has his residence or principal place of business within one of the Contracting States, proceedings shall be brought against him in the courts of that Contracting State.

### Article 3

Subject to Articles 4 and 5, if an applicant for a European patent has his residence or principal place of business outside the Contracting States, and if the party claiming the right to the grant of the European patent has his residence or principal place of business within one of the Contracting States, the courts of the latter State shall have exclusive jurisdiction.

## Article 4

Subject to Article 5, if the subject-matter of a European patent application is the invention of an employee, the courts of the Contracting State, if any, whose law determines the right to the European patent pursuant to Article 60, paragraph 1, second sentence, of the Convention, shall have exclusive jurisdiction over proceedings between the employee and the employer.

## Article 5

(1) If the parties to a dispute concerning the right to the grant of a European patent have concluded an agreement, either in writing or verbally with written confirmation, to the effect that a court or the courts of a particular Contracting State shall decide on such a dispute, the court or courts of that State shall have exclusive jurisdiction.

(2) However, if the parties are an employee and his employer, paragraph 1 shall only apply in so far as the national law governing the contract of employment allows the agreement in question.

## Article 6

In cases where neither Articles 2 to 4 nor Article 5, paragraph 1, apply, the courts of the Federal Republic of Germany shall have exclusive jurisdiction.

## Article 7

The courts of Contracting States before which claims referred to in Article 1 are brought shall of their own motion decide whether or not they have jurisdiction pursuant to Articles 2 to 6.

## Article 8

(1) In the event of proceedings based on the same claim and between the same parties being brought before courts of different Contracting States, the court to which a later application is made shall of its own motion decline jurisdiction in favour of the court to which an earlier application was made.

(2) In the event of the jurisdiction of the court to which an earlier application is made being challenged, the court to which a later application is made shall stay the proceedings until the other court takes a final decision.

### Section II—Recognition

## Article 9

(1) Subject to the provisions of Article 11, paragraph 2, final decisions given in any Contracting State on the right to the grant of a European patent in respect of one or more of the Contracting States designated in the European patent application shall be recognised without requiring a special procedure in the other Contracting States.

(2) The jurisdiction of the court whose decision is to be recognised and the validity of such decision may not be reviewed.

## Article 10

Article 9, paragraph 1, shall not be applicable where:

(a) an applicant for a European patent who has not contested a claim proves that the document initiating the proceedings was not notified to him regularly and sufficiently early for him to defend himself; or

(b)    an applicant proves that the decision is incompatible with another decision given in a Contracting State in proceedings between the same parties which were started before those in which the decision to be recognised was given.

## Article 11

**(1)**    In relations between any Contracting States the provisions of this Protocol shall prevail over any conflicting provisions of other agreements on jurisdiction or the recognition of judgments.

**(2)**    This Protocol shall not affect the implementation of any agreement between a Contracting State and a State which is not bound by the Protocol.

# 35. PARTIES TO THE EUROPEAN PATENT CONVENTION

**Status on May 4, 2021**

---

Albania
Austria
Belgium
Bulgaria
Croatia
Cyprus
Czech Republic
Denmark
Estonia
Finland
France
Germany
Greece
Hungary
Iceland
Ireland
Italy
Latvia
Liechtenstein
Lithuania
Luxembourg
Malta
Monaco
Netherlands
North Macedonia
Norway
Poland
Portugal
Romania
San Marino
Serbia
Slovakia
Slovenia
Spain
Sweden
Switzerland
Turkey
United Kingdom

# 36. PATENT LAW TREATY

Adopted at Geneva June 1, 2000

## Article 1

### Abbreviated Expressions

For the purposes of this Treaty, unless expressly stated otherwise:

(i)   "Office" means the authority of a Contracting Party entrusted with the granting of patents or with other matters covered by this Treaty;

(ii)  "application" means an application for the grant of a patent, as referred to in Article 3;

(iii) "patent" means a patent as referred to in Article 3;

(iv)  references to a "person" shall be construed as including, in particular, a natural person and a legal entity;

(v)   "communication" means any application, or any request, declaration, document, correspondence or other information relating to an application or patent, whether relating to a procedure under this Treaty or not, which is filed with the Office;

(vi)  "records of the Office" means the collection of information maintained by the Office, relating to and including the applications filed with, and the patents granted by, that Office or another authority with effect for the Contracting Party concerned, irrespective of the medium in which such information is maintained;

(vii) "recordation" means any act of including information in the records of the Office;

(viii) "applicant" means the person whom the records of the Office show, pursuant to the applicable law, as the person who is applying for the patent, or as another person who is filing or prosecuting the application;

(ix)  "owner" means the person whom the records of the Office show as the owner of the patent;

(x)   "representative" means a representative under the applicable law;

(xi)  "signature" means any means of self-identification;

(xii) "a language accepted by the Office" means any one language accepted by the Office for the relevant procedure before the Office;

(xiii) "translation" means a translation into a language or, where appropriate, a transliteration into an alphabet or character set, accepted by the Office;

(xiv) "procedure before the Office" means any procedure in proceedings before the Office with respect to an application or patent;

(xv)  except where the context indicates otherwise, words in the singular include the plural, and *vice versa*, and masculine personal pronouns include the feminine;

(xvi) "Paris Convention" means the Paris Convention for the Protection of Industrial Property, signed on March 20, 1883, as revised and amended;

(xvii) "Patent Cooperation Treaty" means the Patent Cooperation Treaty, signed on June 19, 1970, together with the Regulations and the Administrative Instructions under that Treaty, as revised, amended and modified;

(xviii) "Contracting Party" means any State or inter-governmental organization that is party to this Treaty;

(xix) "applicable law" means, where the Contracting Party is a State, the law of that State and, where the Contracting Party is an intergovernmental organization, the legal enactments under which that intergovernmental organization operates;

(xx) "instrument of ratification" shall be construed as including instruments of acceptance or approval;

(xxi) "Organization" means the World Intellectual Property Organization;

(xxii) "International Bureau" means the International Bureau of the Organization;

(xxiii) "Director General" means the Director General of the Organization.

## Article 2

### General Principles

(1) [*More Favorable Requirements*] A Contracting Party shall be free to provide for requirements which, from the viewpoint of applicants and owners, are more favorable than the requirements referred to in this Treaty and the Regulations, other than Article 5.

(2) [*No Regulation of Substantive Patent Law*] Nothing in this Treaty or the Regulations is intended to be construed as prescribing anything that would limit the freedom of a Contracting Party to prescribe such requirements of the applicable substantive law relating to patents as it desires.

## Article 3

### Applications and Patents to Which the Treaty Applies

(1) [*Applications*]

(a) The provisions of this Treaty and the Regulations shall apply to national and regional applications for patents for invention and for invention and for patents of addition, which are filed with or for the Office of a Contracting Party, and which are:

(i) types of applications permitted to be filed as international applications under the Patent Cooperation Treaty;

(ii) divisional applications of the types of applications referred to in item (i), for patents for invention or for patents of addition, as referred to in Article 4G(1) or (2) of the Paris Convention.

(b) Subject to the provisions of the Patent Cooperation Treaty, the provisions of this Treaty and the Regulations shall apply to international applications, for patents for invention and for patents of addition, under the Patent Cooperation Treaty:

(i) in respect of the time limits applicable under Articles 22 and 39(1) of the Patent Cooperation Treaty in the Office of a Contracting Party;

(ii) in respect of any procedure commenced on or after the date on which processing or examination of the international application may start under Article 23 or 40 of that Treaty.

(2) [*Patents*] The provisions of this Treaty and the Regulations shall apply to national and regional patents for invention, and to national and regional patents of addition, which have been granted with effect for a Contracting Party.

## Article 4

### Security Exception

Nothing in this Treaty and the Regulations shall limit the freedom of a Contracting Party to take any action it deems necessary for the preservation of essential security interests.

## Article 5

## Filing Date

(1) [*Elements of Application*]

(a) Except as otherwise prescribed in the Regulations, and subject to paragraphs (2) to (8), a Contracting Party shall provide that the filing date of an application shall be the date on which its Office has received all of the following elements, filed, at the option of the applicant, on paper or as otherwise permitted by the Office for the purposes of the filing date:

(i) an express or implicit indication to the effect that the elements are intended to be an application;

(ii) indications allowing the identity of the applicant to be established or allowing the applicant to be contacted by the Office;

(iii) a part which on the face of it appears to be a description.

(b) A Contracting Party may, for the purposes of the filing date, accept a drawing as the element referred to in subparagraph (a)(iii).

(c) For the purposes of the filing date, a Contracting Party may require both information allowing the identity of the applicant to be established and information allowing the applicant to be contacted by the Office, or it may accept evidence allowing the identity of the applicant to be established or allowing the applicant to be contacted by the Office, as the element referred to in subparagraph (a)(ii).

(2) [*Language*]

(a) A Contracting Party may require that the indications referred to in paragraph (1)(a)(i) and (ii) be in a language accepted by the Office.

(b) The part referred to in paragraph (1)(a)(iii) may, for the purposes of the filing date, be filed in any language.

(3) [*Notification*] Where the application does not comply with one or more of the requirements applied by the Contracting Party under paragraphs (1) and (2), the Office shall, as soon as practicable, notify the applicant, giving the opportunity to comply with any such requirement, and to make observations, within the time limit prescribed in the Regulations.

(4) [*Subsequent Compliance with Requirements*]

(a) Where one or more of the requirements applied by the Contracting Party under paragraphs (1) and (2) are not complied with in the application as initially filed, the filing date shall, subject to subparagraph (b) and paragraph (6), be the date on which all of the requirements applied by the Contracting Party under paragraphs (1) and (2) are subsequently complied with.

(b) A Contracting Party may provide that, where one or more of the requirements referred to in subparagraph (a) are not complied with within the time limit prescribed in the Regulations, the application shall be deemed not to have been filed. Where the application is deemed not to have been filed, the Office shall notify the applicant accordingly, indicating the reasons therefor.

(5) [*Notification Concerning Missing Part of Description or Drawing*] Where, in establishing the filing date, the Office finds that a part of the description appears to be missing from the application, or that the application refers to a drawing which appears to be missing from the application, the Office shall promptly notify the applicant accordingly.

(6) [*Filing Date Where Missing Part of Description or Drawing Is Filed*]

(a) Where a missing part of the description or a missing drawing is filed with the Office within the time limit prescribed in the Regulations, that part of the description or drawing shall be included in the application, and, subject to subparagraphs (b) and (c), the filing date shall be the date on which the Office has received that part of the description or that drawing, or the date on which all of the requirements applied by the Contracting Party under paragraphs (1) and (2) are complied with, whichever is later.

(b) Where the missing part of the description or the missing drawing is filed under subparagraph (a) to rectify its omission from an application which, at the date on which one or more elements referred to in paragraph (1)(a) were first received by the Office, claims the priority of an earlier application, the filing date shall, upon the request of the applicant filed within a time limit prescribed in the Regulations, and subject to the requirements prescribed in the Regulations, be the date on which all the requirements applied by the Contracting Party under paragraphs (1) and (2) are complied with.

(c) Where the missing part of the description or the missing drawing filed under subparagraph (a) is withdrawn within a time limit fixed by the Contracting Party, the filing date shall be the date on which the requirements applied by the Contracting Party under paragraphs (1) and (2) are complied with.

(7) [*Replacing Description and Drawings by Reference to a Previously Filed Application*]

(a) Subject to the requirements prescribed in the Regulations, a reference, made upon the filing of the application, in a language accepted by the Office, to a previously filed application shall, for the purposes of the filing date of the application, replace the description and any drawings.

(b) Where the requirements referred to in subparagraph (a) are not complied with, the application may be deemed not to have been filed. Where the application is deemed not to have been filed, the Office shall notify the applicant accordingly, indicating the reasons therefor.

(8) [*Exceptions*] Nothing in this Article shall limit:

(i) the right of an applicant under Article 4G(1) or (2) of the Paris Convention to preserve, as the date of a divisional application referred to in that Article, the date of the initial application referred to in that Article and the benefit of the right of priority, if any;

(ii) the freedom of a Contracting Party to apply any requirements necessary to accord the benefit of the filing date of an earlier application to an application of any type prescribed in the Regulations.

# Article 6

## Application

(1) [*Form or Contents of Application*] Except where otherwise provided for by this Treaty, no Contracting Party shall require compliance with any requirement relating to the form or contents of an application different from or additional to:

(i) the requirements relating to form or contents which are provided for in respect of international applications under the Patent Cooperation Treaty;

(ii) the requirements relating to form or contents compliance with which, under the Patent Cooperation Treaty, may be required by the Office of, or acting for, any State party to that Treaty once the processing or examination of an international application, as referred to in Article 23 or 40 of the said Treaty, has started;

(iii) any further requirements prescribed in the Regulations.

(2) [*Request Form*]

(a) A Contracting Party may require that the contents of an application which correspond to the contents of the request of an international application under the Patent Cooperation Treaty be presented on a request Form prescribed by that Contracting Party. A Contracting Party may also require that any further contents allowed under paragraph (1)(ii) or prescribed in the Regulations pursuant to paragraph (1)(iii) be contained in that request Form.

(b)   Notwithstanding subparagraph (a), and subject to Article 8(1), a Contracting Party shall accept the presentation of the contents referred to in subparagraph (a) on a request Form provided for in the Regulations.

(3)   [*Translation*] A Contracting Party may require a translation of any part of the application that is not in a language accepted by its Office. A Contracting Party may also require a translation of the parts of the application, as prescribed in the Regulations, that are in a language accepted by the Office, into any other languages accepted by that Office.

(4)   [*Fees*] A Contracting Party may require that fees be paid in respect of the application. A Contracting Party may apply the provisions of the Patent Cooperation Treaty relating to payment of application fees.

(5)   [*Priority Document*] Where the priority of an earlier application is claimed, a Contracting Party may require that a copy of the earlier application, and a translation where the earlier application is not in a language accepted by the Office, be filed in accordance with the requirements prescribed in the Regulations.

(6)   [*Evidence*] A Contracting Party may require that evidence in respect of any matter referred to in paragraph (1) or (2) or in a declaration of priority, or any translation referred to in paragraph (3) or (5), be filed with its Office in the course of the processing of the application only where that Office may reasonably doubt the veracity of that matter or the accuracy of that translation.

(7)   [*Notification*] Where one or more of the requirements applied by the Contracting Party under paragraphs (1) to (6) are not complied with, the Office shall notify the applicant, giving the opportunity to comply with any such requirement, and to make observations, within the time limit prescribed in the Regulations.

(8)   [*Non-Compliance with Requirements*]

(a)   Where one or more of the requirements applied by the Contracting Party under paragraphs (1) to (6) are not complied with within the time limit prescribed in the Regulations, the Contracting Party may, subject to subparagraph (b) and Articles 5 and 10, apply such sanction as is provided for in its law.

(b)   Where any requirement applied by the Contracting Party under paragraph (1), (5) or (6) in respect of a priority claim is not complied with within the time limit prescribed in the Regulations, the priority claim may, subject to Article 13, be deemed non-existent. Subject to Article 5(7)(b), no other sanctions may be applied.

## Article 7

### Representation

(1)   [*Representatives*]

(a)   A Contracting Party may require that a representative appointed for the purposes of any procedure before the Office:

(i)   have the right, under the applicable law, to practice before the Office in respect of applications and patents;

(ii)   provide, as his address, an address on a territory prescribed by the Contracting Party.

(b)   Subject to subparagraph (c), an act, with respect to any procedure before the Office, by or in relation to a representative who complies with the requirements applied by the Contracting Party under subparagraph (a), shall have the effect of an act by or in relation to the applicant, owner or other interested person who appointed that representative.

(c)   A Contracting Party may provide that, in the case of an oath or declaration or the revocation of a power of attorney, the signature of a representative shall not have the effect of the signature of the applicant, owner or other interested person who appointed that representative.

(2) [*Mandatory Representation*]

(a) A Contracting Party may require that an applicant, owner or other interested person appoint a representative for the purposes of any procedure before the Office, except that an assignee of an application, an applicant, owner or other interested person may act himself before the Office for the following procedures:

(i) the filing of an application for the purposes of the filing date;

(ii) the mere payment of a fee;

(iii) any other procedure as prescribed in the Regulations;

(iv) the issue of a receipt or notification by the Office in respect of any procedure referred to in items (i) to (iii).

(b) A maintenance fee may be paid by any person.

(3) [*Appointment of Representative*] A Contracting Party shall accept that the appointment of the representative be filed with the Office in a manner prescribed in the Regulations.

(4) [*Prohibition of Other Requirements*] No Contracting Party may require that formal requirements other than those referred to in paragraphs (1) to (3) be complied with in respect of the matters dealt with in those paragraphs, except where otherwise provided for by this Treaty or prescribed in the Regulations.

(5) [*Notification*] Where one or more of the requirements applied by the Contracting Party under paragraphs (1) to (3) are not complied with, the Office shall notify the assignee of the application, applicant, owner or other interested person, giving the opportunity to comply with any such requirement, and to make observations, within the time limit prescribed in the Regulations.

(6) [*Non-Compliance with Requirements*] Where one or more of the requirements applied by the Contracting Party under paragraphs (1) to (3) are not complied with within the time limit prescribed in the Regulations, the Contracting Party may apply such sanction as is provided for in its law.

## Article 8

## Communications; Addresses

(1) [*Form and Means of Transmittal of Communications*]

(a) Except for the establishment of a filing date under Article 5(1), and subject to Article 6(1), the Regulations shall, subject to subparagraphs (b) to (d), set out the requirements which a Contracting Party shall be permitted to apply as regards the form and means of transmittal of communications.

(b) No Contracting Party shall be obliged to accept the filing of communications other than on paper.

(c) No Contracting Party shall be obliged to exclude the filing of communications on paper.

(d) A Contracting Party shall accept the filing of communications on paper for the purpose of complying with a time limit.

(2) [*Language of Communications*] A Contracting Party may, except where otherwise provided for by this Treaty or the Regulations, require that a communication be in a language accepted by the Office.

(3) [*Model International Forms*] Notwithstanding paragraph (1)(a), and subject to paragraph (1)(b) and Article 6(2)(b), a Contracting Party shall accept the presentation of the contents of a communication on a Form which corresponds to a Model International Form in respect of such a communication provided for in the Regulations, if any.

(4)  [*Signature of Communications*]

(a)  Where a Contracting Party requires a signature for the purposes of any communication, that Contracting Party shall accept any signature that complies with the requirements prescribed in the Regulations.

(b)  No Contracting Party may require the attestation, notarization, authentication, legalization or other certification of any signature which is communicated to its Office, except in respect of any quasi-judicial proceedings or as prescribed in the Regulations.

(c)  Subject to subparagraph (b), a Contracting Party may require that evidence be filed with the Office only where the Office may reasonably doubt the authenticity of any signature.

(5)  [*Indications in Communications*] A Contracting Party may require that any communication contain one or more indications prescribed in the Regulations.

(6)  [*Address for Correspondence, Address for Legal Service and Other Address*] A Contracting Party may, subject to any provisions prescribed in the Regulations, require that an applicant, owner or other interested person indicate in any communication:

(i)  an address for correspondence;

(ii)  an address for legal service;

(iii)  any other address provided for in the Regulations.

(7)  [*Notification*] Where one or more of the requirements applied by the Contracting Party under paragraphs (1) to (6) are not complied with in respect of communications, the Office shall notify the applicant, owner or other interested person, giving the opportunity to comply with any such requirement, and to make observations, within the time limit prescribed in the Regulations.

(8)  [*Non-Compliance with Requirements*] Where one or more of the requirements applied by the Contracting Party under paragraphs (1) to (6) are not complied with within the time limit prescribed in the Regulations, the Contracting Party may, subject to Articles 5 and 10 and to any exceptions prescribed in the Regulations, apply such sanction as is provided for in its law.

## Article 9

### Notifications

(1)  [*Sufficient Notification*] Any notification under this Treaty or the Regulations which is sent by the Office to an address for correspondence or address for legal service indicated under Article 8(6), or any other address provided for in the Regulations for the purpose of this provision, and which complies with the provisions with respect to that notification, shall constitute a sufficient notification for the purposes of this Treaty and the Regulations.

(2)  [*If Indications Allowing Contact Were Not Filed*] Nothing in this Treaty and in the Regulations shall oblige a Contracting Party to send a notification to an applicant, owner or other interested person, if indications allowing that applicant, owner or other interested person to be contacted have not been filed with the Office.

(3)  [*Failure to Notify*] Subject to Article 10(1), where an Office does not notify an applicant, owner or other interested person of a failure to comply with any requirement under this Treaty or the Regulations, that absence of notification does not relieve that applicant, owner or other interested person of the obligation to comply with that requirement.

## Article 10

### Validity of Patent; Revocation

(1)  [*Validity of Patent Not Affected by Non-Compliance with Certain Formal Requirements*] Non-compliance with one or more of the formal requirements referred to in Articles 6(1), (2), (4) and (5) and

8(1) to (4) with respect to an application may not be a ground for revocation or invalidation of a patent, either totally or in part, except where the non-compliance with the formal requirement occurred as a result of a fraudulent intention.

(2)  *[Opportunity to Make Observations, Amendments or Corrections in Case of Intended Revocation or Invalidation]* A patent may not be revoked or invalidated, either totally or in part, without the owner being given the opportunity to make observations on the intended revocation or invalidation, and to make amendments and corrections where permitted under the applicable law, within a reasonable time limit.

(3)  *[No Obligation for Special Procedures]* Paragraphs (1) and (2) do not create any obligation to put in place judicial procedures for the enforcement of patent rights distinct from those for the enforcement of law in general.

## Article 11

### Relief in Respect of Time Limits

(1)  *[Extension of Time Limits]* A Contracting Party may provide for the extension, for the period prescribed in the Regulations, of a time limit fixed by the Office for an action in a procedure before the Office in respect of an application or a patent, if a request to that effect is made to the Office in accordance with the requirements prescribed in the Regulations, and the request is filed, at the option of the Contracting Party:

 (i)  prior to the expiration of the time limit; or

 (ii)  after the expiration of the time limit, and within the time limit prescribed in the Regulations.

(2)  *[Continued Processing]* Where an applicant or owner has failed to comply with a time limit fixed by the Office of a Contracting Party for an action in a procedure before the Office in respect of an application or a patent, and that Contracting Party does not provide for extension of a time limit under paragraph (1)(ii), the Contracting Party shall provide for continued processing with respect to the application or patent and, if necessary, reinstatement of the rights of the applicant or owner with respect to that application or patent, if:

 (i)  a request to that effect is made to the Office in accordance with the requirements prescribed in the Regulations;

 (ii)  the request is filed, and all of the requirements in respect of which the time limit for the action concerned applied are complied with, within the time limit prescribed in the Regulations.

(3)  *[Exceptions]* No Contracting Party shall be required to provide for the relief referred to in paragraph (1) or (2) with respect to the exceptions prescribed in the Regulations.

(4)  *[Fees]* A Contracting Party may require that a fee be paid in respect of a request under paragraph (1) or (2).

(5)  *[Prohibition of Other Requirements]* No Contracting Party may require that requirements other than those referred to in paragraphs (1) to (4) be complied with in respect of the relief provided for under paragraph (1) or (2), except where otherwise provided for by this Treaty or prescribed in the Regulations.

(6)  *[Opportunity to Make Observations in Case of Intended Refusal]* A request under paragraph (1) or (2) may not be refused without the applicant or owner being given the opportunity to make observations on the intended refusal within a reasonable time limit.

## Article 12

### Reinstatement of Rights after a Finding of Due
### Care or Unintentionality by the Office

(1) [*Request*] A Contracting Party shall provide that, where an applicant or owner has failed to comply with a time limit for an action in a procedure before the Office, and that failure has the direct consequence of causing a loss of rights with respect to an application or patent, the Office shall reinstate the rights of the applicant or owner with respect to the application or patent concerned, if:

(i) a request to that effect is made to the Office in accordance with the requirements prescribed in the Regulations;

(ii) the request is filed, and all of the requirements in respect of which the time limit for the said action applied are complied with, within the time limit prescribed in the Regulations;

(iii) the request states the reasons for the failure to comply with the time limit; and

(iv) the Office finds that the failure to comply with the time limit occurred in spite of due care required by the circumstances having been taken or, at the option of the Contracting Party, that any delay was unintentional.

(2) [*Exceptions*] No Contracting Party shall be required to provide for the reinstatement of rights under paragraph (1) with respect to the exceptions prescribed in the Regulations.

(3) [*Fees*] A Contracting Party may require that a fee be paid in respect of a request under paragraph (1).

(4) [*Evidence*] A Contracting Party may require that a declaration or other evidence in support of the reasons referred to in paragraph (1)(iii) be filed with the Office within a time limit fixed by the Office.

(5) [*Opportunity to Make Observations in Case of Intended Refusal*] A request under paragraph (1) may not be refused, totally or in part, without the requesting party being given the opportunity to make observations on the intended refusal within a reasonable time limit.

## Article 13

### Correction or Addition of Priority Claim; Restoration of Priority Right

(1) [*Correction or Addition of Priority Claim*] Except where otherwise prescribed in the Regulations, a Contracting Party shall provide for the correction or addition of a priority claim with respect to an application ("the subsequent application"), if:

(i) a request to that effect is made to the Office in accordance with the requirements prescribed in the Regulations;

(ii) the request is filed within the time limit prescribed in the Regulations; and

(iii) the filing date of the subsequent application is not later than the date of the expiration of the priority period calculated from the filing date of the earliest application whose priority is claimed.

(2) [*Delayed Filing of the Subsequent Application*] Taking into consideration Article 15, a Contracting Party shall provide that, where an application ("the subsequent application") which claims or could have claimed the priority of an earlier application has a filing date which is later than the date on which the priority period expired, but within the time limit prescribed in the Regulations, the Office shall restore the right of priority, if:

(i) a request to that effect is made to the Office in accordance with the requirements prescribed in the Regulations;

(ii) the request is filed within the time limit prescribed in the Regulations;

(iii) the request states the reasons for the failure to comply with the priority period; and

(iv) the Office finds that the failure to file the subsequent application within the priority period occurred in spite of due care required by the circumstances having been taken or, at the option of the Contracting Party, was unintentional.

(3) *[Failure to File a Copy of Earlier Application]* A Contracting Party shall provide that, where a copy of an earlier application required under Article 6(5) is not filed with the Office within the time limit prescribed in the Regulations pursuant to Article 6, the Office shall restore the right of priority, if:

(i) a request to that effect is made to the Office in accordance with the requirements prescribed in the Regulations;

(ii) the request is filed within the time limit for filing the copy of the earlier application prescribed in the Regulations pursuant to Article 6(5);

(iii) the Office finds that the request for the copy to be provided had been filed with the Office with which the earlier application was filed, within the time limit prescribed in the Regulations; and

(iv) a copy of the earlier application is filed within the time limit prescribed in the Regulations.

(4) *[Fees]* A Contracting Party may require that a fee be paid in respect of a request under paragraphs (1) to (3).

(5) *[Evidence]* A Contracting Party may require that a declaration or other evidence in support of the reasons referred to in paragraph (2)(iii) be filed with the Office within a time limit fixed by the Office.

(6) *[Opportunity to Make Observations in Case of Intended Refusal]* A request under paragraphs (1) to (3) may not be refused, totally or in part, without the requesting party being given the opportunity to make observations on the intended refusal within a reasonable time limit.

**Article 14**

**Regulations**

(1) *[Content]*

(a) The Regulations annexed to this Treaty provide rules concerning:

(i) matters which this Treaty expressly provides are to be "prescribed in the Regulations";

(ii) details useful in the implementation of the provisions of this Treaty;

(iii) administrative requirements, matters or procedures.

(b) The Regulations also provide rules concerning the formal requirements which a Contracting Party shall be permitted to apply in respect of requests for:

(i) recordation of change in name or address;

(ii) recordation of change in applicant or owner;

(iii) recordation of a license or a security interest;

(iv) correction of a mistake.

(c) The Regulations also provide for the establishment of Model International Forms, and for the establishment of a request Form for the purposes of Article 6(2)(b), by the Assembly, with the assistance of the International Bureau.

(2) *[Amending the Regulations]* Subject to paragraph (3), any amendment of the Regulations shall require three-fourths of the votes cast.

(3) [*Requirement of Unanimity*]

(a)   The Regulations may specify provisions of the Regulations which may be amended only by unanimity.

(b)   Any amendment of the Regulations resulting in the addition of provisions to, or the deletion of provisions from, the provisions specified in the Regulations pursuant to subparagraph (a) shall require unanimity.

(c)   In determining whether unanimity is attained, only votes actually cast shall be taken into consideration. Abstentions shall not be considered as votes.

(4)   [*Conflict Between the Treaty and the Regulations*] In the case of conflict between the provisions of this Treaty and those of the Regulations, the former shall prevail.

## Article 15

## Relation to the Paris Convention

(1)   [*Obligation to Comply with the Paris Convention*] Each Contracting Party shall comply with the provisions of the Paris Convention which concern patents.

(2)   [*Obligations and Rights Under the Paris Convention*]

(a)   Nothing in this Treaty shall derogate from obligations that Contracting Parties have to each other under the Paris Convention.

(b)   Nothing in this Treaty shall derogate from rights that applicants and owners enjoy under the Paris Convention.

## Article 16

## Effect of Revisions, Amendments and Modifications
## of the Patent Cooperation Treaty

(1)   [*Applicability of Revisions, Amendments and Modifications of the Patent Cooperation Treaty*] Subject to paragraph (2), any revision, amendment or modification of the Patent Cooperation Treaty made after June 2, 2000, which is consistent with the Articles of this Treaty, shall apply for the purposes of this Treaty and the Regulations if the Assembly so decides, in the particular case, by three-fourths of the votes cast.

(2)   [*Non-Applicability of Transitional Provisions of the Patent Cooperation Treaty*] Any provision of the Patent Cooperation Treaty, by virtue of which a revised, amended or modified provision of that Treaty does not apply to a State party to it, or to the Office of or acting for such a State, for as long as the latter provision is incompatible with the law applied by that State or Office, shall not apply for the purposes of this Treaty and the Regulations.

## Article 17

## Assembly

(1)   [*Composition*]

(a) The Contracting Parties shall have an Assembly.

(b) Each Contracting Party shall be represented in the Assembly by one delegate, who may be assisted by alternate delegates, advisors and experts. Each delegate may represent only one Contracting Party.

(2)   [*Tasks*] The Assembly shall:

(i)   deal with matters concerning the maintenance and development of this Treaty and the application and operation of this Treaty;

(ii)   establish Model International Forms, and the request Form, referred to in Article 14(1)(c), with the assistance of the International Bureau;

(iii)   amend the Regulations;

(iv)   determine the conditions for the date of application of each Model International Form, and the request Form, referred to in item (ii), and each amendment referred to in item (iii);

(v)   decide, pursuant to Article 16(1), whether any revision, amendment or modification of the Patent Cooperation Treaty shall apply for the purposes of this Treaty and the Regulations;

(vi)   perform such other functions as are appropriate under this Treaty.

(3)   [*Quorum*]

(a)   One-half of the members of the Assembly which are States shall constitute a quorum.

(b)   Notwithstanding subparagraph (a), if, in any session, the number of the members of the Assembly which are States and are represented is less than one-half but equal to or more than one-third of the members of the Assembly which are States, the Assembly may make decisions but, with the exception of decisions concerning its own procedure, all such decisions shall take effect only if the conditions set forth hereinafter are fulfilled. The International Bureau shall communicate the said decisions to the members of the Assembly which are States and were not represented and shall invite them to express in writing their vote or abstention within a period of three months from the date of the communication. If, at the expiration of this period, the number of such members having thus expressed their vote or abstention attains the number of the members which was lacking for attaining the quorum in the session itself, such decisions shall take effect, provided that at the same time the required majority still obtains.

(4)   [*Taking Decisions in the Assembly*]

(a)   The Assembly shall endeavor to take its decisions by consensus.

(b)   Where a decision cannot be arrived at by consensus, the matter at issue shall be decided by voting. In such a case:

(i)   each Contracting Party that is a State shall have one vote and shall vote only in its own name; and

(ii)   any Contracting Party that is an intergovernmental organization may participate in the vote, in place of its Member States, with a number of votes equal to the number of its Member States which are party to this Treaty. No such intergovernmental organization shall participate in the vote if any one of its Member States exercises its right to vote and *vice versa*. In addition, no such intergovernmental organization shall participate in the vote if any one of its Member States party to this Treaty is a Member State of another such intergovernmental organization and that other intergovernmental organization participates in that vote.

(5)   [*Majorities*]

(a)   Subject to Articles 14(2) and (3), 16(1) and 19(3), the decisions of the Assembly shall require two-thirds of the votes cast.

(b)   In determining whether the required majority is attained, only votes actually cast shall be taken into consideration. Abstentions shall not be considered as votes.

(6)   [*Sessions*] The Assembly shall meet in ordinary session once every two years upon convocation by the Director General.

(7)   [*Rules of Procedure*] The Assembly shall establish its own rules of procedure, including rules for the convocation of extraordinary sessions.

## Article 18

### International Bureau

(1) [*Administrative Tasks*]

(a) The International Bureau shall perform the administrative tasks concerning this Treaty.

(b) In particular, the International Bureau shall prepare the meetings and provide the secretariat of the Assembly and of such committees of experts and working groups as may be established by the Assembly.

(2) [*Meetings Other than Sessions of the Assembly*] The Director General shall convene any committee and working group established by the Assembly.

(3) [*Role of the International Bureau in the Assembly and Other Meetings*]

(a) The Director General and persons designated by the Director General shall participate, without the right to vote, in all meetings of the Assembly, the committees and working groups established by the Assembly.

(b) The Director General or a staff member designated by the Director General shall be ex officio secretary of the Assembly, and of the committees and working groups referred to in subparagraph (a).

(4) [*Conferences*]

(a) The International Bureau shall, in accordance with the directions of the Assembly, make the preparations for any revision conferences.

(b) The International Bureau may consult with member States of the Organization, intergovernmental organizations and international and national non-governmental organizations concerning the said preparations.

(c) The Director General and persons designated by the Director General shall take part, without the right to vote, in the discussions at revision conferences.

(5) [*Other Tasks*] The International Bureau shall carry out any other tasks assigned to it in relation to this Treaty.

## Article 19

### Revisions

(1) [*Revision of the Treaty*] Subject to paragraph (2), this Treaty may be revised by a conference of the Contracting Parties. The convocation of any revision conference shall be decided by the Assembly.

(2) [*Revision or Amendment of Certain Provisions of the Treaty*] Article 17(2) and (6) may be amended either by a revision conference, or by the Assembly according to the provisions of paragraph (3).

(3) [*Amendment by the Assembly of Certain Provisions of the Treaty*]

(a) Proposals for the amendment by the Assembly of Article 17(2) and (6) may be initiated by any Contracting Party or by the Director General. Such proposals shall be communicated by the Director General to the Contracting Parties at least six months in advance of their consideration by the Assembly.

(b) Adoption of any amendment to the provisions referred to in subparagraph (a) shall require three-fourths of the votes cast.

(c) Any amendment to the provisions referred to in subparagraph (a) shall enter into force one month after written notifications of acceptance, effected in accordance with their respective constitutional processes, have been received by the Director General from three-fourths of the Contracting Parties which were members of the Assembly at the time the Assembly adopted the amendment. Any amendment to the said provisions thus accepted shall bind all the Contracting Parties at the time the amendment enters into force, and States and intergovernmental organizations which become Contracting Parties at a subsequent date.

## Article 20

### Becoming Party to the Treaty

(1) [*States*] Any State which is party to the Paris Convention or which is a member of the Organization, and in respect of which patents may be granted, either through the State's own Office or through the Office of another State or intergovernmental organization, may become party to this Treaty.

(2) [*Intergovernmental Organizations*] Any intergovernmental organization may become party to this Treaty if at least one member State of that intergovernmental organization is party to the Paris Convention or a member of the Organization, and the intergovernmental organization declares that it has been duly authorized, in accordance with its internal procedures, to become party to this Treaty, and declares that:

    (i)    it is competent to grant patents with effect for its member States; or

    (ii)   it is competent in respect of, and has its own legislation binding on all its member States concerning, matters covered by this Treaty, and it has, or has charged, a regional Office for the purpose of granting patents with effect in its territory in accordance with that legislation.

Subject to paragraph (3), any such declaration shall be made at the time of the deposit of the instrument of ratification or accession.

(3) [*Regional Patent Organizations*] The European Patent Organization, the Eurasian Patent Organization and the African Regional Industrial Property Organization, having made the declaration referred to in paragraph (2)(i) or (ii) in the Diplomatic Conference that has adopted this Treaty, may become party to this Treaty as an intergovernmental organization, if it declares, at the time of the deposit of the instrument of ratification or accession that it has been duly authorized, in accordance with its internal procedures, to become party to this Treaty.

(4) [*Ratification or Accession*] Any State or intergovernmental organization satisfying the requirements in paragraph (1), (2) or (3) may deposit:

    (i)    an instrument of ratification if it has signed this Treaty; or

    (ii)   an instrument of accession if it has not signed this Treaty.

## Article 21

### Entry into Force; Effective Dates of Ratifications and Accessions

(1) [*Entry into Force of this Treaty*] This Treaty shall enter into force three months after ten instruments of ratification or accession by States have been deposited with the Director General.

(2) [*Effective Dates of Ratifications and Accessions*] This Treaty shall bind:

    (i)    the ten States referred to in paragraph (1), from the date on which this Treaty has entered into force;

    (ii)   each other State, from the expiration of three months after the date on which the State has deposited its instrument of ratification or accession with the Director General, or from any later date indicated in that instrument, but no later than six months after the date of such deposit;

    (iii) each of the European Patent Organization, the Eurasian Patent Organization and the African Regional Industrial Property Organization, from the expiration of three months after the deposit of its instrument of ratification or accession, or from any later date indicated in that instrument, but no later than six months after the date of such deposit, if such instrument has been deposited after the entry into force of this Treaty according to paragraph (1), or three months after the entry into force of this Treaty if such instrument has been deposited before the entry into force of this Treaty;

(iv) any other intergovernmental organization that is eligible to become party to this Treaty, from the expiration of three months after the deposit of its instrument of ratification or accession, or from any later date indicated in that instrument, but no later than six months after the date of such deposit.

## Article 22

### Application of the Treaty to Existing Applications and Patents

(1)  [*Principle*] Subject to paragraph (2), a Contracting Party shall apply the provisions of this Treaty and the Regulations, other than Articles 5 and 6(1) and (2) and related Regulations, to applications which are pending, and to patents which are in force, on the date on which this Treaty binds that Contracting Party under Article 21.

(2)  [*Procedures*] No Contracting Party shall be obliged to apply the provisions of this Treaty and the Regulations to any procedure in proceedings with respect to applications and patents referred to in paragraph (1), if such procedure commenced before the date on which this Treaty binds that Contracting Party under Article 21.

## Article 23

### Reservations

(1)  [*Reservation*] Any State or intergovernmental organization may declare through a reservation that the provisions of Article 6(1) shall not apply to any requirement relating to unity of invention applicable under the Patent Cooperation Treaty to an international application.

(2)  [*Modalities*] Any reservation under paragraph (1) shall be made in a declaration accompanying the instrument of ratification of, or accession to, this Treaty of the State or intergovernmental organization making the reservation.

(3)  [*Withdrawal*] Any reservation under paragraph (1) may be withdrawn at any time.

(4)  [*Prohibition of Other Reservations*] No reservation to this Treaty other than the reservation allowed under paragraph (1) shall be permitted.

## Article 24

### Denunciation of the Treaty

(1)  [*Notification*] Any Contracting Party may denounce this Treaty by notification addressed to the Director General.

(2)  [*Effective Date*] Any denunciation shall take effect one year from the date on which the Director General has received the notification or at any later date indicated in the notification. It shall not affect the application of this Treaty to any application pending or any patent in force in respect of the denouncing Contracting Party at the time of the coming into effect of the denunciation.

## Article 25

### Languages of the Treaty

(1)  [*Authentic Texts*] This Treaty is signed in a single original in the English, Arabic, Chinese, French, Russian and Spanish languages, all texts being equally and exclusively authentic.

(2)  [*Official Texts*] An official text in any language other than those referred to in paragraph (1) shall be established by the Director General, after consultation with the interested parties. For the purposes

of this paragraph, interested party means any State which is party to the Treaty, or is eligible to become party to the Treaty under Article 20(1), whose official language, or one of whose official languages, is involved, and the European Patent Organization, the Eurasian Patent Organization and the African Regional Industrial Property Organization and any other intergovernmental organization that is party to the Treaty, or may become party to the Treaty, if one of its official languages is involved.

(3)    [*Authentic Texts to Prevail*] In case of differences of opinion on interpretation between authentic and official texts, the authentic texts shall prevail.

## Article 26

### Signature of the Treaty

The Treaty shall remain open for signature by any State that is eligible for becoming party to the Treaty under Article 20(1) and by the European Patent Organization, the Eurasian Patent Organization and the African Regional Industrial Property Organization at the headquarters of the Organization for one year after its adoption.

## Article 27

### Depositary; Registration

(1)    [*Depositary*] The Director General is the depositary of this Treaty.

(2)    [*Registration*] The Director General shall register this Treaty with the Secretariat of the United Nations.

# 37.  PARTIES TO THE PATENT LAW TREATY*

(Geneva, 2000)

**Status on May 4, 2021**

| State | Date on which State became party to the Treaty |
|---|---|
| Albania | May 17, 2010 |
| Antigua and Barbuda | June 25, 2019 |
| Armenia | September 17, 2013 |
| Australia | March 16, 2009 |
| Bahrain | December 15, 2005 |
| Belarus | October 21, 2016 |
| Bosnia and Herzegovina | May 9, 2012 |
| Canada | October 30, 2019 |
| Croatia | April 28, 2005 |
| Democratic People's Republic of Korea | August 22, 2018 |
| Denmark | April 28, 2005 |
| Estonia | April 28, 2005 |
| Finland | March 6, 2006 |
| France | January 5, 2010 |
| Hungary | March 12, 2008 |
| Ireland | May 27, 2012 |
| Japan | June 11, 2016 |
| Kazakhstan[2] | October 19, 2011 |
| Kyrgyzstan | April 28, 2005 |
| Latvia | June 12, 2010 |
| Liberia | January 4, 2017 |
| Liechtenstein | December 18, 2009 |
| Lithuania | February 3, 2012 |
| Montenegro | March 9, 2012 |
| Netherlands | December 27, 2010 |
| Nigeria | April 28, 2005 |
| North Macedonia | April 22, 2010 |
| Oman | October 16, 2007 |
| Republic of Moldova | April 28, 2005 |
| Romania | April 28, 2005 |
| Russian Federation[2] | August 12, 2009 |
| Saudi Arabia | August 3, 2013 |
| Serbia | August 20, 2010 |

---

\* Document originally produced by the World Intellectual Property Organization (WIPO), the owner of the copyright. Published with the permission of the World Intellectual Property Organization.

## PARTIES TO THE PATENT LAW TREATY

| State | Date on which State became party to the Treaty |
| --- | --- |
| Slovakia | April 28, 2005 |
| Slovenia | April 28, 2005 |
| Spain | November 6, 2013 |
| Sweden | December 27, 2007 |
| Switzerland | July 1, 2008 |
| Turkmenistan | July 19, 2021 |
| Ukraine | April 28, 2005 |

(Total: 43 States)

---

[1] Entered into force on April 28, 2005.

[2] With the reservation under Article 23(1).

[3] Ratification in respect of the United Kingdom of Great Britain and Northern Ireland and the Isle of Man.

# 38.  INTERNATIONAL CONVENTION FOR THE PROTECTION OF NEW VARIETIES OF PLANTS

of December 2, 1961

as revised at Geneva on November 10, 1972, on
October 23, 1978, and on March 19, 1991

(1991 Act)

## LIST OF ARTICLES

---

# CHAPTER I
# DEFINITIONS

## Article 1

### Definitions

For the purposes of this Act:

(i)    "this Convention" means the present (1991) Act of the International Convention for the Protection of New Varieties of Plants;

(ii)    "Act of 1961/1972" means the International Convention for the Protection of New Varieties of Plants of December 2, 1961, as amended by the Additional Act of November 10, 1972;

(iii)   "Act of 1978" means the Act of October 23, 1978, of the International Convention for the Protection of New Varieties of Plants;

(iv)   "breeder" means

—    the person who bred, or discovered and developed, a variety,

—    the person who is the employer of the aforementioned person or who has commissioned the latter's work, where the laws of the relevant Contracting Party so provide, or

—    the successor in title of the first or second aforementioned person, as the case may be;

(v)    "breeder's right" means the right of the breeder provided for in this Convention;

(vi)  "variety" means a plant grouping within a single botanical taxon of the lowest known rank, which grouping, irrespective of whether the conditions for the grant of a breeder's right are fully met, can be

— defined by the expression of the characteristics resulting from a given genotype or combination of genotypes,

— distinguished from any other plant grouping by the expression of at least one of the said characteristics and

— considered as a unit with regard to its suitability for being propagated unchanged;

(vii)  "Contracting Party" means a State or an intergovernmental organization party to this Convention;

(viii) "territory," in relation to a Contracting Party, means, where the Contracting Party is a State, the territory of that State and, where the Contracting Party is an intergovernmental organization, the territory in which the constituting treaty of that intergovernmental organization applies;

(ix)  "authority" means the authority referred to in Article 30(1)(ii);

(x)  "Union" means the Union for the Protection of New Varieties of Plants founded by the Act of 1961 and further mentioned in the Act of 1972, the Act of 1978 and in this Convention;

(xi)  "member of the Union" means a State party to the Act of 1961/1972 or the Act of 1978, or a Contracting Party.

## CHAPTER II
## GENERAL OBLIGATIONS OF THE CONTRACTING PARTIES

### Article 2

### Basic Obligation of the Contracting Parties

Each Contracting Party shall grant and protect breeders' rights.

### Article 3

### Genera and Species to be Protected

(1)  Each Contracting Party which is bound by the Act of 1961/1972 or the Act of 1978 shall apply the provisions of this Convention,

(i)  at the date on which it becomes bound by this Convention, to all plant genera and species to which it applies, on the said date, the provisions of the Act of 1961/1972 or the Act of 1978 and,

(ii)  at the latest by the expiration of a period of five years after the said date, to all plant genera and species.

(2)  Each Contracting Party which is not bound by the Act of 1961/1972 or the Act of 1978 shall apply the provisions of this Convention,

(i)  at the date on which it becomes bound by this Convention, to at least 15 plant genera or species and,

(ii)  at the latest by the expiration of a period of 10 years from the said date, to all plant genera and species.

## Article 4

### National Treatment

(1)    Without prejudice to the rights specified in this Convention, nationals of a Contracting Party as well as natural persons resident and legal entities having their registered offices within the territory of a Contracting Party shall, insofar as the grant and protection of breeders' rights are concerned, enjoy within the territory of each other Contracting Party the same treatment as is accorded or may hereafter be accorded by the laws of each such other Contracting Party to its own nationals, provided that the said nationals, natural persons or legal entities comply with the conditions and formalities imposed on the nationals of the said other Contracting Party.

(2)    For the purposes of the preceding paragraph, "nationals" means, where the Contracting Party is a State, the nationals of that State and, where the Contracting Party is an intergovernmental organization, the nationals of the States which are members of that organization.

## CHAPTER III
## CONDITIONS FOR THE GRANT OF THE BREEDER'S RIGHT

## Article 5

### Conditions of Protection

(1)    The breeder's right shall be granted where the variety is

    (i)    new,

    (ii)   distinct,

    (iii)  uniform and

    (iv)   stable.

(2)    The grant of the breeder's right shall not be subject to any further or different conditions, provided that the variety is designated by a denomination in accordance with the provisions of Article 20, that the applicant complies with the formalities provided for by the law of the Contracting Party with whose authority the application has been filed and that he pays the required fees.

## Article 6

### Novelty

(1)    The variety shall be deemed to be new if, at the date of filing of the application for a breeder's right, propagating or harvested material of the variety has not been sold or otherwise disposed of to others, by or with the consent of the breeder, for purposes of exploitation of the variety

    (i)    in the territory of the Contracting Party in which the application has been filed earlier than one year before that date and

    (ii)   in a territory other than that of the Contracting Party in which the application has been filed earlier than four years or, in the case of trees or of vines, earlier than six years before the said date.

(2)    Where a Contracting Party applies this Convention to a plant genus or species to which it did not previously apply this Convention or an earlier Act, it may consider a variety of recent creation existing at the date of such extension of protection to satisfy the condition of novelty defined in paragraph (1) even where the sale or disposal to others described in that paragraph took place earlier than the time limits defined in that paragraph.

(3)    For the purposes of paragraph (1), all the Contracting Parties which are member States of one and the same intergovernmental organization may act jointly, where the regulations of that organization so require, to assimilate acts done on the territories of the States members of that

organization to acts done on their own territories and, should they do so, shall notify the Secretary-General accordingly.

## Article 7

### Distinctness

The variety shall be deemed to be distinct if it is clearly distinguishable from any other variety whose existence is a matter of common knowledge at the time of the filing of the application. In particular, the filing of an application for the granting of a breeder's right or for the entering of another variety in an official register of varieties, in any country, shall be deemed to render that other variety a matter of common knowledge from the date of the application, provided that the application leads to the granting of a breeder's right or to the entering of the said other variety in the official register of varieties, as the case may be.

## Article 8

### Uniformity

The variety shall be deemed to be uniform if, subject to the variation that may be expected from the particular features of its propagation, it is sufficiently uniform in its relevant characteristics.

## Article 9

### Stability

The variety shall be deemed to be stable if its relevant characteristics remain unchanged after repeated propagation or, in the case of a particular cycle of propagation, at the end of each such cycle.

## CHAPTER IV
## APPLICATION FOR THE GRANT OF THE BREEDER'S RIGHT

## Article 10

### Filing of Applications

(1) The breeder may choose the Contracting Party with whose authority he wishes to file his first application for a breeder's right.

(2) The breeder may apply to the authorities of other Contracting Parties for the grant of breeders' rights without waiting for the grant to him of a breeder's right by the authority of the Contracting Party with which the first application was filed.

(3) No Contracting Party shall refuse to grant a breeder's right or limit its duration on the ground that protection for the same variety has not been applied for, has been refused or has expired in any other State or intergovernmental organization.

## Article 11

### Right of Priority

(1) Any breeder who has duly filed an application for the protection of a variety in one of the Contracting Parties (the "first application") shall, for the purpose of filing an application for the grant of a breeder's right for the same variety with the authority of any other Contracting Party (the "subsequent application"), enjoy a right of priority for a period of 12 months. This period shall be computed from the date of filing of the first application. The day of filing shall not be included in the latter period.

(2) In order to benefit from the right of priority, the breeder shall, in the subsequent application, claim the priority of the first application. The authority with which the subsequent application has been filed may require the breeder to furnish, within a period of not less than three months from the

filing date of the subsequent application, a copy of the documents which constitute the first application, certified to be a true copy by the authority with which that application was filed, and samples or other evidence that the variety which is the subject matter of both applications is the same.

(3)   The breeder shall be allowed a period of two years after the expiration of the period of priority or, where the first application is rejected or withdrawn, an appropriate time after such rejection or withdrawal, in which to furnish, to the authority of the Contracting Party with which he has filed the subsequent application, any necessary information, document or material required for the purpose of the examination under Article 12, as required by the laws of that Contracting Party.

(4)   Events occurring within the period provided for in paragraph (1), such as the filing of another application or the publication or use of the variety that is the subject of the first application, shall not constitute a ground for rejecting the subsequent application. Such events shall also not give rise to any third-party right.

## Article 12

### Examination of the Application

Any decision to grant a breeder's right shall require an examination for compliance with the conditions under Articles 5 to 9. In the course of the examination, the authority may grow the variety or carry out other necessary tests, cause the growing of the variety or the carrying out of other necessary tests, or take into account the results of growing tests or other trials which have already been carried out. For the purposes of examination, the authority may require the breeder to furnish all the necessary information, documents or material.

## Article 13

### Provisional Protection

Each Contracting Party shall provide measures designed to safeguard the interests of the breeder during the period between the filing or the publication of the application for the grant of a breeder's right and the grant of that right. Such measures shall have the effect that the holder of a breeder's right shall at least be entitled to equitable remuneration from any person who, during the said period, has carried out acts which, once the right is granted, require the breeder's authorization as provided in Article 14. A Contracting Party may provide that the said measures shall only take effect in relation to persons whom the breeder has notified of the filing of the application.

## CHAPTER V
## THE RIGHTS OF THE BREEDER

## Article 14

### Scope of the Breeder's Right

(1)   *(a)*   Subject to Articles 15 and 16, the following acts in respect of the propagating material of the protected variety shall require the authorization of the breeder:

(i)   production or reproduction (multiplication),

(ii)   conditioning for the purpose of propagation,

(iii)   offering for sale,

(iv)   selling or other marketing,

(v)   exporting,

(vi)   importing,

(vii)   stocking for any of the purposes mentioned in (i) to (vi), above.

*(b)*   The breeder may make his authorization subject to conditions and limitations.

(2)   Subject to Articles 15 and 16, the acts referred to in items (i) to (vii) of paragraph (1)*(a)* in respect of harvested material, including entire plants and parts of plants, obtained through the unauthorized use of propagating material of the protected variety shall require the authorization of the breeder, unless the breeder has had reasonable opportunity to exercise his right in relation to the said propagating material.

(3)   Each Contracting Party may provide that, subject to Articles 15 and 16, the acts referred to in items (i) to (vii) of paragraph (1)*(a)* in respect of products made directly from harvested material of the protected variety falling within the provisions of paragraph (2) through the unauthorized use of the said harvested material shall require the authorization of the breeder, unless the breeder has had reasonable opportunity to exercise his right in relation to the said harvested material.

(4)   Each Contracting Party may provide that, subject to Articles 15 and 16, acts other than those referred to in items (i) to (vii) of paragraph (1)*(a)* shall also require the authorization of the breeder.

(5)   *(a)*   The provisions of paragraphs (1) to (4) shall also apply in relation to

(i)   varieties which are essentially derived from the protected variety, where the protected variety is not itself an essentially derived variety,

(ii)   varieties which are not clearly distinguishable in accordance with Article 7 from the protected variety and

(iii)   varieties whose production requires the repeated use of the protected variety.

*(b)*   For the purposes of subparagraph *(a)*(i), a variety shall be deemed to be essentially derived from another variety ("the initial variety") when

(i)   it is predominantly derived from the initial variety, or from a variety that is itself predominantly derived from the initial variety, while retaining the expression of the essential characteristics that result from the genotype or combination of genotypes of the initial variety,

(ii)   it is clearly distinguishable from the initial variety and

(iii)   except for the differences which result from the act of derivation, it conforms to the initial variety in the expression of the essential characteristics that result from the genotype or combination of genotypes of the initial variety.

*(c)*   Essentially derived varieties may be obtained for example by the selection of a natural or induced mutant, or of a somaclonal variant, the selection of a variant individual from plants of the initial variety, backcrossing, or transformation by genetic engineering.

## Article 15

### Exceptions to the Breeder's Right

(1)   The breeder's right shall not extend to

(i)   acts done privately and for non-commercial purposes,

(ii)   acts done for experimental purposes and

(iii)   acts done for the purpose of breeding other varieties, and, except where the provisions of Article 14(5) apply, acts referred to in Article 14(1) to (4) in respect of such other varieties.

(2)   Notwithstanding Article 14, each Contracting Party may, within reasonable limits and subject to the safeguarding of the legitimate interests of the breeder, restrict the breeder's right in relation to any variety in order to permit farmers to use for propagating purposes, on their own

holdings, the product of the harvest which they have obtained by planting, on their own holdings, the protected variety or a variety covered by Article 14(5)*(a)*(i) or (ii).

## Article 16

### Exhaustion of the Breeder's Right

(1) The breeder's right shall not extend to acts concerning any material of the protected variety, or of a variety covered by the provisions of Article 14(5), which has been sold or otherwise marketed by the breeder or with his consent in the territory of the Contracting Party concerned, or any material derived from the said material, unless such acts

(i) involve further propagation of the variety in question or

(ii) involve an export of material of the variety, which enables the propagation of the variety, into a country which does not protect varieties of the plant genus or species to which the variety belongs, except where the exported material is for final consumption purposes.

(2) For the purposes of paragraph (1), "material" means, in relation to a variety,

(i) propagating material of any kind,

(ii) harvested material, including entire plants and parts of plants, and

(iii) any product made directly from the harvested material.

(3) For the purposes of paragraph (1), all the Contracting Parties which are member States of one and the same intergovernmental organization may act jointly, where the regulations of that organization so require, to assimilate acts done on the territories of the States members of that organization to acts done on their own territories and, should they do so, shall notify the Secretary-General accordingly.

## Article 17

### Restrictions on the Exercise of the Breeder's Right

(1) Except where expressly provided in this Convention, no Contracting Party may restrict the free exercise of a breeder's right for reasons other than of public interest.

(2) When any such restriction has the effect of authorizing a third party to perform any act for which the breeder's authorization is required, the Contracting Party concerned shall take all measures necessary to ensure that the breeder receives equitable remuneration.

## Article 18

### Measures Regulating Commerce

The breeder's right shall be independent of any measure taken by a Contracting Party to regulate within its territory the production, certification and marketing of material of varieties or the importing or exporting of such material. In any case, such measures shall not affect the application of the provisions of this Convention.

## Article 19

### Duration of the Breeder's Right

(1) The breeder's right shall be granted for a fixed period.

(2) The said period shall not be shorter than 20 years from the date of the grant of the breeder's right. For trees and vines, the said period shall not be shorter than 25 years from the said date.

## CHAPTER VI
## VARIETY DENOMINATION

### Article 20

### Variety Denomination

(1)  *(a)*  The variety shall be designated by a denomination which will be its generic designation.

*(b)*  Each Contracting Party shall ensure that, subject to paragraph (4), no rights in the designation registered as the denomination of the variety shall hamper the free use of the denomination in connection with the variety, even after the expiration of the breeder's right.

(2)  The denomination must enable the variety to be identified. It may not consist solely of figures except where this is an established practice for designating varieties. It must not be liable to mislead or to cause confusion concerning the characteristics, value or identity of the variety or the identity of the breeder. In particular, it must be different from every denomination which designates, in the territory of any Contracting Party, an existing variety of the same plant species or of a closely related species.

(3)  The denomination of the variety shall be submitted by the breeder to the authority. If it is found that the denomination does not satisfy the requirements of paragraph (2), the authority shall refuse to register it and shall require the breeder to propose another denomination within a prescribed period. The denomination shall be registered by the authority at the same time as the breeder's right is granted.

(4)  Prior rights of third persons shall not be affected. If, by reason of a prior right, the use of the denomination of a variety is forbidden to a person who, in accordance with the provisions of paragraph (7), is obliged to use it, the authority shall require the breeder to submit another denomination for the variety.

(5)  A variety must be submitted to all Contracting Parties under the same denomination. The authority of each Contracting Party shall register the denomination so submitted, unless it considers the denomination unsuitable within its territory. In the latter case, it shall require the breeder to submit another denomination.

(6)  The authority of a Contracting Party shall ensure that the authorities of all the other Contracting Parties are informed of matters concerning variety denominations, in particular the submission, registration and cancellation of denominations. Any authority may address its observations, if any, on the registration of a denomination to the authority which communicated that denomination.

(7)  Any person who, within the territory of one of the Contracting Parties, offers for sale or markets propagating material of a variety protected within the said territory shall be obliged to use the denomination of that variety, even after the expiration of the breeder's right in that variety, except where, in accordance with the provisions of paragraph (4), prior rights prevent such use.

(8)  When a variety is offered for sale or marketed, it shall be permitted to associate a trademark, trade name or other similar indication with a registered variety denomination. If such an indication is so associated, the denomination must nevertheless be easily recognizable.

## CHAPTER VII
## NULLITY AND CANCELLATION OF THE BREEDER'S RIGHT

### Article 21

### Nullity of the Breeder's Right

(1)  Each Contracting Party shall declare a breeder's right granted by it null and void when it is established

(i)   that the conditions laid down in Articles 6 or 7 were not complied with at the time of the grant of the breeder's right,

(ii)   that, where the grant of the breeder's right has been essentially based upon information and documents furnished by the breeder, the conditions laid down in Articles 8 or 9 were not complied with at the time of the grant of the breeder's right, or

(iii)   that the breeder's right has been granted to a person who is not entitled to it, unless it is transferred to the person who is so entitled.

(2)   No breeder's right shall be declared null and void for reasons other than those referred to in paragraph (1).

## Article 22

### Cancellation of the Breeder's Right

(1)   *(a)*   Each Contracting Party may cancel a breeder's right granted by it if it is established that the conditions laid down in Articles 8 or 9 are no longer fulfilled.

*(b)*   Furthermore, each Contracting Party may cancel a breeder's right granted by it if, after being requested to do so and within a prescribed period,

(i)   the breeder does not provide the authority with the information, documents or material deemed necessary for verifying the maintenance of the variety,

(ii)   the breeder fails to pay such fees as may be payable to keep his right in force, or

(iii)   the breeder does not propose, where the denomination of the variety is cancelled after the grant of the right, another suitable denomination.

(2)   No breeder's right shall be cancelled for reasons other than those referred to in paragraph (1).

## CHAPTER VIII
## THE UNION

### Article 23

### Members

The Contracting Parties shall be members of the Union.

### Article 24

### Legal Status and Seat

(1)   The Union has legal personality.

(2)   The Union enjoys on the territory of each Contracting Party, in conformity with the laws applicable in the said territory, such legal capacity as may be necessary for the fulfillment of the objectives of the Union and for the exercise of its functions.

(3)   The seat of the Union and its permanent organs are at Geneva.

(4)   The Union has a headquarters agreement with the Swiss Confederation.

### Article 25

### Organs

The permanent organs of the Union are the Council and the Office of the Union.

## Article 26

### The Council

(1)   The Council shall consist of the representatives of the members of the Union. Each member of the Union shall appoint one representative to the Council and one alternate. Representatives or alternates may be accompanied by assistants or advisers.

(2)   The Council shall elect a President and a first Vice-President from among its members. It may elect other Vice-Presidents. The first Vice-President shall take the place of the President if the latter is unable to officiate. The President shall hold office for three years.

(3)   The Council shall meet upon convocation by its President. An ordinary session of the Council shall be held annually. In addition, the President may convene the Council at his discretion; he shall convene it, within a period of three months, if one-third of the members of the Union so request.

(4)   States not members of the Union may be invited as observers to meetings of the Council. Other observers, as well as experts, may also be invited to such meetings.

(5)   The tasks of the Council shall be to:

(i)   study appropriate measures to safeguard the interests and to encourage the development of the Union;

(ii)   establish its rules of procedure;

(iii) appoint the Secretary-General and, if it finds it necessary, a Vice Secretary-General and determine the terms of appointment of each;

(iv)   examine an annual report on the activities of the Union and lay down the program for its future work;

(v)   give to the Secretary-General all necessary directions for the accomplishment of the tasks of the Union;

(vi)   establish the administrative and financial regulations of the Union;

(vii) examine and approve the budget of the Union and fix the contribution of each member of the Union;

(viii) examine and approve the accounts presented by the Secretary-General;

(ix)   fix the date and place of the conferences referred to in Article 38 and take the measures necessary for their preparation; and

(x)   in general, take all necessary decisions to ensure the efficient functioning of the Union.

(6)   *(a)*   Each member of the Union that is a State shall have one vote in the Council.

*(b)*   Any Contracting Party that is an intergovernmental organization may, in matters within its competence, exercise the rights to vote of its member States that are members of the Union. Such an intergovernmental organization shall not exercise the rights to vote of its member States if its member States exercise their right to vote, and vice versa.

(7)   Any decision of the Council shall require a simple majority of the votes cast, provided that any decision of the Council under paragraphs (5)(ii), (vi) and (vii), and under Articles 28(3), 29(5)*(b)* and 38(1) shall require three-fourths of the votes cast. Abstentions shall not be considered as votes.

### Article 27

### The Office of the Union

(1)   The Office of the Union shall carry out all the duties and tasks entrusted to it by the Council. It shall be under the direction of the Secretary-General.

(2) The Secretary-General shall be responsible to the Council; he shall be responsible for carrying out the decisions of the Council. He shall submit the budget of the Union for the approval of the Council and shall be responsible for its implementation. He shall make reports to the Council on his administration and the activities and financial position of the Union.

(3) Subject to the provisions of Article 26(5)(iii), the conditions of appointment and employment of the staff necessary for the efficient performance of the tasks of the Office of the Union shall be fixed in the administrative and financial regulations.

## Article 28

### Languages

(1) The English, French, German and Spanish languages shall be used by the Office of the Union in carrying out its duties.

(2) Meetings of the Council and of revision conferences shall be held in the four languages.

(3) The Council may decide that further languages shall be used.

## Article 29

### Finances

(1) The expenses of the Union shall be met from

    (i) the annual contributions of the States members of the Union,

    (ii) payments received for services rendered,

    (iii) miscellaneous receipts.

(2) *(a)* The share of each State member of the Union in the total amount of the annual contributions shall be determined by reference to the total expenditure to be met from the contributions of the States members of the Union and to the number of contribution units applicable to it under paragraph (3). The said share shall be computed according to paragraph (4).

*(b)* The number of contribution units shall be expressed in whole numbers or fractions thereof, provided that no fraction shall be smaller than one-fifth.

(3) *(a)* The number of contribution units applicable to any member of the Union which is party to the Act of 1961/1972 or the Act of 1978 on the date on which it becomes bound by this Convention shall be the same as the number applicable to it immediately before the said date.

*(b)* Any other State member of the Union shall, on joining the Union, indicate, in a declaration addressed to the Secretary-General, the number of contribution units applicable to it.

*(c)* Any State member of the Union may, at any time, indicate, in a declaration addressed to the Secretary-General, a number of contribution units different from the number applicable to it under subparagraph *(a)* or *(b)*. Such declaration, if made during the first six months of a calendar year, shall take effect from the beginning of the subsequent calendar year; otherwise, it shall take effect from the beginning of the second calendar year which follows the year in which the declaration was made.

(4) *(a)* For each budgetary period, the amount corresponding to one contribution unit shall be obtained by dividing the total amount of the expenditure to be met in that period from the contributions of the States members of the Union by the total number of units applicable to those States members of the Union.

*(b)* The amount of the contribution of each State member of the Union shall be obtained by multiplying the amount corresponding to one contribution unit by the number of contribution units applicable to that State member of the Union.

(5)   *(a)*   A State member of the Union which is in arrears in the payment of its contributions may not, subject to subparagraph *(b)*, exercise its right to vote in the Council if the amount of its arrears equals or exceeds the amount of the contribution due from it for the preceding full year. The suspension of the right to vote shall not relieve such State member of the Union of its obligations under this Convention and shall not deprive it of any other rights thereunder.

      *(b)*   The Council may allow the said State member of the Union to continue to exercise its right to vote if, and as long as, the Council is satisfied that the delay in payment is due to exceptional and unavoidable circumstances.

(6)   The auditing of the accounts of the Union shall be effected by a State member of the Union as provided in the administrative and financial regulations. Such State member of the Union shall be designated, with its agreement, by the Council.

(7)   Any Contracting Party which is an intergovernmental organization shall not be obliged to pay contributions. If, nevertheless, it chooses to pay contributions, the provisions of paragraphs (1) to (4) shall be applied accordingly.

## CHAPTER IX
## IMPLEMENTATION OF THE CONVENTION; OTHER AGREEMENTS

### Article 30

### Implementation of the Convention

(1)   Each Contracting Party shall adopt all measures necessary for the implementation of this Convention; in particular, it shall:

    (i)   provide for appropriate legal remedies for the effective enforcement of breeders' rights;

    (ii)   maintain an authority entrusted with the task of granting breeders' rights or entrust the said task to an authority maintained by another Contracting Party;

    (iii) ensure that the public is informed through the regular publication of information concerning

    —   applications for and grants of breeders' rights, and

    —   proposed and approved denominations.

(2)   It shall be understood that, on depositing its instrument of ratification, acceptance, approval or accession, as the case may be, each State or intergovernmental organization must be in a position, under its laws, to give effect to the provisions of this Convention.

### Article 31

### Relations Between Contracting Parties and States Bound by Earlier Acts

(1)   Between States members of the Union which are bound both by this Convention and any earlier Act of the Convention, only this Convention shall apply.

(2)   Any State member of the Union not bound by this Convention may declare, in a notification addressed to the Secretary-General, that, in its relations with each member of the Union bound only by this Convention, it will apply the latest Act by which it is bound. As from the expiration of one month after the date of such notification and until the State member of the Union making the declaration becomes bound by this Convention, the said member of the Union shall apply the latest Act by which it is bound in its relations with each of the members of the Union bound only by this Convention, whereas the latter shall apply this Convention in respect of the former.

## Article 32

### Special Agreements

Members of the Union reserve the right to conclude among themselves special agreements for the protection of varieties, insofar as such agreements do not contravene the provisions of this Convention.

## CHAPTER X
## FINAL PROVISIONS

### Article 33

### Signature

This Convention shall be open for signature by any State which is a member of the Union at the date of its adoption. It shall remain open for signature until March 31, 1992.

### Article 34

### Ratification, Acceptance or Approval; Accession

(1) *(a)* Any State may, as provided in this Article, become party to this Convention.

*(b)* Any intergovernmental organization may, as provided in this Article, become party to this Convention if it

(i) has competence in respect of matters governed by this Convention,

(ii) has its own legislation providing for the grant and protection of breeders' rights binding on all its member States and

(iii) has been duly authorized, in accordance with its internal procedures, to accede to this Convention.

(2) Any State which has signed this Convention shall become party to this Convention by depositing an instrument of ratification, acceptance or approval of this Convention. Any State which has not signed this Convention and any intergovernmental organization shall become party to this Convention by depositing an instrument of accession to this Convention. Instruments of ratification, acceptance, approval or accession shall be deposited with the Secretary-General.

(3) Any State which is not a member of the Union and any intergovernmental organization shall, before depositing its instrument of accession, ask the Council to advise it in respect of the conformity of its laws with the provisions of this Convention. If the decision embodying the advice is positive, the instrument of accession may be deposited.

### Article 35

### Reservations

(1) Subject to paragraph (2), no reservations to this Convention are permitted.

(2) *(a)* Notwithstanding the provisions of Article 3(1), any State which, at the time of becoming party to this Convention, is a party to the Act of 1978 and which, as far as varieties reproduced asexually are concerned, provides for protection by an industrial property title other than a breeder's right shall have the right to continue to do so without applying this Convention to those varieties.

*(b)* Any State making use of the said right shall, at the time of depositing its instrument of ratification, acceptance, approval or accession, as the case may be, notify the Secretary-General accordingly. The same State may, at any time, withdraw the said notification.

## Article 36

### Communications Concerning Legislation and the Genera and Species Protected; Information to be Published

(1) When depositing its instrument of ratification, acceptance or approval of or accession to this Convention, as the case may be, any State or intergovernmental organization shall notify the Secretary-General of

(i)  its legislation governing breeder's rights and

(ii)  the list of plant genera and species to which, on the date on which it will become bound by this Convention, it will apply the provisions of this Convention.

(2) Each Contracting Party shall promptly notify the Secretary-General of

(i)  any changes in its legislation governing breeders' rights and

(ii)  any extension of the application of this Convention to additional plant genera and species.

(3) The Secretary-General shall, on the basis of communications received from each Contracting Party concerned, publish information on

(i)  the legislation governing breeders' rights and any changes in that legislation, and

(ii)  the list of plant genera and species referred to in paragraph (1)(ii) and any extension referred to in paragraph (2)(ii).

## Article 37

### Entry into Force; Closing of Earlier Acts

(1) This Convention shall enter into force one month after five States have deposited their instruments of ratification, acceptance, approval or accession, as the case may be, provided that at least three of the said instruments have been deposited by States party to the Act of 1961/1972 or the Act of 1978.

(2) Any State not covered by paragraph (1) or any intergovernmental organization shall become bound by this Convention one month after the date on which it has deposited its instrument of ratification, acceptance, approval or accession, as the case may be.

(3) No instrument of accession to the Act of 1978 may be deposited after the entry into force of this Convention according to paragraph (1), except that any State that, in conformity with the established practice of the General Assembly of the United Nations, is regarded as a developing country may deposit such an instrument until December 31, 1995, and that any other State may deposit such an instrument until December 31, 1993, even if this Convention enters into force before that date.

## Article 38

### Revision of the Convention

(1) This Convention may be revised by a conference of the members of the Union. The convocation of such conference shall be decided by the Council.

(2) The proceedings of a conference shall be effective only if at least half of the States members of the Union are represented at it. A majority of three-quarters of the States members of the Union present and voting at the conference shall be required for the adoption of any revision.

## Article 39

### Denunciation

(1) Any Contracting Party may denounce this Convention by notification addressed to the Secretary-General. The Secretary-General shall promptly notify all members of the Union of the receipt of that notification.

(2) Notification of the denunciation of this Convention shall be deemed also to constitute notification of the denunciation of any earlier Act by which the Contracting Party denouncing this Convention is bound.

(3) The denunciation shall take effect at the end of the calendar year following the year in which the notification was received by the Secretary-General.

(4) The denunciation shall not affect any rights acquired in a variety by reason of this Convention or any earlier Act prior to the date on which the denunciation becomes effective.

## Article 40

### Preservation of Existing Rights

This Convention shall not limit existing breeders' rights under the laws of Contracting Parties or by reason of any earlier Act or any agreement other than this Convention concluded between members of the Union.

## Article 41

### Original and Official Texts of the Convention

(1) This Convention shall be signed in a single original in the English, French and German languages, the French text prevailing in case of any discrepancy among the various texts. The original shall be deposited with the Secretary-General.

(2) The Secretary-General shall, after consultation with the interested Governments, establish official texts of this Convention in the Arabic, Dutch, Italian, Japanese and Spanish languages and such other languages as the Council may designate.

## Article 42

### Depositary Functions

(1) The Secretary-General shall transmit certified copies of this Convention to all States and intergovernmental organizations which were represented in the Diplomatic Conference that adopted this Convention and, on request, to any other State or intergovernmental organization.

(2) The Secretary-General shall register this Convention with the Secretariat of the United Nations.

### Resolution on Article 14(5)

The Diplomatic Conference for the Revision of the International Convention for the Protection of New Varieties of Plants held from March 4 to 19, 1991, requests the Secretary-General of UPOV to start work immediately after the Conference on the establishment of draft standard guidelines, for adoption by the Council of UPOV, on essentially derived varieties.

### Recommendation Relating to Article 15(2)

The Diplomatic Conference recommends that the provisions laid down in Article 15(2) of the International Convention for the Protection of New Varieties of Plants of December 2, 1961, as Revised at Geneva on November 10, 1972, on October 23, 1978, and on March 19, 1991, should not be read so as to be intended to open the possibility of extending the practice commonly called "farmer's privilege" to sectors of agricultural or horticultural production in which such a privilege is not a common practice on the territory of the Contracting Party concerned.

### Common Statement Relating to Article 34

The Diplomatic Conference noted and accepted a declaration by the Delegation of Denmark and a declaration by the Delegation of the Netherlands according to which the Convention adopted by the Diplomatic Conference will not, upon its ratification, acceptance, approval or accession by Denmark or the Netherlands, be automatically applicable, in the case of Denmark, in Greenland and the Faroe Islands and, in the case of the Netherlands, in Aruba and the Netherlands Antilles. The said Convention will only apply in the said territories if and when Denmark or the Netherlands, as the case may be, expressly so notifies the Secretary-General.

# 39.  PARTIES TO THE INTERNATIONAL CONVENTION FOR THE PROTECTION OF NEW VARIETIES OF PLANTS*

International Convention for the Protection of New Varieties of Plants

UPOV Convention (1961), as revised at Geneva (1972, 1978 and 1991)

**Status on May 4, 2021**

| State/Organization | Date on which State/Organization became member of UPOV | Latest Act[1] of the Convention to which State/Organization is party and date on which State/Organization became party to that Act |
| --- | --- | --- |
| African Intellectual Property Organization[2] | July 10, 2014 | 1991 Act ......... July 10, 2014 |
| Albania | October 15, 2005 | 1991 Act ......... October 15, 2005 |
| Argentina | December 25, 1994 | 1978 Act ......... December 25, 1994 |
| Australia | March 1, 1989 | 1991 Act ......... January 20, 2000 |
| Austria | July 14, 1994 | 1991 Act ......... July 1, 2004 |
| Azerbaijan | December 9, 2004 | 1991 Act ......... December 9, 2004 |
| Belarus | January 5, 2003 | 1991 Act ......... January 5, 2003 |
| Belgium[3] | December 5, 1976 | 1991 Act ......... June 2, 2019 |
| Bolivia (Plurinational State of) | May 21, 1999 | 1978 Act ......... May 21, 1999 |
| Bosnia and Herzegovina | November 10, 2017 | 1991 Act ......... November 10, 2017 |
| Brazil | May 23, 1999 | 1978 Act ......... May 23, 1999 |
| Bulgaria | April 24, 1998 | 1991 Act ......... April 24, 1998 |
| Canada | March 4, 1991 | 1991 Act ......... July 19, 2015 |
| Chile | January 5, 1996 | 1978 Act ......... January 5, 1996 |
| China | April 23, 1999 | 1978 Act[4] ......... April 23, 1999 |
| Colombia | September 13, 1996 | 1978 Act ......... September 13, 1996 |
| Costa Rica | January 12, 2009 | 1991 Act ......... January 12, 2009 |
| Croatia | September 1, 2001 | 1991 Act ......... September 1, 2001 |
| Czech Republic | January 1, 1993 | 1991 Act ......... November 24, 2002 |
| Denmark[5] | October 6, 1968 | 1991 Act ......... April 24, 1998 |
| Dominican Republic | June 16, 2007 | 1991 Act ......... June 16, 2007 |
| Ecuador | August 8, 1997 | 1978 Act ......... August 8, 1997 |
| Egypt | December 1, 2019 | 1991 Act ......... December 1, 2019 |
| Estonia | September 24, 2000 | 1991 Act ......... September 24, 2000 |
| European Union[6] | July 29, 2005 | 1991 Act ......... July 29, 2005 |
| Finland | April 16, 1993 | 1991 Act ......... July 20, 2001 |
| France | October 3, 1971 | 1991 Act ......... May 27, 2012 |
| Georgia | November 29, 2008 | 1991 Act ......... November 29, 2008 |

*  Document originally produced by the World Intellectual Property Organization (WIPO), the owner of the copyright. Published with the permission of the World Intellectual Property Organization.

| State/Organization | Date on which State/Organization became member of UPOV | Latest Act[1] of the Convention to which State/Organization is party and date on which State/Organization became party to that Act |
| --- | --- | --- |
| Germany | August 10, 1968 | 1991 Act ......... July 25, 1998 |
| Hungary | April 16, 1983 | 1991 Act ......... January 1, 2003 |
| Iceland | May 3, 2006 | 1991 Act ......... May 3, 2006 |
| Ireland | November 8, 1981 | 1991 Act ......... January 8, 2012 |
| Israel | December 12, 1979 | 1991 Act ......... April 24, 1998 |
| Italy | July 1, 1977 | 1978 Act ......... May 28, 1986 |
| Japan | September 3, 1982 | 1991 Act ......... December 24, 1998 |
| Jordan | October 24, 2004 | 1991 Act ......... October 24, 2004 |
| Kenya | May 13, 1999 | 1991 Act ......... May 11, 2016 |
| Kyrgyzstan | June 26, 2000 | 1991 Act ......... June 26, 2000 |
| Latvia | August 30, 2002 | 1991 Act ......... August 30, 2002 |
| Lithuania | December 10, 2003 | 1991 Act ......... December 10, 2003 |
| Mexico | August 9, 1997 | 1978 Act ......... August 9, 1997 |
| Montenegro | September 24, 2015 | 1991 Act ......... September 24, 2015 |
| Morocco | October 8, 2006 | 1991 Act ......... October 8, 2006 |
| Netherlands | August 10, 1968 | 1991 Act[7] ......... April 24, 1998 |
| New Zealand | November 8, 1981 | 1978 Act ......... November 8, 1981 |
| Nicaragua | September 6, 2001 | 1978 Act ......... September 6, 2001 |
| North Macedonia | May 4, 2011 | 1991 Act ......... May 4, 2011 |
| Norway | September 13, 1993 | 1978 Act ......... September 13, 1993 |
| Oman | November 22, 2009 | 1991 Act ......... November 22, 2009 |
| Panama | May 23, 1999 | 1991 Act ......... November 22, 2012 |
| Paraguay | February 8, 1997 | 1978 Act ......... February 8, 1997 |
| Peru | August 8, 2011 | 1991 Act ......... August 8, 2011 |
| Poland | November 11, 1989 | 1991 Act ......... August 15, 2003 |
| Portugal | October 14, 1995 | 1978 Act ......... October 14, 1995 |
| Republic of Korea | January 7, 2002 | 1991 Act ......... January 7, 2002 |
| Republic of Moldova | October 28, 1998 | 1991 Act ......... October 28, 1998 |
| Romania | March 16, 2001 | 1991 Act ......... March 16, 2001 |
| Russian Federation | April 24, 1998 | 1991 Act ......... April 24, 1998 |
| Saint Vincent and the Grenadines | March 22,2021 | 1991 Act ......... March 22,2021 |
| Serbia | January 5, 2013 | 1991 Act ......... January 5, 2013 |
| Singapore | July 30, 2004 | 1991 Act ......... July 30, 2004 |
| Slovakia | January 1, 1993 | 1991 Act ......... June 12, 2009 |
| Slovenia | July 29, 1999 | 1991 Act ......... July 29, 1999 |
| South Africa | November 6, 1977 | 1978 Act ......... November 8, 1981 |
| Spain | May 18, 1980 | 1991 Act ......... July 18, 2007 |
| Sweden | December 17, 1971 | 1991 Act ......... April 24, 1998 |
| Switzerland | July 10, 1977 | 1991 Act ......... September 1, 2008 |

| State/Organization | Date on which State/Organization became member of UPOV | Latest Act[1] of the Convention to which State/Organization is party and date on which State/Organization became party to that Act |
|---|---|---|
| Trinidad and Tobago | January 30, 1998 | 1978 Act .......... January 30, 1998 |
| Tunisia | August 31, 2003 | 1991 Act .......... August 31, 2003 |
| Turkey | November 18, 2007 | 1991 Act .......... November 18, 2007 |
| Ukraine | November 3, 1995 | 1991 Act .......... January 19, 2007 |
| United Kingdom | August 10, 1968 | 1991 Act .......... January 3, 1999 |
| United Republic of Tanzania | November 22, 2015 | 1991 Act .......... November 22, 2015 |
| United States of America | November 8, 1981 | 1991 Act[8] .......... February 22, 1999 |
| Uruguay | November 13, 1994 | 1978 Act .......... November 13, 1994 |
| Uzbekistan | November 14, 2004 | 1991 Act .......... November 14, 2004 |
| Viet Nam | December 24, 2006 | 1991 Act .......... December 24, 2006 |

(Total: 77)

---

\* The International Union for the Protection of New Varieties of Plants (UPOV), established by the International Convention for the Protection of New Varieties of Plants, is an independent intergovernmental organization having legal personality. Pursuant to an agreement concluded between the World Intellectual Property Organization (WIPO) and UPOV, the Director General of WIPO is the Secretary-General of UPOV and WIPO provides administrative services to UPOV.

[1] "1961/1972 Act" means the International Convention for the Protection of New Varieties of Plants of December 2, 1961, as amended by the Additional Act of November 10, 1972; "1978 Act" means the Act of October 23, 1978, of the Convention; "1991 Act" means the Act of March 19, 1991, of the Convention.

[2] Operates a plant breeders' rights system which covers the territory of its 17 member States (member States of OAPI: Benin, Burkina Faso, Cameroon, Central African Republic, Chad, Comoros, Congo, Côte d'Ivoire, Equatorial Guinea, Gabon, Guinea, Guinea-Bissau, Mali, Mauritania, Niger, Senegal, Togo).

[3] With a notification under Article 34(2) of the 1978 Act.

[4] With a declaration that the 1978 Act is not applicable to Hong Kong, China.

[5] With a declaration that the Convention of 1961, the Additional Act of 1972, the 1978 Act and the 1991 Act are not applicable to Greenland and the Faroe Islands.

[6] Operates a plant breeders' rights system which covers the territory of its 27 member States and until December 31, 2020, the United Kingdom (member States of the European Union: Austria, Belgium, Bulgaria, Croatia, Cyprus, Czech Republic, Denmark, Estonia, Finland, France, Germany, Greece, Hungary, Ireland, Italy, Latvia, Lithuania, Luxembourg, Malta, Netherlands, Poland, Portugal, Romania, Slovakia, Slovenia, Spain, Sweden).

[7] Ratification for the Kingdom in Europe.

[8] With a reservation pursuant to Article 35(2) of the 1991 Act.

# TRADEMARKS AND GEOGRAPHICAL INDICATIONS

---

## 40. MADRID AGREEMENT CONCERNING THE INTERNATIONAL REGISTRATION OF MARKS OF APRIL 14, 1891

as revised at Brussels on December 14, 1900, at Washington on June 2, 1911, at The Hague on November 6, 1925, at London on June 2, 1934, at Nice on June 15, 1957, and at Stockholm on July 14, 1967, and as amended on September 28, 1979

### Article 1

(1) The countries to which this Agreement applies constitute a Special Union for the International registration of marks.

(2) Nationals of any of the contracting countries may, in all the other countries party to this Agreement, secure protection for their marks applicable to goods or services, registered in the country of origin, by filing the said marks at the International Bureau of Intellectual Property (hereinafter designated as "the International Bureau") referred to in the Convention establishing the World Intellectual Property Organization (hereinafter designated as "the Organization"), through the intermediary of the Office of the said country of origin.

(3) Shall be considered the country of origin the country of the Special Union where the applicant has a real and effective industrial or commercial establishment; if he has no such establishment in a country of the Special Union, the country of the Special Union where he has his domicile; if he has no domicile within the Special Union but is a national of a country of the Special Union, the country of which he is a national.

### Article 2

Nationals of countries not having acceded to this Agreement who, within the territory of the Special Union constituted by the said Agreement, satisfy the conditions specified in Article 3 of the Paris Convention for the Protection of Industrial Property shall be treated in the same manner as nationals of the contracting countries.

### Article 3

(1) Every application for international registration must be presented on the form prescribed by the Regulations; the Office of the country of origin of the mark shall certify that the particulars appearing in such application correspond to the particulars in the national register, and shall mention the dates and numbers of the filing and registration of the mark in the country of origin and also the date of the application for international registration.

(2) The applicant must indicate the goods or services in respect of which protection of the mark is claimed and also, if possible, the corresponding class or classes according to the classification established by the Nice Agreement concerning the International Classification of Goods and Services for the Purposes of the Registration of Marks. If the applicant does not give such indication, the International Bureau shall classify the goods or services in the appropriate classes of the said classification. The indication of classes given by the applicant shall be subject to control by the International Bureau, which shall exercise the said control in association with the national

Office. In the event of disagreement between the national Office and the International Bureau, the opinion of the latter shall prevail.

(3) If the applicant claims color as a distinctive feature of his mark, he shall be required:

1. to state the fact, and to file with his application a notice specifying the color or the combination of colors claimed;

2. to append to his application copies in color of the said mark, which shall be attached to the notification given by the International Bureau. The number of such copies shall be fixed by the Regulations.

(4) The International Bureau shall register immediately the marks filed in accordance with Article 1. The registration shall bear the date of the application for international registration in the country of origin, provided that the application has been received by the International Bureau within a period of two months from that date. If the application has not been received within that period, the International Bureau shall record it as at the date on which it received the said application. The International Bureau shall notify such registration without delay to the Offices concerned. Registered marks shall be published in a periodical journal issued by the International Bureau, on the basis of the particulars contained in the application for registration. In the case of marks comprising a figurative element or a special form of writing, the Regulations shall determine whether a printing block must be supplied by the applicant.

(5) With a view to the publicity to be given in the contracting countries to registered marks, each Office shall receive from the International Bureau a number of copies of the said publication free of charge and a number of copies at a reduced price, in proportion to the number of units mentioned in Article 16(4)(a) of the Paris Convention for the Protection of Industrial Property, under the conditions fixed by the Regulations. Such publicity shall be deemed in all the contracting countries to be sufficient, and no other publicity may be required of the applicant.

## Article 3*bis*

(1) Any contracting country may, at any time, notify the Director General of the Organization (hereinafter designated as "the Director General") in writing that the protection resulting from the international registration shall extend to that country only at the express request of the proprietor of the mark.

(2) Such notification shall not take effect until six months after the date of the communication thereof by the Director General to the other contracting countries.

## Article 3*ter*

(1) Any request for extension of the protection resulting from the international registration to a country which has availed itself of the right provided for in Article 3*bis* must be specially mentioned in the application referred to in Article 3(1).

(2) Any request for territorial extension made subsequently to the international registration must be presented through the intermediary of the Office of the country of origin on a form prescribed by the Regulations. It shall be immediately registered by the International Bureau, which shall notify it without delay to the Office or Offices concerned. It shall be published in the periodical journal issued by the International Bureau. Such territorial extension shall be effective from the date on which it has been recorded in the International Register; it shall cease to be valid on the expiration of the international registration of the mark to which it relates.

## Article 4

(1) From the date of the registration so effected at the International Bureau in accordance with the provisions of Articles 3 and 3*ter*, the protection of the mark in each of the contracting countries concerned shall be the same as if the mark had been filed therein direct. The indication of classes

of goods or services provided for in Article 3 shall not bind the contracting countries with regard to the determination of the scope of the protection of the mark.

(2) Every mark which has been the subject of an international registration shall enjoy the right of priority provided for by Article 4 of the Paris Convention for the Protection of Industrial Property, without requiring compliance with the formalities prescribed in Section D of that Article.

## Article 4*bis*

(1) When a mark already filed in one or more of the contracting countries is later registered by the International Bureau in the name of the same proprietor or his successor in title, the international registration shall be deemed to have replaced the earlier national registrations, without prejudice to any rights acquired by reason of such earlier registrations.

(2) The national Office shall, upon request, be required to take note in its registers of the international registration.

## Article 5

(1) In countries where the legislation so authorizes, Offices notified by the International Bureau of the registration of a mark or of a request for extension of protection made in accordance with Article 3*ter* shall have the right to declare that protection cannot be granted to such mark in their territory. Any such refusal can be based only on the grounds which would apply, under the Paris Convention for the Protection of Industrial Property, in the case of a mark filed for national registration. However, protection may not be refused, even partially, by reason only that national legislation would not permit registration except in a limited number of classes or for a limited number of goods or services.

(2) Offices wishing to exercise such right must give notice of their refusal to the International Bureau, together with a statement of all grounds, within the period prescribed by their domestic law and, at the latest, before the expiration of one year from the date of the international registration of the mark or of the request for extension of protection made in accordance with Article 3*ter*.

(3) The International Bureau shall, without delay, transmit to the Office of the country of origin and to the proprietor of the mark, or to his agent if an agent has been mentioned to the Bureau by the said Office, one of the copies of the declaration of refusal so notified. The interested party shall have the same remedies as if the mark had been filed by him direct in the country where protection is refused.

(4) The grounds for refusing a mark shall be communicated by the International Bureau to any interested party who may so request.

(5) Offices which, within the aforesaid maximum period of one year, have not communicated to the International Bureau any provisional or final decision of refusal with regard to the registration of a mark or a request for extension of protection shall lose the benefit of the right provided for in paragraph (1) of this Article with respect to the mark in question.

(6) Invalidation of an international mark may not be pronounced by the competent authorities without the proprietor of the mark having, in good time, been afforded the opportunity of defending his rights. Invalidation shall be notified to the International Bureau.

## Article 5*bis*

Documentary evidence of the legitimacy of the use of certain elements incorporated in a mark, such as armorial bearings, escutcheons, portraits, honorary distinctions, titles, trade names, names of persons other than the name of the applicant, or other like inscriptions, which might be required by the Offices of the contracting countries shall be exempt from any legalization or certification other than that of the Office of the country of origin.

## Article *5ter*

(1) The International Bureau shall issue to any person applying therefor, subject to a fee fixed by the Regulations, a copy of the entries in the Register relating to a specific mark.

(2) The International Bureau may also, upon payment, undertake searches for anticipation among international marks.

(3) Extracts from the International Register requested with a view to their production in one of the contracting countries shall be exempt from all legalization.

## Article 6

(1) Registration of a mark at the International Bureau is effected for twenty years, with the possibility of renewal under the conditions specified in Article 7.

(2) Upon expiration of a period of five years from the date of the international registration, such registration shall become independent of the national mark registered earlier in the country of origin, subject to the following provisions.

(3) The protection resulting from the international registration, whether or not it has been the subject of a transfer, may no longer be invoked, in whole or in part, if, within five years from the date of the international registration, the national mark, registered earlier in the country of origin in accordance with Article 1, no longer enjoys, in whole or in part, legal protection in that country. This provision shall also apply when legal protection has later ceased as the result of an action begun before the expiration of the period of five years.

(4) In the case of voluntary or ex officio cancellation, the Office of the country of origin shall request the cancellation of the mark at the International Bureau, and the latter shall effect the cancellation. In the case of judicial action, the said Office shall send to the International Bureau, ex officio or at the request of the plaintiff, a copy of the complaint or any other documentary evidence that an action has begun, and also of the final decision of the court; the Bureau shall enter notice thereof in the International Register.

## Article 7

(1) Any registration may be renewed for a period of twenty years from the expiration of the preceding period, by payment only of the basic fee and, where necessary, of the supplementary and complementary fees provided for in Article 8(2).

(2) Renewal may not include any change in relation to the previous registration in its latest form.

(3) The first renewal effected under the provisions of the Nice Act of June 15, 1957, or of this Act, shall include an indication of the classes of the International Classification to which the registration relates.

(4) Six months before the expiration of the term of protection, the International Bureau shall, by sending an unofficial notice, remind the proprietor of the mark and his agent of the exact date of expiration.

(5) Subject to the payment of a surcharge fixed by the Regulations, a period of grace of six months shall be granted for renewal of the international registration.

## Article 8

(1) The Office of the country of origin may fix, at its own discretion, and collect, for its own benefit, a national fee which it may require from the proprietor of the mark in respect of which international registration or renewal is applied for.

(2) Registration of a mark at the International Bureau shall be subject to the advance payment of an international fee which shall include:

*(a)* a basic fee;

*(b)* a supplementary fee for each class of the International Classification, beyond three, into which the goods or services to which the mark is applied will fall;

*(c)* a complementary fee for any request for extension of protection under Article 3*ter.*

(3) However, the supplementary fee specified in paragraph (2)(b) may, without prejudice to the date of registration, be paid within a period fixed by the Regulations if the number of classes of goods or services has been fixed or disputed by the International Bureau. If, upon expiration of the said period, the supplementary fee has not been paid or the list of goods or services has not been reduced to the required extent by the applicant, the application for international registration shall be deemed to have been abandoned.

(4) The annual returns from the various receipts from international registration, with the exception of those provided for under (b) and (c) of paragraph (2), shall he divided equally among the countries party to this Act by the International Bureau, after deduction of the expenses and charges necessitated by the implementation of the said Act. If, at the time this Act enters into force, a country has not yet ratified or acceded to the said Act, it shall be entitled, until the date on which its ratification or accession becomes effective, to a share of the excess receipts calculated on the basis of that earlier Act which is applicable to it.

(5) The amounts derived from the supplementary fees provided for in paragraph (2)(b) shall be divided at the expiration of each year among the countries party to this Act or to the Nice Act of June 15, 1957, in proportion to the number of marks for which protection has been applied for in each of them during that year, this number being multiplied, in the case of countries which make a preliminary examination, by a coefficient which shall be determined by the Regulations. If, at the time this Act enters into force, a country has not yet ratified or acceded to the said Act, it shall be entitled, until the date on which its ratification or accession becomes effective, to a share of the amounts calculated on the basis of the Nice Act.

(6) The amounts derived from the complementary fees provided for in paragraph (2)(c) shall be divided according to the requirements of paragraph (5) among the countries availing themselves of the right provided for in Article 3*bis.* If, at the time this Act enters into force, a country has not yet ratified or acceded to the said Act, it shall be entitled, until the date on which its ratification or accession becomes effective, to a share of the amounts calculated on the basis of the Nice Act.

## Article 8*bis*

The person in whose name the international registration stands may at any time renounce protection in one or more of the contracting countries by means of a declaration filed with the Office of his own country, for communication to the International Bureau, which shall notify accordingly the countries in respect of which renunciation has been made. Renunciation shall not be subject to any fee.

## Article 9

(1) The Office of the country of the person in whose name the international registration stands shall likewise notify the International Bureau of all annulments, cancellations, renunciations, transfers, and other changes made in the entry of the mark in the national register, if such changes also affect the international registration.

(2) The Bureau shall record those changes in the International Register, shall notify them in turn to the Offices of the contracting countries, and shall publish them in its journal.

(3) A similar procedure shall be followed when the person in whose name the international registration stands requests a reduction of the list of goods or services to which the registration applies.

(4) Such transactions may be subject to a fee, which shall be fixed by the Regulations.

(5) The subsequent addition of new goods or services to the said list can be obtained only by filing a new application as prescribed in Article 3.

(6) The substitution of one of the goods or services for another shall be treated as an addition.

## Article 9*bis*

(1) When a mark registered in the International Register is transferred to a person established in a contracting country other than the country of the person in whose name the international registration stands, the transfer shall be notified to the International Bureau by the Office of the latter country. The International Bureau shall record the transfer, shall notify the other Offices thereof, and shall publish it in its journal. If the transfer has been effected before the expiration of a period of five years from the international registration, the International Bureau shall seek the consent of the Office of the country of the new proprietor, and shall publish, if possible, the date and registration number of the mark in the country of the new proprietor.

(2) No transfer of a mark registered in the International Register for the benefit of a person who is not entitled to file an international mark shall be recorded.

(3) When it has not been possible to record a transfer in the International Register, either because the country of the new proprietor has refused its consent or because the said transfer has been made for the benefit of a person who is not entitled to apply for international registration, the Office of the country of the former proprietor shall have the right to demand that the International Bureau cancel the mark in its Register.

## Article 9*ter*

(1) If the assignment of an international mark for part only of the registered goods or services is notified to the International Bureau, the Bureau shall record it in its Register. Each of the contracting countries shall have the right to refuse to recognize the validity of such assignment if the goods or services included in the part so assigned are similar to those in respect of which the mark remains registered for the benefit of the assignor.

(2) The International Bureau shall likewise record the assignment of an international mark in respect of one or several of the contracting countries only.

(3) If, in the above cases, a change occurs in the country of the proprietor, the Office of the country to which the new proprietor belongs shall, if the international mark has been transferred before the expiration of a period of five years from the international registration, give its consent as required by Article 9*bis*.

(4) The provisions of the foregoing paragraphs shall apply subject to Article 6*quater* of the Paris Convention for the Protection of Industrial Property.

## Article 9*quater*

(1) If several countries of the Special Union agree to effect the unification of their domestic legislation's on marks, they may notify the Director General:

   (a) that a common Office shall be substituted for the national Office of each of them, and

   (b) that the whole of their respective territories shall be deemed to be a single country for the purposes of the application of all or part of the provisions preceding this Article.

(2) Such notification shall not take effect until six months after the date of the communication thereof by the Director General to the other contracting countries.

**Article 10**

(1)

(a) The Special Union shall have an Assembly consisting of those countries which have ratified or acceded to this Act.

(b) The Government of each country shall be represented by one delegate, who may be assisted by alternate delegates, advisors, and experts.

(c) The expenses of each delegation shall be borne by the Government which has appointed it, except for the travel expenses and the subsistence allowance of one delegate for each member country, which shall be paid from the funds of the Special Union.

(2)

(a) The Assembly shall:

   (i) deal with all matters concerning the maintenance and development of the Special Union and the implementation of this Agreement;

   (ii) give directions to the International Bureau concerning the preparation for conferences of revision, due account being taken of any comments made by those countries of the Special Union which have not ratified or acceded to this Act;

   (iii) modify the Regulations, including the fixation of the amounts of the fees referred to in Article 8(2) and other fees relating to international registration;

   (iv) review and approve the reports and activities of the Director General concerning the Special Union, and give him all necessary instructions concerning matters within the competence of the Special Union;

   (v) determine the program and adopt the biennial budget of the Special Union, and approve its final accounts;

   (vi) adopt the financial regulations of the Special Union;

   (vii) establish such committees of experts and working groups as it may deem necessary to achieve the objectives of the Special Union;

   (viii) determine which countries not members of the Special Union and which intergovernmental and international non-governmental organizations shall be admitted to its meetings as observers;

   (ix) adopt amendments to Articles 10 to 13;

   (x) take any other appropriate action designed to further the objectives of the Special Union;

   (xi) perform such other functions as are appropriate under this Agreement.

(b) With respect to matters which are of interest also to other Unions administered by the Organization, the Assembly shall make its decisions after having heard the advice of the Coordination Committee of the Organization.

(3)

(a) Each country member of the Assembly shall have one vote.

(b) One-half of the countries members of the Assembly shall constitute a quorum.

(c) Notwithstanding the provisions of subparagraph (b), if, in any session, the number of countries represented is less than one-half but equal to or more than one-third of the countries members of the Assembly, the Assembly may make decisions but, with the exception of decisions concerning its own procedure, all such decisions shall take effect only if the conditions set forth hereinafter are fulfilled. The International Bureau shall communicate the said decisions to the countries members of the Assembly which were not represented and shall invite them to express in writing their vote or abstention within a period of three months from the date of the communication. If, at the expiration of this period, the number of countries having thus expressed their vote or abstention attains the number of countries which was lacking for attaining the quorum in the session itself, such decisions shall take effect provided that at the same time the required majority still obtains.

*(d)* Subject to the provisions of Article 13(2), the decisions of the Assembly shall require two-thirds of the votes cast.

*(e)* Abstentions shall not be considered as votes.

*(f)* A delegate may represent, and vote in the name of, one country only.

*(g)* Countries of the Special Union not members of the Assembly shall be admitted to the meetings of the latter as observers.

(4)

*(a)* The Assembly shall meet once in every second calendar year in ordinary session upon convocation by the Director General and, in the absence of exceptional circumstances, during the same period and at the same place as the General Assembly of the Organization.

*(b)* The Assembly shall meet in extraordinary session upon convocation by the Director General, at the request of one-fourth of the countries members of the Assembly.

*(c)* The agenda of each session shall be prepared by the Director General.

(5) The Assembly shall adopt its own rules of procedure.

## Article 11

(1)

*(a)* International registration and related duties, as well as all other administrative tasks concerning the Special Union, shall be performed by the International Bureau.

*(b)* In particular, the International Bureau shall prepare the meetings and provide the secretariat of the Assembly and of such committees of experts and working groups as may have been established by the Assembly.

*(c)* The Director General shall be the chief executive of the Special Union and shall represent the Special Union.

(2) The Director General and any staff member designated by him shall participate, without the right to vote, in all meetings of the Assembly and of such committees of experts or working groups as may have been established by the Assembly. The Director General, or a staff member designated by him, shall be ex officio secretary of those bodies.

(3)

*(a)* The International Bureau shall, in accordance with the directions of the Assembly, make the preparations for the conferences of revision of the provisions of the Agreement other than Articles 10 to 13.

*(b)* The International Bureau may consult with intergovernmental and international non-governmental organizations concerning preparations for conferences of revision.

*(c)* The Director General and persons designated by him shall take part, without the right to vote, in the discussions at those conferences.

(4) The International Bureau shall carry out any other tasks assigned to it.

## Article 12

(1)

(a) The Special Union shall have a budget.

(b) The budget of the Special Union shall include the income and expenses proper to the Special Union, its contribution to the budget of expenses common to the Unions, and, where applicable, the sum made available to the budget of the Conference of the Organization.

(c) Expenses not attributable exclusively to the Special Union but also to one or more other Unions administered by the Organization shall be considered as expenses common to the Unions. The share of the Special Union in such common expenses shall be in proportion to the interest the Special Union has in them.

(2) The budget of the Special Union shall be established with due regard to the requirements of coordination with the budgets of the other Unions administered by the Organization.

(3) The budget of the Special Union shall be financed from the following sources:

(i) international registration fees and other fees and charges due for other services rendered by the International Bureau in relation to the Special Union;

(ii) sale of, or royalties on, the publications of the International Bureau concerning the Special Union;

(iii) gifts, bequests, and subventions;

(iv) rents, interests, and other miscellaneous income.

(4)

(a) The amounts of the fees referred to in Article 8(2) and other fees relating to international registration shall be fixed by the Assembly on the proposal of the Director General.

(b) The amounts of such fees shall be so fixed that the revenues of the Special Union from fees, other than the supplementary and complementary fees referred to in Article 8(2)(b) and (cu), and other sources shall be at least sufficient to cover the expenses of the International Bureau concerning the Special Union.

(c) If the budget is not adopted before the beginning of a new financial period, it shall be at the same level as the budget of the previous year, as provided in the financial regulations.

(5) Subject to the provisions of paragraph (4)(a), the amount of fees and charges due for other services rendered by the International Bureau in relation to the Special Union shall be established, and shall be reported to the Assembly, by the Director General.

(6)

(a) The Special Union shall have a working capital fund which shall be constituted by a single payment made by each country of the Special Union. If the fund becomes insufficient, the Assembly shall decide to increase it.

(b) The amount of the initial payment of each country to the said fund or of its participation in the increase thereof shall be a proportion of the contribution of that country as a member of the Paris Union for the Protection of Industrial Property to the budget of the said Union for the year in which the fund is established or the decision to increase it is made.

(c) The proportion and the terms of payment shall be fixed by the Assembly on the proposal of the Director General and after it has beard the advice of the Coordination Committee of the Organization.

(d) As long as the Assembly authorizes the use of the reserve fund of the Special Union as a working capital fund, the Assembly may suspend the application of the provisions of subparagraphs (a), (b), and (c).

(7)

(a) In the headquarters agreement concluded with the country on the territory of which the Organization has its headquarters, it shall be provided that, whenever the working capital fund is insufficient, such country shall grant advances. The amount of those advances and the conditions on which they are granted shall be the subject of separate agreements, in each case, between such country and the Organization.

(b) The country referred to in subparagraph (a) and the Organization shall each have the right to denounce the obligation to grant advances, by written notification. Denunciation shall take effect three years after the end of the year in which it has been notified.

(8) The auditing of the accounts shall be effected by one or more of the countries of the Special Union or by external auditors, as provided in the financial regulations. They shall be designated, with their agreement, by the Assembly.

## Article 13

(1) Proposals for the amendment of Articles 10, 11, 12, and the present Article, may be initiated by any country member of the Assembly, or by the Director General. Such proposals shall be communicated by the Director General to the member countries of the Assembly at least six months in advance of their consideration by the Assembly.

(2) Amendments to the Articles referred to in paragraph (1) shall be adopted by the Assembly. Adoption shall require three-fourths of the votes cast, provided that any amendment to Article 10, and to the present paragraph, shall require four-fifths of the votes cast.

(3) Any amendment to the Articles referred to in paragraph (1) shall enter into force one month after written notifications of acceptance, effected in accordance with their respective constitutional processes, have been received by the Director General from three-fourths of the countries members of the Assembly at the time it adopted the amendment. Any amendment to the said Articles thus accepted shall bind all the countries which are members of the Assembly at the time the amendment enters into force, or which become members thereof at a subsequent date.

## Article 14

(1) Any country of the Special Union which has signed this Act may ratify it, and, if it has not signed it, may accede to it.

(2)

(a) Any country outside the Special Union which is party to the Paris Convention for the Protection of Industrial Property may accede to this Act and thereby become a member of the Special Union.

(b) As soon as the International Bureau is informed that such a country has acceded to this Act, it shall address to the Office of that country, in accordance with Article 3, a collective notification of the marks which, at that time, enjoy international protection.

(c) Such notification shall, of itself, ensure to the said marks the benefits of the foregoing provisions in the territory of the said country, and shall mark the commencement of the period of one year during which the Office concerned may make the declaration provided for in Article 5.

(d) However, any such country may, in acceding to this Act, declare that, except in the case of international marks which have already been the subject in that country of an earlier identical national registration still in force, and which shall be immediately recognized upon the request of the interested parties, application of this Act shall be limited to marks registered from the date on which its accession enters into force.

(e) Such declaration shall dispense the International Bureau from making the collective notification referred to above. The International Bureau shall notify only those marks in respect of which it receives, within a period of one year from the accession of the new country, a request, with the necessary particulars, to take advantage of the exception provided for in subparagraph (d).

(f) The International Bureau shall not make the collective notification to such countries as declare, in acceding to this Act, that they are availing themselves of the right provided for in Article 35*bis*. The said countries may also declare at the same time that the application of this Act shall be limited to marks registered from the day on which their accessions enter into force; however, such limitation shall not affect international marks which have already been the subject of an earlier identical national registration in those countries, and which could give rise to requests for extension of protection made and notified in accordance with Articles 3*ter* and 8(2)(c).

(g) Registrations of marks which have been the subject of one of the notifications provided for in this paragraph shall be regarded as replacing registrations effected direct in the new contracting country before the date of entry into force of its accession.

(3) Instruments of ratification and accession shall be deposited with the Director General.

(4)

(a) With respect to the first five countries which have deposited their instruments of ratification or accession, this Act shall enter into force three months after the deposit of the fifth such instrument.

(b) With respect to any other country, this Act shall enter into force three months after the date on which its ratification or accession has been notified by the Director General, unless a subsequent date has been indicated in the instrument of ratification or accession. In the latter case, this Act shall enter into force with respect to that country on the date thus indicated.

(5) Ratification or accession shall automatically entail acceptance of all the clauses and admission to all the advantages of this Act.

(6) After the entry into force of this Act, a country may accede to the Nice Act of June 15, 1957, only in conjunction with ratification of, or accession to, this Act. Accession to Acts earlier than the Nice Act shall not be permitted, not even in conjunction with ratification of, or accession to, this Act.

(7) The provisions of Article 24 of the Paris Convention for the Protection of Industrial Property shall apply to this Agreement.

## Article 15

(1) This Agreement shall remain in force without limitation as to time.

(2) Any country may denounce this Act by notification addressed to the Director General. Such denunciation shall constitute also denunciation of all earlier Acts and shall affect only the country making it, the Agreement remaining in full force and effect as regards the other countries of the Special Union.

(3) Denunciation shall take effect one year after the day on which the Director General has received the notification.

(4) The right of denunciation provided for by this Article shall not be exercised by any country before the expiration of five years from the date upon which it becomes a member of the Special Union.

(5) International marks registered up to the date on which denunciation becomes effective, and not refused within the period of one year provided for in Article 5, shall continue, throughout the period of international protection, to enjoy the same protection as if they had been filed direct in the denouncing country.

### Article 16

(1)

    *(a)* This Act shall, as regards the relations between the countries of the Special Union by which it has been ratified or acceded to, replace, as from the day on which it enters into force with respect to them, the Madrid Agreement of 1891, in its texts earlier than this Act.

    *(b)* However, any country of the Special Union which has ratified or acceded to this Act shall remain bound by the earlier texts which it has not previously denounced by virtue of Article 12(4) of the Nice Act of June 15, 1957, as regards its relations with countries which have not ratified or acceded to this Act.

(2) Countries outside the Special Union which become party to this Act shall apply it to international registrations effected at the International Bureau through the intermediary of the national Office of any country of the Special Union not party to this Act, provided that such registrations satisfy, with respect to the said countries, the requirements of this Act. With regard to international registrations effected at the International Bureau through the intermediary of the national Offices of the said countries outside the Special Union which become party to this Act, such countries recognize that the aforesaid country of the Special Union may demand compliance with the requirements of the most recent Act to which it is party.

### Article 17

(1)

    *(a)* This Act shall be signed in a single copy in the French language and shall be deposited with the Government of Sweden.

    *(b)* Official texts shall be established by the Director General, after consultation with the interested Governments, in such other languages as the Assembly may designate.

(2) This Act shall remain open for signature at Stockholm until January 13, 1968.

(3) The Director General shall transmit two copies, certified by the Government of Sweden, of the signed text of this Act to the Governments of all countries of the Special Union and, on request, to the Government of any other country.

(4) The Director General shall register this Act with the Secretariat of the United Nations.

(5) The Director General shall notify the Governments of all countries of the Special Union of signatures, deposits of instruments of ratification or accession and any declarations included in such instruments, entry into force of any provisions of this Act, notifications of denunciation, and notifications pursuant to Articles 3bis, 9quater, 13, 14(7), and 15(2).

### Article 18

(1) Until the first Director General assumes office, references in this Act to the International Bureau of the Organization or to the Director General shall be construed as references to the Bureau of the Union established by the Paris Convention for the Protection of Industrial Property or its Director, respectively.

(2) Countries of the Special Union not having ratified or acceded to this Act may, until five years after the entry into force of the Convention establishing the Organization, exercise, if they so desire, the rights provided for under Articles 10 to 13 of this Act as if they were bound by those

Articles. Any country desiring to exercise such rights shall give written notification to that effect to the Director General; such notification shall be effective from the date of its receipt. Such countries shall be deemed to be members of the Assembly until the expiration of the said period.

# 41. PROTOCOL RELATING TO THE MADRID AGREEMENT CONCERNING THE INTERNATIONAL REGISTRATION OF MARKS

Signed at Madrid on June 28, 1989, amended on
October 3, 2006 and on November 12, 2007

## Article 1

### Membership in the Madrid Union

The States party to this Protocol (hereinafter referred to as "the Contracting States"), even where they are not party to the Madrid Agreement Concerning the International Registration of Marks as revised at Stockholm in 1967 and as amended in 1979 (hereinafter referred to as "the Madrid (Stockholm) Agreement"), and the organizations referred to in Article 14(1)(b) which are party to this Protocol (hereinafter referred to as "the Contracting Organizations") shall be members of the same Union of which countries party to the Madrid (Stockholm) Agreement are members. Any reference in this Protocol to "Contracting Parties" shall be construed as a reference to both Contracting States and Contracting Organizations.

## Article 2

### Securing Protection through International Registration

(1) Where an application for the registration of a mark has been filed with the Office of a Contracting Party, or where a mark has been registered in the register of the Office of a Contracting Party, the person in whose name that application (hereinafter referred to as "the basic application") or that registration (hereinafter referred to as "the basic registration") stands may, subject to the provisions of this Protocol, secure protection for his mark in the territory of the Contracting Parties, by obtaining the registration of that mark in the register of the International Bureau of the World Intellectual Property Organization (hereinafter referred to as "the international registration," "the International Register," "the International Bureau" and "the Organization," respectively), provided that,

(i) where the basic application has been filed with the Office of a Contracting State or where the basic registration has been made by such an Office, the person in whose name that application or registration stands is a national of that Contracting State, or is domiciled, or has a real and effective industrial or commercial establishment, in the said Contracting State,

(ii) where the basic application has been filed with the Office of a Contracting Organization or where the basic registration has been made by such an Office, the person in whose name that application or registration stands is a national of a State member of that Contracting Organization, or is domiciled, or has a real and effective industrial or commercial establishment, in the territory of the said Contracting Organization.

(2) The application for international registration (hereinafter referred to as "the international application") shall be filed with the International Bureau through the intermediary of the Office with which the basic application was filed or by which the basic registration was made (hereinafter referred to as "the Office of origin"), as the case may be.

(3) Any reference in this Protocol to an "Office" or an "Office of a Contracting Party" shall be construed as a reference to the office that is in charge, on behalf of a Contracting Party, of the registration of marks, and any reference in this Protocol to "marks" shall be construed as a reference to trademarks and service marks.

(4) For the purposes of this Protocol, "territory of a Contracting Party" means, where the Contracting Party is a State, the territory of that State and, where the Contracting Party is an intergovernmental organization, the territory in which the constituting treaty of that intergovernmental organization applies.

## Article 3

### International Application

(1) Every international application under this Protocol shall be presented on the form prescribed by the Regulations. The Office of origin shall certify that the particulars appearing in the international application correspond to the particulars appearing, at the time of the certification, in the basic application or basic registration, as the case may be. Furthermore, the said Office shall indicate,

(i) in the case of a basic application, the date and number of that application,

(ii) in the case of a basic registration, the date and number of that registration as well as the date and number of the application from which the basic registration resulted.

The Office of origin shall also indicate the date of the international application.

(2) The applicant must indicate the goods and services in respect of which protection of the mark is claimed and also, if possible, the corresponding class or classes according to the classification established by the Nice Agreement Concerning the International Classification of Goods and Services for the Purposes of the Registration of Marks. If the applicant does not give such indication, the International Bureau shall classify the goods and services in the appropriate classes of the said classification. The indication of classes given by the applicant shall be subject to control by the International Bureau, which shall exercise the said control in association with the Office of origin. In the event of disagreement between the said Office and the International Bureau, the opinion of the latter shall prevail.

(3) If the applicant claims color as a distinctive feature of his mark, he shall be required

(i) to state the fact, and to file with his international application a notice specifying the color or the combination of colors claimed;

(ii) to append to his international application copies in color of the said mark, which shall be attached to the notifications given by the International Bureau; the number of such copies shall be fixed by the Regulations.

(4) The International Bureau shall register immediately the marks filed in accordance with Article 2. The international registration shall bear the date on which the international application was received in the Office of origin, provided that the international application has been received by the International Bureau within a period of two months from that date. If the international application has not been received within that period, the international registration shall bear the date on which the said international application was received by the International Bureau. The International Bureau shall notify the international registration without delay to the Offices concerned. Marks registered in the International Register shall be published in a periodical gazette issued by the International Bureau, on the basis of the particulars contained in the international application.

(5) With a view to the publicity to be given to marks registered in the International Register, each Office shall receive from the International Bureau a number of copies of the said gazette free of charge and a number of copies at a reduced price, under the conditions fixed by the Assembly referred to in Article 10 (hereinafter referred to as "the Assembly"). Such publicity shall be deemed to be sufficient for the purposes of all the Contracting Parties, and no other publicity may be required of the holder of the international registration.

## Article 3*bis*

### Territorial Effect

The protection resulting from the international registration shall extend to any Contracting Party only at the request of the person who files the international application or who is the holder of the international registration. However, no such request can be made with respect to the Contracting Party whose Office is the Office of origin.

## Article 3*ter*

### Request for "Territorial Extension"

(1) Any request for extension of the protection resulting from the international registration to any Contracting Party shall be specially mentioned in the international application.

(2) A request for territorial extension may also be made subsequently to the international registration. Any such request shall be presented on the form prescribed by the Regulations. It shall be immediately recorded by the International Bureau, which shall notify such recordal without delay to the Office or Offices concerned. Such recordal shall be published in the periodical gazette of the International Bureau. Such territorial extension shall be effective from the date on which it has been recorded in the International Register; it shall cease to be valid on the expiry of the international registration to which it relates.

## Article 4

### Effects of International Registration

(1) (a) From the date of the registration or recordal effected in accordance with the provisions of Articles 3 and 3*ter*, the protection of the mark in each of the Contracting Parties concerned shall be the same as if the mark had been deposited direct with the Office of that Contracting Party. If no refusal has been notified to the International Bureau in accordance with Article 5(1) and 5(2) or if a refusal notified in accordance with the said Article has been withdrawn subsequently, the protection of the mark in the Contracting Party concerned shall, as from the said date, be the same as if the mark had been registered by the Office of that Contracting Party.

(b) The indication of classes of goods and services provided for in Article 3 shall not bind the Contracting Parties with regard to the determination of the scope of the protection of the mark.

(2) Every international registration shall enjoy the right of priority provided for by Article 4 of the Paris Convention for the Protection of Industrial Property, without it being necessary to comply with the formalities prescribed in Section 4.D.

## Article 4*bis*

### Replacement of a National or Regional Registration by an International Registration

(1) Where a mark that is the subject of a national or regional registration in the Office of a Contracting Party is also the subject of an international registration and both registrations stand in the name of the same person, the international registration is deemed to replace the national or regional registration, without prejudice to any rights acquired by virtue of the latter, provided that

(i) the protection resulting from the international registration extends to the said Contracting Party under Article 3*ter*(1) or 3*ter*(2),

(ii) all the goods and services listed in the national or regional registration are also listed in the international registration in respect of the said Contracting Party,

(iii) such extension takes effect after the date of the national or regional registration.

(2) The Office referred to in paragraph (1) shall, upon request, be required to take note in its register of the international registration.

## Article 5

### Refusal and Invalidation of Effects of International Registration in Respect of Certain Contracting Parties

(1) Where the applicable legislation so authorizes, any Office of a Contracting Party which has been notified by the International Bureau of an extension to that Contracting Party, under Article 3*ter*(1) or 3*ter*(2), of the protection resulting from the international registration shall have the right to declare in a notification of refusal that protection cannot be granted in the said Contracting Party to the mark which is the subject of such extension. Any such refusal can be based only on the grounds which would apply, under the Paris Convention for the Protection of Industrial Property, in the case of a mark deposited direct with the Office which notifies the refusal. However, protection may not be refused, even partially, by reason only that the applicable legislation would permit registration only in a limited number of classes or for a limited number of goods or services.

(2) (a) Any Office wishing to exercise such right shall notify its refusal to the International Bureau, together with a statement of all grounds, within the period prescribed by the law applicable to that Office and at the latest, subject to subparagraphs (b) and (c), before the expiry of one year from the date on which the notification of the extension referred to in paragraph (1) has been sent to that Office by the International Bureau.

(b) Notwithstanding subparagraph (a), any Contracting Party may declare that, for international registrations made under this Protocol, the time limit of one year referred to in subparagraph (a) is replaced by 18 months.

(c) Such declaration may also specify that, when a refusal of protection may result from an opposition to the granting of protection, such refusal may be notified by the Office of the said Contracting Party to the International Bureau after the expiry of the 18-month time limit. Such an Office may, with respect to any given international registration, notify a refusal of protection after the expiry of the 18-month time limit, but only if

(i) it has, before the expiry of the 18-month time limit, informed the International Bureau of the possibility that oppositions may be filed after the expiry of the 18-month time limit, and

(ii) the notification of the refusal based on an opposition is made within a time limit of not more than seven months from the date on which the opposition period begins; if the opposition period expires before this time limit of seven months, the notification must be made within a time limit of one month from the expiry of the opposition period.

(d) Any declaration under subparagraphs (b) or (c) may be made in the instruments referred to in Article 14(2), and the effective date of the declaration shall be the same as the date of entry into force of this Protocol with respect to the State or intergovernmental organization having made the declaration. Any such declaration may also be made later, in which case the declaration shall have effect three months after its receipt by the Director General of the Organization (hereinafter referred to as "the Director General"), or at any later date indicated in the declaration, in respect of any international registration whose date is the same as or is later than the effective date of the declaration.

(e) Upon the expiry of a period of ten years from the entry into force of this Protocol, the Assembly shall examine the operation of the system established by subparagraphs (a) to (d). Thereafter, the provisions of the said subparagraphs may be modified by a unanimous decision of the Assembly.

(3) The International Bureau shall, without delay, transmit one of the copies of the notification of refusal to the holder of the international registration. The said holder shall have the same remedies as if the mark had been deposited by him direct with the Office which has notified its refusal. Where the International Bureau has received information under paragraph (2)(c)(i), it shall, without delay, transmit the said information to the holder of the international registration.

(4) The grounds for refusing a mark shall be communicated by the International Bureau to any interested party who may so request.

(5) Any Office which has not notified, with respect to a given international registration, any provisional or final refusal to the International Bureau in accordance with paragraphs (1) and (2) shall, with respect to that international registration, lose the benefit of the right provided for in paragraph (1).

(6) Invalidation, by the competent authorities of a Contracting Party, of the effects, in the territory of that Contracting Party, of an international registration may not be pronounced without the holder of such international registration having, in good time, been afforded the opportunity of defending his rights. Invalidation shall be notified to the International Bureau.

## Article 5*bis*

### Documentary Evidence of Legitimacy of Use of Certain Elements of the Mark

Documentary evidence of the legitimacy of the use of certain elements incorporated in a mark, such as armorial bearings, escutcheons, portraits, honorary distinctions, titles, trade names, names of persons other than the name of the applicant, or other like inscriptions, which might be required by the Offices of the Contracting Parties shall be exempt from any legalization as well as from any certification other than that of the Office of origin.

## Article 5*ter*

### Copies of Entries in International Register; Searches for Anticipations; Extracts from International Register

(1) The International Bureau shall issue to any person applying therefor, upon the payment of a fee fixed by the Regulations, a copy of the entries in the International Register concerning a specific mark.

(2) The International Bureau may also, upon payment, undertake searches for anticipation's among marks that are the subject of international registrations.

(3) Extracts from the International Register requested with a view to their production in one of the Contracting Parties shall be exempt from any legalization.

## Article 6

### Period of Validity of International Registration; Dependence and Independence of International Registration

(1) Registration of a mark at the International Bureau is effected for ten years, with the possibility of renewal under the conditions specified in Article 7.

(2)   Upon expiry of a period of five years from the date of the international registration, such registration shall become independent of the basic application or the registration resulting therefrom, or of the basic registration, as the case may be, subject to the following provisions.

(3)   The protection resulting from the international registration, whether or not it has been the subject of a transfer, may no longer be invoked if, before the expiry of five years from the date of the international registration, the basic application or the registration resulting therefrom, or the basic registration, as the case may be, has been withdrawn, has lapsed, has been renounced or has been the subject of a final decision of rejection, revocation, cancellation or invalidation, in respect of all or some of the goods and services listed in the international registration. The same applies if

　　　(i)    an appeal against a decision refusing the effects of the basic application,

　　　(ii)   an action requesting the withdrawal of the basic application or the revocation, cancellation or invalidation of the registration resulting from the basic application or of the basic registration, or

　　　(iii)  an opposition to the basic application

results, after the expiry of the five-year period, in a final decision of rejection, revocation, cancellation or invalidation, or ordering the withdrawal, of the basic application, or the registration resulting therefrom, or the basic registration, as the case may be, provided that such appeal, action or opposition had begun before the expiry of the said period. The same also applies if the basic application is withdrawn, or the registration resulting from the basic application or the basic registration is renounced, after the expiry of the five-year period, provided that, at the time of the withdrawal or renunciation, the said application or registration was the subject of a proceeding referred to in item (i), (ii) or (iii) and that such proceeding had begun before the expiry of the said period.

(4)   The Office of origin shall, as prescribed in the Regulations, notify the International Bureau of the facts and decisions relevant under paragraph (3), and the International Bureau shall, as prescribed in the Regulations, notify the interested parties and effect any publication accordingly. The Office of origin shall, where applicable, request the International Bureau to cancel, to the extent applicable, the international registration, and the International Bureau shall proceed accordingly.

## Article 7

### Renewal of International Registration

(1)   Any international registration may be renewed for a period of ten years from the expiry of the preceding period, by the mere payment of the basic fee and, subject to Article 8(7), of the supplementary and complementary fees provided for in Article 8(2).

(2)   Renewal may not bring about any change in the international registration in its latest form.

(3)   Six months before the expiry of the term of protection, the International Bureau shall, by sending an unofficial notice, remind the holder of the international registration and his representative, if any, of the exact date of expiry.

(4)   Subject to the payment of a surcharge fixed by the Regulations, a period of grace of six months shall be allowed for renewal of the international registration.

## Article 8

### Fees for International Application and Registration

(1)   The Office of origin may fix, at its own discretion, and collect, for its own benefit, a fee which it may require from the applicant for international registration or from the holder of the

international registration in connection with the filing of the international application or the renewal of the international registration.

(2) Registration of a mark at the International Bureau shall be subject to the advance payment of an international fee which shall, subject to the provisions of paragraph (7)(a), include,

(i) a basic fee;

(ii) a supplementary fee for each class of the International Classification, beyond three, into which the goods or services to which the mark is applied will fall;

(iii) a complementary fee for any request for extension of protection under Article 3*ter*.

(3) However, the supplementary fee specified in paragraph (2)(ii) may, without prejudice to the date of the international registration, be paid within the period fixed by the Regulations if the number of classes of goods or services has been fixed or disputed by the International Bureau. If, upon expiry of the said period, the supplementary fee has not been paid or the list of goods or services has not been reduced to the required extent by the applicant, the international application shall be deemed to have been abandoned.

(4) The annual product of the various receipts from international registration, with the exception of the receipts derived from the fees mentioned in paragraph (2)(ii) and (2)(iii), shall be divided equally among the Contracting Parties by the International Bureau, after deduction of the expenses and charges necessitated by the implementation of this Protocol.

(5) The amounts derived from the supplementary fees provided for in paragraph (2)(ii) shall be divided, at the expiry of each year, among the interested Contracting Parties in proportion to the number of marks for which protection has been applied for in each of them during that year, this number being multiplied, in the case of Contracting Parties which make an examination, by a coefficient which shall be determined by the Regulations.

(6) The amounts derived from the complementary fees provided for in paragraph (2)(iii) shall be divided according to the same rules as those provided for in paragraph (5).

(7)

(a) Any Contracting Party may declare that, in connection with each international registration in which it is mentioned under Article 3*ter*, and in connection with the renewal of any such international registration, it wants to receive, instead of a share in the revenue produced by the supplementary and complementary fees, a fee (hereinafter referred to as "the individual fee") whose amount shall be indicated in the declaration, and can be changed in further declarations, but may not be higher than the equivalent of the amount which the said Contracting Party's Office would be entitled to receive from an applicant for a ten-year registration, or from the holder of a registration for a ten-year renewal of that registration, of the mark in the register of the said Office, the said amount being diminished by the savings resulting from the international procedure. Where such an individual fee is payable,

(i) no supplementary fees referred to in paragraph (2)(ii) shall be payable if only Contracting Parties which have made a declaration under this subparagraph are mentioned under Article 3*ter*, and

(ii) no complementary fee referred to in paragraph (2)(iii) shall be payable in respect of any Contracting Party which has made a declaration under this subparagraph.

(b) Any declaration under subparagraph (a) may be made in the instruments referred to in Article 14(2), and the effective date of the declaration shall be the same as the date of entry into force of this Protocol with respect to the State or intergovernmental organization having made the declaration. Any such declaration may also be made later, in which case the declaration shall have effect three months after its receipt by the Director General, or at any later date indicated in the declaration, in respect of any international registration whose date is the same as or is later than the effective date of the declaration.

## Article 9

### Recordal of Change in the Ownership
### of an International Registration

At the request of the person in whose name the international registration stands, or at the request of an interested Office made ex officio or at the request of an interested person, the International Bureau shall record in the International Register any change in the ownership of that registration, in respect of all or some of the Contracting Parties in whose territories the said registration has effect and in respect of all or some of the goods and services listed in the registration, provided that the new holder is a person who, under Article 2(1), is entitled to file international applications.

## Article 9*bis*

### Recordal of Certain Matters Concerning
### an International Registration

The International Bureau shall record in the International Register

(i)    any change in the name or address of the holder of the international registration,

(ii)   the appointment of a representative of the holder of the international registration and any other relevant fact concerning such representative,

(iii)  any limitation, in respect of all or some of the Contracting Parties, of the goods and services listed in the international registration,

(iv)   any renunciation, cancellation or invalidation of the international registration in respect of all or some of the Contracting Parties,

(v)    any other relevant fact, identified in the Regulations, concerning the rights in a mark that is the subject of an international registration.

## Article 9*ter*

### Fees for Certain Recordals

Any recordal under Article 9 or under Article 9bis may be subject to the payment of a fee.

## Article 9*quater*

### Common Office of Several Contracting States

(1)   If several Contracting States agree to effect the unification of their domestic legislations on marks, they may notify the Director General

(i)    that a common Office shall be substituted for the national Office of each of them, and

(ii)   that the whole of their respective territories shall be deemed to be a single State for the purposes of the application of all or part of the provisions preceding this Article as well as the provisions of Articles 9*quinquies* and 9*sexies*.

(2)   Such notification shall not take effect until three months after the date of the communication thereof by the Director General to the other Contracting Parties.

## Article 9*quinquies*

### Transformation of an International Registration
### into National or Regional Applications

Where, in the event that the international registration is cancelled at the request of the Office of origin under Article 6(4), in respect of all or some of the goods and services listed in the said registration, the person who was the holder of the international registration files an application for the registration of the same mark with the Office of any of the Contracting Parties in the territory of which the international registration had effect, that application shall be treated as if it had been filed on the date of the international registration according to Article 3(4) or on the date of recordal of the territorial extension according to Article 3ter(2) and, if the international registration enjoyed priority, shall enjoy the same priority, provided that

(i) such application is filed within three months from the date on which the international registration was cancelled,

(ii) the goods and services listed in the application are in fact covered by the list of goods and services contained in the international registration in respect of the Contracting Party concerned, and

(iii) such application complies with all the requirements of the applicable law, including the requirements concerning fees.

## Article 9*sexies*

### Relations Between States Party to both this Protocol and the Madrid (Stockholm) Agreement

(1) (a) This Protocol alone shall be applicable as regards the mutual relations of States party to both this Protocol and the Madrid (Stockholm) Agreement.

(b) Notwithstanding subparagraph (a), a declaration made under Article 5(2)(b), Article 5(2)(c) or Article 8(7) of this Protocol, by a State party to both this Protocol and the Madrid (Stockholm) Agreement, shall have no effect in the relations with another State party to both this Protocol and the Madrid (Stockholm) Agreement.

(2) The Assembly shall, after the expiry of a period of three years from September 1, 2008, review the application of paragraph (1)(b) and may, at any time thereafter, either repeal it or restrict its scope, by a three-fourths majority. In the vote of the Assembly, only those States which are party to both the Madrid (Stockholm) Agreement and this Protocol shall have the right to participate.

## Article 10

### Assembly

(1) (a) The Contracting Parties shall be members of the same Assembly as the countries party to the Madrid (Stockholm) Agreement.

(b) Each Contracting Party shall be represented in that Assembly by one delegate, who may be assisted by alternate delegates, advisors, and experts.

(c) The expenses of each delegation shall be borne by the Contracting Party which has appointed it, except for the travel expenses and the subsistence allowance of one delegate for each Contracting Party, which shall be paid from the funds of the Union.

(2) The Assembly shall, in addition to the functions which it has under the Madrid (Stockholm) Agreement, also

(i) deal with all matters concerning the implementation of this Protocol;

(ii) give directions to the International Bureau concerning the preparation for conferences of revision of this Protocol, due account being taken of any comments made by those countries of the Union which are not party to this Protocol;

(iii) adopt and modify the provisions of the Regulations concerning the implementation of this Protocol;

(iv) perform such other functions as are appropriate under this Protocol.

(3)   (a)   Each Contracting Party shall have one vote in the Assembly. On matters concerning only countries that are party to the Madrid (Stockholm) Agreement, Contracting Parties that are not party to the said Agreement shall not have the right to vote, whereas, on matters concerning only Contracting Parties, only the latter shall have the right to vote.

     (b)   One-half of the members of the Assembly which have the right to vote on a given matter shall constitute the quorum for the purposes of the vote on that matter.

     (c)   Notwithstanding the provisions of subparagraph (b), if, in any session, the number of the members of the Assembly having the right to vote on a given matter which are represented is less than one-half but equal to or more than one-third of the members of the Assembly having the right to vote on that matter, the Assembly may make decisions but, with the exception of decisions concerning its own procedure, all such decisions shall take effect only if the conditions set forth hereinafter are fulfilled. The International Bureau shall communicate the said decisions to the members of the Assembly having the right to vote on the said matter which were not represented and shall invite them to express in writing their vote or abstention within a period of three months from the date of the communication. If, at the expiry of this period, the number of such members having thus expressed their vote or abstention attains the number of the members which was lacking for attaining the quorum in the session itself, such decisions shall take effect provided that at the same time the required majority still obtains.

     (d)   Subject to the provisions of Articles 5(2)(e), 9*sexies*(2), 12 and 13(2), the decisions of the Assembly shall require two-thirds of the votes cast.

     (e)   Abstentions shall not be considered as votes.

     (f)   A delegate may represent, and vote in the name of, one member of the Assembly only.

(4)   In addition to meeting in ordinary sessions and extraordinary sessions as provided for by the Madrid (Stockholm) Agreement, the Assembly shall meet in extraordinary session upon convocation by the Director General, at the request of one-fourth of the members of the Assembly having the right to vote on the matters proposed to be included in the agenda of the session. The agenda of such an extraordinary session shall be prepared by the Director General.

## Article 11

### International Bureau

(1)   International registration and related duties, as well as all other administrative tasks, under or concerning this Protocol, shall be performed by the International Bureau.

(2)   (a)   The International Bureau shall, in accordance with the directions of the Assembly, make the preparations for the conferences of revision of this Protocol.

     (b)   The International Bureau may consult with intergovernmental and international non-governmental organizations concerning preparations for such conferences of revision.

     (c)   The Director General and persons designated by him shall take part, without the right to vote, in the discussions at such conferences of revision.

(3)   The International Bureau shall carry out any other tasks assigned to it in relation to this Protocol.

## Article 12

### Finances

As far as Contracting Parties are concerned, the finances of the Union shall be governed by the same provisions as those contained in Article 12 of the Madrid (Stockholm) Agreement, provided that any reference to Article 8 of the said Agreement shall be deemed to be a reference to Article 8 of this Protocol. Furthermore, for the purposes of Article 12(6)(b) of the said Agreement, Contracting

Organizations shall, subject to a unanimous decision to the contrary by the Assembly, be considered to belong to contribution class I (one) under the Paris Convention for the Protection of Industrial Property.

## Article 13

### Amendment of Certain Articles of the Protocol

(1) Proposals for the amendment of Articles 10, 11, 12, and the present Article, may be initiated by any Contracting Party, or by the Director General. Such proposals shall be communicated by the Director General to the Contracting Parties at least six months in advance of their consideration by the Assembly.

(2) Amendments to the Articles referred to in paragraph (1) shall be adopted by the Assembly. Adoption shall require three-fourths of the votes cast, provided that any amendment to Article 10, and to the present paragraph, shall require four-fifths of the votes cast.

(3) Any amendment to the Articles referred to in paragraph (1) shall enter into force one month after written notifications of acceptance, effected in accordance with their respective constitutional processes, have been received by the Director General from three-fourths of those States and intergovernmental organizations which, at the time the amendment was adopted, were members of the Assembly and had the right to vote on the amendment. Any amendment to the said Articles thus accepted shall bind all the States and intergovernmental organizations which are Contracting Parties at the time the amendment enters into force, or which become Contracting Parties at a subsequent date.

## Article 14

### Becoming Party to the Protocol; Entry into Force

(1) (a) Any State that is a party to the Paris Convention for the Protection of Industrial Property may become party to this Protocol.

(b) Furthermore, any intergovernmental organization may also become party to this Protocol where the following conditions are fulfilled:

(i) at least one of the member States of that organization is a party to the Paris Convention for the Protection of Industrial Property;

(ii) that organization has a regional Office for the purposes of registering marks with effect in the territory of the organization, provided that such Office is not the subject of a notification under Article 9*quater*.

(2) Any State or organization referred to in paragraph (1) may sign this Protocol. Any such State or organization may, if it has signed this Protocol, deposit an instrument of ratification, acceptance or approval of this Protocol or, if it has not signed this Protocol, deposit an instrument of accession to this Protocol.

(3) The instruments referred to in paragraph (2) shall be deposited with the Director General.

(4) (a) This Protocol shall enter into force three months after four instruments of ratification, acceptance, approval or accession have been deposited, provided that at least one of those instruments has been deposited by a country party to the Madrid (Stockholm) Agreement and at least one other of those instruments has been deposited by a State not party to the Madrid (Stockholm) Agreement or by any of the organizations referred to in paragraph (1)(b).

(b) With respect to any other State or organization referred to in paragraph (1), this Protocol shall enter into force three months after the date on which its ratification, acceptance, approval or accession has been notified by the Director General.

(5)  Any State or organization referred to in paragraph (1) may, when depositing its instrument of ratification, acceptance or approval of, or accession to, this Protocol, declare that the protection resulting from any international registration effected under this Protocol before the date of entry into force of this Protocol with respect to it cannot be extended to it.

## Article 15

### Denunciation

(1)  This Protocol shall remain in force without limitation as to time.

(2)  Any Contracting Party may denounce this Protocol by notification addressed to the Director General.

(3)  Denunciation shall take effect one year after the day on which the Director General has received the notification.

(4)  The right of denunciation provided for by this Article shall not be exercised by any Contracting Party before the expiry of five years from the date upon which this Protocol entered into force with respect to that Contracting Party.

(5)  (a)  Where a mark is the subject of an international registration having effect in the denouncing State or intergovernmental organization at the date on which the denunciation becomes effective, the holder of such registration may file an application for the registration of the same mark with the Office of the denouncing State or intergovernmental organization, which shall be treated as if it had been filed on the date of the international registration according to Article 3(4) or on the date of recordal of the territorial extension according to Article 3*ter*(2) and, if the international registration enjoyed priority, enjoy the same priority, provided that

   (i)  such application is filed within two years from the date on which the denunciation became effective,

   (ii)  the goods and services listed in the application are in fact covered by the list of goods and services contained in the international registration in respect of the denouncing State or intergovernmental organization, and

   (iii)  such application complies with all the requirements of the applicable law, including the requirements concerning fees.

   (b)  The provisions of subparagraph (a) shall also apply in respect of any mark that is the subject of an international registration having effect in Contracting Parties other than the denouncing State or intergovernmental organization at the date on which denunciation becomes effective and whose holder, because of the denunciation, is no longer entitled to file international applications under Article 2(1).

## Article 16

### Signature; Languages; Depositary Functions

(1)

   (a)  This Protocol shall be signed in a single copy in the English, French and Spanish languages, and shall be deposited with the Director General when it ceases to be open for signature at Madrid. The texts in the three languages shall be equally authentic.

   (b)  Official texts of this Protocol shall be established by the Director General, after consultation with the interested governments and organizations, in the Arabic, Chinese, German, Italian, Japanese, Portuguese and Russian languages, and in such other languages as the Assembly may designate.

(2) This Protocol shall remain open for signature at Madrid until December 31, 1989.

(3) The Director General shall transmit two copies, certified by the Government of Spain, of the signed texts of this Protocol to all States and intergovernmental organizations that may become party to this Protocol.

(4) The Director General shall register this Protocol with the Secretariat of the United Nations.

(5) The Director General shall notify all States and international organizations that may become or are party to this Protocol of signatures, deposits of instruments of ratification, acceptance, approval or accession, the entry into force of this Protocol and any amendment thereto, any notification of denunciation and any declaration provided for in this Protocol.

# 42. PARTIES TO THE MADRID AGREEMENT AND THE MADRID PROTOCOL*

Madrid Agreement Concerning the International Registration of
Marks Madrid Agreement (Marks) (1891), revised at Brussels (1900),
Washington (1911), The Hague (1925), London (1934), Nice (1957)
and Stockholm (1967), and amended in 1979 and Protocol Relating
to the Madrid Agreement Concerning the International
Registration of Marks Madrid Protocol (1989),
amended in 2006 and 2007
(Madrid Union)[1]

**Status on May 4, 2021**

| State/IGO | Date on which State became party to the Madrid Agreement[2] | Date on which State/IGO became party to the Madrid Protocol (1989) |
|---|---|---|
| Afghanistan | – | June 26, 2018 |
| African Intellectual Property Organization (OAPI) | – | March 5, 2015[5,6] |
| Albania | October 4, 1995 | July 30, 2003 |
| Algeria | July 5, 1972 | October 31, 2015[5] |
| Antigua and Barbuda | – | March 17, 2000[5,6] |
| Armenia | December 25, 1991 | October 19, 2000[6,10] |
| Australia | – | July 11, 2001[5,6] |
| Austria | January 1, 1909 | April 13, 1999 |
| Azerbaijan | December 25, 1995 | April 15, 2007 |
| Bahrain | – | December 15, 2005[10] |
| Belarus | December 25, 1991 | January 18, 2002[6,10] |
| Belgium | July 15, 1892[3] | April 1, 1998[3,6] |
| Bhutan | August 4, 2000 | August 4, 2000 |
| Bosnia and Herzegovina | March 1, 1992 | January 27, 2009 |
| Botswana | – | December 5, 2006 |
| Brazil | – | October 2, 2019[5,6,8] |
| Brunei Darussalam | – | January 6, 2017[5,6] |
| Bulgaria | August 1, 1985 | October 2, 2001[6] |
| Cambodia | – | June 5, 2015[5,6] |
| Canada | – | June 17, 2019[5,6] |
| China | October 4, 1989[4] | December 1, 1995[4,5] |
| Colombia | – | August 29, 2012[5,6] |
| Croatia | October 8, 1991 | January 23, 2004 |
| Cuba | December 6, 1989 | December 26, 1995 |

---

# PARTIES TO THE MADRID AGREEMENT & PROTOCOL

| State/IGO | Date on which State became party to the Madrid Agreement[2] | Date on which State/IGO became party to the Madrid Protocol (1989) |
|---|---|---|
| Cyprus | November 4, 2003 | November 4, 2003[5] |
| Czech Republic | January 1, 1993 | September 25, 1996 |
| Democratic People's Republic of Korea | June 10, 1980 | October 3, 1996 |
| Denmark | – | February 13, 1996[5,6,7] |
| Egypt | July 1, 1952 | September 3, 2009 |
| Estonia | – | November 18, 1998[5,6,8] |
| Eswatini | December 14, 1998 | December 14, 1998 |
| European Union | – | October 1, 2004[6,10] |
| Finland | – | April 1, 1996[5,6] |
| France | July 15, 1892[9] | November 7, 1997[9] |
| Gambia | – | December 18, 2015[5,6] |
| Georgia | – | August 20, 1998[6,10] |
| Germany | December 1, 1922 | March 20, 1996 |
| Ghana | – | September 16, 2008[5,6] |
| Greece | – | August 10, 2000[5,6] |
| Hungary | January 1, 1909 | October 3, 1997 |
| Iceland | – | April 15, 1997[6,10] |
| India | – | July 8, 2013[5,6,8] |
| Indonesia | – | January 2, 2018[6,10] |
| Iran (Islamic Republic of) | December 25, 2003 | December 25, 2003[5] |
| Ireland | – | October 19, 2001[5,6] |
| Israel | – | September 1, 2010[5,6] |
| Italy | October 15, 1894 | April 17, 2000[5,6] |
| Japan | – | March 14, 2000[6,10] |
| Kazakhstan | December 25, 1991 | December 8, 2010 |
| Kenya | June 26, 1998 | June 26, 1998[5,6] |
| Kyrgyzstan | December 25, 1991 | June 17, 2004[6] |
| Lao People's Democratic Republic | – | March 7, 2016[6,10] |
| Latvia | January 1, 1995 | January 5, 2000 |
| Lesotho | February 12, 1999 | February 12, 1999 |
| Liberia | December 25, 1995 | December 11, 2009 |
| Liechtenstein | July 14, 1933 | March 17, 1998 |
| Lithuania | – | November 15, 1997[5] |
| Luxembourg | September 1, 1924[3] | April 1, 1998[3,6] |
| Madagascar | – | April 28, 2008[10] |
| Malawi | – | December 25, 2018[5] |
| Malaysia | – | December 27, 2019[5,6] |
| Mexico | – | February 19, 2013[6,10] |
| Monaco | April 29, 1956 | September 27, 1996 |

424

| State/IGO | Date on which State became party to the Madrid Agreement[2] | Date on which State/IGO became party to the Madrid Protocol (1989) |
|---|---|---|
| Mongolia | April 21, 1985 | June 16, 2001 |
| Montenegro | June 3, 2006 | June 3, 2006 |
| Morocco | July 30, 1917 | October 8, 1999[6] |
| Mozambique | October 7, 1998 | October 7, 1998 |
| Namibia | June 30, 2004 | June 30, 2004[8] |
| Netherlands | March 1, 1893[3,11] | April 1, 1998[3,6,11] |
| New Zealand | – | December 10, 2012[5,6,12] |
| North Macedonia | September 8, 1991 | August 30, 2002 |
| Norway | – | March 29, 1996[5,6] |
| Oman | – | October 16, 2007[10] |
| Pakistan | – | May 24, 2021[5,6] |
| Philippines | – | July 25, 2012[5,6,8] |
| Poland | March 18, 1991 | March 4, 1997[10] |
| Portugal | October 31, 1893 | March 20, 1997 |
| Republic of Korea | – | April 10, 2003[5,6] |
| Republic of Moldova | December 25, 1991 | December 1, 1997[6] |
| Romania | October 6, 1920 | July 28, 1998 |
| Russian Federation | July 1, 1976[13] | June 10, 1997 |
| Rwanda | – | August 17, 2013 |
| Samoa | – | March 4, 2019[5,6] |
| San Marino | September 25, 1960 | September 12, 2007[6,10] |
| Sao Tome and Principe | – | December 8, 2008 |
| Serbia[14] | April 27, 1992 | February 17, 1998 |
| Sierra Leone | June 17, 1997 | December 28, 1999 |
| Singapore | – | October 31, 2000[5,6] |
| Slovakia | January 1, 1993 | September 13, 1997[10] |
| Slovenia | June 25, 1991 | March 12, 1998 |
| Spain | July 15, 1892 | December 1, 1995 |
| Sudan | May 16, 1984 | February 16, 2010 |
| Sweden | – | December 1, 1995[5,6] |
| Switzerland | July 15, 1892 | May 1, 1997[6,10] |
| Syrian Arab Republic | – | August 5, 2004[5] |
| Tajikistan | December 25, 1991 | June 30, 2011[6,10] |
| Thailand | – | November 7, 2017[5,6] |
| Trinidad and Tobago | – | January 12, 2021[5,6] |
| Tunisia | – | October 16, 2013[5,6] |
| Turkey | – | January 1, 1999[5,6] |
| Turkmenistan | – | September 28, 1999[6,10] |
| Ukraine | December 25, 1991 | December 29, 2000[5,6] |

## PARTIES TO THE MADRID AGREEMENT & PROTOCOL

| State/IGO | Date on which State became party to the Madrid Agreement[2] | Date on which State/IGO became party to the Madrid Protocol (1989) |
|---|---|---|
| United Kingdom | – | December 1, 1995[5,6,15,16] |
| United States of America | – | November 2, 2003[5,6] |
| Uzbekistan | – | December 27, 2006[6,10] |
| Viet Nam | March 8, 1949 | July 11, 2006[6] |
| Zambia | – | November 15, 2001[6] |
| Zimbabwe | – | March 11, 2015[5,6] |
| Total: (108) | (55) | (108) |

[1]  The Madrid Union is composed of the States party to the Madrid Agreement and the Contracting Parties to the Madrid Protocol.

[2]  All the States party to the Madrid Agreement have declared, under Article 3bis of the Nice or Stockholm Act, that the protection arising from international registration shall not extend to them unless the proprietor of the mark so requests.

[3]  The territories of Belgium, Luxembourg and the Kingdom of the Netherlands in Europe are to be deemed a single country, for the application of the Madrid Agreement as from January 1, 1971, and for the application of the Protocol as from April 1, 1998.

[4]  Not applicable to either Hong Kong, China or Macao, China.

[5]  In accordance with Article 5(2)(b) and (c) of the Protocol, this Contracting Party has declared that the time limit to notify a refusal of protection shall be 18 months and that, where a refusal of protection results from an opposition to the granting of protection, such refusal may be notified after the expiry of the 18-month time limit.

[6]  In accordance with Article 8(7)(a) of the Protocol, this Contracting Party has declared that, in connection with each request for territorial extension to it of the protection of an international registration and the renewal of any such international registration, it wants to receive an individual fee, instead of a share in the revenue produced by the supplementary and complementary fees.

[7]  Applicable to Greenland as of January 11, 2011 and the Faroe Islands as of April 13, 2016.

[8]  In accordance with Article 14(5) of the Protocol, this Contracting Party has declared that the protection resulting from any international registration effected under this Protocol before the date of entry into force of this Protocol with respect to it cannot be extended to it.

[9]  Including all Overseas Departments and Territories.

[10]  In accordance with Article 5(2)(b) of the Protocol, this Contracting Party has declared that the time limit to notify a refusal of protection shall be 18 months.

[11]  The instrument of ratification of the Stockholm Act and the instrument of acceptance of the Protocol were deposited for the Kingdom in Europe. The Netherlands extended the application of the Madrid Protocol to the Netherlands Antilles with effect from April 28, 2003. The Netherlands Antilles ceased to exist on October 10, 2010. As from that date, the Protocol continues to apply to Curaçao and Sint Maarten. The Protocol also continues to apply to the islands of Bonaire, Sint Eustatius and Saba which, with effect from October 10, 2010, have become part of the territory of the Kingdom of the Netherlands in Europe.

[12]  With a declaration that this accession shall not extend to Tokelau unless and until a declaration to this effect is lodged by the Government of New Zealand with the depositary on the basis of appropriate consultation with that territory.

[13]  Date of accession by the Soviet Union, continued by the Russian Federation as from December 25, 1991.

[14]  Serbia is the continuing State from Serbia and Montenegro as from June 3, 2006.

[15]  Ratification in respect of the United Kingdom and the Isle of Man.

[16]  The United Kingdom extended the application of the Madrid Protocol to the territories of Gibraltar and the Bailiwick of Guernsey with effect from January 1, 2021.

# 43. TRADEMARK LAW TREATY

Adopted at Geneva October 27, 1994

## Article 1

### Abbreviated Expressions

For the purposes of this Treaty, unless expressly stated otherwise:

(i)     "Office" means the agency entrusted by a Contracting Party with the registration of marks;

(ii)    "registration" means the registration of a mark by an Office;

(iii)   "application" means an application for registration;

(iv)    references to a "person" shall be construed as references to both a natural person and a legal entity;

(v)     "holder" means the person whom the register of marks shows as the holder of the registration;

(vi)    "register of marks" means the collection of data maintained by an Office, which includes the contents of all registrations and all data recorded in respect of all registrations, irrespective of the medium in which such data are stored;

(vii)   "Paris Convention" means the Paris Convention for the Protection of Industrial Property, signed at Paris on March 20, 1883, as revised and amended;

(viii)  "Nice Classification" means the classification established by the Nice Agreement Concerning the International Classification of Goods and Services for the Purposes of the Registration of Marks, signed at Nice on June 15, 1957, as revised and amended;

(ix)    "Contracting Party" means any State or intergovernmental organization party to this Treaty;

(x)     references to an "instrument of ratification" shall be construed as including references to instruments of acceptance and approval;

(xi)    "Organization" means the World Intellectual Property Organization;

(xii)   "Director General" means the Director General of the Organization;

(xiii)  "Regulations" means the Regulations under this Treaty that are referred to in Article 17.

## Article 2

### Marks to Which the Treaty Applies

(1)

(a)     This Treaty shall apply to marks consisting of visible signs, provided that only those Contracting Parties which accept for registration three-dimensional marks shall be obliged to apply this Treaty to such marks.

(b)     This Treaty shall not apply to hologram marks and to marks not consisting of visible signs, in particular, sound marks and olfactory marks.

(2)

(a)     This Treaty shall apply to marks relating to goods (trademarks) or services (service marks) or both goods and services.

(b)     This Treaty shall not apply to collective marks, certification marks and guarantee marks.

## Article 3

## Application

(1)

   (a)   Any Contracting Party may require that an application contain some or all of the following indications or elements:

       (i)   a request for registration;

       (ii)   the name and address of the applicant;

       (iii)   the name of a State of which the applicant is a national if he is the national of any State, the name of a State in which the applicant has his domicile, if any, and the name of a State in which the applicant has a real and effective industrial or commercial establishment, if any;

       (iv)   where the applicant is a legal entity, the legal nature of that legal entity and the State, and, where applicable, the territorial unit within that State, under the law of which the said legal entity has been organized;

       (v)   where the applicant has a representative, the name and address of that representative;

       (vi)   where an address for service is required under Article 4(2)(b), such address;

       (vii)   where the applicant wishes to take advantage of the priority of an earlier application, a declaration claiming the priority of that earlier application, together with indications and evidence in support of the declaration of priority that may be required pursuant to Article 4 of the Paris Convention;

       (viii)   where the applicant wishes to take advantage of any protection resulting from the display of goods and/or services in an exhibition, a declaration to that effect, together with indications in support of that declaration, as required by the law of the Contracting Party;

       (ix)   where the Office of the Contracting Party uses characters (letters and numbers) that it considers as being standard and where the applicant wishes that the mark be registered and published in standard characters, a statement to that effect;

       (x)   where the applicant wishes to claim color as a distinctive feature of the mark, a statement to that effect as well as the name or names of the color or colors claimed and an indication, in respect of each color, of the principal parts of the mark which are in that color;

       (xi)   where the mark is a three-dimensional mark, a statement to that effect;

       (xii)   one or more reproductions of the mark;

       (xiii)   a transliteration of the mark or of certain parts of the mark;

       (xiv)   a translation of the mark or of certain parts of the mark;

       (xv)   the names of the goods and/or services for which the registration is sought, grouped according to the classes of the Nice Classification, each group preceded by the number of the class of that Classification to which that group of goods or services belongs and presented in the order of the classes of the said Classification;

       (xvi)   a signature by the person specified in paragraph (4);

       (xvii)   a declaration of intention to use the mark, as required by the law of the Contracting Party.

(b)   The applicant may file, instead of or in addition to the declaration of intention to use the mark referred to in subparagraph (a)(xvii), a declaration of actual use of the mark and evidence to that effect, as required by the law of the Contracting Party.

(c)   Any Contracting Party may require that, in respect of the application, fees be paid to the Office.

(2)   As regards the requirements concerning the presentation of the application, no Contracting Party shall refuse the application,

(i)   where the application is presented in writing on paper, if it is presented, subject to paragraph (3), on a form corresponding to the application Form provided for in the Regulations,

(ii)   where the Contracting Party allows the transmittal of communications to the Office by telefacsimile and the application is so transmitted, if the paper copy resulting from such transmittal corresponds, subject to paragraph (3), to the application Form referred to in item (i).

(3)   Any Contracting Party may require that the application be in the language, or in one of the languages, admitted by the Office. Where the Office admits more than one language, the applicant may be required to comply with any other language requirement applicable with respect to the Office, provided that the application may not be required to be in more than one language.

(4)

(a)   The signature referred to in paragraph (1)(a)(xvi) may be the signature of the applicant or the signature of his representative.

(b)   Notwithstanding subparagraph (a), any Contracting Party may require that the declarations referred to in paragraph (1)(a)(xvii) and (1)(b) be signed by the applicant himself even if he has a representative.

(5)   One and the same application may relate to several goods and/or services, irrespective of whether they belong to one class or to several classes of the Nice Classification.

(6)   Any Contracting Party may require that, where a declaration of intention to use has been filed under paragraph (1)(a)(xvii), the applicant furnish to the Office within a time limit fixed in its law, subject to the minimum time limit prescribed in the Regulations, evidence of the actual use of the mark, as required by the said law.

(7)   No Contracting Party may demand that requirements other than those referred to in paragraphs (1) to (4) and (6) be complied with in respect of the application. In particular, the following may not be required in respect of the application throughout its pendency:

(i)   the furnishing of any certificate of, or extract from, a register of commerce;

(ii)   an indication of the applicant's carrying on of an industrial or commercial activity, as well as the furnishing of evidence to that effect;

(iii)   an indication of the applicant's carrying on of an activity corresponding to the goods and/or services listed in the application, as well as the furnishing of evidence to that effect;

(iv)   the furnishing of evidence to the effect that the mark has been registered in the register of marks of another Contracting Party or of a State party to the Paris Convention which is not a Contracting Party, except where the applicant claims the application of Article 6*quinquies* of the Paris Convention.

(8)   Any Contracting Party may require that evidence be furnished to the Office in the course of the examination of the application where the Office may reasonably doubt the veracity of any indication or element contained in the application.

## Article 4

### Representation; Address for Service

(1)   Any Contracting Party may require that any person appointed as representative for the purposes of any procedure before the Office be a representative admitted to practice before the Office.

(2)

(a)   Any Contracting Party may require that, for the purposes of any procedure before the Office, any person who has neither a domicile nor a real and effective industrial or commercial establishment on its territory be represented by a representative.

(b)   Any Contracting Party may, to the extent that it does not require representation in accordance with subparagraph (a), require that, for the purposes of any procedure before the Office, any person who has neither a domicile nor a real and effective industrial or commercial establishment on its territory have an address for service on that territory.

(3)

(a)   Whenever a Contracting Party allows or requires an applicant, a holder or any other interested person to be represented by a representative before the Office, it may require that the representative be appointed in a separate communication (hereinafter referred to as "power of attorney") indicating the name of, and signed by, the applicant, the holder or the other person, as the case may be.

(b)   The power of attorney may relate to one or more applications and/or registrations identified in the power of attorney or, subject to any exception indicated by the appointing person, to all existing and future applications and/or registrations of that person.

(c)   The power of attorney may limit the powers of the representative to certain acts. Any Contracting Party may require that any power of attorney under which the representative has the right to withdraw an application or to surrender a registration contain an express indication to that effect.

(d)   Where a communication is submitted to the Office by a person who refers to himself in the communication as a representative but where the Office is, at the time of the receipt of the communication, not in possession of the required power of attorney, the Contracting Party may require that the power of attorney be submitted to the Office within the time limit fixed by the Contracting Party, subject to the minimum time limit prescribed in the Regulations. Any Contracting Party may provide that, where the power of attorney has not been submitted to the Office within the time limit fixed by the Contracting Party, the communication by the said person shall have no effect.

(e)   As regards the requirements concerning the presentation and contents of the power of attorney, no Contracting Party shall refuse the effects of the power of attorney,

(i)    where the power of attorney is presented in writing on paper, if it is presented, subject to paragraph (4), on a form corresponding to the power of attorney Form provided for in the Regulations,

(ii)   where the Contracting Party allows the transmittal of communications to the Office by telefacsimile and the power of attorney is so transmitted, if the paper copy resulting from such transmittal corresponds, subject to paragraph (4), to the power of attorney Form referred to in item (i).

(4)   Any Contracting Party may require that the power of attorney be in the language, or in one of the languages, admitted by the Office.

(5) Any Contracting Party may require that any communication made to the Office by a representative for the purposes of a procedure before the Office contain a reference to the power of attorney on the basis of which the representative acts.

(6) No Contracting Party may demand that requirements other than those referred to in paragraphs (3) to (5) be complied with in respect of the matters dealt with in those paragraphs.

(7) Any Contracting Party may require that evidence be furnished to the Office where the Office may reasonably doubt the veracity of any indication contained in any communication referred to in paragraphs (2) to (5).

## Article 5

### Filing Date

(1)

(a) Subject to subparagraph (b) and paragraph (2), a Contracting Party shall accord as the filing date of an application the date on which the Office received the following indications and elements in the language required under Article 3(3):

 (i) an express or implicit indication that the registration of a mark is sought;

 (ii) indications allowing the identity of the applicant to be established;

 (iii) indications sufficient to contact the applicant or his representative, if any, by mail;

 (iv) a sufficiently clear reproduction of the mark whose registration is sought;

 (v) the list of the goods and/or services for which the registration is sought;

 (vi) where Article 3(1)(a)(xvii) or 3(1)(b) applies, the declaration referred to in Article 3(1)(a)(xvii) or the declaration and evidence referred to in Article 3(1)(b), respectively, as required by the law of the Contracting Party, those declarations being, if so required by the said law, signed by the applicant himself even if he has a representative.

(b) Any Contracting Party may accord as the filing date of the application the date on which the Office received only some, rather than all, of the indications and elements referred to in subparagraph (a) or received them in a language other than the language required under Article 3(3).

(2)

(a) A Contracting Party may provide that no filing date shall be accorded until the required fees are paid.

(b) A Contracting Party may apply the requirement referred to in subparagraph (a) only if it applied such requirement at the time of becoming party to this Treaty.

(3) The modalities of, and time limits for, corrections under paragraphs (1) and (2) shall be fixed in the Regulations.

(4) No Contracting Party may demand that requirements other than those referred to in paragraphs (1) and (2) be complied with in respect of the filing date.

## Article 6

### Single Registration for Goods and/or Services in Several Classes

Where goods and/or services belonging to several classes of the Nice Classification have been included in one and the same application, such an application shall result in one and the same registration.

## Article 7

### Division of Application and Registration

(1)

    (a)   Any application listing several goods and/or services (hereinafter referred to as "initial application") may,

        (i)   at least until the decision by the Office on the registration of the mark,

        (ii)  during any opposition proceedings against the decision of the Office to register the mark,

        (iii) during any appeal proceedings against the decision on the registration of the mark,

        be divided by the applicant or at his request into two or more applications (hereinafter referred to as "divisional applications") by distributing among the latter the goods and/or services listed in the initial application. The divisional applications shall preserve the filing date of the initial application and the benefit of the right of priority, if any.

    (b)   Any Contracting Party shall, subject to subparagraph (a), be free to establish requirements for the division of an application, including the payment of fees.

(2)   Paragraph (1) shall apply, *mutatis mutandis*, with respect to a division of a registration. Such a division shall be permitted

        (i)   during any proceedings in which the validity of the registration is challenged before the Office by a third party,

        (ii)  during any appeal proceedings against a decision taken by the Office during the former proceedings,

provided that a Contracting Party may exclude the possibility of the division of registrations if its law allows third parties to oppose the registration of a mark before the mark is registered.

## Article 8

### Signature

(1)   Where a communication to the Office of a Contracting Party is on paper and a signature is required, that Contracting Party

        (i)   shall, subject to item (iii), accept a handwritten signature,

        (ii)  shall be free to allow, instead of a handwritten signature, the use of other forms of signature, such as a printed or stamped signature, or the use of a seal,

        (iii) may, where the natural person who signs the communication is its national and such person's address is in its territory, require that a seal be used instead of a handwritten signature,

        (iv) may, where a seal is used, require that the seal be accompanied by an indication in letters of the name of the natural person whose seal is used.

(2)

    (a)   Where a Contracting Party allows the transmittal of communications to the Office by telefacsimile, it shall consider the communication signed if, on the printout produced by the telefacsimile, the reproduction of the signature, or the reproduction of the seal together with, where required under paragraph (1)(iv), the indication in letters of the name of the natural person whose seal is used, appears.

(b) The Contracting Party referred to in subparagraph (a) may require that the paper whose reproduction was transmitted by telefacsimile be filed with the Office within a certain period, subject to the minimum period prescribed in the Regulations.

(3) Where a Contracting Party allows the transmittal of communications to the Office by electronic means, it shall consider the communication signed if the latter identifies the sender of the communication by electronic means as prescribed by the Contracting Party.

(4) No Contracting Party may require the attestation, notarization, authentication, legalization or other certification of any signature or other means of self-identification referred to in the preceding paragraphs, except, if the law of the Contracting Party so provides, where the signature concerns the surrender of a registration.

## Article 9

### Classification of Goods and/or Services

(1) Each registration and any publication effected by an Office which concerns an application or registration and which indicates goods and/or services shall indicate the goods and/or services by their names, grouped according to the classes of the Nice Classification, and each group shall be preceded by the number of the class of that Classification to which that group of goods or services belongs and shall be presented in the order of the classes of the said Classification.

(2)

(a) Goods or services may not be considered as being similar to each other on the ground that, in any registration or publication by the Office, they appear in the same class of the Nice Classification.

(b) Goods or services may not be considered as being dissimilar from each other on the ground that, in any registration or publication by the Office, they appear in different classes of the Nice Classification.

## Article 10

### Changes in Names or Addresses

(1)

(a) Where there is no change in the person of the holder but there is a change in his name and/or address, each Contracting Party shall accept that a request for the recordal of the change by the Office in its register of marks be made in a communication signed by the holder or his representative and indicating the registration number of the registration concerned and the change to be recorded. As regards the requirements concerning the presentation of the request, no Contracting Party shall refuse the request,

(i) where the request is presented in writing on paper, if it is presented, subject to subparagraph (c), on a form corresponding to the request Form provided for in the Regulations,

(ii) where the Contracting Party allows the transmittal of communications to the Office by telefacsimile and the request is so transmitted, if the paper copy resulting from such transmittal corresponds, subject to subparagraph (c), to the request Form referred to in item (i).

(b) Any Contracting Party may require that the request indicate

(i) the name and address of the holder;

(ii) where the holder has a representative, the name and address of that representative;

(iii) where the holder has an address for service, such address.

(c)  Any Contracting Party may require that the request be in the language, or in one of the languages, admitted by the Office.

(d)  Any Contracting Party may require that, in respect of the request, a fee be paid to the Office.

(e)  A single request shall be sufficient even where the change relates to more than one registration, provided that the registration numbers of all registrations concerned are indicated in the request.

(2)  Paragraph (1) shall apply, *mutatis mutandis*, where the change concerns an application or applications, or both an application or applications and a registration or registrations, provided that, where the application number of any application concerned has not yet been issued or is not known to the applicant or his representative, the request otherwise identifies that application as prescribed in the Regulations.

(3)  Paragraph (1) shall apply, *mutatis mutandis*, to any change in the name or address of the representative, if any, and to any change relating to the address for service, if any.

(4)  No Contracting Party may demand that requirements other than those referred to in paragraphs (1) to (3) be complied with in respect of the request referred to in this Article. In particular, the furnishing of any certificate concerning the change may not be required.

(5)  Any Contracting Party may require that evidence be furnished to the Office where the Office may reasonably doubt the veracity of any indication contained in the request.

## Article 11

### Change in Ownership

(1)

(a)  Where there is a change in the person of the holder, each Contracting Party shall accept that a request for the recordal of the change by the Office in its register of marks be made in a communication signed by the holder or his representative, or by the person who acquired the ownership (hereinafter referred to as "new owner") or his representative, and indicating the registration number of the registration concerned and the change to be recorded. As regards the requirements concerning the presentation of the request, no Contracting Party shall refuse the request,

  (i)  where the request is presented in writing on paper, if it is presented, subject to paragraph (2)(a), on a form corresponding to the request Form provided for in the Regulations,

  (ii)  where the Contracting Party allows the transmittal of communications to the Office by telefacsimile and the request is so transmitted, if the paper copy resulting from such transmittal corresponds, subject to paragraph (2)(a), to the request Form referred to in item (i).

(b)  Where the change in ownership results from a contract, any Contracting Party may require that the request indicate that fact and be accompanied, at the option of the requesting party, by one of the following:

  (i)  a copy of the contract, which copy may be required to be certified, by a notary public or any other competent public authority, as being in conformity with the original contract;

  (ii)  an extract of the contract showing the change in ownership, which extract may be required to be certified, by a notary public or any other competent public authority, as being a true extract of the contract;

  (iii)  an uncertified certificate of transfer drawn up in the form and with the content as prescribed in the Regulations and signed by both the holder and the new owner;

(iv) an uncertified transfer document drawn up in the form and with the content as prescribed in the Regulations and signed by both the holder and the new owner.

(c) Where the change in ownership results from a merger, any Contracting Party may require that the request indicate that fact and be accompanied by a copy of a document, which document originates from the competent authority and evidences the merger, such as a copy of an extract from a register of commerce, and that that copy be certified by the authority which issued the document or by a notary public or any other competent public authority, as being in conformity with the original document.

(d) Where there is a change in the person of one or more but not all of several co-holders and such change in ownership results from a contract or a merger, any Contracting Party may require that any co-holder in respect of which there is no change in ownership give his express consent to the change in ownership in a document signed by him.

(e) Where the change in ownership does not result from a contract or a merger but from another ground, for example, from operation of law or a court decision, any Contracting Party may require that the request indicate that fact and be accompanied by a copy of a document evidencing the change and that that copy be certified as being in conformity with the original document by the authority which issued the document or by a notary public or any other competent public authority.

(f) Any Contracting Party may require that the request indicate

(i) the name and address of the holder;

(ii) the name and address of the new owner;

(iii) the name of a State of which the new owner is a national if he is the national of any State, the name of a State in which the new owner has his domicile, if any, and the name of a State in which the new owner has a real and effective industrial or commercial establishment, if any;

(iv) where the new owner is a legal entity, the legal nature of that legal entity and the State, and, where applicable, the territorial unit within that State, under the law of which the said legal entity has been organized;

(v) where the holder has a representative, the name and address of that representative;

(vi) where the holder has an address for service, such address;

(vii) where the new owner has a representative, the name and address of that representative;

(viii) where the new owner is required to have an address for service under Article 4(2)(b), such address.

(g) Any Contracting Party may require that, in respect of the request, a fee be paid to the Office.

(h) A single request shall be sufficient even where the change relates to more than one registration, provided that the holder and the new owner are the same for each registration and that the registration numbers of all registrations concerned are indicated in the request.

(i) Where the change of ownership does not affect all the goods and/or services listed in the holder's registration, and the applicable law allows the recording of such change, the Office shall create a separate registration referring to the goods and/or services in respect of which the ownership has changed.

(2)

(a) Any Contracting Party may require that the request, the certificate of transfer or the transfer document referred to in paragraph (1) be in the language, or in one of the languages, admitted by the Office.

(b)   Any Contracting Party may require that, if the documents referred to in paragraph (1)(b)(i) and (1)(b)(ii), (1)(c) and (1)(e) are not in the language, or in one of the languages, admitted by the Office, the request be accompanied by a translation or a certified translation of the required document in the language, or in one of the languages, admitted by the Office.

(3)   Paragraphs (1) and (2) shall apply, mutatis mutandis, where the change in ownership concerns an application or applications, or both an application or applications and a registration or registrations, provided that, where the application number of any application concerned has not yet been issued or is not known to the applicant or his representative, the request otherwise identifies that application as prescribed in the Regulations.

(4)   No Contracting Party may demand that requirements other than those referred to in paragraphs (1) to (3) be complied with in respect of the request referred to in this Article. In particular, the following may not be required:

(i)   subject to paragraph (1)(c), the furnishing of any certificate of, or extract from, a register of commerce;

(ii)   an indication of the new owner's carrying on of an industrial or commercial activity, as well as the furnishing of evidence to that effect;

(iii)   an indication of the new owner's carrying on of an activity corresponding to the goods and/or services affected by the change in ownership, as well as the furnishing of evidence to either effect;

(iv)   an indication that the holder transferred, entirely or in part, his business or the relevant goodwill to the new owner, as well as the furnishing of evidence to either effect.

(5)   Any Contracting Party may require that evidence, or further evidence where paragraph (1)(c) or (1)(e) applies, be furnished to the Office where that Office may reasonably doubt the veracity of any indication contained in the request or in any document referred to in the present Article.

## Article 12

### Correction of a Mistake

(1)

(a)   Each Contracting Party shall accept that the request for the correction of a mistake which was made in the application or other request communicated to the Office and which mistake is reflected in its register of marks and/or any publication by the Office be made in a communication signed by the holder or his representative and indicating the registration number of the registration concerned, the mistake to be corrected and the correction to be entered. As regards the requirements concerning the presentation of the request, no Contracting Party shall refuse the request,

(i)   where the request is presented in writing on paper, if it is presented, subject to subparagraph (c), on a form corresponding to the request Form provided for in the Regulations,

(ii)   where the Contracting Party allows the transmittal of communications to the Office by telefacsimile and the request is so transmitted, if the paper copy resulting from such transmittal corresponds, subject to subparagraph (c), to the request Form referred to in item (i).

(b)   Any Contracting Party may require that the request indicate

(i)   the name and address of the holder;

(ii)   where the holder has a representative, the name and address of that representative;

(iii)   where the holder has an address for service, such address.

(c)   Any Contracting Party may require that the request be in the language, or in one of the languages, admitted by the Office.

(d)   Any Contracting Party may require that, in respect of the request, a fee be paid to the Office.

(e)   A single request shall be sufficient even where the correction relates to more than one registration of the same person, provided that the mistake and the requested correction are the same for each registration and that the registration numbers of all registrations concerned are indicated in the request.

(2)   Paragraph (1) shall apply, *mutatis mutandis*, where the mistake concerns an application or applications, or both an application or applications and a registration or registrations, provided that, where the application number of any application concerned has not yet been issued or is not known to the applicant or his representative, the request otherwise identifies that application as prescribed in the Regulations.

(3)   No Contracting Party may demand that requirements other than those referred to in paragraphs (1) and (2) be complied with in respect of the request referred to in this Article.

(4)   Any Contracting Party may require that evidence be furnished to the Office where the Office may reasonably doubt that the alleged mistake is in fact a mistake.

(5)   The Office of a Contracting Party shall correct its own mistakes, *ex officio* or upon request, for no fee.

(6)   No Contracting Party shall be obliged to apply paragraphs (1), (2) and (5) to any mistake which cannot be corrected under its law.

## Article 13

### Duration and Renewal of Registration

(1)

(a)   Any Contracting Party may require that the renewal of a registration be subject to the filing of a request and that such request contain some or all of the following indications:

(i)    an indication that renewal is sought;

(ii)   the name and address of the holder;

(iii)  the registration number of the registration concerned;

(iv)  at the option of the Contracting Party, the filing date of the application which resulted in the registration concerned or the registration date of the registration concerned;

(v)   where the holder has a representative, the name and address of that representative;

(vi)  where the holder has an address for service, such address;

(vii) where the Contracting Party allows the renewal of a registration to be made for some only of the goods and/or services which are recorded in the register of marks and such a renewal is requested, the names of the recorded goods and/or services for which the renewal is requested or the names of the recorded goods and/or services for which the renewal is not requested, grouped according to the classes of the Nice Classification, each group preceded by the number of the class of that Classification to which that group of goods or services belongs and presented in the order of the classes of the said Classification;

(viii) where a Contracting Party allows a request for renewal to be filed by a person other than the holder or his representative and the request is filed by such a person, the name and address of that person;

> (ix)  a signature by the holder or his representative or, where item (viii) applies, a signature by the person referred to in that item.
>
> (b)  Any Contracting Party may require that, in respect of the request for renewal, a fee be paid to the Office. Once the fee has been paid in respect of the initial period of the registration or of any renewal period, no further payment may be required for the maintenance of the registration in respect of that period. Fees associated with the furnishing of a declaration and/or evidence of use shall not be regarded, for the purposes of this subparagraph, as payments required for the maintenance of the registration and shall not be affected by this subparagraph.
>
> (c)  Any Contracting Party may require that the request for renewal be presented, and the corresponding fee referred to in subparagraph (b) be paid, to the Office within the period fixed by the law of the Contracting Party, subject to the minimum periods prescribed in the Regulations.

(2)  As regards the requirements concerning the presentation of the request for renewal, no Contracting Party shall refuse the request,

> (i)  where the request is presented in writing on paper, if it is presented, subject to paragraph (3), on a form corresponding to the request Form provided for in the Regulations,
>
> (ii)  where the Contracting Party allows the transmittal of communications to the Office by telefacsimile and the request is so transmitted, if the paper copy resulting from such transmittal corresponds, subject to paragraph (3), to the request Form referred to in item (i).

(3)  Any Contracting Party may require that the request for renewal be in the language, or in one of the languages, admitted by the Office.

(4)  No Contracting Party may demand that requirements other than those referred to in paragraphs (1) to (3) be complied with in respect of the request for renewal. In particular, the following may not be required:

> (i)  any reproduction or other identification of the mark;
>
> (ii)  the furnishing of evidence to the effect that the mark has been registered, or that its registration has been renewed, in the register of marks of any other Contracting Party;
>
> (iii)  the furnishing of a declaration and/or evidence concerning use of the mark.

(5)  Any Contracting Party may require that evidence be furnished to the Office in the course of the examination of the request for renewal where the Office may reasonably doubt the veracity of any indication or element contained in the request for renewal.

(6)  No Office of a Contracting Party may, for the purposes of effecting the renewal, examine the registration as to substance.

(7)  The duration of the initial period of the registration, and the duration of each renewal period, shall be 10 years.

## Article 14

### Observations in Case of Intended Refusal

An application or a request under Articles 10 to 13 may not be refused totally or in part by an Office without giving the applicant or the requesting party, as the case may be, an opportunity to make observations on the intended refusal within a reasonable time limit.

## Article 15

### Obligation to Comply with the Paris Convention

Any Contracting Party shall comply with the provisions of the Paris Convention which concern marks.

## Article 16

### Service Marks

Any Contracting Party shall register service marks and apply to such marks the provisions of the Paris Convention which concern trademarks.

## Article 17

### Regulations

(1)

    (a)   The Regulations annexed to this Treaty provide rules concerning

        (i)   matters which this Treaty expressly provides to be "prescribed in the Regulations";

        (ii)   any details useful in the implementation of the provisions of this Treaty;

        (iii)   any administrative requirements, matters or procedures.

    (b)   The Regulations also contain Model International Forms.

(2)   In the case of conflict between the provisions of this Treaty and those of the Regulations, the former shall prevail.

## Article 18

### Revision; Protocols

(1)   This Treaty may be revised by a diplomatic conference.

(2)   For the purposes of further developing the harmonization of laws on marks, protocols may be adopted by a diplomatic conference insofar as those protocols do not contravene the provisions of this Treaty.

## Article 19

### Becoming Party to the Treaty

(1)   The following entities may sign and, subject to paragraphs (2) and (3) and Article 20(1) and 20(3), become party to this Treaty:

        (i)   any State member of the Organization in respect of which marks may be registered with its own Office;

        (ii)   any intergovernmental organization which maintains an Office in which marks may be registered with effect in the territory in which the constituting treaty of the intergovernmental organization applies, in all its member States or in those of its member States which are designated for such purpose in the relevant application, provided that all the member States of the intergovernmental organization are members of the Organization;

        (iii)   any State member of the Organization in respect of which marks may be registered only through the Office of another specified State that is a member of the Organization;

      (iv)   any State member of the Organization in respect of which marks may be registered only through the Office maintained by an intergovernmental organization of which that State is a member;

      (v)   any State member of the Organization in respect of which marks may be registered only through an Office common to a group of States members of the Organization.

(2)   Any entity referred to in paragraph (1) may deposit

      (i)   an instrument of ratification, if it has signed this Treaty,

      (ii)   an instrument of accession, if it has not signed this Treaty.

(3)

   (a)   Subject to subparagraph (b), the effective date of the deposit of an instrument of ratification or accession shall be,

      (i)   in the case of a State referred to in paragraph (1)(i), the date on which the instrument of that State is deposited;

      (ii)   in the case of an intergovernmental organization, the date on which the instrument of that intergovernmental organization is deposited;

      (iii)   in the case of a State referred to in paragraph (1)(iii), the date on which the following condition is fulfilled: the instrument of that State has been deposited and the instrument of the other, specified State has been deposited;

      (iv)   in the case of a State referred to in paragraph (1)(iv), the date applicable under (ii), above;

      (v)   in the case of a State member of a group of States referred to in paragraph (1)(v), the date on which the instruments of all the States members of the group have been deposited.

   (b)   Any instrument of ratification or accession (referred to in this subparagraph as "instrument") of a State may be accompanied by a declaration making it a condition to its being considered as deposited that the instrument of one other State or one intergovernmental organization, or the instruments of two other States, or the instruments of one other State and one intergovernmental organization, specified by name and eligible to become party to this Treaty, is or are also deposited. The instrument containing such a declaration shall be considered to have been deposited on the day on which the condition indicated in the declaration is fulfilled. However, when the deposit of any instrument specified in the declaration is, itself, accompanied by a declaration of the said kind, that instrument shall be considered as deposited on the day on which the condition specified in the latter declaration is fulfilled.

   (c)   Any declaration made under paragraph (b) may be withdrawn, in its entirety or in part, at any time. Any such withdrawal shall become effective on the date on which the notification of withdrawal is received by the Director General.

### Article 20

### Effective Date of Ratifications and Accessions

(1)   For the purposes of this Article, only instruments of ratification or accession that are deposited by entities referred to in Article 19(1) and that have an effective date according to Article 19(3) shall be taken into consideration.

(2)   This Treaty shall enter into force three months after five States have deposited their instruments of ratification or accession.

(3)   Any entity not covered by paragraph (2) shall become bound by this Treaty three months after the date on which it has deposited its instrument of ratification or accession.

## Article 21

### Reservations

(1)   Any State or intergovernmental organization may declare through a reservation that, notwithstanding Article 2(1)(a) and 2(2)(a), any of the provisions of Articles 3(1) and 3(2), 5, 7, 11 and 13 shall not apply to associated marks, defensive marks or derivative marks. Such reservation shall specify those of the aforementioned provisions to which the reservation relates.

(2)   Any reservation under paragraph (1) shall be made in a declaration accompanying the instrument of ratification of, or accession to, this Treaty of the State or intergovernmental organization making the reservation.

(3)   Any reservation under paragraph (1) may be withdrawn at any time.

(4)   No reservation to this Treaty other than the reservation allowed under paragraph (1) shall be permitted.

## Article 22

### Transitional Provisions

(1)

  (a)  Any State or intergovernmental organization may declare that, notwithstanding Article 3(5), an application may be filed with the Office only in respect of goods or services which belong to one class of the Nice Classification.

  (b)  Any State or intergovernmental organization may declare that, notwithstanding Article 6, where goods and/or services belonging to several classes of the Nice Classification have been included in one and the same application, such application shall result in two or more registrations in the register of marks, provided that each and every such registration shall bear a reference to all other such registrations resulting from the said application.

  (c)  Any State or intergovernmental organization that has made a declaration under subparagraph (a) may declare that, notwithstanding Article 7(1), no application may be divided.

(2)   Any State or intergovernmental organization may declare that, notwithstanding Article 4(3)(b), a power of attorney may only relate to one application or one registration.

(3)   Any State or intergovernmental organization may declare that, notwithstanding Article 8(4), the signature of a power of attorney or the signature by the applicant of an application may be required to be the subject of an attestation, notarization, authentication, legalization or other certification.

(4)   Any State or intergovernmental organization may declare that, notwithstanding Article 10(1)(e), 10(2) and 10(3), Article 11(1)(h) and 11(3) and Article 12(1)(e) and 12(2), a request for the recordal of a change in name and/or address, a request for the recordal of a change in ownership and a request for the correction of a mistake may only relate to one application or one registration.

(5)   Any State or intergovernmental organization may declare that, notwithstanding Article 13(4)(iii), it will require, on the occasion of renewal, the furnishing of a declaration and/or of evidence concerning use of the mark.

(6)   Any State or intergovernmental organization may declare that, notwithstanding Article 13(6), the Office may, on the occasion of the first renewal of a registration covering services, examine such registration as to substance, provided that such examination shall be limited to the elimination of multiple registrations based on applications filed during a period of six months following the entry

into force of the law of such State or organization that introduced, before the entry into force of this Treaty, the possibility of registering service marks.

(7)

    (a)    A State or an intergovernmental organization may make a declaration under paragraphs (1) to (6) only if, at the time of depositing its instrument of ratification of, or accession to, this Treaty, the continued application of its law would, without such a declaration, be contrary to the relevant provisions of this Treaty.

    (b)    Any declaration under paragraphs (1) to (6) shall accompany the instrument of ratification of, or accession to, this Treaty of the State or intergovernmental organization making the declaration.

    (c)    Any declaration made under paragraphs (1) to (6) may be withdrawn at any time.

(8)

    (a)    Subject to subparagraph (c), any declaration made under paragraphs (1) to (6) by a State regarded as a developing country in conformity with the established practice of the General Assembly of the United Nations, or by an intergovernmental organization each member of which is such a State, shall lose its effect at the end of a period of eight years from the date of entry into force of this Treaty.

    (b)    Subject to subparagraph (c), any declaration made under paragraphs (1) to (6) by a State other than a State referred to in subparagraph (a), or by an intergovernmental organization other than an intergovernmental organization referred to in subparagraph (a), shall lose its effect at the end of a period of six years from the date of entry into force of this Treaty.

    (c)    Where a declaration made under paragraphs (1) to (6) has not been withdrawn under paragraph (7)(c), or has not lost its effect under subparagraph (a) or (b), before October 28, 2004, it shall lose its effect on October 28, 2004.

(9)    Until December 31, 1999, any State which, on the date of the adoption of this Treaty, is a member of the International (Paris) Union for the Protection of Industrial Property without being a member of the Organization may, notwithstanding Article 19(1)(i), become a party to this Treaty if marks may be registered with its own Office.

## Article 23

### Denunciation of the Treaty

(1)    Any Contracting Party may denounce this Treaty by notification addressed to the Director General.

(2)    Denunciation shall take effect one year from the date on which the Director General has received the notification. It shall not affect the application of this Treaty to any application pending or any mark registered in respect of the denouncing Contracting Party at the time of the expiration of the said one-year period, provided that the denouncing Contracting Party may, after the expiration of the said one-year period, discontinue applying this Treaty to any registration as from the date on which that registration is due for renewal.

## Article 24

### Languages of the Treaty; Signature

(1)

    (a)    This Treaty shall be signed in a single original in the English, Arabic, Chinese, French, Russian and Spanish languages, all texts being equally authentic.

(b)   At the request of a Contracting Party, an official text in a language not referred to in subparagraph (a) that is an official language of that Contracting Party shall be established by the Director General after consultation with the said Contracting Party and any other interested Contracting Party.

(2)   This Treaty shall remain open for signature at the headquarters of the Organization for one year after its adoption.

## Article 25

### Depositary

The Director General shall be the depositary of this Treaty.

# 44. PARTIES TO THE TRADEMARK LAW TREATY*

(Geneva, 1994)

**Status on May 4, 2021**

| State | Date on which State became party to the Treaty |
|---|---|
| Australia | January 21, 1998 |
| Bahrain | March 18, 2007 |
| Belgium | August 11, 2012 |
| Bosnia and Herzegovina | December 22, 2006 |
| Burkina Faso | Not yet in force[1] |
| Chile | August 5, 2011 |
| Colombia | April 13, 2012 |
| Costa Rica | October 17, 2008 |
| Croatia | July 4, 2006 |
| Cyprus | April 17, 1997 |
| Czech Republic | August 1, 1996 |
| Denmark | January 28, 1998[2] |
| Dominican Republic | December 13, 2011 |
| Egypt | October 7, 1999 |
| El Salvador | November 14, 2008 |
| Estonia | January 7, 2003 |
| France | December 15, 2006 |
| Germany | October 16, 2004 |
| Guatemala | December 12, 2016 |
| Guinea | Not yet in force |
| Honduras | April 22, 2008 |
| Hungary | November 26, 1998 |
| Indonesia | September 5, 1997 |
| Ireland | October 13, 1999 |
| Italy | April 26, 2011 |
| Japan[3] | April 1, 1997 |
| Kazakhstan | November 7, 2002 |
| Kyrgyzstan | August 15, 2002 |
| Latvia | December 28, 1999 |
| Liechtenstein | March 17, 1998 |
| Lithuania | April 27, 1998 |
| Luxembourg | August 11, 2012 |
| Monaco | September 27, 1996 |

## PARTIES TO THE TRADEMARK LAW TREATY

| State | Date on which State became party to the Treaty |
|---|---|
| Montenegro | June 3, 2006 |
| Morocco | July 6, 2009 |
| Netherlands[4] | August 11, 2012[5] |
| Nicaragua | September 22, 2009 |
| Oman | October 16, 2007 |
| Panama | September 7, 2012 |
| Peru | November 6, 2009 |
| Republic of Korea | February 25, 2003 |
| Republic of Moldova | August 1, 1996 |
| Romania | July 28, 1998 |
| Russian Federation | May 11, 1998 |
| Serbia[6] | September 15, 1998 |
| Slovakia | July 9, 1997 |
| Slovenia | May 26, 2002 |
| Spain[7] | March 17, 1999 |
| Sri Lanka[8] | August 1, 1996 |
| Switzerland | May 1, 1997 |
| Trinidad and Tobago | April 16, 1998 |
| Turkey | January 1, 2005 |
| Ukraine | August 1, 1996 |
| United Kingdom[9] | August 1, 1996 |
| United States of America | August 12, 2000 |
| Uzbekistan | September 4, 1998 |

(Total: 54 States)

---

[1]   This State will become bound by the Treaty three months after the deposit of the instrument of accession of the African Intellectual Property Organization (OAPI).

[2]   Not applicable to the Faroe Islands and to Greenland.

[3]   With the reservation provided for in Article 21(1), in respect of defensive marks, and the declaration in Article 22(6).

[4]   Ratification for the Kingdom in Europe, the Netherlands Antilles and Aruba. The Netherlands Antilles ceased to exist on October 10, 2010. As from that date, the Treaty continues to apply to Curaçao and Sint Maarten. The Treaty also continues to apply to the islands of Bonaire, Sint Eustatius and Saba which, with effect from October 10, 2010, have become part of the territory of the Kingdom of the Netherlands in Europe.

[5]   The Netherlands Antilles and Aruba became bound by the Treaty as from December 19, 1996 and the Kingdom of the Netherlands in Europe, on August 11, 2012, three months after the deposit of the instrument of ratification of Luxembourg.

[6]   Serbia is the continuing State from Serbia and Montenegro as from June 3, 2006.

[7]   With the reservation provided for in Article 21(1), in respect of derivative marks, and the declarations in Article 22(1)(a) and (c), (2) and (5).

[8]   With the declarations provided for in Article 22(1)(a) and (c), (2) and (4).

[9]   In respect of the United Kingdom of Great Britain and Northern Ireland and the Isle of Man.

# 45.  SINGAPORE TRADEMARK TREATY

Singapore Treaty on the Law of Trademarks

Singapore, 2006

## Article 1

### Abbreviated Expressions

For the purposes of this Treaty, unless expressly stated otherwise:

(i)   "Office" means the agency entrusted by a Contracting Party with the registration of marks;

(ii)  "registration" means the registration of a mark by an Office;

(iii) "application" means an application for registration;

(iv)  "communication" means any application, or any request, declaration, correspondence or other information relating to an application or a registration, which is filed with the Office;

(v)   references to a "person" shall be construed as references to both a natural person and a legal entity;

(vi)  "holder" means the person whom the register of marks shows as the holder of the registration;

(vii) "register of marks" means the collection of data maintained by an Office, which includes the contents of all registrations and all data recorded in respect of all registrations, irrespective of the medium in which such data are stored;

(viii)"procedure before the Office" means any procedure in proceedings before the Office with respect to an application or a registration;

(ix)  "Paris Convention" means the Paris Convention for the Protection of Industrial Property, signed at Paris on March 20, 1883, as revised and amended;

(x)   "Nice Classification" means the classification established by the Nice Agreement Concerning the International Classification of Goods and Services for the Purposes of the Registration of Marks, signed at Nice on June 15, 1957, as revised and amended;

(xi)  "license" means a license for the use of a mark under the law of a Contracting Party;

(xii) "licensee" means the person to whom a license has been granted;

(xiii)"Contracting Party" means any State or intergovernmental organization party to this Treaty;

(xiv) "Diplomatic Conference" means the convocation of Contracting Parties for the purpose of revising or amending the Treaty;

(xv)  "Assembly" means the Assembly referred to in Article 23;

(xvi) references to an "instrument of ratification" shall be construed as including references to instruments of acceptance and approval;

(xvii) "Organization" means the World Intellectual Property Organization;

(xviii) "International Bureau" means the International Bureau of the Organization;

(xix) "Director General" means the Director General of the Organization;

(xx)  "Regulations" means the Regulations under this Treaty that are referred to in Article 22;

(xxi) references to an "Article" or to a "paragraph", "subparagraph" or "item" of an Article shall be construed as including references to the corresponding rule(s) under the Regulations;

(xxii) "TLT 1994" means the Trademark Law Treaty done at Geneva on October 27, 1994.

## Article 2

### Marks to Which the Treaty Applies

(1)    [*Nature of Marks*] Any Contracting Party shall apply this Treaty to marks consisting of signs that can be registered as marks under its law.

(2)    [*Kinds of Marks*]

(a)    This Treaty shall apply to marks relating to goods (trademarks) or services (service marks) or both goods and services.

(b)    This Treaty shall not apply to collective marks, certification marks and guarantee marks.

## Article 3

### Application

(1)    [*Indications or Elements Contained in or Accompanying an Application; Fee*]

(a)    Any Contracting Party may require that an application contain some or all of the following indications or elements:

   (i)    a request for registration;

   (ii)   the name and address of the applicant;

   (iii)  the name of a State of which the applicant is a national if he/she is the national of any State, the name of a State in which the applicant has his/her domicile, if any, and the name of a State in which the applicant has a real and effective industrial or commercial establishment, if any;

   (iv)   where the applicant is a legal entity, the legal nature of that legal entity and the State, and, where applicable, the territorial unit within that State, under the law of which the said legal entity has been organized;

   (v)    where the applicant has a representative, the name and address of that representative;

   (vi)   where an address for service is required under Article 4(2)(b), such address;

   (vii)  where the applicant wishes to take advantage of the priority of an earlier application, a declaration claiming the priority of that earlier application, together with indications and evidence in support of the declaration of priority that may be required pursuant to Article 4 of the Paris Convention;

   (viii) where the applicant wishes to take advantage of any protection resulting from the display of goods and/or services in an exhibition, a declaration to that effect, together with indications in support of that declaration, as required by the law of the Contracting Party;

   (ix)   at least one representation of the mark, as prescribed in the Regulations;

   (x)    where applicable, a statement, as prescribed in the Regulations, indicating the type of mark as well as any specific requirements applicable to that type of mark;

   (xi)   where applicable, a statement, as prescribed in the Regulations, indicating that the applicant wishes that the mark be registered and published in the standard characters used by the Office;

   (xii)  where applicable, a statement, as prescribed in the Regulations, indicating that the applicant wishes to claim color as a distinctive feature of the mark;

   (xiii) a transliteration of the mark or of certain parts of the mark;

(xiv) a translation of the mark or of certain parts of the mark;

(xv) the names of the goods and/or services for which the registration is sought, grouped according to the classes of the Nice Classification, each group preceded by the number of the class of that Classification to which that group of goods or services belongs and presented in the order of the classes of the said Classification;

(xvi) a declaration of intention to use the mark, as required by the law of the Contracting Party.

(b)    The applicant may file, instead of or in addition to the declaration of intention to use the mark referred to in subparagraph (a)(xvi), a declaration of actual use of the mark and evidence to that effect, as required by the law of the Contracting Party.

(c)    Any Contracting Party may require that, in respect of the application, fees be paid to the Office.

(2)    [*Single Application for Goods and/or Services in Several Classes*] One and the same application may relate to several goods and/or services, irrespective of whether they belong to one class or to several classes of the Nice Classification.

(3)    [*Actual Use*] Any Contracting Party may require that, where a declaration of intention to use has been filed under paragraph (1)(a)(xvi), the applicant furnish to the Office within a time limit fixed in its law, subject to the minimum time limit prescribed in the Regulations, evidence of the actual use of the mark, as required by the said law.

(4)    [*Prohibition of Other Requirements*] No Contracting Party may demand that requirements other than those referred to in paragraphs (1) and (3) and in Article 8 be complied with in respect of the application. In particular, the following may not be required in respect of the application throughout its pendency:

(i)    the furnishing of any certificate of, or extract from, a register of commerce;

(ii)    an indication of the applicant's carrying on of an industrial or commercial activity, as well as the furnishing of evidence to that effect;

(iii)    an indication of the applicant's carrying on of an activity corresponding to the goods and/or services listed in the application, as well as the furnishing of evidence to that effect;

(iv)    the furnishing of evidence to the effect that the mark has been registered in the register of marks of another Contracting Party or of a State party to the Paris Convention which is not a Contracting Party, except where the applicant claims the application of Article 6*quinquies* of the Paris Convention.

(5)    [*Evidence*] Any Contracting Party may require that evidence be furnished to the Office in the course of the examination of the application where the Office may reasonably doubt the veracity of any indication or element contained in the application.

### Article 4

### Representation; Address for Service

(1)    [*Representatives Admitted to Practice*]

(a)    Any Contracting Party may require that a representative appointed for the purposes of any procedure before the Office

(i)    have the right, under the applicable law, to practice before the Office in respect of applications and registrations and, where applicable, be admitted to practice before the Office;

(ii)    provide, as its address, an address on a territory prescribed by the Contracting Party.

(b)   An act, with respect to any procedure before the Office, by or in relation to a representative who complies with the requirements applied by the Contracting Party under subparagraph (a), shall have the effect of an act by or in relation to the applicant, holder or other interested person who appointed that representative.

(2)   [*Mandatory Representation; Address for Service*]

(a)   Any Contracting Party may require that, for the purposes of any procedure before the Office, an applicant, holder or other interested person who has neither a domicile nor a real and effective industrial or commercial establishment on its territory be represented by a representative.

(b)   Any Contracting Party may, to the extent that it does not require representation in accordance with subparagraph (a), require that, for the purposes of any procedure before the Office, an applicant, holder or other interested person who has neither a domicile nor a real and effective industrial or commercial establishment on its territory have an address for service on that territory.

(3)   [*Power of Attorney*]

(a)   Whenever a Contracting Party allows or requires an applicant, a holder or any other interested person to be represented by a representative before the Office, it may require that the representative be appointed in a separate communication (hereinafter referred to as "power of attorney") indicating the name of the applicant, the holder or the other person, as the case may be.

(b)   The power of attorney may relate to one or more applications and/or registrations identified in the power of attorney or, subject to any exception indicated by the appointing person, to all existing and future applications and/or registrations of that person.

(c)   The power of attorney may limit the powers of the representative to certain acts. Any Contracting Party may require that any power of attorney under which the representative has the right to withdraw an application or to surrender a registration contain an express indication to that effect.

(d)   Where a communication is submitted to the Office by a person who refers to itself in the communication as a representative but where the Office is, at the time of the receipt of the communication, not in possession of the required power of attorney, the Contracting Party may require that the power of attorney be submitted to the Office within the time limit fixed by the Contracting Party, subject to the minimum time limit prescribed in the Regulations. Any Contracting Party may provide that, where the power of attorney has not been submitted to the Office within the time limit fixed by the Contracting Party, the communication by the said person shall have no effect.

(4)   [*Reference to Power of Attorney*] Any Contracting Party may require that any communication made to the Office by a representative for the purposes of a procedure before the Office contain a reference to the power of attorney on the basis of which the representative acts.

(5)   [*Prohibition of Other Requirements*] No Contracting Party may demand that requirements other than those referred to in paragraphs (3) and (4) and in Article 8 be complied with in respect of the matters dealt with in those paragraphs.

(6)   [*Evidence*] Any Contracting Party may require that evidence be furnished to the Office where the Office may reasonably doubt the veracity of any indication contained in any communication referred to in paragraphs (3) and (4).

## Article 5

### Filing Date

(1)    [*Permitted Requirements*]

(a)    Subject to subparagraph (b) and paragraph (2), a Contracting Party shall accord as the filing date of an application the date on which the Office received the following indications and elements in the language required under Article 8(2):

(i)    an express or implicit indication that the registration of a mark is sought;

(ii)    indications allowing the identity of the applicant to be established;

(iii)    indications allowing the applicant or its representative, if any, to be contacted by the Office;

(iv)    a sufficiently clear representation of the mark whose registration is sought;

(v)    the list of the goods and/or services for which the registration is sought;

(vi)    where Article 3(1)(a)(xvi) or (b) applies, the declaration referred to in Article 3(1)(a)(xvi) or the declaration and evidence referred to in Article 3(1)(b), respectively, as required by the law of the Contracting Party.

(b)    Any Contracting Party may accord as the filing date of the application the date on which the Office received only some, rather than all, of the indications and elements referred to in subparagraph (a) or received them in a language other than the language required under Article 8(2).

(2)    [*Permitted Additional Requirement*]

(a)    A Contracting Party may provide that no filing date shall be accorded until the required fees are paid.

(b)    A Contracting Party may apply the requirement referred to in subparagraph (a) only if it applied such requirement at the time of becoming party to this Treaty.

(3)    [*Corrections and Time Limits*] The modalities of, and time limits for, corrections under paragraphs (1) and (2) shall be fixed in the Regulations.

(4)    [*Prohibition of Other Requirements*] No Contracting Party may demand that requirements other than those referred to in paragraphs (1) and (2) be complied with in respect of the filing date.

## Article 6

### Single Registration for Goods and/or Services in Several Classes

Where goods and/or services belonging to several classes of the Nice Classification have been included in one and the same application, such an application shall result in one and the same registration.

## Article 7

### Division of Application and Registration

(1)    [*Division of Application*]

(a)    Any application listing several goods and/or services (hereinafter referred to as "initial application") may,

(i)    at least until the decision by the Office on the registration of the mark,

(ii)    during any opposition proceedings against the decision of the Office to register the mark,

(iii)   during any appeal proceedings against the decision on the registration of the mark,

be divided by the applicant or at its request into two or more applications (hereinafter referred to as "divisional applications") by distributing among the latter the goods and/or services listed in the initial application. The divisional applications shall preserve the filing date of the initial application and the benefit of the right of priority, if any.

(b)   Any Contracting Party shall, subject to subparagraph (a), be free to establish requirements for the division of an application, including the payment of fees.

(2)   [*Division of Registration*] Paragraph (1) shall apply, *mutatis mutandis*, with respect to a division of a registration. Such a division shall be permitted

(i)   during any proceedings in which the validity of the registration is challenged before the Office by a third party,

(ii)   during any appeal proceedings against a decision taken by the Office during the former proceedings,

provided that a Contracting Party may exclude the possibility of the division of registrations if its law allows third parties to oppose the registration of a mark before the mark is registered.

## Article 8

### Communications

(1)   [*Means of Transmittal and Form of Communications*] Any Contracting Party may choose the means of transmittal of communications and whether it accepts communications on paper, communications in electronic form or any other form of communication.

(2)   [*Language of Communications*]

(a)   Any Contracting Party may require that any communication be in a language admitted by the Office. Where the Office admits more than one language, the applicant, holder or other interested person may be required to comply with any other language requirement applicable with respect to the Office, provided that no indication or element of the communication may be required to be in more than one language.

(b)   No Contracting Party may require the attestation, notarization, authentication, legalization or any other certification of any translation of a communication other than as provided under this Treaty.

(c)   Where a Contracting Party does not require a communication to be in a language admitted by its Office, the Office may require that a translation of that communication by an official translator or a representative, into a language admitted by the Office, be supplied within a reasonable time limit.

(3)   [*Signature of Communications on Paper*]

(a)   Any Contracting Party may require that a communication on paper be signed by the applicant, holder or other interested person. Where a Contracting Party requires a communication on paper to be signed, that Contracting Party shall accept any signature that complies with the requirements prescribed in the Regulations.

(b)   No Contracting Party may require the attestation, notarization, authentication, legalization or other certification of any signature except, where the law of the Contracting Party so provides, if the signature concerns the surrender of a registration.

(c)   Notwithstanding subparagraph (b), a Contracting Party may require that evidence be filed with the Office where the Office may reasonably doubt the authenticity of any signature of a communication on paper.

(4) [*Communications Filed in Electronic Form or by Electronic Means of Transmittal*] Where a Contracting Party permits the filing of communications in electronic form or by electronic means of transmittal, it may require that any such communications comply with the requirements prescribed in the Regulations.

(5) [*Presentation of a Communication*] Any Contracting Party shall accept the presentation of a communication the content of which corresponds to the relevant Model International Form, if any, provided for in the Regulations.

(6) [*Prohibition of Other Requirements*] No Contracting Party may demand that, in respect of paragraphs (1) to (5), requirements other than those referred to in this Article be complied with.

(7) [*Means of Communication with Representative*] Nothing in this Article regulates the means of communication between an applicant, holder or other interested person and its representative.

## Article 9

### Classification of Goods and/or Services

(1) [*Indications of Goods and/or Services*] Each registration and any publication effected by an Office which concerns an application or registration and which indicates goods and/or services shall indicate the goods and/or services by their names, grouped according to the classes of the Nice Classification, and each group shall be preceded by the number of the class of that Classification to which that group of goods or services belongs and shall be presented in the order of the classes of the said Classification.

(2) [*Goods or Services in the Same Class or in Different Classes*]

(a) Goods or services may not be considered as being similar to each other on the ground that, in any registration or publication by the Office, they appear in the same class of the Nice Classification.

(b) Goods or services may not be considered as being dissimilar from each other on the ground that, in any registration or publication by the Office, they appear in different classes of the Nice Classification.

## Article 10

### Changes in Names or Addresses

(1) [*Changes in the Name or Address of the Holder*]

(a) Where there is no change in the person of the holder but there is a change in its name and/or address, each Contracting Party shall accept that a request for the recordal of the change by the Office in its register of marks be made by the holder in a communication indicating the registration number of the registration concerned and the change to be recorded.

(b) Any Contracting Party may require that the request indicate

(i) the name and address of the holder;

(ii) where the holder has a representative, the name and address of that representative;

(iii) where the holder has an address for service, such address.

(c) Any Contracting Party may require that, in respect of the request, a fee be paid to the Office.

(d) A single request shall be sufficient even where the change relates to more than one registration, provided that the registration numbers of all registrations concerned are indicated in the request.

(2) [*Change in the Name or Address of the Applicant*] Paragraph (1) shall apply, *mutatis mutandis*, where the change concerns an application or applications, or both an application or

applications and a registration or registrations, provided that, where the application number of any application concerned has not yet been issued or is not known to the applicant or its representative, the request otherwise identifies that application as prescribed in the Regulations.

(3)   [*Change in the Name or Address of the Representative or in the Address for Service*] Paragraph (1) shall apply, *mutatis mutandis*, to any change in the name or address of the representative, if any, and to any change relating to the address for service, if any.

(4)   [*Prohibition of Other Requirements*] No Contracting Party may demand that requirements other than those referred to in paragraphs (1) to (3) and in Article 8 be complied with in respect of the request referred to in this Article. In particular, the furnishing of any certificate concerning the change may not be required.

(5)   [*Evidence*] Any Contracting Party may require that evidence be furnished to the Office where the Office may reasonably doubt the veracity of any indication contained in the request.

## Article 11

### Change in Ownership

(1)   [*Change in the Ownership of a Registration*]

(a)   Where there is a change in the person of the holder, each Contracting Party shall accept that a request for the recordal of the change by the Office in its register of marks be made by the holder or by the person who acquired the ownership (hereinafter referred to as "new owner") in a communication indicating the registration number of the registration concerned and the change to be recorded.

(b)   Where the change in ownership results from a contract, any Contracting Party may require that the request indicate that fact and be accompanied, at the option of the requesting party, by one of the following:

(i)   a copy of the contract, which copy may be required to be certified, by a notary public or any other competent public authority, as being in conformity with the original contract;

(ii)   an extract of the contract showing the change in ownership, which extract may be required to be certified, by a notary public or any other competent public authority, as being a true extract of the contract;

(iii)   an uncertified certificate of transfer drawn up in the form and with the content as prescribed in the Regulations and signed by both the holder and the new owner;

(iv)   an uncertified transfer document drawn up in the form and with the content as prescribed in the Regulations and signed by both the holder and the new owner.

(c)   Where the change in ownership results from a merger, any Contracting Party may require that the request indicate that fact and be accompanied by a copy of a document, which document originates from the competent authority and evidences the merger, such as a copy of an extract from a register of commerce, and that that copy be certified by the authority which issued the document or by a notary public or any other competent public authority, as being in conformity with the original document.

(d)   Where there is a change in the person of one or more but not all of several co-holders and such change in ownership results from a contract or a merger, any Contracting Party may require that any co-holder in respect of which there is no change in ownership give its express consent to the change in ownership in a document signed by it.

(e)   Where the change in ownership does not result from a contract or a merger but from another ground, for example, from operation of law or a court decision, any Contracting Party may require that the request indicate that fact and be accompanied by a copy of a document evidencing the change and that that copy be certified as being in conformity with the original document by the authority which issued the document or by a notary public or any other competent public authority.

(f)     Any Contracting Party may require that the request indicate

(i)     the name and address of the holder;

(ii)    the name and address of the new owner;

(iii)   the name of a State of which the new owner is a national if he/she is the national of any State, the name of a State in which the new owner has his/her domicile, if any, and the name of a State in which the new owner has a real and effective industrial or commercial establishment, if any;

(iv)    where the new owner is a legal entity, the legal nature of that legal entity and the State, and, where applicable, the territorial unit within that State, under the law of which the said legal entity has been organized;

(v)     where the holder has a representative, the name and address of that representative;

(vi)    where the holder has an address for service, such address;

(vii)   where the new owner has a representative, the name and address of that representative;

(viii)  where the new owner is required to have an address for service under Article 4(2)(b), such address.

(g)     Any Contracting Party may require that, in respect of the request, a fee be paid to the Office.

(h)     A single request shall be sufficient even where the change relates to more than one registration, provided that the holder and the new owner are the same for each registration and that the registration numbers of all registrations concerned are indicated in the request.

(i)     Where the change of ownership does not affect all the goods and/or services listed in the holder's registration, and the applicable law allows the recording of such change, the Office shall create a separate registration referring to the goods and/or services in respect of which the ownership has changed.

(2)     [*Change in the Ownership of an Application*] Paragraph (1) shall apply, *mutatis mutandis*, where the change in ownership concerns an application or applications, or both an application or applications and a registration or registrations, provided that, where the application number of any application concerned has not yet been issued or is not known to the applicant or its representative, the request otherwise identifies that application as prescribed in the Regulations.

(3)     [*Prohibition of Other Requirements*] No Contracting Party may demand that requirements other than those referred to in paragraphs (1) and (2) and in Article 8 be complied with in respect of the request referred to in this Article. In particular, the following may not be required:

(i)     subject to paragraph (1)(c), the furnishing of any certificate of, or extract from, a register of commerce;

(ii)    an indication of the new owner's carrying on of an industrial or commercial activity, as well as the furnishing of evidence to that effect;

(iii)   an indication of the new owner's carrying on of an activity corresponding to the goods and/or services affected by the change in ownership, as well as the furnishing of evidence to either effect;

(iv)    an indication that the holder transferred, entirely or in part, its business or the relevant goodwill to the new owner, as well as the furnishing of evidence to either effect.

(4)     [*Evidence*] Any Contracting Party may require that evidence, or further evidence where paragraph (1)(c) or (e) applies, be furnished to the Office where that Office may reasonably doubt the

veracity of any indication contained in the request or in any document referred to in the present Article.

## Article 12

## Correction of a Mistake

(1)   [*Correction of a Mistake in Respect of a Registration*]

(a)   Each Contracting Party shall accept that the request for the correction of a mistake which was made in the application or other request communicated to the Office and which mistake is reflected in its register of marks and/or any publication by the Office be made by the holder in a communication indicating the registration number of the registration concerned, the mistake to be corrected and the correction to be entered.

(b)   Any Contracting Party may require that the request indicate

   (i)   the name and address of the holder;

   (ii)   where the holder has a representative, the name and address of that representative;

   (iii)   where the holder has an address for service, such address.

(c)   Any Contracting Party may require that, in respect of the request, a fee be paid to the Office.

(d)   A single request shall be sufficient even where the correction relates to more than one registration of the same person, provided that the mistake and the requested correction are the same for each registration and that the registration numbers of all registrations concerned are indicated in the request.

(2)   [*Correction of a Mistake in Respect of an Application*] Paragraph (1) shall apply, *mutatis mutandis*, where the mistake concerns an application or applications, or both an application or applications and a registration or registrations, provided that, where the application number of any application concerned has not yet been issued or is not known to the applicant or its representative, the request otherwise identifies that application as prescribed in the Regulations.

(3)   [*Prohibition of Other Requirements*] No Contracting Party may demand that requirements other than those referred to in paragraphs (1) and (2) and in Article 8 be complied with in respect of the request referred to in this Article.

(4)   [*Evidence*] Any Contracting Party may require that evidence be furnished to the Office where the Office may reasonably doubt that the alleged mistake is in fact a mistake.

(5)   [*Mistakes Made by the Office*] The Office of a Contracting Party shall correct its own mistakes, *ex officio* or upon request, for no fee.

(6)   [*Uncorrectable Mistakes*] No Contracting Party shall be obliged to apply paragraphs (1), (2) and (5) to any mistake which cannot be corrected under its law.

## Article 13

## Duration and Renewal of Registration

(1)   [*Indications or Elements Contained in or Accompanying a Request for Renewal; Fee*]

(a)   Any Contracting Party may require that the renewal of a registration be subject to the filing of a request and that such request contain some or all of the following indications:

   (i)   an indication that renewal is sought;

   (ii)   the name and address of the holder;

   (iii)   the registration number of the registration concerned;

(iv)  at the option of the Contracting Party, the filing date of the application which resulted in the registration concerned or the registration date of the registration concerned;

(v)  where the holder has a representative, the name and address of that representative;

(vi)  where the holder has an address for service, such address;

(vii)  where the Contracting Party allows the renewal of a registration to be made for some only of the goods and/or services which are recorded in the register of marks and such a renewal is requested, the names of the recorded goods and/or services for which the renewal is requested or the names of the recorded goods and/or services for which the renewal is not requested, grouped according to the classes of the Nice Classification, each group preceded by the number of the class of that Classification to which that group of goods or services belongs and presented in the order of the classes of the said Classification;

(viii) where a Contracting Party allows a request for renewal to be filed by a person other than the holder or its representative and the request is filed by such a person, the name and address of that person.

(b)  Any Contracting Party may require that, in respect of the request for renewal, a fee be paid to the Office. Once the fee has been paid in respect of the initial period of the registration or of any renewal period, no further payment may be required for the maintenance of the registration in respect of that period. Fees associated with the furnishing of a declaration and/or evidence of use shall not be regarded, for the purposes of this subparagraph, as payments required for the maintenance of the registration and shall not be affected by this subparagraph.

(c)  Any Contracting Party may require that the request for renewal be presented, and the corresponding fee referred to in subparagraph (b) be paid, to the Office within the period fixed by the law of the Contracting Party, subject to the minimum periods prescribed in the Regulations.

(2)  [*Prohibition of Other Requirements*] No Contracting Party may demand that requirements other than those referred to in paragraph (1) and in Article 8 be complied with in respect of the request for renewal. In particular, the following may not be required:

(i)  any representation or other identification of the mark;

(ii)  the furnishing of evidence to the effect that the mark has been registered, or that its registration has been renewed, in any other register of marks;

(iii) the furnishing of a declaration and/or evidence concerning use of the mark.

(3)  [*Evidence*] Any Contracting Party may require that evidence be furnished to the Office in the course of the examination of the request for renewal where the Office may reasonably doubt the veracity of any indication or element contained in the request for renewal.

(4)  [*Prohibition of Substantive Examination*] No Office of a Contracting Party may, for the purposes of effecting the renewal, examine the registration as to substance.

(5)  [*Duration*] The duration of the initial period of the registration, and the duration of each renewal period, shall be 10 years.

## Article 14

### Relief Measures in Case of Failure to Comply with Time Limits

(1)  [*Relief Measure Before the Expiry of a Time Limit*] A Contracting Party may provide for the extension of a time limit for an action in a procedure before the Office in respect of an application or a registration, if a request to that effect is filed with the Office prior to the expiry of the time limit.

(2)  [*Relief Measures After the Expiry of a Time Limit*] Where an applicant, holder or other interested person has failed to comply with a time limit ("the time limit concerned") for an action in a procedure before the Office of a Contracting Party in respect of an application or a registration, the

Contracting Party shall provide for one or more of the following relief measures, in accordance with the requirements prescribed in the Regulations, if a request to that effect is filed with the Office:

(i)  extension of the time limit concerned for the period prescribed in the Regulations;

(ii)  continued processing with respect to the application or registration;

(iii)  reinstatement of the rights of the applicant, holder or other interested person with respect to the application or registration if the Office finds that the failure to comply with the time limit concerned occurred in spite of due care required by the circumstances having been taken or, at the option of the Contracting Party, that the failure was unintentional.

(3)  [*Exceptions*] No Contracting Party shall be required to provide for any of the relief measures referred to in paragraph (2) with respect to the exceptions prescribed in the Regulations.

(4)  [*Fee*] Any Contracting Party may require that a fee be paid in respect of any of the relief measures referred to in paragraphs (1) and (2).

(5)  [*Prohibition of Other Requirements*] No Contracting Party may demand that requirements other than those referred to in this Article and in Article 8 be complied with in respect of any of the relief measures referred to in paragraph (2).

## Article 15

### Obligation to Comply with the Paris Convention

Any Contracting Party shall comply with the provisions of the Paris Convention which concern marks.

## Article 16

### Service Marks

Any Contracting Party shall register service marks and apply to such marks the provisions of the Paris Convention which concern trademarks.

## Article 17

### Request for Recordal of a License

(1)  [*Requirements Concerning the Request for Recordal*] Where the law of a Contracting Party provides for the recordal of a license with its Office, that Contracting Party may require that the request for recordal

(i)  be filed in accordance with the requirements prescribed in the Regulations, and

(ii)  be accompanied by the supporting documents prescribed in the Regulations.

(2)  [*Fee*] Any Contracting Party may require that, in respect of the recordal of a license, a fee be paid to the Office.

(3)  [*Single Request Relating to Several Registrations*] A single request shall be sufficient even where the license relates to more than one registration, provided that the registration numbers of all registrations concerned are indicated in the request, the holder and the licensee are the same for all registrations, and the request indicates the scope of the license in accordance with the Regulations with respect to all registrations.

(4)  [*Prohibition of Other Requirements*]

(a)  No Contracting Party may demand that requirements other than those referred to in paragraphs (1) to (3) and in Article 8 be complied with in respect of the recordal of a license with its Office. In particular, the following may not be required:

(i)    the furnishing of the registration certificate of the mark which is the subject of the license;

(ii)   the furnishing of the license contract or a translation of it;

(iii)  an indication of the financial terms of the license contract.

(b)   Subparagraph (a) is without prejudice to any obligations existing under the law of a Contracting Party concerning the disclosure of information for purposes other than the recording of the license in the register of marks.

(5)   *[Evidence]* Any Contracting Party may require that evidence be furnished to the Office where the Office may reasonably doubt the veracity of any indication contained in the request or in any document referred to in the Regulations.

(6)   *[Requests Relating to Applications]* Paragraphs (1) to (5) shall apply, *mutatis mutandis,* to requests for recordal of a license for an application, where the law of a Contracting Party provides for such recordal.

## Article 18

### Request for Amendment or Cancellation of the Recordal of a License

(1)   *[Requirements Concerning the Request]* Where the law of a Contracting Party provides for the recordal of a license with its Office, that Contracting Party may require that the request for amendment or cancellation of the recordal of a license

(i)    be filed in accordance with the requirements prescribed in the Regulations, and

(ii)   be accompanied by the supporting documents prescribed in the Regulations.

(2)   *[Other Requirements]* Article 17(2) to (6) shall apply, *mutatis mutandis,* to requests for amendment or cancellation of the recordal of a license.

## Article 19

### Effects of the Non-Recordal of a License

(1)   *[Validity of the Registration and Protection of the Mark]* The non-recordal of a license with the Office or with any other authority of the Contracting Party shall not affect the validity of the registration of the mark which is the subject of the license or the protection of that mark.

(2)   *[Certain Rights of the Licensee]* A Contracting Party may not require the recordal of a license as a condition for any right that the licensee may have under the law of that Contracting Party to join infringement proceedings initiated by the holder or to obtain, by way of such proceedings, damages resulting from an infringement of the mark which is the subject of the license.

(3)   *[Use of a Mark Where License Is Not Recorded]* A Contracting Party may not require the recordal of a license as a condition for the use of a mark by a licensee to be deemed to constitute use by the holder in proceedings relating to the acquisition, maintenance and enforcement of marks.

## Article 20

### Indication of the License

Where the law of a Contracting Party requires an indication that the mark is used under a license, full or partial non-compliance with that requirement shall not affect the validity of the registration of the mark which is the subject of the license or the protection of that mark, and shall not affect the application of Article 19(3).

## Article 21

### Observations in Case of Intended Refusal

An application under Article 3 or a request under Articles 7, 10 to 14, 17 and 18 may not be refused totally or in part by an Office without giving the applicant or the requesting party, as the case may be, an opportunity to make observations on the intended refusal within a reasonable time limit. In respect of Article 14, no Office shall be required to give an opportunity to make observations where the person requesting the relief measure has already had an opportunity to present an observation on the facts on which the decision is to be based.

## Article 22

### Regulations

(1)   [*Content*]

(a)   The Regulations annexed to this Treaty provide rules concerning

    (i)   matters which this Treaty expressly provides to be "prescribed in the Regulations";

    (ii)   any details useful in the implementation of the provisions of this Treaty;

    (iii)  any administrative requirements, matters or procedures.

(b)   The Regulations also contain Model International Forms.

(2)   [*Amending the Regulations*] Subject to paragraph (3), any amendment of the Regulations shall require three-fourths of the votes cast.

(3)   [*Requirement of Unanimity*]

(a)   The Regulations may specify provisions of the Regulations which may be amended only by unanimity.

(b)   Any amendment of the Regulations resulting in the addition of provisions to, or the deletion of provisions from, the provisions specified in the Regulations pursuant to subparagraph (a) shall require unanimity.

(c)   In determining whether unanimity is attained, only votes actually cast shall be taken into consideration. Abstentions shall not be considered as votes.

(4)   [*Conflict Between the Treaty and the Regulations*] In the case of conflict between the provisions of this Treaty and those of the Regulations, the former shall prevail.

## Article 23

### Assembly

(1)   [*Composition*]

(a)   The Contracting Parties shall have an Assembly.

(b)   Each Contracting Party shall be represented in the Assembly by one delegate, who may be assisted by alternate delegates, advisors and experts. Each delegate may represent only one Contracting Party.

(2)   [*Tasks*] The Assembly shall

    (i)   deal with matters concerning the development of this Treaty;

    (ii)   amend the Regulations, including the Model International Forms;

    (iii)  determine the conditions for the date of application of each amendment referred to in item (ii);

(iv)   perform such other functions as are appropriate to implementing the provisions of this Treaty.

(3)   [*Quorum*]

(a)   One-half of the members of the Assembly which are States shall constitute a quorum.

(b)   Notwithstanding subparagraph (a), if, in any session, the number of the members of the Assembly which are States and are represented is less than one-half but equal to or more than one-third of the members of the Assembly which are States, the Assembly may make decisions but, with the exception of decisions concerning its own procedure, all such decisions shall take effect only if the conditions set forth hereinafter are fulfilled. The International Bureau shall communicate the said decisions to the members of the Assembly which are States and were not represented and shall invite them to express in writing their vote or abstention within a period of three months from the date of the communication. If, at the expiration of this period, the number of such members having thus expressed their vote or abstention attains the number of the members which was lacking for attaining the quorum in the session itself, such decisions shall take effect, provided that at the same time the required majority still obtains.

(4)   [*Taking Decisions in the Assembly*]

(a)   The Assembly shall endeavor to take its decisions by consensus.

(b)   Where a decision cannot be arrived at by consensus, the matter at issue shall be decided by voting. In such a case,

   (i)   each Contracting Party that is a State shall have one vote and shall vote only in its own name; and

   (ii)   any Contracting Party that is an intergovernmental organization may participate in the vote, in place of its Member States, with a number of votes equal to the number of its Member States which are party to this Treaty. No such intergovernmental organization shall participate in the vote if any one of its Member States exercises its right to vote and vice versa. In addition, no such intergovernmental organization shall participate in the vote if any one of its Member States party to this Treaty is a Member State of another such intergovernmental organization and that other intergovernmental organization participates in that vote.

(5)   [*Majorities*]

(a)   Subject to Articles 22(2) and (3), the decisions of the Assembly shall require two-thirds of the votes cast.

(b)   In determining whether the required majority is attained, only votes actually cast shall be taken into consideration. Abstentions shall not be considered as votes.

(6)   [*Sessions*] The Assembly shall meet upon convocation by the Director General and, in the absence of exceptional circumstances, during the same period and at the same place as the General Assembly of the Organization.

(7)   [*Rules of Procedure*] The Assembly shall establish its own rules of procedure, including rules for the convocation of extraordinary sessions.

## Article 24

### International Bureau

(1)   [*Administrative Tasks*]

(a)   The International Bureau shall perform the administrative tasks concerning this Treaty.

(b)   In particular, the International Bureau shall prepare the meetings and provide the secretariat of the Assembly and of such committees of experts and working groups as may be established by the Assembly.

(2)   [*Meetings Other than Sessions of the Assembly*] The Director General shall convene any committee and working group established by the Assembly.

(3)   [*Role of the International Bureau in the Assembly and Other Meetings*]

(a)   The Director General and persons designated by the Director General shall participate, without the right to vote, in all meetings of the Assembly, the committees and working groups established by the Assembly.

(b)   The Director General or a staff member designated by the Director General shall be *ex officio* secretary of the Assembly, and of the committees and working groups referred to in subparagraph (a).

(4)   [*Conferences*]

(a)   The International Bureau shall, in accordance with the directions of the Assembly, make the preparations for any revision conferences.

(b)   The International Bureau may consult with Member States of the Organization, intergovernmental organizations and international and national non-governmental organizations concerning the said preparations.

(c)   The Director General and persons designated by the Director General shall take part, without the right to vote, in the discussions at revision conferences.

(5)   [*Other Tasks*] The International Bureau shall carry out any other tasks assigned to it in relation to this Treaty.

## Article 25

### Revision or Amendment

This Treaty may only be revised or amended by a diplomatic conference. The convocation of any diplomatic conference shall be decided by the Assembly.

## Article 26

### Becoming Party to the Treaty

(1)   [*Eligibility*] The following entities may sign and, subject to paragraphs (2) and (3) and Article 28(1) and (3), become party to this Treaty:

(i)   any State member of the Organization in respect of which marks may be registered with its own Office;

(ii)   any intergovernmental organization which maintains an Office in which marks may be registered with effect in the territory in which the constituting treaty of the intergovernmental organization applies, in all its Member States or in those of its Member States which are designated for such purpose in the relevant application, provided that all the Member States of the intergovernmental organization are members of the Organization;

(iii)   any State member of the Organization in respect of which marks may be registered only through the Office of another specified State that is a member of the Organization;

(iv)   any State member of the Organization in respect of which marks may be registered only through the Office maintained by an intergovernmental organization of which that State is a member;

(v)    any State member of the Organization in respect of which marks may be registered only through an Office common to a group of States members of the Organization.

(2)    [*Ratification or Accession*] Any entity referred to in paragraph (1) may deposit

(i)    an instrument of ratification, if it has signed this Treaty,

(ii)    an instrument of accession, if it has not signed this Treaty.

(3)    [*Effective Date of Deposit*] The effective date of the deposit of an instrument of ratification or accession shall be,

(i)    in the case of a State referred to in paragraph (1)(i), the date on which the instrument of that State is deposited;

(ii)    in the case of an intergovernmental organization, the date on which the instrument of that intergovernmental organization is deposited;

(iii)    in the case of a State referred to in paragraph (1)(iii), the date on which the following condition is fulfilled: the instrument of that State has been deposited and the instrument of the other, specified State has been deposited;

(iv)    in the case of a State referred to in paragraph (1)(iv), the date applicable under item (ii), above;

(v)    in the case of a State member of a group of States referred to in paragraph (1)(v), the date on which the instruments of all the States members of the group have been deposited.

## Article 27

### Application of the TLT 1994 and This Treaty

(1)    [*Relations Between Contracting Parties to Both This Treaty and the TLT 1994*] This Treaty alone shall be applicable as regards the mutual relations of Contracting Parties to both this Treaty and the TLT 1994.

(2)    [*Relations Between Contracting Parties to This Treaty and Contracting Parties to the TLT 1994 That Are Not Party to This Treaty*] Any Contracting Party to both this Treaty and the TLT 1994 shall continue to apply the TLT 1994 in its relations with Contracting Parties to the TLT 1994 that are not party to this Treaty.

## Article 28

### Entry into Force; Effective Date of Ratifications and Accessions

(1)    [*Instruments to Be Taken into Consideration*] For the purposes of this Article, only instruments of ratification or accession that are deposited by entities referred to in Article 26(1) and that have an effective date according to Article 26(3) shall be taken into consideration.

(2)    [*Entry into Force of the Treaty*] This Treaty shall enter into force three months after ten States or intergovernmental organizations referred to in Article 26(1)(ii) have deposited their instruments of ratification or accession.

(3)    [*Entry into Force of Ratifications and Accessions Subsequent to the Entry into Force of the Treaty*] Any entity not covered by paragraph (2) shall become bound by this Treaty three months after the date on which it has deposited its instrument of ratification or accession.

## Article 29

### Reservations

(1)    [*Special Kinds of Marks*] Any State or intergovernmental organization may declare through a reservation that, notwithstanding Article 2(1) and (2)(a), any of the provisions of Articles 3(1), 5, 7,

8(5), 11 and 13 shall not apply to associated marks, defensive marks or derivative marks. Such reservation shall specify those of the aforementioned provisions to which the reservation relates.

(2) [*Multiple-class Registration*] Any State or intergovernmental organization, whose legislation at the date of adoption of this Treaty provides for a multiple-class registration for goods and for a multiple-class registration for services may, when acceding to this Treaty, declare through a reservation that the provisions of Article 6 shall not apply.

(3) [*Substantive Examination on the Occasion of Renewal*] Any State or intergovernmental organization may declare through a reservation that, notwithstanding Article 13(4), the Office may, on the occasion of the first renewal of a registration covering services, examine such registration as to substance, provided that such examination shall be limited to the elimination of multiple registrations based on applications filed during a period of six months following the entry into force of the law of such State or organization that introduced, before the entry into force of this Treaty, the possibility of registering service marks.

(4) [*Certain Rights of the Licensee*] Any State or intergovernmental organization may declare through a reservation that, notwithstanding Article 19(2), it requires the recordal of a license as a condition for any right that the licensee may have under the law of that State or intergovernmental organization to join infringement proceedings initiated by the holder or to obtain, by way of such proceedings, damages resulting from an infringement of the mark which is the subject of the license.

(5) [*Modalities*] Any reservation under paragraphs (1), (2), (3) or (4) shall be made in a declaration accompanying the instrument of ratification of, or accession to, this Treaty of the State or intergovernmental organization making the reservation.

(6) [*Withdrawal*] Any reservation under paragraphs (1), (2), (3) or (4) may be withdrawn at any time.

(7) [*Prohibition of Other Reservations*] No reservation to this Treaty other than the reservations allowed under paragraphs (1), (2), (3) and (4) shall be permitted.

## Article 30

### Denunciation of the Treaty

(1) [*Notification*] Any Contracting Party may denounce this Treaty by notification addressed to the Director General.

(2) [*Effective Date*] Denunciation shall take effect one year from the date on which the Director General has received the notification. It shall not affect the application of this Treaty to any application pending or any mark registered in respect of the denouncing Contracting Party at the time of the expiration of the said one-year period, provided that the denouncing Contracting Party may, after the expiration of the said one-year period, discontinue applying this Treaty to any registration as from the date on which that registration is due for renewal.

## Article 31

### Languages of the Treaty; Signature

(1) [*Original Texts; Official Texts*]

(a) This Treaty shall be signed in a single original in the English, Arabic, Chinese, French, Russian and Spanish languages, all texts being equally authentic.

(b) An official text in a language not referred to in subparagraph (a) that is an official language of a Contracting Party shall be established by the Director General after consultation with the said Contracting Party and any other interested Contracting Party.

(2) [*Time Limit for Signature*] This Treaty shall remain open for signature at the headquarters of the Organization for one year after its adoption.

## Article 32

### Depositary

The Director General shall be the depositary of this Treaty.

# 46. PARTIES TO THE SINGAPORE TRADEMARK TREATY*

Singapore Treaty on the Law of Trademarks

(Singapore, 2006)

**Status on May 4, 2021**

| State/IGO | Date on which State/IGO became party to the Treaty |
|---|---|
| Afghanistan | May 14, 2017 |
| African Intellectual Property Organization (OAPI)[1,2] | February 13, 2016 |
| Armenia | September 17, 2013 |
| Australia | March 16, 2009 |
| Belarus | May 13, 2014 |
| Belgium | January 8, 2014 |
| Benelux Organization for Intellectual Property | January 8, 2014 |
| Benin | February 13, 2016 |
| Bulgaria[1] | March 16, 2009 |
| Canada | June 17, 2019 |
| Croatia | April 13, 2011 |
| Democratic People's Republic of Korea | September 13, 2016 |
| Denmark[3] | March 16, 2009 |
| Estonia | August 14, 2009 |
| Finland | August 7, 2019 |
| France | November 28, 2009 |
| Germany | September 20, 2013 |
| Iceland | December 14, 2012 |
| Iraq | November 29, 2014 |
| Ireland | March 21, 2016 |
| Italy | September 21, 2010 |
| Japan[4] | June 11, 2016 |
| Kazakhstan | September 5, 2012 |
| Kyrgyzstan | March 16, 2009 |
| Latvia | March 16, 2009 |
| Liechtenstein | March 3, 2010 |
| Lithuania | August 14, 2013 |
| Luxembourg | January 8, 2014 |

---

# PARTIES TO THE SINGAPORE TRADEMARK TREATY

| State/IGO | Date on which State/IGO became party to the Treaty |
| --- | --- |
| Mali............................................ | February 13, 2016 |
| Mongolia ..................................... | March 3, 2011 |
| Netherlands[5]................................ | January 8, 2014 |
| New Zealand[6] ............................. | December 10, 2012 |
| North Macedonia........................... | October 6, 2010 |
| Peru............................................. | December 27, 2018 |
| Poland.......................................... | July 2, 2009 |
| Republic of Korea ......................... | July 1, 2016 |
| Republic of Moldova ...................... | March 16, 2009 |
| Romania....................................... | March 16, 2009 |
| Russian Federation ....................... | December 18, 2009 |
| Serbia.......................................... | November 19, 2010 |
| Singapore..................................... | March 16, 2009 |
| Slovakia ...................................... | May 16, 2010 |
| Spain[1]........................................ | May 18, 2009 |
| Sweden......................................... | December 16, 2011 |
| Switzerland................................... | March 16, 2009 |
| Tajikistan..................................... | December 26, 2014 |
| Trinidad and Tobago...................... | January 4, 2020 |
| Ukraine........................................ | May 24, 2010 |
| United Kingdom ............................ | June 21, 2012 |
| United States of America.............. | March 16, 2009 |
| Uruguay[1] .................................... | April 29, 2020 |

(Total: 51)

---

[1] With the declaration provided for in Article 29(4).

[2] With the declaration provided for in Article 29(2).

[3] Not applicable to the Faroe Islands nor to Greenland.

[4] With the declaration provided for in Article 29(1).

[5] Accession for the Kingdom in Europe and the Netherlands Antilles. The Netherlands Antilles ceased to exist on October 10, 2010. As from that date, the Treaty continues to apply to Curaçao and Sint Maarten. The Treaty also continues to apply to the islands of Bonaire, Sint Eustatius and Saba which, with effect from October 10, 2010, have become part of the territory of the Kingdom of the Netherlands in Europe.

[6] This ratification shall not extend to Tokelau unless and until a Declaration to this effect is lodged by the Government of New Zealand with the Depositary on the basis of appropriate consultation with that territory.

# 47. LISBON AGREEMENT FOR THE PROTECTION OF APPELLATIONS OF ORIGIN AND THEIR INTERNATIONAL REGISTRATION

of October 31, 1958, as revised at Stockholm on July 14, 1967,
and as amended on September 28, 1979

## Article 1

(1)   The countries to which this Agreement applies constitute a Special Union within the framework of the Union for the Protection of Industrial Property.

(2)   They undertake to protect on their territories, in accordance with the terms of this Agreement, the appellations of origin of products of the other countries of the Special Union, recognized and protected as such in the country of origin and registered at the International Bureau of Intellectual Property (hereinafter designated as "the International Bureau" or "the Bureau") referred to in the Convention establishing the World Intellectual Property Organization (hereinafter designated as "the Organization").

## Article 2

(1)   In this Agreement, "appellation of origin" means the geographical name of a country, region, or locality, which serves to designate a product originating therein, the quality and characteristics of which are due exclusively or essentially to the geographical environment, including natural and human factors.

(2)   The country of origin is the country whose name, or the country in which is situated the region or locality whose name, constitutes the appellation of origin which has given the product its reputation.

## Article 3

Protection shall be ensured against any usurpation or imitation, even if the true origin of the product is indicated or if the appellation is used in translated form or accompanied by terms such as "kind," "type," "make," "imitation," or the like.

## Article 4

The provisions of this Agreement shall in no way exclude the protection already granted to appellations of origin in each of the countries of the Special Union by virtue of other international instruments, such as the Paris Convention of March 20, 1883, for the Protection of Industrial Property and its subsequent revisions, and the Madrid Agreement of April 14, 1891, for the Repression of False or Deceptive Indications of Source on Goods and its subsequent revisions, or by virtue of national legislation or court decisions.

## Article 5

(1)   The registration of appellations of origin shall be effected at the International Bureau, at the request of the Offices of the countries of the Special Union, in the name of any natural persons or legal entities, public or private, having, according to their national legislation, a right to use such appellations.

(2)   The International Bureau shall, without delay, notify the Offices of the various countries of the Special Union of such registrations, and shall publish them in a periodical.

(3)   The Office of any country may declare that it cannot ensure the protection of an appellation of origin whose registration has been notified to it, but only in so far as its declaration is notified to the

International Bureau, together with an indication of the grounds therefor, within a period of one year from the receipt of the notification of registration, and provided that such declaration is not detrimental, in the country concerned, to the other forms of protection of the appellation which the owner thereof may be entitled to claim under Article 4, above.

(4)   Such declaration may not be opposed by the Offices of the countries of the Union after the expiration of the period of one year provided for in the foregoing paragraph.

(5)   The International Bureau shall, as soon as possible, notify the Office of the country of origin of any declaration made under the terms of paragraph (3) by the Office of another country. The interested party, when informed by his national Office of the declaration made by another country, may resort, in that other country, to all the judicial and administrative remedies open to the nationals of that country.

(6)   If an appellation which has been granted protection in a given country pursuant to notification of its international registration has already been used by third parties in that country from a date prior to such notification, the competent Office of the said country shall have the right to grant to such third parties a period not exceeding two years to terminate such use, on condition that it advise the International Bureau accordingly during the three months following the expiration of the period of one year provided for in paragraph (3), above.

### Article 6

An appellation which has been granted protection in one of the countries of the Special Union pursuant to the procedure under Article 5 cannot, in that country, be deemed to have become generic, as long as it is protected as an appellation of origin in the country of origin.

### Article 7

(1)   Registration effected at the International Bureau in conformity with Article 5 shall ensure, without renewal, protection for the whole of the period referred to in the foregoing Article.

(2)   A single fee shall be paid for the registration of each appellation of origin.

### Article 8

Legal action required for ensuring the protection of appellations of origin may be taken in each of the countries of the Special Union under the provisions of the national legislation:

1.   at the instance of the competent Office or at the request of the public prosecutor;

2.   by any interested party, whether a natural person or a legal entity, whether public or private.

### Article 9

(1)

(a)   The Special Union shall have an Assembly consisting of those countries which have ratified or acceded to this Act.

(b)   The Government of each country shall be represented by one delegate, who may be assisted by alternate delegates, advisors, and experts.

(c)   The expenses of each delegation shall be borne by the Government which has appointed it.

(2)

(a)   The Assembly shall:

(i)   deal with all matters concerning the maintenance and development of the Special Union and the implementation of this Agreement;

(ii) give directions to the International Bureau concerning the preparation for conferences of revision, due account being taken of any comments made by those countries of the Special Union which have not ratified or acceded to this Act;

(iii) modify the Regulations, including the fixation of the amount of the fee referred to in Article 7(2) and other fees relating to international registration;

(iv) review and approve the reports and activities of the Director General of the Organization (hereinafter designated as "the Director General") concerning the Special Union, and give him all necessary instructions concerning matters within the competence of the Special Union;

(v) determine the program and adopt the biennial budget of the Special Union, and approve its final accounts;

(vi) adopt the financial regulations of the Special Union;

(vii) establish such committees of experts and working groups as it may deem necessary to achieve the objectives of the Special Union;

(viii) determine which countries not members of the Special Union and which intergovernmental and international non-governmental organizations shall be admitted to its meetings as observers;

(ix) adopt amendments to Article 9 to Article 12;

(x) take any other appropriate action designed to further the objectives of the Special Union;

(xi) perform such other functions as are appropriate under this Agreement.

(b) With respect to matters which are of interest also to other Unions administered by the Organization, the Assembly shall make its decisions after having heard the advice of the Coordination Committee of the Organization.

(3)

(a) Each country member of the Assembly shall have one vote.

(b) One-half of the countries members of the Assembly shall constitute a quorum.

(c) Notwithstanding the provisions of subparagraph (b), if, in any session, the number of countries represented is less than one-half but equal to or more than one-third of the countries members of the Assembly, the Assembly may make decisions but, with the exception of decisions concerning its own procedure, all such decisions shall take effect only if the conditions set forth hereinafter are fulfilled. The International Bureau shall communicate the said decisions to the countries members of the Assembly which were not represented and shall invite them to express in writing their vote or abstention within a period of three months from the date of the communication. If, at the expiration of this period, the number of countries having thus expressed their vote or abstention attains the number of countries which was lacking for attaining the quorum in the session itself, such decisions shall take effect provided that at the same time the required majority still obtains.

(d) Subject to the provisions of Article 12(2), the decisions of the Assembly shall require two-thirds of the votes cast.

(e) Abstentions shall not be considered as votes.

(f) A delegate may represent, and vote in the name of, one country only.

(g) Countries of the Special Union not members of the Assembly shall be admitted to the meetings of the latter as observers.

(4)

    (a)   The Assembly shall meet once in every second calendar year in ordinary session upon convocation by the Director General and, in the absence of exceptional circumstances, during the same period and at the same place as the General Assembly of the Organization.

    (b)   The Assembly shall meet in extraordinary session upon convocation by the Director General, at the request of one-fourth of the countries members of the Assembly.

    (c)   The agenda of each session shall be prepared by the Director General.

(5)   The Assembly shall adopt its own rules of procedure.

## Article 10

(1)

    (a)   International registration and related duties, as well as all other administrative tasks concerning the Special Union, shall be performed by the International Bureau.

    (b)   In particular, the International Bureau shall prepare the meetings and provide the secretariat of the Assembly and of such committees of experts and working groups as may have been established by the Assembly.

    (c)   The Director General shall be the chief executive of the Special Union and shall represent the Special Union.

(2)   The Director General and any staff member designated by him shall participate, without the right to vote, in all meetings of the Assembly and of such committees of experts or working groups as may have been established by the Assembly. The Director General, or a staff member designated by him, shall be *ex officio* secretary of those bodies.

(3)

    (a)   The International Bureau shall, in accordance with the directions of the Assembly, make the preparations for the conferences of revision of the provisions of the Agreement other than Article 9 to Article 12.

    (b)   The International Bureau may consult with intergovernmental and international non-governmental organizations concerning preparations for conferences of revision.

    (c)   The Director General and persons designated by him shall take part, without the right to vote, in the discussions at those conferences.

(4)   The International Bureau shall carry out any other tasks assigned to it.

## Article 11

(1)

    (a)   The Special Union shall have a budget.

    (b)   The budget of the Special Union shall include the income and expenses proper to the Special Union, its contribution to the budget of expenses common to the Unions, and, where applicable, the sum made available to the budget of the Conference of the Organization.

    (c)   Expenses not attributable exclusively to the Special Union but also to one or more other Unions administered by the Organization shall be considered as expenses common to the Unions. The share of the Special Union in such common expenses shall be in proportion to the interest the Special Union has in them.

(2)   The budget of the Special Union shall be established with due regard to the requirements of coordination with the budgets of the other Unions administered by the Organization.

(3)   The budget of the Special Union shall be financed from the following sources:

    (i)   international registration fees collected under Article 7(2) and other fees and charges due for other services rendered by the International Bureau in relation to the Special Union;

    (ii)   sale of, or royalties on, the publications of the International Bureau concerning the Special Union;

    (iii)   gifts, bequests, and subventions;

    (iv)   rents, interests, and other miscellaneous income;

    (v)   contributions of the countries of the Special Union, if and to the extent to which receipts from the sources indicated in items (i) to (iv) do not suffice to cover the expenses of the Special Union.

(4)

    (a)   The amount of the fee referred to in Article 7(2) shall be fixed by the Assembly on the proposal of the Director General.

    (b)   The amount of the said fee shall be so fixed that the revenue of the Special Union should, under normal circumstances, be sufficient to cover the expenses of the International Bureau for maintaining the international registration service, without requiring payment of the contributions referred to in paragraph (3)(v), above.

(5)

    (a)   For the purpose of establishing its contribution referred to in paragraph (3)(v), each country of the Special Union shall belong to the same class as it belongs to in the Paris Union for the Protection of Industrial Property, and shall pay its annual contributions on the basis of the same number of units as is fixed for that class in that Union.

    (b)   The annual contribution of each country of the Special Union shall be an amount in the same proportion to the total sum to be contributed to the budget of the Special Union by all countries as the number of its units is to the total of the units of all contributing countries.

    (c)   The date on which contributions are to be paid shall be fixed by the Assembly.

    (d)   A country which is in arrears in the payment of its contributions may not exercise its right to vote in any of the organs of the Special Union if the amount of its arrears equals or exceeds the amount of the contributions due from it for the preceding two full years. However, any organ of the Union may allow such a country to continue to exercise its right to vote in that organ if, and as long as, it is satisfied that the delay in payment is due to exceptional and unavoidable circumstances.

    (e)   If the budget is not adopted before the beginning of a new financial period, it shall be at the same level as the budget of the previous year, as provided in the financial regulations.

(6)   Subject to the provisions of paragraph (4)(a), the amount of fees and charges due for other services rendered by the International Bureau in relation to the Special Union shall be established, and shall be reported to the Assembly, by the Director General.

(7)

    (a)   The Special Union shall have a working capital fund which shall be constituted by a single payment made by each country of the Special Union. If the fund becomes insufficient, the Assembly shall decide to increase it.

    (b)   The amount of the initial payment of each country to the said fund or of its participation in the increase thereof shall be a proportion of the contribution of that country as a member of the Paris Union for the Protection of Industrial Property to the budget of the said Union for the year in which the fund is established or the decision to increase it is made.

(c)    The proportion and the terms of payment shall be fixed by the Assembly on the proposal of the Director General and after it has heard the advice of the Coordination Committee of the Organization.

(8)

(a)    In the headquarters agreement concluded with the country on the territory of which the Organization has its headquarters, it shall be provided that, whenever the working capital fund is insufficient, such country shall grant advances. The amount of those advances and the conditions on which they are granted shall be the subject of separate agreements, in each case, between such country and the Organization.

(b)    The country referred to in subparagraph (a) and the Organization shall each have the right to denounce the obligation to grant advances, by written notification. Denunciation shall take effect three years after the end of the year in which it has been notified.

(9)    The auditing of the accounts shall be effected by one or more of the countries of the Special Union or by external auditors, as provided in the financial regulations. They shall be designated, with their agreement, by the Assembly.

## Article 12

(1)    Proposals for the amendment of Article 9, Article 10, Article 11, and the present Article, may be initiated by any country member of the Assembly, or by the Director General. Such proposals shall be communicated by the Director General to the member countries of the Assembly at least six months in advance of their consideration by the Assembly.

(2)    Amendments to the Articles referred to in paragraph (1) shall be adopted by the Assembly. Adoption shall require three-fourths of the votes cast, provided that any amendment to Article 9, and to the present paragraph, shall require four-fifths of the votes cast.

(3)    Any amendment to the Articles referred to in paragraph (1) shall enter into force one month after written notifications of acceptance, effected in accordance with their respective constitutional processes, have been received by the Director General from three-fourths of the countries members of the Assembly at the time it adopted the amendment. Any amendment to the said Articles thus accepted shall bind all the countries which are members of the Assembly at the time the amendment enters into force, or which become members thereof at a subsequent date, provided that any amendment increasing the financial obligations of countries of the Special Union shall bind only those countries which have notified their acceptance of such amendment.

## Article 13

(1)    The details for carrying out this Agreement are fixed in the Regulations.

(2)    This Agreement may be revised by conferences held between the delegates of the countries of the Special Union.

## Article 14

(1)    Any country of the Special Union which has signed this Act may ratify it, and, if it has not signed it, may accede to it.

(2)

(a)    Any country outside the Special Union which is party to the Paris Convention for the Protection of Industrial Property may accede to this Act and thereby become a member of the Special Union.

(b)   Notification of accession shall, of itself, ensure, in the territory of the acceding country, the benefits of the foregoing provisions to appellations of origin which, at the time of accession, are the subject of international registration.

(c)   However, any country acceding to this Agreement may, within a period of one year, declare in regard to which appellations of origin, already registered at the International Bureau, it wishes to exercise the right provided for in Article 5(3).

(3)   Instruments of ratification and accession shall be deposited with the Director General.

(4)   The provisions of Article 24 of the Paris Convention for the Protection of Industrial Property shall apply to this Agreement.

(5)

(a)   With respect to the first five countries which have deposited their instruments of ratification or accession, this Act shall enter into force three months after the deposit of the fifth such instrument.

(b)   With respect to any other country, this Act shall enter into force three months after the date on which its ratification or accession has been notified by the Director General, unless a subsequent date has been indicated in the instrument of ratification or accession. In the latter case, this Act shall enter into force with respect to that country on the date thus indicated.

(6)   Ratification or accession shall automatically entail acceptance of all the clauses and admission to all the advantages of this Act.

(7)   After the entry into force of this Act, a country may accede to the original Act of October 31, 1958, of this Agreement only in conjunction with ratification of, or accession to, this Act.

## Article 15

(1)   This Agreement shall remain in force as long as five countries at least are party to it.

(2)   Any country may denounce this Act by notification addressed to the Director General. Such denunciation shall constitute also denunciation of the original Act of October 31, 1958, of this Agreement and shall affect only the country making it, the Agreement remaining in full force and effect as regards the other countries of the Special Union.

(3)   Denunciation shall take effect one year after the day on which the Director General has received the notification.

(4)   The right of denunciation provided for by this Article shall not be exercised by any country before the expiration of five years from the date upon which it becomes a member of the Special Union.

## Article 16

(1)

(a)   This Act shall, as regards the relations between the countries of the Special Union by which it has been ratified or acceded to, replace the original Act of October 31, 1958.

(b)   However, any country of the Special Union which has ratified or acceded to this Act shall be bound by the original Act of October 31, 1958, as regards its relations with countries of the Special Union which have not ratified or acceded to this Act.

(2)   Countries outside the Special Union which become party to this Act shall apply it to international registrations of appellations of origin effected at the International Bureau at the request of the Office of any country of the Special Union not party to this Act, provided that such registrations satisfy, with respect to the said countries, the requirements of this Act. With regard to international registrations effected at the International Bureau at the request of the Offices of the said countries outside the

Special Union which become party to this Act, such countries recognize that the aforesaid country of the Special Union may demand compliance with the requirements of the original Act of October 31, 1958.

## Article 17

(1)

    (a)   This Act shall be signed in a single copy in the French language and shall be deposited with the Government of Sweden.

    (b)   Official texts shall be established by the Director General, after consultation with the interested Governments, in such other languages as the Assembly may designate.

(2)   This Act shall remain open for signature at Stockholm until January 13, 1968.

(3)   The Director General shall transmit two copies, certified by the Government of Sweden, of the signed text of this Act to the Governments of all countries of the Special Union and, on request, to the Government of any other country.

(4)   The Director General shall register this Act with the Secretariat of the United Nations.

(5)   The Director General shall notify the Governments of all countries of the Special Union of signatures, deposits of instruments of ratification or accession, entry into force of any provisions of this Act, denunciations, and declarations pursuant to Article 14(2)(c) and Article 14(4).

## Article 18

(1)   Until the first Director General assumes office, references in this Act to the International Bureau of the Organization or to the Director General shall be construed as references to the Bureau of the Union established by the Paris Convention for the Protection of Industrial Property or its Director, respectively.

(2)   Countries of the Special Union not having ratified or acceded to this Act may, until five years after the entry into force of the Convention establishing the Organization, exercise, if they so desire, the rights provided for under Article 9 to Article 12 of this Act as if they were bound by those Articles. Any country desiring to exercise such rights shall give written notification to that effect to the Director General; such notification shall be effective from the date of its receipt. Such countries shall be deemed to be members of the Assembly until the expiration of the said period.

# 48. PARTIES TO THE LISBON AGREEMENT FOR THE PROTECTION OF APPELLATIONS OF ORIGIN AND THEIR INTERNATIONAL REGISTRATION*

Lisbon Agreement (1958), revised at Stockholm (1967),
and amended in 1979 (Lisbon Union)

**Status on May 4, 2021**

| State | Date on which State became party to the Stockholm (or Lisbon) Act | | Date on which State/IGO became party to the Geneva Act |
|---|---|---|---|
| Albania | Stockholm: | May 8, 2019 | February 26, 2020 |
| Algeria | Stockholm: | October 31, 1973 | - |
| Bosnia and Herzegovina | Stockholm: | July 4, 2013 | - |
| Bulgaria | Stockholm: | August 12, 1975 | - |
| Burkina Faso | Stockholm: | September 2, 1975 | - |
| Cambodia[1] | - | - | February 26, 2020 |
| Congo | Stockholm: | November 16, 1977 | - |
| Costa Rica | Stockholm: | July 30, 1997 | - |
| Côte d'Ivoire | - | - | Not yet in force[2] |
| Cuba | Stockholm: | April 8, 1975 | - |
| Czech Republic | Stockholm: | January 1, 1993 | - |
| Democratic People's Republic of Korea | Stockholm: | January 4, 2005 | February 26, 2020 |
| Dominican Republic | Stockholm: | January 17, 2020 | - |
| European Union[3,4] | - | - | February 26, 2020 |
| France[5] | Stockholm: | August 12, 1975 | April 21, 2021 |
| Gabon | Stockholm: | June 10, 1975 | - |
| Georgia | Stockholm: | September 23, 2004 | - |
| Haiti | Lisbon: | September 25, 1966 | - |
| Hungary | Stockholm: | October 31, 1973 | - |
| Iran (Islamic Republic of) | Stockholm: | March 9, 2006 | - |
| Israel | Stockholm: | October 31, 1973 | - |
| Italy | Stockholm: | April 24, 1977 | - |
| Lao People's Democratic Republic | - | - | February 20, 2021 |
| Mexico | Stockholm: | January 26, 2001 | - |
| Montenegro | Stockholm: | June 3, 2006 | - |
| Nicaragua | Stockholm: | June 15, 2006 | - |
| North Macedonia | Stockholm: | October 6, 2010 | - |
| Oman | - | - | June 30, 2021 |
| Peru | Stockholm: | May 16, 2005 | - |

---

* Document originally produced by the World Intellectual Property Organization (WIPO), the owner of the copyright. Published with the permission of the World Intellectual Property Organization.

## PARTIES TO THE LISBON AGREEMENT

| State | Date on which State became party to the Stockholm (or Lisbon) Act | | Date on which State/IGO became party to the Geneva Act |
|---|---|---|---|
| Portugal | Stockholm: | April 17, 1991 | - |
| Republic of Moldova | Stockholm: | April 5, 2001 | - |
| Samoa[1,6] | - | - | February 26, 2020 |
| Serbia[7] | Stockholm: | June 1, 1999 | - |
| Slovakia | Stockholm: | January 1, 1993 | - |
| Togo | Stockholm: | April 30, 1975 | - |
| Tunisia | Stockholm: | October 31, 1973 | - |
| (Total: 35) | (30) | | (8) |

---

[1]  In accordance with Article 7(4) of the Geneva Act of the Lisbon Agreement, this Contracting Party has declared that it wants to receive an individual fee to cover its cost of substantive examination of each international registration.

[2]  In accordance with Article 28(3)(b), the accession by Côte d'Ivoire shall enter into force three months after the date of the deposit by the African Intellectual Property Organization (OAPI) of its instrument of accession.

[3]  In accordance with Article 28(1)(iii) of the Geneva Act of the Lisbon Agreement, the European Union has been duly authorized, in accordance with its internal procedures, to become party to this Act and, under the constituting treaties of the European Union, legislation applies under which regional titles of protection can be obtained in respect of geographical indications.

[4]  The European Union avails itself of the possibility provided for in Article 29(4) of the Geneva Act of the Lisbon Agreement to extend by one year the time limit referred to in Article 15(1) of the Act, and the periods referred to in Article 17 of the Geneva Act, in accordance with the procedures specified in the Common Regulations.

[5]  Including all Overseas Departments and Territories.

[6]  In accordance with Article 7(4) of the Geneva Act of the Lisbon Agreement, this Contracting Party has declared that it requires an administrative fee relating to the use by the beneficiaries of the appellation of origin or the geographical indication in that Contracting Party.

[7]  Serbia is the continuing State from Serbia and Montenegro as from June 3, 2006.

# INDUSTRIAL DESIGN

## 49. HAGUE AGREEMENT CONCERNING THE INTERNATIONAL DEPOSIT OF INDUSTRIAL DESIGNS

of November 6, 1925

The Hague Act of November 28, 1960

### Article 1

(1)  The contracting States constitute a Special Union for the international deposit of industrial designs.

(2)  Only States members of the International Union for the Protection of Industrial Property may become party to this Agreement.

### Article 2

For the purposes of this Agreement:

"1925 Agreement" shall mean the Hague Agreement concerning the International Deposit of Industrial Designs of November 6, 1925;

"1934 Agreement" shall mean the Hague Agreement concerning the International Deposit of Industrial Designs of November 6, 1925, as revised at London on June 2, 1934;

"this Agreement" or "the present Agreement" shall mean the Hague Agreement concerning the International Deposit of Industrial Designs as established by the present Act;

"Regulations" shall mean the Regulations for carrying out this Agreement;

"International Bureau" shall mean the Bureau of the International Union for the Protection of Industrial Property;

"international deposit" shall mean a deposit made at the International Bureau;

"national deposit" shall mean a deposit made at the national Office of a contracting State;

"multiple deposit" shall mean a deposit including several designs;

"State of origin of an international deposit" shall mean the contracting State in which the applicant has a real and effective industrial or commercial establishment or, if the applicant has such establishments in several contracting States, the contracting State which he has indicated in his application; if the applicant has no such establishment in any contracting State, the contracting State in which he has his domicile; if he has no domicile in a contracting State, the contracting State of which he is a national;

"State having a novelty examination" shall mean a contracting State the domestic law of which provides for a system which involves a preliminary *ex officio* search and examination by its national Office as to the novelty of each deposited design.

## Article 3

Nationals of contracting States and persons who, without being nationals of any contracting State, are domiciled or have a real and effective industrial or commercial establishment in the territory of a contracting State may deposit designs at the International Bureau.

## Article 4

(1)   International deposit may be made at the International Bureau:

1.   direct, or

2.   through the intermediary of the national Office of a contracting State if the law of that State so permits.

(2)   The domestic law of any contracting State may require that international deposits of which it is deemed to be the State of origin shall be made through its national Office. Non-compliance with this requirement shall not prejudice the effects of the international deposit in the other contracting States.

## Article 5

(1)   The international deposit shall consist of an application and one or more photographs or other graphic representations of the design, and shall involve payment of the fees prescribed by the Regulations.

(2)   The application shall contain:

1.   a list of the contracting States in which the applicant requests that the international deposit shall have effect;

2.   the designation of the article or articles in which it is intended to incorporate the design;

3.   if the applicant wishes to claim the priority provided for in Article 9, an indication of the date, the State, and the number of the deposit giving rise to the right of priority;

4.   such other particulars as the Regulations may prescribe.

(3)   (a)   In addition, the application may contain:

1.   a short description of characteristic features of the design;

2.   a declaration as to who is the true creator of the design;

3.   a request for deferment of publication as provided in Article 6(4).

(b)   The application may be accompanied also by samples or models of the article or articles incorporating the design.

(4)   A multiple deposit may include several designs intended to be incorporated in articles included in the same class of the International Design Classification referred to in Article 21(2)4.

## Article 6

(1)   The International Bureau shall maintain the International Design Register and shall register international deposits therein.

(2)   The international deposit shall be deemed to have been made on the date on which the International Bureau received the application in due form, the fees payable with the application, and the photograph or photographs or other graphic representations of the design, or, if the International Bureau received them on different dates, on the last of these dates. The registration shall bear the same date.

(3)

    (a)   For each international deposit, the International Bureau shall publish in a periodical bulletin:

        1.   reproductions in black and white or, at the request of the applicant, in color of the deposited photographs or other graphic representations;

        2.   the date of the international deposit;

        3.   the particulars prescribed by the Regulations.

    (b)   The International Bureau shall send the periodical bulletin to the national Offices as soon as possible.

(4)

    (a)   The publication referred to in paragraph (3)(a) shall, at the request of the applicant, be deferred for such period as he may request. The said period may not exceed twelve months from the date of the international deposit. However, if priority is claimed, the starting date of such period shall be the priority date.

    (b)   At any time during the period referred to in subparagraph (a), the applicant may request immediate publication or may withdraw his deposit. Withdrawal of the deposit may be limited to one or a few only of the contracting States and, in the case of a multiple deposit, to some only of the designs included therein.

    (c)   If the applicant fails to pay within the proper time the fees payable before the expiration of the period referred to in subparagraph (a), the International Bureau shall cancel the deposit and shall not effect the publication referred to in paragraph (3)(a).

    (d)   Until the expiration of the period referred to in subparagraph (a), the International Bureau shall keep in confidence the registration of deposits made subject to deferred publication, and the public shall have no access to any documents or articles concerning such deposits. These provisions shall apply without limitation as to time if the applicant has withdrawn his deposit before the expiration of the said period.

(5)   Except as provided in paragraph (4), the Register and all documents and articles filed with the International Bureau shall be open to inspection by the public.

## Article 7

(1)

    (a)   A deposit registered at the International Bureau shall have the same effect in each of the contracting States designated by the applicant in his application as if all the formalities required by the domestic law for the grant of protection had been complied with by the applicant and as if all administrative acts required to that end had been accomplished by the Office of such State.

    (b)   Subject to the provisions of Article 11, the protection of designs the deposit of which has been registered at the International Bureau is governed in each contracting State by those provisions of the domestic law which are applicable in that State to designs for which protection has been claimed on the basis of a national deposit and in respect of which all formalities and administrative acts have been complied with and accomplished.

(2)   An international deposit shall have no effect in the State of origin if the laws of that State so provide.

## Article 8

(1)   Notwithstanding the provisions of Article 7, the national Office of a contracting State whose domestic law provides that the national Office may, on the basis of an administrative *ex officio* examination or pursuant to an opposition by a third party, refuse protection shall, in case of refusal, notify the International Bureau within six months that the design does not meet the requirements of its domestic law other than the formalities and administrative acts referred to in Article 7(1). If no such refusal is notified within a period of six months the international deposit shall become effective in that State as from the date of that deposit. However, in a contracting State having a novelty examination, the international deposit, while retaining its priority, shall, if no refusal is notified within a period of six months, become effective from the expiration of the said period unless the domestic law provides for an earlier date for deposits made with its national Office.

(2)   The period of six months referred to in paragraph (1) shall be computed from the date on which the national Office receives the issue of the periodical bulletin in which the registration of the international deposit has been published. The national Office shall communicate that date to any person so requesting.

(3)   The applicant shall have the same remedies against the refusal of the national Office referred to in paragraph (1) as if he had deposited his design in that Office; in any case, the refusal shall be subject to a request for re-examination or appeal. Notification of such refusal shall indicate:

1. the reasons for which it has been found that the design does not meet the requirements of the domestic law;

2. the date referred to in paragraph (2);

3. the time allowed for a request for re-examination or appeal;

4. the authority to which such request or appeal may be addressed.

(4)

(a)   The national Office of a contracting State whose domestic law contains provisions of the kind referred to in paragraph (1) requiring a declaration as to who is the true creator of the design or a description of the design may provide that, upon request and within a period of not less than sixty days from the dispatch of such a request by the said Office, the applicant shall file in the language of the application filed with the International Bureau:

1.   a declaration as to who is the true creator of the design;

2.   a short description emphasizing the essential characteristic features of the design as shown by the photographs or other graphic representations.

(b)   No fees shall be charged by a national Office in connection with the filing of such declarations or descriptions, or for their possible publication by that national Office.

(5)

(a)   Any contracting State whose domestic law contains provisions of the kind referred to in paragraph (1) shall notify the International Bureau accordingly.

(b)   If, under its legislation, a contracting State has several systems for the protection of designs one of which provides for novelty examination, the provisions of this Agreement concerning States having a novelty examination shall apply only to the said system.

## Article 9

If the international deposit of a design is made within six months of the first deposit of the same design in a State member of the International Union for the Protection of Industrial Property, and if priority is claimed for the international deposit, the priority date shall be that of the first deposit.

## Article 10

(1)   An international deposit may be renewed every five years by payment only, during the last year of each period of five years, of the renewal fees prescribed by the Regulations.

(2)   Subject to the payment of a surcharge fixed by the Regulations, a period of grace of six months shall be granted for renewal of the international deposit.

(3)   At the time of paying the renewal fees, the international deposit number must be indicated and also, if renewal is not to be effected for all the contracting States for which the deposit is about to expire, those of the contracting States for which the renewal is to be effected.

(4)   Renewal may be limited to some only of the designs included in a multiple deposit.

(5)   The International Bureau shall record and publish renewals.

## Article 11

(1)

(a)   The term of protection granted by a contracting State to designs which have been the subject of an international deposit shall not be less than:

1.   ten years from the date of the international deposit if the deposit has been renewed;

2.   five years from the date of the international deposit in the absence of renewal.

(b)   However, if, under the provisions of the domestic law of a contracting State having a novelty examination, protection commences at a date later than that of the international deposit, the minimum terms provided for in subparagraph (a) shall be computed from the date at which protection commences in that State. The fact that the international deposit is not renewed or is renewed only once shall in no way affect the minimum terms of protection thus defined.

(2)   If the domestic law of a contracting State provides, in respect of designs which have been the subject of a national deposit, for protection whose duration, with or without renewal, is longer than ten years, protection of the same duration shall, on the basis of the international deposit and its renewals, be granted in that State to designs which have been the subject of an international deposit.

(3)   A contracting State may, under its domestic law, limit the term of protection of designs which have been the subject of an international deposit to the terms provided for in paragraph (1).

(4)   Subject to the provisions of paragraph (1)(b), protection in a contracting State shall terminate at the date of expiration of the international deposit, unless the domestic law of that State provides that protection shall continue after the date of expiration of the international deposit.

## Article 12

(1)   The International Bureau shall record and publish changes affecting ownership of a design which is the subject of an international deposit in force. It is understood that transfer of ownership may be limited to the rights arising from the international deposit in one or a few only of the contracting States and, in the case of a multiple deposit, to some only of the designs included therein.

(2)   The recording referred to in paragraph (1) shall have the same effect as if it had been made in the national Offices of the contracting States.

## Article 13

(1)   The owner of an international deposit may, by means of a declaration addressed to the International Bureau, renounce his rights in respect of all or some only of the contracting States and, in the case of a multiple deposit, in respect of some only of the designs included therein.

(2)   The International Bureau shall record and publish such declaration.

### Article 14

(1)   No contracting State may, as a condition of recognition of the right to protection, require that the article incorporating the design bear a sign or notice concerning the deposit of the design.

(2)   If the domestic law of a contracting State provides for a notice on the article for any other purpose, such State shall regard such requirement as satisfied if all the articles offered to the public with the authorization of the owner of the rights in the design, or the tags attached to such articles, bear the international design notice.

(3)   The international design notice shall consist of the symbol (D) (a capital D in a circle) accompanied by:

1.   the year of the international deposit and the name, or the usual abbreviation of the name, of the depositor, or

2.   the number of the international deposit.

(4)   The mere appearance of the international design notice on the article or the tags shall in no case be interpreted as implying a waiver of protection by virtue of copyright or on any other grounds, whenever, in the absence of such notice, such protection may be claimed.

### Article 15

(1)   The fees prescribed by the Regulations shall consist of:

1.   fees for the International Bureau;

2.   fees for the contracting States designated by the applicant, namely:

   *(a)*   a fee for each contracting State;

   *(b)*   a fee for each contracting State having a novelty examination and requiring the payment of a fee for such examination.

(2)   Any fees paid in respect of one and the same deposit for a contracting State under paragraph (1)2(a), shall be deducted from the amount of the fee referred to in paragraph (1)2(b), if the latter fee becomes payable for the same State.

### Article 16

(1)   The fees for contracting States referred to in Article 15(1)2, shall be collected by the International Bureau and paid over annually to the contracting States designated by the applicant.

(2)

(a)   Any contracting State may notify the International Bureau that it waives its right to the supplementary fees referred to in Article 15(1)2(a), in respect of international deposits of which any other contracting State making a similar waiver is deemed to be the State of origin.

(b)   Such State may make a similar waiver in respect of international deposits of which it is itself deemed to be the State of origin.

### Article 17

The Regulations shall govern the details concerning the implementation of this Agreement and in particular:

1.   the languages and the number of copies in which the application for deposit must be filed, and the data to be supplied in the application;

2.     the amounts and the dates and method of payment of the fees for the International Bureau and for the States, including the limits imposed on the fee for contracting States having a novelty examination;

3.     the number, size, and other characteristics, of the photographs or other graphic representations of each design deposited;

4.     the length of the description of characteristic features of the design;

5.     the limits within which and conditions under which samples or models of the articles incorporating the design may accompany the application;

6.     the number of designs that may be included in a multiple deposit and other conditions governing multiple deposits;

7.     all matters relating to the publication and distribution of the periodical bulletin referred to in Article 6(3)(a), including the number of copies of the bulletin which shall be given free of charge to the national Offices and the number of copies which may be sold at a reduced price to such Offices;

8.     the procedure for notification by contracting States of any refusal provided for under Article 8(1), and the procedure for communication and publication of such refusals by the International Bureau;

9.     the conditions for recording and publication by the International Bureau of the changes affecting the ownership of a design referred to in Article 12(1), and for the renunciations referred to in Article 13;

10.    the disposal of documents and articles concerning deposits for which the possibility of renewal has ceased to exist.

## Article 18

The provisions of this Agreement shall not preclude the making of a claim to the benefit of any greater protection which may be granted by domestic legislation in a contracting State, nor shall they affect in any way the protection accorded to works of art and works of applied art by international copyright treaties and conventions.

## Article 19

The fees of the International Bureau for services provided for by this Agreement shall be fixed in such a manner:

(a)    that the proceeds therefrom cover all the expenses of the International Design Service and all those necessitated by the preparation and holding of meetings of the International Design Committee or conferences for the revision of this Agreement;

(b)    that they allow for the maintenance of the reserve fund referred to in Article 20.

## Article 20

(1)    There shall be a reserve fund of 250,000 Swiss francs. The amount of the reserve fund may be modified by the International Design Committee referred to in Article 21.

(2)    The reserve fund shall be replenished by the surplus receipts of the International Design Service.

(3)

(a)    However, at the time of the entry into force of this Agreement, the reserve fund shall be constituted by a single contribution paid by each contracting State and computed in proportion to the number of units corresponding to the class to which it belongs by virtue of Article 13(8) of the Paris Convention for the Protection of Industrial Property.

(b)   States which become party to this Agreement after it enters into force shall also pay a single contribution. The contribution shall be computed according to the principles formulated in the preceding subparagraph, so that all States, whatever the date of their becoming party to the Agreement, shall pay the same contribution per unit.

(4)   When the amount of the reserve fund exceeds the fixed ceiling, the surplus shall be periodically distributed among the contracting States, in proportion to the single contribution paid by each, up to the maximum amount of that contribution.

(5)   When the single contributions have been fully reimbursed, the International Design Committee may decide that States subsequently becoming party to the Agreement shall not be required to pay the single contribution.

## Article 21

(1)   There shall be an International Design Committee consisting of representatives of all the contracting States.

(2)   The Committee shall have the following duties and powers:

1.   to draw up its own rules of procedure;

2.   to amend the Regulations;

3.   to modify the ceiling of the reserve fund referred to in Article 20;

4.   to establish the International Design Classification;

5.   to study matters concerning the application and possible revision of this Agreement;

6.   to study all other matters concerning the international protection of designs;

7.   to approve the yearly management reports of the International Bureau and to give general instructions to the International Bureau concerning the discharge of the duties assigned to it under this Agreement;

8.   to draw up a report on the foreseeable expenditure of the International Bureau for each triennial period to come.

(3)   The decisions of the Committee shall require four-fifths of the votes of its members present or represented and voting in the case of items (2)1, (2)2, (2)3, and (2)4, and a simple majority in all other cases. Abstentions shall not be considered as votes.

(4)   The Committee shall be convened by the Director of the International Bureau:

1.   at least once every three years;

2.   at any time at the request of one-third of the contracting States, or, if deemed necessary, upon the initiative of the Director of the International Bureau or the Government of the Swiss Confederation.

(5)   The travel expenses and subsistence allowances of members of the Committee shall be borne by their respective Governments.

## Article 22

(1)   The Regulations may be amended either by the Committee as prescribed in Article 21(2)2, or in accordance with the written procedure provided for in paragraph (2), below.

(2)   In the case of written procedure, amendments shall be proposed by the Director of the International Bureau in a circular letter addressed to the Government of each contracting State. The amendments shall be regarded as adopted if, within one year from their communication, no contracting State has raised an objection.

## Article 23

(1)   This Agreement shall remain open for signature until December 31, 1961.

(2)   It shall be ratified and the instruments of ratification shall be deposited with the Government of the Netherlands.

## Article 24

(1)   States members of the International Union for the Protection of Industrial Property which have not signed this Agreement may accede thereto.

(2)   Such accessions shall be notified through diplomatic channels to the Government of the Swiss Confederation, and by the latter to the Governments of all contracting States.

## Article 25

(1)   Each contracting State undertakes to provide for the protection of industrial designs and to adopt, in accordance with its constitution, the measures necessary to ensure the application of this Agreement.

(2)   At the time a contracting State deposits its instrument of ratification or accession, it must be in a position under its domestic law to give effect to the provisions of this Agreement.

## Article 26

(1)   This Agreement shall enter into force one month after the date on which the Government of the Swiss Confederation has dispatched a notification to the contracting States of the deposit of ten instruments of ratification or accession, at least four of which are those of States which, at the date of the present Agreement, are not party either to the 1925 Agreement or to the 1934 Agreement.

(2)   Thereafter, the deposit of instruments of ratification and accession shall be notified to the contracting States by the Government of the Swiss Confederation. Such ratifications and accessions shall become effective one month after the date of the dispatch of such notification unless, in the case of accession, a later date is indicated in the instrument of accession.

## Article 27

Any contracting State may at any time notify the Government of the Swiss Confederation that this Agreement shall also apply to all or part of those territories for the external relations of which it is responsible. Thereupon, the Government of the Swiss Confederation shall communicate such notification to the contracting States and the Agreement shall apply also to the said territories one month after the dispatch of the communication by the Government of the Swiss Confederation to the contracting States unless a later date is indicated in the notification.

## Article 28

(1)   Any contracting State may, by notification addressed to the Government of the Swiss Confederation, denounce this Agreement in its own name and on behalf of all or part of the territories designated in the notification under Article 27. Such notification shall take effect one year after its receipt by the Government of the Swiss Confederation.

(2)   Denunciation shall not relieve any contracting State of its obligations under this Agreement in respect of designs deposited at the International Bureau prior to the date on which the denunciation takes effect.

## Article 29

(1)   This Agreement shall be submitted to periodical revision with a view to the introduction of amendments designed to improve the protection resulting from the international deposit of designs.

(2)   Revision conferences shall be called at the request of the International Design Committee or of not less than one-half of the contracting States.

## Article 30

(1)   Two or more contracting States may at any time notify the Government of the Swiss Confederation that, subject to the conditions indicated in the notification:

  1.    a common Office shall be substituted for the national Office of each of them;

  2.    they shall be deemed to be a single State for the purposes of the application of Articles 2 to 17 of this Agreement.

(2)   Such notification shall not take effect until six months after the date of dispatch of the communication thereof by the Government of the Swiss Confederation to the other contracting States.

## Article 31

(1)   This Agreement alone shall be applicable as regards the mutual relations of States party to both the present Agreement and the 1925 Agreement or the 1934 Agreement. However, such States shall, in their mutual relations, apply the 1925 Agreement or the 1934 Agreement, as the case may be, to designs deposited at the International Bureau prior to the date on which the present Agreement becomes applicable as regards their mutual relations.

(2)

  (a)   Any State party to both the present Agreement and the 1925 Agreement shall continue to apply the 1925 Agreement in its relations with States party only to the 1925 Agreement, unless the said State has denounced the 1925 Agreement.

  (b)   Any State party to both the present Agreement and the 1934 Agreement shall continue to apply the 1934 Agreement in its relations with States party only to the 1934 Agreement, unless the said State has denounced the 1934 Agreement.

(3)   States party to the present Agreement only shall not be bound to States which, without being party to the present Agreement, are party to the 1925 Agreement or the 1934 Agreement.

## Article 32

(1)   Signature and ratification of, or accession to, the present Agreement by a State party, at the date of this Agreement, to the 1925 Agreement or the 1934 Agreement shall be deemed to include signature and ratification of, or accession to, the Protocol annexed to the present Agreement, unless such State makes an express declaration to the contrary at the time of signing or depositing its instrument of accession.

(2)   Any contracting State having made the declaration referred to in paragraph (1), or any other contracting State not party to the 1925 Agreement or the 1934 Agreement, may sign or accede to the Protocol annexed to this Agreement. At the time of signing or depositing its instrument of accession, it may declare that it does not consider itself bound by the provisions of paragraphs 1(2)(a) or 1(2)(b) of the Protocol; in such case, the other States party to the Protocol shall be under no obligation to apply, in their relations with that State, the provisions mentioned in such declaration. The provisions of Articles 23 to 28 inclusive shall apply by analogy.

## Article 33

This Act shall be signed in a single copy which shall be deposited in the archives of the Government of the Netherlands. A certified copy shall be transmitted by the latter to the Government of each State which has signed or acceded to this Agreement.

## PROTOCOL

*This protocol is not yet in force.*

States party to this Protocol have agreed as follows:

(1)   The provisions of this Protocol shall apply to designs which have been the subject of an international deposit and of which one of the States party to this Protocol is deemed to be the State of origin.

(2)   In respect of designs referred to in paragraph (1), above:

    (a)   the term of protection granted by States party to this Protocol to the designs referred to in paragraph (1) shall not be less than fifteen years from the date provided for in paragraphs 11(1)(a) or 11(1)(b), as the case may be;

    (b)   the appearance of a notice on the articles incorporating the designs or on the tags attached thereto shall in no case be required by the States party to this Protocol, either for the exercise in their territories of rights arising from the international deposit, or for any other purpose.

# 50. HAGUE AGREEMENT CONCERNING THE INTERNATIONAL REGISTRATION OF INDUSTRIAL DESIGNS

Geneva Act of July 2, 1999

## INTRODUCTORY PROVISIONS

### Article 1

### Abbreviated Expressions

For the purposes of this Act:

(i)   "the Hague Agreement" means the Hague Agreement Concerning the International Deposit of Industrial Designs, henceforth renamed the Hague Agreement Concerning the International Registration of Industrial Designs;

(ii)   "this Act" means the Hague Agreement as established by the present Act;

(iii)  "Regulations" means the Regulations under this Act;

(iv)   "prescribed" means prescribed in the Regulations;

(v)   "Paris Convention" means the Paris Convention for the Protection of Industrial Property, signed at Paris on March 20, 1883, as revised and amended;

(vi)   "international registration" means the international registration of an industrial design effected according to this Act;

(vii)  "international application" means an application for international registration;

(viii) "International Register" means the official collection of data concerning international registrations maintained by the International Bureau, which data this Act or the Regulations require or permit to be recorded, regardless of the medium in which such data are stored;

(ix)   "person" means a natural person or a legal entity;

(x)   "applicant" means the person in whose name an international application is filed;

(xi)   "holder" means the person in whose name an international registration is recorded in the International Register;

(xii)  "intergovernmental organization" means an intergovernmental organization eligible to become party to this Act in accordance with Article 27(1)(ii);

(xiii) "Contracting Party" means any State or intergovernmental organization party to this Act;

(xiv)  "applicant's Contracting Party" means the Contracting Party or one of the Contracting Parties from which the applicant derives its entitlement to file an international application by virtue of satisfying, in relation to that Contracting Party, at least one of the conditions specified in Article 3; where there are two or more Contracting Parties from which the applicant may, under Article 3, derive its entitlement to file an international application, "applicant's Contracting Party" means the one which, among those Contracting Parties, is indicated as such in the international application;

(xv)  "territory of a Contracting Party" means, where the Contracting Party is a State, the territory of that State and, where the Contracting Party is an intergovernmental organization, the territory in which the constituent treaty of that intergovernmental organization applies;

(xvi) "Office" means the agency entrusted by a Contracting Party with the grant of protection for industrial designs with effect in the territory of that Contracting Party;

(xvii)   "Examining Office" means an Office which *ex officio* examines applications filed with it for the protection of industrial designs at least to determine whether the industrial designs satisfy the condition of novelty;

(xviii)   "designation" means a request that an international registration have effect in a Contracting Party; it also means the recording, in the International Register, of that request;

(xix)   "designated Contracting Party" and "designated Office" means the Contracting Party and the Office of the Contracting Party, respectively, to which a designation applies;

(xx)   "1934 Act" means the Act signed at London on June 2, 1934, of the Hague Agreement;

(xxi)   "1960 Act" means the Act signed at The Hague on November 28, 1960, of the Hague Agreement;

(xxii)   "1961 Additional Act" means the Act signed at Monaco on November 18, 1961, additional to the 1934 Act;

(xxiii)   "Complementary Act of 1967" means the Complementary Act signed at Stockholm on July 14, 1967, as amended, of the Hague Agreement;

(xxiv)   "Union" means the Hague Union established by the Hague Agreement of November 6, 1925, and maintained by the 1934 and 1960 Acts, the 1961 Additional Act, the Complementary Act of 1967 and this Act;

(xxv)   "Assembly" means the Assembly referred to in Article 21(1)(a) or any body replacing that Assembly;

(xxvi)   "Organization" means the World Intellectual Property Organization;

(xxvii)   "Director General" means the Director General of the Organization;

(xxviii)   "International Bureau" means the International Bureau of the Organization;

(xxix)   "instrument of ratification" shall be construed as including instruments of acceptance or approval.

## Article 2

### Applicability of Other Protection Accorded by Laws of Contracting Parties and by Certain International Treaties

(1)   [*Laws of Contracting Parties and Certain International Treaties*] The provisions of this Act shall not affect the application of any greater protection which may be accorded by the law of a Contracting Party, nor shall they affect in any way the protection accorded to works of art and works of applied art by international copyright treaties and conventions, or the protection accorded to industrial designs under the Agreement on Trade-Related Aspects of Intellectual Property Rights annexed to the Agreement Establishing the World Trade Organization.

(2)   [*Obligation to Comply with the Paris Convention*] Each Contracting Party shall comply with the provisions of the Paris Convention which concern industrial designs.

## CHAPTER I

### INTERNATIONAL APPLICATION AND INTERNATIONAL REGISTRATION

### Article 3

### Entitlement to File an International Application

Any person that is a national of a State that is a Contracting Party or of a State member of an intergovernmental organization that is a Contracting Party, or that has a domicile, a habitual residence or a real and effective industrial or commercial establishment in the territory of a Contracting Party, shall be entitled to file an international application.

## Article 4

### Procedure for Filing the International Application

(1) [*Direct or Indirect Filing*]

(a)   The international application may be filed, at the option of the applicant, either directly with the International Bureau or through the Office of the applicant's Contracting Party.

(b)   Notwithstanding subparagraph (a), any Contracting Party may, in a declaration, notify the Director General that international applications may not be filed through its Office.

(2) [*Transmittal Fee in Case of Indirect Filing*] The Office of any Contracting Party may require that the applicant pay a transmittal fee to it, for its own benefit, in respect of any international application filed through it.

## Article 5

### Contents of the International Application

(1) [*Mandatory Contents of the International Application*] The international application shall be in the prescribed language or one of the prescribed languages and shall contain or be accompanied by

(i)   a request for international registration under this Act;

(ii)   the prescribed data concerning the applicant;

(iii)   the prescribed number of copies of a reproduction or, at the choice of the applicant, of several different reproductions of the industrial design that is the subject of the international application, presented in the prescribed manner; however, where the industrial design is two-dimensional and a request for deferment of publication is made in accordance with paragraph (5), the international application may, instead of containing reproductions, be accompanied by the prescribed number of specimens of the industrial design;

(iv)   an indication of the product or products which constitute the industrial design or in relation to which the industrial design is to be used, as prescribed;

(v)   an indication of the designated Contracting Parties;

(vi)   the prescribed fees;

(vii)   any other prescribed particulars.

(2) [*Additional Mandatory Contents of the International Application*]

(a)   Any Contracting Party whose Office is an Examining Office and whose law, at the time it becomes party to this Act, requires that an application for the grant of protection to an industrial design contain any of the elements specified in subparagraph (b) in order for that application to be accorded a filing date under that law may, in a declaration, notify the Director General of those elements.

(b)   The elements that may be notified pursuant to subparagraph (a) are the following:

(i)   indications concerning the identity of the creator of the industrial design that is the subject of that application;

(ii)   a brief description of the reproduction or of the characteristic features of the industrial design that is the subject of that application;

(iii)   a claim.

(c)   Where the international application contains the designation of a Contracting Party that has made a notification under subparagraph (a), it shall also contain, in the prescribed manner, any element that was the subject of that notification.

(3) [*Other Possible Contents of the International Application*] The international application may contain or be accompanied by such other elements as are specified in the Regulations.

(4) [*Several Industrial Designs in the Same International Application*] Subject to such conditions as may be prescribed, an international application may include two or more industrial designs.

(5) [*Request for Deferred Publication*] The international application may contain a request for deferment of publication.

## Article 6

### Priority

(1) [*Claiming of Priority*]

(a) The international application may contain a declaration claiming, under Article 4 of the Paris Convention, the priority of one or more earlier applications filed in or for any country party to that Convention or any Member of the World Trade Organization.

(b) The Regulations may provide that the declaration referred to in subparagraph (a) may be made after the filing of the international application. In such case, the Regulations shall prescribe the latest time by which such declaration may be made.

(2) [*International Application Serving as a Basis for Claiming Priority*] The international application shall, as from its filing date and whatever may be its subsequent fate, be equivalent to a regular filing within the meaning of Article 4 of the Paris Convention.

## Article 7

### Designation Fees

(1) [*Prescribed Designation Fee*] The prescribed fees shall include, subject to paragraph (2), a designation fee for each designated Contracting Party.

(2) [*Individual Designation Fee*] Any Contracting Party whose Office is an Examining Office and any Contracting Party that is an intergovernmental organization may, in a declaration, notify the Director General that, in connection with any international application in which it is designated, and in connection with the renewal of any international registration resulting from such an international application, the prescribed designation fee referred to in paragraph (1) shall be replaced by an individual designation fee, whose amount shall be indicated in the declaration and can be changed in further declarations. The said amount may be fixed by the said Contracting Party for the initial term of protection and for each term of renewal or for the maximum period of protection allowed by the Contracting Party concerned. However, it may not be higher than the equivalent of the amount which the Office of that Contracting Party would be entitled to receive from an applicant for a grant of protection for an equivalent period to the same number of industrial designs, that amount being diminished by the savings resulting from the international procedure.

(3) [*Transfer of Designation Fees*] The designation fees referred to in paragraphs (1) and (2) shall be transferred by the International Bureau to the Contracting Parties in respect of which those fees were paid.

## Article 8

### Correction of Irregularities

(1) [*Examination of the International Application*] If the International Bureau finds that the international application does not, at the time of its receipt by the International Bureau, fulfill the requirements of this Act and the Regulations, it shall invite the applicant to make the required corrections within the prescribed time limit.

(2) [*Irregularities Not Corrected*]

(a) If the applicant does not comply with the invitation within the prescribed time limit, the international application shall, subject to subparagraph (b), be considered abandoned.

(b) In the case of an irregularity which relates to Article 5(2) or to a special requirement notified to the Director General by a Contracting Party in accordance with the Regulations, if the applicant does not comply with the invitation within the prescribed time limit, the international application shall be deemed not to contain the designation of that Contracting Party.

## Article 9

### Filing Date of the International Application

(1) [*International Application Filed Directly*] Where the international application is filed directly with the International Bureau, the filing date shall, subject to paragraph (3), be the date on which the International Bureau receives the international application.

(2) [*International Application Filed Indirectly*] Where the international application is filed through the Office of the applicant's Contracting Party, the filing date shall be determined as prescribed.

(3) [*International Application with Certain Irregularities*] Where the international application has, on the date on which it is received by the International Bureau, an irregularity which is prescribed as an irregularity entailing a postponement of the filing date of the international application, the filing date shall be the date on which the correction of such irregularity is received by the International Bureau.

## Article 10

### International Registration, Date of the International Registration, Publication and Confidential Copies of the International Registration

(1) [*International Registration*] The International Bureau shall register each industrial design that is the subject of an international application immediately upon receipt by it of the international application or, where corrections are invited under Article 8, immediately upon receipt of the required corrections. The registration shall be effected whether or not publication is deferred under Article 11.

(2) [*Date of the International Registration*]

(a) Subject to subparagraph (b), the date of the international registration shall be the filing date of the international application.

(b) Where the international application has, on the date on which it is received by the International Bureau, an irregularity which relates to Article 5(2), the date of the international registration shall be the date on which the correction of such irregularity is received by the International Bureau or the filing date of the international application, whichever is the later.

(3) [*Publication*]

(a) The international registration shall be published by the International Bureau. Such publication shall be deemed in all Contracting Parties to be sufficient publicity, and no other publicity may be required of the holder.

(b) The International Bureau shall send a copy of the publication of the international registration to each designated Office.

(4) [*Maintenance of Confidentiality Before Publication*] Subject to paragraph (5) and Article 11(4)(b), the International Bureau shall keep in confidence each international application and each international registration until publication.

(5) [*Confidential Copies*]

(a)   The International Bureau shall, immediately after registration has been effected, send a copy of the international registration, along with any relevant statement, document or specimen accompanying the international application, to each Office that has notified the International Bureau that it wishes to receive such a copy and has been designated in the international application.

(b)   The Office shall, until publication of the international registration by the International Bureau, keep in confidence each international registration of which a copy has been sent to it by the International Bureau and may use the said copy only for the purpose of the examination of the international registration and of applications for the protection of industrial designs filed in or for the Contracting Party for which the Office is competent. In particular, it may not divulge the contents of any such international registration to any person outside the Office other than the holder of that international registration, except for the purposes of an administrative or legal proceeding involving a conflict over entitlement to file the international application on which the international registration is based. In the case of such an administrative or legal proceeding, the contents of the international registration may only be disclosed in confidence to the parties involved in the proceeding who shall be bound to respect the confidentiality of the disclosure.

## Article 11

### Deferment of Publication

(1)   [*Provisions of Laws of Contracting Parties Concerning Deferment of Publication*]

(a)   Where the law of a Contracting Party provides for the deferment of the publication of an industrial design for a period which is less than the prescribed period, that Contracting Party shall, in a declaration, notify the Director General of the allowable period of deferment.

(b)   Where the law of a Contracting Party does not provide for the deferment of the publication of an industrial design, the Contracting Party shall, in a declaration, notify the Director General of that fact.

(2)   [*Deferment of Publication*] Where the international application contains a request for deferment of publication, the publication shall take place,

(i)   where none of the Contracting Parties designated in the international application has made a declaration under paragraph (1), at the expiry of the prescribed period or,

(ii)   where any of the Contracting Parties designated in the international application has made a declaration under paragraph (1)(a), at the expiry of the period notified in such declaration or, where there is more than one such designated Contracting Party, at the expiry of the shortest period notified in their declarations.

(3)   [*Treatment of Requests for Deferment Where Deferment Is Not Possible Under Applicable Law*] Where deferment of publication has been requested and any of the Contracting Parties designated in the international application has made a declaration under paragraph (1)(b) that deferment of publication is not possible under its law,

(i)   subject to item (ii), the International Bureau shall notify the applicant accordingly; if, within the prescribed period, the applicant does not, by notice in writing to the International Bureau, withdraw the designation of the said Contracting Party, the International Bureau shall disregard the request for deferment of publication;

(ii)   where, instead of containing reproductions of the industrial design, the international application was accompanied by specimens of the industrial design, the International Bureau shall disregard the designation of the said Contracting Party and shall notify the applicant accordingly.

(4)   [*Request for Earlier Publication or for Special Access to the International Registration*]

(a)   At any time during the period of deferment applicable under paragraph (2), the holder may request publication of any or all of the industrial designs that are the subject of the international registration, in which case the period of deferment in respect of such industrial design or designs shall be considered to have expired on the date of receipt of such request by the International Bureau.

(b)   The holder may also, at any time during the period of deferment applicable under paragraph (2), request the International Bureau to provide a third party specified by the holder with an extract from, or to allow such a party access to, any or all of the industrial designs that are the subject of the international registration.

(5)   [*Renunciation and Limitation*]

(a)   If, at any time during the period of deferment applicable under paragraph (2), the holder renounces the international registration in respect of all the designated Contracting Parties, the industrial design or designs that are the subject of the international registration shall not be published.

(b)   If, at any time during the period of deferment applicable under paragraph (2), the holder limits the international registration, in respect of all of the designated Contracting Parties, to one or some of the industrial designs that are the subject of the international registration, the other industrial design or designs that are the subject of the international registration shall not be published.

(6)   [*Publication and Furnishing of Reproductions*]

(a)   At the expiration of any period of deferment applicable under the provisions of this Article, the International Bureau shall, subject to the payment of the prescribed fees, publish the international registration. If such fees are not paid as prescribed, the international registration shall be canceled and publication shall not take place.

(b)   Where the international application was accompanied by one or more specimens of the industrial design in accordance with Article 5(1)(iii), the holder shall submit the prescribed number of copies of a reproduction of each industrial design that is the subject of that application to the International Bureau within the prescribed time limit. To the extent that the holder does not do so, the international registration shall be canceled and publication shall not take place.

## Article 12

### Refusal

(1)   [*Right to Refuse*] The Office of any designated Contracting Party may, where the conditions for the grant of protection under the law of that Contracting Party are not met in respect of any or all of the industrial designs that are the subject of an international registration, refuse the effects, in part or in whole, of the international registration in the territory of the said Contracting Party, provided that no Office may refuse the effects, in part or in whole, of any international registration on the ground that requirements relating to the form or contents of the international application that are provided for in this Act or the Regulations or are additional to, or different from, those requirements have not been satisfied under the law of the Contracting Party concerned.

(2)   [*Notification of Refusal*]

(a)   The refusal of the effects of an international registration shall be communicated by the Office to the International Bureau in a notification of refusal within the prescribed period.

(b)   Any notification of refusal shall state all the grounds on which the refusal is based.

(3)   [*Transmission of Notification of Refusal; Remedies*]

(a)   The International Bureau shall, without delay, transmit a copy of the notification of refusal to the holder.

(b) The holder shall enjoy the same remedies as if any industrial design that is the subject of the international registration had been the subject of an application for the grant of protection under the law applicable to the Office that communicated the refusal. Such remedies shall at least consist of the possibility of a re-examination or a review of the refusal or an appeal against the refusal.

(4) [*Withdrawal of Refusal*] Any refusal may be withdrawn, in part or in whole, at any time by the Office that communicated it.

## Article 13

### Special Requirements Concerning Unity of Design

(1) [*Notification of Special Requirements*] Any Contracting Party whose law, at the time it becomes party to this Act, requires that designs that are the subject of the same application conform to a requirement of unity of design, unity of production or unity of use, or belong to the same set or composition of items, or that only one independent and distinct design may be claimed in a single application, may, in a declaration, notify the Director General accordingly. However, no such declaration shall affect the right of an applicant to include two or more industrial designs in an international application in accordance with Article 5(4), even if the application designates the Contracting Party that has made the declaration.

(2) [*Effect of Declaration*] Any such declaration shall enable the Office of the Contracting Party that has made it to refuse the effects of the international registration pursuant to Article 12(1) pending compliance with the requirement notified by that Contracting Party.

(3) [*Further Fees Payable on Division of Registration*] Where, following a notification of refusal in accordance with paragraph (2), an international registration is divided before the Office concerned in order to overcome a ground of refusal stated in the notification, that Office shall be entitled to charge a fee in respect of each additional international application that would have been necessary in order to avoid that ground of refusal.

## Article 14

### Effects of the International Registration

(1) [*Effect as Application Under Applicable Law*] The international registration shall, from the date of the international registration, have at least the same effect in each designated Contracting Party as a regularly-filed application for the grant of protection of the industrial design under the law of that Contracting Party.

(2) [*Effect as Grant of Protection Under Applicable Law*]

(a) In each designated Contracting Party the Office of which has not communicated a refusal in accordance with Article 12, the international registration shall have the same effect as a grant of protection for the industrial design under the law of that Contracting Party at the latest from the date of expiration of the period allowed for it to communicate a refusal or, where a Contracting Party has made a corresponding declaration under the Regulations, at the latest at the time specified in that declaration.

(b) Where the Office of a designated Contracting Party has communicated a refusal and has subsequently withdrawn, in part or in whole, that refusal, the international registration shall, to the extent that the refusal is withdrawn, have the same effect in that Contracting Party as a grant of protection for the industrial design under the law of the said Contracting Party at the latest from the date on which the refusal was withdrawn.

(c) The effect given to the international registration under this paragraph shall apply to the industrial design or designs that are the subject of that registration as received from the

International Bureau by the designated Office or, where applicable, as amended in the procedure before that Office.

(3)  [*Declaration Concerning Effect of Designation of Applicant's Contracting Party*]

(a)  Any Contracting Party whose Office is an Examining Office may, in a declaration, notify the Director General that, where it is the applicant's Contracting Party, the designation of that Contracting Party in an international registration shall have no effect.

(b)  Where a Contracting Party having made the declaration referred to in subparagraph (a) is indicated in an international application both as the applicant's Contracting Party and as a designated Contracting Party, the International Bureau shall disregard the designation of that Contracting Party.

## Article 15

## Invalidation

(1)  [*Requirement of Opportunity of Defense*] Invalidation, by the competent authorities of a designated Contracting Party, of the effects, in part or in whole, in the territory of that Contracting Party, of the international registration may not be pronounced without the holder having, in good time, been afforded the opportunity of defending his rights.

(2)  [*Notification of Invalidation*] The Office of the Contracting Party in whose territory the effects of the international registration have been invalidated shall, where it is aware of the invalidation, notify it to the International Bureau.

## Article 16

## Recording of Changes and Other Matters Concerning International Registrations

(1)  [*Recording of Changes and Other Matters*] The International Bureau shall, as prescribed, record in the International Register

(i)  any change in ownership of the international registration, in respect of any or all of the designated Contracting Parties and in respect of any or all of the industrial designs that are the subject of the international registration, provided that the new owner is entitled to file an international application under Article 3,

(ii)  any change in the name or address of the holder,

(iii)  the appointment of a representative of the applicant or holder and any other relevant fact concerning such representative,

(iv)  any renunciation, by the holder, of the international registration, in respect of any or all of the designated Contracting Parties,

(v)  any limitation, by the holder, of the international registration, in respect of any or all of the designated Contracting Parties, to one or some of the industrial designs that are the subject of the international registration,

(vi)  any invalidation, by the competent authorities of a designated Contracting Party, of the effects, in the territory of that Contracting Party, of the international registration in respect of any or all of the industrial designs that are the subject of the international registration,

(vii)  any other relevant fact, identified in the Regulations, concerning the rights in any or all of the industrial designs that are the subject of the international registration.

(2)  [*Effect of Recording in International Register*] Any recording referred to in items (i), (ii), (iv), (v), (vi) and (vii) of paragraph (1) shall have the same effect as if it had been made in the Register of the Office of each of the Contracting Parties concerned, except that a Contracting Party may, in a declaration, notify the Director General that a recording referred to in item (i) of paragraph (1) shall

not have that effect in that Contracting Party until the Office of that Contracting Party has received the statements or documents specified in that declaration.

(3)    [*Fees*] Any recording made under paragraph (1) may be subject to the payment of a fee.

(4)    [*Publication*] The International Bureau shall publish a notice concerning any recording made under paragraph (1). It shall send a copy of the publication of the notice to the Office of each of the Contracting Parties concerned.

## Article 17

### Initial Term and Renewal of the International
### Registration and Duration of Protection

(1)    [*Initial Term of the International Registration*] The international registration shall be effected for an initial term of five years counted from the date of the international registration.

(2)    [*Renewal of the International Registration*] The international registration may be renewed for additional terms of five years, in accordance with the prescribed procedure and subject to the payment of the prescribed fees.

(3)    [*Duration of Protection in Designated Contracting Parties*]

(a)    Provided that the international registration is renewed, and subject to subparagraph (b), the duration of protection shall, in each of the designated Contracting Parties, be 15 years counted from the date of the international registration.

(b)    Where the law of a designated Contracting Party provides for a duration of protection of more than 15 years for an industrial design for which protection has been granted under that law, the duration of protection shall, provided that the international registration is renewed, be the same as that provided for by the law of that Contracting Party.

(c)    Each Contracting Party shall, in a declaration, notify the Director General of the maximum duration of protection provided for by its law.

(4)    [*Possibility of Limited Renewal*] The renewal of the international registration may be effected for any or all of the designated Contracting Parties and for any or all of the industrial designs that are the subject of the international registration.

(5)    [*Recording and Publication of Renewal*] The International Bureau shall record renewals in the International Register and publish a notice to that effect. It shall send a copy of the publication of the notice to the Office of each of the Contracting Parties concerned.

## Article 18

### Information Concerning Published International Registrations

(1)    [*Access to Information*] The International Bureau shall supply to any person applying therefor, upon the payment of the prescribed fee, extracts from the International Register, or information concerning the contents of the International Register, in respect of any published international registration.

(2)    [*Exemption from Legalization*] Extracts from the International Register supplied by the International Bureau shall be exempt from any requirement of legalization in each Contracting Party.

## CHAPTER II

## ADMINISTRATIVE PROVISIONS

### Article 19

### Common Office of Several States

(1)   [*Notification of Common Office*] If several States intending to become party to this Act have effected, or if several States party to this Act agree to effect, the unification of their domestic legislation on industrial designs, they may notify the Director General

(i)    that a common Office shall be substituted for the national Office of each of them, and

(ii)   that the whole of their respective territories to which the unified legislation applies shall be deemed to be a single Contracting Party for the purposes of the application of Articles 1, 3 to 18 and 31 of this Act.

(2)   [*Time at Which Notification Is to Be Made*] The notification referred to in paragraph (1) shall be made,

(i)    in the case of States intending to become party to this Act, at the time of the deposit of the instruments referred to in Article 27(2);

(ii)   in the case of States party to this Act, at any time after the unification of their domestic legislation has been effected.

(3)   [*Date of Entry into Effect of the Notification*] The notification referred to in paragraphs (1) and (2) shall take effect,

(i)    in the case of States intending to become party to this Act, at the time such States become bound by this Act;

(ii)   in the case of States party to this Act, three months after the date of the communication thereof by the Director General to the other Contracting Parties or at any later date indicated in the notification.

### Article 20

### Membership of the Hague Union

The Contracting Parties shall be members of the same Union as the States party to the 1934 Act or the 1960 Act.

### Article 21

### Assembly

(1)   [*Composition*]

(a)   The Contracting Parties shall be members of the same Assembly as the States bound by Article 2 of the Complementary Act of 1967.

(b)   Each member of the Assembly shall be represented in the Assembly by one delegate, who may be assisted by alternate delegates, advisors and experts, and each delegate may represent only one Contracting Party.

(c)   Members of the Union that are not members of the Assembly shall be admitted to the meetings of the Assembly as observers.

(2)   [*Tasks*]

(a)   The Assembly shall

(i)    deal with all matters concerning the maintenance and development of the Union and the implementation of this Act;

(ii)    exercise such rights and perform such tasks as are specifically conferred upon it or assigned to it under this Act or the Complementary Act of 1967;

(iii)    give directions to the Director General concerning the preparations for conferences of revision and decide the convocation of any such conference;

(iv)    amend the Regulations;

(v)    review and approve the reports and activities of the Director General concerning the Union, and give the Director General all necessary instructions concerning matters within the competence of the Union;

(vi)    determine the program and adopt the biennial budget of the Union, and approve its final accounts;

(vii)    adopt the financial regulations of the Union;

(viii)establish such committees and working groups as it deems appropriate to achieve the objectives of the Union;

(ix)    subject to paragraph (1)(c), determine which States, intergovernmental organizations and non-governmental organizations shall be admitted to its meetings as observers;

(x)    take any other appropriate action to further the objectives of the Union and perform any other functions as are appropriate under this Act.

(b)    With respect to matters which are also of interest to other Unions administered by the Organization, the Assembly shall make its decisions after having heard the advice of the Coordination Committee of the Organization.

(3)    [*Quorum*]

(a)    One-half of the members of the Assembly which are States and have the right to vote on a given matter shall constitute a quorum for the purposes of the vote on that matter.

(b)    Notwithstanding the provisions of subparagraph (a), if, in any session, the number of the members of the Assembly which are States, have the right to vote on a given matter and are represented is less than one-half but equal to or more than one-third of the members of the Assembly which are States and have the right to vote on that matter, the Assembly may make decisions but, with the exception of decisions concerning its own procedure, all such decisions shall take effect only if the conditions set forth hereinafter are fulfilled. The International Bureau shall communicate the said decisions to the members of the Assembly which are States, have the right to vote on the said matter and were not represented and shall invite them to express in writing their vote or abstention within a period of three months from the date of the communication. If, at the expiration of this period, the number of such members having thus expressed their vote or abstention attains the number of the members which was lacking for attaining the quorum in the session itself, such decisions shall take effect provided that at the same time the required majority still obtains.

(4)    [*Taking Decisions in the Assembly*]

(a)    The Assembly shall endeavor to take its decisions by consensus.

(b)    Where a decision cannot be arrived at by consensus, the matter at issue shall be decided by voting. In such a case,

(i)    each Contracting Party that is a State shall have one vote and shall vote only in its own name, and

(ii)   any Contracting Party that is an intergovernmental organization may vote, in place of its Member States, with a number of votes equal to the number of its Member States which are party to this Act, and no such intergovernmental organization shall participate in the vote if any one of its Member States exercises its right to vote, and vice versa.

(c)   On matters concerning only States that are bound by Article 2 of the Complementary Act of 1967, Contracting Parties that are not bound by the said Article shall not have the right to vote, whereas, on matters concerning only Contracting Parties, only the latter shall have the right to vote.

(5)   [*Majorities*]

(a)   Subject to Articles 24(2) and 26(2), the decisions of the Assembly shall require two-thirds of the votes cast.

(b)   Abstentions shall not be considered as votes.

(6)   [*Sessions*]

(a)   The Assembly shall meet once in every second calendar year in ordinary session upon convocation by the Director General and, in the absence of exceptional circumstances, during the same period and at the same place as the General Assembly of the Organization.

(b)   The Assembly shall meet in extraordinary session upon convocation by the Director General, either at the request of one-fourth of the members of the Assembly or on the Director General's own initiative.

(c)   The agenda of each session shall be prepared by the Director General.

(7)   [*Rules of Procedure*] The Assembly shall adopt its own rules of procedure.

## Article 22

### International Bureau

(1)   [*Administrative Tasks*]

(a)   International registration and related duties, as well as all other administrative tasks concerning the Union, shall be performed by the International Bureau.

(b)   In particular, the International Bureau shall prepare the meetings and provide the secretariat of the Assembly and of such committees of experts and working groups as may be established by the Assembly.

(2)   [*Director General*] The Director General shall be the chief executive of the Union and shall represent the Union.

(3)   [*Meetings Other than Sessions of the Assembly*] The Director General shall convene any committee and working group established by the Assembly and all other meetings dealing with matters of concern to the Union.

(4)   [*Role of the International Bureau in the Assembly and Other Meetings*]

(a)   The Director General and persons designated by the Director General shall participate, without the right to vote, in all meetings of the Assembly, the committees and working groups established by the Assembly, and any other meetings convened by the Director General under the aegis of the Union.

(b)   The Director General or a staff member designated by the Director General shall be ex officio secretary of the Assembly, and of the committees, working groups and other meetings referred to in subparagraph (a).

(5)   [*Conferences*]

(a)   The International Bureau shall, in accordance with the directions of the Assembly, make the preparations for any revision conferences.

(b)   The International Bureau may consult with intergovernmental organizations and international and national non-governmental organizations concerning the said preparations.

(c)   The Director General and persons designated by the Director General shall take part, without the right to vote, in the discussions at revision conferences.

(6)   [*Other Tasks*] The International Bureau shall carry out any other tasks assigned to it in relation to this Act.

## Article 23

### Finances

(1)   [*Budget*]

(a)   The Union shall have a budget.

(b)   The budget of the Union shall include the income and expenses proper to the Union and its contribution to the budget of expenses common to the Unions administered by the Organization.

(c)   Expenses not attributable exclusively to the Union but also to one or more other Unions administered by the Organization shall be considered to be expenses common to the Unions. The share of the Union in such common expenses shall be in proportion to the interest the Union has in them.

(2)   [*Coordination with Budgets of Other Unions*] The budget of the Union shall be established with due regard to the requirements of coordination with the budgets of the other Unions administered by the Organization.

(3)   [*Sources of Financing of the Budget*] The budget of the Union shall be financed from the following sources:

(i)    fees relating to international registrations;

(ii)   charges due for other services rendered by the International Bureau in relation to the Union;

(iii)  sale of, or royalties on, the publications of the International Bureau concerning the Union;

(iv)   gifts, bequests and subventions;

(v)    rents, interests and other miscellaneous income.

(4)   [*Fixing of Fees and Charges; Level of the Budget*]

(a)   The amounts of the fees referred to in paragraph (3)(i) shall be fixed by the Assembly on the proposal of the Director General. Charges referred to in paragraph 3(ii) shall be established by the Director General and shall be provisionally applied subject to approval by the Assembly at its next session.

(b)   The amounts of the fees referred to in paragraph (3)(i) shall be so fixed that the revenues of the Union from fees and other sources shall be at least sufficient to cover all the expenses of the International Bureau concerning the Union.

(c)   If the budget is not adopted before the beginning of a new financial period, it shall be at the same level as the budget of the previous year, as provided in the financial regulations.

(5)   [*Working Capital Fund*] The Union shall have a working capital fund which shall be constituted by the excess receipts and, if such excess does not suffice, by a single payment made by each member of the Union. If the fund becomes insufficient, the Assembly shall decide to increase it. The proportion and the terms of payment shall be fixed by the Assembly on the proposal of the Director General.

(6)    [*Advances by Host State*]

(a)    In the headquarters agreement concluded with the State on the territory of which the Organization has its headquarters, it shall be provided that, whenever the working capital fund is insufficient, such State shall grant advances. The amount of those advances and the conditions on which they are granted shall be the subject of separate agreements, in each case, between such State and the Organization.

(b)    The State referred to in subparagraph (a) and the Organization shall each have the right to denounce the obligation to grant advances, by written notification. Denunciation shall take effect three years after the end of the year in which it has been notified.

(7)    [*Auditing of Accounts*] The auditing of the accounts shall be effected by one or more of the States members of the Union or by external auditors, as provided in the financial regulations. They shall be designated, with their agreement, by the Assembly.

## Article 24

### Regulations

(1)    [*Subject Matter*] The Regulations shall govern the details of the implementation of this Act. They shall, in particular, include provisions concerning

(i)    matters which this Act expressly provides are to be prescribed;

(ii)    further details concerning, or any details useful in the implementation of, the provisions of this Act;

(iii)    any administrative requirements, matters or procedures.

(2)    [*Amendment of Certain Provisions of the Regulations*]

(a)    The Regulations may specify that certain provisions of the Regulations may be amended only by unanimity or only by a four-fifths majority.

(b)    In order for the requirement of unanimity or a four-fifths majority no longer to apply in the future to the amendment of a provision of the Regulations, unanimity shall be required.

(c)    In order for the requirement of unanimity or a four-fifths majority to apply in the future to the amendment of a provision of the Regulations, a four-fifths majority shall be required.

(3)    [*Conflict Between This Act and the Regulations*] In the case of conflict between the provisions of this Act and those of the Regulations, the former shall prevail.

## CHAPTER III
### REVISION AND AMENDMENT

## Article 25

### Revision of This Act

(1)    [*Revision Conferences*] This Act may be revised by a conference of the Contracting Parties.

(2)    [*Revision or Amendment of Certain Articles*] Articles 21, 22, 23 and 26 may be amended either by a revision conference or by the Assembly according to the provisions of Article 26.

## Article 26

### Amendment of Certain Articles by the Assembly

(1)    [*Proposals for Amendment*]

(a)    Proposals for the amendment by the Assembly of Articles 21, 22, 23 and this Article may be initiated by any Contracting Party or by the Director General.

(b)    Such proposals shall be communicated by the Director General to the Contracting Parties at least six months in advance of their consideration by the Assembly.

(2)    [*Majorities*] Adoption of any amendment to the Articles referred to in paragraph (1) shall require a three-fourths majority, except that adoption of any amendment to Article 21 or to the present paragraph shall require a four-fifths majority.

(3)    [*Entry into Force*]

(a)    Except where subparagraph (b) applies, any amendment to the Articles referred to in paragraph (1) shall enter into force one month after written notifications of acceptance, effected in accordance with their respective constitutional processes, have been received by the Director General from three-fourths of those Contracting Parties which, at the time the amendment was adopted, were members of the Assembly and had the right to vote on that amendment.

(b)    Any amendment to Article 21(3) or (4) or to this subparagraph shall not enter into force if, within six months of its adoption by the Assembly, any Contracting Party notifies the Director General that it does not accept such amendment.

(c)    Any amendment which enters into force in accordance with the provisions of this paragraph shall bind all the States and intergovernmental organizations which are Contracting Parties at the time the amendment enters into force, or which become Contracting Parties at a subsequent date.

## CHAPTER IV
## FINAL PROVISIONS

### Article 27

### Becoming Party to This Act

(1)    [*Eligibility*] Subject to paragraphs (2) and (3) and Article 28,

(i)    any State member of the Organization may sign and become party to this Act;

(ii)    any intergovernmental organization which maintains an Office in which protection of industrial designs may be obtained with effect in the territory in which the constituting treaty of the intergovernmental organization applies may sign and become party to this Act, provided that at least one of the member States of the intergovernmental organization is a member of the Organization and provided that such Office is not the subject of a notification under Article 19.

(2)    [*Ratification or Accession*] Any State or intergovernmental organization referred to in paragraph (1) may deposit

(i)    an instrument of ratification if it has signed this Act, or

(ii)    an instrument of accession if it has not signed this Act.

(3)    [*Effective Date of Deposit*]

(a)    Subject to subparagraphs (b) to (d), the effective date of the deposit of an instrument of ratification or accession shall be the date on which that instrument is deposited.

(b)    The effective date of the deposit of the instrument of ratification or accession of any State in respect of which protection of industrial designs may be obtained only through the Office maintained by an intergovernmental organization of which that State is a member shall be the date on which the instrument of that intergovernmental organization is deposited if that date is later than the date on which the instrument of the said State has been deposited.

(c)    The effective date of the deposit of any instrument of ratification or accession containing or accompanied by the notification referred to in Article 19 shall be the date on which the last of the instruments of the States members of the group of States having made the said notification is deposited.

(d)   Any instrument of ratification or accession of a State may contain or be accompanied by a declaration making it a condition to its being considered as deposited that the instrument of one other State or one intergovernmental organization, or the instruments of two other States, or the instruments of one other State and one intergovernmental organization, specified by name and eligible to become party to this Act, is or are also deposited. The instrument containing or accompanied by such a declaration shall be considered to have been deposited on the day on which the condition indicated in the declaration is fulfilled. However, when an instrument specified in the declaration itself contains, or is itself accompanied by, a declaration of the said kind, that instrument shall be considered as deposited on the day on which the condition specified in the latter declaration is fulfilled.

(e)   Any declaration made under paragraph (d) may be withdrawn, in its entirety or in part, at any time. Any such withdrawal shall become effective on the date on which the notification of withdrawal is received by the Director General.

## Article 28

### Effective Date of Ratifications and Accessions

(1)   [*Instruments to Be Taken into Consideration*] For the purposes of this Article, only instruments of ratification or accession that are deposited by States or intergovernmental organizations referred to in Article 27(1) and that have an effective date according to Article 27(3) shall be taken into consideration.

(2)   [*Entry into Force of This Act*] This Act shall enter into force three months after six States have deposited their instruments of ratification or accession, provided that, according to the most recent annual statistics collected by the International Bureau, at least three of those States fulfill at least one of the following conditions:

(i)   at least **3,000** applications for the protection of industrial designs have been filed in or for the State concerned, or

(ii)   at least **1,000** applications for the protection of industrial designs have been filed in or for the State concerned by residents of States other than that State.

(3)   [*Entry into Force of Ratifications and Accessions*]

(a)   Any State or intergovernmental organization that has deposited its instrument of ratification or accession three months or more before the date of entry into force of this Act shall become bound by this Act on the date of entry into force of this Act.

(b)   Any other State or intergovernmental organization shall become bound by this Act three months after the date on which it has deposited its instrument of ratification or accession or at any later date indicated in that instrument.

## Article 29

### Prohibition of Reservations

No reservations to this Act are permitted.

## Article 30

### Declarations Made by Contracting Parties

(1)   [*Time at Which Declarations May Be Made*] Any declaration under Articles 4(1)(b), 5(2)(a), 7(2), 11(1), 13(1), 14(3), 16(2) or 17(3)(c) may be made

(i)    at the time of the deposit of an instrument referred to in Article 27(2), in which case it shall become effective on the date on which the State or intergovernmental organization having made the declaration becomes bound by this Act, or

(ii)    after the deposit of an instrument referred to in Article 27(2), in which case it shall become effective three months after the date of its receipt by the Director General or at any later date indicated in the declaration but shall apply only in respect of any international registration whose date of international registration is the same as, or is later than, the effective date of the declaration.

(2)    [*Declarations by States Having a Common Office*] Notwithstanding paragraph (1), any declaration referred to in that paragraph that has been made by a State which has, with another State or other States, notified the Director General under Article 19(1) of the substitution of a common Office for their national Offices shall become effective only if that other State or those other States makes or make a corresponding declaration or corresponding declarations.

(3)    [*Withdrawal of Declarations*] Any declaration referred to in paragraph (1) may be withdrawn at any time by notification addressed to the Director General. Such withdrawal shall take effect three months after the date on which the Director General has received the notification or at any later date indicated in the notification. In the case of a declaration made under Article 7(2), the withdrawal shall not affect international applications filed prior to the coming into effect of the said withdrawal.

## Article 31

### Applicability of the 1934 and 1960 Acts

(1)    [*Relations Between States Party to Both This Act and the 1934 or 1960 Acts*] This Act alone shall be applicable as regards the mutual relations of States party to both this Act and the 1934 Act or the 1960 Act. However, such States shall, in their mutual relations, apply the 1934 Act or the 1960 Act, as the case may be, to industrial designs deposited at the International Bureau prior to the date on which this Act becomes applicable as regards their mutual relations.

(2)    [*Relations Between States Party to Both This Act and the 1934 or 1960 Acts and States Party to the 1934 or 1960 Acts Without Being Party to This Act*]

(a)    Any State that is party to both this Act and the 1934 Act shall continue to apply the 1934 Act in its relations with States that are party to the 1934 Act without being party to the 1960 Act or this Act.

(b)    Any State that is party to both this Act and the 1960 Act shall continue to apply the 1960 Act in its relations with States that are party to the 1960 Act without being party to this Act.

## Article 32

### Denunciation of This Act

(1)    [*Notification*] Any Contracting Party may denounce this Act by notification addressed to the Director General.

(2)    [*Effective Date*] Denunciation shall take effect one year after the date on which the Director General has received the notification or at any later date indicated in the notification. It shall not affect the application of this Act to any international application pending and any international registration in force in respect of the denouncing Contracting Party at the time of the coming into effect of the denunciation.

## Article 33

### Languages of This Act; Signature

(1)  [*Original Texts; Official Texts*]

(a)  This Act shall be signed in a single original in the English, Arabic, Chinese, French, Russian and Spanish languages, all texts being equally authentic.

(b)  Official texts shall be established by the Director General, after consultation with the interested Governments, in such other languages as the Assembly may designate.

(2)  [*Time Limit for Signature*] This Act shall remain open for signature at the headquarters of the Organization for one year after its adoption.

## Article 34

### Depositary

The Director General shall be the depositary of this Act.

### Agreed Statements by the Diplomatic Conference Regarding the Geneva Act and the Regulations under the Geneva Act

1.  When adopting Article 12(4), Article 14(2)(b) and Rule 18(4), the Diplomatic Conference understood that a withdrawal of refusal by an Office that has communicated a notification of refusal may take the form of a statement to the effect that the Office concerned has decided to accept the effects of the international registration in respect of the industrial designs, or some of the industrial designs, to which the notification of refusal related. It was also understood that an Office may, within the period allowed for communicating a notification of refusal, send a statement to the effect that it has decided to accept the effects of the international registration even where it has not communicated such a notification of refusal.

2.  When adopting Article 10, the Diplomatic Conference understood that nothing in this Article precludes access to the international application or the international registration by the applicant or the holder or a person having the consent of the applicant or the holder.

# 51. PARTIES TO THE HAGUE AGREEMENT CONCERNING THE INTERNATIONAL DEPOSIT OF INDUSTRIAL DESIGNS/THE HAGUE AGREEMENT CONCERNING THE INTERNATIONAL REGISTRATION OF INDUSTRIAL DESIGNS*

## Status on May 4, 2021

| State/IGO | Date on which State became party to the Hague Act | Date on which State became party to the Complementary Act of Stockholm | Date on which State/IGO became party to the Geneva Act |
|---|---|---|---|
| African Intellectual Property Organization (OAPI)............ | – | – | September 16, 2008 |
| Albania.................................. | March 19, 2007 | March 19, 2007 | May 19, 2007 |
| Armenia ................................ | – | – | July 13, 2007 |
| Azerbaijan............................. | – | – | December 8, 2010 |
| Belarus.................................. | – | – | July 19, 2021 |
| Belgium⁵................................ | August 1, 1984 | May 28, 1979 | December 18, 2018 |
| Belize.................................... | July 12, 2003 | July 12, 2003 | February 9, 2019 |
| Benin..................................... | November 2, 1986 | January 2, 1987 | – |
| Bosnia and Herzegovina........ | – | – | December 24, 2008 |
| Botswana............................... | – | – | December 5, 2006 |
| Brunei Darussalam ............... | – | – | December 24, 2013 |
| Bulgaria ............................... | December 11, 1996 | December 11, 1996 | October 7, 2008 |
| Cambodia .............................. | – | – | February 25, 2017 |
| Canada .................................. | – | – | November 5, 2018 |
| Côte d'Ivoire.......................... | May 30, 1993 | May 30, 1993 | – |
| Croatia .................................. | February 12, 2004 | February 12, 2004 | April 12, 2004 |
| Democratic People's Republic of Korea................ | May 27, 1992 | May 27, 1992 | September 13, 2016 |
| Denmark ............................... | – | – | December 9, 2008⁶ |
| Egypt..................................... | – | – | August 27, 2004 |
| Estonia .................................. | – | – | December 23, 2003 |
| European Union..................... | – | – | January 1, 2008 |
| Finland.................................. | – | – | May 1, 2011 |
| France⁷.................................. | August 1, 1984 | September 27, 1975 | March 18, 2007 |
| Gabon .................................... | August 18, 2003 | August 18, 2003 | – |
| Georgia.................................. | August 1, 2003 | August 1, 2003 | December 23, 2003 |
| Germany ................................ | August 1, 1984 | September 27, 1975 | February 13, 2010 |

---

* Document originally produced by the World Intellectual Property Organization (WIPO), the owner of the copyright. Published with the permission of the World Intellectual Property Organization.

| State/IGO | Date on which State became party to the Hague Act | Date on which State became party to the Complementary Act of Stockholm | Date on which State/IGO became party to the Geneva Act |
|---|---|---|---|
| Ghana | – | – | September 16, 2008 |
| | April 18, 1997 | April 18, 1997 | – |
| Hungary[8] | August 1, 1984 | April 7, 1984 | May 1, 2004 |
| Iceland | – | – | December 23, 2003 |
| Israel | – | – | January 3, 2020 |
| Italy | June 13, 1987 | August 13, 1987 | – |
| Japan | – | – | May 13, 2015 |
| Kyrgyzstan | March 17, 2003 | March 17, 2003 | December 23, 2003 |
| Latvia | – | – | July 26, 2005 |
| Liechtenstein | August 1, 1984 | September 27, 1975 | December 23, 2003 |
| Lithuania | – | – | September 26, 2008 |
| Luxembourg[5] | August 1, 1984 | May 28, 1979 | December 18, 2018 |
| Mali | September 7, 2006 | September 7, 2006 | – |
| Mexico | – | – | June 6, 2020 |
| Monaco | August 1, 1984 | September 27, 1975 | June 9, 2011 |
| Mongolia | April 12, 1997 | April 12, 1997 | January 19, 2008 |
| Montenegro | June 3, 2006 | June 3, 2006 | March 5, 2012 |
| Morocco | October 13, 1999 | October 13, 1999 | – |
| Namibia | – | – | June 30, 2004 |
| Netherlands[5] | August 1, 1984[9] | May 28, 1979[9] | December 18, 2018[9] |
| Niger | September 20, 2004 | September 20, 2004 | – |
| North Macedonia | March 18, 1997 | March 18, 1997 | March 22, 2006 |
| Norway | – | – | June 17, 2010 |
| Oman | – | – | March 4, 2009 |
| Poland | – | – | July 2, 2009 |
| Republic of Korea | – | – | July 1, 2014 |
| Republic of Moldova | March 14, 1994 | March 14, 1994 | December 23, 2003 |
| Romania | July 18, 1992 | July 18, 1992 | December 23, 2003 |
| Russian Federation | – | – | February 28, 2018 |
| Rwanda | – | – | August 31, 2011 |
| Samoa | – | – | January 2, 2020 |
| San Marino | – | – | January 26, 2019 |
| Sao Tome and Principe | – | – | December 8, 2008 |
| Senegal | August 1, 1984 | June 30, 1984 | – |
| Serbia[10] | December 30, 1993 | December 30, 1993 | December 9, 2009 |
| Singapore | – | – | April 17, 2005 |
| Slovenia | January 13, 1995 | January 13, 1995 | December 23, 2003 |
| Spain | – | – | December 23, 2003 |
| Suriname | August 1, 1984 | February 23, 1977 | September 10, 2020 |

## PARTIES TO THE HAGUE AGREEMENT

| State/IGO | Date on which State became party to the Hague Act | Date on which State became party to the Complementary Act of Stockholm | Date on which State/IGO became party to the Geneva Act |
|---|---|---|---|
| Switzerland............................ | August 1, 1984 | September 27, 1975 | December 23, 2003 |
| Syrian Arab Republic ............ | – | – | May 7, 2008 |
| Tajikistan............................... | – | – | March 21, 2012 |
| Tunisia .................................. | – | – | June 13, 2012 |
| Turkey.................................... | – | – | January 1, 2005 |
| Turkmenistan ........................ | – | – | March 16, 2016 |
| Ukraine ................................. | August 28, 2002 | August 28, 2002 | December 23, 2003 |
| United Kingdom[11]................. | – | – | June 13, 2018 |
| United States of America ...... | – | – | May 13, 2015 |
| Viet Nam................................ | – | – | December 30, 2019 |
| | | | |
| (Total: 75) | (34) | (34) | (66) |

---

[1]  The Geneva (1999) Act of the Hague Agreement Concerning the International Registration of Industrial Designs was adopted on July 2, 1999. The Geneva Act entered into force on December 23, 2003.

[2]  The termination of the London Act, as well as of the Additional Act of Monaco, became effective on October 18, 2016, three months after the Director General received the required instruments of acceptance of termination by 11 Contracting Parties, following the earlier denunciation of the London Act by the three other Contracting Parties, which became effective on June 3, 2010, November 19, 2010, and December 13, 2011, respectively, (see Hague Notification No. 130).

[3]  The Protocol to the Hague Act (1960) is not yet in force. It has been ratified by or acceded to by the following States: Belgium, France, Germany, Italy, Liechtenstein, Monaco, Morocco, Netherlands and Switzerland.

[4]  The Protocol of Geneva (1975), in accordance with Article 11(2)(a) thereof, ceased to have effect as of August 1, 1984; however, as provided by Article 11(2)(b), States bound by the Protocol (Belgium (as from April 1, 1979), France (as from February 18, 1980), Germany (as from December 26, 1981), Hungary (as from April 7, 1984), Liechtenstein (as from April 1, 1979), Luxembourg (as from April 1, 1979), Monaco (as from March 5, 1981), Netherlands (as from April 1, 1979), Senegal (as from June 30, 1984), Suriname (as from April 1, 1979) and Switzerland (as from April 1, 1979)) are not relieved of their obligations thereunder in respect of industrial designs whose date of international deposit is prior to August 1, 1984.

[5]  The territories of Belgium, Luxembourg and the Netherlands in Europe are, for the application of the Hague Agreement, to be deemed a single country.

[6]  Applicable to Greenland as of January 11, 2011 and the Faroe Islands as of April 13, 2016.

[7]  Including all Overseas Departments and Territories.

[8]  With the declaration that Hungary does not consider itself bound by the Protocol annexed to the Hague Act (1960). The London Act ceased to be effective in respect of Hungary as of February 1, 2005.

[9]  Ratification for the Kingdom in Europe.

[10]  Serbia is the continuing State from Serbia and Montenegro as from June 3, 2006.

[11]  In respect of the United Kingdom of Great Britain and Northern Ireland and the Isle of Man.

# EUROPEAN UNION DIRECTIVES AND REGULATIONS

---

## 52. TREATY ON THE FUNCTIONING OF THE EUROPEAN UNION— SELECTED PROVISIONS

(consolidated version as of December 1, 2009,
amended by the Treaty of Lisbon)

PART THREE
UNION POLICIES AND INTERNAL ACTIONS

TITLE II
FREE MOVEMENT OF GOODS

CHAPTER 3
PROHIBITION OF QUANTITATIVE RESTRICTIONS
BETWEEN MEMBER STATES

### *Article 34*

(ex Article 28 TEC)

Quantitative restrictions on imports and all measures having equivalent effect shall be prohibited between Member States.

### *Article 35*

(ex Article 29 TEC)

Quantitative restrictions on exports, and all measures having equivalent effect, shall be prohibited between Member States.

### *Article 36*

(ex Article 30 TEC)

The provisions of Articles 34 and 35 shall not preclude prohibitions or restrictions on imports, exports or goods in transit justified on grounds of public morality, public policy or public security; the protection of health and life of humans, animals or plants; the protection of national treasures possessing artistic, historic or archaeological value; or the protection of industrial and commercial property. Such prohibitions or restrictions shall not, however, constitute a means of arbitrary discrimination or a disguised restriction on trade between Member States.

### *Article 37*

(ex Article 31 TEC)

1.    Member States shall adjust any State monopolies of a commercial character so as to ensure that no discrimination regarding the conditions under which goods are procured and marketed exists between nationals of Member States.

The provisions of this Article shall apply to any body through which a Member State, in law or in fact, either directly or indirectly supervises, determines or appreciably influences imports or exports between Member States. These provisions shall likewise apply to monopolies delegated by the State to others.

2. Member States shall refrain from introducing any new measure which is contrary to the principles laid down in paragraph 1 or which restricts the scope of the articles dealing with the prohibition of customs duties and quantitative restrictions between Member States.

3. If a State monopoly of a commercial character has rules which are designed to make it easier to dispose of agricultural products or obtain for them the best return, steps should be taken in applying the rules contained in this Article to ensure equivalent safeguards for the employment and standard of living of the producers concerned.

TITLE VII
COMMON RULES ON COMPETITION, TAXATION
AND APPROXIMATION OF LAWS

CHAPTER 1
RULES ON COMPETITION

SECTION 1
RULES APPLYING TO UNDERTAKINGS

*Article 101*

(ex Article 81 TEC)

1. The following shall be prohibited as incompatible with the internal market: all agreements between undertakings, decisions by associations of undertakings and concerted practices which may affect trade between Member States and which have as their object or effect the prevention, restriction or distortion of competition within the internal market, and in particular those which:

(a) directly or indirectly fix purchase or selling prices or any other trading conditions;

(b) limit or control production, markets, technical development, or investment;

(c) share markets or sources of supply;

(d) apply dissimilar conditions to equivalent transactions with other trading parties, thereby placing them at a competitive disadvantage;

(e) make the conclusion of contracts subject to acceptance by the other parties of supplementary obligations which, by their nature or according to commercial usage, have no connection with the subject of such contracts.

2. Any agreements or decisions prohibited pursuant to this Article shall be automatically void.

3. The provisions of paragraph 1 may, however, be declared inapplicable in the case of:

—any agreement or category of agreements between undertakings,

—any decision or category of decisions by associations of undertakings,

—any concerted practice or category of concerted practices,

which contributes to improving the production or distribution of goods or to promoting technical or economic progress, while allowing consumers a fair share of the resulting benefit, and which does not:

(a) impose on the undertakings concerned restrictions which are not indispensable to the attainment of these objectives;

(b) afford such undertakings the possibility of eliminating competition in respect of a substantial part of the products in question.

## Article 102

### (ex Article 82 TEC)

Any abuse by one or more undertakings of a dominant position within the internal market or in a substantial part of it shall be prohibited as incompatible with the internal market in so far as it may affect trade between Member States.

Such abuse may, in particular, consist in:

(a)  directly or indirectly imposing unfair purchase or selling prices or other unfair trading conditions;

(b)  limiting production, markets or technical development to the prejudice of consumers;

(c)  applying dissimilar conditions to equivalent transactions with other trading parties, thereby placing them at a competitive disadvantage;

(d)  making the conclusion of contracts subject to acceptance by the other parties of supplementary obligations which, by their nature or according to commercial usage, have no connection with the subject of such contracts.

## Article 106

### (ex Article 86 TEC)

1.  In the case of public undertakings and undertakings to which Member States grant special or exclusive rights, Member States shall neither enact nor maintain in force any measure contrary to the rules contained in the Treaties, in particular to those rules provided for in Article 18 and Articles 101 to 109.

2.  Undertakings entrusted with the operation of services of general economic interest or having the character of a revenue-producing monopoly shall be subject to the rules contained in the Treaties, in particular to the rules on competition, in so far as the application of such rules does not obstruct the performance, in law or in fact, of the particular tasks assigned to them. The development of trade must not be affected to such an extent as would be contrary to the interests of the Union.

3.  The Commission shall ensure the application of the provisions of this Article and shall, where necessary, address appropriate directives or decisions to Member States.

# 53. SOFTWARE DIRECTIVE

**DIRECTIVE 2009/24/EC OF THE EUROPEAN PARLIAMENT**
**AND OF THE COUNCIL**
**of 23 April 2009**
**on the legal protection of computer programs**

**(codified version)**

**(Text with EEA relevance)***

. . . Whereas:

(1)   The content of Council Directive 91/250/EEC of 14 May 1991 on the legal protection of computer programs has been amended. In the interests of clarity and rationality the said Directive should be codified.

(2)   The development of computer programs requires the investment of considerable human, technical and financial resources while computer programs can be copied at a fraction of the cost needed to develop them independently.

(3)   Computer programs are playing an increasingly important role in a broad range of industries and computer program technology can accordingly be considered as being of fundamental importance for the Community's industrial development.

(4)   Certain differences in the legal protection of computer programs offered by the laws of the Member States have direct and negative effects on the functioning of the internal market as regards computer programs.

(5)   Existing differences having such effects need to be removed and new ones prevented from arising, while differences not adversely affecting the functioning of the internal market to a substantial degree need not be removed or prevented from arising. . . .

(7)   For the purpose of this Directive, the term "computer program" shall include programs in any form, including those which are incorporated into hardware. This term also includes preparatory design work leading to the development of a computer program provided that the nature of the preparatory work is such that a computer program can result from it at a later stage.

(8)   In respect of the criteria to be applied in determining whether or not a computer program is an original work, no tests as to the qualitative or aesthetic merits of the program should be applied.

(9)   The Community is fully committed to the promotion of international standardisation.

(10)   The function of a computer program is to communicate and work together with other components of a computer system and with users and, for this purpose, a logical and, where appropriate, physical interconnection and interaction is required to permit all elements of software and hardware to work with other software and hardware and with users in all the ways in which they are intended to function. The parts of the program which provide for such interconnection and interaction between elements of software and hardware are generally known as "interfaces". This functional interconnection and interaction is generally known as "interoperability"; such interoperability can be defined as the ability to exchange information and mutually to use the information which has been exchanged.

(11)   For the avoidance of doubt, it has to be made clear that only the expression of a computer program is protected and that ideas and principles which underlie any element of a program, including those which underlie its interfaces, are not protected by copyright under this Directive. In accordance with this principle of copyright, to the extent that logic, algorithms and programming languages comprise

---

\*   Footnotes, some recitals, and annexes omitted.

ideas and principles, those ideas and principles are not protected under this Directive. In accordance with the legislation and case-law of the Member States and the international copyright conventions, the expression of those ideas and principles is to be protected by copyright.

(12) For the purposes of this Directive, the term "rental" means the making available for use, for a limited period of time and for profit-making purposes, of a computer program or a copy thereof. This term does not include public lending, which, accordingly, remains outside the scope of this Directive.

(13) The exclusive rights of the author to prevent the unauthorised reproduction of his work should be subject to a limited exception in the case of a computer program to allow the reproduction technically necessary for the use of that program by the lawful acquirer. This means that the acts of loading and running necessary for the use of a copy of a program which has been lawfully acquired, and the act of correction of its errors, may not be prohibited by contract. In the absence of specific contractual provisions, including when a copy of the program has been sold, any other act necessary for the use of the copy of a program may be performed in accordance with its intended purpose by a lawful acquirer of that copy.

(14) A person having a right to use a computer program should not be prevented from performing acts necessary to observe, study or test the functioning of the program, provided that those acts do not infringe the copyright in the program.

(15) The unauthorised reproduction, translation, adaptation or transformation of the form of the code in which a copy of a computer program has been made available constitutes an infringement of the exclusive rights of the author. Nevertheless, circumstances may exist when such a reproduction of the code and translation of its form are indispensable to obtain the necessary information to achieve the interoperability of an independently created program with other programs. It has therefore to be considered that, in these limited circumstances only, performance of the acts of reproduction and translation by or on behalf of a person having a right to use a copy of the program is legitimate and compatible with fair practice and must therefore be deemed not to require the authorisation of the rightholder. An objective of this exception is to make it possible to connect all components of a computer system, including those of different manufacturers, so that they can work together. Such an exception to the author's exclusive rights may not be used in a way which prejudices the legitimate interests of the rightholder or which conflicts with a normal exploitation of the program.

(16) Protection of computer programs under copyright laws should be without prejudice to the application, in appropriate cases, of other forms of protection. However, any contractual provisions contrary to the provisions of this Directive laid down in respect of decompilation or to the exceptions provided for by this Directive with regard to the making of a back-up copy or to observation, study or testing of the functioning of a program should be null and void. . . .

## Article 1

### Object of protection

1.    In accordance with the provisions of this Directive, Member States shall protect computer programs, by copyright, as literary works within the meaning of the Berne Convention for the Protection of Literary and Artistic Works. For the purposes of this Directive, the term "computer programs" shall include their preparatory design material.

2.    Protection in accordance with this Directive shall apply to the expression in any form of a computer program. Ideas and principles which underlie any element of a computer program, including those which underlie its interfaces, are not protected by copyright under this Directive.

3.    A computer program shall be protected if it is original in the sense that it is the author's own intellectual creation. No other criteria shall be applied to determine its eligibility for protection.

4.    The provisions of this Directive shall apply also to programs created before 1 January 1993, without prejudice to any acts concluded and rights acquired before that date.

## *Article 2*

### Authorship of computer programs

1.    The author of a computer program shall be the natural person or group of natural persons who has created the program or, where the legislation of the Member State permits, the legal person designated as the rightholder by that legislation.

Where collective works are recognised by the legislation of a Member State, the person considered by the legislation of the Member State to have created the work shall be deemed to be its author.

2.    In respect of a computer program created by a group of natural persons jointly, the exclusive rights shall be owned jointly.

3.    Where a computer program is created by an employee in the execution of his duties or following the instructions given by his employer, the employer exclusively shall be entitled to exercise all economic rights in the program so created, unless otherwise provided by contract.

## *Article 3*

### Beneficiaries of protection

Protection shall be granted to all natural or legal persons eligible under national copyright legislation as applied to literary works.

## *Article 4*

### Restricted acts

1.    Subject to the provisions of Articles 5 and 6, the exclusive rights of the rightholder within the meaning of Article 2 shall include the right to do or to authorise:

(a)    the permanent or temporary reproduction of a computer program by any means and in any form, in part or in whole; in so far as loading, displaying, running, transmission or storage of the computer program necessitate such reproduction, such acts shall be subject to authorisation by the rightholder;

(b)    the translation, adaptation, arrangement and any other alteration of a computer program and the reproduction of the results thereof, without prejudice to the rights of the person who alters the program;

(c)    any form of distribution to the public, including the rental, of the original computer program or of copies thereof.

2.    The first sale in the Community of a copy of a program by the rightholder or with his consent shall exhaust the distribution right within the Community of that copy, with the exception of the right to control further rental of the program or a copy thereof.

## *Article 5*

### Exceptions to the restricted acts

1.    In the absence of specific contractual provisions, the acts referred to in points (a) and (b) of Article 4(1) shall not require authorisation by the rightholder where they are necessary for the use of the computer program by the lawful acquirer in accordance with its intended purpose, including for error correction.

2.    The making of a back-up copy by a person having a right to use the computer program may not be prevented by contract in so far as it is necessary for that use.

3.    The person having a right to use a copy of a computer program shall be entitled, without the authorisation of the rightholder, to observe, study or test the functioning of the program in order to

determine the ideas and principles which underlie any element of the program if he does so while performing any of the acts of loading, displaying, running, transmitting or storing the program which he is entitled to do.

*Article 6*

**Decompilation**

1.    The authorisation of the rightholder shall not be required where reproduction of the code and translation of its form within the meaning of points (a) and (b) of Article 4(1) are indispensable to obtain the information necessary to achieve the interoperability of an independently created computer program with other programs, provided that the following conditions are met:

(a)    those acts are performed by the licensee or by another person having a right to use a copy of a program, or on their behalf by a person authorised to do so;

(b)    the information necessary to achieve interoperability has not previously been readily available to the persons referred to in point (a); and

(c)    those acts are confined to the parts of the original program which are necessary in order to achieve interoperability.

2.    The provisions of paragraph 1 shall not permit the information obtained through its application:

(a)    to be used for goals other than to achieve the interoperability of the independently created computer program;

(b)    to be given to others, except when necessary for the interoperability of the independently created computer program; or

(c)    to be used for the development, production or marketing of a computer program substantially similar in its expression, or for any other act which infringes copyright.

3.    In accordance with the provisions of the Berne Convention for the protection of Literary and Artistic Works, the provisions of this Article may not be interpreted in such a way as to allow its application to be used in a manner which unreasonably prejudices the rightholder's legitimate interests or conflicts with a normal exploitation of the computer program.

*Article 7*

**Special measures of protection**

1.    Without prejudice to the provisions of Articles 4, 5 and 6, Member States shall provide, in accordance with their national legislation, appropriate remedies against a person committing any of the following acts:

(a)    any act of putting into circulation a copy of a computer program knowing, or having reason to believe, that it is an infringing copy;

(b)    the possession, for commercial purposes, of a copy of a computer program knowing, or having reason to believe, that it is an infringing copy;

(c)    any act of putting into circulation, or the possession for commercial purposes of, any means the sole intended purpose of which is to facilitate the unauthorised removal or circumvention of any technical device which may have been applied to protect a computer program.

2.    Any infringing copy of a computer program shall be liable to seizure in accordance with the legislation of the Member State concerned.

3.    Member States may provide for the seizure of any means referred to in point (c) of paragraph 1.

*Article 8*

## Continued application of other legal provisions

The provisions of this Directive shall be without prejudice to any other legal provisions such as those concerning patent rights, trade-marks, unfair competition, trade secrets, protection of semi-conductor products or the law of contract.

Any contractual provisions contrary to Article 6 or to the exceptions provided for in Article 5(2) and (3) shall be null and void.

*Article 9*

## Communication

Member States shall communicate to the Commission the provisions of national law adopted in the field governed by this Directive.

*Article 10*

## Repeal

Directive 91/250/EEC, as amended by the Directive indicated in Annex I, Part A, is repealed, without prejudice to the obligations of the Member States relating to the time-limits for transposition into national law of the Directives set out in Annex I, Part B.

References to the repealed Directive shall be construed as references to this Directive and shall be read in accordance with the correlation table in Annex II.

*Article 11*

## Entry into force

This Directive shall enter into force on the 20th day following its publication in the Official Journal of the European Union.

*Article 12*

## Addressees

This Directive is addressed to the Member States.

Done at Strasbourg, 23 April 2009.

# 54. COPYRIGHT TERM DIRECTIVE

**DIRECTIVE 2006/116/EC OF THE EUROPEAN PARLIAMENT
AND OF THE COUNCIL
of 12 December 2006
on the term of protection of copyright and certain related rights**

**(codified version, as amended)***

... Whereas:

(1)   Council Directive 93/98/EEC of 29 October 1993 harmonising the term of protection of copyright and certain related rights has been substantially amended. In the interests of clarity and rationality the said Directive should be codified. ...

(6)   The minimum term of protection laid down by the Berne Convention, namely the life of the author and 50 years after his death, was intended to provide protection for the author and the first two generations of his descendants. The average lifespan in the Community has grown longer, to the point where this term is no longer sufficient to cover two generations.

(7)   Certain Member States have granted a term longer than 50 years after the death of the author in order to offset the effects of the world wars on the exploitation of authors' works.

(8)   For the protection of related rights certain Member States have introduced a term of 50 years after lawful publication or lawful communication to the public. ...

(11)  The level of protection of copyright and related rights should be high, since those rights are fundamental to intellectual creation. Their protection ensures the maintenance and development of creativity in the interest of authors, cultural industries, consumers and society as a whole.

(12)  In order to establish a high level of protection which at the same time meets the requirements of the internal market and the need to establish a legal environment conducive to the harmonious development of literary and artistic creation in the Community, the term of protection for copyright should be harmonised at 70 years after the death of the author or 70 years after the work is lawfully made available to the public, and for related rights at 50 years after the event which sets the term running. ...

(16)  The protection of photographs in the Member States is the subject of varying regimes. A photographic work within the meaning of the Berne Convention is to be considered original if it is the author's own intellectual creation reflecting his personality, no other criteria such as merit or purpose being taken into account. The protection of other photographs should be left to national law.

(17)  In order to avoid differences in the term of protection as regards related rights it is necessary to provide the same starting point for the calculation of the term throughout the Community. The performance, fixation, transmission, lawful publication, and lawful communication to the public, that is to say the means of making a subject of a related right perceptible in all appropriate ways to persons in general, should be taken into account for the calculation of the term of protection regardless of the country where this performance, fixation, transmission, lawful publication, or lawful communication to the public takes place. ...

(25)  Respect of acquired rights and legitimate expectations is part of the Community legal order. Member States may provide in particular that in certain circumstances the copyright and related rights which are revived pursuant to this Directive may not give rise to payments by persons who undertook in good faith the exploitation of the works at the time when such works lay within the public domain. ...

---

\*   Footnotes, some recitals, and annexes omitted.

*Article 1*

### Duration of authors' rights

1.    The rights of an author of a literary or artistic work within the meaning of Article 2 of the Berne Convention shall run for the life of the author and for 70 years after his death, irrespective of the date when the work is lawfully made available to the public.

2.    In the case of a work of joint authorship, the term referred to in paragraph 1 shall be calculated from the death of the last surviving author.

3.    In the case of anonymous or pseudonymous works, the term of protection shall run for 70 years after the work is lawfully made available to the public. However, when the pseudonym adopted by the author leaves no doubt as to his identity, or if the author discloses his identity during the period referred to in the first sentence, the term of protection applicable shall be that laid down in paragraph 1.

4.    Where a Member State provides for particular provisions on copyright in respect of collective works or for a legal person to be designated as the rightholder, the term of protection shall be calculated according to the provisions of paragraph 3, except if the natural persons who have created the work are identified as such in the versions of the work which are made available to the public. This paragraph is without prejudice to the rights of identified authors whose identifiable contributions are included in such works, to which contributions paragraph 1 or 2 shall apply.

5.    Where a work is published in volumes, parts, instalments, issues or episodes and the term of protection runs from the time when the work was lawfully made available to the public, the term of protection shall run for each such item separately.

6.    In the case of works for which the term of protection is not calculated from the death of the author or authors and which have not been lawfully made available to the public within 70 years from their creation, the protection shall terminate.

7.    The term of protection of a musical composition with words shall expire 70 years after the death of the last of the following persons to survive, whether or not those persons are designated as co-authors: the author of the lyrics and the composer of the musical composition, provided that both contributions were specifically created for the respective musical composition with words.

*Article 2*

### Cinematographic or audiovisual works

1.    The principal director of a cinematographic or audiovisual work shall be considered as its author or one of its authors. Member States shall be free to designate other co-authors.

2.    The term of protection of cinematographic or audiovisual works shall expire 70 years after the death of the last of the following persons to survive, whether or not these persons are designated as co-authors: the principal director, the author of the screenplay, the author of the dialogue and the composer of music specifically created for use in the cinematographic or audiovisual work.

*Article 3*

### Duration of related rights

1.    The rights of performers shall expire 50 years after the date of the performance. However,

—    if a fixation of the performance otherwise than in a phonogram is lawfully published or lawfully communicated to the public within this period, the rights shall expire 50 years from the date of the first such publication or the first such communication to the public, whichever is the earlier,

— if a fixation of the performance in a phonogram is lawfully published or lawfully communicated to the public within this period, the rights shall expire **70** years from the date of the first such publication or the first such communication to the public, whichever is the earlier.

2.     The rights of producers of phonograms shall expire **50** years after the fixation is made. However, if the phonogram has been lawfully published within this period, the said rights shall expire **70** years from the date of the first lawful publication. If no lawful publication has taken place within the period mentioned in the first sentence, and if the phonogram has been lawfully communicated to the public within this period, the said rights shall expire **70** years from the date of the first lawful communication to the public.

However, this paragraph shall not have the effect of protecting anew the rights of producers of phonograms where, through the expiry of the term of protection granted them pursuant to Article 3(2) of Directive 93/98/EEC in its version before amendment by Directive 2001/29/EEC, they were no longer protected on 22 December 2002.

2a.     If, **50** years after the phonogram was lawfully published or, failing such publication, **50** years after it was lawfully communicated to the public, the phonogram producer does not offer copies of the phonogram for sale in sufficient quantity or does not make it available to the public, by wire or wireless means, in such a way that members of the public may access it from a place and at a time individually chosen by them, the performer may terminate the contract by which the performer has transferred or assigned his rights in the fixation of his performance to a phonogram producer (hereinafter a "contract on transfer or assignment"). The right to terminate the contract on transfer or assignment may be exercised if the producer, within a year from the notification by the performer of his intention to terminate the contract on transfer or assignment pursuant to the previous sentence, fails to carry out both of the acts of exploitation referred to in that sentence. This right to terminate may not be waived by the performer. Where a phonogram contains the fixation of the performances of a plurality of performers, they may terminate their contracts on transfer or assignment in accordance with applicable national law. If the contract on transfer or assignment is terminated pursuant to this paragraph, the rights of the phonogram producer in the phonogram shall expire.

2b.     Where a contract on transfer or assignment gives the performer a right to claim a non-recurring remuneration, the performer shall have the right to obtain an annual supplementary remuneration from the phonogram producer for each full year immediately following the 50th year after the phonogram was lawfully published or, failing such publication, the 50th year after it was lawfully communicated to the public. The right to obtain such annual supplementary remuneration may not be waived by the performer.

2c.     The overall amount to be set aside by a phonogram producer for payment of the annual supplementary remuneration referred to in paragraph 2b shall correspond to **20 %** of the revenue which the phonogram producer has derived, during the year preceding that for which the said remuneration is paid, from the reproduction, distribution and making available of the phonogram in question, following the 50th year after it was lawfully published or, failing such publication, the 50th year after it was lawfully communicated to the public.

Member States shall ensure that phonogram producers are required on request to provide to performers who are entitled to the annual supplementary remuneration referred to in paragraph 2b any information which may be necessary in order to secure payment of that remuneration.

2d.     Member States shall ensure that the right to obtain an annual supplementary remuneration as referred to in paragraph 2b is administered by collecting societies.

2e.     Where a performer is entitled to recurring payments, neither advance payments nor any contractually defined deductions shall be deducted from the payments made to the performer following the 50th year after the phonogram was lawfully published or, failing such publication, the 50th year after it was lawfully communicated to the public.

3.   The rights of producers of the first fixation of a film shall expire 50 years after the fixation is made. However, if the film is lawfully published or lawfully communicated to the public during this period, the rights shall expire 50 years from the date of the first such publication or the first such communication to the public, whichever is the earlier. The term 'film' shall designate a cinematographic or audiovisual work or moving images, whether or not accompanied by sound.

4.   The rights of broadcasting organisations shall expire 50 years after the first transmission of a broadcast, whether this broadcast is transmitted by wire or over the air, including by cable or satellite.

## *Article 4*

### Protection of previously unpublished works

Any person who, after the expiry of copyright protection, for the first time lawfully publishes or lawfully communicates to the public a previously unpublished work, shall benefit from a protection equivalent to the economic rights of the author. The term of protection of such rights shall be 25 years from the time when the work was first lawfully published or lawfully communicated to the public.

## *Article 5*

### Critical and scientific publications

Member States may protect critical and scientific publications of works which have come into the public domain. The maximum term of protection of such rights shall be 30 years from the time when the publication was first lawfully published.

## *Article 6*

### Protection of photographs

Photographs which are original in the sense that they are the author's own intellectual creation shall be protected in accordance with Article 1. No other criteria shall be applied to determine their eligibility for protection. Member States may provide for the protection of other photographs.

## *Article 7*

### Protection vis-à-vis third countries

1.   Where the country of origin of a work, within the meaning of the Berne Convention, is a third country, and the author of the work is not a Community national, the term of protection granted by the Member States shall expire on the date of expiry of the protection granted in the country of origin of the work, but may not exceed the term laid down in Article 1.

2.   The terms of protection laid down in Article 3 shall also apply in the case of rightholders who are not Community nationals, provided Member States grant them protection. However, without prejudice to the international obligations of the Member States, the term of protection granted by Member States shall expire no later than the date of expiry of the protection granted in the country of which the rightholder is a national and may not exceed the term laid down in Article 3.

3.   Member States which, on 29 October 1993, in particular pursuant to their international obligations, granted a longer term of protection than that which would result from the provisions of paragraphs 1 and 2 may maintain this protection until the conclusion of international agreements on the term of protection of copyright or related rights.

## *Article 8*

### Calculation of terms

The terms laid down in this Directive shall be calculated from the first day of January of the year following the event which gives rise to them.

## Article 9

### Moral rights

This Directive shall be without prejudice to the provisions of the Member States regulating moral rights.

## Article 10

### Application in time

1.    Where a term of protection which is longer than the corresponding term provided for by this Directive was already running in a Member State on 1 July 1995, this Directive shall not have the effect of shortening that term of protection in that Member State.

2.    The terms of protection provided for in this Directive shall apply to all works and subject matter which were protected in at least one Member State on the date referred to in paragraph 1, pursuant to national provisions on copyright or related rights, or which meet the criteria for protection under [Council Directive 92/100/EEC of 19 November 1992 on rental right and lending right and on certain rights related to copyright in the field of intellectual property].

3.    This Directive shall be without prejudice to any acts of exploitation performed before the date referred to in paragraph 1. Member States shall adopt the necessary provisions to protect in particular acquired rights of third parties.

4.    Member States need not apply the provisions of Article 2(1) to cinematographic or audiovisual works created before 1 July 1994.

5.    Article 3(1) to (2e) in the version thereof in force on 31 October 2011 shall apply to fixations of performances and phonograms in regard to which the performer and the phonogram producer are still protected, by virtue of those provisions in the version thereof in force on 30 October 2011, as at 1 November 2013 and to fixations of performances and phonograms which come into being after that date.

6.    Article 1(7) shall apply to musical compositions with words of which at least the musical composition or the lyrics are protected in at least one Member State on 1 November 2013, and to musical compositions with words which come into being after that date.

The first subparagraph of this paragraph shall be without prejudice to any acts of exploitation performed before 1 November 2013. Member States shall adopt the necessary provisions to protect, in particular, acquired rights of third parties.

## Article 10a

### Transitional measures

1.    In the absence of clear contractual indications to the contrary, a contract on transfer or assignment concluded before 1 November 2013 shall be deemed to continue to produce its effects beyond the moment at which, by virtue of Article 3(1) in the version thereof in force on 30 October 2011, the performer would no longer be protected.

2.    Member States may provide that contracts on transfer or assignment which entitle a performer to recurring payments and which are concluded before 1 November 2013 can be modified following the 50th year after the phonogram was lawfully published or, failing such publication, the 50th year after it was lawfully communicated to the public.

## Article 11

### Notification and communication

1.  Member States shall immediately notify the Commission of any governmental plan to grant new related rights, including the basic reasons for their introduction and the term of protection envisaged.

2.  Member States shall communicate to the Commission the texts of the provisions of internal law which they adopt in the field governed by this Directive.

## Article 12

### Repeal

Directive 93/98/EEC is hereby repealed, without prejudice to the obligations of the Member States relating to the time-limits for transposition into national law, as set out in Part B of Annex I, of the Directives, and their application.

References made to the repealed Directive shall be construed as being made to this Directive and should be read in accordance with the correlation table in Annex II.

## Article 13

### Entry into force

This Directive shall enter into force on the twentieth day following that of its publication in the *Official Journal of the European Union*.

## Article 14

### Addressees

This Directive is addressed to the Member States.

# 55. RENTAL AND LENDING RIGHTS DIRECTIVE

**DIRECTIVE 2006/115/EC OF THE EUROPEAN PARLIAMENT**
**AND OF THE COUNCIL**
**of 12 December 2006**
**on rental right and lending right and on certain rights**
**related to copyright in the field of intellectual property**

**(codified version)\***

. . . Whereas:

(1) Council Directive 92/100/EEC of 19 November 1992 on rental right and lending right and on certain rights related to copyright in the field of intellectual property has been substantially amended several times. In the interests of clarity and rationality the said Directive should be codified.

(2) Rental and lending of copyright works and the subject matter of related rights protection is playing an increasingly important role in particular for authors, performers and producers of phonograms and films. Piracy is becoming an increasing threat. . . .

(10) It is desirable, with a view to clarity, to exclude from rental and lending within the meaning of this Directive certain forms of making available, as for instance making available phonograms or films for the purpose of public performance or broadcasting, making available for the purpose of exhibition, or making available for on-the-spot reference use. Lending within the meaning of this Directive should not include making available between establishments which are accessible to the public.

(11) Where lending by an establishment accessible to the public gives rise to a payment the amount of which does not go beyond what is necessary to cover the operating costs of the establishment, there is no direct or indirect economic or commercial advantage within the meaning of this Directive.

(12) It is necessary to introduce arrangements ensuring that an unwaivable equitable remuneration is obtained by authors and performers who must remain able to entrust the administration of this right to collecting societies representing them.

(13) The equitable remuneration may be paid on the basis of one or several payments at any time on or after the conclusion of the contract. It should take account of the importance of the contribution of the authors and performers concerned to the phonogram or film. . . .

(15) The provisions laid down in this Directive as to rights related to copyright should not prevent Member States from extending to those exclusive rights the presumption provided for in this Directive with regard to contracts concerning film production concluded individually or collectively by performers with a film producer. Furthermore, those provisions should not prevent Member States from providing for a rebuttable presumption of the authorisation of exploitation in respect of the exclusive rights of performers provided for in the relevant provisions of this Directive, in so far as such presumption is compatible with the International Convention for the Protection of Performers, Producers of Phonograms and Broadcasting Organisations (hereinafter referred to as the Rome Convention).

(16) Member States should be able to provide for more far-reaching protection for owners of rights related to copyright than that required by the provisions laid down in this Directive in respect of broadcasting and communication to the public.

(17) The harmonised rental and lending rights and the harmonised protection in the field of rights related to copyright should not be exercised in a way which constitutes a disguised restriction on trade between Member States or in a way which is contrary to the rule of media exploitation chronology, as recognised in the judgment handed down in *Société Cinéthèque v. FNCF*. . . .

---

\*    Footnotes, some recitals, and annexes omitted.

## CHAPTER I
## RENTAL AND LENDING RIGHT

*Article 1*

### Object of harmonisation

1.    In accordance with the provisions of this Chapter, Member States shall provide, subject to Article 6, a right to authorise or prohibit the rental and lending of originals and copies of copyright works, and other subject matter as set out in Article 3(1).

2.    The rights referred to in paragraph 1 shall not be exhausted by any sale or other act of distribution of originals and copies of copyright works and other subject matter as set out in Article 3(1).

*Article 2*

### Definitions

1.    For the purposes of this Directive the following definitions shall apply:

(a)    "rental" means making available for use, for a limited period of time and for direct or indirect economic or commercial advantage;

(b)    "lending" means making available for use, for a limited period of time and not for direct or indirect economic or commercial advantage, when it is made through establishments which are accessible to the public;

(c)    "film" means a cinematographic or audiovisual work or moving images, whether or not accompanied by sound.

2.    The principal director of a cinematographic or audiovisual work shall be considered as its author or one of its authors. Member States may provide for others to be considered as its co-authors.

*Article 3*

### Rightholders and subject matter of rental and lending right

1.    The exclusive right to authorise or prohibit rental and lending shall belong to the following:

(a)    the author in respect of the original and copies of his work;

(b)    the performer in respect of fixations of his performance;

(c)    the phonogram producer in respect of his phonograms;

(d)    the producer of the first fixation of a film in respect of the original and copies of his film.

2.    This Directive shall not cover rental and lending rights in relation to buildings and to works of applied art.

3.    The rights referred to in paragraph 1 may be transferred, assigned or subject to the granting of contractual licences.

4.    Without prejudice to paragraph 6, when a contract concerning film production is concluded, individually or collectively, by performers with a film producer, the performer covered by this contract shall be presumed, subject to contractual clauses to the contrary, to have transferred his rental right, subject to Article 5.

5.    Member States may provide for a similar presumption as set out in paragraph 4 with respect to authors.

6.    Member States may provide that the signing of a contract concluded between a performer and a film producer concerning the production of a film has the effect of authorising rental, provided that

such contract provides for an equitable remuneration within the meaning of Article 5. Member States may also provide that this paragraph shall apply mutatis mutandis to the rights included in Chapter II.

*Article 4*

### Rental of computer programs

This Directive shall be without prejudice to Article 4(c) of Council Directive 91/250/EEC of 14 May 1991 on the legal protection of computer programs.

*Article 5*

### Unwaivable right to equitable remuneration

1.   Where an author or performer has transferred or assigned his rental right concerning a phonogram or an original or copy of a film to a phonogram or film producer, that author or performer shall retain the right to obtain an equitable remuneration for the rental.

2.   The right to obtain an equitable remuneration for rental cannot be waived by authors or performers.

3.   The administration of this right to obtain an equitable remuneration may be entrusted to collecting societies representing authors or performers.

4.   Member States may regulate whether and to what extent administration by collecting societies of the right to obtain an equitable remuneration may be imposed, as well as the question from whom this remuneration may be claimed or collected.

*Article 6*

### Derogation from the exclusive public lending right

1.   Member States may derogate from the exclusive right provided for in Article 1 in respect of public lending, provided that at least authors obtain a remuneration for such lending. Member States shall be free to determine this remuneration taking account of their cultural promotion objectives.

2.   Where Member States do not apply the exclusive lending right provided for in Article 1 as regards phonograms, films and computer programs, they shall introduce, at least for authors, a remuneration.

3.   Member States may exempt certain categories of establishments from the payment of the remuneration referred to in paragraphs 1 and 2.

CHAPTER II
### RIGHTS RELATED TO COPYRIGHT

*Article 7*

### Fixation right

1.   Member States shall provide for performers the exclusive right to authorise or prohibit the fixation of their performances.

2.   Member States shall provide for broadcasting organisations the exclusive right to authorise or prohibit the fixation of their broadcasts, whether these broadcasts are transmitted by wire or over the air, including by cable or satellite.

3.   A cable distributor shall not have the right provided for in paragraph 2 where it merely retransmits by cable the broadcasts of broadcasting organisations.

*Article 8*

**Broadcasting and communication to the public**

1.    Member States shall provide for performers the exclusive right to authorise or prohibit the broadcasting by wireless means and the communication to the public of their performances, except where the performance is itself already a broadcast performance or is made from a fixation.

2.    Member States shall provide a right in order to ensure that a single equitable remuneration is paid by the user, if a phonogram published for commercial purposes, or a reproduction of such phonogram, is used for broadcasting by wireless means or for any communication to the public, and to ensure that this remuneration is shared between the relevant performers and phonogram producers. Member States may, in the absence of agreement between the performers and phonogram producers, lay down the conditions as to the sharing of this remuneration between them.

3.    Member States shall provide for broadcasting organisations the exclusive right to authorise or prohibit the rebroadcasting of their broadcasts by wireless means, as well as the communication to the public of their broadcasts if such communication is made in places accessible to the public against payment of an entrance fee.

*Article 9*

**Distribution right**

1.    Member States shall provide the exclusive right to make available to the public, by sale or otherwise, the objects indicated in points (a) to (d), including copies thereof, hereinafter "the distribution right":

(a)    for performers, in respect of fixations of their performances;

(b)    for phonogram producers, in respect of their phonograms;

(c)    for producers of the first fixations of films, in respect of the original and copies of their films;

(d)    for broadcasting organisations, in respect of fixations of their broadcasts as set out in Article 7(2).

2.    The distribution right shall not be exhausted within the Community in respect of an object as referred to in paragraph 1, except where the first sale in the Community of that object is made by the rightholder or with his consent.

3.    The distribution right shall be without prejudice to the specific provisions of Chapter I, in particular Article 1(2).

4.    The distribution right may be transferred, assigned or subject to the granting of contractual licences.

*Article 10*

**Limitations to rights**

1.    Member States may provide for limitations to the rights referred to in this Chapter in respect of:

(a)    private use;

(b)    use of short excerpts in connection with the reporting of current events;

(c)    ephemeral fixation by a broadcasting organisation by means of its own facilities and for its own broadcasts;

(d)    use solely for the purposes of teaching or scientific research.

2.    Irrespective of paragraph 1, any Member State may provide for the same kinds of limitations with regard to the protection of performers, producers of phonograms, broadcasting organisations and

of producers of the first fixations of films, as it provides for in connection with the protection of copyright in literary and artistic works.

However, compulsory licences may be provided for only to the extent to which they are compatible with the Rome Convention.

3.    The limitations referred to in paragraphs 1 and 2 shall be applied only in certain special cases which do not conflict with a normal exploitation of the subject matter and do not unreasonably prejudice the legitimate interests of the rightholder.

## CHAPTER III
## COMMON PROVISIONS

### *Article 11*

### Application in time

1.    This Directive shall apply in respect of all copyright works, performances, phonograms, broadcasts and first fixations of films referred to in this Directive which were, on 1 July 1994, still protected by the legislation of the Member States in the field of copyright and related rights or which met the criteria for protection under this Directive on that date.

2.    This Directive shall apply without prejudice to any acts of exploitation performed before 1 July 1994.

3.    Member States may provide that the rightholders are deemed to have given their authorisation to the rental or lending of an object referred to in points (a) to (d) of Article 3(1) which is proven to have been made available to third parties for this purpose or to have been acquired before 1 July 1994.

However, in particular where such an object is a digital recording, Member States may provide that rightholders shall have a right to obtain an adequate remuneration for the rental or lending of that object.

4.    Member States need not apply the provisions of Article 2(2) to cinematographic or audiovisual works created before 1 July 1994.

5.    This Directive shall, without prejudice to paragraph 3 and subject to paragraph 7, not affect any contracts concluded before 19 November 1992.

6.    Member States may provide, subject to the provisions of paragraph 7, that when rightholders who acquire new rights under the national provisions adopted in implementation of this Directive have, before 1 July 1994, given their consent for exploitation, they shall be presumed to have transferred the new exclusive rights.

7.    For contracts concluded before 1 July 1994, the unwaivable right to an equitable remuneration provided for in Article 5 shall apply only where authors or performers or those representing them have submitted a request to that effect before 1 January 1997. In the absence of agreement between rightholders concerning the level of remuneration, Member States may fix the level of equitable remuneration.

### *Article 12*

### Relation between copyright and related rights

Protection of copyright-related rights under this Directive shall leave intact and shall in no way affect the protection of copyright.

*Article 13*

## Communication

Member States shall communicate to the Commission the main provisions of national law adopted in the field covered by this Directive.

*Article 14*

## Repeal

Directive 92/100/EEC is hereby repealed, without prejudice to the obligations of the Member States relating to the time-limits for transposition into national law of the Directives as set out in Part B of Annex I.

References made to the repealed Directive shall be construed as being made to this Directive and should be read in accordance with the correlation table in Annex II.

*Article 15*

## Entry into force

This Directive shall enter into force on the twentieth day following that of its publication in the Official Journal of the European Union.

*Article 16*

## Addressees

This Directive is addressed to the Member States.

Done at Strasbourg, 12 December 2006.

# 56.  RESALE RIGHT DIRECTIVE

**DIRECTIVE 2001/84/EC OF THE EUROPEAN PARLIAMENT
AND OF THE COUNCIL
of 27 September 2001
on the resale right for the benefit of the author of an original work of art***

. . . Whereas:

(1)   In the field of copyright, the resale right is an unassignable and inalienable right, enjoyed by the author of an original work of graphic or plastic art, to an economic interest in successive sales of the work concerned.

(2)   The resale right is a right of a productive character which enables the author/artist to receive consideration for successive transfers of the work. The subject-matter of the resale right is the physical work, namely the medium in which the protected work is incorporated.

(3)   The resale right is intended to ensure that authors of graphic and plastic works of art share in the economic success of their original works of art. It helps to redress the balance between the economic situation of authors of graphic and plastic works of art and that of other creators who benefit from successive exploitations of their works.

(4)   The resale right forms an integral part of copyright and is an essential prerogative for authors. The imposition of such a right in all Member States meets the need for providing creators with an adequate and standard level of protection.

(5)   Under Article 151(4) of the Treaty the Community is to take cultural aspects into account in its action under other provisions of the Treaty.

(6)   The Berne Convention for the Protection of Literary and Artistic Works provides that the resale right is available only if legislation in the country to which the author belongs so permits. The right is therefore optional and subject to the rule of reciprocity. It follows from the case-law of the Court of Justice of the European Communities on the application of the principle of non-discrimination laid down in Article 12 of the Treaty, as shown in the judgment of 20 October 1993 in Joined Cases C-92/92 and C-326/92 Phil Collins and Others, that domestic provisions containing reciprocity clauses cannot be relied upon in order to deny nationals of other Member States rights conferred on national authors. The application of such clauses in the Community context runs counter to the principle of equal treatment resulting from the prohibition of any discrimination on grounds of nationality. . . .

(19) It should be made clear that the harmonisation brought about by this Directive does not apply to original manuscripts of writers and composers. . . .

(29) Enjoyment of the resale right should be restricted to Community nationals as well as to foreign authors whose countries afford such protection to authors who are nationals of Member States. A Member State should have the option of extending enjoyment of this right to foreign authors who have their habitual residence in that Member State. . . .

## CHAPTER I
## SCOPE

*Article 1*

### Subject matter of the resale right

1.   Member States shall provide, for the benefit of the author of an original work of art, a resale right, to be defined as an inalienable right, which cannot be waived, even in advance, to receive a

---

*   Footnotes and some recitals omitted.

royalty based on the sale price obtained for any resale of the work, subsequent to the first transfer of the work by the author.

2.    The right referred to in paragraph 1 shall apply to all acts of resale involving as sellers, buyers or intermediaries art market professionals, such as salesrooms, art galleries and, in general, any dealers in works of art.

3.    Member States may provide that the right referred to in paragraph 1 shall not apply to acts of resale where the seller has acquired the work directly from the author less than three years before that resale and where the resale price does not exceed EUR 10 000.

4.    The royalty shall be payable by the seller. Member States may provide that one of the natural or legal persons referred to in paragraph 2 other than the seller shall alone be liable or shall share liability with the seller for payment of the royalty.

*Article 2*

**Works of art to which the resale right relates**

1.    For the purposes of this Directive, "original work of art" means works of graphic or plastic art such as pictures, collages, paintings, drawings, engravings, prints, lithographs, sculptures, tapestries, ceramics, glassware and photographs, provided they are made by the artist himself or are copies considered to be original works of art.

2.    Copies of works of art covered by this Directive, which have been made in limited numbers by the artist himself or under his authority, shall be considered to be original works of art for the purposes of this Directive. Such copies will normally have been numbered, signed or otherwise duly authorised by the artist.

CHAPTER II
**PARTICULAR PROVISIONS**

*Article 3*

**Threshold**

1.    It shall be for the Member States to set a minimum sale price from which the sales referred to in Article 1 shall be subject to resale right.

2.    This minimum sale price may not under any circumstances exceed EUR 3 000.

*Article 4*

**Rates**

1.    The royalty provided for in Article 1 shall be set at the following rates:

   (a)    4% for the portion of the sale price up to EUR 50 000;

   (b)    3% for the portion of the sale price from EUR 50 000,01 to EUR 200 000;

   (c)    1% for the portion of the sale price from EUR 200 000,01 to EUR 350 000;

   (d)    0,5% for the portion of the sale price from EUR 350 000,01 to EUR 500 000;

   (e)    0,25% for the portion of the sale price exceeding EUR 500 000.

However, the total amount of the royalty may not exceed EUR 12 500.

2.    By way of derogation from paragraph 1, Member States may apply a rate of 5% for the portion of the sale price referred to in paragraph 1(a).

3.   If the minimum sale price set should be lower than EUR 3 000, the Member State shall also determine the rate applicable to the portion of the sale price up to EUR 3 000; this rate may not be lower than 4%.

## Article 5

### Calculation basis

The sale prices referred to in Articles 3 and 4 are net of tax.

## Article 6

### Persons entitled to receive royalties

1.   The royalty provided for under Article 1 shall be payable to the author of the work and, subject to Article 8(2), after his death to those entitled under him/her.

2.   Member States may provide for compulsory or optional collective management of the royalty provided for under Article 1.

## Article 7

### Third-country nationals entitled to receive royalties

1.   Member States shall provide that authors who are nationals of third countries and, subject to Article 8(2), their successors in title shall enjoy the resale right in accordance with this Directive and the legislation of the Member State concerned only if legislation in the country of which the author or his/her successor in title is a national permits resale right protection in that country for authors from the Member States and their successors in title.

2.   On the basis of information provided by the Member States, the Commission shall publish as soon as possible an indicative list of those third countries which fulfil the condition set out in paragraph 1. This list shall be kept up to date.

3.   Any Member State may treat authors who are not nationals of a Member State but who have their habitual residence in that Member State in the same way as its own nationals for the purpose of resale right protection.

## Article 8

### Term of protection of the resale right

1.   The term of protection of the resale right shall correspond to that laid down in Article 1 of Directive 93/98/EEC.

2.   By way of derogation from paragraph 1, those Member States which do not apply the resale right on (the entry into force date referred to in Article 13), shall not be required, for a period expiring not later than 1 January 2010, to apply the resale right for the benefit of those entitled under the artist after his/her death.

3.   A Member State to which paragraph 2 applies may have up to two more years, if necessary to enable the economic operators in that Member State to adapt gradually to the resale right system while maintaining their economic viability, before it is required to apply the resale right for the benefit of those entitled under the artist after his/her death. At least 12 months before the end of the period referred to in paragraph 2, the Member State concerned shall inform the Commission giving its reasons, so that the Commission can give an opinion, after appropriate consultations, within three months following the receipt of such information. If the Member State does not follow the opinion of the Commission, it shall within one month inform the Commission and justify its decision. The notification and justification of the Member State and the opinion of the Commission shall be

published in the Official Journal of the European Communities and forwarded to the European Parliament.

4.    In the event of the successful conclusion, within the periods referred to in Article 8(2) and (3), of international negotiations aimed at extending the resale right at international level, the Commission shall submit appropriate proposals.

## Article 9

### Right to obtain information

The Member States shall provide that for a period of three years after the resale, the persons entitled under Article 6 may require from any art market professional mentioned in Article 1(2) to furnish any information that may be necessary in order to secure payment of royalties in respect of the resale.

## CHAPTER III
## FINAL PROVISIONS

### Article 10

### Application in time

This Directive shall apply in respect of all original works of art as defined in Article 2 which, on 1 January 2006, are still protected by the legislation of the Member States in the field of copyright or meet the criteria for protection under the provisions of this Directive at that date.

### Article 11

### Revision clause

1.    The Commission shall submit to the European Parliament, the Council and the Economic and Social Committee not later than 1 January 2009 and every four years thereafter a report on the implementation and the effect of this Directive, paying particular attention to the competitiveness of the market in modern and contemporary art in the Community, especially as regards the position of the Community in relation to relevant markets that do not apply the resale right and the fostering of artistic creativity and the management procedures in the Member States. It shall examine in particular its impact on the internal market and the effect of the introduction of the resale right in those Member States that did not apply the right in national law prior to the entry into force of this Directive. Where appropriate, the Commission shall submit proposals for adapting the minimum threshold and the rates of royalty to take account of changes in the sector, proposals relating to the maximum amount laid down in Article 4(1) and any other proposal it may deem necessary in order to enhance the effectiveness of this Directive.

2.    A Contact Committee is hereby established. It shall be composed of representatives of the competent authorities of the Member States. It shall be chaired by a representative of the Commission and shall meet either on the initiative of the Chairman or at the request of the delegation of a Member State.

3.    The task of the Committee shall be as follows:

—    to organise consultations on all questions deriving from application of this Directive,

—    to facilitate the exchange of information between the Commission and the Member States on relevant developments in the art market in the Community.

*Article 12*

### Implementation

1.    Member States shall bring into force the laws, regulations and administrative provisions necessary to comply with this Directive before 1 January 2006. They shall forthwith inform the Commission thereof.

When Member States adopt these measures, they shall contain a reference to this Directive or shall be accompanied by such reference on the occasion of their official publication. The methods of making such a reference shall be laid down by the Member States.

2.    Member States shall communicate to the Commission the provisions of national law which they adopt in the field covered by this Directive.

*Article 13*

### Entry into force

This Directive shall enter into force on the day of its publication in the Official Journal of the European Communities.

*Article 14*

### Addressees

This Directive is addressed to the Member States.

Done at Brussels, 27 September 2001.

# 57. ORPHAN WORKS DIRECTIVE

## DIRECTIVE 2012/28/EU OF THE EUROPEAN PARLIAMENT AND OF THE COUNCIL
### of 25 October 2012
### on certain permitted uses of orphan works

### (Text with EEA relevance)*

. . . Whereas: . . .

(3)   Creating a legal framework to facilitate the digitisation and dissemination of works and other subject-matter which are protected by copyright or related rights and for which no rightholder is identified or for which the rightholder, even if identified, is not located—so-called orphan works—is a key action of the Digital Agenda for Europe, as set out in the Communication from the Commission entitled "A Digital Agenda for Europe". This Directive targets the specific problem of the legal determination of orphan work status and its consequences in terms of the permitted users and permitted uses of works or phonograms considered to be orphan works.

(4)   This Directive is without prejudice to specific solutions being developed in the Member States to address larger mass digitisation issues, such as in the case of so-called "out-of-commerce" works. Such solutions take into account the specificities of different types of content and different users and build upon the consensus of the relevant stakeholders. This approach has also been followed in the Memorandum of Understanding on key principles on the digitisation and making available of out-of-commerce works, signed on 20 September 2011 by representatives of European libraries, authors, publishers and collecting societies and witnessed by the Commission. This Directive is without prejudice to that Memorandum of Understanding, which calls on Member States and the Commission to ensure that voluntary agreements concluded between users, rightholders and collective rights management organisations to licence the use of out-of-commerce works on the basis of the principles contained therein benefit from the requisite legal certainty in a national and cross-border context. . . .

(12) For reasons of international comity, this Directive should apply only to works and phonograms that are first published in the territory of a Member State or, in the absence of publication, first broadcast in the territory of a Member State or, in the absence of publication or broadcast, made publicly accessible by the beneficiaries of this Directive with the consent of the rightholders. In the latter case, this Directive should only apply provided that it is reasonable to assume that the rightholders would not oppose the use allowed by this Directive. . . .

(22) Contractual arrangements may play a role in fostering the digitisation of European cultural heritage, it being understood that publicly accessible libraries, educational establishments and museums, as well as archives, film or audio heritage institutions and public-service broadcasting organisations, should be allowed, with a view to undertaking the uses permitted under this Directive, to conclude agreements with commercial partners for the digitisation and making available to the public of orphan works. Those agreements may include financial contributions by such partners. Such agreements should not impose any restrictions on the beneficiaries of this Directive as to their use of orphan works and should not grant the commercial partner any rights to use, or control the use of, the orphan works. . . .

(24) This Directive is without prejudice to the arrangements in the Member States concerning the management of rights such as extended collective licences, legal presumptions of representation or transfer, collective management or similar arrangements or a combination of them, including for mass digitisation. . . .

---

*   Footnotes and some recitals omitted.

*Article 1*

**Subject-matter and scope**

1.   This Directive concerns certain uses made of orphan works by publicly accessible libraries, educational establishments and museums, as well as by archives, film or audio heritage institutions and public-service broadcasting organisations, established in the Member States, in order to achieve aims related to their public-interest missions.

2.   This Directive applies to:

(a)   works published in the form of books, journals, newspapers, magazines or other writings contained in the collections of publicly accessible libraries, educational establishments or museums as well as in the collections of archives or of film or audio heritage institutions;

(b)   cinematographic or audiovisual works and phonograms contained in the collections of publicly accessible libraries, educational establishments or museums as well as in the collections of archives or of film or audio heritage institutions; and

(c)   cinematographic or audiovisual works and phonograms produced by public-service broadcasting organisations up to and including 31 December 2002 and contained in their archives;

which are protected by copyright or related rights and which are first published in a Member State or, in the absence of publication, first broadcast in a Member State.

3.   This Directive also applies to works and phonograms referred to in paragraph 2 which have never been published or broadcast but which have been made publicly accessible by the organisations referred to in paragraph 1 with the consent of the rightholders, provided that it is reasonable to assume that the rightholders would not oppose the uses referred to in Article 6. Member States may limit the application of this paragraph to works and phonograms which have been deposited with those organisations before 29 October 2014.

4.   This Directive shall also apply to works and other protected subject-matter that are embedded or incorporated in, or constitute an integral part of, the works or phonograms referred to in paragraphs 2 and 3.

5.   This Directive does not interfere with any arrangements concerning the management of rights at national level.

*Article 2*

**Orphan works**

1.   A work or a phonogram shall be considered an orphan work if none of the rightholders in that work or phonogram is identified or, even if one or more of them is identified, none is located despite a diligent search for the rightholders having been carried out and recorded in accordance with Article 3.

2.   Where there is more than one rightholder in a work or phonogram, and not all of them have been identified or, even if identified, located after a diligent search has been carried out and recorded in accordance with Article 3, the work or phonogram may be used in accordance with this Directive provided that the rightholders that have been identified and located have, in relation to the rights they hold, authorised the organisations referred to in Article 1(1) to carry out the acts of reproduction and making available to the public covered respectively by Articles 2 and 3 of Directive 2001/29/EC.

3.   Paragraph 2 shall be without prejudice to the rights in the work or phonogram of rightholders that have been identified and located.

4.   Article 5 shall apply mutatis mutandis to the rightholders that have not been identified and located in the works referred to in paragraph 2.

5.    This Directive shall be without prejudice to national provisions on anonymous or pseudonymous works.

## Article 3

### Diligent search

1.    For the purposes of establishing whether a work or phonogram is an orphan work, the organisations referred to in Article 1(1) shall ensure that a diligent search is carried out in good faith in respect of each work or other protected subject-matter, by consulting the appropriate sources for the category of works and other protected subject-matter in question. The diligent search shall be carried out prior to the use of the work or phonogram.

2.    The sources that are appropriate for each category of works or phonogram in question shall be determined by each Member State, in consultation with rightholders and users, and shall include at least the relevant sources listed in the Annex.

3.    A diligent search shall be carried out in the Member State of first publication or, in the absence of publication, first broadcast, except in the case of cinematographic or audiovisual works the producer of which has his headquarters or habitual residence in a Member State, in which case the diligent search shall be carried out in the Member State of his headquarters or habitual residence.

In the case referred to in Article 1(3), the diligent search shall be carried out in the Member State where the organisation that made the work or phonogram publicly accessible with the consent of the rightholder is established.

4.    If there is evidence to suggest that relevant information on rightholders is to be found in other countries, sources of information available in those other countries shall also be consulted.

5.    Member States shall ensure that the organisations referred to in Article 1(1) maintain records of their diligent searches and that those organisations provide the following information to the competent national authorities:

(a)    the results of the diligent searches that the organisations have carried out and which have led to the conclusion that a work or a phonogram is considered an orphan work;

(b)    the use that the organisations make of orphan works in accordance with this Directive;

(c)    any change, pursuant to Article 5, of the orphan work status of works and phonograms that the organisations use;

(d)    the relevant contact information of the organisation concerned.

6.    Member States shall take the necessary measures to ensure that the information referred to in paragraph 5 is recorded in a single publicly accessible online database established and managed by the Office for Harmonization in the Internal Market ("the Office") in accordance with Regulation (EU) No 386/2012. To that end, they shall forward that information to the Office without delay upon receiving it from the organisations referred to in Article 1(1).

## Article 4

### Mutual recognition of orphan work status

A work or phonogram which is considered an orphan work according to Article 2 in a Member State shall be considered an orphan work in all Member States. That work or phonogram may be used and accessed in accordance with this Directive in all Member States. This also applies to works and phonograms referred to in Article 2(2) in so far as the rights of the non-identified or non-located rightholders are concerned.

*Article 5*

## End of orphan work status

Member States shall ensure that a rightholder in a work or phonogram considered to be an orphan work has, at any time, the possibility of putting an end to the orphan work status in so far as his rights are concerned.

*Article 6*

## Permitted uses of orphan works

1.　Member States shall provide for an exception or limitation to the right of reproduction and the right of making available to the public provided for respectively in Articles 2 and 3 of Directive 2001/29/EC to ensure that the organisations referred to in Article 1(1) are permitted to use orphan works contained in their collections in the following ways:

(a)　by making the orphan work available to the public, within the meaning of Article 3 of Directive 2001/29/EC;

(b)　by acts of reproduction, within the meaning of Article 2 of Directive 2001/29/EC, for the purposes of digitisation, making available, indexing, cataloguing, preservation or restoration.

2.　The organisations referred to in Article 1(1) shall use an orphan work in accordance with paragraph 1 of this Article only in order to achieve aims related to their public-interest missions, in particular the preservation of, the restoration of, and the provision of cultural and educational access to, works and phonograms contained in their collection. The organisations may generate revenues in the course of such uses, for the exclusive purpose of covering their costs of digitising orphan works and making them available to the public.

3.　Member States shall ensure that the organisations referred to in Article 1(1) indicate the name of identified authors and other rightholders in any use of an orphan work.

4.　This Directive is without prejudice to the freedom of contract of such organisations in the pursuit of their public-interest missions, particularly in respect of public-private partnership agreements.

5.　Member States shall provide that a fair compensation is due to rightholders that put an end to the orphan work status of their works or other protected subject-matter for the use that has been made by the organisations referred to in Article 1(1) of such works and other protected subject-matter in accordance with paragraph 1 of this Article. Member States shall be free to determine the circumstances under which the payment of such compensation may be organised. The level of the compensation shall be determined, within the limits imposed by Union law, by the law of the Member State in which the organisation which uses the orphan work in question is established.

*Article 7*

## Continued application of other legal provisions

This Directive shall be without prejudice to provisions concerning, in particular, patent rights, trade marks, design rights, utility models, the topographies of semi-conductor products, type faces, conditional access, access to cable of broadcasting services, the protection of national treasures, legal deposit requirements, laws on restrictive practices and unfair competition, trade secrets, security, confidentiality, data protection and privacy, access to public documents, the law of contract, and rules on the freedom of the press and freedom of expression in the media.

*Article 8*

## Application in time

1.　This Directive shall apply in respect of all works and phonograms referred to in Article 1 which are protected by the Member States' legislation in the field of copyright on or after 29 October 2014.

2.     This Directive shall apply without prejudice to any acts concluded and rights acquired before 29 October 2014.

## *Article 9*

### Transposition

1.     Member States shall bring into force the laws, regulations and administrative provisions necessary to comply with this Directive by 29 October 2014. They shall forthwith communicate to the Commission the text of those provisions.

When Member States adopt those provisions, they shall contain a reference to this Directive or shall be accompanied by such a reference on the occasion of their official publication. The methods of making such reference shall be laid down by Member States.

2.     Member States shall communicate to the Commission the text of the main provisions of national law which they adopt in the field covered by this Directive.

## *Article 10*

### Review clause

The Commission shall keep under constant review the development of rights information sources and shall by 29 October 2015, and at annual intervals thereafter, submit a report concerning the possible inclusion in the scope of application of this Directive of publishers and of works or other protected subject-matter not currently included in its scope, and in particular stand-alone photographs and other images.

By 29 October 2015, the Commission shall submit to the European Parliament, the Council and the European Economic and Social Committee a report on the application of this Directive, in the light of the development of digital libraries.

When necessary, in particular to ensure the functioning of the internal market, the Commission shall submit proposals for amendment of this Directive.

A Member State that has valid reasons to consider that the implementation of this Directive hinders one of the national arrangements concerning the management of rights referred to in Article 1(5) may bring the matter to the attention of the Commission together with all relevant evidence. The Commission shall take such evidence into account when drawing up the report referred to in the second paragraph of this Article and when assessing whether it is necessary to submit proposals for amendment of this Directive.

## *Article 11*

### Entry into force

This Directive shall enter into force on the day following that of its publication in the Official Journal of the European Union.

## *Article 12*

### Addressees

This Directive is addressed to the Member States.

Done at Strasbourg, 25 October 2012.

ANNEX

The sources referred to in Article 3(2) include the following:

(1)  for published books:

(a)  legal deposit, library catalogues and authority files maintained by libraries and other institutions;

(b)  the publishers' and authors' associations in the respective country;

(c)  existing databases and registries, WATCH (Writers, Artists and their Copyright Holders), the ISBN (International Standard Book Number) and databases listing books in print;

(d)  the databases of the relevant collecting societies, in particular reproduction rights organisations;

(e)  sources that integrate multiple databases and registries, including VIAF (Virtual International Authority Files) and ARROW (Accessible Registries of Rights Information and Orphan Works);

(2)  for newspapers, magazines, journals and periodicals:

(a)  the ISSN (International Standard Serial Number) for periodical publications;

(b)  indexes and catalogues from library holdings and collections;

(c)  legal deposit;

(d)  the publishers' associations and the authors' and journalists' associations in the respective country;

(e)  the databases of relevant collecting societies including reproduction rights organisations;

(3)  for visual works, including fine art, photography, illustration, design, architecture, sketches of the latter works and other such works that are contained in books, journals, newspapers and magazines or other works:

(a)  the sources referred to in points (1) and (2);

(b)  the databases of the relevant collecting societies, in particular for visual arts, and including reproduction rights organisations;

(c)  the databases of picture agencies, where applicable;

(4)  for audiovisual works and phonograms:

(a)  legal deposit;

(b)  the producers' associations in the respective country;

(c)  databases of film or audio heritage institutions and national libraries;

(d)  databases with relevant standards and identifiers such as ISAN (International Standard Audiovisual Number) for audiovisual material, ISWC (International Standard Music Work Code) for musical works and ISRC (International Standard Recording Code) for phonograms;

(e)  the databases of the relevant collecting societies, in particular for authors, performers, phonogram producers and audiovisual producers;

(f)  credits and other information appearing on the work's packaging;

(g)  databases of other relevant associations representing a specific category of rightholders.

# 58. VISUALLY IMPAIRED PERSONS DIRECTIVE

## DIRECTIVE (EU) 2017/1564 OF THE EUROPEAN PARLIAMENT AND OF THE COUNCIL

### of 13 September 2017

**on certain permitted uses of certain works and other subject matter protected by copyright and related rights for the benefit of persons who are blind, visually impaired or otherwise print-disabled and amending Directive 2001/29/EC on the harmonisation of certain aspects of copyright and related rights in the information society***

. . . Whereas:

(1) Union legal acts in the area of copyright and related rights provide legal certainty and a high level of protection for rightholders, and constitute a harmonised legal framework. That framework contributes to the proper functioning of the internal market and stimulates innovation, creation, investment and the production of new content, including in the digital environment. It also aims to promote access to knowledge and culture by protecting works and other subject matter and by permitting exceptions or limitations that are in the public interest. A fair balance of rights and interests between rightholders and users should be safeguarded. . . .

(3) Persons who are blind, visually impaired or otherwise print-disabled continue to face many barriers to accessing books and other printed material which are protected by copyright and related rights. Taking into consideration the rights of blind, visually impaired or otherwise print-disabled persons as recognised in the Charter of Fundamental Rights of the European Union (the 'Charter') and the United Nations Convention on the Rights of Persons with Disabilities (the 'UNCRPD'), measures should be taken to increase the availability of books and other printed material in accessible formats, and to improve their circulation in the internal market.

(4) The Marrakesh Treaty to Facilitate Access to Published Works for Persons Who Are Blind, Visually Impaired, or Otherwise Print Disabled (the 'Marrakesh Treaty') was signed on behalf of the Union on 30 April 2014. . . .

(6) This Directive implements the obligations that the Union has to meet under the Marrakesh Treaty in a harmonised manner, with a view to ensuring that the corresponding measures are applied consistently throughout the internal market. This Directive should therefore provide for a mandatory exception to the rights that are harmonised by Union law and are relevant for the uses and works covered by the Marrakesh Treaty. Such rights include, in particular, the rights of reproduction, communication to the public, making available to the public, distribution and lending, as provided for in Directives 2001/29/EC, 2006/115/EC and 2009/24/EC, as well as the corresponding rights provided for in Directive 96/9/EC. As the scope of the exceptions or limitations required by the Marrakesh Treaty also includes works in audio form, like audiobooks, the mandatory exception provided for under this Directive should also apply to related rights.

(7) This Directive concerns persons who are blind, persons who have a visual impairment which cannot be improved so as to give them visual function substantially equivalent to that of a person who has no such impairment, persons who have a perceptual or reading disability, including dyslexia or any other learning disability preventing them from reading printed works to substantially the same degree as persons without such disability, and persons who are unable, due to a physical disability, to hold or manipulate a book or to focus or move the eyes to the extent that would be normally acceptable for reading, insofar as, as a result of such impairments or disabilities, those persons are unable to read printed works to substantially the same degree as

---

\* Footnotes and some recitals omitted.

persons without such impairments or disabilities. This Directive therefore aims to improve the availability of books, including e-books, journals, newspapers, magazines and other kinds of writing, notation, including sheet music, and other printed material, including in audio form, whether digital or analogue, online or offline, in formats that make those works and other subject matter accessible to those persons to substantially the same degree as to persons without such impairment or disability. Accessible formats include, for example, Braille, large print, adapted e-books, audio books and radio broadcasts.

(8) The mandatory exception provided for in this Directive should limit the right of reproduction so as to allow for any act that is necessary in order to make changes to or convert or adapt a work or other subject matter in such a way as to produce an accessible format copy that makes it possible for beneficiary persons to access that work or other subject matter. This includes providing the necessary means to navigate information in an accessible format copy. It also includes changes that might be required in cases in which the format of a work or of other subject matter is already accessible to certain beneficiary persons while it might not be accessible to other beneficiary persons, due to different impairments or disabilities, or the different degree of such impairments or disabilities. . . .

(10) The exception provided for in this Directive should allow authorised entities to make and disseminate, online and offline within the Union, accessible format copies of works or other subject matter covered by this Directive. This Directive should not impose an obligation on authorised entities to make and disseminate such copies.

(11) It should be possible for accessible format copies made in one Member State to be available in all Member States, in order to ensure their greater availability across the internal market. This would reduce the demand for duplication of work in producing accessible format copies of one and the same work or other subject matter across the Union, thus generating savings and efficiency gains. This Directive should therefore ensure that accessible format copies made by authorised entities in any Member State can be circulated and accessed by beneficiary persons and authorised entities throughout the Union. In order to foster such cross-border exchange and to facilitate authorised entities' mutual identification and cooperation, the voluntary sharing of information regarding the names and contact details of authorised entities established in the Union, including websites if available, should be encouraged. Member States should therefore provide the information received from authorised entities to the Commission. This should not imply an obligation for Member States to check the completeness and accuracy of such information or its compliance with their national law transposing this Directive. Such information should be made available online by the Commission on a central information access point at Union level. This would also assist authorised entities, as well as beneficiary persons and rightholders in contacting authorised entities to receive further information, in line with the provisions set out in this Directive and in Regulation (EU) 2017/1563 of the European Parliament and of the Council. The aforementioned central information access point should be complementary to the information access point to be established by the International Bureau of the World Intellectual Property Organisation (WIPO), as provided for in the Marrakesh Treaty, aiming to facilitate the identification of, and cooperation among, authorised entities at international level. . . .

(13) Authorisation or recognition requirements that Member States may apply to authorised entities, such as those relating to the provision of services of a general nature to beneficiary persons, should not have the effect of preventing entities that are covered by the definition of authorised entity under this Directive from undertaking the uses allowed under this Directive.

(14) In view of the specific nature of the exception provided for under this Directive, its specific scope and the need for legal certainty for its beneficiaries, Member States should not be allowed to impose additional requirements for the application of the exception, such as the prior verification of the commercial availability of works in accessible formats, other than those laid down in this Directive. Member States should only be allowed to provide for compensation schemes regarding

the permitted uses of works or other subject matter by authorised entities. In order to avoid burdens for beneficiary persons, prevent barriers to the cross-border dissemination of accessible format copies and excessive requirements on authorised entities, it is important that the possibility for Member States to provide for such compensation schemes be limited. Consequently, compensation schemes should not require payments by beneficiary persons. They should only apply to uses by authorised entities established in the territory of the Member State providing for such a scheme, and they should not require payments by authorised entities established in other Member States or third countries that are parties to the Marrakesh Treaty. Member States should ensure that there are not more burdensome requirements for the cross-border exchange of accessible format copies under such compensation schemes than for non-cross border situations, including with regard to the form and possible level of compensation. When determining the level of compensation, due account should be taken of the non-profit nature of the activities of authorised entities, of the public interest objectives pursued by this Directive, of the interests of beneficiaries of the exception, of the possible harm to rightholders and of the need to ensure cross-border dissemination of accessible format copies. Account should also be taken of the particular circumstances of each case, resulting from the making of a particular accessible format copy. Where the harm to a rightholder is minimal, no obligation for payment of compensation should arise. . . .

(16) The UNCRPD, to which the Union is a party, guarantees persons with disabilities the right of access to information and education and the right to participate in cultural, economic and social life, on an equal basis with others. The UNCRPD requires parties to the Convention to take all appropriate steps, in accordance with international law, to ensure that laws protecting intellectual property rights do not constitute an unreasonable or discriminatory barrier to access by persons with disabilities to cultural materials.

(17) Under the Charter, all forms of discrimination, including on grounds of disability, are prohibited and the right of persons with disabilities to benefit from measures designed to ensure their independence, social and occupational integration and participation in the life of the community is recognised and respected by the Union.

(18) With the adoption of this Directive, the Union aims to ensure that beneficiary persons have access to books and other printed material in accessible formats across the internal market. Accordingly, this Directive is an essential first step in improving access to works for persons with disabilities. . . .

(20) Member States should be allowed to continue to provide for an exception or limitation for the benefit of persons with a disability in cases which are not covered by this Directive, in particular as regards works and other subject matter and disabilities other than those covered by this Directive, pursuant to point (b) of Article 5(3) of Directive 2001/29/EC. This Directive does not prevent Member States from providing for exceptions or limitations to rights that are not harmonised in the copyright framework of the Union. . . .

(22) The Marrakesh Treaty imposes certain obligations regarding the exchange of accessible format copies between the Union and third countries that are parties to that Treaty. The measures taken by the Union to fulfil those obligations are contained in Regulation (EU) 2017/1563 which should be read in conjunction with this Directive. . . .

*Article 1*

### Subject matter and scope

This Directive aims to further harmonise Union law applicable to copyright and related rights in the framework of the internal market, by establishing rules on the use of certain works and other subject matter without the authorisation of the rightholder, for the benefit of persons who are blind, visually impaired or otherwise print-disabled.

*Article 2*

**Definitions**

For the purposes of this Directive the following definitions apply:

(1) 'work or other subject matter' means a work in the form of a book, journal, newspaper, magazine or other kind of writing, notation, including sheet music, and related illustrations, in any media, including in audio form such as audiobooks and in digital format, which is protected by copyright or related rights and which is published or otherwise lawfully made publicly available;

(2) 'beneficiary person' means, regardless of any other disabilities, a person who:

    (a) is blind;

    (b) has a visual impairment which cannot be improved so as to give the person visual function substantially equivalent to that of a person who has no such impairment, and who is, as a result, unable to read printed works to substantially the same degree as a person without such an impairment;

    (c) has a perceptual or reading disability and is, as a result, unable to read printed works to substantially the same degree as a person without such disability; or

    (d) is otherwise unable, due to a physical disability, to hold or manipulate a book or to focus or move their eyes to the extent that would be normally acceptable for reading.

(3) 'accessible format copy' means a copy of a work or other subject matter in an alternative manner or form that gives a beneficiary person access to the work or other subject matter, including allowing such person to have access as feasibly and comfortably as a person without any of the impairments or disabilities referred to in point 2;

(4) 'authorised entity' means an entity that is authorised or recognised by a Member State to provide education, instructional training, adaptive reading or information access to beneficiary persons on a non-profit basis. It also includes a public institution or non-profit organisation that provides the same services to beneficiary persons as one of its primary activities, institutional obligations or as part of its public-interest missions.

*Article 3*

**Permitted uses**

1. Member States shall provide for an exception to the effect that no authorisation of the rightholder of any copyright or related right in a work or other subject matter is required pursuant to Articles 5 and 7 of Directive 96/9/EC, Articles 2, 3 and 4 of Directive 2001/29/EC, Article 1(1), Article 8(2) and (3) and Article 9 of Directive 2006/115/EC and Article 4 of Directive 2009/24/EC for any act necessary for:

(a) a beneficiary person, or a person acting on their behalf, to make an accessible format copy of a work or other subject matter to which the beneficiary person has lawful access for the exclusive use of the beneficiary person; and

(b) an authorised entity to make an accessible format copy of a work or other subject matter to which it has lawful access, or to communicate, make available, distribute or lend an accessible format copy to a beneficiary person or another authorised entity on a non-profit basis for the purpose of exclusive use by a beneficiary person.

2. Member States shall ensure that each accessible format copy respects the integrity of the work or other subject matter, with due consideration given to the changes required to make the work or other subject matter accessible in the alternative format.

3. The exception provided for in paragraph 1 shall only be applied in certain special cases which do not conflict with a normal exploitation of the work or other subject matter and do not unreasonably prejudice the legitimate interests of the rightholder.

4. The first, third and fifth subparagraphs of Article 6(4) of Directive 2001/29/EC shall apply to the exception provided for in paragraph 1 of this Article.

5. Member States shall ensure that the exception provided for in paragraph 1 cannot be overridden by contract.

6. Member States may provide that uses permitted under this Directive, if undertaken by authorised entities established in their territory, be subject to compensation schemes within the limits provided for in this Directive.

*Article 4*

### Accessible format copies in the internal market

Member States shall ensure that an authorised entity established in their territory may carry out the acts referred to in point (b) of Article 3(1) for a beneficiary person or another authorised entity established in any Member State. Member States shall also ensure that a beneficiary person or an authorised entity established in their territory may obtain or may have access to an accessible format copy from an authorised entity established in any Member State.

*Article 5*

### Obligations of authorised entities

1. Member States shall provide that an authorised entity established in their territory carrying out the acts referred to in Article 4 establishes and follows its own practices to ensure that it:

(a) distributes, communicates and makes available accessible format copies only to beneficiary persons or other authorised entities;

(b) takes appropriate steps to discourage the unauthorised reproduction, distribution, communication to the public or making available to the public of accessible format copies;

(c) demonstrates due care in, and maintains records of, its handling of works or other subject matter and of accessible format copies thereof; and

(d) publishes and updates, on its website if appropriate, or through other online or offline channels, information on how it complies with the obligations laid down in points (a) to (c).

Member States shall ensure that the practices referred to in the first subparagraph are established and followed in full respect of the rules applicable to the processing of personal data of beneficiary persons referred to in Article 7.

2. Member States shall ensure that an authorised entity established in their territory carrying out the acts referred to in Article 4 provides the following information in an accessible way, on request, to beneficiary persons, other authorised entities or rightholders:

(a) the list of works or other subject matter for which it has accessible format copies and the available formats; and

(b) the name and contact details of the authorised entities with which it has engaged in the exchange of accessible format copies pursuant to Article 4.

*Article 6*

**Transparency and exchange of information**

1. Member States shall encourage authorised entities established in their territory carrying out the acts referred to in Article 4 of this Directive and Articles 3 and 4 of Regulation (EU) 2017/1563 to communicate to them, on a voluntary basis, their names and contact details.

2. Member States shall provide the information they have received pursuant to paragraph 1 to the Commission. The Commission shall make such information publicly available online on a central information access point and keep it up to date.

*Article 7*

**Protection of personal data**

The processing of personal data carried out within the framework of this Directive shall be carried out in compliance with Directives 95/46/EC and 2002/58/EC.

*Article 8*

**Amendment to Directive 2001/29/EC**

. . .

*Article 9*

**Report**

By 11 October 2020, the Commission shall present a report to the European Parliament, the Council and the European Economic and Social Committee on the availability, in accessible formats, of works and other subject matter other than those defined in point 1 of Article 2 for beneficiary persons, and of works and other subject matter for persons with disabilities other than those referred to in point 2 of Article 2, in the internal market. The report shall take into account developments concerning relevant technology and shall contain an assessment of the appropriateness of broadening the scope of this Directive in order to improve access to other types of works and other subject matter and to improve access for persons with disabilities other than those covered by this Directive.

*Article 10*

**Review**

1. By 11 October 2023, the Commission shall carry out an evaluation of this Directive and present the main findings in a report to the European Parliament, the Council and the European Economic and Social Committee, accompanied, where appropriate, by proposals for amending this Directive. Such evaluation shall include an assessment of the impact of compensation schemes, provided for by Member States pursuant to Article 3(6), on the availability of accessible format copies for beneficiary persons and on their cross-border exchange. The Commission's report shall take into account the views of relevant civil society actors and of non-governmental organisations, including organisations representing persons with disabilities and those representing older persons.

2. Member States shall provide the Commission with the necessary information for the preparation of the report referred to in paragraph 1 of this Article and the preparation of the report referred to in Article 9.

3. A Member State that has valid reasons to consider that the implementation of this Directive has had a significant negative impact on the commercial availability of works or other subject matter in accessible formats for beneficiary persons may bring the matter to the attention of the Commission providing all relevant evidence. The Commission shall take that evidence into account when drawing up the report referred to in paragraph 1.

*Article 11*

**Transposition**

1.    Member States shall bring into force the laws, regulations and administrative provisions necessary to comply with this Directive by 11 October 2018. They shall immediately inform the Commission thereof.

When Member States adopt those measures, they shall contain a reference to this Directive or be accompanied by such a reference on the occasion of their official publication. The methods of making such reference shall be laid down by Member States.

2.    Member States shall communicate to the Commission the text of the main measures of national law which they adopt in the field covered by this Directive.

*Article 12*

**Entry into force**

This Directive shall enter into force on the twentieth day following that of its publication in the Official Journal of the European Union.

*Article 13*

**Addressees**

This Directive is addressed to the Member States.

Done at Strasbourg, 13 September 2017.

# 59. VISUALLY IMPAIRED PERSONS REGULATION

### REGULATION (EU) 2017/1563 OF THE EUROPEAN PARLIAMENT AND OF THE COUNCIL

### of 13 September 2017

**on the cross-border exchange between the Union and third countries of accessible format copies of certain works and other subject matter protected by copyright and related rights for the benefit of persons who are blind, visually impaired or otherwise print-disabled***

. . . Whereas:

(1) The Marrakesh Treaty to Facilitate Access to Published Works for Persons Who Are Blind, Visually Impaired, or Otherwise Print Disabled (the 'Marrakesh Treaty') was signed on behalf of the Union on 30 April 2014. . . .

(2) The beneficiaries of the Marrakesh Treaty are persons who are blind, persons who have a visual impairment which cannot be improved so as to give them visual function substantially equivalent to that of a person who has no such impairment, persons who have a perceptual or reading disability, including dyslexia or any other learning disability preventing them from reading printed works to substantially the same degree as persons without such disability, and persons who are unable, due to a physical disability, to hold or manipulate a book or to focus or move the eyes to the extent that would be normally acceptable for reading, insofar as, as a result of such impairments or disabilities, those persons are unable to read printed works to substantially the same degree as persons without such impairments or disabilities. . . .

(5) Directive (EU) 2017/1564 of the European Parliament and of the Council aims to implement the obligations that the Union has to meet under the Marrakesh Treaty in a harmonised manner in order to improve the availability of accessible format copies for beneficiary persons in all of the Member States of the Union and the circulation of such copies within the internal market, and requires Member States to introduce a mandatory exception to certain rights that are harmonised by Union law. This Regulation aims to implement the obligations under the Marrakesh Treaty with respect to the export and import arrangements for accessible format copies for non-commercial purposes for the benefit of beneficiary persons between the Union and third countries that are parties to the Marrakesh Treaty, and to lay down the conditions for such export and import in a uniform manner within the field harmonised by Directives 2001/29/EC and (EU) 2017/1564 in order to ensure that those measures are applied consistently throughout the internal market and do not jeopardise the harmonisation of exclusive rights and exceptions contained within those Directives.

(6) This Regulation should ensure that accessible format copies of books, including e-books, journals, newspapers, magazines and other kinds of writing, notation, including sheet music, and other printed material, including in audio form, whether digital or analogue, which have been made in any Member State in accordance with the national provisions adopted pursuant to Directive (EU) 2017/1564 can be distributed, communicated, or made available, to a beneficiary person or authorised entity, as referred to in the Marrakesh Treaty, in third countries that are parties to the Marrakesh Treaty. Accessible formats include, for example, Braille, large print, adapted e-books, audio books and radio broadcasts. Taking into account the 'non-commercial objective of the Marrakesh Treaty', the distribution, communication to the public or making available to the public of accessible format copies to persons who are blind, visually impaired or otherwise print-

---

disabled or to authorised entities in the third country should only be carried out on a non-profit basis by authorised entities established in a Member State.

(7) This Regulation should also allow for the importation of, and access to, accessible format copies made in accordance with the implementation of the Marrakesh Treaty, from a third country, by beneficiary persons in the Union and authorised entities established in a Member State, for non-commercial purposes for the benefit of persons who are blind, visually impaired or otherwise print-disabled. It should be possible for those accessible format copies to circulate in the internal market under the same conditions as accessible format copies made in the Union in accordance with Directive (EU) 2017/1564. . . .

(10) The United Nations Convention on the Rights of Persons with Disabilities (the 'UNCRPD'), to which the Union is a party, guarantees persons with disabilities the right of access to information and education and the right to participate in cultural, economic and social life, on an equal basis with others. The UNCRPD requires parties to the Convention to take all appropriate steps, in accordance with international law, to ensure that laws protecting intellectual property rights do not constitute an unreasonable or discriminatory barrier to access by persons with disabilities to cultural materials.

(11) Under the Charter, all forms of discrimination, including on grounds of disability, are prohibited and the right of persons with disabilities to benefit from measures designed to ensure their independence, social and occupational integration and participation in the life of the community is recognised and respected by the Union. . . .

### Article 1

### Subject matter and scope

This Regulation lays down uniform rules on the cross-border exchange of accessible format copies of certain works and other subject matter between the Union and third countries that are parties to the Marrakesh Treaty without the authorisation of the rightholder, for the benefit of persons who are blind, visually impaired or otherwise print-disabled, within the field harmonised by Directives 2001/29/EC and (EU) 2017/1564, in order to prevent jeopardising the harmonisation of exclusive rights and exceptions in the internal market.

### Article 2

### Definitions

For the purposes of this Regulation the following definitions apply:

(1) 'work or other subject matter' means a work in the form of a book, journal, newspaper, magazine or other kind of writing, notation, including sheet music, and related illustrations, in any media, including in audio form such as audiobooks and in digital format, which is protected by copyright or related rights and which is published or otherwise lawfully made publicly available;

(2) 'beneficiary person' means, regardless of any other disabilities, a person who:

    (a) is blind;

    (b) has a visual impairment which cannot be improved so as to give the person visual function substantially equivalent to that of a person who has no such impairment, and who is, as a result, unable to read printed works to substantially the same degree as a person without such an impairment;

    (c) has a perceptual or reading disability and is, as a result, unable to read printed works to substantially the same degree as a person without such disability; or

    (d) is otherwise unable, due to a physical disability, to hold or manipulate a book or to focus or move their eyes to the extent that would be normally acceptable for reading.

(3) 'accessible format copy' means a copy of a work or other subject matter in an alternative manner or form that gives a beneficiary person access to the work or other subject matter, including allowing such person to have access as feasibly and comfortably as a person without any of the impairments or disabilities referred to in point 2;

(4) 'authorised entity established in a Member State' means an entity that is authorised or recognised by a Member State to provide education, instructional training, adaptive reading or information access to beneficiary persons on a non-profit basis. It also includes a public institution or non-profit organisation that provides the same services to beneficiary persons as one of its primary activities, institutional obligations or as part of its public-interest missions.

## Article 3

### Export of accessible format copies to third countries

An authorised entity established in a Member State may distribute, communicate or make available to beneficiary persons or to an authorised entity established in a third country that is a party to the Marrakesh Treaty an accessible format copy of a work or other subject matter made in accordance with the national legislation adopted pursuant to Directive (EU) 2017/1564.

## Article 4

### Import of accessible format copies from third countries

A beneficiary person or an authorised entity established in a Member State may import or otherwise obtain or access and thereafter use, in accordance with the national legislation adopted pursuant to Directive (EU) 2017/1564, an accessible format copy of a work or other subject matter that has been distributed, communicated or made available to beneficiary persons or to authorised entities, by an authorised entity in a third country that is a party to the Marrakesh Treaty.

## Article 5

### Obligations of authorised entities

1. An authorised entity established in a Member State carrying out the acts referred to in Articles 3 and 4 shall establish and follow its own practices to ensure that it:

(a) distributes, communicates and makes available accessible format copies only to beneficiary persons or other authorised entities;

(b) takes appropriate steps to discourage the unauthorised reproduction, distribution, communication to the public and making available to the public of accessible format copies;

(c) demonstrates due care in, and maintains records of, its handling of works or other subject matter and of accessible format copies thereof; and

(d) publishes and updates, on its website if appropriate, or through other online or offline channels, information on how it complies with the obligations laid down in points (a) to (c).

An authorised entity established in a Member State shall establish and follow the practices referred to in the first subparagraph in full respect of the rules applicable to the processing of personal data of beneficiary persons referred to in Article 6.

2. An authorised entity established in a Member State carrying out the acts referred to in Articles 3 and 4 shall provide the following information in an accessible way, on request, to beneficiary persons, other authorised entities or rightholders:

(a) the list of works or other subject matter for which it has accessible format copies and the available formats; and

(b)  the name and contact details of the authorised entities with which it has engaged in the exchange of accessible format copies pursuant to Articles 3 and 4.

## *Article 6*

### **Protection of personal data**

The processing of personal data carried out within the framework of this Regulation shall be carried out in compliance with Directives 95/46/EC and 2002/58/EC.

## *Article 7*

### **Review**

By 11 October 2023, the Commission shall carry out an evaluation of this Regulation and present the main findings in a report to the European Parliament, the Council and the European Economic and Social Committee, accompanied, where appropriate, by proposals for amending this Regulation.

Member States shall provide the Commission with the necessary information for the preparation of the evaluation report.

## *Article 8*

### **Entry into force and application**

This Regulation shall enter into force on the twentieth day following that of its publication in the *Official Journal of the European Union.*

It shall apply from 12 October 2018.

This Regulation shall be binding in its entirety and directly applicable in all Member States.

Done at Strasbourg, 13 September 2017.

# 60. SATELLITE AND CABLE DIRECTIVE

## COUNCIL DIRECTIVE 93/83/EEC
### of 27 September 1993
### on the coordination of certain rules concerning copyright and rights related to copyright applicable to satellite broadcasting and cable retransmission

### (as amended)*

. . . (3)  Whereas broadcasts transmitted across frontiers within the Community, in particular by satellite and cable, are one of the most important ways of pursuing these Community objectives, which are at the same time political, economic, social, cultural and legal;

(4)  Whereas the Council has already adopted Directive 89/552/EEC of 3 October 1989 on the coordination of certain provisions laid down by law, regulation or administrative action in Member States concerning the pursuit of television broadcasting activities (4), which makes provision for the promotion of the distribution and production of European television programmes and for advertising and sponsorship, the protection of minors and the right of reply;

(5)  Whereas, however, the achievement of these objectives in respect of cross-border satellite broadcasting and the cable retransmission of programmes from other Member States is currently still obstructed by a series of differences between national rules of copyright and some degree of legal uncertainty; whereas this means that holders of rights are exposed to the threat of seeing their works exploited without payment of remuneration or that the individual holders of exclusive rights in various Member States block the exploitation of their rights; whereas the legal uncertainty in particular constitutes a direct obstacle in the free circulation of programmes within the Community;

(6)  Whereas a distinction is currently drawn for copyright purposes between communication to the public by direct satellite and communication to the public by communications satellite; whereas, since individual reception is possible and affordable nowadays with both types of satellite, there is no longer any justification for this differing legal treatment;

(7)  Whereas the free broadcasting of programmes is further impeded by the current legal uncertainty over whether broadcasting by a satellite whose signals can be received directly affects the rights in the country of transmission only or in all countries of reception together; whereas, since communications satellites and direct satellites are treated alike for copyright purposes, this legal uncertainty now affects almost all programmes broadcast in the Community by satellite;

(8)  Whereas, furthermore, legal certainty, which is a prerequisite for the free movement of broadcasts within the Community, is missing where programmes transmitted across frontiers are fed into and retransmitted through cable networks;

(9)  Whereas the development of the acquisition of rights on a contractual basis by authorization is already making a vigorous contribution to the creation of the desired European audiovisual area; whereas the continuation of such contractual agreements should be ensured and their smooth application in practice should be promoted wherever possible;

(10) Whereas at present cable operators in particular cannot be sure that they have actually acquired all the programme rights covered by such an agreement;

(11) Whereas, lastly, parties in different Member States are not all similarly bound by obligations which prevent them from refusing without valid reason to negotiate on the acquisition of the rights necessary for cable distribution or allowing such negotiations to fail; . . .

---

\*    Footnotes and some recitals omitted.

(29) Whereas the exemption provided for in Article 10 should not limit the choice of holders of rights to transfer their rights to a collecting society and thereby have a direct share in the remuneration paid by the cable distributor for cable retransmission; . . .

CHAPTER I
**DEFINITIONS**

*Article 1*

**Definitions**

1. For the purpose of this Directive, "satellite" means any satellite operating on frequency bands which, under telecommunications law, are reserved for the broadcast of signals for reception by the public or which are reserved for closed, point-to-point communication. In the latter case, however, the circumstances in which individual reception of the signals takes place must be comparable to those which apply in the first case.

2. (a) For the purpose of this Directive, "communication to the public by satellite" means the act of introducing, under the control and responsibility of the broadcasting organization, the programme-carrying signals intended for reception by the public into an uninterrupted chain of communication leading to the satellite and down towards the earth.

   (b) The act of communication to the public by satellite occurs solely in the Member State where, under the control and responsibility of the broadcasting organization, the programme-carrying signals are introduced into an uninterrupted chain of communication leading to the satellite and down towards the earth.

   (c) If the programme-carrying signals are encrypted, then there is communication to the public by satellite on condition that the means for decrypting the broadcast are provided to the public by the broadcasting organization or with its consent.

   (d) Where an act of communication to the public by satellite occurs in a non-Community State which does not provide the level of protection provided for under Chapter II,

   (i) if the programme-carrying signals are transmitted to the satellite from an uplink situation situated in a Member State, that act of communication to the public by satellite shall be deemed to have occurred in that Member State and the rights provided for under Chapter II shall be exercisable against the person operating the uplink station; or

   (ii) if there is no use of an uplink station situated in a Member State but a broadcasting organization established in a Member State has commissioned the act of communication to the public by satellite, that act shall be deemed to have occured in the Member State in which the broadcasting organization has its principal establishment in the Community and the rights provided for under Chapter II shall be exercisable against the broadcasting organization.

3. For the purposes of this Directive, "cable retransmission" means the simultaneous, unaltered and unabridged retransmission by a cable or microwave system for reception by the public of an initial transmission from another Member State, by wire or over the air, including that by satellite, of television or radio programmes intended for reception by the public, regardless of how the operator of a cable retransmission service obtains the programme-carrying signals from the broadcasting organisation for the purpose of retransmission.

4. For the purposes of this Directive "collecting society" means any organization which manages or administers copyright or rights related to copyright as its sole purpose or as one of its main purposes.

5. For the purposes of this Directive, the principal director of a cinematographic or audiovisual work shall be considered as its author or one of its authors. Member States may provide for others to be considered as its co-authors.

CHAPTER II
## BROADCASTING OF PROGRAMMES BY SATELLITE

*Article 2*

### Broadcasting right

Member States shall provide an exclusive right for the author to authorize the communication to the public by satellite of copyright works, subject to the provisions set out in this chapter.

*Article 3*

### Acquisition of broadcasting rights

1.    Member States shall ensure that the authorization referred to in Article 2 may be acquired only be agreement.

2.    A Member State may provide that a collective agreement between a collecting society and a broadcasting organization concerning a given category of works may be extended to rightholders of the same category who are not represented by the collecting society, provided that:

—    the communication to the public by satellite simulcasts a terrestrial broadcast by the same broadcaster,

and

—    the unrepresented rightholder shall, at any time, have the possibility of excluding the extension of the collective agreement to his works and of exercising his rights either individually or collectively.

3.    Paragraph 2 shall not apply to cinematographic works, including works created by a process analogous to cinematography.

4.    Where the law of a Member State provides for the extension of a collective agreement in accordance with the provisions of paragraph 2, that Member States shall inform the Commission which broadcasting organizations are entitled to avail themselves of that law. The Commission shall publish this information in the Official Journal of the European Communities (C series).

*Article 4*

### Rights of performers, phonogram producers and broadcasting organizations

1.    For the purposes of communication to the public by satellite, the rights of performers, phonogram producers and broadcasting organizations shall be protected in accordance with the provisions of Articles 6, 7, 8 and 10 of Directive 92/100/EEC.

2.    For the purposes of paragraph 1, "broadcasting by wireless means" in Directive 92/100/EEC shall be understood as including communication to the public by satellite.

3.    With regard to the exercise of the rights referred to in paragraph 1, Articles 2(7) and 12 of Directive 92/100/EEC shall apply.

*Article 5*

### Relation between copyright and related rights

Protection of copyright-related rights under this Directive shall leave intact and shall in no way affect the protection of copyright.

## Article 6

### Minimum protection

1.   Member States may provide for more far-reaching protection for holders of rights related to copyright than that required by Article 8 of Directive 92/100/EEC.

2.   In applying paragraph 1 Member States shall observe the definitions contained in Article 1(1) and (2).

## Article 7

### Transitional provisions

1.   With regard to the application in time of the rights referred to in Article 4(1) of this Directive, Article 13(1), (2), (6) and (7) of Directive 92/100/EEC shall apply. Article 13(4) and (5) of Directive 92/100/EEC shall apply mutatis mutandis.

2.   Agreements concerning the exploitation of works and other protected subject matter which are in force on the date mentioned in Article 14(1) shall be subject to the provisions of Articles 1(2), 2 and 3 as from 1 January 2000 if they expire after that date.

3.   When an international co-production agreement concluded before the date mentioned in Article 14(1) between a co-producer from a Member State and one or more co-producers from other Member States or third countries expressly provides for a system of division of exploitation rights between the co-producers by geographical areas for all means of communication to the public, without distinguishing the arrangement applicable to communication to the public by satellite from the provisions applicable to the other means of communication, and where communication to the public by satellite of the co-production would prejudice the exclusivity, in particular the language exclusivity, of one of the co-producers or his assignees in a given territory, the authorization by one of the co-producers or his assignees for a communication to the public by satellite shall require the prior consent of the holder of that exclusivity, whether co-producer or assignee.

### CHAPTER III
### CABLE RETRANSMISSION

## Article 8

### Cable retransmission right

1.   Member States shall ensure that when programmes from other Member States are retransmitted by cable in their territory the applicable copyright and related rights are observed and that such retransmission takes place on the basis of individual or collective contractual agreements between copyright owners, holders of related rights and cable operators.

2.   Notwithstanding paragraph 1, Member States may retain until 31 December 1997 such statutory licence systems which are in operation or expressly provided for by national law on 31 July 1991.

## Article 9

### Exercise of the cable retransmission right

1.   Member States shall ensure that the right of copyright owners and holders or related rights to grant or refuse authorization to a cable operator for a cable retransmission may be exercised only through a collecting society.

2.   Where a rightholder has not transferred the management of his rights to a collecting society, the collecting society which manages rights of the same category shall be deemed to be mandated to manage his rights. Where more than one collecting society manages rights of that category, the rightholder shall be free to choose which of those collecting societies is deemed to be mandated to manage his rights. A rightholder referred to in this paragraph shall have the same rights and

obligations resulting from the agreement between the cable operator and the collecting society which is deemed to be mandated to manage his rights as the rightholders who have mandated that collecting society and he shall be able to claim those rights within a period, to be fixed by the Member State concerned, which shall not be shorter than three years from the date of the cable retransmission which includes his work or other protected subject matter.

3.    A Member State may provide that, when a right-holder authorizes the initial transmission within its territory of a work or other protected subject matter, he shall be deemed to have agreed not to exercise his cable retransmission rights on an individual basis but to exercise them in accordance with the provisions of this Directive.

## *Article 10*

### Exercise of the cable retransmission right by broadcasting organizations

Member States shall ensure that Article 9 does not apply to the rights exercised by a broadcasting organization in respect of its own transmission, irrespective of whether the rights concerned are its own or have been transferred to it by other copyright owners and/or holders of related rights.

## *Article 11*

### Mediators

1.    Where no agreement is concluded regarding authorization of the cable retransmission of a broadcast. Member States shall ensure that either party may call upon the assistance of one or more mediators.

2.    The task of the mediators shall be to provide assistance with negotiation. They may also submit proposals to the parties.

3.    It shall be assumed that all the parties accept a proposal as referred to in paragraph 2 if none of them expresses its opposition within a period of three months. Notice of the proposal and of any opposition thereto shall be served on the parties concerned in accordance with the applicable rules concerning the service of legal documents.

4.    The mediators shall be so selected that their independence and impartiality are beyond reasonable doubt.

## *Article 12*

### Prevention of the abuse of negotiating positions

1.    Member States shall ensure by means of civil or administrative law, as appropriate, that the parties enter and conduct negotiations regarding authorization for cable retransmission in good faith and do not prevent or hinder negotiation without valid justification.

2.    A Member State which, on the date mentioned in Article 14(1), has a body with jurisdiction in its territory over cases where the right to retransmit a programme by cable to the public in that Member State has been unreasonably refused or offered on unreasonable terms by a broadcasting organization may retain that body.

3.    Paragraph 2 shall apply for a transitional period of eight years from the date mentioned in Article 14(1).

## CHAPTER IV
### GENERAL PROVISIONS

*Article 13*

### Collective administration of rights

This Directive shall be without prejudice to the regulation of the activities of collecting societies by the Member States.

*Article 14*

### Final provisions

1.     Member States shall bring into force the laws, regulations and administrative provisions necessary to comply with this Directive before 1 January 1995. They shall immediately inform the Commission thereof.

When Member States adopt these measures, the latter shall contain a reference to this Directive or shall be accompanied by such reference at the time of their official publication. The methods of making such a reference shall be laid down by the Member States.

2.     Member States shall communicate to the Commission the provisions of national law which they adopt in the field covered by this Directive.

3.     Not later than 1 January 2000, the Commission shall submit to the European Parliament, the Council and the Economic and Social Committee a report on the application of this Directive and, if necessary, make further proposals to adapt it to developments in the audio and audiovisual sector.

*Article 15*

This Directive is addressed to the Member States.

# 61. INFORMATION SOCIETY DIRECTIVE

### DIRECTIVE 2001/29/EC OF THE EUROPEAN PARLIAMENT
### AND OF THE COUNCIL
### of 22 May 2001
### on the harmonisation of certain aspects of copyright
### and related rights in the information society

### (as amended)\*

. . . Whereas:

(1)   The Treaty provides for the establishment of an internal market and the institution of a system ensuring that competition in the internal market is not distorted. Harmonisation of the laws of the Member States on copyright and related rights contributes to the achievement of these objectives. . . .

(16)   Liability for activities in the network environment concerns not only copyright and related rights but also other areas, such as defamation, misleading advertising, or infringement of trademarks, and is addressed horizontally in Directive 2000/31/EC of the European Parliament and of the Council of 8 June 2000 on certain legal aspects of information society services, in particular electronic commerce, in the internal market ("Directive on electronic commerce"), which clarifies and harmonises various legal issues relating to information society services including electronic commerce. This Directive should be implemented within a timescale similar to that for the implementation of the Directive on electronic commerce, since that Directive provides a harmonised framework of principles and provisions relevant inter alia to important parts of this Directive. This Directive is without prejudice to provisions relating to liability in that Directive.

(17)   It is necessary, especially in the light of the requirements arising out of the digital environment, to ensure that collecting societies achieve a higher level of rationalisation and transparency with regard to compliance with competition rules. . . .

(23)   This Directive should harmonise further the author's right of communication to the public. This right should be understood in a broad sense covering all communication to the public not present at the place where the communication originates. This right should cover any such transmission or retransmission of a work to the public by wire or wireless means, including broadcasting. This right should not cover any other acts.

(24)   The right to make available to the public subject-matter referred to in Article 3(2) should be understood as covering all acts of making available such subject-matter to members of the public not present at the place where the act of making available originates, and as not covering any other acts.

(25)   The legal uncertainty regarding the nature and the level of protection of acts of on-demand transmission of copyright works and subject-matter protected by related rights over networks should be overcome by providing for harmonised protection at Community level. It should be made clear that all rightholders recognised by this Directive should have an exclusive right to make available to the public copyright works or any other subject-matter by way of interactive on-demand transmissions. Such interactive on-demand transmissions are characterised by the fact that members of the public may access them from a place and at a time individually chosen by them.

(26)   With regard to the making available in on-demand services by broadcasters of their radio or television productions incorporating music from commercial phonograms as an integral part thereof, collective licensing arrangements are to be encouraged in order to facilitate the clearance of the rights concerned.

---

\*   Footnotes and some recitals omitted.

(27) The mere provision of physical facilities for enabling or making a communication does not in itself amount to communication within the meaning of this Directive.

(28) Copyright protection under this Directive includes the exclusive right to control distribution of the work incorporated in a tangible article. The first sale in the Community of the original of a work or copies thereof by the rightholder or with his consent exhausts the right to control resale of that object in the Community. This right should not be exhausted in respect of the original or of copies thereof sold by the rightholder or with his consent outside the Community. Rental and lending rights for authors have been established in Directive 92/100/EEC. The distribution right provided for in this Directive is without prejudice to the provisions relating to the rental and lending rights contained in Chapter I of that Directive.

(29) The question of exhaustion does not arise in the case of services and on-line services in particular. This also applies with regard to a material copy of a work or other subject-matter made by a user of such a service with the consent of the rightholder. Therefore, the same applies to rental and lending of the original and copies of works or other subject-matter which are services by nature. Unlike CD-ROM or CD-I, where the intellectual property is incorporated in a material medium, namely an item of goods, every on-line service is in fact an act which should be subject to authorisation where the copyright or related right so provides. . . .

(35) In certain cases of exceptions or limitations, rightholders should receive fair compensation to compensate them adequately for the use made of their protected works or other subject-matter. When determining the form, detailed arrangements and possible level of such fair compensation, account should be taken of the particular circumstances of each case. When evaluating these circumstances, a valuable criterion would be the possible harm to the rightholders resulting from the act in question. In cases where rightholders have already received payment in some other form, for instance as part of a licence fee, no specific or separate payment may be due. The level of fair compensation should take full account of the degree of use of technological protection measures referred to in this Directive. In certain situations where the prejudice to the rightholder would be minimal, no obligation for payment may arise.

(36) The Member States may provide for fair compensation for rightholders also when applying the optional provisions on exceptions or limitations which do not require such compensation. . . .

(42) When applying the exception or limitation for non-commercial educational and scientific research purposes, including distance learning, the non-commercial nature of the activity in question should be determined by that activity as such. The organisational structure and the means of funding of the establishment concerned are not the decisive factors in this respect.

(43) It is in any case important for the Member States to adopt all necessary measures to facilitate access to works by persons suffering from a disability which constitutes an obstacle to the use of the works themselves, and to pay particular attention to accessible formats. . . .

(54) Important progress has been made in the international standardisation of technical systems of identification of works and protected subject-matter in digital format. In an increasingly networked environment, differences between technological measures could lead to an incompatibility of systems within the Community. Compatibility and interoperability of the different systems should be encouraged. It would be highly desirable to encourage the development of global systems.

(55) Technological development will facilitate the distribution of works, notably on networks, and this will entail the need for rightholders to identify better the work or other subject-matter, the author or any other rightholder, and to provide information about the terms and conditions of use of the work or other subject-matter in order to render easier the management of rights attached to them. Rightholders should be encouraged to use markings indicating, in addition to the information referred to above, inter alia their authorisation when putting works or other subject-matter on networks. . . .

## CHAPTER I
## OBJECTIVE AND SCOPE

*Article 1*

### Scope

1.   This Directive concerns the legal protection of copyright and related rights in the framework of the internal market, with particular emphasis on the information society.

2.   Except in the cases referred to in Article 11, this Directive shall leave intact and shall in no way affect existing Community provisions relating to:

(a)   the legal protection of computer programs;

(b)   rental right, lending right and certain rights related to copyright in the field of intellectual property;

(c)   copyright and related rights applicable to broadcasting of programmes by satellite and cable retransmission;

(d)   the term of protection of copyright and certain related rights;

(e)   the legal protection of databases.

## CHAPTER II
## RIGHTS AND EXCEPTIONS

*Article 2*

### Reproduction right

Member States shall provide for the exclusive right to authorise or prohibit direct or indirect, temporary or permanent reproduction by any means and in any form, in whole or in part:

(a)   for authors, of their works;

(b)   for performers, of fixations of their performances;

(c)   for phonogram producers, of their phonograms;

(d)   for the producers of the first fixations of films, in respect of the original and copies of their films;

(e)   for broadcasting organisations, of fixations of their broadcasts, whether those broadcasts are transmitted by wire or over the air, including by cable or satellite.

*Article 3*

### Right of communication to the public of works and right
### of making available to the public other subject-matter

1.   Member States shall provide authors with the exclusive right to authorise or prohibit any communication to the public of their works, by wire or wireless means, including the making available to the public of their works in such a way that members of the public may access them from a place and at a time individually chosen by them.

2.   Member States shall provide for the exclusive right to authorise or prohibit the making available to the public, by wire or wireless means, in such a way that members of the public may access them from a place and at a time individually chosen by them:

(a)   for performers, of fixations of their performances;

(b)   for phonogram producers, of their phonograms;

(c)   for the producers of the first fixations of films, of the original and copies of their films;

(d)   for broadcasting organisations, of fixations of their broadcasts, whether these broadcasts are transmitted by wire or over the air, including by cable or satellite.

3.   The rights referred to in paragraphs 1 and 2 shall not be exhausted by any act of communication to the public or making available to the public as set out in this Article.

*Article 4*

**Distribution right**

1.   Member States shall provide for authors, in respect of the original of their works or of copies thereof, the exclusive right to authorise or prohibit any form of distribution to the public by sale or otherwise.

2.   The distribution right shall not be exhausted within the Community in respect of the original or copies of the work, except where the first sale or other transfer of ownership in the Community of that object is made by the rightholder or with his consent.

*Article 5*

**Exceptions and limitations**

1.   Temporary acts of reproduction referred to in Article 2, which are transient or incidental, which are an integral and essential part of a technological process and the sole purpose of which is to enable:

(a)   a transmission in a network between third parties by an intermediary, or

(b)   a lawful use

of a work or other subject-matter to be made, and which have no independent economic significance, shall be exempted from the reproduction right provided for in Article 2.

2.   Member States may provide for exceptions or limitations to the reproduction right provided for in Article 2 in the following cases:

(a)   in respect of reproductions on paper or any similar medium, effected by the use of any kind of photographic technique or by some other process having similar effects, with the exception of sheet music, provided that the rightholders receive fair compensation;

(b)   in respect of reproductions on any medium made by a natural person for private use and for ends that are neither directly nor indirectly commercial, on condition that the rightholders receive fair compensation which takes account of the application or non-application of technological measures referred to in Article 6 to the work or subject-matter concerned;

(c)   in respect of specific acts of reproduction made by publicly accessible libraries, educational establishments or museums, or by archives, which are not for direct or indirect economic or commercial advantage, without prejudice to the exceptions and limitations provided for in Directive (EU) 2019/790 of the European Parliament and of the Council;

(d)   in respect of ephemeral recordings of works made by broadcasting organisations by means of their own facilities and for their own broadcasts; the preservation of these recordings in official archives may, on the grounds of their exceptional documentary character, be permitted;

(e)   in respect of reproductions of broadcasts made by social institutions pursuing non-commercial purposes, such as hospitals or prisons, on condition that the rightholders receive fair compensation.

3.   Member States may provide for exceptions or limitations to the rights provided for in Articles 2 and 3 in the following cases:

(a)   use for the sole purpose of illustration for teaching or scientific research, as long as the source, including the author's name, is indicated, unless this turns out to be impossible and to the extent justified by the non-commercial purpose to be achieved, without prejudice to the exceptions and limitations provided for in Directive (EU) 2019/790;

(b)   uses, for the benefit of people with a disability, which are directly related to the disability and of a non-commercial nature, to the extent required by the specific disability, without prejudice to the obligations of Member States under Directive (EU) 2017/1564 of the European Parliament and of the Council;

(c)   reproduction by the press, communication to the public or making available of published articles on current economic, political or religious topics or of broadcast works or other subject-matter of the same character, in cases where such use is not expressly reserved, and as long as the source, including the author's name, is indicated, or use of works or other subject-matter in connection with the reporting of current events, to the extent justified by the informatory purpose and as long as the source, including the author's name, is indicated, unless this turns out to be impossible;

(d)   quotations for purposes such as criticism or review, provided that they relate to a work or other subject-matter which has already been lawfully made available to the public, that, unless this turns out to be impossible, the source, including the author's name, is indicated, and that their use is in accordance with fair practice, and to the extent required by the specific purpose;

(e)   use for the purposes of public security or to ensure the proper performance or reporting of administrative, parliamentary or judicial proceedings;

(f)   use of political speeches as well as extracts of public lectures or similar works or subject-matter to the extent justified by the informatory purpose and provided that the source, including the author's name, is indicated, except where this turns out to be impossible;

(g)   use during religious celebrations or official celebrations organised by a public authority;

(h)   use of works, such as works of architecture or sculpture, made to be located permanently in public places;

(i)   incidental inclusion of a work or other subject-matter in other material;

(j)   use for the purpose of advertising the public exhibition or sale of artistic works, to the extent necessary to promote the event, excluding any other commercial use;

(k)   use for the purpose of caricature, parody or pastiche;

(*l*)   use in connection with the demonstration or repair of equipment;

(m)   use of an artistic work in the form of a building or a drawing or plan of a building for the purposes of reconstructing the building;

(n)   use by communication or making available, for the purpose of research or private study, to individual members of the public by dedicated terminals on the premises of establishments referred to in paragraph 2(c) of works and other subject-matter not subject to purchase or licensing terms which are contained in their collections;

(*o*)   use in certain other cases of minor importance where exceptions or limitations already exist under national law, provided that they only concern analogue uses and do not affect the free circulation of goods and services within the Community, without prejudice to the other exceptions and limitations contained in this Article.

4.    Where the Member States may provide for an exception or limitation to the right of reproduction pursuant to paragraphs 2 and 3, they may provide similarly for an exception or limitation to the right of distribution as referred to in Article 4 to the extent justified by the purpose of the authorised act of reproduction.

5.    The exceptions and limitations provided for in paragraphs 1, 2, 3 and 4 shall only be applied in certain special cases which do not conflict with a normal exploitation of the work or other subject-matter and do not unreasonably prejudice the legitimate interests of the rightholder.

## CHAPTER III
## PROTECTION OF TECHNOLOGICAL MEASURES
## AND RIGHTS-MANAGEMENT INFORMATION

### Article 6

### Obligations as to technological measures

1.    Member States shall provide adequate legal protection against the circumvention of any effective technological measures, which the person concerned carries out in the knowledge, or with reasonable grounds to know, that he or she is pursuing that objective.

2.    Member States shall provide adequate legal protection against the manufacture, import, distribution, sale, rental, advertisement for sale or rental, or possession for commercial purposes of devices, products or components or the provision of services which:

(a)    are promoted, advertised or marketed for the purpose of circumvention of, or

(b)    have only a limited commercially significant purpose or use other than to circumvent, or

(c)    are primarily designed, produced, adapted or performed for the purpose of enabling or facilitating the circumvention of,

any effective technological measures.

3.    For the purposes of this Directive, the expression "technological measures" means any technology, device or component that, in the normal course of its operation, is designed to prevent or restrict acts, in respect of works or other subject-matter, which are not authorised by the rightholder of any copyright or any right related to copyright as provided for by law or the sui generis right provided for in Chapter III of Directive 96/9/EC. Technological measures shall be deemed "effective" where the use of a protected work or other subject-matter is controlled by the rightholders through application of an access control or protection process, such as encryption, scrambling or other transformation of the work or other subject-matter or a copy control mechanism, which achieves the protection objective.

4.    Notwithstanding the legal protection provided for in paragraph 1, in the absence of voluntary measures taken by rightholders, including agreements between rightholders and other parties concerned, Member States shall take appropriate measures to ensure that rightholders make available to the beneficiary of an exception or limitation provided for in national law in accordance with Article 5(2)(a), (2)(c), (2)(d), (2)(e), (3)(a), (3)(b) or (3)(e) the means of benefiting from that exception or limitation, to the extent necessary to benefit from that exception or limitation and where that beneficiary has legal access to the protected work or subject-matter concerned.

A Member State may also take such measures in respect of a beneficiary of an exception or limitation provided for in accordance with Article 5(2)(b), unless reproduction for private use has already been made possible by rightholders to the extent necessary to benefit from the exception or limitation concerned and in accordance with the provisions of Article 5(2)(b) and (5), without preventing rightholders from adopting adequate measures regarding the number of reproductions in accordance with these provisions.

The technological measures applied voluntarily by rightholders, including those applied in implementation of voluntary agreements, and technological measures applied in implementation of the measures taken by Member States, shall enjoy the legal protection provided for in paragraph 1.

The provisions of the first and second subparagraphs shall not apply to works or other subject-matter made available to the public on agreed contractual terms in such a way that members of the public may access them from a place and at a time individually chosen by them.

When this Article is applied in the context of Directives 92/100/EEC and 96/9/EC, this paragraph shall apply mutatis mutandis.

## Article 7

### Obligations concerning rights-management information

1.   Member States shall provide for adequate legal protection against any person knowingly performing without authority any of the following acts:

(a)   the removal or alteration of any electronic rights-management information;

(b)   the distribution, importation for distribution, broadcasting, communication or making available to the public of works or other subject-matter protected under this Directive or under Chapter III of Directive 96/9/EC from which electronic rights-management information has been removed or altered without authority,

if such person knows, or has reasonable grounds to know, that by so doing he is inducing, enabling, facilitating or concealing an infringement of any copyright or any rights related to copyright as provided by law, or of the sui generis right provided for in Chapter III of Directive 96/9/EC.

2.   For the purposes of this Directive, the expression "rights-management information" means any information provided by rightholders which identifies the work or other subject-matter referred to in this Directive or covered by the sui generis right provided for in Chapter III of Directive 96/9/EC, the author or any other rightholder, or information about the terms and conditions of use of the work or other subject-matter, and any numbers or codes that represent such information.

The first subparagraph shall apply when any of these items of information is associated with a copy of, or appears in connection with the communication to the public of, a work or other subject-matter referred to in this Directive or covered by the sui generis right provided for in Chapter III of Directive 96/9/EC.

## CHAPTER IV
## COMMON PROVISIONS

## Article 8

### Sanctions and remedies

1.   Member States shall provide appropriate sanctions and remedies in respect of infringements of the rights and obligations set out in this Directive and shall take all the measures necessary to ensure that those sanctions and remedies are applied. The sanctions thus provided for shall be effective, proportionate and dissuasive.

2.   Each Member State shall take the measures necessary to ensure that rightholders whose interests are affected by an infringing activity carried out on its territory can bring an action for damages and/or apply for an injunction and, where appropriate, for the seizure of infringing material as well as of devices, products or components referred to in Article 6(2).

3.   Member States shall ensure that rightholders are in a position to apply for an injunction against intermediaries whose services are used by a third party to infringe a copyright or related right.

## Article 9

### Continued application of other legal provisions

This Directive shall be without prejudice to provisions concerning in particular patent rights, trade marks, design rights, utility models, topographies of semi-conductor products, type faces, conditional access, access to cable of broadcasting services, protection of national treasures, legal deposit requirements, laws on restrictive practices and unfair competition, trade secrets, security, confidentiality, data protection and privacy, access to public documents, the law of contract.

## Article 10

### Application over time

1.   The provisions of this Directive shall apply in respect of all works and other subject-matter referred to in this Directive which are, on 22 December 2002, protected by the Member States' legislation in the field of copyright and related rights, or which meet the criteria for protection under the provisions of this Directive or the provisions referred to in Article 1(2).

2.   This Directive shall apply without prejudice to any acts concluded and rights acquired before 22 December 2002.

## Article 11

### Technical adaptations

1.   Directive 92/100/EEC is hereby amended as follows:

(a)   Article 7 shall be deleted;

(b)   Article 10(3) shall be replaced by the following: "3. The limitations shall only be applied in certain special cases which do not conflict with a normal exploitation of the subject-matter and do not unreasonably prejudice the legitimate interests of the rightholder."

2.   Article 3(2) of Directive 93/98/EEC shall be replaced by the following:

"2. The rights of producers of phonograms shall expire 50 years after the fixation is made. However, if the phonogram has been lawfully published within this period, the said rights shall expire 50 years from the date of the first lawful publication. If no lawful publication has taken place within the period mentioned in the first sentence, and if the phonogram has been lawfully communicated to the public within this period, the said rights shall expire 50 years from the date of the first lawful communication to the public.

However, where through the expiry of the term of protection granted pursuant to this paragraph in its version before amendment by Directive 2001/29/EC of the European Parliament and of the Council of 22 May 2001 on the harmonisation of certain aspects of copyright and related rights in the information society the rights of producers of phonograms are no longer protected on 22 December 2002, this paragraph shall not have the effect of protecting those rights anew."

## Article 12

### Final provisions

1.   Not later than 22 December 2004 and every three years thereafter, the Commission shall submit to the European Parliament, the Council and the Economic and Social Committee a report on the application of this Directive, in which, inter alia, on the basis of specific information supplied by the Member States, it shall examine in particular the application of Articles 5, 6 and 8 in the light of the development of the digital market. In the case of Article 6, it shall examine in particular whether that Article confers a sufficient level of protection and whether acts which are permitted by law are being adversely affected by the use of effective technological measures. Where necessary, in particular to ensure the functioning of the internal market pursuant to Article 14 of the Treaty, it shall submit proposals for amendments to this Directive.

2.   Protection of rights related to copyright under this Directive shall leave intact and shall in no way affect the protection of copyright.

3.   A contact committee is hereby established. It shall be composed of representatives of the competent authorities of the Member States. It shall be chaired by a representative of the Commission and shall meet either on the initiative of the chairman or at the request of the delegation of a Member State.

4.   The tasks of the committee shall be as follows:

(a)   to examine the impact of this Directive on the functioning of the internal market, and to highlight any difficulties;

(b)   to organise consultations on all questions deriving from the application of this Directive;

(c)   to facilitate the exchange of information on relevant developments in legislation and case-law, as well as relevant economic, social, cultural and technological developments;

(d)   to act as a forum for the assessment of the digital market in works and other items, including private copying and the use of technological measures;

(e)   to examine the impact of the transposition of Directive (EU) 2019/790 on the functioning of the internal market and to highlight any transposition difficulties;

(f)   to facilitate the exchange of information on relevant developments in legislation and case law as well as on the practical application of the measures taken by Member States to implement Directive (EU) 2019/790;

(g)   to discuss any other questions arising from the application of Directive (EU) 2019/790.

*Article 13*

**Implementation**

1.   Member States shall bring into force the laws, regulations and administrative provisions necessary to comply with this Directive before 22 December 2002. They shall forthwith inform the Commission thereof.

When Member States adopt these measures, they shall contain a reference to this Directive or shall be accompanied by such reference on the occasion of their official publication. The methods of making such reference shall be laid down by Member States.

2.   Member States shall communicate to the Commission the text of the provisions of domestic law which they adopt in the field governed by this Directive.

*Article 14*

**Entry into force**

This Directive shall enter into force on the day of its publication in the Official Journal of the European Communities.

*Article 15*

**Addressees**

This Directive is addressed to the Member States.

# 62. ELECTRONIC COMMERCE DIRECTIVE

## DIRECTIVE 2000/31/EC OF THE EUROPEAN PARLIAMENT AND OF THE COUNCIL
### of 8 June 2000
### on certain legal aspects of information society services, in particular electronic commerce, in the Internal Market*

... Whereas: ...

(19) The place at which a service provider is established should be determined in conformity with the case-law of the Court of Justice according to which the concept of establishment involves the actual pursuit of an economic activity through a fixed establishment for an indefinite period; this requirement is also fulfilled where a company is constituted for a given period; the place of establishment of a company providing services via an Internet website is not the place at which the technology supporting its website is located or the place at which its website is accessible but the place where it pursues its economic activity; in cases where a provider has several places of establishment it is important to determine from which place of establishment the service concerned is provided; in cases where it is difficult to determine from which of several places of establishment a given service is provided, this is the place where the provider has the centre of his activities relating to this particular service.

(20) The definition of "recipient of a service" covers all types of usage of information society services, both by persons who provide information on open networks such as the Internet and by persons who seek information on the Internet for private or professional reasons. ...

(23) This Directive neither aims to establish additional rules on private international law relating to conflicts of law nor does it deal with the jurisdiction of Courts; provisions of the applicable law designated by rules of private international law must not restrict the freedom to provide information society services as established in this Directive. ...

(40) Both existing and emerging disparities in Member States' legislation and case-law concerning liability of service providers acting as intermediaries prevent the smooth functioning of the internal market, in particular by impairing the development of cross-border services and producing distortions of competition; service providers have a duty to act, under certain circumstances, with a view to preventing or stopping illegal activities; this Directive should constitute the appropriate basis for the development of rapid and reliable procedures for removing and disabling access to illegal information; such mechanisms could be developed on the basis of voluntary agreements between all parties concerned and should be encouraged by Member States; it is in the interest of all parties involved in the provision of information society services to adopt and implement such procedures; the provisions of this Directive relating to liability should not preclude the development and effective operation, by the different interested parties, of technical systems of protection and identification and of technical surveillance instruments made possible by digital technology within the limits laid down by Directives 95/46/EC and 97/66/EC.

(41) This Directive strikes a balance between the different interests at stake and establishes principles upon which industry agreements and standards can be based.

(42) The exemptions from liability established in this Directive cover only cases where the activity of the information society service provider is limited to the technical process of operating and giving access to a communication network over which information made available by third parties is transmitted or temporarily stored, for the sole purpose of making the transmission more efficient; this activity is of a mere technical, automatic and passive nature, which implies that the information society service provider has neither knowledge of nor control over the information which is transmitted or stored.

---

\* Footnotes and some recitals omitted.

(43) A service provider can benefit from the exemptions for "mere conduit" and for "caching" when he is in no way involved with the information transmitted; this requires among other things that he does not modify the information that he transmits; this requirement does not cover manipulations of a technical nature which take place in the course of the transmission as they do not alter the integrity of the information contained in the transmission.

(44) A service provider who deliberately collaborates with one of the recipients of his service in order to undertake illegal acts goes beyond the activities of "mere conduit" or "caching" and as a result cannot benefit from the liability exemptions established for these activities.

(45) The limitations of the liability of intermediary service providers established in this Directive do not affect the possibility of injunctions of different kinds; such injunctions can in particular consist of orders by courts or administrative authorities requiring the termination or prevention of any infringement, including the removal of illegal information or the disabling of access to it.

(46) In order to benefit from a limitation of liability, the provider of an information society service, consisting of the storage of information, upon obtaining actual knowledge or awareness of illegal activities has to act expeditiously to remove or to disable access to the information concerned; the removal or disabling of access has to be undertaken in the observance of the principle of freedom of expression and of procedures established for this purpose at national level; this Directive does not affect Member States' possibility of establishing specific requirements which must be fulfilled expeditiously prior to the removal or disabling of information.

(47) Member States are prevented from imposing a monitoring obligation on service providers only with respect to obligations of a general nature; this does not concern monitoring obligations in a specific case and, in particular, does not affect orders by national authorities in accordance with national legislation.

(48) This Directive does not affect the possibility for Member States of requiring service providers, who host information provided by recipients of their service, to apply duties of care, which can reasonably be expected from them and which are specified by national law, in order to detect and prevent certain types of illegal activities.

(49) Member States and the Commission are to encourage the drawing-up of codes of conduct; this is not to impair the voluntary nature of such codes and the possibility for interested parties of deciding freely whether to adhere to such codes.

(50) It is important that the proposed directive on the harmonisation of certain aspects of copyright and related rights in the information society and this Directive come into force within a similar time scale with a view to establishing a clear framework of rules relevant to the issue of liability of intermediaries for copyright and relating rights infringements at Community level. . . .

(57) The Court of Justice has consistently held that a Member State retains the right to take measures against a service provider that is established in another Member State but directs all or most of his activity to the territory of the first Member State if the choice of establishment was made with a view to evading the legislation that would have applied to the provider had he been established on the territory of the first Member State.

(58) This Directive should not apply to services supplied by service providers established in a third country; in view of the global dimension of electronic commerce, it is, however, appropriate to ensure that the Community rules are consistent with international rules; this Directive is without prejudice to the results of discussions within international organisations (amongst others WTO, OECD, Uncitral) on legal issues. . . .

## CHAPTER I
## GENERAL PROVISIONS

*Article 1*

### Objective and scope

1.    This Directive seeks to contribute to the proper functioning of the internal market by ensuring the free movement of information society services between the Member States.

2.    This Directive approximates, to the extent necessary for the achievement of the objective set out in paragraph 1, certain national provisions on information society services relating to the internal market, the establishment of service providers, commercial communications, electronic contracts, the liability of intermediaries, codes of conduct, out-of-court dispute settlements, court actions and cooperation between Member States.

3.    This Directive complements Community law applicable to information society services without prejudice to the level of protection for, in particular, public health and consumer interests, as established by Community acts and national legislation implementing them in so far as this does not restrict the freedom to provide information society services.

4.    This Directive does not establish additional rules on private international law nor does it deal with the jurisdiction of Courts.

5.    This Directive shall not apply to:

(a)    the field of taxation;

(b)    questions relating to information society services covered by Directives 95/46/EC and 97/66/EC;

(c)    questions relating to agreements or practices governed by cartel law;

(d)    the following activities of information society services:

— the activities of notaries or equivalent professions to the extent that they involve a direct and specific connection with the exercise of public authority,

— the representation of a client and defence of his interests before the courts,

— gambling activities which involve wagering a stake with monetary value in games of chance, including lotteries and betting transactions.

6.    This Directive does not affect measures taken at Community or national level, in the respect of Community law, in order to promote cultural and linguistic diversity and to ensure the defence of pluralism.

*Article 2*

### Definitions

For the purpose of this Directive, the following terms shall bear the following meanings:

(a)    "information society services": services within the meaning of Article 1(2) of Directive 98/34/EC as amended by Directive 98/48/EC;

(b)    "service provider": any natural or legal person providing an information society service;

(c)    "established service provider": a service provider who effectively pursues an economic activity using a fixed establishment for an indefinite period. The presence and use of the technical means and technologies required to provide the service do not, in themselves, constitute an establishment of the provider;

(d)   "recipient of the service": any natural or legal person who, for professional ends or otherwise, uses an information society service, in particular for the purposes of seeking information or making it accessible;

(e)   "consumer": any natural person who is acting for purposes which are outside his or her trade, business or profession;

(f)   "commercial communication": any form of communication designed to promote, directly or indirectly, the goods, services or image of a company, organisation or person pursuing a commercial, industrial or craft activity or exercising a regulated profession. The following do not in themselves constitute commercial communications:

— information allowing direct access to the activity of the company, organisation or person, in particular a domain name or an electronic-mail address,

— communications relating to the goods, services or image of the company, organisation or person compiled in an independent manner, particularly when this is without financial consideration;

(g)   "regulated profession": any profession within the meaning of either Article 1(d) of Council Directive 89/48/EEC of 21 December 1988 on a general system for the recognition of higher-education diplomas awarded on completion of professional education and training of at least three-years' duration or of Article 1(f) of Council Directive 92/51/EEC of 18 June 1992 on a second general system for the recognition of professional education and training to supplement Directive 89/48/EEC;

(h)   "coordinated field": requirements laid down in Member States' legal systems applicable to information society service providers or information society services, regardless of whether they are of a general nature or specifically designed for them.

(i)   The coordinated field concerns requirements with which the service provider has to comply in respect of:

— the taking up of the activity of an information society service, such as requirements concerning qualifications, authorisation or notification,

— the pursuit of the activity of an information society service, such as requirements concerning the behaviour of the service provider, requirements regarding the quality or content of the service including those applicable to advertising and contracts, or requirements concerning the liability of the service provider;

(ii)   The coordinated field does not cover requirements such as:

— requirements applicable to goods as such,

— requirements applicable to the delivery of goods,

— requirements applicable to services not provided by electronic means.

*Article 3*

**Internal market**

1.   Each Member State shall ensure that the information society services provided by a service provider established on its territory comply with the national provisions applicable in the Member State in question which fall within the coordinated field.

2.   Member States may not, for reasons falling within the coordinated field, restrict the freedom to provide information society services from another Member State.

3.   Paragraphs 1 and 2 shall not apply to the fields referred to in the Annex.

4.    Member States may take measures to derogate from paragraph 2 in respect of a given information society service if the following conditions are fulfilled:

(a)    the measures shall be:

  (i)    necessary for one of the following reasons:

    —    public policy, in particular the prevention, investigation, detection and prosecution of criminal offences, including the protection of minors and the fight against any incitement to hatred on grounds of race, sex, religion or nationality, and violations of human dignity concerning individual persons,

    —    the protection of public health,

    —    public security, including the safeguarding of national security and defence,

    —    the protection of consumers, including investors;

  (ii)    taken against a given information society service which prejudices the objectives referred to in point (i) or which presents a serious and grave risk of prejudice to those objectives;

  (iii)    proportionate to those objectives;

(b)    before taking the measures in question and without prejudice to court proceedings, including preliminary proceedings and acts carried out in the framework of a criminal investigation, the Member State has:

    —    asked the Member State referred to in paragraph 1 to take measures and the latter did not take such measures, or they were inadequate,

    —    notified the Commission and the Member State referred to in paragraph 1 of its intention to take such measures.

5.    Member States may, in the case of urgency, derogate from the conditions stipulated in paragraph 4(b). Where this is the case, the measures shall be notified in the shortest possible time to the Commission and to the Member State referred to in paragraph 1, indicating the reasons for which the Member State considers that there is urgency.

6.    Without prejudice to the Member State's possibility of proceeding with the measures in question, the Commission shall examine the compatibility of the notified measures with Community law in the shortest possible time; where it comes to the conclusion that the measure is incompatible with Community law, the Commission shall ask the Member State in question to refrain from taking any proposed measures or urgently to put an end to the measures in question.

## CHAPTER II
## PRINCIPLES

Section 1

### Establishment and information requirements

*Article 4*

### Principle excluding prior authorisation

1.    Member States shall ensure that the taking up and pursuit of the activity of an information society service provider may not be made subject to prior authorisation or any other requirement having equivalent effect.

2.    Paragraph 1 shall be without prejudice to authorisation schemes which are not specifically and exclusively targeted at information society services, or which are covered by Directive 97/13/EC of the European Parliament and of the Council of 10 April 1997 on a common framework for general authorisations and individual licences in the field of telecommunications services.

*Article 5*

### General information to be provided

1. In addition to other information requirements established by Community law, Member States shall ensure that the service provider shall render easily, directly and permanently accessible to the recipients of the service and competent authorities, at least the following information:

(a) the name of the service provider;

(b) the geographic address at which the service provider is established;

(c) the details of the service provider, including his electronic mail address, which allow him to be contacted rapidly and communicated with in a direct and effective manner;

(d) where the service provider is registered in a trade or similar public register, the trade register in which the service provider is entered and his registration number, or equivalent means of identification in that register;

(e) where the activity is subject to an authorisation scheme, the particulars of the relevant supervisory authority;

(f) as concerns the regulated professions:

— any professional body or similar institution with which the service provider is registered,

— the professional title and the Member State where it has been granted,

— a reference to the applicable professional rules in the Member State of establishment and the means to access them;

(g) where the service provider undertakes an activity that is subject to VAT, the identification number referred to in Article 22(1) of the sixth Council Directive 77/388/EEC of 17 May 1977 on the harmonisation of the laws of the Member States relating to turnover taxes—Common system of value added tax: uniform basis of assessment.

2. In addition to other information requirements established by Community law, Member States shall at least ensure that, where information society services refer to prices, these are to be indicated clearly and unambiguously and, in particular, must indicate whether they are inclusive of tax and delivery costs.

Section 2

### Commercial communications

*Article 6*

### Information to be provided

In addition to other information requirements established by Community law, Member States shall ensure that commercial communications which are part of, or constitute, an information society service comply at least with the following conditions:

(a) the commercial communication shall be clearly identifiable as such;

(b) the natural or legal person on whose behalf the commercial communication is made shall be clearly identifiable;

(c) promotional offers, such as discounts, premiums and gifts, where permitted in the Member State where the service provider is established, shall be clearly identifiable as such, and the conditions which are to be met to qualify for them shall be easily accessible and be presented clearly and unambiguously;

(d)   promotional competitions or games, where permitted in the Member State where the service provider is established, shall be clearly identifiable as such, and the conditions for participation shall be easily accessible and be presented clearly and unambiguously.

## *Article 7*

### Unsolicited commercial communication

1.   In addition to other requirements established by Community law, Member States which permit unsolicited commercial communication by electronic mail shall ensure that such commercial communication by a service provider established in their territory shall be identifiable clearly and unambiguously as such as soon as it is received by the recipient.

2.   Without prejudice to Directive 97/7/EC and Directive 97/66/EC, Member States shall take measures to ensure that service providers undertaking unsolicited commercial communications by electronic mail consult regularly and respect the opt-out registers in which natural persons not wishing to receive such commercial communications can register themselves.

## *Article 8*

### Regulated professions

1.   Member States shall ensure that the use of commercial communications which are part of, or constitute, an information society service provided by a member of a regulated profession is permitted subject to compliance with the professional rules regarding, in particular, the independence, dignity and honour of the profession, professional secrecy and fairness towards clients and other members of the profession.

2.   Without prejudice to the autonomy of professional bodies and associations, Member States and the Commission shall encourage professional associations and bodies to establish codes of conduct at Community level in order to determine the types of information that can be given for the purposes of commercial communication in conformity with the rules referred to in paragraph 1.

3.   When drawing up proposals for Community initiatives which may become necessary to ensure the proper functioning of the Internal Market with regard to the information referred to in paragraph 2, the Commission shall take due account of codes of conduct applicable at Community level and shall act in close cooperation with the relevant professional associations and bodies.

4.   This Directive shall apply in addition to Community Directives concerning access to, and the exercise of, activities of the regulated professions.

### Section 3

### Contracts concluded by electronic means

## *Article 9*

### Treatment of contracts

1.   Member States shall ensure that their legal system allows contracts to be concluded by electronic means. Member States shall in particular ensure that the legal requirements applicable to the contractual process neither create obstacles for the use of electronic contracts nor result in such contracts being deprived of legal effectiveness and validity on account of their having been made by electronic means.

2.   Member States may lay down that paragraph 1 shall not apply to all or certain contracts falling into one of the following categories:

(a)   contracts that create or transfer rights in real estate, except for rental rights;

(b)   contracts requiring by law the involvement of courts, public authorities or professions exercising public authority;

(c)   contracts of suretyship granted and on collateral securities furnished by persons acting for purposes outside their trade, business or profession;

(d)   contracts governed by family law or by the law of succession.

3.   Member States shall indicate to the Commission the categories referred to in paragraph 2 to which they do not apply paragraph 1. Member States shall submit to the Commission every five years a report on the application of paragraph 2 explaining the reasons why they consider it necessary to maintain the category referred to in paragraph 2(b) to which they do not apply paragraph 1.

*Article 10*

**Information to be provided**

1.   In addition to other information requirements established by Community law, Member States shall ensure, except when otherwise agreed by parties who are not consumers, that at least the following information is given by the service provider clearly, comprehensibly and unambiguously and prior to the order being placed by the recipient of the service:

(a)   the different technical steps to follow to conclude the contract;

(b)   whether or not the concluded contract will be filed by the service provider and whether it will be accessible;

(c)   the technical means for identifying and correcting input errors prior to the placing of the order;

(d)   the languages offered for the conclusion of the contract.

2.   Member States shall ensure that, except when otherwise agreed by parties who are not consumers, the service provider indicates any relevant codes of conduct to which he subscribes and information on how those codes can be consulted electronically.

3.   Contract terms and general conditions provided to the recipient must be made available in a way that allows him to store and reproduce them.

4.   Paragraphs 1 and 2 shall not apply to contracts concluded exclusively by exchange of electronic mail or by equivalent individual communications.

*Article 11*

**Placing of the order**

1.   Member States shall ensure, except when otherwise agreed by parties who are not consumers, that in cases where the recipient of the service places his order through technological means, the following principles apply:

—   the service provider has to acknowledge the receipt of the recipient's order without undue delay and by electronic means,

—   the order and the acknowledgement of receipt are deemed to be received when the parties to whom they are addressed are able to access them.

2.   Member States shall ensure that, except when otherwise agreed by parties who are not consumers, the service provider makes available to the recipient of the service appropriate, effective and accessible technical means allowing him to identify and correct input errors, prior to the placing of the order.

3.   Paragraph 1, first indent, and paragraph 2 shall not apply to contracts concluded exclusively by exchange of electronic mail or by equivalent individual communications.

Section 4

**Liability of intermediary service providers**

*Article 12*

**"Mere conduit"**

1. Where an information society service is provided that consists of the transmission in a communication network of information provided by a recipient of the service, or the provision of access to a communication network, Member States shall ensure that the service provider is not liable for the information transmitted, on condition that the provider:

(a) does not initiate the transmission;

(b) does not select the receiver of the transmission; and

(c) does not select or modify the information contained in the transmission.

2. The acts of transmission and of provision of access referred to in paragraph 1 include the automatic, intermediate and transient storage of the information transmitted in so far as this takes place for the sole purpose of carrying out the transmission in the communication network, and provided that the information is not stored for any period longer than is reasonably necessary for the transmission.

3. This Article shall not affect the possibility for a court or administrative authority, in accordance with Member States' legal systems, of requiring the service provider to terminate or prevent an infringement.

*Article 13*

**"Caching"**

1. Where an information society service is provided that consists of the transmission in a communication network of information provided by a recipient of the service, Member States shall ensure that the service provider is not liable for the automatic, intermediate and temporary storage of that information, performed for the sole purpose of making more efficient the information's onward transmission to other recipients of the service upon their request, on condition that:

(a) the provider does not modify the information;

(b) the provider complies with conditions on access to the information;

(c) the provider complies with rules regarding the updating of the information, specified in a manner widely recognised and used by industry;

(d) the provider does not interfere with the lawful use of technology, widely recognised and used by industry, to obtain data on the use of the information; and

(e) the provider acts expeditiously to remove or to disable access to the information it has stored upon obtaining actual knowledge of the fact that the information at the initial source of the transmission has been removed from the network, or access to it has been disabled, or that a court or an administrative authority has ordered such removal or disablement.

2. This Article shall not affect the possibility for a court or administrative authority, in accordance with Member States' legal systems, of requiring the service provider to terminate or prevent an infringement.

## *Article 14*

### Hosting

1.    Where an information society service is provided that consists of the storage of information provided by a recipient of the service, Member States shall ensure that the service provider is not liable for the information stored at the request of a recipient of the service, on condition that:

(a)    the provider does not have actual knowledge of illegal activity or information and, as regards claims for damages, is not aware of facts or circumstances from which the illegal activity or information is apparent; or

(b)    the provider, upon obtaining such knowledge or awareness, acts expeditiously to remove or to disable access to the information.

2.    Paragraph 1 shall not apply when the recipient of the service is acting under the authority or the control of the provider.

3.    This Article shall not affect the possibility for a court or administrative authority, in accordance with Member States' legal systems, of requiring the service provider to terminate or prevent an infringement, nor does it affect the possibility for Member States of establishing procedures governing the removal or disabling of access to information.

## *Article 15*

### No general obligation to monitor

1.    Member States shall not impose a general obligation on providers, when providing the services covered by Articles 12, 13 and 14, to monitor the information which they transmit or store, nor a general obligation actively to seek facts or circumstances indicating illegal activity.

2.    Member States may establish obligations for information society service providers promptly to inform the competent public authorities of alleged illegal activities undertaken or information provided by recipients of their service or obligations to communicate to the competent authorities, at their request, information enabling the identification of recipients of their service with whom they have storage agreements.

## CHAPTER III
## IMPLEMENTATION

## *Article 16*

### Codes of conduct

1.    Member States and the Commission shall encourage:

(a)    the drawing up of codes of conduct at Community level, by trade, professional and consumer associations or organisations, designed to contribute to the proper implementation of Articles 5 to 15;

(b)    the voluntary transmission of draft codes of conduct at national or Community level to the Commission;

(c)    the accessibility of these codes of conduct in the Community languages by electronic means;

(d)    the communication to the Member States and the Commission, by trade, professional and consumer associations or organisations, of their assessment of the application of their codes of conduct and their impact upon practices, habits or customs relating to electronic commerce;

(e)    the drawing up of codes of conduct regarding the protection of minors and human dignity.

2.    Member States and the Commission shall encourage the involvement of associations or organisations representing consumers in the drafting and implementation of codes of conduct affecting

their interests and drawn up in accordance with paragraph 1(a). Where appropriate, to take account of their specific needs, associations representing the visually impaired and disabled should be consulted.

## Article 17

### Out-of-court dispute settlement

1.    Member States shall ensure that, in the event of disagreement between an information society service provider and the recipient of the service, their legislation does not hamper the use of out-of-court schemes, available under national law, for dispute settlement, including appropriate electronic means.

2.    Member States shall encourage bodies responsible for the out-of-court settlement of, in particular, consumer disputes to operate in a way which provides adequate procedural guarantees for the parties concerned.

3.    Member States shall encourage bodies responsible for out-of-court dispute settlement to inform the Commission of the significant decisions they take regarding information society services and to transmit any other information on the practices, usages or customs relating to electronic commerce.

## Article 18

### Court actions

1.    Member States shall ensure that court actions available under national law concerning information society services' activities allow for the rapid adoption of measures, including interim measures, designed to terminate any alleged infringement and to prevent any further impairment of the interests involved.

2.    The Annex to Directive 98/27/EC shall be supplemented as follows:

"11. Directive 2000/31/EC of the European Parliament and of the Council of 8 June 2000 on certain legal aspects on information society services, in particular electronic commerce, in the internal market (Directive on electronic commerce) (OJ L 178, 17.7.2000, p. 1)."

## Article 19

### Cooperation

1.    Member States shall have adequate means of supervision and investigation necessary to implement this Directive effectively and shall ensure that service providers supply them with the requisite information.

2.    Member States shall cooperate with other Member States; they shall, to that end, appoint one or several contact points, whose details they shall communicate to the other Member States and to the Commission.

3.    Member States shall, as quickly as possible, and in conformity with national law, provide the assistance and information requested by other Member States or by the Commission, including by appropriate electronic means.

4.    Member States shall establish contact points which shall be accessible at least by electronic means and from which recipients and service providers may:

(a)    obtain general information on contractual rights and obligations as well as on the complaint and redress mechanisms available in the event of disputes, including practical aspects involved in the use of such mechanisms;

(b)    obtain the details of authorities, associations or organisations from which they may obtain further information or practical assistance.

5.    Member States shall encourage the communication to the Commission of any significant administrative or judicial decisions taken in their territory regarding disputes relating to information society services and practices, usages and customs relating to electronic commerce. The Commission shall communicate these decisions to the other Member States.

## Article 20

### Sanctions

Member States shall determine the sanctions applicable to infringements of national provisions adopted pursuant to this Directive and shall take all measures necessary to ensure that they are enforced. The sanctions they provide for shall be effective, proportionate and dissuasive.

## CHAPTER IV
## FINAL PROVISIONS

### Article 21

### Re-examination

1.    Before 17 July 2003, and thereafter every two years, the Commission shall submit to the European Parliament, the Council and the Economic and Social Committee a report on the application of this Directive, accompanied, where necessary, by proposals for adapting it to legal, technical and economic developments in the field of information society services, in particular with respect to crime prevention, the protection of minors, consumer protection and to the proper functioning of the internal market.

2.    In examining the need for an adaptation of this Directive, the report shall in particular analyse the need for proposals concerning the liability of providers of hyperlinks and location tool services, "notice and take down" procedures and the attribution of liability following the taking down of content. The report shall also analyse the need for additional conditions for the exemption from liability, provided for in Articles 12 and 13, in the light of technical developments, and the possibility of applying the internal market principles to unsolicited commercial communications by electronic mail.

### Article 22

### Transposition

1.    Member States shall bring into force the laws, regulations and administrative provisions necessary to comply with this Directive before 17 January 2002. They shall forthwith inform the Commission thereof.

2.    When Member States adopt the measures referred to in paragraph 1, these shall contain a reference to this Directive or shall be accompanied by such reference at the time of their official publication. The methods of making such reference shall be laid down by Member States.

### Article 23

### Entry into force

This Directive shall enter into force on the day of its publication in the *Official Journal of the European Communities*.

### Article 24

### Addressees

This Directive is addressed to the Member States.

Done at Luxemburg, 8 June 2000.

# 63. DIGITAL SINGLE MARKET DIRECTIVE

**DIRECTIVE (EU) 2019/790 OF THE EUROPEAN PARLIAMENT
AND OF THE COUNCIL
of 17 April 2019
on copyright and related rights in the Digital Single Market
and amending Directives 96/9/EC and 2001/29/EC**

**(Text with EEA relevance)***

. . . Whereas: . . .

(3) Rapid technological developments continue to transform the way works and other subject matter are created, produced, distributed and exploited. New business models and new actors continue to emerge. Relevant legislation needs to be future-proof so as not to restrict technological development. The objectives and the principles laid down by the Union copyright framework remain sound. However, legal uncertainty remains, for both rightholders and users, as regards certain uses, including cross-border uses, of works and other subject matter in the digital environment. . . .

(6) The exceptions and limitations provided for in this Directive seek to achieve a fair balance between the rights and interests of authors and other rightholders, on the one hand, and of users on the other. They can be applied only in certain special cases that do not conflict with the normal exploitation of the works or other subject matter and do not unreasonably prejudice the legitimate interests of the rightholders.

(8) New technologies enable the automated computational analysis of information in digital form, such as text, sounds, images or data, generally known as text and data mining. Text and data mining makes the processing of large amounts of information with a view to gaining new knowledge and discovering new trends possible. Text and data mining technologies are prevalent across the digital economy; however, there is widespread acknowledgment that text and data mining can, in particular, benefit the research community and, in so doing, support innovation. Such technologies benefit universities and other research organisations, as well as cultural heritage institutions since they could also carry out research in the context of their main activities. However, in the Union, such organisations and institutions are confronted with legal uncertainty as to the extent to which they can perform text and data mining of content. In certain instances, text and data mining can involve acts protected by copyright, by the sui generis database right or by both, in particular, the reproduction of works or other subject matter, the extraction of contents from a database or both which occur for example when the data are normalised in the process of text and data mining. Where no exception or limitation applies, an authorisation to undertake such acts is required from rightholders.

(10) Union law provides for certain exceptions and limitations covering uses for scientific research purposes which may apply to acts of text and data mining. However, those exceptions and limitations are optional and not fully adapted to the use of technologies in scientific research. Moreover, where researchers have lawful access to content, for example through subscriptions to publications or open access licences, the terms of the licences could exclude text and data mining. As research is increasingly carried out with the assistance of digital technology, there is a risk that the Union's competitive position as a research area will suffer, unless steps are taken to address the legal uncertainty concerning text and data mining.

(11) The legal uncertainty concerning text and data mining should be addressed by providing for a mandatory exception for universities and other research organisations, as well as for cultural heritage institutions, to the exclusive right of reproduction and to the right to prevent extraction

---

\* Footnotes and some recitals omitted.

from a database. In line with the existing Union research policy, which encourages universities and research institutes to collaborate with the private sector, research organisations should also benefit from such an exception when their research activities are carried out in the framework of public-private partnerships. While research organisations and cultural heritage institutions should continue to be the beneficiaries of that exception, they should also be able to rely on their private partners for carrying out text and data mining, including by using their technological tools.

(12) Research organisations across the Union encompass a wide variety of entities the primary goal of which is to conduct scientific research or to do so together with the provision of educational services. The term 'scientific research' within the meaning of this Directive should be understood to cover both the natural sciences and the human sciences. Due to the diversity of such entities, it is important to have a common understanding of research organisations. They should for example cover, in addition to universities or other higher education institutions and their libraries, also entities such as research institutes and hospitals that carry out research. Despite different legal forms and structures, research organisations in the Member States generally have in common that they act either on a not-for-profit basis or in the context of a public-interest mission recognised by the State. Such a public-interest mission could, for example, be reflected through public funding or through provisions in national laws or public contracts. Conversely, organisations upon which commercial undertakings have a decisive influence allowing such undertakings to exercise control because of structural situations, such as through their quality of shareholder or member, which could result in preferential access to the results of the research, should not be considered research organisations for the purposes of this Directive.

(13) Cultural heritage institutions should be understood as covering publicly accessible libraries and museums regardless of the type of works or other subject matter that they hold in their permanent collections, as well as archives, film or audio heritage institutions. They should also be understood to include, inter alia, national libraries and national archives, and, as far as their archives and publicly accessible libraries are concerned, educational establishments, research organisations and public sector broadcasting organisations.

(14) Research organisations and cultural heritage institutions, including the persons attached thereto, should be covered by the text and data mining exception with regard to content to which they have lawful access. Lawful access should be understood as covering access to content based on an open access policy or through contractual arrangements between rightholders and research organisations or cultural heritage institutions, such as subscriptions, or through other lawful means. For instance, in the case of subscriptions taken by research organisations or cultural heritage institutions, the persons attached thereto and covered by those subscriptions should be deemed to have lawful access. Lawful access should also cover access to content that is freely available online.

(15) Research organisations and cultural heritage institutions could in certain cases, for example for subsequent verification of scientific research results, need to retain copies made under the exception for the purposes of carrying out text and data mining. In such cases, the copies should be stored in a secure environment. Member States should be free to decide, at national level and after discussions with relevant stakeholders, on further specific arrangements for retaining the copies, including the ability to appoint trusted bodies for the purpose of storing such copies. In order not to unduly restrict the application of the exception, such arrangements should be proportionate and limited to what is needed for retaining the copies in a safe manner and preventing unauthorised use. . . .

(16) In view of a potentially high number of access requests to, and downloads of, their works or other subject matter, rightholders should be allowed to apply measures when there is a risk that the security and integrity of their systems or databases could be jeopardised. Such measures could, for example, be used to ensure that only persons having lawful access to their data can access them, including through IP address validation or user authentication. Those measures should

remain proportionate to the risks involved, and should not exceed what is necessary to pursue the objective of ensuring the security and integrity of the system and should not undermine the effective application of the exception.

(17) In view of the nature and scope of the exception, which is limited to entities carrying out scientific research, any potential harm created to rightholders through this exception would be minimal. Member States should, therefore, not provide for compensation for rightholders as regards uses under the text and data mining exceptions introduced by this Directive.

(18) In addition to their significance in the context of scientific research, text and data mining techniques are widely used both by private and public entities to analyse large amounts of data in different areas of life and for various purposes, including for government services, complex business decisions and the development of new applications or technologies. Rightholders should remain able to license the uses of their works or other subject matter falling outside the scope of the mandatory exception provided for in this Directive for text and data mining for the purposes of scientific research and of the existing exceptions and limitations provided for in Directive 2001/29/EC. At the same time, consideration should be given to the fact that users of text and data mining could be faced with legal uncertainty as to whether reproductions and extractions made for the purposes of text and data mining can be carried out on lawfully accessed works or other subject matter, in particular when the reproductions or extractions made for the purposes of the technical process do not fulfil all the conditions of the existing exception for temporary acts of reproduction provided for in Article 5(1) of Directive 2001/29/EC. In order to provide for more legal certainty in such cases and to encourage innovation also in the private sector, this Directive should provide, under certain conditions, for an exception or limitation for reproductions and extractions of works or other subject matter, for the purposes of text and data mining, and allow the copies made to be retained for as long as is necessary for those text and data mining purposes.

This exception or limitation should only apply where the work or other subject matter is accessed lawfully by the beneficiary, including when it has been made available to the public online, and insofar as the rightholders have not reserved in an appropriate manner the rights to make reproductions and extractions for text and data mining. In the case of content that has been made publicly available online, it should only be considered appropriate to reserve those rights by the use of machine-readable means, including metadata and terms and conditions of a website or a service. Other uses should not be affected by the reservation of rights for the purposes of text and data mining. In other cases, it can be appropriate to reserve the rights by other means, such as contractual agreements or a unilateral declaration. Rightholders should be able to apply measures to ensure that their reservations in this regard are respected. This exception or limitation should leave intact the mandatory exception for text and data mining for scientific research purposes provided for in this Directive, as well as the existing exception for temporary acts of reproduction provided for in Article 5(1) of Directive 2001/29/EC.

(19) Article 5(3)(a) of Directive 2001/29/EC allows Member States to introduce an exception or limitation to the rights of reproduction, communication to the public and making available to the public of works or other subject matter in such a way that members of the public may access them from a place and a time individually chosen by them, for the sole purpose of illustration for teaching. In addition, Articles 6(2)(b) and 9(b) of Directive 96/9/EC permit the use of a database and the extraction of a substantial part of its contents for the purpose of illustration for teaching. The scope of those exceptions or limitations as they apply to digital uses is unclear. In addition, there is a lack of clarity as to whether those exceptions or limitations would apply where teaching is provided online and at a distance. Moreover, the existing legal framework does not provide for a cross-border effect. This situation could hamper the development of digitally supported teaching activities and distance learning. Therefore, the introduction of a new mandatory exception or limitation is necessary to ensure that educational establishments benefit from full legal certainty when using works or other subject matter in digital teaching activities, including online and across borders.

(20) While distance learning and cross-border education programmes are mostly developed at higher education level, digital tools and resources are increasingly used at all education levels, in particular to improve and enrich the learning experience. The exception or limitation provided for in this Directive should, therefore, benefit all educational establishments recognised by a Member State, including those involved in primary, secondary, vocational and higher education. It should apply only to the extent that the uses are justified by the non-commercial purpose of the particular teaching activity. The organisational structure and the means of funding of an educational establishment should not be the decisive factors in determining whether the activity is non-commercial in nature.

(21) The exception or limitation provided for in this Directive for the sole purpose of illustration for teaching should be understood as covering digital uses of works or other subject matter to support, enrich or complement the teaching, including learning activities. The distribution of software allowed under that exception or limitation should be limited to digital transmission of software. In most cases, the concept of illustration would, therefore, imply the use only of parts or extracts of works, which should not substitute for the purchase of materials primarily intended for the educational market. When implementing the exception or limitation, Member States should remain free to specify, for the different types of works or other subject matter, in a balanced manner, the proportion of a work or other subject matter that can be used for the sole purpose of illustration for teaching. Uses allowed under the exception or limitation should be understood to cover the specific accessibility needs of persons with a disability in the context of illustration for teaching.

(22) The use of works or other subject matter under the exception or limitation for the sole purpose of illustration for teaching provided for in this Directive should only take place in the context of teaching and learning activities carried out under the responsibility of educational establishments, including during examinations or teaching activities that take place outside the premises of educational establishments, for example in a museum, library or another cultural heritage institution, and should be limited to what is necessary for the purpose of such activities. The exception or limitation should cover both uses of works or other subject matter made in the classroom or in other venues through digital means, for example electronic whiteboards or digital devices which might be connected to the internet, as well as uses made at a distance through secure electronic environments, such as in the context of online courses or access to teaching material complementing a given course. Secure electronic environments should be understood as digital teaching and learning environments access to which is limited to an educational establishment's teaching staff and to pupils or students enrolled in a study programme, in particular through appropriate authentication procedures including password-based authentication.

(23) Different arrangements, based on the implementation of the exception or limitation provided for in Directive 2001/29/EC or on licensing agreements covering further uses, are in place in a number of Member States in order to facilitate educational uses of works and other subject matter. Such arrangements have usually been developed taking account of the needs of educational establishments and of different levels of education. While it is essential to harmonise the scope of the new mandatory exception or limitation in relation to digital uses and cross-border teaching activities, the arrangements for implementation can vary from one Member State to another, to the extent that they do not hamper the effective application of the exception or limitation or cross-border uses. Member States should, for example, remain free to require that the use of works or other subject matter respect the moral rights of authors and performers. This should allow Member States to build on the existing arrangements concluded at national level. In particular, Member States could decide to subject the application of the exception or limitation, fully or partially, to the availability of suitable licences, covering at least the same uses as those allowed under the exception or limitation. Member States should ensure that where licences cover only partially the uses allowed under the exception or limitation, all the other uses remain subject to the exception or limitation.

Member States could, for example, use this mechanism to give precedence to licences for material that is primarily intended for the educational market or licences for sheet music. In order to avoid that subjecting the application of the exception to the availability of licences results in legal uncertainty or an administrative burden for educational establishments, Member States adopting such an approach should take concrete measures to ensure that licensing schemes allowing digital uses of works or other subject matter for the purpose of illustration for teaching are easily available, and that educational establishments are aware of the existence of such licensing schemes. Such licensing schemes should meet the needs of educational establishments. Information tools aimed at ensuring that existing licensing schemes are visible could also be developed. Such schemes could, for example, be based on collective licensing or on extended collective licensing, in order to avoid educational establishments having to negotiate individually with rightholders. In order to guarantee legal certainty, Member States should specify under which conditions an educational establishment can use protected works or other subject matter under that exception and, conversely, when it should act under a licensing scheme.

(24) Member States should remain free to provide that rightholders receive fair compensation for the digital uses of their works or other subject matter under the exception or limitation provided for in this Directive for illustration for teaching. In setting the level of fair compensation, due account should be taken, inter alia, of Member States' educational objectives and of the harm to rightholders. Member States that decide to provide for fair compensation should encourage the use of systems that do not create an administrative burden for educational establishments.

(25) Cultural heritage institutions are engaged in the preservation of their collections for future generations. An act of preservation of a work or other subject matter in the collection of a cultural heritage institution might require a reproduction and consequently require the authorisation of the relevant rightholders. Digital technologies offer new ways of preserving the heritage contained in those collections but they also create new challenges. In view of those new challenges, it is necessary to adapt the existing legal framework by providing for a mandatory exception to the right of reproduction in order to allow such acts of preservation by such institutions.

(26) The existence of different approaches in the Member States with regard to acts of reproduction for preservation by cultural heritage institutions hampers cross-border cooperation, the sharing of means of preservation and the establishment of cross-border preservation networks in the internal market by such institutions, leading to an inefficient use of resources. That can have a negative impact on the preservation of cultural heritage.

(27) Member States should, therefore, be required to provide for an exception to permit cultural heritage institutions to reproduce works and other subject matter permanently in their collections for preservation purposes, for example to address technological obsolescence or the degradation of original supports or to insure such works and other subject matter. Such an exception should allow the making of copies by the appropriate preservation tool, means or technology, in any format or medium, in the required number, at any point in the life of a work or other subject matter and to the extent required for preservation purposes. Acts of reproduction undertaken by cultural heritage institutions for purposes other than the preservation of works and other subject matter in their permanent collections should remain subject to the authorisation of rightholders, unless permitted by other exceptions or limitations provided for in Union law.

(28) Cultural heritage institutions do not necessarily have the technical means or expertise to undertake the acts required to preserve their collections themselves, particularly in the digital environment, and might, therefore, have recourse to the assistance of other cultural institutions and other third parties for that purpose. Under the exception for preservation purposes provided for by this Directive, cultural heritage institutions should be allowed to rely on third parties acting on their behalf and under their responsibility, including those that are based in other Member States, for the making of copies.

(29) For the purposes of this Directive, works and other subject matter should be considered to be permanently in the collection of a cultural heritage institution when copies of such works or other subject matter are owned or permanently held by that institution, for example as a result of a transfer of ownership or a licence agreement, legal deposit obligations or permanent custody arrangements.

(30) Cultural heritage institutions should benefit from a clear framework for the digitisation and dissemination, including across borders, of works or other subject matter that are considered to be out of commerce for the purposes of this Directive. However, the particular characteristics of the collections of out-of-commerce works or other subject matter, together with the amount of works and other subject matter involved in mass digitisation projects, mean that obtaining the prior authorisation of the individual rightholders can be very difficult. This can be due, for example, to the age of the works or other subject matter, their limited commercial value or the fact that they were never intended for commercial use or that they have never been exploited commercially. It is therefore necessary to provide for measures to facilitate certain uses of out-of-commerce works or other subject matter that are permanently in the collections of cultural heritage institutions.

(31) All Member States should have legal mechanisms in place allowing licences issued by relevant and sufficiently representative collective management organisations to cultural heritage institutions, for certain uses of out-of-commerce works or other subject matter, to also apply to the rights of rightholders that have not mandated a representative collective management organisation in that regard. It should be possible, pursuant to this Directive, for such licences to cover all Member States.

(32) The provisions on collective licensing of out-of-commerce works or other subject matter introduced by this Directive might not provide a solution for all cases in which cultural heritage institutions encounter difficulties in obtaining all the necessary authorisations from rightholders for the use of such out-of-commerce works or other subject matter. That could be the case for example, where there is no practice of collective management of rights for a certain type of work or other subject matter or where the relevant collective management organisation is not sufficiently representative for the category of the rightholders and of the rights concerned. In such particular instances, it should be possible for cultural heritage institutions to make out-of-commerce works or other subject matter that are permanently in their collection available online in all Member States under a harmonised exception or limitation to copyright and related rights. It is important that uses under such exception or limitation only take place when certain conditions, in particular as regards the availability of licensing solutions, are fulfilled. A lack of agreement on the conditions of the licence should not be interpreted as a lack of availability of licensing solutions.

(33) Member States should, within the framework provided for in this Directive, have flexibility in choosing the specific type of licensing mechanism, such as extended collective licensing or presumptions of representation, that they put in place for the use of out-of-commerce works or other subject matter by cultural heritage institutions, in accordance with their legal traditions, practices or circumstances. Member States should also have flexibility in determining what the requirements for collective management organisations to be sufficiently representative are, as long as that determination is based on a significant number of rightholders in the relevant type of works or other subject matter having given a mandate allowing the licensing of the relevant type of use. Member States should be free to establish specific rules applicable to cases in which more than one collective management organisation is representative for the relevant works or other subject matter, requiring for example joint licences or an agreement between the relevant organisations. . . .

(35) Appropriate safeguards should be available for all rightholders, who should be given the opportunity of excluding the application of the licensing mechanisms and of the exception or limitation, introduced by this Directive for the use of out-of-commerce works or other subject matter, in relation to all their works or other subject matter, in relation to all licences or all uses

under the exception or limitation, in relation to particular works or other subject matter, or in relation to particular licences or uses under the exception or limitation, at any time before or during the term of the licence or before or during the use under the exception or limitation. Conditions governing those licensing mechanisms should not affect their practical relevance for cultural heritage institutions. It is important that, where a rightholder excludes the application of such mechanisms or of such exception or limitation to one or more works or other subject matter, any ongoing uses are terminated within a reasonable period, and, where they take place under a collective licence, that the collective management organisation once informed ceases to issue licences covering the uses concerned. Such exclusion by rightholders should not affect their claims to remuneration for the actual use of the work or other subject matter under the licence.

(36) This Directive does not affect the ability of Member States to decide who is to have legal responsibility as regards the compliance of the licensing of out-of-commerce works or other subject matter, and of their use, with the conditions set out in this Directive, and as regards the compliance of the parties concerned with the terms of those licences.

(37) Considering the variety of works and other subject matter in the collections of cultural heritage institutions, it is important that the licensing mechanisms and the exception or limitation provided for by this Directive are available and can be used in practice for different types of works and other subject matter, including photographs, software, phonograms, audiovisual works and unique works of art, including where they have never been commercially available. Never-in-commerce works can include posters, leaflets, trench journals or amateur audiovisual works, but also unpublished works or other subject matter, without prejudice to other applicable legal constraints, such as national rules on moral rights. When a work or other subject matter is available in any of its different versions, such as subsequent editions of literary works and alternate cuts of cinematographic works, or in any of its different manifestations, such as digital and printed formats of the same work, that work or other subject matter should not be considered out of commerce. Conversely, the commercial availability of adaptations, including other language versions or audiovisual adaptations of a literary work, should not preclude a work or other subject matter from being deemed to be out of commerce in a given language. In order to reflect the specificities of different types of works and other subject matter as regards modes of publication and distribution, and to facilitate the usability of those mechanisms, specific requirements and procedures might have to be established for the practical application of those licensing mechanisms, such as a requirement for a certain time period to have elapsed since the work or other subject matter was first commercially available. It is appropriate that Member States consult rightholders, cultural heritage institutions and collective management organisations when establishing such requirements and procedures.

(38) When determining whether works or other subject matter are out of commerce, a reasonable effort should be required to assess their availability to the public in the customary channels of commerce, taking into account the characteristics of the particular work or other subject matter or of the particular set of works or other subject matter. Member States should be free to determine the allocation of responsibilities for making that reasonable effort. The reasonable effort should not have to involve repeated action over time but it should nevertheless involve taking account of any easily accessible evidence of upcoming availability of works or other subject matter in the customary channels of commerce. A work-by-work assessment should only be required where that is considered reasonable in view of the availability of relevant information, the likelihood of commercial availability and the expected transaction cost. Verification of availability of a work or other subject matter should normally take place in the Member State where the cultural heritage institution is established, unless verification across borders is considered reasonable, for example in cases where there is easily available information that a literary work was first published in a given language version in another Member State. In many cases, the out-of-commerce status of a set of works or other subject matter could be determined through a proportionate mechanism, such as sampling. The limited availability of a work or other subject matter, such as its availability in second-hand shops, or the theoretical possibility that a

licence for a work or other subject matter could be obtained should not be considered as availability to the public in the customary channels of commerce.

(39) For reasons of international comity, the licensing mechanism and the exception or limitation provided for in this Directive for the digitisation and dissemination of out-of-commerce works or other subject matter should not apply to sets of out-of-commerce works or other subject matter where there is evidence available to presume that they predominantly consist of works or other subject matter of third countries, unless the collective management organisation concerned is sufficiently representative for that third country, for example via a representation agreement. That assessment could be based on the evidence available following the making of the reasonable effort to determine whether the works or other subject matter are out of commerce, without the need to search for further evidence. A work-by-work assessment of the origin of out-of-commerce works or other subject matter should only be required insofar as it is also required for making the reasonable effort to determine whether they are commercially available.

(40) Contracting cultural heritage institutions and collective management organisations should remain free to agree on the territorial scope of licences, including the option of covering all Member States, the licence fee and the uses allowed. Uses covered by such licences should not be for profit-making purposes, including where copies are distributed by the cultural heritage institution, such as in the case of promotional material about an exhibition. At the same time, given that the digitisation of the collections of cultural heritage institutions can entail significant investments, any licences granted under the mechanism provided for in this Directive should not prevent cultural heritage institutions from covering the costs of the licence and the costs of digitising and disseminating the works or other subject matter covered by the licence.

(41) Information regarding the ongoing and future use of out-of-commerce works and other subject matter by cultural heritage institutions on the basis of this Directive and the arrangements in place for all rightholders to exclude the application of licences or of the exception or limitation to their works or other subject matter should be adequately publicised both before and during the use under a licence or under the exception or limitation, as appropriate. Such publicising is particularly important when uses take place across borders in the internal market. It is therefore appropriate to provide for the creation of a single publicly accessible online portal for the Union in order to make such information available to the public for a reasonable period of time before the use takes place. Such portal should make it easier for rightholders to exclude the application of licences or of the exception or limitation to their works or other subject matter. Under Regulation (EU) No 386/2012 of the European Parliament and of the Council, the European Union Intellectual Property Office is entrusted with certain tasks and activities, financed by making use of its own budgetary means and aimed at facilitating and supporting the activities of national authorities, the private sector and Union institutions in the fight against, including the prevention of, infringement of intellectual property rights. It is therefore appropriate to rely on that Office to establish and manage the portal making such information available. . . .

(45) Given the nature of some uses, together with the usually large amount of works or other subject matter involved, the transaction cost of individual rights clearance with every rightholder concerned is prohibitively high. As a result, it is unlikely that, without effective collective licensing mechanisms, all the transactions in the areas concerned that are required to enable the use of such works or other subject matter would take place. Extended collective licensing by collective management organisations and similar mechanisms can make it possible to conclude agreements in those areas where collective licensing based on an authorisation by rightholders does not provide an exhaustive solution for covering all works or other subject matter to be used. Such mechanisms complement collective management of rights based on individual authorisation by rightholders, by providing full legal certainty to users in certain cases. At the same time, they provide an opportunity to rightholders to benefit from the legitimate use of their works.

(46) Given the increasing importance of the ability to offer flexible licensing schemes in the digital age, and the increasing use of such schemes, Member States should be able to provide for licensing

mechanisms which permit collective management organisations to conclude licences, on a voluntary basis, irrespective of whether all rightholders have authorised the organisation concerned to do so. Member States should have the ability to maintain and introduce such mechanisms in accordance with their national traditions, practices or circumstances, subject to the safeguards provided for in this Directive and in compliance with Union law and the international obligations of the Union. Such mechanisms should only have effect in the territory of the Member State concerned, unless otherwise provided for in Union law. Member States should have flexibility in choosing the specific type of mechanism allowing licences for works or other subject matter to extend to the rights of rightholders that have not authorised the organisation that concludes the agreement, provided that such mechanism is in compliance with Union law, including with the rules on collective management of rights provided for in Directive 2014/26/EU. In particular, such mechanisms should also ensure that Article 7 of Directive 2014/26/EU applies to rightholders that are not members of the organisation that concludes the agreement. Such mechanisms could include extended collective licensing, legal mandates and presumptions of representation. The provisions of this Directive concerning collective licensing should not affect the existing ability of Member States to apply mandatory collective management of rights or other collective licensing mechanisms with an extended effect, such as that included in Article 3 of Council Directive 93/83/EEC.

(47) It is important that mechanisms of collective licensing with an extended effect are only applied in well-defined areas of use, in which obtaining authorisation from rightholders on an individual basis is typically onerous and impractical to a degree that makes the required licensing transaction, namely one involving a licence that covers all rightholders concerned, unlikely to occur due to the nature of the use or of the types of works or other subject matter concerned. Such mechanisms should be based on objective, transparent and non-discriminatory criteria as regards the treatment of rightholders, including rightholders who are not members of the collective management organisation. In particular, the mere fact that the rightholders affected are not nationals or residents of, or established in, the Member State of the user who is seeking a licence, should not be in itself a reason to consider the clearance of rights to be so onerous and impractical as to justify the use of such mechanisms. It is equally important that the licensed use neither affect adversely the economic value of the relevant rights nor deprive rightholders of significant commercial benefits.

(48) Member States should ensure that appropriate safeguards are in place to protect the legitimate interests of rightholders that have not mandated the organisation offering the licence and that those safeguards apply in a non-discriminatory manner. Specifically, in order to justify the extended effect of the mechanisms, such an organisation should be, on the basis of authorisations from rightholders, sufficiently representative of the types of works or other subject matter and of the rights which are the subject of the licence. . . .

In order to ensure that rightholders can easily regain control of their works, and prevent any uses of their works that would be prejudicial to their interests, it is essential that rightholders be given an effective opportunity to exclude the application of such mechanisms to their works or other subject matter for all uses and works or other subject matter, or for specific uses and works or other subject matter, including before the conclusion of a licence and during the term of the licence. In such cases, any ongoing use should be terminated within a reasonable period. Such exclusion by rightholders should not affect their claims for remuneration for the actual use of the work or other subject matter under the licence. Member States should also be able to decide that additional measures are appropriate to protect rightholders. Such additional measures could include, for example, encouraging the exchange of information among collective management organisations and other interested parties across the Union to raise awareness about such mechanisms and the option available to rightholders to exclude their works or other subject matter from those mechanisms.

(49) Member States should ensure that the purpose and scope of any licence granted as a result of mechanisms of collective licensing with an extended effect, as well as the possible uses, should

always be carefully and clearly defined in law or, if the underlying law is a general provision, in the licensing practices applied as a result of such general provisions, or in the licences granted. The ability to operate a licence under such mechanisms should also be limited to collective management organisations that are subject to national law implementing Directive 2014/26/EU. . . .

(51) Video-on-demand services have the potential to play a decisive role in the dissemination of audiovisual works across the Union. However, the availability of such works, in particular European works, on video-on-demand services remains limited. Agreements on the online exploitation of such works can be difficult to conclude due to issues related to the licensing of rights. Such issues could, for instance, arise when the holder of the rights for a given territory has a low economic incentive to exploit a work online and does not license or holds back the online rights, which can lead to audiovisual works being unavailable on video-on-demand services. Other issues could relate to windows of exploitation.

(52) To facilitate the licensing of rights in audiovisual works to video-on-demand services, Member States should be required to provide for a negotiation mechanism allowing parties willing to conclude an agreement to rely on the assistance of an impartial body or of one or more mediators. For that purpose, Member States should be allowed either to establish a new body or rely on an existing one that fulfils the conditions established by this Directive. Member States should be able to designate one or more competent bodies or mediators. The body or the mediators should meet with the parties and help with the negotiations by providing professional, impartial and external advice. Where a negotiation involves parties from different Member States and where those parties decide to rely on the negotiation mechanism, the parties should agree beforehand on the competent Member State. The body or the mediators could meet with the parties to facilitate the start of negotiations or in the course of the negotiations to facilitate the conclusion of an agreement. Participation in that negotiation mechanism and the subsequent conclusion of agreements should be voluntary and should not affect the parties' contractual freedom. Member States should be free to decide on the specific functioning of the negotiation mechanism, including the timing and duration of the assistance to negotiations and the bearing of the costs. Member States should ensure that administrative and financial burdens remain proportionate to guarantee the efficiency of the negotiation mechanism. Without it being an obligation for them, Member States should encourage dialogue between representative organisations.

(53) The expiry of the term of protection of a work entails the entry of that work into the public domain and the expiry of the rights that Union copyright law provides in relation to that work. In the field of visual arts, the circulation of faithful reproductions of works in the public domain contributes to the access to and promotion of culture, and the access to cultural heritage. In the digital environment, the protection of such reproductions through copyright or related rights is inconsistent with the expiry of the copyright protection of works. In addition, differences between the national copyright laws governing the protection of such reproductions give rise to legal uncertainty and affect the cross-border dissemination of works of visual arts in the public domain. Certain reproductions of works of visual arts in the public domain should, therefore, not be protected by copyright or related rights. All of that should not prevent cultural heritage institutions from selling reproductions, such as postcards.

(54) A free and pluralist press is essential to ensure quality journalism and citizens' access to information. It provides a fundamental contribution to public debate and the proper functioning of a democratic society. The wide availability of press publications online has given rise to the emergence of new online services, such as news aggregators or media monitoring services, for which the reuse of press publications constitutes an important part of their business models and a source of revenue. Publishers of press publications are facing problems in licensing the online use of their publications to the providers of those kinds of services, making it more difficult for them to recoup their investments. In the absence of recognition of publishers of press publications as rightholders, the licensing and enforcement of rights in press publications regarding online

uses by information society service providers in the digital environment are often complex and inefficient.

(55) The organisational and financial contribution of publishers in producing press publications needs to be recognised and further encouraged to ensure the sustainability of the publishing industry and thereby foster the availability of reliable information. It is therefore necessary to provide at Union level for harmonised legal protection for press publications in respect of online uses by information society service providers, which leaves the existing copyright rules in Union law applicable to private or non-commercial uses of press publications by individual users unaffected, including where such users share press publications online. Such protection should be effectively guaranteed through the introduction, in Union law, of rights related to copyright for the reproduction and making available to the public of press publications of publishers established in a Member State in respect of online uses by information society service providers within the meaning of Directive (EU) 2015/1535 of the European Parliament and of the Council. The legal protection for press publications provided for by this Directive should benefit publishers that are established in a Member State and have their registered office, central administration or principal place of business within the Union.

The concept of publisher of press publications should be understood as covering service providers, such as news publishers or news agencies, when they publish press publications within the meaning of this Directive.

(56) For the purposes of this Directive, it is necessary to define the concept of 'press publication' so that it only covers journalistic publications, published in any media, including on paper, in the context of an economic activity that constitutes a provision of services under Union law. The press publications that should be covered include, for instance, daily newspapers, weekly or monthly magazines of general or special interest, including subscription-based magazines, and news websites. Press publications contain mostly literary works, but increasingly include other types of works and other subject matter, in particular photographs and videos. Periodical publications published for scientific or academic purposes, such as scientific journals, should not be covered by the protection granted to press publications under this Directive. Neither should that protection apply to websites, such as blogs, that provide information as part of an activity that is not carried out under the initiative, editorial responsibility and control of a service provider, such as a news publisher.

(57) The rights granted to the publishers of press publications under this Directive should have the same scope as the rights of reproduction and making available to the public provided for in Directive 2001/29/EC, insofar as online uses by information society service providers are concerned. The rights granted to publishers of press publications should not extend to acts of hyperlinking. They should also not extend to mere facts reported in press publications. The rights granted to publishers of press publications under this Directive should also be subject to the same provisions on exceptions and limitations as those applicable to the rights provided for in Directive 2001/29/EC, including the exception in the case of quotations for purposes such as criticism or review provided for in Article 5(3)(d) of that Directive.

(58) The use of press publications by information society service providers can consist of the use of entire publications or articles but also of parts of press publications. Such uses of parts of press publications have also gained economic relevance. At the same time, the use of individual words or very short extracts of press publications by information society service providers may not undermine the investments made by publishers of press publications in the production of content. Therefore, it is appropriate to provide that the use of individual words or very short extracts of press publications should not fall within the scope of the rights provided for in this Directive. Taking into account the massive aggregation and use of press publications by information society service providers, it is important that the exclusion of very short extracts be interpreted in such a way as not to affect the effectiveness of the rights provided for in this Directive.

(59) The protection granted to publishers of press publications under this Directive should not affect the rights of the authors and other rightholders in the works and other subject matter incorporated therein, including as regards the extent to which authors and other rightholders can exploit their works or other subject matter independently from the press publication in which they are incorporated. Publishers of press publications should, therefore, not be able to invoke the protection granted to them under this Directive against authors and other rightholders or against other authorised users of the same works or other subject matter. That should be without prejudice to contractual arrangements concluded between the publishers of press publications, on the one hand, and authors and other rightholders, on the other. Authors whose works are incorporated in a press publication should be entitled to an appropriate share of the revenues that press publishers receive for the use of their press publications by information society service providers. That should be without prejudice to national laws on ownership or exercise of rights in the context of employment contracts, provided that such laws are in compliance with Union law.

(60) Publishers, including those of press publications, books or scientific publications and music publications, often operate on the basis of the transfer of authors' rights by means of contractual agreements or statutory provisions. In that context, publishers make an investment with a view to the exploitation of the works contained in their publications and can in some instances be deprived of revenues where such works are used under exceptions or limitations such as those for private copying and reprography, including the corresponding existing national schemes for reprography in the Member States, or under public lending schemes. In several Member States, compensation for uses under those exceptions or limitations is shared between authors and publishers. In order to take account of this situation and to improve legal certainty for all parties concerned, this Directive allows Member States that have existing schemes for the sharing of compensation between authors and publishers to maintain them. That is particularly important for Member States that had such compensation-sharing mechanisms before 12 November 2015, although in other Member States compensation is not shared and is due solely to authors in accordance with national cultural policies. While this Directive should apply in a non-discriminatory way to all Member States, it should respect the traditions in this area and not oblige Member States that do not currently have such compensation-sharing schemes to introduce them. It should not affect existing or future arrangements in Member States regarding remuneration in the context of public lending.

It should also leave national arrangements relating to the management of rights and to remuneration rights unaffected, provided that they are in compliance with Union law. All Member States should be allowed but not obliged to provide that, where authors have transferred or licensed their rights to a publisher or otherwise contribute with their works to a publication, and there are systems in place to compensate for the harm caused to them by an exception or limitation, including through collective management organisations that jointly represent authors and publishers, publishers are entitled to a share of such compensation. Member States should remain free to determine how publishers are to substantiate their claims for compensation or remuneration, and to lay down the conditions for the sharing of such compensation or remuneration between authors and publishers in accordance with their national systems.

(61) In recent years, the functioning of the online content market has gained in complexity. Online content-sharing services providing access to a large amount of copyright-protected content uploaded by their users have become a main source of access to content online. Online services are a means of providing wider access to cultural and creative works and offer great opportunities for cultural and creative industries to develop new business models. However, although they enable diversity and ease of access to content, they also generate challenges when copyright-protected content is uploaded without prior authorisation from rightholders. Legal uncertainty exists as to whether the providers of such services engage in copyright-relevant acts, and need to obtain authorisation from rightholders for content uploaded by their users who do not hold the relevant rights in the uploaded content, without prejudice to the application of exceptions and

limitations provided for in Union law. That uncertainty affects the ability of rightholders to determine whether, and under which conditions, their works and other subject matter are used, as well as their ability to obtain appropriate remuneration for such use. It is therefore important to foster the development of the licensing market between rightholders and online content-sharing service providers. Those licensing agreements should be fair and keep a reasonable balance between both parties. Rightholders should receive appropriate remuneration for the use of their works or other subject matter. However, as contractual freedom should not be affected by those provisions, rightholders should not be obliged to give an authorisation or to conclude licensing agreements.

(62) Certain information society services, as part of their normal use, are designed to give access to the public to copyright-protected content or other subject matter uploaded by their users. The definition of an online content-sharing service provider laid down in this Directive should target only online services that play an important role on the online content market by competing with other online content services, such as online audio and video streaming services, for the same audiences. The services covered by this Directive are services, the main or one of the main purposes of which is to store and enable users to upload and share a large amount of copyright-protected content with the purpose of obtaining profit therefrom, either directly or indirectly, by organising it and promoting it in order to attract a larger audience, including by categorising it and using targeted promotion within it. Such services should not include services that have a main purpose other than that of enabling users to upload and share a large amount of copyright-protected content with the purpose of obtaining profit from that activity. The latter services include, for instance, electronic communication services within the meaning of Directive (EU) 2018/1972 of the European Parliament and of the Council, as well as providers of business-to-business cloud services and cloud services, which allow users to upload content for their own use, such as cyberlockers, or online marketplaces the main activity of which is online retail, and not giving access to copyright-protected content.

Providers of services such as open source software development and sharing platforms, not-for-profit scientific or educational repositories as well as not-for-profit online encyclopedias should also be excluded from the definition of online content-sharing service provider. Finally, in order to ensure a high level of copyright protection, the liability exemption mechanism provided for in this Directive should not apply to service providers the main purpose of which is to engage in or to facilitate copyright piracy.

(63) The assessment of whether an online content-sharing service provider stores and gives access to a large amount of copyright-protected content should be made on a case-by-case basis and should take account of a combination of elements, such as the audience of the service and the number of files of copyright-protected content uploaded by the users of the service.

(64) It is appropriate to clarify in this Directive that online content-sharing service providers perform an act of communication to the public or of making available to the public when they give the public access to copyright-protected works or other protected subject matter uploaded by their users. Consequently, online content-sharing service providers should obtain an authorisation, including via a licensing agreement, from the relevant rightholders. This does not affect the concept of communication to the public or of making available to the public elsewhere under Union law, nor does it affect the possible application of Article 3(1) and (2) of Directive 2001/29/EC to other service providers using copyright-protected content.

(65) When online content-sharing service providers are liable for acts of communication to the public or making available to the public under the conditions laid down in this Directive, Article 14(1) of Directive 2000/31/EC should not apply to the liability arising from the provision of this Directive on the use of protected content by online content-sharing service providers. That should not affect the application of Article 14(1) of Directive 2000/31/EC to such service providers for purposes falling outside the scope of this Directive.

(66) Taking into account the fact that online content-sharing service providers give access to content which is not uploaded by them but by their users, it is appropriate to provide for a specific liability mechanism for the purposes of this Directive for cases in which no authorisation has been granted. That should be without prejudice to remedies under national law for cases other than liability for copyright infringements and to national courts or administrative authorities being able to issue injunctions in compliance with Union law. In particular, the specific regime applicable to new online content-sharing service providers with an annual turnover below EUR 10 million, of which the average number of monthly unique visitors in the Union does not exceed 5 million, should not affect the availability of remedies under Union and national law. Where no authorisation has been granted to service providers, they should make their best efforts in accordance with high industry standards of professional diligence to avoid the availability on their services of unauthorised works and other subject matter, as identified by the relevant rightholders. For that purpose, rightholders should provide the service providers with relevant and necessary information taking into account, among other factors, the size of rightholders and the type of their works and other subject matter. The steps taken by online content-sharing service providers in cooperation with rightholders should not lead to the prevention of the availability of non-infringing content, including works or other protected subject matter the use of which is covered by a licensing agreement, or an exception or limitation to copyright and related rights. Steps taken by such service providers should, therefore, not affect users who are using the online content-sharing services in order to lawfully upload and access information on such services.

In addition, the obligations established in this Directive should not lead to Member States imposing a general monitoring obligation. When assessing whether an online content-sharing service provider has made its best efforts in accordance with the high industry standards of professional diligence, account should be taken of whether the service provider has taken all the steps that would be taken by a diligent operator to achieve the result of preventing the availability of unauthorised works or other subject matter on its website, taking into account best industry practices and the effectiveness of the steps taken in light of all relevant factors and developments, as well as the principle of proportionality. For the purposes of that assessment, a number of elements should be considered, such as the size of the service, the evolving state of the art as regards existing means, including potential future developments, to avoid the availability of different types of content and the cost of such means for the services. Different means to avoid the availability of unauthorised copyright-protected content could be appropriate and proportionate depending on the type of content, and, therefore, it cannot be excluded that in some cases availability of unauthorised content can only be avoided upon notification of rightholders. Any steps taken by service providers should be effective with regard to the objectives pursued but should not go beyond what is necessary to achieve the objective of avoiding and discontinuing the availability of unauthorised works and other subject matter.

If unauthorised works and other subject matter become available despite the best efforts made in cooperation with rightholders, as required by this Directive, the online content-sharing service providers should be liable in relation to the specific works and other subject matter for which they have received the relevant and necessary information from rightholders, unless those providers demonstrate that they have made their best efforts in accordance with high industry standards of professional diligence.

In addition, where specific unauthorised works or other subject matter have become available on online content-sharing services, including irrespective of whether the best efforts were made and regardless of whether rightholders have made available the relevant and necessary information in advance, the online content-sharing service providers should be liable for unauthorised acts of communication to the public of works or other subject matter, when, upon receiving a sufficiently substantiated notice, they fail to act expeditiously to disable access to, or to remove from their websites, the notified works or other subject matter. Additionally, such online content-sharing service providers should also be liable if they fail to demonstrate that they have made their best efforts to prevent the future uploading of specific unauthorised works, based on relevant and necessary information provided by rightholders for that purpose.

Where rightholders do not provide online content-sharing service providers with the relevant and necessary information on their specific works or other subject matter, or where no notification concerning the disabling of access to, or the removal of, specific unauthorised works or other subject matter has been provided by rightholders, and, as a result, those service providers cannot make their best efforts to avoid the availability of unauthorised content on their services, in accordance with high industry standards of professional diligence, such service providers should not be liable for unauthorised acts of communication to the public or of making available to the public of such unidentified works or other subject matter.

(67) Similar to Article 16(2) of Directive 2014/26/EU, this Directive provides for rules as regards new online services. The rules provided for in this Directive are intended to take into account the specific case of start-up companies working with user uploads to develop new business models. The specific regime applicable to new service providers with a small turnover and audience should benefit genuinely new businesses, and should therefore cease to apply three years after their services first became available online in the Union. That regime should not be abused by arrangements aimed at extending its benefits beyond the first three years. In particular, it should not apply to newly created services or to services provided under a new name but which pursue the activity of an already existing online content-sharing service provider which could not benefit or no longer benefits from that regime.

(68) Online content-sharing service providers should be transparent with rightholders with regard to the steps taken in the context of cooperation. As various actions could be undertaken by online content-sharing service providers, they should provide rightholders, at the request of rightholders, with adequate information on the type of actions undertaken and the way in which they are undertaken. Such information should be sufficiently specific to provide enough transparency to rightholders, without affecting business secrets of online content-sharing service providers. Service providers should, however, not be required to provide rightholders with detailed and individualised information for each work or other subject matter identified. That should be without prejudice to contractual arrangements, which could contain more specific provisions on the information to be provided where agreements are concluded between service providers and rightholders.

(69) Where online content-sharing service providers obtain authorisations, including through licensing agreements, for the use on their service of content uploaded by the users of the service, those authorisations should also cover the copyright relevant acts in respect of uploads by users within the scope of the authorisation granted to the service providers, but only in cases where those users act for non-commercial purposes, such as sharing their content without any profit-making purpose, or where the revenue generated by their uploads is not significant in relation to the copyright relevant acts of the users covered by such authorisations. Where rightholders have explicitly authorised users to upload and make available works or other subject matter on an online content-sharing service, the act of communication to the public of the service provider is authorised within the scope of the authorisation granted by the rightholder. However, there should be no presumption in favour of online content-sharing service providers that their users have cleared all relevant rights.

(70) The steps taken by online content-sharing service providers in cooperation with rightholders should be without prejudice to the application of exceptions or limitations to copyright, including, in particular, those which guarantee the freedom of expression of users. Users should be allowed to upload and make available content generated by users for the specific purposes of quotation, criticism, review, caricature, parody or pastiche. That is particularly important for the purposes of striking a balance between the fundamental rights laid down in the Charter of Fundamental Rights of the European Union ('the Charter'), in particular the freedom of expression and the freedom of the arts, and the right to property, including intellectual property. Those exceptions

and limitations should, therefore, be made mandatory in order to ensure that users receive uniform protection across the Union. It is important to ensure that online content-sharing service providers operate an effective complaint and redress mechanism to support use for such specific purposes.

Online content-sharing service providers should also put in place effective and expeditious complaint and redress mechanisms allowing users to complain about the steps taken with regard to their uploads, in particular where they could benefit from an exception or limitation to copyright in relation to an upload to which access has been disabled or that has been removed. Any complaint filed under such mechanisms should be processed without undue delay and be subject to human review. When rightholders request the service providers to take action against uploads by users, such as disabling access to or removing content uploaded, such rightholders should duly justify their requests. Moreover, cooperation should not lead to any identification of individual users nor to the processing of personal data, except in accordance with Directive 2002/58/EC of the European Parliament and of the Council and Regulation (EU) 2016/679 of the European Parliament and of the Council. Member States should also ensure that users have access to out-of-court redress mechanisms for the settlement of disputes. Such mechanisms should allow disputes to be settled impartially. Users should also have access to a court or another relevant judicial authority to assert the use of an exception or limitation to copyright and related rights.

(71) As soon as possible after the date of entry into force of this Directive, the Commission, in cooperation with Member States, should organise dialogues between stakeholders to ensure uniform application of the obligation of cooperation between online content-sharing service providers and rightholders and to establish best practices with regard to the appropriate industry standards of professional diligence. For that purpose, the Commission should consult relevant stakeholders, including users' organisations and technology providers, and take into account developments on the market. Users' organisations should also have access to information on actions carried out by online content-sharing service providers to manage content online.

(72) Authors and performers tend to be in the weaker contractual position when they grant a licence or transfer their rights, including through their own companies, for the purposes of exploitation in return for remuneration, and those natural persons need the protection provided for by this Directive to be able to fully benefit from the rights harmonised under Union law. That need for protection does not arise where the contractual counterpart acts as an end user and does not exploit the work or performance itself, which could, for instance, be the case in some employment contracts.

(73) The remuneration of authors and performers should be appropriate and proportionate to the actual or potential economic value of the licensed or transferred rights, taking into account the author's or performer's contribution to the overall work or other subject matter and all other circumstances of the case, such as market practices or the actual exploitation of the work. A lump sum payment can also constitute proportionate remuneration but it should not be the rule. Member States should have the freedom to define specific cases for the application of lump sums, taking into account the specificities of each sector. Member States should be free to implement the principle of appropriate and proportionate remuneration through different existing or newly introduced mechanisms, which could include collective bargaining and other mechanisms, provided that such mechanisms are in conformity with applicable Union law.

(74) Authors and performers need information to assess the economic value of rights of theirs that are harmonised under Union law. This is especially the case where natural persons grant a licence or a transfer of rights for the purposes of exploitation in return for remuneration. That need does not arise where the exploitation has ceased, or where the author or performer has granted a licence to the general public without remuneration.

(75) As authors and performers tend to be in the weaker contractual position when they grant licences or transfer their rights, they need information to assess the continued economic value of their

rights, compared to the remuneration received for their licence or transfer, but they often face a lack of transparency. Therefore, the sharing of adequate and accurate information by their contractual counterparts or their successors in title is important for the transparency and balance in the system governing the remuneration of authors and performers. That information should be up-to-date to allow access to recent data, relevant to the exploitation of the work or performance, and comprehensive in a way that it covers all sources of revenues relevant to the case, including, where applicable, merchandising revenues. As long as exploitation is ongoing, contractual counterparts of authors and performers should provide information available to them on all modes of exploitation and on all relevant revenues worldwide with a regularity that is appropriate in the relevant sector, but at least annually. The information should be provided in a manner that is comprehensible to the author or performer and it should allow the effective assessment of the economic value of the rights in question. The transparency obligation should nevertheless apply only where copyright relevant rights are concerned. The processing of personal data, such as contact details and information on remuneration, that are necessary to keep authors and performers informed in relation to the exploitation of their works and performances, should be carried out in accordance with Article 6(1)(c) of Regulation (EU) 2016/679.

(76) In order to ensure that exploitation-related information is duly provided to authors and performers also in cases where the rights have been sub-licensed to other parties who exploit the rights, this Directive entitles authors and performers to request additional relevant information on the exploitation of the rights, in cases where the first contractual counterpart has provided the information available to them, but that information is not sufficient to assess the economic value of their rights. That request should be made either directly to sub-licensees or through the contractual counterparts of authors and performers. Authors and performers, and their contractual counterparts, should be able to agree to keep the shared information confidential, but authors and performers should always be able to use the shared information for the purpose of exercising their rights under this Directive. Member States should have the option, in compliance with Union law, to provide for further measures to ensure transparency for authors and performers.

(77) When implementing the transparency obligation provided for in this Directive, Member States should take into account the specificities of different content sectors, such as those of the music sector, the audiovisual sector and the publishing sector, and all relevant stakeholders should be involved when deciding on such sector-specific obligations. Where relevant, the significance of the contribution of authors and performers to the overall work or performance should also be considered. Collective bargaining should be considered as an option for the relevant stakeholders to reach an agreement regarding transparency. Such agreements should ensure that authors and performers have the same level of transparency as or a higher level of transparency than the minimum requirements provided for in this Directive. . . .

(78) Certain contracts for the exploitation of rights harmonised at Union level are of long duration, offering few opportunities for authors and performers to renegotiate them with their contractual counterparts or their successors in title in the event that the economic value of the rights turns out to be significantly higher than initially estimated. Accordingly, without prejudice to the law applicable to contracts in Member States, a remuneration adjustment mechanism should be provided for as regards cases where the remuneration originally agreed under a licence or a transfer of rights clearly becomes disproportionately low compared to the relevant revenues derived from the subsequent exploitation of the work or fixation of the performance by the contractual counterpart of the author or performer. All revenues relevant to the case in question, including, where applicable, merchandising revenues, should be taken into account for the assessment of whether the remuneration is disproportionately low. The assessment of the situation should take account of the specific circumstances of each case, including the contribution of the author or performer, as well as of the specificities and remuneration practices in the different content sectors, and whether the contract is based on a collective bargaining agreement. Representatives of authors and performers duly mandated in accordance with

national law in compliance with Union law, should be able to provide assistance to one or more authors or performers in relation to requests for the adjustment of the contracts, also taking into account the interests of other authors or performers where relevant.

Those representatives should protect the identity of the represented authors and performers for as long as that is possible. Where the parties do not agree on the adjustment of the remuneration, the author or performer should be entitled to bring a claim before a court or other competent authority. Such mechanism should not apply to contracts concluded by entities defined in Article 3(a) and (b) of Directive 2014/26/EU or by other entities subject to national rules implementing Directive 2014/26/EU.

(79) Authors and performers are often reluctant to enforce their rights against their contractual partners before a court or tribunal. Member States should therefore provide for an alternative dispute resolution procedure that addresses claims by authors and performers, or by their representatives on their behalf, related to obligations of transparency and the contract adjustment mechanism. For that purpose, Member States should be able to either establish a new body or mechanism, or rely on an existing one that fulfils the conditions established by this Directive, irrespective of whether those bodies or mechanisms are industry-led or public, including when part of the national judiciary system. Member States should have flexibility in deciding how the costs of the dispute resolution procedure are to be allocated. Such alternative dispute resolution procedure should be without prejudice to the right of parties to assert and defend their rights by bringing an action before a court.

(80) When authors and performers license or transfer their rights, they expect their work or performance to be exploited. However, it could be the case that works or performances that have been licensed or transferred are not exploited at all. Where those rights have been transferred on an exclusive basis, authors and performers cannot turn to another partner to exploit their works or performances. In such a case, and after a reasonable period of time has elapsed, authors and performers should be able to benefit from a mechanism for the revocation of rights allowing them to transfer or license their rights to another person. As exploitation of works or performances can vary depending on the sectors, specific provisions could be laid down at national level in order to take into account the specificities of the sectors, such as the audiovisual sector, or of the works or performances, in particular providing for time frames for the right of revocation. In order to protect the legitimate interests of licensees and transferees of rights and to prevent abuses, and taking into account that a certain amount of time is needed before a work or performance is actually exploited, authors and performers should be able to exercise the right of revocation in accordance with certain procedural requirements and only after a certain period of time following the conclusion of the licence or of the transfer agreement. Member States should be allowed to regulate the exercise of the right of revocation in the case of works or performances involving more than one author or performer, taking into account the relative importance of the individual contributions.

(81) The provisions regarding transparency, contract adjustment mechanisms and alternative dispute resolution procedures laid down in this Directive should be of a mandatory nature, and parties should not be able to derogate from those provisions, whether in contracts between authors, performers and their contractual counterparts, or in agreements between those counterparts and third parties, such as non-disclosure agreements. . . .

## TITLE I
## GENERAL PROVISIONS

*Article 1*

### Subject matter and scope

1.   This Directive lays down rules which aim to harmonise further Union law applicable to copyright and related rights in the framework of the internal market, taking into account, in particular, digital and cross-border uses of protected content. It also lays down rules on exceptions and limitations to copyright and related rights, on the facilitation of licences, as well as rules which aim to ensure a well-functioning marketplace for the exploitation of works and other subject matter.

2.   Except in the cases referred to in Article 24, this Directive shall leave intact and shall in no way affect existing rules laid down in the directives currently in force in this area, in particular Directives 96/9/EC, 2000/31/EC, 2001/29/EC, 2006/115/EC, 2009/24/EC, 2012/28/EU and 2014/26/EU.

*Article 2*

### Definitions

For the purposes of this Directive, the following definitions apply:

(1)   'research organisation' means a university, including its libraries, a research institute or any other entity, the primary goal of which is to conduct scientific research or to carry out educational activities involving also the conduct of scientific research:

(a)   on a not-for-profit basis or by reinvesting all the profits in its scientific research; or

(b)   pursuant to a public interest mission recognised by a Member State;

in such a way that the access to the results generated by such scientific research cannot be enjoyed on a preferential basis by an undertaking that exercises a decisive influence upon such organisation;

(2)   'text and data mining' means any automated analytical technique aimed at analysing text and data in digital form in order to generate information which includes but is not limited to patterns, trends and correlations;

(3)   'cultural heritage institution' means a publicly accessible library or museum, an archive or a film or audio heritage institution;

(4)   'press publication' means a collection composed mainly of literary works of a journalistic nature, but which can also include other works or other subject matter, and which:

(a)   constitutes an individual item within a periodical or regularly updated publication under a single title, such as a newspaper or a general or special interest magazine;

(b)   has the purpose of providing the general public with information related to news or other topics; and

(c)   is published in any media under the initiative, editorial responsibility and control of a service provider.

Periodicals that are published for scientific or academic purposes, such as scientific journals, are not press publications for the purposes of this Directive;

(5)   'information society service' means a service within the meaning of point (b) of Article 1(1) of Directive (EU) 2015/1535;

(6)   'online content-sharing service provider' means a provider of an information society service of which the main or one of the main purposes is to store and give the public access to a large amount

of copyright-protected works or other protected subject matter uploaded by its users, which it organises and promotes for profit-making purposes.

Providers of services, such as not-for-profit online encyclopedias, not-for-profit educational and scientific repositories, open source software-developing and-sharing platforms, providers of electronic communications services as defined in Directive (EU) 2018/1972, online marketplaces, business-to-business cloud services and cloud services that allow users to upload content for their own use, are not 'online content-sharing service providers' within the meaning of this Directive.

## TITLE II
## MEASURES TO ADAPT EXCEPTIONS AND LIMITATIONS TO THE DIGITAL AND CROSS-BORDER ENVIRONMENT

*Article 3*

### Text and data mining for the purposes of scientific research

1.    Member States shall provide for an exception to the rights provided for in Article 5(a) and Article 7(1) of Directive 96/9/EC, Article 2 of Directive 2001/29/EC, and Article 15(1) of this Directive for reproductions and extractions made by research organisations and cultural heritage institutions in order to carry out, for the purposes of scientific research, text and data mining of works or other subject matter to which they have lawful access.

2.    Copies of works or other subject matter made in compliance with paragraph 1 shall be stored with an appropriate level of security and may be retained for the purposes of scientific research, including for the verification of research results.

3.    Rightholders shall be allowed to apply measures to ensure the security and integrity of the networks and databases where the works or other subject matter are hosted. Such measures shall not go beyond what is necessary to achieve that objective.

4.    Member States shall encourage rightholders, research organisations and cultural heritage institutions to define commonly agreed best practices concerning the application of the obligation and of the measures referred to in paragraphs 2 and 3 respectively.

*Article 4*

### Exception or limitation for text and data mining

1.    Member States shall provide for an exception or limitation to the rights provided for in Article 5(a) and Article 7(1) of Directive 96/9/EC, Article 2 of Directive 2001/29/EC, Article 4(1)(a) and (b) of Directive 2009/24/EC and Article 15(1) of this Directive for reproductions and extractions of lawfully accessible works and other subject matter for the purposes of text and data mining.

2.    Reproductions and extractions made pursuant to paragraph 1 may be retained for as long as is necessary for the purposes of text and data mining.

3.    The exception or limitation provided for in paragraph 1 shall apply on condition that the use of works and other subject matter referred to in that paragraph has not been expressly reserved by their rightholders in an appropriate manner, such as machine-readable means in the case of content made publicly available online.

4.    This Article shall not affect the application of Article 3 of this Directive.

*Article 5*

## Use of works and other subject matter in digital and cross-border teaching activities

1.    Member States shall provide for an exception or limitation to the rights provided for in Article 5(a), (b), (d) and (e) and Article 7(1) of Directive 96/9/EC, Articles 2 and 3 of Directive 2001/29/EC, Article 4(1) of Directive 2009/24/EC and Article 15(1) of this Directive in order to allow the digital use of works and other subject matter for the sole purpose of illustration for teaching, to the extent justified by the non-commercial purpose to be achieved, on condition that such use:

(a)    takes place under the responsibility of an educational establishment, on its premises or at other venues, or through a secure electronic environment accessible only by the educational establishment's pupils or students and teaching staff; and

(b)    is accompanied by the indication of the source, including the author's name, unless this turns out to be impossible.

2.    Notwithstanding Article 7(1), Member States may provide that the exception or limitation adopted pursuant to paragraph 1 does not apply or does not apply as regards specific uses or types of works or other subject matter, such as material that is primarily intended for the educational market or sheet music, to the extent that suitable licences authorising the acts referred to in paragraph 1 of this Article and covering the needs and specificities of educational establishments are easily available on the market.

Member States that decide to avail of the first subparagraph of this paragraph shall take the necessary measures to ensure that the licences authorising the acts referred to in paragraph 1 of this Article are available and visible in an appropriate manner for educational establishments.

3.    The use of works and other subject matter for the sole purpose of illustration for teaching through secure electronic environments undertaken in compliance with the provisions of national law adopted pursuant to this Article shall be deemed to occur solely in the Member State where the educational establishment is established.

4.    Member States may provide for fair compensation for rightholders for the use of their works or other subject matter pursuant to paragraph 1.

*Article 6*

## Preservation of cultural heritage

Member States shall provide for an exception to the rights provided for in Article 5(a) and Article 7(1) of Directive 96/9/EC, Article 2 of Directive 2001/29/EC, Article 4(1)(a) of Directive 2009/24/EC and Article 15(1) of this Directive, in order to allow cultural heritage institutions to make copies of any works or other subject matter that are permanently in their collections, in any format or medium, for purposes of preservation of such works or other subject matter and to the extent necessary for such preservation.

*Article 7*

## Common provisions

1.    Any contractual provision contrary to the exceptions provided for in Articles 3, 5 and 6 shall be unenforceable.

2.    Article 5(5) of Directive 2001/29/EC shall apply to the exceptions and limitations provided for under this Title. The first, third and fifth subparagraphs of Article 6(4) of Directive 2001/29/EC shall apply to Articles 3 to 6 of this Directive.

## TITLE III
## MEASURES TO IMPROVE LICENSING PRACTICES
## AND ENSURE WIDER ACCESS TO CONTENT

### CHAPTER 1
*Out-of-commerce works and other subject matter*

*Article 8*

### Use of out-of-commerce works and other subject
### matter by cultural heritage institutions

1.   Member States shall provide that a collective management organisation, in accordance with its mandates from rightholders, may conclude a non-exclusive licence for non-commercial purposes with a cultural heritage institution for the reproduction, distribution, communication to the public or making available to the public of out-of-commerce works or other subject matter that are permanently in the collection of the institution, irrespective of whether all rightholders covered by the licence have mandated the collective management organisation, on condition that:

(a)   the collective management organisation is, on the basis of its mandates, sufficiently representative of rightholders in the relevant type of works or other subject matter and of the rights that are the subject of the licence; and

(b)   all rightholders are guaranteed equal treatment in relation to the terms of the licence.

2.   Member States shall provide for an exception or limitation to the rights provided for in Article 5(a), (b), (d) and (e) and Article 7(1) of Directive 96/9/EC, Articles 2 and 3 of Directive 2001/29/EC, Article 4(1) of Directive 2009/24/EC, and Article 15(1) of this Directive, in order to allow cultural heritage institutions to make available, for non-commercial purposes, out-of-commerce works or other subject matter that are permanently in their collections, on condition that:

(a)   the name of the author or any other identifiable rightholder is indicated, unless this turns out to be impossible; and

(b)   such works or other subject matter are made available on non-commercial websites.

3.   Member States shall provide that the exception or limitation provided for in paragraph 2 only applies to types of works or other subject matter for which no collective management organisation that fulfils the condition set out in point (a) of paragraph 1 exists.

4.   Member States shall provide that all rightholders may, at any time, easily and effectively, exclude their works or other subject matter from the licensing mechanism set out in paragraph 1 or from the application of the exception or limitation provided for in paragraph 2, either in general or in specific cases, including after the conclusion of a licence or after the beginning of the use concerned.

5.   A work or other subject matter shall be deemed to be out of commerce when it can be presumed in good faith that the whole work or other subject matter is not available to the public through customary channels of commerce, after a reasonable effort has been made to determine whether it is available to the public.

Member States may provide for specific requirements, such as a cut-off date, to determine whether works and other subject matter can be licensed in accordance with paragraph 1 or used under the exception or limitation provided for in paragraph 2. Such requirements shall not extend beyond what is necessary and reasonable, and shall not preclude being able to determine that a set of works or other subject matter as a whole is out of commerce, when it is reasonable to presume that all works or other subject matter are out of commerce.

6.   Member States shall provide that the licences referred to in paragraph 1 are to be sought from a collective management organisation that is representative for the Member State where the cultural heritage institution is established.

7.   This Article shall not apply to sets of out-of-commerce works or other subject matter if, on the basis of the reasonable effort referred to in paragraph 5, there is evidence that such sets predominantly consist of:

(a)   works or other subject matter, other than cinematographic or audiovisual works, first published or, in the absence of publication, first broadcast in a third country;

(b)   cinematographic or audiovisual works, of which the producers have their headquarters or habitual residence in a third country; or

(c)   works or other subject matter of third country nationals, where after a reasonable effort no Member State or third country could be determined pursuant to points (a) and (b).

By way of derogation from the first subparagraph, this Article shall apply where the collective management organisation is sufficiently representative, within the meaning of point (a) of paragraph 1, of rightholders of the relevant third country.

## Article 9

### Cross-border uses

1.   Member States shall ensure that licences granted in accordance with Article 8 may allow the use of out-of-commerce works or other subject matter by cultural heritage institutions in any Member State.

2.   The uses of works and other subject matter under the exception or limitation provided for in Article 8(2) shall be deemed to occur solely in the Member State where the cultural heritage institution undertaking that use is established.

## Article 10

### Publicity measures

1.   Member States shall ensure that information from cultural heritage institutions, collective management organisations or relevant public authorities, for the purposes of the identification of the out-of-commerce works or other subject matter, covered by a licence granted in accordance with Article 8(1), or used under the exception or limitation provided for in Article 8(2), as well as information about the options available to rightholders as referred to in Article 8(4), and, as soon as it is available and where relevant, information on the parties to the licence, the territories covered and the uses, is made permanently, easily and effectively accessible on a public single online portal from at least six months before the works or other subject matter are distributed, communicated to the public or made available to the public in accordance with the licence or under the exception or limitation.

The portal shall be established and managed by the European Union Intellectual Property Office in accordance with Regulation (EU) No 386/2012.

2.   Member States shall provide that, if necessary for the general awareness of rightholders, additional appropriate publicity measures are taken regarding the ability of collective management organisations to license works or other subject matter in accordance with Article 8, the licences granted, the uses under the exception or limitation provided for in Article 8(2) and the options available to rightholders as referred to in Article 8(4).

The appropriate publicity measures referred to in the first subparagraph of this paragraph shall be taken in the Member State where the licence is sought in accordance with Article 8(1) or, for uses under the exception or limitation provided for in Article 8(2), in the Member State where the cultural heritage institution is established. If there is evidence, such as the origin of the works or other subject matter, to suggest that the awareness of rightholders could be more efficiently raised in other Member States or third countries, such publicity measures shall also cover those Member States and third countries.

*Article 11*

### Stakeholder dialogue

Member States shall consult rightholders, collective management organisations and cultural heritage institutions in each sector before establishing specific requirements pursuant to Article 8(5), and shall encourage regular dialogue between representative users' and rightholders' organisations, including collective management organisations, and any other relevant stakeholder organisations, on a sector-specific basis, to foster the relevance and usability of the licensing mechanisms set out in Article 8(1) and to ensure that the safeguards for rightholders referred to in this Chapter are effective.

### CHAPTER 2
#### *Measures to facilitate collective licensing*

*Article 12*

### Collective licensing with an extended effect

1.  Member States may provide, as far as the use on their territory is concerned and subject to the safeguards provided for in this Article, that where a collective management organisation that is subject to the national rules implementing Directive 2014/26/EU, in accordance with its mandates from rightholders, enters into a licensing agreement for the exploitation of works or other subject matter:

(a)  such an agreement can be extended to apply to the rights of rightholders who have not authorised that collective management organisation to represent them by way of assignment, licence or any other contractual arrangement; or

(b)  with respect to such an agreement, the organisation has a legal mandate or is presumed to represent rightholders who have not authorised the organisation accordingly.

2.  Member States shall ensure that the licensing mechanism referred to in paragraph 1 is only applied within well-defined areas of use, where obtaining authorisations from rightholders on an individual basis is typically onerous and impractical to a degree that makes the required licensing transaction unlikely, due to the nature of the use or of the types of works or other subject matter concerned, and shall ensure that such licensing mechanism safeguards the legitimate interests of rightholders.

3.  For the purposes of paragraph 1, Member States shall provide for the following safeguards:

(a)  the collective management organisation is, on the basis of its mandates, sufficiently representative of rightholders in the relevant type of works or other subject matter and of the rights which are the subject of the licence, for the relevant Member State;

(b)  all rightholders are guaranteed equal treatment, including in relation to the terms of the licence;

(c)  rightholders who have not authorised the organisation granting the licence may at any time easily and effectively exclude their works or other subject matter from the licensing mechanism established in accordance with this Article; and

(d)  appropriate publicity measures are taken, starting from a reasonable period before the works or other subject matter are used under the licence, to inform rightholders about the ability of the collective management organisation to license works or other subject matter, about the licensing taking place in accordance with this Article and about the options available to rightholders as referred to in point (c). Publicity measures shall be effective without the need to inform each rightholder individually.

4. This Article does not affect the application of collective licensing mechanisms with an extended effect in accordance with other provisions of Union law, including provisions that allow exceptions or limitations.

This Article shall not apply to mandatory collective management of rights.

Article 7 of Directive 2014/26/EU shall apply to the licensing mechanism provided for in this Article.

5. Where a Member State provides in its national law for a licensing mechanism in accordance with this Article, that Member State shall inform the Commission about the scope of the corresponding national provisions, about the purposes and types of licences that may be introduced under those provisions, about the contact details of organisations issuing licences in accordance with that licensing mechanism, and about the means by which information on the licensing and on the options available to rightholders as referred to in point (c) of paragraph 3 can be obtained. The Commission shall publish that information.

6. Based on the information received pursuant to paragraph 5 of this Article and on the discussions within the contact committee established in Article 12(3) of Directive 2001/29/EC, the Commission shall, by 10 April 2021, submit to the European Parliament and to the Council a report on the use in the Union of the licensing mechanisms referred to in paragraph 1 of this Article, their impact on licensing and rightholders, including rightholders who are not members of the organisation granting the licences or who are nationals of, or resident in, another Member State, their effectiveness in facilitating the dissemination of cultural content, and their impact on the internal market, including the cross-border provision of services and competition. That report shall be accompanied, if appropriate, by a legislative proposal, including as regards the cross-border effect of such national mechanisms.

## CHAPTER 3
### *Access to and availability of audiovisual works on video-on-demand platforms*

#### Article 13

#### Negotiation mechanism

Member States shall ensure that parties facing difficulties related to the licensing of rights when seeking to conclude an agreement for the purpose of making available audiovisual works on video-on-demand services may rely on the assistance of an impartial body or of mediators. The impartial body established or designated by a Member State for the purpose of this Article and mediators shall provide assistance to the parties with their negotiations and help the parties reach agreements, including, where appropriate, by submitting proposals to them.

Member States shall notify the Commission of the body or mediators referred to in the first paragraph no later than 7 June 2021. Where Member States have chosen to rely on mediation, the notification to the Commission shall at least include, when available, the source where relevant information on the mediators entrusted can be found.

## CHAPTER 4
### *Works of visual art in the public domain*

*Article 14*

### Works of visual art in the public domain

Member States shall provide that, when the term of protection of a work of visual art has expired, any material resulting from an act of reproduction of that work is not subject to copyright or related rights, unless the material resulting from that act of reproduction is original in the sense that it is the author's own intellectual creation.

## TITLE IV
## MEASURES TO ACHIEVE A WELL-FUNCTIONING MARKETPLACE FOR COPYRIGHT

## CHAPTER 1
### *Rights in publications*

*Article 15*

### Protection of press publications concerning online uses

1.　Member States shall provide publishers of press publications established in a Member State with the rights provided for in Article 2 and Article 3(2) of Directive 2001/29/EC for the online use of their press publications by information society service providers.

The rights provided for in the first subparagraph shall not apply to private or non-commercial uses of press publications by individual users.

The protection granted under the first subparagraph shall not apply to acts of hyperlinking.

The rights provided for in the first subparagraph shall not apply in respect of the use of individual words or very short extracts of a press publication.

2.　The rights provided for in paragraph 1 shall leave intact and shall in no way affect any rights provided for in Union law to authors and other rightholders, in respect of the works and other subject matter incorporated in a press publication. The rights provided for in paragraph 1 shall not be invoked against those authors and other rightholders and, in particular, shall not deprive them of their right to exploit their works and other subject matter independently from the press publication in which they are incorporated.

When a work or other subject matter is incorporated in a press publication on the basis of a non-exclusive licence, the rights provided for in paragraph 1 shall not be invoked to prohibit the use by other authorised users. The rights provided for in paragraph 1 shall not be invoked to prohibit the use of works or other subject matter for which protection has expired.

3.　Articles 5 to 8 of Directive 2001/29/EC, Directive 2012/28/EU and Directive (EU) 2017/1564 of the European Parliament of the Council shall apply mutatis mutandis in respect of the rights provided for in paragraph 1 of this Article.

4.　The rights provided for in paragraph 1 shall expire two years after the press publication is published. That term shall be calculated from 1 January of the year following the date on which that press publication is published.

Paragraph 1 shall not apply to press publications first published before 6 June 2019.

5.    Member States shall provide that authors of works incorporated in a press publication receive an appropriate share of the revenues that press publishers receive for the use of their press publications by information society service providers.

## Article 16

### Claims to fair compensation

Member States may provide that where an author has transferred or licensed a right to a publisher, such a transfer or licence constitutes a sufficient legal basis for the publisher to be entitled to a share of the compensation for the use of the work made under an exception or limitation to the transferred or licensed right.

The first paragraph shall be without prejudice to existing and future arrangements in Member States concerning public lending rights.

## CHAPTER 2
### *Certain uses of protected content by online services*

## Article 17

### Use of protected content by online content-sharing service providers

1.    Member States shall provide that an online content-sharing service provider performs an act of communication to the public or an act of making available to the public for the purposes of this Directive when it gives the public access to copyright-protected works or other protected subject matter uploaded by its users.

An online content-sharing service provider shall therefore obtain an authorisation from the rightholders referred to in Article 3(1) and (2) of Directive 2001/29/EC, for instance by concluding a licensing agreement, in order to communicate to the public or make available to the public works or other subject matter.

2.    Member States shall provide that, where an online content-sharing service provider obtains an authorisation, for instance by concluding a licensing agreement, that authorisation shall also cover acts carried out by users of the services falling within the scope of Article 3 of Directive 2001/29/EC when they are not acting on a commercial basis or where their activity does not generate significant revenues.

3.    When an online content-sharing service provider performs an act of communication to the public or an act of making available to the public under the conditions laid down in this Directive, the limitation of liability established in Article 14(1) of Directive 2000/31/EC shall not apply to the situations covered by this Article.

The first subparagraph of this paragraph shall not affect the possible application of Article 14(1) of Directive 2000/31/EC to those service providers for purposes falling outside the scope of this Directive.

4.    If no authorisation is granted, online content-sharing service providers shall be liable for unauthorised acts of communication to the public, including making available to the public, of copyright-protected works and other subject matter, unless the service providers demonstrate that they have:

(a)    made best efforts to obtain an authorisation, and

(b)    made, in accordance with high industry standards of professional diligence, best efforts to ensure the unavailability of specific works and other subject matter for which the rightholders have provided the service providers with the relevant and necessary information; and in any event (c)　acted expeditiously, upon receiving a sufficiently substantiated notice from the rightholders, to disable access to, or to remove from their websites, the notified works or other subject matter, and made best efforts to prevent their future uploads in accordance with point (b).

5.　In determining whether the service provider has complied with its obligations under paragraph 4, and in light of the principle of proportionality, the following elements, among others, shall be taken into account:

(a)　the type, the audience and the size of the service and the type of works or other subject matter uploaded by the users of the service; and

(b)　the availability of suitable and effective means and their cost for service providers.

6.　Member States shall provide that, in respect of new online content-sharing service providers the services of which have been available to the public in the Union for less than three years and which have an annual turnover below EUR 10 million, calculated in accordance with Commission Recommendation 2003/361/EC, the conditions under the liability regime set out in paragraph 4 are limited to compliance with point (a) of paragraph 4 and to acting expeditiously, upon receiving a sufficiently substantiated notice, to disable access to the notified works or other subject matter or to remove those works or other subject matter from their websites.

Where the average number of monthly unique visitors of such service providers exceeds 5 million, calculated on the basis of the previous calendar year, they shall also demonstrate that they have made best efforts to prevent further uploads of the notified works and other subject matter for which the rightholders have provided relevant and necessary information.

7.　The cooperation between online content-sharing service providers and rightholders shall not result in the prevention of the availability of works or other subject matter uploaded by users, which do not infringe copyright and related rights, including where such works or other subject matter are covered by an exception or limitation.

Member States shall ensure that users in each Member State are able to rely on any of the following existing exceptions or limitations when uploading and making available content generated by users on online content-sharing services:

(a)　quotation, criticism, review;

(b)　use for the purpose of caricature, parody or pastiche.

8.　The application of this Article shall not lead to any general monitoring obligation.

Member States shall provide that online content-sharing service providers provide rightholders, at their request, with adequate information on the functioning of their practices with regard to the cooperation referred to in paragraph 4 and, where licensing agreements are concluded between service providers and rightholders, information on the use of content covered by the agreements.

9.　Member States shall provide that online content-sharing service providers put in place an effective and expeditious complaint and redress mechanism that is available to users of their services in the event of disputes over the disabling of access to, or the removal of, works or other subject matter uploaded by them.

Where rightholders request to have access to their specific works or other subject matter disabled or to have those works or other subject matter removed, they shall duly justify the reasons for their requests. Complaints submitted under the mechanism provided for in the first subparagraph shall be processed without undue delay, and decisions to disable access to or remove uploaded content shall be subject to human review. Member States shall also ensure that out-of-court redress mechanisms are available for the settlement of disputes. Such mechanisms shall enable disputes to be settled impartially and shall not deprive the user of the legal protection afforded by national law, without prejudice to the rights of users to have recourse to efficient judicial remedies. In particular, Member States shall ensure that users have access to a court or another relevant judicial authority to assert the use of an exception or limitation to copyright and related rights.

This Directive shall in no way affect legitimate uses, such as uses under exceptions or limitations provided for in Union law, and shall not lead to any identification of individual users nor to the processing of personal data, except in accordance with Directive 2002/58/EC and Regulation (EU) 2016/679.

Online content-sharing service providers shall inform their users in their terms and conditions that they can use works and other subject matter under exceptions or limitations to copyright and related rights provided for in Union law.

10. As of 6 June 2019 the Commission, in cooperation with the Member States, shall organise stakeholder dialogues to discuss best practices for cooperation between online content-sharing service providers and rightholders. The Commission shall, in consultation with online content-sharing service providers, rightholders, users' organisations and other relevant stakeholders, and taking into account the results of the stakeholder dialogues, issue guidance on the application of this Article, in particular regarding the cooperation referred to in paragraph 4. When discussing best practices, special account shall be taken, among other things, of the need to balance fundamental rights and of the use of exceptions and limitations. For the purpose of the stakeholder dialogues, users' organisations shall have access to adequate information from online content-sharing service providers on the functioning of their practices with regard to paragraph 4.

## CHAPTER 3
### *Fair remuneration in exploitation contracts of authors and performers*

#### Article 18

### Principle of appropriate and proportionate remuneration

1. Member States shall ensure that where authors and performers license or transfer their exclusive rights for the exploitation of their works or other subject matter, they are entitled to receive appropriate and proportionate remuneration.

2. In the implementation in national law of the principle set out in paragraph 1, Member States shall be free to use different mechanisms and take into account the principle of contractual freedom and a fair balance of rights and interests.

#### Article 19

### Transparency obligation

1. Member States shall ensure that authors and performers receive on a regular basis, at least once a year, and taking into account the specificities of each sector, up to date, relevant and comprehensive information on the exploitation of their works and performances from the parties to whom they have licensed or transferred their rights, or their successors in title, in particular as regards modes of exploitation, all revenues generated and remuneration due.

2. Member States shall ensure that, where the rights referred to in paragraph 1 have subsequently been licensed, authors and performers or their representatives shall, at their request, receive from sub-licensees additional information, in the event that their first contractual counterpart does not hold all the information that would be necessary for the purposes of paragraph 1.

Where that additional information is requested, the first contractual counterpart of authors and performers shall provide information on the identity of those sub-licensees.

Member States may provide that any request to sub-licensees pursuant to the first subparagraph is made directly or indirectly through the contractual counterpart of the author or the performer.

3. The obligation set out in paragraph 1 shall be proportionate and effective in ensuring a high level of transparency in every sector. Member States may provide that in duly justified cases where the administrative burden resulting from the obligation set out in paragraph 1 would become

disproportionate in the light of the revenues generated by the exploitation of the work or performance, the obligation is limited to the types and level of information that can reasonably be expected in such cases.

4.     Member States may decide that the obligation set out in paragraph 1 of this Article does not apply when the contribution of the author or performer is not significant having regard to the overall work or performance, unless the author or performer demonstrates that he or she requires the information for the exercise of his or her rights under Article 20(1) and requests the information for that purpose.

5.     Member States may provide that, for agreements subject to or based on collective bargaining agreements, the transparency rules of the relevant collective bargaining agreement are applicable, on condition that those rules meet the criteria provided for in paragraphs 1 to 4.

6.     Where Article 18 of Directive 2014/26/EU is applicable, the obligation laid down in paragraph 1 of this Article shall not apply in respect of agreements concluded by entities defined in Article 3(a) and (b) of that Directive or by other entities subject to the national rules implementing that Directive.

*Article 20*

### Contract adjustment mechanism

1.     Member States shall ensure that, in the absence of an applicable collective bargaining agreement providing for a mechanism comparable to that set out in this Article, authors and performers or their representatives are entitled to claim additional, appropriate and fair remuneration from the party with whom they entered into a contract for the exploitation of their rights, or from the successors in title of such party, when the remuneration originally agreed turns out to be disproportionately low compared to all the subsequent relevant revenues derived from the exploitation of the works or performances.

2.     Paragraph 1 of this Article shall not apply to agreements concluded by entities defined in Article 3(a) and (b) of Directive 2014/26/EU or by other entities that are already subject to the national rules implementing that Directive.

*Article 21*

### Alternative dispute resolution procedure

Member States shall provide that disputes concerning the transparency obligation under Article 19 and the contract adjustment mechanism under Article 20 may be submitted to a voluntary, alternative dispute resolution procedure. Member States shall ensure that representative organisations of authors and performers may initiate such procedures at the specific request of one or more authors or performers.

*Article 22*

### Right of revocation

1.     Member States shall ensure that where an author or a performer has licensed or transferred his or her rights in a work or other protected subject matter on an exclusive basis, the author or performer may revoke in whole or in part the licence or the transfer of rights where there is a lack of exploitation of that work or other protected subject matter.

2.     Specific provisions for the revocation mechanism provided for in paragraph 1 may be provided for in national law, taking into account the following:

(a)     the specificities of the different sectors and the different types of works and performances; and

(b)     where a work or other subject matter contains the contribution of more than one author or performer, the relative importance of the individual contributions, and the legitimate interests of all authors and performers affected by the application of the revocation mechanism by an individual author or performer.

Member States may exclude works or other subject matter from the application of the revocation mechanism if such works or other subject matter usually contain contributions of a plurality of authors or performers.

Member States may provide that the revocation mechanism can only apply within a specific time frame, where such restriction is duly justified by the specificities of the sector or of the type of work or other subject matter concerned.

Member States may provide that authors or performers can choose to terminate the exclusivity of the contract instead of revoking the licence or transfer of the rights.

3.    Member States shall provide that the revocation provided for in paragraph 1 may only be exercised after a reasonable time following the conclusion of the licence or the transfer of the rights. The author or performer shall notify the person to whom the rights have been licensed or transferred and set an appropriate deadline by which the exploitation of the licensed or transferred rights is to take place. After the expiry of that deadline, the author or performer may choose to terminate the exclusivity of the contract instead of revoking the licence or the transfer of the rights.

4.    Paragraph 1 shall not apply if the lack of exploitation is predominantly due to circumstances that the author or the performer can reasonably be expected to remedy.

5.    Member States may provide that any contractual provision derogating from the revocation mechanism provided for in paragraph 1 is enforceable only if it is based on a collective bargaining agreement.

## *Article 23*

### Common provisions

1.    Member States shall ensure that any contractual provision that prevents compliance with Articles 19, 20 and 21 shall be unenforceable in relation to authors and performers.

2.    Members States shall provide that Articles 18 to 22 of this Directive do not apply to authors of a computer program within the meaning of Article 2 of Directive 2009/24/EC.

## TITLE V
## FINAL PROVISIONS

### *Article 24*

### Amendments to Directives 96/9/EC and 2001/29/EC

. . .

### *Article 25*

### Relationship with exceptions and limitations provided for in other directives

Member States may adopt or maintain in force broader provisions, compatible with the exceptions and limitations provided for in Directives 96/9/EC and 2001/29/EC, for uses or fields covered by the exceptions or limitations provided for in this Directive.

### *Article 26*

### Application in time

1.    This Directive shall apply in respect of all works and other subject matter that are protected by national law in the field of copyright on or after 7 June 2021.

2.    This Directive shall apply without prejudice to any acts concluded and rights acquired before 7 June 2021.

## Article 27

### Transitional provision

Agreements for the licence or transfer of rights of authors and performers shall be subject to the transparency obligation set out in Article 19 as from 7 June 2022.

## Article 28

### Protection of personal data

The processing of personal data carried out within the framework of this Directive shall be carried out in compliance with Directive 2002/58/EC and Regulation (EU) 2016/679.

## Article 29

### Transposition

1.    Member States shall bring into force the laws, regulations and administrative provisions necessary to comply with this Directive by 7 June 2021. They shall immediately inform the Commission thereof.

When Member States adopt those provisions, they shall contain a reference to this Directive or be accompanied by such a reference on the occasion of their official publication. The methods of making such reference shall be laid down by Member States.

2.    Member States shall communicate to the Commission the text of the main provisions of national law which they adopt in the field covered by this Directive.

## Article 30

### Review

1.    No sooner than 7 June 2026, the Commission shall carry out a review of this Directive and present a report on the main findings to the European Parliament, the Council and the European Economic and Social Committee.

The Commission shall, by 7 June 2024, assess the impact of the specific liability regime set out in Article 17 applicable to online content-sharing service providers that have an annual turnover of less than EUR 10 million and the services of which have been available to the public in the Union for less than three years under Article 17(6) and, if appropriate, take action in accordance with the conclusions of its assessment.

2.    Member States shall provide the Commission with the necessary information for the preparation of the report referred to in paragraph 1.

## Article 31

### Entry into force

This Directive shall enter into force on the twentieth day following that of its publication in the *Official Journal of the European Union*.

*Article 32*

**Addressees**

This Directive is addressed to the Member States.

Done at Strasbourg, 17 April 2019.

# 64. PORTABILITY REGULATION

### REGULATION (EU) 2017/1128 OF THE EUROPEAN PARLIAMENT AND OF THE COUNCIL
### of 14 June 2017
### on cross-border portability of online content services in the internal market

### (Text with EEA relevance)*

... Whereas: ...

(1) Seamless access throughout the Union to online content services that are lawfully provided to consumers in their Member State of residence is important for the smooth functioning of the internal market and for the effective application of the principles of free movement of persons and services. Since the internal market comprises an area without internal borders relying, inter alia, on the free movement of persons and services, it is necessary to ensure that consumers can use portable online content services which offer access to content such as music, games, films, entertainment programmes or sports events, not only in their Member State of residence but also when they are temporarily present in another Member State for purposes such as leisure, travel, business trips or learning mobility. Therefore, barriers that hamper access to and use of such online content services in such cases should be eliminated.

(2) The technological developments that have led to a proliferation of portable devices such as laptops, tablets and smartphones are increasingly facilitating the use of online content services by providing access to them regardless of the location of consumers. There is a rapidly growing demand on the part of consumers for access to content and innovative online services not only in their Member State of residence but also when they are temporarily present in another Member State.

(3) Consumers increasingly enter into contractual arrangements with service providers for the provision of online content services. However, consumers that are temporarily present in a Member State other than their Member State of residence often cannot continue to access and use the online content services that they have lawfully acquired the right to access and use in their Member State of residence.

(4) There are a number of barriers which hinder the provision of online content services to consumers temporarily present in a Member State other than their Member State of residence. Certain online services include content such as music, games, films or entertainment programmes which are protected by copyright or related rights under Union law. At present, the barriers to cross-border portability of online content services differ from one sector to another. The barriers stem from the fact that the rights for the transmission of content protected by copyright or related rights, such as audiovisual works, are often licensed on a territorial basis, as well as from the fact that providers of online content services might choose to serve specific markets only.

(5) The same applies to content, such as sports events, which is not protected by copyright or related rights under Union law but which could be protected by copyright or related rights under national law or by virtue of other specific national legislation and which is often also licensed by the organisers of such events or offered by providers of online content services on a territorial basis. Transmissions of such content by broadcasting organisations are protected by related rights which have been harmonised at Union level. Moreover, transmissions of such content often include copyright-protected elements such as music, opening or closing video sequences or graphics. Also, certain aspects of transmissions of such content, specifically those relating to broadcasting events of major importance for society as well as to short news reports on events of

---

* Footnotes and some recitals omitted.

high interest to the public, have been harmonised by Directive 2010/13/EU of the European Parliament and of the Council. Finally, audiovisual media services within the meaning of Directive 2010/13/EU include services which provide access to content such as sports events, news or current affairs.

(6) Increasingly, online content services are marketed in a package in which content which is not protected by copyright or related rights is not separable from content which is protected by copyright or related rights without substantially lessening the value of the service provided to consumers. This is especially the case with premium content such as sports events or other events of significant interest to consumers. In order to enable providers of online content services to provide to consumers full access to their online content services when consumers are temporarily present in a Member State other than their Member State of residence, it is indispensable that this Regulation also covers such content used by online content services and therefore that it applies to audiovisual media services within the meaning of Directive 2010/13/EU as well as to transmissions of broadcasting organisations in their entirety. . . .

(8) It is essential that providers of online content services that make use of works or other protected subject-matter, such as books, audiovisual works, recorded music or broadcasts have the right to use such content for the relevant territories.

(9) The transmission by providers of online content services of content that is protected by copyright or related rights requires the authorisation of the relevant rightholders, such as authors, performers, producers or broadcasting organisations, regarding the content included in the transmission. This is equally true when such transmission takes place for the purpose of allowing a consumer to carry out a download in order to use an online content service.

(10) The acquisition of a licence for relevant rights is not always possible, in particular when rights in content are licensed on an exclusive basis. In order to ensure that territorial exclusivity is effectively complied with, providers of online content services often undertake, in their licence contracts with rightholders, including broadcasting organisations or events organisers, to prevent their subscribers from accessing and using their services outside the territory for which the providers hold the licence. Such contractual restrictions imposed on providers require them to take measures such as disallowing access to their services from internet protocol (IP) addresses located outside the territory concerned. Therefore, one of the obstacles to the cross-border portability of online content services is to be found in the contracts concluded between the providers of online content services and their subscribers, which reflect the territorial restriction clauses included in contracts concluded between those providers and the rightholders.

(11) The case law of the Court of Justice of the European Union should be taken into account when balancing the objective of protecting intellectual property rights with the fundamental freedoms guaranteed by the Treaty on the Functioning of the European Union (TFEU).

(12) Therefore, the objective of this Regulation is to adapt the harmonised legal framework on copyright and related rights and to provide a common approach to the provision of online content services to subscribers temporarily present in a Member State other than their Member State of residence by removing barriers to cross-border portability of online content services which are lawfully provided. This Regulation should ensure cross-border portability of online content services in all sectors concerned and hence provide consumers with an additional means of accessing online content lawfully, without affecting the high level of protection guaranteed by copyright and related rights in the Union, without changing the existing licensing models, such as territorial licensing, and without affecting the existing financing mechanisms. The concept of cross-border portability of online content services should be distinguished from that of cross-border access by consumers to online content services provided in a Member State other than their Member State of residence, which is not covered by this Regulation. . . .

(14) This Regulation defines several concepts necessary for its application, including the Member State of residence. The Member State of residence should be determined taking into account the

objectives of this Regulation and the necessity to ensure its uniform application in the Union. The definition of the Member State of residence implies that the subscriber has his or her actual and stable residence in that Member State. A provider of an online content service who has verified the Member State of residence in accordance with this Regulation should be allowed to assume, for the purposes of this Regulation, that the Member State of residence as verified is the only Member State of residence of the subscriber. Providers should not be obliged to verify whether their subscribers are also subscribers to an online content service in another Member State.

(15) This Regulation should apply to online content services that providers, after having obtained the relevant rights from rightholders in a given territory, provide to their subscribers on the basis of a contract, by any means including streaming, downloading, through applications or any other technique which allows use of that content. For the purposes of this Regulation, the term contract should be regarded as covering any agreement between a provider and a subscriber, including any arrangement by which the subscriber accepts the provider's terms and conditions for the provision of online content services, whether against payment of money or without such payment. A registration to receive content alerts or a mere acceptance of HTML cookies should not be regarded as a contract for the provision of online content services for the purposes of this Regulation.

(16) An online service which is not an audiovisual media service within the meaning of Directive 2010/13/EU and which uses works, other protected subject-matter or transmissions of broadcasting organisations in a merely ancillary manner should not be covered by this Regulation. Such services include websites that use works or other protected subject-matter only in an ancillary manner such as graphical elements or music used as background, where the main purpose of such websites is, for example, the sale of goods.

(17) This Regulation should apply only to online content services which subscribers can effectively access and use in their Member State of residence without being limited to a specific location, as it is not appropriate to require providers of online content services that do not offer portable online content services in the Member State of residence of a subscriber to do so across borders.

(18) This Regulation should apply to online content services which are provided against payment of money. Providers of such services are in a position to verify the Member State of residence of their subscribers. The right to use an online content service should be regarded as acquired against payment of money, whether such payment is made directly to the provider of the online content service, or to another party such as a provider offering a package combining an electronic communications service and an online content service operated by another provider. For the purposes of this Regulation, the payment of a mandatory fee for public broadcasting services should not be regarded as a payment of money for an online content service.

(19) Providers of online content services should not subject their subscribers to any additional charges for the provision of cross-border portability of online content services in accordance with this Regulation. It is possible however that subscribers, in order to access and use online content services in Member States other than their Member State of residence, could be subject to fees payable to operators of electronic communications networks used to access such services.

(20) Providers of online content services which are provided without payment of money generally do not verify the Member State of residence of their subscribers. The inclusion of such online content services in the scope of this Regulation would involve a major change to the way those services are delivered and involve disproportionate costs. However, the exclusion of those services from the scope of this Regulation would mean that providers of those services would not be able to take advantage of the legal mechanism which is provided for in this Regulation and which enables providers of online content services to offer cross-border portability of such services, even when they decide to invest in means that allow them to verify their subscribers' Member State of residence. Accordingly, providers of online content services which are provided without payment of money should be able to opt to be included in the scope of this Regulation provided that they comply with the requirements on the verification of the Member State of residence of their

subscribers. If such providers exercise that option, they should comply with the same obligations as imposed under this Regulation upon the providers of online content services which are provided against payment of money. Furthermore, they should inform the subscribers, the relevant holders of copyright and related rights and the relevant holders of any other rights in the content of the online content service of their decision to exercise that option in a timely manner. Such information could be provided on the provider's website.

(21) In order to ensure the cross-border portability of online content services, it is necessary to require providers of online content services covered by this Regulation to enable subscribers to use such services in the Member State in which they are temporarily present in the same manner as in their Member State of residence. Subscribers should have access to online content services offering the same content on the same range and number of devices, for the same number of users and with the same range of functionalities as those offered in their Member State of residence. It is essential that the obligation to provide cross-border portability of online content services be mandatory and therefore the parties should not be able to exclude it, derogate from it or vary its effect. Any action by a provider which would prevent subscribers from accessing or using the service while temporarily present in a Member State other than their Member State of residence, for example restrictions to the functionalities of the service or to the quality of its delivery should be considered to be a circumvention of the obligation to provide cross-border portability of online content services and therefore contrary to this Regulation.

(22) Requiring that the delivery of online content services to subscribers temporarily present in a Member State other than their Member State of residence be of the same quality as in the Member State of residence could result in high costs for providers of online content services and thus ultimately for subscribers. Therefore, it is not appropriate for this Regulation to require that providers ensure a quality of delivery of such services that would be beyond the quality available via the local online access chosen by a subscriber while temporarily present in another Member State. In such cases the provider should not be liable if the quality of delivery of the service is lower. Nevertheless, if the provider expressly guarantees a certain quality of delivery to subscribers while temporarily present in another Member State, it should be bound by that guarantee. The provider, on the basis of the information in its possession, should provide its subscribers in advance with information concerning the quality of delivery of an online content service in Member States other than their Member State of residence, in particular the fact that the quality of delivery could differ from that applicable in their Member State of residence. The provider should not be under an obligation to actively seek information on the quality of delivery of a service in Member States other than the subscriber's Member State of residence. The relevant information could be provided on the provider's website.

(23) In order to ensure that providers of online content services covered by this Regulation comply with the obligation to provide cross-border portability of their services, without acquiring the relevant rights in another Member State, it is necessary to stipulate that those providers should always be entitled to provide such services to subscribers when they are temporarily present in a Member State other than their Member State of residence. This should be achieved by establishing that the provision of, access to and use of such online content services should be deemed to occur in the subscriber's Member State of residence. This legal mechanism should apply for the sole purpose of ensuring the cross-border portability of online content services. An online content service should be considered to be provided lawfully if both the service and the content are provided in a lawful manner in the Member State of residence. This Regulation, and in particular the legal mechanism by which the provision of, access to and use of an online content service are deemed to occur in the subscriber's Member State of residence, does not prevent a provider from enabling the subscriber to additionally access and use the content lawfully offered by the provider in the Member State where the subscriber is temporarily present.

(24) For the licensing of copyright or related rights, the legal mechanism laid down in this Regulation means that relevant acts of reproduction, communication to the public and making available of works and other protected subject-matter, as well as the acts of extraction or re-utilization in

relation to databases protected by sui generis rights, which occur when the service is provided to subscribers when they are temporarily present in a Member State other than their Member State of residence, should be deemed to occur in the subscribers' Member State of residence. Providers of online content services covered by this Regulation, therefore, should be deemed to carry out such acts on the basis of the respective authorisations from the rightholders concerned for the Member State of residence of their subscribers. Whenever providers have the right to carry out acts of communication to the public or reproduction in their subscribers' Member State of residence on the basis of an authorisation from the rightholders concerned, subscribers who are temporarily present in a Member State other than their Member State of residence should be able to access and use the service and where necessary carry out any relevant acts of reproduction, such as downloading, which they would be entitled to do in their Member State of residence. The provision of an online content service by providers to subscribers temporarily present in a Member State other than their Member State of residence and the access to and use of the service by such subscribers in accordance with this Regulation should not constitute a breach of copyright or related rights or any other rights relevant for the provision of, access to and use of the online content service.

(25) Providers of online content services covered by this Regulation should not be liable for the breach of any contractual provisions that are contrary to the obligation to enable their subscribers to use such services in the Member State in which they are temporarily present. Therefore, clauses in contracts designed to prohibit or limit the cross-border portability of such online content services should be unenforceable. The providers and holders of rights relevant for the provision of online content services should not be allowed to circumvent the application of this Regulation by choosing the law of a third country as the law applicable to contracts between them. The same should apply to contracts concluded between providers and subscribers.

(26) This Regulation should enable subscribers to enjoy online content services to which they have subscribed in their Member State of residence when they are temporarily present in another Member State. Subscribers should be eligible for cross-border portability of online content services only if they reside in a Member State of the Union. Therefore, this Regulation should oblige providers of online content services to make use of reasonable, proportionate and effective means in order to verify the Member State of residence of their subscribers. To that end, providers should use the means of verification listed in this Regulation. This does not preclude agreement between providers and rightholders on those means of verification within the limits of this Regulation. The objective of the list is to provide legal certainty as to the means of verification to be used by providers as well as to limit interference with subscribers' privacy. In each case, account should be taken of the effectiveness and proportionality of a particular means of verification in a given Member State and for a given type of online content service. Unless the subscriber's Member State of residence can be verified with sufficient certainty on the basis of a single means of verification, providers should rely on two means of verification. In cases where the provider has reasonable doubts concerning the subscriber's Member State of residence, the provider should be able to repeat the verification of the subscriber's Member State of residence. The provider should implement the necessary technical and organisational measures required under applicable data protection rules for the processing of personal data collected for the purpose of verification of the subscriber's Member State of residence under this Regulation. Examples of such measures include providing transparent information to the individuals about the methods used for, and the purpose of, the verification, and appropriate security measures.

(27) In order to verify the subscriber's Member State of residence, the provider of an online content service should rely, if possible, on information which is in the provider's possession, such as billing information. As regards contracts concluded prior to the date of application of this Regulation and as regards the verification carried out upon renewal of a contract, the provider should be allowed to request the subscriber to provide the information necessary to verify the subscriber's Member State of residence only when it cannot be determined on the basis of information which is already in the provider's possession.

(28) IP address checks performed under this Regulation should be conducted in accordance with Directives 95/46/EC and 2002/58/EC of the European Parliament and of the Council. In addition, for the purpose of verification of the subscriber's Member State of residence what matters is not the precise location of the subscriber, but rather the Member State in which the subscriber is accessing the service. Accordingly, data on the subscriber's precise location or any other personal data should neither be collected nor processed for that purpose. Where the provider has reasonable doubts concerning the subscriber's Member State of residence and carries out an IP address check to verify the Member State of residence, the sole purpose of such checks should be to establish whether the subscriber is accessing or using the online content service within or outside the Member State of residence. Therefore, in such cases, the data resulting from the checking of IP addresses should only be collected in binary format and in compliance with applicable data protection rules. The provider should not exceed that level of detail.

(29) A holder of copyright, related rights, or any other rights in the content of an online content service should remain able to exercise contractual freedom to authorise such content to be provided, accessed and used under this Regulation without verification of the Member State of residence. This can be particularly relevant in sectors such as music and e-books. Each rightholder should be able to take such decisions freely when entering into contracts with providers of online content services. Contracts between providers and rightholders should not restrict the possibility for rightholders to withdraw such authorisation subject to giving reasonable notice to the provider. The authorisation given by an individual rightholder does not as such release the provider from the obligation to verify the subscriber's Member State of residence. It is only in cases where all the holders of copyright, related rights or any other rights in the content used by the provider decide to authorise their content to be provided, accessed and used without verification of the subscriber's Member State of residence that the obligation to verify should not apply, and the contract between the provider and the subscriber for the provision of an online content service should be used to determine the latter's Member State of residence. All other aspects of this Regulation should remain applicable in such cases. . . .

(31) Contracts under which content is licensed are usually concluded for a relatively long duration. Consequently, and in order to ensure that all consumers residing in the Union can enjoy cross-border portability of online content services on an equal basis in time and without any undue delay, this Regulation should also apply to contracts concluded and rights acquired before the date of its application if those contracts and rights are relevant for the cross-border portability of an online content service provided after that date. Such application of this Regulation is also necessary in order to ensure a level playing field for providers of online content services covered by this Regulation operating in the internal market, particularly for SMEs, by enabling providers that concluded contracts with rightholders for a long duration to offer cross-border portability to their subscribers, independently of the provider's ability to renegotiate such contracts. Moreover, such application of this Regulation should ensure that when providers make arrangements necessary for the cross-border portability of their services, they will be able to offer such portability with regard to the entirety of their online content. This should also apply to providers of online content services that offer packages combining electronic communications services and online content services. Finally, such application of this Regulation should also allow rightholders not to have to renegotiate their existing licensing contracts in order to enable providers to offer cross-border portability of their services.

(32) Accordingly, since this Regulation will apply to some contracts concluded and rights acquired before the date of its application, it is also appropriate to provide for a reasonable period between the date of entry into force of this Regulation and the date of its application, so as to allow rightholders and providers of online content services covered by this Regulation to make the arrangements necessary to adapt to the new situation, as well as to allow providers to amend the terms of use of their services. Changes to the terms of use of online content services offered in packages combining an electronic communications service and an online content service that are made strictly in order to comply with the requirements of this Regulation should not trigger for

subscribers any right under national laws transposing the regulatory framework for electronic communications networks and services to withdraw from contracts for the provision of such electronic communications services.

(33) This Regulation is aimed at improving competitiveness by fostering innovation in online content services and attracting more consumers. This Regulation should not affect the application of the rules of competition, and in particular Articles 101 and 102 TFEU. The rules provided for in this Regulation should not be used to restrict competition in a manner contrary to the TFEU. . . .

## *Article 1*

### Subject matter and scope

1.    This Regulation introduces a common approach in the Union to the cross-border portability of online content services, by ensuring that subscribers to portable online content services which are lawfully provided in their Member State of residence can access and use those services when temporarily present in a Member State other than their Member State of residence.

2.    This Regulation shall not apply to the field of taxation.

## *Article 2*

### Definitions

For the purposes of this Regulation, the following definitions apply:

(1)   'subscriber' means any consumer who, on the basis of a contract for the provision of an online content service with a provider whether against payment of money or without such payment, is entitled to access and use such service in the Member State of residence;

(2)   'consumer' means any natural person who, in contracts covered by this Regulation, is acting for purposes which are outside that person's trade, business, craft or profession;

(3)   'Member State of residence' means the Member State, determined on the basis of Article 5, where the subscriber has his or her actual and stable residence;

(4)   'temporarily present in a Member State' means being present in a Member State other than the Member State of residence for a limited period of time;

(5)   'online content service' means a service as defined in Articles 56 and 57 TFEU that a provider lawfully provides to subscribers in their Member State of residence on agreed terms and online, which is portable and which is:

  (i)   an audiovisual media service as defined in point (a) of Article 1 of Directive 2010/13/EU, or

  (ii)  a service the main feature of which is the provision of access to, and the use of, works, other protected subject-matter or transmissions of broadcasting organisations, whether in a linear or an on-demand manner;

(6)   'portable' means a feature of an online content service whereby subscribers can effectively access and use the online content service in their Member State of residence without being limited to a specific location.

## *Article 3*

### Obligation to enable cross-border portability of online content services

1.    The provider of an online content service provided against payment of money shall enable a subscriber who is temporarily present in a Member State to access and use the online content service in the same manner as in the Member State of residence, including by providing access to the same content, on the same range and number of devices, for the same number of users and with the same range of functionalities.

2.    The provider shall not impose any additional charges on the subscriber for the access to and the use of the online content service pursuant to paragraph 1.

3.    The obligation set out in paragraph 1 shall not extend to any quality requirements applicable to the delivery of an online content service that the provider is subject to when providing that service in the Member State of residence, unless otherwise expressly agreed between the provider and the subscriber.

The provider shall not take any action to reduce the quality of delivery of the online content service when providing the online content service in accordance with paragraph 1.

4.    The provider shall, on the basis of the information in its possession, provide the subscriber with information concerning the quality of delivery of the online content service provided in accordance with paragraph 1. The information shall be provided to the subscriber prior to providing the online content service in accordance with paragraph 1 and by means which are adequate and proportionate.

## Article 4

### Localisation of the provision of, access to and use of online content services

The provision of an online content service under this Regulation to a subscriber who is temporarily present in a Member State, as well as the access to and the use of that service by the subscriber, shall be deemed to occur solely in the subscriber's Member State of residence.

## Article 5

### Verification of the Member State of residence

1.    At the conclusion and upon the renewal of a contract for the provision of an online content service provided against payment of money, the provider shall verify the Member State of residence of the subscriber by using not more than two of the following means of verification and shall ensure that the means used are reasonable, proportionate and effective:

(a)    an identity card, electronic means of identification, in particular those falling under the electronic identification schemes notified in accordance with Regulation (EU) No 910/2014 of the European Parliament and of the Council, or any other valid identity document confirming the subscriber's Member State of residence;

(b)    payment details such as the bank account or credit or debit card number of the subscriber;

(c)    the place of installation of a set top box, a decoder or a similar device used for supply of services to the subscriber;

(d)    the payment by the subscriber of a licence fee for other services provided in the Member State, such as public service broadcasting;

(e)    an internet or telephone service supply contract or any similar type of contract linking the subscriber to the Member State;

(f)    registration on local electoral rolls, if the information concerned is publicly available;

(g)    payment of local taxes, if the information concerned is publicly available;

(h)    a utility bill of the subscriber linking the subscriber to the Member State;

(i)    the billing address or the postal address of the subscriber;

(j)    a declaration by the subscriber confirming the subscriber's address in the Member State;

(k)    an internet protocol (IP) address check, to identify the Member State where the subscriber accesses the online content service.

The means of verification under points (i) to (k) shall only be used in combination with one of the means of verification under points (a) to (h), unless the postal address under point (i) is included in a publicly available official register.

2.　If the provider has reasonable doubts about the subscriber's Member State of residence in the course of the duration of the contract for the provision of an online content service, the provider may repeat the verification of the Member State of residence of the subscriber, in accordance with paragraph 1. In such a case, however, the means of verification under point (k) may be used as a sole means. Data resulting from the use of the means of verification under point (k) shall be collected in binary format only.

3.　The provider shall be entitled to request the subscriber to provide the information necessary to determine the subscriber's Member State of residence in accordance with paragraphs 1 and 2. If the subscriber fails to provide that information, and as a result the provider is unable to verify the subscriber's Member State of residence, the provider shall not, on the basis of this Regulation, enable the subscriber to access or use the online content service when the subscriber is temporarily present in a Member State.

4.　The holders of copyright or related rights or those holding any other rights in the content of an online content service may authorise the provision of, access to and use of their content under this Regulation without verification of the Member State of residence. In such cases, the contract between the provider and the subscriber for the provision of an online content service shall be sufficient to determine the subscriber's Member State of residence.

The holders of copyright or related rights or those holding any other rights in the content of an online content service shall be entitled to withdraw the authorisation given pursuant to the first subparagraph subject to giving reasonable notice to the provider.

5.　The contract between the provider and the holders of copyright or related rights or those holding any other rights in the content of an online content service shall not restrict the possibility for such holders of rights to withdraw the authorisation referred to in paragraph 4.

## *Article 6*

### Cross-border portability of online content services provided without payment of money

1.　The provider of an online content service provided without payment of money may decide to enable its subscribers who are temporarily present in a Member State to access and use the online content service on condition that the provider verifies the subscriber's Member State of residence in accordance with this Regulation.

2.　The provider shall inform its subscribers, the relevant holders of copyright and related rights and the relevant holders of any other rights in the content of the online content service of its decision to provide the online content service in accordance with paragraph 1, prior to providing that service. The information shall be provided by means which are adequate and proportionate.

3.　This Regulation shall apply to providers that provide an online content service in accordance with paragraph 1.

## *Article 7*

### Contractual provisions

1.　Any contractual provisions, including those between providers of online content services and holders of copyright or related rights or those holding any other rights in the content of online content services, as well as those between such providers and their subscribers, which are contrary to this Regulation, including those which prohibit cross-border portability of online content services or limit such portability to a specific time period, shall be unenforceable.

2.    This Regulation shall apply irrespective of the law applicable to contracts concluded between providers of online content services and holders of copyright or related rights or those holding any other rights in the content of online content services, or to contracts concluded between such providers and their subscribers.

## Article 8

### Protection of personal data

1.    The processing of personal data carried out within the framework of this Regulation including, in particular, for the purposes of verification of the subscriber's Member State of residence under Article 5, shall be carried out in compliance with Directives 95/46/EC and 2002/58/EC. In particular, the use of the means of verification in accordance with Article 5 and any processing of personal data under this Regulation, shall be limited to what is necessary and proportionate in order to achieve its purpose.

2.    Data collected pursuant to Article 5 shall be used solely for the purpose of verifying the subscriber's Member State of residence. They shall not be communicated, transferred, shared, licensed or otherwise transmitted or disclosed to holders of copyright or related rights or to those holding any other rights in the content of online content services, or to any other third parties.

3.    Data collected pursuant to Article 5 shall not be stored by the provider of an online content service longer than necessary to complete a verification of a subscriber's Member State of residence pursuant to Article 5(1) or (2). On completion of each verification, the data shall be immediately and irreversibly destroyed.

## Article 9

### Application to existing contracts and rights acquired

1.    This Regulation shall apply also to contracts concluded and rights acquired before the date of its application if they are relevant for the provision of, access to and use of an online content service, in accordance with Articles 3 and 6, after that date.

2.    By 21 May 2018, the provider of an online content service provided against payment of money shall verify, in accordance with this Regulation, the Member State of residence of those subscribers who concluded contracts for the provision of the online content service before that date.

Within two months of the date upon which the provider of an online content service provided without payment of money first provides the service in accordance with Article 6, the provider shall verify, in accordance with this Regulation, the Member State of residence of those subscribers who concluded contracts for the provision of the online content service before that date.

## Article 10

### Review

By 21 March 2021, and as required thereafter, the Commission shall assess the application of this Regulation in the light of legal, technological and economic developments, and submit to the European Parliament and to the Council a report thereon.

The report referred to in the first paragraph shall include, inter alia, an assessment of the application of the verification means of the Member State of residence referred to in Article 5, taking into account newly developed technologies, industry standards and practices, and, if necessary, consider the need for a review. The report shall pay special attention to the impact of this Regulation on SMEs and the protection of personal data. The Commission's report shall be accompanied, if appropriate, by a legislative proposal.

## *Article 11*

### Final provisions

1.    This Regulation shall enter into force on the twentieth day following that of its publication in the Official Journal of the European Union.

2.    It shall apply from 20 March 2018.

This Regulation shall be binding in its entirety and directly applicable in all Member States.

Done at Strasbourg, 14 June 2017.

# 65.  ENFORCEMENT DIRECTIVE

**DIRECTIVE 2004/48/EC OF THE EUROPEAN PARLIAMENT
AND OF THE COUNCIL
of 29 April 2004
on the enforcement of intellectual property rights**

**(Text with EEA relevance)***

. . . Whereas: . . .

(2)   The protection of intellectual property should allow the inventor or creator to derive a legitimate profit from his/her invention or creation. It should also allow the widest possible dissemination of works, ideas and new know-how. At the same time, it should not hamper freedom of expression, the free movement of information, or the protection of personal data, including on the Internet.

(3)   However, without effective means of enforcing intellectual property rights, innovation and creativity are discouraged and investment diminished. It is therefore necessary to ensure that the substantive law on intellectual property, which is nowadays largely part of the *acquis communautaire*, is applied effectively in the Community. In this respect, the means of enforcing intellectual property rights are of paramount importance for the success of the internal market. . . .

(7)   It emerges from the consultations held by the Commission on this question that, in the Member States, and despite the TRIPS Agreement, there are still major disparities as regards the means of enforcing intellectual property rights. For instance, the arrangements for applying provisional measures, which are used in particular to preserve evidence, the calculation of damages, or the arrangements for applying injunctions, vary widely from one Member State to another. In some Member States, there are no measures, procedures and remedies such as the right of information and the recall, at the infringer's expense, of the infringing goods placed on the market.

(8)   The disparities between the systems of the Member States as regards the means of enforcing intellectual property rights are prejudicial to the proper functioning of the Internal Market and make it impossible to ensure that intellectual property rights enjoy an equivalent level of protection throughout the Community. This situation does not promote free movement within the internal market or create an environment conducive to healthy competition. . . .

(13)  It is necessary to define the scope of this Directive as widely as possible in order to encompass all the intellectual property rights covered by Community provisions in this field and/or by the national law of the Member State concerned. Nevertheless, that requirement does not affect the possibility, on the part of those Member States which so wish, to extend, for internal purposes, the provisions of this Directive to include acts involving unfair competition, including parasitic copies, or similar activities.

(14)  The measures provided for in Articles 6(2), 8(1) and 9(2) need to be applied only in respect of acts carried out on a commercial scale. This is without prejudice to the possibility for Member States to apply those measures also in respect of other acts. Acts carried out on a commercial scale are those carried out for direct or indirect economic or commercial advantage; this would normally exclude acts carried out by end consumers acting in good faith. . . .

(17)  The measures, procedures and remedies provided for in this Directive should be determined in each case in such a manner as to take due account of the specific characteristics of that case, including the specific features of each intellectual property right and, where appropriate, the intentional or unintentional character of the infringement.

(18)  The persons entitled to request application of those measures, procedures and remedies should be not only the rightholders but also persons who have a direct interest and legal standing in so far as permitted by and in accordance with the applicable law, which may include professional organisations

---

\*   Footnotes and some recitals omitted.

in charge of the management of those rights or for the defence of the collective and individual interests for which they are responsible.

(19) Since copyright exists from the creation of a work and does not require formal registration, it is appropriate to adopt the rule laid down in Article 15 of the Berne Convention, which establishes the presumption whereby the author of a literary or artistic work is regarded as such if his/her name appears on the work. A similar presumption should be applied to the owners of related rights since it is often the holder of a related right, such as a phonogram producer, who will seek to defend rights and engage in fighting acts of piracy. . . .

(26) With a view to compensating for the prejudice suffered as a result of an infringement committed by an infringer who engaged in an activity in the knowledge, or with reasonable grounds for knowing, that it would give rise to such an infringement, the amount of damages awarded to the rightholder should take account of all appropriate aspects, such as loss of earnings incurred by the rightholder, or unfair profits made by the infringer and, where appropriate, any moral prejudice caused to the rightholder. As an alternative, for example where it would be difficult to determine the amount of the actual prejudice suffered, the amount of the damages might be derived from elements such as the royalties or fees which would have been due if the infringer had requested authorisation to use the intellectual property right in question. The aim is not to introduce an obligation to provide for punitive damages but to allow for compensation based on an objective criterion while taking account of the expenses incurred by the rightholder, such as the costs of identification and research. . . .

(29) Industry should take an active part in the fight against piracy and counterfeiting. The development of codes of conduct in the circles directly affected is a supplementary means of bolstering the regulatory framework. The Member States, in collaboration with the Commission, should encourage the development of codes of conduct in general. Monitoring of the manufacture of optical discs, particularly by means of an identification code embedded in discs produced in the Community, helps to limit infringements of intellectual property rights in this sector, which suffers from piracy on a large scale. However, these technical protection measures should not be misused to protect markets and prevent parallel imports. . . .

## CHAPTER I
## OBJECTIVE AND SCOPE

### *Article 1*

### Subject matter

This Directive concerns the measures, procedures and remedies necessary to ensure the enforcement of intellectual property rights. For the purposes of this Directive, the term "intellectual property rights" includes industrial property rights.

### *Article 2*

### Scope

1.    Without prejudice to the means which are or may be provided for in Community or national legislation, in so far as those means may be more favourable for rightholders, the measures, procedures and remedies provided for by this Directive shall apply, in accordance with Article 3, to any infringement of intellectual property rights as provided for by Community law and/or by the national law of the Member State concerned.

2.    This Directive shall be without prejudice to the specific provisions on the enforcement of rights and on exceptions contained in Community legislation concerning copyright and rights related to copyright, notably those found in Directive 91/250/EEC and, in particular, Article 7 thereof or in Directive 2001/29/EC and, in particular, Articles 2 to 6 and Article 8 thereof.

3.   This Directive shall not affect:

(a)   the Community provisions governing the substantive law on intellectual property, Directive 95/46/EC, Directive 1999/93/EC or Directive 2000/31/EC, in general, and Articles 12 to 15 of Directive 2000/31/EC in particular;

(b)   Member States' international obligations and notably the TRIPS Agreement, including those relating to criminal procedures and penalties;

(c)   any national provisions in Member States relating to criminal procedures or penalties in respect of infringement of intellectual property rights.

CHAPTER II
## MEASURES, PROCEDURES AND REMEDIES

Section 1

### *General provisions*

*Article 3*

### General obligation

1.   Member States shall provide for the measures, procedures and remedies necessary to ensure the enforcement of the intellectual property rights covered by this Directive. Those measures, procedures and remedies shall be fair and equitable and shall not be unnecessarily complicated or costly, or entail unreasonable time-limits or unwarranted delays.

2.   Those measures, procedures and remedies shall also be effective, proportionate and dissuasive and shall be applied in such a manner as to avoid the creation of barriers to legitimate trade and to provide for safeguards against their abuse.

*Article 4*

### Persons entitled to apply for the application of the measures, procedures and remedies

Member States shall recognise as persons entitled to seek application of the measures, procedures and remedies referred to in this chapter:

(a)   the holders of intellectual property rights, in accordance with the provisions of the applicable law;

(b)   all other persons authorised to use those rights, in particular licensees, in so far as permitted by and in accordance with the provisions of the applicable law;

(c)   intellectual property collective rights-management bodies which are regularly recognised as having a right to represent holders of intellectual property rights, in so far as permitted by and in accordance with the provisions of the applicable law;

(d)   professional defence bodies which are regularly recognised as having a right to represent holders of intellectual property rights, in so far as permitted by and in accordance with the provisions of the applicable law.

*Article 5*

### Presumption of authorship or ownership

For the purposes of applying the measures, procedures and remedies provided for in this Directive,

637

(a)   for the author of a literary or artistic work, in the absence of proof to the contrary, to be regarded as such, and consequently to be entitled to institute infringement proceedings, it shall be sufficient for his/her name to appear on the work in the usual manner;

(b)   the provision under (a) shall apply *mutatis mutandis* to the holders of rights related to copyright with regard to their protected subject matter.

Section 2

*Evidence*

*Article 6*

**Evidence**

1.    Member States shall ensure that, on application by a party which has presented reasonably available evidence sufficient to support its claims, and has, in substantiating those claims, specified evidence which lies in the control of the opposing party, the competent judicial authorities may order that such evidence be presented by the opposing party, subject to the protection of confidential information. For the purposes of this paragraph, Member States may provide that a reasonable sample of a substantial number of copies of a work or any other protected object be considered by the competent judicial authorities to constitute reasonable evidence.

2.    Under the same conditions, in the case of an infringement committed on a commercial scale Member States shall take such measures as are necessary to enable the competent judicial authorities to order, where appropriate, on application by a party, the communication of banking, financial or commercial documents under the control of the opposing party, subject to the protection of confidential information.

*Article 7*

**Measures for preserving evidence**

1.    Member States shall ensure that, even before the commencement of proceedings on the merits of the case, the competent judicial authorities may, on application by a party who has presented reasonably available evidence to support his/her claims that his/her intellectual property right has been infringed or is about to be infringed, order prompt and effective provisional measures to preserve relevant evidence in respect of the alleged infringement, subject to the protection of confidential information. Such measures may include the detailed description, with or without the taking of samples, or the physical seizure of the infringing goods, and, in appropriate cases, the materials and implements used in the production and/or distribution of these goods and the documents relating thereto. Those measures shall be taken, if necessary without the other party having been heard, in particular where any delay is likely to cause irreparable harm to the rightholder or where there is a demonstrable risk of evidence being destroyed.

Where measures to preserve evidence are adopted without the other party having been heard, the parties affected shall be given notice, without delay after the execution of the measures at the latest. A review, including a right to be heard, shall take place upon request of the parties affected with a view to deciding, within a reasonable period after the notification of the measures, whether the measures shall be modified, revoked or confirmed.

2.    Member States shall ensure that the measures to preserve evidence may be subject to the lodging by the applicant of adequate security or an equivalent assurance intended to ensure compensation for any prejudice suffered by the defendant as provided for in paragraph 4.

3.    Member States shall ensure that the measures to preserve evidence are revoked or otherwise cease to have effect, upon request of the defendant, without prejudice to the damages which may be claimed, if the applicant does not institute, within a reasonable period, proceedings leading to a decision on the merits of the case before the competent judicial authority, the period to be determined

by the judicial authority ordering the measures where the law of a Member State so permits or, in the absence of such determination, within a period not exceeding 20 working days or 31 calendar days, whichever is the longer.

4.    Where the measures to preserve evidence are revoked, or where they lapse due to any act or omission by the applicant, or where it is subsequently found that there has been no infringement or threat of infringement of an intellectual property right, the judicial authorities shall have the authority to order the applicant, upon request of the defendant, to provide the defendant appropriate compensation for any injury caused by those measures.

5.    Member States may take measures to protect witnesses' identity.

Section 3

*Right of information*

*Article 8*

**Right of information**

1.    Member States shall ensure that, in the context of proceedings concerning an infringement of an intellectual property right and in response to a justified and proportionate request of the claimant, the competent judicial authorities may order that information on the origin and distribution networks of the goods or services which infringe an intellectual property right be provided by the infringer and/or any other person who:

(a)    was found in possession of the infringing goods on a commercial scale;

(b)    was found to be using the infringing services on a commercial scale;

(c)    was found to be providing on a commercial scale services used in infringing activities; or

(d)    was indicated by the person referred to in point (a), (b) or (c) as being involved in the production, manufacture or distribution of the goods or the provision of the services.

2.    The information referred to in paragraph 1 shall, as appropriate, comprise:

(a)    the names and addresses of the producers, manufacturers, distributors, suppliers and other previous holders of the goods or services, as well as the intended wholesalers and retailers;

(b)    information on the quantities produced, manufactured, delivered, received or ordered, as well as the price obtained for the goods or services in question.

3.    Paragraphs 1 and 2 shall apply without prejudice to other statutory provisions which:

(a)    grant the rightholder rights to receive fuller information;

(b)    govern the use in civil or criminal proceedings of the information communicated pursuant to this Article;

(c)    govern responsibility for misuse of the right of information; or

(d)    afford an opportunity for refusing to provide information which would force the person referred to in paragraph 1 to admit to his/her own participation or that of his/her close relatives in an infringement of an intellectual property right; or

(e)    govern the protection of confidentiality of information sources or the processing of personal data.

Section 4

*Provisional and precautionary measures*

*Article 9*

**Provisional and precautionary measures**

1.    Member States shall ensure that the judicial authorities may, at the request of the applicant:

(a)   issue against the alleged infringer an interlocutory injunction intended to prevent any imminent infringement of an intellectual property right, or to forbid, on a provisional basis and subject, where appropriate, to a recurring penalty payment where provided for by national law, the continuation of the alleged infringements of that right, or to make such continuation subject to the lodging of guarantees intended to ensure the compensation of the rightholder; an interlocutory injunction may also be issued, under the same conditions, against an intermediary whose services are being used by a third party to infringe an intellectual property right; injunctions against intermediaries whose services are used by a third party to infringe a copyright or a related right are covered by Directive 2001/29/EC;

(b)   order the seizure or delivery up of the goods suspected of infringing an intellectual property right so as to prevent their entry into or movement within the channels of commerce.

2.    In the case of an infringement committed on a commercial scale, the Member States shall ensure that, if the injured party demonstrates circumstances likely to endanger the recovery of damages, the judicial authorities may order the precautionary seizure of the movable and immovable property of the alleged infringer, including the blocking of his/her bank accounts and other assets. To that end, the competent authorities may order the communication of bank, financial or commercial documents, or appropriate access to the relevant information.

3.    The judicial authorities shall, in respect of the measures referred to in paragraphs 1 and 2, have the authority to require the applicant to provide any reasonably available evidence in order to satisfy themselves with a sufficient degree of certainty that the applicant is the rightholder and that the applicant's right is being infringed, or that such infringement is imminent.

4.    Member States shall ensure that the provisional measures referred to in paragraphs 1 and 2 may, in appropriate cases, be taken without the defendant having been heard, in particular where any delay would cause irreparable harm to the rightholder. In that event, the parties shall be so informed without delay after the execution of the measures at the latest. A review, including a right to be heard, shall take place upon request of the defendant with a view to deciding, within a reasonable time after notification of the measures, whether those measures shall be modified, revoked or confirmed.

5.    Member States shall ensure that the provisional measures referred to in paragraphs 1 and 2 are revoked or otherwise cease to have effect, upon request of the defendant, if the applicant does not institute, within a reasonable period, proceedings leading to a decision on the merits of the case before the competent judicial authority, the period to be determined by the judicial authority ordering the measures where the law of a Member State so permits or, in the absence of such determination, within a period not exceeding 20 working days or 31 calendar days, whichever is the longer.

6.    The competent judicial authorities may make the provisional measures referred to in paragraphs 1 and 2 subject to the lodging by the applicant of adequate security or an equivalent assurance intended to ensure compensation for any prejudice suffered by the defendant as provided for in paragraph 7.

7.    Where the provisional measures are revoked or where they lapse due to any act or omission by the applicant, or where it is subsequently found that there has been no infringement or threat of infringement of an intellectual property right, the judicial authorities shall have the authority to order the applicant, upon request of the defendant, to provide the defendant appropriate compensation for any injury caused by those measures.

640

Section 5

*Measures resulting from a decision on the merits of the case*

*Article 10*

**Corrective measures**

1.    Without prejudice to any damages due to the rightholder by reason of the infringement, and without compensation of any sort, Member States shall ensure that the competent judicial authorities may order, at the request of the applicant, that appropriate measures be taken with regard to goods that they have found to be infringing an intellectual property right and, in appropriate cases, with regard to materials and implements principally used in the creation or manufacture of those goods. Such measures shall include:

(a)    recall from the channels of commerce;

(b)    definitive removal from the channels of commerce; or

(c)    destruction.

2.    The judicial authorities shall order that those measures be carried out at the expense of the infringer, unless particular reasons are invoked for not doing so.

3.    In considering a request for corrective measures, the need for proportionality between the seriousness of the infringement and the remedies ordered as well as the interests of third parties shall be taken into account.

*Article 11*

**Injunctions**

Member States shall ensure that, where a judicial decision is taken finding an infringement of an intellectual property right, the judicial authorities may issue against the infringer an injunction aimed at prohibiting the continuation of the infringement. Where provided for by national law, non-compliance with an injunction shall, where appropriate, be subject to a recurring penalty payment, with a view to ensuring compliance. Member States shall also ensure that rightholders are in a position to apply for an injunction against intermediaries whose services are used by a third party to infringe an intellectual property right, without prejudice to Article 8(3) of Directive 2001/29/EC.

*Article 12*

**Alternative measures**

Member States may provide that, in appropriate cases and at the request of the person liable to be subject to the measures provided for in this section, the competent judicial authorities may order pecuniary compensation to be paid to the injured party instead of applying the measures provided for in this section if that person acted unintentionally and without negligence, if execution of the measures in question would cause him/her disproportionate harm and if pecuniary compensation to the injured party appears reasonably satisfactory.

Section 6

*Damages and legal costs*

*Article 13*

**Damages**

1.    Member States shall ensure that the competent judicial authorities, on application of the injured party, order the infringer who knowingly, or with reasonable grounds to know, engaged in an

infringing activity, to pay the rightholder damages appropriate to the actual prejudice suffered by him/her as a result of the infringement.

When the judicial authorities set the damages:

(a)   they shall take into account all appropriate aspects, such as the negative economic consequences, including lost profits, which the injured party has suffered, any unfair profits made by the infringer and, in appropriate cases, elements other than economic factors, such as the moral prejudice caused to the rightholder by the infringement; or

(b)   as an alternative to (a), they may, in appropriate cases, set the damages as a lump sum on the basis of elements such as at least the amount of royalties or fees which would have been due if the infringer had requested authorisation to use the intellectual property right in question.

2.   Where the infringer did not knowingly, or with reasonable grounds know, engage in infringing activity, Member States may lay down that the judicial authorities may order the recovery of profits or the payment of damages, which may be pre-established.

*Article 14*

### Legal costs

Member States shall ensure that reasonable and proportionate legal costs and other expenses incurred by the successful party shall, as a general rule, be borne by the unsuccessful party, unless equity does not allow this.

Section 7

### *Publicity measures*

*Article 15*

### Publication of judicial decisions

Member States shall ensure that, in legal proceedings instituted for infringement of an intellectual property right, the judicial authorities may order, at the request of the applicant and at the expense of the infringer, appropriate measures for the dissemination of the information concerning the decision, including displaying the decision and publishing it in full or in part. Member States may provide for other additional publicity measures which are appropriate to the particular circumstances, including prominent advertising.

## CHAPTER III
## SANCTIONS BY MEMBER STATES

*Article 16*

### Sanctions by Member States

Without prejudice to the civil and administrative measures, procedures and remedies laid down by this Directive, Member States may apply other appropriate sanctions in cases where intellectual property rights have been infringed.

CHAPTER IV
## CODES OF CONDUCT AND ADMINISTRATIVE COOPERATION

*Article 17*

### Codes of conduct

Member States shall encourage:

(a)   the development by trade or professional associations or organisations of codes of conduct at Community level aimed at contributing towards the enforcement of the intellectual property rights, particularly by recommending the use on optical discs of a code enabling the identification of the origin of their manufacture;

(b)   the submission to the Commission of draft codes of conduct at national and Community level and of any evaluations of the application of these codes of conduct.

*Article 18*

### Assessment

1.   Three years after the date laid down in Article 20(1), each Member State shall submit to the Commission a report on the implementation of this Directive.

On the basis of those reports, the Commission shall draw up a report on the application of this Directive, including an assessment of the effectiveness of the measures taken, as well as an evaluation of its impact on innovation and the development of the information society. That report shall then be transmitted to the European Parliament, the Council and the European Economic and Social Committee. It shall be accompanied, if necessary and in the light of developments in the Community legal order, by proposals for amendments to this Directive.

2.   Member States shall provide the Commission with all the aid and assistance it may need when drawing up the report referred to in the second subparagraph of paragraph 1.

*Article 19*

### Exchange of information and correspondents

For the purpose of promoting cooperation, including the exchange of information, among Member States and between Member States and the Commission, each Member State shall designate one or more national correspondents for any question relating to the implementation of the measures provided for by this Directive. It shall communicate the details of the national correspondent(s) to the other Member States and to the Commission.

CHAPTER V
## FINAL PROVISIONS

*Article 20*

### Implementation

1.   Member States shall bring into force the laws, regulations and administrative provisions necessary to comply with this Directive by **29 April 2006**. They shall forthwith inform the Commission thereof.

When Member States adopt these measures, they shall contain a reference to this Directive or shall be accompanied by such reference on the occasion of their official publication. The methods of making such reference shall be laid down by Member States.

2.   Member States shall communicate to the Commission the texts of the provisions of national law which they adopt in the field governed by this Directive.

*Article 21*

**Entry into force**

This Directive shall enter into force on the 20th day following that of its publication in the *Official Journal of the European Union*.

*Article 22*

**Addressees**

This Directive is addressed to the Member States.

Done at Brussels, 29 April 2004.

# 66. REGULATION ON THE EU TRADEMARK

**REGULATION (EU) 2017/1001 OF THE EUROPEAN PARLIAMENT
AND OF THE COUNCIL
of 14 June 2017
on the European Union trade mark**

**(codification)**

**(Text with EEA relevance)\***

Whereas:

(1) Council Regulation (EC) No 207/2009 has been substantially amended several times. In the interests of clarity and rationality, that Regulation should be codified.

(2) Council Regulation (EC) No 40/94, which was codified in 2009 as Regulation (EC) No 207/2009, created a system of trade mark protection specific to the Union which provided for the protection of trade marks at the level of the Union, in parallel to the protection of trade marks available at the level of the Member States in accordance with the national trade mark systems, harmonised by Council Directive 89/104/EEC, which was codified as Directive 2008/95/EC of the European Parliament and of the Council.

(3) It is desirable to promote throughout the Union a harmonious development of economic activities and a continuous and balanced expansion by completing an internal market which functions properly and offers conditions which are similar to those obtaining in a national market. In order to establish a market of this kind and make it increasingly a single market, not only should barriers to free movement of goods and services be removed and arrangements be instituted which ensure that competition is not distorted, but, in addition, legal conditions should be laid down which enable undertakings to adapt their activities to the scale of the Union, whether in manufacturing and distributing goods or in providing services. For those purposes, trade marks enabling the products and services of undertakings to be distinguished by identical means throughout the entire Union, regardless of frontiers, should feature amongst the legal instruments which undertakings have at their disposal.

(4) For the purpose of pursuing the Union's said objectives it would appear necessary to provide for Union arrangements for trade marks whereby undertakings can by means of one procedural system obtain EU trade marks to which uniform protection is given and which produce their effects throughout the entire area of the Union. The principle of the unitary character of the EU trade mark thus stated should apply unless otherwise provided for in this Regulation.

(5) The barrier of territoriality of the rights conferred on proprietors of trade marks by the laws of the Member States cannot be removed by approximation of laws. In order to open up unrestricted economic activity in the whole of the internal market for the benefit of undertakings, it should be possible to register trade marks which are governed by a uniform Union law directly applicable in all Member States. . . .

(7) The Union law relating to trade marks nevertheless does not replace the laws of the Member States on trade marks. It would not in fact appear to be justified to require undertakings to apply for registration of their trade marks as EU trade marks. . . .

---

\*   Footnotes, some recitals, and annexes omitted.

## CHAPTER I
## GENERAL PROVISIONS

### Article 1

### EU trade mark

1.    A trade mark for goods or services which is registered in accordance with the conditions contained in this Regulation and in the manner herein provided is hereinafter referred to as a 'European Union trade mark ("EU trade mark")'.

2.    An EU trade mark shall have a unitary character. It shall have equal effect throughout the Union: it shall not be registered, transferred or surrendered or be the subject of a decision revoking the rights of the proprietor or declaring it invalid, nor shall its use be prohibited, save in respect of the whole Union. This principle shall apply unless otherwise provided for in this Regulation.

### Article 2

### Office

1.    A European Union Intellectual Property Office ('the Office') is established.

2.    All references in Union law to the Office for Harmonization in the Internal Market (Trade Marks and Designs) shall be read as references to the Office.

### Article 3

### Capacity to act

For the purpose of implementing this Regulation, companies or firms and other legal bodies shall be regarded as legal persons if, under the terms of the law governing them, they have the capacity in their own name to have rights and obligations of all kinds, to make contracts or accomplish other legal acts, and to sue and be sued.

## CHAPTER II
## THE LAW RELATING TO TRADE MARKS

### SECTION 1

### Definition of an EU trade mark and obtaining an EU trade mark

### Article 4

### Signs of which an EU trade mark may consist

An EU trade mark may consist of any signs, in particular words, including personal names, or designs, letters, numerals, colours, the shape of goods or of the packaging of goods, or sounds, provided that such signs are capable of:

(a)    distinguishing the goods or services of one undertaking from those of other undertakings; and

(b)    being represented on the Register of European Union trade marks ('the Register'), in a manner which enables the competent authorities and the public to determine the clear and precise subject matter of the protection afforded to its proprietor.

*Article 5*

### Persons who can be proprietors of EU trade marks

Any natural or legal person, including authorities established under public law, may be the proprietor of an EU trade mark.

*Article 6*

### Means whereby an EU trade mark is obtained

An EU trade mark shall be obtained by registration.

*Article 7*

### Absolute grounds for refusal

1.  The following shall not be registered:

(a)  signs which do not conform to the requirements of Article 4;

(b)  trade marks which are devoid of any distinctive character;

(c)  trade marks which consist exclusively of signs or indications which may serve, in trade, to designate the kind, quality, quantity, intended purpose, value, geographical origin or the time of production of the goods or of rendering of the service, or other characteristics of the goods or service;

(d)  trade marks which consist exclusively of signs or indications which have become customary in the current language or in the bona fide and established practices of the trade;

(e)  signs which consist exclusively of:

(i)  the shape, or another characteristic, which results from the nature of the goods themselves;

(ii)  the shape, or another characteristic, of goods which is necessary to obtain a technical result;

(iii)  the shape, or another characteristic, which gives substantial value to the goods;

(f)  trade marks which are contrary to public policy or to accepted principles of morality;

(g)  trade marks which are of such a nature as to deceive the public, for instance as to the nature, quality or geographical origin of the goods or service;

(h)  trade marks which have not been authorised by the competent authorities and are to be refused pursuant to Article 6*ter* of the Paris Convention for the Protection of Industrial Property ('Paris Convention');

(i)  trade marks which include badges, emblems or escutcheons other than those covered by Article 6*ter* of the Paris Convention and which are of particular public interest, unless the consent of the competent authority to their registration has been given;

(j)  trade marks which are excluded from registration, pursuant to Union legislation or national law or to international agreements to which the Union or the Member State concerned is party, providing for protection of designations of origin and geographical indications;

(k)  trade marks which are excluded from registration pursuant to Union legislation or international agreements to which the Union is party, providing for protection of traditional terms for wine;

(*l*)  trade marks which are excluded from registration pursuant to Union legislation or international agreements to which the Union is party, providing for protection of traditional specialities guaranteed;

(m)  trade marks which consist of, or reproduce in their essential elements, an earlier plant variety denomination registered in accordance with Union legislation or national law, or international agreements to which the Union or the Member State concerned is a party, providing for protection of plant variety rights, and which are in respect of plant varieties of the same or closely related species.

2.  Paragraph 1 shall apply notwithstanding that the grounds of non-registrability obtain in only part of the Union.

3.  Paragraph 1(b), (c) and (d) shall not apply if the trade mark has become distinctive in relation to the goods or services for which registration is requested as a consequence of the use which has been made of it.

*Article 8*

### Relative grounds for refusal

1.  Upon opposition by the proprietor of an earlier trade mark, the trade mark applied for shall not be registered:

(a)  if it is identical with the earlier trade mark and the goods or services for which registration is applied for are identical with the goods or services for which the earlier trade mark is protected;

(b)  if, because of its identity with, or similarity to, the earlier trade mark and the identity or similarity of the goods or services covered by the trade marks there exists a likelihood of confusion on the part of the public in the territory in which the earlier trade mark is protected; the likelihood of confusion includes the likelihood of association with the earlier trade mark.

2.  For the purposes of paragraph 1, 'earlier trade mark' means:

(a)  trade marks of the following kinds with a date of application for registration which is earlier than the date of application for registration of the EU trade mark, taking account, where appropriate, of the priorities claimed in respect of those trade marks:

  (i)  EU trade marks;

  (ii)  trade marks registered in a Member State, or, in the case of Belgium, the Netherlands or Luxembourg, at the Benelux Office for Intellectual Property;

  (iii)  trade marks registered under international arrangements which have effect in a Member State;

  (iv)  trade marks registered under international arrangements which have effect in the Union;

(b)  applications for the trade marks referred to in point (a), subject to their registration;

(c)  trade marks which, on the date of application for registration of the EU trade mark, or, where appropriate, of the priority claimed in respect of the application for registration of the EU trade mark, are well known in a Member State, in the sense in which the words 'well known' are used in Article 6*bis* of the Paris Convention.

3.  Upon opposition by the proprietor of the trade mark, a trade mark shall not be registered where an agent or representative of the proprietor of the trade mark applies for registration thereof in his own name without the proprietor's consent, unless the agent or representative justifies his action.

4.  Upon opposition by the proprietor of a non-registered trade mark or of another sign used in the course of trade of more than mere local significance, the trade mark applied for shall not be

registered where and to the extent that, pursuant to Union legislation or the law of the Member State governing that sign:

(a) rights to that sign were acquired prior to the date of application for registration of the EU trade mark, or the date of the priority claimed for the application for registration of the EU trade mark;

(b) that sign confers on its proprietor the right to prohibit the use of a subsequent trade mark.

5. Upon opposition by the proprietor of a registered earlier trade mark within the meaning of paragraph 2, the trade mark applied for shall not be registered where it is identical with, or similar to, an earlier trade mark, irrespective of whether the goods or services for which it is applied are identical with, similar to or not similar to those for which the earlier trade mark is registered, where, in the case of an earlier EU trade mark, the trade mark has a reputation in the Union or, in the case of an earlier national trade mark, the trade mark has a reputation in the Member State concerned, and where the use without due cause of the trade mark applied for would take unfair advantage of, or be detrimental to, the distinctive character or the repute of the earlier trade mark.

6. Upon opposition by any person authorised under the relevant law to exercise the rights arising from a designation of origin or a geographical indication, the trade mark applied for shall not be registered where and to the extent that, pursuant to the Union legislation or national law providing for the protection of designations of origin or geographical indications:

(i) an application for a designation of origin or a geographical indication had already been submitted, in accordance with Union legislation or national law, prior to the date of application for registration of the EU trade mark or the date of the priority claimed for the application, subject to its subsequent registration;

(ii) that designation of origin or geographical indication confers the right to prohibit the use of a subsequent trade mark.

## SECTION 2

### *Effects of an EU trade mark*

### Article 9

### Rights conferred by an EU trade mark

1. The registration of an EU trade mark shall confer on the proprietor exclusive rights therein.

2. Without prejudice to the rights of proprietors acquired before the filing date or the priority date of the EU trade mark, the proprietor of that EU trade mark shall be entitled to prevent all third parties not having his consent from using in the course of trade, in relation to goods or services, any sign where:

(a) the sign is identical with the EU trade mark and is used in relation to goods or services which are identical with those for which the EU trade mark is registered;

(b) the sign is identical with, or similar to, the EU trade mark and is used in relation to goods or services which are identical with, or similar to, the goods or services for which the EU trade mark is registered, if there exists a likelihood of confusion on the part of the public; the likelihood of confusion includes the likelihood of association between the sign and the trade mark;

(c) the sign is identical with, or similar to, the EU trade mark irrespective of whether it is used in relation to goods or services which are identical with, similar to or not similar to those for which the EU trade mark is registered, where the latter has a reputation in the Union and where use of that sign without due cause takes unfair advantage of, or is detrimental to, the distinctive character or the repute of the EU trade mark.

3.     The following, in particular, may be prohibited under paragraph 2:

(a)    affixing the sign to the goods or to the packaging of those goods;

(b)    offering the goods, putting them on the market, or stocking them for those purposes under the sign, or offering or supplying services thereunder;

(c)    importing or exporting the goods under the sign;

(d)    using the sign as a trade or company name or part of a trade or company name;

(e)    using the sign on business papers and in advertising;

(f)    using the sign in comparative advertising in a manner that is contrary to Directive 2006/114/EC.

4.     Without prejudice to the rights of proprietors acquired before the filing date or the priority date of the EU trade mark, the proprietor of that EU trade mark shall also be entitled to prevent all third parties from bringing goods, in the course of trade, into the Union without being released for free circulation there, where such goods, including packaging, come from third countries and bear without authorisation a trade mark which is identical with the EU trade mark registered in respect of such goods, or which cannot be distinguished in its essential aspects from that trade mark.

The entitlement of the proprietor of an EU trade mark pursuant to the first subparagraph shall lapse if, during the proceedings to determine whether the EU trade mark has been infringed, initiated in accordance with Regulation (EU) No 608/2013, evidence is provided by the declarant or the holder of the goods that the proprietor of the EU trade mark is not entitled to prohibit the placing of the goods on the market in the country of final destination.

## *Article 10*

### Right to prohibit preparatory acts in relation
### to the use of packaging or other means

Where the risk exists that the packaging, labels, tags, security or authenticity features or devices or any other means to which the mark is affixed could be used in relation to goods or services and such use would constitute an infringement of the rights of the proprietor of an EU trade mark under Article 9(2) and (3), the proprietor of that trade mark shall have the right to prohibit the following acts if carried out in the course of trade:

(a)    affixing a sign identical with, or similar to, the EU trade mark on packaging, labels, tags, security or authenticity features or devices or any other means to which the mark may be affixed;

(b)    offering or placing on the market, or stocking for those purposes, or importing or exporting, packaging, labels, tags, security or authenticity features or devices or any other means to which the mark is affixed.

## *Article 11*

### Date from which rights against third parties prevail

1.     The rights conferred by an EU trade mark shall prevail against third parties from the date of publication of the registration of the trade mark.

2.     Reasonable compensation may be claimed in respect of acts occurring after the date of publication of an EU trade mark application, where those acts would, after publication of the registration of the trade mark, be prohibited by virtue of that publication.

3.     A court seised of a case shall not decide upon the merits of that case until the registration has been published.

*Article 12*

### Reproduction of an EU trade mark in a dictionary

If the reproduction of an EU trade mark in a dictionary, encyclopaedia or similar reference work gives the impression that it constitutes the generic name of the goods or services for which the trade mark is registered, the publisher of the work shall, at the request of the proprietor of the EU trade mark, ensure that the reproduction of the trade mark at the latest in the next edition of the publication is accompanied by an indication that it is a registered trade mark.

*Article 13*

### Prohibition of the use of an EU trade mark registered in the name of an agent or representative

Where an EU trade mark is registered in the name of the agent or representative of a person who is the proprietor of that trade mark, without the proprietor's authorisation, the latter shall be entitled to oppose the use of his mark by his agent or representative if he has not authorised such use, unless the agent or representative justifies his action.

*Article 14*

### Limitation of the effects of an EU trade mark

1.   An EU trade mark shall not entitle the proprietor to prohibit a third party from using, in the course of trade:

(a)   the name or address of the third party, where that third party is a natural person;

(b)   signs or indications which are not distinctive or which concern the kind, quality, quantity, intended purpose, value, geographical origin, the time of production of goods or of rendering of the service, or other characteristics of the goods or services;

(c)   the EU trade mark for the purpose of identifying or referring to goods or services as those of the proprietor of that trade mark, in particular, where the use of that trade mark is necessary to indicate the intended purpose of a product or service, in particular as accessories or spare parts.

2.   Paragraph 1 shall only apply where the use made by the third party is in accordance with honest practices in industrial or commercial matters.

*Article 15*

### Exhaustion of the rights conferred by an EU trade mark

1.   An EU trade mark shall not entitle the proprietor to prohibit its use in relation to goods which have been put on the market in the European Economic Area under that trade mark by the proprietor or with his consent.

2.   Paragraph 1 shall not apply where there exist legitimate reasons for the proprietor to oppose further commercialisation of the goods, especially where the condition of the goods is changed or impaired after they have been put on the market.

*Article 16*

### Intervening right of the proprietor of a later registered trade mark as a defence in infringement proceedings

1.   In infringement proceedings, the proprietor of an EU trade mark shall not be entitled to prohibit the use of a later registered EU trade mark where that later trade mark would not be declared invalid pursuant to Article 60(1), (3) or (4), Article 61(1) or (2), or Article 64(2) of this Regulation.

2.    In infringement proceedings, the proprietor of an EU trade mark shall not be entitled to prohibit the use of a later registered national trade mark where that later registered national trade mark would not be declared invalid pursuant to Article 8 or Article 9(1) or (2), or Article 46(3) of Directive (EU) 2015/2436 of the European Parliament and of the Council.

3.    Where the proprietor of an EU trade mark is not entitled to prohibit the use of a later registered trade mark pursuant to paragraph 1 or 2, the proprietor of that later registered trade mark shall not be entitled to prohibit the use of that earlier EU trade mark in infringement proceedings.

*Article 17*

**Complementary application of national law relating to infringement**

1.    The effects of EU trade marks shall be governed solely by the provisions of this Regulation. In other respects, infringement of an EU trade mark shall be governed by the national law relating to infringement of a national trade mark in accordance with the provisions of Chapter X.

2.    This Regulation shall not prevent actions concerning an EU trade mark being brought under the law of Member States relating in particular to civil liability and unfair competition.

3.    The rules of procedure to be applied shall be determined in accordance with the provisions of Chapter X.

## SECTION 3

*Use of an EU trade mark*

*Article 18*

**Use of an EU trade mark**

1.    If, within a period of five years following registration, the proprietor has not put the EU trade mark to genuine use in the Union in connection with the goods or services in respect of which it is registered, or if such use has been suspended during an uninterrupted period of five years, the EU trade mark shall be subject to the sanctions provided for in this Regulation, unless there are proper reasons for non-use.

The following shall also constitute use within the meaning of the first subparagraph:

(a)    use of the EU trade mark in a form differing in elements which do not alter the distinctive character of the mark in the form in which it was registered, regardless of whether or not the trade mark in the form as used is also registered in the name of the proprietor;

(b)    affixing of the EU trade mark to goods or to the packaging thereof in the Union solely for export purposes.

2.    Use of the EU trade mark with the consent of the proprietor shall be deemed to constitute use by the proprietor.

## SECTION 4

*EU trade marks as objects of property*

*Article 19*

**Dealing with EU trade marks as national trade marks**

1.    Unless Articles 20 to 28 provide otherwise, an EU trade mark as an object of property shall be dealt with in its entirety, and for the whole area of the Union, as a national trade mark registered in the Member State in which, according to the Register:

(a)   the proprietor has his seat or his domicile on the relevant date;

(b)   where point (a) does not apply, the proprietor has an establishment on the relevant date.

2.   In cases which are not provided for by paragraph 1, the Member State referred to in that paragraph shall be the Member State in which the seat of the Office is situated.

3.   If two or more persons are mentioned in the Register as joint proprietors, paragraph 1 shall apply to the joint proprietor first mentioned; failing this, it shall apply to the subsequent joint proprietors in the order in which they are mentioned. Where paragraph 1 does not apply to any of the joint proprietors, paragraph 2 shall apply.

*Article 20*

**Transfer**

1.   An EU trade mark may be transferred, separately from any transfer of the undertaking, in respect of some or all of the goods or services for which it is registered.

2.   A transfer of the whole of the undertaking shall include the transfer of the EU trade mark except where, in accordance with the law governing the transfer, there is agreement to the contrary or circumstances clearly dictate otherwise. This provision shall apply to the contractual obligation to transfer the undertaking.

3.   Without prejudice to paragraph 2, an assignment of the EU trade mark shall be made in writing and shall require the signature of the parties to the contract, except when it is a result of a judgment; otherwise it shall be void.

4.   On request of one of the parties a transfer shall be entered in the Register and published.

5.   An application for registration of a transfer shall contain information to identify the EU trade mark, the new proprietor, the goods and services to which the transfer relates, as well as documents duly establishing the transfer in accordance with paragraphs 2 and 3. The application may further contain, where applicable, information to identify the representative of the new proprietor.

6.   The Commission shall adopt implementing acts specifying:

(a)   the details to be contained in the application for registration of a transfer;

(b)   the kind of documentation required to establish a transfer, taking account of the agreements given by the registered proprietor and the successor in title;

(c)   the details of how to process applications for partial transfers, ensuring that the goods and services in the remaining registration and the new registration do not overlap and that a separate file, including a new registration number, is established for the new registration.

Those implementing acts shall be adopted in accordance with the examination procedure referred to in Article 207(2).

7.   Where the conditions applicable to the registration of a transfer, as laid down in paragraphs 1, 2 and 3, or in the implementing acts referred to in paragraph 6, are not fulfilled, the Office shall notify the applicant of the deficiencies. If the deficiencies are not remedied within a period to be specified by the Office, it shall reject the application for registration of the transfer.

8.   A single application for registration of a transfer may be submitted for two or more trade marks, provided that the registered proprietor and the successor in title are the same in each case.

9.   Paragraphs 5 to 8 shall also apply to applications for EU trade marks.

10.   In the case of a partial transfer, any application made by the original proprietor pending with regard to the original registration shall be deemed to be pending with regard to the remaining registration and the new registration. Where such application is subject to the payment of fees and

those fees have been paid by the original proprietor, the new proprietor shall not be liable to pay any additional fees with regard to such application.

11.  As long as the transfer has not been entered in the Register, the successor in title may not invoke the rights arising from the registration of the EU trade mark.

12.  Where there are time limits to be observed vis-à-vis the Office, the successor in title may make the corresponding statements to the Office once the request for registration of the transfer has been received by the Office.

13.  All documents which require notification to the proprietor of the EU trade mark in accordance with Article 98 shall be addressed to the person registered as proprietor.

## Article 21

### Transfer of a trade mark registered in the name of an agent

1.  Where an EU trade mark is registered in the name of the agent or representative of a person who is the proprietor of that trade mark, without the proprietor's authorisation, the latter shall be entitled to demand the assignment of the EU trade mark in his favour, unless such agent or representative justifies his action.

2.  The proprietor may submit a request for assignment pursuant to paragraph 1 of this Article to the following:

(a)  the Office, pursuant to Article 60(1)(b), instead of an application for a declaration of invalidity;

(b)  a European Union trade mark court ('EU trade mark court') as referred to in Article 123, instead of a counterclaim for a declaration of invalidity based on Article 128(1).

## Article 22

### *Rights* in rem

1.  An EU trade mark may, independently of the undertaking, be given as security or be the subject of rights *in rem*.

2.  At the request of one of the parties, the rights referred to in paragraph 1 or the transfer of those rights shall be entered in the Register and published.

3.  An entry in the Register effected pursuant to paragraph 2 shall be cancelled or modified at the request of one of the parties.

## Article 23

### Levy of execution

1.  An EU trade mark may be levied in execution.

2.  As regards the procedure for levy of execution in respect of an EU trade mark, the courts and authorities of the Member States determined in accordance with Article 19 shall have exclusive jurisdiction.

3.  On request of one the parties, the levy of execution shall be entered in the Register and published.

4.  An entry in the Register effected pursuant to paragraph 3 shall be cancelled or modified at the request of one of the parties.

## Article 24

### Insolvency proceedings

1.    The only insolvency proceedings in which an EU trade mark may be involved are those opened in the Member State in the territory of which the debtor has his centre of main interests.

However, where the debtor is an insurance undertaking or a credit institution as defined in Directive 2009/138/EC of the European Parliament and of the Council and Directive 2001/24/EC of the European Parliament and of the Council, respectively, the only insolvency proceedings in which an EU trade mark may be involved are those opened in the Member State where that undertaking or institution has been authorised.

2.    In the case of joint proprietorship of an EU trade mark, paragraph 1 shall apply to the share of the joint proprietor.

3.    Where an EU trade mark is involved in insolvency proceedings, on request of the competent national authority an entry to this effect shall be made in the Register and published in the European Union Trade Marks Bulletin referred to in Article 116.

## Article 25

### Licensing

1.    An EU trade mark may be licensed for some or all of the goods or services for which it is registered and for the whole or part of the Union. A licence may be exclusive or non-exclusive.

2.    The proprietor of an EU trade mark may invoke the rights conferred by that trade mark against a licensee who contravenes any provision in his licensing contract with regard to:

(a)    its duration;

(b)    the form covered by the registration in which the trade mark may be used;

(c)    the scope of the goods or services for which the licence is granted;

(d)    the territory in which the trade mark may be affixed; or

(e)    the quality of the goods manufactured or of the services provided by the licensee.

3.    Without prejudice to the provisions of the licensing contract, the licensee may bring proceedings for infringement of an EU trade mark only if its proprietor consents thereto. However, the holder of an exclusive licence may bring such proceedings if the proprietor of the trade mark, after formal notice, does not himself bring infringement proceedings within an appropriate period.

4.    A licensee shall, for the purpose of obtaining compensation for damage suffered by him, be entitled to intervene in infringement proceedings brought by the proprietor of the EU trade mark.

5.    On request of one of the parties the grant or transfer of a licence in respect of an EU trade mark shall be entered in the Register and published.

6.    An entry in the Register effected pursuant to paragraph 5 shall be cancelled or modified at the request of one of the parties.

## Article 26

### Procedure for entering licences and other rights in the Register

1.    Article 20(5) and (6) and the rules adopted pursuant to it and Article 20(8) shall apply *mutatis mutandis* to the registration of a right *in rem* or transfer of a right *in rem* as referred to in Article 22(2), the levy of execution as referred to in Article 23(3), the involvement in insolvency proceedings as referred to in Article 24(3), as well as to the registration of a licence or transfer of a licence as referred to in Article 25(5), subject to the following:

(a) the requirement relating to the identification of goods and services to which the transfer relates shall not apply in respect of a request for registration of a right *in rem*, of a levy of execution or of insolvency proceedings;

(b) the requirement relating to the documents proving the transfer shall not apply where the request is made by the proprietor of the EU trade mark.

2. The application for registration of the rights referred to in paragraph 1 shall not be deemed to have been filed until the required fee has been paid.

3. The application for registration of a licence may contain a request to record a licence in the Register as one or more of the following:

(a) an exclusive licence;

(b) a sub-licence in the event that the licence is granted by a licensee whose licence is recorded in the Register;

(c) a licence limited to only part of the goods or services for which the mark is registered;

(d) a licence limited to part of the Union;

(e) a temporary licence.

Where a request is made to record the licence as a licence listed in points (c), (d) and (e) of the first subparagraph, the application for registration of a licence shall indicate the goods and services, the part of the Union and the time period for which the licence is granted.

4. Where the conditions applicable to registration, as laid down in Articles 22 to 25, in paragraphs 1 and 3 of this Article and in the other applicable rules adopted pursuant to this Regulation, are not fulfilled, the Office shall notify the applicant of the deficiency. If the deficiency is not corrected within a period specified by the Office, it shall reject the application for registration.

5. Paragraphs 1 and 3 shall apply *mutatis mutandis* to applications for EU trade marks.

*Article 27*

**Effects vis-à-vis third parties**

1. Legal acts referred to in Articles 20, 22 and 25 concerning an EU trade mark shall have effects vis-à-vis third parties in all the Member States only after entry in the Register. Nevertheless, such an act, before it is so entered, shall have effect vis-à-vis third parties who have acquired rights in the trade mark after the date of that act but who knew of the act at the date on which the rights were acquired.

2. Paragraph 1 shall not apply in the case of a person who acquires the EU trade mark or a right concerning the EU trade mark by way of transfer of the whole of the undertaking or by any other universal succession.

3. The effects vis-à-vis third parties of the legal acts referred to in Article 23 shall be governed by the law of the Member State determined in accordance with Article 19.

4. Until such time as common rules for the Member States in the field of bankruptcy enter into force, the effects vis-à-vis third parties of bankruptcy or similar proceedings shall be governed by the law of the Member State in which such proceedings are first brought within the meaning of national law or of conventions applicable in this field.

*Article 28*

**The application for an EU trade mark as an object of property**

Articles 19 to 27 shall apply to applications for EU trade marks.

## Article 29

### Procedure for cancelling or modifying the entry in the Register of licences and other rights

1.    A registration effected under Article 26(1) shall be cancelled or modified at the request of one of the persons concerned.

2.    The application shall contain the registration number of the EU trade mark concerned and the particulars of the right for which registration is requested to be cancelled or modified.

3.    The application for cancellation of a licence, a right *in rem* or an enforcement measure shall not be deemed to have been filed until the required fee has been paid.

4.    The application shall be accompanied by documents showing that the registered right no longer exists or that the licensee or the holder of another right consents to the cancellation or modification of the registration.

5.    Where the requirements for cancellation or modification of the registration are not satisfied, the Office shall notify the applicant of the deficiency. If the deficiency is not corrected within a period to be specified by the Office, it shall reject the application for cancellation or modification of the registration.

6.    Paragraphs 1 to 5 of this Article shall apply *mutatis mutandis* to entries made in the files pursuant to Article 26(5).

## CHAPTER III
## APPLICATION FOR EU TRADE MARKS

## SECTION 1

### *Filing of applications and the conditions which govern them*

### Article 30

### Filing of applications

1.    An application for an EU trade mark shall be filed at the Office.

2.    The Office shall issue to the applicant, without delay, a receipt which shall include at least the file number, a representation, description or other identification of the mark, the nature and the number of the documents and the date of their receipt. That receipt may be issued by electronic means.

### Article 31

### Conditions with which applications must comply

1.    An application for an EU trade mark shall contain:

(a)    a request for the registration of an EU trade mark;

(b)    information identifying the applicant;

(c)    a list of the goods or services in respect of which the registration is requested;

(d)    a representation of the mark, which satisfies the requirements set out in Article 4(b).

2.    The application for an EU trade mark shall be subject to the payment of the application fee covering one class of goods or services and, where appropriate, of one or more class fees for each class of goods and services exceeding the first class and, where applicable, the search fee.

3.     In addition to the requirements referred to in paragraphs 1 and 2, an application for an EU trade mark shall comply with the formal requirements laid down in this Regulation and in the implementing acts adopted pursuant to it. If those conditions provide for the trade mark to be represented electronically, the Executive Director may determine the formats and maximum size of such an electronic file.

4.     The Commission shall adopt implementing acts specifying the details to be contained in the application. Those implementing acts shall be adopted in accordance with the examination procedure referred to in Article 207(2).

*Article 32*

**Date of filing**

The date of filing of an EU trade mark application shall be the date on which the documents containing the information specified in Article 31(1) are filed with the Office by the applicant, subject to payment of the application fee within one month of filing those documents.

*Article 33*

**Designation and classification of goods and services**

1.     Goods and services in respect of which trade mark registration is applied for shall be classified in conformity with the system of classification established by the Nice Agreement Concerning the International Classification of Goods and Services for the Purposes of the Registration of Marks of 15 June 1957 ('the Nice Classification').

2.     The goods and services for which the protection of the trade mark is sought shall be identified by the applicant with sufficient clarity and precision to enable the competent authorities and economic operators, on that sole basis, to determine the extent of the protection sought.

3.     For the purposes of paragraph 2, the general indications included in the class headings of the Nice Classification or other general terms may be used, provided that they comply with the requisite standards of clarity and precision set out in this Article.

4.     The Office shall reject an application in respect of indications or terms which are unclear or imprecise, where the applicant does not suggest an acceptable wording within a period set by the Office to that effect.

5.     The use of general terms, including the general indications of the class headings of the Nice Classification, shall be interpreted as including all the goods or services clearly covered by the literal meaning of the indication or term. The use of such terms or indications shall not be interpreted as comprising a claim to goods or services which cannot be so understood.

6.     Where the applicant requests registration for more than one class, the applicant shall group the goods and services according to the classes of the Nice Classification, each group being preceded by the number of the class to which that group of goods or services belongs, and shall present them in the order of the classes.

7.     Goods and services shall not be regarded as being similar to each other on the ground that they appear in the same class under the Nice Classification. Goods and services shall not be regarded as being dissimilar from each other on the ground that they appear in different classes under the Nice Classification.

8.     Proprietors of EU trade marks applied for before 22 June 2012 which are registered in respect of the entire heading of a Nice class may declare that their intention on the date of filing had been to seek protection in respect of goods or services beyond those covered by the literal meaning of the heading of that class, provided that the goods or services so designated are included in the alphabetical list for that class in the edition of the Nice Classification in force at the date of filing.

The declaration shall be filed at the Office by 24 September 2016, and shall indicate, in a clear, precise and specific manner, the goods and services, other than those clearly covered by the literal meaning of the indications of the class heading, originally covered by the proprietor's intention. The Office shall take appropriate measures to amend the Register accordingly. The possibility to make a declaration in accordance with the first subparagraph of this paragraph shall be without prejudice to the application of Article 18, Article 47(2), Article 58(1)(a), and Article 64(2).

EU trade marks for which no declaration is filed within the period referred to in the second subparagraph shall be deemed to extend, as from the expiry of that period, only to goods or services clearly covered by the literal meaning of the indications included in the heading of the relevant class.

9.    Where the register is amended, the exclusive rights conferred by the EU trade mark under Article 9 shall not prevent a third party from continuing to use a trade mark in relation to goods or services where and to the extent that the use of the trade mark for those goods or services:

(a)    commenced before the register was amended; and

(b)    did not infringe the proprietor's rights based on the literal meaning of the record of the goods and services in the register at that time.

In addition, the amendment of the list of goods or services recorded in the register shall not give the proprietor of the EU trade mark the right to oppose or to apply for a declaration of invalidity of a later trade mark where and to the extent that:

(a)    the later trade mark was either in use, or an application had been made to register the trade mark, for goods or services before the register was amended; and

(b)    the use of the trade mark in relation to those goods or services did not infringe, or would not have infringed, the proprietor's rights based on the literal meaning of the record of the goods and services in the register at that time.

## SECTION 2

### Priority

### Article 34

### Right of priority

1.    A person who has duly filed an application for a trade mark in or in respect of any State party to the Paris Convention or to the Agreement establishing the World Trade Organisation, or his successors in title, shall enjoy, for the purpose of filing an EU trade mark application for the same trade mark in respect of goods or services which are identical with or contained within those for which the application has been filed, a right of priority during a period of six months from the date of filing of the first application.

2.    Every filing that is equivalent to a regular national filing under the national law of the State where it was made or under bilateral or multilateral agreements shall be recognised as giving rise to a right of priority.

3.    By a regular national filing is meant any filing that is sufficient to establish the date on which the application was filed, whatever may be the outcome of the application.

4.    A subsequent application for a trade mark which was the subject of a previous first application in respect of the same goods or services and which is filed in or in respect of the same State shall be considered as the first application for the purposes of determining priority, provided that, at the date of filing of the subsequent application, the previous application has been withdrawn, abandoned or refused, without being open to public inspection and without leaving any rights outstanding, and has not served as a basis for claiming a right of priority. The previous application may not thereafter serve as a basis for claiming a right of priority.

5.    If the first filing has been made in a State which is not a party to the Paris Convention or to the Agreement establishing the World Trade Organisation, paragraphs 1 to 4 shall apply only in so far as that State, according to published findings, grants, on the basis of the first filing made at the Office and subject to conditions equivalent to those laid down in this Regulation, a right of priority having equivalent effect. The Executive Director shall, where necessary, request the Commission to consider enquiring as to whether a State within the meaning of the first sentence accords that reciprocal treatment. If the Commission determines that reciprocal treatment in accordance with the first sentence is accorded, it shall publish a communication to that effect in the *Official Journal of the European Union.*

6.    Paragraph 5 shall apply from the date of publication in the *Official Journal of the European Union* of the communication determining that reciprocal treatment is accorded, unless the communication states an earlier date from which it is applicable. It shall cease to apply from the date of publication in the *Official Journal of the European Union* of a communication of the Commission to the effect that reciprocal treatment is no longer accorded, unless the communication states an earlier date from which it is applicable.

7.    Communications as referred to in paragraphs 5 and 6 shall also be published in the Official Journal of the Office.

## Article 35

### Claiming priority

1.    Priority claims shall be filed together with the EU trade mark application and shall include the date, number and country of the previous application. The documentation in support of priority claims shall be filed within three months of the filing date.

2.    The Commission shall adopt implementing acts specifying the kind of documentation to be filed for claiming the priority of a previous application in accordance with paragraph 1 of this Article. Those implementing acts shall be adopted in accordance with the examination procedure referred to in Article 207(2).

3.    The Executive Director may determine that the documentation to be provided by the applicant in support of the priority claim may consist of less than what is required under the specifications adopted in accordance with paragraph 2, provided that the information required is available to the Office from other sources.

## Article 36

### Effect of priority right

The right of priority shall have the effect that the date of priority shall count as the date of filing of the EU trade mark application for the purposes of establishing which rights take precedence.

## Article 37

### Equivalence of Union filing with national filing

An EU trade mark application which has been accorded a date of filing shall, in the Member States, be equivalent to a regular national filing, where appropriate with the priority claimed for the EU trade mark application.

## SECTION 3
### *Exhibition priority*

### Article 38
### Exhibition priority

1.    If an applicant for an EU trade mark has displayed goods or services under the mark applied for, at an official or officially recognised international exhibition falling within the terms of the Convention relating to international exhibitions signed at Paris on 22 November 1928 and last revised on 30 November 1972, he may, if he files the application within a period of six months of the date of the first display of the goods or services under the mark applied for, claim a right of priority from that date within the meaning of Article 36. The priority claim shall be filed together with the EU trade mark application.

2.    An applicant who wishes to claim priority pursuant to paragraph 1 shall file evidence of the display of goods or services under the mark applied for within three months of the filing date.

3.    An exhibition priority granted in a Member State or in a third country shall not extend the period of priority laid down in Article 34.

4.    The Commission shall adopt implementing acts specifying the type and details of evidence to be filed for claiming an exhibition priority in accordance with paragraph 2 of this Article. Those implementing acts shall be adopted in accordance with the examination procedure referred to in Article 207(2).

## SECTION 4
### *Seniority of a national trade mark*

### Article 39
### Claiming seniority of a national trade mark in an application for an EU trade mark or subsequent to the filing of the application

1.    The proprietor of an earlier trade mark registered in a Member State, including a trade mark registered in the Benelux countries, or registered under international arrangements having effect in a Member State, who applies for an identical trade mark for registration as an EU trade mark for goods or services which are identical with or contained within those for which the earlier trade mark has been registered, may claim for the EU trade mark the seniority of the earlier trade mark in respect of the Member State in or for which it is registered.

2.    Seniority claims shall either be filed together with the EU trade mark application or within two months of the filing date of the application, and shall include the Member State or Member States in or for which the mark is registered, the number and the filing date of the relevant registration, and the goods and services for which the mark is registered. Where the seniority of one or more registered earlier trade marks is claimed in the application, the documentation in support of the seniority claim shall be filed within three months of the filing date. Where the applicant wishes to claim the seniority subsequent to the filing of the application, the documentation in support of the seniority claim shall be submitted to the Office within three months of receipt of the seniority claim.

3.    Seniority shall have the sole effect under this Regulation that, where the proprietor of the EU trade mark surrenders the earlier trade mark or allows it to lapse, he shall be deemed to continue to have the same rights as he would have had if the earlier trade mark had continued to be registered.

4.    The seniority claimed for the EU trade mark shall lapse where the earlier trade mark the seniority of which is claimed is declared to be invalid or revoked. Where the earlier trade mark is

revoked, the seniority shall lapse provided that the revocation takes effect prior to the filing date or priority date of that EU trade mark.

5.   The Office shall inform the Benelux Office for Intellectual Property or the central industrial property office of the Member State concerned of the effective claiming of seniority.

6.   The Commission shall adopt implementing acts specifying the kind of documentation to be filed for claiming the seniority of a national trade mark or a trade mark registered under international agreements having effect in a Member State in accordance with paragraph 2 of this Article. Those implementing acts shall be adopted in accordance with the examination procedure referred to in Article 207(2).

7.   The Executive Director may determine that the documentation to be provided by the applicant in support of the seniority claim may consist of less than what is required under the specifications adopted in accordance with paragraph 6, provided that the information required is available to the Office from other sources.

*Article 40*

### Claiming seniority of a national trade mark after registration of an EU trade mark

1.   The proprietor of an EU trade mark who is the proprietor of an earlier identical trade mark registered in a Member State, including a trade mark registered in the Benelux countries or of an earlier identical trade mark, with an international registration effective in a Member State, for goods or services which are identical to those for which the earlier trade mark has been registered, or contained within them, may claim the seniority of the earlier trade mark in respect of the Member State in or for which it was registered.

2.   Seniority claims filed pursuant to paragraph 1 of this Article shall include the registration number of the EU trade mark, the name and address of its proprietor, the Member State or Member States in or for which the earlier mark is registered, the number and the filing date of the relevant registration, the goods and services for which the mark is registered and those in respect of which seniority is claimed, and supporting documentation as provided for in the rules adopted pursuant to Article 39(6).

3.   If the requirements governing the claiming of seniority are not fulfilled, the Office shall communicate the deficiency to the proprietor of the EU trade mark. If the deficiency is not remedied within a period to be specified by the Office, the Office shall reject the claim.

4.   Article 39(3), (4), (5) and (7) shall apply.

## CHAPTER IV
## REGISTRATION PROCEDURE

### SECTION 1
### *Examination of applications*

*Article 41*

### Examination of the conditions of filing

1.   The Office shall examine whether:

(a)   the EU trade mark application satisfies the requirements for the accordance of a date of filing in accordance with Article 32;

(b)    the EU trade mark application complies with the conditions and requirements referred to in Article 31(3);

(c)    where appropriate, the class fees have been paid within the prescribed period.

2.    Where the EU trade mark application does not satisfy the requirements referred to in paragraph 1, the Office shall request the applicant to remedy the deficiencies or the default on payment within two months of the receipt of the notification.

3.    If the deficiencies or the default on payment established pursuant to paragraph 1(a) are not remedied within this period, the application shall not be dealt with as an EU trade mark application. If the applicant complies with the Office's request, the Office shall accord as the date of filing of the application the date on which the deficiencies or the default on payment established are remedied.

4.    If the deficiencies established pursuant to paragraph 1(b) are not remedied within the prescribed period, the Office shall refuse the application.

5.    If the default on payment established pursuant to paragraph 1(c) is not remedied within the prescribed period, the application shall be deemed to be withdrawn unless it is clear which categories of goods or services the amount paid is intended to cover. In the absence of other criteria to determine which classes are intended to be covered, the Office shall take the classes in the order of the classification. The application shall be deemed to have been withdrawn with regard to those classes for which the class fees have not been paid or have not been paid in full.

6.    Failure to satisfy the requirements concerning the claim to priority shall result in loss of the right of priority for the application.

7.    Failure to satisfy the requirements concerning the claiming of seniority of a national trade mark shall result in loss of that right for the application.

8.    Where failure to satisfy the requirements referred to in paragraph 1(b) and (c) concerns only some of the goods or services, the Office shall refuse the application, or the right of priority or the right of seniority shall be lost, only in so far as those goods and services are concerned.

## *Article 42*

### Examination as to absolute grounds for refusal

1.    Where, under Article 7, a trade mark is ineligible for registration in respect of some or all of the goods or services covered by the EU trade mark application, the application shall be refused as regards those goods or services.

2.    The application shall not be refused before the applicant has been allowed the opportunity to withdraw or amend the application or to submit his observations. To this effect, the Office shall notify the applicant of the grounds for refusing registration and shall specify a period within which he may withdraw or amend the application or submit his observations. Where the applicant fails to overcome the grounds for refusing registration, the Office shall refuse registration in whole or in part.

## *SECTION 2*

### *Search*

## *Article 43*

### Search report

1.    The Office shall, at the request of the applicant for the EU trade mark when filing the application, draw up a European Union search report ('EU search report') citing those earlier EU trade marks or EU trade mark applications discovered which may be invoked under Article 8 against the registration of the EU trade mark applied for.

2.     Where, at the time of filing an EU trade mark application, the applicant requests that a search report be prepared by the central industrial property offices of the Member States and where the appropriate search fee has been paid within the time limit for the payment of the filing fee, the Office shall transmit without delay a copy of the EU trade mark application to the central industrial property office of each Member State which has informed the Office of its decision to operate a search in its own register of trade marks in respect of EU trade mark applications.

3.     Each of the central industrial property offices of the Member States referred to in paragraph 2 shall communicate a search report which shall either cite any earlier national trade marks, national trade mark applications or trade marks registered under international agreements, having effect in the Member State or Member States concerned, which have been discovered and which may be invoked under Article 8 against the registration of the EU trade mark applied for, or state that the search has revealed no such rights.

4.     The Office, after consulting the Management Board provided for in Article 153 ('the Management Board'), shall establish the contents and modalities for the reports.

5.     The Office shall pay an amount to each central industrial property office for each search report provided in accordance with paragraph 3. The amount, which shall be the same for each office, shall be fixed by the Budget Committee by means of a decision adopted by a majority of three quarters of the representatives of the Member States.

6.     The Office shall transmit to the applicant for the EU trade mark the EU search report requested and any requested national search reports received.

7.     Upon publication of the EU trade mark application, the Office shall inform the proprietors of any earlier EU trade marks or EU trade mark applications cited in the EU search report of the publication of the EU trade mark application. The latter shall apply irrespective of whether the applicant has requested to receive the EU search report, unless the proprietor of an earlier registration or application requests not to receive the notification.


## SECTION 3

### Publication of the application

*Article 44*

**Publication of the application**

1.     If the conditions which the application for an EU trade mark is required to satisfy have been fulfilled, the application shall be published for the purposes of Article 46 to the extent that it has not been refused pursuant to Article 42. The publication of the application shall be without prejudice to information already made available to the public otherwise in accordance with this Regulation or acts adopted pursuant to this Regulation.

2.     Where, after publication, the application is refused pursuant to Article 42, the decision that it has been refused shall be published upon becoming final.

3.     Where the publication of the application contains an error attributable to the Office, the Office shall of its own motion or at the request of the applicant correct the error and publish the correction.

The rules adopted pursuant to Article 49(3) shall apply *mutatis mutandis* where a correction is requested by the applicant.

4.     Article 46(2) shall also apply where the correction concerns the list of goods or services or the representation of the mark.

5.    The Commission shall adopt implementing acts laying down the details to be contained in the publication of the application. Those implementing acts shall be adopted in accordance with the examination procedure referred to in Article 207(2).

## SECTION 4

### *Observations by third parties and opposition*

### Article 45

### Observations by third parties

1.    Any natural or legal person and any group or body representing manufacturers, producers, suppliers of services, traders or consumers may submit to the Office written observations, explaining on which grounds, under Articles 5 and 7, the trade mark should not be registered *ex officio.*

Persons and groups or bodies as referred to in the first subparagraph shall not be parties to the proceedings before the Office.

2.    Third party observations shall be submitted before the end of the opposition period or, where an opposition against the trade mark has been filed, before the final decision on the opposition is taken.

3.    The submission referred to in paragraph 1 shall be without prejudice to the right of the Office to re-open the examination of absolute grounds on its own initiative at any time before registration, where appropriate.

4.    The observations referred to in paragraph 1 shall be communicated to the applicant who may comment on them.

### Article 46

### Opposition

1.    Within a period of three months following the publication of an EU trade mark application, notice of opposition to registration of the trade mark may be given on the grounds that it may not be registered under Article 8:

(a)   by the proprietors of earlier trade marks referred to in Article 8(2) as well as licensees authorised by the proprietors of those trade marks, in respect of Article 8(1) and (5);

(b)   by the proprietors of trade marks referred to in Article 8(3);

(c)   by the proprietors of earlier marks or signs referred to in Article 8(4) and by persons authorised under the relevant national law to exercise these rights;

(d)   by the persons authorised under the relevant Union legislation or national law to exercise the rights referred to in Article 8(6).

2.    Notice of opposition to registration of the trade mark may also be given, subject to the conditions laid down in paragraph 1, in the event of the publication of an amended application in accordance with the second sentence of Article 49(2).

3.    Opposition shall be expressed in writing, and shall specify the grounds on which it is made. It shall not be considered as duly entered until the opposition fee has been paid.

4.    Within a period to be fixed by the Office, the opponent may submit facts, evidence and arguments in support of his case.

*Article 47*

**Examination of opposition**

1.    In the examination of the opposition the Office shall invite the parties, as often as necessary, to file observations, within a period set by the Office, on communications from the other parties or issued by itself.

2.    If the applicant so requests, the proprietor of an earlier EU trade mark who has given notice of opposition shall furnish proof that, during the five-year period preceding the date of filing or the date of priority of the EU trade mark application, the earlier EU trade mark has been put to genuine use in the Union in connection with the goods or services in respect of which it is registered and which he cites as justification for his opposition, or that there are proper reasons for non-use, provided that the earlier EU trade mark has at that date been registered for not less than five years. In the absence of proof to this effect, the opposition shall be rejected. If the earlier EU trade mark has been used in relation to only part of the goods or services for which it is registered it shall, for the purposes of the examination of the opposition, be deemed to be registered in respect only of that part of the goods or services.

3.    Paragraph 2 shall apply to earlier national trade marks referred to in Article 8(2)(a), by substituting use in the Member State in which the earlier national trade mark is protected for use in the Union.

4.    The Office may, if it thinks fit, invite the parties to make a friendly settlement.

5.    If examination of the opposition reveals that the trade mark may not be registered in respect of some or all of the goods or services for which the EU trade mark application has been made, the application shall be refused in respect of those goods or services. Otherwise the opposition shall be rejected.

6.    The decision refusing the application shall be published upon becoming final.

*Article 48*

**Delegation of powers**

The Commission is empowered to adopt delegated acts in accordance with Article 208 specifying the details of the procedure for filing and examining an opposition set out in Articles 46 and 47.

## SECTION 5

### *Withdrawal, restriction, amendment and division of the application*

*Article 49*

**Withdrawal, restriction and amendment of the application**

1.    The applicant may at any time withdraw his EU trade mark application or restrict the list of goods or services contained therein. Where the application has already been published, the withdrawal or restriction shall also be published.

2.    In other respects, an EU trade mark application may be amended, upon request of the applicant, only by correcting the name and address of the applicant, errors of wording or of copying, or obvious mistakes, provided that such correction does not substantially change the trade mark or extend the list of goods or services. Where the amendments affect the representation of the trade mark or the list of goods or services and are made after publication of the application, the trade mark application shall be published as amended.

3.    The Commission is empowered to adopt delegated acts in accordance with Article 208 specifying the details of the procedure governing the amendment of the application.

## Article 50

### Division of the application

1.   The applicant may divide the application by declaring that some of the goods or services included in the original application will be the subject of one or more divisional applications. The goods or services in the divisional application shall not overlap with the goods or services which remain in the original application or those which are included in other divisional applications.

2.   The declaration of division shall not be admissible:

(a)   if, where an opposition has been entered against the original application, such a divisional application has the effect of introducing a division amongst the goods or services against which the opposition has been directed, until the decision of the Opposition Division has become final or the opposition proceedings are finally terminated otherwise;

(b)   before the date of filing referred to in Article 32 has been accorded by the Office and during the opposition period provided for in Article 46(1).

3.   The declaration of division shall be subject to a fee. The declaration shall be deemed not to have been made until the fee has been paid.

4.   Where the Office finds that the requirements laid down in paragraph 1 and in the rules adopted pursuant to paragraph 9(a) are not fulfilled, it shall invite the applicant to remedy the deficiencies within a period to be specified by the Office. If the deficiencies are not remedied before the time limit expires, the Office shall refuse the declaration of division.

5.   The division shall take effect on the date on which it is recorded in the files kept by the Office concerning the original application.

6.   All requests and applications submitted and all fees paid with regard to the original application prior to the date on which the Office receives the declaration of division are deemed also to have been submitted or paid with regard to the divisional application or applications. The fees for the original application which have been duly paid prior to the date on which the declaration of division is received shall not be refunded.

7.   The divisional application shall preserve the filing date and any priority date and seniority date of the original application.

8.   Where the declaration of division relates to an application which has already been published pursuant to Article 44, the division shall be published. The divisional application shall be published. The publication shall not open a new period for the filing of oppositions.

9.   The Commission shall adopt implementing acts specifying:

(a)   the details to be contained in a declaration of the division of an application made pursuant to paragraph 1;

(b)   the details as to how to process a declaration of the division of an application, ensuring that a separate file, including a new application number, is established for the divisional application;

(c)   the details to be contained in the publication of the divisional application pursuant to paragraph 8.

Those implementing acts shall be adopted in accordance with the examination procedure referred to in Article 207(2).

## SECTION 6
### *Registration*

*Article 51*

### Registration

1.     Where an application meets the requirements set out in this Regulation and where no notice of opposition has been given within the period referred to in Article 46(1) or where any opposition entered has been finally disposed of by withdrawal, rejection or other disposition, the trade mark and the particulars referred to in Article 111(2) shall be recorded in the Register. The registration shall be published.

2.     The Office shall issue a certificate of registration. That certificate may be issued by electronic means. The Office shall provide certified or uncertified copies of the certificate subject to the payment of a fee, where those copies are issued other than by electronic means.

3.     The Commission shall adopt implementing acts specifying the details to be contained in and the form of the certificate of registration referred to in paragraph 2 of this Article. Those implementing acts shall be adopted in accordance with the examination procedure referred to in Article 207(2).

## CHAPTER V
## DURATION, RENEWAL, ALTERATION AND DIVISION OF EU TRADE MARKS

*Article 52*

### Duration of registration

EU trade marks shall be registered for a period of 10 years from the date of filing of the application. Registration may be renewed in accordance with Article 53 for further periods of 10 years.

*Article 53*

### Renewal

1.     Registration of the EU trade mark shall be renewed at the request of the proprietor of the EU trade mark or any person expressly authorised by him, provided that the fees have been paid.

2.     The Office shall inform the proprietor of the EU trade mark, and any person having a registered right in respect of the EU trade mark, of the expiry of the registration at least six months before the said expiry. Failure to give such information shall not involve the responsibility of the Office and shall not affect the expiry of the registration.

3.     The request for renewal shall be submitted in the six-month period prior to the expiry of the registration. The basic fee for the renewal and, where appropriate, one or more class fees for each class of goods or services exceeding the first one shall also be paid within this period. Failing this, the request may be submitted and the fees paid within a further period of six months following the expiry of registration, provided that an additional fee for late payment of the renewal fee or late submission of the request for renewal is paid within this further period.

4.     The request for renewal shall include:

(a)     the name of the person requesting renewal;

(b)     the registration number of the EU trade mark to be renewed;

(c)     if the renewal is requested for only part of the registered goods and services, an indication of those classes or those goods and services for which renewal is requested, or those classes or those goods and services for which renewal is not requested, grouped according to the classes of the Nice classification, each group being preceded by the number of the class of that classification to which that group of goods or services belongs, and presented in the order of classes of that classification.

If the payment referred to in paragraph 3 is made, it shall be deemed to constitute a request for renewal provided that it contains all necessary indications to establish the purpose of the payment.

5.    Where the request is submitted or the fees paid in respect of only some of the goods or services for which the EU trade mark is registered, registration shall be renewed for those goods or services only. Where the fees paid are insufficient to cover all the classes of goods and services for which renewal is requested, registration shall be renewed if it is clear which class or classes are to be covered. In the absence of other criteria, the Office shall take the classes into account in the order of classification.

6.    Renewal shall take effect from the day following the date on which the existing registration expires. The renewal shall be registered.

7.    Where the request for renewal is filed within the periods provided for in paragraph 3, but the other conditions governing renewal provided for in this Article are not satisfied, the Office shall inform the applicant of the deficiencies found.

8.    Where a request for renewal is not submitted or is submitted after the expiry of the period provided for in paragraph 3, or where the fees are not paid or are paid only after the period in question has expired, or where the deficiencies referred to in paragraph 7 are not remedied within that period, the Office shall determine that the registration has expired and shall notify the proprietor of the EU trade mark accordingly. Where the determination has become final, the Office shall cancel the mark from the register. The cancellation shall take effect from the day following the date on which the existing registration expired. Where the renewal fees have been paid but the registration is not renewed, those fees shall be refunded.

9.    A single request for renewal may be submitted for two or more marks, upon payment of the required fees for each of the marks, provided that the proprietors or the representatives are the same in each case.

## *Article 54*

### **Alteration**

1.    The EU trade mark shall not be altered in the Register during the period of registration or on renewal thereof.

2.    Nevertheless, where the EU trade mark includes the name and address of the proprietor, any alteration thereof not substantially affecting the identity of the trade mark as originally registered may be registered at the request of the proprietor.

3.    The request for alteration shall include the element of the mark to be altered and that element in its altered version.

The Commission shall adopt implementing acts specifying the details to be contained in the request for alteration. Those implementing acts shall be adopted in accordance with the examination procedure referred to in Article 207(2).

4.    The request shall be deemed not to have been filed until the required fee has been paid. If the fee has not been paid or has not been paid in full, the Office shall inform the applicant accordingly. A single request may be made for the alteration of the same element in two or more registrations of the same proprietor. The required fee shall be paid in respect of each registration to be altered. If the requirements governing the alteration of the registration are not fulfilled, the Office shall communicate the deficiency to the applicant. If the deficiency is not remedied within a period to be specified by the Office, the Office shall reject the request.

5.    The publication of the registration of the alteration shall contain a representation of the EU trade mark as altered. Third parties whose rights may be affected by the alteration may challenge the registration thereof within the period of three months following publication. Articles 46 and 47 and rules adopted pursuant to Article 48 shall apply to the publication of the registration of the alteration.

*Article 55*

### Change of the name or address

1.    A change of the name or address of the proprietor of the EU trade mark which is not an alteration of the EU trade mark pursuant to Article 54(2) and which is not the consequence of a whole or partial transfer of the EU trade mark shall, at the request of the proprietor, be recorded in the Register.

The Commission shall adopt implementing acts specifying the details to be contained in a request for the change of name or address pursuant to the first subparagraph of this paragraph. Those implementing acts shall be adopted in accordance with the examination procedure referred to in Article 207(2).

2.    A single request may be made for the change of the name or address in respect of two or more registrations of the same proprietor.

3.    If the requirements governing the recording of a change are not fulfilled, the Office shall communicate the deficiency to the proprietor of the EU trade mark. If the deficiency is not remedied within a period to be specified by the Office, the Office shall reject the request.

4.    Paragraphs 1, 2 and 3 shall also apply to a change of the name or address of the registered representative.

5.    Paragraphs 1 to 4 shall apply to applications for EU trade marks. The change shall be recorded in the files kept by the Office on the EU trade mark application.

*Article 56*

### Division of the registration

1.    The proprietor of the EU trade mark may divide the registration by declaring that some of the goods or services included in the original registration will be the subject of one or more divisional registrations. The goods or services in the divisional registration shall not overlap with the goods or services which remain in the original registration or those which are included in other divisional registrations.

2.    The declaration of division shall not be admissible:

(a)    if, where an application for revocation of rights or for a declaration of invalidity has been entered at the Office against the original registration, such a divisional declaration has the effect of introducing a division amongst the goods or services against which the application for revocation of rights or for a declaration of invalidity is directed, until the decision of the Cancellation Division has become final or the proceedings are finally terminated otherwise;

(b)    if, where a counterclaim for revocation or for a declaration of invalidity has been entered in a case before an EU trade mark court, such a divisional declaration has the effect of introducing a division amongst the goods or services against which the counterclaim is directed, until the mention of the EU trade mark court's judgment is recorded in the Register pursuant to Article 128(6).

3.    If the requirements laid down in paragraph 1 and pursuant to the implementing acts referred to in paragraph 8 are not fulfilled, or the list of goods and services which form the divisional registration overlap with the goods and services which remain in the original registration, the Office

shall invite the proprietor of the EU trade mark to remedy the deficiencies within such period as it may specify. If the deficiencies are not remedied before the period expires, the Office shall refuse the declaration of division.

4.  The declaration of division shall be subject to a fee. The declaration shall be deemed not to have been made until the fee has been paid.

5.  The division shall take effect on the date on which it is entered in the Register.

6.  All requests and applications submitted and all fees paid with regard to the original registration prior to the date on which the Office receives the declaration of division shall be deemed also to have been submitted or paid with regard to the divisional registration or registrations. The fees for the original registration which have been duly paid prior to the date on which the declaration of division is received shall not be refunded.

7.  The divisional registration shall preserve the filing date and any priority date and seniority date of the original registration.

8.  The Commission shall adopt implementing acts specifying:

(a)  the details to be contained in a declaration of the division of a registration pursuant to paragraph 1;

(b)  the details as how to process a declaration of the division of a registration, ensuring that a separate file, including a new registration number, is established for the divisional registration.

Those implementing acts shall be adopted in accordance with the examination procedure referred to in Article 207(2).

<h1 style="text-align:center">CHAPTER VI<br>SURRENDER, REVOCATION AND INVALIDITY</h1>

<h2 style="text-align:center">SECTION 1</h2>

<h3 style="text-align:center">Surrender</h3>

Article 57

<h3 style="text-align:center">Surrender</h3>

1.  An EU trade mark may be surrendered in respect of some or all of the goods or services for which it is registered.

2.  The surrender shall be declared to the Office in writing by the proprietor of the trade mark. It shall not have effect until it has been entered in the Register. The validity of the surrender of an EU trade mark which is declared to the Office subsequent to the submission of an application for revocation of that trade mark pursuant to Article 63(1) shall be conditional upon the final rejection or withdrawal of the application for revocation.

3.  Surrender shall be entered only with the agreement of the proprietor of a right relating to the EU trade mark and which is entered in the Register. If a licence has been registered, surrender shall be entered in the Register only if the proprietor of the EU trade mark proves that he has informed the licensee of his intention to surrender. The entry of the surrender shall be made on expiry of the three-month period after the date on which the proprietor satisfies the Office that he has informed the licensee of his intention to surrender, or before the expiry of that period, as soon as he proves that the licensee has given his consent.

4.    If the requirements governing surrender are not fulfilled, the Office shall communicate the deficiencies to the declarant. If the deficiencies are not remedied within a period to be specified by the Office, the Office shall reject the entry of surrender in the Register.

5.    The Commission shall adopt implementing acts specifying the details to be contained in a declaration of surrender pursuant to paragraph 2 of this Article and the kind of documentation required to establish a third party's agreement pursuant to paragraph 3 of this Article. Those implementing acts shall be adopted in accordance with the examination procedure referred to in Article 207(2).

## SECTION 2

### *Grounds for revocation*

#### *Article 58*

#### Grounds for revocation

1.    The rights of the proprietor of the EU trade mark shall be declared to be revoked on application to the Office or on the basis of a counterclaim in infringement proceedings:

(a)    if, within a continuous period of five years, the trade mark has not been put to genuine use in the Union in connection with the goods or services in respect of which it is registered, and there are no proper reasons for non-use; however, no person may claim that the proprietor's rights in an EU trade mark should be revoked where, during the interval between expiry of the five-year period and filing of the application or counterclaim, genuine use of the trade mark has been started or resumed; the commencement or resumption of use within a period of three months preceding the filing of the application or counterclaim which began at the earliest on expiry of the continuous period of five years of non-use shall, however, be disregarded where preparations for the commencement or resumption occur only after the proprietor becomes aware that the application or counterclaim may be filed;

(b)    if, in consequence of acts or inactivity of the proprietor, the trade mark has become the common name in the trade for a product or service in respect of which it is registered;

(c)    if, in consequence of the use made of the trade mark by the proprietor of the trade mark or with his consent in respect of the goods or services for which it is registered, the trade mark is liable to mislead the public, particularly as to the nature, quality or geographical origin of those goods or services.

2.    Where the grounds for revocation of rights exist in respect of only some of the goods or services for which the EU trade mark is registered, the rights of the proprietor shall be declared to be revoked in respect of those goods or services only.

## SECTION 3

### *Grounds for invalidity*

#### *Article 59*

#### Absolute grounds for invalidity

1.    An EU trade mark shall be declared invalid on application to the Office or on the basis of a counterclaim in infringement proceedings:

(a)    where the EU trade mark has been registered contrary to the provisions of Article 7;

(b)    where the applicant was acting in bad faith when he filed the application for the trade mark.

2.    Where the EU trade mark has been registered in breach of the provisions of Article 7(1)(b), (c) or (d), it may nevertheless not be declared invalid if, in consequence of the use which has been made of it, it has after registration acquired a distinctive character in relation to the goods or services for which it is registered.

3.    Where the ground for invalidity exists in respect of only some of the goods or services for which the EU trade mark is registered, the trade mark shall be declared invalid as regards those goods or services only.

*Article 60*

### Relative grounds for invalidity

1.    An EU trade mark shall be declared invalid on application to the Office or on the basis of a counterclaim in infringement proceedings:

(a)    where there is an earlier trade mark as referred to in Article 8(2) and the conditions set out in paragraph 1 or 5 of that Article are fulfilled;

(b)    where there is a trade mark as referred to in Article 8(3) and the conditions set out in that paragraph are fulfilled;

(c)    where there is an earlier right as referred to in Article 8(4) and the conditions set out in that paragraph are fulfilled;

(d)    where there is an earlier designation of origin or geographical indication as referred to in Article 8(6) and the conditions set out in that paragraph are fulfilled.

All the conditions referred to in the first subparagraph shall be fulfilled at the filing date or the priority date of the EU trade mark.

2.    An EU trade mark shall also be declared invalid on application to the Office or on the basis of a counterclaim in infringement proceedings where the use of such trade mark may be prohibited pursuant to another earlier right under the Union legislation or national law governing its protection, and in particular:

(a)    a right to a name;

(b)    a right of personal portrayal;

(c)    a copyright;

(d)    an industrial property right.

3.    An EU trade mark may not be declared invalid where the proprietor of a right referred to in paragraph 1 or 2 consents expressly to the registration of the EU trade mark before submission of the application for a declaration of invalidity or the counterclaim.

4.    Where the proprietor of one of the rights referred to in paragraph 1 or 2 has previously applied for a declaration that an EU trade mark is invalid or made a counterclaim in infringement proceedings, he may not submit a new application for a declaration of invalidity or lodge a counterclaim on the basis of another of the said rights which he could have invoked in support of his first application or counterclaim.

5.    Article 59(3) shall apply.

*Article 61*

### Limitation in consequence of acquiescence

1.    Where the proprietor of an EU trade mark has acquiesced, for a period of five successive years, in the use of a later EU trade mark in the Union while being aware of such use, he shall no longer be entitled on the basis of the earlier trade mark to apply for a declaration that the later trade

mark is invalid in respect of the goods or services for which the later trade mark has been used, unless registration of the later EU trade mark was applied for in bad faith.

2. Where the proprietor of an earlier national trade mark as referred to in Article 8(2) or of another earlier sign referred to in Article 8(4) has acquiesced, for a period of five successive years, in the use of a later EU trade mark in the Member State in which the earlier trade mark or the other earlier sign is protected while being aware of such use, he shall no longer be entitled on the basis of the earlier trade mark or of the other earlier sign to apply for a declaration that the later trade mark is invalid in respect of the goods or services for which the later trade mark has been used, unless registration of the later EU trade mark was applied for in bad faith.

3. In the cases referred to in paragraphs 1 and 2, the proprietor of a later EU trade mark shall not be entitled to oppose the use of the earlier right, even though that right may no longer be invoked against the later EU trade mark.

## SECTION 4

### Consequences of revocation and invalidity

### Article 62

### Consequences of revocation and invalidity

1. The EU trade mark shall be deemed not to have had, as from the date of the application for revocation or of the counterclaim, the effects specified in this Regulation, to the extent that the rights of the proprietor have been revoked. An earlier date, on which one of the grounds for revocation occurred, may be fixed in the decision at the request of one of the parties.

2. The EU trade mark shall be deemed not to have had, as from the outset, the effects specified in this Regulation, to the extent that the trade mark has been declared invalid.

3. Subject to the national provisions relating either to claims for compensation for damage caused by negligence or lack of good faith on the part of the proprietor of the trade mark, or to unjust enrichment, the retroactive effect of revocation or invalidity of the trade mark shall not affect:

(a) any decision on infringement which has acquired the authority of a final decision and been enforced prior to the revocation or invalidity decision;

(b) any contract concluded prior to the revocation or invalidity decision, in so far as it has been performed before that decision; however, repayment, to an extent justified by the circumstances, of sums paid under the relevant contract may be claimed on grounds of equity.

## SECTION 5

### Proceedings in the office in relation to revocation or invalidity

### Article 63

### Application for revocation or for a declaration of invalidity

1. An application for revocation of the rights of the proprietor of an EU trade mark or for a declaration that the trade mark is invalid may be submitted to the Office:

(a) where Articles 58 and 59 apply, by any natural or legal person and any group or body set up for the purpose of representing the interests of manufacturers, producers, suppliers of services, traders or consumers, which, under the terms of the law governing it, has the capacity in its own name to sue and be sued;

(b) where Article 60(1) applies, by the persons referred to in Article 46(1);

(c) where Article 60(2) applies, by the owners of the earlier rights referred to in that provision or by the persons who are entitled under Union legislation or the law of the Member State concerned to exercise the rights in question.

2. The application shall be filed in a written reasoned statement. It shall not be deemed to have been filed until the fee has been paid.

3. An application for revocation or for a declaration of invalidity shall be inadmissible where an application relating to the same subject matter and cause of action, and involving the same parties, has been adjudicated on its merits, either by the Office or by an EU trade mark court as referred to in Article 123, and the decision of the Office or that court on that application has acquired the authority of a final decision.

## Article 64

### Examination of the application

1. On the examination of the application for revocation of rights or for a declaration of invalidity, the Office shall invite the parties, as often as necessary, to file observations, within a period to be fixed by the Office, on communications from the other parties or issued by itself.

2. If the proprietor of the EU trade mark so requests, the proprietor of an earlier EU trade mark, being a party to the invalidity proceedings, shall furnish proof that, during the period of five years preceding the date of the application for a declaration of invalidity, the earlier EU trade mark has been put to genuine use in the Union in connection with the goods or services in respect of which it is registered and which the proprietor of that earlier trade mark cites as justification for his application, or that there are proper reasons for non-use, provided that the earlier EU trade mark has at that date been registered for not less than five years. If, at the date on which the EU trade mark application was filed or at the priority date of the EU trade mark application, the earlier EU trade mark had been registered for not less than five years, the proprietor of the earlier EU trade mark shall furnish proof that, in addition, the conditions set out in Article 47(2) were satisfied at that date. In the absence of proof to this effect, the application for a declaration of invalidity shall be rejected. If the earlier EU trade mark has been used only in relation to part of the goods or services for which it is registered, it shall, for the purpose of the examination of the application for a declaration of invalidity, be deemed to be registered in respect of that part of the goods or services only.

3. Paragraph 2 shall apply to earlier national trade marks referred to in Article 8(2)(a), by substituting use in the Member State in which the earlier national trade mark is protected for use in the Union.

4. The Office may, if it thinks fit, invite the parties to make a friendly settlement.

5. If the examination of the application for revocation of rights or for a declaration of invalidity reveals that the trade mark should not have been registered in respect of some or all of the goods or services for which it is registered, the rights of the proprietor of the EU trade mark shall be revoked or it shall be declared invalid in respect of those goods or services. Otherwise the application for revocation of rights or for a declaration of invalidity shall be rejected.

6. A record of the Office's decision on the application for revocation of rights or for a declaration of invalidity shall be entered in the Register once it has become final.

## Article 65

### Delegation of powers

The Commission is empowered to adopt delegated acts in accordance with Article 208 specifying the details of the procedures governing the revocation and declaration of invalidity of an EU trade mark as referred to in Articles 63 and 64, as well as the transfer of an EU trade mark registered in the name of an agent as referred to in Article 21.

## CHAPTER VII
## APPEALS

*Article 66*

### Decisions subject to appeal

1.    An appeal shall lie from decisions of any of the decision-making instances of the Office listed in points (a) to (d) of Article 159, and, where appropriate, point (f) of that Article. Those decisions shall take effect only as from the date of expiration of the appeal period referred to in Article 68. The filing of the appeal shall have suspensive effect.

2.    A decision which does not terminate proceedings as regards one of the parties can only be appealed together with the final decision, unless the decision allows separate appeal.

*Article 67*

### Persons entitled to appeal and to be parties to appeal proceedings

Any party to proceedings adversely affected by a decision may appeal. Any other parties to the proceedings shall be parties to the appeal proceedings as of right.

*Article 68*

### Time limit and form of appeal

1.    Notice of appeal shall be filed in writing at the Office within two months of the date of notification of the decision. The notice shall be deemed to have been filed only when the fee for appeal has been paid. It shall be filed in the language of the proceedings in which the decision subject to appeal was taken. Within four months of the date of notification of the decision, a written statement setting out the grounds of appeal shall be filed.

2.    In *inter partes* proceedings, the defendant may, in his response, seek a decision annulling or altering the contested decision on a point not raised in the appeal. Such submissions shall cease to have effect should the appellant discontinue the proceedings.

*Article 69*

### Revision of decisions in ex parte cases

1.    If the party which has lodged the appeal is the sole party to the procedure, and if the department whose decision is contested considers the appeal to be admissible and well founded, the department shall rectify its decision.

2.    If the decision is not rectified within one month of receipt of the statement of grounds, the appeal shall be remitted to the Board of Appeal without delay, and without comment as to its merit.

*Article 70*

### Examination of appeals

1.    If the appeal is admissible, the Board of Appeal shall examine whether the appeal is allowable.

2.    In the examination of the appeal, the Board of Appeal shall invite the parties, as often as necessary, to file observations, within a period to be fixed by the Board of Appeal, on communications from the other parties or issued by itself.

## Article 71

### Decisions in respect of appeals

1.    Following the examination as to the allowability of the appeal, the Board of Appeal shall decide on the appeal. The Board of Appeal may either exercise any power within the competence of the department which was responsible for the decision appealed or remit the case to that department for further prosecution.

2.    If the Board of Appeal remits the case for further prosecution to the department whose decision was appealed, that department shall be bound by the *ratio decidendi* of the Board of Appeal, in so far as the facts are the same.

3.    The decisions of the Board of Appeal shall take effect only as from the date of expiry of the period referred to in Article 72(5) or, if an action has been brought before the General Court within that period, as from the date of dismissal of such action or of any appeal filed with the Court of Justice against the decision of the General Court.

## Article 72

### Actions before the Court of Justice

1.    Actions may be brought before the General Court against decisions of the Boards of Appeal in relation to appeals.

2.    The action may be brought on grounds of lack of competence, infringement of an essential procedural requirement, infringement of the TFEU, infringement of this Regulation or of any rule of law relating to their application or misuse of power.

3.    The General Court shall have jurisdiction to annul or to alter the contested decision.

4.    The action shall be open to any party to proceedings before the Board of Appeal adversely affected by its decision.

5.    The action shall be brought before the General Court within two months of the date of notification of the decision of the Board of Appeal.

6.    The Office shall take the necessary measures to comply with the judgment of the General Court or, in the event of an appeal against that judgment, the Court of Justice.

## Article 73

### Delegation of powers

The Commission is empowered to adopt delegated acts in accordance with Article 208 specifying:

(a)    the formal content of the notice of appeal referred to in Article 68 and the procedure for the filing and the examination of an appeal;

(b)    the formal content and form of the Board of Appeal's decisions as referred to in Article 71;

(c)    the reimbursement of the appeal fee referred to in Article 68.

# CHAPTER VIII
## SPECIFIC PROVISIONS ON EUROPEAN UNION COLLECTIVE MARKS AND CERTIFICATION MARKS

### SECTION 1
### EU collective marks

### Article 74

### EU collective marks

1.    A European Union collective mark ('EU collective mark') shall be an EU trade mark which is described as such when the mark is applied for and is capable of distinguishing the goods or services of the members of the association which is the proprietor of the mark from those of other undertakings. Associations of manufacturers, producers, suppliers of services, or traders which, under the terms of the law governing them, have the capacity in their own name to have rights and obligations of all kinds, to make contracts or accomplish other legal acts, and to sue and be sued, as well as legal persons governed by public law, may apply for EU collective marks.

2.    By way of derogation from Article 7(1)(c), signs or indications which may serve, in trade, to designate the geographical origin of the goods or services may constitute EU collective marks within the meaning of paragraph 1. An EU collective mark shall not entitle the proprietor to prohibit a third party from using in the course of trade such signs or indications, provided that he uses them in accordance with honest practices in industrial or commercial matters; in particular, such a mark shall not be invoked against a third party who is entitled to use a geographical name.

3.    Chapters I to VII and IX to XIV shall apply to EU collective marks to the extent that this section does not provide otherwise.

### Article 75

### Regulations governing use of an EU collective mark

1.    An applicant for an EU collective mark shall submit regulations governing use within two months of the date of filing.

2.    The regulations governing use shall specify the persons authorised to use the mark, the conditions of membership of the association and, where they exist, the conditions of use of the mark, including sanctions. The regulations governing use of a mark referred to in Article 74(2) shall authorise any person whose goods or services originate in the geographical area concerned to become a member of the association which is the proprietor of the mark.

3.    The Commission shall adopt implementing acts specifying the details to be contained in the regulations referred to in paragraph 2 of this Article. Those implementing acts shall be adopted in accordance with the examination procedure referred to in Article 207(2).

### Article 76

### Refusal of the application

1.    In addition to the grounds for refusal of an EU trade mark application provided for in Articles 41 and 42, an application for an EU collective mark shall be refused where the provisions of Articles 74 or 75 are not satisfied, or where the regulations governing use are contrary to public policy or to accepted principles of morality.

2.    An application for an EU collective mark shall also be refused if the public is liable to be misled as regards the character or the significance of the mark, in particular if it is likely to be taken to be something other than a collective mark.

3.    An application shall not be refused if the applicant, as a result of amendment of the regulations governing use, meets the requirements of paragraphs 1 and 2.

## Article 77

### Observations by third parties

Where written observations on an EU collective mark are submitted to the Office pursuant to Article 45, those observations may also be based on the particular grounds on which the application for an EU collective mark should be refused pursuant to Article 76.

## Article 78

### Use of marks

Use of an EU collective mark by any person who has authority to use it shall satisfy the requirements of this Regulation, provided that the other conditions which this Regulation imposes with regard to the use of EU trade marks are fulfilled.

## Article 79

### Amendment of the regulations governing use of the EU collective mark

1.    The proprietor of an EU collective mark shall submit to the Office any amended regulations governing use.

2.    The amendment shall not be mentioned in the Register if the amended regulations do not satisfy the requirements of Article 75 or involve one of the grounds for refusal referred to in Article 76.

3.    Written observations made in accordance with Article 77 may also be submitted with regard to amended regulations governing use.

4.    For the purposes of applying this Regulation, amendments to the regulations governing use shall take effect only from the date of entry of the mention of the amendment in the Register.

## Article 80

### Persons who are entitled to bring an action for infringement

1.    The provisions of Article 25(3) and (4) concerning the rights of licensees shall apply to every person who has authority to use an EU collective mark.

2.    The proprietor of an EU collective mark shall be entitled to claim compensation on behalf of persons who have authority to use the mark where they have sustained damage in consequence of unauthorised use of the mark.

## Article 81

### Grounds for revocation

Apart from the grounds for revocation provided for in Article 58, the rights of the proprietor of an EU collective mark shall be revoked on application to the Office or on the basis of a counterclaim in infringement proceedings, if:

(a)    the proprietor does not take reasonable steps to prevent the mark being used in a manner incompatible with the conditions of use, where these exist, laid down in the regulations governing use, amendments to which have, where appropriate, been mentioned in the Register;

(b)    the manner in which the mark has been used by the proprietor has caused it to become liable to mislead the public in the manner referred to in Article 76(2);

(c) an amendment to the regulations governing use of the mark has been mentioned in the Register in breach of the provisions of Article 79(2), unless the proprietor of the mark, by further amending the regulations governing use, complies with the requirements of those provisions.

*Article 82*

### Grounds for invalidity

Apart from the grounds for invalidity provided for in Articles 59 and 60, an EU collective mark which is registered in breach of the provisions of Article 76 shall be declared invalid on application to the Office or on the basis of a counterclaim in infringement proceedings, unless the proprietor of the mark, by amending the regulations governing use, complies with the requirements of those provisions.

## SECTION 2

### *EU certification marks*

*Article 83*

### EU certification marks

1. An EU certification mark shall be an EU trade mark which is described as such when the mark is applied for and is capable of distinguishing goods or services which are certified by the proprietor of the mark in respect of material, mode of manufacture of goods or performance of services, quality, accuracy or other characteristics, with the exception of geographical origin, from goods and services which are not so certified.

2. Any natural or legal person, including institutions, authorities and bodies governed by public law, may apply for EU certification marks provided that such person does not carry on a business involving the supply of goods or services of the kind certified.

3. Chapters I to VII and IX to XIV shall apply to EU certification marks to the extent that this Section does not provide otherwise.

*Article 84*

### Regulations governing use of an EU certification mark

1. An applicant for an EU certification mark shall submit regulations governing the use of the EU certification mark within two months of the date of filing.

2. The regulations governing use shall specify the persons authorised to use the mark, the characteristics to be certified by the mark, how the certifying body is to test those characteristics and to supervise the use of the mark. Those regulations shall also specify the conditions of use of the mark, including sanctions.

3. The Commission shall adopt implementing acts specifying the details to be contained in the regulations referred to in paragraph 2 of this Article. Those implementing acts shall be adopted in accordance with the examination procedure referred to in Article 207(2).

*Article 85*

### Refusal of the application

1. In addition to the grounds for refusal of an EU trade mark application provided for in Articles 41 and 42, an application for an EU certification mark shall be refused where the conditions set out in Articles 83 and 84 are not satisfied, or where the regulations governing use are contrary to public policy or to accepted principles of morality.

2. An application for an EU certification mark shall also be refused if the public is liable to be misled as regards the character or the significance of the mark, in particular if it is likely to be taken to be something other than a certification mark.

3. An application shall not be refused if the applicant, as a result of an amendment of the regulations governing use, meets the requirements of paragraphs 1 and 2.

## Article 86

### Observations by third parties

Where written observations on an EU certification mark are submitted to the Office pursuant to Article 45, those observations may also be based on the particular grounds on which the application for an EU certification mark should be refused pursuant to Article 85.

## Article 87

### Use of the EU certification mark

Use of an EU certification mark by any person who has authority to use it pursuant to the regulations governing use referred to in Article 84 shall satisfy the requirements of this Regulation, provided that the other conditions laid down in this Regulation with regard to the use of EU trade marks are fulfilled.

## Article 88

### Amendment of the regulations governing use of the EU certification mark

1. The proprietor of an EU certification mark shall submit to the Office any amended regulations governing use.

2. Amendments shall not be mentioned in the Register where the regulations as amended do not satisfy the requirements of Article 84 or involve one of the grounds for refusal referred to in Article 85.

3. Written observations in accordance with Article 86 may also be submitted with regard to amended regulations governing use.

4. For the purposes of this Regulation, amendments to the regulations governing use shall take effect only as from the date of entry of the mention of the amendment in the Register.

## Article 89

### Transfer

By way of derogation from Article 20(1), an EU certification mark may only be transferred to a person who meets the requirements of Article 83(2).

## Article 90

### Persons who are entitled to bring an action for infringement

1. Only the proprietor of an EU certification mark, or any person specifically authorised by him to that effect, shall be entitled to bring an action for infringement.

2. The proprietor of an EU certification mark shall be entitled to claim compensation on behalf of persons who have authority to use the mark where they have sustained damage as a consequence of unauthorised use of the mark.

## Article 91

### Grounds for revocation

In addition to the grounds for revocation provided for in Article 58, the rights of the proprietor of an EU certification mark shall be revoked on application to the Office or on the basis of a counterclaim in infringement proceedings, where any of the following conditions is fulfilled:

(a) the proprietor no longer complies with the requirements set out in Article 83(2);

(b) the proprietor does not take reasonable steps to prevent the EU certification mark being used in a manner that is incompatible with the conditions of use laid down in the regulations governing use, amendments to which have, where appropriate, been mentioned in the Register;

(c) the manner in which the EU certification mark has been used by the proprietor has caused it to become liable to mislead the public in the manner referred to in Article 85(2);

(d) an amendment to the regulations governing use of the EU certification mark has been mentioned in the Register in breach of Article 88(2), unless the proprietor of the mark, by further amending the regulations governing use, complies with the requirements of that Article.

## Article 92

### Grounds for invalidity

In addition to the grounds for invalidity provided for in Articles 59 and 60, an EU certification mark which is registered in breach of Article 85 shall be declared invalid on application to the Office or on the basis of a counterclaim in infringement proceedings, unless the proprietor of the EU certification mark, by amending the regulations governing use, complies with the requirements of Article 85.

## Article 93

### Conversion

Without prejudice to Article 139(2), conversion of an application for an EU certification mark or of a registered EU certification mark shall not take place where the national law of the Member State concerned does not provide for the registration of guarantee or certification marks pursuant to Article 28 of Directive (EU) 2015/2436.

## CHAPTER IX
## PROCEDURE

### SECTION 1

### *General provisions*

### Article 94

### Decisions and communications of the Office

1.    Decisions of the Office shall state the reasons on which they are based. They shall be based only on reasons or evidence on which the parties concerned have had an opportunity to present their comments. Where oral proceedings are held before the Office, the decision may be given orally. Subsequently, the decision shall be notified in writing to the parties.

2.    Any decision, communication or notice from the Office shall indicate the department or division of the Office as well as the name or the names of the official or officials responsible. They shall be signed by that official or those officials, or, instead of a signature, carry a printed or stamped seal of the Office. The Executive Director may determine that other means of identifying the department or division of the Office and the name of the official or officials responsible, or an identification other than a seal, may be used where decisions, communications or notices from the Office are transmitted by telecopier or any other technical means of communication.

3.    Decisions of the Office which are open to appeal shall be accompanied by a written communication indicating that any notice of appeal is to be filed in writing at the Office within two months of the date of notification of the decision in question. The communications shall also draw the attention of the parties to the provisions laid down in Articles 66, 67 and 68. The parties may not plead any failure on the part of the Office to communicate the availability of appeal proceedings.

## *Article 95*

### Examination of the facts by the Office of its own motion

1.    In proceedings before it the Office shall examine the facts of its own motion; however, in proceedings relating to relative grounds for refusal of registration, the Office shall be restricted in this examination to the facts, evidence and arguments provided by the parties and the relief sought. In invalidity proceedings pursuant to Article 59, the Office shall limit its examination to the grounds and arguments submitted by the parties.

2.    The Office may disregard facts or evidence which are not submitted in due time by the parties concerned.

## *Article 96*

### Oral proceedings

1.    If the Office considers that oral proceedings would be expedient they shall be held either at the instance of the Office or at the request of any party to the proceedings.

2.    Oral proceedings before the examiners, the Opposition Division and the Department in charge of the Register shall not be public.

3.    Oral proceedings, including delivery of the decision, shall be public before the Cancellation Division and the Boards of Appeal, in so far as the department before which the proceedings are taking place does not decide otherwise in cases where admission of the public could have serious and unjustified disadvantages, in particular for a party to the proceedings.

4.    The Commission is empowered to adopt delegated acts in accordance with Article 208 specifying the detailed arrangements for oral proceedings, including the detailed arrangements for the use of languages in accordance with Article 146.

## *Article 97*

### Taking of evidence

1.    In any proceedings before the Office, the means of giving or obtaining evidence shall include the following:

(a)   hearing the parties;

(b)   requests for information;

(c)   the production of documents and items of evidence;

(d)   hearing witnesses;

(e)   opinions by experts;

(f)     statements in writing sworn or affirmed or having a similar effect under the law of the State in which the statement is drawn up.

2.     The relevant department may commission one of its members to examine the evidence adduced.

3.     If the Office considers it necessary for a party, witness or expert to give evidence orally, it shall issue a summons to the person concerned to appear before it. The period of notice provided in such summons shall be at least one month, unless they agree to a shorter period.

4.     The parties shall be informed of the hearing of a witness or expert before the Office. They shall have the right to be present and to put questions to the witness or expert.

5.     The Executive Director shall determine the amounts of expenses to be paid, including advances, as regards the costs of taking of evidence as referred to in this Article.

6.     The Commission is empowered to adopt delegated acts in accordance with Article 208 specifying the detailed arrangements for the taking of evidence.

## *Article 98*

### Notification

1.     The Office shall, as a matter of course, notify those concerned of decisions and summonses and of any notice or other communication from which a time limit is reckoned, or of which those concerned are to be notified under other provisions of this Regulation or of acts adopted pursuant to this Regulation, or of which notification has been ordered by the Executive Director.

2.     The Executive Director may determine which documents other than decisions subject to a time limit for appeal and summonses shall be notified by registered letter with proof of delivery.

3.     Notification may be effected by different means, including by electronic means. The details regarding electronic means shall be determined by the Executive Director.

4.     Where notification is to be effected by public notice, the Executive Director shall determine how the public notice is to be given and shall fix the beginning of the one-month period on the expiry of which the document shall be deemed to have been notified.

5.     The Commission is empowered to adopt delegated acts in accordance with Article 208 specifying the detailed arrangements for notification.

## *Article 99*

### Notification of loss of rights

Where the Office finds that the loss of any rights results from this Regulation or acts adopted pursuant to this Regulation, without any decision having been taken, it shall communicate this to the person concerned in accordance with Article 98. The latter may apply for a decision on the matter within two months of notification of the communication, if he considers that the finding of the Office is incorrect. The Office shall adopt such a decision only where it disagrees with the person requesting it; otherwise the Office shall amend its finding and inform the person requesting the decision.

## *Article 100*

### Communications to the Office

1.     Communications addressed to the Office may be effected by electronic means. The Executive Director shall determine to what extent and under which technical conditions those communications may be submitted electronically.

2.     The Commission is empowered to adopt delegated acts in accordance with Article 208 specifying the rules on the means of communication, including the electronic means of communication,

to be used by the parties to proceedings before the Office and the forms to be made available by the Office.

## Article 101

### Time limits

1.     Time limits shall be laid down in terms of full years, months, weeks or days. Calculation shall start on the day following the day on which the relevant event occurred. The duration of time limits shall be no less than one month and no more than six months.

2.     The Executive Director shall determine, before the commencement of each calendar year, the days on which the Office is not open for receipt of documents or on which ordinary post is not delivered in the locality in which the Office is located.

3.     The Executive Director shall determine the duration of the period of interruption in the case of a general interruption in the delivery of post in the Member State where the Office is located or, in the case of an actual interruption of the Office's connection to admitted electronic means of communication.

4.     If an exceptional occurrence, such as a natural disaster or strike, interrupts or interferes with proper communication from the parties to the proceedings to the Office or vice-versa, the Executive Director may determine that for parties to the proceedings having their residence or registered office in the Member State concerned or who have appointed a representative with a place of business in the Member State concerned all time limits that otherwise would expire on or after the date of commencement of such occurrence, as determined by him, shall extend until a date to be determined by him. When determining that date, he shall assess when the exceptional occurrence comes to an end. If the occurrence affects the seat of the Office, such determination of the Executive Director shall specify that it applies in respect of all parties to the proceedings.

5.     The Commission is empowered to adopt delegated acts in accordance with Article 208 specifying the details regarding the calculation and duration of time limits.

## Article 102

### Correction of errors and manifest oversights

1.     The Office shall correct any linguistic errors or errors of transcription and manifest oversights in its decisions, or technical errors attributable to it in registering an EU trade mark or in publishing the registration of its own motion or at the request of a party.

2.     Where the correction of errors in the registration of an EU trade mark or the publication of the registration is requested by the proprietor, Article 55 shall apply *mutatis mutandis*.

3.     Corrections of errors in the registration of an EU trade mark and in the publication of the registration shall be published by the Office.

## Article 103

### Revocation of decisions

1.     Where the Office has made an entry in the Register or taken a decision which contains an obvious error attributable to the Office, it shall ensure that the entry is cancelled or the decision is revoked. Where there is only one party to the proceedings and the entry or the act affects its rights, cancellation or revocation shall be determined even if the error was not evident to the party.

2.     Cancellation or revocation as referred to in paragraph 1 shall be determined, *ex officio* or at the request of one of the parties to the proceedings, by the department which made the entry or took the decision. The cancellation of the entry in the Register or the revocation of the decision shall be effected within one year of the date on which the entry was made in the Register or that decision was

taken, after consultation with the parties to the proceedings and any proprietor of rights to the EU trade mark in question that are entered in the Register. The Office shall keep records of any such cancellation or revocation.

3.     The Commission is empowered to adopt delegated acts in accordance with Article 208 specifying the procedure for the revocation of a decision or for the cancellation of an entry in the Register.

4.     This Article shall be without prejudice to the right of the parties to submit an appeal under Articles 66 and 72, or to the possibility of correcting errors and manifest oversights under Article 102. Where an appeal has been filed against a decision of the Office containing an error, the appeal proceedings shall become devoid of purpose upon revocation by the Office of its decision pursuant to paragraph 1 of this Article. In the latter case, the appeal fee shall be reimbursed to the appellant.

*Article 104*

### Restitutio in integrum

1.     The applicant for or proprietor of an EU trade mark or any other party to proceedings before the Office who, in spite of all due care required by the circumstances having been taken, was unable to comply with a time limit vis-à-vis the Office shall, upon application, have his rights re-established if the obstacle to compliance has the direct consequence, by virtue of the provisions of this Regulation, of causing the loss of any right or means of redress.

2.     The application shall be filed in writing within two months of the removal of the obstacle to compliance with the time limit. The omitted act shall be completed within this period. The application shall only be admissible within the year immediately following the expiry of the unobserved time limit. In the case of non-submission of the request for renewal of registration or of non-payment of a renewal fee, the further period of six months provided in the third sentence of Article 53(3) shall be deducted from the period of one year.

3.     The application shall state the grounds on which it is based and shall set out the facts on which it relies. It shall not be deemed to be filed until the fee for re-establishment of rights has been paid.

4.     The department competent to decide on the omitted act shall decide upon the application.

5.     This Article shall not be applicable to the time limits referred to in paragraph 2 of this Article, Article 46(1) and (3) and Article 105.

6.     Where the applicant for or proprietor of an EU trade mark has his rights re-established, he may not invoke his rights vis-à-vis a third party who, in good faith, has put goods on the market or supplied services under a sign which is identical with, or similar to, the EU trade mark in the course of the period between the loss of rights in the application or in the EU trade mark and publication of the mention of re-establishment of those rights.

7.     A third party who may avail himself of the provisions of paragraph 6 may bring third party proceedings against the decision re-establishing the rights of the applicant for or proprietor of an EU trade mark within a period of two months as from the date of publication of the mention of re-establishment of those rights.

8.     Nothing in this Article shall limit the right of a Member State to grant *restitutio in integrum* in respect of time limits provided for in this Regulation and to be observed vis-à-vis the authorities of such State.

## Article 105

### Continuation of proceedings

1.    An applicant for or proprietor of an EU trade mark or any other party to proceedings before the Office who has omitted to observe a time limit vis-à-vis the Office may, upon request, obtain the continuation of proceedings, provided that at the time the request is made the omitted act has been carried out. The request for continuation of proceedings shall be admissible only if it is submitted within two months of the expiry of the unobserved time limit. The request shall not be deemed to have been filed until the fee for continuation of the proceedings has been paid.

2.    This Article shall not apply to the time limits laid down in Article 32, Article 34(1), Article 38(1), Article 41(2), Article 46(1) and (3), Article 53(3), Article 68, Article 72(5), Article 104(2) and Article 139, or to the time limits laid down in paragraph 1 of this Article or the time limit for claiming seniority pursuant to Article 39 after the application has been filed.

3.    The department competent to decide on the omitted act shall decide upon the application.

4.    If the Office accepts the application, the consequences of having failed to observe the time limit shall be deemed not to have occurred. If a decision has been taken between the expiry of that time limit and the request for the continuation of proceedings, the department competent to decide on the omitted act shall review the decision and, where completion of the omitted act itself is sufficient, take a different decision. If, following the review, the Office concludes that the original decision does not require to be altered, it shall confirm that decision in writing.

5.    If the Office rejects the application, the fee shall be refunded.

## Article 106

### Interruption of proceedings

1.    Proceedings before the Office shall be interrupted:

(a)    in the event of the death or legal incapacity of the applicant for, or proprietor of, an EU trade mark or of the person authorised by national law to act on his behalf. To the extent that that death or incapacity does not affect the authorisation of a representative appointed under Article 120, proceedings shall be interrupted only on application by such representative;

(b)    in the event of the applicant for, or proprietor of, an EU trade mark being prevented, for legal reasons resulting from action taken against his property, from continuing the proceedings before the Office;

(c)    in the event of the death or legal incapacity of the representative of an applicant for, or proprietor of, an EU trade mark, or of that representative being prevented, for legal reasons resulting from action taken against his property, from continuing the proceedings before the Office.

2.    Proceedings before the Office shall be resumed as soon as the identity of the person authorised to continue them has been established.

3.    The Commission is empowered to adopt delegated acts in accordance with Article 208 specifying the detailed arrangements for the resumption of proceedings before the Office.

## Article 107

### Reference to general principles

In the absence of procedural provisions in this Regulation or in acts adopted pursuant to this Regulation, the Office shall take into account the principles of procedural law generally recognised in the Member States.

## *Article 108*

### Termination of financial obligations

1.     Rights of the Office to the payment of a fee shall be extinguished after four years from the end of the calendar year in which the fee fell due.

2.     Rights against the Office for the refunding of fees or sums of money paid in excess of a fee shall be extinguished after four years from the end of the calendar year in which the right arose.

3.     The period laid down in paragraphs 1 and 2 shall be interrupted, in the case covered by paragraph 1, by a request for payment of the fee, and in the case covered by paragraph 2, by a reasoned claim in writing. On interruption it shall begin again immediately and shall end at the latest six years after the end of the year in which it originally began, unless, in the meantime, judicial proceedings to enforce the right have begun; in this case the period shall end at the earliest one year after the judgment has acquired the authority of a final decision.

## *SECTION 2*

### *Costs*

## *Article 109*

### Costs

1.     The losing party in opposition proceedings, proceedings for revocation, proceedings for a declaration of invalidity or appeal proceedings shall bear the fees paid by the other party. Without prejudice to Article 146(7), the losing party shall also bear all costs incurred by the other party that are essential to the proceedings, including travel and subsistence and the remuneration of a representative within the meaning of Article 120(1), within the limits of the scales set for each category of costs in the implementing act to be adopted in accordance with paragraph 2 of this Article. The fees to be borne by the losing party shall be limited to the fees paid by the other party for opposition, for an application for revocation or for a declaration of invalidity of the EU trade mark and for appeal.

2.     The Commission shall adopt implementing acts specifying the maximum rates for costs essential to the proceedings and actually incurred by the successful party. Those implementing acts shall be adopted in accordance with the examination procedure referred to in Article 207(2).

When specifying such amounts with respect to travel and subsistence costs, the Commission shall take into account the distance between the place of residence or business of the party, representative or witness or expert and the place where the oral proceedings are held, the procedural stage at which the costs have been incurred, and, as far as costs of representation within the meaning of Article 120(1) are concerned, the need to ensure that the obligation to bear the costs may not be misused for tactical reasons by the other party. Subsistence expenses shall be calculated in accordance with the Staff Regulations of Officials of the Union and the Conditions of Employment of Other Servants of the Union, laid down in Council Regulation (EEC, Euratom, ECSC) No 259/68 ('the Staff Regulations' and 'Conditions of Employment' respectively).

The losing party shall bear the costs for one opposing party only and, where applicable, one representative only.

3.     However, where each party succeeds on some and fails on other heads, or if reasons of equity so dictate, the Opposition Division, Cancellation Division or Board of Appeal shall decide a different apportionment of costs.

4.     The party who terminates the proceedings by withdrawing the EU trade mark application, the opposition, the application for revocation of rights, the application for a declaration of invalidity or the appeal, or by not renewing registration of the EU trade mark or by surrendering the EU trade

mark, shall bear the fees and the costs incurred by the other party as stipulated in paragraphs 1 and 3.

5.     Where a case does not proceed to judgment the costs shall be at the discretion of the Opposition Division, Cancellation Division or Board of Appeal.

6.     Where the parties conclude before the Opposition Division, Cancellation Division or Board of Appeal a settlement of costs differing from that provided for in paragraphs 1 to 5, the department concerned shall take note of that agreement.

7.     The Opposition Division or Cancellation Division or Board of Appeal shall fix the amount of the costs to be paid pursuant to paragraphs 1 to 6 of this Article when the costs to be paid are limited to the fees paid to the Office and the representation costs. In all other cases, the registry of the Board of Appeal or a member of the staff of the Opposition Division or Cancellation Division shall fix, on request, the amount of the costs to be reimbursed. The request shall be admissible only for the period of two months following the date on which the decision for which an application was made for the costs to be fixed becomes final and shall be accompanied by a bill and supporting evidence. For the costs of representation pursuant to Article 120(1), an assurance by the representative that the costs have been incurred shall be sufficient. For other costs, it shall be sufficient if their plausibility is established. Where the amount of the costs is fixed pursuant to the first sentence of this paragraph, representation costs shall be awarded at the level laid down in the implementing act adopted pursuant to paragraph 2 of this Article and irrespective of whether they have been actually incurred.

8.     The decision on the fixing of costs, stating the reasons on which it is based, may be reviewed by a decision of the Opposition Division or Cancellation Division or Board of Appeal on a request filed within one month of the date of notification of the awarding of costs. It shall not be deemed to be filed until the fee for reviewing the amount of the costs has been paid. The Opposition Division, the Cancellation Division or the Board of Appeal, as the case may be, shall take a decision on the request for a review of the decision on the fixing of costs without oral proceedings.

*Article 110*

**Enforcement of decisions fixing the amount of costs**

1.     Any final decision of the Office fixing the amount of costs shall be enforceable.

2.     Enforcement shall be governed by the rules of civil procedure in force in the State in the territory of which it is carried out. Each Member State shall designate a single authority responsible for verifying the authenticity of the decision referred to in paragraph 1 and shall communicate its contact details to the Office, the Court of Justice and the Commission. The order for the enforcement of the decision shall be appended to the decision by that authority, with the verification of the authenticity of the decision as the sole formality.

3.     When these formalities have been completed on application by the party concerned, the latter may proceed to enforcement in accordance with the national law, by bringing the matter directly before the competent authority.

4.     Enforcement may be suspended only by a decision of the Court of Justice. However, the courts of the country concerned shall have jurisdiction over complaints that enforcement is being carried out in an irregular manner.

## SECTION 3

### *Information which may be made available to the public and to the authorities of the Member States*

*Article 111*

### Register of EU trade marks

1.    The Office shall keep a Register of EU trade marks which it shall keep up to date.

2.    The Register shall contain the following entries relating to EU trade mark applications and registrations:

(a)   the date of filing the application;

(b)   the file number of the application;

(c)   the date of the publication of the application;

(d)   the name and address of the applicant;

(e)   the name and business address of the representative, other than a representative as referred to in the first sentence of Article 119(3);

(f)   the representation of the mark, with indications as to its nature; and, where applicable, a description of the mark;

(g)   an indication of the goods and services by their names;

(h)   particulars of claims of priority pursuant to Article 35;

(i)   particulars of claims of exhibition priority pursuant to Article 38;

(j)   particulars of claims of seniority of a registered earlier trade mark as referred to in Article 39;

(k)   a statement that the mark has become distinctive in consequence of the use which has been made of it, pursuant to Article 7(3);

(*l*)   an indication that the mark is a collective mark;

(m)  an indication that the mark is a certification mark;

(n)   the language in which the application was filed and the second language which the applicant has indicated in his application, pursuant to Article 146(3);

(*o*)   the date of registration of the mark in the Register and the registration number;

(p)   a statement that the application is the result of a transformation of an international registration designating the Union, pursuant to Article 204 of this Regulation, together with the date of the international registration pursuant to Article 3(4) of the Madrid Protocol or the date on which the territorial extension to the Union made subsequent to the international registration pursuant to Article 3ter(2) of the Madrid Protocol was recorded and, where applicable, the date of priority of the international registration.

3.    The Register shall also contain the following entries, each accompanied by the date of recording of such entry:

(a)   changes in the name, address or nationality of the proprietor of an EU trade mark or a change in the State in which he is domiciled or has his seat or establishment;

(b)   changes in the name or business address of the representative, other than a representative as referred to in the first sentence of Article 119(3);

(c)    where a new representative is appointed, the name and business address of that representative;

(d)    amendments and alterations of the mark, pursuant to Articles 49 and 54, and corrections of errors;

(e)    notice of amendments to the regulations governing the use of the collective mark pursuant to Article 79;

(f)    particulars of claims of seniority of a registered earlier trade mark as referred to in Article 39, pursuant to Article 40;

(g)    total or partial transfers pursuant to Article 20;

(h)    creation or transfer of a right *in rem* pursuant to Article 22, and the nature of the right *in rem*;

(i)    levy of execution pursuant to Article 23 and insolvency proceedings pursuant to Article 24;

(j)    the grant or transfer of a licence pursuant to Article 25 and, where applicable, the type of licence;

(k)    renewal of a registration pursuant to Article 53, the date from which it takes effect and any restrictions pursuant to Article 53(4);

(*l*)    a record of a determination of the expiry of a registration pursuant to Article 53;

(m)    declarations of withdrawal or surrender by the proprietor of the mark pursuant to Articles 49 and 57 respectively;

(n)    the date of submission and the particulars of an opposition pursuant to Article 46, of an application pursuant to Article 63, or a counterclaim pursuant to Article 128(4) for revocation or for a declaration of invalidity, or of an appeal pursuant to Article 68;

(o)    the date and content of a decision on an opposition, on an application or counterclaim pursuant to Article 64(6) or the third sentence of Article 128(6), or on an appeal pursuant to Article 71;

(p)    a record of the receipt of a request for conversion pursuant to Article 140(2);

(q)    the cancellation of the representative recorded pursuant to point (e) of paragraph 2 of this Article;

(r)    the cancellation of the seniority of a national mark;

(s)    the modification to or cancellation from the Register of the items referred to in points (h), (i) and (j) of this paragraph;

(t)    the replacement of the EU trade mark by an international registration pursuant to Article 197;

(u)    the date and number of international registrations based on the EU trade mark application which has been registered as an EU trade mark pursuant to Article 185(1);

(v)    the date and number of international registrations based on the EU trade mark pursuant to Article 185(2);

(w)    the division of an application pursuant to Article 50 and the division of a registration pursuant to Article 56, together with the items referred to in paragraph 2 of this Article in respect of the divisional registration, as well as the list of goods and services of the original registration as amended;

(x)    the revocation of a decision or an entry in the Register pursuant to Article 103, where the revocation concerns a decision or entry which has been published;

(y)  notice of amendments to the regulations governing the use of the EU certification mark pursuant to Article 88.

4.  The Executive Director may determine that items other than those referred to in paragraphs 2 and 3 of this Article are to be entered in the Register, subject to Article 149(4).

5.  The Register may be maintained in electronic form. The Office shall collect, organise, make public and store the items referred to in paragraphs 2 and 3, including any personal data, for the purposes laid down in paragraph 8. The Office shall keep the register easily accessible for public inspection.

6.  The proprietor of an EU trade mark shall be notified of any change in the Register.

7.  The Office shall provide certified or uncertified extracts from the Register on request and on payment of a fee.

8.  The processing of the data concerning the entries set out in paragraphs 2 and 3, including any personal data, shall take place for the purposes of:

(a)  administering the applications and/or registrations as described in this Regulation and acts adopted pursuant to it;

(b)  maintaining a public register for inspection by, and the information of, public authorities and economic operators, in order to enable them to exercise the rights conferred on them by this Regulation and be informed about the existence of prior rights belonging to third parties; and

(c)  producing reports and statistics enabling the Office to optimise its operations and improve the functioning of the system.

9.  All the data, including personal data, concerning the entries in paragraphs 2 and 3 shall be considered to be of public interest and may be accessed by any third party. For reasons of legal certainty, the entries in the Register shall be kept for an indefinite period of time.

*Article 112*

### Database

1.  In addition to the obligation to keep a Register within the meaning of Article 111, the Office shall collect and store in an electronic database all the particulars provided by applicants or any other party to the proceedings pursuant to this Regulation or acts adopted pursuant to it.

2.  The electronic database may include personal data, beyond those included in the Register pursuant to Article 111, to the extent that such particulars are required by this Regulation or by acts adopted pursuant to it. The collection, storage and processing of such data shall serve the purposes of:

(a)  administering the applications and/or registrations as described in this Regulation and in acts adopted pursuant to it;

(b)  accessing the information necessary for conducting the relevant proceedings more easily and efficiently;

(c)  communicating with the applicants and other parties to the proceedings;

(d)  producing reports and statistics enabling the Office to optimise its operations and improve the functioning of the system.

3.  The Executive Director shall determine the conditions of access to the electronic database and the manner in which its contents, other than the personal data referred to in paragraph 2 of this Article but including those listed in Article 111, may be made available in machine-readable form, including the charge for such access.

4.    Access to the personal data referred to in paragraph 2 shall be restricted and such data shall not be made publicly available unless the party concerned has given his express consent.

5.    All data shall be kept indefinitely. However, the party concerned may request the removal of any personal data from the database after 18 months from the expiry of the EU trade mark or the closure of the relevant *inter partes* procedure. The party concerned shall have the right to obtain the correction of inaccurate or erroneous data at any time.

## Article 113

### Online access to decisions

1.    The decisions of the Office shall be made available online for the information and consultation of the general public in the interest of transparency and predictability. Any party to the proceedings that led to the adoption of the decision may request the removal of any personal data included in the decision.

2.    The Office may provide online access to judgments of national and Union courts related to its tasks in order to raise public awareness of intellectual property matters and promote convergence of practices. The Office shall respect the conditions of the initial publication with regard to personal data.

## Article 114

### Inspection of files

1.    The files relating to EU trade mark applications which have not yet been published shall not be made available for inspection without the consent of the applicant.

2.    Any person who can prove that the applicant for an EU trade mark has stated that after the trade mark has been registered he will invoke the rights under it against him may obtain inspection of the files prior to the publication of that application and without the consent of the applicant.

3.    Subsequent to the publication of the EU trade mark application, the files relating to such application and the resulting trade mark may be inspected on request.

4.    Where the files are inspected pursuant to paragraph 2 or 3 of this Article, documents relating to exclusion or objection pursuant to Article 169, draft decisions and opinions, and all other internal documents used for the preparation of decisions and opinions, as well as parts of the file which the party concerned showed a special interest in keeping confidential before the request for inspection of the files was made, unless inspection of such parts of the file is justified by overriding, legitimate interests of the party seeking inspection, may be withheld from inspection.

5.    Inspection of the files of EU trade mark applications and of registered EU trade marks shall be of the original document, or of copies thereof, or of technical means of storage if the files are stored in this way. The Executive Director shall determine the means of inspection.

6.    Where inspection of files takes place as provided for in paragraph 7, the request for inspection of the files shall not be deemed to have been made until the required fee has been paid. No fee shall be payable if inspection of technical means of storage takes place online.

7.    Inspection of the files shall take place at the premises of the Office. On request, inspection of the files shall be effected by means of issuing copies of file documents. The issuing of such copies shall be conditional on the payment of a fee. The Office shall also issue on request certified or uncertified copies of the application for an EU trade mark upon payment of a fee.

8.    The files kept by the Office relating to international registrations designating the Union may be inspected on request as from the date of publication referred to in Article 190(1), in accordance with the conditions laid down in paragraphs 1, 3 and 4 of this Article.

9.     Subject to the restrictions provided for in paragraph 4, the Office may, on request, communicate information from any file of an EU trade mark applied for or of a registered EU trade mark, subject to payment of a fee. However, the Office may require the exercise of the option to obtain inspection of the file itself should it deem this to be appropriate in view of the quantity of information to be supplied.

*Article 115*

### Keeping of files

1.     The Office shall keep the files of any procedure relating to an EU trade mark application or EU trade mark registration. The Executive Director shall determine the form in which those files shall be kept.

2.     Where the files are kept in electronic format, the electronic files, or back-up copies thereof, shall be kept indefinitely. The original documents filed by parties to the proceedings, and forming the basis of such electronic files, shall be disposed of after a period following their reception by the Office, which shall be determined by the Executive Director.

3.     Where and to the extent that files or parts of the files are kept in any form other than electronically, documents or items of evidence constituting part of such files shall be kept for at least five years from the end of the year in which the application is rejected or withdrawn or is deemed to be withdrawn, the registration of the EU trade mark expires completely pursuant to Article 53, the complete surrender of the EU trade mark is registered pursuant to Article 57, or the EU trade mark is completely removed from the Register pursuant to Article 64(6) or 128(6).

*Article 116*

### Periodical publications

1.     The Office shall periodically publish:

(a)     a European Union Trade Marks Bulletin containing publications of applications and of entries made in the Register as well as other particulars relating to applications or registrations of EU trade marks the publication of which is required under this Regulation or by acts adopted pursuant to it;

(b)     an Official Journal of the Office containing notices and information of a general character issued by the Executive Director, as well as any other information relevant to this Regulation or its implementation.

The publications referred to in points (a) and (b) of the first subparagraph may be effected by electronic means.

2.     The European Union Trade Marks Bulletin shall be published in a manner and at a frequency to be determined by the Executive Director.

3.     The Official Journal of the Office shall be published in the languages of the Office. However, the Executive Director may determine that certain items shall be published in the Official Journal of the Office in the official languages of the Union.

4.     The Commission shall adopt implementing acts specifying:

(a)     the date to be taken as the date of publication in the European Union Trade Marks Bulletin;

(b)     the manner of publication of entries regarding the registration of a trade mark which do not contain changes as compared to the publication of the application;

(c)     the forms in which editions of the Official Journal of the Office may be made available to the public.

Those implementing acts shall be adopted in accordance with the examination procedure referred to in Article 207(2).

## Article 117

### Administrative cooperation

1.    Unless otherwise provided in this Regulation or in national laws, the Office and the courts or authorities of the Member States shall on request give assistance to each other by communicating information or opening files for inspection. Where the Office lays files open to inspection by courts, Public Prosecutors' Offices or central industrial property offices, the inspection shall not be subject to the restrictions laid down in Article 114.

2.    The Office shall not charge fees for the communication of information or the opening of files for inspection.

3.    The Commission shall adopt implementing acts specifying the detailed arrangements as to how the Office and the authorities of the Member States are to exchange information between each other and open files for inspection, taking into account the restrictions to which the inspection of files relating to EU trade mark applications or registrations is subject, pursuant to Article 114, when it is opened to third parties. Those implementing acts shall be adopted in accordance with the examination procedure referred to in Article 207(2).

## Article 118

### Exchange of publications

1.    The Office and the central industrial property offices of the Member States shall despatch to each other on request and for their own use one or more copies of their respective publications free of charge.

2.    The Office may conclude agreements relating to the exchange or supply of publications.

## SECTION 4

### *Representation*

## Article 119

### General principles of representation

1.    Subject to the provisions of paragraph 2, no person shall be compelled to be represented before the Office.

2.    Without prejudice to the second sentence of paragraph 3 of this Article, natural or legal persons having neither their domicile nor their principal place of business or a real and effective industrial or commercial establishment in the European Economic Area shall be represented before the Office in accordance with Article 120(1) in all proceedings provided for by this Regulation, other than the filing of an application for an EU trade mark.

3.    Natural or legal persons having their domicile or principal place of business or a real and effective industrial or commercial establishment in the European Economic Area may be represented before the Office by an employee. An employee of a legal person to which this paragraph applies may also represent other legal persons which have economic connections with the first legal person, even if those other legal persons have neither their domicile nor their principal place of business nor a real and effective industrial or commercial establishment within the European Economic Area. Employees who represent persons, within the meaning of this paragraph, shall, at the request of the Office or, where appropriate, of the party to the proceedings, file with it a signed authorisation for insertion in the files.

4.     Where there is more than one applicant or more than one third party acting in common, a common representative shall be appointed.

## Article 120

### Professional representatives

1.     Representation of natural or legal persons before the Office may only be undertaken by:

(a)     a legal practitioner qualified in one of the Member States of the European Economic Area and having his place of business within the European Economic Area, to the extent that he is entitled, within the said Member State, to act as a representative in trade mark matters;

(b)     professional representatives whose names appear on the list maintained for this purpose by the Office.

Representatives acting before the Office shall, at the request of the Office or, where appropriate, of the other party to the proceedings, file with it a signed authorisation for insertion on the files.

2.     Any natural person who fulfils the following conditions may be entered on the list of professional representatives:

(a)     being a national of one of the Member States of the European Economic Area;

(b)     having his place of business or employment in the European Economic Area;

(c)     being entitled to represent natural or legal persons in trade mark matters before the Benelux Office for Intellectual Property or before the central industrial property office of a Member State of the European Economic Area. Where, in the State concerned, the entitlement is not conditional upon the requirement of special professional qualifications, persons applying to be entered on the list who act in trade mark matters before the Benelux Office for Intellectual Property or those central industrial property offices shall have habitually so acted for at least five years. However, persons whose professional qualification to represent natural or legal persons in trade mark matters before the Benelux Office for Intellectual Property or those central industrial property offices is officially recognised in accordance with the regulations laid down by the State concerned shall not be required to have exercised the profession.

3.     Entry shall be effected upon request, accompanied by a certificate furnished by the central industrial property office of the Member State concerned, indicating that the conditions laid down in paragraph 2 are fulfilled.

4.     The Executive Director may grant an exemption from:

(a)     the requirement in the second sentence of paragraph 2(c), if the applicant furnishes proof that he has acquired the requisite qualification in another way;

(b)     the requirement set out in paragraph 2(a) in the case of highly qualified professionals, provided that the requirements set out in paragraph 2(b) and (c) are fulfilled.

5.     A person may be removed from the list of professional representatives at his request or when no longer in a capacity to represent. The amendments of the list of professional representatives shall be published in the Official Journal of the Office.

## Article 121

### Delegation of powers

The Commission is empowered to adopt delegated acts in accordance with Article 208 specifying:

(a)     the conditions and the procedure for the appointment of a common representative as referred to in Article 119(4);

(b) the conditions under which employees referred to in Article 119(3) and professional representatives referred to in Article 120(1) shall file with the Office a signed authorisation in order to undertake representation, and the content of that authorisation;

(c) the circumstances in which a person may be removed from the list of professional representatives referred to in Article 120(5).

# CHAPTER X
## JURISDICTION AND PROCEDURE IN LEGAL ACTIONS RELATING TO EU TRADE MARKS

### SECTION 1

*Application of Union rules on jurisdiction and the recognition and enforcement of judgments in civil and commercial matters*

*Article 122*

**Application of Union rules on jurisdiction and the recognition and enforcement of judgments in civil and commercial matters**

1.   Unless otherwise specified in this Regulation, the Union rules on jurisdiction and the recognition and enforcement of judgments in civil and commercial matters shall apply to proceedings relating to EU trade marks and applications for EU trade marks, as well as to proceedings relating to simultaneous and successive actions on the basis of EU trade marks and national trade marks.

2.   In the case of proceedings in respect of the actions and claims referred to in Article 124:

(a) Articles 4 and 6, points 1, 2, 3 and 5 of Article 7 and Article 35 of Regulation (EU) No 1215/2012 shall not apply;

(b) Articles 25 and 26 of Regulation (EU) No 1215/2012 shall apply subject to the limitations in Article 125(4) of this Regulation;

(c) the provisions of Chapter II of Regulation (EU) No 1215/2012 which are applicable to persons domiciled in a Member State shall also be applicable to persons who do not have a domicile in any Member State but have an establishment therein.

3.   References in this Regulation to Regulation (EU) No 1215/2012 shall include, where appropriate, the Agreement between the European Community and the Kingdom of Denmark on jurisdiction and the recognition and enforcement of judgments in civil and commercial matters done on 19 October 2005.

### SECTION 2

*Disputes concerning the infringement and validity of EU trade marks*

*Article 123*

**EU trade mark courts**

1.   The Member States shall designate in their territories as limited a number as possible of national courts and tribunals of first and second instance, which shall perform the functions assigned to them by this Regulation.

2.   Any change made in the number, names or territorial jurisdiction of the courts included in the list of EU trade mark courts communicated by a Member State to the Commission in accordance

with Article 95(2) of Regulation (EC) No 207/2009 shall be notified without delay by the Member State concerned to the Commission.

3.      The information referred to in paragraph 2 shall be notified by the Commission to the Member States and published in the *Official Journal of the European Union*.

## Article 124

### Jurisdiction over infringement and validity

The EU trade mark courts shall have exclusive jurisdiction:

(a)      for all infringement actions and—if they are permitted under national law—actions in respect of threatened infringement relating to EU trade marks;

(b)      for actions for declaration of non-infringement, if they are permitted under national law;

(c)      for all actions brought as a result of acts referred to in Article 11(2);

(d)      for counterclaims for revocation or for a declaration of invalidity of the EU trade mark pursuant to Article 128.

## Article 125

### International jurisdiction

1.      Subject to the provisions of this Regulation as well as to any provisions of Regulation (EU) No 1215/2012 applicable by virtue of Article 122, proceedings in respect of the actions and claims referred to in Article 124 shall be brought in the courts of the Member State in which the defendant is domiciled or, if he is not domiciled in any of the Member States, in which he has an establishment.

2.      If the defendant is neither domiciled nor has an establishment in any of the Member States, such proceedings shall be brought in the courts of the Member State in which the plaintiff is domiciled or, if he is not domiciled in any of the Member States, in which he has an establishment.

3.      If neither the defendant nor the plaintiff is so domiciled or has such an establishment, such proceedings shall be brought in the courts of the Member State where the Office has its seat.

4.      Notwithstanding the provisions of paragraphs 1, 2 and 3:

(a)      Article 25 of Regulation (EU) No 1215/2012 shall apply if the parties agree that a different EU trade mark court shall have jurisdiction;

(b)      Article 26 of Regulation (EU) No 1215/2012 shall apply if the defendant enters an appearance before a different EU trade mark court.

5.      Proceedings in respect of the actions and claims referred to in Article 124, with the exception of actions for a declaration of non-infringement of an EU trade mark, may also be brought in the courts of the Member State in which the act of infringement has been committed or threatened, or in which an act referred to in Article 11(2) has been committed.

## Article 126

### Extent of jurisdiction

1.      An EU trade mark court whose jurisdiction is based on Article 125(1) to (4) shall have jurisdiction in respect of:

(a)      acts of infringement committed or threatened within the territory of any of the Member States;

(b)      acts referred to in Article 11(2) committed within the territory of any of the Member States.

2.    An EU trade mark court whose jurisdiction is based on Article 125(5) shall have jurisdiction only in respect of acts committed or threatened within the territory of the Member State in which that court is situated.

## Article 127

### Presumption of validity—Defence as to the merits

1.    The EU trade mark courts shall treat the EU trade mark as valid unless its validity is put in issue by the defendant with a counterclaim for revocation or for a declaration of invalidity.

2.    The validity of an EU trade mark may not be put in issue in an action for a declaration of non-infringement.

3.    In the actions referred to in points (a) and (c) of Article 124, a plea relating to revocation of the EU trade mark submitted otherwise than by way of a counterclaim shall be admissible where the defendant claims that the EU trade mark could be revoked for lack of genuine use at the time the infringement action was brought.

## Article 128

### Counterclaims

1.    A counterclaim for revocation or for a declaration of invalidity may only be based on the grounds for revocation or invalidity mentioned in this Regulation.

2.    An EU trade mark court shall reject a counterclaim for revocation or for a declaration of invalidity if a decision taken by the Office relating to the same subject matter and cause of action and involving the same parties has already become final.

3.    If the counterclaim is brought in a legal action to which the proprietor of the trade mark is not already a party, he shall be informed thereof and may be joined as a party to the action in accordance with the conditions set out in national law.

4.    The EU trade mark court with which a counterclaim for revocation or for a declaration of invalidity of the EU trade mark has been filed shall not proceed with the examination of the counterclaim, until either the interested party or the court has informed the Office of the date on which the counterclaim was filed. The Office shall record that information in the Register. If an application for revocation or for a declaration of invalidity of the EU trade mark had already been filed before the Office before the counterclaim was filed, the court shall be informed thereof by the Office and stay the proceedings in accordance with Article 132(1) until the decision on the application is final or the application is withdrawn.

5.    Article 64(2) to (5) shall apply.

6.    Where an EU trade mark court has given a judgment which has become final on a counterclaim for revocation or for a declaration of invalidity of an EU trade mark, a copy of the judgment shall be sent to the Office without delay, either by the court or by any of the parties to the national proceedings. The Office or any other interested party may request information about such transmission. The Office shall mention the judgment in the Register and shall take the necessary measures to comply with its operative part.

7.    The EU trade mark court hearing a counterclaim for revocation or for a declaration of invalidity may stay the proceedings on application by the proprietor of the EU trade mark and after hearing the other parties and may request the defendant to submit an application for revocation or for a declaration of invalidity to the Office within a time limit which it shall determine. If the application is not made within the time limit, the proceedings shall continue; the counterclaim shall be deemed withdrawn. Article 132(3) shall apply.

### *Article 129*

### Applicable law

1.     The EU trade mark courts shall apply the provisions of this Regulation.

2.     On all trade mark matters not covered by this Regulation, the relevant EU trade mark court shall apply the applicable national law.

3.     Unless otherwise provided for in this Regulation, an EU trade mark court shall apply the rules of procedure governing the same type of action relating to a national trade mark in the Member State in which the court is located.

### *Article 130*

### Sanctions

1.     Where an EU trade mark court finds that the defendant has infringed or threatened to infringe an EU trade mark, it shall, unless there are special reasons for not doing so, issue an order prohibiting the defendant from proceeding with the acts which infringed or would infringe the EU trade mark. It shall also take such measures in accordance with its national law as are aimed at ensuring that this prohibition is complied with.

2.     The EU trade mark court may also apply measures or orders available under the applicable law which it deems appropriate in the circumstances of the case.

### *Article 131*

### Provisional and protective measures

1.     Application may be made to the courts of a Member State, including EU trade mark courts, for such provisional, including protective, measures in respect of an EU trade mark or EU trade mark application as may be available under the law of that State in respect of a national trade mark, even if, under this Regulation, an EU trade mark court of another Member State has jurisdiction as to the substance of the matter.

2.     An EU trade mark court whose jurisdiction is based on Article 125(1), (2), (3) or (4) shall have jurisdiction to grant provisional and protective measures which, subject to any necessary procedure for recognition and enforcement pursuant to Chapter III of Regulation (EU) No 1215/2012, are applicable in the territory of any Member State. No other court shall have such jurisdiction.

### *Article 132*

### Specific rules on related actions

1.     An EU trade mark court hearing an action referred to in Article 124 other than an action for a declaration of non-infringement shall, unless there are special grounds for continuing the hearing, of its own motion after hearing the parties or at the request of one of the parties and after hearing the other parties, stay the proceedings where the validity of the EU trade mark is already in issue before another EU trade mark court on account of a counterclaim or where an application for revocation or for a declaration of invalidity has already been filed at the Office.

2.     The Office, when hearing an application for revocation or for a declaration of invalidity shall, unless there are special grounds for continuing the hearing, of its own motion after hearing the parties or at the request of one of the parties and after hearing the other parties, stay the proceedings where the validity of the EU trade mark is already in issue on account of a counterclaim before an EU trade mark court. However, if one of the parties to the proceedings before the EU trade mark court so requests, the court may, after hearing the other parties to these proceedings, stay the proceedings. The Office shall in this instance continue the proceedings pending before it.

3.   Where the EU trade mark court stays the proceedings it may order provisional and protective measures for the duration of the stay.

## Article 133

### Jurisdiction of EU trade mark courts of second instance—Further appeal

1.   An appeal to the EU trade mark courts of second instance shall lie from judgments of the EU trade mark courts of first instance in respect of proceedings arising from the actions and claims referred to in Article 124.

2.   The conditions under which an appeal may be lodged with an EU trade mark court of second instance shall be determined by the national law of the Member State in which that court is located.

3.   The national rules concerning further appeal shall be applicable in respect of judgments of EU trade mark courts of second instance.

## SECTION 3

### *Other disputes concerning EU trade marks*

### Article 134

### Supplementary provisions on the jurisdiction of national courts other than EU trade mark courts

1.   Within the Member State whose courts have jurisdiction under Article 122(1) those courts shall have jurisdiction for actions other than those referred to in Article 124, which would have jurisdiction *ratione loci* and *ratione materiae* in the case of actions relating to a national trade mark registered in that State.

2.   Actions relating to an EU trade mark, other than those referred to in Article 124, for which no court has jurisdiction under Article 122(1) and paragraph 1 of this Article may be heard before the courts of the Member State in which the Office has its seat.

### Article 135

### Obligation of the national court

A national court which is dealing with an action relating to an EU trade mark, other than the action referred to in Article 124, shall treat the EU trade mark as valid.

## CHAPTER XI
## EFFECTS ON THE LAWS OF THE MEMBER STATES

## SECTION 1

### *Civil actions on the basis of more than one trade mark*

### Article 136

### Simultaneous and successive civil actions on the basis of EU trade marks and national trade marks

1.   Where actions for infringement involving the same cause of action and between the same parties are brought in the courts of different Member States, one seised on the basis of an EU trade mark and the other seised on the basis of a national trade mark:

(a) the court other than the court first seised shall of its own motion decline jurisdiction in favour of that court where the trade marks concerned are identical and valid for identical goods or services. The court which would be required to decline jurisdiction may stay its proceedings if the jurisdiction of the other court is contested;

(b) the court other than the court first seised may stay its proceedings where the trade marks concerned are identical and valid for similar goods or services and where the trade marks concerned are similar and valid for identical or similar goods or services.

2. The court hearing an action for infringement on the basis of an EU trade mark shall reject the action if a final judgment on the merits has been given on the same cause of action and between the same parties on the basis of an identical national trade mark valid for identical goods or services.

3. The court hearing an action for infringement on the basis of a national trade mark shall reject the action if a final judgment on the merits has been given on the same cause of action and between the same parties on the basis of an identical EU trade mark valid for identical goods or services.

4. Paragraphs 1, 2 and 3 shall not apply in respect of provisional, including protective, measures.

## SECTION 2

### *Application of national laws for the purpose of prohibiting the use of EU trade marks*

### *Article 137*

### Prohibition of use of EU trade marks

1. This Regulation shall, unless otherwise provided for, not affect the right existing under the laws of the Member States to invoke claims for infringement of earlier rights within the meaning of Article 8 or Article 60(2) in relation to the use of a later EU trade mark. Claims for infringement of earlier rights within the meaning of Article 8(2) and (4) may, however, no longer be invoked if the proprietor of the earlier right may no longer apply for a declaration that the EU trade mark is invalid in accordance with Article 61(2).

2. This Regulation shall, unless otherwise provided for, not affect the right to bring proceedings under the civil, administrative or criminal law of a Member State or under provisions of Union law for the purpose of prohibiting the use of an EU trade mark to the extent that the use of a national trade mark may be prohibited under the law of that Member State or under Union law.

### *Article 138*

### Prior rights applicable to particular localities

1. The proprietor of an earlier right which only applies to a particular locality may oppose the use of the EU trade mark in the territory where his right is protected in so far as the law of the Member State concerned so permits.

2. Paragraph 1 shall cease to apply if the proprietor of the earlier right has acquiesced in the use of the EU trade mark in the territory where his right is protected for a period of five successive years, being aware of such use, unless the EU trade mark was applied for in bad faith.

3. The proprietor of the EU trade mark shall not be entitled to oppose use of the right referred to in paragraph 1 even though that right may no longer be invoked against the EU trade mark.

## *Conversion into a national trade mark application*

### *Article 139*

### Request for the application of national procedure

1. The applicant for or proprietor of an EU trade mark may request the conversion of his EU trade mark application or EU trade mark into a national trade mark application:

(a) to the extent that the EU trade mark application is refused, withdrawn, or deemed to be withdrawn;

(b) to the extent that the EU trade mark ceases to have effect.

2. Conversion shall not take place:

(a) where the rights of the proprietor of the EU trade mark have been revoked on the grounds of non-use, unless in the Member State for which conversion is requested the EU trade mark has been put to use which would be considered to be genuine use under the laws of that Member State;

(b) for the purpose of protection in a Member State in which, in accordance with the decision of the Office or of the national court, grounds for refusal of registration or grounds for revocation or invalidity apply to the EU trade mark application or EU trade mark.

3. The national trade mark application resulting from the conversion of an EU trade mark application or an EU trade mark shall enjoy in respect of the Member State concerned the date of filing or the date of priority of that application or trade mark and, where appropriate, the seniority of a trade mark of that State claimed under Articles 39 or 40.

4. In cases where an EU trade mark application is deemed to be withdrawn, the Office shall send to the applicant a communication fixing a period of three months from the date of that communication in which a request for conversion may be filed.

5. Where the EU trade mark application is withdrawn or the EU trade mark ceases to have effect as a result of a surrender being recorded or of failure to renew the registration, the request for conversion shall be filed within three months of the date on which the EU trade mark application has been withdrawn or on which the EU trade mark ceases to have effect.

6. Where the EU trade mark application is refused by decision of the Office or where the EU trade mark ceases to have effect as a result of a decision of the Office or of an EU trade mark court, the request for conversion shall be filed within three months of the date on which that decision acquired the authority of a final decision.

7. The effect referred to in Article 37 shall lapse if the request is not filed in due time.

### *Article 140*

### Submission, publication and transmission of the request for conversion

1. A request for conversion shall be filed with the Office within the relevant period pursuant to Article 139(4), (5) or (6), and shall include an indication of the grounds for conversion in accordance with Article 139(1)(a) or (b), the Member States in respect of which conversion is requested, and the goods and services subject to conversion. Where conversion is requested following a failure to renew the registration, the period of three months provided for in Article 139(5) shall begin to run on the day following the last day on which the request for renewal can be presented pursuant to Article 53(3). The request for conversion shall not be deemed to be filed until the conversion fee has been paid.

2.    Where the request for conversion relates to an EU trade mark application which has already been published or where the request for conversion relates to an EU trade mark, receipt of any such request shall be recorded in the Register and the request for conversion shall be published.

3.    The Office shall check whether the conversion requested fulfils the conditions set out in this Regulation, in particular Article 139(1), (2), (4), (5) and (6), and paragraph 1 of this Article, together with the formal conditions specified in the implementing act adopted pursuant to paragraph 6 of this Article. If the conditions governing the request are not fulfilled, the Office shall notify the applicant of the deficiencies. If the deficiencies are not remedied within a period to be specified by the Office, the Office shall reject the request for conversion. Where Article 139(2) applies, the Office shall reject the request for conversion as inadmissible only with respect to those Member States for which conversion is excluded under that provision. Where the conversion fee has not been paid within the relevant period of three months pursuant to Article 139(4), (5) or (6), the Office shall inform the applicant that the request for conversion is deemed not to have been filed.

4.    If the Office or an EU trade mark court has refused the EU trade mark application or has declared the EU trade mark invalid on absolute grounds by reference to the language of a Member State, conversion shall be excluded under Article 139(2) for all the Member States in which that language is one of the official languages. If the Office or an EU trade mark court has refused the EU trade mark application or has declared the EU trade mark invalid on absolute grounds which are found to apply throughout the Union or on account of an earlier EU trade mark or other Union industrial property right, conversion shall be excluded under Article 139(2) for all Member States.

5.    Where the request for conversion complies with the requirements referred to in paragraph 3 of this Article, the Office shall transmit the request for conversion and the data referred to in Article 111(2) to the central industrial property offices of the Member States, including the Benelux Office for Intellectual Property, for which the request has been found admissible. The Office shall inform the applicant of the date of transmission.

6.    The Commission shall adopt implementing acts specifying:

(a)    the details to be contained in a request for conversion of an EU trade mark application or a registered EU trade mark into a national trade mark application pursuant to paragraph 1;

(b)    the details which are to be contained in the publication of the request for conversion pursuant to paragraph 2.

Those implementing acts shall be adopted in accordance with the examination procedure referred to in Article 207(2).

## *Article 141*

### Formal requirements for conversion

1.    Any central industrial property office to which the request for conversion is transmitted may obtain from the Office any additional information concerning the request enabling that office to make a decision regarding the national trade mark resulting from the conversion.

2.    An EU trade mark application or an EU trade mark transmitted in accordance with Article 140 shall not be subject to formal requirements of national law which are different from or additional to those provided for in this Regulation or in acts adopted pursuant to this Regulation.

3.    Any central industrial property office to which the request is transmitted may require that the applicant shall, within not less than two months:

(a)    pay the national application fee;

(b)    file a translation in one of the official languages of the State in question of the request and of the documents accompanying it;

(c)    indicate an address for service in the State in question;

(d) supply a representation of the trade mark in the number of copies specified by the State in question.

## CHAPTER XII
## THE OFFICE

...

## CHAPTER XIII
## INTERNATIONAL REGISTRATION OF MARKS

### *SECTION I*

### *General provisions*

*Article 182*

### Application of provisions

Unless otherwise specified in this chapter, this Regulation and the acts adopted pursuant to this Regulation shall apply to applications for international registrations under the Madrid Protocol ('international applications'), based on an application for an EU trade mark or on an EU trade mark and to registrations of marks in the international register maintained by the International Bureau of the World Intellectual Property Organisation ('international registrations' and 'the International Bureau', respectively) designating the Union.

### *SECTION 2*

### *International registration on the basis of applications for an EU trade mark and of EU trade marks*

*Article 183*

### Filing of an international application

1. International applications pursuant to Article 3 of the Madrid Protocol based on an application for an EU trade mark or on an EU trade mark shall be filed at the Office.

2. Where an international application is filed before the mark on which the international registration is to be based has been registered as an EU trade mark, the applicant for the international registration shall indicate whether the international registration is to be based on an EU trade mark application or registration. Where the international registration is to be based on an EU trade mark once it is registered, the international application shall be deemed to have been received at the Office on the date of registration of the EU trade mark. ...

*Article 187*

### Request for territorial extension subsequent to international registration

1. A request for territorial extension made subsequent to an international registration pursuant to Article 3*ter*(2) of the Madrid Protocol may be filed through the intermediary of the Office. The request shall be filed in the language in which the international application was filed pursuant to Article 184 of this Regulation. It shall include indications to substantiate the entitlement to make a designation in accordance with Article 2(1)(ii) and Article 3*ter*(2) of the Madrid Protocol. The Office shall inform the applicant requesting the territorial extension of the date on which the request for territorial extension was received.

2.    The Commission shall adopt implementing acts specifying the detailed requirements regarding the request for territorial extension pursuant to paragraph 1 of this Article. Those implementing acts shall be adopted in accordance with the examination procedure referred to in Article 207(2).

3.    Where the request for territorial extension made subsequent to the international registration does not comply with the requirements set out in paragraph 1 and in the implementing act adopted pursuant to paragraph 2, the Office shall invite the applicant to remedy the deficiencies found within such time limit as it may specify. If the deficiencies are not remedied within the time limit fixed by the Office, the Office shall refuse to forward the request to the International Bureau. The Office shall not refuse to forward the request to the International Bureau before the applicant has had the opportunity to correct any deficiency detected in the request.

4.    The Office shall forward the request for territorial extension made subsequent to the international registration to the International Bureau as soon as the requirements referred to in paragraph 3 are complied with. ...

## SECTION 3

### *International registrations designating the Union*

### Article 189

#### Effects of international registrations designating the Union

1.    An international registration designating the Union shall, from the date of its registration pursuant to Article 3(4) of the Madrid Protocol or from the date of the subsequent designation of the Union pursuant to Article 3*ter*(2) of the Madrid Protocol, have the same effect as an application for an EU trade mark.

2.    If no refusal has been notified in accordance with Article 5(1) and (2) of the Madrid Protocol or if any such refusal has been withdrawn, the international registration of a mark designating the Union shall, from the date referred to in paragraph 1, have the same effect as the registration of a mark as an EU trade mark.

3.    For the purposes of applying Article 11 of this Regulation, publication of the particulars of the international registration designating the Union pursuant to Article 190(1) shall take the place of publication of an EU trade mark application, and publication pursuant to Article 190(2) shall take the place of publication of the registration of an EU trade mark. ...

### Article 203

#### Use of a mark subject of an international registration

For the purposes of applying Article 18(1), Article 47(2), Article 58(1)(a) and Article 64(2), the date of publication pursuant to Article 190(2) shall take the place of the date of registration for the purpose of establishing the date as from which the mark which is the subject of an international registration designating the Union shall be put to genuine use in the Union.

### Article 204

#### Transformation

1.    Subject to paragraph 2, the provisions applicable to EU trade mark applications shall apply *mutatis mutandis* to applications for transformation of an international registration into an EU trade mark application pursuant to Article 9*quinquies* of the Madrid Protocol. ...

## CHAPTER XIV
## FINAL PROVISIONS

...

*Article 211*

### Repeal

Regulation (EC) No **207/2009** is repealed.

References to the repealed Regulation shall be construed as references to this Regulation and shall be read in accordance with the correlation table in Annex III.

*Article 212*

### Entry into force

This Regulation shall enter into force on the twentieth day following that of its publication in the *Official Journal of the European Union*.

It shall apply from 1 October 2017.

This Regulation shall be binding in its entirety and directly applicable in all Member States.

Done at Strasbourg, 14 June 2017.

# 67. TRADEMARK DIRECTIVE

## DIRECTIVE (EU) 2015/2436 OF THE EUROPEAN PARLIAMENT AND OF THE COUNCIL
### of 16 December 2015
### to approximate the laws of the Member States relating to trade marks

### (Recast)

### (Text with EEA relevance)*

... Whereas: ...

(2)  Directive 2008/95/EC has harmonised central provisions of substantive trade mark law which at the time of adoption were considered as most directly affecting the functioning of the internal market by impeding the free movement of goods and the freedom to provide services in the Union.

(3)  Trade mark protection in the Member States coexists with protection available at Union level through European Union trade marks ('EU trade marks') which are unitary in character and valid throughout the Union as laid down in Council Regulation (EC) No 207/2009. The coexistence and balance of trade mark systems at national and Union level in fact constitutes a cornerstone of the Union's approach to intellectual property protection. ...

(6)  The Commission concluded in its communication of 24 May 2011 entitled 'A single market for intellectual property rights' that in order to meet increased demands from stakeholders for faster, higher quality, more streamlined trade mark registration systems, which are also more consistent, user friendly, publicly accessible and technologically up to date, there is a necessity to modernise the trade mark system in the Union as a whole and adapt it to the internet era. ...

(9)  For the purpose of making trade mark registrations throughout the Union easier to obtain and administer, it is essential to approximate not only provisions of substantive law but also procedural rules. Therefore, the principal procedural rules in the area of trade mark registration in the Member States and in the EU trade mark system should be aligned. As regards procedures under national law, it is sufficient to lay down general principles, leaving the Member States free to establish more specific rules.

(10) It is essential to ensure that registered trade marks enjoy the same protection under the legal systems of all the Member States. In line with the extensive protection granted to EU trade marks which have a reputation in the Union, extensive protection should also be granted at national level to all registered trade marks which have a reputation in the Member State concerned.

(11) This Directive should not deprive the Member States of the right to continue to protect trade marks acquired through use but should take them into account only with regard to their relationship with trade marks acquired by registration.

(12) Attainment of the objectives of this approximation of laws requires that the conditions for obtaining and continuing to hold a registered trade mark be, in general, identical in all Member States.

(13) To this end, it is necessary to list examples of signs which are capable of constituting a trade mark, provided that such signs are capable of distinguishing the goods or services of one undertaking from those of other undertakings. In order to fulfil the objectives of the registration system for trade marks, namely to ensure legal certainty and sound administration, it is also essential to require that the sign is capable of being represented in a manner which is clear, precise, self-contained, easily accessible, intelligible, durable and objective. A sign should therefore be permitted to be represented in any appropriate form using generally available technology, and thus not necessarily by graphic means, as long as the representation offers satisfactory guarantees to that effect.

---

*    Footnotes, some recitals, and annexes omitted.

(14) Furthermore, the grounds for refusal or invalidity concerning the trade mark itself, including the absence of any distinctive character, or concerning conflicts between the trade mark and earlier rights, should be listed in an exhaustive manner, even if some of those grounds are listed as an option for the Member States which should therefore be able to maintain or introduce them in their legislation. . . .

(16) The protection afforded by the registered trade mark, the function of which is in particular to guarantee the trade mark as an indication of origin, should be absolute in the event of there being identity between the mark and the corresponding sign and the goods or services. The protection should apply also in the case of similarity between the mark and the sign and the goods or services. It is indispensable to give an interpretation of the concept of similarity in relation to the likelihood of confusion. The likelihood of confusion, the appreciation of which depends on numerous elements and, in particular, on the recognition of the trade mark on the market, the association which can be made with the used or registered sign, the degree of similarity between the trade mark and the sign and between the goods or services identified, should constitute the specific condition for such protection. The ways in which a likelihood of confusion can be established, and in particular the onus of proof in that regard, should be a matter for national procedural rules which should not be prejudiced by this Directive. . . .

(18) It is appropriate to provide that an infringement of a trade mark can only be established if there is a finding that the infringing mark or sign is used in the course of trade for the purposes of distinguishing goods or services. Use of the sign for purposes other than for distinguishing goods or services should be subject to the provisions of national law. . . .

(21) In order to strengthen trade mark protection and combat counterfeiting more effectively, and in line with international obligations of the Member States under the World Trade Organisation (WTO) framework, in particular Article V of the General Agreement on Tariffs and Trade on freedom of transit and, as regards generic medicines, the 'Declaration on the TRIPS Agreement and public health' adopted by the Doha WTO Ministerial Conference on 14 November 2001, the proprietor of a trade mark should be entitled to prevent third parties from bringing goods, in the course of trade, into the Member State where the trade mark is registered without being released for free circulation there, where such goods come from third countries and bear without authorisation a trade mark which is identical or essentially identical with the trade mark registered in respect of such goods.

(22) To this effect, it should be permissible for trade mark proprietors to prevent the entry of infringing goods and their placement in all customs situations, including, in particular transit, transhipment, warehousing, free zones, temporary storage, inward processing or temporary admission, also when such goods are not intended to be placed on the market of the Member State concerned. In performing customs controls, the customs authorities should make use of the powers and procedures laid down in Regulation (EU) No 608/2013 of the European Parliament and of the Council, also at the request of the right holders. In particular, the customs authorities should carry out the relevant controls on the basis of risk analysis criteria.

(23) In order to reconcile the need to ensure the effective enforcement of trade mark rights with the necessity to avoid hampering the free flow of trade in legitimate goods, the entitlement of the proprietor of the trade mark should lapse where, during the subsequent proceedings initiated before the judicial or other authority competent to take a substantive decision on whether the registered trade mark has been infringed, the declarant or the holder of the goods is able to prove that the proprietor of the registered trade mark is not entitled to prohibit the placing of the goods on the market in the country of final destination. . . .

(25) Appropriate measures should be taken with a view to ensuring the smooth transit of generic medicines. With respect to international non-proprietary names (INN) as globally recognised generic names for active substances in pharmaceutical preparations, it is vital to take due account of the existing limitations on the effect of trade mark rights. Consequently, the proprietor of a trade mark should not have the right to prevent a third party from bringing goods into a Member State where the trade mark is registered without being released for free circulation there based upon similarities between the INN for the active ingredient in the medicines and the trade mark. . . .

(27) The exclusive rights conferred by a trade mark should not entitle the proprietor to prohibit the use of signs or indications by third parties which are used fairly and thus in accordance with honest practices in industrial and commercial matters. In order to create equal conditions for trade names and trade marks against the background that trade names are regularly granted unrestricted protection against later trade marks, such use should only be considered to include the use of the personal name of the third party. Such use should further permit the use of descriptive or non-distinctive signs or indications in general. Furthermore, the proprietor should not be entitled to prevent the fair and honest use of the mark for the purpose of identifying or referring to the goods or services as those of the proprietor. Use of a trade mark by third parties to draw the consumer's attention to the resale of genuine goods that were originally sold by, or with the consent of, the proprietor of the trade mark in the Union should be considered as being fair as long as it is at the same time in accordance with honest practices in industrial and commercial matters. Use of a trade mark by third parties for the purpose of artistic expression should be considered as being fair as long as it is at the same time in accordance with honest practices in industrial and commercial matters. Furthermore, this Directive should be applied in a way that ensures full respect for fundamental rights and freedoms, and in particular the freedom of expression.

(28) It follows from the principle of free movement of goods that the proprietor of a trade mark should not be entitled to prohibit its use by a third party in relation to goods which have been put into circulation in the Union, under the trade mark, by him or with his consent, unless the proprietor has legitimate reasons to oppose further commercialisation of the goods. . . .

(35) Collective trade marks have proven a useful instrument for promoting goods or services with specific common properties. It is therefore appropriate to subject national collective trade marks to rules similar to the rules applicable to European Union collective marks. . . .

## CHAPTER 1
## GENERAL PROVISIONS

### *Article 1*

### Scope

This Directive applies to every trade mark in respect of goods or services which is the subject of registration or of an application for registration in a Member State as an individual trade mark, a guarantee or certification mark or a collective mark, or which is the subject of a registration or an application for registration in the Benelux Office for Intellectual Property or of an international registration having effect in a Member State.

### *Article 2*

### Definitions

For the purpose of this Directive, the following definitions apply:

(a)  'office' means the central industrial property office of the Member State or the Benelux Office for Intellectual Property, entrusted with the registration of trade marks;

(b)  'register' means the register of trade marks kept by an office.

## CHAPTER 2

### SUBSTANTIVE LAW ON TRADE MARKS

#### SECTION 1

#### *Signs of which a trade mark may consist*

*Article 3*

#### Signs of which a trade mark may consist

A trade mark may consist of any signs, in particular words, including personal names, or designs, letters, numerals, colours, the shape of goods or of the packaging of goods, or sounds, provided that such signs are capable of:

(a) distinguishing the goods or services of one undertaking from those of other undertakings; and

(b) being represented on the register in a manner which enables the competent authorities and the public to determine the clear and precise subject matter of the protection afforded to its proprietor.

#### SECTION 2

#### *Grounds for refusal or invalidity*

*Article 4*

#### Absolute grounds for refusal or invalidity

1.    The following shall not be registered or, if registered, shall be liable to be declared invalid:

(a) signs which cannot constitute a trade mark;

(b) trade marks which are devoid of any distinctive character;

(c) trade marks which consist exclusively of signs or indications which may serve, in trade, to designate the kind, quality, quantity, intended purpose, value, geographical origin, or the time of production of the goods or of rendering of the service, or other characteristics of the goods or services;

(d) trade marks which consist exclusively of signs or indications which have become customary in the current language or in the bona fide and established practices of the trade;

(e) signs which consist exclusively of:

(i) the shape, or another characteristic, which results from the nature of the goods themselves;

(ii) the shape, or another characteristic, of goods which is necessary to obtain a technical result;

(iii) the shape, or another characteristic, which gives substantial value to the goods;

(f) trade marks which are contrary to public policy or to accepted principles of morality;

(g) trade marks which are of such a nature as to deceive the public, for instance, as to the nature, quality or geographical origin of the goods or service;

(h) trade marks which have not been authorised by the competent authorities and are to be refused or invalidated pursuant to Article 6ter of the Paris Convention;

(i) trade marks which are excluded from registration pursuant to Union legislation or the national law of the Member State concerned, or to international agreements to which the Union or the

Member State concerned is party, providing for protection of designations of origin and geographical indications;

(j) trade marks which are excluded from registration pursuant to Union legislation or international agreements to which the Union is party, providing for protection of traditional terms for wine;

(k) trade marks which are excluded from registration pursuant to Union legislation or international agreements to which the Union is party, providing for protection of traditional specialities guaranteed;

(l) trade marks which consist of, or reproduce in their essential elements, an earlier plant variety denomination registered in accordance with Union legislation or the national law of the Member State concerned, or international agreements to which the Union or the Member State concerned is party, providing protection for plant variety rights, and which are in respect of plant varieties of the same or closely related species.

2. A trade mark shall be liable to be declared invalid where the application for registration of the trade mark was made in bad faith by the applicant. Any Member State may also provide that such a trade mark is not to be registered.

3. Any Member State may provide that a trade mark is not to be registered or, if registered, is liable to be declared invalid where and to the extent that:

(a) the use of that trade mark may be prohibited pursuant to provisions of law other than trade mark law of the Member State concerned or of the Union;

(b) the trade mark includes a sign of high symbolic value, in particular a religious symbol;

(c) the trade mark includes badges, emblems and escutcheons other than those covered by Article 6ter of the Paris Convention and which are of public interest, unless the consent of the competent authority to their registration has been given in conformity with the law of the Member State.

4. A trade mark shall not be refused registration in accordance with paragraph 1(b), (c) or (d) if, before the date of application for registration, following the use which has been made of it, it has acquired a distinctive character. A trade mark shall not be declared invalid for the same reasons if, before the date of application for a declaration of invalidity, following the use which has been made of it, it has acquired a distinctive character.

5. Any Member State may provide that paragraph 4 is also to apply where the distinctive character was acquired after the date of application for registration but before the date of registration.

## Article 5

### Relative grounds for refusal or invalidity

1. A trade mark shall not be registered or, if registered, shall be liable to be declared invalid where:

(a) it is identical with an earlier trade mark, and the goods or services for which the trade mark is applied for or is registered are identical with the goods or services for which the earlier trade mark is protected;

(b) because of its identity with, or similarity to, the earlier trade mark and the identity or similarity of the goods or services covered by the trade marks, there exists a likelihood of confusion on the part of the public; the likelihood of confusion includes the likelihood of association with the earlier trade mark.

2. 'Earlier trade marks' within the meaning of paragraph 1 means:

(a) trade marks of the following kinds with a date of application for registration which is earlier than the date of application for registration of the trade mark, taking account, where appropriate, of the priorities claimed in respect of those trade marks:

    (i)     EU trade marks;

    (ii)    trade marks registered in the Member State concerned or, in the case of Belgium, Luxembourg or the Netherlands, at the Benelux Office for Intellectual Property;

    (iii)   trade marks registered under international arrangements which have effect in the Member State concerned;

(b)    EU trade marks which validly claim seniority, in accordance with Regulation (EC) No 207/2009, of a trade mark referred to in points (a)(ii) and (iii), even when the latter trade mark has been surrendered or allowed to lapse;

(c)    applications for the trade marks referred to in points (a) and (b), subject to their registration;

(d)    trade marks which, on the date of application for registration of the trade mark, or, where appropriate, of the priority claimed in respect of the application for registration of the trade mark, are well known in the Member State concerned, in the sense in which the words 'well-known' are used in Article 6bis of the Paris Convention.

3.     Furthermore, a trade mark shall not be registered or, if registered, shall be liable to be declared invalid where:

(a)    it is identical with, or similar to, an earlier trade mark irrespective of whether the goods or services for which it is applied or registered are identical with, similar to or not similar to those for which the earlier trade mark is registered, where the earlier trade mark has a reputation in the Member State in respect of which registration is applied for or in which the trade mark is registered or, in the case of an EU trade mark, has a reputation in the Union and the use of the later trade mark without due cause would take unfair advantage of, or be detrimental to, the distinctive character or the repute of the earlier trade mark;

(b)    an agent or representative of the proprietor of the trade mark applies for registration thereof in his own name without the proprietor's authorisation, unless the agent or representative justifies his action;

(c)    and to the extent that, pursuant to Union legislation or the law of the Member State concerned providing for protection of designations of origin and geographical indications:

    (i)     an application for a designation of origin or a geographical indication had already been submitted in accordance with Union legislation or the law of the Member State concerned prior to the date of application for registration of the trade mark or the date of the priority claimed for the application, subject to its subsequent registration;

    (ii)    that designation of origin or geographical indication confers on the person authorised under the relevant law to exercise the rights arising therefrom the right to prohibit the use of a subsequent trade mark.

4.     Any Member State may provide that a trade mark is not to be registered or, if registered, is liable to be declared invalid where, and to the extent that:

(a)    rights to a non-registered trade mark or to another sign used in the course of trade were acquired prior to the date of application for registration of the subsequent trade mark, or the date of the priority claimed for the application for registration of the subsequent trade mark, and that non-registered trade mark or other sign confers on its proprietor the right to prohibit the use of a subsequent trade mark;

(b)    the use of the trade mark may be prohibited by virtue of an earlier right, other than the rights referred to in paragraph 2 and point (a) of this paragraph, and in particular:

    (i)    a right to a name;

    (ii)   a right of personal portrayal;

    (iii)  a copyright;

    (iv)  an industrial property right;

    (c)   the trade mark is liable to be confused with an earlier trade mark protected abroad, provided that, at the date of the application, the applicant was acting in bad faith.

5.    The Member States shall ensure that in appropriate circumstances there is no obligation to refuse registration or to declare a trade mark invalid where the proprietor of the earlier trade mark or other earlier right consents to the registration of the later trade mark.

6.    Any Member State may provide that, by way of derogation from paragraphs 1 to 5, the grounds for refusal of registration or invalidity in force in that Member State prior to the date of the entry into force of the provisions necessary to comply with Directive 89/104/EEC are to apply to trade marks for which an application has been made prior to that date.

## Article 6

### Establishment *a posteriori* of invalidity or revocation of a trade mark

Where the seniority of a national trade mark or of a trade mark registered under international arrangements having effect in the Member State, which has been surrendered or allowed to lapse, is claimed for an EU trade mark, the invalidity or revocation of the trade mark providing the basis for the seniority claim may be established *a posteriori*, provided that the invalidity or revocation could have been declared at the time the mark was surrendered or allowed to lapse. In such a case, the seniority shall cease to produce its effects.

## Article 7

### Grounds for refusal or invalidity relating to only some of the goods or services

Where grounds for refusal of registration or for invalidity of a trade mark exist in respect of only some of the goods or services for which that trade mark has been applied or registered, refusal of registration or invalidity shall cover those goods or services only.

## Article 8

### Lack of distinctive character or of reputation of an earlier trade mark precluding a declaration of invalidity of a registered trade mark

An application for a declaration of invalidity on the basis of an earlier trade mark shall not succeed at the date of application for invalidation if it would not have been successful at the filing date or the priority date of the later trade mark for any of the following reasons:

    (a)   the earlier trade mark, liable to be declared invalid pursuant to Article 4(1)(b), (c) or (d), had not yet acquired a distinctive character as referred to in Article 4(4);

    (b)   the application for a declaration of invalidity is based on Article 5(1)(b) and the earlier trade mark had not yet become sufficiently distinctive to support a finding of likelihood of confusion within the meaning of Article 5(1)(b);

    (c)   the application for a declaration of invalidity is based on Article 5(3)(a) and the earlier trade mark had not yet acquired a reputation within the meaning of Article 5(3)(a).

*Article 9*

## Preclusion of a declaration of invalidity due to acquiescence

1.    Where, in a Member State, the proprietor of an earlier trade mark as referred to in Article 5(2) or Article 5(3)(a) has acquiesced, for a period of five successive years, in the use of a later trade mark registered in that Member State while being aware of such use, that proprietor shall no longer be entitled on the basis of the earlier trade mark to apply for a declaration that the later trade mark is invalid in respect of the goods or services for which the later trade mark has been used, unless registration of the later trade mark was applied for in bad faith.

2.    Member States may provide that paragraph 1 of this Article is to apply to the proprietor of any other earlier right referred to in Article 5(4)(a) or (b).

3.    In the cases referred to in paragraphs 1 and 2, the proprietor of a later registered trade mark shall not be entitled to oppose the use of the earlier right, even though that right may no longer be invoked against the later trade mark.

## SECTION 3

### Rights conferred and limitations

*Article 10*

## Rights conferred by a trade mark

1.    The registration of a trade mark shall confer on the proprietor exclusive rights therein.

2.    Without prejudice to the rights of proprietors acquired before the filing date or the priority date of the registered trade mark, the proprietor of that registered trade mark shall be entitled to prevent all third parties not having his consent from using in the course of trade, in relation to goods or services, any sign where:

    (a)    the sign is identical with the trade mark and is used in relation to goods or services which are identical with those for which the trade mark is registered;

    (b)    the sign is identical with, or similar to, the trade mark and is used in relation to goods or services which are identical with, or similar to, the goods or services for which the trade mark is registered, if there exists a likelihood of confusion on the part of the public; the likelihood of confusion includes the likelihood of association between the sign and the trade mark;

    (c)    the sign is identical with, or similar to, the trade mark irrespective of whether it is used in relation to goods or services which are identical with, similar to, or not similar to, those for which the trade mark is registered, where the latter has a reputation in the Member State and where use of that sign without due cause takes unfair advantage of, or is detrimental to, the distinctive character or the repute of the trade mark.

3.    The following, in particular, may be prohibited under paragraph 2:

    (a)    affixing the sign to the goods or to the packaging thereof;

    (b)    offering the goods or putting them on the market, or stocking them for those purposes, under the sign, or offering or supplying services thereunder;

    (c)    importing or exporting the goods under the sign;

    (d)    using the sign as a trade or company name or part of a trade or company name;

    (e)    using the sign on business papers and in advertising;

    (f)    using the sign in comparative advertising in a manner that is contrary to Directive 2006/114/EC.

4.    Without prejudice to the rights of proprietors acquired before the filing date or the priority date of the registered trade mark, the proprietor of that registered trade mark shall also be entitled to prevent all third parties from bringing goods, in the course of trade, into the Member State where the trade mark is registered, without being released for free circulation there, where such goods, including the packaging thereof, come from third countries and bear without authorisation a trade mark which is identical with the trade mark registered in respect of such goods, or which cannot be distinguished in its essential aspects from that trade mark.

The entitlement of the trade mark proprietor pursuant to the first subparagraph shall lapse if, during the proceedings to determine whether the registered trade mark has been infringed, initiated in accordance with Regulation (EU) No 608/2013, evidence is provided by the declarant or the holder of the goods that the proprietor of the registered trade mark is not entitled to prohibit the placing of the goods on the market in the country of final destination.

5.    Where, under the law of a Member State, the use of a sign under the conditions referred to in paragraph 2 (b) or (c) could not be prohibited before the date of entry into force of the provisions necessary to comply with Directive 89/104/EEC in the Member State concerned, the rights conferred by the trade mark may not be relied on to prevent the continued use of the sign.

6.    Paragraphs 1, 2, 3 and 5 shall not affect provisions in any Member State relating to the protection against the use of a sign other than use for the purposes of distinguishing goods or services, where use of that sign without due cause takes unfair advantage of, or is detrimental to, the distinctive character or the repute of the trade mark.

### *Article 11*

### The right to prohibit preparatory acts in relation to the use of packaging or other means

Where the risk exists that the packaging, labels, tags, security or authenticity features or devices, or any other means to which the trade mark is affixed, could be used in relation to goods or services and that use would constitute an infringement of the rights of the proprietor of a trade mark under Article 10(2) and (3), the proprietor of that trade mark shall have the right to prohibit the following acts if carried out in the course of trade:

(a)    affixing a sign identical with, or similar to, the trade mark on packaging, labels, tags, security or authenticity features or devices, or any other means to which the mark may be affixed;

(b)    offering or placing on the market, or stocking for those purposes, or importing or exporting, packaging, labels, tags, security or authenticity features or devices, or any other means to which the mark is affixed.

### *Article 12*

### Reproduction of trade marks in dictionaries

If the reproduction of a trade mark in a dictionary, encyclopaedia or similar reference work, in print or electronic form, gives the impression that it constitutes the generic name of the goods or services for which the trade mark is registered, the publisher of the work shall, at the request of the proprietor of the trade mark, ensure that the reproduction of the trade mark is, without delay, and in the case of works in printed form at the latest in the next edition of the publication, accompanied by an indication that it is a registered trade mark.

*Article 13*

### Prohibition of the use of a trade mark registered in the name of an agent or representative

1. Where a trade mark is registered in the name of the agent or representative of a person who is the proprietor of that trade mark, without the proprietor's consent, the latter shall be entitled to do either or both of the following:

(a) oppose the use of the trade mark by his agent or representative;

(b) demand the assignment of the trade mark in his favour.

2. Paragraph 1 shall not apply where the agent or representative justifies his action.

*Article 14*

### Limitation of the effects of a trade mark

1. A trade mark shall not entitle the proprietor to prohibit a third party from using, in the course of trade:

(a) the name or address of the third party, where that third party is a natural person;

(b) signs or indications which are not distinctive or which concern the kind, quality, quantity, intended purpose, value, geographical origin, the time of production of goods or of rendering of the service, or other characteristics of goods or services;

(c) the trade mark for the purpose of identifying or referring to goods or services as those of the proprietor of that trade mark, in particular, where the use of the trade mark is necessary to indicate the intended purpose of a product or service, in particular as accessories or spare parts.

2. Paragraph 1 shall only apply where the use made by the third party is in accordance with honest practices in industrial or commercial matters.

3. A trade mark shall not entitle the proprietor to prohibit a third party from using, in the course of trade, an earlier right which only applies in a particular locality, if that right is recognised by the law of the Member State in question and the use of that right is within the limits of the territory in which it is recognised.

*Article 15*

### Exhaustion of the rights conferred by a trade mark

1. A trade mark shall not entitle the proprietor to prohibit its use in relation to goods which have been put on the market in the Union under that trade mark by the proprietor or with the proprietor's consent.

2. Paragraph 1 shall not apply where there exist legitimate reasons for the proprietor to oppose further commercialisation of the goods, especially where the condition of the goods is changed or impaired after they have been put on the market.

*Article 16*

### Use of trade marks

1. If, within a period of five years following the date of the completion of the registration procedure, the proprietor has not put the trade mark to genuine use in the Member State in connection with the goods or services in respect of which it is registered, or if such use has been suspended during a continuous five-year period, the trade mark shall be subject to the limits and sanctions provided for in Article 17, Article 19(1), Article 44(1) and (2), and Article 46(3) and (4), unless there are proper reasons for non-use.

2.    Where a Member State provides for opposition proceedings following registration, the five-year period referred to in paragraph 1 shall be calculated from the date when the mark can no longer be opposed or, in the event that an opposition has been lodged, from the date when a decision terminating the opposition proceedings became final or the opposition was withdrawn.

3.    With regard to trade marks registered under international arrangements and having effect in the Member State, the five-year period referred to in paragraph 1 shall be calculated from the date when the mark can no longer be rejected or opposed. Where an opposition has been lodged or when an objection on absolute or relative grounds has been notified, the period shall be calculated from the date when a decision terminating the opposition proceedings or a ruling on absolute or relative grounds for refusal became final or the opposition was withdrawn.

4.    The date of commencement of the five-year period, as referred to in paragraphs 1 and 2, shall be entered in the register.

5.    The following shall also constitute use within the meaning of paragraph 1:

(a)    use of the trade mark in a form differing in elements which do not alter the distinctive character of the mark in the form in which it was registered, regardless of whether or not the trade mark in the form as used is also registered in the name of the proprietor;

(b)    affixing of the trade mark to goods or to the packaging thereof in the Member State concerned solely for export purposes.

6.    Use of the trade mark with the consent of the proprietor shall be deemed to constitute use by the proprietor.

### *Article 17*

### Non-use as defence in infringement proceedings

The proprietor of a trade mark shall be entitled to prohibit the use of a sign only to the extent that the proprietor's rights are not liable to be revoked pursuant to Article 19 at the time the infringement action is brought. If the defendant so requests, the proprietor of the trade mark shall furnish proof that, during the five-year period preceding the date of bringing the action, the trade mark has been put to genuine use as provided in Article 16 in connection with the goods or services in respect of which it is registered and which are cited as justification for the action, or that there are proper reasons for non-use, provided that the registration procedure of the trade mark has at the date of bringing the action been completed for not less than five years.

### *Article 18*

### Intervening right of the proprietor of a later registered trade mark as defence in infringement proceedings

1.    In infringement proceedings, the proprietor of a trade mark shall not be entitled to prohibit the use of a later registered mark where that later trade mark would not be declared invalid pursuant to Article 8, Article 9(1) or (2) or Article 46(3).

2.    In infringement proceedings, the proprietor of a trade mark shall not be entitled to prohibit the use of a later registered EU trade mark where that later trade mark would not be declared invalid pursuant to Article 53(1), (3) or (4), 54(1) or (2) or 57(2) of Regulation (EC) No 207/2009.

3.    Where the proprietor of a trade mark is not entitled to prohibit the use of a later registered trade mark pursuant to paragraph 1 or 2, the proprietor of that later registered trade mark shall not be entitled to prohibit the use of the earlier trade mark in infringement proceedings, even though that earlier right may no longer be invoked against the later trade mark.

## SECTION 4

### *Revocation of trade mark rights*

#### Article 19

#### Absence of genuine use as ground for revocation

1.    A trade mark shall be liable to revocation if, within a continuous five-year period, it has not been put to genuine use in the Member State in connection with the goods or services in respect of which it is registered, and there are no proper reasons for non-use.

2.    No person may claim that the proprietor's rights in a trade mark should be revoked where, during the interval between expiry of the five-year period and filing of the application for revocation, genuine use of the trade mark has been started or resumed.

3.    The commencement or resumption of use within the three-month period preceding the filing of the application for revocation which began at the earliest on expiry of the continuous five-year period of non-use shall be disregarded where preparations for the commencement or resumption occur only after the proprietor becomes aware that the application for revocation may be filed.

#### Article 20

#### Trade mark having become generic or misleading indication as grounds for revocation

A trade mark shall be liable to revocation if, after the date on which it was registered:

    (a)   as a result of acts or inactivity of the proprietor, it has become the common name in the trade for a product or service in respect of which it is registered;

    (b)   as a result of the use made of it by the proprietor of the trade mark or with the proprietor's consent in respect of the goods or services for which it is registered, it is liable to mislead the public, particularly as to the nature, quality or geographical origin of those goods or services.

#### Article 21

#### Revocation relating to only some of the goods or services

Where grounds for revocation of a trade mark exist in respect of only some of the goods or services for which that trade mark has been registered, revocation shall cover those goods or services only.

## SECTION 5

### *Trade marks as objects of property*

#### Article 22

#### Transfer of registered trade marks

1.    A trade mark may be transferred, separately from any transfer of the undertaking, in respect of some or all of the goods or services for which it is registered.

2.    A transfer of the whole of the undertaking shall include the transfer of the trade mark except where there is agreement to the contrary or circumstances clearly dictate otherwise. This provision shall apply to the contractual obligation to transfer the undertaking.

3.    Member States shall have procedures in place to allow for the recordal of transfers in their registers.

*Article 23*

### *Rights* in rem

1.    A trade mark may, independently of the undertaking, be given as security or be the subject of rights *in rem*.

2.    Member States shall have procedures in place to allow for the recordal of rights *in rem* in their registers.

*Article 24*

### Levy of execution

1.    A trade mark may be levied in execution.

2.    Member States shall have procedures in place to allow for the recordal of levy of execution in their registers.

*Article 25*

### Licensing

1.    A trade mark may be licensed for some or all of the goods or services for which it is registered and for the whole or part of the Member State concerned. A licence may be exclusive or non-exclusive.

2.    The proprietor of a trade mark may invoke the rights conferred by that trade mark against a licensee who contravenes any provision in his licensing contract with regard to:

(a)    its duration;

(b)    the form covered by the registration in which the trade mark may be used;

(c)    the scope of the goods or services for which the licence is granted;

(d)    the territory in which the trade mark may be affixed; or

(e)    the quality of the goods manufactured or of the services provided by the licensee.

3.    Without prejudice to the provisions of the licensing contract, the licensee may bring proceedings for infringement of a trade mark only if its proprietor consents thereto. However, the holder of an exclusive licence may bring such proceedings if the proprietor of the trade mark, after formal notice, does not himself bring infringement proceedings within an appropriate period.

4.    A licensee shall, for the purpose of obtaining compensation for damage suffered by him, be entitled to intervene in infringement proceedings brought by the proprietor of the trade mark.

5.    Member States shall have procedures in place to allow for the recordal of licences in their registers.

*Article 26*

### Applications for a trade mark as an object of property

Articles 22 to 25 shall apply to applications for trade marks.

## SECTION 6

### *Guarantee or certification marks and collective marks*

*Article 27*

## Definitions

For the purposes of this Directive, the following definitions apply:

(a) 'guarantee or certification mark' means a trade mark which is described as such when the mark is applied for and is capable of distinguishing goods or services which are certified by the proprietor of the mark in respect of material, mode of manufacture of goods or performance of services, quality, accuracy or other characteristics, from goods and services which are not so certified;

(b) 'collective mark' means a trade mark which is described as such when the mark is applied for and is capable of distinguishing the goods or services of the members of an association which is the proprietor of the mark from the goods or services of other undertakings.

*Article 28*

## Guarantee or certification marks

1. Member States may provide for the registration of guarantee or certification marks.

2. Any natural or legal person, including institutions, authorities and bodies governed by public law, may apply for guarantee or certification marks provided that such person does not carry on a business involving the supply of goods or services of the kind certified.

Member States may provide that a guarantee or certification mark is not to be registered unless the applicant is competent to certify the goods or services for which the mark is to be registered.

3. Member States may provide that guarantee or certification marks are not to be registered, or are to be revoked or declared invalid, on grounds other than those specified in Articles 4, 19 and 20, where the function of those marks so requires.

4. By way of derogation from Article 4(1)(c), Member States may provide that signs or indications which may serve, in trade, to designate the geographical origin of the goods or services may constitute guarantee or certification marks. Such a guarantee or certification mark shall not entitle the proprietor to prohibit a third party from using in the course of trade such signs or indications, provided that third party uses them in accordance with honest practices in industrial or commercial matters. In particular, such a mark may not be invoked against a third party who is entitled to use a geographical name.

5. The requirements laid down in Article 16 shall be satisfied where genuine use of a guarantee or certification mark in accordance with Article 16 is made by any person who has the authority to use it.

*Article 29*

## Collective marks

1. Member States shall provide for the registration of collective marks.

2. Associations of manufacturers, producers, suppliers of services or traders, which, under the terms of the law governing them, have the capacity in their own name to have rights and obligations, to make contracts or accomplish other legal acts, and to sue and be sued, as well as legal persons governed by public law, may apply for collective marks.

3. By way of derogation from Article 4(1)(c), Member States may provide that signs or indications which may serve, in trade, to designate the geographical origin of the goods or services may constitute collective marks. Such a collective mark shall not entitle the proprietor to prohibit a third party from

using, in the course of trade, such signs or indications, provided that third party uses them in accordance with honest practices in industrial or commercial matters. In particular, such a mark may not be invoked against a third party who is entitled to use a geographical name.

## Article 30

### Regulations governing use of a collective mark

1.   An applicant for a collective mark shall submit the regulations governing its use to the office.

2.   The regulations governing use shall specify at least the persons authorised to use the mark, the conditions of membership of the association and the conditions of use of the mark, including sanctions. The regulations governing use of a mark referred to in Article 29(3) shall authorise any person whose goods or services originate in the geographical area concerned to become a member of the association which is the proprietor of the mark, provided that the person fulfils all the other conditions of the regulations.

## Article 31

### Refusal of an application

1.   In addition to the grounds for refusal of a trade mark application provided for in Article 4, where appropriate with the exception of Article 4(1)(c) concerning signs or indications which may serve, in trade, to designate the geographical origin of the goods or services, and Article 5,and without prejudice to the right of an office not to undertake examination *ex officio* of relative grounds, an application for a collective mark shall be refused where the provisions of point (b) of Article 27, Article 29 or Article 30 are not satisfied, or where the regulations governing use of that collective mark are contrary to public policy or to accepted principles of morality.

2.   An application for a collective mark shall also be refused if the public is liable to be misled as regards the character or the significance of the mark, in particular if it is likely to be taken to be something other than a collective mark.

3.   An application shall not be refused if the applicant, as a result of amendment of the regulations governing use of the collective mark, meets the requirements referred to in paragraphs 1 and 2.

## Article 32

### Use of collective marks

The requirements of Article 16 shall be satisfied where genuine use of a collective mark in accordance with that Article is made by any person who has authority to use it.

## Article 33

### Amendments to the regulations governing use of a collective mark

1.   The proprietor of a collective mark shall submit to the office any amended regulations governing use.

2.   Amendments to the regulations governing use shall be mentioned in the register unless the amended regulations do not satisfy the requirements of Article 30 or involve one of the grounds for refusal referred to in Article 31.

3.   For the purposes of this Directive, amendments to the regulations governing use shall take effect only from the date of entry of the mention of those amendments in the register.

*Article 34*

### Persons entitled to bring an action for infringement

1.    Article 25(3) and (4) shall apply to every person who has the authority to use a collective mark.

2.    The proprietor of a collective mark shall be entitled to claim compensation on behalf of persons who have authority to use the mark where those persons have sustained damage as a result of unauthorised use of the mark.

*Article 35*

### Additional grounds for revocation

In addition to the grounds for revocation provided for in Articles 19 and 20, the rights of the proprietor of a collective mark shall be revoked on the following grounds:

(a)    the proprietor does not take reasonable steps to prevent the mark being used in a manner that is incompatible with the conditions of use laid down in the regulations governing use, including any amendments thereto mentioned in the register;

(b)    the manner in which the mark has been used by authorised persons has caused it to become liable to mislead the public in the manner referred to in Article 31(2);

(c)    an amendment to the regulations governing use of the mark has been mentioned in the register in breach of Article 33(2), unless the proprietor of the mark, by further amending the regulations governing use, complies with the requirements of that Article.

*Article 36*

### Additional grounds for invalidity

In addition to the grounds for invalidity provided for in Article 4, where appropriate with the exception of Article 4(1)(c) concerning signs or indications which may serve, in trade, to designate the geographical origin of the goods or services, and Article 5, a collective mark which is registered in breach of Article 31 shall be declared invalid unless the proprietor of the mark, by amending the regulations governing use, complies with the requirements of Article 31.

## CHAPTER 3
## PROCEDURES

*SECTION 1*

### *Application and registration*

*Article 37*

### Application requirements

1.    An application for registration of a trade mark shall contain at least all of the following:

(a)    a request for registration;

(b)    information identifying the applicant;

(c)    a list of the goods or services in respect of which the registration is requested;

(d)    a representation of the trade mark, which satisfies the requirements set out in point (b) of Article 3.

2.    The application for a trade mark shall be subject to the payment of a fee determined by the Member State concerned.

## Article 38

### Date of filing

1.    The date of filing of a trade mark application shall be the date on which the documents containing the information specified in Article 37(1) are filed with the office by the applicant.

2.    Member States may, in addition, provide that the accordance of the date of filing is to be subject to the payment of a fee as referred to in Article 37(2).

## Article 39

### Designation and classification of goods and services

1.    The goods and services in respect of which trade mark registration is applied for shall be classified in conformity with the system of classification established by the Nice Agreement Concerning the International Classification of Goods and Services for the Purposes of the Registration of Marks of 15 June 1957 ('the Nice Classification').

2.    The goods and services for which protection is sought shall be identified by the applicant with sufficient clarity and precision to enable the competent authorities and economic operators, on that sole basis, to determine the extent of the protection sought.

3.    For the purposes of paragraph 2, the general indications included in the class headings of the Nice Classification or other general terms may be used, provided that they comply with the requisite standards of clarity and precision set out in this Article.

4.    The office shall reject an application in respect of indications or terms which are unclear or imprecise, where the applicant does not suggest an acceptable wording within a period set by the office to that effect.

5.    The use of general terms, including the general indications of the class headings of the Nice Classification, shall be interpreted as including all the goods or services clearly covered by the literal meaning of the indication or term. The use of such terms or indications shall not be interpreted as comprising a claim to goods or services which cannot be so understood.

6.    Where the applicant requests registration for more than one class, the applicant shall group the goods and services according to the classes of the Nice Classification, each group being preceded by the number of the class to which that group of goods or services belongs, and shall present them in the order of the classes.

7.    Goods and services shall not be regarded as being similar to each other on the ground that they appear in the same class under the Nice Classification. Goods and services shall not be regarded as being dissimilar from each other on the ground that they appear in different classes under the Nice Classification.

## Article 40

### Observations by third parties

1.    Member States may provide that prior to registration of a trade mark, any natural or legal person and any group or body representing manufacturers, producers, suppliers of services, traders or consumers may submit to the office written observations, explaining on which grounds the trade mark should not be registered *ex officio*.

Persons and groups or bodies, as referred to in the first subparagraph, shall not be parties to the proceedings before the office.

2. In addition to the grounds referred to in paragraph 1 of this Article, any natural or legal person and any group or body representing manufacturers, producers, suppliers of services, traders or consumers may submit to the office written observations based on the particular grounds on which the application for a collective mark should be refused under Article 31(1) and (2). This provision may be extended to cover certification and guarantee marks where regulated in Member States.

*Article 41*

### Division of applications and registrations

The applicant or proprietor may divide a national trade mark application or registration into two or more separate applications or registrations by sending a declaration to the office and indicating for each divisional application or registration the goods or services covered by the original application or registration which are to be covered by the divisional applications or registrations.

*Article 42*

### Class fees

Member States may provide that the application and renewal of a trade mark is to be subject to an additional fee for each class of goods and services beyond the first class.

*SECTION 2*

### *Procedures for opposition, revocation and invalidity*

*Article 43*

### Opposition procedure

1. Member States shall provide for an efficient and expeditious administrative procedure before their offices for opposing the registration of a trade mark application on the grounds provided for in Article 5.

2. The administrative procedure referred to in paragraph 1 of this Article shall at least provide that the proprietor of an earlier trade mark as referred to in Article 5(2) and Article 5(3)(a), and the person authorised under the relevant law to exercise the rights arising from a protected designation of origin or geographical indication as referred to in Article 5(3)(c) shall be entitled to file a notice of opposition. A notice of opposition may be filed on the basis of one or more earlier rights, provided that they all belong to the same proprietor, and on the basis of part or the totality of the goods or services in respect of which the earlier right is protected or applied for, and may be directed against part or the totality of the goods or services in respect of which the contested mark is applied for.

3. The parties shall be granted, at their joint request, a minimum of two months in the opposition proceedings in order to allow for the possibility of a friendly settlement between the opposing party and the applicant.

*Article 44*

### Non-use as defence in opposition proceedings

1. In opposition proceedings pursuant to Article 43, where at the filing date or date of priority of the later trade mark, the five-year period within which the earlier trade mark must have been put to genuine use as provided for in Article 16 had expired, at the request of the applicant, the proprietor of the earlier trade mark who has given notice of opposition shall furnish proof that the earlier trade mark has been put to genuine use as provided for in Article 16 during the five-year period preceding the filing date or date of priority of the later trade mark, or that proper reasons for non-use existed. In the absence of proof to this effect, the opposition shall be rejected.

2.    If the earlier trade mark has been used in relation to only part of the goods or services for which it is registered, it shall, for the purpose of the examination of the opposition as provided for in paragraph 1, be deemed to be registered in respect of that part of the goods or services only.

3.    Paragraphs 1 and 2 of this Article shall also apply where the earlier trade mark is an EU trade mark. In such a case, the genuine use of the EU trade mark shall be determined in accordance with Article 15 of Regulation (EC) No 207/2009.

*Article 45*

### Procedure for revocation or declaration of invalidity

1.    Without prejudice to the right of the parties to appeal to the courts, Member States shall provide for an efficient and expeditious administrative procedure before their offices for the revocation or declaration of invalidity of a trade mark.

2.    The administrative procedure for revocation shall provide that the trade mark is to be revoked on the grounds provided for in Articles 19 and 20.

3.    The administrative procedure for invalidity shall provide that the trade mark is to be declared invalid at least on the following grounds:

(a)    the trade mark should not have been registered because it does not comply with the requirements provided for in Article 4;

(b)    the trade mark should not have been registered because of the existence of an earlier right within the meaning of Article 5(1) to (3).

4.    The administrative procedure shall provide that at least the following are to be entitled to file an application for revocation or for a declaration of invalidity:

(a)    in the case of paragraph 2 and paragraph 3(a), any natural or legal person and any group or body set up for the purpose of representing the interests of manufacturers, producers, suppliers of services, traders or consumers, and which, under the terms of the law governing it, has the capacity to sue in its own name and to be sued;

(b)    in the case of paragraph 3(b) of this Article, the proprietor of an earlier trade mark as referred to in Article 5(2) and Article 5(3)(a), and the person authorised under the relevant law to exercise the rights arising from a protected designation of origin or geographical indication as referred to in Article 5(3)(c).

5.    An application for revocation or for a declaration of invalidity may be directed against a part or the totality of the goods or services in respect of which the contested mark is registered.

6.    An application for a declaration of invalidity may be filed on the basis of one or more earlier rights, provided they all belong to the same proprietor.

*Article 46*

### Non-use as a defence in proceedings seeking a declaration of invalidity

1.    In proceedings for a declaration of invalidity based on a registered trade mark with an earlier filing date or priority date, if the proprietor of the later trade mark so requests, the proprietor of the earlier trade mark shall furnish proof that, during the five-year period preceding the date of the application for a declaration of invalidity, the earlier trade mark has been put to genuine use, as provided for in Article 16, in connection with the goods or services in respect of which it is registered and which are cited as justification for the application, or that there are proper reasons for non-use, provided that the registration process of the earlier trade mark has at the date of the application for a declaration of invalidity been completed for not less than five years.

2.    Where, at the filing date or date of priority of the later trade mark, the five-year period within which the earlier trade mark was to have been put to genuine use, as provided for in Article 16, had expired, the proprietor of the earlier trade mark shall, in addition to the proof required under paragraph 1 of this Article, furnish proof that the trade mark was put to genuine use during the five-year period preceding the filing date or date of priority, or that proper reasons for non-use existed.

3.    In the absence of the proof referred to in paragraphs 1 and 2, an application for a declaration of invalidity on the basis of an earlier trade mark shall be rejected.

4.    If the earlier trade mark has been used in accordance with Article 16 in relation to only part of the goods or services for which it is registered, it shall, for the purpose of the examination of the application for a declaration of invalidity, be deemed to be registered in respect of that part of the goods or services only.

5.    Paragraphs 1 to 4 of this Article shall also apply where the earlier trade mark is an EU trade mark. In such a case, genuine use of the EU trade mark shall be determined in accordance with Article 15 of Regulation (EC) No 207/2009.

*Article 47*

### Consequences of revocation and invalidity

1.    A registered trade mark shall be deemed not to have had, as from the date of the application for revocation, the effects specified in this Directive, to the extent that the rights of the proprietor have been revoked. An earlier date, on which one of the grounds for revocation occurred, may be fixed in the decision on the application for revocation, at the request of one of the parties.

2.    A registered trade mark shall be deemed not to have had, as from the outset, the effects specified in this Directive, to the extent that the trade mark has been declared invalid.

*SECTION 3*

### *Duration and renewal of registration*

*Article 48*

### Duration of registration

1.    Trade marks shall be registered for a period of 10 years from the date of filing of the application.

2.    Registration may be renewed in accordance with Article 49 for further 10-year periods.

*Article 49*

### Renewal

1.    Registration of a trade mark shall be renewed at the request of the proprietor of the trade mark or any person authorised to do so by law or by contract, provided that the renewal fees have been paid. Member States may provide that receipt of payment of the renewal fees is to be deemed to constitute such a request.

2.    The office shall inform the proprietor of the trade mark of the expiry of the registration at least six months before the said expiry. The office shall not be held liable if it fails to give such information.

3.    The request for renewal shall be submitted and the renewal fees shall be paid within a period of at least six months immediately preceding the expiry of the registration. Failing that, the request may be submitted within a further period of six months immediately following the expiry of the registration or of the subsequent renewal thereof. The renewal fees and an additional fee shall be paid within that further period.

4.    Where the request is submitted or the fees paid in respect of only some of the goods or services for which the trade mark is registered, registration shall be renewed for those goods or services only.

5.    Renewal shall take effect from the day following the date on which the existing registration expires. The renewal shall be recorded in the register.

## SECTION 4

### *Communication with the office*

### *Article 50*

### Communication with the office

Parties to the proceedings or, where appointed, their representatives, shall designate an official address for all official communication with the office. Member States shall have the right to require that such an official address be situated in the European Economic Area.

## CHAPTER 4

## ADMINISTRATIVE COOPERATION

### *Article 51*

### Cooperation in the area of trade mark registration and administration

The offices shall be free to cooperate effectively with each other and with the European Union Intellectual Property Office in order to promote convergence of practices and tools in relation to the examination and registration of trade marks.

### *Article 52*

### Cooperation in other areas

The offices shall be free to cooperate effectively with each other and with the European Union Intellectual Property Office in all areas of their activities other than those referred to in Article 51 which are of relevance for the protection of trade marks in the Union.

## CHAPTER 5

## FINAL PROVISIONS

### *Article 53*

### Data protection

The processing of any personal data carried out in the Member States in the framework of this Directive shall be subject to national law implementing Directive 95/46/EC.

### *Article 54*

### Transposition

1.    Member States shall bring into force the laws, regulations and administrative provisions necessary to comply with Articles 3 to 6, Articles 8 to 14, Articles 16, 17 and 18, Articles 22 to 39, Article 41, Articles 43 and 44 and Articles 46 to 50 by 14 January 2019. Member States shall bring into force the laws, regulations and administrative provisions to comply with Article 45 by 14 January 2023. They shall immediately communicate the text of those measures to the Commission.

When Member States adopt those measures, they shall contain a reference to this Directive or be accompanied by such a reference on the occasion of their official publication. They shall also include a statement that references in existing laws, regulations and administrative provisions to the Directive repealed by this Directive shall be construed as references to this Directive. Member States shall determine how such reference is to be made and how that statement is to be formulated.

2.    Member States shall communicate to the Commission the text of the main provisions of national law which they adopt in the field covered by this Directive.

## *Article 55*

### Repeal

Directive 2008/95/EC is repealed with effect from 15 January 2019, without prejudice to the obligations of the Member States relating to the time limit for the transposition into national law of Directive 89/104/EEC set out in Part B of Annex I to Directive 2008/95/EC.

References to the repealed Directive shall be construed as references to this Directive and shall be read in accordance with the correlation table in the Annex.

## *Article 56*

### Entry into Force

This Directive shall enter into force on the twentieth day following that of its publication in the *Official Journal of the European Union*.

Articles 1, 7, 15, 19, 20 and 21 shall apply from 15 January 2019.

## *Article 57*

### Addressees

This Directive is addressed to the Member States.

# 68. SEMICONDUCTOR DIRECTIVE

**COUNCIL DIRECTIVE of 16 December 1986
on the legal protection of topographies of
semiconductor products (87/54/EEC)***

. . .

## CHAPTER 1
## Definitions

*Article 1*

1. For the purposes of this Directive:

   (a)  a "semiconductor product" shall mean the final or an intermediate form of any product:

      (i)  consisting of a body of material which includes a layer of semiconducting material; and

      (ii)  having one or more other layers composed of conducting, insulating or semiconducting material, the layers being arranged in accordance with a predetermined three-dimensional pattern; and

      (iii)  intended to perform, exclusively or together with other functions, an electronic function;

   (b)  the "topography" of a semiconductor product shall mean a series of related images, however fixed or encoded;

      (i)  representing the three-dimensional pattern of the layers of which a semiconductor product is composed; and

      (ii)  in which series, each image has the pattern or part of the pattern of a surface of the semiconductor product at any stage of its manufacture;

   (c)  "commercial exploitation" means the sale, rental, leasing or any other method of commercial distribution, or an offer for these purposes. However, for the purposes of Articles 3(4), 4(1), 7(1), (3) and (4) "commercial exploitation" shall not include exploitation under conditions of confidentiality to the extent that no further distribution to third parties occurs, except where exploitation of a topography takes place under conditions of confidentiality required by a measure taken in conformity with Article 223(1)(b) of the Treaty.

2. The Council acting by qualified majority on a proposal from the Commission, may amend paragraph 1(a)(i) and (ii) in order to adapt these provisions in the light of technical progress.

## CHAPTER 2
## Protection of topographies of semiconductor products

*Article 2*

1. Member States shall protect the topographies of semiconductor products by adopting legislative provisions conferring exclusive rights in accordance with the provisions of the Directive.

2. The topography of a semiconductor product shall be protected in so far as it satisfies the conditions that it is the result of its creator's own intellectual effort and is not commonplace in the semiconductor industry. Where the topography of a semiconductor product consists of elements that are commonplace in the semiconductor industry, it shall be protected only to the extent that the combination of such elements, taken as a whole, fulfils the abovementioned conditions.

---

\*  Footnotes and recitals omitted.

*Article 3*

1.    Subject to paragraphs 2 to 5, the right to protection shall apply in favour of persons who are the creators of the topographies of semiconductor products.

2.    Member States may provide that,

(a)  where a topography is created in the course of the creator's employment, the right to protection shall apply in favour of the creator's employer unless the terms of employment provide to the contrary;

(b)  where a topography is created under a contract other than a contract of employment, the right to protection shall apply in favour of a party to the contract by whom the topography has been commissioned, unless the contract provides to the contrary.

3.    (a) As regards the persons referred to in paragraph 1, the right to protection shall apply in favour of natural persons who are nationals of a Member State or who have their habitual residence on the territory of a Member State.

(b)  Where Member States make provision in accordance with paragraph 2, the right to protection shall apply in favour of:

(i)   natural persons who are nationals of a Member State or who have their habitual residence on the territory of a Member State;

(ii)  companies or other legal persons which have a real and effective industrial or commercial establishment on the territory of a Member State.

4.    Where no right to protection exists in accordance with other provisions of this Article, the right to protection shall also apply in favour of the persons referred to in paragraph 3(b)(i) and (ii) who:

(a)  first commercially exploit within a Member State a topography which has not yet been exploited commercially anywhere in the world; and

(b)  have been exclusively authorized to exploit commercially the topography throughout the Community by the person entitled to dispose of it.

5.    The right to protection shall also apply in favour of the successors in title of the persons mentioned in paragraphs 1 to 4.

6.    Subject to paragraph 7, Member States may negotiate and conclude agreements or understandings with third States and multilateral Conventions concerning the legal protection of topographies of semiconductor products whilst respecting Community law and in particular the rules laid down in this Directive.

7.    Member States may enter into negotiations which third States with a view to extending the right to protection to persons who do not benefit from the right to protection according to the provisions of this Directive. Member States who enter into such negotiations shall inform the Commission thereof.

When a Member State wishes to extend protection to persons who otherwise do not benefit from the right to protection according to the provisions of this Directive or to conclude an agreement or understanding on the extension of protection with a non-Member State it shall notify the Commission. The Commission shall inform the other Member States thereof. The Member State shall hold the extension of protection or the conclusion of the agreement or understanding in abeyance for one month from the date on which it notifies the Commission. However, if within that period the Commission notifies the Member State concerned of its intention to submit a proposal to the Council for all Member States to extend protection in respect of the persons or non-Member State concerned, the Member State shall hold the extension of protection or the conclusion of the agreement or understanding in abeyance for a period of two months from the date of the notification by the Member State.

Where, before the end of this two-month period, the Commission submits such a proposal to the Council, the Member State shall hold the extension of protection or the conclusion of the agreement or understanding in abeyance for a further period of four months from the date on which the proposal was submitted.

In the absence of a Commission notification or proposal or a Council decision within the time limits prescribed above, the Member State may extend protection or conclude the agreement or understanding.

A proposal by the Commission to extend protection, whether or not it is made following a notification by a Member State in accordance with the preceding paragraphs shall be adopted by the Council acting by qualified majority.

A Decision of the Council on the basis of a Commission proposal shall not prevent a Member State from extending protection to persons, in addition to those to benefit from protection in all Member States, who were included in the envisaged extension, agreement or understanding as notified, unless the Council acting by qualified majority has decided otherwise.

8.    Commission proposals and Council decisions pursuant to paragraph 7 shall be published for information in the Official Journal of the European Communities.

## *Article 4*

1.    Member States may provide that the exclusive rights conferred in conformity with Article 2 shall not come into existence or shall no longer apply to the topography of a semiconductor product unless an application for registration in due form has been filed with a public authority within two years of its first commercial exploitation. Member States may require in addition to such registration that material identifying or exemplifying the topography or any combination thereof has been deposited with a public authority, as well as a statement as to the date of first commercial exploitation of the topography where it precedes the date of the application for registration.

2.    Member States shall ensure that material deposited in conformity with paragraph 1 is not made available to the public where it is a trade secret. This provision shall be without prejudice to the disclosure of such material pursuant to an order of a court or other competent authority to persons involved in litigation concerning the validity or infringement of the exclusive rights referred to in Article 2.

3.    Member States may require that transfers of rights in protected topographies be registered.

4.    Member States may subject registration and deposit in accordance with paragraphs 1 and 3 to the payment of fees not exceeding their administrative costs.

5.    Conditions prescribing the fulfillment of additional formalities for obtaining or maintaining protection shall not be admitted.

6.    Member States which require registration shall provide for legal remedies in favour of a person having the right to protection in accordance with the provisions of this Directive who can prove that another person has applied for or obtained the registration of a topography without his authorization.

## *Article 5*

1.    The exclusive rights referred to in Article 2 shall include the rights to authorize or prohibit any of the following acts:

(a)    reproduction of a topography in so far as it is protected under Article 2 (2);

(b)    commercial exploitation or the importation for that purpose of a topography or of a semiconductor product manufactured by using the topography.

2.    Notwithstanding paragraph 1, a Member State pay permit the reproduction of a topography privately for non commercial aims.

3.   The exclusive rights referred to in paragraph 1(a) shall not apply to reproduction for the purpose of analyzing, evaluating or teaching the concepts, processes, systems or techniques embodied in the topography or the topography itself.

4.   The exclusive rights referred to in paragraph 1 shall not extend to any such act in relation to a topography meeting the requirements of Article 2(2) and created on the basis of an analysis and evaluation of another topography, carried out in conformity with paragraph 3.

5.   The exclusive rights to authorize or prohibit the acts specified in paragraph 1(b) shall not apply to any such act committed after the topography or the semiconductor product has been put on the market in a Member State by the person entitled to authorize its marketing or with his consent.

6.   A person who, when he acquires a semiconductor product, does not know, or has no reasonable grounds to believe, that the product is protected by an exclusive right conferred by a Member State in conformity with this Directive shall not be prevented from commercially exploiting that product.

However, for acts committed after that person knows, or has reasonable grounds to believe, that the semiconductor product is so protected, Member States shall ensure that on the demand of the rightholder a tribunal may require, in accordance with the provisions of the national law applicable, the payment of adequate remuneration.

7.   The provisions of paragraph 6 shall apply to the successors in title of the person referred to in the first sentence of that paragraph.

## Article 6

Member States shall not subject the exclusive rights referred to in Article 2 to licences granted, for the sole reason that a certain period of time has elapsed, automatically, and by operation of law.

## Article 7

1.   Member States shall provide that the exclusive rights referred to in Article 2 shall come into existence:

(a)   where registration is the condition for the coming into existence of the exclusive rights in accordance with Article 4, on the earlier of the following dates:

(i)   the date when the topography is first commercially exploited anywhere in the world;

(ii)   the date when an application or registration has been filed in due form; or

(b)   when the topography is first commercially exploited anywhere in the world; or

(c)   when the topography is first fixed or encoded.

2.   Where the exclusive rights come into existence in accordance with paragraph 1(a) or (b), the Member States shall provide, for the period prior to those rights coming into existence, legal remedies in favour of a person having the right to protection in accordance with the provisions of this Directive who can prove that another person has fraudulently reproduced or commercially exploited or imported for that purpose a topography. This paragraph shall be without prejudice to legal remedies made available to enforce the exclusive rights conferred in conformity with Article 2.

3.   The exclusive rights shall come to an end 10 years from the end of the calendar year in which the topography is first commercially exploited anywhere in the world or, where registration is a condition for the coming into existence or continuing application of the exclusive rights, 10 years from the earlier of the following dates:

(a)   the end of the calendar year in which the topography is first commercially exploited anywhere in the world;

(b)   the end of the calendar year in which the application for registration has been filed in due form.

4.    Where a topography has not been commercially exploited anywhere in the world within a period of 15 years from its first fixation or encoding, any exclusive rights in existence pursuant to paragraph 1 shall come to an end and no new exclusive rights shall come into existence unless an application for registration in due form has been filed within that period in those Member States where registration is a condition for the coming into existence or continuing application of the exclusive rights.

### *Article 8*

The protection granted to the topographies of semiconductor products in accordance with Article 2 shall not extend to any concept, process, system, technique or encoded information embodied in the topography other than the topography itself.

### *Article 9*

Where the legislation of Member States provides that semiconductor products manufactured using protected topographies may carry an indication, the indication to be used shall be a capital T as follows: T, "T", [T], T, T* or T.

## CHAPTER 3
## Continued application of other legal provisions

### *Article 10*

1.    The provisions of this Directive shall be without prejudice to legal provisions concerning patent and utility model rights.

2.    The provisions of this Directive shall be without prejudice:

(a)    to rights conferred by the Member States in fulfillment of their obligations under international agreements, including provisions extending such rights to nationals of, or residents in, the territory of the Member State concerned;

(b)    to the law of copyright in Member States, restricting the reproduction of drawing or other artistic representations of topographies by copying them in two dimensions.

3.    Protection granted by national law to topographies of semiconductor products fixed or encoded before the entry into force of the national provisions enacting the Directive, but no later than the date set out in Article 11(1), shall not be affected by the provisions of this Directive.

## CHAPTER 4
## Final provisions

### *Article 11*

1.    Member States shall bring into force the laws, regulations or administrative provisions necessary to comply with this Directive by 7 November 1987.

2.    Member States shall ensure that they communicate to the Commission the texts of the main provisions of national law which they adopt in the field covered by this Directive.

### *Article 12*

This Directive is addressed to the Member States.

Done at Brussels, 16 December 1986.

# 69.  DATABASE DIRECTIVE

**DIRECTIVE 96/9/EC OF THE EUROPEAN PARLIAMENT
AND OF THE COUNCIL
of 11 March 1996
on the legal protection of databases**

**(as amended)**\*

. . . (5)    Whereas copyright remains an appropriate form of exclusive right for authors who have created databases;

(6)    Whereas, nevertheless, in the absence of a harmonized system of unfair-competition legislation or of case-law, other measures are required in addition to prevent the unauthorized extraction and/or re-utilization of the contents of a database;

(7)    Whereas the making of databases requires the investment of considerable human, technical and financial resources while such databases can be copied or accessed at a fraction of the cost needed to design them independently; . . .

(13) Whereas this Directive protects collections, sometimes called "compilations", of works, data or other materials which are arranged, stored and accessed by means which include electronic, electromagnetic or electro-optical processes or analogous processes;

(14) Whereas protection under this Directive should be extended to cover non-electronic databases;

(15) Whereas the criteria used to determine whether a database should be protected by copyright should be defined to the fact that the selection or the arrangement of the contents of the database is the author's own intellectual creation; whereas such protection should cover the structure of the database;

(16) Whereas no criterion other than originality in the sense of the author's intellectual creation should be applied to determine the eligibility of the database for copyright protection, and in particular no aesthetic or qualitative criteria should be applied;

(17) Whereas the term "database" should be understood to include literary, artistic, musical or other collections of works or collections of other material such as texts, sound, images, numbers, facts, and data; whereas it should cover collections of independent works, data or other materials which are systematically or methodically arranged and can be individually accessed; whereas this means that a recording or an audiovisual, cinematographic, literary or musical work as such does not fall within the scope of this Directive; . . .

(19) Whereas, as a rule, the compilation of several recordings of musical performances on a CD does not come within the scope of this Directive, both because, as a compilation, it does not meet the conditions for copyright protection and because it does not represent a substantial enough investment to be eligible under the sui generis right;

(20) Whereas protection under this Directive may also apply to the materials necessary for the operation or consultation of certain databases such as thesaurus and indexation systems;

(21) Whereas the protection provided for in this Directive relates to databases in which works, data or other materials have been arranged systematically or methodically; whereas it is not necessary for those materials to have been physically stored in an organized manner;

(22) Whereas electronic databases within the meaning of this Directive may also include devices such as CD-ROM and CD-i;

---

\*    Footnotes and some recitals omitted.

(23) Whereas the term "database" should not be taken to extend to computer programs used in the making or operation of a database, which are protected by Council Directive 91/250/EEC of 14 May 1991 on the legal protection of computer programs; . . .

(26) Whereas works protected by copyright and subject matter protected by related rights, which are incorporated into a database, remain nevertheless protected by the respective exclusive rights and may not be incorporated into, or extracted from, the database without the permission of the rightholder or his successors in title;

(27) Whereas copyright in such works and related rights in subject matter thus incorporated into a database are in no way affected by the existence of a separate right in the selection or arrangement of these works and subject matter in a database;

(28) Whereas the moral rights of the natural person who created the database belong to the author and should be exercised according to the legislation of the Member States and the provisions of the Berne Convention for the Protection of Literary and Artistic Works; whereas such moral rights remain outside the scope of this Directive; . . .

(33) Whereas the question of exhaustion of the right of distribution does not arise in the case of on-line databases, which come within the field of provision of services; whereas this also applies with regard to a material copy of such a database made by the user of such a service with the consent of the rightholder; whereas, unlike CD-ROM or CD-i, where the intellectual property is incorporated in a material medium, namely an item of goods, every on-line service is in fact an act which will have to be subject to authorization where the copyright so provides;

(34) Whereas, nevertheless, once the rightholder has chosen to make available a copy of the database to a user, whether by an on-line service or by other means of distribution, that lawful user must be able to access and use the database for the purposes and in the way set out in the agreement with the rightholder, even if such access and use necessitate performance of otherwise restricted acts; . . .

(36) Whereas the term "scientific research" within the meaning of this Directive covers both the natural sciences and the human sciences; . . .

(41) Whereas the objective of the sui generis right is to give the maker of a database the option of preventing the unauthorized extraction and/or re-utilization of all or a substantial part of the contents of that database; whereas the maker of a database is the person who takes the initiative and the risk of investing; whereas this excludes subcontractors in particular from the definition of maker;

(42) Whereas the special right to prevent unauthorized extraction and/or re-utilization relates to acts by the user which go beyond his legitimate rights and thereby harm the investment; whereas the right to prohibit extraction and/or re-utilization of all or a substantial part of the contents relates not only to the manufacture of a parasitical competing product but also to any user who, through his acts, causes significant detriment, evaluated qualitatively or quantitatively, to the investment;

(43) Whereas, in the case of on-line transmission, the right to prohibit re-utilization is not exhausted either as regards the database or as regards a material copy of the database or of part thereof made by the addressee of the transmission with the consent of the rightholder;

(44) Whereas, when on-screen display of the contents of a database necessitates the permanent or temporary transfer of all or a substantial part of such contents to another medium, that act should be subject to authorization by the rightholder;

(45) Whereas the right to prevent unauthorized extraction and/or re-utilization does not in any way constitute an extension of copyright protection to mere facts or data; . . .

(47) Whereas, in the interests of competition between suppliers of information products and services, protection by the sui generis right must not be afforded in such a way as to facilitate abuses of a dominant position, in particular as regards the creation and distribution of new products and services which have an intellectual, documentary, technical, economic or commercial added value; whereas,

therefore, the provisions of this Directive are without prejudice to the application of Community or national competition rules; . . .

(53) Whereas the burden of proof regarding the date of completion of the making of a database lies with the maker of the database;

(54) Whereas the burden of proof that the criteria exist for concluding that a substantial modification of the contents of a database is to be regarded as a substantial new investment lies with the maker of the database resulting from such investment;

(55) Whereas a substantial new investment involving a new term of protection may include a substantial verification of the contents of the database;

(56) Whereas the right to prevent unauthorized extraction and/or re-utilization in respect of a database should apply to databases whose makers are nationals or habitual residents of third countries or to those produced by legal persons not established in a Member State, within the meaning of the Treaty, only if such third countries offer comparable protection to databases produced by nationals of a Member State or persons who have their habitual residence in the territory of the Community; . . .

## CHAPTER I
## SCOPE

### *Article 1*

### Scope

1. This Directive concerns the legal protection of databases in any form.

2. For the purposes of this Directive, "database" shall mean a collection of independent works, data or other materials arranged in a systematic or methodical way and individually accessible by electronic or other means.

3. Protection under this Directive shall not apply to computer programs used in the making or operation of databases accessible by electronic means.

### *Article 2*

### Limitations on the scope

This Directive shall apply without prejudice to Community provisions relating to:

(a)   the legal protection of computer programs;

(b)   rental right, lending right and certain rights related to copyright in the field of intellectual property;

(c)   the term of protection of copyright and certain related rights.

## CHAPTER II
## COPYRIGHT

### *Article 3*

### Object of protection

1. In accordance with this Directive, databases which, by reason of the selection or arrangement of their contents, constitute the author's own intellectual creation shall be protected as such by copyright. No other criteria shall be applied to determine their eligibility for that protection.

2. The copyright protection of databases provided for by this Directive shall not extend to their contents and shall be without prejudice to any rights subsisting in those contents themselves.

*Article 4*

## Database authorship

1.    The author of a database shall be the natural person or group of natural persons who created the base or, where the legislation of the Member States so permits, the legal person designated as the rightholder by that legislation.

2.    Where collective works are recognized by the legislation of a Member State, the economic rights shall be owned by the person holding the copyright.

3.    In respect of a database created by a group of natural persons jointly, the exclusive rights shall be owned jointly.

*Article 5*

## Restricted acts

In respect of the expression of the database which is protectable by copyright, the author of a database shall have the exclusive right to carry out or to authorize:

(a)    temporary or permanent reproduction by any means and in any form, in whole or in part;

(b)    translation, adaptation, arrangement and any other alteration;

(c)    any form of distribution to the public of the database or of copies thereof. The first sale in the Community of a copy of the database by the rightholder or with his consent shall exhaust the right to control resale of that copy within the Community;

(d)    any communication, display or performance to the public;

(e)    any reproduction, distribution, communication, display or performance to the public of the results of the acts referred to in (b).

*Article 6*

## Exceptions to restricted acts

1.    The performance by the lawful user of a database or of a copy thereof of any of the acts listed in Article 5 which is necessary for the purposes of access to the contents of the databases and normal use of the contents by the lawful user shall not require the authorization of the author of the database. Where the lawful user is authorized to use only part of the database, this provision shall apply only to that part.

2.    Member States shall have the option of providing for limitations on the rights set out in Article 5 in the following cases:

(a)    in the case of reproduction for private purposes of a non-electronic database;

(b)    where there is use for the sole purpose of illustration for teaching or scientific research, as long as the source is indicated and to the extent justified by the non-commercial purpose to be achieved, without prejudice to the exceptions and limitations provided for in Directive (EU) 2019/790 of the European Parliament and of the Council;

(c)    where there is use for the purposes of public security of for the purposes of an administrative or judicial procedure;

(d)    where other exceptions to copyright which are traditionally authorized under national law are involved, without prejudice to points (a), (b) and (c).

3.    In accordance with the Berne Convention for the protection of Literary and Artistic Works, this Article may not be interpreted in such a way as to allow its application to be used in a manner which

unreasonably prejudices the rightholder's legitimate interests or conflicts with normal exploitation of the database.

## CHAPTER III
## SUI GENERIS RIGHT

### *Article 7*

### Object of protection

1.    Member States shall provide for a right for the maker of a database which shows that there has been qualitatively and/or quantitatively a substantial investment in either the obtaining, verification or presentation of the contents to prevent extraction and/or re-utilization of the whole or of a substantial part, evaluated qualitatively and/or quantitatively, of the contents of that database.

2.    For the purposes of this Chapter:

(a)   "extraction" shall mean the permanent or temporary transfer of all or a substantial part of the contents of a database to another medium by any means or in any form;

(b)   "re-utilization" shall mean any form of making available to the public all or a substantial part of the contents of a database by the distribution of copies, by renting, by on-line or other forms of transmission. The first sale of a copy of a database within the Community by the rightholder or with his consent shall exhaust the right to control resale of that copy within the Community;

Public lending is not an act of extraction or re-utilization.

3.    The right referred to in paragraph 1 may be transferred, assigned or granted under contractual licence.

4.    The right provided for in paragraph 1 shall apply irrespective of the eligibility of that database for protection by copyright or by other rights. Moreover, it shall apply irrespective of eligibility of the contents of that database for protection by copyright or by other rights. Protection of databases under the right provided for in paragraph 1 shall be without prejudice to rights existing in respect of their contents.

5.    The repeated and systematic extraction and/or re-utilization of insubstantial parts of the contents of the database implying acts which conflict with a normal exploitation of that database or which unreasonably prejudice the legitimate interests of the maker of the database shall not be permitted.

### *Article 8*

### Rights and obligations of lawful users

1.    The maker of a database which is made available to the public in whatever manner may not prevent a lawful user of the database from extracting and/or re-utilizing insubstantial parts of its contents, evaluated qualitatively and/or quantitatively, for any purposes whatsoever. Where the lawful user is authorized to extract and/or re-utilize only part of the database, this paragraph shall apply only to that part.

2.    A lawful user of a database which is made available to the public in whatever manner may not perform acts which conflict with normal exploitation of the database or unreasonably prejudice the legitimate interests of the maker of the database.

3.    A lawful user of a database which is made available to the public in any manner may not cause prejudice to the holder of a copyright or related right in respect of the works or subject matter contained in the database.

## Article 9

### Exceptions to the sui generis right

Member States may stipulate that lawful users of a database which is made available to the public in whatever manner may, without the authorization of its maker, extract or re-utilize a substantial part of its contents:

(a)   in the case of extraction for private purposes of the contents of a non-electronic database;

(b)   in the case of extraction for the purposes of illustration for teaching or scientific research, as long as the source is indicated and to the extent justified by the non-commercial purpose to be achieved, without prejudice to the exceptions and limitations provided for in Directive (EU) 2019/790;

(c)   in the case of extraction and/or re-utilization for the purposes of public security or an administrative or judicial procedure.

## Article 10

### Term of protection

1.   The right provided for in Article 7 shall run from the date of completion of the making of the database. It shall expire fifteen years from the first of January of the year following the date of completion.

2.   In the case of a database which is made available to the public in whatever manner before expiry of the period provided for in paragraph 1, the term of protection by that right shall expire fifteen years from the first of January of the year following the date when the database was first made available to the public.

3.   Any substantial change, evaluated qualitatively or quantitatively, to the contents of a database, including any substantial change resulting from the accumulation of successive additions, deletions or alterations, which would result in the database being considered to be a substantial new investment, evaluated qualitatively or quantitatively, shall qualify the database resulting from that investment for its own term of protection.

## Article 11

### Beneficiaries of protection under the sui generis right

1.   The right provided for in Article 7 shall apply to database whose makers or rightholders are nationals of a Member State or who have their habitual residence in the territory of the Community.

2.   Paragraph 1 shall also apply to companies and firms formed in accordance with the law of a Member State and having their registered office, central administration or principal place of business within the Community; however, where such a company or firm has only its registered office in the territory of the Community, its operations must be genuinely linked on an ongoing basis with the economy of a Member State.

3.   Agreements extending the right provided for in Article 7 to databases made in third countries and falling outside the provisions of paragraphs 1 and 2 shall be concluded by the Council acting on a proposal from the Commission. The term of any protection extended to databases by virtue of that procedure shall not exceed that available pursuant to Article 10.

## CHAPTER IV
## COMMON PROVISIONS

*Article 12*

**Remedies**

Member States shall provide appropriate remedies in respect of infringements of the rights provided for in this Directive.

*Article 13*

**Continued application of other legal provisions**

This Directive shall be without prejudice to provisions concerning in particular copyright, rights related to copyright or any other rights or obligations subsisting in the data, works or other materials incorporated into a database, patent rights, trade marks, design rights, the protection of national treasures, laws on restrictive practices and unfair competition, trade secrets, security, confidentiality, data protection and privacy, access to public documents, and the law of contract.

*Article 14*

**Application over time**

1.    Protection pursuant to this Directive as regards copyright shall also be available in respect of databases created prior to the date referred to Article 16(1) which on that date fulfil the requirements laid down in this Directive as regards copyright protection of databases.

2.    Notwithstanding paragraph 1, where a database protected under copyright arrangements in a Member State on the date of publication of this Directive does not fulfil the eligibility criteria for copyright protection laid down in Article 3(1), this Directive shall not result in any curtailing in that Member State of the remaining term of protection afforded under those arrangements.

3.    Protection pursuant to the provisions of this Directive as regards the right provided for in Article 7 shall also be available in respect of databases the making of which was completed not more than fifteen years prior to the date referred to in Article 16(1) and which on that date fulfil the requirements laid down in Article 7.

4.    The protection provided for in paragraphs 1 and 3 shall be without prejudice to any acts concluded and rights acquired before the date referred to in those paragraphs.

5.    In the case of a database the making of which was completed not more than fifteen years prior to the date referred to in Article 16(1), the term of protection by the right provided for in Article 7 shall expire fifteen years from the first of January following that date.

*Article 15*

**Binding nature of certain provisions**

Any contractual provision contrary to Articles 6(1) and 8 shall be null and void.

*Article 16*

**Final provisions**

1.    Member States shall bring into force the laws, regulations and administrative provisions necessary to comply with this Directive before 1 January 1998.

When Member States adopt these provisions, they shall contain a reference to this Directive or shall be accompanied by such reference on the occasion of their official publication. The methods of making such reference shall be laid down by Member States.

2.     Member States shall communicate to the Commission the text of the provisions of domestic law which they adopt in the field governed by this Directive.

3.     Not later than at the end of the third year after the date refered to in paragraph 1, and every three years thereafter, the Commission shall submit to the European Parliament, the Council and the Economic and Social Committee a report on the application of this Directive, in which, inter alia, on the basis of specific information supplied by the Member States, it shall examine in particular the application of the sui generis right, including Articles 8 and 9, and shall verify especially whether the application of this right has led to abuse of a dominant position or other interference with free competition which would justify appropriate measures being taken, including the establishment of non-voluntary licensing arrangements. Where necessary, it shall submit proposals for adjustment of this Directive in line with developments in the area of databases.

*Article 17*

This Directive is addressed to the Member States.

# 70. BIOTECHNOLOGY INVENTION DIRECTIVE

## DIRECTIVE 98/44/EC OF THE EUROPEAN PARLIAMENT
## AND OF THE COUNCIL
### of 6 July 1998
#### on the legal protection of biotechnological inventions*

. . . (8)    Whereas legal protection of biotechnological inventions does not necessitate the creation of a separate body of law in place of the rules of national patent law; whereas the rules of national patent law remain the essential basis for the legal protection of biotechnological inventions given that they must be adapted or added to in certain specific respects in order to take adequate account of technological developments involving biological material which also fulfil the requirements for patentability; . . .

(16) Whereas patent law must be applied so as to respect the fundamental principles safeguarding the dignity and integrity of the person; whereas it is important to assert the principle that the human body, at any stage in its formation or development, including germ cells, and the simple discovery of one of its elements or one of its products, including the sequence or partial sequence of a human gene, cannot be patented; whereas these principles are in line with the criteria of patentability proper to patent law, whereby a mere discovery cannot be patented;

(17) Whereas significant progress in the treatment of diseases has already been made thanks to the existence of medicinal products derived from elements isolated from the human body and/or otherwise produced, such medicinal products resulting from technical processes aimed at obtaining elements similar in structure to those existing naturally in the human body and whereas, consequently, research aimed at obtaining and isolating such elements valuable to medicinal production should be encouraged by means of the patent system; . . .

(20) Whereas, therefore, it should be made clear that an invention based on an element isolated from the human body or otherwise produced by means of a technical process, which is susceptible of industrial application, is not excluded from patentability, even where the structure of that element is identical to that of a natural element, given that the rights conferred by the patent do not extend to the human body and its elements in their natural environment;

(21) Whereas such an element isolated from the human body or otherwise produced is not excluded from patentability since it is, for example, the result of technical processes used to identify, purify and classify it and to reproduce it outside the human body, techniques which human beings alone are capable of putting into practice and which nature is incapable of accomplishing by itself;

(22) Whereas the discussion on the patentability of sequences or partial sequences of genes is controversial; whereas, according to this Directive, the granting of a patent for inventions which concern such sequences or partial sequences should be subject to the same criteria of patentability as in all other areas of technology: novelty, inventive step and industrial application; whereas the industrial application of a sequence or partial sequence must be disclosed in the patent application as filed;

(23) Whereas a mere DNA sequence without indication of a function does not contain any technical information and is therefore not a patentable invention;

(24) Whereas, in order to comply with the industrial application criterion it is necessary in cases where a sequence or partial sequence of a gene is used to produce a protein or part of a protein, to specify which protein or part of a protein is produced or what function it performs;

---

\*    Footnotes and some recitals omitted.

(25) Whereas, for the purposes of interpreting rights conferred by a patent, when sequences overlap only in parts which are not essential to the invention, each sequence will be considered as an independent sequence in patent law terms;

(26) Whereas if an invention is based on biological material of human origin or if it uses such material, where a patent application is filed, the person from whose body the material is taken must have had an opportunity of expressing free and informed consent thereto, in accordance with national law;

(27) Whereas if an invention is based on biological material of plant or animal origin or if it uses such material, the patent application should, where appropriate, include information on the geographical origin of such material, if known; whereas this is without prejudice to the processing of patent applications or the validity of rights arising from granted patents; . . .

(38) Whereas the operative part of this Directive should also include an illustrative list of inventions excluded from patentability so as to provide national courts and patent offices with a general guide to interpreting the reference to *ordre public* and morality; whereas this list obviously cannot presume to be exhaustive; whereas processes, the use of which offend against human dignity, such as processes to produce chimeras from germ cells or totipotent cells of humans and animals, are obviously also excluded from patentability;

(39) Whereas *ordre public* and morality correspond in particular to ethical or moral principles recognised in a Member State, respect for which is particularly important in the field of biotechnology in view of the potential scope of inventions in this field and their inherent relationship to living matter; whereas such ethical or moral principles supplement the standard legal examinations under patent law regardless of the technical field of the invention;

(40) Whereas there is a consensus within the Community that interventions in the human germ line and the cloning of human beings offends against *ordre public* and morality; whereas it is therefore important to exclude unequivocally from patentability processes for modifying the germ line genetic identity of human beings and processes for cloning human beings;

(41) Whereas a process for cloning human beings may be defined as any process, including techniques of embryo splitting, designed to create a human being with the same nuclear genetic information as another living or deceased human being;

(42) Whereas, moreover, uses of human embryos for industrial or commercial purposes must also be excluded from patentability; whereas in any case such exclusion does not affect inventions for therapeutic or diagnostic purposes which are applied to the human embryo and are useful to it; . . .

(45) Whereas processes for modifying the genetic identity of animals which are likely to cause them suffering without any substantial medical benefit in terms of research, prevention, diagnosis or therapy to man or animal, and also animals resulting from such processes, must be excluded from patentability; . . .

## CHAPTER I
### Patentability

*Article 1*

1.    Member States shall protect biotechnological inventions under national patent law. They shall, if necessary, adjust their national patent law to take account of the provisions of this Directive.

2.    This Directive shall be without prejudice to the obligations of the Member States pursuant to international agreements, and in particular the TRIPs Agreement and the Convention on Biological Diversity.

## Article 2

1.  For the purposes of this Directive,

    (a) "biological material" means any material containing genetic information and capable of reproducing itself or being reproduced in a biological system;

    (b) "microbiological process" means any process involving or performed upon or resulting in microbiological material.

2.  A process for the production of plants or animals is essentially biological if it consists entirely of natural phenomena such as crossing or selection.

3.  The concept of "plant variety" is defined by Article 5 of Regulation (EC) No 2100/94.

## Article 3

1.  For the purposes of this Directive, inventions which are new, which involve an inventive step and which are susceptible of industrial application shall be patentable even if they concern a product consisting of or containing biological material or a process by means of which biological material is produced, processed or used.

2.  Biological material which is isolated from its natural environment or produced by means of a technical process may be the subject of an invention even if it previously occurred in nature.

## Article 4

1.  The following shall not be patentable:

    (a) plant and animal varieties;

    (b) essentially biological processes for the production of plants or animals.

2.  Inventions which concern plants or animals shall be patentable if the technical feasibility of the invention is not confined to a particular plant or animal variety.

3.  Paragraph 1(b) shall be without prejudice to the patentability of inventions which concern a microbiological or other technical process or a product obtained by means of such a process.

## Article 5

1.  The human body, at the various stages of its formation and development, and the simple discovery of one of its elements, including the sequence or partial sequence of a gene, cannot constitute patentable inventions.

2.  An element isolated from the human body or otherwise produced by means of a technical process, including the sequence or partial sequence of a gene, may constitute a patentable invention, even if the structure of that element is identical to that of a natural element.

3.  The industrial application of a sequence or a partial sequence of a gene must be disclosed in the patent application.

## Article 6

1.  Inventions shall be considered unpatentable where their commercial exploitation would be contrary to *ordre public* or morality; however, exploitation shall not be deemed to be so contrary merely because it is prohibited by law or regulation.

2.  On the basis of paragraph 1, the following, in particular, shall be considered unpatentable:

    (a) processes for cloning human beings;

    (b) processes for modifying the germ line genetic identity of human beings;

(c)    uses of human embryos for industrial or commercial purposes;

(d)    processes for modifying the genetic identity of animals which are likely to cause them suffering without any substantial medical benefit to man or animal, and also animals resulting from such processes.

*Article 7*

The Commission's European Group on Ethics in Science and New Technologies evaluates all ethical aspects of biotechnology.

## CHAPTER II
### Scope of protection

*Article 8*

1.    The protection conferred by a patent on a biological material possessing specific characteristics as a result of the invention shall extend to any biological material derived from that biological material through propagation or multiplication in an identical or divergent form and possessing those same characteristics.

2.    The protection conferred by a patent on a process that enables a biological material to be produced possessing specific characteristics as a result of the invention shall extend to biological material directly obtained through that process and to any other biological material derived from the directly obtained biological material through propagation or multiplication in an identical or divergent form and possessing those same characteristics.

*Article 9*

The protection conferred by a patent on a product containing or consisting of genetic information shall extend to all material, save as provided in Article 5(1), in which the product in incorporated and in which the genetic information is contained and performs its function.

*Article 10*

The protection referred to in Articles 8 and 9 shall not extend to biological material obtained from the propagation or multiplication of biological material placed on the market in the territory of a Member State by the holder of the patent or with his consent, where the multiplication or propagation necessarily results from the application for which the biological material was marketed, provided that the material obtained is not subsequently used for other propagation or multiplication.

*Article 11*

1.    By way of derogation from Articles 8 and 9, the sale or other form of commercialisation of plant propagating material to a farmer by the holder of the patent or with his consent for agricultural use implies authorisation for the farmer to use the product of his harvest for propagation or multiplication by him on his own farm, the extent and conditions of this derogation corresponding to those under Article 14 of Regulation (EC) No 2100/94.

2.    By way of derogation from Articles 8 and 9, the sale or any other form of commercialisation of breeding stock or other animal reproductive material to a farmer by the holder of the patent or with his consent implies authorisation for the farmer to use the protected livestock for an agricultural purpose. This includes making the animal or other animal reproductive material available for the purposes of pursuing his agricultural activity but not sale within the framework or for the purpose of a commercial reproduction activity.

3.    The extent and the conditions of the derogation provided for in paragraph 2 shall be determined by national laws, regulations and practices.

## CHAPTER III
## Compulsory cross-licensing

*Article 12*

1.    Where a breeder cannot acquire or exploit a plant variety right without infringing a prior patent, he may apply for a compulsory licence for non-exclusive use of the invention protected by the patent inasmuch as the licence is necessary for the exploitation of the plant variety to be protected, subject to payment of an appropriate royalty. Member States shall provide that, where such a licence is granted, the holder of the patent will be entitled to a cross-licence on reasonable terms to use the protected variety.

2.    Where the holder of a patent concerning a biotechnological invention cannot exploit it without infringing a prior plant variety right, he may apply for a compulsory licence for non-exclusive use of the plant variety protected by that right, subject to payment of an appropriate royalty. Member States shall provide that, where such a licence is granted, the holder of the variety right will be entitled to a cross-licence on reasonable terms to use the protected invention.

3.    Applicants for the licences referred to in paragraphs 1 and 2 must demonstrate that:

(a)    they have applied unsuccessfully to the holder of the patent or of the plant variety right to obtain a contractual licence;

(b)    the plant variety or the invention constitutes significant technical progress of considerable economic interest compared with the invention claimed in the patent or the protected plant variety.

4.    Each Member State shall designate the authority or authorities responsible for granting the licence. Where a licence for a plant variety can be granted only by the Community Plant Variety Office, Article 29 of Regulation (EC) No 2100/94 shall apply.

## CHAPTER IV
## Deposit, access and re-deposit of a biological material

*Article 13*

1.    Where an invention involves the use of or concerns biological material which is not available to the public and which cannot be described in a patent application in such a manner as to enable the invention to be reproduced by a person skilled in the art, the description shall be considered inadequate for the purposes of patent law unless:

(a)    the biological material has been deposited no later than the date on which the patent application was filed with a recognised depositary institution. At least the international depositary authorities which acquired this status by virtue of Article 7 of the Budapest Treaty of 28 April 1977 on the international recognition of the deposit of micro-organisms for the purposes of patent procedure, hereinafter referred to as the "Budapest Treaty", shall be recognised;

(b)    the application as filed contains such relevant information as is available to the applicant on the characteristics of the biological material deposited;

(c)    the patent application states the name of the depository institution and the accession number.

2.    Access to the deposited biological material shall be provided through the supply of a sample:

(a)    up to the first publication of the patent application, only to those persons who are authorised under national patent law;

(b)    between the first publication of the application and the granting of the patent, to anyone requesting it or, if the applicant so requests, only to an independent expert;

(c)  after the patent has been granted, and notwithstanding revocation or cancellation of the patent, to anyone requesting it.

3.  The sample shall be supplied only if the person requesting it undertakes, for the term during which the patent is in force:

(a)  not to make it or any material derived from it available to third parties; and

(b)  not to use it or any material derived from it except for experimental purposes, unless the applicant for or proprietor of the patent, as applicable, expressly waives such an undertaking.

4.  At the applicant's request, where an application is refused or withdrawn, access to the deposited material shall be limited to an independent expert for **20** years from the date on which the patent application was filed. In that case, paragraph 3 shall apply.

5.  The applicant's requests referred to in point (b) of paragraph 2 and in paragraph 4 may only be made up to the date on which the technical preparations for publishing the patent application are deemed to have been completed.

*Article 14*

1.  If the biological material deposited in accordance with Article 13 ceases to be available from the recognised depositary institution, a new deposit of the material shall be permitted on the same terms as those laid down in the Budapest Treaty.

2.  Any new deposit shall be accompanied by a statement signed by the depositor certifying that the newly deposited biological material is the same as that originally deposited.

## CHAPTER V
### Final provisions

*Article 15*

1.  Member States shall bring into force the laws, regulations and administrative provisions necessary to comply with this Directive not later than 30 July 2000. They shall forthwith inform the Commission thereof.

When Member States adopt these measures, they shall contain a reference to this Directive or shall be accompanied by such reference on the occasion of their official publication. The methods of making such reference shall be laid down by Member States.

2.  Member States shall communicate to the Commission the text of the provisions of national law which they adopt in the field covered by this Directive.

*Article 16*

The Commission shall send the European Parliament and the Council:

(a)  every five years as from the date specified in Article 15(1) a report on any problems encountered with regard to the relationship between this Directive and international agreements on the protection of human rights to which the Member States have acceded;

(b)  within two years of entry into force of this Directive, a report assessing the implications for basic genetic engineering research of failure to publish, or late publication of, papers on subjects which could be patentable;

(c)  annually as from the date specified in Article 15(1), a report on the development and implications of patent law in the field of biotechnology and genetic engineering.

*Article 17*

This Directive shall enter into force on the day of its publication in the Official Journal of the European Communities.

*Article 18*

This Directive is addressed to the Member States.

Done at Brussels, 6 July 1998.

# 71. REGULATION IMPLEMENTING THE UNITARY PATENT

### REGULATION (EU) NO 1257/2012 OF THE EUROPEAN PARLIAMENT AND OF THE COUNCIL
### of 17 December 2012
### implementing enhanced cooperation in the area of the creation of unitary patent protection*

. . . Whereas: . . .

(4) Unitary patent protection will foster scientific and technological advances and the functioning of the internal market by making access to the patent system easier, less costly and legally secure. It will also improve the level of patent protection by making it possible to obtain uniform patent protection in the participating Member States and eliminate costs and complexity for undertakings throughout the Union. It should be available to proprietors of a European patent from both the participating Member States and from other States, regardless of their nationality, residence or place of establishment.

(5) The Convention on the Grant of European Patents of 5 October 1973, as revised on 17 December 1991 and on 29 November 2000 (hereinafter "EPC"), established the European Patent Organisation and entrusted it with the task of granting European patents. This task is carried out by the European Patent Office (hereinafter "EPO"). A European patent granted by the EPO should, at the request of the patent proprietor, benefit from unitary effect by virtue of this Regulation in the participating Member States. Such a patent is hereinafter referred to as a "European patent with unitary effect". . . .

(7) Unitary patent protection should be achieved by attributing unitary effect to European patents in the post-grant phase by virtue of this Regulation and in respect of all the participating Member States. The main feature of a European patent with unitary effect should be its unitary character, i.e. providing uniform protection and having equal effect in all the participating Member States. Consequently, a European patent with unitary effect should only be limited, transferred or revoked, or lapse, in respect of all the participating Member States. It should be possible for a European patent with unitary effect to be licensed in respect of the whole or part of the territories of the participating Member States. To ensure the uniform substantive scope of protection conferred by unitary patent protection, only European patents that have been granted for all the participating Member States with the same set of claims should benefit from unitary effect. Finally, the unitary effect attributed to a European patent should have an accessory nature and should be deemed not to have arisen to the extent that the basic European patent has been revoked or limited.

(8) In accordance with the general principles of patent law and Article 64(1) of the EPC, unitary patent protection should take effect retroactively in the participating Member States as from the date of publication of the mention of the grant of the European patent in the European Patent Bulletin. Where unitary patent protection takes effect, the participating Member States should ensure that the European patent is deemed not to have taken effect on their territory as a national patent, so as to avoid any duplication of patent protection.

(9) The European patent with unitary effect should confer on its proprietor the right to prevent any third party from committing acts against which the patent provides protection. This should be ensured through the establishment of a Unified Patent Court. In matters not covered by this Regulation or by Council Regulation (EU) No 1260/2012 of 17 December 2012 implementing enhanced cooperation in the area of unitary patent protection with regard to the applicable translation arrangements [3], the provisions of the EPC, the Agreement on a Unified Patent Court, including its provisions defining the

---

\*    Footnotes and some recitals omitted.

scope of that right and its limitations, and national law, including rules of private international law, should apply.

(10) Compulsory licences for European patents with unitary effect should be governed by the laws of the participating Member States as regards their respective territories. . . .

(12) In accordance with the case-law of the Court of Justice of the European Union, the principle of the exhaustion of rights should also be applied to European patents with unitary effect. Therefore, rights conferred by a European patent with unitary effect should not extend to acts concerning the product covered by that patent which are carried out within the participating Member States after that product has been placed on the market in the Union by the patent proprietor. . . .

(24) Jurisdiction in respect of European patents with unitary effect should be established and governed by an instrument setting up a unified patent litigation system for European patents and European patents with unitary effect.

(25) Establishing a Unified Patent Court to hear cases concerning the European patent with unitary effect is essential in order to ensure the proper functioning of that patent, consistency of case-law and hence legal certainty, and cost-effectiveness for patent proprietors. It is therefore of paramount importance that the participating Member States ratify the Agreement on a Unified Patent Court in accordance with their national constitutional and parliamentary procedures and take the necessary steps for that Court to become operational as soon as possible.

(26) This Regulation should be without prejudice to the right of the participating Member States to grant national patents and should not replace the participating Member States' laws on patents. Patent applicants should remain free to obtain either a national patent, a European patent with unitary effect, a European patent taking effect in one or more of the Contracting States to the EPC or a European patent with unitary effect validated in addition in one or more other Contracting States to the EPC which are not among the participating Member States. . . .

## CHAPTER I

## GENERAL PROVISIONS

### Article 1

#### Subject matter

1.     This Regulation implements enhanced cooperation in the area of the creation of unitary patent protection, authorised by Decision 2011/167/EU.

2.     This Regulation constitutes a special agreement within the meaning of Article 142 of the Convention on the Grant of European Patents of 5 October 1973, as revised on 17 December 1991 and on 29 November 2000 (hereinafter "EPC").

### Article 2

#### Definitions

For the purposes of this Regulation, the following definitions shall apply:

(a)     "Participating Member State" means a Member State which participates in enhanced cooperation in the area of the creation of unitary patent protection by virtue of Decision 2011/167/EU, or by virtue of a decision adopted in accordance with the second or third subparagraph of Article 331(1) of the TFEU, at the time the request for unitary effect as referred to in Article 9 is made;

(b)     "European patent" means a patent granted by the European Patent Office (hereinafter "EPO") under the rules and procedures laid down in the EPC;

(c)     "European patent with unitary effect" means a European patent which benefits from unitary effect in the participating Member States by virtue of this Regulation;

(d)   "European Patent Register" means the register kept by the EPO under Article 127 of the EPC;

(e)   "Register for unitary patent protection" means the register constituting part of the European Patent Register in which the unitary effect and any limitation, licence, transfer, revocation or lapse of a European patent with unitary effect are registered;

(f)   "European Patent Bulletin" means the periodical publication provided for in Article 129 of the EPC.

## *Article 3*

### **European patent with unitary effect**

1.   A European patent granted with the same set of claims in respect of all the participating Member States shall benefit from unitary effect in the participating Member States provided that its unitary effect has been registered in the Register for unitary patent protection.

A European patent granted with different sets of claims for different participating Member States shall not benefit from unitary effect.

2.   A European patent with unitary effect shall have a unitary character. It shall provide uniform protection and shall have equal effect in all the participating Member States.

It may only be limited, transferred or revoked, or lapse, in respect of all the participating Member States.

It may be licensed in respect of the whole or part of the territories of the participating Member States.

3.   The unitary effect of a European patent shall be deemed not to have arisen to the extent that the European patent has been revoked or limited.

## *Article 4*

### **Date of effect**

1.   A European patent with unitary effect shall take effect in the participating Member States on the date of publication by the EPO of the mention of the grant of the European patent in the European Patent Bulletin.

2.   The participating Member States shall take the necessary measures to ensure that, where the unitary effect of a European patent has been registered and extends to their territory, that European patent is deemed not to have taken effect as a national patent in their territory on the date of publication of the mention of the grant in the European Patent Bulletin.

## CHAPTER II

### EFFECTS OF A EUROPEAN PATENT WITH UNITARY EFFECT

## *Article 5*

### **Uniform protection**

1.   The European patent with unitary effect shall confer on its proprietor the right to prevent any third party from committing acts against which that patent provides protection throughout the territories of the participating Member States in which it has unitary effect, subject to applicable limitations.

2.   The scope of that right and its limitations shall be uniform in all participating Member States in which the patent has unitary effect.

3.   The acts against which the patent provides protection referred to in paragraph 1 and the applicable limitations shall be those defined by the law applied to European patents with unitary effect

in the participating Member State whose national law is applicable to the European patent with unitary effect as an object of property in accordance with Article 7.

4.    In its report referred to in Article 16(1), the Commission shall evaluate the functioning of the applicable limitations and shall, where necessary, make appropriate proposals.

## *Article 6*

### Exhaustion of the rights conferred by a European patent with unitary effect

The rights conferred by a European patent with unitary effect shall not extend to acts concerning a product covered by that patent which are carried out within the participating Member States in which that patent has unitary effect after that product has been placed on the market in the Union by, or with the consent of, the patent proprietor, unless there are legitimate grounds for the patent proprietor to oppose further commercialisation of the product.

## CHAPTER III

## A EUROPEAN PATENT WITH UNITARY EFFECT AS AN OBJECT OF PROPERTY

### *Article 7*

### Treating a European patent with unitary effect as a national patent

1.    A European patent with unitary effect as an object of property shall be treated in its entirety and in all the participating Member States as a national patent of the participating Member State in which that patent has unitary effect and in which, according to the European Patent Register:

(a)   the applicant had his residence or principal place of business on the date of filing of the application for the European patent; or

(b)   where point (a) does not apply, the applicant had a place of business on the date of filing of the application for the European patent.

2.    Where two or more persons are entered in the European Patent Register as joint applicants, point (a) of paragraph 1 shall apply to the joint applicant indicated first. Where this is not possible, point (a) of paragraph 1 shall apply to the next joint applicant indicated in the order of entry. Where point (a) of paragraph 1 does not apply to any of the joint applicants, point (b) of paragraph 1 shall apply accordingly.

3.    Where no applicant had his residence, principal place of business or place of business in a participating Member State in which that patent has unitary effect for the purposes of paragraphs 1 or 2, the European patent with unitary effect as an object of property shall be treated in its entirety and in all the participating Member States as a national patent of the State where the European Patent Organisation has its headquarters in accordance with Article 6(1) of the EPC.

4.    The acquisition of a right may not be dependent on any entry in a national patent register.

### *Article 8*

### Licences of right

1.    The proprietor of a European patent with unitary effect may file a statement with the EPO to the effect that the proprietor is prepared to allow any person to use the invention as a licensee in return for appropriate consideration.

2.    A licence obtained under this Regulation shall be treated as a contractual licence.

CHAPTER IV

## INSTITUTIONAL PROVISIONS

*Article 9*

### Administrative tasks in the framework of the European Patent Organisation

1.   The participating Member States shall, within the meaning of Article 143 of the EPC, give the EPO the following tasks, to be carried out in accordance with the internal rules of the EPO:

(a)   to administer requests for unitary effect by proprietors of European patents;

(b)   to include the Register for unitary patent protection within the European Patent Register and to administer the Register for unitary patent protection;

(c)   to receive and register statements on licensing referred to in Article 8, their withdrawal and licensing commitments undertaken by the proprietor of the European patent with unitary effect in international standardisation bodies;

(d)   to publish the translations referred to in Article 6 of Regulation (EU) No 1260/2012 during the transitional period referred to in that Article;

(e)   to collect and administer renewal fees for European patents with unitary effect, in respect of the years following the year in which the mention of the grant is published in the European Patent Bulletin; to collect and administer additional fees for late payment of renewal fees where such late payment is made within six months of the due date, as well as to distribute part of the collected renewal fees to the participating Member States;

(f)   to administer the compensation scheme for the reimbursement of translation costs referred to in Article 5 of Regulation (EU) No 1260/2012;

(g)   to ensure that a request for unitary effect by a proprietor of a European patent is submitted in the language of the proceedings as defined in Article 14(3) of the EPC no later than one month after the mention of the grant is published in the European Patent Bulletin; and

(h)   to ensure that the unitary effect is indicated in the Register for unitary patent protection, where a request for unitary effect has been filed and, during the transitional period provided for in Article 6 of Regulation (EU) No 1260/2012, has been submitted together with the translations referred to in that Article, and that the EPO is informed of any limitations, licences, transfers or revocations of European patents with unitary effect.

2.   The participating Member States shall ensure compliance with this Regulation in fulfilling their international obligations undertaken in the EPC and shall cooperate to that end. In their capacity as Contracting States to the EPC, the participating Member States shall ensure the governance and supervision of the activities related to the tasks referred to in paragraph 1 of this Article and shall ensure the setting of the level of renewal fees in accordance with Article 12 of this Regulation and the setting of the share of distribution of the renewal fees in accordance with Article 13 of this Regulation.

To that end they shall set up a select committee of the Administrative Council of the European Patent Organisation (hereinafter "Select Committee") within the meaning of Article 145 of the EPC.

The Select Committee shall consist of the representatives of the participating Member States and a representative of the Commission as an observer, as well as alternates who will represent them in their absence. The members of the Select Committee may be assisted by advisers or experts.

Decisions of the Select Committee shall be taken with due regard for the position of the Commission and in accordance with the rules laid down in Article 35(2) of the EPC.

3.   The participating Member States shall ensure effective legal protection before a competent court of one or several participating Member States against the decisions of the EPO in carrying out the tasks referred to in paragraph 1.

## CHAPTER V
## FINANCIAL PROVISIONS

*Article 10*

### Principle on expenses

The expenses incurred by the EPO in carrying out the additional tasks given to it, within the meaning of Article 143 of the EPC, by the participating Member States shall be covered by the fees generated by the European patents with unitary effect.

*Article 11*

### Renewal fees

1. Renewal fees for European patents with unitary effect and additional fees for their late payment shall be paid to the European Patent Organisation by the patent proprietor. Those fees shall be due in respect of the years following the year in which the mention of the grant of the European patent which benefits from unitary effect is published in the European Patent Bulletin.

2. A European patent with unitary effect shall lapse if a renewal fee and, where applicable, any additional fee have not been paid in due time.

3. Renewal fees which fall due after receipt of the statement referred to in Article 8(1) shall be reduced.

*Article 12*

### Level of renewal fees

1. Renewal fees for European patents with unitary effect shall be:

   (a)   progressive throughout the term of the unitary patent protection;

   (b)   sufficient to cover all costs associated with the grant of the European patent and the administration of the unitary patent protection; and

   (c)   sufficient, together with the fees to be paid to the European Patent Organisation during the pre-grant stage, to ensure a balanced budget of the European Patent Organisation.

2. The level of the renewal fees shall be set, taking into account, among others, the situation of specific entities such as small and medium-sized enterprises, with the aim of:

   (a)   facilitating innovation and fostering the competitiveness of European businesses;

   (b)   reflecting the size of the market covered by the patent; and

   (c)   being similar to the level of the national renewal fees for an average European patent taking effect in the participating Member States at the time the level of the renewal fees is first set.

3. In order to attain the objectives set out in this Chapter, the level of renewal fees shall be set at a level that:

   (a)   is equivalent to the level of the renewal fee to be paid for the average geographical coverage of current European patents;

   (b)   reflects the renewal rate of current European patents; and

   (c)   reflects the number of requests for unitary effect.

## Article 13

### Distribution

1.    The EPO shall retain 50 per cent of the renewal fees referred to in Article 11 paid for European patents with unitary effect. The remaining amount shall be distributed to the participating Member States in accordance with the share of distribution of the renewal fees set pursuant to Article 9(2).

2.    In order to attain the objectives set out in this Chapter, the share of distribution of renewal fees among the participating Member States shall be based on the following fair, equitable and relevant criteria:

(a)    the number of patent applications;

(b)    the size of the market, while ensuring a minimum amount to be distributed to each participating Member State;

(c)    compensation to the participating Member States which have:

(i)    an official language other than one of the official languages of the EPO;

(ii)    a disproportionately low level of patenting activity; and/or

(iii)    acquired membership of the European Patent Organisation relatively recently.

## CHAPTER VI

## FINAL PROVISIONS

### Article 14

### Cooperation between the Commission and the EPO

The Commission shall establish a close cooperation through a working agreement with the EPO in the fields covered by this Regulation. This cooperation shall include regular exchanges of views on the functioning of the working agreement and, in particular, on the issue of renewal fees and their impact on the budget of the European Patent Organisation.

### Article 15

### Application of competition law and the law relating to unfair competition

This Regulation shall be without prejudice to the application of competition law and the law relating to unfair competition.

### Article 16

### Report on the operation of this Regulation

1.    Not later than three years from the date on which the first European patent with unitary effect takes effect, and every five years thereafter, the Commission shall present to the European Parliament and the Council a report on the operation of this Regulation and, where necessary, make appropriate proposals for amending it.

2.    The Commission shall regularly submit to the European Parliament and the Council reports on the functioning of the renewal fees referred to in Article 11, with particular emphasis on compliance with Article 12.

### Article 17

### Notification by the participating Member States

1.    The participating Member States shall notify the Commission of the measures adopted in accordance with Article 9 by the date of application of this Regulation.

2.   Each participating Member State shall notify the Commission of the measures adopted in accordance with Article 4(2) by the date of application of this Regulation or, in the case of a participating Member State in which the Unified Patent Court does not have exclusive jurisdiction with regard to European patents with unitary effect on the date of application of this Regulation, by the date from which the Unified Patent Court has such exclusive jurisdiction in that participating Member State.

## Article 18

### Entry into force and application

1.   This Regulation shall enter into force on the twentieth day following that of its publication in the Official Journal of the European Union.

2.   It shall apply from 1 January 2014 or the date of entry into force of the Agreement on a Unified Patent Court (the "Agreement"), whichever is the later.

By way of derogation from Articles 3(1), 3(2) and 4(1), a European patent for which unitary effect is registered in the Register for unitary patent protection shall have unitary effect only in those participating Member States in which the Unified Patent Court has exclusive jurisdiction with regard to European patents with unitary effect at the date of registration.

3.   Each participating Member State shall notify the Commission of its ratification of the Agreement at the time of deposit of its ratification instrument. The Commission shall publish in the Official Journal of the European Union the date of entry into force of the Agreement and a list of the Member States who have ratified the Agreement at the date of entry into force. The Commission shall thereafter regularly update the list of the participating Member States which have ratified the Agreement and shall publish such updated list in the Official Journal of the European Union.

4.   The participating Member States shall ensure that the measures referred to in Article 9 are in place by the date of application of this Regulation.

5.   Each participating Member State shall ensure that the measures referred to in Article 4(2) are in place by the date of application of this Regulation or, in the case of a participating Member State in which the Unified Patent Court does not have exclusive jurisdiction with regard to European patents with unitary effect on the date of application of this Regulation, by the date from which the Unified Patent Court has such exclusive jurisdiction in that participating Member State.

6.   Unitary patent protection may be requested for any European patent granted on or after the date of application of this Regulation.

This Regulation shall be binding in its entirety and directly applicable in the participating Member States in accordance with the Treaties.

Done at Brussels, 17 December 2012.

# 72. AGREEMENT ON A UNIFIED PATENT COURT

Agreement on a Unified Patent Court—
Selected Provisions*

. . .

## PART I
## GENERAL AND INSTITUTIONAL PROVISIONS
### CHAPTER I
### GENERAL PROVISIONS

*Article 1*

### Unified Patent Court

A Unified Patent Court for the settlement of disputes relating to European patents and European patents with unitary effect is hereby established.

The Unified Patent Court shall be a court common to the Contracting Member States and thus subject to the same obligations under Union law as any national court of the Contracting Member States.

*Article 2*

### Definitions

For the purposes of this Agreement:

(a)  "Court" means the Unified Patent Court created by this Agreement.

(b)  "Member State" means a Member State of the European Union.

(c)  "Contracting Member State" means a Member State party to this Agreement.

(d)  "EPC" means the Convention on the Grant of European Patents of 5 October 1973, including any subsequent amendments.

(e)  "European patent" means a patent granted under the provisions of the EPC, which does not benefit from unitary effect by virtue of Regulation (EU) No 1257/2012.

(f)  "European patent with unitary effect" means a patent granted under the provisions of the EPC which benefits from unitary effect by virtue of Regulation (EU) No 1257/2012.

(g)  "Patent" means a European patent and/or a European patent with unitary effect.

(h)  "Supplementary protection certificate" means a supplementary protection certificate granted under Regulation (EC) No 469/2009 or under Regulation (EC) No 1610/96.

(i)  "Statute" means the Statute of the Court as set out in Annex I, which shall be an integral part of this Agreement.

(j)  "Rules of Procedure" means the Rules of Procedure of the Court, as established in accordance with Article 41.

---

\*  Footnotes, the preamble, and some provisions omitted.

*Article 3*

### Scope of application

This Agreement shall apply to any:

(a)   European patent with unitary effect;

(b)   supplementary protection certificate issued for a product protected by a patent;

(c)   European patent which has not yet lapsed at the date of entry into force of this Agreement or was granted after that date, without prejudice to Article 83; and

(d)   European patent application which is pending at the date of entry into force of this Agreement or which is filed after that date, without prejudice to Article 83.

*Article 4*

### Legal status

(1)   The Court shall have legal personality in each Contracting Member State and shall enjoy the most extensive legal capacity accorded to legal persons under the national law of that State.

(2)   The Court shall be represented by the President of the Court of Appeal who shall be elected in accordance with the Statute.

*Article 5*

### Liability

(1)   The contractual liability of the Court shall be governed by the law applicable to the contract in question in accordance with Regulation (EC) No. 593/2008 (Rome I), where applicable, or failing that in accordance with the law of the Member State of the court seized.

(2)   The non-contractual liability of the Court in respect of any damage caused by it or its staff in the performance of their duties, to the extent that it is not a civil and commercial matter within the meaning of Regulation (EC) No. 864/2007 (Rome II), shall be governed by the law of the Contracting Member State in which the damage occurred. This provision is without prejudice to the application of Article 22.

(3)   The court with jurisdiction to settle disputes under paragraph 2 shall be a court of the Contracting Member State in which the damage occurred.

CHAPTER II

## INSTITUTIONAL PROVISIONS

*Article 6*

### The Court

(1)   The Court shall comprise a Court of First Instance, a Court of Appeal and a Registry.

(2)   The Court shall perform the functions assigned to it by this Agreement.

*Article 7*

### The Court of First Instance

(1)   The Court of First Instance shall comprise a central division as well as local and regional divisions.

(2)   The central division shall have its seat in Paris, with sections in London and Munich. The cases before the central division shall be distributed in accordance with Annex II, which shall form an integral part of this Agreement.

(3)   A local division shall be set up in a Contracting Member State upon its request in accordance with the Statute. A Contracting Member State hosting a local division shall designate its seat.

(4)   An additional local division shall be set up in a Contracting Member State upon its request for every one hundred patent cases per calendar year that have been commenced in that Contracting Member State during three successive years prior to or subsequent to the date of entry into force of this Agreement. The number of local divisions in one Contracting Member State shall not exceed four.

(5)   A regional division shall be set up for two or more Contracting Member States, upon their request in accordance with the Statute. Such Contracting Member States shall designate the seat of the division concerned. The regional division may hear cases in multiple locations.

## Article 8

### Composition of the panels of the Court of First Instance

(1)   Any panel of the Court of First Instance shall have a multinational composition. Without prejudice to paragraph 5 of this Article and to Article 33(3)(a), it shall sit in a composition of three judges.

(2)   Any panel of a local division in a Contracting Member State where, during a period of three successive years prior or subsequent to the entry into force of this Agreement, less than fifty patent cases per calendar year on average have been commenced shall sit in a composition of one legally qualified judge who is a national of the Contracting Member State hosting the local division concerned and two legally qualified judges who are not nationals of the Contracting Member State concerned and are allocated from the Pool of Judges in accordance with Article 18(3) on a case by case basis.

(3)   Notwithstanding paragraph 2, any panel of a local division in a Contracting Member State where, during a period of three successive years prior or subsequent to the entry into force of this Agreement, fifty or more patent cases per calendar year on average have been commenced, shall sit in a composition of two legally qualified judges who are nationals of the Contracting Member State hosting the local division concerned and one legally qualified judge who is not a national of the Contracting Member State concerned and is allocated from the Pool of Judges in accordance with Article 18(3). Such third judge shall serve at the local division on a long term basis, where this is necessary for the efficient functioning of divisions with a high work load.

(4)   Any panel of a regional division shall sit in a composition of two legally qualified judges chosen from a regional list of judges, who shall be nationals of the Contracting Member States concerned, and one legally qualified judge who shall not be a national of the Contracting Member States concerned and who shall be allocated from the Pool of Judges in accordance with Article 18(3).

(5)   Upon request by one of the parties, any panel of a local or regional division shall request the President of the Court of First Instance to allocate from the Pool of Judges in accordance with

Article 18(3) an additional technically qualified judge with qualifications and experience in the field of technology concerned. Moreover, any panel of a local or regional division may, after having heard the parties, submit such request on its own initiative, where it deems this appropriate.

In cases where such a technically qualified judge is allocated, no further technically qualified judge may be allocated under Article 33(3)(a).

(6)   Any panel of the central division shall sit in a composition of two legally qualified judges who are nationals of different Contracting Member States and one technically qualified judge allocated from the Pool of Judges in accordance with Article 18(3) with qualifications and experience in the field of technology concerned. However, any panel of the central division dealing with actions under Article

32(1)(i) shall sit in a composition of three legally qualified judges who are nationals of different Contracting Member States.

(7) Notwithstanding paragraphs 1 to 6 and in accordance with the Rules of Procedure, parties may agree to have their case heard by a single legally qualified judge.

(8) Any panel of the Court of First Instance shall be chaired by a legally qualified judge.

*Article 9*

### The Court of Appeal

(1) Any panel of the Court of Appeal shall sit in a multinational composition of five judges. It shall sit in a composition of three legally qualified judges who are nationals of different Contracting Member States and two technically qualified judges with qualifications and experience in the field of technology concerned. Those technically qualified judges shall be assigned to the panel by the President of the Court of Appeal from the pool of judges in accordance with Article 18.

(2) Notwithstanding paragraph 1, a panel dealing with actions under Article 32(1)(i) shall sit in a composition of three legally qualified judges who are nationals of different Contracting Member States.

(3) Any panel of the Court of Appeal shall be chaired by a legally qualified judge.

(4) The panels of the Court of Appeal shall be set up in accordance with the Statute.

(5) The Court of Appeal shall have its seat in Luxembourg.

*Article 10*

### The Registry

(1) A Registry shall be set up at the seat of the Court of Appeal. It shall be managed by the Registrar and perform the functions assigned to it in accordance with the Statute. Subject to conditions set out in this Agreement and the Rules of Procedure, the register kept by the Registry shall be public.

(2) Sub-registries shall be set up at all divisions of the Court of First Instance.

(3) The Registry shall keep records of all cases before the Court. Upon filing, the sub-registry concerned shall notify every case to the Registry.

(4) The Court shall appoint the Registrar in accordance with Article 22 of the Statute and lay down the rules governing the Registrar's service.

. . .

## CHAPTER III

## JUDGES OF THE COURT

*Article 15*

### Eligibility criteria for the appointment of judges

(1) The Court shall comprise both legally qualified judges and technically qualified judges. Judges shall ensure the highest standards of competence and shall have proven experience in the field of patent litigation.

(2) Legally qualified judges shall possess the qualifications required for appointment to judicial offices in a Contracting Member State.

(3) Technically qualified judges shall have a university degree and proven expertise in a field of technology. They shall also have proven knowledge of civil law and procedure relevant in patent litigation.

. . .

## CHAPTER IV

## THE PRIMACY OF UNION LAW, LIABILITY AND RESPONSIBILITY OF THE CONTRACTING MEMBER STATES

*Article 20*

### Primacy of and respect for Union law

The Court shall apply Union law in its entirety and shall respect its primacy.

*Article 21*

### Requests for preliminary rulings

As a court common to the Contracting Member States and as part of their judicial system, the Court shall cooperate with the Court of Justice of the European Union to ensure the correct application and uniform interpretation of Union law, as any national court, in accordance with Article 267 TFEU in particular. Decisions of the Court of Justice of the European Union shall be binding on the Court.

*Article 22*

### Liability for damage caused by infringements of Union law

(1)   The Contracting Member States are jointly and severally liable for damage resulting from an infringement of Union law by the Court of Appeal, in accordance with Union law concerning non-contractual liability of Member States for damage caused by their national courts breaching Union law.

(2)   An action for such damages shall be brought against the Contracting Member State where the claimant has its residence or principal place of business or, in the absence of residence or principal place of business, place of business, before the competent authority of that Contracting Member State. Where the claimant does not have its residence, or principal place of business or, in the absence of residence or principal place of business, place of business in a Contracting Member State, the claimant may bring such an action against the Contracting Member State where the Court of Appeal has its seat, before the competent authority of that Contracting Member State.

The competent authority shall apply the *lex fori*, with the exception of its private international law, to all questions not regulated by Union law or by this Agreement. The claimant shall be entitled to obtain the entire amount of damages awarded by the competent authority from the Contracting Member State against which the action was brought.

(3)   The Contracting Member State that has paid damages is entitled to obtain proportional contribution, established in accordance with the method laid down in Article 37(3) and (4), from the other Contracting Member States. The detailed rules governing the Contracting Member States' contribution under this paragraph shall be determined by the Administrative Committee.

*Article 23*

### Responsibility of the Contracting Member States

Actions of the Court are directly attributable to each Contracting Member State individually, including for the purposes of Articles 258, 259 and 260 TFEU, and to all Contracting Member States collectively.

## CHAPTER V

## SOURCES OF LAW AND SUBSTANTIVE LAW

*Article 24*

### Sources of law

(1) In full compliance with Article 20, when hearing a case brought before it under this Agreement, the Court shall base its decisions on:

(a) Union law, including Regulation (EU) No 1257/2012 and Regulation (EU) No 1260/2012;

(b) this Agreement;

(c) the EPC;

(d) other international agreements applicable to patents and binding on all the Contracting Member States; and

(e) national law.

(2) To the extent that the Court shall base its decisions on national law, including where relevant the law of non-contracting States, the applicable law shall be determined:

(a) by directly applicable provisions of Union law containing private international law rules, or

(b) in the absence of directly applicable provisions of Union law or where the latter do not apply, by international instruments containing private international law rules; or

(c) in the absence of provisions referred to in points (a) and (b), by national provisions on private international law as determined by the Court.

(3) The law of non-contracting States shall apply when designated by application of the rules referred to in paragraph 2, in particular in relation to Articles 25 to 28, 54, 55, 64, 68 and 72.

*Article 25*

### Right to prevent the direct use of the invention

A patent shall confer on its proprietor the right to prevent any third party not having the proprietor's consent from the following:

(a) making, offering, placing on the market or using a product which is the subject matter of the patent, or importing or storing the product for those purposes;

(b) using a process which is the subject matter of the patent or, where the third party knows, or should have known, that the use of the process is prohibited without the consent of the patent proprietor, offering the process for use within the territory of the Contracting Member States in which that patent has effect;

(c) offering, placing on the market, using, or importing or storing for those purposes a product obtained directly by a process which is the subject matter of the patent.

*Article 26*

### Right to prevent the indirect use of the invention

(1) A patent shall confer on its proprietor the right to prevent any third party not having the proprietor's consent from supplying or offering to supply, within the territory of the Contracting Member States in which that patent has effect, any person other than a party entitled to exploit the patented invention, with means, relating to an essential element of that invention, for putting it into effect therein, when the third party knows, or should have known, that those means are suitable and intended for putting that invention into effect.

(2)　Paragraph 1 shall not apply when the means are staple commercial products, except where the third party induces the person supplied to perform any of the acts prohibited by Article 25.

(3)　Persons performing the acts referred to in Article 27(a) to (e) shall not be considered to be parties entitled to exploit the invention within the meaning of paragraph 1.

*Article 27*

**Limitations of the effects of a patent**

The rights conferred by a patent shall not extend to any of the following:

(a)　acts done privately and for non-commercial purposes;

(b)　acts done for experimental purposes relating to the subject matter of the patented invention;

(c)　the use of biological material for the purpose of breeding, or discovering and developing other plant varieties;

(d)　the acts allowed pursuant to Article 13(6) of Directive 2001/82/EC or Article 10(6) of Directive 2001/83/EC in respect of any patent covering the product within the meaning of either of those Directives;

(e)　the extemporaneous preparation by a pharmacy, for individual cases, of a medicine in accordance with a medical prescription or acts concerning the medicine so prepared;

(f)　the use of the patented invention on board vessels of countries of the International Union for the Protection of Industrial Property (Paris Union) or members of the World Trade Organisation, other than those Contracting Member States in which that patent has effect, in the body of such vessel, in the machinery, tackle, gear and other accessories, when such vessels temporarily or accidentally enter the waters of a Contracting Member State in which that patent has effect, provided that the invention is used there exclusively for the needs of the vessel;

(g)　the use of the patented invention in the construction or operation of aircraft or land vehicles or other means of transport of countries of the International Union for the Protection of Industrial Property (Paris Union) or members of the World Trade Organisation, other than those Contracting Member States in which that patent has effect, or of accessories to such aircraft or land vehicles, when these temporarily or accidentally enter the territory of a Contracting Member State in which that patent has effect;

(h)　the acts specified in Article 27 of the Convention on International Civil Aviation of 7 December 19441, where these acts concern the aircraft of a country party to that Convention other than a Contracting Member State in which that patent has effect;

(i)　the use by a farmer of the product of his harvest for propagation or multiplication by him on his own holding, provided that the plant propagating material was sold or otherwise commercialised to the farmer by or with the consent of the patent proprietor for agricultural use. The extent and the conditions for this use correspond to those under Article 14 of Regulation (EC) No. 2100/94;

(j)　the use by a farmer of protected livestock for an agricultural purpose, provided that the breeding stock or other animal reproductive material were sold or otherwise commercialized to the farmer by or with the consent of the patent proprietor. Such use includes making the animal or other animal reproductive material available for the purposes of pursuing the farmer's agricultural activity, but not the sale thereof within the framework of, or for the purpose of, a commercial reproductive activity;

(k)　the acts and the use of the obtained information as allowed under Articles 5 and 6 of Directive 2009/24/EC, in particular, by its provisions on decompilation and interoperability; and

(*l*)　the acts allowed pursuant to Article 10 of Directive 98/44/EC.

*Article 28*

### Right based on prior use of the invention

Any person, who, if a national patent had been granted in respect of an invention, would have had, in a Contracting Member State, a right based on prior use of that invention or a right of personal possession of that invention, shall enjoy, in that Contracting Member State, the same rights in respect of a patent for the same invention.

*Article 29*

### Exhaustion of the rights conferred by a European patent

The rights conferred by a European patent shall not extend to acts concerning a product covered by that patent after that product has been placed on the market in the European Union by, or with the consent of, the patent proprietor, unless there are legitimate grounds for the patent proprietor to oppose further commercialization of the product.

*Article 30*

### Effects of supplementary protection certificates

A supplementary protection certificate shall confer the same rights as conferred by the patent and shall be subject to the same limitations and the same obligations.

## CHAPTER VI

## INTERNATIONAL JURISDICTION AND COMPETENCE

*Article 31*

### International jurisdiction

The international jurisdiction of the Court shall be established in accordance with Regulation (EU) No 1215/2012 or, where applicable, on the basis of the Convention on jurisdiction and the recognition and enforcement of judgments in civil and commercial matters (Lugano Convention).

*Article 32*

### Competence of the Court

(1)    The Court shall have exclusive competence in respect of:

(a)    actions for actual or threatened infringements of patents and supplementary protection certificates and related defences, including counterclaims concerning licences;

(b)    actions for declarations of non-infringement of patents and supplementary protection certificates;

(c)    actions for provisional and protective measures and injunctions;

(d)    actions for revocation of patents and for declaration of invalidity of supplementary protection certificates;

(e)    counterclaims for revocation of patents and for declaration of invalidity of supplementary protection certificates;

(f)    actions for damages or compensation derived from the provisional protection conferred by a published European patent application;

(g)    actions relating to the use of the invention prior to the granting of the patent or to the right based on prior use of the invention;

(h)   actions for compensation for licences on the basis of Article 8 of Regulation (EU) No 1257/2012; and

(i)   actions concerning decisions of the European Patent Office in carrying out the tasks referred to in Article 9 of Regulation (EU) No 1257/2012.

(2)   The national courts of the Contracting Member States shall remain competent for actions relating to patents and supplementary protection certificates which do not come within the exclusive competence of the Court.

## Article 33

### Competence of the divisions of the Court of First Instance

(1)   Without prejudice to paragraph 7 of this Article, actions referred to in Article 32(1)(a), (c), (f) and (g) shall be brought before:

(a)   the local division hosted by the Contracting Member State where the actual or threatened infringement has occurred or may occur, or the regional division in which that Contracting Member State participates; or

(b)   the local division hosted by the Contracting Member State where the defendant or, in the case of multiple defendants, one of the defendants has its residence, or principal place of business, or in the absence of residence or principal place of business, its place of business, or the regional division in which that Contracting Member State participates. An action may be brought against multiple defendants only where the defendants have a commercial relationship and where the action relates to the same alleged infringement.

Actions referred to in Article 32(1)(h) shall be brought before the local or regional division in accordance with point (b) of the first subparagraph.

Actions against defendants having their residence, or principal place of business or, in the absence of residence or principal place of business, their place of business, outside the territory of the Contracting Member States shall be brought before the local or regional division in accordance with point (a) of the first subparagraph or before the central division.

If the Contracting Member State concerned does not host a local division and does not participate in a regional division, actions shall be brought before the central division.

(2)   If an action referred to in Article 32(1)(a), (c), (f), (g) or (h) is pending before a division of the Court of First Instance, any action referred to in Article 32(1)(a), (c), (f), (g) or (h) between the same parties on the same patent may not be brought before any other division.

If an action referred to in Article 32(1)(a) is pending before a regional division and the infringement has occurred in the territories of three or more regional divisions, the regional division concerned shall, at the request of the defendant, refer the case to the central division.

In case an action between the same parties on the same patent is brought before several different divisions, the division first seized shall be competent for the whole case and any division seized later shall declare the action inadmissible in accordance with the Rules of Procedure.

(3)   A counterclaim for revocation as referred to in Article 32(1)(e) may be brought in the case of an action for infringement as referred to in Article 32(1)(a). The local or regional division concerned shall, after having heard the parties, have the discretion either to:

(a)   proceed with both the action for infringement and with the counterclaim for revocation and request the President of the Court of First Instance to allocate from the Pool of Judges in accordance with Article 18(3) a technically qualified judge with qualifications and experience in the field of technology concerned.

(b)   refer the counterclaim for revocation for decision to the central division and suspend or proceed with the action for infringement; or

(c)   with the agreement of the parties, refer the case for decision to the central division.

(4) Actions referred to in Article 32(1)(b) and (d) shall be brought before the central division.

If, however, an action for infringement as referred to in Article 32(1)(a) between the same parties relating to the same patent has been brought before a local or a regional division, these actions may only be brought before the same local or regional division.

(5)   If an action for revocation as referred to in Article 32(1)(d) is pending before the central division, an action for infringement as referred to in Article 32(1)(a) between the same parties relating to the same patent may be brought before any division in accordance with paragraph 1 of this Article or before the central division. The local or regional division concerned shall have the discretion to proceed in accordance with paragraph 3 of this Article.

(6)   An action for declaration of non-infringement as referred to in Article 32(1)(b) pending before the central division shall be stayed once an infringement action as referred to in Article 32(1)(a) between the same parties or between the holder of an exclusive licence and the party requesting a declaration of non-infringement relating to the same patent is brought before a local or regional division within three months of the date on which the action was initiated before the central division.

(7)   Parties may agree to bring actions referred to in Article 32(1)(a) to (h) before the division of their choice, including the central division.

(8)   Actions referred to in Article 32(1)(d) and (e) can be brought without the applicant having to file notice of opposition with the European Patent Office.

(9)   Actions referred to in Article 32(1)(i) shall be brought before the central division.

(10) A party shall inform the Court of any pending revocation, limitation or opposition proceedings before the European Patent Office, and of any request for accelerated processing before the European Patent Office. The Court may stay its proceedings when a rapid decision may be expected from the European Patent Office.

*Article 34*

### Territorial scope of decisions

Decisions of the Court shall cover, in the case of a European patent, the territory of those Contracting Member States for which the European patent has effect.

CHAPTER VII

## PATENT MEDIATION AND ARBITRATION

*Article 35*

### Patent mediation and arbitration centre

(1)   A patent mediation and arbitration centre ("the Centre") is hereby established. It shall have its seats in Ljubljana and Lisbon.

(2)   The Centre shall provide facilities for mediation and arbitration of patent disputes falling within the scope of this Agreement. Article 82 shall apply mutatis mutandis to any settlement reached through the use of the facilities of the Centre, including through mediation. However, a patent may not be revoked or limited in mediation or arbitration proceedings.

(3)   The Centre shall establish Mediation and Arbitration Rules.

(4)   The Centre shall draw up a list of mediators and arbitrators to assist the parties in the settlement of their dispute.

. . .

## Article 46

### Legal capacity

Any natural or legal person, or any body equivalent to a legal person entitled to initiate proceedings in accordance with its national law, shall have the capacity to be a party to the proceedings before the Court.

## Article 47

### Parties

(1)   The patent proprietor shall be entitled to bring actions before the Court.

(2)   Unless the licensing agreement provides otherwise, the holder of an exclusive licence in respect of a patent shall be entitled to bring actions before the Court under the same circumstances as the patent proprietor, provided that the patent proprietor is given prior notice.

(3)   The holder of a non-exclusive licence shall not be entitled to bring actions before the Court, unless the patent proprietor is given prior notice and in so far as expressly permitted by the licence agreement.

(4)   In actions brought by a licence holder, the patent proprietor shall be entitled to join the action before the Court.

(5)   The validity of a patent cannot be contested in an action for infringement brought by the holder of a licence where the patent proprietor does not take part in the proceedings. The party in an action for infringement wanting to contest the validity of a patent shall have to bring actions against the patent proprietor.

(6)   Any other natural or legal person, or any body entitled to bring actions in accordance with its national law, who is concerned by a patent, may bring actions in accordance with the Rules of Procedure.

(7)   Any natural or legal person, or any body entitled to bring actions in accordance with its national law and who is affected by a decision of the European Patent Office in carrying out the tasks referred to in Article 9 of Regulation (EU) No 1257/2012 is entitled to bring actions under Article 32(1)(i).

. . .

## CHAPTER III

### PROCEEDINGS BEFORE THE COURT

## Article 52

### Written, interim and oral procedures

(1)   The proceedings before the Court shall consist of a written, an interim and an oral procedure, in accordance with the Rules of Procedure. All procedures shall be organized in a flexible and balanced manner.

(2)   In the interim procedure, after the written procedure and if appropriate, the judge acting as Rapporteur, subject to a mandate of the full panel, shall be responsible for convening an interim hearing. That judge shall in particular explore with the parties the possibility for a settlement, including through mediation, and/or arbitration, by using the facilities of the Centre referred to in Article 35.

(3)   The oral procedure shall give parties the opportunity to explain properly their arguments.

The Court may, with the agreement of the parties, dispense with the oral hearing.

*Article 53*

### Means of evidence

(1)   In proceedings before the Court, the means of giving or obtaining evidence shall include in particular the following:

   (a)   hearing the parties;

   (b)   requests for information;

   (c)   production of documents;

   (d)   hearing witnesses;

   (e)   opinions by experts;

   (f)   inspection;

   (g)   comparative tests or experiments;

   (h)   sworn statements in writing (affidavits).

(2)   The Rules of Procedure shall govern the procedure for taking such evidence. Questioning of witnesses and experts shall be under the control of the Court and be limited to what is necessary.

*Article 54*

### Burden of proof

Without prejudice to Article 24(2) and (3), the burden of the proof of facts shall be on the party relying on those facts.

*Article 55*

### Reversal of burden of proof

(1)   Without prejudice to Article 24(2) and (3), if the subject-matter of a patent is a process for obtaining a new product, the identical product when produced without the consent of the patent proprietor shall, in the absence of proof to the contrary, be deemed to have been obtained by the patented process.

(2)   The principle set out in paragraph 1 shall also apply where there is a substantial likelihood that the identical product was made by the patented process and the patent proprietor has been unable, despite reasonable efforts, to determine the process actually used for such identical product.

   (3)   In the adduction of proof to the contrary, the legitimate interests of the defendant in protecting its manufacturing and trade secrets shall be taken into account.

. . .

## CHAPTER IV

### POWERS OF THE COURT

. . .

*Article 59*

### Order to produce evidence

(1)   At the request of a party which has presented reasonably available evidence sufficient to support its claims and has, in substantiating those claims, specified evidence which lies in the control of the opposing party or a third party, the Court may order the opposing party or a third party to present such evidence, subject to the protection of confidential information. Such order shall not result in an obligation of self-incrimination.

(2)   At the request of a party the Court may order, under the same conditions as specified in paragraph 1, the communication of banking, financial or commercial documents under the control of the opposing party, subject to the protection of confidential information.

## Article 60

### Order to preserve evidence and to inspect premises

(1)   At the request of the applicant which has presented reasonably available evidence to support the claim that the patent has been infringed or is about to be infringed the Court may, even before the commencement of proceedings on the merits of the case, order prompt and effective provisional measures to preserve relevant evidence in respect of the alleged infringement, subject to the protection of confidential information.

(2)   Such measures may include the detailed description, with or without the taking of samples, or the physical seizure of the infringing products, and, in appropriate cases, the materials and implements used in the production and/or distribution of those products and the documents relating thereto.

(3)   The Court may, even before the commencement of proceedings on the merits of the case, at the request of the applicant who has presented evidence to support the claim that the patent has been infringed or is about to be infringed, order the inspection of premises. Such inspection of premises shall be conducted by a person appointed by the Court in accordance with the Rules of Procedure.

(4)   At the inspection of the premises the applicant shall not be present itself but may be represented by an independent professional practitioner whose name has to be specified in the Court's order.

(5)   Measures shall be ordered, if necessary without the other party having been heard, in particular where any delay is likely to cause irreparable harm to the proprietor of the patent, or where there is a demonstrable risk of evidence being destroyed.

(6)   Where measures to preserve evidence or inspect premises are ordered without the other party in the case having been heard, the parties affected shall be given notice, without delay and at the latest immediately after the execution of the measures. A review, including a right to be heard, shall take place upon request of the parties affected with a view to deciding, within a reasonable period after the notification of the measures, whether the measures are to be modified, revoked or confirmed.

(7)   The measures to preserve evidence may be subject to the lodging by the applicant of adequate security or an equivalent assurance intended to ensure compensation for any prejudice suffered by the defendant as provided for in paragraph 9.

(8)   The Court shall ensure that the measures to preserve evidence are revoked or otherwise cease to have effect, at the defendant's request, without prejudice to the damages which may be claimed, if the applicant does not bring, within a period not exceeding 31 calendar days or 20 working days, whichever is the longer, action leading to a decision on the merits of the case before the Court.

(9)   Where the measures to preserve evidence are revoked, or where they lapse due to any act or omission by the applicant, or where it is subsequently found that there has been no infringement or threat of infringement of the patent, the Court may order the applicant, at the defendant's request, to provide the defendant with appropriate compensation for any damage suffered as a result of those measures.

## Article 61

### Freezing orders

(1)   At the request of the applicant which has presented reasonably available evidence to support the claim that the patent has been infringed or is about to be infringed the Court may, even before the commencement of proceedings on the merits of the case, order a party not to remove from its

jurisdiction any assets located therein, or not to deal in any assets, whether located within its jurisdiction or not.

(2)   Article 60(5) to (9) shall apply by analogy to the measures referred to in this Article.

*Article 62*

### Provisional and protective measures

(1)   The Court may, by way of order, grant injunctions against an alleged infringer or against an intermediary whose services are used by the alleged infringer, intended to prevent any imminent infringement, to prohibit, on a provisional basis and subject, where appropriate, to a recurring penalty payment, the continuation of the alleged infringement or to make such continuation subject to the lodging of guarantees intended to ensure the compensation of the right holder.

(2)   The Court shall have the discretion to weigh up the interests of the parties and in particular to take into account the potential harm for either of the parties resulting from the granting or the refusal of the injunction.

(3)   The Court may also order the seizure or delivery up of the products suspected of infringing a patent so as to prevent their entry into, or movement, within the channels of commerce. If the applicant demonstrates circumstances likely to endanger the recovery of damages, the Court may order the precautionary seizure of the movable and immovable property of the alleged infringer, including the blocking of the bank accounts and of other assets of the alleged infringer.

(4)   The Court may, in respect of the measures referred to in paragraphs 1 and 3, require the applicant to provide any reasonable evidence in order to satisfy itself with a sufficient degree of certainty that the applicant is the right holder and that the applicant's right is being infringed, or that such infringement is imminent.

(5)   Article 60(5) to (9) shall apply by analogy to the measures referred to in this Article.

*Article 63*

### Permanent injunctions

(1) Where a decision is taken finding an infringement of a patent, the Court may grant an injunction against the infringer aimed at prohibiting the continuation of the infringement. The Court may also grant such injunction against an intermediary whose services are being used by a third party to infringe a patent.

(2) Where appropriate, non-compliance with the injunction referred to in paragraph 1 shall be subject to a recurring penalty payment payable to the Court.

*Article 64*

### Corrective measures in infringement proceedings

(1)   Without prejudice to any damages due to the injured party by reason of the infringement, and without compensation of any sort, the Court may order, at the request of the applicant, that appropriate measures be taken with regard to products found to be infringing a patent and, in appropriate cases, with regard to materials and implements principally used in the creation or manufacture of those products.

(2)   Such measures shall include:

  (a)   a declaration of infringement;

  (b)   recalling the products from the channels of commerce;

  (c)   depriving the product of its infringing property;

(d)  definitively removing the products from the channels of commerce; or

(e)  the destruction of the products and/or of the materials and implements concerned.

(3)  The Court shall order that those measures be carried out at the expense of the infringer, unless particular reasons are invoked for not doing so.

(4)  In considering a request for corrective measures pursuant to this Article, the Court shall take into account the need for proportionality between the seriousness of the infringement and the remedies to be ordered, the willingness of the infringer to convert the materials into a noninfringing state, as well as the interests of third parties.

## Article 65

### Decision on the validity of a patent

(1)  The Court shall decide on the validity of a patent on the basis of an action for revocation or a counterclaim for revocation.

(2)  The Court may revoke a patent, either entirely or partly, only on the grounds referred to in Articles 138(1) and 139(2) of the EPC.

(3)  Without prejudice to Article 138(3) of the EPC, if the grounds for revocation affect the patent only in part, the patent shall be limited by a corresponding amendment of the claims and revoked in part.

(4)  To the extent that a patent has been revoked it shall be deemed not to have had, from the outset, the effects specified in Articles 64 and 67 of the EPC.

(5)  Where the Court, in a final decision, revokes a patent, either entirely or partly, it shall send a copy of the decision to the European Patent Office and, with respect to a European patent, to the national patent office of any Contracting Member State concerned.

## Article 66

### Powers of the Court concerning decisions of the European Patent Office

(1)  In actions brought under Article 32(1)(i), the Court may exercise any power entrusted on the European Patent Office in accordance with Article 9 of Regulation (EU) No 1257/2012, including the rectification of the Register for unitary patent protection.

(2)  In actions brought under Article 32(1)(i) the parties shall, by way of derogation from Article 69, bear their own costs.

## Article 67

### Power to order the communication of information

(1)  The Court may, in response to a justified and proportionate request of the applicant and in accordance with the Rules of Procedure, order an infringer to inform the applicant of:

(a)  the origin and distribution channels of the infringing products or processes;

(b)  the quantities produced, manufactured, delivered, received or ordered, as well as the price obtained for the infringing products; and

(c)  the identity of any third person involved in the production or distribution of the infringing products or in the use of the infringing process.

(2)  The Court may, in accordance with the Rules of Procedure, also order any third party who:

(a)  was found in the possession of the infringing products on a commercial scale or to be using an infringing process on a commercial scale;

(b)  was found to be providing on a commercial scale services used in infringing activities; or

(c)   was indicated by the person referred to in points (a) or (b) as being involved in the production, manufacture or distribution of the infringing products or processes or in the provision of the services, to provide the applicant with the information referred to in paragraph 1.

*Article 68*

### Award of damages

(1)   The Court shall, at the request of the injured party, order the infringer who knowingly, or with reasonable grounds to know, engaged in a patent infringing activity, to pay the injured party damages appropriate to the harm actually suffered by that party as a result of the infringement.

(2)   The injured party shall, to the extent possible, be placed in the position it would have been in if no infringement had taken place. The infringer shall not benefit from the infringement.

However, damages shall not be punitive.

(3)   When the Court sets the damages:

(a)   it shall take into account all appropriate aspects, such as the negative economic consequences, including lost profits, which the injured party has suffered, any unfair profits made by the infringer and, in appropriate cases, elements other than economic factors, such as the moral prejudice caused to the injured party by the infringement; or

(b)   as an alternative to point (a), it may, in appropriate cases, set the damages as a lump sum on the basis of elements such as at least the amount of the royalties or fees which would have been due if the infringer had requested authorisation to use the patent in question.

(4)   Where the infringer did not knowingly, or with reasonable grounds to know, engage in the infringing activity, the Court may order the recovery of profits or the payment of compensation.

*Article 69*

### Legal costs

(1)   Reasonable and proportionate legal costs and other expenses incurred by the successful party shall, as a general rule, be borne by the unsuccessful party, unless equity requires otherwise, up to a ceiling set in accordance with the Rules of Procedure.

(2)   Where a party succeeds only in part or in exceptional circumstances, the Court may order that costs be apportioned equitably or that the parties bear their own costs.

(3)   A party should bear any unnecessary costs it has caused the Court or another party.

(4)   At the request of the defendant, the Court may order the applicant to provide adequate security for the legal costs and other expenses incurred by the defendant which the applicant may be liable to bear, in particular in the cases referred to in Articles 59 to 62.

*Article 70*

### Court fees

(1)   Parties to proceedings before the Court shall pay court fees.

(2)   Court fees shall be paid in advance, unless the Rules of Procedure provide otherwise. Any party which has not paid a prescribed court fee may be excluded from further participation in the proceedings.

## Article 71

### Legal aid

(1)   A party who is a natural person and who is unable to meet the costs of the proceedings, either wholly or in part, may at any time apply for legal aid. The conditions for granting of legal aid shall be laid down in the Rules of Procedure.

(2)   The Court shall decide whether legal aid should be granted in full or in part, or whether it should be refused, in accordance with the Rules of Procedure.

(3)   On a proposal from the Court, the Administrative Committee shall set the level of legal aid and the rules on bearing the costs thereof.

## Article 72

### Period of limitation

Without prejudice to Article 24(2) and (3), actions relating to all forms of financial compensation may not be brought more than five years after the date on which the applicant became aware, or had reasonable grounds to become aware, of the last fact justifying the action.

## CHAPTER V

### APPEALS

## Article 73

### Appeal

(1)   An appeal against a decision of the Court of First Instance may be brought before the Court of Appeal by any party which has been unsuccessful, in whole or in part, in its submissions, within two months of the date of the notification of the decision.

(2)   An appeal against an order of the Court of First Instance may be brought before the Court of Appeal by any party which has been unsuccessful, in whole or in part, in its submissions:

(a)   for the orders referred to in Articles 49(5), 59 to 62 and 67 within 15 calendar days of the notification of the order to the applicant ;

(b)   for other orders than the orders referred to in point (a):

(i)   together with the appeal against the decision, or

(ii)   where the Court grants leave to appeal, within 15 days of the notification of the Court's decision to that effect.

(3)   The appeal against a decision or an order of the Court of First Instance may be based on points of law and matters of fact.

(4)   New facts and new evidence may only be introduced in accordance with the Rules of Procedure and where the submission thereof by the party concerned could not reasonably have been expected during proceedings before the Court of First Instance.

## Article 74

### Effects of an appeal

(1)   An appeal shall not have suspensive effect unless the Court of Appeal decides otherwise at the motivated request of one of the parties. The Rules of Procedure shall guarantee that such a decision is taken without delay.

(2)   Notwithstanding paragraph 1, an appeal against a decision on actions or counterclaims for revocation and on actions based on Article 32(1)(i) shall always have suspensive effect.

(3)    An appeal against an order referred to in Articles 49(5), 59 to 62 or 67 shall not prevent the continuation of the main proceedings . However, the Court of First Instance shall not give a decision in the main proceedings before the decision of the Court of Appeal concerning an appealed order has been given.

## Article 75

### Decision on appeal and referral back

(1)    If an appeal pursuant to Article 73 is well-founded, the Court of Appeal shall revoke the decision of the Court of First Instance and give a final decision. The Court of Appeal may in exceptional cases and in accordance with the Rules of Procedure refer the case back to the Court of First Instance for decision.

(2)    Where a case is referred back to the Court of First Instance pursuant to paragraph 1, the Court of First Instance shall be bound by the decision of the Court of Appeal on points of law.

## CHAPTER VI

## DECISIONS

## Article 76

### Basis for decisions and right to be heard

(1)    The Court shall decide in accordance with the requests submitted by the parties and shall not award more than is requested.

(2)    Decisions on the merits may only be based on grounds, facts and evidence, which were submitted by the parties or introduced into the procedure by an order of the Court and on which the parties have had an opportunity to present their comments.

(3)    The Court shall evaluate evidence freely and independently.

## Article 77

### Formal requirements

(1)    Decisions and orders of the Court shall be reasoned and shall be given in writing in accordance with the Rules of Procedure.

(2)    Decisions and orders of the Court shall be delivered in the language of proceedings.

## Article 78

### Decisions of the Court and dissenting opinions

(1)    Decisions and orders of the Court shall be taken by a majority of the panel, in accordance with the Statute. In case of equal votes, the vote of the presiding judge shall prevail.

(2)    In exceptional circumstances, any judge of the panel may express a dissenting opinion separately from the decision of the Court.

## Article 79

### Settlement

The parties may, at any time in the course of proceedings, conclude their case by way of settlement, which shall be confirmed by a decision of the Court. A patent may not be revoked or limited by way of settlement.

## Article 80

### Publication of decisions

The Court may order, at the request of the applicant and at the expense of the infringer, appropriate measures for the dissemination of information concerning the Court's decision, including displaying the decision and publishing it in full or in part in public media.

## Article 81

### Rehearing

(1) A request for rehearing after a final decision of the Court may exceptionally be granted by the Court of Appeal in the following circumstances:

(a) on discovery of a fact by the party requesting the rehearing, which is of such a nature as to be a decisive factor and which, when the decision was given, was unknown to the party requesting the rehearing; such request may only be granted on the basis of an act which was held, by a final decision of a national court, to constitute a criminal offence; or

(b) in the event of a fundamental procedural defect, in particular when a defendant who did not appear before the Court was not served with the document initiating the proceedings or an equivalent document in sufficient time and in such a way as to enable him to arrange for the defence.

(2) A request for a rehearing shall be filed within 10 years of the date of the decision but not later than two months from the date of the discovery of the new fact or of the procedural defect. Such request shall not have suspensive effect unless the Court of Appeal decides otherwise.

(3) If the request for a rehearing is well-founded, the Court of Appeal shall set aside, in whole or in part, the decision under review and re-open the proceedings for a new trial and decision, in accordance with the Rules of Procedure.

(4) Persons using patents which are the subject-matter of a decision under review and who act in good faith should be allowed to continue using such patents.

## Article 82

### Enforcement of decisions and orders

(1) Decisions and orders of the Court shall be enforceable in any Contracting Member State. An order for the enforcement of a decision shall be appended to the decision by the Court.

(2) Where appropriate, the enforcement of a decision may be subject to the provision of security or an equivalent assurance to ensure compensation for any damage suffered, in particular in the case of injunctions.

(3) Without prejudice to this Agreement and the Statute, enforcement procedures shall be governed by the law of the Contracting Member State where the enforcement takes place. Any decision of the Court shall be enforced under the same conditions as a decision given in the Contracting Member State where the enforcement takes place.

(4) If a party does not comply with the terms of an order of the Court, that party may be sanctioned with a recurring penalty payment payable to the Court. The individual penalty shall be proportionate to the importance of the order to be enforced and shall be without prejudice to the party's right to claim damages or security.

. . .

*AGREEMENT ON A UNIFIED PATENT COURT*

## PART V
## FINAL PROVISIONS

*Article 84*

### Signature, ratification and accession

(1)   This Agreement shall be open for signature by any Member State on 19 February 2013.

(2)   This Agreement shall be subject to ratification in accordance with the respective constitutional requirements of the Member States. Instruments of ratification shall be deposited with the General Secretariat of the Council of the European Union (hereinafter referred to as "the depositary").

(3)   Each Member State having signed this Agreement shall notify the European Commission of its ratification of the Agreement at the time of the deposit of its ratification instrument pursuant to Article 18(3) of Regulation (EU) No 1257/2012.

(4)   This Agreement shall be open to accession by any Member State. Instruments of accession shall be deposited with the depositary.

. . .


*Article 86*

### Duration of the Agreement

This Agreement shall be of unlimited duration.

*Article 87*

### Revision

(1)   Either seven years after the entry into force of this Agreement or once 2000 infringement cases have been decided by the Court, whichever is the later point in time, and if necessary at regular intervals thereafter, a broad consultation with the users of the patent system shall be carried out by the Administrative Committee on the functioning, efficiency and cost effectiveness of the Court and on the trust and confidence of users of the patent system in the quality of the Court's decisions. On the basis of this consultation and an opinion of the Court, the Administrative Committee may decide to revise this Agreement with a view to improving the functioning of the Court.

(2)   The Administrative Committee may amend this Agreement to bring it into line with an international treaty relating to patents or Union law.

(3)   A decision of the Administrative Committee taken on the basis of paragraphs 1 and 2 shall not take effect if a Contracting Member State declares within twelve months of the date of the decision, on the basis of its relevant internal decision-making procedures, that it does not wish to be bound by the decision. In this case, a Review Conference of the Contracting Member States shall be convened.

. . .


*Article 89*

### Entry into force

(1)   This Agreement shall enter into force on 1 January 2014 or on the first day of the fourth month after the deposit of the thirteenth instrument of ratification or accession in accordance with Article 84, including the three Member States in which the highest number of European patents had effect in the year preceding the year in which the signature of the Agreement takes place or on the first day of the fourth month after the date of entry into force of the amendments to Regulation (EU) No 1215/2012 concerning its relationship with this Agreement, whichever is the latest.

(2)   Any ratification or accession after the entry into force of this Agreement shall take effect on the first day of the fourth month after the deposit of the instrument of ratification or accession.

In witness whereof the undersigned, being duly authorised thereto, have signed this Agreement,

Done at Brussels on 19 February 2013 in English, French and German, all three texts being equally authentic, in a single copy which shall be deposited in the archives of the General Secretariat of the Council of the European Union.

# 73. REGULATION ON COMMUNITY DESIGNS

## COUNCIL REGULATION (EC) No 6/2002
## of 12 December 2001
## on Community designs

(amended by Council Regulation No 1891/2006 of 18 December 2006
amending Regulations (EC) No 6/2002 and (EC) No 40/94)*

. . . Whereas: . . .

(2) Only the Benelux countries have introduced a uniform design protection law. In all the other Member States the protection of designs is a matter for the relevant national law and is confined to the territory of the Member State concerned. Identical designs may be therefore protected differently in different Member States and for the benefit of different owners. This inevitably leads to conflicts in the course of trade between Member States. . . .

(4) The effect of design protection being limited to the territory of the individual Member States whether or not their laws are approximated, leads to a possible division of the internal market with respect to products incorporating a design which is the subject of national rights held by different individuals, and hence constitutes an obstacle to the free movement of goods.

(5) This calls for the creation of a Community design which is directly applicable in each Member State, because only in this way will it be possible to obtain, through one application made to the Office for Harmonisation in the Internal Market (Trade Marks and Design) in accordance with a single procedure under one law, one design right for one area encompassing all Member States. . . .

(10) Technological innovation should not be hampered by granting design protection to features dictated solely by a technical function. It is understood that this does not entail that a design must have an aesthetic quality. Likewise, the interoperability of products of different makes should not be hindered by extending protection to the design of mechanical fittings. Consequently, those features of a design which are excluded from protection for those reasons should not be taken into consideration for the purpose of assessing whether other features of the design fulfil the requirements for protection.

(11) The mechanical fittings of modular products may nevertheless constitute an important element of the innovative characteristics of modular products and present a major marketing asset, and therefore should be eligible for protection.

(12) Protection should not be extended to those component parts which are not visible during normal use of a product, nor to those features of such part which are not visible when the part is mounted, or which would not, in themselves, fulfil the requirements as to novelty and individual character. Therefore, those features of design which are excluded from protection for these reasons should not be taken into consideration for the purpose of assessing whether other features of the design fulfil the requirements for protection.

(13) Full-scale approximation of the laws of the Member States on the use of protected designs for the purpose of permitting the repair of a complex product so as to restore its original appearance, where the design is applied to or incorporated in a product which constitutes a component part of a complex product upon whose appearance the protected design is dependent, could not be achieved through Directive 98/71/EC. Within the framework of the conciliation procedure on the said Directive, the Commission undertook to review the consequences of the provisions of that Directive three years after the deadline for transposition of the Directive in particular for the industrial sectors which are most affected. Under these circumstances, it is appropriate not to confer any protection as a Community design for a design which is applied to or incorporated in a product which constitutes a component part of a complex product upon whose appearance the design is dependent and which is used for the

---

* Footnotes and some recitals and articles omitted.

purpose of the repair of a complex product so as to restore its original appearance, until the Council has decided its policy on this issue on the basis of a Commission proposal.

(14) The assessment as to whether a design has individual character should be based on whether the overall impression produced on an informed user viewing the design clearly differs from that produced on him by the existing design corpus, taking into consideration the nature of the product to which the design is applied or in which it is incorporated, and in particular the industrial sector to which it belongs and the degree of freedom of the designer in developing the design. . . .

(29) It is essential that the rights conferred by a Community design can be enforced in an efficient manner throughout the territory of the Community.

(30) The litigation system should avoid as far as possible "forum shopping". It is therefore necessary to establish clear rules of international jurisdiction.

(31) This Regulation does not preclude the application to designs protected by Community designs of the industrial property laws or other relevant laws of the Member States, such as those relating to design protection acquired by registration or those relating to unregistered designs, trade marks, patents and utility models, unfair competition or civil liability.

(32) In the absence of the complete harmonisation of copyright law, it is important to establish the principle of cumulation of protection under the Community design and under copyright law, whilst leaving Member States free to establish the extent of copyright protection and the conditions under which such protection is conferred. . . .

TITLE I
**GENERAL PROVISIONS**

*Article 1*

**Community design**

1.    A design which complies with the conditions contained in this Regulation is hereinafter referred to as a "Community design".

2.    A design shall be protected:

(a)   by an "unregistered Community design", if made available to the public in the manner provided for in this Regulation;

(b)   by a "registered Community design", if registered in the manner provided for in this Regulation.

3.    A Community design shall have a unitary character. It shall have equal effect throughout the Community. It shall not be registered, transferred or surrendered or be the subject of a decision declaring it invalid, nor shall its use be prohibited, save in respect of the whole Community. This principle and its implications shall apply unless otherwise provided in this Regulation.

*Article 2*

**Office**

The Office for Harmonisation in the Internal Market (Trade Marks and Designs), hereinafter referred to as "the Office", instituted by Council Regulation (EC) No 40/94 of 20 December 1993 on the Community trade mark, hereinafter referred to as the "Regulation on the Community trade mark", shall carry out the tasks entrusted to it by this Regulation.

TITLE II
## THE LAW RELATING TO DESIGNS
Section 1
### Requirements for protection

*Article 3*

### Definitions

For the purposes of this Regulation:

(a)  "design" means the appearance of the whole or a part of a product resulting from the features of, in particular, the lines, contours, colours, shape, texture and/or materials of the product itself and/or its ornamentation;

(b)  "product" means any industrial or handicraft item, including *inter alia* parts intended to be assembled into a complex product, packaging, get-up, graphic symbols and typographic typefaces, but excluding computer programs;

(c)  "complex product" means a product which is composed of multiple components which can be replaced permitting disassembly and re-assembly of the product.

*Article 4*

### Requirements for protection

1.  A design shall be protected by a Community design to the extent that it is new and has individual character.

2.  A design applied to or incorporated in a product which constitutes a component part of a complex product shall only be considered to be new and to have individual character:

(a)  if the component part, once it has been incorporated into the complex product, remains visible during normal use of the latter; and

(b)  to the extent that those visible features of the component part fulfil in themselves the requirements as to novelty and individual character.

3.  "Normal use" within the meaning of paragraph (2)(a) shall mean use by the end user, excluding maintenance, servicing or repair work.

*Article 5*

### Novelty

1.  A design shall be considered to be new if no identical design has been made available to the public:

(a)  in the case of an unregistered Community design, before the date on which the design for which protection is claimed has first been made available to the public;

(b)  in the case of a registered Community design, before the date of filing of the application for registration of the design for which protection is claimed, or, if priority is claimed, the date of priority.

2.  Designs shall be deemed to be identical if their features differ only in immaterial details.

*Article 6*

## Individual character

1.    A design shall be considered to have individual character if the overall impression it produces on the informed user differs from the overall impression produced on such a user by any design which has been made available to the public:

(a)   in the case of an unregistered Community design, before the date on which the design for which protection is claimed has first been made available to the public;

(b)   in the case of a registered Community design, before the date of filing the application for registration or, if a priority is claimed, the date of priority.

2.    In assessing individual character, the degree of freedom of the designer in developing the design shall be taken into consideration.

*Article 7*

## Disclosure

1.    For the purpose of applying Articles 5 and 6, a design shall be deemed to have been made available to the public if it has been published following registration or otherwise, or exhibited, used in trade or otherwise disclosed, before the date referred to in Articles 5(1)(a) and 6(1)(a) or in Articles 5(1)(b) and 6(1)(b), as the case may be, except where these events could not reasonably have become known in the normal course of business to the circles specialised in the sector concerned, operating within the Community. The design shall not, however, be deemed to have been made available to the public for the sole reason that it has been disclosed to a third person under explicit or implicit conditions of confidentiality.

2.    A disclosure shall not be taken into consideration for the purpose of applying Articles 5 and 6 and if a design for which protection is claimed under a registered Community design has been made available to the public:

(a)   by the designer, his successor in title, or a third person as a result of information provided or action taken by the designer or his successor in title; and

(b)   during the 12-month period preceding the date of filing of the application or, if a priority is claimed, the date of priority.

3.    Paragraph 2 shall also apply if the design has been made available to the public as a consequence of an abuse in relation to the designer or his successor in title.

*Article 8*

## Designs dictated by their technical function
## and designs of interconnections

1.    A Community design shall not subsist in features of appearance of a product which are solely dictated by its technical function.

2.    A Community design shall not subsist in features of appearance of a product which must necessarily be reproduced in their exact form and dimensions in order to permit the product in which the design is incorporated or to which it is applied to be mechanically connected to or placed in, around or against another product so that either product may perform its function.

3.    Notwithstanding paragraph 2, a Community design shall under the conditions set out in Articles 5 and 6 subsist in a design serving the purpose of allowing the multiple assembly or connection of mutually interchangeable products within a modular system.

## Article 9

### Designs contrary to public policy or morality

A Community design shall not subsist in a design which is contrary to public policy or to accepted principles of morality.

### Section 2

### Scope and term of protection

### Article 10

### Scope of protection

1. The scope of the protection conferred by a Community design shall include any design which does not produce on the informed user a different overall impression.

2. In assessing the scope of protection, the degree of freedom of the designer in developing his design shall be taken into consideration.

### Article 11

### Commencement and term of protection of the unregistered Community design

1. A design which meets the requirements under Section 1 shall be protected by an unregistered Community design for a period of three years as from the date on which the design was first made available to the public within the Community.

2. For the purpose of paragraph 1, a design shall be deemed to have been made available to the public within the Community if it has been published, exhibited, used in trade or otherwise disclosed in such a way that, in the normal course of business, these events could reasonably have become known to the circles specialised in the sector concerned, operating within the Community. The design shall not, however, be deemed to have been made available to the public for the sole reason that it has been disclosed to a third person under explicit or implicit conditions of confidentiality.

### Article 12

### Commencement and term of protection of the registered Community design

Upon registration by the Office, a design which meets the requirements under Section 1 shall be protected by a registered Community design for a period of five years as from the date of the filing of the application. The right holder may have the term of protection renewed for one or more periods of five years each, up to a total term of 25 years from the date of filing.

### Article 13

### Renewal

1. Registration of the registered Community design shall be renewed at the request of the right holder or of any person expressly authorised by him, provided that the renewal fee has been paid.

2. The Office shall inform the right holder of the registered Community design and any person having a right entered in the register of Community designs, referred to in Article 72, hereafter referred to as the "register" in respect of the registered Community design, of the expiry of the registration in good time before the said expiry. Failure to give such information shall not involve the responsibility of the Office.

3. The request for renewal shall be submitted and the renewal fee paid within a period of six months ending on the last day of the month in which protection ends. Failing this, the request may be

submitted and the fee paid within a further period of six months from the day referred to in the first sentence, provided that an additional fee is paid within this further period.

4.     Renewal shall take effect from the day following the date on which the existing registration expires. The renewal shall be entered in the register.

Section 3

**Right to the Community design**

*Article 14*

**Right to the Community design**

1.     The right to the Community design shall vest in the designer or his successor in title.

2.     If two or more persons have jointly developed a design, the right to the Community design shall vest in them jointly.

3.     However, where a design is developed by an employee in the execution of his duties or following the instructions given by his employer, the right to the Community design shall vest in the employer, unless otherwise agreed or specified under national law.

*Article 15*

**Claims relating to the entitlement to a Community design**

1.     If an unregistered Community design is disclosed or claimed by, or a registered Community design has been applied for or registered in the name of, a person who is not entitled to it under Article 14, the person entitled to it under that provision may, without prejudice to any other remedy which may be open to him, claim to become recognised as the legitimate holder of the Community design.

2.     Where a person is jointly entitled to a Community design, that person may, in accordance with paragraph 1, claim to become recognised as joint holder.

3.     Legal proceedings under paragraphs 1 or 2 shall be barred three years after the date of publication of a registered Community design or the date of disclosure of an unregistered Community design. This provision shall not apply if the person who is not entitled to the Community design was acting in bad faith at the time when such design was applied for or disclosed or was assigned to him.

4.     In the case of a registered Community design, the following shall be entered in the register:

(a)     the mention that legal proceedings under paragraph 1 have been instituted;

(b)     the final decision or any other termination of the proceedings;

(c)     any change in the ownership of the registered Community design resulting from the final decision.

*Article 16*

**Effects of a judgement on entitlement to a registered Community design**

1.     Where there is a complete change of ownership of a registered Community design as a result of legal proceedings under Article 15(1), licences and other rights shall lapse upon the entering in the register of the person entitled.

2.     If, before the institution of the legal proceedings under Article 15(1) has been registered, the holder of the registered Community design or a licensee has exploited the design within the Community or made serious and effective preparations to do so, he may continue such exploitation provided that he requests within the period prescribed by the implementing regulation a non-exclusive licence from the new holder whose name is entered in the register. The licence shall be granted for a reasonable period and upon reasonable terms.

3.    Paragraph 2 shall not apply if the holder of the registered Community design or the licensee was acting in bad faith at the time when he began to exploit the design or to make preparations to do so.

*Article 17*

**Presumption in favour of the registered holder of the design**

The person in whose name the registered Community design is registered or, prior to registration, the person in whose name the application is filed, shall be deemed to be the person entitled in any proceedings before the Office as well as in any other proceedings.

*Article 18*

**Right of the designer to be cited**

The designer shall have the right, in the same way as the applicant for or the holder of a registered Community design, to be cited as such before the Office and in the register. If the design is the result of teamwork, the citation of the team may replace the citation of the individual designers.

Section 4

**Effects of the Community design**

*Article 19*

**Rights conferred by the Community design**

1.    A registered Community design shall confer on its holder the exclusive right to use it and to prevent any third party not having his consent from using it. The aforementioned use shall cover, in particular, the making, offering, putting on the market, importing, exporting or using of a product in which the design is incorporated or to which it is applied, or stocking such a product for those purposes.

2.    An unregistered Community design shall, however, confer on its holder the right to prevent the acts referred to in paragraph 1 only if the contested use results from copying the protected design.

The contested use shall not be deemed to result from copying the protected design if it results from an independent work of creation by a designer who may be reasonably thought not to be familiar with the design made available to the public by the holder.

3.    Paragraph 2 shall also apply to a registered Community design subject to deferment of publication as long as the relevant entries in the register and the file have not been made available to the public in accordance with Article 50(4).

*Article 20*

**Limitation of the rights conferred by a Community design**

1.    The rights conferred by a Community design shall not be exercised in respect of:

(a)    acts done privately and for non-commercial purposes;

(b)    acts done for experimental purposes;

(c)    acts of reproduction for the purpose of making citations or of teaching, provided that such acts are compatible with fair trade practice and do not unduly prejudice the normal exploitation of the design, and that mention is made of the source.

2.    In addition, the rights conferred by a Community design shall not be exercised in respect of:

(a)    the equipment on ships and aircraft registered in a third country when these temporarily enter the territory of the Community;

(b)    the importation in the Community of spare parts and accessories for the purpose of repairing such craft;

(c)    the execution of repairs on such craft.

*Article 21*

### Exhaustion of rights

The rights conferred by a Community design shall not extend to acts relating to a product in which a design included within the scope of protection of the Community design is incorporated or to which it is applied, when the product has been put on the market in the Community by the holder of the Community design or with his consent.

*Article 22*

### Rights of prior use in respect of a registered Community design

1.    A right of prior use shall exist for any third person who can establish that before the date of filing of the application, or, if a priority is claimed, before the date of priority, he has in good faith commenced use within the Community, or has made serious and effective preparations to that end, of a design included within the scope of protection of a registered Community design, which has not been copied from the latter.

2.    The right of prior use shall entitle the third person to exploit the design for the purposes for which its use had been effected, or for which serious and effective preparations had been made, before the filing or priority date of the registered Community design.

3.    The right of prior use shall not extend to granting a licence to another person to exploit the design.

4.    The right of prior use cannot be transferred except, where the third person is a business, along with that part of the business in the course of which the act was done or the preparations were made.

*Article 23*

### Government use

Any provision in the law of a Member State allowing use of national designs by or for the government may be applied to Community designs, but only to the extent that the use is necessary for essential defence or security needs.

Section 5

### Invalidity

*Article 24*

### Declaration of invalidity

1.    A registered Community design shall be declared invalid on application to the Office in accordance with the procedure in Titles VI and VII or by a Community design court on the basis of a counterclaim in infringement proceedings.

2.    A Community design may be declared invalid even after the Community design has lapsed or has been surrendered.

3.    An unregistered Community design shall be declared invalid by a Community design court on application to such a court or on the basis of a counterclaim in infringement proceedings.

## Article 25

### Grounds for invalidity

1. A Community design may be declared invalid only in the following cases:

(a) if the design does not correspond to the definition under Article 3(a);

(b) if it does not fulfil the requirements of Articles 4 to 9;

(c) if, by virtue of a court decision, the right holder is not entitled to the Community design under Article 14;

(d) if the Community design is in conflict with a prior design which has been made available to the public after the date of filing of the application or, if priority is claimed, the date of priority of the Community design, and which is protected from a date prior to the said date

(i) by a registered Community design or an application for such a design, or

(ii) by a registered design right of a Member State, or by an application for such a right, or

(iii) by a design right registered under the Geneva Act of the Hague Agreement concerning the international registration of industrial designs, adopted in Geneva on 2 July 1999, hereinafter referred to as "the Geneva Act", which was approved by Council Decision 954/2006 and which has effect in the Community, or by an application for such a right;

(e) if a distinctive sign is used in a subsequent design, and Community law or the law of the Member State governing that sign confers on the right holder of the sign the right to prohibit such use;

(f) if the design constitutes an unauthorised use of a work protected under the copyright law of a Member State;

(g) if the design constitutes an improper use of any of the items listed in Article 6ter of the "Paris Convention" for the Protection of Industrial Property hereafter referred to as the "Paris Convention", or of badges, emblems and escutcheons other than those covered by the said Article 6ter and which are of particular public interest in a Member State.

2. The ground provided for in paragraph (1)(c) may be invoked solely by the person who is entitled to the Community design under Article 14.

3. The grounds provided for in paragraph (1)(d), (e) and (f) may be invoked solely by the applicant for or holder of the earlier right.

4. The ground provided for in paragraph (1)(g) may be invoked solely by the person or entity concerned by the use.

5. Paragraphs 3 and 4 shall be without prejudice to the freedom of Member States to provide that the grounds provided for in paragraphs 1(d) and (g) may also be invoked by the appropriate authority of the Member State in question on its own initiative.

6. A registered Community design which has been declared invalid pursuant to paragraph (1)(b), (e), (f) or (g) may be maintained in an amended form, if in that form it complies with the requirements for protection and the identity of the design is retained. "Maintenance" in an amended form may include registration accompanied by a partial disclaimer by the holder of the registered Community design or entry in the register of a court decision or a decision by the Office declaring the partial invalidity of the registered Community design.

## Article 26

### Consequences of invalidity

1. A Community design shall be deemed not to have had, as from the outset, the effects specified in this Regulation, to the extent that it has been declared invalid.

2.   Subject to the national provisions relating either to claims for compensation for damage caused by negligence or lack of good faith on the part of the holder of the Community design, or to unjust enrichment, the retroactive effect of invalidity of the Community design shall not affect:

(a)   any decision on infringement which has acquired the authority of a final decision and been enforced prior to the invalidity decision;

(b)   any contract concluded prior to the invalidity decision, in so far as it has been performed before the decision; however, repayment, to an extent justified by the circumstances, of sums paid under the relevant contract may be claimed on grounds of equity.

TITLE III

**COMMUNITY DESIGNS AS OBJECTS OF PROPERTY**

*Article 27*

**Dealing with Community designs as national design rights**

1.   Unless Articles 28, 29, 30, 31 and 32 provide otherwise, a Community design as an object of property shall be dealt with in its entirety, and for the whole area of the Community, as a national design right of the Member State in which:

(a)   the holder has his seat or his domicile on the relevant date; or

(b)   where point (a) does not apply, the holder has an establishment on the relevant date.

2.   In the case of a registered Community design, paragraph 1 shall apply according to the entries in the register.

3.   In the case of joint holders, if two or more of them fulfil the condition under paragraph 1, the Member State referred to in that paragraph shall be determined:

(a)   in the case of an unregistered Community design, by reference to the relevant joint holder designated by them by common agreement;

(b)   in the case of a registered Community design, by reference to the first of the relevant joint holders in the order in which they are mentioned in the register.

4.   Where paragraphs 1, 2 and 3 do not apply, the Member State referred to in paragraph 1 shall be the Member State in which the seat of the Office is situated.

*Article 28*

**Transfer of the registered Community design**

The transfer of a registered Community design shall be subject to the following provisions:

(a)   at the request of one of the parties, a transfer shall be entered in the register and published;

(b)   until such time as the transfer has been entered in the register, the successor in title may not invoke the rights arising from the registration of the Community design;

(c)   where there are time limits to be observed in dealings with the Office, the successor in title may make the corresponding statements to the Office once the request for registration of the transfer has been received by the Office;

(d)   all documents which by virtue of Article 66 require notification to the holder of the registered Community design shall be addressed by the Office to the person registered as holder or his representative, if one has been appointed.

## Article 29

### Rights in rem on a registered Community design

1.    A registered Community design may be given as security or be the subject of rights in rem.

2.    On request of one of the parties, the rights mentioned in paragraph 1 shall be entered in the register and published.

## Article 30

### Levy of execution

1.    A registered Community design may be levied in execution.

2.    As regards the procedure for levy of execution in respect of a registered Community design, the courts and authorities of the Member State determined in accordance with Article 27 shall have exclusive jurisdiction.

3.    On request of one of the parties, levy of execution shall be entered in the register and published.

## Article 31

### Insolvency proceedings

1.    The only insolvency proceedings in which a Community design may be involved shall be those opened in the Member State within the territory of which the centre of a debtor's main interests is situated.

2.    In the case of joint proprietorship of a Community design, paragraph 1 shall apply to the share of the joint proprietor.

3.    Where a Community design is involved in insolvency proceedings, on request of the competent national authority an entry to this effect shall be made in the register and published in the Community Designs Bulletin referred to in Article 73(1).

## Article 32

### Licensing

1.    A Community design may be licensed for the whole or part of the Community. A licence may be exclusive or non-exclusive.

2.    Without prejudice to any legal proceedings based on the law of contract, the holder may invoke the rights conferred by the Community design against a licensee who contravenes any provision in his licensing contract with regard to its duration, the form in which the design may be used, the range of products for which the licence is granted and the quality of products manufactured by the licensee.

3.    Without prejudice to the provisions of the licensing contract, the licensee may bring proceedings for infringement of a Community design only if the right holder consents thereto. However, the holder of an exclusive licence may bring such proceedings if the right holder in the Community design, having been given notice to do so, does not himself bring infringement proceedings within an appropriate period.

4.    A licensee shall, for the purpose of obtaining compensation for damage suffered by him, be entitled to intervene in an infringement action brought by the right holder in a Community design.

5.    In the case of a registered Community design, the grant or transfer of a licence in respect of such right shall, at the request of one of the parties, be entered in the register and published.

### Article 33

### Effects vis-à-vis third parties

1.     The effects vis-à-vis third parties of the legal acts referred to in Articles 28, 29, 30 and 32 shall be governed by the law of the Member State determined in accordance with Article 27.

2.     However, as regards registered Community designs, legal acts referred to in Articles 28, 29 and 32 shall only have effect vis-à-vis third parties in all the Member States after entry in the register. Nevertheless, such an act, before it is so entered, shall have effect vis-à-vis third parties who have acquired rights in the registered Community design after the date of that act but who knew of the act at the date on which the rights were acquired.

3.     Paragraph 2 shall not apply to a person who acquires the registered Community design or a right concerning the registered Community design by way of transfer of the whole of the undertaking or by any other universal succession.

4.     Until such time as common rules for the Member States in the field of insolvency enter into force, the effects vis-à-vis third parties of insolvency proceedings shall be governed by the law of the Member State in which such proceedings are first brought under the national law or the regulations applicable in this field.

### Article 34

### The application for a registered Community design as an object of property

1.     An application for a registered Community design as an object of property shall be dealt with in its entirety, and for the whole area of the Community, as a national design right of the Member State determined in accordance with Article 27.

2.     Articles 28, 29, 30, 31, 32 and 33 shall apply mutatis mutandis to applications for registered Community designs. Where the effect of one of these provisions is conditional upon an entry in the register, that formality shall be performed upon registration of the resulting registered Community design.

### TITLE IV
### APPLICATION FOR A REGISTERED COMMUNITY DESIGN
### Section 1
### Filing of applications and the conditions which govern them

### Article 35

### Filing and forwarding of applications

1.     An application for a registered Community design shall be filed, at the option of the applicant:

    (a)    at the Office; or

    (b)    at the central industrial property office of a Member State; or

    (c)    in the Benelux countries, at the Benelux Design Office.

2.     Where the application is filed at the central industrial property office of a Member State or at the Benelux Design Office, that office shall take all steps to forward the application to the Office within two weeks after filing. It may charge the applicant a fee which shall not exceed the administrative costs of receiving and forwarding the application.

3.     As soon as the Office has received an application which has been forwarded by a central industrial property office of a Member State or by the Benelux Design Office, it shall inform the applicant accordingly, indicating the date of its receipt at the Office.

4.    No less than 10 years after the entry into force of this Regulation, the Commission shall draw up a report on the operation of the system of filing applications for registered Community designs, accompanied by any proposals for revision that it may deem appropriate.

## Article 36

### Conditions with which applications must comply

1.    An application for a registered Community design shall contain:

(a)    a request for registration;

(b)    information identifying the applicant;

(c)    a representation of the design suitable for reproduction. However, if the object of the application is a two-dimensional design and the application contains a request for deferment of publication in accordance with Article 50, the representation of the design may be replaced by a specimen.

2.    The application shall further contain an indication of the products in which the design is intended to be incorporated or to which it is intended to be applied.

3.    In addition, the application may contain:

(a)    a description explaining the representation or the specimen;

(b)    a request for deferment of publication of the registration in accordance with Article 50;

(c)    information identifying the representative if the applicant has appointed one;

(d)    the classification of the products in which the design is intended to be incorporated or to which it is intended to be applied according to class;

(e)    the citation of the designer or of the team of designers or a statement under the applicant's responsibility that the designer or the team of designers has waived the right to be cited.

4.    The application shall be subject to the payment of the registration fee and the publication fee. Where a request for deferment under paragraph 3(b) is filed, the publication fee shall be replaced by the fee for deferment of publication.

5.    The application shall comply with the conditions laid down in the implementing regulation.

6.    The information contained in the elements mentioned in paragraph 2 and in paragraph 3(a) and (d) shall not affect the scope of protection of the design as such.

## Article 37

### Multiple applications

1.    Several designs may be combined in one multiple application for registered Community designs. Except in cases of ornamentation, this possibility is subject to the condition that the products in which the designs are intended to be incorporated or to which they are intended to be applied all belong to the same class of the International Classification for Industrial Designs.

2.    Besides the fees referred to in Article 36(4), the multiple application shall be subject to payment of an additional registration fee and an additional publication fee. Where the multiple application contains a request for deferment of publication, the additional publication fee shall be replaced by the additional fee for deferment of publication. The additional fees shall correspond to a percentage of the basic fees for each additional design.

3.    The multiple application shall comply with the conditions of presentation laid down in the implementing regulation.

4.   Each of the designs contained in a multiple application or registration may be dealt with separately from the others for the purpose of applying this Regulation. It may in particular, separately from the others, be enforced, licensed, be the subject of a right in rem, a levy of execution or insolvency proceedings, be surrendered, renewed or assigned, be the subject of deferred publication or be declared invalid. A multiple application or registration may be divided into separate applications or registrations only under the conditions set out in the implementing regulation.

*Article 38*

### Date of filing

1.   The date of filing of an application for a registered Community design shall be the date on which documents containing the information specified in Article 36(1) are filed with the Office by the applicant, or, if the application has been filed with the central industrial property office of a Member State or with the Benelux Design Office, with that office.

2.   By derogation from paragraph 1, the date of filing of an application filed with the central industrial property office of a Member State or with the Benelux Design Office and reaching the Office more than two months after the date on which documents containing the information specified in Article 36(1) have been filed shall be the date of receipt of such documents by the Office.

*Article 39*

### Equivalence of Community filing with national filing

An application for a registered Community design which has been accorded a date of filing shall, in the Member States, be equivalent to a regular national filing, including where appropriate the priority claimed for the said application.

*Article 40*

### Classification

For the purpose of this Regulation, use shall be made of the Annex to the Agreement establishing an International Classification for Industrial Designs, signed at Locarno on 8 October 1968.

Section 2

### Priority

*Article 41*

### Right of priority

1.   A person who has duly filed an application for a design right or for a utility model in or for any State party to the Paris Convention for the Protection of Industrial Property, or to the Agreement establishing the World Trade Organisation, or his successors in title, shall enjoy, for the purpose of filing an application for a registered Community design in respect of the same design or utility model, a right of priority of six months from the date of filing of the first application.

2.   Every filing that is equivalent to a regular national filing under the national law of the State where it was made or under bilateral or multilateral agreements shall be recognised as giving rise to a right of priority.

3.   "Regular national filing" means any filing that is sufficient to establish the date on which the application was filed, whatever may be the outcome of the application.

4.   A subsequent application for a design which was the subject of a previous first application, and which is filed in or in respect of the same State, shall be considered as the first application for the purpose of determining priority, provided that, at the date of the filing of the subsequent application, the previous application has been withdrawn, abandoned or refused without being open to public

inspection and without leaving any rights outstanding, and has not served as a basis for claiming priority. The previous application may not thereafter serve as a basis for claiming a right of priority.

5.    If the first filing has been made in a State which is not a party to the Paris Convention, or to the Agreement establishing the World Trade Organisation, paragraphs 1 to 4 shall apply only in so far as that State, according to published findings, grants, on the basis of a filing made at the Office and subject to conditions equivalent to those laid down in this Regulation, a right of priority having equivalent effect.

## *Article 42*

### Claiming priority

An applicant for a registered Community design desiring to take advantage of the priority of a previous application shall file a declaration of priority and a copy of the previous application. If the language of the latter is not one of the languages of the Office, the Office may require a translation of the previous application in one of those languages.

## *Article 43*

### Effect of priority right

The effect of the right of priority shall be that the date of priority shall count as the date of the filing of the application for a registered Community design for the purpose of Articles 5, 6, 7, 22, 25(1)(d) and 50(1).

## *Article 44*

### Exhibition priority

1.    If an applicant for a registered Community design has disclosed products in which the design is incorporated, or to which it is applied, at an official or officially recognised international exhibition falling within the terms of the Convention on International Exhibitions signed in Paris on 22 November 1928 and last revised on 30 November 1972, he may, if he files the application within a period of six months from the date of the first disclosure of such products, claim a right of priority from that date within the meaning of Article 43.

2.    An applicant who wishes to claim priority pursuant to paragraph 1, under the conditions laid down in the implementing regulation, must file evidence that he has disclosed at an exhibition the products in or to which the design is incorporated or applied.

3.    An exhibition priority granted in a Member State or in a third country does not extend the period of priority laid down in Article 41.

## TITLE V
## REGISTRATION PROCEDURE

## *Article 45*

### Examination as to formal requirements for filing

1.    The Office shall examine whether the application complies with the requirements laid down in Article 36(1) for the accordance of a date of filing.

2.    The Office shall examine whether:

(a)    the application complies with the other requirements laid down in Article 36(2), (3), (4) and (5) and, in the case of a multiple application, Article 37(1) and (2);

(b)    the application meets the formal requirements laid down in the implementing regulation for the implementation of Articles 36 and 37;

(c)   the requirements of Article 77(2) are satisfied;

(d)   the requirements concerning the claim to priority are satisfied, if a priority is claimed.

3.   The conditions for the examination as to the formal requirements for filing shall be laid down in the implementing regulation.

## *Article 46*

### Remediable deficiencies

1.   Where, in carrying out the examination under Article 45, the Office notes that there are deficiencies which may be corrected, the Office shall request the applicant to remedy them within the prescribed period.

2.   If the deficiencies concern the requirements referred to in Article 36(1) and the applicant complies with the Office's request within the prescribed period, the Office shall accord as the date of filing the date on which the deficiencies are remedied. If the deficiencies are not remedied within the prescribed period, the application shall not be dealt with as an application for a registered Community design.

3.   If the deficiencies concern the requirements, including the payment of fees, as referred to in Article 45(2)(a), (b) and (c) and the applicant complies with the Office's request within the prescribed period, the Office shall accord as the date of filing the date on which the application was originally filed. If the deficiencies or the default in payment are not remedied within the prescribed period, the Office shall refuse the application.

4.   If the deficiencies concern the requirements referred to in Article 45(2)(d), failure to remedy them within the prescribed period shall result in the loss of the right of priority for the application.

## *Article 47*

### Grounds for non-registrability

1.   If the Office, in carrying out the examination pursuant to Article 45, notices that the design for which protection is sought:

(a)   does not correspond to the definition under Article 3(a); or

(b)   is contrary to public policy or to accepted principles of morality, it shall refuse the application.

2.   The application shall not be refused before the applicant has been allowed the opportunity of withdrawing or amending the application or of submitting his observations.

## *Article 48*

### Registration

If the requirements that an application for a registered Community design must satisfy have been fulfilled and to the extent that the application has not been refused by virtue of Article 47, the Office shall register the application in the Community design Register as a registered Community design. The registration shall bear the date of filing of the application referred to in Article 38.

## *Article 49*

### Publication

Upon registration, the Office shall publish the registered Community design in the Community Designs Bulletin as mentioned in Article 73(1). The contents of the publication shall be set out in the implementing regulation.

## Article 50

### Deferment of publication

1.   The applicant for a registered Community design may request, when filing the application, that the publication of the registered Community design be deferred for a period of 30 months from the date of filing the application or, if a priority is claimed, from the date of priority.

2.   Upon such request, where the conditions set out in Article 48 are satisfied, the registered Community design shall be registered, but neither the representation of the design nor any file relating to the application shall, subject to Article 74(2), be open to public inspection.

3.   The Office shall publish in the Community Designs Bulletin a mention of the deferment of the publication of the registered Community design. The mention shall be accompanied by information identifying the right holder in the registered Community design, the date of filing the application and any other particulars prescribed by the implementing regulation.

4.   At the expiry of the period of deferment, or at any earlier date on request by the right holder, the Office shall open to public inspection all the entries in the register and the file relating to the application and shall publish the registered Community design in the Community Designs Bulletin, provided that, within the time limit laid down in the implementing regulation:

(a)   the publication fee and, in the event of a multiple application, the additional publication fee are paid;

(b)   where use has been made of the option pursuant to Article 36(1)(c), the right holder has filed with the Office a representation of the design.

If the right holder fails to comply with these requirements, the registered Community design shall be deemed from the outset not to have had the effects specified in this Regulation.

5.   In the case of multiple applications, paragraph 4 need only be applied to some of the designs included therein.

6.   The institution of legal proceedings on the basis of a registered Community design during the period of deferment of publication shall be subject to the condition that the information contained in the register and in the file relating to the application has been communicated to the person against whom the action is brought.

## TITLE VI
### SURRENDER AND INVALIDITY OF THE REGISTERED COMMUNITY DESIGN

## Article 51

### Surrender

1.   The surrender of a registered Community design shall be declared to the Office in writing by the right holder. It shall not have effect until it has been entered in the register.

2.   If a Community design which is subject to deferment of publication is surrendered it shall be deemed from the outset not to have had the effects specified in this Regulation.

3.   A registered Community design may be partially surrendered provided that its amended form complies with the requirements for protection and the identity of the design is retained.

4.   Surrender shall be registered only with the agreement of the proprietor of a right entered in the register. If a licence has been registered, surrender shall be entered in the register only if the right holder in the registered Community design proves that he has informed the licensee of his intention to surrender. This entry shall be made on expiry of the period prescribed by the implementing regulation.

5.    If an action pursuant to Article 14 relating to the entitlement to a registered Community design has been brought before a Community design court, the Office shall not enter the surrender in the register without the agreement of the claimant.

## Article 52

### Application for a declaration of invalidity

1.    Subject to Article 25(2), (3), (4) and (5), any natural or legal person, as well as a public authority empowered to do so, may submit to the Office an application for a declaration of invalidity of a registered Community design.

2.    The application shall be filed in a written reasoned statement. It shall not be deemed to have been filed until the fee for an application for a declaration of invalidity has been paid.

3.    An application for a declaration of invalidity shall not be admissible if an application relating to the same subject matter and cause of action, and involving the same parties, has been adjudicated on by a Community design court and has acquired the authority of a final decision.

## Article 53

### Examination of the application

1.    If the Office finds that the application for a declaration of invalidity is admissible, the Office shall examine whether the grounds for invalidity referred to in Article 25 prejudice the maintenance of the registered Community design.

2.    In the examination of the application, which shall be conducted in accordance with the implementing regulation, the Office shall invite the parties, as often as necessary, to file observations, within a period to be fixed by the Office, on communications from the other parties or issued by itself.

3.    The decision declaring the registered Community design invalid shall be entered in the register upon becoming final.

## Article 54

### Participation in the proceedings of the alleged infringer

1.    In the event of an application for a declaration of invalidity of a registered Community design being filed, and as long as no final decision has been taken by the Office, any third party who proves that proceedings for infringement of the same design have been instituted against him may be joined as a party in the invalidity proceedings on request submitted within three months of the date on which the infringement proceedings were instituted.

    The same shall apply in respect of any third party who proves both that the right holder of the Community design has requested that he cease an alleged infringement of the design and that he has instituted proceedings for a court ruling that he is not infringing the Community design.

2.    The request to be joined as a party shall be filed in a written reasoned statement. It shall not be deemed to have been filed until the invalidity fee, referred to in Article 52(2), has been paid. Thereafter the request shall, subject to any exceptions laid down in the implementing regulation, be treated as an application for a declaration of invalidity.

## TITLE VII
## APPEALS

*Article 55*

### Decisions subject to appeal

1.    An appeal shall lie from decisions of the examiners, the Administration of Trade Marks and Designs and Legal Division and Invalidity Divisions. It shall have suspensive effect.

2.    A decision which does not terminate proceedings as regards one of the parties can only be appealed together with the final decision, unless the decision allows separate appeal.

*Article 56*

### Persons entitled to appeal and to be parties to appeal proceedings

Any party to proceedings adversely affected by a decision may appeal. Any other parties to the proceedings shall be parties to the appeal proceedings as of right.

*Article 57*

### Time limit and form of appeal

Notice of appeal must be filed in writing at the Office within two months after the date of notification of the decision appealed from. The notice shall be deemed to have been filed only when the fee for appeal has been paid. Within four months after the date of notification of the decision, a written statement setting out the grounds of appeal must be filed.

*Article 58*

### Interlocutory revision

1.    If the department whose decision is contested considers the appeal to be admissible and well founded, it shall rectify its decision. This shall not apply where the appellant is opposed by another party to the proceedings.

2.    If the decision is not rectified within one month after receipt of the statement of grounds, the appeal shall be remitted to the Board of Appeal without delay and without comment as to its merits.

*Article 59*

### Examination of appeals

1.    If the appeal is admissible, the Board of Appeal shall examine whether the appeal is to be allowed.

2.    In the examination of the appeal, the Board of Appeal shall invite the parties, as often as necessary, to file observations, within a period to be fixed by the Board of Appeal, on communications from the other parties or issued by itself.

*Article 60*

### Decisions in respect of appeals

1.    Following the examination as to the merits of the appeal, the Board of Appeal shall decide on the appeal. The Board of Appeal may either exercise any power within the competence of the department which was responsible for the decision appealed against or remit the case to that department for further prosecution.

2.    If the Board of Appeal remits the case for further prosecution to the department whose decision was appealed, that department shall be bound by the ratio decidendi of the Board of Appeal, in so far as the facts are the same.

3.    The decisions of the Boards of Appeal shall take effect only from the date of expiry of the period referred to in Article 61(5) or, if an action has been brought before the Court of Justice within that period, from the date of rejection of such action.

### *Article 61*

### Actions before the Court of Justice

1.    Actions may be brought before the Court of Justice against decisions of the Boards of Appeal on appeals.

2.    The action may be brought on grounds of lack of competence, infringement of an essential procedural requirement, infringement of the Treaty, of this Regulation or of any rule of law relating to their application or misuse of power.

3.    The Court of Justice has jurisdiction to annul or to alter the contested decision.

4.    The action shall be open to any party to proceedings before the Board of Appeal adversely affected by its decision.

5.    The action shall be brought before the Court of Justice within two months of the date of notification of the decision of the Board of Appeal.

6.    The Office shall be required to take the necessary measures to comply with the judgment of the Court of Justice.

### TITLE VIII
### PROCEDURE BEFORE THE OFFICE
Section 1
### General provisions

### *Article 62*

### Statement of reasons on which decisions are based

Decisions of the Office shall state the reasons on which they are based. They shall be based only on reasons or evidence on which the parties concerned have had an opportunity to present their comments.

### *Article 63*

### Examination of the facts by the Office of its own motion

1.    In proceedings before it the Office shall examine the facts of its own motion. However, in proceedings relating to a declaration of invalidity, the Office shall be restricted in this examination to the facts, evidence and arguments provided by the parties and the relief sought.

2.    The Office may disregard facts or evidence which are not submitted in due time by the parties concerned.

### *Article 64*

### Oral proceedings

1.    If the Office considers that oral proceedings would be expedient, they shall be held either at the instance of the Office or at the request of any party to the proceedings.

2.    Oral proceedings, including delivery of the decision, shall be public, unless the department before which the proceedings are taking place decides otherwise in cases where admission of the public could have serious and unjustified disadvantages, in particular for a party to the proceedings.

*Article 65*

**Taking of evidence**

1.    In any proceedings before the Office the means of giving or obtaining evidence shall include the following:

(a)    hearing the parties;

(b)    requests for information;

(c)    the production of documents and items of evidence;

(d)    hearing witnesses;

(e)    opinions by experts;

(f)    statements in writing, sworn or affirmed or having a similar effect under the law of the State in which the statement is drawn up.

2.    The relevant department of the Office may commission one of its members to examine the evidence adduced.

3.    If the Office considers it necessary for a party, witness or expert to give evidence orally, it shall issue a summons to the person concerned to appear before it.

4.    The parties shall be informed of the hearing of a witness or expert before the Office. They shall have the right to be present and to put questions to the witness or expert.

*Article 66*

**Notification**

The Office shall, as a matter of course, notify those concerned of decisions and summonses and of any notice or other communication from which a time limit is reckoned, or of which those concerned must be notified under other provisions of this Regulation or of the implementing regulation, or of which notification has been ordered by the President of the Office.

*Article 67*

**Restitutio in integrum**

1.    The applicant for or holder of a registered Community design or any other party to proceedings before the Office who, in spite of all due care required by the circumstances having been taken, was unable to observe a time limit vis-à-vis the Office shall, upon application, have his rights re-established if the non-observance in question has the direct consequence, by virtue of the provisions of this Regulation, of causing the loss of any rights or means of redress.

2.    The application must be filed in writing within two months of the removal of the cause of non-compliance with the time limit. The omitted act must be completed within this period. The application shall only be admissible within the year immediately following the expiry of the unobserved time limit. In the case of non-submission of the request for renewal of registration or of non-payment of a renewal fee, the further period of six months provided for in the second sentence of Article 13(3) shall be deducted from the period of one year.

3.    The application must state the grounds on which it is based and must set out the facts on which it relies. It shall not be deemed to be filed until the fee for the re-establishment of rights has been paid.

4.    The department competent to decide on the omitted act shall decide upon the application.

5.    The provisions of this Article shall not be applicable to the time limits referred to in paragraph 2 and Article 41(1).

6.    Where the applicant for or holder of a registered Community design has his rights re-established, he may not invoke his rights vis-à-vis a third party who, in good faith, in the course of the period between the loss of rights in the application for or registration of the registered Community design and publication of the mention of re-establishment of those rights, has put on the market products in which a design included within the scope of protection of the registered Community design is incorporated or to which it is applied.

7.    A third party who may avail himself of the provisions of paragraph 6 may bring third party proceedings against the decision re-establishing the rights of the applicant for or holder of the registered Community design within a period of two months as from the date of publication of the mention of re-establishment of those rights.

8.    Nothing in this Article shall limit the right of a Member State to grant restitutio in integrum in respect of time limits provided for in this Regulation and to be complied with vis-à-vis the authorities of such State.

*Article 68*

**Reference to general principles**

In the absence of procedural provisions in this Regulation, the implementing regulation, the fees regulation or the rules of procedure of the Boards of Appeal, the Office shall take into account the principles of procedural law generally recognised in the Member States.

*Article 69*

**Termination of financial obligations**

1.    Rights of the Office to the payment of fees shall be barred four years from the end of the calendar year in which the fee fell due.

2.    Rights against the Office for the refunding of fees or sums of money paid in excess of a fee shall be barred after four years from the end of the calendar year in which the right arose.

3.    The periods laid down in paragraphs 1 and 2 shall be interrupted, in the case covered by paragraph 1, by a request for payment of the fee and, in the case covered by paragraph 2, by a reasoned claim in writing. On interruption it shall begin again immediately and shall end at the latest six years after the end of the year in which it originally began, unless in the meantime judicial proceedings to enforce the right have begun. In this case the period shall end at the earliest one year after the judgment has acquired the authority of a final decision.

Section 2

**Costs**

*Article 70*

**Apportionment of costs**

1.    The losing party in proceedings for a declaration of invalidity of a registered Community design or appeal proceedings shall bear the fees incurred by the other party as well as all costs incurred by him essential to the proceedings, including travel and subsistence and the remuneration of an agent, adviser or advocate, within the limits of scales set for each category of costs under the conditions laid down in the implementing regulation.

2.    However, where each party succeeds on some and fails on other heads, or if reasons of equity so dictate, the Invalidity Division or Board of Appeal shall decide a different apportionment of costs.

3.    A party who terminates the proceedings by surrendering the registered Community design or by not renewing its registration or by withdrawing the application for a declaration of invalidity or the appeal, shall bear the fees and the costs incurred by the other party as stipulated in paragraphs 1 and 2.

4.    Where a case does not proceed to judgment, the costs shall be at the discretion of the Invalidity Division or Board of Appeal.

5.    Where the parties conclude before the Invalidity Division or Board of Appeal a settlement of costs differing from that provided for in paragraphs 1, 2, 3 and 4, the body concerned shall take note of that agreement.

6.    On request, the registry of the Invalidity Division or Board of Appeal shall fix the amount of the costs to be paid pursuant to the preceding paragraphs. The amount so determined may be reviewed by a decision of the Invalidity Division or Board of Appeal on a request filed within the period prescribed by the implementing regulation.

*Article 71*

### Enforcement of decisions fixing the amount of costs

1.    Any final decision of the Office fixing the amount of costs shall be enforceable.

2.    Enforcement shall be governed by the rules of civil procedure in force in the State in the territory of which it is carried out. The order for its enforcement shall be appended to the decision, without any other formality than verification of the authenticity of the decision, by the national authority which the government of each Member State shall designate for this purpose and shall make known to the Office and to the Court of Justice.

3.    When these formalities have been completed on application by the party concerned, the latter may proceed to enforcement in accordance with the national law, by bringing the matter directly before the competent authority.

4.    Enforcement may be suspended only by a decision of the Court of Justice. However, the courts of the Member State concerned shall have jurisdiction over complaints that enforcement is being carried out in an irregular manner

Section 3

### Informing the public and the official authorities of the Member States

*Article 72*

### Register of Community designs

The Office shall keep a register to be known as the register of Community designs, which shall contain those particulars of which the registration is provided for by this Regulation or by the implementing regulation. The register shall be open to public inspection, except to the extent that Article 50(2) provides otherwise.

*Article 73*

### Periodical publications

1.    This Office shall periodically publish a Community Designs Bulletin containing entries open to public inspection in the register as well as other particulars the publication of which is prescribed by this Regulation or by the implementing regulation.

2.    Notices and information of a general character issued by the President of the Office, as well as any other information relevant to this Regulation or its implementation, shall be published in the Official Journal of the Office.

*Article 74*

**Inspection of files**

1.    The files relating to applications for registered Community designs which have not yet been published or the files relating to registered Community designs which are subject to deferment of publication in accordance with Article 50 or which, being subject to such deferment, have been surrendered before or on the expiry of that period, shall not be made available for inspection without the consent of the applicant for or the right holder in the registered Community design.

2.    Any person who can establish a legitimate interest may inspect a file without the consent of the applicant for or holder of the registered Community design prior to the publication or after the surrender of the latter in the case provided for in paragraph 1.

This shall in particular apply if the interested person proves that the applicant for or the holder of the registered Community design has taken steps with a view to invoking against him the right under the registered Community design.

3.    Subsequent to the publication of the registered Community design, the file may be inspected on request.

4.    However, where a file is inspected pursuant to paragraph 2 or 3, certain documents in the file may be withheld from inspection in accordance with the provisions of the implementing regulation.

*Article 75*

**Administrative cooperation**

Unless otherwise provided in this Regulation or in national laws, the Office and the courts or authorities of the Member States shall on request give assistance to each other by communicating information or opening files for inspection.

Where the Office opens files to inspection by courts, public prosecutors' offices or central industrial property offices, the inspection shall not be subject to the restrictions laid down in Article 74.

*Article 76*

**Exchange of publications**

1.    The Office and the central industrial property offices of the Member States shall despatch to each other on request and for their own use one or more copies of their respective publications free of charge.

2.    The Office may conclude agreements relating to the exchange or supply of publications.

Section 4

**Representation**

*Article 77*

**General principles of representation**

1.    Subject to paragraph 2, no person shall be compelled to be represented before the Office.

2.    Without prejudice to the second subparagraph of paragraph 3, natural or legal persons not having either their domicile or their principal place of business or a real and effective industrial or commercial establishment in the Community must be represented before the Office in accordance with Article 78(1) in all proceedings before the Office established by this Regulation, other than in filing an application for a registered Community design; the implementing regulation may permit other exceptions.

3.    Natural or legal persons having their domicile or principal place of business or a real and effective industrial or commercial establishment in the Community may be represented before the Office by one of their employees, who must file with it a signed authorisation for inclusion in the files, the details of which are set out in the implementing regulation.

An employee of a legal person to which this paragraph applies may also represent other legal persons which have economic connections with the first legal person, even if those other legal persons have neither their domicile nor their principal place of business nor a real and effective industrial or commercial establishment within the Community.

*Article 78*

**Professional representation**

1.    Representation of natural or legal persons in proceedings before the Office under this Regulation may only be undertaken by:

(a)    any legal practitioner qualified in one of the Member States and having his place of business within the Community, to the extent that he is entitled, within the said State, to act as a representative in industrial property matters; or

(b)    any professional representatives whose name has been entered on the list of professional representatives referred to in Article 89(1)(b) of the Regulation on the Community trade mark; or

(c)    persons whose names are entered on the special list of professional representatives for design matters referred to in paragraph 4.

2.    The persons referred to in paragraph 1(c) shall only be entitled to represent third persons in proceedings on design matters before the Office.

3.    The implementing regulation shall provide whether and under what conditions representatives must file with the Office a signed authorisation for insertion on the files.

4.    Any natural person may be entered on the special list of professional representatives in design matters, if he fulfils the following conditions:

(a)    he must be a national of one of the Member States;

(b)    he must have his place of business or employment in the Community;

(c)    he must be entitled to represent natural or legal persons in design matters before the central industrial property office of a Member State or before the Benelux Design Office. Where, in that State, the entitlement to represent in design matters is not conditional upon the requirement of special professional qualifications, persons applying to be entered on the list must have habitually acted in design matters before the central industrial property office of the said State for at least five years. However, persons whose professional qualification to represent natural or legal persons in design matters before the central industrial property office of one of the Member States is officially recognised in accordance with the regulations laid by such State shall not be subject to the condition of having exercised the profession.

5.    Entry on the list referred to in paragraph 4 shall be effected upon request, accompanied by a certificate furnished by the central industrial property office of the Member State concerned, which must indicate that the conditions laid down in the said paragraph are fulfilled.

6.    The President of the Office may grant exemption from:

(a)    the requirement of paragraph 4(a) in special circumstances;

(b)    the requirement of paragraph 4(c), second sentence, if the applicant furnishes proof that he has acquired the requisite qualification in another way.

7.    The conditions under which a person may be removed from the list shall be laid down in the implementing regulation.

## TITLE IX
## JURISDICTION AND PROCEDURE IN LEGAL ACTIONS RELATING TO COMMUNITY DESIGNS

### Section 1

### Jurisdiction and enforcement

*Article 79*

### Application of the Convention on Jurisdiction and Enforcement

1.    Unless otherwise specified in this Regulation, the Convention on Jurisdiction and the Enforcement of Judgements in Civil and Commercial Matters, signed in Brussels on 27 September 1968, hereinafter referred to as the "Convention on Jurisdiction and Enforcement", shall apply to proceedings relating to Community designs and applications for registered Community designs, as well as to proceedings relating to actions on the basis of Community designs and national designs enjoying simultaneous protection.

2.    The provisions of the Convention on Jurisdiction and Enforcement which are rendered applicable by the paragraph 1 shall have effect in respect of any Member State solely in the text which is in force in respect of that State at any given time.

3.    In the event of proceedings in respect of the actions and claims referred to in Article 85:

(a)    Articles 2, 4, 5(1), (3), (4) and (5), 16(4) and 24 of the Convention on Jurisdiction and Enforcement shall not apply;

(b)    Articles 17 and 18 of that Convention shall apply subject to the limitations in Article 82(4) of this Regulation;

(c)    the provisions of Title II of that Convention which are applicable to persons domiciled in a Member State shall also be applicable to persons who do not have a domicile in any Member State but have an establishment therein.

4.    The provisions of the Convention on Jurisdiction and Enforcement shall not have effect in respect of any Member State for which that Convention has not yet entered into force. Until such entry into force, proceedings referred to in paragraph 1 shall be governed in such a Member State by any bilateral or multilateral convention governing its relationship with another Member State concerned, or, if no such convention exists, by its domestic law on jurisdiction, recognition and enforcement of decisions.

### Section 2

### Disputes concerning the infringement and validity of Community designs

*Article 80*

### Community design courts

1.    The Member States shall designate in their territories as limited a number as possible of national courts and tribunals of first and second instance (Community design courts) which shall perform the functions assigned to them by this Regulation.

2.    Each Member State shall communicate to the Commission not later than 6 March 2005 a list of Community design courts, indicating their names and their territorial jurisdiction.

3.    Any change made after communication of the list referred to in paragraph 2 in the number, names or territorial jurisdiction of the Community design courts shall be notified without delay by the Member State concerned to the Commission.

4.    The information referred to in paragraphs 2 and 3 shall be notified by the Commission to the Member States and published in the Official Journal of the European Communities.

5.    As long as a Member State has not communicated the list as stipulated in paragraph 2, jurisdiction for any proceedings resulting from an action covered by Article 81 for which the courts of that State have jurisdiction pursuant to Article 82 shall lie with that court of the State in question which would have jurisdiction ratione loci and ratione materiae in the case of proceedings relating to a national design right of that State.

*Article 81*

### Jurisdiction over infringement and validity

The Community design courts shall have exclusive jurisdiction:

(a)    for infringement actions and—if they are permitted under national law—actions in respect of threatened infringement of Community designs;

(b)    for actions for declaration of non-infringement of Community designs, if they are permitted under national law;

(c)    for actions for a declaration of invalidity of an unregistered Community design;

(d)    for counterclaims for a declaration of invalidity of a Community design raised in connection with actions under (a).

*Article 82*

### International jurisdiction

1.    Subject to the provisions of this Regulation and to any provisions of the Convention on Jurisdiction and Enforcement applicable by virtue of Article 79, proceedings in respect of the actions and claims referred to in Article 81 shall be brought in the courts of the Member State in which the defendant is domiciled or, if he is not domiciled in any of the Member States, in any Member State in which he has an establishment.

2.    If the defendant is neither domiciled nor has an establishment in any of the Member States, such proceedings shall be brought in the courts of the Member State in which the plaintiff is domiciled or, if he is not domiciled in any of the Member States, in any Member State in which he has an establishment.

3.    If neither the defendant nor the plaintiff is so domiciled or has such an establishment, such proceedings shall be brought in the courts of the Member State where the Office has its seat.

4.    Notwithstanding paragraphs 1, 2 and 3:

(a)    Article 17 of the Convention on Jurisdiction and Enforcement shall apply if the parties agree that a different Community design court shall have jurisdiction;

(b)    Article 18 of that Convention shall apply if the defendant enters an appearance before a different Community design court.

5.    Proceedings in respect of the actions and claims referred to in Article 81(a) and (d) may also be brought in the courts of the Member State in which the act of infringement has been committed or threatened.

## Article 83

### Extent of jurisdiction on infringement

1.    A Community design court whose jurisdiction is based on Article 82(1), (2) (3) or (4) shall have jurisdiction in respect of acts of infringement committed or threatened within the territory of any of the Member States.

2.    A Community design court whose jurisdiction is based on Article 82(5) shall have jurisdiction only in respect of acts of infringement committed or threatened within the territory of the Member State in which that court is situated.

## Article 84

### Action or counterclaim for a declaration of invalidity of a Community design

1.    An action or a counterclaim for a declaration of invalidity of a Community design may only be based on the grounds for invalidity mentioned in Article 25.

2.    In the cases referred to in Article 25(2), (3), (4) and (5) the action or the counterclaim may be brought solely by the person entitled under those provisions.

3.    If the counterclaim is brought in a legal action to which the right holder of the Community design is not already a party, he shall be informed thereof and may be joined as a party to the action in accordance with the conditions set out in the law of the Member State where the court is situated.

4.    The validity of a Community design may not be put in issue in an action for a declaration of non-infringement.

## Article 85

### Presumption of validity—defence as to the merits

1.    In proceedings in respect of an infringement action or an action for threatened infringement of a registered Community design, the Community design court shall treat the Community design as valid. Validity may be challenged only with a counterclaim for a declaration of invalidity. However, a plea relating to the invalidity of a Community design, submitted otherwise than by way of counterclaim, shall be admissible in so far as the defendant claims that the Community design could be declared invalid on account of an earlier national design right, within the meaning of Article 25(1)(d), belonging to him.

2.    In proceedings in respect of an infringement action or an action for threatened infringement of an unregistered Community design, the Community design court shall treat the Community design as valid if the right holder produces proof that the conditions laid down in Article 11 have been met and indicates what constitutes the individual character of his Community design. However, the defendant may contest its validity by way of a plea or with a counterclaim for a declaration of invalidity.

## Article 86

### Judgements of invalidity

1.    Where in a proceeding before a Community design court the Community design has been put in issue by way of a counterclaim for a declaration of invalidity:

(a)    if any of the grounds mentioned in Article 25 are found to prejudice the maintenance of the Community design, the court shall declare the Community design invalid;

(b)    if none of the grounds mentioned in Article 25 is found to prejudice the maintenance of the Community design, the court shall reject the counterclaim.

2.     The Community design court with which a counterclaim for a declaration of invalidity of a registered Community design has been filed shall inform the Office of the date on which the counterclaim was filed. The latter shall record this fact in the register.

3.     The Community design court hearing a counterclaim for a declaration of invalidity of a registered Community design may, on application by the right holder of the registered Community design and after hearing the other parties, stay the proceedings and request the defendant to submit an application for a declaration of invalidity to the Office within a time limit which the court shall determine. If the application is not made within the time limit, the proceedings shall continue; the counterclaim shall be deemed withdrawn. Article 91(3) shall apply.

4.     Where a Community design court has given a judgment which has become final on a counterclaim for a declaration of invalidity of a registered Community design, a copy of the judgment shall be sent to the Office. Any party may request information about such transmission. The Office shall mention the judgment in the register in accordance with the provisions of the implementing regulation.

5.     No counterclaim for a declaration of invalidity of a registered Community design may be made if an application relating to the same subject matter and cause of action, and involving the same parties, has already been determined by the Office in a decision which has become final.

## Article 87

### Effects of the judgement on invalidity

When it has become final, a judgment of a Community design court declaring a Community design invalid shall have in all the Member States the effects specified in Article 26.

## Article 88

### Applicable law

1.     The Community design courts shall apply the provisions of this Regulation.

2.     On all matters not covered by this Regulation, a Community design court shall apply its national law, including its private international law.

3.     Unless otherwise provided in this Regulation, a Community design court shall apply the rules of procedure governing the same type of action relating to a national design right in the Member State where it is situated.

## Article 89

### Sanctions in actions for infringement

1.     Where in an action for infringement or for threatened infringement a Community design court finds that the defendant has infringed or threatened to infringe a Community design, it shall, unless there are special reasons for not doing so, order the following measures:

(a)     an order prohibiting the defendant from proceeding with the acts which have infringed or would infringe the Community design;

(b)     an order to seize the infringing products;

(c)     an order to seize materials and implements predominantly used in order to manufacture the infringing goods, if their owner knew the effect for which such use was intended or if such effect would have been obvious in the circumstances;

(d)     any order imposing other sanctions appropriate under the circumstances which are provided by the law of the Member State in which the acts of infringement or threatened infringement are committed, including its private international law.

2.    The Community design court shall take such measures in accordance with its national law as are aimed at ensuring that the orders referred to in paragraph 1 are complied with.

*Article 90*

**Provisional measures, including protective measures**

1.    Application may be made to the courts of a Member State, including Community design courts, for such provisional measures, including protective measures, in respect of a Community design as may be available under the law of that State in respect of national design rights even if, under this Regulation, a Community design court of another Member State has jurisdiction as to the substance of the matter.

2.    In proceedings relating to provisional measures, including protective measures, a plea otherwise than by way of counterclaim relating to the invalidity of a Community design submitted by the defendant shall be admissible. Article 85(2) shall, however, apply mutatis mutandis.

3.    A Community design court whose jurisdiction is based on Article 82(1), (2), (3) or (4) shall have jurisdiction to grant provisional measures, including protective measures, which, subject to any necessary procedure for recognition and enforcement pursuant to Title III of the Convention on Jurisdiction and Enforcement, are applicable in the territory of any Member State. No other court shall have such jurisdiction.

*Article 91*

**Specific rules on related actions**

1.    A Community design court hearing an action referred to in Article 81, other than an action for a declaration of non-infringement, shall, unless there are special grounds for continuing the hearing, of its own motion after hearing the parties, or at the request of one of the parties and after hearing the other parties, stay the proceedings where the validity of the Community design is already in issue before another Community design court on account of a counterclaim or, in the case of a registered Community design, where an application for a declaration of invalidity has already been filed at the Office.

2.    The Office, when hearing an application for a declaration of invalidity of a registered Community design, shall, unless there are special grounds for continuing the hearing, of its own motion after hearing the parties, or at the request of one of the parties and after hearing the other parties, stay the proceedings where the validity of the registered Community design is already in issue on account of a counterclaim before a Community design court. However, if one of the parties to the proceedings before the Community design court so requests, the court may, after hearing the other parties to these proceedings, stay the proceedings. The Office shall in this instance continue the proceedings pending before it.

3.    Where the Community design court stays the proceedings it may order provisional measures, including protective measures, for the duration of the stay.

*Article 92*

**Jurisdiction of Community design courts of second instance—further appeal**

1.    An appeal to the Community design courts of second instance shall lie from judgments of the Community design courts of first instance in respect of proceedings arising from the actions and claims referred to in Article 81.

2.    The conditions under which an appeal may be lodged with a Community design court of second instance shall be determined by the national law of the Member State in which that court is located.

3.    The national rules concerning further appeal shall be applicable in respect of judgments of Community design courts of second instance.

Section 3

## Other disputes concerning Community designs

*Article 93*

## Supplementary provisions on the jurisdiction of national courts other than Community design courts

1.    Within the Member State whose courts have jurisdiction under Article 79(1) or (4), those courts shall have jurisdiction for actions relating to Community designs other than those referred to in Article 81 which would have jurisdiction ratione loci and ratione materiae in the case of actions relating to a national design right in that State.

2.    Actions relating to a Community design, other than those referred to in Article 81, for which no court has jurisdiction pursuant to Article 79(1) and (4) and paragraph 1 of this Article may be heard before the courts of the Member State in which the Office has its seat.

*Article 94*

## Obligation of the national court

A national court which is dealing with an action relating to a Community design other than the actions referred to in Article 81 shall treat the design as valid. Articles 85(2) and 90(2) shall, however, apply mutatis mutandis.

## TITLE X
## EFFECTS ON THE LAWS OF THE MEMBER STATES

*Article 95*

## Parallel actions on the basis of Community designs and national design rights

1.    Where actions for infringement or for threatened infringement involving the same cause of action and between the same parties are brought before the courts of different Member States, one seized on the basis of a Community design and the other seized on the basis of a national design right providing simultaneous protection, the court other than the court first seized shall of its own motion decline jurisdiction in favour of that court. The court which would be required to decline jurisdiction may stay its proceedings if the jurisdiction of the other court is contested.

2.    The Community design court hearing an action for infringement or threatened infringement on the basis of a Community design shall reject the action if a final judgment on the merits has been given on the same cause of action and between the same parties on the basis of a design right providing simultaneous protection.

3.    The court hearing an action for infringement or for threatened infringement on the basis of a national design right shall reject the action if a final judgment on the merits has been given on the same cause of action and between the same parties on the basis of a Community design providing simultaneous protection.

4.    Paragraphs 1, 2 and 3 shall not apply in respect of provisional measures, including protective measures.

*Article 96*

## Relationship to other forms of protection under national law

1.    The provisions of this Regulation shall be without prejudice to any provisions of Community law or of the law of the Member States concerned relating to unregistered designs, trade marks or other distinctive signs, patents and utility models, typefaces, civil liability and unfair competition.

2.    A design protected by a Community design shall also be eligible for protection under the law of copyright of Member States as from the date on which the design was created or fixed in any form. The extent to which, and the conditions under which, such a protection is conferred, including the level of originality required, shall be determined by each Member State.

## TITLE XI
## SUPPLEMENTARY PROVISIONS CONCERNING THE OFFICE

. . .

### *Article 99*

### Publication and register

1.    All information the publication of which is prescribed by this Regulation or the implementing regulation shall be published in all the official languages of the Community.

2.    All entries in the Register of Community designs shall be made in all the official languages of the Community.

3.    In cases of doubt, the text in the language of the Office in which the application for a registered Community design was filed shall be authentic. If the application was filed in an official language of the Community other than one of the languages of the Office, the text in the second language indicated by the applicant shall be authentic. . . .

### Section 2

### Procedures

### *Article 102*

### Competence

For taking decisions in connection with the procedures laid down in this Regulation the following shall be competent:

(a)   examiners;

(b)   the Administration of Trade Marks and Designs and Legal Division;

(c)   Invalidity Divisions;

(d)   Boards of Appeal.

### *Article 103*

### Examiners

An examiner shall be responsible for taking decisions on behalf of the Office in relation to an application for a registered Community design.

### *Article 104*

### The Administration of Trade Marks and Designs and Legal Division

1.    The Administration of Trade Marks and Legal Division provided for by Article 128 of the Regulation on the Community trade mark shall become the Administration of Trade Marks and Designs and Legal Division.

2.    In addition to the powers conferred upon it by the Regulation on the Community trade mark, it shall be responsible for taking those decisions required by this Regulation which do not fall within the competence of an examiner or an Invalidity Division. It shall in particular be responsible for decisions in respect of entries in the register.

## Article 105

### Invalidity Divisions

1.  An Invalidity Division shall be responsible for taking decisions in relation to applications for declarations of invalidity of registered Community designs.

2.  An Invalidity Division shall consist of three members. At least one of the members must be legally qualified.

## Article 106

### Boards of Appeal

In addition to the powers conferred upon it by Article 131 of the Regulation on the Community trade mark, the Boards of Appeal instituted by that Regulation shall be responsible for deciding on appeals from decisions of the examiners, the Invalidity Divisions and from the decisions of the Administration of Trade Marks and Designs and Legal Division as regards their decisions concerning Community designs.

## TITLE XIa
## INTERNATIONAL REGISTRATION OF DESIGNS

### Section 1

### General provisions

## Article 106a

### Application of provisions

1.  Unless otherwise specified in this title, this Regulation and any Regulations implementing this Regulation adopted pursuant to Article 109 shall apply, mutatis mutandis, to registrations of industrial designs in the international register maintained by the International Bureau of the World Intellectual Property Organisation (hereinafter referred to as "international registration" and "the International Bureau") designating the Community, under the Geneva Act.

2.  Any recording of an international registration designating the Community in the International Register shall have the same effect as if it had been made in the register of Community designs of the Office, and any publication of an international registration designating the Community in the Bulletin of the International Bureau shall have the same effect as if it had been published in the Community Designs Bulletin.

### Section 2

### International registrations designating the Community

## Article 106b

### Procedure for filing the international application

International applications pursuant to Article 4(1) of the Geneva Act shall be filed directly at the International Bureau.

## Article 106c

### Designation fees

The prescribed designation fees referred to in Article 7(1) of the Geneva Act are replaced by an individual designation fee.

*Article 106d*

**Effects of international registration designating the European Community**

1.    An international registration designating the Community shall, from the date of its registration referred to in Article 10(2) of the Geneva Act, have the same effect as an application for a registered Community design.

2.    If no refusal has been notified or if any such refusal has been withdrawn, the international registration of a design designating the Community shall, from the date referred to in paragraph 1, have the same effect as the registration of a design as a registered Community design.

3.    The Office shall provide information on international registrations referred to in paragraph 2, in accordance with the conditions laid down in the Implementing Regulation.

*Article 106e*

**Refusal**

1.    The Office shall communicate to the International Bureau a notification of refusal not later than six months from the date of publication of the international registration, if in carrying out an examination of an international registration, the Office notices that the design for which protection is sought does not correspond to the definition under Article 3(a), or is contrary to public policy or to accepted principles of morality.

The notification shall state the grounds on which the refusal is based.

2.    The effects of an international registration in the Community shall not be refused before the holder has been allowed the opportunity of renouncing the international registration in respect of the Community or of submitting observations.

3.    The conditions for the examination as to the grounds for refusal shall be laid down in the Implementing Regulation.

*Article 106f*

**Invalidation of the effects of an international registration**

1.    The effects of an international registration in the Community may be declared invalid partly or in whole in accordance with the procedure in Titles VI and VII or by a Community design court on the basis of a counterclaim in infringement proceedings.

2.    Where the Office is aware of the invalidation, it shall notify it to the International Bureau.

TITLE XII
**FINAL PROVISIONS**

*Article 107*

**Implementing regulation**

1.    The rules implementing this Regulation shall be adopted in an implementing regulation.

2.    In addition to the fees already provided for in this Regulation, fees shall be charged, in accordance with the detailed rules of application laid down in the implementing regulation and in a fees regulation, in the cases listed below:

   (a)   late payment of the registration fee;

   (b)   late payment of the publication fee;

   (c)   late payment of the fee for deferment of publication;

   (d)   late payment of additional fees for multiple applications;

(e)   issue of a copy of the certificate of registration;

(f)   registration of the transfer of a registered Community design;

(g)   registration of a licence or another right in respect of a registered Community design;

(h)   cancellation of the registration of a licence or another right;

(i)   issue of an extract from the register;

(j)   inspection of the files;

(k)   issue of copies of file documents;

(*l*)   communication of information in a file;

(m)   review of the determination of the procedural costs to be refunded;

(n)   issue of certified copies of the application.

3.    The implementing regulation and the fees regulation shall be adopted and amended in accordance with the procedure laid down in Article 109(2).

## *Article 108*

### Rules of procedure of the Boards of Appeal

The rules of procedure of the Boards of Appeal shall apply to appeals heard by those Boards under this Regulation, without prejudice to any necessary adjustment or additional provision, adopted in accordance with the procedure laid down in Article 109(2).

## *Article 109*

### Committee

1.    The Commission shall be assisted by a Committee.

2.    Where reference is made to this paragraph, Articles 5 and 7 of Decision 1999/468/EC shall apply. The period laid down in Article 5(6) of Decision 1999/468/EC shall be set at three months.

3.    The Committee shall adopt its rules of procedure.

## *Article 110*

### Transitional provision

1.    Until such time as amendments to this Regulation enter into force on a proposal from the Commission on this subject, protection as a Community design shall not exist for a design which constitutes a component part of a complex product used within the meaning of Article 19(1) for the purpose of the repair of that complex product so as to restore its original appearance.

2.    The proposal from the Commission referred to in paragraph 1 shall be submitted together with, and take into consideration, any changes which the Commission shall propose on the same subject pursuant to Article 18 of Directive 98/71/EC.

## *Article 110a*

### Provisions relating to the enlargement of the Community

. . .

*Article 111*

**Entry into force**

1.    This Regulation shall enter into force on the 60th day following its publication in the Official Journal of the European Communities.

2.    Applications for registered Community designs may be filed at the Office from the date fixed by the Administrative Board on the recommendation of the President of the Office.

3.    Applications for registered Community designs filed within three months before the date referred to in paragraph 2 shall be deemed to have been filed on that date.

This Regulation shall be binding in its entirety and directly applicable in all Member States.

Done at Brussels, 12 December 2001.

# 74.  DESIGN DIRECTIVE

**DIRECTIVE 98/71/EC OF THE EUROPEAN PARLIAMENT
AND OF THE COUNCIL
of 13 October 1998
on the legal protection of designs*\***

. . . (6)    Whereas Member States should accordingly remain free to fix the procedural provisions concerning registration, renewal and invalidation of design rights and provisions concerning the effects of such invalidity;

(7)    Whereas this Directive does not exclude the application to designs of national or Community legislation providing for protection other than that conferred by registration or publication as design, such as legislation relating to unregistered design rights, trade marks, patents and utility models, unfair competition or civil liability;

(8)    Whereas, in the absence of harmonisation of copyright law, it is important to establish the principle of cumulation of protection under specific registered design protection law and under copyright law, whilst leaving Member States free to establish the extent of copyright protection and the conditions under which such protection is conferred; . . .

(10) Whereas it is essential, in order to facilitate the free movement of goods, to ensure in principle that registered design rights confer upon the right holder equivalent protection in all Member States;

(11) Whereas protection is conferred by way of registration upon the right holder for those design features of a product, in whole or in part, which are shown visibly in an application and made available to the public by way of publication or consultation of the relevant file;

(12) Whereas protection should not be extended to those component parts which are not visible during normal use of a product, or to those features of such part which are not visible when the part is mounted, or which would not, in themselves, fulfil the requirements as to novelty and individual character; whereas features of design which are excluded from protection for these reasons should not be taken into consideration for the purpose of assessing whether other features of the design fulfil the requirements for protection;

(13) Whereas the assessment as to whether a design has individual character should be based on whether the overall impression produced on an informed user viewing the design clearly differs from that produced on him by the existing design corpus, taking into consideration the nature of the product to which the design is applied or in which it is incorporated, and in particular the industrial sector to which it belongs and the degree of freedom of the designer in developing the design;

(14) Whereas technological innovation should not be hampered by granting design protection to features dictated solely by a technical function; whereas it is understood that this does not entail that a design must have an aesthetic quality; whereas, likewise, the interoperability of products of different makes should not be hindered by extending protection to the design of mechanical fittings; whereas features of a design which are excluded from protection for these reasons should not be taken into consideration for the purpose of assessing whether other features of the design fulfil the requirements for protection;

(15) Whereas the mechanical fittings of modular products may nevertheless constitute an important element of the innovative characteristics of modular products and present a major marketing asset and therefore should be eligible for protection;

---

\*    Footnotes and some recitals omitted.

(16) Whereas a design right shall not subsist in a design which is contrary to public policy or to accepted principles of morality; whereas this Directive does not constitute a harmonisation of national concepts of public policy or accepted principles of morality; . . .

*Article 1*

## Definitions

For the purpose of this Directive:

(a) "design" means the appearance of the whole or a part of a product resulting from the features of, in particular, the lines, contours, colours, shape, texture and/or materials of the product itself and/or its ornamentation;

(b) "product" means any industrial or handicraft item, including inter alia parts intended to be assembled into a complex product, packaging, get-up, graphic symbols and typographic typefaces, but excluding computer programs;

(c) "complex product" means a product which is composed of multiple components which can be replaced permitting disassembly and reassembly of the product.

*Article 2*

## Scope of application

1. This Directive shall apply to:

(a) design rights registered with the central industrial property offices of the Member States;

(b) design rights registered at the Benelux Design Office;

(c) design rights registered under international arrangements which have effect in a Member State;

(d) applications for design rights referred to under (a), (b) and (c).

2. For the purpose of this Directive, design registration shall also comprise the publication following filing of the design with the industrial property office of a Member State in which such publication has the effect of bringing a design right into existence.

*Article 3*

## Protection requirements

1. Member States shall protect designs by registration, and shall confer exclusive rights upon their holders in accordance with the provisions of this Directive.

2. A design shall be protected by a design right to the extent that it is new and has individual character.

3. A design applied to or incorporated in a product which constitutes a component part of a complex product shall only be considered to be new and to have individual character:

(a) if the component part, once it has been incorporated into the complex product, remains visible during normal use of the latter, and

(b) to the extent that those visible features of the component part fulfil in themselves the requirements as to novelty and individual character.

4. "Normal use" within the meaning of paragraph (3)(a) shall mean use by the end user, excluding maintenance, servicing or repair work.

## Article 4

## Novelty

A design shall be considered new if no identical design has been made available to the public before the date of filing of the application for registration or, if priority is claimed, the date of priority. Designs shall be deemed to be identical if their features differ only in immaterial details.

## Article 5

## Individual character

1.    A design shall be considered to have individual character if the overall impression it produces on the informed user differs from the overall impression produced on such a user by any design which has been made available to the public before the date of filing of the application for registration or, if priority is claimed, the date of priority.

2.    In assessing individual character, the degree of freedom of the designer in developing the design shall be taken into consideration.

## Article 6

## Disclosure

1.    For the purpose of applying Articles 4 and 5, a design shall be deemed to have been made available to the public if it has been published following registration or otherwise, or exhibited, used in trade or otherwise disclosed, except where these events could not reasonably have become known in the normal course of business to the circles specialised in the sector concerned, operating within the Community, before the date of filing of the application for registration or, if priority is claimed, the date of priority. The design shall not, however, be deemed to have been made available to the public for the sole reason that it has been disclosed to a third person under explicit or implicit conditions of confidentiality.

2.    A disclosure shall not be taken into consideration for the purpose of applying Articles 4 and 5 if a design for which protection is claimed under a registered design right of a Member State has been made available to the public:

(a)    by the designer, his successor in title, or a third person as a result of information provided or action taken by the designer, or his successor in title; and

(b)    during the 12-month period preceding the date of filing of the application or, if priority is claimed, the date of priority.

3.    Paragraph 2 shall also apply if the design has been made available to the public as a consequence of an abuse in relation to the designer or his successor in title.

## Article 7

## Designs dictated by their technical function
## and designs of interconnections

1.    A design right shall not subsist in features of appearance of a product which are solely dictated by its technical function.

2.    A design right shall not subsist in features of appearance of a product which must necessarily be reproduced in their exact form and dimensions in order to permit the product in which the design is incorporated or to which it is applied to be mechanically connected to or placed in, around or against another product so that either product may perform its function.

3. Notwithstanding paragraph 2, a design right shall, under the conditions set out in Articles 4 and 5, subsist in a design serving the purpose of allowing multiple assembly or connection of mutually interchangeable products within a modular system.

## Article 8

### Designs contrary to public policy or morality

A design right shall not subsist in a design which is contrary to public policy or to accepted principles of morality.

## Article 9

### Scope of protection

1. The scope of the protection conferred by a design right shall include any design which does not produce on the informed user a different overall impression.

2. In assessing the scope of protection, the degree of freedom of the designer in developing his design shall be taken into consideration.

## Article 10

### Term of protection

Upon registration, a design which meets the requirements of Article 3(2) shall be protected by a design right for one or more periods of five years from the date of filing of the application. The right holder may have the term of protection renewed for one or more periods of five years each, up to a total term of 25 years from the date of filing.

## Article 11

### Invalidity or refusal of registration

1. A design shall be refused registration, or, if the design has been registered, the design right shall be declared invalid:

   (a) if the design is not a design within the meaning of Article 1(a); or

   (b) if it does not fulfil the requirements of Articles 3 to 8; or

   (c) if the applicant for or the holder of the design right is not entitled to it under the law of the Member State concerned; or

   (d) if the design is in conflict with a prior design which has been made available to the public after the date of filing of the application or, if priority is claimed, the date of priority, and which is protected from a date prior to the said date by a registered Community design or an application for a registered Community design or by a design right of the Member State concerned, or by an application for such a right.

2. Any Member State may provide that a design shall be refused registration, or, if the design has been registered, that the design right shall be declared invalid:

   (a) if a distinctive sign is used in a subsequent design, and Community law or the law of the Member State concerned governing that sign confers on the right holder of the sign the right to prohibit such use; or

   (b) if the design constitutes an unauthorised use of a work protected under the copyright law of the Member State concerned; or

   (c) if the design constitutes an improper use of any of the items listed in Article 6b of the Paris Convention for the Protection of Industrial Property, or of badges, emblems and escutcheons other than those covered by Article 6b of the said Convention which are of particular public interest in the Member State concerned.

3.    The ground provided for in paragraph 1(c) may be invoked solely by the person who is entitled to the design right under the law of the Member State concerned.

4.    The grounds provided for in paragraph 1(d) and in paragraph 2(a) and (b) may be invoked solely by the applicant for or the holder of the conflicting right.

5.    The ground provided for in paragraph 2(c) may be invoked solely by the person or entity concerned by the use.

6.    Paragraphs 4 and 5 shall be without prejudice to the freedom of Member States to provide that the grounds provided for in paragraphs 1(d) and 2(c) may also be invoked by the appropriate authority of the Member State in question on its own initiative.

7.    When a design has been refused registration or a design right has been declared invalid pursuant to paragraph 1(b) or to paragraph 2, the design may be registered or the design right maintained in an amended form, if in that form it complies with the requirements for protection and the identity of the design is retained. Registration or maintenance in an amended form may include registration accompanied by a partial disclaimer by the holder of the design right or entry in the design Register of a court decision declaring the partial invalidity of the design right.

8.    Any Member State may provide that, by way of derogation from paragraphs 1 to 7, the grounds for refusal of registration or for invalidation in force in that State prior to the date on which the provisions necessary to comply with this Directive enter into force shall apply to design applications which have been made prior to that date and to resulting registrations.

9.    A design right may be declared invalid even after it has lapsed or has been surrendered.

## Article 12

### Rights conferred by the design right

1.    The registration of a design shall confer on its holder the exclusive right to use it and to prevent any third party not having his consent from using it. The aforementioned use shall cover, in particular, the making, offering, putting on the market, importing, exporting or using of a product in which the design is incorporated or to which it is applied, or stocking such a product for those purposes.

2.    Where, under the law of a Member State, acts referred to in paragraph 1 could not be prevented before the date on which the provisions necessary to comply with this Directive entered into force, the rights conferred by the design right may not be invoked to prevent continuation of such acts by any person who had begun such acts prior to that date.

## Article 13

### Limitation of the rights conferred by the design right

1.    The rights conferred by a design right upon registration shall not be exercised in respect of:

(a)    acts done privately and for non-commercial purposes;

(b)    acts done for experimental purposes;

(c)    acts of reproduction for the purposes of making citations or of teaching, provided that such acts are compatible with fair trade practice and do not unduly prejudice the normal exploitation of the design, and that mention is made of the source.

2.    In addition, the rights conferred by a design right upon registration shall not be exercised in respect of:

(a)    the equipment on ships and aircraft registered in another country when these temporarily enter the territory of the Member State concerned;

(b)   the importation in the Member State concerned of spare parts and accessories for the purpose of repairing such craft;

(c)   the execution of repairs on such craft.

*Article 14*

**Transitional provision**

Until such time as amendments to this Directive are adopted on a proposal from the Commission in accordance with the provisions of Article 18, Member States shall maintain in force their existing legal provisions relating to the use of the design of a component part used for the purpose of the repair of a complex product so as to restore its original appearance and shall introduce changes to those provisions only if the purpose is to liberalise the market for such parts.

*Article 15*

**Exhaustion of rights**

The rights conferred by a design right upon registration shall not extend to acts relating to a product in which a design included within the scope of protection of the design right is incorporated or to which it is applied, when the product has been put on the market in the Community by the holder of the design right or with his consent.

*Article 16*

**Relationship to other forms of protection**

The provisions of this Directive shall be without prejudice to any provisions of Community law or of the law of the Member State concerned relating to unregistered design rights, trade marks or other distinctive signs, patents and utility models, typefaces, civil liability or unfair competition.

*Article 17*

**Relationship to copyright**

A design protected by a design right registered in or in respect of a Member State in accordance with this Directive shall also be eligible for protection under the law of copyright of that State as from the date on which the design was created or fixed in any form. The extent to which, and the conditions under which, such a protection is conferred, including the level of originality required, shall be determined by each Member State.

*Article 18*

**Revision**

Three years after the implementation date specified in Article 19, the Commission shall submit an analysis of the consequences of the provisions of this Directive for Community industry, in particular the industrial sectors which are most affected, particularly manufacturers of complex products and component parts, for consumers, for competition and for the functioning of the internal market. At the latest one year later the Commission shall propose to the European Parliament and the Council any changes to this Directive needed to complete the internal market in respect of component parts of complex products and any other changes which it considers necessary in light of its consultations with the parties most affected.

## Article 19

### Implementation

1.    Member States shall bring into force the laws, regulations or administrative provisions necessary to comply with this Directive not later than 28 October 2001.

When Member States adopt these provisions, they shall contain a reference to this Directive or shall be accompanied by such reference on the occasion of their official publication. The methods of making such reference shall be laid down by Member States.

2.    Member States shall communicate to the Commission the provisions of national law which they adopt in the field governed by this Directive.

## Article 20

### Entry into force

This Directive shall enter into force on the 20th day following its publication in the Official Journal of the European Communities.

## Article 21

### Addressees

This Directive is addressed to the Member States.

Done at Luxembourg, 13 October 1998.